AMERICAN ENTERTAINMENT

AMERICAN ENTERTAINMENT

A UNIQUE HISTORY OF POPULAR SHOW BUSINESS

BY JOSEPH CSIDA AND JUNE BUNDY CSIDA

with a special remembrance
of Billboard's *founder, W.H. Donaldson,*
by his grandson, Roger S. Littleford, Jr.

Executive Editor, Lee Zhito

A Billboard Book

This book is dedicated to the memory
of our good friend Dick Jablow who sang
"It's Only a Shanty in Old Shanty Town"
better than any attorney in the world.

Copyright © 1978 by Watson-Guptill Publications

First published 1978 in New York by Watson-Guptill Publications,
a division of Billboard Publications, Inc.,
1515 Broadway, New York, N.Y. 10036

Library of Congress Cataloging in Publication Data

Csida, Joseph.
  American entertainment.

  (A Billboard book)
  "With a special remembrance of Billboard's founder,
W. H. Donaldson, by his grandson, Roger S.
Littleford, Jr."
  Bibliography: p.
  Includes index.
  1. Performing arts—United States—History.
I. Csida, June Bundy, joint author. II. Title.
PN2221.C75   790.2'0973   78-15415
ISBN 0-8320-7506-0

Manufactured in U.S.A.

First Printing, 1978

CONTENTS

PART ONE 1700—1893

THE SHOW BUSINESS PIONEERS   18

Despite the dawn-to-dark drudgery and hardships of daily life, puritanical pressures, laws against presenting or acting in plays, the dangers and difficulties of travel, and almost nonexistent communications in pre-revolutionary colonial times, small groups of men and women created theatre, trained animals, performed acrobatic feats, danced and made music. They were the show business pioneers.

Even before the Civil War and Lincoln's murder, there were Shakespearean productions, wagon shows and magic lantern presentations, circuses, minstrel shows and show boats. After the war the show business pioneers, in increasing numbers, continued to bring joy, excitement and laughter to the troubled nation. Vaudeville blossomed; Thomas Alva Edison invented the phonograph. American entertainment grew as the new nation grew.

PART TWO 1894—1904

THE MAD, MERRY MIX OF
LIVE SHOW BUSINESS   68

The peep show machines in the kinetoscope parlors and, later, the nickelodeons and electric theatres, were moderately successful. The Victor Talking Machine Company was suffering growing pains. But it was the heyday of live show business. Theatres, opera houses, academies of music opened in almost every city and town across the country. Show business's first powerful trust stabilized the theatre, and then "milked" it. The three Barrymores made their debuts. Hard-driving showmen took over vaudeville and ruthlessly brought it to new peaks of prosperity. Minstrelsy and burlesque boomed. Barnum and Bailey and the Ringlings were the giants of the circus world.

Marconi transmitted the human voice by wireless. No one recognized radio's incubation. Few considered Caruso's first recordings and *The Great Train Robbery* as signals that mechanical show business would one day become a mounting threat to the live forms.

PART THREE 1905–1918

OF TRUSTS AND STARS 140

Trusts dominated show business. In vaudeville, Keith-Albee ruled. In the theatre, the Shuberts used Sarah Bernhardt as the spearhead in their battles against Klaw and Erlanger. Independent movie producers—in their wars against each other and against the mighty Motion Picture Patents Company trust—soon used the box office magnetism of "Little Mary" and "The Tramp" as prime weapons. The lure of the stars, the success of the new full length feature films (among them D. W. Griffith's *The Birth of a Nation*) and magnificent new theatres made motion pictures the dominant area of American entertainment.

Some of the older forms of show business, such as minstrelsy, waned and died. The first night clubs appeared. The Ringlings bought out their rivals, Barnum and Bailey. But the sensation of the outdoor show business was the aeroplane. At the end of World War I, the government attempted to gain control of that modern new miracle, radio . . . and almost did!

PART FOUR 1919–1946

THE SOUND OF A NEW SHOW BUSINESS 216

Technological improvements in recording temporarily saved the recording industry when radio threatened its existence. Then talking movies and the radio networks devastated the recording industry once again—and cut severely into every area of show business. Indeed, for a brief time, the movies and radio even seemed immune to the Great Depression. But eventually all of American entertainment, the entire economy, suffered greatly. Vaudeville dwindled and died.

At the Depression's end, William Paley's upstart CBS network seriously challenged David Sarnoff's NBC. Once again records made a surprising comeback. The big bands played through their span of glory. Mobster Bugsy Siegel "mid-wifed" a new live entertainment capital in the Las Vegas desert. The legitimate theatre and outdoor show areas found their own special niches. At the end of World War II, General Sarnoff stepped up his $50,000,000 drive to make television a factor in American entertainment—and American life.

PART FIVE 1947—1977

TECHNOLOGY, CONGLOMERATES AND SUPERSTARS 324

Television encountered obstacles: a Government freeze and total lack of cooperation from the movies. Classic Sarnoff-Paley confrontations continued in radio, and then spread to TV and records. Technology was at the heart of these battles. After the freeze, the sale of black and white TV sets zoomed and color TV was also introduced. Cable TV plodded ahead. When United Paramount's Leonard Goldenson bought ABC, he brought the first major film producers into television and set up a three-way network competition. By the 1970s, TV was filmdom's best customer, as well as its arch rival.

Conglomerates took over much of show business. Scores of superstars had multi-million dollar annual incomes. Disney created the first theme park. The discotheque vogue erupted.

Technological advances continued. Over 10,000,000 homes became cable TV subscribers; over-the-air pay TV moved ahead; videocassettes were off to a flying start; and new TV stations were transmitting signals via satellite. No one knew where show business was heading. But in every phase of American entertainment box-office records were falling like trees in a forest beset by berserk lumberjacks.

PART SIX THERE WAS ALWAYS MUSIC

CODA 384

In every phase of the nation's life, beginning with religious and political songs, and in every area of show business, there was always music. The earliest traveling shows—whether circuses or carnivals, minstrel companies, dramatic, vaudeville or burlesque presentations—all had their music makers. As the decades passed, music not only played an integral part in the development of movies, radio and television but also emerged as a major American entertainment form in its own right. Incredible twists and turns of fortune marked popular music's evolution from the day in 1743 when Benjamin Franklin heard good "musick" on a visit to Bethlehem, the Pennsylvania colonial settlement, to the contemporary pop, country and rock music of today. Hundreds of fascinating writers, stars, styles, producers, publishers and promoters contributed to the magical story of music.

BACKGROUND AND ACKNOWLEDGMENTS

Our bibliography testifies to the fact that there is no scarcity of works that deal with any single area of American entertainment. But until now there has been no book which presents the entire history of popular show business in the United States (omitting only cultural and classical entertainment forms such as ballet and opera) from before the American Revolution to the beginning of 1978.

We decided to put together the story and the interrelationships of *all* phases of American show business because we have been fascinated with, and have worked in, one area or another of popular entertainment all our lives. The many years we worked as reporters, reviewers, and editors of *Billboard*—America's oldest show business trade paper—gave us the opportunity to observe developments in American entertainment first hand on a daily basis. Our own supplementary activities in script and other writing, record and television show production, talent management, music publishing, and in administrative posts with various record and other show business organizations supplied us with additional pertinent data and expertise.

Thomas Alva Edison, 1877

PERSONAL EXPERIENCE PLUS RESEARCH

Our experiences working on *Billboard* as well as in show business itself gave us a sound base on which to construct our history of American entertainment. What we required beyond that, of course, was exhaustive research. This research took three forms. The first involved reading close to 200 books which are itemized in the bibliography. The second was to check numerous issues of key show business trade papers. And the third was to conduct continuing formal and informal interviews on a multitude of show business matters with friends and contacts in all branches of entertainment whom we had developed over the years.

The importance of the industry trade press as a basic source cannot be overstated. Our own years of involvement in American entertainment have made us fully aware of the significant part show business publications have played, and continue to play, in the development of the entertainment fields they cover. The meaningful contributions that have been made down through the years by the founders of these journals have been particularly significant.

ADROIT ADDUCENT ATHLETESS
MITE MOOREE
GREATEST MUSCULAR LADY
IN THE WORLD

Mite Mooree, 1911

Hurricane, the Trotting Ostrich, 1914

THE TRADE PRESS FOUNDERS

From the day he launched *Variety* in 1905, Sime Silverman had a continuing impact on show business. Sol Taishoff founded *Broadcasting* in 1931, and he and his publication have made their presence felt in both radio and television ever since. William H. Donaldson founded *Billboard* in 1894, and in his own quiet way he profoundly affected the development of show business. A number of examples of how Bill Donaldson and *Billboard* played a key part in American entertainment's evolution are cited in the introduction to this book which follows these acknowledgments. This special remembrance was written by Bill Donaldson's grandson, Roger S. Littleford, Jr. Roger, himself, was one of the editors who followed in his granddad's footsteps and contributed to sustaining *Billboard*'s role in the growth of show business.

By a stroke of good fortune, Lee Zhito, current editor-in-chief and publisher of *Billboard,* approached us at the time we were writing a first draft of our history. He suggested that we use original material from *Billboard* to highlight our story of American entertainment. We have used original material from *Billboard* not only in that manner, but we have also scanned the microfilm copies and/or bound volumes of all issues back to November, 1894, and utilized the wealth of factual information we found there.

However, *Billboard* discontinued its coverage of outdoor show business in the 1950s and covered these entertainment areas in new publications, *Fun Spot* and *Amusement Business*. Subsequently *Billboard*'s coverage focused on all the indoor show business branches primarily as they related to music, records and tape. At that point, to augment our historical research we checked an increasing number of issues of daily and weekly *Variety, Hollywood Reporter, Broadcasting* and other entertainment industry journals.

ORIGINAL MATERIAL REPRODUCTIONS

While the reproductions of original *Billboard* material naturally do not constitute a sequential or total history in themselves, they do give *American Entertainment* the unique, piquant flavor of each historical period which the narrative article of each of the book's six parts describes. These advertisements, stories, editorials, photos and drawings are reproduced here exactly as they appeared in the weekly issues of *Billboard.*

They provide highlights of entertainment history from the days of the wagon shows and the panstereoramas through the present, as witnessed and described by the people who lived through those periods. Nothing that a present-day author might write could capture the flavor of the earlier originals, with their archaic, colloquial language and often quaint graphics.

The history of American entertainment is presented as one consecutive narrative, which has been divided into six chronological parts. If each of the articles in these parts is read in sequence—without pausing to savor the original *Billboard* material or study the capsule histories—the articles constitute an interpretive, comprehensive history of popular show business.

Francis LeMaire, 1915

THE CODED CHRONOLOGY AND CAPSULE HISTORIES

Each of the articles in the six parts is followed by brief descriptions or "Highlights" of the original *Billboard* material. These *Billboard* items are then reproduced immediately following the "Highlights." And there is a chronology to serve as a handy, year-by-year reference to key events, the more interesting developments and even the titillating trivia of each show business period—all coded by category. This chronology is a capsule history of American show business.

ACKNOWLEDGMENTS

It is obvious that a book such as *American Entertainment* could not possibly have been put together and written without the help of many people. We owe a deep vote of thanks to the hundreds of showmen and showwomen, actors and performers, writers, directors and other craftsmen, producers and promoters, press agents and booking agents, talent managers and corporation executives who shared their experiences with us down through the years.

We are also indebted, of course, to the authors of the show business books we have consulted. And to every person who ever worked on *Billboard*, from William H. Donaldson, himself, to his grandsons, William Donaldson Littleford, chairman and chief executive officer of Billboard Publications and Roger S. Littleford, Jr., who served many years in key editorial and management positions.

We owe thanks, as well, to the editors and writers on daily and weekly *Variety, Hollywood Reporter, Broadcasting, Down Beat* and other publications we consulted.

SELZNICK PICTURES

Joseph Schenck
PRESENTS
NORMA
TALMADGE
AT THE HEAD OF HER
OWN PRODUCING COMPANY
IN
"THE PRICE SHE PAID"
BY
DAVID GRAHAM PHILLIPS

1916

Actual Scene, Chapter Three, "The Diamond From the Sky."

The Big, Amazing Scene Makes Audiences Gasp!

THE DIAMOND FROM THE SKY

A Picturized Romantic Novel
By Roy L. McCardell

1915

Martin Block, 1945

10

Thanks also to our publisher, Jules Perel of Watson-Guptill and our editor, Diane Hines in Los Angeles who worked closely with us from the very beginning, and to Kathie Ness, Watson-Guptill's managing editor in New York. Thanks are also due to our art director, Bert Johnson and his associates, Jeanne Vlazny and Arlene Ben-Lulu. They, and our manuscript typist, Celeste Mitchell, all contributed to making the task of putting together *American Entertainment* a pleasurable one.

We should say a word about omissions. Telling the story of all of popular show business in 448 pages was difficult. We found ourselves constantly agonizing over whether or not a specific incident should or should not be included. Space limitations obviously made it impossible to include every important and/or interesting event or personality. We tried to include as many as possible either in the narrative history, the original *Billboard* material, or the capsule histories. No doubt we have missed some. For any such omissions we offer our regrets.

We hope you will enjoy *American Entertainment* as a story—the first complete history of the fascinating business of show business, as well as a comprehensive reference work.

Joseph Csida and
June Bundy Csida
Malibu, Ca., 1978

Okeh catalog cover, 1926

Tom Mix and Tony, 1934

Lana Turner and Artie Shaw, 1939

11

WILLIAM H. DONALDSON
Founder, Editor and Publisher of *Billboard*
April 19, 1864–August 1, 1925

A MAN WHO LOVED SHOW BUSINESS

A SPECIAL REMEMBRANCE
BY ROGER S. LITTLEFORD, JR.

My granddad, William H. Donaldson, the man who founded *Billboard,* America's oldest entertainment trade-paper, was an imposing figure—tall, robust, with beautiful brown hair, a full beard and a ruddy complexion. But the feature most vivid in my mind—even after fifty years—is still the twinkle in his eyes when he told us stories. He was an artful and exuberant storyteller. I was thirteen, the oldest of the four Littleford grandchildren, when he died on August 1, 1925. The grandchildren included my sister, Jane; my brother, William Donaldson Littleford; and my youngest sister, Marjorie, just two years old. Marjorie, of course, was too young to understand, but brother Bill was eleven and Jane was twelve, and deep sorrow and grieving filled our hearts and our home.

As we grew up, we learned more and more about our beloved maternal grandfather. Our mother, Marjorie, and dad, Roger, Sr., filled in gaps in our youthful memories with revealing vignettes. Bill Donaldson was a Presbyterian when he married Episcopalian Jennie Hasson and converted to that faith himself. My dad told me, when I was older, that what Granddad liked best about Episcopalian St. Andrew's Parish was that one could join the Rector in an occasional Scotch or Bourbon, a pleasantry frowned upon by the more rigid Presbyterians.

THE RIFLE NEVER USED

A few years after Granddad's death, my father presented brother Bill and me with a very special gift, our late grandfather's Savage #202 Big Game Rifle. Dad told us the gun had never been fired. Granddad had purchased it for a hunting outing with some cronies in the mountains of North Carolina. He later told Dad that the first time he had a stag in his sights all he could see were the soft beautiful eyes of the beast. He could not pull the trigger. Granddad spent the remainder of the trip at the card table and in the kitchen of the lodge.

By the time Bill Donaldson died in 1925, *Billboard* was a prosperous show business trade newspaper. Granddad and Granny were living in comfort in Sarasota, Fla., near their dear friends, Charles and Edith Ringling and the John Ringlings. Granddad still kept a sharp eye on the paper. Each week he sent a "marked" copy of the current issue with comments and criticisms to the editors and other key executives in New York. But brother Bill, our sisters and I knew little about how and why *Billboard* was founded, or its history since 1894.

It was not until 1934, when Bill and I both joined *Billboard,* that we began to get the first glimmerings of how deeply our granddad had loved show business and what a vast portion of his life was dedicated to it. Until we went through back issues and dug up W. H. Donaldson's memos

---

FROM MAY 4, 1918 ISSUE

FINE!

Keith's Palace Theater, New York City, was filled to overflowing with actors, actresses and artists April 23 last.

Altho the meeting was called for 11 a.m., they began arriving as early as 10:15, and at the appointed hour not a seat was vacant, while standing room was at a premium.

Winthrop Ames and E. H. Sothern, bearers of a message from General John J. Pershing in France to the profession in America, were there to deliver it.

It proved to be a call for volunteers to entertain our soldier boys in France.

There was to be no pay.

Only troopship passage could be extended them and barracks accommodation, together with the plainest hotels, were to be their portion over there.

It was strongly hinted that they might expect not only inconvenience, but hardship and privation behind the lines.

And yet, when George M. Cohan, who presided, called for those who would enlist to stand up, every one of these generous, warmhearted souls, who have given, given and given again, given their services, given their money, given their leisure—all of them rose as one person.

Ah, but it was fine!

Not one of them hesitated, sought to qualify his assent, to impose conditions or exact the slightest special consideration.

They rose eagerly, enthusiastically, and, with shining faces, joyously tendered themselves.

Who could do more?

What other class or classes of people stand ready to do half as much?

As the writer reviewed the impressive scene he was moved in spite of himself. His eyes dimmed and a lump formed in his throat. When his wife, who was with him, remarked ecstatically, "How splendid!" he stalled—dropped his hat and pretended to be engrossed in recovering it—but it was because he could not trust himself to speak—he was afraid if he did his voice might break.

But he was very happy—the big gob of fat—and very proud, too.

For is it not a great privilege and honor to serve such people, to enjoy the confidence and esteem of very many of them, and, in a way, to represent and speak for them?

Be assured that there is one guy that thinks so. He is very sure of it. He's the fellow that the older members of The Billboard's staff call "W. H." and the youngsters dub "the old man."

Even before the meeting he had frequently declared that he would not change places with the President, but since—well, he would not swap now even with Mr. McAdoo's railroad pass perquisites thrown in.

FROM AUG. 15, 1925 ISSUE

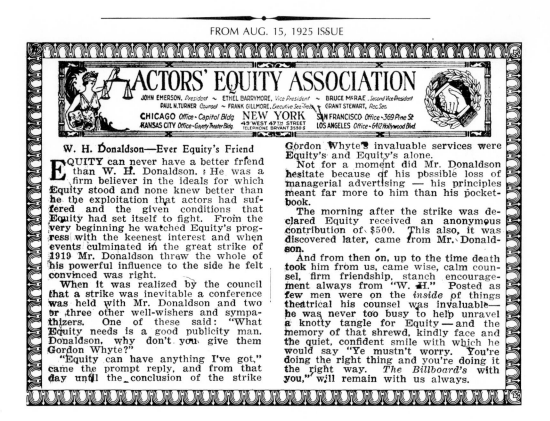

ACTORS' EQUITY ASSOCIATION

JOHN EMERSON, *President* ~ ETHEL BARRYMORE, *Vice President* ~ BRUCE MᶜRAE, *Second Vice President*
PAUL N. TURNER *Counsel* ~ FRANK GILLMORE, *Executive Sec-Treas* ~ GRANT STEWART, *Rec.Sec.*

CHICAGO *Office - Capitol Bldg.*   **NEW YORK**   SAN FRANCISCO *Office - 369 Pine St.*
KANSAS CITY *Office - Gayety Theater Bldg.*   45 WEST 47ᵀᴴ STREET   LOS ANGELES *Office - 6412 Hollywood Blvd.*
    TELEPHONE BRYANT 3550 S

W. H. Donaldson—Ever Equity's Friend

EQUITY can never have a better friend than W. H. Donaldson. He was a firm believer in the ideals for which Equity stood and none knew better than he the exploitation that actors had suffered and the given conditions that Equity had set itself to fight. From the very beginning he watched Equity's progress with the keenest interest and when events culminated in the great strike of 1919 Mr. Donaldson threw the whole of his powerful influence to the side he felt convinced was right.

When it was realized by the council that a strike was inevitable a conference was held with Mr. Donaldson and two or three other well-wishers and sympathizers. One of these said: "What Equity needs is a good publicity man. Donaldson, why don't you give them Gordon Whyte?"

"Equity can have anything I've got," came the prompt reply, and from that day until the conclusion of the strike Gordon Whyte's invaluable services were Equity's and Equity's alone.

Not for a moment did Mr. Donaldson hesitate because of his possible loss of managerial advertising — his principles meant far more to him than his pocketbook.

The morning after the strike was declared Equity received an anonymous contribution of $500. This also, it was discovered later, came from Mr. Donaldson.

And from then on, up to the time death took him from us, came wise, calm counsel, firm friendship, stanch encouragement always from "W. H." Posted as few men were on the *inside* of things theatrical his counsel was invaluable—he was never too busy to help unravel a knotty tangle for Equity — and the memory of that shrewd, kindly face and the quiet, confident smile with which he would say "Ye mustn't worry. You're doing the right thing and you're doing it the right way. *The Billboard's* with you," will remain with us always.

---

to various staff members and his correspondence, we had no idea of the hardships and financial sacrifices both he and Granny had endured in the first decade of the paper's life. Granddad worked a very hard, full day in his father's (William Mills Donaldson) Donaldson Lithographing Company in Newport, Ky. Evenings and week-ends he worked long and late to turn out *Billboard*. (A friend, James Hennegan, co-founded the publication with Granddad but sold out his interest in the paper to Bill Donaldson in an amicable settlement soon after it was launched.)

THE EARLY STRUGGLE

For the first eight years, until 1902, Bill Donaldson wrote practically every word of the paper himself, sold ads, laid it out, and took it through production. Jennie Donaldson worked by his side, handling circulation, hand-addressing subscriber copies, and performing sundry administrative and clerical functions. Virtually every penny Bill Donaldson made on his lithographing job, plus other assets, went into the struggling publication.

Granddad founded *Billboard* on a basic principle of humanity, i.e., every person needs a "home base," a "place" he may share with others of like interests. In his work with his dad's lithographing firm, he had come to know many of the "billposters," and the owners and managers of the travelling circuses, carnivals, vaudeville, dramatic, minstrel and other shows who were the major users of the colorful lithograph posters. All these people were itinerants, many of whom had no permanent address and no way of communicating with one another.

PERMANENT ADDRESS: *BILLBOARD*

One of the earliest features in *Billboard* was the "Letter List." *Billboard* readers would use *Billboard's* address as their own permanent address, and *Billboard* would either forward their mail to them upon request or hold it at the *Billboard* office where they could pick it up. There was no charge for this service. By 1914, more than 42,000 performers, agents and other showmen were using one of the *Billboard* offices in Cincinnati, New York, Chicago, St. Louis or San Francisco as their permanent address. The *Billboard* Letters department was forwarding between 1100 and 1250 letters per day to show people.

The "Letter List" was only the first of literally scores of practical and valuable service features developed by Bill Donaldson. The bedrock upon which *Billboard* was built was the philosophy of helping show people on all levels and fostering the growth of the entertainment industry. The editorials accompanying this remembrance—telling how Zat Zam found the daughter he hadn't seen for nineteen years and the plea for help for ailing Professor Harry Tyler of Tyler's Mastodon Dog Circus—are two examples.

BILLBOARD CRUSADES

While editor of the paper, Bill Donaldson conducted editorial campaigns to fight elements and practices he considered harmful to American entertainment and gave aggressive and unqualified support to causes he considered in the best interests of show business. In every area of entertainment he battled tirelessly, frequently at great cost to

FROM DEC. 21, 1912 ISSUE

OUTDOOR SHOW-MEN HONOR THE PUBLISHER OF THE BILLBOARD

W. H. Donaldson Unanimously Elected Honorary President

Of Outdoor Showmen of the World Christmas Celebration

Everything Set for Greatest Event of Kind Ever Held

New York, Dec. 16.—William H. Donaldson, proprietor of The Billboard and life-long exponent of the outdoor amusement world in general, was today befittingly honored by the Executive Committee of the Outdoor Showmen of the World's Christmas Dinner and Ball when they elected him unanimously as their honorary president.

It was the consensus of opinion on the part of the fourteen executives assembled that no one so much as the owner of Old Billyboy deserves this dignity, and it was for that reason that the meeting was temporarily adjourned in order that the body could go en masse to the Hotel Astor, where Mr. Donaldson has been living the past three weeks, so as to acquaint him with the honorary post voted him. The meeting was then called to order in the offices of the general manager of the Hotel Astor and Mr. Donaldson brought in to the council chamber. Chairman Frank P. Spellman delivered the address and in part stated that the honorary presidency had been voted him not only because no other character in the United States had a better right to the title, but also because this was one time where the showmen were not going to pay him his respects in the form of flowers on his casket, but instead were going to extend him his just rewards while he yet lived and could appreciate in this world the high and unlimited esteem that the entire outdoor show world bears him.

himself, against showmen who purveyed smut or practiced corruption. The editorial, "Our Moving Picture Reviews," is just one example of Bill Donaldson's unrelenting editorial war against what he considered to be filth in entertainment. He waged similar campaigns in never-ending, although sometimes futile, efforts to clean up carnival and circus graft and indecent performances in burlesque, night clubs and the theatre. At the same time, he was outspokenly against "blue-nose" censorship.

He gave whole-hearted and unselfish support to the actors in their struggles against the managers. In 1925, upon his death, Frank Gilmore, Executive Secretary and Treasurer of Actors' Equity Association, wrote of Bill Donaldson's support of the successful 1919 actors' strike:

Not for a moment did he hesitate (to support the actors) *because of his possible loss of managerial advertising—his principles meant far more to him than his pocketbook.*

HOSPITALS AND PUBLIC DEFENDERS

In 1912, the Outdoor Showmen of the World made Bill Donaldson their honorary president and Frank Spellman, chairman of that organization, praised Donaldson for the many successful campaigns he had conducted for the betterment of outdoor showmen. Among these were the fund raising drive which had created an outdoor showmen's ward in the American Theatrical Hospital, and the sustained and aggressive editorial crusade which resulted in the creation of an office of Public Defender in many cities across the country.

The latter campaign was the deep-reaching, far-sighted kind of trade journalism rarely encountered now or then. Aware that impoverished, travelling show people often ran into venal prejudices on the part of townspeople and were frequently arrested, tried and convicted without adequate

FROM MAR. 13, 1915 ISSUE

LETTER FROM THE FIRST PUBLIC DEFENDER, HON. WALTON J. WOOD

Los Angeles, Cal., Feb. 19, 1915.

The Billboard Publishing Co.,
Cincinnati, O.:

Gentlemen—In furthering your campaign for the creation of the office of Public Defender it will probably be of interest to note that on February 12, 1915, the lawyers of Orange County, composing the **Orange County Bar Association,** by a vote of 24 to 2, asked the county representatives in the State Legislature not only to bring about the passage of the Public Defender law, but make a special effort to have it apply to Orange County.

The bill now pending before the **California Legislature** provides for the office of Public Defender in each of the ten most populous counties. Orange County is fourteenth on the list. The Orange County Bar Association wants to have the office in still other counties so that Orange County will have a Public Defender. Orange County is one of the counties near Los Angeles County.

Very truly yours,

WALTON J. WOOD.

FROM MAR. 20, 1915 ISSUE

A CLIPPING AND A LETTER

Meridian, Miss., Feb. 27.—The recent grand jury, according to information, failed to find indictments against Dave and Kearney Smith, charged with the killing of Eddie Durham.

The two Smith brothers were charged with killing Eddie Durham, a showman, during the recent fair. A difficulty arose on the midway and following the difficulty one of the Smiths cut Durham's throat with a razor. At a preliminary hearing both were bound over under bond, but the grand jury evidently thought the killing was justifiable, as no indictment was returned.

Dear Sir—Am enclosing you clipping from Montgomery Advertiser of yesterday, which ought to be of interest to you and every carnival man in the country.

According to the way I heard the story this young man was a canvas man on the Girl Show with K. G. Barkoot's Carnival, which played the last fair here, Meridian, Miss. The yaps mentioned in this article insulted the girls while they were ballyhooing, and when the young fellow remonstrated with them they pulled him off the ballyhoo and cut his throat. The people about Meridian evidently thought their conduct was rude enough to indict them, or it may be that some one connected with the show was there to push the case against them, but as soon as the thing blowed over a little they were turned loose—"they hadn't done nothing but killed one of them 'ere pesky showfolks."

Now, it looks to me, being interested in showfolks, as though something was rotten. It also looks to me as though the next trick that went into Meridian were taking their lives in their hands, for with this as an incentive to lead them on the populace would not feel right until it had shown them—said showfolks—where they stood, and as this bunch got away with it so will the next ones.

That old stuff about the "Grift and the Girl Shows" does not hold good in this case, as every one knows what kind of an outfit K. G. has. It is merely the spirit manifested all over the country that carnival people are little better than tramps, and that home guards can go as far as they like with them—insult the women and beat up or kill the men—and get away with it.

While I never expect to see a Public Defender in this part of the country, I would feel a lot better if there had been a Public Prosecutor to see into this case.

Hoping The Billboard is finally successful in its campaign for a Public Defender, to the end that such as this may become a thing of the past, I am as ever,

Sincerely yours,

TOM P. NELSON.

BOOST FOR THE PUBLIC DEFENDER

representation by defense counsel, Bill Donaldson carried on a successful crusade in *Billboard* to persuade communities to make the services of public defenders available free of charge. He editorialized consistently in behalf of numerous causes beyond show business's immediate boundaries. In a 1912 editorial on the issue of women's suffrage, he wrote:

If benefits will accrue to women from suffrage, actresses will share in them. There is no excuse, therefore, for their not taking an interest in the subject, and a lively interest at that.

FIRST RECOGNITION OF BLACK SHOWMEN

Women's rights were only one of his social concerns. He was acutely conscious of the discrimination against blacks and other minority groups. In 1920, he inaugurated a special department in *Billboard* devoted exclusively to giving recognition and encouragement to blacks in all branches of show business. James Albert Jackson, whom Bill Donaldson described as "a Negro writer of attainments and distinction," was appointed editor of the new depart-

FROM JAN. 1, 1916 ISSUE

THE BILLBOARD REUNITES FATHER AND DAUGHTER AFTER NINETEEN YEARS

The Billboard is in receipt of the following letter from Zat Zam, the magician and illusionist:

Editor Billboard:

I want to thank you for being a messenger of joy for me, for through your paper I have found my daughter, who was separated from me nineteen years ago.

In October a letter was advertised for me in The Billboard, and when I received it noticed it was from one Mrs. Arnette, who said that good old Flo Wallace had told her, before she died, that Zat Zam was the first knife thrower in America, and that The Billboard could locate theatrical people. The letter did not explain who Mrs. Arnette is, but after answering the letter and getting a reply I find she is my long lost daughter, who was married about five years ago. It certainly means a bright Christmas for me, and I feel very grateful to The Billboard. Yours truly,

ZAT ZAM.

ment. It was the first department of its kind in entertainment history.

As the years went by and brother Bill and I worked in positions of increasing responsibility in various departments of *Billboard,* we met and worked with many who had known Granddad. We learned how undiscriminating and total was his affection for all show people. On the daily short walk from his office on 42nd Street in New York to the Astor Hotel on 44th Street—where he joined friends for lunch in the Hunting Room—Bill Donaldson would pause and say hello to a dozen or more actors and other showmen. Invariably a number of them were down on their luck. As unobtrusively as he attempted to handle the delicate "handshakes," Granddad nevertheless became known as a "soft touch." The lunch-time stroll cost between $10 and $20 per day in handouts.

THE TELL-TALE PALACE MEETING

Perhaps the most touching admission from Bill Donaldson himself of how much he loved show people—and how proud he was to speak to and for them through *Billboard*—was a short editorial he wrote following a meeting at the Palace Theatre in New York when George M. Cohan called for show people to volunteer to serve in World War I.

Granddad was normally a quiet, reserved, almost shy man. He usually kept emotions well concealed. But in the editorial, "Fine!", for once, his love of show business and show people was beautifully exposed.

Much has transpired in the fifty-two years since Bill Donaldson's death. In a manner almost mystical, his publishing policies have been perpetuated by a series of dedicated editors, reporters, administrators and employees in every department. American entertainment grew to dimensions hardly conceivable a half century ago. *Billboard* found it could best service its show business constituency by creating separate publications for the outdoor phases of entertainment, and thus were born *Fun Spot* and *Amusement Business*. Then the phenomenal evolution of the pre-recorded and tape music industries, plus other economic factors, dictated that *Billboard* should cover television, radio, theatres, motion pictures, et al. primarily as they related to the music/record/tape areas of entertainment.

But the *Billboard* of 1894 and the decades that followed under Granddad's affectionate and inspired leadership—and those who carried on in his tradition—made its own unique contributions to American entertainment. The reproductions of original *Billboard* material that Joe and June Csida have selected to add a touch of unique spice to their exhaustively researched history of popular show business is ample evidence of this.

I think our granddad, Bill Donaldson—a man who truly loved show business—would be proud of his work and the work of those of us who followed.

PROF. HARRY C. TYLER
An "Oldtimer," Destitute and in Ill Health, Needs Help

To those of you "oldtimers" upon whom fortune has smiled and you youngsters who have everything before you and who may, when your hair whitens, your eyes grow dim and the candle of life burns low, be in sore distress, this is written with the hope that it will provoke a bit of that big-heartedness and charity for which showfolks are noted.

About the time of the opening of the San Francisco Exposition there came to this city an old man seeking work, a man whose name at one time appeared in type larger than others on the program, but whose age prevented him from securing a position and whose pride prohibited him from disclosing his identity.

Shortly after his arrival he was stricken with dysentery and locomotor ataxia and was taken to the public hospital, where he has lain in an iron cot, staring at the white ceiling, for six long months.

A man whose life had been devoted to bringing joy and happiness to countless thousands is now destitute and alone with no one to give him that which he so freely gave to others.

Harry C. Tyler's Mastodon Dog Circus was a feature on many an old program and Harry Tyler's career has seen him interlocutor with the old Arnold Bros.' Minstrels, with Billy Emerson, with the John H. Murray Wagon Show, with the Great Wallace Show, the original Howe's Great London Show, the Barnum & Bailey Show, Ringling Show and with the Sells-Floto Show the first season out, usually with dogs and ponies and acting as ringmaster or announcer. In 1902 he lost his nineteen dogs and two monkeys in a fire at Krug's Park, Omaha, then later secured a position as treasurer at Manhattan Beach, Denver.

So much is true and is past.

Now for the future.

Who will give Harry Tyler a job? He doesn't want a position, just a job so he can earn a living. Taking tickets or something that will not require too much activity. And who will send him a bit of change? Not much, a dime, two bits, the price of one of your cigars or your next drink, so that he may have transportation to his job when he leaves the hospital.

And remember his early days were as bright and as full of hope as yours are now. The future is before all of us and should misfortune overtake us in our old age may the world be charitable to us.

Address all letters to Harry C. Tyler, Bed 6, Ward H, City & County Hospital, San Francisco, Cal.

OUR MOVING PICTURE REVIEWS

ARE HONEST, TRUTHFUL AND DEVOID OF ALL BIAS AND PREJUDICE SAVE IN CASE OF THE PANDERING FILTH FILM, WHICH WE SWAT TO THE VERY BEST OF OUR ABILITY EVERY TIME WE GET THE CHANCE

That our policy is appreciated by real showmen is evidenced by the following letter to the Circulation Audit Committee of the Associated Motion Picture Advertisers (Inc.) by Manager Buckley of the Ellsworth Theater, Kansas City, Mo.:

"Gentlemen—It has been brought to my attention that you are making a test of what trade papers the exhibitors most depend upon, and I am taking this opportunity of advising you that in my opinion The Billboard with its fine weekly reviews is the most satisfactory and reliable viewed from every angle. I am and have been a reader of The Billboard for a great many years, when I was business manager of the Willis Wood Theater, Kansas City, Mo., and now in my connection with the Ellsworth Theater, presenting high-class motion pictures.

"I find The Billboard the most useful of papers and shall continue to benefit from it every week.

"Yours very truly."

That that same policy is not appreciated by the manufacturers is evidenced by our advertising pages.

It has been evident this long while that the producing companies deemed this policy wrong, but as it is constructive and on the square we think the companies are wrong and the policy right.

Hence we shall stick to it.

We shall probably lose what little M. P. advertising we have left, but there is going to be at least one paper in the field that will be believable and on the level with exhibitors.

PART ONE

1700–1893

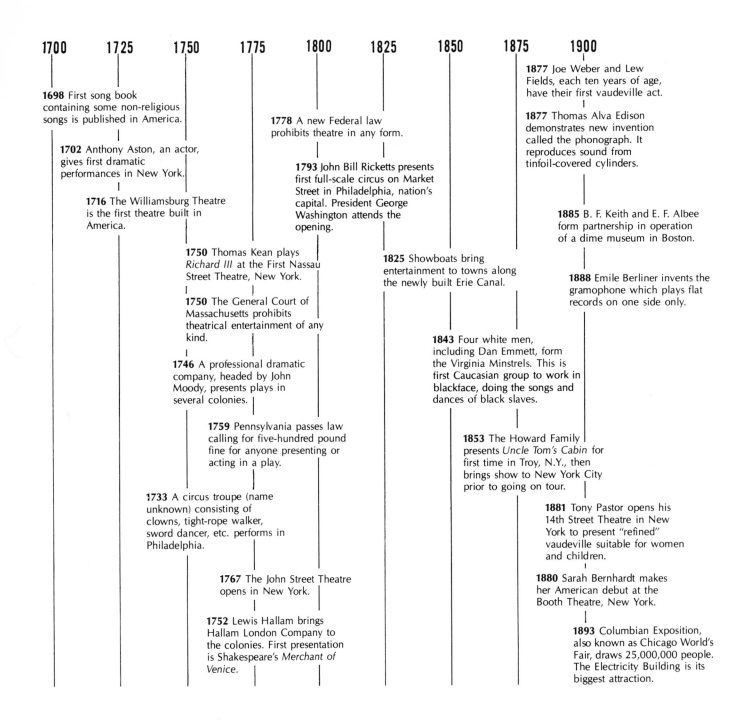

1700   1725   1750   1775   1800   1825   1850   1875   1900

1877 Joe Weber and Lew Fields, each ten years of age, have their first vaudeville act.

1698 First song book containing some non-religious songs is published in America.

1877 Thomas Alva Edison demonstrates new invention called the phonograph. It reproduces sound from tinfoil-covered cylinders.

1778 A new Federal law prohibits theatre in any form.

1702 Anthony Aston, an actor, gives first dramatic performances in New York.

1793 John Bill Ricketts presents first full-scale circus on Market Street in Philadelphia, nation's capital. President George Washington attends the opening.

1716 The Williamsburg Theatre is the first theatre built in America.

1885 B. F. Keith and E. F. Albee form partnership in operation of a dime museum in Boston.

1750 Thomas Kean plays *Richard III* at the First Nassau Street Theatre, New York.

1825 Showboats bring entertainment to towns along the newly built Erie Canal.

1888 Emile Berliner invents the gramophone which plays flat records on one side only.

1750 The General Court of Massachusetts prohibits theatrical entertainment of any kind.

1746 A professional dramatic company, headed by John Moody, presents plays in several colonies.

1843 Four white men, including Dan Emmett, form the Virginia Minstrels. This is first Caucasian group to work in blackface, doing the songs and dances of black slaves.

1759 Pennsylvania passes law calling for five-hundred pound fine for anyone presenting or acting in a play.

1853 The Howard Family presents *Uncle Tom's Cabin* for first time in Troy, N.Y., then brings show to New York City prior to going on tour.

1733 A circus troupe (name unknown) consisting of clowns, tight-rope walker, sword dancer, etc. performs in Philadelphia.

1881 Tony Pastor opens his 14th Street Theatre in New York to present "refined" vaudeville suitable for women and children.

1767 The John Street Theatre opens in New York.

1880 Sarah Bernhardt makes her American debut at the Booth Theatre, New York.

1752 Lewis Hallam brings Hallam London Company to the colonies. First presentation is Shakespeare's *Merchant of Venice*.

1893 Columbian Exposition, also known as Chicago World's Fair, draws 25,000,000 people. The Electricity Building is its biggest attraction.

THE SHOW BUSINESS PIONEERS

Social life was bare and spiritless beyond the possibility of description. Opportunities for pleasure would hardly satisfy the common laborer of two centuries later.

That was historian William B. Weeden's description of early New England, specifically Boston in 1706. Less than forty years later in 1743 Benjamin Franklin wrote,

The first Drudgery of Settling new Colonies, which confines the Attention of the People to mere Necessaries is now pretty well over; and there are many in every Province in Circumstances that set them at Ease, and afford leisure to cultivate the finer Arts.

The astute Mr. F. was overstating the situation. By 1775 popular, live show business—circuses, vaudeville, burlesque, minstrelsy, theatre and music—as Americans came to know it through the years was still almost non-existent.

Some evidence of the existence of popular entertainment in post-Colonial times is found in a *Billboard* report dealing with a Franklin contemporary, Thomas Jefferson. Jefferson was not only the third president of the United States and the author of the Declaration of Independence, he was also a meticulous keeper of records and a careful man with a shilling.

The report said, in part:

. . . . it appears that the great Virginian must have subscribed to a personal declaration of independence as to his pleasures and indulgences, for the tell-tale records he left behind prove that he was not prejudiced against amusements any more than he was averse to the good things in life. . . . Anything in the nature of a show or entertainment appealed to his taste. He was a regular theatre-goer, wherever opportunity offered either in Virginia, Philadelphia or Paris.

Here are some of the entertainment entries in Jefferson's diaries from 1771 to 1786:

Paid for hearing the musical glasses, 3 shillings; paid for Dutch dancing and singing, 2 shillings, 3d; paid for seeing puppet show, 2 shillings, 6d; paid for two tickets to see the balloon, 15 shillings; paid for seeing a learned pig, 1 shilling.

THE BIRTH OF AMERICA

In tracing the extraordinarily difficult birth of American show business from its earliest days, it is oddly appropriate to note that the granting of the first charter to the Virginia Company and their financing of the first American colony constituted much the same procedure used in creating and bankrolling a major musical comedy or drama on New York's Broadway: moneyed people would buy shares in a company to enable a producer (explorer) to develop a property, which would hopefully earn great returns. Each share in the Virginia Company entitled the holder to an acre of land in the new colony, and great returns were, indeed, to come.

Everyone knows of the hardships that were endured by the early Colonists who founded Jamestown in 1607, followed by the Pilgrims in 1620 and then scores of others. These settlers had to be hardy, practical people, indeed. Singing, dancing, playacting, comicking, juggling, or tumbling were far from the average man's thoughts. Show business types were not sorely needed.

Yet, in spite of the full-time job of chopping a habitat out of the awesome forests, in spite of death by disease and tomahawk, the population of the earliest colonies grew, and more and more settlements were opened up.

DIVERSE PEOPLES, DIVERSE CUSTOMS

The diversity of the types of people who settled the colonies accounts for the later diversity in the types of entertainment that appeared in America. Historian Abbott Emerson Smith summed it up:

The Colonies were a haven for the Godly, a refuge for the oppressed, a challenge to the adventurous but particularly (in regard to) indentured servants, they were also the last resort of scoundrels, men and women who were dirty and lazy, rough, ignorant, lewd and often criminal.

Members of this motley group, nevertheless, made a contribution to the growth of the struggling nation. Indeed there are numerous cases of distinguished American show business folk who descended from these early notorious emigrés.

For example, one of the first to set up paid-admission museums in America—long before P. T. Barnum—was Charles Wilson Peale. Peale was also a fine painter and a pioneer collector of scientific lore and materials. His father was an embezzler who was shipped to the colonies from a British jail.

By 1641 more than 50,000 English settlers had reached the New World. Seventy-five years later, by 1716, the number had increased to 435,000. In that period took place a series of emigrations which most historians agree was a major factor in ultimately shaping the character of the country still to be named the United States of America.

Hundreds of thousands of non-English people came to the continent. Among other nationalities, Germans from the Rhineland, Moravia and elsewhere came. This particular ethnic group provides a good example of how the customs of each arriving group of peoples contributed to the diversity of American entertainment.

The Moravian Germans, some of whom settled in Pennsylvania communities such as Bethlehem and Nazareth, probably brought the first extensive band music to the New World. Benjamin Franklin, after a visit to Bethlehem, wrote:

I heard good Musick, the Organ being accompanied with Violins, Hautboys, Flutes and Clarinets.

One of the Moravian musicians, Johann Friedrich Peter, was a composer of string quartets and is generally recognized as the "father" of chamber music in America. The Moravians are also credited with bringing the first trombones to America, and developing the use of the harp, the harpsichord, and the clavichord.

It was a Moravian custom to have flautists and drummers go into the fields with the harvesters. When a Moravian family, aided by neighbors, completed building a new home, the feat was heralded with trumpet fanfares. The infusion of customs of this kind was meaningful in the development of the musical phase of American show business and may be further appreciated when contrasted with the attitude of the early English Puritan settlers toward instrumental or vocal music making. The Puritans, of course, considered such music an utter frivolity—a sin.

RELIGIOUS BELIEFS AND ENTERTAINMENT

The varying religious backgrounds of the settlers of diverse ethnic origins created widely differing attitudes toward entertainment of any form, and of course, had a bearing on American show business's destiny. In 1776, out of a total of 2,500,000 colonists approximately 500,000 were Church of England. More than 1,000,000 were members of such Calvinist denominations as Puritan Congregationalist, Dutch and German Reformed Church, and Presbyterian. Other thriving religious groups were the Quakers, the Pietists, the Baptists, the Methodists, and Lutherans. Less than one per-

cent (approximately 2,000) were Jews and about ten percent (25,000) Roman Catholics.

OTHER OBSTACLES TO ENTERTAINMENT'S GROWTH

Another factor hindering the growth of American entertainment was the very sparse population through the last half of the eighteenth century scattered among small towns and settlements the length and breadth of the colonies. In 1752 Baltimore, for example, was a village of about one hundred people, twenty-five houses, two inns, and a church.

Even as late as 1790 when the first Federal Census was taken, less than 120,000 of the total population of 3,929,000 lived in cities of over 10,000 people. The most populated cities were Philadelphia (40,000), New York (25,000), Boston (16,000) and Charleston in the South with 12,000.

But small numbers of people and their prejudices were, of course, not the only reasons for American show business's incredibly difficult struggle to come into being. As many historians have told us, the rigors of daily living back then are almost beyond our twentieth-century comprehension.

Another great difficulty was getting from one place to another. All through the eighteenth century travel by land was tortuous and dangerous. One traveled on horseback, or via horse and carriage, through deep woods and forests, finding bad roads, if any at all. Boat was the preferred method of transportation. Benjamin Franklin traveled from Philadelphia to Boston by sea and it took him two days. The Philadelphia-Lancaster Turnpike wasn't begun until 1790. The Cumberland Turnpike, running from Cumberland, Maryland (near Baltimore) to Ohio, Indiana, and Illinois wasn't completed until many years later.

There was also scant communication. The first newspaper wasn't produced until a man named Benjamin Harris turned out "Publick Occurences" in Boston in 1690. But he was soon shut down for running a story saying the English army had made an alliance with "miserable savages." By the time the Colonies decided to fight for their independence in late 1775 there were thirty-seven newspapers.

A sparse and scattered population, poor transportation and communication, religious scruples, and the incredible hardships of daily life all worked as impediments to the emergence of American entertainment. But somehow, show business did manage to survive and eventually flourish in diverse ways and in varying forms.

ENTERTAINMENT IN PRE-COLONIAL TIMES

In the several decades preceding the fateful year before the Colonies declared their Independence, small numbers of individuals and groups, possibly as few as two or three hundred persons in all, represented whatever show business there was.

In Philadelphia a band of wandering players (jugglers, magicians, and such) gave performances which might have passed for early vaudeville. A bearded , dirty trapper came out of the forest bordering a new settlement with a bear he had trained, and showed its talents in the village square. A sailor, freshly arrived in a seaport colony, earned his rum or Madeira in the local Inn by displaying his pet monkey. In 1716 a lion was put on display in Boston. In 1721 in the same progressive city, an entrepreneur showed a camel, and in 1733 a polar bear. In Philadelphia a complete circus troupe—including clowns, tight-rope walkers, sword dancers and other "artistes"—gave its first performance. Nowhere were the names of these pioneer show folk recorded.

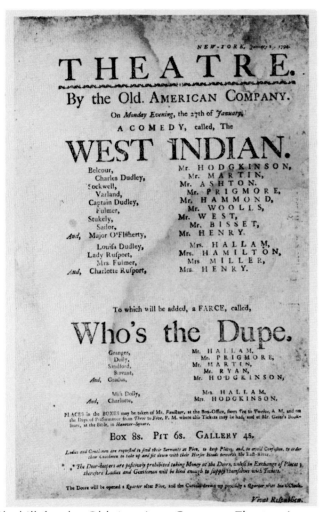

Playbill for the Old American Company Theatre, January, 1794. Courtesy Museum of the City of New York.

EARLY THEATRE

Historians of the theatre were apparently more industrious and concerned. Or perhaps there was simply more theatre. At any rate, records indicate that as early as 1702 an English actor named Anthony Aston performed in New York. In 1746 a professional company under the directorship of John Moody worked in several settlements. On March 5, 1750 Thomas Kean played Richard III at the First Nassau Street Theatre in New York.

And the man who is generally conceded to be responsible for bringing full-fledged professional theatre to America, Lewis Hallam, an English actor-manager, brought his Hallam London Company to the Colonies in 1752. Their first performance was Shakespeare's *Merchant of Venice* at the Williamsburg Theatre in Virginia.

The early theatrical companies were almost exclusively made up of English actors, since few Americans aspired to the stage. The troupes traveled in covered wagons, which served as sleeping quarters as well as transportation. A *Billboard* historian described a typical traveling dramatic company:

These players appeared in a first piece full of strong situations, broadsword combats and rantings of the leading man, all of which pleased the audience. Every act had a good strong death scene at the end and the audience was never appeased until all the dead appeared before the curtain in full response to the encores. The drama was followed by a short farce.

Very few towns had any halls for the players to act in, and they had to take any empty room they could find, which was generally the dining room of the tavern. Sometimes they had to take the blacksmith shop, utilizing soap boxes, barrels and pails for seats.

In the first half of the nineteenth century villages and towns on the waterfront were regularly visited by what were then called "floating theaters," later showboats. The Erie Canal, completed in 1825, brought entertainment to towns between Albany and Buffalo, and soon similar theatrical companies were "showboating" up and down the Ohio and Mississippi Rivers as well.

There is a *Billboard* report on the most successful play before, during, and after the Civil War, *Uncle Tom's Cabin*:

The Howard family were the first of the old school actors to play this piece. They staged the adaptation which had been made from Harriet Beecher Stowe's book by George Aitken. They opened with it in Troy, New York, where it had a run of over three months. From there they took it to the National Theater in New York where they gave their first performance on July 18, 1853. After the New York run they took the play entour.

George C. Howard acted as St. Clair, and he made an ideal southern planter. On and off the stage he invariably wore a black broadcloth frock coat with brass buttons, and he always had on lavender trousers. So when he was on the streets of the town where he was playing, people who had seen him would recognize him at once and would say, "There goes Eva's father.". . . Mrs. Howard was Topsy and there has never been any one yet to equal her in the character. Little Cordella, her daughter, was a born actress. I have never seen anything more natural and beautiful than the way in which she played little Eva. She required no

Poster for Jay Rial's
Ideal Uncle Tom's Cabin.
Courtesy Museum of
the City of New York

training for it. It came natural to her . . . Green C. Germon acted Uncle Tom. . .

There were literally hundreds of theatrical companies, (some extraordinarily proficient, some atrocious and amateurish) which toured *Uncle Tom's Cabin* well into the early part of the twentieth century. It is said that Mrs. Stowe never made a penny from the dramatic adaptation.

STRUGGLES OF THE EARLY THEATRE

The theatre struggled not only against the "Drudgery . . . which confined the Attention of the People to mere Necessaries," but in some colonies it was actually forbidden by law. In 1750 the General Court of Massachusetts passed an Act prohibiting stage plays and theatrical entertainment of any kind. In Pennsylvania in 1759 the House of Representatives passed a law stipulating that anyone presenting or acting in a play would be fined 500 pounds. A similar law was enacted in Rhode Island two years later. Until 1775 Virginia and Maryland were the only two colonies which did not have anti-theatre laws at one time or another. In 1778 with the Colonial forces fighting for life and liberty, the Federal Congress adopted a law prohibiting theatre in any form.

MUSIC AS A VICE

Even music, that integral ingredient of virtually every segment of show business, faced fierce religious resistance in many of the Colonies. A special sketch tracing the course of music through all segments of show business from the very beginning of American entertainment is presented in Part Six, but an incident in 1700 illustrates the attitude of the period toward music as a whole.

In 1640, the first song book called *The Bay Psalm Book* was published. Another edition of it was printed in 1698. The tunes in the 1698 edition were largely adapted from yet another music book, published in England in 1674, called *Introduction to the Skill of Music* by John Playford. It contained such non-religious songs as, "John, Come Kiss Me Now".

Yet in 1700 in the Massachusetts Bay Colony, a Reverend Walter Roxbury called the communal singing which went on in church, at town meetings, and other social gatherings "a mere disorderly noise, left to the mercy of every unskillful throat to chop and alter." The reason for the chopping and altering, of course, was that everyone was singing by ear, as he or she remembered the psalm or hymn as it was sung by his or her parents. Singing by note was considered sinful, even sacrilegious, by many.

POPULAR SONGS

Prejudice and intolerance, however, were no more effective in halting the growth and influence of music in American entertainment—and in American life, for that matter—than in any other sector of show business.

Two song classics are fine examples of the persistence of music in American life. One, "Yankee Doodle," is identified with the Revolution which gave the nation its birth; the other, "Dixie," became a battle hymn of the Confederacy in the war which tore the young country apart.

"Yankee Doodle" had a most complex, difficult-to-trace origin and development. France, Spain, Holland, Hungary, and of course, England and America itself were all involved in the life of the song at one time, or in one way or another. Many historians and musicologists have their own versions of the background of the song. "Dixie," with such lines as ". . . in Dixieland, I'll take my stand, to live and die in Dixie" seems a natural song of battle, but it was actually written by a northern minstrel man, Dan Emmett, who had no war in mind at all. Emmett wrote the song as a "walk-around" tune for Bryant's Minstrels, while he was appearing with that famed company in New York City in 1859.

22

MINSTREL SHOWS

Minstrelsy, according to some historians, started in 1828. A *Billboard* historian writes:

Two old darkies, long years ago, way back in 1828, can justly lay claim to be the originators of negro minstrelsy in this country.

First was an old darky in New Orleans, known by every one in the city in those days as 'Old Corn Meal'. He could be seen from morning till night with his old horse and cart going about the city selling cornmeal, and most every evening he would draw up in front of the old Planters' Hotel, the well-known hostelry of those days, and pick up many a sixpence singing old negro melodies as they were sung by the negroes of the South in those early days.

The other one was an old darky known all up and down the Mississippi and Ohio Rivers from New Orleans to Cincinnati as Picayune Butler. He would sing those old eccentric negro songs, accompanying himself on a banjo that he made himself.

In the pre–Civil War period and for some time afterwards minstrelsy was a major form of American entertainment.

VAUDEVILLE

Vaudeville, of course, played a major role in American show business. There are probably no two persons in early show business history who so thoroughly personified vaudeville—both as performers and managers or producers—as Joe Weber and Lew Fields. In 1904, after twenty-seven years, the two dissolved their partnership, which started like this,. according to a *Billboard* interview with Lew Fields himself:

Joe Weber and I first met in the Allen Street public school in New York City, when we were ten years old. We both had a fancy for clog dancing and it was this mutual liking that drew us together. During recess and after school hours we would practice dancing, and every time we could we would sneak off to the London Theatre and gaze with awe upon the performers from our seats in the gallery. We resolved to be actors too and it was not long before we made our first appearance on the stage.

From the pennies we could scrape together we each bought a pair of green knickerbockers, a white waist, black stockings, dancing clogs and a derby hat. Then we were ready to make our debut as dancers and singers. We had a song, words of our own composition, music cribbed, which we called "The Land of the Shamrock Green." Just listen to the chorus:

Here we are, an Irish pair,
Without any troubles or care;
We're here once more to make people roar
Before we go to the ball.

Well, Joe and I make our first appearance at this benefit and we received such praise from a very slim audience, that we felt we were cut out for actors.

The team's first paid engagement in 1877 was at Morris and Hickman's East Side Museum on Chatham Square. And they got three dollars for the job.

They broke into a major vaudeville booker's office by sending in word that they had found a "new curiosity," a Chinaman with only one eye in the middle of his forehead. This canard won them a hearing, and eventually a booking with the agent. Their careers virtually ran parallel with the growth of vaudeville in America.

PANORAMAS, PANSTEREORAMAS, MAGIC LANTERN SHOWS

Long before either minstrelsy or vaudeville there were the wagon shows featuring panoramas, panstereoramas and magic lantern performances. These showmen were actually the pioneers of the motion picture industry. Indeed, one of them, Jim Bonheur, claimed to have passed on to Thomas Edison the basic idea for what became the kinetoscope.

One of the traveling panorama showmen, later turned *Billboard* historian, told of becoming a client of young Abraham Lincoln of the firm of Herndon & Lincoln in Springfield, Illinois. The theatrical Joseph Jefferson family also was represented by attorney Lincoln. In yet a third report in this section, Harry Hawks, who played the title role in *American Cousin* and a young actress, sitting in her backstage dressing room at the Ford theatre, recount their stories of the night of President Lincoln's assassination by actor John Wilkes Booth.

CIRCUSES, FAIRS, WILD WEST SHOWS

In each area of American show business, a small—a very small—number of pioneers led the way.

Street fairs, county fairs, and then vast expositions developed; the circus went from one ring to three and Wild West shows were born and proliferated.

The pioneers of such shows were little known and unheralded, but among them were such giants as P. T. Barnum and Buffalo Bill, Dan Emmett and Dan Rice, and Weber and Fields. Whether famous or little known, they all made their contributions to American entertainment's growth.

And now follows the unique story of those pioneer show people and their descendants as reflected in the pages of the world's oldest entertainment publication, *The Billboard*. Its stories, editorials, advertisements and features provide an informal but very real history of the tribulations and the triumphs of these show folk as told by themselves and the people who reported on their activities.

The first such stories that follow cover the period from before the Revolutionary War until after the Civil War.

Each of the essays telling the complete story of American Entertainment will be followed by reproductions of such original material as published in *Billboard*.

ORIGINAL BILLBOARD MATERIAL 1700–1893
HIGHLIGHTS

THE LAST WORDS LINCOLN HEARD 52

"... Well, I know enough to turn you inside out, woman. You darned old sockdollinger of a man trap." Those were the last words Abraham Lincoln heard spoken just before he was shot, according to W. Harry Hawks, who uttered those lines in the title role in *American Cousin* at the Ford Theatre the night of the assassination. Here is Hawks' version of the tragic episode as published in *Billboard*. Kathryne Evans, playing one of the servants, was sitting in the Green Room when the shot was fired, and she gives her impression in another *Billboard* story.

STREET AND COUNTY FAIRS 53

From the times of the ancient Hebrews and Greeks through the period of the Louisiana Exposition, fairs have been a source of entertainment in small towns and large cities throughout the nation.

EARLY CIRCUS DAYS 55

The Howes' Brothers Great North American Circus in 1826 and the arrival of the elephant, "Old Bet," on Hackaliah Bailey's sailing vessel in 1821 were among the historic episodes of the early days of the American circus.

WILD WEST SHOWS' FIRST COWBOY 58

Wild West shows soon became a major part of early American show business. The Buffalo Bill (Wm. F. Cody) extravaganza was one of the most successful of all. Here is the tale of the first American cowboy featured by the show—Buck Taylor, one-time opera singer.

THE BARNUM CAREER—HITS AND FLOPS 59

Acknowledged one of the greatest showmen of all time was Phineas T. Barnum. His first business ventures starting in 1835 were far from successful, but ultimately his triumphs made show business history.

THOMAS JEFFERSON'S
ENTERTAINMENT EXPENDITURES

FROM MAY 28, 1904 ISSUE

THE DAY OF THE PEEP SHOW.

The late Paul Licester Ford, historian and novelist, presents Thomas Jefferson in "Undress" in liberal quotations from the memoranda of the distinguished statesman, who faithfully set down his most trival expenditures. From these accounts. It appears that the great Virginian must have subscribed to a personal declaration of independence as to his pleasures and indulgencies, for e tell tale records he left behind, prove that he was not prejudiced against amusements anymore than he was adverse to the good things of life. Ford writes: "He must have had as good stock of wine as any man in the country," and charges appear in detail that the political leader provided a good table of olden time extravagancies, including such luxuries as pine-apples, oysters, venison, partridges, watermelons, peaches, oranges, etc. "Still another means of spending money seems to have tempted him strongly. Anything in the nature of an entertainment or show appealed to his tasts." He was a regular theatre-goer, wherever opportunity offered either in Virginia, Philadelphia or Paris. Jefferson's methodical memoranda records in his methodical way:

1771—Paid for hearing the musical glasses, 3 shillings.
Paid for seeing the aligator, 1 shilling, 3d.
Paid for Dutch dancing and singing, 2 shilling, 3d.
A lively year that!
1772—Paid for seeing puppet show, 2 shillings, 6d.
1783—Paid for 2 tickets to see balloon, 15 shillings.
It is to be hoped that the balloon went up and that there was no postponement on account of bad weather.
1786—Paid for seeing figure of King of Prussia, 12 francs.
Paid for seeing a learned pig, 1 shilling.
1790—Paid for seeing a congar from Paraguay, 1 shilling.

The shows of Jefferson's time were very small affairs and probably the exhibition of the aligator, the learned pig and the congar, were infrequent. Altogether they might have been financially, "The success of the season," in the minds and pockets of the pioneer capitalists controlling such rare novelties. The musical glasses and the Dutch singing and dancing, must have been quite out of the usual line, and each an "Engagement extraordinary."

FROM OCT. 14, 1905 ISSUE

DUMMY ALLEN

The Eccentric Old-time Actor

By Doctor Judd.

Dummy Allen, who was he? the reader will say. One might travel for years in this country, and then not find a person who ever saw or heard of him; still, there was such a man. Twenty-five or thirty years ago I saw his grace in the grounds of the Dramatic Fund Association at Cypress Hills

Thomas Jefferson. From a print engraved by A. Desmoyers.
Courtesy Museum of the City of New York.

cemetery, New York, Dummy, or Andrew J. Allen, died in 1853. On his modest tombstone is the following remarkable inscription, with name and dates of birth and death:

"From the cradle he was a scholar—exceeding wise, fair spoken and pusuading. Lofty and sour to them that loved him; but to those men that sought him sweet as summer."

This eccentric individual, Dummy Allen, as he was called most all his lifetime, was born in New York in 1776; his father and mother were members of a Thespian troupe that came from England a few years before his birth. Dummy went upon the stage when a boy about ten years old, at the old John Street Theatre in New York. He was one of the incense boys in Romeo and Juliet (before the funeral pageant in that play was dispensed with), and from this circumstance used to boast in his old age that he was the "father of the American stage," being as he claimed, the oldest living performer. But he was such an inveterate old humbug that his stories were little credited, although this one might have been true. In 1815-16 he was semi-attached to the old Green Street Theatre, at Albany, N. Y.

Here at that time he sang the first negro song ever heard in an American theatre. He was playing the character of a negro in the play, The Battle of Lake Champlain, and the song of which we will only give a specimen of the first two verses:

"Backside Albany, stan' Lake Champlain—
Little pond, half full o' water;
Platteburg dar too close 'pon de main,
Town small, he grow bigger here-arter.
.   .   .   .
"On Lake Champlain Uncle Sam set he boat,
An' Massa McDonough he sail 'em;
While General Macomb make Platteburg he home
Wid de army whose courage nebber fall 'em."

Dummy, or as he named himself in after life, Andrew Jackson Allen, was a kind of a Jack-of-all-trades about a theatre, and as it can be easily imagined, he was never much of an actor, although, it is said, he could play Goldfinch tolerably well and was noted as Caleb Quotem. He was afflicted with a chronic catarrh which caused him to speak in a peculiar manner.

He was partially deaf, and was quite annoying to those with whom he played, who not infrequently revenged themselves by misleading him with inaudible movements of the lips during a performance, to which he thought he must reply, his speeches often being thus introduced quite malapropos. It was the hardest thing in the world to get him to hear anything about a little bill he owed. "I say, Mr. Allen, can you settle that little account to-day?"

"T'ank you, t'ank you," was the reply, with the politest of bows, "I neber takes any-tink pefore my meals," and on he would march.

He was noted all over the United States for his "gags" and benefits. Once he advertised a grand balloon ascension to take place from a yard on Washington avenue, when two aeronauts, Monsieur Gageromo and Mademoiselle Prysiremo, would take a flight through the air. The adventurous foreigners proved to be two cats dressed in the prevailing style, and strapped to the balloon. Dummy managed generally to celebrate the 8th of January every year by a performance of The Battle of New Orleans, in which he impersonated General Jackson, one of the two only great men, who, according to Dummy's ideas, ever lived. As we have said before, he is supposed to have named himself after the old hero, and was never tired of sounding his praises.

The other semi-god whom Dummy worshipped was Edwin Forrest, who took a fancy to the old man, and made him his costumer, dresser and traveling companion for years. To hear Dummy talk, one would suppose that "de poy" (he always called Forrest "the boy") owed most of his greatness to the man who made his wardrobe. Dummy did have excellent taste in such matters. Dummy was also the inventor, or claimed to be, of a kind of gold and silver leather much used in theatrical representations. In his opinion, that silver leather did quite as much for Forrest as Dr. Bird or any other of the playwrights. Forrest used to humor him in this, and other of his hobbies. When traveling with the tragedian in Europe on one occasion, some of the minor actors of the theatre gave a dinner, to which Dummy was invited. In reply to a toast complimentary to America, Dummy made a few remarks, in which he spoke of "the boy as the greatest actor of the age."

"Where," he shouted, "is there another equal to him? Where!" he exclaimed in highest tragic tones, "will you find him." An excited individual, carried away by the eloquence of the speaker, expressed his assent by shouting "Hear! hear!" after the usual English fashion. Dummy, taking the response as a literal reply to his question, shouted in return:

"Where? Show me the man!"

"Hear! hear!" was heard from several voices.

"Where?" roared Dummy, now thoroughly excited and angry. "Where is he? Show me the man; bring him up."

"Hear! hear!"

"Where?"

"Hear! hear!' again resounded through the room.

The excitement increased till Dummy, enraged at their boast of a man they could not produce, rushed from the room, exclaiming: "I should like to see the man that can beat the boy!"

Once when Dummy was on his way to Albany from the western part of the state, with Forrest's wardrobe in charge, he had the usual luck to run out of cash. Calling for a gin cocktail, a cigar and a sheet of paper, he sat down and wrote a thrilling description of his capture by the Esquimaux while on a sealing expedition, and his sufferings unutterable while residing with them for many years, concluding with some account of his escape and the announcement that he would, by particular desire, exhibit on the following day only, the largest and most splendid collection of war dresses and arms of the Esquimaux ever exposed to a civilized community. The next day the large dining-room of the hotel was crowded with curious citizens, who had paid two shillings each, and were admiring the splendid dresses for Richard, Hamlet, Othello, Lear, The Gladiator and Metamora, the shields, stage swords, etc., etc., belonging to Edwin Forrest, and which Dummy gravely informed them were the regular outfits of the northern warriors. After, for some cause not made public, Dummy and Forrest parted company; the former set up a restaurant near the Bowery Theatre, New York.

Dummy, at this time, was a man well advanced in life, tall and erect in person, with firmly conpressed features, an eye like a hawk's, nose slightly Romanesque, hair mottled gray. He wore a funny white hat, a coat of blue with bright brass buttons, and carried a knobby cane. He generally spoke in a sharp, decisive manner, often giving wrong answers, and invariably mistaking the drift of the person with whom he was con-

Interior of the John Street Theatre, 1767. Courtesy Museum of the City of New York.

versing. He took snuff constantly. Why he was called "Dummy" was a wonder, for he was one of the most loquacious men living. No one could ever bear him down in argument—his invariable clincher being an emphatic thump with his cane. He had a sublime contempt for all English stars, and could never listen to their praises with patience.

The great actor, Edwin Forrest, made Dummy his costumer, dresser and traveling companion.

One day John Pavey met the announcement that an extraordinary attraction had been engaged for the coming season. "'Traction," rejoined Dummy. "What sort of 'traction? Legs, I s'pose; that's the thig down-a-days. The bore you cad hubbug the beople, the bedder." "Legs!" said John, rubbing his hands with satisfaction, "image not. Better than that." (Then speaking confidentially through his hands.) "We've secured Macready?" "Bah!" said Dummy with contempt; "he's dobody—can't speak decet Igglish—mere mounteback, sir—mere mounteback," and here he took snuff fiercely.

"Well, mounteback or no mounteback," said Pavey, "he's sure to draw a great card, sir." "Ag," said Dummy, with importance, "can draw a cart, eh? Bedder stick to his trade, then—pay him much bedder," and with a conclusive thump of his stick, he turned away and entered his restaurant.

Dummy was an excellent cook; two fancy dishes, "calapash" and "cala-

pee" are remembered to this day. The calapash was made of old cheese, codfish, onions, mustard, rum and wine; the calapee was the same, with the addition of cabbage. It is difficult to say which was the most in demand. He set all the actors about the Bowery wild at one time with his delicious turtle soup, which was served upon certain days, week after week, to the infinite relish by the actors, and all the gourmants in the vicinity. The day when it was to be had was conspcuously advertised the day previous, by the doomed turtle in person, who was allowed to promenade, at the end of a long string, up and down the sidewalk in front of his restaurant. The next morning he had disappeared, and at noon green turtle soup was ready. After a time it was noticed that while the soup was uniformly good, the turtles were uniform also; that, in fact, they were all as near alike as the Corsican Brothers, or the Two Dromios—nearer, if anything. One day some envious observer put a private mark on his turtleship, which was strangely reproduced on his successors. The fact then leaked, that with a cheap and regular supply of calves heads and one display turtle, Dummy had fed the epicures on turtle soup for months, and the turtle was alive yet.

Dummy's last public appearance was at the old Broadway Theatre (near Broom street), which he opened for a benefit, July 26, 1851, when he played Goldfinch and Silvester Daggerwood, with imitations of George Frederick Cooke, wearing the identical costume in which the giant of the stage had appeared forty years previous, the same suit, doubtless, that hung behind the bar in Dean street and which was probably about as genuine as the famous turtle soup. Two years later, 1853, Dummy crossed the Dark River of Death.

27

UNCLE TOM'S CABIN
AND OTHER EARLY THEATRE

FROM DEC. 2, 1905 ISSUE

INTRODUCTION
OF THE DRAMA
INTO AMERICA

By DR. JUDD.

THE Hallam's Company of Comedians were the first reputable theatrical company ever seen on the American Continent, they came to this country from England in the year 1752. Of all the actors who preceded Hallam's Company, next to nothing is known. They strutted their little hour upon the stage, no doubt affording amusement to thousands and then were heard of no more, only the names of a few have come down to us, and with meagre information as to their performances.

We have extended our researches much beyond the middle of the eighteenth century, and to whom belongs the honor of founding the theatre in the new world, where the first play was produced, what it was, and who performed it, are questions which though answered with great exactness of detail by some writers, are still open to debate and likely always to remain so. In the year 1744 John Moody, an Englishman, with a small company of actors left London for America, and first landed at the Island of Jamaica. Here Moody stopped with his company, played for three years and made a small fortune. He then returned to England and recruited a second company, but instead of coming back with them was induced by Garrick to remain at Drury Lane, where he became celebrated as an Irish actor. However, a few members of the company came over and landed at Boston in 1749. Probably it may have been these actors who, about this time, shocked all New England by playing, with the assistance of volunteer talent, Otway's tragedy of The Orphan, or Unhappy Marriage, at a coffee house in State street, Boston, a proceeding which led the great and general court of Massachusetts to pass an act in March, 1750, to prevent stage plays and other theatrical entertainments.

And, presumably, they were the same company of actors which produced the same play and others in Nassau street, New York, in 1750. They announced themselves as English players. History not knowing their names, there is no reason but these actors should have the credit of being the advance guard of the great thespian army which has since crossed the ocean to America, and of the Hallams, to whom is due the credit of founding the drama in this country by the large company of professional actors they brought into the new world.

In the year 1752, William Hallam, manager of the Goodman's Fields Theatre, London, England, formed a company of actors, ten in all, including the apprentices He put his brother, Lewis Hallam, a low comedian, in charge of the company. Lewis' wife, a beautiful woman of somewhat remarkable histronic ability, was leading lady, and in after years became a great favorite in New York and Philadelphia.

Over twenty plays were selected and cast before Lewis Hallam and his company left London for America, on the Charming Sally, a tobacco ship returning light for a cargo. James Higby was first male player for this band, and also acted as stage manager. Day after day as the old ship plowed through the sea, on her unsteady deck during the long voyage of over sixty days, he diligently rehearsed the actors in the plays with which they purposed to cheer the hearts of people in the new world.

Williamsburg, Va., was the destination of the Charming Sally, with its burden of actors, and not much of anything else besides a few boxes of books, silks, satins, shoes, and European nicknacks for the merchants and the gentlemen of the Virginia colony.

Williamsburg, then the capital of Virginia, was also where the Hallams were to open their colonial theatrical career. They chose the capital of Virginia because they had learned that the inhabitants of that colony were known to be rich, leisurely and society loving people, with enough of refinement to enjoy plays, and with few religious scruples against anything that tended to interest and amuse the upper classes. Long before this period and long afterward, the reading of plays, romances and operas was a pastime in Virginia country houses. The readings might be by the private tutor, and many of the young men of those days prided themselves on being good elocutionists. It was a pastime that filled out rainy days, Sunday afternoons, and when a fiddler could not be had for evening dances.

Williamsburg was somewhat of a disappointment to the Hallams when they first landed. There were not more than twelve hundred inhabitants, white and black, in the town, and there were only about fifteen or twenty "gentlemen's" families resident in the village. Most of the buildings were very insignificant, without it was the capital and the so-called "palace" of the governor, and the William and Mary College, the second oldest college in the United States, which was opened in 1693. There was also the old Bruton parish church, erected in 1678.

In the outskirts of the village the actors rented a warehouse and fitted it up for a theatre. The seats were classified into boxes, pit and gallery, all on the same floor. They had brought some scenery with them from England, and the stage was built at the end of the warehouse. They had to use tallow dips for the foot lights, and also to light the building. Before the time arrived for the opening of the theatre the company became much more discouraged than at first. The old warehouse was right in the woods, and during the still hours of the day, hardly did they see a person stirring in the village. They could hear the singing of bird in the trees, and it looked to them that they had come on a fool's errand to act dramas in the woods. But when the opening night of the theatre came, Sept. 5, 1752, the whole scene was changed like a work of magic. The road leading into Williamsburg were thronged with out-of-date vehicles of every sort, driven by negroes and filled with gayly dressed ladies, whose gallants rode on horseback by their side. The treasury was well replenished, the theatre was crowded, and Shakespeare was acted on the continent for the first time by a trained and competent company.

John Singleton, one of the actors wrote and spoke the following prologue on this, the opening night:

To this New World, from famed Britania's shore,
Through boist'rous seas where foaming billows roar;
The Muse, who Britons charmed for many an age,
Now send her servants forth to tread your stage;
Britain's own race, though far removed to show
Patterns of every virtue they should know,
The Muse's friends, we hope will join our cause,
And crown our best endeavors with applause.

The Merchant of Venice and for the after piece Garrick's farce of Lethe were then played. At the close, the actors found themselves surrounded by groups of planters congratulating them, and, after the old Virginia fashion, offering them the hospitality of their houses. The actor folks soon found that the capacity of their theatre was not large enough to accommodate the throng of people who came to patronize them.

Lewis Hallam, jr., or, as he was called in those days, Lewis Hallam, the second, was the son of Lewis Hallam, the manager of this company. Young Hallam was about sixteen when his father opened with his theatre at Williamsburg, and it was on the opening night that he tried to make his debut. He had one line to speak, but when he found himself in the presence of the audience he was stage struck. He stood motionless and speechless until, bursting into tears, he walked off the stage, making a most inglorious exit. But, nevertheless, before his fathers' company left Williamsburg, he tried it again, and in after years filled a unique place in the history of the American theatre. He was the first star ever known to American playgoers, and the first leading actor whose debut and early experiences were American. He was the foremost actor in America for fifteen years or more before the revolution, and he was the first dramatic manager in New York after the Independence of the United States had been established.

Lewis Hallam, the second, retired from management in 1797, but continued to play in various places in America until his death in Philadelphia, in 1808, at seventy-two years of age.

In the year 1751, one year before Hallam's Company of C o m e d i a n s opened at Williamsburg, Va., the frontier was threatened by the French and Indians, and frequent attacks and dep-

Lewis Hallam, Jr. (1740–1808).
Courtesy Museum of the City of New York.

redations occurred, necessitating some provisions for the public safety. The colony was accordingly divided into military districts, to each of which an adjutant general was appointed, with the rank of major and a salary of £150 per annum. George Washington, who was then about twenty years of age, receiving one of these appoints went to Williamsburg, and entered with zeal on the study of military tactics and strategy, chiefly under Adjutant Muse, a Virginian, and Jacob Van Beaem, a Dutch soldier of fortune. These studies were interrupted by excursion to Barbadoes with his uncle, Lawrence Washington, who was sent thither by his physician. During this trip George had an attack of smallpox . Recovering from this, he returned to Williamsburg to resume his studies about the same time that the Hallams opened their theatre.

Long years after this—the Revolutionary war had been fought, peace declared, George Washington was serving his first term as President of the United States—when in the winter of 1796 Lewis Hallam, the second, was playing at the old Chestnut Street Theatre, Philadelphia. On this occasion he had the pleasure of meeting George Washington, and in their conversation Washington told him that he was present on the opening night of his father's theatre at Williamsburg, witnessed his failure in making his debut, and that many an evening after he was at the old warehouse enjoying the plays, songs and farces of the Hallam comedians.

Not only was George Washington first in war, first in peace, first in the hearts of his countrymen; but was also one of the first to witness the first introduction of the drama into America.

FROM JAN. 17, 1903 ISSUE

THE STAGE ONE HUNDRED YEARS AGO

Some Interesting Facts Concerning Theatrical Events in America a Century Past—Peculiar Customs Existing in the Olden Days

THE OLDEST PLAY BILL

By FRANK WINCH.

Who founded the theatre in America? What was the play, and where? Ever think of this —most interesting, yet ever, try to answer these questions.

In this present-day mad rush for achievements, we seldom turn the backward page—to-day's and to-morrow's events hold our strictest attention. The average theatregoer knows nothing of early theatrical days, the average actor knows no more.

In its inception the American stage was hedged by narrow-gauged prejudices; few of us realize the difficulties under which the actor labored. A backward glance of a hundred years reveals much that should interest the amusement loving public.

Such historians of stage lore as may be found generally accredited Thomas Kean with being the first American Richard. The theatre was in Nassau street, New York, and date of production was March 5, 1750.

About this time Kean was associated with Murray, and it is thought that they were the two young Englishmen that shocked New England beyond measure.

They gave a performance of The Orphan, or Unhappy Marriage, at a coffee-house in State street, Boston, and on its heels the State of Massachusetts passed an act in 1750, "To prevent stage plays and other theatrical entertainments." Parenthetically it may be observed that Boston hasn't quite recovered yet!

There are some who give Hallam credit for founding the American stage, but this seems to be offset by virtue of an old newspaper clipping, which indicates that Hallam and his players produced The Merchant of Venice at Williamsburg, capital of Virginia, on September 5, 1752.

The following playbill is of peculiar interest, as it is one of the oldest in existence:

"BY AUTHORITY.
On Friday evening, the 9th of December, 1785, the Theatre in the City of Albany
Will be Opened
With an occasional Prologue
By Mr. Allen.
After which he will present a Comedy in two acts, called,
CROSS PURPOSES.

Mr. Grubb and Robin	Mr. Moore
George Bevil	Mr. Bentley
Harry Bevil	Mr. Warsdale
Servant	Mr. Bellair
Chapeau, F. Bevil & Consol	Mr. Allen
Emily	Mrs. Moore
Housemaid	Mrs. Bentley
Mrs. Grubb	Mrs. Allen

After the Comedy,
An Eulogy on Free Masonry,
By Brother Moore,
To be followed by a Dance called
LA POLONESE.
To conclude with a Comedy of three acts, written by Shakespeare, called,
CATHARINE AND PETRUCHIO,
or
THE TAMING OF THE SHREW.

FROM MARCH 17, 1906 ISSUE

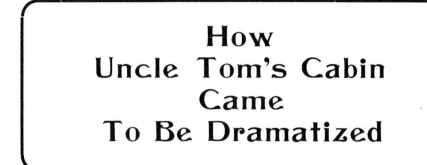

How Uncle Tom's Cabin Came To Be Dramatized

By DOCTOR JUDD.

(Written for The Billboard.)

IT was only a short time after Harriet Beecher Stowe's famous story, Uncle Tom's Cabin was out, that it was seen to contain dramatic possibilities, and Charley Taylor, long connected with Purdy's National Theatre in Chatham street, New York, was among the first to grasp at them, and on August 24, 1852, produced the first version seen in New York.. It was hastily written, a mere "catch-house" affair (as he afterward acknowledged), ignoring Topsy and Eva altogether. It was all Uncle Tom and George Harris. Meantime, the "Uncle Tom," by which is meant the version that has kept the stage till the present day, grew into being at the Troy Museum under singular and interesting circumstances. George C. Howard was the manager of the theatre at the time, and had been for a year or so. The play of the evening was Oliver Twist, in the adaptation of which was a child's character, that of Little Dick, the sick pauper boy, who takes a tearful farewell of Oliver as he runs away from the poorhouse. Without any idea that she would be more than a "dummy," it was suggested that Little Cordelia, the manager's four-year-old daughter, be dressed as Little Dick, and placed behind the paling for Oliver to talk to; but when at rehearsal, the mother, Mrs. G. C. Howard who was playing Oliver, caught the baby up and went through the scenes the little thing responded just in the proper place, "Dood by—tum again." "Well, now," said Mrs. Howard, "if she is going to do anything like that, better teach her the lines." And, accordingly, during the day, in her mothers' lap little Cordelia was taught the speeches of Little Dick. Night came; the fat baby face was skillfully painted to represent consumption, and duly clad in her brother's suit, and with a little spade in her hand, Cordelia Howard made her first appearance on any stage.

UPON THE STAGE

On came the fugitive Oliver, while Cordelia, according to direction, dug vigorously at the pile of dirt dumped in the corner. "I'm running away, Dick," said Oliver. "Lunning away, is you?" replied the little chit. Then, with a full perception of the character, but with the most self-possessed oblivion of the written words, the child gave, in her own language, the sense of the scene:

"I'll come back and see you some day, Dick," said Mrs. Howard, as Oliver.

"It yont be no use, Olly, dear," sobbed the little actress, "when oo tum back, I yont be digging 'ittle graves, I'll be all dead an' in a 'ittle grave by myself." This, in a voice, trembling with feigned emotion, yet clear as a bell, and distinctly heard by every person in the building. Such a shower of tears as swept over that theatre! Actors and auditors were alike affected. The Oliver (naturally enough) broke down, but Cordelia's hit and her parent's fortunes were made from that very night.

It was at once decided that such infantile emotional talent as this, must not be wasted, and Mr. Howard began looking about for some appropriate channel through which to present it to the public. The whole country was talking about the book, "Uncle Toms' Cabin," and thousands of eyes were being moistened at Eva's saint-like sayings. "The very part for our Cordelia said George Howard, her father!"

George L. Aiken, a cousin of the Howards, undertook the work of dramatization, and with Mr. Howard's advice and assistance in less than a week it was a thing accomplished. It was produced in Troy, N. Y., September, 1852, and had the amazing run of one hundred nights. The play was cast in Troy, in part as follows: Eva, Cordelia Howard; Topsy, Mrs. George C. Howard; St. Clair, Mr. George C. Howard; George Harris, G. L. Aiken; Phineas Fletcher, C. K. Fox; Gumption Cute, W. J. LeMoyne; Uncle Tom, G. C. Germore. From Troy the Howards went to Albany, N. Y., and on July 18, 1853, brought out the piece at Purdy's National Theatre, where it ran almost uninterruptedly until May 13, 1854.

Mr. Howard was one of the first to introduce one play entertainments. That is, until the advent of Uncle Tom in New York, no evening at the theatre in those days was thought complete without an afterpiece, or a little ballet dancing. When Mr. Howard told the manager Uncle Tom must

constitute the entire performance, he flouted the idea; said that he would have to shut up in a week. But Howard carried his point, and the theatre didn't shut up. People came to the theatre by the hundreds who were never inside its doors before, and the Howards played Uncle Tom over three hundred times during that engagement.

Some of these old-time players are still living. Cordelia Howard is now residing in Cambridge, Mass. Mrs. Howard, her mother, is still alive and a hearty old lady. W. J. LeMoyne is still acting. All the other members of the old company are dead. The death of George C. Howard occurred Jan. 18, 1887, and with it ended the theatrical career of the Howard's in Uncle Tom.

FROM AUG. 13, 1904 ISSUE

Old Theatrical Days
DESCRIBED AND ILLUSTRATED

BY DOCTOR JUDD

All who have witnessed a performance of The Lights 'o London will remember the celebrated Jarvis Family, and the manner in which they traveled about the country in a gypsy-like vehicle, stopping here and there to give their unexcelled interpretations of the tragic and comic creations of the day. In the same manner the drama was first presented in the small towns throughout the United States. The manager and his actors traveled and slept in their covered wagon in much the same manner as did the Jarvis family of fiction. These companies were generally made up of English actors, for in those days very few Americans aspired to historionic honors. The actors and the plays were a good deal like those described by Dickens in his various works. As was the custom in England, these players appeared in a first piece full of strong situations, broadsword combats and rantings of the leading man, all of which pleased the audience. Every act had a good, strong death scene at the end and the audience was never appeased until all the dead appeared before the curtain, in response to the encores. The drama was followed by a short farce.

Very few towns had any halls for the players to act in, and they had to take any empty room they could find, which was generally the dining-room of the tavern. Sometimes they had to take the blacksmith shop, utilizing soap boxes, barrels, pails, etc. for seats.

Many an anecdote has been told of the old time strolling theatrical troupes that were perambulating this country during the last century. One of the old time story-telling actors with whom the writer of this article came in contact in his early traveling life and listened to was Sol Smith, in those days one of the brightest of American comedians, and one of the earliest of the American managers in the Southwest. He was also one of the pioneer traveling stars in the theatrical firmament.

He could tell an anecdote lightly and brightly and with a charm peculiar to many of the men of the old school theatrical profession.

Sol Smith, or Old Sol, as he was called by everybody in those days of long ago, was an uncle of Sol Smith Russell, the comedian who died a few years ago.

Old Sol used to say when he was in a story-telling mood, that he made his first appearance on the dramatic stage In a Coffin. When Sol was 14 years old or thereabouts, he was working in his uncle's store at Albany, N. Y. About this time, 1814, John Bernard, an actor of considerable celebrity both in England and in this country, opened a theatre at Albany, and Sol, when he could raise the wherewith, attended. Sol was stage struck, and when the customers came to his uncle's store for sugars and calicoes, they would find Sol hidden under the counter studying Shakespeare.

A magnificent presentation of Richard, the Third, was advertised to be put on one night at the theatre. Sol was short of cash just at this time. His uncle was a deacon in the church and was opposed to theatres. He called theatres the devil's playhouse, and would not give Sol money to attend them but Sol thought he must see Richard, the Third. As he had no money to pay his way through the front door, he went in by the way of the back door when it was unguarded, and concealed himself up over the stage in the carpenters' gallery. Here by peeping down upon

---

Very few towns had any halls for the players to act in .... Sometimes they had to take the blacksmith shop, utilizing soap boxes, barrels, pails, etc. for seats.

---

the stage he could see all that was going on. Sol was enjoying the play until the second or third act, when he heard some men making their way directly to his hiding place.

He had just time enough to pop into a large box that was near by and close the door (or lid). The men were after this box. It was King Henry's coffin. He felt himself being conveyed down stairs and then placed upon the bier. Sol lay quiet as the injured King would have lain had he been in Sol's place. The bier was carried by four supernumeraries onto the stage, followed by weeping Lady Anna and all the court. Little did the lady imagine she was weeping over a living corpse. When the procession moved off the stage to Whitefriars to inter the King (or Sol), the men of the bier dumped their precious burden up against the wall, but since it left Sol head down, he let out an unearthly yell. The four supernumeraries were so frightened and terrified to hear such an unearthly voice issuing from the coffin, which they supposed to be empty, that they quickly made their escape out of the back door. One of them never returned to the theatre, but joined the church and afterwards prepared himself for the ministry and never spared the theatre or theatrical people in his sermons, telling his hearers that he had a most mysterious warning when he was a young man.

Sol finally became a "super" at the theatre, and one night was blackened up with a plentiful supply of burnt cork and oil to make himself a fit associate of the renowned Three-Fingered Jack. It being late when the performance concluded, he forgot to wash his face previous to returning home, and went to bed, black as he was, and in the morning as usual on such occasions, overslept himself. A servant was sent up-stairs to awaken him, she seeing a black face peeping from under the bed clothes ran down stairs three steps at a time, and declared there was a nigger in Sol's bed. This announcement brought the whole family to his room; an explanation was inevitable. He visited the playhouse no more that winter.

In a few years after this, 1820, Sol had drifted out West, and was working in a printing shop at Vincennes, Ind., when Alexander Drake with his theatre came along. Sol made application to Manager Drake for an engagement and was accepted, and here began Sol's theatrical career.

"The Drake Family came to this country from England in the fore part of the last

---

century. Alexander Drake, his wife, and his sons and daughters were all actors. They brought with them the English custom of traveling across the country in covered vans. On the top of the family chaise was carried their wardrobe, which they changed about to meet the exegencies that arose in costuming the dramas of the times. After hanging the limited scenery they carried, this wonderful family, with the aid of necessary supernumeraries, presented such plays as Othello, Virginius, Long Tom Coffin, Love's Sacrifice, etc. The drama was always followed by a short farce. For years the Drakes toured the East, but as the West opened up they drifted to Ohio and Indiana. The elder Drake was a Christian gentleman. He said grace before each meal, conducted family prayers, and lived a life that thespians of to-day would do well to pattern after. There was always a Bible in the old, covered wagon. After touring Ohio and Indiana for a number of years, Manager Drake finally began to hunger for a field further West, so he moved on with his old covered wagon and his actors' company towards the setting sun to the region of the scalping-knife and the tamahawk, where they broke the histrionic ice, and, like the proverbial bird, caught the meandering worm and filled their coffers. Their fame did not perish with them, as to-day they are known in the dramatic profession as the pioneers of the drama in the South-west and the upper Mississippi. When Sol Smith joined the Drakes the company consisted of only six actors. These were the times when one actor doubled and played many parts.

Sol has often related his experiences with the Drakes, a company so limited in numbers, but who grappled successfully with Pizarro, The Poor Gentleman, and other equally full plays. When they were playing the above play, Pizarro, he was the Spanish army entire, and he also had to officiate as High Priest of the Sun, then lose both of his eyes, and feel his way guided by a little boy, through the heat of the battle, to tell the audience what they must imagine but could not see. Afterwards, his sight being restored and his black cloak dropped, he acted as sentinel over Alonzo. Besides this, he was obliged to find the sleeping child; fight a blow or two with Rolla, fire off three guns at him, while crossing the bridge; beat the alarm drum, and do at least two-thirds of the shouting. He said that his exertions were nothing in comparsion with those of the Drakes, particularly Sam Drake, who frequently played two or three parts in one play, and after being killed in the last scene, was obliged to fall far enough off the stage and creep around in front to play slow music on his violin as the old muslin curtain descended, for he was also the whole orchestra.

While Sol was jogging over the country with the Drakes in their covered vans and wagons, stopping in towns to play a night or two, they at one time were arrested for being pirates. This was on one of their journeys from Steubenville, Ohio to Pittsburg, Pa., when they had put up for the night at a very small village on the Virginia side, about midway between the two places. At the supper table the conversation of the company turned on the performances of the night previous at Steubenville, which had consisted, among other things, of the pantomine of Don Juan. The landlady and the waitress were very much attracted by the conversation, and in going back and forth to bring in the eatables they snatched up only a part of the actors' conversation. They heard Manager Drake say, "I observed that Davis, after murdering Don Guzman and Don Ferdinand, was too slow in getting to Sea-there was time enough for the whole town to be alarmed—that the combat with Ferdinand was shockingly bad, and that if he did not improve in fighting, he had better leave the profession." Sam Drake remarked of Lucas that he had murdered Doctor Pangloss a few nights before, and that there was no use of his trying to play the part. A good deal of similar chit-chat took place, to hear which did the waiting maid and landlady "seriously incline." In the meantime, the landlord and the idlers around the tavern had been out to the barn inspecting the actors' wagons and saw hanging up on the inside of the baggage wagon, guns, pistols, swords, etc. which the actors used on the stage. After the actors had retired for the night, the landlord, the villagers and the women folks put this and that together and came to the conclusion that the actors were a band of escaping pirates. They sent a man over to the country

IN YE OLDEN DAYS.

seat for the sheriff to come over and arrest them. In the morning when the actors were about to continue their journey, they were surprised to see quite a crowd collected about their wagons, and as they started, a man with long whiskers and some of the others stepped up and seizing their horses by the bridles, ordered them to stop. Big Whiskers addressing the actors said. "Strangers, you are in old Virginia, and you mus'n't think of getting off. We don't mean to let pirates pass through here, no way, no how." "Pirates!" exclaimed Manager Drake. "Do you take us for pirates?" "No," answered Whiskers, "We don't take you at all, but the sheriff will." "What reason have you for thinking us pirates?" Manager Drake ventured to ask. What reason!" Whiskers was still the spokesman— That's a good one! In the first place, what can honest people do with such a heap of plunder as you are toting in these wagons? Nextly, your confessions last night before Peggy Duncan and the landlord's wife while you were all eating supper. Don't one of you men like to have been taken before he escaped to the ship, after killing two Dons? Didn't you threaten to discharge him, because he fought so bad? Then that 'ere doctor whom one of your people murdered 'tother night in Steubenville, Dr. Panglosh, I believe was his name." Soon the sheriff arrived and being a man who had seen more of the outside world took it all in, and roared with laughter. He took Whiskers and the others aside and explained that they were actors, instead of pirates.

In the first half of the last century not a few of the newly settled towns and cities along American waterways depended for dramatic entertainments on floating theatres. These enterprises first attracted notice in connection with the growth of commerce along the Erie Canal, in New York State, but the idea soon spread to the Ohio and Mississippi Rivers.

In the early history of the drama in America there is no chapter more curious than those days when, in the absence of railroads, enterprising thespians utilized the great rivers and waterways to supply the newly settled towns along their banks with theatrical entertainment.

The Erie Canal was completed in 1825, and it was a success from the very start, contributing largely to the growth of the towns between Albany and Buffalo. For a long time it was the great artery of passage as well as freight traffic between the northwestern sections of the United States and the newly settled states — what was then called the West. Light packet boats, drawn by frequently changed horses which were made to proceed at a trot, made the trip from Albany to Buffalo, 363 miles, in three and a half days.

New towns sprang up along the banks of the canal and the older towns took a new impulse and grew very fast. The inhabitants began to desire amusements, but in most of the towns theatre companies coming along could not find halls or suitable rooms to play in. They were barred out of the churches, which could be rented only by lecturers and concert companies.

About 1836 Henry Butler, an old theatrical manager, saw no reason why the Erie Canal could not be utilized for the amusement business as well as carrying passengers and freight. He had previously been up and down the Mohawk valley with his theatre company and had found difficulty in finding rooms to play in, so he conceived the idea of fitting up a canal-boat for a traveling theatre, and in the same year he started for Troy, N. Y., with his floating theatre and museum, stopping from one day to a week in a place, according to its size. In the daytime he exhibited only the museum part of his "show," which contained all the usual concomitants— stuffed birds, lions, tigers, Washington, Napoleon, Captain Kidd, the Twelve Apostles in wax, etc. In the evening his small company of thespians gave performances on the little stage erected at the end of the boat.

> **Henry Butler, an old theatrical manager, saw no reason why the Erie Canal could not be utilized for the amusement business, as well as carrying passengers and freight.**

He had among his actors Jack Turner, who had a reputation for playing sailor parts, and the company would present such plays as Black-eyed Susan, Long Tom Coffin, and other dramas of the sea. Butler sailed up and down the raging canal with his playship in this manner for a number of years till he went blind; but he stuck to his old boat, which he finally turned entirely into a museum. Although blind, he could be found at all exhibition hours in his little box office dispensing tickets to adults for one shilling, and to children under a certain age for sixpence. He had no way of telling a child's age except by ascertaining the height. This he would do by feeling for their heads. If that useful appendage came under his conception of the six cents line, the owner got in at children's prices. The boys used to fool him by stooping, consequently he often touched and passed judgment on heads out of their proper sphere.

In these river towns old people may be found to-day who will recall their younger days, and will declare that they saw better acting in the old boat performances than they see in the luxurious theatres of to-day. Many long to see again those old thespians on the little stage built upon one end of the boat, the muslin curtain, the tallow candles for footlights. They would like to sit once more on the hard board seats stretched from one side of the boat to the other. The only undesirable seats on the boat were under the blazing tallow-dropping chandelier, which consisted of a circular hoop with tallow dips, hanging over the audience from the ceiling of the old boat.

Another floating theatre famous in its day was that built and managed for a number of years by William Chapman, Sr., who was born in England in 1764. When quite a young man he joined Richardson's Traveling Theatre, which at that time was one of the principal exhibitions of its kind visiting the fairs throughout England, traveling, exhibiting and lodging in their own vans. In 1803 he made his first appearance on the London stage as Sir Bertram, in The Jew. In 1827 he came to America, and September 14 of the same year he appeared at the Broadway Theatre, New York, as Billy Lackaday in Sweethearts and Wives. The next year he brought over to this country his family, wife, sons and daughters, who had all followed in the footsteps of their father and had adopted the same profession. Shortly after Chapman formed a company of thespians, consisting of his folks and others, which he called the Chapman Family, and started for the Southwest. At Pittsburg, Pa., they made a long stop, and for the want of a hall or suitable room, they played in the dining-room of the Old Red Lion hotel. While in Pittsburg one Captain Brown built for them a floating theatre, which was the first of the kind that played up and down the Ohio and Mississippi Rivers, visiting all the principal towns. He died on his boat in 1839 and was buried at Manchester, Mississippi. Mrs. Chapman then undertook the management and conducted it very successfully for a number of years.

FROM SEPT. 10, 1904 ISSUE

THE OLD SCHOOL ACTORS.

The Drama Before and After the Civil War.

By Doctor Judd.

The few remaining actors who trod the theatre boards far back in the early or middle part of the last century can recall with the deepest pleasure the days that have gone, although these days were often fraught with hardship and deprivations which few actors of today can recognize. But since those days years have gone swiftly by, and have brought wondrous changes. Could the old actors of the fifties then have fallen into a Rip Van Winkle sleep, and awaken today, no amount of evidence would convince them that this is the same country they knew and over which they perambulated in the long ago. In no time or country in the world have such wondrous changes taken place in so short a space of time. The old halls have given place to the modern opera houses that have sprung up like mushrooms all over the country.

* * *

Garry Hough, an old-time actor and traveling theatrical manager, who in the early days was touring the western countries with a small company in a covered wagon, stopping here and there to present Uncle Tom's Cabin to the eager public, anxious to witness this play, told when relating his reminiscences that when he was knocking about the country with his company in his early days, getting plenty of experience and not much of anything else, they had played Hamlet, Macbeth, Damon and Pythias in a blacksmith shop, and that they had a curtain, which was about all they did have that bore any semblance to a playhouse. Soap boxes, barrels, pails, etc., made good orchestra chairs, and the hard dirt floor of the shop made a stage true to nature.

A great many theatres in the early days were not known as theatres, but were called museums instead. Nearly all of them had small collections of wax figures, stuffed birds and animals. In order that there could be some excuse for the use of the word museum, a great many old-time theatre-goers had an idea that this stock of oddities and ill-appointed and very dubitable curiosities, took the stigma off from their attending the theatrical part of the show.

* * *

The successful theatrical managers of today sink into utter insignificence when compared with the doings of that old distinguished individual and theatrical manager, John S. Potter, who flourished in this country from the thirties to the sixties. There was not a town from New York to Ohio and Michigan, nor on the western waters from Cincinnati to New Orleans that did not have some experience with him: not a steamboat captain nor a tavern-keeper in any town accessible to theatrical enterprises but retained "notes" of remembrances of him.

Manager Potter built and fitted up more theatres and traveled a greater number of miles with large companies than any other manager of those days ever thought of traveling. He at one time took a company of twenty-two persons from Cleveland, O., to Richmond, Va., with but seventy-five cents in his pocket to start with.

One time in the forties Manager Potter arrived in St. Louis with his company of thespians on his way to Chicago. The captain of the boat which brought him from Memphis swore that the baggage should not be taken away until the passage and freight bills were paid. This was in the forenoon, and before night Potter had the whole company and property shipped on board a Galena boat. The captain who brought him to St. Louis accepting his notes for the debt, and besides that, indorsed notes for him to pay, not only the passage of his company to Galena, but across the country to Chicago.

Potter was blest with a weakness in a nerve of one of his eyes from which a tear was always involuntarily starting and rolling down his cheek on timely occasions when he was pouring his tale of woe into the hall owner's, landlord's and steamboat captain's ears. This weakness was the source of Potter's strength. No person was ever found who could resist that "tear."

The great Napoleon in his day moved his armies from one place to another with some speed, but he had the means. Potter moved his army from one extremity of the country to the other whenever he had a streak of bad luck without any means whatever, except that "tear."

The successful theatrical managers of today sink into utter insignificance when compared with John S. Potter. The-Man-With-A-Tear-In-His-Eye was an epithet that clung to Potter till he passed away.

In the fifties Manager Potter opened a theatre during the legislative session at the capital of one of the southern states. Potter, as usual, was low in funds, therefore he borrowed $50 from a lawyer of the place with a solemn promise that the amount should be returned out of the first night's receipts. The time passed on until nearly to the end of the legislative period and the theatrical season and no sign of the $50 appeared to be forthcoming, though the debtor had been "often requested" to refund. In the meantime reports of Potter's facility in "putting off" duns reached the lawyer's ears, and in a merry mood he laid a wager with some friends that he would visit the manager in his box office and would not depart without his money. If he failed he was to set up the wine. To secure himself against the possibility of failure, the attorney armed himself with a cowhide and a pair of pistols, and entered the sanctum. His friends stationed themselves near the premises and within hearing. At first loud words were heard between the debtor and the creditor, but gradually the voices of the dun and the dunned sank into a low tone of friendly converse. In a short time the attorney sallied forth and encountered his friends, who were in waiting. Addressing his friends, he said: "Come on, the wine will have to be set up by me. I've lost." "Oh, then," said one friend, "you didn't get your fifty dollars?" "Get my fifty dollars!" answered the loser of the wager. "Get my fifty! I would like to see the man that could get fifty out of him. Curse the fellow! I went in there determined to have the money or take it out of his hide, and before I left—I am almost ashamed to own it—hang me, if he didn't borrow another fifty of me." That tear did the business once more. When Potter was in hard luck and could not carry around a large company of actors to fill the cast of the play, he himself would take the leading part and also other parts, doubling, thribbling and quadrupling characters to an enormous extent in tragedies, comedies, farces innumerable.

In the fifties and sixties Potter was one of the early pioneers to establish theatres throughout California, Oregon, Nevada, Utah, and in the Cherokee Nation. The sobriquet, The-Man-With-A-Tear-In-His-Eye clung to Potter till he passed away from this earth.

* * *

The palmy days of the drama in this country commenced along in the forties, when the Eastern, Southern and some of our Western cities had fairly well appointed theatres. By the middle of the century most of the places throughout the United States that called themselves cities also had their own theatres. Most of them had stock companies, which supported the stars, who then traveled without companies.

These old theatres were run as a theatre should be, and the actors were actors in every sense of the word. The pieces presented were legitimate. The "Slap-stick" and hurrah comedians of today were never dreamed of by those actors of the old school. Every star had his or her lengthy repertoire of heavy, legitimate dramas, high comedies and tragedies, in all of which every member of the home company was expected to be perfect. It was hard lines for the actors. A different piece was put on each night. and those in the cast often studied until the day was dawning, and then managed to arise and get to the theatre for the morning rehearsal. To get along easily these old "legits" had to be perfect in 30 or 40 different plays.

Many actors who were drudging away in these old theatres became shining lights of the dramatic profession, and for years afterwards remembered vividly the well trodden boards of their old playhouses, and the old school, old style in manner in which the drama was ground out. If any youth of today, who is aspiring to a theatrical career behind the glittering footlights and canvass trees, could go back and have a week's engagement in any of those theatres, it would knock all the notions of being an Irving or a Mansfield out of his noddle in short order.

The most successful and popular American play that was being produced on our stage before and after the Civil War and even to this day, was Uncle Tom's Cabin.

The Howard family were the first of the old school actors to play this piece. They staged the adaptation which had been made from Mrs. Stowe's book by Geo. L. Aitken. They opened with it in Troy, New York, where it had a run of over three months. From there they took it to the National Theatre in New York, where they gave their first performance on July 18, 1853. After the New York run, they took the play entour.

George C. Howard acted St. Clair, and made an ideal southern planter. On and off the stage he invariably wore a black broadcloth frock coat with brass buttons, and he always had on lavender trousers. So, when he was around the hotels and on the streets of the towns where he was playing, people who had seen him at the theatre would recognize him at once and would say, "There goes Eva's father." Mrs. Howard was Topsy, and there has never been any one yet to equal her in the character. Little Cordelia, her daughter, was a born actress. I have never seen anything more natural and beautiful than the way in which she played little Eva. She required no training for it; it came natural to her. Many a time I have seen a big crowd following her when she was out on the streets or at the stores shopping with her mother. They wanted to get a peep at little Eva with her long, golden hair.

The rest of the cast had in it Green C. Germon, who acted Uncle Tom; Geo. L. Fox, who afterwards became the famous pantomimist, Humpty Dumpty, played Phineas Fletcher; his brother, Charles K. Fox, took the part of that droll individual, Gumption Cute. George Harris was played by Samuel M. Siple, and Eliza, by Mrs. W. G. Jones. N. B. Clark was Simon Legree. W. J. Le Moyne, who was with the Howard family when they first produced the play at Troy, created and acted the part of Deacon Perry. In 1857 the Howards went to England under the management of P. T. Barnum, where it made a tremendous hit.

On returning from England the Howards played Uncle Tom in St. Louis and Cincinnati. A few of the southern towns wouldn't tolerate the piece. It was performed in Baltimore, but Washington had to be avoided for fear of a riot. The pleadings of little Eva were listened to in many a case where some had come intending to interrupt and disturb the performance. Many slave owners having pet slaves beheld the play and went away wondering if slavery was just the thing. Managers in many cases were afraid to book the play at their theatres. Even the Howards' first appearance in New York had been accomplished with difficulty, owing to the timidity of the various playhouses.

FROM DEC. 1, 1934 ISSUE

The New York Theatrical Season 1854~1855

By EUGENE BURR

The days of 1854-'55 were the days of star repertory, combined with what amounted to permanent stock companies. The old repertory system had died out under the popular weight of traveling stars. Regular stock had not yet sprung up under the master hands of the New York managers of the late 1800s. Stars traveled alone or with a few of their chief leads over the land and were supported in their engagements by the permanent local company. Stars brought their own repertory with them, and, except in the intervals between star engagements, the always-present afterpieces were often the only things upon which the permanent company could try its individual hand.

Tours made money in those days—tours to principal cities with their own permanent supporting companies or barnstorming sessions to the one-night stands. They could last well over a year—sometimes several years—and all players of note indulged in them.

New York was far from being the theatrical center of the land, but it was representative, since all of the best played there sooner or later. A cross-section of New York, with its methods of production and the types of plays produced, would therefore be a cross-section of the country, the theatrical enterprises of which were so many, so far-flung and so universal that it would be a hopeless task to try to unravel and describe them.

Let's turn to New York then and see what its theatrical fare was during the fall of 1854, just 40 years before the founding of The Billboard.

The Broadway Theater, regarded as the home of stars, opened for the season on August 21, with George H. Barrett succeeding Thomas Barry as stage manager, N. B. Clarke as prompter, La Manna as leader of the orchestra, Heister as chief scenic artist, John Furze as machinist, S. Wallis as props and Mrs. Wallis in charge of costumes. It opened feebly, with repertory featuring Henry Farren and Louisa Howard. two comparative unknowns.

The season really got under way August 28 with the engagement of Jean Davenport, who established herself as the first of the really great Camilles. The sad adventures of the lady of the camellias ran for no less than 12 nights—and without an afterpiece!—which made it a tremendous success. It was followed on September 11 by another Davenport, E. L., an extremely versatile actor, and therefore not quite as popular as some of his more personality-bound brethren.

The big engagement, however, began September 18, when the large, sonorous, powerful and impressive Forrest appeared in his rigid repertoire. Forrest by this time had boiled his plays down to a certain few favorites, opening as Richelieu and running thru the rest. The engagement lasted until October 9.

Then the house went musical for the singing of Louisa Pyne, a homely but charming and lovely voiced warbler, who was probably the greatest sensation since Jenny Lind. She was supported by Harrison, a crystal-clear tenor, who looked something like William Powell, and by her sister Susan,

the repertory including La Somnambula, The Bohemian Girl, Maritana, Fra Diavolo and The Crown Diamonds. The Pynes, incidentally, were aunts of no less a stage personage than Mrs. Thomas Whiffen.

Meanwhile the regular company had supported the dramatic stars and had appeared in a long list of afterpieces. One player, Davidge, even supported the Pynes in their musical engagement. He, along with Josephine Gougenheim, was the standby in the afterpieces. Miss Gougenheim during the season far outdistanced her sister Adelaide, who was also a member of the company. They were a pair of lovely lasses, according to reports.

Back to the drama, the house next had an engagement of Agnes Robertson, a young sensation of the season before, who seemed to specialize in boys' parts and whose charm won her huge acclaim. It was at her benefit on November 10 (almost exactly 40 years before the founding of The Billboard) that the great Dion Boucicault made his New York debut as an actor, appearing as Sir Charles Coldstream in Used Up.

The middle season was taken up with return engagements: The Harrison-Pyne troupe, Miss Davenport in another week of Camille, and then at last a long engagement of the Pynes, from December 18 to February 19, in which the big hit was a musical version of Cinderella, which ran a full month, less a few nights' intermission because of the hoarseness of the star.

The rest of the season had E. L. Davenport again; his wife, Fanny Vining, and both of them together—plus a late engagement of Mr. and Mrs. Barney Williams, huge popular favorites, with Barney playing honest Irishmen and his wife Yankee maidens. They, of course, had their own special repertory.

The Gougenheim sisters went to California early in June, taking a benefit before they left.

Wallack's (J. W. Wallack, manager and star) opened September 7, for a season of its famous "old comedies," with The Irish Heiress and A Phenomenon in a Smock Frock. The company had played together for a long while, and Wallack's was regarded as the finest home of "old comedy" in the land.

Two important debuts marked the beginning of the season. J. H. Stoddart, the younger, long a fixture on the New York stage, appeared the first night, remaining with the company at a salary of $15 a week. And on the second night Douglas Stewart (better known as E. A. Sothern) made his Wallack's debut in Old Heads and Young Hearts. He had previously appeared in Barnum's Museum.

Brougham was a standby at Wallack's, along with many other well-known players. The repertory included The School for Scandal, She Stoops To Conquer, A Bold Stroke for a Husband and others, along with plays of a somewhat later vintage and just a few novelties.

September 25 Wallack himself swung into action with his repertory, including Much Ado, London Assurance, Spring and Autumn, Don Caesar de Bazan and others. A successful revival of The Brigand served to introduce Rosa Bennett, an English actress who stayed for but one season, and who scored her biggest success a little later in The Sisters, adapted by Fitz-James O'Brien from the French. Another O'Brien play, a two-acter called A Gentleman From Ireland, was frequently given on the same bill as

Lester Wallack's full-length success, Two to One. Audiences in those days got their money's worth.

O'Brien, incidentally, is an interesting figure in his own right. He was the first of New York's Greenwich Village bohemians.

The runs of Two to One and The Sisters took the house to January 13. (We could envy such runs even now.) Then came the most pretentious production of the season, Bulwer's Night and Morning, adapted to the stage by Brougham, the actor. In early spring there was a succession of the old comedies that the company did so well, including The Road to Ruin, The School for Scandal, The Rivals, Town and Country, She Would and She Would Not and many others, while in late spring there were a few new pieces, none very important.

Burton's, still popular, but hard pressed by Wallack's, opened September 4, turning from its "old comedies" to modern farce—and with excellent early-season success. According to Prof. G. C. D. Odell, whose great Annals of the New York Stage is a priceless reference, Burton advertised, rather wistfully, at the start of the season: "A new and extensive parquet has been constructed; the house has been fresh painted, carpeted and matted, and all the seats newly upholstered. New ventilators have been opened in all parts of the house. The company will, as usual, be the best in America."

The early season showed various Burton revivals and new pieces, the only visiting star being J. H. Stoddart the elder (father of the lad who was making his debut at Wallack's), a Scotch actor who flopped rather dismally as Sir Anthony Absolute. Early October saw the annual engagement of Henry Placide, while all the while, doing yeoman service, was Kate Saxon. She even appeared as Bob Nettles in To Parents and Guardians, which was almost the personal property of Agnes Robertson, at the Broadway.

Popular was a play called Ben Bolt (based on the ballad), which had a character named Mary Moonlight, a forerunner, perhaps, of Benn Levy's Sarah Moonlight. She was played by Marian Macarthy, who made her debut at Burton's October 16, and who stayed to play leads, including Ariel in The Tempest.

The Upper 10 and the Lower 20 ... was a horrific problem drama of a bad wife, sleazy lover, a trusting husband and a great deal of death.

A big success was scored by The Upper 10 and the Lower 20, by T. DeWalden, an actor, which was a horrific problem drama of a bad wife, sleazy lover, a trusting husband and a great deal of death. It offered a new type of role for Burton. And then came another huge popular success with Boucicault's local skit, Apollo in New York, which often played with the previous drama as a double bill. The depths plumbed by these 1854 farces can be shown by Apollo's cast of characters: "Jupiter, disguised as Sandy Hook, Mrs. Partington, etc."; "Apollo, or Apollini, a grand Italian tenor"; "Mars, as a Bowery fireman"; "Mercury, as a penny-a-liner"; "Cupid, as a newsboy"; "New York, one side as Fifth avenue, one side as the Bowery, and one side as something else"; "Mrs. Screecher Crowe"; "Abby Fulsome"; "Juno (Hell Gate)."

Burton played Jupiter—including a burlesque of Mrs. Partington in a Woman's-Rights-Convention scene; Miss Macarthy was Apollo, while New York, a seemingly difficult but expansive part, was played by Johnston.

FROM MARCH 21, 1908 ISSUE

A Player's Memories

By John W. Blaisdell

THE first production, at Niblo's, of The Black Crook, created a great sensation. The ballets were elaborate, and they appealed to different nationalities because of the characteristic dances of each nation, in which the premieres were of the country represented, be it American, French, English, Italian, Spanish or German. The Reverend Mr. Smythe, who preached at Cooper Institute to immense crowds, attacked the extravaganza and especially its ballet, for what he called its indecency.

The New York Herald gave wide publicity to these attacks, and it was found that The Herald had, in fact, engaged Mr. Smythe for the express purpose of making attacks upon The Black Crook, and, as a consequence, it was stated in all of Niblo's programs and posters, "This theatre does not advertise in The New York Herald." These notes, together with the preacher's lectures, roused the curiosity of the public, and the production had a long and very successful run. The fortunes of the managers were made. This was, perhaps, the first time that the abuse of a play served to make it an unqualified success as a financial venture.

The dramatic members of the original cast of The Black Crook, leaving out singers and dancers, etc., have all passed to the Great Beyond, with two exceptions, George Boniface, of New York, and myself.

During the war I was engaged by John Owens to play at his theatre in Washington. I remember the trouble of Mr. Owens in procuring a substitute to take his place at the front. The first one he engaged took the $300 bounty paid him by Mr. Owens and disappeared. So another had to be found, and when I arrived in Washington Mr. Owens had just secured another substitute, paying him $300. With the full determination that he should not escape, Mr. Owens brought the man to the dressing room, where he was kept until after the performance, as he could not be sworn in until the next morning. When the play was over, Mr. Owens said to me. "Blaisdell, I am going to take this man out to supper, and fix him so that he can be kept in sight till morning. I want you to go along."

We had supper, and the substitute was given all he could eat and drink. We had determined to sit up all night, and now we walked down Pennsylvania avenue after the supper. A friend of Mr. Owens spoke to him and asked him to come to his place of business, to pass the time. This friend proved to be an undertaker, and, the weather being warm, we all sat in chairs just outside of his establishment. In time, the substitute, overcome by the different concoctions he had taken, fell asleep.

Our host offered the hospitalities of his back room, and the man was carried there and laid on the floor, where he was left to have his sleep out, while we still sat on guard in front of the place.

Just after daylight we heard a terrific scream, and rushing to the back room, we discovered that the substitute had escaped through a back window. Waking up, he had found himself between two dead men, and with one great yell, he had fled, and was never seen again. Here was Mr. Owens, again, without a substitute, but, fortunately, a few days after this second failure, President Lincoln issued a proclamation that no more men were needed.

The fortunes of war brought me another adventure at the close of my experience in Washington as a member of Mr. Owens' company. During the run of The French Spy, with Isabella Cubus as the Spy, Charles Barron, Fred Meader, Shirley France, of the National Theatre, started on a jaunt to Mt. Vernon. We secured passes from the Provo Marshal, and started. Mr. Meader and Mr. Barron in a buggy, and Mr. France and myself on horseback. South of Alexandria we found the roads in a very bad condition, and we did not reach Mt. Vernon until late in the afternoon. Returning, we did not reach Alexandria until it was quite dark. We were halted outside of the city, and our passes were demanded, enforced by the display of business-like looking muskets. These papers, though signed all right by the Provost Marshal, were not good after six o'clock p. m. Our buggy was searched, our saddles were taken from us, and we were marched as prisoners into Alexandria. There we were detained until seven o'clock. When we at last reached Washington, and went to our respective theatres, other actors were on the stage in our places, and we were summarily discharged. Mr. Barron, Mr. France and Mr. Meader were, after explaining on the following day, reinstated. Not so with me. Mr. Owens was very angry at me, called me into the office and paid me my salary in full. We had been in arrears with salaries for two weeks, and I considered myself a lucky man, as, on the following night, the theatre closed for good, the other members of our Mt. Vernon journey remaining unpaid, like the rest of the company. I have reason to believe that the seeming severity with me was through good-natured regard for me on the part of Mr. Owens.

From Washington I went to St. Louis, opening with Edwin Booth at Deagle's Theatre, now the Grand Opera House. Here there was, from time to time a break in the payment of salaries, notwithstanding the first-class attractions of the house, and the splendid business that sometimes came to it. Lucille Western played to small houses there, and she was followed by Joseph Jefferson in Rip Van Winkle. The business was magnificent, and I began to hope that my four weeks' areas of salary would be paid. Immediately following Mr. Jefferson's opening I was offered an engagement as leading juvenile at Woods'' Museum, in Chicago, and, being released by Manager Burnett, and paid my full salary to date, I bade St. Louis good-bye, and on the following morning started for Chicago.

The Boston Museum had, for years, the leading stock company in America. In those days each actor was engaged for a line of business beginning with the general utility man; next came the first and second old man, juvenile, leading juvenile, heavy and leading man. The ladies were first and second walking lady, first and second soubrette, first and second old woman, juvenile lady, heavy and leading lady. These I have named with least first and the best last, taking note of that promised day of Holy Writ, when the first shall be last and the last first.

We played stock plays, which included comedies, farces, tragedies and melodramas. At times stars would come—the better class of stars, and then the young men and women of the companies who supported them, had an opportunity of seeing the methods and studying them, of the best actors and actresses on the stage. These opportunities, together with the strict discipline of the stage director, were sure to make something of even mediocre talent.

The Black Crook, 1866. Costumes worn by the Costas Ballet troupe.
Courtesy Museum of the City of New York.

After I had been five years with the company at the munificent salary of $3 per week, our efficient manager, W. H. Smith, retired, and E. F. Keach became our manager for the season. A benefit was given at our theatre, for Mr. Bass, a very noted actor of the time, and who appeared on this occasion as the principal character in The Last Man. Mr. E. L. Davenport appeared in the double bill, playing the leading part in The Honeymoon, and I had the small part of Lopez. Before the night of this performance I had asked Mr. Keach for an increase of salary, but had been refused. After the day Mr. Davenport took me aside, and asked me if I was engaged for the following season. He was at that time the manager of the Howard Athenaeum. The next morning I again asked Mr. Keach for a raise in salary, which he again refused. I then called upon Mr. Davenport, who astonished me with an offer of $10 a week for the following season, to open with Lucullus, in Damon and Pythias, Mr. Davenport playing the part of Damon.

So I got a chance to play a character in which I could make use of my long and meagerly paid apprenticeship. On the first night, at the end of one of the scenes, there was a call for Damon. Mr. Davenport took me with him before the curtain, patted me on the head, and said, "This is my boy," and from that moment I felt as one inspired in my art.

John McCullough was a member of the Howard Athenaeum Company under Mr. Davenport's management, and here he got his first start on the road along which he traveled so far, toward the heights of his profession. Mr. Davenport was playing the part of Robert Laundry, in The Dead Heart, and during the run of the play he was disabled by a severe attack of the gout. He contemplated closing the theatre for a few nights, or until his recovery. John McCullough, who was a minor member of the company, asked Mr. Davenport to allow him to play the part, saying that he was perfect in the lines. Lawrence Barrett, who was the Abbe Latour of the cast, interceded in McCullough's behalf, and Mr. Davenport gave his consent. McCullough made a decided impression upon his audiences, and from that time his rise was rapid. Edwin Forest, a few weeks later, engaged him to play opposite parts to him. After Mr. Forest's death, McCullough secured many of his plays, giving them with great success. His brilliant career was ended during an engagement at McVicker's Theatre, in Chicago, where he was stricken with paresis.

During the Civil War I remained with Mr. Davenport, and played such parts as were given me, a round of characters embracing almost everything from the polished villain to the injured and magnanimous hero. Just before the end of the war we produced a play called the Battle of Bull Run. I was cast for the character of Sergeant Frank Bromwell, the avenger of Colonel Ellsworth, who was shot at Alexandria, Va., by a man named Jackson, early in the war.

Edwin Forrest played a long engagement at Niblo's . . . Much has been said of Mr. Forrest's surly disposition and brutality to his brother and sister professionals . . . a reputation surely undeserved.

E. L. Davenport was one of the greatest of American actors. He was of the old school, of course, and his broad and strong method and his original personality filled the stage. His influence upon those playing with him was telling. He saw the beginning of the line of

JOHN W. BLAISDELL.

American tragedians that was to follow him, McCullough, Edwin Booth, Barrett, and was one of Forrest's early contemporaries. In character he was lovable. I have given an instance or two of his dealing with me, when I was an obscure member of his company. To him I look as the most inspiring among the stage people with whom I came in contact in my early years, if not in all of those I passed upon the boards of the theatre.

Three members of the Howard Athenaeum Company were chosen to join the great combination which had been formed for Niblo's Garden, New York City, and I was one of the three. The combination included E. L. Davenport, William Wheatley, J. W. Wallack, John E. Owens, Harry and Thomas Placide, Harry Langdon, Edward Lamb, C. Kingsland, Charles Barron and myself. The women players were Mrs. E. L. Davenport, Julia Bennett Barrow, Mrs. J. W. Wallack, Jr., Henrietta Irving, Sophia Gimber Kuhn, and Josephine Henry.

Our programs would prove interesting reading to theatregoers, now. One night we would play Hamlet with Wallack as the Ghost, Wheatley as Hamlet, and Davenport as Laertes. Another night would be given Speed the Plow, with many of the leading members in minor parts, E. L. Davenport, for example, one of our greatest tragedians, taking the part of a Judge, with only a few lines.

While this combination was playing at Niblo's, John E. Owens produced there his play, Solon Shingle. Owens himself played Solon Shingle. J. W. Wallack, Jr., John Ellsley, E. L. Davenport, the Prosecuting Attorney, William Wheatley, Charles Otis, and the other members of the company filled out the cast.

The play was a tremendous success, and it was followed by many other memorable productions. The Enchantress received its original presentation here, with Caroline Richings in the title role, Kate Bateman as Leah, Edwin Adams as Rudolph, and J. W. Wallack, Jr., as Nathan. This was followed by Bel Domino with Madame Vestvali in the male character of Bel Domino. Charles Dillon played his celebrated role of Belphager.

The first performance in America of The Dukes Motto, was at this theatre, and the play aroused such enthusiasm as its subsequent career of popularity justified. Lagadare was played by William Wheatley and James Collins, known in those days as "Paddy" Collins, and who brought the play to America, played Carrickfergus. In the cast was Mr. Seymore, father of the celebrated stage manager, Willie Seymore. During the run of the production, Mr. Wheatley was seriously ill, and Mr. Collins, who had always had an ambition to play the part of Lagadare, got the opportunity. Mr. Seymore playing Mr. Collins' part of Carrickfergus.

It was at this time that the Nation was shaken by the tragedy of President Lincoln's death. Our theatre was, of course, closed. I heard the story that our orchestra leader, Mr. Cooke, being asked one night why the theatre was closed, replied that Mr. Wheatley, who played Lagadare, was ill, and Mr. Collins undertook to play the part of Lagadare, and Seymore undertook to play the part of Carrickfergus, and the two undertakers buried the piece.

Edwin Forrest played a long engagement at Niblo's, and then my long acquaintance with him begun. Much has been said and written of Mr. Forrest's surly disposition and brutality to his brother and sister profesisonals, and he has been given a reputation which was surely undeserved. While he was a strict disciplinarian, and would not tolerate inattention to business under any circumstances, he always had a word of encouragement for deserving strugglers, however humble the position they held. Forrest was with the general public in his great admiration at one time, of General George B. McClellan, the war hero. One morning, while we were rehearsing Damon and Pythias, in the scene where the soldiers rush on the stage, headed by Procius, shouting "On to the Citadel, on to the Citadel," Forrest, in an irritable manner said: "Now, follow me, and shout, 'On to the Citadel, on to the Citadel,' as if you had George B. McClellan at your head." This exhortation had its due effect, and each supernumerary tried to outdo the other, not only in voice, but in action.

Edwin Forrest was a sorely tried, and unhappy man. He showed sometimes the effects of the "Slings and arrows of outrageous fortune," in his irritability and uncertainty of temper, but the stories of his "brutality," are in my belief, gross exaggerations of the moods and expressions of a man sorely tormented, and harassed. He was always ready to aid the young aspirant, and the following incident, which has been related since, as belonging to more than one theatrical light really occurred during Forrest's engagement at Niblo's. One morning, while we were rehearsing Jack Cade, one of the young men had a speech of two or three lines which he spoke without proper force or expression. Mr. Forrest said, "Here, young man, that will not do. I'll read your lines for you." This he did in an impressive and telling manner. "There, do it that way," he ended by saying. The young actor replied, "Mr. Forrest, if I could do it that way, I would not be here at 25 cents a night."

Forrest received this sally with appreciation and delight.

FROM JULY 30, 1904 ISSUE

LIKE THIRTY CENTS

Seem the Former Expenses of a Dramatic Production.

In these days of extravagant theatrical expenditure it is interesting to study the cost of performances given years ago. An industrious delver has found the record of some Eighteenth Century performances that are in marked contrast to the amounts spend to-day.

A performance of Hamlet given in September, 1735, in London, cost $300, and the expenses of the night were $85. The orchestra cost $17.50, the advertisements in a newspaper 4, and for the service of two soldiers who stood at either side of the proscenium arch to keep order, the sum of $3.50 was paid. The candles that illuminated the theatre cost $15.

Sometimes in those economical days there were expenditures unknown now. When the Princ and the Princess of Wales, for instance, attended a performance of Jane Shore, the manager was compelled to tip all the flunkeys that came in the royal retinue, and the cost of that was $50.

Although some elaborate pantomimes were produced in those days, the scene painters received small salaries. The best known of all these, an Italian imported to London on account of his skill in constructing scenery, was the highest paid of the scene painters. He was able to get only $25 a week.

Some of the expenditures for costumes seemed extravagant to that age, although the prices would be rather moderate now. Much emphasis was laid on the cost of a gown and cape made for a popular actor of the day, for which $120 was paid. A crown for King Lear, on the other hand, cost only $175, while for $125 the costumes for all the dancers in the opera of Diocleton were obtained.

In those days $700 was looked upon as an uncommonly good house. Salaries were low, for the highest recorded is $80 a week. That was much above the average, which was about $35 for the principal actors.

FROM DEC. 3, 1904 ISSUE

ACTORS' SALARIES IN THE '40S.

A writer, in 1840, commenting on the state of the drama, asserts that the first blow to the destruction of the great theaters "has been the extraordinary increase in the demands of all kinds of actors;" and, to illustrate the injustice of the salaries then given, gives the following statistics of the salaries paid to actors of a preceding generation: "Munden, Fawcett, Quick, Edwin, Jack Johnstone and their class received £14 a week; William Lewis, a superb comedian, £20 a week; Matthews, in 1812, wrote, 'Now to my offer, which I think stupendous and magnificent, £17 a week;' Miss O'Neill, after achieving a good provincial reputation, received £15 at Covent Garden, and never more than £20; Cooke was paid £20 a week; Mrs. Jordon, £31 10s a week; Dowton, £12 and never more than £20 a week; Miss Stephens, £20 a week. All these actors were first rate, but, looking down the list, we find Macready, in 1839, receiving £25 a night; Power (1840), £120 a week; Farren, at the same period, £40 a week; Liston, who began at £17 a week, ended by receiving £20 a night, and Miss Ellen Tree, certainly a pretty and popular actress, was engaged by the Drury Lane manager, when lessee of both theaters, to play for both, for £15 a week. She then went to America, returned after two seasons, and even after this rustication. she comes, demands, and even actually obtains £25 a night." The same writer says that were it not for the management, the dramatic author would receive larger sums for his plays; and instances the money paid to authors in the days of Kemble and Suett by quoting Coleman, who received £1,000 for John Bull; Morton, £1,000 for Town and Country; Mrs. Inchbald, £800 for Wives as They Were, and Reynolds, for two works in one season (The Blind Bargain and Out of Place), £1,000."

FROM JULY 9, 1904 ISSUE

STAGE DANCING.

Its Growth and Developement. Early Forms of Terpsichorean Exercise.

Dancing is of very ancient origin, and in the absence of proof to the contrary, we may well suppose the Garden of Eden to have witnessed the first dance, crude thought it may have been, on the morning of creation. The Hindoos claim that the art of dancing was taught to their women by one Asporas, a mythological female who came to earth about the ninth Avator. But be this as it may, dancing in the East has ever been in the hands, or rather—feet of its women. In many Oriental countries dancing girls seem to have been an exclusive prerogative of royalty.

In India the nauch-girls, like the geishas of Japan, form a distinct class, and are trained from childhood in the art. Before the English conquest every great temple kept its troupe of dancing girls and the freizes in the old temples show that the nauch-girls were familiar with every feature of the serpentine dance.

The women called almas and ghawazee are the best modern representatives of the ancient Egyptian singers and dancers. They dance precisely the same dance that was danced in Pharaoli's time, as proved by paintings on the walls of the tombs. In making the voyage from Egypt to Chicago in 1892 it gained the name of couchee-couchee, by which it is commonly known throughout the Occident.

Modern comic opera has made the dress and dance of the geishas of Japan too well known to need comment, but to see the true geishas in all her native loveliness one must journey to the flowery kingdom.

Skirt dancing in this country began a dozen or fifteen years ago, when the London Gaiety Girls came to America. Several members of this company danced in accordion skirts with comparatively few yards of silk in them. The dance took at once, and since has been so extensively improved upon that to-day one of the Gaity Girls who first danced it would, unless she had progressed with the dance, have difficulty in recognizing it as the same sort of thing. It may have been Loie Fuller who first realized the possibilities of a voluminous silk skirt in connection with colored lights. Perhaps not, but the fact is that some one saw them and others have developed them until today the skirt dance is a matter of an extensive lighting equipment, an artistic blending of colors under those lights, yards and yards of silk of the finest and lightest texture, and a woman with the necessary muscular training to wave the skirt about for a space of several minutes.

In the sixteenth and seventeenth centuries dancing was a part of the educational training of all persons of rank as a means to the end of graceful carriage, and is regarded by most of the best actors of today as a necessary part of the preparation for a successful stage career. Madam Bernhardt has said that it took her two years of hard work to acquire the graceful stage walk for which she is noted.

The premier dansense on the stage today are usually graduates of the school connected with the Paris Opera or La Scala in Milan. There are also private schools in New York, most of which are managed by performers who have retired, perhaps with the memory of a brilliant career before the footlights, or the applause of the Moline Rouge ringing in their ears.

FROM JULY 23, 1904 ISSUE

ENCORE, 1752?

We have no record of when the encore was introduced into this country, although it is very probable and likely that it came about the same time as the first theatrical performance. This was in the year 1752. It is not necessary to say that the custom took root quickly in this country. The fact would be in keeping with the quick perception and enthusiasm of the American patrons. In America the encore has grown so rapidly that it, at times, assumes the character of a nuisance, much to the discomfort of a moderate conservative. Few managers have dared to try to root it out, though once in a while a half-hearted attempt seems to be made. On the programs of the old Theatre Comique, down at 444 Broadway, New York City, was this legend, perhaps hereditary: "On account of the length of the program only two encores can be allowed." Certainly there was no attempt to enforce the alleged rule, so probably the Comique can not be cited as a theatre where any real attempt was made to suppress the sometimes designated nuisance.

Evidently one of the causes for the prevalence of the encore is the fact that an encore granted generally gives rise to another and so on, thus extending a good performance indefinitely. It is said that—in Paris—encores are the result of the actions of paid promoters of applause, but this falls without the true encore—a repetition demanded by an audience because of the ability exhibited by the actor or performer. The encore should result from true applause. True applause should be inspired by exhibited devotion to art.

• • •

FROM NOV. 28, 1903 ISSUE

DE WOLF HOPPER,

The huge comic opera singer who can truthfully say, "I enjoy life hugely." Mr. Hopper's father had thought DeWolf cut out for the bar, and his mother was persuaded, after seeing him in his first night with Edward Harrigan in The Blackbird, that he had better go back to the law. Mr. Hopper had made a hit that night with the gallery. He has a big voice, and in making his point he shouted for all he was worth, and the applause he drew from the upper regions filled him with delight. It was evident that it was all off with Blackstone. His decision proved to be correct, and the stage is Mr. Hopper's proper sphere. He appeared in Hazel Kirke as Pittacus Green in 1884 in the Madison Square Theatre company under Daniel Frohman, and Owen Hathaway in May Blossom. Annie Louise Cary was the first to suggest that he had a voice, which was seconded by Miss Georgie Cayvan. To Luigi Meola he lays the credit for his musical training and to Mr. Mackay for the technique and mechanism of acting. Save for the lessons in learning the steps of the waltz in his youth, Mr. Hopper has acquired directly his skill as a dancer.

Mr. Hopper was born in New York City March 30, 1858. The name De Wolf given him in baptism was his mother's maiden name, and she was of the family of De Wolf, whose daughters and nieces have become Tiffanys, Perrys, Lawrences and Aspinwalls. The old homestead at Bristol, R. I., is one of the quaintest among the ancient mansions of the country, with a wide hall through the center of the house. Mr. Hopper's father was a lawyer, from whom the stage evidently was not an inheritance. Mr. Pickwick has been the successful vehicle for Mr. Hopper for the past two seasons with the reputation of a Broadway run for three months.

FROM JAN. 31, 1903 ISSUE

THE JEFFERSON FAMILY.

No name is more closely linked with stage history of the past as well as the stage to-day than that of Jefferson. "Rip Van Winkle" is one of the stage's perennial jewels, holding the subtle power of making any audience the better for the seeing.

Some interesting facts follow relating to the Jefferson family.

Thomas Jefferson, a young man of 18, rode to London in 1746, on one of his father's farm horses and there met David Garrick, the greatest actor of his time. Jefferson was the wit of Ripton, Yorkshire, and it was there that he first made the acquaintance of Garrick, who was struck with the genius of Jefferson, and proposed his going on the stage with him, which he accepted.

This was the foundation of the Jefferson family of actors. Jefferson died in 1807. His family consisted of a wife and two sons; the youngest became a minister, and the elder, Joseph Jefferson the Second, an actor, who was born in 1774. Having some difficulty with his father's second wife, he left England and came to America, arriving in 1797. Joseph Jefferson found lodgings in New York, with a Mrs. Fortune. She had two daughters, one Euphemia, who became the young comedian's wife, the other married William Warren, the father of the celebrated and much beloved comedian of the Boston Museum. This is where these two talented families of actors became related.

Joseph Jefferson II left England and came to America in 1797, founding America's first great theatrical family.

FROM NOV. 7, 1903 ISSUE

JEFFERSON REMINISCENT.

At the close of the performance of Rip Van Winkle, at Powers' Theatre, Chicago, Sept. 28, Joseph Jefferson, responding to a curtain call, delivered an address in which, apropos of the centennial celebration now in progress, he grew reminiscent and said he not only played Rip Van Winkle here 35 years ago, but was married in Chicago, and his son was born in Chicago during the great conflagration which destroyed the city.

"But there is something still further back," said he, "for I acted in this city 64 years ago. My father was one of the first managers in Chicago, and with a small company of actors, myself among that number, being a boy 10 years old, we landed in front of the then mere village of Chicago, which numbered about 4,000 inhabitants. We acted here for the season, and I need not tell you that when I return here year after year I feel like a veritable Rip Van Winkle indeed."

Mr. Jefferson then told how, in the old days, when prejudice against actors was great, the Town Council of Springfield, Ill., had placed a prohibitory tax on theatrical performances, and his father's company, stranded in that town, would have been unable to give a performance had not a young lawyer volunteered to arrange matters with the city fathers. That young lawyer was Abraham Lincoln. Mr. Jefferson also told an anecdote of former Governor Richard Oglesby, of Illinois, relating how, when Oglesby was a lad of 15 years he was so fascinated by the performances given by the elder Jefferson's company that he ran away to join the company in Galena, Ill., but was persuaded to return to his home.

FROM MAR. 14, 1903 ISSUE

BIRTHDAY CELEBRATION.

February 20th, Joseph Jefferson reached his seventy-fourth year. He was given an elaborate spread at Cragin's Hotel, Jacksonville, Fla. After the breakfast, Mr. Cragin gave the following toast. Gentlemen: Another year has passed, and again this party gathers to congratulate and cheer our dear old friend as he reaches another mile-stone on life's journey. No, that simile is not a happy one. The idea of a journey brings to the mind visions of weariness, of dust, of general discomfort, of an unpleasant thing, the sooner ended the better. The picture I see to-day is not that of a weary, dusty travler, but of a gentle, happy nature, sauntering along life's sunny autumn afternoon, picking a flower here, stopping there to sketch a bit of landscape, or here again to do a kindly deed or say a loving word. As he sees his little group of friends gathered to greet him at the mile-stone, he says—with a merry twinkle of his eye that the whole world knows so well, "God bless my soul, gentlemen, is it possible that I am seventy-four years old to-day? He surely knows how to grow old gracefully, or rather how to glide along life's pathway without growing old at all. In his beauty sleep of twenty years in the Catskills, or in the discovery of Ponce de Leon's fountain of perpetual youth here in Florida, he has learned how to grow younger with each added year. We drink his health and sincerely echo the wish that he may "live long and prosper."

•••

FROM FEB. 28, 1903 ISSUE

HISTORIC

Old Front Street Theatre in Baltimore, Md., Will be Remodeled.

Mr. James L. Kernan, the well known owner and managers of theaters, has purchased the historic Front Street Theatre in Baltimore, Md. Several capitalists are associated with him and intend to improve the building which will give it a seating capacity of 4,000 to 5,000 persons. The object of purchasing this theater is to present large spectacular productions as there is no stage of sufficient size to accomodate their large productions. This theater will form a link to a large chain of theaters that will be conducted for this purpose.

Mr. Kernan has also secured control of the Empire Theater in Washington, D. C. and the attractions that appear at the Lyceum Theater will be transfered to the Empire. The Lyceum Theater will be enlarged so that the spectacular productions can be presented there.

The Front Street Theater is linked with the history of the Union. The present building was erected in 1838 and within its historic walls some of the most memorable of Presidential nominating conventions were held, and the brightest stars that ever shone in the theatrical firmament received their greatest triumph there. Stephen A. Douglas was nominated for President in this house in the stormy political times which preceeded those troublesome times in 1864, and President Lincoln was nominated for re-election to the President chair in 1864 in the same place.

The original Front Street Theater was built in 1829 by Charles Grover, a well known architect, and was at the time considered the finest playhouse in the country. On the afternoon of February 3, 1838, while an English troupe was on the stage the theater caught fire. The building was totally destroyed. In the same year the structure was rebuilt andd opened December 3. Mrs. Frank Drew made her stage debut as the Duke of York, to the elder Booth's "Richard III," in 1842. On the night of December 8, 1850, Jenny Lind, the great singer, made her first appearance in this city, under the management of P. T. Barnum. The most extravagent prices were paid for seats. Four concerts were given and 12½ cents was charged merely for admission to the auction sale of seats. The concerts netted $60,000.

Charlotte Cushman, Macrady, Cornilia Jefferson, James Wills, J. K. Field, Mrs. Henry Eberle were among the famous stars who appeared at this house. At the close of the war George Kunkel leased the house and ran a series of melodramas. Kunkel was followed by the late Col. William E. Sims who in turn was succeeded by Daniel A. Kelley.

In 1895 the house was leased by the Hebrew Stock Company, which ran the place until December 27, 1895, when ocurred the frightful catastrophe in which 23 persons were trampled to death and many more were injured. On that night the house was crowded and the curtain was about to go up, when some one in searching for a leaking gas pipe struck a match. A cry of fire was followed by a wild rush for the doors. Since then the building has been idle. Rough boards bar the entrance to the old house and rats chase each other over the stage once pressed by the first of the greatest tragedicans, comedians and vocalists.   S. S.

TWO HISTORIC ALL-TIME SONG HITS

FROM JAN. 16, 1904 ISSUE

THE HISTORY OF DIXIE.

They will never get Dixie accepted in a rewritten form. It is impossible to attain any such purpose with the song ingrained in the hearts of millions as Dixie is. It is about as near realization as had been the efforts to write a national anthem to order. Dixie was written by Emmet in 1859 as a walk-around for Bryant's Minstrels in New York, with which he was appearing. Here are his words:

I wish I was in de land of cotton,
Old times dar am not forgotten.
        Look away, look away,
        Look away, Dixie land.
In Dixie land where I was born in,
Early on one frosty morning,
        Look away, look away,
        Look away, Dixie land,
        Look away, Dixie land.
            CHORUS.
Den I wish I was in Dixie,
    *Hooray! Hooray!
    In Dixie land
    I'll take my stand.
To live and die in Dixie.
Away, away, away down South in Dixie.
Away, away, away down South in Dixie.

Some of the lines are very apropos to the Southern cause, and this largely explains why this song became the war cry of the South. Although Dan Emmet was a Northern man, Old Times Dar Am Not Forgotten and In Dixie Land I'll Take My stand, to Live and Die in Dixie are among these lines that, written merely for amusement, became so historically significant.

"Dixie" was written in 1859 by Dan Emmett as a walk-around for Bryant's Minstrels in New York . . . the song became the war cry of the South.

Dan Emmet is still alive and has passed his eightieth year, living at Mount Vernon, O. He and Sam Sanford, who makes his home in Brooklyn with his son, are probably the only minstrel pioneers still alive. Emmet is respected by burnt cork men as one of the four who began it.

FROM AUG. 6, 1904 ISSUE

SEVERAL COUNTRIES CLAIM YANKEE DOODLE.

It is said that France, Holland and Spain, besides our own country lay claim to the famous melody—Yankee Doodle.

Buckingham Smith, while secretary of the American Legation at Madrid, in 1858, wrote to an American gentleman that "Yankee Doodle's" music bore a strong resemblance to a popular air of Biscay and that a professor from Northern Spain had recognized it as being much like the ancient sword dance played on solemn occasions by the people of San Sebastin.

"The professor says the tune varies in those provinces," wrote Mr. Smith, "and he purposes in a couple of months to give me the changes as they are to be found in the different towns. Our national air certainly has its origin in the music of the free Pyrenees. The first strains are identically those of the heroic Danza Esparta, of brave old Biscay."

To checkmate Mr. Smith's enthusiastic claim for the origin of the tune, one has Louis Kossuth's account of his countrymen's behavior when, traveling with him on the Mississippi, they first heard Americans sing "Yankee Doodle." He writes that his companions straightway fell to capering and dancing, for they recognized an air familiar to them and which they had heard in old Hungary.

Again, both the French and the Dutch lay claim to the melody. For the south of France knew it as an old vinting song, while in the land of dikes, according to the tale of one old Hollander, in the days when the Dutch harvesters received for wages as much buttermilk as they could drink and a tenth of the grain, they reaped to this old tune, singing the words:—

Yanker, dudel, doodle down,
    Diddle, dudel, lanther.
Yankee viver, voover vown,
    Boter milk and tanther.

Besides being thus surprisingly at home on the Continent, from the North Sea to the Mediterranean, the music is likewise English property. The earliest trace of it in print is in "Walsh's Collection of Dances for the year 1750." Here it is written in 6-8 times, and is known as "Fisher's Jig." But besides being used under this name as a dance tune, it had had for years before 1750 been crooned by English mothers to their babies to the nursery verses.—

Lucy Locket lost her pocket,
    Kitty Fisher found it.
Nothing in it, nothing on it
    But the binding round it.

And there was a variant form wherein the unfortunate lass whose loss is exploited was Lydia, not Lucy, and of whose pocket 'twas
        Not a bit of money in it—
        Only binding round it.

It is noticeable that the name "Fisher" occurs in both jig and rhyme. This is not without significance, for Kitty Fisher was a real personage, of some notoriety.

The tune (Yankee Doodle) is carried back to 1650, the days of Roundhead and Cavalier. . . . Cromwell rode in to Oxford on a diminutive steed with his single plume fastened into a knot, which was called a macaroni. Thus the Cavaliers sang derisively:
*Yankee Doodle came to town
Upon a Kentish pony;
He stuck a feather in his hat
And called it macaroni*

Thus the tune is carried back another hundred years to 1650, the days of Roundhead and Cavalier. Credence may then well be given to the tradition which makes Cromwell the conspicuous figure in the stanza:—
Yankee Doodle came to town
    Upon a Kentish pony;
He stuck a feather in his hat
    And called it macaroni.

The origination of the lines story says, was after the time of the uprising against Charles, Cromwell once rode in to Oxford mounted upon a diminutive steed which may well have been Kentish—since horses of that extraction are so small—with his single plume fastened into a sort of knot which was derisively called a macaroni. In ridicule of the figure thus cut by the Puritan leader the Cavaliers sang the lines quoted.

There is another tale told in England attesting the popularity of "Fisher's Jig." This runs that about the middle of the eighteenth century there stood in London, in the city proper, in the neighborhood of Bow Bells, a church with a musical clock. This daily at the hour of twelve played, among several melodies, the air of "Yankee Doodle." Fifty years ago an interested American tried to trace the story to its source and learn the locality of the clock, but his quest was vain. Nothing indefinite could be learned, and no trace of the building could be found. The simple story that such a thing had been was all that time had bequeathed.

The tune having been thus familiar in the mother country, it is not surprising that it should have been brought across the water in Colonial days. Nor, perhaps, in view of its extraordinary popularity on the European continent, ought surprise to be expressed that the simple air should have laid such a strong hold on the young nation. Yet the circumstances of its birth are of dramatic interest, and strikingly similar to the Cromwell part of the tune's English history.

OLD CORN MEAL, DADDY RICE,
DAN EMMETT AND MINSTRELSY

FROM DEC. 6, 1902 ISSUE

THE ORIGINATORS OF NEGRO MINSTRELSY
by DR. JUDD
WHO WAS FOR 6 YEARS
TREASURER E.P. CHRISTY'S MINSTRELS

Two old darkies, long years ago, away back in 1828, can justly claim to be the originators of negro minstrelsy in this country.

First was an old darky in New Orleans, known by every one in that city in those days as "Old Corn Meal." He could be seen from morning till night with his old horse and cart going about the city selling cornmeal, and most every evening he would draw up in front of the old Planters' Hotel, the well-known hostelry of those days, and pick up many a sixpence singing old negro melodies as they were sung by the negroes of the South in those early days. The other one was an old darky known all up and down the Mississippi and Ohio Rivers, from New Orleans to Cincinnati, as Picayune Butler. He would sing those old eccentric negro songs, accompanying himself on a banjo that he made himself.

In these years there was traveling with Purdy Brown's Theater a clown named George Nichols. He was very original and wrote all his own comic songs and many funny anecdotes and stories, etc. Nichols had run across these old darkies and heard them sing their odd songs, and he jotted them down and then rewrote them, and made more of a song out of them; he would then black up and sing these songs with the Theater. Among the most popular that he rearranged and sang himself, and sung by other negro minstrels long after Nichols' death, were, "Zip Coon" and "Clare de Kitchen." Nichols also heard "Old Corn Meal" sing some version of "Jim Crow." He rewrote that and sang it with a blackened face, with the Theater.

Old Daddy Rice has always had the credit of being the first one to sing and jump "Jim Crow." He was not the first to sing it, but was the first one to give it its popularity. Daddy Rice had been connected in some minor capacity with a traveling theater that toured the West and South. He picked this song up and put a peculiar step to it of his own. Along in the year 1830 he got an engagement to sing "Jim Crow" between the acts at the old National Theater, Cincinnati, and it took like wildfire. The theater was packed night after night. Sol Smith was the star then playing there, but it was hard to tell which was the star, Daddy Rice or Sol Smith. Rice then went on to the Eastern cities and made quite a fortune in the United States and England by singing the song of "Jim Crow."

Up to 1841 we had no regularly organized minstrel troupes ... but in '41 the Virginia Serenaders with Dan Emmett ... and the Virginia Minstrels — the foundation of the Original Christy Minstrels — were formed.

Up to the year 1841 we had no regularly organized minstrel troupes, but in this year there were two companies organized about the same time. The first was the Virginia Serenaders, consisting of Dan Emmet, Billy Whitlock, Dick Pelham and Frank Bowers, only four all told. They gave the whole show, music and all. They played in New York, Boston and other Eastern cities with great success. They then went to Engand. While in London they performed at the St. James Theater, and so great was the demand to see them that they gave morning performances, and were frequently solicited to give their entertainment at private houses of the highest nobility. During the success of the Virginia Serenaders in Europe they were called to Windsor Castle by special command of Her Majesty, Queen Victoria. For this they each received a splendid crest ring as a token of her appreciation. Some time later they returned to America.

The other company was the Virginia Minstrels, which was the foundation of the Original Christy Minstrels. They were organized in Tiffin, O., in the winter of 1841, by a man named Yale, a house painter by trade, and a banjo player when in the minstrel business. He had been out with Joe Pentland's Circus the year before, and a minstrel performer coming along by the name of Lansing Durand, they planned a negro show. Yale went to work and painted a set of large banners, with pictures of negro minstrels going through their different performances, to hang up in front of the place wherever they would exhibit. They did not have big show bills in those days. About the time they got their banners done, E. P. Christy came along to Tiffin with his sleight-of-hand show. He had a man with him by the name of Weldon, who was the magician, and a boy about 14 years old to act as confederate to the magician. This boy's name was George Harrington, afterwards the famous George Christy. He was a very good jig dancer at this time, and had danced in public a number of times at the old Eagle Street Theater, Buffalo, N. Y., a year or so before this.

Christy had been doing a very poor business with his legerdemain show, and at Tiffin it was no better, and there disbanded. Christy went back to his home, then in Buffalo, N. Y., and Yale and Durand induced Christy to let the boy, George Harrington, remain with them and help them out with their show. Christy had in some kind of a way adopted him, or had some agreement with his folks to bring him up. He let him remain with Yale, and now, with the addition of Harrington and another fellow that they picked up over at Milan, O., by the name of Ed. Marks, who could sing negro songs and play the triangle, the Virginia Minstrels opened their show one evening in December, 1841, in the old town hall over a wagon shop at Tiffin. They then started out on the road with good and bad luck, more of the latter than of the former. They landed in Buffalo a few months afterwards without a cent in the whole party, and Yale having had enough of the negro show business, went back to house painting and sold for the sum of $16 to E. P. Christy the entire outfit of the negro show, consisting of only the three banners that he had painted. Now E. P. Christy, with the assistance of Lansing Durand, Tom Vaughn and Young

Harrington (he was now called on the small bills George Christy), opened as the Virginia Minstrels at a small hall on Water street, in Buffalo, March 22, 1842. Soon after leaving Buffalo they reorganized. Emom Dickerson, Richard M. Hooley and Zeke Backus were added to the party, and they called themselves the Original Christy Minstrels, E. P. Christy, manager. They then traveled all over the United States, were successful and became very popular. George Christy got to be the star of the party. He was the first one to do the wench business, and in this line we have never had his equal. He was the original Lucy Long and Cachuca. The Christys first appeared for a short time in New York in 1846, at the Palmo Opera House. On their second or third appearance in New York, in 1847, they located permanently at the old Mechanics' Hall, 472 Broadway, and remained here seven years.

In 1854, E. P. Christy retired from the business. Shortly before this, George Christy left E. P. Christy and went with Henry Wood as partner. Wood was running an opposition party of minstrels at 444 Broadway.

From now on minstrel troupes sprang up very fast. Instead of having four, five or six performers in a company, they began to have twelve, then twenty-five, and now minstrel troupes advertise fifty and one hundred. Of the old pioneers or originators of negro minstrelsy all are dead and gone but one, Dan Emmett, who was with the Virginia Serenaders.

E. P. Christy, in the year 1862, while in a fit of temporary insanity, jumped out of the second-story window of his residence in New York, and died a few days afterwards. George Christy died in New York in 1868.

Although all these old minstrel performers have passed away from the checkered and exciting scenes of life, and their faces will no more be seen before the footlights, and their limbs are cold and motionless, and their voices are hushed forever, still their memories will remain green in the hearts of many who are still living and have listened to their good old-time songs, stories, music and funny antics.

A few years ago I met in Chicago Dan Emmett, famous as a negro minstrel to playgoers of two generations, and it was he who, a year or so before our Civil War, wrote and composed "Dixie," the soul-stirring negro melody which served as the rallying song in both the Northern and Southern Armies. Emmett was born in Norwalk, O., 'way back in the 20s, and when a boy his father, who was a blacksmith, moved with his family to Morris, O, and opened a blacksmith shop. Young Daniel went to work in the shop with his father, blowing the bellows and helped around, but blacksmithing had no charms for him. He was a natural born musician, and had great talent for music, and when a boy he played the violin to perfection, and always had his violin with him, and when there was no work for him, he would get out in front of the blacksmith shop and play, and soon would have a crowd of the villagers around him listening. But one day Daniel was missed from his home and the village. He went off with old Sam Stickney's Circus, which was then showing in that section. He was a man grown before he ever returned to his native village. He had in the meantime gained quite a reputation as a musician in his line.

Along in the year of 1859, I was in Springfield, Mass., and at the same hotel where I was stopping was also stopping Dan Bryant's Minstrels. Dan Emmett was with them as musical composer. It was a cold, dismal Sunday, and no one wanted to be out. The minstrel troupe was quartered on the same hall that I was; some were trying to sleep, while others were trying to read, but Dan Emmett, who had a room at the end of the hall, kept up such a variety of mixed up tunes on his violin that the minstrel boys would call to him, "For pity sakes, Dan, stop that noise and let us sleep." After awhile we heard Dan dancing around in his room and yelling, "I have

E. P. Christy, in a fit of temporary insanity, jumped out of a second-story window and died a few days afterwards.

got it, I have got it." The boys rushed to his room to see what he had got. It was that Sunday afternoon that he composed "Dixie." The next evening the Bryants used it in their walk around. All minstrel troupes in those days closed their entertainment with a walk around, and they were always anxious to get something new and lively. "Dixie" took like wildfire, and before the Bryants returned to their own hall in New York, the boys were whistling it on the streets. In New York the Bryants had a theater of their own for many years, where prosperity smiled upon them from 1857 to 1867. They held forth at No. 472 Broadway nightly the year round, only when they went out in the summer on a short trip through the country. Their hall was little like the cozy playhouses of today. It had formerly been a church, and it was filled up with wooden pews for seats. On Sunday it served as a house of worship. The auditorium proper was a long way from the street, and was reached by a narrow entrance hall. Here at this old hall they would clear in profits, year after year $25,-000 to $30,000; but after they moved up town minstrelsy was losing in favor with the public, and when in 1875 Dan Bryant died, he did not have much of the wherewith to leave behind him.

Although these old minstrel performers have passed away ... their memories will remain green in the hearts of many who listened to their good old-time songs, stories, music, and funny antics.

FROM AUG. 23, 1902 ISSUE

VAGRANT.

Charles Howard, Once a Leader in the Burnt-Cork World, Sent to Bayview Asylum.

Bare-footed and tattered, Charles Howard, the famous old-time minstrel, was picked up on East Preston street, Baltimore, Md., on the night of July 30 by an officer of the Northeastern District, and the following morning Justice Lewis sent him to Bayview Asylum on the charge of vagrancy.

"Thank you," said the old man, when sentence was passed, for he knew that fate had nothing better in store for him, and the disposition of the case was the best that could be made.

He was bare-footed when found by the officer, and home was a place which had

long been forgotten by the minstrel. His clothes were ragged and one foot and leg were bandaged. He had been receiving medical treatment at the Johns Hopkins dispensary, and the malady, he thought, was erysipelas.

Howard was one of the original minstrels, and was familiar to all the theater-goers of a generation ago. He traveled with his troupe from city to city, and was well known everywhere. Baltimore, however, has always been his home, and when his days before the footlights were over he became stage manager at the Monumental, or Central Theater, as it was then called.

Like many others who pursue the same means of livelihood, he was prodigal of his money, and when his career was ended he had very little saved. This little soon disappeared.

When arrested, he gave his age as sixty-five years, but those who remember him believe him to be much older. He has taken the part of Uncle Tom in "Uncle Tom's Cabin," and many of the minstrel troupes of a generation ago included him in their roster.

Frank Brower

Dan Emmett

VARIETY AND VAUDEVILLE PIONEERS

FROM NOV. 5, 1904 ISSUE

WEBER AND FIELDS' PARTNERSHIP.

If the partnership between Joe Weber and Lew Fields had continued until next January it would have covered a period of twenty-seven years.

No other theatrical team had worked together so long, with the exception of McIntyre and Heath, the blackface vaudeville comedians. Harrigan and Hart were partners many years and so where Robson and Crane, but neither pair stayed together so long as Weber and Fields.

"Twenty-seven years is a long time to be business partners and friends," said Mr. Fields recently. "Joe Weber and I first met in the Allen street public school, New York City, when we were ten years old. We both had a fancy for clog dancing and it was this mutual liking that drew us together.

"During recess and after school hours we would practice dancing, and every time we could we would sneak off to the London Theatre and gaze with awe upon the performers from our seats in the gallery. We resolved to be actors, too, and it was not long before we made our first appearance on the stage.

"The Elks' Serenaders was the name selected by five East Side young men who banded together and gave themselves a benefit at what was then known as Turner's Hall, on the Bowery. Wanting the opportunity to see what we could do in public, Joe and I volunteered our services.

"From the pennies we could scrape together we each bought a pair of green knickerbockers, a white waist, black stockings, dancing clogs and a derby hat. Then we were ready to make our debut as dancers and singers.

"We had a song, words of our own composition, music cribbed, which we called The Land of the Shamrock Green. Just listen to the chorus:

Here we are, an Irish pair,
Without any troubles or care;
We're one more to make people roar
Before we go to the hall.

"Well, Joe and I made our first appearance at this benefit and we received much praise from a very slim audience that we felt we were cut out but for actors. At that benefit we decided upon our vocation, and we vowed that neither one of us would do any other sort except dance and sing. The Lord knows we did not look like the two Irish boys our song told about, but our first audience didn't care whether we came from Ireland or Jerusalem.

"We played at three or four benefits after this and kept on going to school. Then we were bold and struck out for a job.

"Morris and Hickman's East Side Museum was then on Chatham Square. We demanded an engagement there and were hired for one week at $3 each.

"We went to school in the morning and played hookey in the afternoon while we were billed at the museum. We were billed at the museum as Weber and Fields. We were hired for a second week and the proprietors billed us as Fields and Weber. That was the only time we were billed that way.

"We were pretty well pleased with ourselves after our first two weeks, and we certainly were tickled to know that we were getting paid real money for what we considered fun.

"It wasn't long before we had another engagement. This time it was at the New York, another Bowery museum. The Bowery museums of those days were not very high class places of entertainment; in fact, low class would better describe most of them. It was at the New York that we first saw the possibilities of elaborating our song and dance act.

We were ten years old . . . . We made our debut at Morris and Hickman's East Side Museum on Chatham Square for one week at $3 each.

"Playing at one of the Bowery places was a chap who was called the Paper King. He made all sorts of things out of paper and then presented specimens of his handiwork to the women of the audience as souvenirs.

"One of the things he used to do well was to make tidies out of white paper. He would take a big sheet of white paper, fold it and by tearing pieces out of the fold here and there he would work out a pattern of a tidy.

"The Paper King took a liking to Joe and I and he taught us how to make tidies. As soon as we learned how we added that to our act. While we danced we would tear tidies and then give them to the ladies.

"Well, we played at New York nine weeks and when we ended our stay there we were getting $12.50 each for a week's work. By that time nothing could drive us away from our set purpose of continuing on the stage. We left school and let our parents in on our game.

"We next went to Worth's Museum. This was the best museum on the Bowery. We often changed our act there. If we were not liked as an Irish pair we'd change to a Dutch or a coon pair. It made no difference to us. All we had to do was to change the first line of our song and our costume and make-up.

The Paper King taught us how to make tidies. . . . While we danced, we would tear tidies and give them to the ladies.

"It was at Worth's that Joe was taken off the stage by the Gerry society. We were playing eight or nine times a day and Joe's folks had to promise that they wouldn't allow him to play more than three times each day before the society would allow him to go back to work. He was picked up because he was smaller than I, but after the first interference we were never bothered.

"We'd played the museums for about four years up and down the Bowery, but there was one museum we couldn't seem to break into. That was at Broadway and Ninth Streets, and George H. Bunnell ran it.

"Being off the Bowery it had a higher class of patronage, and Joe and I wanted to play there. We used to write to Bunnell every week asking him for an engagement, but he always sent us back a stamped postal saying, 'All time filled.'

"We made up our minds that we were going to play in that house and we spent considerable time in planning how we were going to do it. Remember we were only youngsters, but we wanted to go ahead.

"We called on Mr. Bunnell one day after we had received his fiftieth stamped postal, telling us all his dates were filled. The man at the door of his office recognized us and suspecting what we were after, told us to go away. He said Mr. Bunnell was too busy to see us.

" 'He ain't too busy,' I said. 'We got a new curiosity for him.'

"The doorkeeper gave Mr. Bunnell our message and we were ushered into his office. He was a very busy man, and he asked curtly what we wanted.

" 'We want to tell you about a curiosity.' said I boldly.

" 'Yes, a one-eyed Chinaman,' broke in Joe.

" 'What's curious about a one-eyed Chinaman?' asked Mr. Bunnell sharply.

" 'But this Chink ain't got any eyes like other Chinks,' said I.

" 'No, he ain't,' said Joe. 'He's only got one eye and it's in the center of his forehead.'

" 'And he wears a black, soft hat pulled down over his face,' said I, 'and he's got a hole cut in the hat so he can see out with his one eye.'

" 'Where is this remarkable Chinaman?' asked the museum man, excited at hearing of such a freak.

" 'We saw him on Mott street and we know the house he lives in,' said I.

" 'Meet me here to-morrow morning and take me to him,' said Mr. Bunnell.

" 'But what do we get for telling you about this curosity?' we asked.

"Mr. Bunnell asked what we wanted. We told him a job, and we went to work at his place the following day.

"Our freak Chinaman never existed and for several days we lived in fear that Mr. Bunnell would ask us to take him to the freak. We strung him along for four weeks about that freak, reporting every once in a while that the Chink was still living in the place we first saw him.

"Everything went along smoothly until Mr. Bunnell called us from the stage one day and told us to hustle into our street clothes. We knew then that the museum manager was going after our freak Chink.

"We got in Mr. Bunnell's carriage and drove to Chinatown. Although we were weak in the knees we decided to bluff as long as we could, and when we reached the Chinese quarter we pointed out a house in Mott street where our freak was supposed to live.

"Just as we were entering the house a Chinaman appeared out of the dark hall and barred our way. We told him what we were in search of, but he would not let us enter the house.

"Mr. Bunnell threatened him and we called him names for barring our way, but he paid no attention to us. I learned later that he was the lookout man for a Chinese gambling house.

"Mr. Bunnell was furious at being balked by the Chink and we drove to the office of the Chinese Consul. Once there Mr. Bunnell did all the talking.

"He told the Consul that he wanted that one-eyed Chinese freak and he was going to have him no matter what it cost. Mr. Bunnell demanded of the Consul that he help him get the man.

" 'Why I never even heard of such a man,' said the Consul, 'and no such person could be here without my knowing it. Some one must be fooling you.'

"Mr. Bunnell looked at us. We couldn't help grinning, for we figured that we had played our first and last engagement at his house.

"He never said a word to us all the way back to the museum. He realized that he had been duped by a couple of youngsters, and he showed he was a good sport by the way he stood for it.

"When he got back to his place he took us off in a corner and said to us:

" 'By gimminently! if you were not a couple of Jews you would not be so bright. Go back to work.'

"We stayed there four weeks longer and Mr. Bunnell always called us his boys after that. We played in his theatre recently and we had a great laugh over our one-eyed freak that never existed.

"The first real theatre Joe and I ever played in was Harry Miner's Bowery. We went there from Mr. Bunnell's for $30 a week. We were still doing the Irish song and dance act and the opening night we drew our salary in the gallery.

"Every boy in our neighborhood turned out to welcome us and we did feel proud. A. H. Sheldon was the stage manager of the Bowery then and it was he who gave us our next lift.

"The Ada Richmond burlesque troupe played at Miner's the week after we did and they were in need of a Dutch comedy team. Sheldon thought we would do and he hunted us up and asked if we could do the work.

"Wel', we got the job and that was the first time we ever did a Dutch turn. We did a knockabout, rough house turn, in which we welted each other with sticks. The program gave an idea of what was expected of us, for in big letters we were billed as The Two Skull Crackers.

"It was in this show that we first introduced our twisted dialect. We made good with the house and the next week we were at Miner's Eighth avenue house.

"There Col. Hopkins, of the Comique, of Providence, asked us to play his house for a week. We demanded $125 for a week's work in Providence, but jumped at Hopkins' final offer of $80. You see that was a clear jump of fifty from what we were getting.

"Providence liked our murder act. It was rough work. Of course we were always well padded, but accidents would happen.

On one occasion he forgot to put on the metallic protector which he wore under his skull pad and I hit him with a cane and opened his scalp. Another time he meant to hit me across the chest and he caught me across the lips.

"When we bled our audiences seemed to like us all the better. We used to be so much used up after our act that we would have to rub each other with alcohol after each performance.

"From Providence we went to Philadelphia, where we were offered an engagement with Carcrosses' Minstrels. Carcross never played a white-faced act in his house and he thought we would be a novelty.

"The opening night we never got a hand. We went to our dressing rooms and were crying when Carcross found us. He was a kindly man, and he began to cheer us up.

" 'Your act didn't go well, boys,' he said. 'My audience didn't seem to understand it. They seem to think your stage fight is real. Now at the end of your argument hereafter shake hands and smile at the audience to show them it is all in fun. Then you must dress different. Go to some second-hand place and buy dress suits. No matter how they fit, get them.'

"We were only too glad to follow the veteran manager's instructions and retain our jobs.

This Chink ain't got any eyes like other Chinks, I said. No, he aint, said Joe. He's only got one eye and it's in the center of his forehead.

We got the dress suits and shook hands after our fight. Then began our first experience in educating an audience.

"We didn't make a single change except the two Carcross advised. In a week his audience had begun to applaud us. Finally we began to get curtains calls, and we became so popular that we stayed there nine months. By the way we were the first team of this kind to wear dress suits on the stage.

"It was pretty smooth sailing after that. We played with many companies and our salary kept on increasing. We began to think of taking out a company of our own and began to save money toward that end. When we did take out a company it was an all-star vaudeville cast and we got the money.

"Nine years ago Joe and I played at Hammerstein's Olympia at $750 a week. It was there that we first got the idea of burlesque. We let others in our plans, but they laughed at us.

"We took the old Imperial anyway and changed its title to our own names. Everybody remembers what we did there. We gave the best show we could get and the best artists.

"To get the best artists we had to pay the highest salaries. We paid De Wolf Hopper $80,000 for his season of eighty weeks with us. Lillian Russell has always received $1,200 a week.

We were billed as the Skull Crackers. . . . On one occasion, Joe forgot to put on the metallic protector he wore under his skull pad and I hit him with a cane and opened his scalp. . . . When we bled, our audiences liked us all the better.

"We kept on advancing all the time when until it got to the point where we could not go any further. I think the public will always go to see a good burlesque, but they seem to be a little tired of the style of the show we have been giving them. However, I won't have to bother about what the public cares for at the music hall hereafter."

"Is there any chances of you and Weber getting getting together again?" Fields was asked.

"Who can tell?" replied the comedian. "Stranger things have happened."

WEBER AND FIELDS REUNITED AFTER LONG SEPARATION

FROM MAY 25, 1907 ISSUE

Editorial Bulletin

SHADES of the mighty! What is more conducive to thoughts of the transitoriness, the ephemerality of man, than a collection of old theatre programs. Tom has long been dead, Dick has risen to the head of his profession, while Harry has turned his ability to the managerial end of the business (to which he is much better suited, and is able to smile magnanimously, albeit with a sort of gloating glee, at his present contemporaries who were used to cut his salary after rehearsal) and now has a long list of attractions to his credit; or perhaps it is theatres in which he is interested.

MARGUERITE, who played the halls (though she is loath to admit it and avoids those who knew her in the days of her struggle for recognition) is now a topliner. It is not generally known that she has two grown sons, but she speaks of them and their accomplishments and achievements with much pride when among her intimates.

What memories those old programs hold . . . the names call up familiar faces, a thousand little incidents are brought out . . . and we laugh at them as we did when they were new and we were younger . . .

JOSEY, poor thing, she of so much beauty and talent, fell the victim of too many suppers after shows and her weakened vitality was not able to withstand an attack of fever that kept her confined to a sanitarium for many months. It was even doubted at one time whether her mind was permanently affected; that mind at whose quickness and wit her friends had marvelled and her enemies had felt the sting; for she had enemies as all beautiful and vivacious women have, some (these were among the women) simply because she was beautiful and vivacious, and others (men, of course) because she had resented their approaches, though they were ready to testify upon oath if need be, that John Jones was not always in his own room when at the hotel, and that if John Jones was absent from the territory in which Josey was playing, James Smith or Dick Brown or some other equally unprincipalled fellow with power to influence a certain manager or booking agent in New York, was the favored one.

AND so it goes. What memories those old programs hold for us. As we run over the list of names and call up the familiar faces a thousand little incidents, buried under the accumulated experiences of years, are brought out and brushed up again and we laugh at them as we did when they were new, and we were many hundreds of days younger, or feel a straining sensation of the throat in tracing the history of those with whom the fates have not been kind.

IT IS a story of many characters, suggesting varied scenes and multifamous plots, that is told by the excellent colleetion of programs that Harry Knapp has preserved from the old Theatre Comique of St. Louis, that made variety history from 1873 to 1878. These programs will be reproduced in The Billboard, beginning with the next issue and running through several numbers. They embrace many names famous in the profession and will be of exceeding interest to all its members.

FROM JUNE 1, 1907 ISSUE

FROM JUNE 1, 1907 ISSUE

HARRY KNAPP'S

Excellent Collection of Old Theatre Programs

Preserved from the Prosperous and History - making Days of the Old Theatre Comique in St. Louis—Is Your Name Here ?

MOST men never realize that the day in which they are living will sometime be a part of history. With that selfishness which characterizes a large majority of the human race, they plod along through life, like the grumpy traveler who thinks only of the dinner waiting him at his destination, seeing nothing, making no enduring observations, picking up no souvenirs. The business man keeps his eye on the main chance, missing many others, perhaps not realizing that other people are interesting—even human—except as he may conflict with them in tactics or come in contact with them in a clever transaction. Artists, authors, actors, even, are often so occupied by the consideration of their own trivial affairs that their perspective of life is narrowed to a minimum of what that term implies.

Harry Knapp is different. While he was business manager and treasurer of the old Theatre Comique, at St. Louis, in those halcyon days of variety from 1873, when the house was named (it had formerly been known as Ben DeBarr's Opera House) till 1878 when it was burned, he was assiduously preserving the weekly handbills containing the programs at that house. The collection is valuable now, after a quarter of a century, embracing, as it does, many names indissolubly associated with the history of variety and the stage in general.

We reproduce those names herewith, as they appeared on the bills. Those who wish to communicate with Mr. Knapp can address him in care of the New York office of The Billboard.

APRIL 15, 1877.
Johnny Allen, specialties; The Whitmans, Joseph, Charlotte and Ferdinand, introducing their hit, entitled, The Old Suwannee River; Miss Clara Sidelle, finest male impersonator in the country; Maurice Lapoint, a pocket edition of Mr. D. S. Wambold; Mlle. Ida Idalie, favorite premiere; Miss Lillie Laurence, first appearance of the dashing corypher; Ballet, Satinella, or The Spirit of Beauty; Sisters Irwin, Florence and May; Thatcher and Hume, songs, dances, etc.; Mr. W. J. Mills, character songs and lightning changes; Miss Mollie Wilson, St. Louis' favorite. To conclude every night with Mr. Johnny Allen's original piece, entitled, Uncle Schneider.

JUNE 10, 1877.
Rollin Howard and his opera bouffe and burlesque company, the leading spirits of which are Miss Blanche Clifton, Miss Marie Sherman, Mr. T. W. Hanshew and John L. Sanford, the great comedian; The Woods, Harry and Fannie; Two Haleys; Parker Sisters, Georgie and Lizzie; the favorites Miss Edna Orr, Mlle. Emaline, Dick Parker and Otto Burbank.

NOVEMBER 5, 1876.
Miss Nully Pieris, songstress; Jas. Maas and Miss Gussie Crayton, in their musical entertainment; Zanfratta, burlesque troupe; Les Postillions, produced under the direction of Signor Tito Cellini, introducing some brilliant dancing; holdovers.

NOVEMBER 19, 1876.
Frank Lewis, the star motto vocalist; C. A. Gardner, the celebrated Dutch artist; Chas. Harris and Lottie Gray, the California comiques; Miss Nully Pieris; The Fostelles, sketch, entitled, Life in the Kitchen; Miss Annie Fox; Homer and Holly; Sanford and Wilson and Parker and Burbank will introduce their great success, The Slipperyelmville Serenaders.

SEPTEMBER 24, 1876.
Cecile La Comte, the beautiful French vocalist; Miss Lena Rivers, in beautiful ballads; The Lawrence Sisters, in their daring trapeze act, The Leap for Life; Miss Annie Fox, vocal gems; Sanford and Wilson, in their sketch, Vegetables and Clams; Murphy and Mack in their new sketch, entitled, The Rafferty Blues; Billy Noonan and Miss Alice Bateman in their comedy statue clog; Manchester and Jennings, in their original sketch, Serenading Under Difficulties; Miss Florence Warner and Miss Marie Swinebrun, the velocipede riders.

Miss Clara Sidelle, finest male impersonator in the country; Rollin Howard and his opera bouffe and burlesque company; Cecile LaComte, the beautiful French vocalist, and the first-class Ethiopian comedian, John Bowman were just a few of the acts, which played the old Theatre Comique . . .

OCTOBER 17, 1875.
Frankie, serio-comic and Motto songstress; Allie Drayton, pleasing song and dance lady; Hurley and Marr; The Levanion Brothers, the greatest gymnasts in the world; Chas. Diamond, song and dance harpist; Murphy and Mack, the great Irish artists; Maggie Weston; Madame Blanche and her troupe of beautiful young ladies; Rouselle Brothers; Prof. Giovanni, the musical artist.

MARCH 19, 1876.
Tom Allen and the inimitable Ned Donnelly, appearing every night in ring costume, in a grand assault d'arms in the celebrated crib scene from Tom and Jerry, or High and Low Life in London; Mr. W. J. Daly, soloist; Fields and Hoey, great musical artists, vocalists and dancers; Miss Emma Jatau and Mr. George W. Brown, gymnasts; Winner Sisters, three in number, characteristic melodies and songs; Murphy and Mack, appearing this week in their original Irish sketch, Trouble in America, introducing their new song, We'll Go Back Again; La Verde Sisters, entirely new selection of songs, dances, etc.; Glenn and Williams, introducing Welch and Rice's original sketch, entitled, Mischievous Boy; Cellini's ballet, The Pas Syrian, introducing our favorite premiere, Miss Frankie Christie and company; Miss Mollie Wilson, in a new selection of serio-comic gems.

MAY 9, 187—.
Shed Le Clair, the wonderful gymnast; Miss Minnie Jackson; Mr. Nick Woodland, with his performing dogs; Miss Mollie Wilson, appearing in new songs; Miss Lottie Brown, popular serio-comic vocalist; Miss Annie Fox, singer; the first-class Ethiopian comedian, John Bowman, Dick Parker, Otto Burbank and Cogill and Cooper will appear in specialties; Rose de Mai, ballet, by Sig Titto Cellini, introducing Mlle. Ida De Vere.

NOVEMBER 14, 1875.
Peak Family, Swiss bell ringers; Delehanty and Cummings; Miss Minnie Loder, La Petite Rosa, J. A. Gulick; Burton Stanley.

NOVEMBER 28, 1875.
Fostelle and Rugby, in their specialty, Borrowed Plumes; Cawthorne Children, Dutch and Ethiopian comedians; Delehanty and Cummings;

THE WAGON SHOWMEN

FROM DEC. 5, 1903 ISSUE

FIFTY YEARS RECOLLECTIONS OF AN OLD AMUSEMENT MANAGER

ANECDOTES ~ STORIES   WAYBACK ~ TALES

BY DOCTOR JUDD

Along in the fifties and up to the commencement of our Civil War, or to 1860, panoramas were very popular in the United States.

They came into vogue in the days when the young people of this land were invited to know that the theatre and stage was a wicked diversion, and all entertainments that they attended must be serious and take some intellectual and instructive form.

The early exhibitors of panoramas headed their advertising bills "A Grand Moral Entertainment," and as they made at once a commodious means of travel and a vehicle of art, they became very popular.

All the old panorama men who catered to the last generation with their exhibitions are fast passing away, and soon they and their shows will be forgotten. Only recently occurred the death at his home, Cambridge, Mass., of Rufus Somerby. He was the only one left, that I can remember, of that long line of panorama exhibitors that were perambulating this country with their exhibitions in the fifties and sixties.

In his earlier manhood he was a handsome and conspicuous figure; later on in his life you might have taken him for a Bishop or a retired General or Statesman of the old blue-dress-coat-and-brass-buttons school.

Some persons of a certain age will remember him kindly as their first "panoramy" man, the master of the painted show, lecturing frequently, with his long stick in his hand, which he used to point out to his audiences the most important objects in the magical picture gallery, called the "Seven Mile Mirror of the World," that he exhibited for so many years to delighted audiences in the leading cities and towns of the United States and Canada.

I first met Rufus Somerby years and years ago out in what was then called the Western Country—Ohio, Michigan, Indiana and Illinois.—when we had but very few railroads and all shows then traveling had to have their own conveyances or take the public stages to get over the country.

• • •

The first panorama exhibition that I traveled with was Bullard's Panorama of New York City.

It was in the early fifties that I went on to New York to go out with it. We had no palace cars in those days to ride in as showmen and theatrical people have today. I left Cleveland Ohio, and crossed the Lake on a schooner, then took the Erie Canal to Albany, and down the Hudson on a steamboat to New York. Traveling on the Erie Canal on a packet boat was the pleasantest part of the trip. It was drawn by three prancing horses, with their driver seated on the rear horse. Some of these pas-

senger packets then running on the Erie Canal were doing a very good business, but the railroad was making great inroads on them and in only a few more years they were tied up along the banks of the canal and stored away in canal basins to rot. This old style of traveling on passenger packet boats had its pleasures and its hardships. One of the latter was when you had to drop down on your hands and knees whenever you heard the man at the rudder call out "low bridge." Down in the cabin you could sit and read with the greatest comfort, gliding along on your route without any noise, except when you would come to a jam of canal boats, then you would hear the words that we have been taught not to use brought forth in the loudest tone of voice possible. It was some years after the railroads got started before you could persuade some of the older people to take the steam cars. They preferred the old and safest way—the packet boat.

BARNUM'S MUSEUM.

Situated for many years at the corner of Ann and Broadway. Variety and circus performances were given here. The place reached the height of its prosperity during the Civil War.

EXTERIOR OF THE HIPPODROME, MADISON SQUARE, 1853.

I remember when on this trip we were plodding along near and alongside of the track of the old Schenectady and Utica Railroad, a train came along and a number of passengers were sitting on the deck of our packet boat and were making all kinds of objections to riding on the steam cars. An old lady spoke up and said, "Yes, they will turn everybody that rides on them into consumption. They go so fast and riding against the wind will ruin a person's lungs." I don't think at that time there were any trains making more than fifteen miles an hour.

The packet boats have had their day and gone. The next generation may see the railroads gone. The day of steam is nearly over, "Electricity is now King." The locomotive and steam engine are becoming obsolete. It will only be a short time now before we will be traveling on our journey through space in electrical airships.

When I arrived in New York I stopped at the Clinton Hotel, corner Beeckman and Nassau streets. It was then conducted by Simeon Leland and his two brothers, Charles and Warren, who were the clerks. In later years I have stopped with the Lelands at some of their mammoth hotels that they have been keeping; but not at such a reasonable price as I did at the old Clinton Hotel, one dollar a day. At this time General Winfield Scott was in New York stopping at this hotel.

On my first evening in the city I went to the old Bowery Theatre.

> The packet boats have had their day. . . . The next generation may see the railroad gone. . . . It will only be a short time before we will be traveling through space in electrical airships.

The most of the next day I spent at Barnum's Museum, which was then at the corner of Broadway and Ann streets. Even to stand on the opposite side of the street and look over to Barnum's Museum was worth the price of the admission. He had big paintings of all known wild animals and curiosities from all parts of the world tacked up between each window, and the whole building was covered with flags of all nations. A brass band was out on the balcony over the entrance playing all day long. Inside of the Museum the Bohemian Troup of Glass Blowers pleased me the most. Also on exhibition were the celebrated Siamese Twins, Chang and Eng. Mailzee Automaton Chess Player was also one of the attractions. I had learned how to play chess a little and sat down and tackled the figure for a game, but it beat me, as it did every one else. In after years I learned how it was all done when I had the same Automaton with an exhibition of my own, and every week I would pay off the little French dwarf who an expert chess player and would crawl inside the figure and manipulate it. He was concealed among the dummy machinery which would be wound up only to deceive the public.

At Castle Garden I remember of seeing Lola Montez, a popular favorite of that day, who came out between the acts and introduced songs and dances. Castle Garden still remains once a fort, then a concert garden, next a shelter for thousands of immigrants and now an acquarium. At Niblo's Garden I witnessed the old and original Ravel Family of Pantomimists. Their equal in this line of business I have never seen. They were all natural born pantomimists. What took my fancy at that time was when Garibaldi Ravel, the father of all the Ravels, was crushed as flat as a pancake by a thing looking like a big grindstone that three or four men rolled out on the stage. It accidentally tipped over and Garibaldi was caught under it. When the huge grindstone was lifted up with the help of more men who were called in, Garibaldi looked lige a great cut-out paper man. A lounge was procured and the paper man was laid on it. Then one of the Ravels rushed out, procured a pair of bellows and commenced to blow it up. The figure gradually assumed its normal shape. Instantly Garibaldi jumped from the lounge a man newly made over and made his customary bow to the audiences.

Where now stands the Fifth Avenue Hotel, I went to see Fraconi's mammoth hippodrome, which had just been brought to this country from Paris by Seth B. Howes.

Bullard's Panorama of New York City that I went out with gave a very faithful representation of the great city as it was in those days. If you were going to give a representation of New York City of today you would have to add a great many yards of canvas to the old panorama. As it was, we took the audience up and down Broadway, down among the shipping through the Five Points and The Bowery. As the panorama would move along, the lecturer would point out with his long lecturing stick the principal buildings. He never failed to notify the audience when they came to A. T. Stewart's marble front store, which was in those days way down Broadway near the City Hall. This would please the ladies who were in the audience, for what lady in those days did not have the ambition that when, if she ever did go to New York, she would pay a visit to the mammoth store. He would also point out the prominent men and well-known people of that day. He would never let Horace Greeley with his white hat, jogging along on his way to the Tribune office, get by without calling the audience's attention to him. No matter if some person had come into prominence since the panorama had been painted, he would point to any figure on the painting and say it was they, and the audience would have to imagine the resemblance.

In 1857 I was in the employ of George K. Goodwin of Boston, Mass. He bought and sold panoramas and also sent them out on the road under other showmen's management. He made a mint of money out of his panorama, "Milton's Paradise Lost." He sent me out with a panorama exhibition, Dr. Kane's Arctic Expedition. We had with this exhibition a great many curosities that came from the Arctic Regions. We had a team of Esquimaux dogs and the sleds that they drew, and while we were in the Eastern country we had Hans Christian, a native Esquimaux boy, whom Dr. Kane brought back to this country with him. The first night that we opened in Boston, Dr. Kane came on from New York, and after the evening entertainment Goodwin gave a supper at the Adams House to Dr. Kane and the press of Boston.

Along that winter we had gotten out west with this panorama and were showing for one week in Springfield, Ill., when an officer of the law came in and put an attachment on our panorama for some debt. I did not want to pay it, if I could get out of it, and was consulting our landlord when he told me I had better go over and see Lincoln & Herndon, lawyers. So I crossed over through the State House grounds to a red brick block and went upstairs through a narrow hall, and found Lincoln & Herndon's law office and went in. There sat a long, lean, lank fellow, leaning back in

INTERIOR OF CASTLE GARDEN IN 1850.

a chair with his coat off and legs upon a desk. He looked to me like an old prairie farmer. I told him I was looking for a lawyer. He said, "Well, I hope you haven't killed anybody." I said "No, but there has been a horse killed and parties want to saddle the pay for it on me and I want to find a lawyer to straighten the thing out." He said once more "I am kind of a lawyer," took my papers and looked at them. It seemed that one of Goodwin's panoramas had been in Springfield the year before and the manager had engaged a horse and wagon to do some street advertising. The horse ran away, broke his leg and had to be killed. Goodwin's manager left town without making any settlement. While he was looking at my papers a man came into the office and said, "Good morning, Mr. Lincoln." He then took the newspaper, The Springfield Republican, that he had been reading when I came in, folded it up, thrust it into a pigeon hole in his desk and said: "Well, this man may have the best of you, but he has put a big price for a horse, especially a dead one." He then looked out of the window in a kind of a dreamy way for a while and then said: "It was about twenty years ago that I rode into this place with all my belongings on a horse that I borrowed of this man's father who now makes a claim against you. I came here to see if I could make a living at law. Now, we will go down to this man's livery stable and see what we can do." He put on his coat, took down from the top of his desk an old slouch hat—I had seen older ones but not much. We went down and saw the man at the livery stable, and it only took Lincoln a few minutes to settle the whole matter satisfactory to both of us. On our way back to his office I paid him for his services, and gave him some complimentary tickets to our entertainment, and that evening he attended it, accompanied by one of his sons.

In a short time the occurrence was practically forgotten, but it returned vividly when I began to read of Abraham Lincoln daily.

There never was on land and sea such color as stared from those canvases (panoramas); the soaring battle smoke, flags in processions, artillery rushing by, so painted that the audiences imagined they heard the clatter ... fires, sunsets, mines exploding, battered forts, the Merrimac, a fabulous marine monster, and the Monitor ....

The early '60's was the palmy days for panoramas of our Civil War. There never was on land and sea such color as stared from those canvases; the soaring battle smoke, flags in processions, artillery rushing by, and so painted that the audiences imagined they heard the clatter, officers waving their swords,—the only function of officers in battle pieces.—fires, sunsets, mines exploding, battered forts, the Merrimac, a fabulous marine monster, and the Monitor, smaller than life; Generals, all painted with long black hair and black whiskers, and their uniforms wondrously spick and shiny; an unusual amount of bayonet charging and hand-to-hand encounters; altogether an endless river of fire and blood. These old panoramas had breathless interest for every spectator, for most all the audience had some friends at the front and the subject was painfully interesting to them.

FROM DEC. 3, 1904 ISSUE

The OLD PANORAMA

By DR. JUDD

There is one branch in the history of the United States neglected by historians; they do not give any account of the old showmen and their shows that were perambulating the country in the early days.

If this generation of amusement-going people could look back and see the exhibitions and entertainments that their forefathers attended they probably would think it took very little to please them, for during the fore part and up to the middle of the last century all shows were very small affairs, compared to those spread out before the public at the present day.

Exhibitors of the early days, traveling over this country, in the absence of railroads, had to utilize the waterways, and where steamboats and canal boats could not go, stage coaches were the only conveyance for towns in the interior. Very few of the towns, outside of the larger cities, had any halls for them to hold forth in, and often they had to take any empty room they could find, which was generally the dining room of the tavern. Rates of travel were high, and it was very expensive for the showman to get his baggage over the country.

The first shows traveling in this country on the pictorial order were the magic lantern or dissolving view exhibitions. These could be carried on in a very small space. There were any number of exhibitors of panstereorama models. These models of a town, country or buildings were made of wood, cork, pasteboard and other substances, showing every part in relief. There were models of Jerusalem, The Lord's Supper, St. Peter's Church at Rome, Mt. Vernon and Washington's Tomb, Windsor Castle, etc.

P. T. Barnum at one time in his early life traveled about the country exhibiting a panstereorama model of Solomon's Temple. He advertised on his small bills that there was $10,000 worth of gold used in the construction of this model. He forgot to add leaf to the word gold in his advertisements.

Yankee Robinson, who in his lifetime was owner of several large circuses and menageries, commenced in the show business as an exhibitor of one of these models, known as The Raising of Lazarus. He traversed the country with it in an old, rickety, one-horse wagon. But poor, old Yankee, with all his ups and downs in the show business, finally died poorer than when he was born.

Panoramas began to make their appearance late in the '40s. About this time P. T. Barnum brought over from London a duplicate of the panorama, The Ascent of Mt. Blanc, which Albert Smith had exhibited for so many years at Egyptian Hall, London. This Albert Smith was manager of Charles Dickens' first reading tours in England. Barnum also brought over from Paris Huldon's Diorama, The Obsequies of Napoleon. This was a very realistic production of that great event on canvas, containing moving pictures of soldiers, horses, ships, barges, etc.

During the '50s there was no end of panoramas traveling illustrating every subject: Bunyan's Pilgrim's Progress, Milton's Paradise Lost, The Revolutionary War, Life of Christ, The Holy Land, The Napoleonic Wars, Dr. Kane's Arctic Expedition, panoramas of London, Paris, Tour of Europe, the McElvoy and Uncle John McElvoy and others with their panoramas of Ireland. Some of the most prominent panoramas that were put on exhibition were really works of art, as they were painted by the best artists in this country and in Europe, which made the cost of them run up into many thousands of dollars, but soon the panorama business was overdone. There was such a demand for them by showmen that firms went into the business of painting panoramas that were mere daubs. After the close of the Civil War panoramas had to take a back seat in the amusement line. Many a curious anecdote related of these old panorama exhibitors could be told if we had the space in this article. Amos Hubbel was a queer old character, who for a number of years exhibited a diorama called The Burning of Moscow. He traveled over the country with it in his own wagon, and did his own advertising after he arrived in a town where he was to exhibit. At night he attended his own door until it was time to commence the exhibition.

Late in the '50s I went to England for P. T. Barnum and brought over to this country Thidon's Theater of Art, a diorama of pictorial, mechanical, animated and moving figures, representations of noted battles that had been fought on land, naval engagements on the high seas and other noted scenes all over the world, with moving figures of men, soldiers, horses, ships, etc. These figures were very nicely cut out of sheet brass, painted natural and lifelike on one side. Each was set with a cogwheel, which ran over a strip of felt, which set the figures into their natural movements when hooked on a revolving belt running in front of the painted scenery. You could show a town, city or street scene, and have a whole army marching through, the natural movements of the limbs of the soldiers, people and horses, and the guns and cannon in the ships and forts were so fixed that the operators behind the scenery could puff smoke through them, and the boom noise would be imitated on a bass drum.

One week in 1860 we were showing in Galena, Ill., and while there we were overhauling the exhibition and needed some leather belting. I went out around town to find some, and I came across a store that had a sign over the door, "Leather Store." I went in, found what I thought would answer the purpose and wanted to take it down to the hall to see if it would work with what I had. The man who waited on me did not seem to want to trust me with the rolls, so he called out to some one in the back part of the store, "Orville, Orville, is Ulysses there? Send him here." Ulysses took one or two rolls, I the rest, and we went to the hall. There I found that even the narrow would not fit into our grooves, so Ulysses, as he had been called, said: "I will take it back to the store. I think they have a machine there that will trim off the edge better than you can do it here, and right after dinner I will bring it back and you can pay me." "All right," said I. After dinner he was back with it, and when he came into the hall we had spread out on the floor lots of our scenery, and all kinds of figures of men, soldiers and horses. "Well, well," he said, "what have you got here, anyway. War, more war." I began to tell him, and I saw him looking intently at a scene that was partly set up into the frame on the exhibition stage. He said: "What is that scene over there?" I told him it was the battle of Buena Vista, in the Mexican War, and I told him the scene leaning against the wall nd the figures around on the floor all went to make up a moving picture of General Scott and his army's triumphal march and grand parade through the principal streets of the City of Mexico. Pulling out another scene, I said: "This is the famous building known as the Hall of the Montezumas, of which General Scott took possession." Then I picked up a figure from the floor, a full uniformed officer on horseback, and said to him: "This is General Winfield Scott." "Yes," he said, "Old Fuss nd Feathers. Can you bring out 'Old Rough and Ready?'" I said, "Yes, here is General Taylor." Then he said he was in and all through the Mexican War. We soon got to work on the belting that he had brought. I paid him, but he lingered around and sat down where we were working putting hooks on the belting. Soon he pulled off his coat, picked up a punch and mallet and went to punching holes in the belt where one of our men had marked them, and then went on telling more bout himself and stories of the Mexican War. It was getting pretty late n the afternoon and almost dark, when a man came into the hall and called out: "Ulysses, Orville wants to know when you are coming back to the store, and wants to know if you have hired out to the show." He looked up, took out his watch and said: "I declare, I did not think it was so late. I must go." I thrust a number of complimentary tickets into his hand and told him to come down to the show. He did and brought his wife and two children.

The afternoon that he helped us he told us that he was formerly of the regular army and was Captain Grant when he left the service, but at that

---

The first shows traveling this country on the pictorial order were the magic lantern exhibitions . . .

---

time he might as well have said he was Captain Jones, as far as it would be of any unusual interest to us. We thought of him only as one with whom we had spent a very pleasant afternoon listening to his stories. We would have some one tell us most every day that they were in the Mexican War or were in some battle that we represented in our exhibition. However, it was only just a few more years when we did begin to think it was a little out of the usual occurrence when we would hear nd read of Gen. Ulysses S. Grant.

FROM DEC. 15, 1900 ISSUE

J. R. BONHEUR.

H. A. BONHEUR.

A. G. BONHEUR.

The Three Bonheurs.

This famous trio have attracted the good public's attention by their originality and unique standing in the profession. Dresden, O., not 100 miles from Cincinnati, is the scene of their boyhood. Their remarkable success as showmen has been almost continuous and unvarying from the time of their first exhibition, which was given at Riley Center, Kan., in 1880, unknown to their most intimate friends in Morris county, where they lived at that time. Their show consisted of a magic-lantern outfit and a camera, to secure their own pictures in case they were successful.

Amos G. Bonheur, then a mere lad, purchased a white mustang from Miss Lida Gillett, sister of the notorious cattle plunger, Grant Gillett, now an exile in Mexico, to go in advance of the show, and carried his posting outfit, with paper for each week's billing, in a pair of leather saddle-bags.

They were so sucessful with their views of Western life, wit Howard A. Bonheur as operator and James R. Bonheur as lecturer, that they soon discarded the mules. A fine wagon was built to order, and four big dapple grays purchased to pull it over the country. The cast-off wagon was black, but the new one was white and gold, with a revel of color and art. This wagon, the birthplace of the marvelous living pictures, having in turn had its palmy days of trooping, now lies dismantled, in wretched deseutude, at the Bonheur Bros.' winter quarters. Jim Bonheur often reverts to those days as the happiest of their career. The charm of the life on the plains was its freedom, its soothing effects of sky and wind, the rolling, wide sweeping scene, and above all, the ever-increasing patronage accorded them at the settlements where even a magic-lantern show was a new thing. Their routes extended into western Missouri, where they frequently met the James boys. They added to their show some real photographic views of the noted bandits, which, after the assassination of Jesse James, proved so valuable an attraction that they went to southern Ohio and Indiana, where their exhibitions netted over $10,000.

There are at least two men in Ohio living to-day who know how Jim Bonheur obtained his first lessons in magic-lantern delineation. At an early age he painted very creditable water-color pictures. One of these water-colors, showing a group of bears at a gringo picnic, was traded, "even up," to a lad of his own age for a pair of big, old-fashioned skates, intending, as he said, to make an ice sled of the runners, because they were so big. But Frank Hindle, better recognized as "Gimlet," coveting the skates because they fit his feet so well, induced young Bonheur to exchange them for a tiny tin box, with a bull's-eye lens and a sperm oil lamp, which "Gimlet" signified was a magic-lantern. Bonheur had never seen one before, and was captivated with the strips of glass, on which were transparent daubs of gorgeous-colored pictures. Both parties were satisfied with their bargain, and the incident of this boyish trade for the little tin lantern certainly had a direct bearing on the whole after lives of the three brothers.

> ## In western Missouri they frequently met the James Boys. They added to their show some real photographic views of the noted bandits.

In 1883, through experiments with a series of glass slides of a bucking broncho, taken at a round-up, Jim Bonheur hit on the solution of the animated picture problem. He took much pride in showing a simple illustration of his idea, produced by only two views of the bucking broncho. By jerking the mechanical dissolver quickly back and forth across the optical centers of the stereopticon, the moving objects were connected in the pictures without any apparent eclipse between the change of postures, and no change whatever apparent in the surrounding landscape. The broncho bounded into the air or struck the earth in rapid succession, according as the jerking back and forth of the dissolver shutter closed and opened the right or left lens.

In January, 1886, while the three brothers were snowbound at Nelson's ranch, in McPherson county, Kansas, Mr. Bonheur submitted his idea in writing, accompanied with diagrams, explaining (to Edison) how unlimited continuous action could be produced on the same general optical principle with a single magic-lantern by passing through its optical system an endless belt of such pictures, each having a slightly advanced movement of the living objects, and referred to Muybridge's method of taking motion pictures, that he suggested might be thus utilized. In this document he credited the invention of the "Dancing Skeleton," which he had studied, to Prof. Pepper, and subsequently learned that Mr. Beale, of Greenwich, Eng., was its inventor. Mr. Bonheur's mistake unchanged remains, however, in the history of the modern animated picture, as published in The Century in 1894, by the Dicksons.

Milton Starr, a literary friend of James R. Bonheur, says, in his writings: "James Watt discovered the expansive power of steam, but other men applied the discovery and perfected the steam engine. The making of the engine was mere carpentry, but the eye that penetrated the secret of nature was the eye of genius. The kinetoscope is one of the most wonderful of Edison's inventions. The man who gave Mr. Edison the idea which that invention embodies is James R. Bonheur, the credit of which is his due in this connection."

Howard Bonheur, who was always the inseparable companion of his elder brother, has a penchant for training animals, and his control over goats, ponies and dogs, of which he has a large collection at the quarters, is remarkable, many of his pets being endowed with very human-like functions, as a result of thought and patient training.   B. B.

FROM AUG. 22, 1903 ISSUE

DEVELOPMENT

Of the Floating Theatre. Managers Expense
Comparatively Nominal. No Town
Licenses. No Hotel Bills.

Leaving Pittsburg the floating theatre steams up the Monongahela River to the towns of the coal miners and steel workers. Returning it continues its journey down the muddy Ohio to the Kanawha, the conditions of navigation, in this instance, being a depth of eight feet of water and a population of 4,000 in the towns along the banks. The route of the boat is next down the Ohio to Cairo and then up the Illinois River to Lasalle, which is only a few hour's railroad ride from Chicago. From Lasalle the playboat steams back to the Mississippi and thence to the vicinity of New Orleans where the theatrical season ends late in the southern winter. Over this route there are thousands of towns in all, with many varied types of people as patrons, including those of the famous Mississippi plantations.

For 25 years past from one to four playboats have been on this long water circuit. Years ago French's floating theatre, one of the originals, presented Uncle Tom's Cabin on the very river over which Eliza escaped on the ice. The water circuit tired of the Uncle Tom show, however, and until recently there has been nothing in the floating theatres except vaudeville.

This year the drama has been revived on water and a version of Faust, full of electricity and life, is being shown before thousands under more novel conditions than surround most theatrical audiences.

The floating theatre is notably independent. It pays no railroad fare, hires no houses, divides no receipts and incurs no hotel bills. From the time the stock company goes aboard the theatre at the beginning of the season until be seen as well as his work can be heard. The company need step on land. Cut off in odd corners of the playboat and the steamer that propels it are the bedrooms of the members of the company. On the steamer is a dining room, where all the people of the floating theatre eat. For amusement there is the wonderful panorama of the river through which the steamer steams lazily during the day.

Towns are close together and many of the jumps of the floating theatre are but 10 miles. An advance agent bills the town and exchanges passes for newspaper notices. For a week before the boat comes the towns blaze like poppy fields with lithographs. Then, about the middle of the day of the show, the calliope fills the air with "Mr. Dooley" or "Dixie." Plantation songs are drowned half sung and everyone pauses to watch the theatre, glistening whitely in the sunshine, coming up the river. It is still so far away that the man who plays the calliope on the upper deck of the puffing steamer cannot be seen as well as his work can be heard. The idle population of the town gathers to meet the steamer at the wharf. As it comes nearer the calliope is hushed and the brass band, perched on the top of the pilot house, begins to play. The crowd on the wharf thickens. With a final bunt the stern-wheel steamer pushes the theatre against the wharf and the demons of the brocken, deckhands for the time, tumble nimbly over the side and tie the theatre fast. The gangway is then placed and the theatre is arrived. From this time until an hour before the show the public is welcome.

Theatregoers of the little river towns have not been educated up to buying their seats by a puzzling diagram and anyway they have plenty of time. They therefore go aboard the theatre and pick out their seats, the first comers dashing eagerly to the seats they want and holding them against later comers until the ticket seller has exchanged his numbered pasteboard for their 25 or 50 cents. Often the playgoers sit in seats to see if they are comfortable before they make a final selection.

Back on the steamer odors of cooking mingle with the smell of sulphur from banked fires under the boilers. The deckhands wash their hands and faces and become actors. The captain stops chewing the tobacco of the sailor man and lights the cigar of the theatrical manager.

"Make fast that for'ard port hawser," he says to a deckhand not yet transformed.

"Put another weight on that No. 3 drop, Mr. Jones, we want that anchor for the boat," he says to the stage carpenter.

When the band comes aft for supper the calliope plays. When the latter music is stopped for more steam the band resumes work and the free concert is continuous until the band's final transformation changes it into the orchestra and the overture is played. There are seats

For a week before the boat comes, the towns blaze like poppy fields with lithographs. Then about the middle of the day of the show, the calliope fills the air with "Mr. Dooley" or "Dixie." Plantation songs are drowned half sung and everyone pauses to watch the theatre, glistening whitely in the sunshine, coming up the river.

for 1,000 people in the floating theatre. On the southern end of the circuit seats or sold "black and white," no colored people being allowed to buy seats at the door except for others. Up north there is no color line.

When night falls the whole outfit, steamer, theatre and all, blazes with electric lights. A dynamo on the steamer supplies plenty of current and the floating theatre is as brilliant with lights as the front of a Broadway playhouse. The steamer proper is closely lashed to the main theatre boat. From the edge of the upper deck of the steamer a search light flashes about over the hills, the trees, the open fields or the mills.

The overture over, the curtain is raised. Between the acts there are vaudeville stunts, for the habit is so strongly fixed along the rivers as on Broadway, and after the last deckhand "devil" has dropped apparently through the bottom of the theatre into the muddy river, the show is continued with a half hour of a vaudeville olio. River towns look for about three hours' entertainment because entertainments do not come often and the appetite is strong.

There are no matinees held on the floating theatre.

THE LAST WORDS LINCOLN HEARD

FROM JULY 20, 1907 ISSUE

SAW LINCOLN SHOT.

Stirring Days of '65 Recalled by Harry Hawk, the Well-known Philadelphia Actor and Elk.

"On the afternoon of Friday, April 14, 1865, I was at the theatre at the rehearsal of a song composed by William Withers, the leader of the orchestra, in honor of President Lincoln, and about 2 o'clock I went out to get some lunch. On the steps of the theatre sat J. Wilkes Booth, reading a letter. I spoke to him, and he started, folded the letter with a muttered 'Damn that woman,' and came with me, and we had a light lunch together.

"I can see him yet, tall, handsome, and gifted. He was dressed all in black and wore a black hat, the same clothing he wore that night at the theatre. He was morose, as he always was, for John Booth, as we called him, was disappointed, and burning with the shame and wrongs of the South, as he bitterly called them. He was insane on that one subject, I am sure, and had he lived to-day would have been credited with a brain storm. He thought the whole South would rise up with open arms to greet him when he committed that awful crime, and in his poor, diseased imagination, he pictured himself as the idol of the Confederacy.

"Well, after we had finished our lunch I returned to the theatre and saw no more of Booth until after the shot had been fired. When the assassination occurred I was alone on the stage, but my back was turned toward the President, and therefore I did not see the actual shooting.

"Mrs. Muzzy, who played the part of Mrs. Mount Chessington in the play, had just discovered that I, as The American Cousin, had destroyed a will which gave me a large fortune, and in anger she cried, 'Sir, it is plain to be seen that you are not accustomed to the manners of good society,' and with this parting shot she flounced out.

" 'Not accustomed to the manners of society?' I replied 'Well, I know enough to turn you inside out, woman. You darned old sockdolliger of a man trap.' Those were the last words that the President heard, for just as I finished them I heard a shot. It was not loud, and I supposed some one had fired a pistol by mistake in the property room. As I turned to go on with my part, not realizing what had taken place, the huse was as silent as the grave for an instant, and then through the quietness came the now famous 'Sic Semper Tyrannis,' followed by a scene of wild confusion.

HAWK WAS ARRESTED.

"Booth was advancing over the stage with a big dagger in his hand, and I took a step toward him, then, as he waved his weapon, I went off the stage, to return a moment later, when I was grasped by Colonel Stewart, who had gained the stage, and who shouted, 'Where is that man?'

" 'By God I don't know,' I shouted in return and then went into the green room. Even then the members of the company did not know who had fired the shot, and were rushing about in wild disorder.

"After this I was arrested and was taken before Mayor Wallach, who held me under $1,000 bail as a witness. This was furnished by Dr. Brown, an undertaker, who afterwards embalmed the body of the President. Dr. Brown took me with him to his home, and at about 3 in the morning I was taken under an escort of six soldiers to the Peterson House, where the members of the Cabinet and other officials were gathered. Here also was the wounded President lying, and it was not until about 7 in the morning that he died. I gave my testimony before Judge Carter, and was allowed to return to my friend's home.

"About a week after this we started to Cincinnati, and as I was told that a military pass was not needed at that time, I was greatly surprised to be arrested at Harrisburg because I was un-

The Assassination of President Lincoln, April 14, 1865.
Courtesy Kenneth M. Newman, The Old Print Shop, Inc., New York.

able to show one. I was held at the State Capitol, while word was sent to Washington that I had been captured. A few days later an order came from Washington: 'Release him (Signed) Stanton,' and even then the officers could not get it into their heads that the Secretary was not letting some valuable prisoner get away, and it was not until fully twenty-four hours later that I was freed. After that for some time, I went under an assumed name, so as not to fall victim to over-zealous officials."

FROM SEPT. 28, 1901 ISSUE

SIX ARE LEFT

Of the Entire Cast of Booth's Company at the Time Lincoln Was Shot.

Findlay, O., Sept. 23.—"The calamity that has just fallen upon the people of the United States recalls to me the night that President Lincoln was shot," said Mrs. Kathryne M. Evans, an actress with the Carner Stock Company, in this city.

"At the time my husband, J. H. Evans, and I were playing with the stock company at Ford's Theater. Laura Keene was playing the leading role, and I was taking the part of Mrs. Sharp, one of the servants. My husband and I were sitting in the green room, waiting for our 'call,' when we heard a shot that we knew was not a part of the play. Everybody rushed frantically to the stage, and as we arrived there we saw the

President's head fall forward on his breast. The members of the company were terribly excited, and refused to believe that the assassin was an actor, much less that it was Booth, as he was loved by every one who knew him.

> **My husband and I were sitting in the green room waiting for our call, when we heard a shot that we knew was not a part of the play.**

" A great gloom fell over all theatrical people that the deed had been committed by one of their number, and many did not go back to Washington for years. My husband and everybody that had been seen in the company during the day was put under arrest, on suspicion of being an accessory to the great crime.

"Of the company that was playing there that night there are but two women and four men alive to-day. I am the only woman of the company still on the stage. There are but two men still before the footlights, M. A. Kennedy and W. J. Ferguson, the latter starring in "A Girl From Japan."

STREET AND COUNTY FAIRS

FROM NOV. 5, 1904 ISSUE

FAIRS—THEIR ORIGIN AND GROWTH.

Fairs and feasts have the same derivation—had their beginning among the Hebrews.

The Olympian Games were held once in four years in honor of Zeus at Olympia.

The competitive exercises consisted of running races. The prize was a wreath from the sacred olive tree in Olympia.

The Pythian Games ranked next to the Olympian; the prize wreath was laurel.

The Nemean and Isthmian had prizes for music and poetry, as well as gymnastics, chariots and horses.

The Games and Festivals of the Romans: of these the most important were the Saturnalia. It was a time of general mirth and feasting; schools were closed; the Senate adjourned; presents were made; wars were forgotten; criminals had certain privileges, and the slaves, whose lives were ordinarily at the mercy of their masters, were permitted to jest with them at table—all this in memory of the free and golden rule of Ancient Saturn.

The fairs of Modern Times may be said to have been inaugurated with the Crystal Palace, London, 1851, lasting 144 days; visitors, 6,039,193; exhibitors, 17,000.

The first Fair in Paris, 1855, lasting 200 days; visitors, 5,162,330; exhibitors, 21,779.

Again in London in 1862 a Fair was held, lasting 171 days; visitors, 6,211,103; exhibitors, 82,653.

1867 Paris repeats her effort (1855), lasting 217 days; visitors, 10,200,000; exhibitors, 50,236. About doubling the number of visitors and more than doubling the exhibitors of her previous effort.

1873 Vienna opened an exhibition of her resources in a World's Fair, lasting 186 days; visitors, 7,254,687; exhibitors, 42,584.

The American Centennial, Philadelphia, 1876, lasting 159 days; visitors, 9,910,916; exhibitors, 60,000.

For the third time (1889) Paris offers to the world an opportunity for competition, and 28,149,353 visitors attended to examine the various products of both nature and art as presented by 55,000 exhibitors a curious paradox here, while the number of exhibitors, up to this time was the smallest the number of visitors was the largest.

1893, America, feeling an increasing debt of gratitude, thought it appropriate to show her appreciation of the discoverer by celebrating the four-hundredth anniversary of the "discovery," with what was very aptly and befittingly styled The Columbian Exposition.

This exposition opened May 1st and lasted till October 30th.

Paid admissions	21,480,141
Free admissions	6,059,380
Total	27,539,521

The largest attendance any one day, October 9th, 756,880.

Total receipts from all sources (including subscriptions to capital stock $5,617,154.33), City of Chicago Bonds ($5,000,000), United States Souvenir Coin appropriations, gate receipts, concession receipts, etc., amounted to $28,787,532.80.

The total disbursements for general operating expenses, construction expenses, and post exposition expenses amounted to $27,291,715.

Up to 1893 this may be ranked easily as the greatest success. It left as a legacy to Chicago its own beautiful sobriquet—The White City.

Passing over the Cotton States and International Exposition, Atlanta, Georgia, 1895; the Tennessee Centennial Exposition, Nashville, 1897, and even the Pan-American or the Buffalo

---

It was a time of mirth and feasting ... The senate adjourned; wars were forgotten; criminals had certain privileges; and slaves were permitted to jest with their masters.

Exposition, we come to a realization of what Bishop Berkeley said so prophetically:

"Westward the course of empire takes its way,
* * * * * * * *

Time's noblest off-spring is the last."

Truly may "The Louisiana Purchase Exposition" be styled "The World's Fair," for here are gathered, systematized, tabulated, and exhibited, all the peoples, products, discoveries, and inventions from the ends of the earth and that, too, through past centuries.

It is hard to describe, to give even the salient points of this great Exposition.

The grounds occupy 1,240 acres, nearly two square miles.

Approximate cost, $50,000,000.

Forty-four States and Territories contributed to it.

These may be grouped in regard to territory, population and taxable wealth, thus:

Square miles, 1,037,735.

Population, 14,572,189.

Wealth, $6,616,642,829.

Over two-thirds of the territory of the United States with its full proportion of population and wealth.

FROM MARCH 20, 1920 ISSUE

Back in the Seventies —

Sitting in the GRAND STAND With Grandpa

By Rob Roy

M OST of us like to turn back the pages of dead yesterdays and live over in our memory the light of other days. Nowhere is this more enjoyable than in recounting the events of the oldtime county fair, when profiteers dared not rule the land and before these great United States followed the example of Russia on the prohibition question. Few of the secretaries, general managers, heads of departments, commissioners of agriculture and other moguls who wear diamonds that shine like locomotive headlights and who annually gather from the four winds that wisdom may ooze from their systems and vibrate from their vocal cords in an effort to enlighten their comrades in the conduct and management of fairs, and who annually sit at banquets where appear the daughters of Eve, arrayed in little more than a side comb and a smile—banquets that would make the Feast of Belshazzar resemble a 20-cent noonday lunch or the handout at a woman's club celebration. Few if any of these present-day officials of fairs would be willing to admit that the oldtime secretary knew anything about fairs, yet he was wise in his day and generation and resourceful as well, for, contrary to general belief, he had something more to do than "hire a band and open his gates."

There was no gathering like the oldtime fair then and there has been no gathering like it since. The reckless abandon of soberminded business men and the removal of much of the restraint of demure maids and modest matrons was noticeable on these annual occasions, which were really after-harvest jubilees. Thousands gathered at these oldtime fairs, it often requiring days to make the journey, the "pilgrims" camping at various points along the route and living in camp style during the entire period of the fair.

THE GRAND STAND WAS NOT MADE OF STEEL AND CONCRETE

T HE grand stands at the fairs attended by our forefathers consisted of two rows of tall poles placed upright about ten feet apart with forks at the tops. More poles were placed in these forks and cedar and other brush was placed on top, forming a delightful shade and shelter. The show ring consisted of saplings placed in forked stakes and invariably formed a circle. There were no restaurants, cookhouses, eating places or pie joints. Great "hampers of grub" were brought by every family and the negroes usually looked after the food and arranged the big spread at the noon hour. There was never a thought of charging anyone for anything to eat. Such a procedure would have brought disgrace on anyone.

ROB ROY

The invitation to dinner was broad and one could eat without money and without price. And what a feast it was. The good mothers and those sainted old black mammies of the South cooked and boiled and baked and stewed and barbecued for many days before the fair that "beef, bull, pig and bear" might adorn their tables. It looked like one big, happy family, for the table linens would meet and form long rows, around which the people, rich and poor, the high and the low, the learned and the unlearned, gathered to enjoy the feast. The journey to the fair resembled in many respects the caravans of old. Down the dusty roads the procession moved, slowly winding its way over hills and thru the valleys like a monster parade. The white people rode in carriages and spring wagons, the "one-hoss shay" being very much in evidence. Along with them came the darkies in wagons, sometimes drawn by oxen, but more often by mules and horses. Behind them came the show stock. Once at the "fair grounds" the animals intended for exhibition were quartered in rail pens, for there were no stables.

SCRUB SIRES WERE SOMETIMES WINNERS IN THE BABY SHOW

Q UITE frequently one hears a latter-day secretary make the boast that his fair was the first to adopt the one judge system. With no desire to discredit the claims of those who honestly believe what they say, it is none the less a fact that the one judge system was in vogue long before some of our present secretaries saw the light of day, and a Czar of Russia in the zenith of his power or the profiteer who rules and reigns today were piker monarchs compared to the one judge dignitaries of the fairs of long ago. Quite frequently he was a leading magistrate of the county in which he resided. He judged the rams, the lambs, the bulls, the boars, the jacks, the mules, the horses, the agricultural products, the fruit of the loom and the spinning wheel and other rick-rack woven, spun, knitted and crocheted by the women, but his crowning glory was when he presided over the baby show and announced before the waiting thousands the winners in these contests between little mites of humanity.

The Guideless Wonder and Diving Horse Combination. The best Fair Attraction on Earth.

EARLY CIRCUS DAYS

FROM APRIL 30, 1904 ISSUE

THE FIRST CIRCUS.

A memorial to the first elephant brought to the United States and to the spot on which the first circus this country ever saw was erected, stands at Somers, Westchester County, New York.

Somers is a quiet little township, with its fertile farms and dreamy valleys, and yet you ask any villager about the odd looking monument, with an elephant surmounting the high column, and his bosom will swell with pride as he tells you the history of the first elephant that ever walked the streets of that place.

The monument, which is near a country inn called the Elephant Hotel, was erected sixty years ago to "Old Bet," which was the elephant's name. Her owner was Hackaliah Bailey. His brother was a sea captain, and one day while taking on a cargo on the Asiatic Coast, he bought the elephant at a bargain and reached New York with her on his sailing vessel in 1821.

It took the vessel many months to sail to New York, and "Old Bet" had no keeper to look after her like the circus beasts do nowadays, but she stood the trip well. She was very fat, as she devoured everything she could put her trunk on. Hackaliah Bailey immediately purchased the elephant on the arrival of his brother and started out to exhibit her. He made "Old Bet" walk all the way to Somerstown, traveling only at night and giving exhibitions in barns during the day, charging 10 cents admission "to see the greatest show elephant on earth."

"Old Bet" proved to be the greatest attraction ever seen. Crowds followed her at night and those who didn't have ten cents ran ahead to the next show place and hid in hay mows until the beast arrived.

On reaching Somers, and where the monument now is, Mr. Bailey put up a tent, and started a circus with the elephant as the main and only attraction and her owner made a barrel of money.

The primitive circus lasted in Somers for months before Mr. Bailey sent "Old Bet" on a tour of the United States.

Keepers overfed and spoiled the elephant and one day she broke her chains and killed one of them. It was shown he had angered her and she was forgiven, and given another chance to live.

While in South Carolina, in 1827, she crushed another keeper to death, then escaped and started on a run across the country. The circus hands chased her twenty miles before they got a fatal bullet in her brain.

FROM AUG. 20, 1904 ISSUE

IN THE DAYS OF THE ONE RING SHOW.

By The Great Henry A. Higgins.

"Hey rube!" that in the circus man's vernacular means "something doin'" to the followers in the trail of the little red wagons. It means to rally round the tent poles just as the call to arms meant life and liberty to the continentals in the days of '76.

But since the passing of the old-time circus men, many of whom retired from the sawdust arena long before the introduction of the high priced European acts, the army of unseen workers is made up of a different type of men.

Seth B. Howes was called the father of the American Circus. He and his brother started in 1826 the first circus under a top canvas.

DAN RICE,

The most famous clown in circus history.

In the early 'sixties', the old Refere house, at the corner of Broadway and Houston streets, was the headquarters for all circus men in New York. In the wintertime there could be seen collected in the sitting room all of the circus proprietors and performers of that day—George F. Bailey, John Robinson, Bill Lake, Hyatt Frost, Van Ahburg and others. Dan Rice, the old clown, would be there, too, with a crowd around him listening to the stories. He was then in his prime.

Spaulding and Rogers' was the finest circus that traveled by railroad. They did not make it pay. Railroading with a circus was too expensive at that time. They did not have things down to such a fine point during the year 1901 as they have now.

There died in Brewster, N. J., one of the early pioneers in the circus business—Seth B. Howes. He was called the father of the American circus. He and his brother Natham A. Howes, and Aaron Turner started in 1826, the first regular circus under a top canvas. They started from Salem, N. Y., and called it The Great North American Circus. They had six wagons and twenty horses, all told, with four musicians in the band. When Howes and Cush-

---

In the Dan Rice and Eldrid time the clown was a man of wit as well as a poet.

---

ing took their circus to Europe they engaged a number of Indians to accompany them, but the Indians reached New York too late to sail with the show and while waiting for another steamer, the syndicate of which Smith and Natham and others were members, sent an agent to the red men and told them that they would be sold into slavery if they went to England. The Indians refused to go, and negroes were engaged to impersonate them and the name flat foot party was given to the schemers. The Indians went out with the Natham Co. circus that season.

Dr. Jas. L. Thayer and his partner, Charley Noyer would come down from Girard, Pa. to the Revere House. Dr. Thayer, at one time, before he had a show of his own, traveled with Dan Rice and played clown, and would take the part of old Dan when the latter was indisposed, which was quite often. Dr. Thayer would make himself up in good imitation of Dan Rice and go in the ring, sing Dan's songs, tell his stories and make speeches. Dan was a good speech maker and threw a good deal of soft soap. He would tell his audience how proud he was to have the honor to show in their town and all that kind of business. Thayer carried out the deception very well for weeks and weeks at a time, and his audience would go home thinking they had seen and heard Dan Rice.

I regret more than anything the passing of the old time clown, the funny boy, who used to stop the action of the whole show to sing several verses of "Oh, Fred tell them to stop," and "Grandfather's Clock." The clowns of the present three ring circuses are no more like the ones of the old days than are th shows themselves. What do they do today? Nothing, except a lot of tomfoolery. Five or six men dress up as clowns, come into the ring, knock one another down, and roll in a heap and that is all there is to it. Now, in the Dan Rice and Eldrid time, the clown was a man of wit as well as a poet, and his verses and jokes were treasured and repeated over and over again by those who saw and heard him. The old-time circus clown could stand as the swap of the ring master's whip, and it was no small part of his duty to be in the center of the sawdust ring and crack jokes as sharp. He was able to give quick and humorous retarts to any remarks hurled suddenly in his direction. From the audience it used tobe, that the clown of our forefathers appealed, not only to the eye of his audience, but the ear also. Nowdays, I suppose, on account of the vast space covered by the three rings, the stage and outer rings, the funny boys have time to do nothing more than catch the eye alone. There is nothing but action, action all the time. It seems to me that the more a clown falls around and tumbles over himself and his fellows and slams around generally, the better the public is pleased. But that is not clowning the clown clown of today as supposed to be nothing more or less than an overgrown kid with common sense left out of his make up. The public wants to laugh when it looks at him and in nine cases out of ten it does. That is the reason the clown of today appeals more to the eye than the ear.

But we old fellows in the business miss his songs and mirthful quips just as we do the fading of the sacred white elephant, that paraded the jungle, known as the nondiscript; the stone man and the maid of the sea. All the old time advance agents, the men who squared themselves with the town authorities for the use of the commons, wrangled with the hotel keepers for lowest rates, jollied the newspaper men and planned to steal marches on their rivals are on the shelf—or headed that way. The old man has been crowded to the wall by the chubby-faced youngster, who not only has a good front but also a novel line of talk and up-to-date methods.

I recall the Robinson and Eldrid combination which headed its heralds in this wise:
"Southern men, Southern women, Southern Horses and Southern Enterprise against the World."
Robinson was a rider and eldred was a clown, both being experienced performers, and they toured the Southland in the winter up to 1856. It was the first tent show to exhibit in Florida and Texas. Circus and menageries did not exhibit together until along in the '50 at one price of admission, and under one tent. About that time, in order to attract the church-going people, George F. Bailey added to his circus several cages of animals and an elephant, Hackaliar.

Bailey, an uncle of George, brought to this country the first elephant, and in 1853, Seth B. Howes imported from Paris the hippodrome of Henri Franconi and several London novelties.

Yankee Robinson, who had more ups and downs than any man in the show business, began business early in life with a one-horse wagon exhibition, in which the feature was the raising of Lazarus. He continued with this for years and at one time owned a large circus, but that in some way went the way of the winds. The following season, however, the old man bobbed up with another show.

Old Hannibal, the elephant and camel were the old animals one could see free in the days of Yankee Robinson. All others were caged in wagons and the small boys had to content themselves with looking at the pictures on the wagons ... fearful works of art ... ponderous beasts tearing men limb from limb; boa constrictors, several hundred feet in length, coiled around half a score of black natives ...

I suppose there are many of the old-timers alive who can remember getting up early in the morning the day the show was to come to town and going out to the edge of town waiting many hours for the one elephant. There was a general eagerness of the youngster to carry water for the big beast, because that meant a free admission to the whole show. Old Hannibol, the elephant and camel were the only animals one could see free of charge in the days of Yankee Robinson. All others were caged in enclosed wagons and the small boys had to content themselves with looking at the pictures on the outside of the wagons. Some of these pictures were fearful and wonderful works of art. They showed ponderous beasts tearing men limb from limb; boaconstructors several hundred feet in length, coiled around half a score of black natives; then there was the golden chariot, drawn by four cream-colored horses and driven by one man. The chariot was the pride of the circus man's heart, and the public considered it of sufficient merit to go miles to see it.

Now, switching off on the horse end of the old-time circus, I will mention that the desire to keep traveling with a circus effects a horse the same as it does the rider, gymnast or general hustler. The smell of the sawdust and tanbark once in the nostrils of a horse that has been in the ring for any time, holds him and he can't get it out of him.

FROM NOV. 9, 1907 ISSUE

The Intelligence of the Old-Time Circus Manager.

His Business Ability Was Way Above Par, and for Enterprise He Was in Advance of the Majority of the Mercantile Community. In His Way, an Explorer and Pathfinder.

By The Late CHARLES H. DAY.

The old-time circus managers were, as a whole, men of character and more than ordinary ability, and conducted their business honorably and aboveboard. Their travels at home and abroad gave them an education not to be found in books. Exploiters and explorers, they assumed risks and profited thereby. They faced dangers on the seas and in the wilds and the Star of Empire never moved so far west that it failed to have a circus wagon hitched to it; and these same old-time circus managers showed the American flag on a centre pole in about every inhabitable spot on earth and still pined for the showman's unrequited, insatiable desire, "new country."

The old-time circus managers of this country, it may be said, discovered advertising. Who ever took any noticeable space in a newspaper until after the circus made the experiment and demonstrated the profit and the possibilities?

Who appropriated the poster to his purpose and adoptd it as almost solely his own? The old-time circus manager.

Who, first, last and all the while, believed in printing ink, in the distribution of the handbill not only locally but for miles and miles around the place of exhibition? The old-time circus manager.

Who first employed men of literary ability to prepare their announcements and secure publicity in the newspaper? The old-time circus manager.

And while these same old-time circus managers were ever alert and venturesome the representative merchants and men of commercial interests were a rather slow lot and not a bit ready to risk their dollars in enterprise or exploitation. In fact, the old-time merchant believed it was beneath his dignity to advertise, so he sat in his counting room and waited for customers to come, as his father and grandfather had done before him. The merchants were a half century behind the circus managers of the time in appreciating and appropriating the increasing methods of publicity discovered and developed by the showmen.

Even the theatrical managers were slow to learn or pattern after the tenters, and it was decades after before the slumbering directors of the drama woke up and realized that the world had moved and that they had not moved with it. The theatrical manager in time came to follow in the wake of the circus manager, but his step was slow and he was ever very far behind in the promotion of publicity.

The cheapening of the process of poster printing by the discovery of the use of the pine block gave a great impetus to circus business and advertising. Joseph Morse, the inventor, had his hands full, as he was both artist and engraver.

And now something of the manner of men who were the pioneers in the circus business in the United States and developed it as fortune favored and capital accrued. They were not an uncouth, ignorant lot, did not wear loud clothes, chew plug tobacco and unloose an oath every other word as they have often been pictured in imaginative literature. They were men of affairs and as for practical knowledge of the general condition of finance and trade throughout the country they were the best posted people in the land. It would never do to take a circus into a section that was not prosperous, and the old-time circus manager rarely made any mistakes in the selection of profitable territory. And now let some of these heroes of the sawdust arena of yore pass in review.

Turner, who left the shoemaker's bench to become an innovator in the circus line and induct

P. T. Barnum in the sawdust. Barnum, the writer, the humorist, lecturer and most famous of showmen, set the pace for rivals for many years. Nat Howes, who put the top on the tent; Seth B. Howes, who sent out the first golden chariot drawn by twenty horses. This same Mr. Howes was always the prime mover in the organization of large enterprises and an extensive importer of wild animals. He was also instrumental in touring a magnificent American circus in England with the cream of the Yankee performers in the ring.

The first of "the flatfoots," the progenitors of the later tribe who succeeded to the heritage, were financiers of great ability. They set out to monopolize the menagerie business and came well nigh doing it. They also aimed to syndicate the shows. June Titus and Angeoine and their associates were making good progress with the scheme when the panic of 1837 made the merging of interests impossible. And this was many years before the time of Rockefeller, Hill, Gould or Harriman.

"General" Rufus Welch went in strong for expensive spectacles. In his tours "the world was an oyster," and he visited many lands and also made a venture in the importation of wild animals, in opposition to "the flatfoot" trust.

Lewis B. Lent, a manager of culture, travel and wide information, founded the famous kid glove show, the New York Circus.

Levi J. North accumulated a fortune in the ring and on the road, built an amphitheatre in Chicago in 1856, and became an alderman of the growing burgh.

P. T. Barnum represented Bridgeport in the Connecticut legislature and also served his city as mayor. "Old" John Robinson ran for mayor of Cincinnati, but failed of election.

"Dr." Gilbert R. Spaulding was one of the brightest of the old-timers. He invented the use of quarter poles, eleven tier seats and extra front seats, and with his associate, Charles J. Rogers, put a floating palace on the Mississippi river and also the water minstrel hall, called The Banjo. Rogers, who was originally an equestrian, was a polished gentleman of the old school, but not so aggressive as his pushing, demonstrative partner.

Isaac A. Van Amburgh, the Lion King, got his fill of glory at home and abroad.

Stone, Rosston and Murray were managers of worth and gentleness in all that word implies.

Hyatt Frost, was a sterling character, a wit, humorist and versifier, who could find lots of fun in an ink bottle.

O. J. Ferguson, many years an associate with Mr. Frost and the Van Amburgh party, a linguist and a show writer of no mean ability.

Col. Dan Rice, the most popular clown, who, having no early advantages of education, under the inspiration of Van Orden, the press agent, took to the books and made good his deficiencies.

John J. Nathans, who during his career as manager and performer visited a good part of the world, and for many years participated in many ventures in about every land under the sun. He was one of the latter day "flatfoots," headed by Avery Smith, whose name was never used in connection with any show of which he was part owner.

George Fox Bailey, of Danbury, Conn. The Turners made Danbury a circus town, and Mr. Bailey—not to be confounded with James A. Bailey, the great—was the son-in-law of a Turner. When "the flatfoots ran the Barnum Show, George F. Bailey was the manager.

Many managers have made the last stand and for whom the band has played "Home, Sweet, Home"—for they are at rest—might be classed as old managers. Adam Forepaugh, Ephraim, Allen and Peter Sells, W. C. Coup, several of the younger associates of P. T. Barnum, and even James A. Bailey, are not to be included in this imperfect reminder of those who actually created the American circus. The circus as it was born in a topless tent, without seats and exhibiting but once a day, grown under the skillful direction of its managers to become the great popular amusement for decades, whose one ring was a plenty and the prodigious innovations of millionaire managers had not been made to present at every performance at enormous expense an army of performers in the presence of a world of people.

Taking into consideration all the conditions, the original American circus managers, under the lead of the Turners, the Howes, Raymond and Waring, "the flatfoots," made rapid progress in the enlargement and improvement of the tent show. At the outset, the population of the entire country was small, but a few cities of any size existed, and New York, Boston and Philadelpuia were little better than large towns. The masses were not in possession of much "cash money," and barter was in vogue in many localities. The people were close fisted, being bred that way, and the larger majority of them puritanical and narrow minded. One might as well be frank about it and out with the truth. Pleasure and recreation was a sin and it was better to weep in woe than to rejoice and be glad.

"The entrance of the theatre is the gateway to hell," said the preacher who inveighed against amusements, "and the ring of the circus is the bottomless pit itself."

FROM MARCH 20, 1920 ISSUE

Francisco Lentini, the three-legged boy

Freaks And What I Know About Them
By Barry Gray

"LET the band play." How often have I heard this familiar expression. And only the side-show manager knows what it means if "the band doesn't play" right on this given signal.

I am requested to give The Billboard readers a little "inside" information on "freaks," and will endeavor to do so without exaggeration or imposition on the sensitive feelings of my many friends of "freakdom."

The first freak I ever had the pleasure of gazing on in wonderment was "Old Zip," Barnum's "What is it?"

To the best of my recollection it was in 1877 at either Worth's or Bunnell's Museum in New York.

Barry Gray

Prof. Hutchings was lecturer there at that time and described "Zip" in flowery language as the "connecting link between human and the ape creation." "Zip" is still on exhibition under the management of Capt. O. K. White, and is still making the same old speeches and playing the fiddle as in days of yore.

I estimate his age at 60 or over. Reports have circulated in late years that the original "Zip" died some time ago and the present "Zip" very cleverly substituted in his stead, but, to the best of my knowledge and belief, the "Zip" we have with us today is "only and original," and is not a "dead one" by any means.

I little thought, when in my boyhood days I saw "Old Zip" and many other wonderful freaks in the days of the dime museums, that I would in later years become closely associated with them. Enough that is interesting and amusing could be related about "Zip" to fill volumes, but, as I have some "nice things" to say about the rest of the freaks, I must confine myself to just a few of the incidents in and around the life of this "happiest of them all."

IN 1896 my wife and I joined the Barnum & Bailey Show with our Marionette act as one of the many side-show attractions, and it was then that I became closely acquainted with some of the world's greatest freaks, including "Zip," "Krao," "Wild Men of Borneo," "Lalloo" (double body boy) and many others.

Ernest Warner, manager of the "Wild Men of Borneo," was lecturer that season with the B. & B. Show. Col. W. D. Hagar had the side-show and other privileges, and Lew Graham had charge of our department.

I was deputized as assistant to Mr. Warner, the lecturer, thereby getting my first real experience as a "demonstrator of freaks."

"Zip" and I, during the "off" hours, would usually indulge in a little "travesty" to the amusement of the butchers and ticket sellers.

One day in a Pennsylvania town, where the "blue laws" prohibiting the exhibition of freaks compelled the show to lay off one or two of them, including "Zip," he was wrapped in a tarpaulin—the day being a rainy, chilly one—and sitting back of our Marionette stage playing solitaire, his favorite pastime.

I had occasion to pass around and back of the stage and gave him the usual "high sign." He mumbled in his guttural manner: "Where go, Barry?" I replied—dramatically—"I'm going down—down—to hell." "Good-by," said "Zip," "I won't see you no more."

Later in the season, or it may have been a later season, the show was due to Sunday in Idaho Falls and the 24-hour man instructed to arrange with a town dentist to be at his office around noon to treat a tooth for one of the showfolk. "Zip's" manager—at that time Ed Maxwell—Captain George Auger and I went with "Zip" to the dentist and found him ready for business, but he couldn't quite figure out what kind of a nondescript he was to operate on, when "Zip" removed his cap and disclosed a small, comical cranium with a knot of wool on the summit of the same.

Maxwell explained, as "Zip" took the chair, that "Zip" had no power of articulation. "Which tooth is it?" asked the dentist. "I don't want to make a mistake and pull the wrong one." The naughty tooth was located finally, and the "ivory jerker" grabbed it firmly with his forceps. A twist or two followed and—that's all. "Zip" yelled: "What the blankety blank you doing, you blankety blank so and so." After the dentist had mustered up sufficient courage to resume his task Maxwell explained that the "pulling of 'Zip's' tooth had restored his voice."

DURING my many years' experience with the tent shows I became well acquainted with "Krao, the Missing Link." Miss Krao, as she is known to her close friends, and Krao Farini, as she is known in private life.

"Krao" is one of the most interesting as well as highest salaried anomalies in the world, and has been on exhibition since girlhood. Her good traits are many; her bad ones none.

Kind, gentle, charitable, thoroly educated and loyal always to her friends and employers.

WILD WEST SHOWS' FIRST COWBOY

FROM SEPT. 1, 1900 ISSUE

Tent Shows.

Before he became a cowboy Buck Taylor was an opera singer . . . he appeared as Ralph Rackstraw in *Pinafore*.

Buck Taylor Dead.

"Buck" Taylor is dead, and with him passes away much of the primitive glory and sensationalism of the American cowboy.

Ned Buntline discovered "Buffalo Bill" (Hon. William F. Cody) away back in 1869 or '70, when the buffalo hunters upon the great Western plains were rapidly giving way to the then more modern cowboy. Until the American bison had been largely exterminated the cattle of the ranchman could not graze at will upon the prairies, and, therefore, there was no need of the rider of the cow pony who afterward became so picturesque a feature of frontier life.

Buntline made a dime-novel hero of "Buffalo Bill," and afterward Colonel Cody took to the stage in a play written by General Burt, of the United States Army, now commanding a brigade in the Philippines. Colonel Cody had served ten years in the playhouse before his at present famous "Wild West" was ever thought of—by the merest accident in the world. Colonel Hamlin, of the Barnum and Bailey Circus, suggested this peculiar and essentially American institution to Colonel Cody, and then "Buck" Taylor and the others of his class became necessary factors in its success.

"Buck" Taylor was really the first American cowboy the public had ever been permitted to gaze upon. Every one had read of this wild and venturesome individual of the broad ranges of the West, but "Buck" was the real thing, picturesque in appearance, sensational in his doings and well deserving the soubriquet "King of Cowboys."

"Buck," whose real name was Berry F. Tatum, his family being one of the oldest and best in Montgomery, Ala., died at the Providence Hospital, Washington, D. C., on Monday, August 20. He was a sergeant in Roosevelt's Rough Riders during the Spanish-American War, and contracted the disease, consumption, of which he died, while in Cuba. Since his return he has been almost unable to attend to any business, although he held a clerkship in the Census Bureau in Washington, having received his appointment through the kindly aid of Governor Roosevelt and Senator Morgan, of Alabama.

He went to Cabin John's Bridge, a suburban resort not far from Washington, last Sunday night, and was taken sick on the veranda of one of the hotels, being found there, gasping for breath and in an almost dying condition, before medical aid could be summoned.

Before he became a cowboy "Buck" Taylor, or Berry F. Tatum, was an opera singer, having appeared as Ralph Rackstraw in "Pinafore" and in other light or comic opera characters. Tiring of the stage, however, he went West, and found employment on one of the ranches in Nebraska, where he afterward became celebrated as one of the most daring cow punchers of the many wild Western rangers. When Colonel Cody undertook the organization of his famous American show "Buck" Taylor became essential to its completeness, and for years was almost as conspicuous and as much applauded in its exhibitions as the famous bison killer himself.

He rode before the Queen at Windsor, and not only received presents from her, but from nearly all of the monarchs of Europe, as expressions of their admiration for his skill and daring as a horseman.

THE BARNUM CAREER — HITS AND FLOPS

FROM NOV. 5, 1904 ISSUE

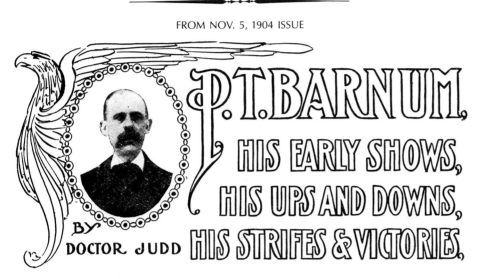

P. T. BARNUM, HIS EARLY SHOWS, HIS UPS AND DOWNS, HIS STRIFES & VICTORIES, BY DOCTOR JUDD

P. T. Barnum, the greatest and most successful showman the United States ever had, was born in the town of Bethel, in the State of Connecticut, July 5, 1810. His father was a tailor, a farmer and a tavernkeeper, all combined. Young Barnum went to school, when he was not driving the cows to and from the pasture, weeding the garden, riding the horse, shelling corn on an old shovel—which was laid on a chair, then sitting on it to hold it down, he would rub the ears of corn over the blade to loosen the kernels. This was the primitive corn sheller and was universally used in those days.

When Barnum was nearly twelve years old, in 1822, he made his first visit to New York City. He hired out to a cattle drover to assist in driving some fat cattle to the metropolis to sell. After five or six days on the road with their cattle they arrived in New York. They put up at the Bull's Head Tavern, where they stayed a week, disposing of their cattle. It was an eventful week for Barnum, wandering, gazing, and spending the dollar that his mother had given him before he left home. In these first wanderings about the city, he often passed the corner of Broadway and Ann Streets, never dreaming of the stir he was destined at a future day to make in that locality as proprietor and manager of the American Museum. After young Barnum returned to his home, like all the great men that we read of, he went to work in a "country store," bartering with the women who brought butter, eggs, beeswax and feathers to exchange for dry goods, and with men who wanted to trade oats, corn, buckwheat, axe-helves, and other commodities for ten penny nails, molasses, or New England rum. He was also obliged to take down the shutters, sweep the store and make the fire.

Barnum's first venture in the show business was in 1835, when he went out to exhibit "Joice Heth," a remarkable negro woman, who was advertised to be one hundred and sixty-one years old, and was formerly the nurse of General Washington, or, as Joice called him, "Her dear little Georgie." Barnum ran across Joice Heth in Philadelphia. A man by the name of Lindsay, from Kentucky, was then exhibiting her, but he had no knack as a showman and wanted to sell out. Barnum borrowed $1,000 and became proprietor of this novel ex-

> **Barnum's first venture in show business was in 1835. . . . He exhibited Joice Heth, a remarkable negro woman, he advertised as 165 years old, and former nurse of George Washington . . .**

hibition, and began the life of a showman. In proof of Joice's extraordinary age and pretensions, Mr. Lindsay had a bill of sale, dated February 15, 1727, conveying Joice Heth, aged fifty-four years from Augustine Washington, father of George Washington, to his sister, and it was further claimed that Joice had long been a nurse in the Washington family. She was called in at the birth of George and clothed the new-born infant.

Barnum took Joice on to New York and opened his exhibition in a vacant room on lower Broadway. Joice was certainly a remarkable curiosity. She looked as if she might be three hundred years old. Her head was covered with a thick bush of grey hair. She was toothless and totally blind, and her eyes had sunk so deeply in the sockets as to have disappeared altogether. She could not walk, and had to lie on a couch day and night. Nevertheless she could talk as long as people would converse with her.

From New York Barnum moved on to Albany with her, but he had hardly gotten back of the money that he had invested in her when she died one day while they were in Albany. It came time to open the exhibition. Joice was on her couch all right, but in one of her usual long and deep sleeps, as the attendants thought, and they knew by experience that it was of no use to try to awaken her. People

were clamoring to enter the exhibition room, so they opened up, and explained to their audiences that she was in one of her long sleeps. Along in the afternoon, an old colored woman who had the courage to feel of Joice, found

In 1836 Barnum connected himself with Aaron Turner's traveling circus company as ticket seller, secretary and treasurer. With this company Barnum saved up enough of the wherewithal to start a small show under a tent, and go South with it. While he was with his show in South Carolina, James Sanford (a negro singer and dancer) suddenly left him, and as Barnum had advertised negro songs, and none of his company were competent to fill Sanford's place, Barnum, so as not to disappoint his audience, blackened himself up and sang the advertised songs, Zip Coon, Old Bob Ridley and Clar de Kitchen. This roll he had to keep until he re-enforced his show with more performers, and among them was a negro singer, but in less than three weeks White, the negro singer, was drowned while crossing the river at Frankfort, Ky. Barnum's business was bad in Kentucky. They crossed over into Ohio, but it was no better. Funds were low and Barnum was obliged to leave pledges here and there in payment for bills. At last he had to pawn his watch and chain to raise funds to Tiffin, O.

Joe Pentland, who had been with Barnum acting as clown, ventriloquist, comic singer, balancer and legerdemain performer, informed Barnum that at Tiffin there was a man by the name of Zacharias Graves, who had funds and wanted to go into the show business. With this man Barnum made a partnership. They enlarged the show, buying more horses, had a new tent made, as his old one was in a very dilapidated condition, had four more wagons and a band chariot built at Tiffin, engaged more performers and musicians and called the show P. T. Barnum's Grand Scientific and Musical Theatre. The writer of this article, whose father at that time had a carriage and her cold unto death. She rushed by the doortender to get out and said to him, "That nigger you have in there is nothin' more than wood or wax, or she is dead." True enough,

Barnum's First Tent.

they found out that all day they had been exhibiting a corpse.

wagon factory at Tiffin, made the wagons for them, and let them have them on part payment, but he never received the balance. After his death, his administrator sent the bill on to Barnum, when he was well established at the American Museum. Barnum immediately remitted the full amount with interest.

Barnum and Graves now started out with their show for the South, exhibiting to good and bad business, more of the latter than of the former. At Vicksburg they sold all of their land conveyances, excepting the band wagon and a few horses, bought a small steamboat, hired the captain and crew, and started down the river to exhibit at places on the way. At Opelousas in the Attakapas country, they disbanded the company, and exchanged the steamer for sugar and molasses. Barnum now started for New York, where he arrived in 1838.

He lost what little money he brought back with him by going in partnership with a German, a manufacturer of paste blacking, water proof paste for leather, Cologne water and bear's grease.

This speculation turned out very bad, worse than the show business. Barnum then went into the Bible business, taking a United States agency for "Sear's Pictorial Illustrations of the Bible," and in six months sold thousands of copies, but irresponsible agents used up all his profits and capital. He then leased and opened the Vauxhall Garden in New York, and gave a variety of performances, including singing, dancing and circus acts. At the close of the season he had only cleared a hundred dollars or so, but this sum was soon exhausted, and with a family consisting of wife and two daughters on his hands and no employment, he was glad to do anything that would keep the wolf from the door. He wrote advertisements and notices for the Bowery Amphitheatre, receiving for the services four dollars a week, which he was very glad to get. He was at the Bowery Amphitheatre in 1841 and he learned that the collection of curiosities comprising Scudder's American Museum at the corner of Broadway and Ann Streets was for sale.

The nucleus of this establishment, Scudder's Museum, was formed in 1810, the year that Barnum was born. It was begun in Chatham Street, and from small beginnings by purchases and to a considerable degree by presents, it had grown to a large and valuable collection. People in all parts of the country had sent in relics and rare curiosities; sea captains for years had brought and deposited strange things from foreign lands. The museum, however, since Mr. Scudder's death had been for several years a losing concern, and the heirs were anxious to sell it. When Mr. Scudder was alive and managed it he made money, and he had been able to leave a large competency of children.

Barnum's First Advance.

The story has often been told of how Barnum bought this museum without any money, only "brass." Barnum bought the museum of the administration for $12,000, payable in seven annual installments, with good security. The museum building belonged to a retired merchant. Barnum went to him to go security for the collection of curiosities and that he should retain the property and all that Bar-

To keep the wolf from the door, Barnum wrote advertisements for the Bowery Amphitheatre for four dollars a week . . .

num should pay in till it was entirely paid for. Barnum took formal possession of the museum December, 1841, and before another December came around he was in full possession of the property as his own, and it was entirely paid for from the profits of the business.

From this time on Barnum's successful enterprises are familiar to most all, as they have been heralded near and far by the press. P. T. Barnum has been dead now for a number of years, but his name is still worth a mint of money to those who have a right to use it.

FROM DEC. 5, 1903 ISSUE

JENNIE LIND'S CONCERT AT MADISON.

There is nothing in the history of Madison, Ind., that caused such a furore as the coming of Jenny Lind, the Swedish nightingale, in 1851. Madison, at that time, was the leading city in Indiana, toward which the people of all Hoosierdom wended their way in search of health and pleasure, and she was fortunate in catching the beautiful song bird, as she sang in but eighteen cities in the United States. The late P. T. Barnum, the great showman, had Miss Lind engaged for the season. She gave thirty-five concerts in New York City, eight in Philadelphia, seven in Boston, one in Providence, four in Baltimore, two in Washington City, one in Richmond, Va., one in Natchez, one in Memphis, five in St. Louis, two in Nashville, three in Louisville, one in Madison, five in Cincinnati, one in Wheeling and one in Pittsburg.

. . . a corps of men put an old frame pork house in Madison, Indiana in condition for the Swedish nightingale, since Madison had no opera house.

While the song bird was in Louisville an enterprising citizen of Madison, named William Wilson, made arrangements with Mr. Barnum for a concert in Madison. Mr. Wilson agreed to take the management in his own hands and pay Mr. Barnum $5,000. As the mail boat from Louisville to Cincinnati would arrive at Madison about sundown and would wait at the wharf until after the concert, Mr. Barnum agreed to the proposition. Mr. Wilson returned home and engaged a corps of men to put an old frame pork house in condition for the reception of the beautiful Swedish nightingale, as Madison at that time had no opera house. It was a one-story structure, about fourteen feet high to the eaves, with an ordinary pitch to the roof, no ceiling to the auditorium, and was about thirty feet wide by one hundred and fifty feet long, occupying the length of half a block. Time was short, but Mr. Wilson was equal to the emergency. The greasy, dirty building was thoroughly mopped, scrubbed and whitewashed. Rough seats were improvised, and many enthusiastic ladies of Madison volunteered to assist in the work of decorating, and soon everything was in readiness.

On Friday evening, April 11, 1851, the mail steamer, Ben Franklin, landed at the Madison wharf, having on board Mlle. Jenny Lind and her troupe, accompanied by Phineas T. Barnum. All Madison turned out and gathered at the wharf to welcome the distinguished visitor, and her advent was hailed by the firing of the cannon, the cheers of the populace and other demonstrations of joy.

Madison being the only city in Indiana in which Miss Lind would sing, reporters and public men from all parts of the state were there. Several fine steamers all laid at the wharf until the concert was over.

Tickets were sold at auction at the "Grand Opera (or Pork) House" before the concert, and the first ticket was sold to Capt. David White for eighty dollars. The remainder of the tickets offered at auction were bought at an average of seven dollars each. Tickets were also sold at different places throughout the town, and gentlemen passed through the crowd on the outside offering them at one dollar, while curbstone tickets were in great demand, as the singing could be plainly heard through the thin weather boarding of the building.

The following is the program rendered:

MLLE. JENNY LIND'S
—ONLY—
GRAND CONCERT,
Friday Evening, April 11, 1851,
in Madison.

PROGRAM.

Part I.

Overture—Italiana in Algeri . . . . .Romini.
Duetto—Voglio dire (L'Elisie d'Amore)
Donizetti.
Signori Salvi and Belletti.
Aria—"I Know That My Redeemer Liveth"
(Messiah) . . . . Handel.
Mlle. Jenny Lind.
Cavatina—Bella Adorata . . . . .Guirmento.
Mercadante.
Signor Salvi.
Scena—Ah non credie . . . . .Sonambula.
Aria—Au non guinge . . . . .Bellini.
Mlle. Jenny Lind.

PART. II.

Overture—Felsenmuhle . . . . .Reissiger.
Duetto—Per Piacer alla Signori (Il Tarrco in
Italia) . . . . Rossini.
Mlle. Jenny Lind and Signor Belletti.
Romanza—Spirito onde Palma (La Favorita)
Donizetta.
Signor Salvi.
Bird Song . . . . .Taulbert.
Mlle. Jenny Lind.
Barcarole—Sulla poppa des mo brik (Prigioni
Edinburgo) . . . . Ricci.
Signor Belletti.
Home, Sweet Home .Bishop.
Mlle. Jenny Lind.
Conductor—Mr. Julius Benedict.

A first-class orchestra, comprising the best talent of New York City, led by Mr. Joseph Burke, and under the direction of Mr. Julius Benedict, was engaged. The receipts of the concert were $3,693.25, leaving Mr. Wilson $1,306.75 short of his agreement, which loss Mr. Barnum stood and let Mr. Wilson down easy in consideration of his enterprise and pluck in assuming such a great responsibility.

Though financially the enterprise in bringing Mlle. Lind to Madison was not a success, it did much toward advertising the town abroad, as every newspaper in the United States had something to say about Jenny Lind singing in a pork house at Madison, some of them even converting it into a slaughter house.

Jenny Lind was truly the greatest and sweetest singer of the nineteenth century. The following tribute to her gives one an idea of the gentleness of character and the angelic inspiration in song that softened the heart of marble and conquered her bitterest rivals:

"Jenny Lind and Grisi were rivals for popular favor in London. Both were invited to sing the same night at a court concert before the queen. Jenny Lind, being the younger, sang first, and was so disturbed by the fierce, scornful look of Grisi that she was at the point of failure, when suddenly an inspiration came to her. The accompanist was striking the final chords. She asked him to rise, and took the vacant seat. Her fingers wandered over the keys in a loving prelude, and then she sang a little prayer which she had loved as a child. She hadn't sung it for years. As she sang she was no longer in the presence of royalty, but singing to loving friends in her fatherland. Softly at first the plaintive notes floated on the air, swelling louder and richer at every moment. The singer seemed to throw her soul into that weird, thrilling, plaintive "prayer."

FROM MAY 4, 1901 ISSUE

Tom Thumb's Baby.

The Countess Magri has been loosing floods of reminiscence in Bridgeport.

This is intelligible when it is understood that the Countess was formerly Mrs. Tom Thumb and lived in Bridgeport. Indeed, just 37 years ago she and her midget husband held their marriage reception here. The host and hostess stood on a marble-topped table, and it was the biggest reception the town ever saw.

Last week the Countess visited the grave of the lamented "Tom Thumb;" likewise that of the late P. T. Barnum, which is opposite it. After she left the cemetery she related for the first time certain passages in the biography of the Tom Thumbs that are worth retelling.

The discerning Mr. Barnum first met Tom Thumb in 1842, when the latter was a boy of eight. His name was Charles Stratton, and his father was a drayman. Mr. Barnum offered the father $3 a week for the use of the boy, and a week later exhibited him in New ork as "General Tom Thumb."

... an innocent little item was smuggled into the English papers to the effect that the Tom Thumbs had a baby son.

Two years later the midget, whose commercial value had meantime greatly increased, was taken to England, presented to the Queen and to other sovereigns. On returning the prosperous little "General" built himself a comfortable home in Bridgeport and subsided for a few years.

In 1862, however, Mr. Barnum met a certain Lavinia Warren, a midget from Middleboro, Mass., then 20 years old. She was promptly installed in his sister's home in New York, and the "General" was invited to meet her.

The romance so fostered developed satisfactorily, and in a few months, to the great edification of the large public that already knew Tom Thumb, his engagement was announced.

On February 10, 1863, they were married in Grace Church by Rev. Thomas House Taylor, and the whole world read about the wedding. Two weeks later they held their historic reception in Bridgeport.

The next year an innocent little item was smuggled into the English papers to the effect that the Tom Thumbs had a baby son. It was widely copied, and by the time Mr. Barnum and his midget charges arrived the British public was worked up to a considerable degree of expectancy as regarded the baby.

In Egyptian Hall, London, they were exhibited all over again—General Tom Thumb, Mrs. Thumb—and the baby.

The performance was repeated all over Europe, and the Thumbs came back richer than they had ever been before.

People have occasionally wondered since then whatever became of that baby! The Countess Magri explains the mystery.

"I never had a baby," she declared last week. "The exhibition baby came from a foundling hospital in the first place, and was renewed as often as we found it necessary. A real baby would have grown. Our first baby—a boy—grew very rapidly.

"At the age of four years he was taller than his father.

"This would never do. Our friends predicted that our son would be a giant and that in a few years his parents would look ridiculous alongside of him.

"We appealed to Mr. Barnum.

"He agreed with us. He thought our baby should not grow. Thus we exhibited English babies in England, French babies in France and German babies in Germany. It was—they were—a great success. Mr. Barnum was a great man."—Bridgeport (Conn.) Cor. N. Y. World.

I never had a baby . . . we exhibited English babies in England; French babies in France; and German babies in Germany . . . they were a great success.

FROM JULY 12, 1902 ISSUE

STILL LIVING

Are Several Descendants of Siamese Twins.

The Siamese Twins are buried in North Carolina in a beautiful spot on a knoll near Mt. Airy on one of the farms which they owned. Several of the descendants of the most famous monstrosity the world has ever known are still living. One of the sons of Eng is a prosperous merchant. The people of that section of North Carolina have many interesting stories to tell about the brothers, whose Anglicized names were Eng and Chang Bunker.

The Siamese twins were born in Siam on April 15, 1811. They were brought to the United States in 1829, and for many years were exhibited all over the civilized world. Barnum and others realizing immense sums of money.

Chang died in January 1875 . . . his brother, Eng was asleep at the time, but was so startled over the death that he died a few hours later.

The brothers were entirely unlike in tastes and disposition. Chang was intemperate and irritable, while Eng was sober and quiet. In August, 1874, Chang suffered a paralytic stroke, but did not die until January, 1875. His brother was asleep at the time, but it is said was so startled over the death of Chang that he died a few hours later. The doctors of those days said that it would be certain death to attempt to disunite them, but in this age they would have been great subjects for the X-rays.

It is a singular coincidence that Millie Christine, the double woman, has purchased a farm in North Carolina not very far from the former home of Chang and Eng.

General Tom Thumb's widow with her new husband Count Magri and his brother Baron Magri.

A CAPSULE HISTORY

A chronology of milestones, interesting events, and some trivia in the history of show business

Entries for all phases of American entertainment are listed chronologically. Individual show business areas are identified by a two-letter code which precedes each entry.

AP —Amusement Parks
BU —Burlesque
CA —Carnivals
CH —Chautauqua
CI —Circus
FA —Fairs
MI —Minstrelsy
MO —Motion Pictures
MU —Music
NC —Night Clubs, Supper Clubs, Cabarets
RA —Radio
RE —Recordings
SH —Showboats
ST —Stereorama and Panstereorama
TH —Legitimate Theatre
TV —Television
VA —Vaudeville
WA —Wagon Shows

Items in this chronology may be discussed in greater detail in the articles that introduce each of the six parts of the book or in the reproductions of news stories, advertisements, etc. from *Billboard*. However, some items are not covered in either the introductory articles or the *Billboard* material, and have been compiled from outside sources (see Bibliography).

1698

MU First song book containing some non-religious songs is published in America.

1702

TH English actor Anthony Aston, also known as Mat Medley, wrote in 1731 that he had visited America in 1701 and acted in New York during 1702 and 1703. Although some historians claim Aston was the first professional actor to appear in America, most believe that professional actors were active here before that period. However, Aston's report is the earliest documented evidence of professional theatrical activity in New York.

1709

MU Bartolomeo Cristofori, a Florentine harpsichord maker, invents the piano.

1716

TH First professional theatre is built by William Levingston in Williamsburg, Va. The theatre, an all-purpose entertainment spot complete with bowling alley, was run by Charles and Mary Stagg, proprietors of a dancing school.

1732

TH *The Recruiting Officer*, by George Farquhar, is presented at the "New" Theatre in New York. It is the earliest documented record of a play performed by professional actors in North America. The comedy stars Thomas Heady, "barber and Peruque [wig] maker to his Honour." John Moody, first to cross the Atlantic with a dramatic company, was also a barber as well as an actor-manager.

1733

CI A circus troupe (name unknown) consisting of clowns, tightrope walkers, sword dancer, etc. performs in Philadelphia.

1750

TH Thomas Kean plays *Richard III* at the First Nassau Street Theatre, New York.

TH A law banning theatrical performance of any kind is enacted by Massachusetts. Although theatre is popular in the South, northern colonies frown on drama, condemning it as "immoral."

1752

TH Hallam London Company, headed by actor-manager Lewis Hallam, arrives in the U.S. from England and opens at the Williamsburg Theatre, Va., with *The Merchant of Venice*. They are America's first popular theatrical troupe.

1758

TH The American Company (originally the Company of Comedians from London) is formed by actor-manager David Douglass and Lewis Hallam's widow.

1759

TH Pennsylvania passes law calling for five-hundred pound fine for anyone presenting or acting in a play.

1761

TH Lewis Hallam Jr. at age twenty-one, who later becomes as famous an actor-manager as his father, is America's first *Hamlet*.

1762

TH Actor-manager David Douglass offers a reward for identity of persons throwing eggs at his players from the gallery. He suspects culprits are disgruntled "on-stage johnnies" who were refused permission to mingle with the actors during a performance — a custom of the day which justifiably irked players.

1767

TH The John Street Theatre, America's leading theatre until 1797, opens Dec. 7 in New York City. The all-wooden structure is painted red and lighted with candles as were most theatres of the time.

TH Three of the most prominent theatrical personalities of the day — David Douglass, Lewis Hallam Jr., and John Henry — form a company to produce plays for the John Street Theatre and other houses. John Henry, a young Irish actor, becomes America's first matinee idol.

TH *Prince of Parthia*, first drama written by a native-born American (Thomas Godfrey) and performed by professionals, is played by David Douglass' company at the Southwark Theatre in Philadelphia.

1768

MU "The Liberty Song" is the first important political song published in America. The lyrics are by John Dickinson, set to melody of another tune, "Hearts of Oak," written by William Boyce. The song protested new duties and taxes.

1770

MU William Billings of Boston, the most prolific composer of "popular" music of the day, publishes his first song book, *The New England Psalm Singer.* He also organizes first singing class in which he teaches singing by note.

1775

TH The British re-open theatres in Boston. During the Revolution, from about 1775 to 1783, the American stage is under the full control of the British military. British General Burgoyne is an avid amateur actor and playwright.

1776

MU Colonial revolutionary war songs are introduced. English melodies with new colonial lyrics are used. "God Save the King" is rewritten into "God Save the Thirteen Colonies"; "The British Grenadiers" new lyrics are "Free America," etc. First all-American songs are "The American Hero" written by Nathaniel Niles and Andrew Law, and "Chester" written by William Billings.

MU William Billings publishes new song book, *The Singing Master's Assistant,* a collection of his songs.

MU First black gospel singing by organized choral groups is heard at newly opened black Baptist church in Petersburg, Virginia.

1778

TH Congress prohibits theatrical entertainment in any form. However, the British occupy most of existing theatres and, for the most part, drama continues to be a popular recreation.

1787

TH *The Contrast,* first comedy written by an American (Royall Tyler) and acted by professionals, is presented by the American Company at the John Street Theatre in New York City.

1789

TH William Dunlap's first play, *The*

Father, is presented. Dunlap is America's first important playwright and a foremost historian of the theatre.

1793

CI John Bill Ricketts presents the first "complete" circus performance in America at an arena he has built in Philadelphia. President George Washington attends the show. Ricketts, a veteran English equestrian, is the star of his own show.

1796

The first critic's circle is formed by a group of prominent literary men who meet after every opening and issue a pooled opinion to the press. One of them is Charles Adams, brother and son of the U.S. Presidents. The critics are despised by many top stars of the day.

1798

TH The first Park Theatre, also known as the New Theatre, opens in New York City. The Park replaced the John Street Theatre as America's most celebrated playhouse and retained that title for more than twenty years. Built of stone, the Park is financed (at more than $130,000) by 113 persons and is first leased by William Dunlap and John Hodgkinson, a leading actor of the 1790s.

MU *The American Musical Miscellany* is published. It contains one hundred songs, familiar melodies all set to new lyrics. It is sold via street-hawkers.

MU "Hail, Columbia," the most popular patriotic song of the day is written. Lyric is by Joseph Hopkinson with the melody written earlier by Philip Phile for tune called "The President's March," which honored George Washington.

1800

MU John Isaac Hawkins invents the upright piano.

1809

TH A Miss Arnold appears with her husband David Poe in *Castle Spectre* at a Boston theatre. Earlier this year, in January, their son, Edgar Allen Poe, is born. The inventor of the detective story also worked as a theatre critic for the *Broadway Journal* in the 1840s.

1810

CI Phineas Taylor Barnum is born July 5 at Bethel, Connecticut.

1815

CI Hackaliah Bailey buys an elephant,

Old Bet, from a ship's captain in New York for $1,000. It is the first pachyderm to be seen in America. He takes Old Bet on tour, charging adults twenty-five cents, children ten cents to see her.

1816

TH The Chestnut Theatre in Philadelphia is the first American playhouse to have gas lights installed in place of candles.

1820

TH England's famous Drury Lane star, Edmund Kean, visits the United States for the first time to perform in a series of Shakespearean dramas and one American play by Payne. He appears first in *Richard III.*

CI Observing the phenomenal success Hackaliah Bailey was having in exhibiting Old Bet, a group of men — Jeremiah Crane, John June, Lewis Titus and Sutton Angevine — form the Zoological Institute, a traveling circus. They have a few mangy wild animals, a couple of acrobats, and a half-dozen farm hands costumed as clowns. The show travels in wagons and performs within a circular canvas wall which they erect at each stop.

1821

TH Junius Brutus Booth, father of Edwin and John Wilkes, arrives in America for the first time. He appears as *Richard III* at the Park Theatre in New York.

1823

TH/MU A musical, *Cleri,* is presented in New York with words by John Howard Payne and music by Henry Bishop. The show's hit song is "Home Sweet Home," based on an Italian melody. A prolific playwright, Payne wrote more than fifty plays, including his most famous work, *Brutus (or The Fall of Tarquin)* when he was only twenty-one.

1825

SH Showboats bring entertainment to towns along the newly built Erie Canal.

1827

TH Seven-year-old Louisa Lane arrives in America and makes her debut as an actress. Ms. Lane later marries John Drew and, in 1860, becomes manager of the Arch Theatre in Philadelphia. The Drews found a theatrical dynasty. Their sons, John and Sidney Drew, become stars. Their daughter, Georgiana, weds actor Maurice Barrymore and has three children — John, Lionel, and Ethel Barrymore.

1828

MI Two black men — known only as

"Old Corn Meal" and Picayune Butler — are credited by some historians with originating minstrelsy in America. Corn Meal — who sold that product — picked up extra money by singing melodies created by blacks in the early days of slavery in front of the old Planters' Hotel in New Orleans.

1830

CI Aaron Turner takes out a circus which plays under a portable round-top tent and has wooden seats on which the audience may sit. A young man named P. T. Barnum works for Turner as a ticket taker and as an occasional black-faced minstrel man.

CI The group of up-state New York neighbors of Hackaliah Bailey, who organized shows ten years earlier, are now virtually a circus "syndicate." They buy up small shows; sign top performers to exclusive long term deals; import animals from Asia and Africa. In next three decades they are the dominant force in the circus world.

1832

TH Fanny Kemble, soon to become one of America's most popular actresses, arrives from England with her father, Charles, (brother of the famous British actress, Mrs. Siddons) and opens in New York. She is also a playwright.

1833

TH American-born black actor Ira Aldridge appears as Othello in England. He becomes a star in Europe but is never seen in America, where blacks are still relegated to minor — if any — parts.

CI Isaac Van Amburgh presents the first wild animal act, featuring lions, tigers, leopards, and panthers at the Richmond Hill Theatre, New York.

1835

CI Barnum buys an elderly black woman slave, Joice Heth. Her owner has documents which support his claim that she is 161 years old and was a slave of the Washington family at the time of President George Washington's birth. In spite of her age, she is coherent and articulate and tells stories about "little Georgie" and sings Negro spirituals. Barnum exhibits her in New York with great success. At her death, an autopsy indicates she was about eighty.

1842

CI Barnum makes a deal with Mr. and Mrs. Sherwood E. Stratton of Bridgeport, Connecticut to manage and exhibit their five-year-old son, Charles, who is twenty-five inches tall and weighs fifteen pounds. Barnum converts young Charles into General Tom Thumb; he makes a fortune with the bright young midget, exhibiting him in the United States and Europe.

1843

MI *The Virginia Minstrels* (four white men, including Dixie composer, Dan Emmett) is formed. This marks the beginning of black-face minstrelsy by white performers, which is based on the singing and dancing of black slaves.

1845

TH *Fashion,* one of the first plays written by an American woman, Anna Cora Mowatt, is presented at the Park Theatre. Although the drama only ran twenty nights, it was considered a hit. In 1924 *Fashion* is revived and runs for 235 performances on Broadway.

1847

RE/MO Thomas Alva Edison — whose lesser inventions included the kinetoscope (basis for the movie industry) and the phonograph — is born in Milan, Ohio on February 11.

1849

TH The leading tragedians of America (Edwin Forrest) and England (William Charles Macready) open in the same play, *Macbeth,* on the same night in New York. Three nights later rowdy supporters of Forrest mob the Astor Place Theatre where Macready is playing. The riot, which kills twenty-two and injures thirty-six, typifies the passionate mood of fans in that era.

TH Charlotte Cushman returns from five years of study in England to become the leading tragedian actress of the day. She is particularly successful in male roles such as *Hamlet.*

1850

CI This year, and in the years immediately preceding and following, Dan Rice is one of the most colorful performer/owners of the early circus days. As a clown and entertainer he is offered as much as $1000 per week by various circus owners. As owner of his own shows, which he toured on land, and via show boats he makes and loses several fortunes.

MU P. T. Barnum takes his first flyer into the straight musical world by importing Jenny Lind, "the Swedish Nightingale," for an American concert tour. Up to this point, Barnum's main claim to fame has been the flamboyant manner in which he promoted various freak attractions, real and/or fake.

1851

SH Gilbert Spalding, owner of a small circus in Albany, New York, builds the most elegant showboat of the day, the *Floating Palace.* It is a huge barge towed by two boats; it has a forty-two foot riding ring, is elegantly appointed, and seats 2,400 people. It costs Spalding more than $40,000. Ten years later the Confederate Army confiscates it and coverts it into a hospital ship.

1853

TH The Howard Family stages first performance of Harriet Beecher Stowe's *Uncle Tom's Cabin* in Troy, N.Y.

1855

MU George Bristow writes *Rip Van Winkle,* the first American grand opera on an American theme.

1856

TH First copyright law designed to protect playwrights is passed by Congress. In addition to giving the author sole rights to print and publish his work, it also gives him "sole right to act, perform, or represent same." However, only the title was filed, not the text. Thus, it was still possible for unethical producers and performers to steal material.

1857

TH Joseph Jefferson III becomes a star in the title role of *Our American Cousin,* which also stars Laura Keene in dual role of actress and manager. The play, written by England's Tom Taylor, was playing at the Ford Theater on the night in 1865 when John Wilkes Booth shot Lincoln.

1859

MU Northern minstrel man Dan Emmett writes "Dixie" as a walk-around tune for Bryant's Minstrels. Not until the Civil War does the song become a battle hymn for the South.

1862

TH Adah Isaacs Menken in a play, *Mazeppa,* creates a sensation by riding a horse bareback and wearing a flesh-colored costume which makes her appear naked.

1863

TH Melodrama is in vogue and that sterling tear-jerker, *East Lynne,* opens at the Winter Garden starring Lucille Western who purchased all rights to the play for $100.

1864

TH Edwin Booth becomes one of the most famous Hamlets in history at New

York's Winter Garden Theatre. Booth is founder of the famous Players Club for actors in New York.

TH In what is believed to be a first and only time, the three Booth brothers perform in *Julius Caesar* at New York's Winter Garden with John Wilkes as Marc Anthony, Edwin as Brutus, and Junius Brutus Jr. as Cassius. Less than five months later, John Wilkes assassinates President Lincoln.

1865

MI First all-black minstrel company, the "Georgia Minstrels," is formed by George Hicks.

1866

TH The first chorus line of 100 girls is featured in the first musical spectacular, *The Black Crook,* which opens at Niblo's Garden. It's a miraculous accident. A European ballet troupe is burned out of a theatre, so Niblo's manager decides to combine its dancers and music, by Charles Barres, with a melodrama plot. New Yorkers love it.

TH Dion Boucicault, Irish-born playwright-actor, writes an adaptation of Washington Irving's *Rip Van Winkle* which opens at the Olympic Theatre, New York. Its star, Joseph Jefferson III, is such a hit that he is still touring with the play thirty-five years later in 1902.

1867

TH Augustin Daly's first original play, *Under the Gaslight,* opens and introduces the plot device of tying an actor to a railroad track. Daly is the king of melodrama from 1860 to 1900. He is also a director and manager, and is the first to team John Drew and Ada Rehan in comedy.

CH England's Charles Dickens is a big hit in this country with his one-man show — readings from his novels.

MU First collection of black spiritual songs is published in New York by Lucy Garrison, William Allen, and Charles Ware.

1870

CI Albert, August, Otto, Alfred Theodore, Charles, and John Ringling (ages eighteen to four respectively) attend the Dan Rice Circus on Rice's showboat at the Mississippi River town of McGregor, Iowa. From that day forward, they are determined to have their own circus.

1871

CI Barnum's "Great Museum, Menagerie, Caravan, Hippodrome and Circus" opens in Brooklyn, New York, April 10. It is the forerunner of the great Barnum and Bailey

circus. Barnum's partner and general manager, William Coup, is largely responsible for its success.

VA H. J. Sargent organizes a group of mixed entertainers called "Sargent's Great Vaudeville Company" in Louisville, Kentucky.

1873

TH Maude Adams makes her stage debut at the age of nine months as *The Lost Child.* She is carried on stage by her actress mother, Annie Adams Kisskadden, at the Mormon Theatre in Salt Lake City, the first playhouse built by a religious sect in America.

1874

CI James A. Bailey — general manager of the Hemmings, Cooper and Whitby Shows, a thriving circus — buys out Hemmings' interest in the show after Whitby is killed by a drunken gunfighter. The show's name is changed to Cooper and Bailey. Bailey is twenty-six years old and this is first show he owns.

CI After Barnum's circus is completely wiped out by a fire at the New York Hippotheatron in New York in 1872, he puts together an even larger show and builds the Great Barnum Hippodrome in New York. It seats 10,000 people. Several years later it is renamed Madison Square Garden.

1876

RA/RE Alexander Graham Bell invents the telephone, proving the practicality of transmitting the human voice over distances.

1877

MO San Francisco photographer Eadweard Muybridge and scientist John Isaacs line up twenty-four cameras and, in sequence, photograph Leland Stanford's race horse running down a track. The result is the first successful photograph of motion.

VA Joe Weber and Lew Fields, each ten years of age, put together their first vaudeville act.

RE Thomas Alva Edison gives one of his key assistants, John Kreusi, a sketch of a device with instructions to "make this"; the device is the phonograph. Kreusi completes the machine in December and Edison recites "Mary Had a Little Lamb" into the machine. Kreusi is amazed, and even Edison is surprised at this first intelligible recording of the human voice.

RE Edison demonstrates the "phonograph" for the editors of the *Scientific American* magazine.

1878

RE Attorney Gardner Hubbard, father-in-law of Alexander Graham Bell, forms a syndicate which arranges with Edison to manufacture and sell the phonograph. They organize the Edison Speaking Phonograph Company in April.

RE Académie des Sciences in Paris opens envelope submitted by inventor Charles Cros, in which Cros sketches and details manner in which a phonograph may be built. Through the years France maintains that Cros is the inventor of the phonograph.

RE Novelty appeal of phonograph is enormous. Edison Speaking Phonograph Company sends trained lecturers across country to play vaudeville theatres, chautauqua tents, lecture halls, showing audiences how to make "phonograms" (as tin foil cylinders are called). By the end of the year the limitations and imperfections of phonogram sound force Edison Speaking Phonograph Company to close. Less than 500 phonographs have been produced.

1879

VA Edward Harrigan and his partner Tony Hart open at the Theatre Comique in *The Mulligan Guard Ball,* first of their famed Mulligan series which blend comedy with song.

TH Edison helps playwright-actor-manager Steele MacKaye install overhead lighting in the Madison Square Theatre, New York, along with such new mechanical innovations as folding seats and an elevator stage.

1880

TH Sarah Bernhardt, the great French star, makes her debut in America as *Adrienne Lecouvreur* at the Booth Theatre, New York. She speaks only French, as she does for the rest of her remarkable career.

RE Chichester Bell and Charles Tainter set up an experimental sound laboratory in Washington, D.C.

CI Barnum sends Bailey a wire offering to buy his baby elephant, Young America, and the mother for $100,000. Bailey rejects the offer and uses enlarged copies of the telegram to promote his show, with the theme: "What Barnum Thinks of Young America, the Baby Elephant!!!" One year later, Barnum has split with William Coup, and he and Bailey go into partnership with show called, "Barnum and London."

1881

CI The Barnum and Bailey Circus — using the slogan, "The Greatest Show on Earth" — makes its debut in New York on March 16.

RE Bell and Tainter construct what they call a graphophone. It utilizes wax cylinders, rather than the tinfoil cylinders Edison had been using. They turn the graphophone over to the Smithsonian Institution in Washington.

VA Tony Pastor opens his 14th Street Theatre in New York presenting "refined" vaudeville. The bill includes Lillie Western, instrumentalist, Ella Wesner, English Music Hall singer; Leland Sisters, vocal duet; Dan Collier, comedy songs; Mack and Ferguson, knockabout comedy act; Frank McNisk, acrobat; and Tony himself, singing a generous number of his thousand-plus repertoire of song favorites.

1882

CI P. T. Barnum buys the famous elephant, Jumbo — twelve feet tall and weighing seven tons — from the London Zoo. Barnum's circus posters made Jumbo appear more than thirty feet tall.

CI Headed by eldest brother, Al — now thirty, and a seasoned juggler, balancer, and tight-rope walker — the Ringling Brothers put together their first really professional show in their barn in Baraboo, Wisc. It is called the "Ringling Brothers Classic and Comic Concert Company."

1883

TH Helena Modjeska, the great Polish actress, stars in the first American performance of Ibsen's *A Doll's House* in Louisville, Ky.

TH Eugene O'Neill's father, James O'Neill, opens as Edmond Dantes in *The Count of Monte Cristo*. The part becomes a life-long career for O'Neill. The public will not accept him in any other role. In later years he even stars in a film of the play.

RA Edison applies for a patent on a method of moving current inside a glass tube from a filament to a plate and back again. It is the basic principle behind the radio tube.

1884

TV In Germany, Paul Nipkow is granted a patent for a whirling disk scanner. The method is later used in the development of television.

CI Veteran circus man, Yankee Robinson, having come upon hard times with his own shows, joins the Ringling Brothers and on May 19 the new "Yankee Robinson and Ringling Brothers Great Double Show" gives its initial performance in Baraboo, Wisc.

1885

VA B.F. Keith and E.F. Albee become partners in the operation of a museum

show in Boston. They de-emphasize freak attractions and feature song and dance and comedy acts, such as Weber and Fields.

TH Levi Shubert (later to become known as Lee) at the age of ten and his younger brother, Sam, age eight, set up in business selling newspapers, shining shoes, and running errands outside the Wieting Opera House in Syracuse, New York. The Shubert family are poverty-stricken Russian immigrants.

TH David Belasco, touring a show called *May Blossom* at the Wieting, hires four children for a scene in the play's first act finale. One of them is Sam Shubert. Belasco becomes Sam's idol.

RA American Telephone and Telegraph Company is organized.

1886

TH Sam Shubert gets job as program boy at Bastable Theatre, Syracuse, quickly rises to assistant treasurer, then treasurer. Jacob Shubert replaces him as part of the team with Levi, still working in front of the Wieting.

MO/RE Having developed the phonograph, Edison considers the possibilities of a machine which will enable one to see as well as hear. Busy with more important problems — such as the magnetic separation of ores — he assigns the picture project to a young assistant, William Kennedy Laurie Dickson.

1887

RE Bell and Tainter sell their patents for the graphophone to a Washington, D.C. syndicate. They form a corporation called The American Graphophone Company, but concentrate on selling their device as an office dictating machine to compete with Edison's reorganized Edison Phonograph Company.

RE A system for coating tape with magnetic particles is developed by Wilhelm Hedic.

RE Emile Berliner secures patent for a laterally recorded flat disk and a player he calls the gramophone. He also creates plating and engraving processes for record manufacture.

1888

RE Multi-millionaire Jesse Lippincott buys Edison's talking machine patents and all sales rights, as well as all sales rights to machines produced by American Graphophone. Lippincott forms North American Phonograph Company, handling both phonograph and graphophone. It is an attempt (typical of the era) to create a monopoly in the talking machine industry.

1889

RE In Vienna, Johannes Brahms makes a cylinder recording.

RE Gianni Bettini, an Italian, living in Paris, patents a device called the micro-reproducer, a recording stylus mounted on metal legs. Its function is to deliver vibrations to and from the stylus with greater fidelity. With this improved reproducer, Bettini begins to record opera and concert stars.

RE North American Phonograph Company licenses more than thirty companies to lease phonographs and graphophones across the country. Among these are the Columbia Phonograph Company headed by Edward Easton.

RE Louis Glass invents a coin-operated device attached to an Edison phonograph which enables a patron for five cents to listen to a record through ear-tubes. He places the new coin-operated entertainment phonographs in penny arcades; they are very successful.

RE With the success of coin-operated listening tube entertainment phonographs in penny arcades, North American Phonograph Company, Edison and Columbia (as well as some smaller firms) begin making "entertainment" cylinders.

MO Edison receives first film strips from George Eastman, who has manufactured a thin, flexible film.

MO Working under Edison, William Kennedy Laurie Dickson utilizes Eastman's new film and invents the sprocket system to move the film through the camera. He also experiments with sound, synchronizing Edison's newly invented phonograph, thereby creating the first sound film.

MO The Edison Kinetoscope is completed. It is a coin-in-the-slot peep show machine. Edison at this stage does not believe a machine which would project a moving picture on a screen would be commercially sound idea.

1890

RE Louis Glass sells his coin-operated phonograph patents to Felix Gottschalk, who organizes the Automatic Phonograph Company and begins to sell the coin-operated listening tubes to struggling North American Phonograph franchises.

1891

TH Playwright Bronson Howard — who along with Clyde Fitch, Belasco and others, introduced "realism" to the American theatre — is a founder of the American Dramatists Club, forerunner of the Dramatists Guild.

RE Edison acquires control of the North

American Phonograph operation. The first players on market sell for $150.

MO Edison applies for a United States patent on the Kinetoscope. His attorneys suggest he secure foreign patents at the same time but he decides against this, considering the $150 it would cost to be more than the patents are worth.

MU Henry Sayers writes "Ta-Ra-Ra-Boom-De-E," first American song with a lyric that makes little sense.

CI Barnum dies at his home in Bridgeport, Conn., April 7.

RE Columbia Phonograph Company is top manufacturer of entertainment cylinders. It issues a ten-page catalog featuring bands, singers, and whistlers. Among most in-demand cylinders for coin-operated machines are whistler John Atlee's performances of "Home Sweet Home" and "The Mockingbird."

1892

CI All seven Ringling brothers are now partners in the show. Al is producer-director; Otto, financial director; Charlie, advertising director; Alf T., the promotion genius; Gus, advance man; Henry, superintendent; and John, general manager. The show now travels on thirty-one railroad cars. It is called "The Ringling Brothers Circus, The World's Greatest Show."

1893

FA The Chicago World's Fair, also known as the Columbian Exposition, opens and runs for six months drawing more than 25,000,000 people at fifty cents each. It is the biggest show of the 1890s; its most popular attraction is the new Electricity Building.

TH The great Italian star Eleonora Duse makes her American debut in *Camille* at the Fifth Avenue Theatre in New York.

TH Sam Shubert becomes treasurer of the Wieting, best threatre in Syracuse, leaving his job as treasurer of the town's second best house, the Grand Opera House. He is eighteen.

VA Albee builds his first theatre in Boston, financed by the Catholic diocese.

MO The world's first movie studio is built by Edison in West Orange, N.J., near his research labs. He names it after the public's slang name for police patrol wagons, "The Black Maria." The studio (which costs $637.67) has a swinging stage which rotates around a pivot post to follow the light of the sun.

MO Fred Ott, Edison's handyman-comedian, stars in the first movie filmed in The Black Maria. It is also the first close-up and features Ott's famous sneeze. Another Edison film produced this year is *The Execution of Mary, Queen of Scots*, complete with a shot of a regal, rolling head.

RE In Copenhagen, Valdemar Poulsen conducts experiments with recording on magnetic wire.

RE Edward Easton and Columbia Phonograph Company acquire control of American Graphophone Company, which holds Tainter-Bell patents.

RE Big cylinder sales run about 300 per day, at fifty-cents per cylinder, five dollars per dozen. Performers get five dollars for each time they successfully record a selection. No royalties.

RE Record industry plagued by pirates who make own duplicates of most popular cylinders, and by hundreds of local machine shop operators who make coin-operated phonographs, violating all patent laws.

RE Edison tells National Phonograph Convention: "I will yet live to see the day when phonographs will be as common in homes as pianos and organs are today."

RE Emile Berliner forms a patent-holding firm, the United States Gramophone Company, to protect patents on his gramophone and the one-sided flat disks it plays. Within a year he produces a gramophone to retail for twelve dollars, and a seven-inch rubber, flat disk with a playing time of two minutes. They sell for fifty cents, five dollars per dozen.

PART TWO

1894–1904

1890   1900   1901   1902   1903   1904   1905

1894 The Holland brothers open ten kinetoscope parlors in New York City. The coin-operated movie peep shows catch on quickly.

1895 Seven leading producers and theatre owner/managers form Klaw and Erlanger, Inc. It becomes known as "the trust" in the legitimate theatre and dominates the theatre for years.

1895 Guglielmo Marconi transmits wireless signals across his large family estate in Bologna, Italy.

1896 Public interest in "refined" vaudeville grows rapidly. Family-style variety challenges legitimate theatre as nation's most popular entertainment.

1896 One of first movie projectors, the Vitascope, makes its debut at the Koster & Bial Music Hall.

1897 Barnum and Bailey Circus goes on five-year European tour. Returns to find Ringling Brothers Shows have become major competitor.

1898 Wagon medicine shows are fast fading from the scene. Only about 150 still travel the country.

1900 B. F. Keith, E. F. Albee, F. F. Proctor and other vaudeville theatre owners and managers form the United Booking office. It becomes key unit in an Albee-dominated vaudeville trust.

1900 White Rats actors' union strikes against vaudeville owners and managers, but strike fails.

1901 Reginald Fessenden successfully transmits the human voice via wireless.

1901 New York City with forty-one theatres becomes the center of the legitimate theatre's world.

1901 Berliner and Johnson form the Victor Talking Machine Company.

1901 Rudolph Wurlitzer Company introduces first coin-operated music machine, the Tonophone.

1902 Enrico Caruso makes first records for His Master's Voice. Phonograph is now looked upon as serious music-reproducing machine, rather than a toy.

1902 Thomas Talley opens the first "Electric Theatre" in Los Angeles and charges 10¢ to see "a vaudeville of motion pictures lasting one hour."

1901-1903 All three Barrymores — Ethel, Lionel, and John — make their Broadway debuts.

1903 602 people die in Iroquois Theatre fire in Chicago. Tragedy marks a turning point in legitimate theatre power struggle between Erlanger and the Shuberts.

1903 Marcus Loew, Adolph Zukor, and the Warner brothers are among early penny arcade and nickelodeon operators.

1903 Public interest in movies is waning seriously when Edwin S. Porter makes *The Great Train Robbery*. It revitalizes the industry.

1903 In the theatre, musicals come into their own. *Wizard of Oz* and *Babes in Toyland* are two of season's hits.

1904 George M. Cohan writes and stars in his first hit show, *Little Johnny Jones*. He becomes outstanding popular star of the era.

1904 Lew Dockstader leaves George Primrose to form his own minstrel company.

1904 Columbia introduces first flat records, playable on both sides.

1904 John Fleming, in England, perfects a glass-bulb detector of radio waves.

THE MAD, MERRY MIX OF LIVE SHOW BUSINESS

It was an explosion—an explosion that was to continue well into the twentieth century. Seventy-six million people inhabited America in 1900, almost double the number of twenty years earlier. In a little more than two decades Philadelphia's population exploded from 674,000 to over 1,000,000; Detroit from 79,500 to 285,000; Atlanta from 21,000 to over 85,000; Los Angeles from 57,000 to 102,000. There were 3,500,000 people living in New York City.

Millions were moving—eastward, westward, north and south. Wagon and boat were no longer the only means of transportation. In 1869 the transcontinental railroad had been joined at Promontory Point, Utah, and by 1898 the United States had half the railroad mileage in the entire world.

SHORTER HOURS, MORE MONEY

There were depressions of sorts in 1873, 1884 and 1894, but they were temporary setbacks. After more than a hundred years of almost unrelieved hardship and unceasing morning-to-night toil, a majority of the work force was putting in only ten hours a day instead of twelve, and the median wage had climbed from fourteen to twenty-three dollars per week.

It was a rough and tough, colorful and chaotic time. Live show business thrived in a mad, merry, disorganized mix. Every town of any size had at least one legitimate theatre, vaudeville or burlesque house, museum, academy of music and/or music hall. The larger cities had several of each. New York was the mecca of live show business, where stars were made and hits originated. "Direct from New York" was a promotion line every touring show sought to use, if there were any pretext for using it at all, and sometimes even if there were none. All kinds of abuses, on the part of actors as well as managers, developed.

Tent shows of every description toured the smaller towns, some still by wagon, some by railroad. Vaudeville and burlesque companies, circuses, carnivals and minstrel shows, and some combinations of all of these toured every town where a dollar could be made.

NEW THEATRES MUSHROOM

New theatres opened by the scores. In a single issue of *Billboard* in 1902, new houses were reported under construction or opening in Techumseh, Nebraska; Huron Lake, Minnesota; Green Isle, Minnesota; Mason City, Iowa; Thief River Falls, Minnesota; Springfield, Ohio; Portsmouth, Ohio; Newhan, Georgia; and Grand Rapids, Michigan.

The new towns and new theatres scrambled for attractions. Cities and their theatres and civic organizations ran ads in *Billboard*, seeking shows and acts. A typical town ad of this type in 1903 read:

> OPEN—TIME
> *Including Opening Date Nov. 25*
> NEW $40,000 THEATRE
> VAN WERT, OHIO
> *In a city of 8000 population, all good spenders. Situated between Lima, O. and Fort Wayne, Ind.*
> $6,000 subscribed for the open date.
> Address all communications to C. B. PEARSON, MGR.
> THE AUDITORIUM   VAN WERT, OHIO

Performers and shows were sought for events which ran the gamut from street fairs to conventions. Poultry shows, food shows, livestock shows, expositions, horse shows, picnics, firemen's tournaments, and Fourth of July celebrations all vied for attractions.

DOUBLE BOOKING, DOUBLE CROSSES

By 1901 New York had forty-one theatres. The more affluent theatre owners in other parts of the country made trips to the big city each July or August and October or November to line up the most important shows and players they could find for the upcoming seasons. They discovered that the New York actors and shows they booked frequently failed to appear. The reason was that the shows' managers sought to put together the most logistically sensible and economical tour they could arrange, without leaving too many open dates. And the method they used to achieve this was to book two, or even three, theatres for the same dates, and

FAIRS   STREET FAIRS   CIRCUS   PARKS   DRAMATIC   BILLPOSTERS

THE BILLBOARD

Volume XIV., No. 10.   CINCINNATI, SATURDAY, MARCH 8, 1902.   Price, 10 Cents. Per Year, $4.00

MISS MAUDE ELLIOTT.
The Only Woman Manager of a Theatrical Exchange in America, a Hustler and an Artiste.

MARCH 8, 1902 ISSUE   MAUDE ELLIOTT

Initially, for a fee, they booked important New York shows and players into theatres and guaranteed their appearance.

In due time, in addition to booking, they also insisted on handling the show's advertising and charged a fee for this. Then they demanded that the theatre owners pay them a percentage of the gross business the show did. This percentage was small in the beginning, but was increased gradually until, in many cases, the trust was collecting as much as 50% of the show's gross, in addition to the booking, advertising, and other fees. This was especially true in the larger cities with a number of theatres, where Erlanger was able to play one theatre against another.

The theatrical trust made millions and Erlanger and his partners dominated the theatre in New York for many years. In 1897, two years after the formation of Klaw and Erlanger's trust, Erlanger made his first deal with three young boys from Syracuse—Levi, Sam, and Jacob Shubert, ages twenty-two, twenty, and sixteen respectively. The Shuberts had just built a new theatre, the Baker in Rochester, N.Y. and Erlanger arranged for the trust to book it for a 5% fee. Before the theatre opened, however, he used his Shubert deal to raise the fees a rival theatre, the Lyceum, was paying. Then he blithely informed the Shuberts he had changed his mind. Their deal was off.

This was only the first encounter between Erlanger and the Shuberts, and at this stage Erlanger was totally unaware that the Shuberts would one not-too-far-off day be formidable foes.

POWERFUL ACTOR/MANAGERS AND NEW STARS

The trust prospered, and the legitimate theatre as a whole thrived as the number-one, glory and gold segment of show business. Star actor/managers such as Minnie Maddern-Fiske, E. H. Sothern, Julia Marlowe, Richard Mansfield and John Drew were immune to the trust's machinations. They could and did fill houses wherever they played, and they had their own organizations to route their shows and handle the box-office. Mrs. Fiske's husband, Harrison Fiske, published the *New York Dramatic Mirror* and produced shows himself. He and David Belasco were among the handful of independent producers who waged constant war against the Klaw and Erlanger forces.

In 1895, the year the trust was formed, Belasco had his first Broadway hit, *The Heart of Maryland*. He wrote the play as well as produced it. It made Mrs. Leslie Carter a star. In 1900 Belasco had two more hits: *Madame Butterfly* and *Naughty Anthony*. He starred Blanche Bates in both these plays.

All three of the Barrymores made their Broadway debuts. In 1901, Ethel, at twenty-one, played her first starring role in *Captain Jinks of the Horse Marines*, a play by one of the most prolific and talented playwrights of the day, Clyde Fitch. Lionel—working with his uncle, John Drew—played a secondary role in *The Second in Command*. John Barry-

then play the one which fitted into their ultimate itinerary most profitably and conveniently.

It was not long before the theatre owners devised a means of protecting themselves against this practice. Instead of booking one show for a specific date, they booked two (or sometimes three) and played the show which arrived in town first. The other one or two were simply stranded. This double and triple booking and double and triple crossing was only one example of the chaotic conditions which existed in this flamboyant era of live show business' heyday.

THE FIRST THEATRICAL TRUST

This era gave rise to the first powerful trust in the history of American entertainment. In 1895 two of the outstanding producer/managers of the day, Charles Frohman and his brother Daniel, met with five other men who held a good deal of control over New York theatrical production and plays, as well as effective control of theatres in almost every major city in the country. These five men were Abe Erlanger, Marc Klaw, Sam Nirdlinger (who changed his name to Nixon), J. F. Zimmerman, and Alfred Hayman. The seven men organized a firm called Klaw and Erlanger, soon known as the theatrical syndicate or trust. The operating head of the trust was Erlanger.

more, who had been pursuing a career as a commercial artist, made his stage debut in 1903 in Fitch's *Glad of It.*

The year 1904 saw the birth of another young star, George M. Cohan, in the third play he wrote (his first big success), *Little Johnny Jones.* The musical score included Cohan's "Give My Regards to Broadway."

Musicals came into their own in the earliest years of the century. *The Wizard of Oz* and Victor Herbert's *Babes in Toyland* were two 1903 hits, and Metropolitan Opera star Fritzi Scheff forsook the opera to make her Broadway debut in the operetta *Babette* that same year.

Other major stars of the day were William Gillette, whose *Sherlock Holmes* was an early theatre classic; Olga Nethersole; Ada Rehan; Maude Adams; and Sarah Bernhardt. All had highly successful starring vehicles.

LONG-RUNNING "TOM" AND RACISM

Theater on the road was something else again. There were hundreds of traveling acting companies whose repertoire and performances left something to be desired artistically, but they all served the purpose of bringing entertainment to a population that was more than ready for it. Even thirty years and more after the Civil War, scores of companies still played *Uncle Tom's Cabin,* occasionally to hostile crowds, and now and then causing riots.

Racism was still rampant. Every year from 1894 to 1905 100 or more black men were lynched. In 1900 a North Carolina congressman, G. H. White (a black) introduced a bill to make the lynching of an American a Federal crime. The bill died in committee, and that year 105 blacks died by vigilante hanging.

Many of the most popular songs of the day were "Coon" songs: "The Phrenologist Coon," "Nobody's Lookin' But de Owl and de Moon," "Ain't Dat Scan'lous." Minstrel shows included *The Hottest Coon in Dixie Company,* and *Richard's Original Pickaninny Cakewalkers.* A favorite throw-the-ball game at carnivals was *Hit the Coon.* Blacks, along with some Indians, were frequently employed as snake eaters—later called "geeks"—in carnival pits.

MINSTRELS PEAK, VAUDE'S BEGINNING

Some blacks had prospered and continued to work in minstrel shows and combination minstrel-variety shows. Minstrelsy, however, had enjoyed its peak era in the years between 1840 and 1880. In the dominant live show business of the day, vaudeville was beginning to come into its own. Up until the closing years of the nineteenth century vaudeville was, for the most part, a bawdy and boisterous form of entertainment featuring dancing girls, suggestive songs, and comedy of the type appreciated by the raucous, brawling, hard-drinking audiences in the honky-tonks of the newly opened Western territories and many of the saloons of the East.

CARL HAGENBECK,
The Dean and High Priest of the Wild Beast Industry.

APRIL 20, 1901 ISSUE   CARL HAGENBECK

Other types of vaudeville acts—such as magicians, acrobats, animal acts, et al.—played as part of a circus program or as after-pieces in legitimate theatres playing drama. Some vaudeville troupes toured the country. But in 1881, Tony Pastor opened a new theatre on 14th Street in New York City and began a policy of "refined" vaudeville, designed to appeal to the entire family.

At the same time, B. F. Keith and E. F. Albee changed the entertainment policies at the dime museums they operated in Boston in the 1890s. They de-emphasized the showing of the freaks and oddities which were until then the main fare in the dime museums and added clean song and dance acts to their programs. Among the earliest acts they played were Joe Weber and Lew Fields, whose youthful years in show business paralleled the growth of vaudeville.

The Keith-Albee policy was so greatly appreciated by the Boston community that in 1893 the Catholic archdiocese financed the building of a new theatre for Albee. It was the first of hundreds of theatres Keith and Albee would own and/or control as vaudeville gradually, in the years to come, replaced the legitimate theatre as America's favorite mass entertainment. Even by 1896, refined or advanced vaudeville was becoming so popular that it was attracting some of the brightest and most ambitious young showmen. Florenz Ziegfeld, for example, was producing the Trocadero

THEATRICAL   CIRCUS   BILLPOSTERS   FAIRS

THE BILLBOARD

Volume XVI. No. 22.   CINCINNATI, MAY 25, 1904.   Price, 10 Cents.
Per Year, $4.00

AL. G. FIELD,
Proprietor of The Al. G. Field Greater Minstrels,
and whose name is synonymous with success.

MAY 28, 1904 ISSUE   AL. G. FIELD

Vaudevilles—a ten-act bill, starring "Sandow the Strong Man and a congress of World Famous Artists and Athletes and comedian Billy Van"—at the Grand Opera House in New York that year.

EARLY MOVIES ON THE VAUDE BILL

In 1896 some vaudeville houses were also adding a new entertainment novelty to their programs. It was called the Vitascope, a device which projected moving pictures onto a screen. It was really an extension of the peep show parlor kinetoscopes, which had been around since 1894, when the first such parlor was opened on Broadway in New York City.

A small handful of people—generally from other industries, such as the fur and the jewelry business—were getting involved in the kinetoscope and projection movie business, but most experienced showmen were too busy making fortunes (or trying to) in the theatre, vaudeville, circuses, carnivals and other established areas of entertainment.

B. F. Keith, for one, saw such a glowing future for properly organized vaudeville that in 1900 he formed the United Booking Office. The UBO was to become a key element in a new vaudeville trust, which rivaled the theatre's Klaw-Erlanger combine (upon which it was modeled) for sheer ruthlessness and money-making capacities.

Vaudeville had not yet reached that stage, but it was singing, dancing and clowning its way into the classic yet profitable state of chaos that screams for well-financed organization and ultimate iron-fisted monopoly. And Keith and his younger partner and general manager, E. F. Albee, were laying and executing careful plans to head up such a monopoly.

ACTION AT THE CARNIVALS

Other segments of live entertainment were more or less active too. Less active were the declining medicine shows. By 1898 fewer than 150 of them still traveled the country. Carnivals, by the hundreds, found all the action they sought in the special events—ranging from street fairs to firemen's tournaments—which were held in virtually every town and city across the country. There were occasional ruckuses between the carnival people and townies, some erupting into violence as extreme as murder. Small-town politicians frequently milked the carnies for license fees and other permits; many carnivals got these fees (and more) back by inviting the locals into the "privilege" car, a private gambling layout where loaded dice and marked cards were not unknown.

A handful of the larger, more affluent carnivals—those which played the major state fairs and other lush events—ran clean shows and took stringent precautions against the gamblers. Some carnivals traveled by railroad car, but the majority still moved via wagon trains.

THE CIRCUS EXPANSION

Circuses went into substantial expansion programs, due primarily to the greatly enlarged audience scattered around the country, and to the new and extensive railroad facilities. By 1891 seven large circuses were traveling by rail. Barnum and Bailey led them with a show which utilized sixty-five railroad cars. The Adam Forepaugh show used fifty-two cars; the Sells Brothers circus, forty-two; the John Robinson show, thirty-five; the Walter L. Main circus, twenty-seven. The Ringling Brothers show at that time required only twenty cars to transport its equipment and personnel. The Great Wallace Shows also used twenty cars.

While the railroads enabled the tented big shows to move more efficiently than ever before, they also represented one of the great risks of the times: train wrecks. On the early railroads car wheels occasionally broke; sections of track weakened or separated; now and then one railroad car clattering along at thirty to forty miles per hour would ram another car standing still, due to poor or inadequate signal planning and execution.

One of the worst of these early wrecks occurred August 6, 1903, when two cars of the Great Wallace Shows collided at Durand, Michigan. Twenty-eight circus people were killed and many others were injured. *Billboard* sponsored a showmen's fund, and a monument was built to commemorate the wreck and those who died in it.

THEATRICAL   CIRCUS   BILLPOSTERS   FAIRS

THE BILLBOARD

Volume XVI, No. 20.   CINCINNATI, MAY 14, 1904.   Price, 10 Cents Per Year, $4.00

EDDIE FOY as PETER POUFFLE
in Piff, Paff, Pouf, which is enjoying a phenomenally successful
run at the Casino Theatre, New York City.

MAY 14, 1904 ISSUE   EDDIE FOY AS PETER POUFFLE

THE RINGLING-BARNUM AND BAILEY COMPETITION

By 1895 the Ringling Brothers had developed their show to the point where they were the major competitive threat to "the Greatest Show on Earth," Barnum and Bailey. The Ringlings' spectacle that year was *Cleopatra,* and it boasted a cast of 1,250, including 300 dancers, 500 mounted Roman soldiers, 200 foot soldiers, plus every animal in the show's menagerie, whether known to the Romans or not.

In 1896, James Bailey bought control of the Adam Forepaugh Circus and worked out a partnership arrangement with the prosperous Sells Brothers show, to combine Forepaugh and Sells. In 1897, Bailey left the American circus scene to the Ringlings and its other domestic competitors, and took the Barnum and Bailey show to England and Europe. The greatest show on earth remained overseas for five consecutive years, through 1902, playing virtually every city of any size in England, Scotland, Wales, Germany, France and several other continental countries. In 1902, Barnum and Bailey returned to find the Ringling Brothers stronger than ever. In addition to outstanding acts of all kinds that Barnum and Bailey had contracted on their European tour, an ad they placed in *Billboard* in 1902 gives

some indication of what they were seeking on their return to America. It read:

> *Wanted*
> *Absolutely the Best, Most Perfect and Most Accomplished Performers and Artists in All Branches and Lines—Equestrian, Aerial, Acrobatic, Gymnastic, Terpsichorean, Athletic, Comic, Grotesque, Sensational Thrill and Wonderful Exhibitions and Performances of Every Kind—Singly, in teams, troupes and whole companies.*

A booking agent, Milton Aborn of New York, in an ad in *Billboard* in that same year offered:

> *3000 Acts—including Arabs, Japanese, Bull Fighters, Hindoo Fakirs, Musicians, Dancers, etc. Everything in the Gymnastic Line, including Aerial Bars, Flying, Casting, High Diving, Ground Acts. Everything in Animal Acts from a Kitten to an Elephant.*

ANIMAL ACTS AND DAREDEVILS

In live show business animal and daredevil acts were favorites. Showmen trained horses, dogs, elks, and pigs to dive off high platforms into water tanks. Trained bears, elephants, horses—even bulls and sheep—as well as wild animals, were featured not only in circuses and vaudeville, but in theatres, parks, and at carnivals and fairs.

The daredevils included the wild animal trainers who worked with lions, tigers, and other savage beasts, as well as balloon ascencionists, high-divers and loop-the-loop riders. A surprisingly large number of the daredevils of the day were women. Scores of them performed dangerous feats of all kinds and were active in many other show business pursuits. There were all-women military brass bands, boxers, wrestlers, bag punchers, club swingers, baseball teams and, of course, dancers and singers, actresses, and chorus girls by the thousands.

Wild west shows, amusement parks, and county and state fairs all prospered.

THE MOST SPECTACULAR SHOW OF ALL

By any standard, the most spectacular show of the 1890s was a fair which ran from May to October of 1893. This was the Columbian Exposition (marking the 400th anniversary of Columbus's discovery of America), but better known as the Chicago World's Fair. Most of the more than 25,000,000 people who paid twenty-five cents each to see the fair came from villages or towns where they still used

FROM JULY 18, 1903 ISSUE   LUCIA MOORE

gas or candles and oil for illumination. To these people the hit of the show was not the exotic troupe of belly dancers working the Cairo Street exhibit, nor even the giant 250-foot wheel, with the thirty glass cabs suspended from its girders. Each of the cabs held sixty people who got a panoramic view of the fair and the surrounding countryside, as the huge wheel, invented by G. W. Ferris, slowly rotated. It was the first Ferris wheel, a ride destined to become a fixture in America's amusement parks, at carnivals, and lesser fairs.

No show, no ride, had the awesome impact on Chicago's fairgoers in 1893 as that of the Electricity Building—a huge, white palace with hundreds of large, arched and rectangular windows and turreted towers. The building was flanked by canals. On the canals glided Venetian gondolas.

GOLD ON ONYX WATERS

The nighttime sight of the brilliant electric lights beaming from the windows of the imposing building—painting shimmering golden paths on the onyx waters of the canal—was truly spectacular. To most of the fair's visitors, it was breathtaking, something they could not have imagined in the most fantastic of all their dreams.

Inside the building various other uses of electric power were demonstrated. Plans had been made to include the kinetoscope and the kinetograph, but the working models were not completed in time for display at the fair.

The man behind all this, of course, was Thomas Alva Edison. It is not hyperbolic to say that Edison was the star of the Chicago World's Fair. The genius from West Orange, N.J., had a greater effect on the evolution of show business—from the dominance of the live forms to the eventual takeover by the mechanical and electronic concepts—than any other man in history.

THE PHONOGRAPH AND KINETOSCOPE

Edison's invention of the phonograph and tin-foil cylinder records in 1877 and his invention of the kinetoscope in 1891 are two easily traced, direct examples of his influence. He also was the indirect cause of certain key entertainment developments as a result of his sometimes erroneous estimates of the commercial application and potential of his inventions. And, on occasion, his frugality created situations in which the course of American entertainment was hindered or halted, and the evolution of show business took unexpected twists and turns.

There was at least one incident in which the work of his fertile brain turned out to be a contributing factor in unseating one theatrical power group, and enabling another to take over—*purely as a matter of unforeseeable fate*. In late 1903, the Klaw and Erlanger trust was at its all-time peak. It controlled more theatres across the country than it could actually handle efficiently. Yet Erlanger pushed relentlessly to add more and more houses.

MASS DEATH AT MR. BLUEBEARD

Then during a matinee in one of the trust's Chicago theatres—the Iroquois, on December 30, 1903—an electric spark ignited a flimsy bit of gauze draped over a piece of scenery. Small clouds of smoke drifted out from the proscenium arch. In seconds ribbons of flame curled around the audience side of the arch. As some backstage people rushed out of exit doors, and wind drafts swept in, more gauze, cloth, canvas, and wood caught fire. Eddie Foy, starring in the musical *Mr. Bluebeard*, was on stage. He stepped down to the footlights.

"Everything is all right," he told the audience, largely a holiday crowd of women with their children. "The theatre is fire-proof. Don't panic." He signaled the orchestra leader in the pit, and the band played a happy tune. But the fire quickly raced up and down the proscenium arch, ate at the drops and flats, and roared out into the house. Six hundred and two people were either trampled or burned to death. An electric spark had caused the worst fire in the history of the theatre, in a key house of the Klaw and Erlanger trust.

THE ANTI-ERLANGER PRESS

Newspapers, not only in Chicago but across the country, denounced Erlanger and the money-hungry theatrical trust. *Life* magazine ran a caricature of a bloated Erlanger, towering before a burning theatre in the background. The trust was accused of disregarding the safety of its patrons by violating existing fire regulations, in order to save the money it would take to meet the requirements of these regulations. In cities across the country theatres were closed down. Many were condemned. New safety requirements were written into law. New theatres had to be built. And many of these signed with the Shuberts rather than Erlanger, whose reputation had been smeared in a most profound and ugly manner by the Iroquois publicity. The electric spark that created the Iroquois fire was a key incident in the downfall of Klaw and Erlanger and the rise of the Shuberts. The press pursued its anti-Erlanger, anti-trust policies aggressively from that point on, and that fact played no small part in later confrontations between the expanding Shuberts and the Klaw and Erlanger operations.

A HIATUS FOR THE PHONOGRAPH

In the earliest years of the twentieth century few recognized the monumental impact Edison's entertainment inventions would have on American show business. He invented the phonograph, and the tin-foil cylindrical records it played, in 1877. After securing patents on it and demonstrating it for the *Scientific American* magazine's editors in 1878, he incorporated the Edison Speaking Phonograph Company, then dropped the whole matter for practical purposes and went on to other projects, which he considered to be far more important. (As indeed they were—one of them being the electric light.)

It was not until ten years later, 1887, that records became an entertainment reality. In that year Emile Berliner invented another "talking" machine, the gramophone, which played laterally recorded, flat disks instead of cylinders. At that stage Edison reactivated his phonograph company. And even then he insisted the phonograph be pushed as a business dictating machine, rather than a medium of musical or spoken entertainment.

His position made good common sense, since the sound reproduced by either the cylindrical or the flat disks—played on either the phonograph or gramophone—was distorted, crackled and popped with static, and had little musical quality. It was not until 1901—when Berliner and an engineer from Camden, N.J., named Eldridge Johnson, formed the Victor Talking Machine Company—that records stood on the threshold of becoming a genuine factor in musical entertainment.

CARUSO'S BIG DEAL

In 1902, Fred Gaisberg, an American producer working for the English branch of the company, *His Master's Voice,* went to Milan and persuaded Enrico Caruso to record ten songs. He paid Caruso the unheard-of price of 100 pounds, against the strict orders of his London headquarters, who felt that price an outrageous figure to pay a singer.

The Caruso sides were released in London that May, timed to coincide with the fabled tenor's first concert appearance at Covent Gardens. They were an overnight success. Soon other leading opera and concert stars followed Caruso's lead and the phonograph became an accepted device for musical reproduction rather than a distorted sound novelty.

THE CYLINDER-FLAT DISK WAR

The early years of the record business were marked by a classic technological battle between Edison's cylindrical disks and Berliner's flat disk, but the total impact of both record types on the era's show business was minimal. Few gave any thought to its ultimate potential as a major, mass market entertainment force. The competition between the cylinder and the flat disk contributed to the popularization of recorded music generally, just as future technological conflicts would continue to stimulate popular interest.

In 1904, the Odeon Record Company in Berlin added another plus to the flat disk by turning out records with material on both sides. Up to that time songs or talk were recorded on one side only. The Columbia Phonograph Company released the first two-sided, flat disks in America later that same year. They retailed for $1.50. But the flat versus cylindrical war raged on. Edison was not only a genius; he was a very stubborn man.

HERE COMES THE PEEP SHOW

The second mechanical form of show business fathered by Edison was the motion picture. In 1889, he completed the first models of the kinetoscope. A talented associate named William Kennedy Laurie Dickson helped him greatly with this invention, since Edison was busy simultaneously with other projects, such as finding ways to separate ores magnetically. The kinetoscope was a film shown in a peep-show machine, activated by insertion of a penny, and operated by turning a crank. Edison's attorneys filed patent applications in 1891. They suggested that Edison ask for European patents as well as patents in the United States. Securing the foreign patents would cost $150. Edison decided this protection wasn't worth that much money, so patents were secured for the United States only.

This frugal decision was partially responsible for making it necessary for the great inventor and his associates to fight a number of bitter and costly lawsuits over patents in the years to come.

In 1894, the Holland brothers opened the first kinetoscope parlor on Broadway in New York City with ten machines. That same year Grey and Otway Latham, brothers from Northcliff, Va., also opened a parlor in New York with six machines. The Lathams did such a fine business that it occurred to them that if someone would produce a screen machine, which would enable them to throw the picture upon a wall or screen, they could have dozens of people see the film at the same time, rather than the one-at-a-time procedure necessitated by the peep-show machines. They proposed the idea to Norman Raff, who managed the Kinetoscope Company for Edison. Raff thought the idea excellent and took it to the wizard. Edison rejected it.

SCREEN MACHINES AND GOLDEN EGGS

If we make this screen machine, he told Raff, *it will spoil everything. We are making these peep show machines and selling a lot of them at a good profit. If we put out a screen machine there will be a use for maybe about ten of them in the whole United States. With that many screen machines you could show the pictures to everybody in the country— and then it would be done. Let's not kill the goose that lays the golden egg.*

Others invented various screen machines as early as 1895. One, the Vitascope, was created by an inventor named Thomas Armat in Washington, D.C. Its promoters made a deal with Edison to use his name as the inventor, since the Edison name was magic at the box-office.

Magic in the peep-show machines of the day were features developed in tie-ups with Barnum and Bailey's "Greatest Show on Earth," and the Buffalo Bill "Wild West Show." From the circus, Edison's company filmed *The Paddle Dance* by Fiji Islanders, *The Dance of Rejoicing* by Samoan Islanders, the *Short Stick Dance* by natives of India, the Hindustan Fakir, and the Cotta Dwarf. Buffalo Bill subjects included Cody himself and Annie Oakley, "the little sure shot," in an exhibition of rifle shooting at glass balls. Comedy subjects were *New Bar Room*, which showed a quarrel in a saloon and "a policeman taking a glass of beer on the sly;" Professor Welton's Boxing Cats; and the Glenroy Brothers, "farcical pugilists in costume."

Non-farcical boxing bouts were also peep-show favorites. In the 1894 crop were a "five round glove contest to a finish" between Hornbacker and Murphy; and Billy Edwards and the Unknown, a boxing bout in five rounds. Prices were generally $12.50 or $15.00 per subject, with prize fight films selling from $20.00 to $25.00 per round.

Edison's earliest catalog also featured "musical records for use on the Kinetophone at $1.50 each."

EDISON'S BIG COMPETITOR

In 1896, William Kennedy Laurie Dickson joined a group of men in forming the American Mutoscope and Biograph Company. It was the intense competition which developed between Edison's motion picture operations and Biograph (the subsequent shortened name of American Mutoscope and Biograph Company) which ultimately led to the forma-

tion of the Motion Picture Patents Company, another of the show business trusts of the early twentieth century.

Soon screen machines and projectors of various kinds became available, and soon enterprising businessmen were not only collecting pennies by the hundreds of thousands from their peep-show kinetoscopes, but also taking in nickels from their store shows. In these store shows, programs of movies were thrown on a screen and generally accompanied by an indefatigable and versatile piano player. In 1902, the first such store show was opened on Main Street in Los Angeles, Calif., by Thomas Talley. He called it the "Electric Theatre" and he charged ten cents for what he advertised as "a vaudeville of motion pictures lasting one hour." Most operators charged five cents.

THE PIONEERS MOVE IN

Among the most successful of the earliest penny arcade kinetoscope operators and store show, electric theatre and nickelodeon impresarios were Harry Warner and his brothers, who opened the Cascade Theatre in New Castle, Pa., in 1903. That same year and in the year or two thereafter, Marcus Loew, his friend Adolph Zukor (both from the fur business), and William Fox were among those who opened nickelodeons in New York City. An early partner of Loew's was a stage actor friend named David Warfield who became one of the biggest stars of his time.

The box-office appeal of the early peep shows and projected films was simply the novelty of seeing people and things move. Occasionally the subject matter would be interesting enough to embellish this basic novelty appeal. Such an instance was the release in 1896 of *The Kiss,* a short one-reeler in which May Irwin and John Rice were filmed kissing each other chastely on the mouth, exactly as they did it in the stage play, *The Widow Jones,* in which they were starring on Broadway. Many people were as shocked at *The Kiss* as some people, years later, would be at *Deep Throat.*

THE EFFECTIVE CHASERS

During the novelty-appeal years of early movies (approximately 1894 through 1902), they became a part of the program in almost all dime museums, amusement parks, and vaudeville theatres—as well as in the penny arcades and the straight all-movie nickelodeons. In the parks, they were shown in small buildings called Kinodromes. In vaudeville, house owners and managers considered the one reel films primarily "chasers," i.e., they hoped the films would persuade people to leave the theatre, rather than stay to see the vaudeville bill a second time. And the films, for the most part, worked very well as chasers.

Few people in the film industry thought in terms of making the movies dramatically interesting. The inventors were busy struggling to improve the quality of the film itself: to eliminate the eye-torturing flicker, to make the film viewable in rooms not utterly dark, and other technical prob-

JULY 9, 1904 ISSUE   FORBES ROBERTSON

tion of its audience. It was a super shot of adrenalin to the lethargic nickelodeon world. It was the first super successful Western. Its unbilled star, George M. Anderson—called Broncho Billy—started his own movie company with George Spoor, and made 372 western one-reelers in seven years.

The movie business had a new life, but it did not soar immediately or uninterruptedly to its place as the number-one form of show business. It was to go through several critical stages in which its future was in doubt.

THE WIRELESS DREAMERS

A third form of electric or mechanical show business was not yet even in the wings, but experimenters and inventors were preparing its birth. Radio would some day, in the not too distant future, have its own incalculable impact on the theatre and vaudeville, and on motion pictures. In strange, paradoxical ways, it would have both negative and positive effects on recorded entertainment. But in the late years of the nineteenth and early years of the twentieth century it was hardly a dream in the minds of a handful of geniuses.

Edison again played a part. In 1883, he devised a method of moving current from a filament to a glass plate and back again, inside a glass tube. This was, and is, the basic principle behind the radio tube. In 1885, the Wizard of Orange actually filed for his only patent in wireless communications. It was granted and he sold it to the Marconi Company.

Guglielmo Marconi must be considered the father of radio. In 1895, as a very young man, he transmitted signals across the length of the huge Marconi family estate in Bologna by wireless. Two years later the Marconi Company was formed in England, and in 1889 Marconi transmitted wireless signals across the English Channel.

In 1901, Reginald Fessenden, a Canadian electrical engineer, successfully transmitted the human voice by wireless. And, in 1904, an Englishman named John Fleming perfected a glass bulb "detector" of radio waves.

NEW TRUSTS, NEW STARS

But radio, for practical purposes, was two decades away. In 1905 the Shuberts were to experience the greatest tragedy of their lives, yet go on to a dominance of the theatre, surpassing that achieved by Klaw and Erlanger. Keith and Albee, particularly the latter, were to play a major part in developing "refined" vaudeville into America's number one mass entertainment medium, by creating a vaudeville monopoly Erlanger or the Shuberts might envy.

The fierce Edison-Biograph battles—inside and out of the courts—was to lead to a motion picture trust which initially stabilized the film, then almost choked it to death.

And all these power struggles led to the creation of new stars, and more varied and absorbing entertainment than America had ever seen before.

lems. The manufacturers were busy suing each other and attempting to find ways to make the one reelers more quickly and economically and get the rate up from the established ten cents per foot price.

PORTER'S ROBBERY

By 1902, the majority of the one-reelers were so dull, and the basic appeal of seeing pictures move was wearing so thin, that the movie industry may well have disappeared into a limbo of momentarily flashy, but basically valueless, freak novelties. Fortunately, in the cosmic way the planet turns, there are always creative people doodling with ideas for utilizing the inventions of the inventors and the facilities manufactured by the wheeler-dealers and financiers.

In the year 1903, one of these was Edwin S. Porter. He was making pictures for the Edison Film Company. He had made one called *The Life of an American Fireman*, which told an interesting enough story, something few films did at all. But, in 1903, he wrote, directed, and produced an eleven-minute film, *The Great Train Robbery*. In it, for the first time in movie history, he used modern film story telling techniques—such as shooting the story out of sequence, with flashbacks and other narrative techniques.

The Great Train Robbery told a complete, exciting story, and told it in a fresh way which held the rapt atten-

ORIGINAL BILLBOARD MATERIAL 1894–1904

HIGHLIGHTS

———————◆•●•◆———————

VAUDEVILLE PERFORMERS, AN ODD COLLECTION   81

"Vaudeville performers," said one writer, "are certainly the oddest collection of entertaining talent ever collected in a modern theatre." There were sixty-seven vaudeville theatres, playing some 700 acts, and "even the most insignificant act on a bill received $40 per week."

A WAR IN BURLESQUE   83

A war was brewing in burlesque. The powerful Empire Circuit with theatres in numerous cities would not play a traveling burlesque company in any of its cities if that company played an opposition house in any city. Non-Empire managers planned to form permanent companies for their houses.

CHANGES IN MINSTRELSY   85

Although many of the pioneer performers and managers of the early minstrel days were dying in the early 1900s, minstrelsy still thrived. Lew Dockstader, J. A. Coburn, Al G. Field, J. S. Hoffman, John W. Vogel, George Primrose, Klaw & Erlanger, and others, presented highly entertaining shows in the black minstrel format but changes were taking place.

SHOESTRING CARNIVALS TO THE ST. LOUIS WORLD'S FAIR   89

In spite of the carnival companies that "were going around the country on a shoestring, and that had a lot of vulgar, immoral, disgusting exhibitions aggregated under a collection of dirty ragged canvas," the legitimate carnivals and the street and county fairs—including the giant St. Louis World's Fair—prospered. Their attractions included everything from Gypsy camps to the Henry J. Pain's spectacles, *The Last Days of Pompei* and *Ancient Rome,* which were so large that they traveled on twenty railroad cars.

THE BOOMING CIRCUSES   91

The 1904 opening of the Barnum & Bailey Circus at Madison Square Garden in New York was a major event of the season, and the review of the show which ran in *Billboard* gives a precise account of its array of acts. Circus gossip covered all manner of activity on the scores of shows which traveled the country.

PERILS OF PERFORMING 117

Occupational hazards were inherent in a number of performances.
Many a balloon ascensionist was killed; many a "loop-the-loop" bicyclist
or motorcyclist was injured or died in a fall.

SOME EARLY STARS 119

The stars had their own unique problems. One was the embarrassment of an
occasional bad review. Another was the sometimes shameful behavior of
admirers. For the most part, aside from their intimate personal problems—
which were not too frequently revealed to the public—they collected their
fabulous salaries and pursued their careers and their glamorous lives. One
jolting exception to this was Maurice Barrymore's insanity and subsequent
death.

FROM MAGIC LANTERNS
TO MOTION PICTURES 131

The potential of motion pictures was little realized in the beginning, but
Edwin S. Porter's *Great Train Robbery*—made in 1903 and widely distributed
in 1904—made clear to many showmen that movies had a great future. There
were even some early experiments with "talking" pictures and color.

VAUDEVILLE PERFORMERS, AN ODD COLLECTION

FROM JAN. 5, 1901 ISSUE

Vaudeville Performers.

The vaudeville performers are certainly the oddest collection of entertaining talent ever collected in a modern theater. The roster reaches from a tragedian in a twenty-minute snip of Shakespeare to a lady with trained lions. There are three shows each day in the continuous houses. These are, the afternoon show, the supper show, the night show. The first begins in the various houses from eleven-thirty to half-past twelve. This show lasts until five o'clock and it employs the full strength of the bill. The supper show runs from five o'clock almost till eight, and consists only of the minor features of the bill. The need of the supper show is a mystery even to some managers; but they will continue it as long as there are so many people who seem to take their supper at noon. The night show comprises the full strength of the bill, and lasts from eight till half-past ten or a quarter before eleven.

The oddest collection of talent in a modern theater ... from a twenty minutes snip of Shakespeare to a lady with trained lions.

The weekly bill of a vaudeville theater usually represents a fair proportion of striking individual turns to a balance of general variety. Dramatic sketches or acrobatic acts which require the full stage alternate with monologists and singers that need only the space of the first entrance. In this way changes of scene are made without delay. For from the moment the house has an audience—and there is always a crowd waiting before the doors are opened—until the last picture is shown on the biograph at night, some act is going on. A bill contains sixteen turns, only eight of which appear in the supper show. Here is an outline of the contents of an average bill:

Two dramatic sketches.
Two teams of acrobats.
Two vocalists, one in character, one straight.
Three or four song-and-dance comedy duos, if sufficiently varied.
One or two monologists.
Two single singers.
Two teams of talking comedians.
Two teams of musical specialists.

The average cost of such a bill is two thousand two hundred dollars for the week. If a manager is spending two thousand five hundred dollars a week for acts, he must do a rushing business. At two thousand two hundred dollars he is safe from worry. One of the best known vaudeville theaters has a seating capacity of twelve hundred. On ordinary days the house is filled in the afternoon and in the evening. The supper show audiences run much lighter.

"In the lightest business we do," said the manager, "we turn the house over twice and a half. In heavy business we turn it over three and a half times. On Saturdays and on holidays we have four and five full houses."

No seats are sold, only admission; and you are entitled to a seat when the usher can find one. Admission costs from twenty-five cents to a dollar, according to the part of the theater. It is not hard to see how the manager may safely invest two thousand two hundred dollars a week in the selection of his bill. This theater is open every day in the year except Sunday.

FROM DEC. 29, 1900 ISSUE

Salaries in Vaudeville.

"Higher salaries are now paid to individual performers in the modern vaudeville than were dreamed of in the old days of the variety show, which was the precursor of refined vaudeville. The most insignificant act in a bill costs at least forty dollars per week. (If you chanced on some of these you might think it would be worth forty to keep them out of the theater.) The less important acts, those that appear in full force at the supper show, cost from fifty to ninety dollars per week. The stalwart remainder which constitutes the real force of the bill receives salaries running from $250 to $1,000 per week. The last is a top-notch figure, and it is reached no oftener than can be helped. Do not forget that these salaries are for engagements of from twenty to fifty-two weeks, according to the value and the luck of performers.

"Competent acts usually can book thirty weeks of the year. Again, at a very popular theater, an act may draw $100 a week, while at a smaller theater the same act will draw only $75. Performers booked only for a small number of weeks in vaudeville often play in the cheap variety houses. These are called hide-away dates. Then many monologists and singers do turns at clubs after theater hours at profitable terms. The late J. W. Kelly, whose salary was at least $300 a week, is known to have earned as much as $700 above this figure at club entertainments. He was worth it—we shall not see his peer in many a long day.

"To compare present conditions with those of the past: A monologist of the J. W. Kelly type usually received $50 a week twenty-five years ago. To-day he can often draw ten times that figure. What is more, his salary is safe, because the vaudeville manager is a conservative man of business, and not of the fly-by-night species that has made theater people the dread of creditors. Again, the average salary for a song and dance team years ago was $70; to-day it is more often $250. A more sensational jump was made by Ching Ling Foo, the Chinese conjurer. A couple of years ago, when he came to this country, he had difficulty in securing an engagement. Finally he was booked for cities

The most insignificant act in a bill costs at least forty dollars a week ... you might think it would be worth forty to keep some of them out of the theater.

outside of New York, at $260 per week, railroad fares not included. His novel magic fetched good houses and the managers boomed him. Eight months later he was being booked at $1,000 per week and railroad fares paid. As an indication of the inducement that leads the legitimate actor into vaudeville, here is the case of William Harcourt and Alice Fisher. Both of them, while not possessing the peculiar endowment of stars, have a certain reputation in leading roles. In the legitimate, it may be ventured, that each of them received from $150 to $200 per week. They played perhaps thirty weeks in the year. In vaudeville they commanded together $500 per week. To be sure, they had to appear twice a day, and for each appearance they spent about an hour in the theater. In the legitimate they must be at least three hours in the theater each night, and there for one or two matinees in the week. Furthermore, in vaudeville they get an amount of advertising that could be had only as stars in the legitimate. They are but a type, and must not be considered an exception.

FROM DEC. 29, 1900 ISSUE

Vaudeville Acts.

"In the United States there are about sixty-seven theaters devoted to vaudeville. There are two in Canada; and two are in process of being in London. With the exception of a few parks, where performances are given only in summer, almost all of these theaters are open the year round.

"Of such theaters, twelve are in Greater New York; seven are in Chicago; in the Eastern States there are thirty-four; in the Middle West and South, twenty-four, and on the Pacific coast there are two. There is none between Omaha and San Francisco.

"In order to keep these houses supplied with performers, from 650 to 700 acts are required. An act may be a sweet girl singing tearful ballads of love and parting; it may be a pair of knockabout comedians; it may be a well-known legitimate actor and his company of three or four; or it may be a man with trained elephants. In answer to this

In order to keep the 67 vaudeville theaters supplied with performers, from 650 to 700 acts are required . . . there is a supply of 1500 acts.

FROM APRIL 20, 1901 ISSUE

VAUDEVILLE THEATERS

Sixty=seven of them in the United States requiring Seven Hundred Acts. ✔ ✔ ✔ ✔

Written by
SMILEY WALKER.

SOME INTERESTING.......
VAUDEVILLE HISTORY.

demand there is a supply of 1,500 acts. Half of this number is made up of people that get along indifferently or not at all. You may be sure that the latter consider the vaudeville business to be in a very bad way.

"As a fact, several millions stand invested in vaudeville to-day. Of the managers, at least one is a millionaire, and he has this advantage over many millionaires, in that he passes nearly all his time on his yacht. His wife has spent a small fortune in collecting pictures of the Madonna and of the Holy Family by old masters. At least ten others have made enough money to convince them of the utter fallacy of the income tax. As a cap of cream to this pudding is the security of a fortune made in vaudeville. In the legitimate a manager has to risk a large slice of his capital frequently twice and sometimes three times in a season of about thirty weeks. Once a vaudeville business has been built the enterprise takes much of the stability of a department store."

Fashionable vaudeville as it is presented at the Columbia under the management of M. C. Anderson has taken such a strong hold upon local theater-goers that a short resume of its history is apropos at this time. The amusement title "vaudeville" is a misleading one to very many of the theater-goers of America. Originally a French word meaning "singers of comic songs," it has become anglicized in the amusement world. To compare vaudeville as it is known to-day with the vaudeville of fifteen years ago would be to invite a comparison between all that is great, artistic and most worthy in the form of amusement with all that is small, devoid of merit and talent, gaudy and cheap. The uplifting of vaudeville in talent and morality, and the broadening of its scope of amusement features, is primarily and mainly traceable to the Association of Vaudeville Managers of the United States. This now great purveyor of vaudeville, perceiving something really new, meritorious and great in the then undiscovered realm of theatrical offerings, started in a moderate way to win from the various legitimate ranks artists of more than ordinary ability in their respective lines. Noting that their efforts won a more than moderate appreciation from their patrons, they persevered in their policy, and, aiming higher and higher, gradually but surely, by great financial inducements, lured from the dramatic, musical and operatic fields the best of those three great professions. Combining this talent with the greatest in the line of gymnastic, equilibristic and trained animal acts, together with other special features which have for their base electric light effects, vaudeville became the entertainment par excellence of the day. In the United States there are about sixty-seven theaters devoted to vaudeville. There are two in Canada, and two are in process of being in London. With the exception of a few parks, where performances are given only in summer, almost all these theaters are open the year round. Of such theaters, 12 are in Greater New York; 7 are in Chicago; in the Eastern States there are 34; in the Middle, West and South 24, and on the Pacific coast there

are 2. There is none between Omaha and San Francisco. In order to keep these houses supplied with performers, from 650 to 700 acts are required. An act may be a sweet girl singing tearful ballads of love and parting; it may be a pair of knockabout comedians; it may be a well-known legitimate actor and his company of three or four; or it may be a man with trained elephants. In answer to this demand there is a supply of 1,500 acts. Half of this number is made up of people that get along indifferently or not at all. You may be sure that the latter consider the vaudeville business to be in a very bad way. As a fact, several millions stand invested in vaudeville to-day. Of the managers, at least several are millionaires. At least ten others have made enough money to convince them of the utter fallacy of the income tax. The naming here of a few celebrities who have been induced to forsake their chosen field of work to enter the new profession of vaudeville will substantiate the claim that no star is too great or salary too high for their consideration. Jessie Bartlett Davis, the famous contralto, formerly the star of the Bostonians, who appeared here lately, receives the munificent sum of $1,000 weekly. Camille d'Arville, who is an early attraction, receives the same amount for her services from the various vaudeville managers in whose houses she sings. Other artists who have played or will play here and in the various other theaters devoted to high-class vaudeville may be mentioned: Camilla Urso; Felix Morris, who has joined the silent majority, and who was a great drawing power in vaudeville; Ovide Musin, A. L. Guille, the famous tenor, who appears here soon; Rose Coghlan, Minnie Seligman, Marie Wainwright, Robert Hilliard, who recently closed an engagement in this city; Maurice Barrymore, Patti Rosa, the daughter of the famous and clever little camedienne, Patti Rosa; Fanny Rice, Cora Tanner, Louis Massen, Pauline Hall, Hilda Thomas, Dorothy Morton, Carroll Johnson, the Nine Nelson Family, Phyllis Allen, Laura Burt, Julia Kingsley, George Thatcher, Robbie Gaylor, Anna Boyd, Lizzie and Vinnie Daly, Digby Bell and Della Fox.

A WAR IN BURLESQUE

FROM DEC. 21, 1901 ISSUE

STOCK COMPANIES

May Be Used in Burlesque Houses Which Are Hurt By the Wheel Scheme.

New York, Dec. 16.—While the rumblings of the storm which broke out recently among the burlesque managers has been a trifle fainter during the past few days, the trouble has not ended by any means, and a new phase has been added to the situation. Several managers who were left out of consideration at the Pittsburg conference met informally, and before the conference had ended it practically was decided to adopt a new policy in some of the houses and thus circumvent the action recently taken.

If the plan discussed is carried out the stock system will be inaugurated at several of the houses. Alphonse J. Meyer, the manager of the Court Street Theater, Buffalo, and Morris Schlesinger, formerly treasurer of that theater, but now business manager of the Bijou Theater, Washington, and two others discussed the situation at great length, and while no definite action could be taken on such short notice the trend of the discussion was decidedly in favor of the stock system. Both the Court Street and Bijou Theaters are feeling the power of the Empire Circuit, the strong Western combination of houses which has decided that a company playing at an opposition house in one city will be barred from the Empire chain of theaters over the entire circuit. Inasmuch as both Buffalo and Washington are represented in the Empire Circuit, the managers of the opposition houses in those cities foresee difficulty in obtaining attractions next season.

Instead of the traveling companies a permanent company is engaged. By giving an entire season in one city performers may be engaged more cheaply. The specialties and burlesques are changed weekly, and experience has shown that the young women of the chorus attract more of a following by remaining in the one place for the season.

> ... Experience has shown that the young women of the chorus attract more of a following by remaining in one place for the season.

So far as can be learned the Empire Circuit and the committee from the Association of Traveling Variety Managers seem likely to score a clean victory in the recent troubles. The Empire Circuit is so strong that the opposition is finding it difficult to successfully combat it.

...

Casino Theater (Sire Bros., Mgrs.)—Anna Held and her trousers, in "The Little Duchess," continues to pack this house. To those who like to look at lace, lingerie and legs there is much to enjoy in this production.

...

Weber and Fields' Music Hall (Weber and Fields, Mgrs.)—Weber and Fields have decided upon a new burlesque, which will be introduced in the near future. They have taken "The Girl and the Judge" for their subject. The burlesque and lyric will be written by Edgar Smith and the incidental music will be composed by John Stromberg. Fay Templeton will burlesque Annie Russell as Winifred Stanton. It is considered that "The Girl and the Judge" is the best play for burlesque purposes since the travesty of "Catherine" 'at the Music Hall.

The various burlesque and vaudeville houses presented bills of unusual merit last week.

FROM DEC. 5, 1903 ISSUE

JOE OPPENHEIMER

And His Merry Mirth-Makers of the

Fay Foster Burlesque Company

THE SEASON'S SENSATIONAL SUCCESS

The Dancing Missionary

EXTEND GREETINGS TO ALL FRIENDS,

FROM JULY 26, 1902 ISSUE

New York Burlesque Stars

can use two Oriental Dancers, one Bally-Hoo Man, Good Skirt Dancer, two Irish Comedians. This is the show that keeps the opponents guessing. Played to more business at the Lafayette Carnival than any other two shows there. The season is booked until January in the best of western and southern cities.

Address F. MONTGOMERY, Deadwood, S. Dakota.

FROM DEC. 7, 1901 ISSUE

VULGAR SHOWS

In the Burlesque Field to Receive a Set-Back From New York Managers.

New York, Dec. 2.—A determined effort to purify the burlesque stage has been inaugurated by Eastern managers. At a meeting of forty-one managers and proprietors of burlesque music halls in the principal cities east of Pittsburg and south of Rochester, held at the Fifth Avenue Hotel last Friday afternoon, a union was organized, to be known as the Managers' Association of Burlesque Theaters of the Eastern Circuit.

The purported object of the movement is to "discourage vulgar, indecent and degrading entertainments and acts, and to prevent further opposition in the cities in which theaters belonging to the organization are located." "Competition by vulgar shows" is given as the meaning of "opposition." In response to a general call, 90 per cent. of the managers or their representatives were in attendance at this meeting, and the following officers were elected for one year: President, George J. Kraus, of the Dewey Theater, this city; vice president, John G. Germon, of the Lyceum Theater, Philadelphia; secretary, William H. Burt, of the New Star Theater, Troy; treasurer, E. D. Miner, of Miner's Eighth Avenue Theater, New York. The association decided to admit the Star Theater of Toronto and the Theater Royal of Montreal, although it did not originally intend to include houses in cities north of Rochester According to President Kraus, the new organization will be a benefit to players as well as to the theaters. He denies that a trust of any kind has been formed, and declares the benefits would be mutual.

The elevating of the burlesque stage is certainly a step in the right direction. It but carries out the idea of evolution, that wrong will right itself in time. The doing away of suggestive exhibitions and the nauseating vulgarity coincident with many burlesque shows I wot of, will tend to eliminate the vitiated tastes of a certain class of theatergoers, and at the same time surround the players with a purer and more wholesome, refined atmosphere.

It is a matter of wonder to me that the people who enjoy clean burlesque have not, of themselves, ere this, arisen in arms and demanded the reforms now set on foot by this new association of managers. Once let the devotee of burlesque become accustomed to clean fun and proper exhibitions, and the oft-repeated excuse made by managers of indecent shows, "We must please the people," will become unnecessary and cease to be effective.

Vulgar burlesque shows must go.
WARREN W. PATRICK.

FROM DEC. 9, 1905 ISSUE

MEN OF CHICAGO THEATRICAL AFFAIRS
NO. 14

SID. J. EUSON

CHANGES IN MINSTRELSY

FROM OCT. 29, 1904 ISSUE

LEW DOCKSTADER.

On the first page of this issue of The Billboard appears an excellent likeness of Mr. Lew Dockstader, owner of the Dockstader Minstrels. Mr. Dockstader has had a long and varied career, and he has his ups and downs which are always necessary for one who treads the boards to fame. He was born in Hartford, Conn., of good old New England stock. As a boy he was always imitating the actors who visited Hartford, and at the age of fifteen he ran away from home and joined a traveling variety show, doing a song and dance. The company dissolved in a little Connecticut town and he was forced to walk to Waterbury, where Skiff and Galford's Minstrels were playing in the town hall. He met Skiff and during the afternoon gave him a sample of his ability, and was immediately engaged to sit on the end of the first part and go in the negro acts of the olio and play bass drum in the band. He stayed with this company till the end of the season, after which he played the variety theatres around Boston. The next year he became leading comedian with a small minstrel company that left New York for a tour through the South. Upon their arrival in Havre de Grace, Md., they found that their manager instead of getting off the train, had continued on a private tour of the South, leaving them broke in the town. Dockstader got to Baltimore, where he met Charlie Dockstader and formed a partnership with him, the act being known as the Dockstader Brothers, Lew and Charlie. After playing dates at different variety theatres, they joined Haverly's Minstrels and stayed with him for two years, and after the close of the engagement dissolved partnership, Lew Dockstader going to Concross' Minstrels, Philadelphia, where he remained for a number of years. His next engagement was with Birch, Wambold and Backus, San Francisco Minstrels at their New York theatre, leaving there to go as principal comedian with a large minstrel company. The next season he went out with his own minstrel company and tried to do away with the street parades, but was unsuccessful, as the public would not accept minstrelsy without its accustomed street parade. After the show closed he went back to New York, where he met Frank Siddell, who had no lack of money, and who backed him in the opening of a permanent minstrel company in that city, securing the old Minstrel Theatre on Broadway, now known as the Princess. During the first two years the theatre was a paying venture, and Dockstader's fame had grown enormous. He went on the road and crossed the continent twice, leaving George Francis Train, the noted comic lecturer, at the theatre, drawing crowded houses. After four years Dockstader gave up the theatre a little behind in his accounts to the extent of $45,000. Going into vaudeville he received the largest salary ever paid a single act, being the feature with Weber and Fields for six months, after which with Vesta Tilley in an all-star vaudeville company, he played the leading theatres in the country. It was during an engagement of four weeks at the Masonic Temple, Chicago, that he met James H. Decker, who secured his signature to a five-year contract to go into minstrelsy. During the fourth year of his contract he decided to go it alone, and present real minstrelsy, with all the southern atmosphere and color and do away with time-worn vaudeville acts. How well he has accomplished this can be measured by the immense success of his new enterprise.

LEW DOCKSTADER,
Proprietor Dockstader's Minstrels.

FROM JAN. 17, 1903 ISSUE

MINSTRELS.

Barlow Bros.' Minstrels want a good high tenor singer. Salary sure. Ticket to right party.

Robert Harty, of the West Minstrels, is singing, "I Feel So Very Lonely," the latest song hit by Fay & Oliver.

Professor Fred. J. Paul, proprietor and manager of Paul's Modern Minstrels, writes as follows from Garrett, Ind.: "Everything in good shape at winterquarters and I have good many of my performers and musicians signed for the coming season. I will open about the middle of April. Following is some of the people engaged—Chas. Foltz, single traps, bass drum in band; Bert Smith, trap drums and masters of popps; Dad Caulkins, tuba and bass; Harry C. Darling, horn and comedian; Professor Tremain, violin and baritone; Texas Smith, trombone; Miss Gertie De Mont, black-face song and dance and illustrated songs; Prof. Fred J. Paul, (that's myself) leader of band and orchestra. I will have something of a novelty in a minstrel first-part, in the way of four ladies on the ends, also a lady interlocutor."

Lew Baldwin's death was a great shock to his friends. Although he had been ailing for weeks before his death, he stuck to his work manfully and few, even of his intimate friends, realized that he was as sick as he was. His complaint was not understood. Various doctors diagnosed in various ways. At first it was thought to be malaria, then it was pronounced jaundice, then auricular appendicitis. It was only after he was forced to go to the hospital at Bloomington that the existence of the cancer was discovered. If he had not been so greatly weakened by the delay he might have stood the operation, but his vitality had been sapped by the sore to such an extent that he had little or no strength left. Lew Baldwin was a good fellow, devoted to his work, loyal to his friends, kind hearted, sanguine and jovial. He made many friends. He will be sorely missed.

Jos. Spencer, of Hilton-Spencer & Hoffman's "America's Youngest Juvenile Minstrels," tells us of the success of their company in the South. Business has been very encouraging, and managers are highly pleased with our show, and we are booking return dates everywhere. We opened at Empire Theater, Philadelphia, to fine business. Our attraction is a novelty, and the audiences who have witnessed our performances are simply dumbfounded at the manner in which the little members of our company handle their parts. Our minstrel first part is rich and up to date, our olio can not be surpassed, and our after-piece is a howling success. At Annapolis, Md., we gave four performances to big business, and our clever comedian, Master Robin Frear, and the little wonder, Miss Anna Ricely, were big favorites. Miss Ricely was the recipient of a number of presents and two large bouquets on Christmas Day.

FROM MARCH 15, 1902 ISSUE

Neil Bryant, the father of black-face minstrelsy, died March 6 in New York, at the age of 71 years. His death follows closely upon those of "Billy" West, John Queen. "Billy" Emerson and "Billy" Rice, all premiers in minstrelsy. When Bryant was told they were dead, he prophesied that he would be next to go. Bryant is one who helped to popularize "Old Folks at Home" and other famous songs.

FROM MARCH 7, 1903 ISSUE

Hilton, Spencer & Hoffman's

AMERICA'S GREATEST, BIGGEST AND BEST

JUVENILE MINSTREL

ORGANIZATION

Second Season pursuing the perennial policy that has made this new venture a novelty—the only one traveling in the world.

Everything Entirely New Next Season

WANTED—For next season, to open August 8th, a positive novelty to feature. Also Musical Act (all artists must be under 17 years of age.) Juvenile Band and Orchestra (8 girls or boys) except director. Tenors basso soloists and chorus singers. Ten boys that have had experience, for first part.

N. B.—None but competent and reliable children need apply. We carry two matrons, so, mothers and fathers, don't ask to see the country. If your letter is not answered, the position you apply for is filled. Press matter or photos to be returned. Managers Southern States, Jersey, Pa., N. Y., Ohio, Indiana, Iowa, Kansas, send in your open time. Permanent address,

J. S. HOFFMAN, Bus. Mgr.

182 Union Ave., Long Branch, N. J.

FROM AUG. 8, 1903 ISSUE

MOBILIZING

For the Opening of the Al. G. Field Greater Minstrels.

All the people engaged for the Al. G. Field Greater Minstrels the coming season are in Columbus, Ohio, engaged in daily rehearsals of the big spectacular production with which Mr. Field hopes to catch the approval and coin of his patrons.

The Parrento Family, of the European contingent, have not become acclimated, consequently they have had several of their members on the sick list.

George A. Pearce, the English tenor, lost all his luggage on the trip between London and Liverpool. He is in a bad fix and has been hustling to keep in society until his bloody traps arrive, as he expressed it.

There will be a wide departure in stereotyped minstrelsy by this company. The first part will be a double one intended to contrast the different styles of stage minstrelsy, namely, the refined and the plantation style. While the minstrel features will predominate, there will be many innovations in the vaudeville portion of the show. The olio, excepting the finale and afterpiece, will be given by European performers. The Leigh Brothers, the Mignani Family, the Parrentos and the Walton Family.

There will be an unusually large singing corps, under the direction of Paul LaLonde. All the vocal music is from the Witmarks, arranged by Shattuck.

J. M. J. Kane is the press agent and representative of Mr. Field in a business way. Will J. Donnelly has charge of the advance work, with J. E. Hatfield as advertising agent. Wm. Thorpe, assistant. The season will open August 10.

FROM DEC. 6, 1902 ISSUE

EDDIE LEONARD.

The subject of the above sketch is Eddie Leonard, who is one of the stars in the Haverly Minstrel Troupe. Being obliged to support his mother at a very early age, Mr. Leonard was unable to secure the education given to those more fortunate and he became an apprentice in a rolling mill in Richmond Va. He learned the trade, and at the same time attracted the attention of his fellow workers by his rich voice. His coon songs and dancing are said to have caused his companions to wonder, and they talked of him. Lew Dockstader's agent, James Decker, chanced to hear of Mr. Leonard, and made a visit to the mills to see him. The result was that he was soon a member of that organization. This was ten years ago. After several years of success with Dockstader, he joined Haverly's Minstrels, and is now, although a young man, a most valuable addition to that company.

FROM FEB. 22, 1902 ISSUE

17-YEARS OF CONTINUOUS SUCCESS-17
THE AL. G. FIELD GREATER MINSTRELS

Combined with the Al. G. Field Big Minstrels

One and Inseparable Herafter. Two Big Companies. One Big Show.

The Oldest Biggest and Best. Recognized as the leading organization of its kind in existence. Playing to more people and more money than any other minstrel show. A record breaker from Maine to California. Never trading on traditions of the past. Always originating for the future.

A Ten Thousand Dollar First Part

$10,000 The Roof Garden; A Night in New York $10,000

The third of the serirs of spectacular productions originated by Al. F. Field. This spectacle will excel in magnificence anything heretofore presented. Original electrical effects. Startling transformations. Bird's eye view of Greater New York from the roof of a skyscraper. Scenes of prominent places in and around New York, including the Brooklyn Bridge, the North River by night and day, moving boats and barges, the "Etruria" leaving the harbor, terminating with the most realistic storm scene ever witnessed.

100 PEOPLE ON THE STAGE IN THIS PRODUCTION 100

NOTICE

The stage production, "The Roof Garden: A Night in New York," has been duly copyrighted by Al. G. Field. Also the designs and models for advertising purposes of the same. Any person using any scene, effect or appliance, or any cut, picture or drawing which has been copyrighted under the title of "The Roof Garden: A Night in New York," will be prosecuted under the laws protecting said copyright and patent.

EMMETT TOMKINS, Attorney.

WANTED

For next season, **A Feature Act**, not less than three persons (other than singing, dancsng or musical). Must be entirely new to our patrons. Salary no object if you have what you we want. **Wanted Solo Singers.** Also chorus singers, two property men and one wardrobe man who can double in band or dancing acts. Also ten buglers who can sing and dance. **Wanted Musicians for Band and Orchestra.** Two strong E Flat Clarinets for brass, double Cello and Viola in orchestra. One Oboe, one French Horn, one Harp. Musicians address **Burt Cutler,** en route. All others **AL. G. FIELD,** Home Office, Spahr Building, Columbus, Ohio. N. B.—No press notices or photos returned.

TO LET ON ROYALTY—"Darkest America." A negro drama descriptive of negro life before and after the war. A truthful portrayal of negro life on the plantation and in the city. No slave drivers, overseers, bloodhounds or Uncle Tom's Cabin business. A clean, wholesome drama in five acts by Frank Dumont. Mr. Dumont has rewritten an entire new third act. New scenery, original music, etc. This drama has been presented successfully three seasons. None but responsible parties need apply.

FOR SALE.—One minstrel first part (set stuff) representing Rotunda of Hotel Colonnade, Paris. One first part setting (hanging stuff) representing "Garden of the Tuilleries." Both first part settings arranged for electrical effects. Can be seen at Armbruster's Scenic Studio, Columbus, O. One of the settings has been used but ten weeks. Appropriate costumes, chair covers and everything complete for an up-to-date minstrel first part setting. Also three sets of band uniforms, one set Roman drill costumes, street parade coats and hats, flags, banners and other wardrobe. Will sell in lots to suit purchaser

Address AL. G. FIELD, 29 West 3d Ave., Columbus, Ohio.

— ◆ — ◆ — ◆ —

FROM AUG. 30, 1902 ISSUE

— FOR RENT —

Harrison BROS. Minstrels

WITH USE OF TITLE AND PAPER

The show stands well throughout the entire South and any person who can manage a real negro show under canvas will find this the opportunity of a life time.

LOOK AT THE IMMENSE LINE OF PAPER. IT IS ALL SPECIAL AND ALL LITHOGRAPHED.

24-Sheet Parade	7-Sheet Streamer	1-Sheet Contortionist	1-2 Sheet Title
9-Sheet Cake Walk	1-Sheet First Part	1-Sheet Cakewalk	1-4 Card Tents
6-Sheet Trademark	1-Sheet Cottonfield	1-Sheet Ben Brown	1-4 Card Portraits
6-Sheet Title	1-Portraits	1-2 Sheet Jackson	1-4 Card Jackson
6-Sheet Plantation	1-Jackson	1-2 Sheet Garret	1-4 Card Washington
6-Sheet Tents	1-Washington	1-2 Sheet Proctor	1-Booklet
6-Sheet Levee	1-Tents	1-2 Sheet Title	1-Program

TENTS, SCENERY, COSTUMES, WARDROBE, UNIFORMS, ETC., all complete (not a thing missing) except the railroad cars, WORTH $1500.00, CAN BE BOUGHT FOR $500.00. This is all the investment required to obtain control of one of the best and strongest minstrel attractions in America. FOR PARTICULARS ADDRESS

ARCH M. DONALDSON,

Treas. Donaldson Litho. Co., Newport, Ky.

— ◆ — ◆ —   — ◆ — ◆ —   — ◆ — ◆ —

FROM MARCH 8, 1902 ISSUE

ONCE MORE

Death Invades Minstrelsy's Ranks, Claiming "Billy" Rice.

Hot Springs, Ark., March 1. The grim monster to-day claimed that popular old minstrel, "Billy" Rice, for its own. Dropsy was the cause of death. For forty-two years Rice was a minstrel, and made big money, but spent it as he got it, resulting in his being penniless at death. There were few playhouses in the country where Rice had not shown, and few people there are who have not either seen or heard of him. He was a whole-souled, genial man—a "good fellow" in the true meaning of the term.

For a long time "Billy" knew his earthly career was rapidly nearing the end, but to the last he retained his jovial manner, and just before Life's curtain rung down, he said: "Tell my friends I am going away back, and they'll find me on the end seat."

FROM JUNE 28, 1902 ISSUE

MINSTREL COMBINATION.

Lew Dockstader and John W. Vogel Have Joined Hands.

John W. Vogel, of Columbus, has formed a combination with Lew Dockstader, the famous minstrel, and the seasons of 1903 and 1904 will see a newly-born Dockstader Minstrel Company on the road, under the very competent management of Mr. Vogel. Both gentlemen are very well known, and the news of their combination will be hailed with delight by every one who loves a minstrel show.

As every lover of black-face fun already knows, George Primrose has announced his intention of retiring from the stage at the conclusion of the coming season. Primrose has for some time been minus a singing voice, and only a pair of extraordinary nimble legs have kept him in minstrelry.

FROM OCT. 18, 1902 ISSUE

OPPOSITION

Between Two Ends of a Well-Known Minstrel Team.

Spurred by the news that his present partner, Lew Dockstader, will head Klaw & Erlanger's Modern Minstrels next season, George Primrose has declared his intention of coming out in opposition with a show which he enthusiastically claims will outshine anything of the kind ever attempted.

The attraction which he is prospecting will be called "Primrose's Gigantic All-Star Minstrels."

That there is ample money to be had for this purpose no one who knows George Primrose and his thriftiness will for a moment doubt. The minstrel is one of the wealthiest men on the stage. His fortune is estimated at six large figures, and if he chooses to spend it he can raise the cash for a production of almost any possible magnitude.

SHOESTRING CARNIVALS TO THE ST. LOUIS WORLD'S FAIR

FROM MARCH 21, 1903 ISSUE

QARNIVALS AND FAIRS.

A FEW TIMELY WORDS ON THE SUBJECT OF ANNUAL URBAN FESTIVITIES. BY WILL S. HECK, GENERAL MANAGER OF THE GENERAL AMUSEMENT CO., OF CINCINNATI, O.

Within the past several years it has been my privilege to contribute frequently to the columns of "The Billboard," on the subject of Street Fairs and Carnivals,

When "The Billboard" came into existence, Street Fairs and Carnivals were comparatively unknown. True, there were several attempts to put on a "Midway" in diferent parts of the country, immediately following the "World's Columbian Exposition." but these earlier attempts were abortive, probably for the reason that the managers of them were incompetent, and had no proper conception of what constituted a well-ordered Midway or Carnival.

While the Carnivals and Street Fairs in this country were no doubt suggested by the bewildering and endless wonders and delights of the original Midway at Chicago, they did not become the fad until 1898. now there are few cities in the United States that do not hold these annual festivities.

In spite of predictions that they would lose their popularity, they have grown steadily in favor, for the reason, as has been explained in these columns, that they advertise cities in a unique and effective manner; that they afford harmless pleasure to the populace, and are not only self-supporting, but profit-making, the profits being used always for some praiseworthy purpose, such as the relief of some charitable institution, the increase of a monument fund, the building of a home for some worthy order, etc.

Of course, there are a number of cities and towns in the United States where it would be impossible to hold a Carnival. I am sorry to say this, but it is true. In these towns and cities, this opposition to Carnivals is due to the fact that Carnivals hitherto have been held in these cities have been held under unpopular local auspices or have been characterized by inferior and immoral attractions.

This is not strange to understand. Take for instance a city where a Carnival has never been held—suppose that a Carnival is organized under the auspices of some organization that does not stand well with the local public; then suppose further that this organization contracts with one of the numerous alleged Carnival companies that are going around over the country on a "shoe string," and that have a lot of vulgar, immoral, disgusting, exhibitions aggregated under a collection of dirty, ragged canvas. The Carnival comes off, and it leaves a stench that reaches from earth to sky, filling the nostrils of the law-abiding public, and arousing their profound disgust. Naturally, they having no experience with legitimate companies, decide that all Carnival aggregations are alike, and that the one that visited their city is a fair sample of the rest. For several years thereafter it is useless to talk Carnival in that city.

FROM MAY 7, 1904 ISSUE

FAIRS STREET FAIRS & EXPOSITIONS

OPENING OF THE WORLD'S FAIR.

The great World's Fair at St. Louis, Mo., opened Saturday, April 30, at 9 o'clock sharp, Central time. President Roosevelt, at his office in Washington, D. C., pressed the electric button that set in motion the machinery of the greatest world's fair ever held. The opening ceremonies were very elaborate, Secretary Taft representing President Roosevelt at St. Louis. Many distinguished foreign personages and several members of the cabinet were present and graced the occasion by short addresses, which lauded highly the management of the Louisiana Purchase Exposition Company and the general thrift and energy of the American toiler.

About 500,000 people witnessed the opening ceremonies. A beautiful warm day marked the opening of the great event, and from the eagerness and the enthusiastic spirit exhibited by those in attendance, the management and the people of St. Louis themselves, the event of which Saturday was the opening day, will be the most important, both international and local, of its kind ever held in the history of the world.

St. Louis now has the eyes of the world upon her and she seems very capable of executing the trust that has been placed in her keeping. In her fold is now exhibited the craft and art of those who excelled the masterpieces of sculpture and the honest products of the farmer and the mechanic and the relicts and curios of nations.

> The great World's Fair opened April 30 at 9 o'clock sharp ... St. Louis now has the eyes of the world upon her and she seems very capable of executing the trust that has been placed in her keeping.

ON THE PIKE AT THE WORLD'S FAIR.

The Irish Industrial Exhibition, or as it is more popularly known, "The Irish Village," is one of the most attractive concessions on the Pike. Its southern facade faces the Court of Honor displaying a reproduction of the Irish Houses of Parliment, Ross Castle and an Irish Round Tower. The gateway of Ross Castle forms the entrance to the Village from the main entrance of the Pike. In the Houses of Parliment there is one of the finest restaurants on the grounds, from the windows of which the guests may obtain a splendid view of the Grand Cascades and illuminations as well as the parades in the Court of Honor.

DETROIT CHOSEN PERMANENT SITE.

After months of argument and discussion the Michigan State Fair has been permanently located at Detroit. Several rival cities presented their claims, their merits were considered by the committee and the result is that Detroit will be the permanent site for the institution. Expressions from several leading live stock men favor the selection of the committee and it is claimed that a majority of the people of the state are of the same opinion.

A committee has been appointed to select a site for the fair, but as yet have not accepted any of the proposals sent in from various parts of the City. The committee consists of Chairman, John T. Shaw, W. T. Anderson, Levi L. Bartour, W. Collier and Lester E. Wise. The committee held a conference with the Michigan Agricultural Society which met May 6.

DISASTROUS FIRE.

The barns and ten valuable trotting and pacing horses were recently destroyed by fire at the Great Northwestern Fair grounds at Sterling, Ill. The horses were owned by J. T. Wilson.

FAIR NOTES.

The Lancaster, Iowa Fair Association has been formed with a capital stock of $100,000.

The amphitheatre at the fair grounds in Maysville, Ky., was unroofed April 25 by the heavy wind.

The Eaton County Fair at Charlotte, Mich., will open their premiums to the state this year, calling themselves the State Fair Jr.

The directors of the Park County Fair Association. of Livingston, Mont., are seeking a permanent site for the fair. A fair will be held this fall.

Frank P. Spellman, of Cleveland, Ohio, will furnish all attractions for the Ohio State Fair to be held at Columbus, Ohio, August 29 to September 3.

The officers and executive committee of the Humboldt County (Iowa) Agricultural Society, have decided to hold their annual fair September 6-9 inclusive at Humboldt.

The St. Paul Galight Co. has arranged to extend their mains to the Minnesota State Fair Grounds and will supply gas for lighting and heating purposes during the state event.

The fair grounds at Lockport, N. Y., will be greatly improved this year. Two new buildings will be erected, the grand stand will be enlarged and a tavern built. The fair is scheduled for September 7-10.

The Independent Fair Association of Hamilton County, Ohio, have commenced preparations for their fair, as the board is confident that the commissioners will grant them the use of the Carthage fair grounds.

The Ionia County Fair Grounds at Ionia, Mich., was under about eight feet of water during the Michigan floods, but everything will be put in shape and a new art hall built to replace the one destroyed by fire about two years ago.

The Hagerstown, Ind., Fair Association is making an effort to raise enough funds to put the grounds in repair. They recently suffered much damage on account of the floods. The fair will not be abandoned if sufficient funds can be raised.

FROM JAN. 17, 1903 ISSUE

SOMETHING NEW.

PET SHOW AND FAIR COMBINED PROMISES BIG SUCCESS.

Mr. A. R. Rogers, owner of the celebrated educated horse, and so well known as president of the Midway Club at the Charleston Exposition, and in connection with his successful management of large exhibitions and fairs, has created a new field, which he calls "pet shows and fairs." The first one ever held he got up and managed at Syracuse lately, and it was a grand success.

The second on his circuit is at Rochester, N. Y., lasting two weeks, March 2-14, and given under the auspices of the Gymnaium Committee of the Young Women's Christian Association, the most popular and largest society in Rochester, during the two weeks. This will be a cat show under the American Cat Club rules, lasting three days, by the Rochester Cat Club, at which 300 cats are expected. A dog show, lasting four days, under the A. K. S. rules by the Rochester Dog Club, at which Spratt is arranging to bench 600 dogs. An automobile and bicycle show; a pony show, by the Pony Club; and, in addition, during the two weeks, there will be a food fair, merchants' fair sportsmen's show. Mr. Rogers certainly has his hands full, and he has promised the Y. W. C. A. $10,000 profit, and has the reputation of always making good. This pet show fair is sure to be a great success. There have been cat shows, dog shows and pet stock shows, but these are the first shows that cover the entire field. Mr. Rogers is a member of most of the kennel clubs, cat and cavey clubs, and there is a big field open in this line, for which he is especially fitted, as his long and successful experience in managing fairs, and his well-known ability as a judge of dogs and cats, makes him thoroughly capable in this new field he has opened.

Beautiful Jim Key, Mr. Rogers' celebrated educated horse, which has the reputation of earning more money than any single show on the road, is resting this winter and being taught new acts. Mr. Rogers has never shown Jim Key in the winter except at the Charleston Exposition.

George La Rose, manager of the La Rose Spectacular Electric Fountain, writes that he has, notwithstanding a rainy season, closed a most successful season of twenty-eight weeks, covering a territory of the central, eastern and northern states, east of the Mississippi River. The attraction is now in Chicago, undergoing the usual yearly improvements, and will be in ship-shape for the early spring opening. Manager, La Rose has been laid up in Chicago two weeks with a severe attack of la grippe, but is once more on his feet and ready for business. He has returned to his home for his vacation.

TWO

BIG PAIN SPECTACLES ON TOUR NEXT SUMMER.

There will be two big traveling Pain spectacles on the road during the coming season—"Last Days of Pompeii" and "Ancient Rome"—each given on a more pretentious scale than any of their predecessors. During the absence of Henry J. Pain, in England, his general manager, H. B. Thearle, is superintending the building of the extensive equipments and organization of the small armies of employes. Both organizations will be twenty-car shows, carrvthing their own portable amphitheaters, electric light plants, seats, stages, pyrotechnist's workshops, etc. The scenic equipment alone of each of these huge spectacles will fill ten cars,

FROM DEC. 5, 1903 ISSUE

EVOLUTION

Of the Spieler and Passing of the Barker.

To the average visitor the different "spielers" at a carnival are not the least of the attractions that interest. Their energetic efforts to interest the crowds that gather in front of their different shows: the ingenious methods of attracting and holding the attention of those who gather outside, are a source of much amusement and diversion to the sightseer. The many shows and attractions of the Southern Carnival Company, which opens at the big autumn carnival and fair here Oct. 12, suggested an interview with Mr. C. A. Doyle, promoter of the carnival company, who has had years of experience in exploiting street fairs, carnivals and expositions. Asked for his opinion yesterday, of "spielers" in general, and those of his aggregation in particular, Mr. Doyle said:

"It is a very delicate subject, for as a class spielers are rather conceited and each one thinks he is in the "top-notch" class. There are spielers and spielers as in every other calling, and that some have more ability than others is a self-evident fact.

"I will say, however, that there is a vast improvement noticeable in the personnel as well as the ability of the modern "exterior exponent," as compared with his prototype of a decade back. They were then called "barkers," and were, as a rule, illiterate, coarse fellows, whose brazen audacity and painful lack of veracity were their distinguishing traits. They were slovenly in dress, lacking in elementary grammar, and their breaths were redolent of bad whisky and their jaws filled with enormous quids of tobacco.

"The composite picture of the average "barker" of that period would show a battered plug hat, a lavish display of cheap jewelry, especially as to length of watch chain, and a vicious looking moustache running down to below the edge of the jaw, plentifully moistened with tobacco juice which trickled down the chin, with an imitation gold headed cane as a pointer, and his 'dicer' cocked on one side of his head. his hair reeking with cheap hair oil, he would proceed to describe the wonders within as represented by the line of banners of impossible 'freaks, monstrosities and curiosities,'

"But today! Time has wrought a great change in the character and ability of the spielers. The managers do all in their power to enlist the services of talented young men of good appearance, who can use good language and lucidly explain, without too much exaggeration, the features of their shows. The salary is quite liberal, and often tempts young men to abandon the legal, medical and other professions to adopt the calling of a show spieler. Many earn handsome incomes by working on percentage, and are able to save enough to pay for a post-graduate course at some of the great universities, and some college students find it a lucrative calling during vacation. Hence it is that young fellows are seen on the outside of shows with a megaphone in one hand and a kid glove in the other."

THE BOOMING CIRCUSES

FROM MARCH 26, 1904 ISSUE

THE GREAT OPENING

Of the "Greatest Show on Earth" in Madison Square Garden.

New York, N. Y., March 20, 1904.—(Special to "The Billboard.")—The two large audiences that assembled in Madison Square Garden Saturday afternoon and Saturday evening, March 19, to witness the opening performances of the Barnum & Bailey Show, were representative of the culture and wealth of the metropolis, and it may be added, characteristic Barnum & Bailey audiences. The show has a traditional and well sustained prestige among the elite, and is framed up with a view to satisfying their fastidious tastes.

At the opening performances the beautiful Garden suggested comparison with a bee hive, that busiest of all places in a proportionate area. The audiences, moreover, that filled every seat from pit to the beautiful glass dome, were enthusiastic from the beginning of the pageant, or spectacle, and their enthusiasm increased and expanded as the performance progressed.

Their enthusiasm was vindicated, for even in the opening performance there was not a single detrimental element, not an instance to mar the beauty or detract from the strength, the splendor, the magnificence of the show. As a conglomerate whole, it is wonderful; as reviewed in individual displays, it is marvelous, and as dissected in separate acts, its effect may be expressed by the combined definition and significance of the two used above.

The success of a show depends as much on attention to minute details as to the conception and execution of the big spectacular acts and surprises. The opening performances of the Barnum & Bailey "Greatest Show on Earth" showed that the most infinitesimal detail had not been neglected or overlooked. The audience appreciated this fact and commented upon it. They expected much. Past performances of the Barnum & Bailey Show in New York have educated their circus tastes and demands up to a standard that requires acts and spectacles of the highest quality, skill and novelty to satiate. They were not disappointed in the performance in Madison Square Garden. On the other hand, they were agreeably surprised, and their delight was signified and expressed in protracted, almost continuous applause. It is safe to say that Madison Square Garden has never echoed and re-echoed to heartier (or better earned) applause than that which greeted the various acts that constitute the best program that even this, the criterion of circuses the world over, has ever offered. The negotiation and selection of performers and subordinates in all branches has been the work of the best judges possible to procure, and they have justified the trust and confidence reposed in them. Their task is a difficult one, but the greatest essential next to their own ability is means—wherewithal —and this has been placed at their disposal. No act is too good for presentation in the program of this leviathan of shows, and salary is always a secondary consideration.

The spectacle, which constitutes the opening display, represents the Durbar at Delhi, when Edward VII. was proclaimed Emperor of India by Lord Curson in the presence of the Duke and Duchess of Connaught. The subject is capable of spectacular display on a most gorgeous scale, and the magnificence with which it was presented, enhanced by the most elaborate trappings that have ever been seen in a circus pageant, provoked thunderous applause and established a standard of excellence that only the high quality of the subsequent performance might have sustained. The costumes of riders and attendants were chosen with the closest attention to harmony and with a manifest disregard to cost. Real silk, actual satin and armor of the finest quality such as might be transferred to the Indian or Hindoo army for use in conflict, glittering and glistening as their wearers moved with the discipline of the best trained infantry is a spectacle in itself, and when strengthened and augmented by the other features of the pageant, appeals to the most aesthetic and hushes the caviler to silence. The spectacle was even grander and more magnificent than what might safely be expected of a show that has established the reputation of the Barnum & Bailey Show in this line.

Display Number 2

Presents three equestrian acts, Rosa Hutterman occupying Ring No. 1, Madame Maranettte, Ring No. 2, and Josephine Koubeck, Ring No. 3. Each act was of the highest standard and consummate skill in control over representatives of the best in equine production.

Display Number 3

Presents a revival of leaping exploits, with novel features. Every leaper is a triple somersault leaper.

The audiences were representative of the culture and wealth of the metropolis.

Display Number 4.

A bareback riding display by Edna Bradna in Ring No. 1; Dollie Julian in Ring No. 2, and Rosa Wentworth in Ring No. 3. Each rider received round after round of applause for her excellent work.

Display Number 5,

"A potpourri of startling and sensational international expert performances," participated in by Lulu Sutcliffe, contortionist; Mons. Forresto, chair pyramid artist, and Shokishi, umbrella kicker in Ring No. 1. The Aurillotti Troupe of bicyclists and young Friskey, juggler ludicrous on stage No. 1; Yokahama, foot juggler and tub kicker, and Percy Clark, hand balancer, in Ring No. 2. The Marvelous contortionists and Charles Clark, juggler, on stage No. 2; the Three Dinns, athletes, and Uniski, Japanese barrel trick artist, in Ring No. 3.

Display Number 6

Three herds of elephants, one in each of the rings, are put through a series of tricks and manoeuvres worthy of animals with much greater intelligence than the pachyderm. They have been well and skillfully trained and their first public performance of the season went off without a perceptible hitch.

Display Number 7.

Shokichi, Japanese wire artist; Alfred and John Campbell, double trapeze exercises; Seigrist and Gibbons, flying ring artists; Uniski and Dikuli, Japanese shoulder perch experts; Nettie Carroll, wire artist; Senor Dian, horizontal bars; Mons. Toto, high wire; Hajataka, high wire and slide for life; Yokohama and Kiku, ladder act.

Display Number 8.

John Rooney, Wilkes Floyd and William Wallett, bareback riding.

Display Number 9.

The Dinus Troupe, the Three Marvelles, the Gruntellas Sisters and the Seven Sutcliffes, acrobats. The work of each of these troupes is marvelously skillful, and elicited great applause.

Display Number 10.

On the programs this is called the children's number, and consists of feats by Manuel Herzog's troupe of stallions, Samuel Watson's dogs, cats and chickens, Col. Magnus Schulte's dogs, Alfred Crandall's mule, Pauline Viola's leaping dogs, antics by Fox and Foxie, clowns, and one of the animal acts is good enough to be featured, and will be reviewed in another number of "The Billboard."

Display Number 11.

The Clarkonians, in aerial acts that for their daring and skill of execution evoke much applause. It is a wonderful act. Lizzie Seabert, aerialist; Frank Smith, trapeze head balancer; Yokohama, Kiku and Jesa, posturing on balanced poles; Cyclo, in the perpendicular cycle whirl, and the Alfonzo troupe of aerialists. Following these acts Solo rides down an inclined ladder on a unicycle.

Display Number 12.

Fred Derrick and William Wallett, the Wentworths and the Rooneys, in double equestrian acts of the highest merit.

Display Number 13.

The Florinze Troupe of acrobats do some of the finest work ever presented. Their somersaults and twisters from shoulder to shoulder are amazing and marvelous.

Display Number 14.

Menage acts by Misses Vonhort and Hirsch in Ring No. 1; Josephine Kouback, Ring No. 2; Herzog Bros., Ring No. 2, and Madame Marantette on the hippodrome track.

Display Number 15.

The Imperial Viennese and the Peerless Potters in aerial work of the greatest skill.

Display Number 16.

Volo rides down a steep incline which curves upward, breaks off and continues forty feet further on. He makes the leap through space and rides down on the other side. The act is sensational and one that stands out most prominently in recollecting the performance.

Display Number 17.

Auillotti "loops the gap," a loop from which the top has been removed. It is the consummation of all that is skillful and daring in bicycle riding.

The performance concludes with a series of dashing races on the hippodrome track, and the spectator goes away with the same sense of appreciation that was expressed by Bishop Potter after the opening matinee: "It is the best show I have ever seen."

The menagerie includes a large variety of all the rarest animals, and the side show presents a collection of freaks that has never been equalled.

A more detailed review of the principal numbers on the program will be published in the next issue of "The Billboard."

WALLACE WRECK FUND.

"The Billboard" has started a subscription list to supplement that of the bosses with the John Robinson Show for the purpose of buying a tombstone for the unidentified victims of the Wallace Show wreck buried at Durand, Mich. As a large amount is not required, we deem it advisable not to accept subscriptions larger than $1.00.

Amount previously reported............$374.00
R. L. Brannan 1.00
W. H. Rice 1.00

CIRCUS GOSSIP.

L. C. Zelleno has not as yet signed for the coming season.

Major E. H. Gosney goes with the Campbell Bros. this season.

Prince Mungo is with Norris & Rowe's side show this season.

Attina, the strong man, has signed with Ringling Brothers.

Wm. Voss is pantomime and juggling clown with Bonheur Bros. show.

King Cole joined Norris & Rowe's side show at Pasadena, Cal., March 7.

Buffalo Bill's Show opens the season on April 25 for another tour of England.

The Great Beno opens at the Memphis Theatre March 21 for two weeks.

J. St. Belmo will have charge of tents with Bonheur Bros. shows this season.

A flock of trained geese will be a side show feature with the Bonheur Bros. show.

The Sells & Downs Show lost a brood of cub lions which were killed by their mother.

D. H. Lano has been engaged to manage Augustus Jones New Empire Railroad Show.

Mr. Willie Sells is at home once more. But how long?—he is seldom still long at a time.

Clyde Riando has signed with Bonheur Bros. as singing, talking and acting principal clown.

E. H. Jones will manage Augustus Jones' New Model Plate Railroad Show this coming season.

Floyd Trover, general agent of the Colorado Grant Wild West Show, was in Cincinnati March 21.

Augustus Jones has sold the Indian Bill Wild West outfit to W. U. Montgomery, of Boone, Ia.

The Wilmarth Family, musicians and comedians, will be with the Bonheur Bros. show season 1904.

Col. Ed Burk, who has been wintering in Oakland, Cal., has come east to join Walter L. Main's advance.

The Sells & Downs show lost a brood of cub lions which were killed by their mother.

Schiller Bros., of Kansas City, Mo., have abandoned their intention of taking out a show this summer.

F. C. Archer has left Leipsic, Ohio, to take up his work as advance agent of Forepaugh-Sells Bros.' Shows.

Augustus Jones has the side show and all the privileges with the Great Texas Bill Wild West, which opens at Boone, Ia.

Karl E. Johnson, saxophonist, now with the Wagner Duo, is engaged for the coming season with the Robinson's Ten Big Shows.

San Kichi, one of the eight Oka Troupe with the Norris & Rowe Shows, broke his wrist at the opening performance in San Jose.

W. H. McFarland, manager No. 2 side show, Forepaugh-Sells, was a caller on "The Billboard" on his way to join the big show.

The Wintermute Brothers recently purchased 189 acres of land adjoining their present winter quarters at Hebron, Wis., the consideration being $10,900.

Prof. P. J. German, season 1901 with Bonheur Bros.; 1902 with Buffalo Bill; 1903 with Barnum & Bailey, will again go on with Bonheur Bros. this year.

A gasoline tank exploded at the Crystal Roof Garden at Jacksonville, Fla., on March 8. A small panic ensued, but no one was injured. The fire was quickly extinguished.

Miss Lotta, daughter of Edw. D. Barnum,

was married to Mr. B. Hanford in Pensacola, Fla., March 14. Mr. Hanford is an officer on the torpedo boat Worden.

Jessie Stumon, of the Stuman Family Band and Orchestra, has been working on a new musical act. She has signed with the vaudeville department of the Sun Bros. big show.

The Stumon family band and orchestra of ten will not be with the Thos. Hargreaves Big Railroad Show the coming season. They have been engaged with Sun Bros. Big Railroad Show.

K. Sugimoto, Jr., a Japanese performer, was attacked in the hold of a steamship traveling from Havana to New Orleans by an infuriated panther. His cries for help were quickly answered, but not before he was terribly torn.

M. L. Clark's combined shows opened March 7 at Alexandria, La., and are now playing Northern Louisiana and Mississippi. The show goes out with two elephants, two camels, ten cages, thirty-five baggage wagons and 145 head of stock.

The popularity and strength of the Norris & Rowe Shows is demonstrated by the fact of their playing a number of towns three times in a year. A notable example of this is the Los Angeles engagement, where they opened to turn away business March 8.

The Ringling Brothers have commenced to remove their animals from their winter dens at Baraboo to regular traveling cages, and will made the first shipment to Chicago on March 20. They will open the season in that city on March 30 at the Coliseum.

J. S. Kritchfield, bandmaster, and C. H. Cooper, musician, of the John H. Sparks Show, were initiated March 5 into the B. P. O. Elks by Lake City (Fla.) Lodge No. 893. As a favor to Tampa Lodge No. 708 Lake City Lodge attended the night performance in a body.

Alfred J. F. Perino, the lion tamer, went insane at Jacksonville, Fla., on March 16. He is the owner of three lions and had just separated from the Sparks Show, with which he was connected for a short time, and had opened a side show in Jacksonville. He hails from London and has been in the circus business for thirty years.

While Hannibal, the untamable lion, was being shipped from San Francisco to the winter quarters of the Norris & Rowe Shows at San Jose, he escaped from the shifting den in which he was being transported and killed a horse which was being shipped in the same car. The horse was the private property of Frank Hall, the lion tamer, who is now giving exhibitions with Hannibal with Norris & Rowe's side show.

The Norris & Rowe Shows opened the season March 2 at San Jose, Cal. As it is the winter quarters of the show, the citizens turned out enmasse and terstified their appreciation by packing the tents to the capacity at both the afternoon and evening performances. The Board of Trade, the members of the Chamber of Commerce, the Eagles and the Elks attended in a body at the evening exhibition and showed gen-

erous appreciation by liberal applause. The performance is given in two rings and upon an elevated stage and is bil..ed as the Norris & Rowe New and Greater Circus. The canvas is new throughout. They carry 65 head of baggage horses, 16 head of ring and hippodrome horses and 76 shetland ponies. There are about 225 people with the show. The train consists of 15 cars. George Wormald is boss canvasman and Frank Ervin is master of transportation. Among the principal acts of the program are the marvelous Belfords, the Flying LeVans, Melnotte, LaNole and Melnotte, the Gardner Family, the Groh Family, Oka Japanese Troupe and the Fairmount Sisters. The best features of the trained animal acts have been retained and many new ones added. The show is moving south through California over the Southern Pacific Coast line, and after showing the orange growing route will return north by the Valley route to San Francisco where they will exhibit for nine day at the Mechanics Pavilion. After the Frisco engagement the route will be up the coast to Oregon and Washington.

Alfred J. F. Perino, the lion tamer, went insane at Jacksonville, Fla., March 16.

WANTED FOR THE

BARNUM & BAILEY

Greatest Show on Earth

FOR THE SPRING SEASON OF 1903 IN THE CITY OF NEW YORK AND THE SUMMER SEASON'S TOUR OF THE AMERICAN CONTINENT.

—— ABSOLUTELY THE BEST, MOST PERFECT AND MOST ACCOMPLISHED ——

Performers and Artists in all Branches and Lines

Equestrian, Aerial, Acrobatic, Gymnastic, Terpsichorean, Atheletic, Comic, Grotesque, Sensational, Thrilling and Wonderful

Exhibitions and Performances of Every Kind

Singly, in teams, troupes or whole companies. The grandest attractions of the world wanted **for the Greatest Show in America.** All the usual features, and in addition thereto every existing novelty or modern attraction of any kind whatsoever. **The Latest, Newest and Freshest Sensations** on the ground, in the air, on horseback or in the realm of wonder earnestly sought and will be most liberally treated with. For all such, special terms will be made and the best accomodations provided. No salary too high; no attraction too dear; no curiosity too costly; nothing too expensive. For absolute novelties never seen under canvas, or positively new to the American people, the **most liberal and extravagant inducements** will be offered, coupled with generous and superior treatment.

ONLY THE BEST OF EVERYTHING WANTED

Comprising in detail, male and female equestrians and riders, sensational aerial artists; novel acrobatic companies, modern gymnastic troupes, expert jugglers, contortionists, specialty artists, tumblers, leapers, freaks, prodigies, curiosities, wonders, marvels, clowns of all kinds, **educated trick and trained animal exhibitions,** vaudeville artists, impersonators, pantomimists, somersaulters, bicyclists, motorists, high kickers, grotesques, humorists, specialists, trapezeists, aerialists, illusionists, strong men and women, menage and high school riders of both sexes, trainers, hippodrome riders and drivers, mechanical devices of all kinds, novel surprises and thrilling features; in fact, **every kind of meritorious performance or exhibition,** exploit, feat, sketch, specialty, novelty or originality, humorous, gay, comic; grand, soul-stirring, noble or exalted that by any possibility can be shown in, adapted to, or, that is qualified for **THE GREATEST SHOW ON EARTH.** To save unnecessary delay in correspondence, state lowest terms in first letter, with full and complete particulars and details, and if new to America. Address, as per route below,

J. A. BAILEY, Managing Director

Auxerre, France, July 13
Troyes, France, July 14-15
Chaumont, France, July 16
Dijon, France, July 17-18
Besanoon, France, July 19-20
Lons-le-Saunier, France, July
21; Bourg, France, July 22; Macon, France, July 23; Chalon-sur-Soane, France, July 24; Le Creusot, France, July 25; Nevers, France, July 26; Bourges, France, July 27-28; Chateauroux, France, July 29; Montluoon, France, July 30; Moulins, France, July 31; Thiers, France, August 1; Clermont-Ferrand, France, August 2-3; Vichy, France, August 4; Roanne France, August 5-6; Saint Etienne, France, 7-8-9-10; Valence, France, August 11; Grenoble, France, August 12-13; Chambery, France, August 14; Geneva, Switzerland, August 15-16-17-18; Lausanne, Switzerland, August 19-20; Fribough Switzerland, August 21; Biel, Switzerland, August 22; Chaux-d-Fond, Switzerland, August 23-24; Bern, Switzerland August 25-26; Luzern, Switzerland, August 27; Zeurich, Switzerland, August 28-29-30-31.

Or Permanent Offices (as below) from where all mail will be forwarded

Room 504 Townsend Buiilding, 1123 Broadway, N. Y. City.   No. 3 Crosby Square, London, E. C., England.

RINGLING BROS.

There exists no more extensive user of billboard space under the sun than this tremendous amusement institution. Their printing contract is prodigious. Last year it approximated $128,000 for posters; as much more was spent for heralds, couriers, booklets, programmes and other matter for house-to-house distribution, to say nothing of cloth banners, dates, excursion bills, newspapers, etc.

It will be readily seen, therefore, that as their season is of but six months duration they are the heaviest advertisers in the world. They can easily double discount any three of the largest mercantile concerns in existence in point of daily expenditure for advertising, and then win out handily with points to spare.

As advertisers, there is only one other concern that approaches them—the Barnum & Bailey Show, which recently abandoned the American field and is now in England.

The success of the Messrs. Ringling has been one of the most remarkable incidents of the age. The growth of their attraction, both financially and in the estimation of the American public, totally eclipses all previous records in the annals of the arena.

Various efforts have been made to explain and account for their great success. Astute observers will contend that it is owing to the fact that this one is a great general agent, the other a great railroad contractor; still another, a wonderful judge of a performance; another, an exceedingly clever press agent, etc.

All attempts to relegate any one of the remarkable gentlemen to any one of the departments of their gigantic institution must prove failures, because no one seperately conducts any one department.

They have individuality in plenty, and their capacities and abilities do run to specialties, but they are always like a deliberative body, working as a committee of the whole.

It occurs to us just here that in this manner may be set at rest much controversy over the special attributes of each. For instance, we will suppose that each of the principal departments is managed by a committee, in which case the various committees would be made up exactly as follows, viz:

Committee on Finance :

Mr. Al. Ringling, | Mr. Alf. T. Ringling,
Mr. Chas. Ringling, | Mr. John Ringling,
Mr. Otto Ringling, Chairman.

Committee on Internal Affairs :

Mr. Chas. Ringling, | Mr. John Ringling,
Mr. Alf. T. Ringling, | Mr. Otto Ringling,
Mr. Al. Ringling, Chairman.

Committee on Appropriations ;

Mr. Alf. T. Ringling, | Mr. Otto Ringling,
Mr. John Ringling, | Mr. Al. Ringling,
Mr. Chas. Ringling, Chairman.

Committee on Ways and Means :

Mr. John Ringling, | Mr. Al. Ringling,
Mr. Otto Ringling, | Mr. Chas. Ringling,
Mr. Alf. T. Ringling, Chairman.

Committee on Foreign Affairs :

Mr. Otto Ringling, | Mr. Chas. Ringling,
Mr. Al. Ringling, | Mr. Alf. T. Ringling,
Mr. John Ringling, Chairman.

There—we believe we are the first to convey to the public a definite idea of how the greatest show in the world is managed. Couple with this the fact that each and every member of the firm is a past master in the intricate art of advertising, make due allowance for their bold and daring aggressiveness, and it is easy to discern the cause of their complete and enviable success.

THE TWO BILLS AND THEIR WILD WEST SPECTACULARS

FROM MAY 30, 1903 ISSUE

LEVYNE'S LETTER.

Giving an Account of His Visit to the Show.
Editor Billboard:

Dear Sir:—As the contents of this letter is a radical departure from my ordinary billposting letter, I trust that your readers will overlook any of the enthusiasm that may enter therein, and not for a moment imagine that I have gone into the circus business.

Pawnee Bill certainly captured the citizens of Cincinnati with his wonderful display of the peculiarities of a peculiar people. It is wonderful to think of the energy displayed by Major Lillie in bringing together from distant parts of the world, Indians, cowboys, Arabs, Japanese, Filipinos, Cossacks' Hindoos, Gauchos and Mexicans, all for the amusement of those who are willing to pay the small pittance to be amused.

Pawnee Bill has surely the best collection of "peculiar" people that was ever brought under canvas and in my visit to the several dressing rooms, the Tower of Babel wasn't in it for a minute. These peculiar people were representatives of their different countries and all the dare devil feats that were ever performed by man can be seen at this show.

Just imagine a half dozen men holding on by their heels to a horse's mane while the animal is going like wild-fire and the rider (I should say the dragger) is dragged around the arena with his head bumping in the grass.

The cowboys seem to be the most popular. I presume that it is on account of their recklessness. How they will rope their ponies and jump on the backs of these wild animals, keeping their seats, is against all known laws of equilibrium.

The monkey drill by the soldiers from the regular army, illustrates the methods of training officers and soldiers to ride without saddle or bridle and mount steeds while going at full speed. I never thought that man could have so little respect for his life as to jeopardize his neck.

For a moment (and for a wonder) there was a lull in the commotion, and out came an antideluvian stage coach, probably the same one in which Horace Greeley poked his head up through the roof and spoke to the driver, on his memorial trip in the West some years ago, only I failed to see the hole.

Here it comes, creeping along: and an old. grey-haired and long-whiskered plainsman riding a buckskin horse with his rifle strapped on his back, and with his keen eyes looking on every side for the red devils. Then all at once, with a hoop and a hellish yell, bursts forth the blanketed Indian, trimmed up in style a la Apache, and they attack the stage, murder the old plainsman just before the cowboys arrive on the scene; but it is needless to say that the latter routed the Indians, and then attended to the burial of the old plainsman, and afterwards ditto the Red Indians, that had bit the grass.

All spectacular plays and Indian shows suggest to me the costumer, but in this Major Little has been careful in giving you something on the order of homemade cooking. Nothing from the costumer in this show. Every rag and garment worn is worn with a made-to-order fit. The clothes are a part of the man. You can see the garments in all their homeliness, containing all the colors of the rainbow, which in his savage mind, is just the proper caper. I personally examined the Indian's wardrobe and found their garments sewn together with sinews of the deer. No needle and thread business in this.

The wild men from Australia, known as the bushmen and boomerang throwers, had on nothing but dirt and hair, and they were the most savage-looking specimens of humanity I ever had the misfortune to look upon. In fact they were too realistic. I could almost imagine that

I could hear them tearing the flesh of their victims that they had captured in war, to appease their appetites.

> ... the bushmen had on nothing but dirt and hair ... they were the most savage-looking specimens of humanity. I could imagine I could hear them tearing the flesh of the victims they had captured in war to appease their appetites.

The Fall of Luzon, participated in by the selfsame soldiers that fought in the battle, is imported especially by Major Lillie. This "fall" was made by the terrific work of the Gatling gun and one could almost hear the bullets rattling against the paper mache fort. Talk about realistic scenes, why the whole thing was so realistic that for a moment I imagined I could speak Spanish.

Golden chariots, highly decorated banners, color novelties and spectacular glimpses of oriental life actual participants of stirring scenes, showing the strenuous life of the hero of many nations.

One of the most interesting numbers on the program was the introduction of the daring Cossack riders in their somber though artistic native costumes. They enter the arena singing their weird yet harmonious melodies, making a circle therein, advancing to the front two of their number execute one of their native dances. They then give an exhibition of daring horsemanship which has made them famous the world over. Luccas, the leader of these Cossack riders, is undoubtedly one of the most daring horsemen in the world.

A pleasing novelty was a quadrille on horseback by Pawnee Bill and Miss May Lillie. They executed wonderful evolutions and displayed eccentric horsemanship; yet it was hardly eccentric as it showed as precise figures as can be found in a ballroom.

In this show you cannot see any tinsel. Everything is home-made and true to life. Every man or squaw dresses the part with the exception of the Australians, who do not dress at all.

Anybody that pays his hard-earned money and leaves this show discontented can get their money back by writing to Yours truly,
M. L. LEVYNE.

FROM APRIL 11, 1903 ISSUE

PAWNEE BILL,
MAJOR GORDON W. LILLIE.
Manager and Proprietor of the Largest Wild West in America.

BUFFALO

THE WORLD'S

THIS YEAR
THE

ORIENT
AND
OCCIDENT

RIDE

**Shoulder to
Shoulder**

IN THE

GREAT
ARENA

Novelty piled
on Novelty and

MORE
to
COME.

BILL'S ROUGH RIDERS

GREATEST EDUCATIONAL EXHIBITION

EMBRACING, AS IT DOES, THE

HERO HORSEMEN OF ALL NATIONS

As well as the strong, sturdy,

Coast Guard
Life Savers

Thus exemplifying all that there is in bold, dashing,

HEROIC MANHOOD

In the saddle and on the seashore.

The great

WILD WEST
..AND..
WILD EAST

Now United Hand-In-Hand.

Step by step the pathfinder has
encircled the globe.
Note the endless array of stir-
ling attractions.

**SQUADRONS OF BRITISH
A BAND OF BOERS
CANADIAN MOUNTED RIFLES
NORTHWEST POLICE
STRATHCONA HORSE
RUSSIAN COSSACKS. BEDOUIN ARABS
WILD WEST COWBOYS. U.S. LIFE SAVERS**

And the

World's Mounted Warriors

Presenting the greatest of all military
spectacles the

Battle of Tien=Tsin

AND

CAPTURE OF PEKIN

With all the exciting episodes incidental to
the rescue of the imprisoned Legations
including the

SCALING :OF: THE CHINESE WALL

And still we have the undisputed public favorites

ANNIE OAKLEY,—JOHNNY BAKER

Indians, Cowboys, Mexicans, Broncos, Stage Coach, Emigrant Train,
and all the familiar features led by the great and only

COL. W. F. CODY—"BUFFALO BILL"

Under the Effective Directorship of MR. NATE SALSBURY.

GRAND ROUGH RIDERS REVIEW

On the morning of Exhibition, leaving the grounds at 9.30 o'clock, and traversing the principal streets

Two Exhibitions Daily, 2 and 8 P. M. Rain or Shine. Admission 50 Cents. Children Under 10 Years 25 Cents
RESERVED SEATS (including admission), $1.00 and may be secured on the morning of the show date, at the usual place

COPYRIGHT 1900
BY
The Courier Co.
BUFFALO,
N.Y.

CINCINNATI,

Reserved Seats on sale at Hawley's Book Store, 410 Vine Street.

Cumminsville Lot.

PARADE, Monday Morning, May 6th, ONLY.

2 Days Only.
Monday &
Tuesday....

MAY 6 and 7

THE DAREDEVILS

FROM JULY 5, 1902 ISSUE

97

FROM JUNE, 1898 ISSUE

BIG FEATURE FOR FAIRS.

A RIFLE EXPERT ON THE HIGH AND LOFTY WIRE.

The strongest and best shooting act ever witnessed in America. It never fails to score a tremendous success, and is received everywhere with overwhelming ovations and enthusiastic applause.

Langslow's performance is unquestionably the marvel of the century, and must be seen to be appreciated.   For time and terms, address,

MONS. LANGSLOW, 334 E. 13th St., NEW YORK.

Something New for the Public

Open Few
Weeks in
Oct. & Nov.

Title of Act and
Apparatus Patented,
Protected and
Copyrighted.

DRAWING
CARD.

A VAN-GOFRE THE LION MOUTH MAN.

Ad. 109 E. 12th St,   New York, N. Y.

TO MANAGERS AND AGENTS:

Absolutely the only act of its kind in the world.   All up-to-date managers shou'd secure this Sensation Novelty for Parks, Fairs, Carnivals and Vaudeville Managers. The Greatest MOUTH BALANCER and EQUILIBRIST FEATURE ATTRACTION.

A Few Open Weeks in October and November.

FROM MAY 31, 1902 ISSUE

THE
Motor Cycle
SENSATION

Four Experts on the Track at the One Time.

Another of **Miss Brandon's** fearless rides. Being paced by a Motor in a Motor Pursuit Race, on a circular track at an angle of 70 degrees. ¡The laws of gravitation defied In doing this Motor Race, the Motor Wonders **Arthur Stone** and **Joe Judge** pace **Frank Armstrong** (who knows no fear as a trick rider) and **Miss Brandon** the demonstrator of Sensational Feats.

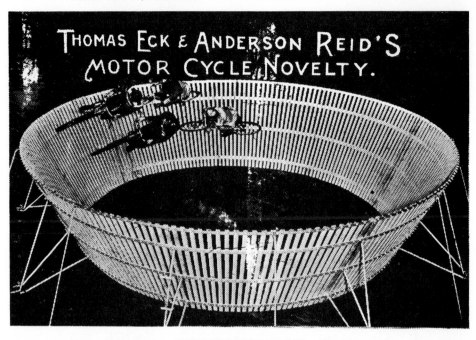

For the above attractions, address all communications to   **J. S. DEVLIN**   **REPRESENTATIVE, ROOM 305, KNICKERBOCKER BUILDING, NEW YORK CITY.**

FROM JULY, 1896 ISSUE

FROM APRIL 12, 1902 ISSUE

The Great Joseph Diavolo is Himself Again

The Dare Devil Rider Wins in His Race with Death.   Now open for Engagements for the Summer.

IN HIS

NEW BICYCLE ACT, "FLIP THE FLAP"

So Desperate that It Disarms Description. Deriding Danger; Defying Death; Putting to Naught all Laws of Gravity. The Sensation of the Twentieth Century. The act commonly known as "Looping the Loop" pales into insignificance compared to Joseph Diavolo's "Flipping the Flap." He "Flips the Flap" on a bicycle carrying a lady on his shoulders. He "Flips tne Flap" oo an Unicycle. He "Flips the Flap" on roller skates, and for a finish makes a sixty-foot dive into a tank or net.

=====SALARY $1,000.00 PER WEEK=====

If you cannot pay the price, don't write. "Looping the Loop" has made all New York talk. "Flipping the Flap" will fill the entire world with wonder. PIRATES TAKE NOTICE!—The above acts are my original creations and at the present time, I am the only individual accomplishing them. If you intend to attempt to imitate these acts, please arrange to have your friends send me obituary notices. Address all communications to

W. W. POWER, SOLE MANAGER OF THE GREAT JOSEPH DIAVOLO NEW YORK CITY.
—————————————STURTEVANT HOTEL—————————————

FROM APRIL 19, 1902 ISSUE

DIAVALO'S OFFER.

Will Loop-the-Loop Blindfolded, or Give Up $1,000.

New York, April 7, 1902.
Editor of "The Billboard:"
Dear Sir—It affords me no small degree of pleasure to inform you and the readers of "The Billboard" that I have so far recovered from my injuries received last September that I am now in shape to resume my professional engagements. In simple justice to myself, I feel duty bound to state a few plain facts relative to my position in regard to the engagement of the so-called "Diavolo" now appearing with a circus at Madison Square Garden, New York City, in a bicycle act called "Loop-the-Loop."

In the first place, I am the original "Diavolo," and first worked under that name with the Pubillones' Circus, Havana, Cuba, in 1899, and any other individual making use of that nom-de-plume is a usurper.

In the second place, I am the sole originator of the bicycle act commonly known as "Loop-the-Loop," and was the first man to ever accomplish the feat successfully.

I have recovered from my injuries and am in shape to resume my professional engagements ...

Last fall I approached Mr. Van Dusen, who at that time was manager of the "Loop" (on which cars were operated) at Coney Island, in regard to the bicycle act of "Looping-the-Loop." He was impressed with the idea, and later the apparatus necessary for the exhibition was constructed in Madison Square Garden under my direction. On Sunday morning, Sept. 7, 1901, before an audience of 300 invited guests, including prominent doctors, newspaper men and police officials, I successfully accomplished the trick of "Looping-the-Loop" three consecutive times. On account of the tardy arrival of several interested parties who came in too late to witness my trial exhibition, I was pressed to make a fourth attempt. My last effort proved disastrous. My "Loop" was only three feet wide (the one now used at the Garden being four times as wide) and as I finished the "Loop" I was thrown from my wheel and sustained the injuries that have confined me in Bellevue Hospital since Sept. 7, up to within a few days ago. During my sojourn in the hospital, the new manager of the "Loop" at Coney Island picked up this man who now styles himself as "Diavolo," and had him under practice for three months down at the Island before presenting the act to the public under my name, "Diavolo."

I am now open for engagements for the coming summer season in my new and more daring act entitled "Flip-the-Flap," which I perform on a bicycle, carrying a lady on my shoulders. I also "Flip-the-Flap" on a unicycle, and, last and more thrilling, on roller-skates. On the finish of my act I make a sixty-foot dive into a tank or net, as the case may be. I use the name of "Flip-the-Flap" for my bicycle act by the permission of Capt. Paul Boynton and Thomas Folks, owners and managers of Sea Lion Park, Coney Island, N. Y. The title and act are duly copyrighted. I have placed my business in the hands of W. W. Power, and

... in my new and more daring act entitled, Flip-the-Flap, I perform on a bicycle, carrying a lady on my shoulders.

will hereafter appear under his sole direction.

To show you that I mean business, I will agree to give any charitable institution in this country the sum of one thousand dollars ($1,000) if I can not duplicate the feat of looping the so-called "Loop-the-Loop" with a bicycle while blindfolded.

Yours very truly,
THE GREAT JOSEPH DIAVOLO.
(The Original.)

HIGH DIVERS:
MEN, WOMEN, HORSES, ELKS

FROM MARCH 22, 1902 ISSUE
NOW OPEN FOR SEASON OF 1902
The Highest Diver Living

The most sensational outdoor attraction ever presented
to the American public.

DANA THOMPSON WORLD'S GREATEST SOMERSAULT HIGH DIVER.

I carry all my own apparatus including tower and tank. Illuminated with
175 incandescent lights. Absolutely nothing to furnish except water.
PERMANENT ADDRESS: MONTGOMERY, ALA., CARE L. L. GILBERT.

FROM APRIL 12, 1902 ISSUE

FROM JULY 16, 1904 ISSUE

LILJENS,

The Only
WOMAN FIRE HIGH DIVER
Of the World,

Has a few open weeks on account of certain parties' misrepresentations.

A BLAZING HIT and Drawing Card of First Magnitude for Parks, Fairs Carnivals, Etc., Etc.

For terms and time, address

614 Wells Street
CHICAGO, ILL.
MARIAN LILJENS,

FROM MAY, 1899 ISSUE

"THE" ATTRACTION FOR COUNTY AND STREET FAIRS, RACE MEETINGS AND RESORTS.

Jones County Agricultural and Mechanical Association.

Monticello, Iowa, August 26, 1898.
To Whom It May Concern :—The famous Diving Elks, owned by W. H. Barnes, of Sioux City, have just closed a four days' contract with the above Association, for which we paid him $500, and I must say that the same has been very cheerfully paid by me, for we have received full value for same by extra attendance. Mr Barnes is a gentleman in every respect and he more than carried out his contract. The people are delighted with the attraction, and I wish to say that the Elks dive of their own free will, and that they are NOT THROWN from any trap or contrivance. They ascend the tower unattended and dive of their own free will. All I can say is that they are a marvelous attraction.   G. E. BISHOP, Secretary.

Address, WILL H. BARNES, Sioux City, Iowa.

PIGS, SHEEP, BULLS, AND A TIGHTROPE WALKING PONY

FROM APRIL 20, 1901 ISSUE

Carl Hagenbeck.

Carl Hagenbeck, the dean and high priest of the wild beast industry, who has agencies in every part of the world where interesting animals are found, and through whose hands pass nearly all of the wild creatures on exhibition in the whole world, is a remarkable man. The collecting and buying of wild beasts has been handed down to him through three generations, which makes his establishment the oldest, as well as the largest, wild beast emporium in the world. As a boy Hagenback received a present of a pair of seals, which he trained and exhibited, and at the present time he maintains in the principal towns and cities of Europe the largest wild beast shows that have ever been organized. Since Mr. Hagenback's triumphant career at the World's Fair he has not been associated with any amusement enterprises on this side of the Atlantic, notwithstanding the fact that various unscrupulous persons have used his trade-mark in an effort to benefit their mediocre performances. But his attention on the other side has been divided continually between his training quarters, his zoological gardens and the show that bears his name. Mr. Hagenback enjoys many distinctions. He was the first man who ever secured any polar bears for exhibition purposes, and when he forged into the interior of Africa and secured some magnificent full-grown elephants his fortune was made. Black, brown, yellow and white men work for him, and they have made his name known to dusky, greasy potentates from the frozen Arctic regions to the torrid zone, and to many barbaric races the name of Hagenback is familiar, some of whom have never heard of Edward VII., the Kaiser, or the President of the United States.

Hagenback's South African headquarters, which is his principal place for collecting specimens of animals that are brought from the rivers and forests of the almost impenetrable wilderness, are about twenty miles north of Cape Town. His buildings cover thirty acres of ground, and are surrounded by a stockade some twenty feet high. Here the animals become accustomed to confinement before they are shipped to Europe. Their prisons are enormously strong and particularly well kept. All the native animals of South and Central Africa are to be found in this corral, and at times, when a fresh lot of captives have been brought in, they make the air fairly reek with their hideous noises. Wild beast taming and handling is, perhaps, the most dangerous occupation in the world, but Mr. Hagenback has become so attached to his vocation that he considers the calling no more hazardous than one in an ordinary walk of life.

FROM AUG. 30, 1901 ISSUE

In the Coils of a Python.

A most thrilling accident happened to a little child, whose name was not secured, at Dexter, Mo., during the soldiers' encampment at that place, Aug. 5 to 15. "Kiko," the snake-man, was due to appear in a short while, and a rush was made for his platform by the crowds of people on the grounds. Among the first to reach the platform was the little girl and her mother. The child rushed to the side of the snake-pit and caught hold, with both hands, of one of the guy ropes which held the canvas pit, in an endeavor to get a good look at the monster reptiles. The rope, which was a looped one, and not intended as a guard rope, slipped under her weight, and she pitched head foremost into the den, among the seething mass of reptiles. The mother immediately fainted, and the excitement of the crowd was intense. No sooner had the child struck the bottom of the pit than one of the pythons, a monster boa constrictor, coiled itself around her fragile body, in a deadly embrace. Calls were made for "Kiko," who was sleeping at the time, but the manager of the show, Chic Davis, attracted by the commingled screams of the crowd, rushed forward, jumped into the pit, and after a lively struggle of a few minutes, succeeded in releasing the child from the coils of the monster's body, and carried her to a place of safety, more scared than hurt. Two of the largest snakes were badly injured by being trampled on by Mr. Davis, their bodies being severely mashed by his shoe heels.

FROM MARCH 2, 1901 ISSUE

Baby Elephant is Dead.

The death of the baby elephant, Ned, at winter quarters in Baraboo, Wis., on the night of Feb. 16, will be a severe loss to those enterprising showmen, the Ringling Brothers. The baby was considered a great prize, and would have proved a great attraction with the show the coming summer. Ever since its birth, the little animal was fed on malted milk at an expense of $10 a week. The Ringlings estimate their loss at $50,000, which is really a very moderate figure. The animal will be mounted and exhibited.

FROM MAY 11, 1901 ISSUE

REMORSE

Was Always Shown by an Elephant when Talked to about a Man he had Killed.

"The elephant is one of the most knowing and kindest of beasts alive," said Chief Trainer "Badger" to the New York Tribune, who boasts he isn't afraid of any elephant that ever swung a trunk.

"There's 'Big Sid,' for instance. He killed poor Patsy Forepaugh a year ago. Why? Because Patsy didn't understand him. He was kind to him when he felt like being so, and when he was out of sorts he wasn't. No matter how I am feeling I never lose my temper with 'Sid.' 'Sid' is sorry for having killed Patsy. He hasn't forgot it. I bet when that old beast is a candidate for a permanent position in some museum, carrying a ton or two of sawdust under his hide, it will be through remorse for his killing Patsy."

Every one laughed at this statement of "Badger's."

"You don't believe it," he continued. "Well, I'll show you that 'Sid' hasn't forgot that incident in his life. Follow me."

The rest of the trainers and those interested followed behind "Badger," and he led them down the walk to where "Sid" was busy tossing and munching hay.

"Badger" approached him, put his arms around his trunk, spoke to him kindly, at the same time patting him with his hand. Then he walked out of reach of the oscillating trunk.

"This is the only time I'm afraid of 'Sid,'" he explained, "for you'll see what I say burns deep in his hide. I've never learned whether it's anger or real contrition which causes him to act so every time I mention Patsy."

Probably out of regard for "Sid,'s" remorse, "Badger" had never mentioned this knowledge of elephant psychology to the other trainers, and they appeared to be as much interested as the witnesses of the scene not attached to the circus.

"Now watch," commanded "Badger," and he called out to the elephant.

"Where's Patsy, 'Sid?'"

The elephant's big ears moved with the alertness of those of a colt at an unfamiliar sound in his stall.

"Where's Patsy?" he repeated.

The elephant flapped his ears, danced around as far as his chains would permit him and swung his trunk viciously round and above his head.

"'Sid' killed Patsy, didn't you, 'Sid?'"

The animal seemed to understand every word the trainer spoke. "Badger" continued repeated the accusation. The elephant tugged at his chains 'til it seemed as if they would snap, and then suddenly gave vent to a terrible roar that reverberated throughout the whole building. At every mention of the name of the dead trainer the roar was repeated, till the whole row of elephants was answering him in a like manner, and the man who superintends the advent of the performers in the rings upstairs ran down and commanded the trainers to stop them, which they did after much difficulty.

"Badger" turned to his listeners:

"There, don't you believe elephants have memory and that 'Sid' is sorry for his act?"

They were obliged to confess they did.

"Now, wait," said "Badger." "You'll notice when the show is over upstairs and the people come down to see the elephants that 'Sid' won't eat. I'll bet that beast won't touch a mouthful of food for the rest of the night."

"Sid" was tempted with all sorts of toothsome morsels by the big crowd around him. They held peanuts and candy in their hands before him, but he never stirred or noticed them. The other elephants reached out their trunks and allowed the crowd to pitch the candy into their mouths, which they opened wide for this purpose. But, then, they hadn't killed a man and they didn't know remorse. Perhaps some day they will.

FROM DEC. 8, 1900 ISSUE

A Wild Animal Farm.

Twenty miles from the town of Bozeman, Idaho, is an establishment devoted entirely to the raising of wild animals. The stock is made up exclusively of the wildest, rarest and most ferocious creatures. This animal farm is owned and operated by Mr. Richard W. Rock, who has spent all his life in the West. As trader, hunter, scout and animal fancier he has been the hero of remarkable exploits Thirty years ago he was a valued scout for Generals Gibbon, Hayden and Howard. He is now the only man in the United States who raises wild animals on a large scale. Many of the big animals find their way from the ranch of "Rocky Mountain Dick," as he is called, to Eastern zoological colections, and some of the rarer specimens have been sent to Europe. He has fifty-two buffalo, three grizzly bears, sixty elk and large numbers of moose, deer and Rocky Mountain sheep and several black and brown bears. These animals are caught with a lasso when the snow is on the ground, secured and hauled to the ranch on sleds. There they have large quarters, but are securely confined. A few have been born in captivity. Mr. Rock has trained a moose to the harness, and it is a common sight to see him drive into Bozeman with his wife in their cart drawn by "Nellie Bly."

THE WOMEN DID IT ALL

FROM OCT. 26, 1901 ISSUE

BUSINESS WOMAN,

As Well as a Clever Actress, is Miss Marie Dressler.

Miss Marie Dressler, whose picture adorns the first page of the current issue of "The Billboard," was born in Coburgh, Canada. Her first hit was when she played the part of Cigarettes in "Under Two Flags," while she was quite young.

She then appeared, and made pronounced hits as Katisha in "The Mikado" and as Queen Isabella in "1492." Her later successes have been in "Madeline, or the Magic Kiss," "Hotel Topsey Turvey" and "The Man in the Moon." Critics are of the opinion that her greatest success was as Flo of the Music Halls in "The Lady Slavey." She is at present at the head of a big company as the Queen of Spain in "The King's Carnival." Last season she starred in the musical comedy, "Miss Prinnt," and made a great reputation throughout the country, being referred to by the best critics as the greatest comedienne in America. She has received many flattering offers to go to England, but has declined. She contemplated taking out her own company this season, but was prevailed upon by the Sire Brothers, of the New York Theater, to accept their offer of $25,000 for her services for the season. Articles to that effect have recently appeared in the New York and out-of-town papers throughout the country. This is undoubtedly one of the largest salaries ever paid to a comedienne. Next season she will star in a production, now being written for her by Sidney Rosenfeld.

The Sire Brothers paid comedienne Marie Dressler $25,000 for the season, but she's looking around for a hotel she can buy and run.

Miss Dressler recently negotiated for the purchase of "Kid" McCoy's hotel at Saratoga, N. Y., intending to run the hotel herself, but she found the property so badly involved that she instructed her attorney not to touch it. However, she has her own ideas about running a hotel, and says she will yet conduct one.

MISS MARIE DRESSLER,
A Capable Actress who is Ambitious to Become a Successful Hotel Proprietress.

FROM DEC. 7, 1901 ISSUE

THE WOMAN IN BILL POSTING.

Here Are Two of Them Who Have Been More Than Successful in Sticking Up Paper.

MRS. CHAS. DUCKETT,
Ottawa, Ill.

That woman's work is no longer confined to the four walls of the home, that she is capable of leading the strenuous life of the twentieth century is fully illustrated in the life of Mrs. Chas. Duckett, the subject of this sketch, whose picture appears herewith.

Mrs. Duckett is a member of the La Salle County Advertising Association, of Ottawa, Ill. Her work, however, is not confined to Ottawa, where the main office is located, but she personally manages a route of forty-one towns, and very often she drives over the route alone, frequently covering fifty miles a day. Some of her experiences would fill a book that would be worth reading, indeed. Aside from her professional work Mrs. Duckett is actively engaged in religious and social undertakings. She is an active member of Christ's Episcopal Church, the I. D. A. and belongs also to the Order of Eastern Stars.

Socially she is a great favorite and is a leader in the social life of Ottawa, which has become very famous throughout the state.

The friends of Mrs. Duckett have all been intensely interested in her work and, naturally, have speculated as to the outcome of such a unique enterprise. To say that she has made a success does not do her justice. Not content with past methods she has introduced into her work many innovations which are decidedly clever and has proved beyond doubt that a conspicuous advertisement is the very life of trade.

DIDN'T STOP

Her Business When Mrs. Root's Bill Posters Went to the Philippines.

Among the most interesting pictures which appear in this very profusely illustrated issue of "The Billboard" are those which accompany this sketch, portraying the energy of one of the most business-like, energetic and progressive women of that most progressive part of this vast land—the West, whose strenuous endeavors amidst a most strenuous life have not only been rewarded in part, but in whole, by success. The lady is Mrs. H. E. Root, of Laramie, Wyoming.

Mrs. Root is the manager of the only opera house in Laramie, as well as the city bill poster of that most thriving town of the West. The house is a handsome little theater with a seating capacity of 700, lighted by electricity, with ample dressing rooms, a stage 48 by 75 feet, thoroughly equipped in every respect and well heated.

Laramie is a city of 9,000 inhabitants, and the whole of the populace are theatergoers. Hence, "the best in the house is not too good for "Riley" in that town, only first-class attractions being given dates to play there.

Besides being the amusement provider for the city of Laramie, Mrs. Root is as well, as I have said, the city bill poster, and distributor, and an ardent member of the I. A. of D. and the A. D. A., and is registered in all the leading lists of the country.

Nothing so well exemplifies the true characteristic western energy of the noble wo-

Mrs. Root is the manager of the only opera house in Laramie, and the city bill poster of that most thriving town of the West.

man, under the most trying circumstances, as the two cuts we present, showing the little lady overseeing the work of her "hands" while posting paper.

A most interesting little story goes with the pictures. At the time of the breaking out of the Spanish-American War, with true patriotic spirit and devotion to duty, all the bill posters in Mrs. Root's employ shouldered their trusty rifles and joined the vanguard bound for the Philippines.

Mrs. Root, with energy and spirit, hired other men, who, however, proved absolutely "green" in bill posting, and incapable of doing the work required of them. Nothing daunted, however, she shouldered her long-handled brush, and with a bucket of paste and the green hands along, proceeded to do the work herself, meanwhile instructing them in the art of putting up bills and posters.

The two pictures show her in the role of the instructress, one while she is upon the ladder posting up paper, her assistants standing by, viewing with evident interest the work she is doing, and endeavoring to teach them.

The war had its many successes, but none was more potent or signal than that won by Mrs. Root in overcoming the difficulties which beset her, in consequence of the desertion from her ranks of the mainsprings of her business—the bill posters.

Mrs. Root has greatly enlarged and increased her plant since those strenuous times, and is now doing as nice a business in that line as many others in much larger cities.

"Nothing succeeds like success," and that Mrs. Root is a success without doubt, goes without the saying.

FROM SEPT. 24, 1904 ISSUE

MADAM LILJENS.

Diving from a height of 65 feet, her body enveloped in flames, is the feat of Madame Liljens, who is thrilling audiences nightly at Riverview Park, Chicago, this summer. This is a unique act for a woman, and more interest would be added if the public were more familiar with the Madame's personality. Possessed of a superbly molded figure, she is striking in appearance, even upon the public thoroughfares, and when she makes her advent, ready to ascend her lofty pedestal, her outlines mark the contour of the perfect physical development in a woman. Her career has been a romantic one. A Russian by birth, she was married while young to a Swedish nobleman. After his death she turned her accomplishments as a swimmer to practical use. She was figured in all the great water shows in recent years and has been rewarded with several medals.

FROM JULY, 1896 ISSUE

America's Famous Death Defying
AERONAUTS.

LeROY SISTERS.

Justly styled the Dauntless Queens of the Air

Now arranging dates with the leading Parks, Summer Resorts, Fairs, Celebrations, etc., for single and double

BALLOON ASCENSIONS,

Balloon Races, Sensational Night Ascensions, all with Parachute Leaps. The greatest drawing attraction in America.

Notice to Managers: We furnish everything complete, take all chances on weather and property and guarantee every ascension as per agreement or don't ask a cent of your money. Furnish all kinds of printing. For terms and particulars, address

LeROY SISTERS,

BILLBOARD ADVERTISING, Cincinnati, O.

FROM DEC. 3, 1904 ISSUE

LOTTIE BLAIR PARKER.

The difficulties of successful play-writing may be imagined when we consider how small is the number of writers for the stage, and of these the women may be counted almost upon the fingers of one hand. These women are today objects of interest in the public eye, and among them Mrs. Lottie Blair Parker is a prominent figure.

In her very early years the theater, plays, actors and actresses were almost unknown quantities to her, for her family were non-theater goers, and were largely imbued with Puritanical prejudices against the playhouse and all that pertains to it. But the future playwright was destined to run counter to all these prejudices by later adopting the stage as a profession. After leaving school she went to Boston and became a member of the Boston Theater Stock Company. Here she worked industriously, playing small parts, and little dreamed that upon this same stage a play from her own pen would one day be enacted. In 1892 Mrs. Parker's first play was produced. It was a dainty little society trifle, which Mr. Daniel Frohman put on at his Lyceum Theater, in New York. Although this was Mrs. Parker's first effort, it was produced without alteration in line or business. Undoubtedly her several years' experience as an actress had given her a valuable knowledge of the practical requirements of play building. Although this play, White Roses, was but a curtain raiser, its merits were so marked and its success so great that it gave Mrs. Parker an immediate standing among dramatic authors. For the encouragement of those who may now be struggling for recognition as playwrights, it is worth noting that, notwithstanding this first real success, Mrs. Parker worked in vain for five years to secure another production. During this period a number of plays were completed, but failed to find purchasers. Among them was the since famous Way Down East. It was five years after White Roses was produced that Mrs. Parker's drama of rural New England was produced. Its success was immediate and lasting. Way Down East was followed by A War Correspondent, which proved an artistic, but not a great financial success, and it was withdrawn from the road. Under Southern Skies was the next offering from Mrs. Parker's pen, and the success of this play, following upon that of Way Down East, has established beyond cavil her right to be numbered among our foremost dramatists. Lights of Home, produced last season at the Fourteenth Street Theater, New York, was a new departure for Mrs. Parker, being a dip into genuine melodrama. It achieved success.

FROM NOV. 5, 1904 ISSUE

ADGIE AND HER FAVORITE LION, PRINCE.

The exhibition by Adgie and her lions is one of the most marvelous animal acts now before the public. Her work is more than putting a pack of dangerous brutes through some trained paces. It is an exhibition of the sublime control of a beautiful and perfectly fearless Spanish woman over the acknowledged king of beasts. Aside from the various tricks she put her lions through Adgie performs a delightful Spanish dance, sings La Paloma and does Delsarte posing surrounded by her savage companions. Once seen her marvelous work is never forgotten.

FROM NOV. 22, 1902 ISSUE

FROM JULY, 1896 ISSUE

FROM SEPT. 28, 1901 ISSUE

HARD LINES

Experienced By the First Woman Who Essayed to Write a Play.

Aphra Behn seems to have been identified positively as the first of the women dramatists, and also the first of what an ungallant Australian writer has described as "pen hens." She was born in England, in the darkest days of the commonwealth, and was lucky enough to be saved from growing up in that atmosphere of hypocrisy which required the license of the restoration to clear and put men once more on a natural basis of life. Her father was dead, but she lived with a relative who had adopted her, and was sent, when Aphra was only a child, to be Lieutenant-Governor of Surinam, or Dutch Guiana. Here she met the chieftain, Orinooko, who was the hero of her first novel, and with whom she is said to have been in love. She saw there the slave trade in its worst horrors.

She returned to England when old enough to marry, and almost immediately took advantage of that privilege, changing for the Dutch name Behn her maiden name of Johnson. She was also taken by this marriage to the court of Charles II, and the monarch had such respect for her ability that he sent her as a spy to Holland when the Dutch war of his reign began, and she lived in Antwerp in that service. It was on her return to England that she decided to put herself into rivalry with the dramatists of the day. Women had begun to act in the theaters in place of boys, and she seems to have determined that one of them would also try to make her way into the company of playwrights.

She was as licentious in all her writings as the worst of the other sex . . . . But foul speech was the habit of the day.

She did not succeed without a long struggle. The atmosphere of the theater was never less suited to a woman's pen. The license of the Restoration dramatists was at its worst. Dryden, Wycherly, Congreve and the rest were translating from French originals, and befouling them brilliantly. They were finding native subjects of drama that could be made just as evil. She came into the theater because she was compelled to earn her living, and for that reason she may be excused for persisting for such a long time in the attempt to do something she should have been ashamed of at any time.

She struggled for a long period before her first drama was produced. That was "The Forced Marriage." It succeeded well enough for her to get another play before the public. The second work was "The Rover," and met with genuine success. It was thought to be the work of a man, and that helped her. In all she wrote seven teen plays, of which "The Rovers," "The Roundheads" and "The City Heiress" were the most successful. She was as licentious in all her writings as the worst of the other sex, and it is agreeable to see how, in that respect, the women who have followed her differ from her. But foul speech was a habit of her day.

When she died, at the age of 49, from overwork, she was buried at Westminster Abbey, where not many of the men dramatists of the period in England rest.

CARRIE NATION,
SALOON SMASHER AND ACTOR!

FROM MARCH 19, 1904 ISSUE

FROM SEPT. 13, 1901 ISSUE

CARRIE NATION

At the Danville Fair.

One of the most successful enclosed street fairs and Midway of the present season, I think, was the Elks' Street Fair and Free Horse Show held in Danville, Ill., Aug. 26 to 31. The main entrance was the finest I have ever seen in all my experience as a promoter.

The exhibit street, while not large, was very attractive and exceedingly lively. Five acts, a company of negro entertainers, the Country Store and a band kept the people busy before entering the Midway. All the shows were furnished by F. W. Gaskill's Midway Company, and did a record-breaking business. The front gate had 37,000 paid admissions, and the Midway got 34,000.

Friday was the "big day," strange to say, but Carrie Nation, with her little hatchet, did it. She was delighted with the fair, with but one exception—an exhibit of a local brewery. This she put out of business in short order. One of th eamusing features of the day was her visit to the "Streets of Cairo." The committee tried their best to keep her out, but she was not to be denied. Every one expected her to cause a riot, but after the performance she mounted the "coochee" platform and delivered an address on dress reform ,something like this:

"Ladies and Gentlemen—You will excuse my appearance, as I have just smashed a dirty old beer joint, and I smell terrible, but I would rather have the dirty stuff on my clothes than to have some one drink it. I can't say that I admire the dance that these women just gave, but it's the dance of their country, and it's all right. I would much rather see women dressed as they are without corsets, than all you women out there laced up with a nasty corset, which squeezes your liver, heart and stomach all out of shape. If I was a young man engaged to be married to a girl, and she wore a corset, I would write and tell her to throw it away or it's all off. I don't wear any corsets, and lots of people admire my shape."

After this, she rode in the Ferris Wheel. "The Statue Turning to Life" was her favorite show, as she visited it three times and finally mounted the bally-hoo stand and advised everyone to pay it a visit. She presented Mr. Montgomery, the door spieler, with one of her hatchets to nail on the ticket box for good luck.

Her price for the day was only $75, and I considered it the cheapest and best drawing-card I ever had.

I am now at Huntsville, Ala., working for the Elks.   W. H. RICE.

FROM SEPT. 7, 1901 ISSUE

Mrs. Nation Lecturing.

Carrie Nation, the Kansas joint smasher, has been liberated, and is now delivering lectures. She has been secured to speak at a number of fairs as the star attraction. Mrs. Nation says she has to earn some money, to pay debts incurred during her crusade. Great crowds have gathered to hear and see her in New York State and Pennsylvania during the past two weeks. She is said by the newspapers to be a very interesting talker, with a voice like a trumpet. Mrs. Nation's tour is under the management of J. E. Furlong, of Rochester, N. Y.

FROM DEC. 26, 1903 ISSUE

NEW YORK.

Third Avenue is up and doing this week. Eighth Avenue last week had the only Monday opening. Third Avenue this week has a debut to counteract that first night. The piece is not exactly a new one, as it had its original production in New York about fifty years ago under its present title, Ten Nights in a Bar Room, but it never had such a star as the present Mrs. Carrie Nation. Mrs. Nation plays the part of Mrs. Hammond and supplies her own lines in the form of a temperance lecture at the death bed of her son Willie. Mrs. Nation wrecks the bar roof scene at each performance, and then passes through the audience and sells miniature hatchets. She is the most daring star we have ever seen, for she talks back to her audience, and Third Avenue is delighted.

UNCLE TOM AND RACISM

FROM DEC. 6, 1902 ISSUE

STETSON'S

BIG DOUBLE SPECTACULAR

Uncle Tom's Cabin Co's, No. 1, 2, 3 & 4

LEON W. WASHBURN, Owner and General Director.

GENERAL OFFICE, 1358 BROADWAY, ROOM 3,   -   -   -   -   -   -   NEW YORK CITY.

The wonderful popularity of Harriet Beecher Stowe's masterpiece all over the United States for the past forty years has led to its production by all kinds of managers with all kinds of actors —good, bad and indifferent. There is magic in the name of Uncle Tom and its capacity to draw the public to see it. This, as pretty much all theatre patrons are aware, has been fully taken advantage of by hordes of irresponsibles and a production by them at once "wild and wooly" has been too often the result. When produced with a proper dramatic cast, coupled with proper scenic and mechanical equipment no such story of American life prior to the great crisis in our national affairs has ever been penned.

LEON W. WASHBURN,
Owner & General Manager of Stetson's
Big "Uncle Tom's Cabin" Co.

For twenty years the Stetson production has been the leading one, steadily advancing each season with the wonderful advancement of stage craft. The rolling stock, parade features, scenic investment and choruses have been steadily added to, while the musical and dramatic roles have been placed in the hands of artists of reputation. Special scenery by Seavey is carried for every scene depicted. A corps of colored singers, cake walkers, dancers and field hands from the cotton belt lend realism. A train of railroad cars especially constructed is required in the transportation of these mammoth companies, while the street demonstration is said to excel anything yet seen in the theatrical world. We are the originators of the 2 bands, 2 Marks, 2 Topsey sand the big parades.

Mr. SAM La PORT,
Mgr. Stetson's "Uncle Tom's Cabin" Co.
No. 4.

Mr. AL GOULD,
Mgr. Stetson's "Uncle Tom's
Cabin" Co., No. 1.

WM. KIBBLE,
Mgr. Stetson's "Uncle Tom's Cabin" Co.
No. 2.

FROM MAY 18, 1901 ISSUE

Gotham Theatricals.

It is an intersting fact that "Uncle Tom's Cabin," the American play which has enjoyed the longest virility, has never paid a cent to Harriet Beecher Stowe., from whose novel it was taken. It paid $150 to the man who dramatized it.

FROM JULY 9, 1904 ISSUE

Tony Pastor's Theatre (Harry Sanderson, Mgr.)—An unusually strong bill is the offering for the week of July 4. Edward M. Favor and Edith Sinclair in the latest offering, Caesar's Angel, head the bill. Mr. and Mrs. Allison, in Minnie from Minnesota; Frey and Fields, in The Wrong Man; Hayes and Winne, the dancing couple; Harry Thompson, presenting Uncle Tom's Cabin, by the Hebrew comedian; Bert Baker, singer; The Gagnoux, jugglers and equilibrists; Sisters DeGraff, singing and dancing specialty; Elwood and Maggie Fenton, change artists; Miss Gertie Gordon, commedienne; The Rock Illustrator. and the American Vitagraph, complete the bill.

FROM JUNE 21, 1902 ISSUE

TIED UP.

"Uncle Tom's Cabin" Company At tached at Waterbury, Conn.

Geo. H. Downing's "Uncle Tom's Cabin" Company, under canvas, in which John L. Sullivan, the once popular pugilist, plays the role of Simon Legree, was recently attached at Waterbury, Conn., at the instance of a creditor, who claims to have loaned Downing $4,500 with which to launch the show. The company had only been on the road eleven days, and had met with considerable opposition from the elements.

The papers of attachment were served about 10 o'clock, and some of the property which was on its way to the car was stopped and taken possession of. It is believed the affair will be amicably settled.

FROM MAY 17, 1902 ISSUE

BARRED OUT.

"Uncle Tom's Cabin" Will Never Be Seen in Louisville Again.

The Daughters of the Confederacy, at Louisville, Ky., are jubilant over their victory in their fight against the presentation in that city in the future of "Uncle Tom's Cabin." The play was seen there two weeks ago, but was so strongly boycotted that it proved a financial frost. Manager Stair, of the Avenue Theater, had booked the attraction some months ahead, and when the bills announcing its coming were posted his office resembled a female seminary Old women, young women, women of doubtful age, pretty women, ugly women, all kinds of women, swarmed in upon him with demands that the engagement be cancelled. This Mr. Stair refused to do, for the reason that such a course would make him liable to a damage suit; but he assured the ladies that he would adopt no measures to force their attendance.

Now Stair announces that "Uncle Tom" will nevermore be seen at his house. Other cities south of the Ohio will likely follow Stair's example. Verily, the days of "Uncle Tom" seem to be numbered in Dixie.

FROM JUNE 6, 1903 ISSUE

TENT PULLED DOWN.

Mob Wrecks Al. W. Martin's Uncle Tom Show Under Canvas.

A riot occurred during the performance of Uncle Tom's Cabin by Al. W. Martin's company under canvas on the lot at the corner of California and Armitage Aves., Chicago, last week, in which the tent was pulled down and even the wardrobe carried by the company was burned by the rioters.

The riot was started by a lot of touts who forced an entrance without paying admission.

The police were called but no arrests were made.

FROM FEB. 22, 1902 ISSUE

FROM AUG. 23, 1902 ISSUE

FROM APRIL 26, 1902 ISSUE

FROM OCT. 31, 1903 ISSUE

FROM DEC. 21, 1901 ISSUE

THE RAGTIME SHOW.

Great Northern (Edward Smith, Mgr.)—After two weeks of Cohan fun, we now have the "Real Coons," Williams and Walker and their ensemble of "ragtime" colored entertainers. Of all the ebony colored comedians that travel, Williams and Walker are the leaders, and their managers always keep their musical show up to an attractive standard. Many new and catchy musical numbers are introduced this year and the entire company is well dressed and immensely amusing, while the vocal end of it is nicely done. The Williams and Walker Company improve each trip.

PERILS OF PERFORMING

FROM AUG., 1899 ISSUE

TRIALS OF THE BALOONIST.

Some of the State Fair managers are constantly looking for new attractions to exhibit, to call out the patrons and fill the grand stands. Formerly, a State fair was run on the principle that the exhibit of vegetables, quilts, fruits, cattle and other stock, with an occasional race of farm horses, was all that was necessary to draw from the farms and cities the people who paid the quarters to see the show. Of late years faster horses have been brought in, and later balloon ascensions have been a feature, the society engaging a ballooon man or woman, hoping that an accident might happen by which a human being would fall from the skies and flatten out the ground in the presence of thousands of applauding citizens, who would go home and say they never had such a good time at a fair. Many societies have felt hurt that the balloonist came down safely, and in some cases where the balloonist has fallen to death a mile or two away from the fair ground, the management has complained and held back the money from the heirs of the deceased, on the grond that the death exhibit was not what they had a right to expect. But the balloon part of an agricultural fair has become too free from casualties to be attractive, and new attractions are sought.

> **In some cases where the baloonist has fallen to death a mile or two away from the fair grounds the management complained that the death exhibit was not what they had a right to expect.**

The Kansas State Fair has a scheme that is worthy of notice. It is proposed to engage the brave Gen. Funston, the redheaded swimming soldier, to duplicate his feat of swimming a river with soldiers at his back, armed with cheese knives, and routing an enemy on the other side, in imitation of his feat in the war in the Philippines. They propose to dig a river on the Kansas prairie, and fill it with seltzer water, and turn the General loose, with the citizens of Kansas watching the show at 50 cents a head. It is not probable that Funston can be induced to give a continuous performance of himself, but if he does, it will open the way for others that have attained distinction in other lines, to be exhibited at State fairs. Mr. Roosevelt, with his rough riders, may be engaged to charge an imaginary San Juan Hill at Des Moines, Iowa, and Mr. Cleveland might be engaged to shoot ducks at Springfield, Ill., or catch a

few stuffed striped bass. The meat packers could be hired to stand up before a State fair audience in Minnesota armed with can openers and open a few cans of roast beef, with clothes pins on their noses. Gen. Eagan who is not engaged in steady employment, could give an exhibition of language and conduct becoming a dismissed officer of the army, and Gen. Alger could give a continuous performance at the Michigan State Fair of patience, that overcomes all obstacles, and enables a hero to keep on in the heroing business notwithstanding his time has expired. If these exhibits are drawing cards at fairs, there will be a chance for all who have attained distinction to keep before the people, and become object lessons to the common herd.

FROM SEPT. 1, 1900 ISSUE

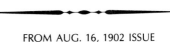

Aeronaut Killed.

Delphos, O., August 22—(Special.)—During the street fair being held in Delphos this week a balloon ascension was arranged for every day. At 2 o'clock this afternoon Harry Davis, an aeronaut of Delphos, made an ascension, one of the prettiest ever seen, and when about 800 feet high he cut loose his parachute, evidently not being aware that the ropes were entangled. He descended to earth at a rapid rate, the parachute failing to open. He struck on a telegraph wire, which checked the fall somewhat, and from there he fell to

the street, his parachute falling on top of him. Not a bone in his body was broken, and he only received a few scratches about the face and shoulders. He was taken to his home, and doctors soon found that he was crushed internally to a pulp, and he died at about 9 o'clock in awful agony. Davis had been making ascensions for about four years, and this was the first accident he had met with. The awful tradegy was witnessed by about 8,000 people. He had been working for G. O. Litt, of Dayton, a street fair promoter.

Fell into a River.

FELL INTO A RIVER.
Niles, Mich., August 22—(Special.)—William Hogan, a well-known balloonist, was probably fatally injured to-day while making an ascension in view of a street carnival crowd of 10,000. Hogan started on his trip at 4 o'clock this afternoon, but in some way the ropes had become entangled and the balloon struck a 60-foot building. Hogan also hit the building with terrific force, but managed to hang on until the airship was about 150 feet from the ground. It then turned over suddenly, dropping Hogan into the St. Joseph River. He would have drowned but for two men who swam out and supported him until rescued by oarsmen.

FROM AUG. 16, 1902 ISSUE

FACED DEATH.

Parachute Jumper Falls into the Patapsco.

Jacob Kelly, who is making balloon ascensions and dropping to earth with a parachute from Riverview Park, near Baltimore, Md., fell into the Patapsco River, entangled in his paraphernalia, and was in danger of drowning on the afternoon of July 30, when he was picked up by the Baltimore American's shipping news tug, "Dispatch."

The people at Riverview assembled about 4 o'clock to watch Kelly sail skyward, clad in green tights and sitting on the trapeze attached to a parachute hanging from the balloon. He soared up and up until he was but a mere speck a mile overhead in the black and gray storm clouds. When Kelly pulled the string that held the parachute to the balloon the big umbrella-like apparatus opened out successfully, but to Kelly's dismay the parachute was caught in a northeasterly wind and began to rapidly drift off shore and out toward the Patapsco River. At the same time the heavens were banked with angry clouds that threatened to burst into a storm at any moment. Kelly was enveloped by the mists until he could see but a few feet away from him, and he feared that the balloon, descending above the parachute, would fall on top of him and smother or drown him in the river.

Nearly everyone at Riverview ran to the southwestern limits of the grounds to watch Kelly as he rapidly descended toward the river, nearly a mile off shore. The fact that the man's life was in danger and that no boats were within a mile of him caused the Baltimore American's tug "Dispatch," headed up the river, to put about to the man's assistance. It is a rule of balloonists to jump and dive clear of the parachute, but for some reason Kelly sat in the trapeze and struck the water with a great splash.

Kelly came up treading water, but he was entangled in the canvas and a rope which had been fastened about his waist and so attached to the apparatus as to prevent him from falling while in the air still held him to the parachute. The balloon dropped about fifty feet from him.

Captain Collison and the crew of the "Dispatch" were soon lending a helping hand and had the tiring man and his apparatus aboard the tug by the time a rowboat put out from Riverview, nearly a mile distant. Kelly could not release himself from the parachute until he was aboard the "Dispatch," when he sat on the deck almost exhausted. He was landed at Riverview, where he was soon himself again.

FROM MAY 3, 1902 ISSUE

DIAVOLO'S UNDERSTUDY

Receives Painful Injuries By a Fall While Doing the "Loop-the-Loop."

Diavolo's understudy, while trying to perfect the trick in practice, during a rehearsal at Madison Square Garden, met with a severe accident. While in the center of the loop he suddenly seemed to lose all control of his balance or equilibrium, and shot clear of the side. The wheel fell full forty-five feet distant, completely wrecked, while he himself fell in a lump, breaking the bottom staging of the loop. His escape from instant death was miraculous. He came off with a sprained ankle and a severely wrenched back.

He avers that he will loop-the-loop for all that, or die in the attempt. Minting the Marvel, who was standing near at hand, smiled and said: "Oh, he'll do it after two or three more good bumps."

It was rather disappointing to all concerned, as many of the trick bicycle riders were at the rehearsal.

FROM JUNE 21, 1902 ISSUE

ANOTHER VICTIM.

Moncrief Injured While Attempting to Loop-the-Loop.

Minneapolis, Minn., June 16.—Clarence Hamilton, known as Moncrief, a trick bicyclist, brought here from New York to "loop-the-loop" at the Elks' Fair, followed the example of his three predecessors and fell from the giant wheel on the inside of which he tried to steer a bicycle. E. Kilpatrick, John Larson and Josiah Dougherty had each been injured in attempting the feat. In his second attempt he left the rim of the big loop just as he neared the top and was riding head downward. He was hurled with terrific force among the spectators and had several ribs fractured. Besides this he received internal injuries. He is now at a hospital in a serious condition.

FROM AUG. 3, 1901 ISSUE

Flaming Acrobat Climbs for Life.

High in the air, his body enveloped in flames, George Devan climbed, hand over hand, forty feet of wire cable, at Sunbury, Pa., July 23, while 3,000 men, women and children alternately prayed, screamed, cried or fainted at the sight. When he did reach safety he was burned so that his recovery is doubtful.

Devan is a traveling aerialist, and goes about the country giving exhibitions for the money he can collect in a hat from the crowd. His feat is to make a long slide down an inclined cable, holding on to a trolley wheel by his teeth, and then make a high dive into a pool of water. It is ordinarily inspiring and exciting to the beholder, but last night he determined to add to it in a spectacular way. He advertised that he would make a human torch of himself when the dive was made.

An immense crowd gathered at the spot and beheld Devan enveloped in petroleum-soaked cotton from head to foot. He had fastened 60 feet of heavy wire cable, 50 feet high in the air at one end and 30 at the other. Over this ran the trolley wheel.

When the time came to perform his act Devan climbed to the highest part of the cable, placed the trolley in his teeth, and just as he launched forth touched a lighted match to his costume. As he swung off the flames shot up and nothing could be seen of him. For 40 feet he slid with lightning swiftness, and it would all have been over in a second if, within 20 feet of the lower end, the trolley had not caught in three broken strands of cable. They held the little wheel, while Devan swung to and fro 40 feet above the heads of the crowd, the cotton blazing fiercely. Men called upon him to jump, while the screams of the women were above everything else. But this would have meant sure death upon the rocks, and it looked as if the man would burn alive, when he reached up, grasped the cable and began to go to the starting point hand over hand. The ascent was slow.

To the staring, breathless crowd below it seemed as if it would last forever. Several times it appeared as if he was weakening, as the flames began to eat into his flesh and the fumes of the kerosene got into his lungs. But he was plucky, and at last managed to gain the little platform from which he started. Here he braced himself and tore away the fragments of the cotton still unburned, and then climbed down to the ground, where he fainted. He was at once removed to a hospital.

The 20th Century Sensation.

LOTTIE BRANDON
THE MOST FEARLESS CYCLIST IN THE WORLD

SOME EARLY STARS

FROM APRIL 6, 1901 ISSUE

Reed, Dead; Barrymore, Insane.

Two incidents in the theatrical world last week cast a gloom over the entire profession. Roland Reed, the comedian died and Maurice Barrymore, the talented actor, became a raving maniac, and had to be sent to Bellevue Hospital, New York. Roland Reed was born in 1852. His first appearance as a star was in 1882 in "Cheek." From that time on he was one of the most popular light comedians in America. The cause of his death was cancer of the stomach, from which he was a sufferer for the past three years. He pluckily fought against death and rallied once or twice sufficiently to go back on the stage, but finally had to succumb to an enemy who has never been conquered. His funeral took place under the direction of the Actor's Society, and in the list of pallbearers were such eminent stage lights as Frank W. Sanger, Milton Nobles, Louis Aldrich, Gus Pitou, John Drew, W. A. Brady and others. The remains were placed temporarily in a vault in Woodlawn Cemetery.

Barrymore looked strange ... he began a wild harangue. The stage manager ordered him off the stage, but he would not obey .... At first the audience stared; then it tittered. At last a woman screamed and the curtain was rung down.

The other pathetic event is the loss of mind of Maurice Barrymore, who had not been himself for several months. His ravings take the form of quotations from well known plays and an egotistical comparison of himself with other actors.

There was a large audience present at the Lion Palace Music Hall in Harlem on Thursday night when Barrymore went insane. They were drawn there chiefly by the not yet departed vogue of the once great actor and in part by the stories of his ardent advocacy of the cause of the White Rats, the organization of vaudeville artists that is warring upon the theatrical trust.

Barrymore looked strange in spite of his make-up. His eyes were large and staring. He looked unkempt and his hands twitched nervously. He stepped to the front of the stage, and, instead of speaking the lines, his monologue, began a wild harangue against the Theatrical Trust. He talked so fast and so indistinctly that only those in the front rows heard the words.

"Down with the trust! Death to the syndicate! Charles Frohman is doomed!"

The stage manager ordered him off the stage, but he either did not hear or would not obey. He went on haranguing, tossing his arms above his head and striding from one side of the stage to the other.

At first the audience stared; then it tittered. At last a woman screamed, and the curtain was rung down.

The actor raved about the White Rats and George Fuller Golden and Charlie Frohman, but seemed to know nothing of the fiasco of his act. He hurried from the theater, and almost ran to the Ft. Lee ferry, at the foot of One Hundred and Thirtieth street, followed by his son John.

FROM NOV. 12, 1904 ISSUE

THE ELDER BARRYMORE IN A DYING CONDITION.

Maurice Barrymore, father of Ethel Barrymore, is reported to be in a dying condition at the Amityville Sanitarium in New York City. His vitality has been marvelous, but it is now at its lowest ebb. His son John, the artist, is constantly with him, but the other son, Lionel, now convalescent from typhoid fever, has not been appraised of the news. It is said that the mind of the once famous actor is almost a blank. Of late he has refused to take food and often does not recognize the nurse in charge. At times he is overtaken with anger and is difficult to control. A large part of his waking hours is spent in reacting the scenes of his former successes, and he repeats the lines in some of the plays which brought thunderous applause from an appreciative audience.

• • •

The DeMille Bros., Cecil and William, have truly inherited the talent of their father for play writing. The brothers have written for Chas. Richman a play called The Genius in which Mr. Richman will star this season and Mr. William DeMille has written Robert Edison's new play which will be presented at the Hudson Theatre early in June.

FROM JAN. 17, 1903 ISSUE

NEW YORK.

THE PASSING SHOW.—MLLE. DUSE TO GIVE "MAGDA."—CRITICS ROAST MRS. LANGTRY.

Four new productions. The opening of the new Majestic Theater and Mme. Duse as "Magda"—first time in New York this season—insures variety and promises to make next week theatrically interesting.

• • •

As anticipated in my last week's letter, the first appearance of Mrs. Langtry, in the 'Crossways,' was the signal for a general all-round roast from the New York critics. The programs disclosed the fact that Mrs. Langtry's gowns were the product of a highly advertised Paris gown factory. Here was item number one for a dramatic critic to dissect or make fun of. Moreover, His Royal Highness, Edward VII., of England, had witnessed the play, and although it is not on record what he thought of it, still the old exaggerated friendship between the lady and the King was one of those juicy items, which however irrelevant to the play itself, offered the dramatic critic such a grand opportunity of spilling ink upon matters more or less imaginary. In result Tuesday's New York papers contain columns calculated to make one almost believe that King Edward wrote and staged this play as some momento of the many happy hours that he and Lilly never spent together, and when the critic, hopelessly forgetting his vocation, was not suggesting that the actress, owing to her age, should now take to nice little starched caps on the crocheting of tidies he would be sizing up the lady "on points" like a sub-editor commenting on the various animal exhibits at an agricultural show,

FROM OCT. 25, 1902 ISSUE

REPLY

Filed to Suit Brought Against Weber and Fields.

Weber and Fields have filed an answer to the suit brought against them by W. H. Walker ("Harry Williams"), in which Walker seeks $1,000 for an alleged breach of contract for the failure of the defendants to give a performance at one of his theaters. The defendants claim that the action is not legal. It is denied that the agreement was in force at the time the suit was brought, it having previously been canceled, it is said. It is alleged that at the time the agreement, or contract, was made three others were also made for performances of different companies. After signing them in July, 1896, it is said, the defendants notified the plaintiffs of their desire to play the Russell Brothers combination in Pittsburg, and the plaintiff wrote that if they did so he would regard all contracts canceled, and later notified them that he had done so. The affidavit is signed by Joseph M. Weber.

OUT OF ORDER.

A Story Told of Jake Simon, the Old-Time Actor.

It is told of Jake Simon, who is playing "Rip Van Winkle," that one winter when making a stand at Jefferson City, Mo., he was given the privilege of the floor of the House of Representatives, a high and unusual favor. Out of that grew an episode that set the whole State to laughing. An intense strain was on, and feeling fierce fight was on that winter between Sedalia and Jefferson City for the State Capital high in the House, where the removal debate was on. The excitement was something awful, and Jake, who is a Jew, got carried away, and jumping upon a desk he shouted: "Misther Speaker." Speaker Russell saw him, and beating thunderously on his desk, roared back: "The gentleman from Jerusalem will please come to order, by G—." That brought down both Jake and the house, and there was immediate adjournment at Jake's expense.

NEW THEATER

Projected for Erie, Pa.—New York Managers Interested.

It is rumored that Erie, Pa., is to have a fine new playhouse, providing a desirable site can be secured. While the project was given inception by Erie people, it has now been taken up by Messrs. Hyde and Beman, of Brooklyn, N. Y.

The house, if carried into construction, will compare favorably with any in this country.

BIG FINISH.

Weber and Fields Offered $120,000 for Last Six Weeks.

It is rumored that Weber and Fields have been offered $120,000 for six weeks. The show syndicate, organized for the purpose, it is said, proposed to give the comedians $20,000 a week for a six weeks tour on the road after the regular season closes at the little Music Hall on Broadway.

Weber and Fields went on a tour seven weeks last season, earning $142,000.

NAT GOODWIN

To Star in "A Midsummer Night's Dream" Next Season.

Nat C. Goodwin will be the star in a brilliant production of "A Midsummer Night's Dream," which Klaw & Erlanger will put on next season. He will play Bottom, and will make this an even more notable Shakesperian effort than his Shylock, which he gave with an all-star cast two seasons ago.

FROM DEC. 1, 1900 ISSUE

Sarah Bernhardt is to receive for every appearance during her present American season the sum of $1,000, which is more than any actress ever got here before. Eleanora Duse, when she was negotiating with an American manager three years ago, demanded that sum for the services of herself and her company. She was to get $1,000 a performance for seven performances a week, and was to pay the actors. Mme. Bernhardt is the only actress speaking a foreign language who ever made money for her managers in this country. But the French actress has never been able to keep any of her earnings. During her last tour here four years ago she sent by cable to Paris her share of the receipts. Sometimes she was paid in small towns, and the rate of transfer by cable was high, but she was never willing to postpone the transfer for a day. The only cash that she carried back with her to France was the sum of $7,000, which was her share of the profits during the week and a half ending the night before she took the steamer. As her jewels, which were taken out of pawn for her American tour, were all pledged again the day after her arrival in Paris, that amount did not last her very long. The cost of the organization may have been understood from the size of the guarantee demanded outside of New York. No less than $4,500 is necessary to cover the cost of every performance. Constant Coquelin is to receive $500 for every performance, which is probably quite as much as he ever earned on any previous tour.

FROM DEC. 7, 1901 ISSUE

BERNHARDT

To Play "Mary, Queen of Scots."

Mme. Bernhardt's latest exploit is to induce Maurice Hewlett to promise a play for her on the subject of Mary, Queen of Scots. To an actress of such power and charm as the "Divine Sarah," the role of the most lovely and luckless of the Stuarts naturally appeals with overwhelming force.

If the play is written it will be done by Bernhardt in English. Since she took Charles Frohman unexpectedly at his word and offered to play an English Romeo to the Juliet of Miss Maude Adams, the great French actress has become possessed of a fierce longing to impersonate other English-speaking characters of the first dramatic rank.

> **Since she (Bernhardt) took Charles Frohman at his word and offered to play an English Romeo to the Juliet of Miss Maude Adams, the great French actress has become possessed of a fierce longing to impersonate other English speaking characters . . . .**

Mr. Hewlett has already displayed talent as a writer of dramatic romances. Miss Clo Graves' version of his "The Forest Lovers" has been successfully produced by Daniel Frohman at the New York. Mr. Sutro is casting "Richard Yea and Nay" into dramatic shape for Beerbohm Tree, and Mr. Hewlett himself is dramatizing one of his "little novels of Italy" for H. B. Irving.

There is no doubt of the readiness with which much of Hewlett's work lends itself to stage uses. But a play for Bernhardt on a theme of such magnitude and complexity as Mary Stuart means a bolder flight. Of all the thousand and one dramas dealing with it, only Schiller's survives, as the vehicle for the personal triumphs of Modjeska.

MAUDE ADAMS.
The Talented Actress whose charming Personality
has been Conducive to Her Great Success.

In another column of this week's "Billboard" appears the picture of Maude Adams, the American star, who last season was the rival of the immortal Sarah Bernhardt in the production of "L'Aiglon." Chas. Frohman, with these two of the world's greatest dramatic celebrities, has formed a combination to present "Romeo and Juliet," which critics believe will overshadow all others. Either lady numbers in the list of admirers thousands who strongly contend for the pre-eminence of their favorite. Last season it was a mooted question as to which gave the most artistic interpretation of "L'Aiglon," and the fact of the combination reveals that either has a very high regard for the other. Madame Bernhardt will devote a large portion of her summer vacation to the study in English of the role, and it may be predicted that her effort as Romeo will be the very strongest of which she is capable. The roles of Romeo and Juliet afford, perhaps, the very best possibility for these ladies to show forth their artistic power and their weight of natural talent. The Juliet of Miss Adams, it is safe to say, will be of such character as to give the Romeo of Madame Bernhardt splendid opportunity for the display of the queenly talent of the French actress. Mr. Charles Frohman, who has engaged this duo of artists, is confident that it will be the winning event of the season. That the engagement will be a profitable one goes without question, and on both sides of the water the two stars will be the center of critical attention.

ANNA HELD,
In the Title-role of the Comic-Opera Success,
Mam'selle Napoleon.

WEBER & HELD.

Joseph Weber, of the erstwhile firm of Weber and Fields, and Florenz Ziegfeld, manager of Anna Held, have entered into a contract whereby the famous comedian and the Parisian nightingale will appear together next season in the theatre formerly known as Weber and Fields' Music Hall.

The new company will be known as the Weber and Ziegfeld Stock Company and the house will be known as Weber's Broadway Music Hall.

The house opens about September 1, and Weber and Held will assume leading roles. The supporting company has not been formed, but it is probable that Charles Bigelow, who was previously engaged to support Miss Held in her next season's tour, will have a leading part.

Edgar Smith, who supplied the librettos for Weber and Fields' Company, has been engaged to act in a like capacity for the new orgaanization.

Miss Anna Held sailed May 29 on the steamship Kaiser Wilhelm der Grosse for her home in Paris. She was accompanied by her husband and manager, Mr. Florence Zeigfeld, and Mr. George Marion, her stage manager. "I am going to Wales shortly after reaching the other side," confided Miss Held before her departure, "and intend to bid for the castle of Adeline Patti, in Wales, which is going to be sold. I want it very much, and I think it would make an ideal home. When I return to beautiful America to fill my next season's engagements I shall have with me the prettiest and most talented chorus girls to be found in France and England. My new piece? Oh, Mr. Harry B. Smith has written a new musical comedy for me. Its title? Probably 'The Little Duchess.'" Friends in throngs crowded to the steamship to bid Miss Held adieu and filled her state-room with flowers.

FROM OCT. 19, 1901 ISSUE

SIR HENRY IRVING.

His Wonderful Strength and Vitality— Refers Feelingly to Our Martyred President.

With sixty years over his head, one can not help marveling at the wonderful vitality of the leading exponent of the drama, Sir Henry Irving. Since the close of his Lyceum season, with the exception of a brief vacation, he has been on tour, playing something like eight parts every week at seven or eight performances, but he hardly even in his younger days performed such a feat as he did recently, traveling more than 500 miles and appearing in two towns.

After playing "Charles I." in Leeds, England, on a Tuesday night, he got up at an early hour the next morning and left Leeds at 7 o'clock for London. Here he drove across the city from King's Cross to Waterloo, and left there about 1 o'clock for Winchester, where he was escorted to Castle Hall. He read scenes from "Becket," in connection with the King Alfred celebration, and made an impromptu speech, in which he said he was proud to take part in the millenary of King Alfred as the representative of the royal institution.

Sir Henry alluded to the dire tragedy which filled the whole world: Mr. McKinley was the avatar of noble purpose and patriotism. . . . His memory shall be green forever in the hearts of all English speaking people.

Sir Henry, who, as may be remembered, wired at once a sympathetic expression on Mr. McKinley's death, could not conclude the speech which he was called upon to make without an allusion to the dire tragedy which filled the whole world with woe and righteous indignation. That he did very neatly and most appropriately. He said:

"May I add that all the race which looks upon King Alfred's memory as a common heritage is in bitter grief for one whom a mourning nation is laying at rest.

"Mr. McKinley was at once the avatar and the emblem of noble purpose, high thought and patriotism. He, like his predecessor of a thousand years ago, though he worked immediately for his own country, worked for all the world, and his memory shall be green forever in the hearts of our loyal and expansive race—of all English-speaking people."

After performing this duty, Sir Henry dined with the mayor and others, and returned to London, going to his flat in Stratton street on the same evening. He left King's Cross early the next day, and returned to Leeds in time to play Shylock in the evening.

Sir Henry leaves London for America on Oct. 6, on the Minnehaha, with Miss Terry and the same company which played during the season at the Lyceum in London, and also during his tour of the English provinces.

FROM DEC. 7, 1901 ISSUE

JENNY LIND'S YOUTH.

The Swedish Nightingale's Struggle from Obscurity to Fame.

 ENNY LIND was baptized as Johanna Lindborg, says a Stockholm letter in the Chicago Record. The nickname by which she became famous was given her in her childhood. Her mother lived in two different tenements in Stockholm, N o . 4 3 Jakobsbergsgatan and No. 32 Mastersamuelgatan, while she was an infant, and it is not definitely known in which she was born. Both claim the honor, but the weight of evidence seems to be in favor of the former, which is on a short street in the manufacturing section of the city and mostly occupied by artisans of various sorts. The other place is on a better street near the center of the manufacturing section.

A Mr. Lindhahl, who holds a position in the Royal Library at Philadelphia, has an interesting collection of letters and documents relating to the early life of Jenny Lind. He has certified copies of the record of her birth and christening and the proceedings of the court, which, when she was fourteen years of age, decided that her parents were unfit persons to have charge of her, and appointed the director of the Opera House as her guardian. He also has a number of autograph letters written when she was a child and afterward when she was a young woman in Paris studying with Mme. Garcia.

One of them, written at the age of eleven, is extremely interesting, for it reveals the poverty of her family and her thoughtfulness in saving expenses for her mother. She says that she must have a new pair of shoes, for the shoemaker has refused to repair her old ones any longer, and tells her mother that she could buy a pair at Drottningholm, where she is stopping—a little village that surrounds the king's palace—a little cheaper than she could get them at Stockholm. The letters from Paris, full of ardor and enthusiasm, tell of her experience there, the compliments that have been paid her, the encouragement she has received and her confidence of success.

There are people still living in Stockholm who knew her intimately, although the greater part of her life was spent in London. Among others is Professor Gunter, a former instructor in the Royal Conservatory of Music, who retired on a pension a few years ago, to whom she was at one time engaged to be married. She jilted him to marry Otto Goldsmith, her accompanist upon her American tour under the management of P. T. Barnum. Mr. Goldsmith is still living in London. Their son is a captain in the British army, and their daughter is married to a prominent business man in London.

When she was ten years old she was apprenticed to the singing master of the Royal Opera in Stockholm, with a number of other girls of her age who had fine voices, and at the age of eighteen made her debut in the opera "Agata" in the Royal Opera House, which was torn down to make room for the new one that stands opposite the palace to-day. It is an institution of which the people of Stockholm are very proud.

FROM JAN. 11, 1902 ISSUE

ETHEL BARRYMORE HERE.

Illinois (W. J. Davis, Mgr.)—The bright young comidienne Ethel Barrymore is here, presenting Clyde Fitch's "fantastic" comedy-drama, "Captain Jinks of the Horse Marines." Miss Barrymore appeared in this play at the Garrick Theater, New York, some 200 nights last season(the longest run of the year, so I understand, and when she opened there again, this past autumn, was again greeted with immense business and, in all probability, remained for another lengthy run if she had not been obliged to make way for other bookings managed by Charles Frohman, besides she had been booked en tour. It is pretty well known that when Ethel Barrymore is recognized as a leading actress she only comes into her own. Her position to-day is her birthright. Her mother was the talented Georgia Drew, whose untimely death bereaved the stage of one of its most brilliant daughters. Her father, Maurice Barrymore, was long an actor of prominence. Her grandmother, Mrs. John Drew, was a favorite with three generations of theatergoers. Her uncle, John Drew, of our day, has long been regarded as one of our leading actors. In fact, all of Miss Barrymore's people, all her relatives as far back as can be remembered have been players. Besides the dramatic talent which belongs to her Miss Barrymore has inherited beauty of face and form—no small part of the actor's equipment. In her appearance the mingling of the family characteristics is pronounced.

Her position today is her birthright. Her mother was the talented Georgia Drew . . . . Her father, Maurice Barrymore, long an actor of prominence . . . . Her grandmother, Mrs. John Drew, a favorite with three generations of theatre-goers. Her uncle, John Drew, long regarded as one of our leading actors.

Although Miss Barrymore has reached distinction before she is 21, she has worked faithfully in the years she has been on the stage. Her debut was made when she played Julia in "The Rivals," with Mrs. Drew. Later she appeared as the maid in "Rosemary," with her uncle. The following year she was in "Secret Service" and went with the company to London. Sir Henry Irving saw her play Odette Tyler's part one night and engaged her for "Peter the Great," written by his son. She also appeared as the daughter in "The Bells," with Mr. Irving. She was also with Annie Russell in "Catherine," and late with John Drew in "The Liars." She then became leading woman in "His Excellency, the Governor," continuing until she blossomed forth as a full-fledged star in "Captain Jinks."

FROM JULY 5, 1902 ISSUE

RESUME

Of the Career of Clyde Fitch, the Playright.

Clyde Fitch, the noted playwright, who has hurried to Berne, Switzerland for treatment by a noted specialist on appendicitis, in hopes of thus avoiding an operation, has already accomplished the work of a lifetime, though he has not yet reached the turning post in years. Mr. Fitch's career has been a strenuous one, his rapidity as a playwright having elicited much comment, and, indeed, considerable adverse criticism in the newspapers and magazines of this country as well as in England. His literary ability was in no way hereditary, his father having been an army officer who was greatly prejudiced against his son's ambition to become a writer, and insisted he should put aside the idea and become an architect. But fate had not so decreed. Ability will assert itself, even under contrary circumstances. Clyde Fitch had the ability and the strength of character to support it. Finally, he brought about a compromise between himself and his father, in which it was agreed that if after three years he was not supporting himself with the pen, he should then put aside his ambition and become an architect. The end of the third year approached, and the proceeds from his literary work had failed to materialize. About this time it chanced that he met a friend, who incidentally mentioned that Richard Mansfield was in need of a play, and could find nothing to suit him. Fitch immediately called on the actor, and "Beau Brummel" was the result of the conference. Its immediate success assured the sale of future plays, which have been dashed off at the average of two a year ever since. The following are the plays that he has written, though no attempt has been made to arrange them in successive order, as it is doubtful whether Mr. Fitch could do this himself: "The Girl and the Indes," "Way of the World," "The Climbers," "Captain Jinks," "Lover's Lane," "Barbara Frietchie," "The Cowboy and the Lady," "Nathan Hale," "The Moth and the Flame," "The Last of the Dandies," "Frederick le Maitre," "The Modern Match," "His Grace De Gramont," "Mistress Betty," "April Weather," "Bessie's Finish," "Pamela's Prodigy," "The Mask Ball," "Bohemia" and "Sapho," the two last-named being adaptations.

FROM SEPT. 27, 1902 ISSUE

BOSTON.

David Warfield's "The Auctioneer" Meets a Cold Reception.

Hollis Street Theater. (Rich, Harris & Frohman, Mgrfl)—Second week of David Warfield in "The Auctioneer." After its long run in New York, I expected a treat. The production is a pronounced failure. The audience sat dumb as marble, and with the exception of one or two laughs the performance failed to gain any applause. Dave Warfield plays a perfect Jew, but not one who touches the heart. His Jew is a grinning and idiotic character. The play is supposed to picture low life, but is inconsistent from start to finish. With a stage production true to life and with a star who has power, pathos and emotion, "The Auctioneer" would be a hit, but as it now stands the managers who have booked it have a gold brick.

FROM SEPT. 13, 1902 ISSUE

BOSTON.

The Four Cohans Open the Boston Museum to Great Business— Colonial Opens Also.

The Boston Museum, (Field, Rich, Harris & Frohman, Mgrs.)—This house opened for the season Labor Day. Every seat in the house was taken, and the Four Cohans gave a rattling show. The town is billed like a circus. I understand that George M. Cohan designs all the advertisinm matter. Whoever does it should be complimented. The company is styled "The Four Cohans." Why don't they say "The Five Cohans" and include Miss Levey, who is Mrs. Geo. M. This is certainly one of the greatest working companies on the road, and they have the material to work with, too—everything bright, witty, sane and sensible, and a winner.

FROM NOV. 1, 1902 ISSUE

John L. Sullivan makes his initial appearance in vaudeville at Hurtig & Seamon's Harlem Music Hall, Nov. 17. He will do a monologue act, a la James J. Corbett. Ben Harris will be his manager.

• • •

Marie Dressler is seriously ill at her apartments in Forty-fourth street, New York. Her manager, Joseph Immerman, has canceled her engagements for the entire season. Miss Dressler was booked in vaudeville for twenty weeks. Fourteen of these weeks were to be spent on the Orpheum Circuit. For her appearances east and west of Chicago $900.

FROM FEB. 7, 1903 ISSUE

The compiling genius has been at work again. He has discovered the published ages of various successful players, and he has sent them journeying out into the world. Here they are:

Mrs. C. H. Gilbert	82
Joseph Jefferson	74
Francesca Janauschek	73
James H. Stoddard	76
Henry Clay Barnabee	70
Ada Rehan	43
Sarah Bernhardt	59
Lillian Russell	42
Thomas Q. Seabrooke	43
Robert Bruce Mantell	49
Frederick Warde	52
Otis Skinner	46
Robert Downing	46
Ellen Terry	55
Rose Coghlan	42
Lulu Glaser	29
Eleanor Duse	44
William Gillette	50
Henry Irving	65
Maude Adams	31
Helena Modjeska	59
Richard Mansfield	46
Nat C. Goodwin	46
Edward H. Sothern	44
De Wolfe Hopper	45
Fransic Wilson	49
Willilam H. Crane	58
Louis James	61
John Drew	50
Ethel Barrymore	24

FROM JAN. 31, 1903 ISSUE

Seldom if ever before in the history of New York has the half-year season in the dramatic world been marked by greater activity than the present. This is largely attributed to the ultra-prosperous condition of the country which always manifests itself in expenditures for luxuries—and amusements are certainly luxuries the way they are managed now-a-days.

Managers are responding liberally to the demands of the public, spending vast sums on great productions that would not have been deemed feasible investments ten years ago, and making hay while the sun shines. There have been few failures and many successes.

> "This business may aptly be likened to sea-sickness," declared Oscar Hammerstein. "A failure is a sad affair while it lasts, but when one gets over the effects of the malady he is ready to launch once more on the dramatic sea, for he is cocksure he will never be taken again."

"This business may aptly be likened to sea-sickness," recently declared Oscar Hammerstein in speaking of managerial uncertainties. "A failure is a sad affair while it lasts, but when one gets over the effects of the malady he is ready to launch once more on the dramatic sea, for he is cock sure he will never be "taken again."

Mr. Hammerstein is world-renowned as a builder of theatres and a manager of mammoth productions and his word is usually accepted as law on the Rialto. He is just now sailing over smooth waters as he has two successes in his playhouses. Viola Allen, at his Victoria, in Hall Caine's "Eternal City," has made money since her opening performance, and David Belasco's "The Darling of the Gods," at the old Hammerstein Theatre Republic (now the Belasco Theatre), is in many respects the most notable melodrama in the country today.

Miss Allen is under the management of Liebler & Co., the same firm, by the way, which is struggling with the tour of Mme. Eleonore Duse, the Italian actress set down by international critics as the greatest living exponent of the naturalistic school of acting. Her tour has not been a pronounced financial success for the reason that, in her endeavor to further Italian art, the actress has insisted upon jamming her depraved D'Annunzio plays down the throats of an unwilling and somewhat unappreciative American public. The Lieblers have "struggled" with the tour and "struggled" hard, not only because of the D'Annunzio plays, however. Mme. Duse has frequently exercised the perogative of a woman and a star and refused to appear at advertised performances for no good reason that the lay mind can fathom. A slight cold, a headache, and even ennui, have sufficed for the calling off of a performance worth $3,000, and that at an hour's notice. George Tyler, the active head of the firm, who, after three weeks of Duse and an equal number of mental indigestion, fled to Europe, still maintains that his foreign star is easy to manage. But as Mme. Duse is to return next season the reason of Mr. Tyler's exterior calm is easy to explain.

Charles Frohman's list of stars were gathered from a different constellation. There is but one "Boss" at a Frohman playhouse and that is Mr. Frohman. In consequence the manager has achieved a number of marked successes during the latter part of the season so far spent. William Faversham's second annual starring venture— this time in "Imprudence"— has not been dwarfed even by his marriage a few weeks ago to Miss Julie Opp. He is now on tour and bids fair to remain on the road the same moneymaker he was on Broadway. Miss Ethel Barrymore, in her two comedies, "A Country Mouse" and "Carrots," gained equal favor and now that the Empire Stock Company has come to its home in the Empire Theatre in its new play, "The Unforeseen," the Frohman coffers will be further replenished.

FROM APRIL 4, 1903 ISSUE

CLEVELAND, O.

The Colonial Doing Splendid Business. Ethel Barrymore at the Opera House. Marie Dressler at the Empire.. Hanlon's Superba at the Lyceum. Other Theatres.

Colonial, (Mr. Marsh, Mgr.) The bill here this week is certainly strictly high class in every sense of the word. Camille D'Arville was warmly received. Mr. R. G. Knowles, monologist made a decided hit with his funny sayings. The rest of the bill is as follows: Merville, Booth & Elmore in The Two Juliets; Leonal Thurber, the Brothers Damm and the Three Rio Brothers in acrobatic acts; Henry Lee, held over from last week; Madison and Wayne in a good sketch. Everything now at this new house is moving in a smooth manner, business is exceedingly good.

Empire Chase's, (C. K. Stevenson, Mgr.) As a headliner, and as an excellent entertainer, we have Marie Dressler for this week. She is a very shapely woman, large and heavy, and her ways immediately captivate an audience. Victor Moore and Pearl Hight have a novel act in, Change Your Act. Le Page is a wonderful jumper; Billy Single Clifford has a fair monologue, the Carmen sisters, banjo players, are good, and especially the sketch presented by Eugene O'Rourke and Nellie Elfing, known as, Parlor A, amusing and interesting and very pleasing, winding up with the Sa-Vans in a laughable act. The show is good.

Opera House. Ethel Barrymore, surrounded by a company of capable artists, and plenty of good scenery, but with a play that doesn't suit the actress. She plays Carrots and a Country Mouse.

Marie Dressler is a very shapely woman, large and heavy, and her ways immediately captivate an audience.

FROM JAN. 9, 1904 ISSUE

Mrs. Lily Langtry gave an elaborate Christmas dinner to her company on Christmas Day at Atlanta, Ga., at the Hotel Piedmont. The dinner was served in the regular English style and all of the meats were brought in great portions just as they are brought from the great burning grills in the London chop shop houses. It was a very sumptuous dinner with all kinds of odd things in the way of trimmings and condiments and dishes made from recipes such as found round Charing Cross way or at "St. Jimmy's" or table d'hotes as far up as High Holburn. The chef became very much interested, naturally, and he made a number of most remarkable things, reaching from soups to English tarts and turnovers, and one of the company made the brandy sauce for the plum pudding from a recipe of his own which he insisted was used by Dr. Johnson and Oliver Goldsmith in the days when Cheshire Chese in Wine Office Court was young. Mrs. Langtry had a number of things to say which she said in the happiest way possible. And there were many responses made from members of the company. The gifts were plentiful to Mrs. Langtry. There were many beautiful bits of jewelry and gem studded ornaments for her dressing table from admirers in two hemispheres. Then there was a couple of grand pianos and two or three automobiles, more or less, and a host of things in between. But if there is anything in appearances, Mrs. Langtry enjoyed the messages of good will quite as much as any of the more pretentious affairs.

FROM MAY 30, 1903 ISSUE

NEW YORK.

Two Important Shakespearian Productions. All Star Performance of Romeo & Juliet. Adler The Yiddish Actor, to be seen as Shylock.

Romeo & Juliet will be presented on Monday night of this week, at the Knickerbocker Theatre, and for the week following, with a matinee on Saturday, under the direction of Liebler & Co. The cast of principals forms a group of players seldom assembled. There is already great interest to see Miss Eleanor Robson as Juliet, while Kyrle Bellew's Romeo, Eben Plympton's Mercutio and W. H. Thompson's Frar up of assured merit. Edwin Arden and Forrest Robinson will play "Paris and Benvolio." The Capulet will be George Clarke; the Montague, Frank C. Bangs; the Tybalt, John E. Kellerd, and the Peter, W. J. Ferguson. The production will be costly.

At the American Theatre, Jacob P. Adler . . . renders the role of Shylock in *The Merchant of Venice* in Yiddish, while the supporting company speak English.

Dan Daly will make his first appearance on the stage as a funny man, in a farce at the Herald Square Theatre this week, in Klaw & Erlanger's production of George V. Hobart and Edward E. Rose's new comic play, John Henry, founded on humorous incidents in Mr. Hobart's popular John Henry books. There is no music in John Henry. In English literature John Henry is the exponent of a new school of slang—not that of the slum, but of the bright up-to-date young American of good society and polite surroundings. It has three acts, the scenes representing the rotunda of a New York hotel, Dove's Nest Villa at Ruraldene, a New York suburb, and the railroad station at that place. Underlying its humorous side there is a very strong sentimental interest, developed by John Henry and Clara J., and "Bunch" Jefferson and Alice Gray, in which Uncle Peter and Aunt Martha Grant, relatives of Clara J., and Uncle William Gray, the uncle of Alice, become involved. The most comic complications of the piece revolve around Dove's Nest Villa at Ruraldene, purchased by "Bunch" Jefferson for the Countess Veccio, an Italian noblewoman.

An interesting dramatic event of this week is the engagement at the American Theatre of Jacob P. Adler as Shylock in The Merchant of Venice. Mr. Adler rendering the role in Yiddish, while the supporting company speak English. Mr. Adler has appealed more directly to the Hebrews of this city, in view of the fact that they were given in the Yiddish language entirely. Mr. Adler has achieved distinction and won high praise for his performances in Yiddish. In physique, bearing and manner, he is not unlike the late Charles Coghlan. His repertoire includes nearly 300 plays, ranging from lightest farce to heaviest tragedy. He was born in Odessa in 1855. Thirty years of his life have been spent on the stage.

Manager George H. Brennan announces a most elaborate production in the way of scenery costumes, properties and electrical effects These have been secured from the Augustin Daly estate. It was originally built by Augustin Daly and used by him during his revival of The Merchant of Venice at Daly's Theatre. His supporting company includes Russ Whytal, Meta Maynard, Elizabeth Woodson, James J. Ryan, Augustus Balfour, Guy Coombs, Sadie Handy, Victor M. De Silke, Robert C. Turner, D. E. Hanlon and George Morton.

FROM AUG. 29, 1903 ISSUE

PLAYERS

And The Productions In Which They Will Be Seen This Season.

The prominent actors and actresses will be placed as follows during the coming season.

Maxine Elliott starring under her own right in Her Own Way, by Clyde Fitch.

Kyrle Bellew in Raffles, a dramatization of The Amateur Cracksman.

Bertha Galland in Dorothy Vernon of Haddon Hall.

Wilton Lackaye in The Pit.

Viola Allen in Twelfth Night.

Richard Mansfield in either Ivan the Terrible or The Garden of Lies, or both. Heidelburg will be used for matinees.

E. H. Sothern in The Proud Prince.

Clia Loftus and Margaret Illington in support of Mr. Sothern.

William Gillette in The Admirable Crichton.

Julia Marlowe in H. V. Esmond's Fools of Nature.

Mrs. Le Moyne in a romantic play of Stanlans Strange.

James K. Hackett in an elaborate production of Alexander the Great.

Mary Mannering in Judith by Ramsey Morris.

Charles Hawtry in The Gordian Knot—probably.

Percy Haswell in the Favor of the Queen.

Sir Henry Irving in Dante, by Sardou.

Ethel Barrymore in Cousin Kate.

Orrin Johnson in Hearts Courageous.

Nat Goodwin in A Midsummer Nights Dream.

Henrietta Crossman in As You Like It. Later she will produce Mary Quite Contrary, by E. W. Pressly.

Nance O'Neil in Lady Macbeth.

Robert Edeson in Soldiers of Fortune. Later he will play The Captain's Interference, by Mrs. Robert Drouet.

Mrs. Langtry in Mrs. Deerings Divorce and The Cross Ways.

Chauncey Olcott in Terrence.

Alice Fischer in Mrs. Jack, until January.

William H. Crane in The Spenders.

Robert Drouet in Blannerhasset.

Amelia Bingham in the Canterbury Tales.

Sadie Martinit in Anna Kerenina.

S. Miller Kent in Fighting Bob.

Maclyn Arbuckle in The County Chairman, by George Ade.

Mildred Holland in The Triumph of an Empress.

Otis Skinner and Ada Rehan appeared in joint productions of Shakespeare's dramas.

Andrew Mack in The Middle of June.

Frederick Warde and Louis James in brief session in Alexander the Great.

Katherine Osterman in Miss Petticoats.

Walter Whiteside in We Are King.

Charles Richman in Captain Barrington.

Marie Tempest in the Marriage of Kitty.

John Drew in a comedy by Henry Arthur Jones.

Maude Adams in a comedy by J. M. Barrie.

William Faversham in The Light that Failed.

Adelaide Thurson in Polly Primrose.

Elsie De Wolfe, late in the winter, in a new Paris comedy.

Elizabeth Kennedy in As You Like It and Camille.

William Collier in a new comedy, Personal.

Edwin Milton Royle and Selma Fetter in My Wife's Husband.

Otis Skinner and Ada Rehan in joint production of Shakespeare's Dramas.

Henry E. Dixey will tour in The Fencing Master.

Ezra Kendal, another season in The Vinegar Buyer.

FROM NOV. 29, 1902 ISSUE

MME. DUSE'S VIEW OF HER ACTING.

Now, what does Signora Duse think of her playing? I had asked her about the pieces in which she is appearing this tour. She had refused to discuss them in any way. That was the domain of the critic. She was merely the actress—the instrument by means of which certain. There was, however, no reason why she should not state which role she preferred in the three dramas by Gabriele d'Annunzio, which form her present repertoire.

"It is Anna in 'La Citta Morta,'" she said. "That appeals to me more than the others. Why? I can't exactly determine. One can not always give reasons for a preference. One sees more in a certain role than in another. Anna, to me, is a creation of infinite pathos. She is sublime in her suffering. Indescribable woe is hers."

"The great joy has been given to me," said Eleanora Duse, "to enter into my roles from the moment I take them up, and to remain in them without effort to the end."

"Do you suffer as Anna suffers, when you are playing the part?" I ascked.

Signora Duse's reply was a remarkable one.

"The great joy has been given to me," she said, "to enter into my roles rrom the moment I take them up and to remain in them without effort till the end."

FROM JULY 30, 1904 ISSUE

WHAT THEY WILL DO THIS SEASON

Richard Mansfield will present a dramatization of Jack London's story, The Sea Wolf. The book is now in the hands of an able playwright.

Viola Allen will continue in Shakspeare, reviving A Winter's Tale, in which she will be seen as Hermoine and Perdita. She will retain Twelfth Night in her repertoire.

Lulu Glaser will be presented in a musical version of When Knighthood Was in Flower. It will be entitled The Madcap Princess. The music is by Ludwig Englander and the words Harry Smith.

Ethel Barrymore will start the season with Cousin Kate, later presenting a Chinese comedy by Mrs Fred Gresac entitled The Third Moon. It is adapted from the French.

Margaret Anglin will be launched as a star in The Eternal Feminine, by Robert Misch.

Fritzi Scheff will sing in Stanislaus Stange's new opera, The Queen of Hearts.

Henry Miller, with Hilda Spong as leading woman, will offer Joseph Entangled.

Ezra Kendall will appear in Weatherbeaten Benson, by E. E. Kidder.

Charles Richman has decided to present The Genius, the maiden effort of the DeMille Boys. He has already tried it. The De Mills are sons of Henry C. DeMille, author of The Charity Ball.

Mrs. Leslie Carter will be seen as Lady Macbeth.

Victor Herbert's new opera, The Enchanted Isue, will be produced early in the season at Boston.

Herbert Kelcey and Effie Shannon will be seen in the German military play Taps.

Amelia Bingham has decided to follow Mansfield's example and will go on tour with an extensive repertoire. Joseph Kilgore and Forrest Robinson will be in her company.

Wilton Lackaye will have The Pit as his principal offering, but will also have in his repertoire Othello, Pillars of Society, King Lear and a revival of Trilby, in which he will play Svengali.

Mr. Chas. Frohman's stars are scheduled as follows:

John Drew opens the season at the Empire in The Duke of Killicrankie and Miss Adams probably will follow him in Jenny. Miss Annie Russell will be seen at the Garrick in Brother Jacques and Mr. Faversham comes to the Hudson in Pinero's Letty. William H. Crane appears at the Criterion in Business Is Business and will be followed by Miss Virginia Harned in a new comedy. Miss Barrymore will appear at the Hudson Theatre in Sunday after her California trip. Later she will be seen in the Esmond play.

Francis Wilson, deserting musical comedy, will appear in a comedy without music early in November. Mrs. Gilbert is to star in the new Fitch play Granny. Henry Miller, after his western tour, comes to the Garrick in Henry Arthur Jones' play. Joseph Entangled. Miss Fay Davis will be seen in R. C. Carton's play, The Rich Mrs. Repton. William Collier, after opening the Criterion, will play The Dictator and On the Quiet at Wyndham's Theatre in London. William Gillette's new play is a comedy in four acts, with the scenes laid in the South. He will appear in it after his tour in The Admirable Crichton.

Mr. Frohman will begin work at once on the Sothern Marlowe tour, which opens Sept. 19 in Chicago. The opening production will be Romeo and Juliet. Miss Bloodgood comes to the Garrick Theatre in Clude Fitch's play, The Coronet of a Duchess.

FROM AUG. 20, 1904 ISSUE

NFW PLAY FOR DAVID WARFIELD.

David Belasco has put an end to the secrecy with which he has guarded the future plans of his star, David Warfield, by announcing that a new play to be called The Music Master and written especially by him, was to be put in rehearsal at once. The author is Charles Klein, although Mr. Belasco has supervised the work and added some striking stage effects of his own.

The report that Mr. Belasco was to risk his latest star in what is known in the vernacular as a "straight part" is unfounded. The Music Master will present him as a striking and familar type, said to be an Italian, in lower east side life. The story in which he will be the leading figure will have a strongly pathetic side.

This new attempt at character building will put Mr. Warfield to a crucial test. He is an actor of pronounced and unique ability, which approaches genius, but all his work heretofore, has been restricted to a very narrow range. His impersonations of lower east side Hebrew types were at first broadly humorous and designed for musical comedy, but Mr. Belasco discovered his marked serious side and placed him on the legitimate stage in The Auctioneer with great success.

Owing to the manner in which he has become identified with impersonations of the Hebrew type, it has been predicted that he would fail, or at least meet with small success in the protrayal of eccentric characters of other races. This year he will be put to the test, and upon the results his future will depend.

Minnie Dupree has been selected for the leading feminine role, and Marie Boles will have another of her eccentric Irish Roles. Other members of the company will be Antionette Walker, Isobel Waldron, Sybel Klein, Campbell Gollan, Archie Boyd and William Boog.

The New York production will be made at the Belasco Theatre on Monday, Sept. 26.

FROM FEB. 7, 1903 ISSUE

WM. H. CRANE AS "DAVID HARUM."

PETER PAN, J. M. Barrie's new five-act play, was produced for the first time tre, Washington, D. C., Tuesday, Oct. tre, Washington, D. C., Tuesday, Oct. 17, with Miss Maude Adams in the leading role. The company was cast as follows:

Peter Pan ....Maude Adams
Mr. Darling ....Ernest Lawford
Mrs. Darling ....Grace Henderson
Wendy Moira Angela Darling........
.... Mildred Morris
John Napoleon Darling....Walter Robinson
Michael Nicholas Darling..Martha McGraw
Nana ....Charles H. Weston
Tinker Bell ....Jane Wren
Tootles ....Violet Rand
Nibs ....Lula Peck
Slightly ....Frances Sedgwick
Curly ....Mabel Kipp
First Twin ....Katherine Kappell
Second Twin ....Ella Gilroy
James Hook ....Ernest Lawford
Smee ....Thomas McGrath
Starkey ....Wallace Jackson
Cookson ....William Henderson
Cecco ....Paul Tharp
Mullins ....Thomas Valentine
Jukes ....Harry Gynette
Noodler ....Frederick Raymond
Great Big Little Panther...Lloyd Carleton
Tiger Lily ....Margaret Gordon
Liza ....Anna Wheaton

The opening in a new play by Maude Adams, which of itself is always a matter of vast theatrical importance, becomes of more interest when the play is made to share high honors with the well known star.

FROM OCT. 29, 1904 ISSUE

LILLIAN RUSSELL SIGNS.

Lillian Russell's stage future is now assured as the noted actress has signed a contract with Sam Shubert for five years. The contract provides that Miss Russell is to be starred during that time in comic opera with what are regarded as the most satisfactory financial arrangements ever made by Miss Russell. Her first appearance under the new management will be in the opera, My Lady Teazle.

For months the question most frequently asked along upper Broadway, New York, has been, "Has Lillian Russell signed yet?" There was much vague inquiry as to her plans for the season, but there was no necessity for haste on her part, and her contract with Sam Shubert, came at the end of only a short period of preliminary negotiation.

Lillian Russell's first appearance under the management of Sam Shubert will be in the opera *My Lady Teazle* . . . a musical adaptation of *The School for Scandal*.

Miss Russell will make her first appearance under the direction of Sam Shubert and will appear at either the Casino or the Lyric. Owing to the sentimental considerations involved her appearance at the Casino will be arranged if there is any possible chance of securing an open date when the preparations for producing the opera in which she is to appear are concluded.

The opera is practically concluded, only a few changes being necessary to adapt the solo arrangements to Miss Russell. The lyrics have been written by John Kendrick Bangs, the book by Roderic Penfield, and the music by A. Baldwin Sloane. It is a musical adaptation of The School for Scandal.

Miss Russell will receive, it is understood, a percentage of the gross receipts and a weekly guarantee of $?,???. The exact amount of the guarantee has not been disclosed.

FROM DEC. 7, 1901 ISSUE

POINTED HINTS

Given By the Veteran, Joe Jefferson, On Stage Realism and Idealism.

St. Louis, Mo., Dec. 1.—Joseph Jefferson, the veteran actor, was the guest of honor at a banquet recently, tendered by the employes of the Parina Mills. He delivered an interesting address on stage realism and referred to a Chicago reporter's interview with him, in which he was quoted as saying that he was going to retire.

"I am going to answer some questions that have been asked during this luncheon," said Mr. Jefferson. "I have been asked my opinion of the two dramatic schools in Paris, one standing for realism and the other for idealism. Realism is carried to great lengths in Paris. If the part of a cook is to be played a real cook must be obtained to take the part. If a fire occurs in the action of the play there must be real smoke.

"One thing they can't have on the stage. That is a shipwreck. No theater would hold the necessary amount of water.

"Some one has asked me to-day why I don't bring my dog on the stage in 'Rip Van Winkle.' I answer that the dog must be suggested, rather than shown. Then each person in the audience can form his own idea of the dog. If I were to bring a real dog on the stage, one man would say, 'I thought Schneider was one of those dachschunds,' and another would say, 'Why, he ought to have been a Newfoundland dog for the part,' and, like as not, some one up in the gallery would whistle and off the dog would go. Anyway, he always would be wagging his tail at the wrong time.

"It would be natural and realistic for a man to sit on the stage reading a paper and never say a word, but I don't know how the audience would take it. Some of them might ask him what he was reading.

"Whistler once said, 'Nature sometimes comes up to art.' I believe in suggestion and imagination, rather than strained realism. 'Should an actor feel his part?' is another question asked. Coquelin and Irving take opposite sides of this, the former that the actor should feel nothing of his character and the latter that he should feel it to tears.

"I answer that it must rest with the actor. He should keep his head cool and his heart warm. As Shakespeare says, 'Let the whirlwind of your passion beget a temperance that shall give it smoothness.'

"I am asked to give the secret of the vigor which has enabled me to remain so long on the stage. It is largely good fortune, but so far as I can name other elements which have contributed to the result, they are sensibility, imagination and industry."

FROM DEC. 3, 1904 ISSUE

JULIA SANDERSON

With Fantana, now Enjoying a Record Run at the Garrick Theatre, Chicago.

FROM DEC. 5, 1903 ISSUE

ABOUT MANSFIELD.

An old letter written by the late Patrick Gilmore, the bandmaster, regarding Richard Mansfield, has just come to light. It reads as follows:

"I have known him (Mansfield) since he was a youth at his mother's home in London, and it was no surprise to me when I heard of his success on the stage in the Parisian Romance first, and afterward in Prince Karl. The son of such a mother could scarcely be anything except a genius. She was a magnificent woman and a great artiste; a dramatic singer of superb power and skill. When I was seeking artists for the Boston jubilee in 1872, Mme. Rudersdorf was recommended to me as the best exponent of oratorio singing, and I found her a superb artiste. She filled my idea of queenliness.

"His road to success was not an easy one, however. One would think that with an artiste mother the stage would be thrown open to him, but it was not. Mme. Rudersdorf, who was a Russian, while Richard's father was an Englishman, had no idea of devoting her son to art, but designed him for mercantile pursuits, and, having settled in Boston, put him to work. Business did not fit his ideal, and he began dabbling in drawing and painting, and showed so much talent that his mother sent him to Europe to pursue his art studies. The stage was his fate, however, and he spent more time in the foyer than in the studio, and finally determined to adopt the profession.

"His mother so strongly opposed this new venture that she cut off his allowance, and he was adrift in London without anyone to depend upon. He stayed there two or three years, with the entree to good society, but with devilish little in his pocket. He has told me that some days about all he ate was what he got from the spreads at receptions and parties. He is a capital entertainer, though, and was in great demand.

"One of his most intimate friends was a son of Hepworth Dixon, who did him several good turns. He got him into the company of a popular entertainer, but his first appearance was a dire failure. Stage fright and discouragement got the upper hand of him, and he failed. He was bounced. D'Oyly Carte had a competitive examination for a comic opera company to play the provinces in Pinafore; Mansfield tried for the captain's part.

"Gilbert and Sullivan and several celebrities were present at the examination and when it came to Mansfield's turn to sing he said he would sing a duet, and he did. He sang a soprano and barytone duet, and they kept him singing and imitating for half an hour. Carte had the part fixed for a friend, but a countess who had been an intimate friend of Richard's mother interposed in his behalf and obtained him the place. It was worth $15 a week, and he kept it until he struck for higher wages. That was treason. Then he went to New York, and I guess you know the rest."

FROM APRIL 27, 1901 ISSUE

Several weeks have passed, and Richard Mansfield has not been engaged in any "eccentric disturbances." Either Mr. Mansfield has experienced a change of heart and is trying to get along amicably with his fellow men or his press agent has overlooked some oddities which very often take a belligerent turn.

FROM DEC. 5, 1903 ISSUE

RICHARD MANSFIELD.

He Is Now Touring in Old Heidelberg, after a Successful New York Engagement.

FROM FEB. 6, 1904 ISSUE

MAXINE ELLIOTT.
Who is this Season Starring in the Latest Clyde Fitch Success
Her Own Way.

FROM FEB. 6, 1904 ISSUE

MISS MAXINE ELLIOTT.

Miss Maxine Elliott, who is starring this season in Clyde Fitch's new comedy, Her Own Way, under the management of Charles B. Dillingham, is noted as being one of the most classically beautiful actresses on the American stage. Miss Elliott was born in Rockford, Me., and went on the stage barely ten years ago, when she was still in her teens. She first applied to Manager A. M. Palmer, who gave her a chance to walk on as an extra girl, without lines, at his theatre. But even here Miss Elliott's commanding beauty and striking personality lifted her above the crowd, and she was given small parts. Afterwards she went to Daly's Theatre, and the late Augustin Daly advanced her rapidly. In 1896 Nat Goodwin selected her to go with him on his Australian tour, and while in the Antipodes the leading woman became ill and Miss Elliott played the

From this business arrangement a sentimental relationship arose between Nat Goodwin and Miss Elliott, which resulted in matrimony. . . .

leading roles. From this business arrangement a sentimental relationship arose between Mr Goodwin and Miss Elliott, which resulted soon afterwards in matrimony and a joint starring tour. This season Miss Elliott and Mr. Goodwin decided for the first time to try separate starring tours. Accordingly Miss Elliott became an individual star, under the management of C. B. Dillingham, and she has just scored the hit of the season in New York in Her Own Way. She will appear in Cincinnati in February.

FROM FEB. 13, 1904 ISSUE

ETHEL BARRYMORE

MISS ETHEL BARRYMORE.

Miss Ethel Barrymore, who is now in a very brilliant tour in the stellar role of Cousin Kate, is the daughter of Maurice and Georgie Drew Barrymore, and consequently the niece of John Drew and granddaughter of Mrs. John Drew, Sr. She was born in Philadelphia, Pa., and received her early education at the Convent of the Notre Dame. At the age of fourteen she left the convent and began to learn the theatrical profession in her grandmother's, Mrs. John Drew, Sr., company, then playing The Rivals. Next she played in The Bauble Shop, and then in Rosemary, after which she went abroad in The Secret Service Company. In London she joined Sir Henry Irving's Lyceum Theatre Company. After a short engagement she returned to this country to take a small part in the cast of His Excellency, the Governor. Her work was beginning to show her fitness for the profession, and she succeeded Miss Jessie Millward in the stellar role when this company went on the road. This was her first attempt as an interpreter of a leading role, and she made a success. She established herself as a star, and the next season Charles Frohman put her forth in the Clyde Fitch comedy, Captain Jinks, in which she essayed the stellar role for two seasons. Last season she won new laurels in the double bill of Carrots and A Country Mouse. Her vehicle this year has afforded her new conquests. Her New York run was remarkable, and the same can be said of her tour. Her season will close the first week in April, as Mr. Frohman has decided to present her in London in May.

DUSTIN FARNUM.
Whose work in The Virginian the past season has placed him among the stars of the first magnitude.

FROM JUNE 18, 1904 ISSUE

DUSTIN FARNUM.

Dustin Farnum, who has scored a decided triumph in the title role of The Virginian, has developed into a star of which even greater things may be expected. He was born in Boston, is twenty-eight years of age, and this is his seventh year on the stage. He began his career, in the way of principal parts, with Margaret Mather and was with her for a year and a half, playing Shakespearean roles. He then spent a year with different stock companies throughout the country, playing everything, mostly heavy parts, however. He next created the role of Chevalier Ramsay, in Marcelle, and after that went with Chauncey Olcott, remaining with him about a season and a half, returning after that to do stock work for a couple

> He has never before played a part like *The Virginian* . . . some of his experiences in the way of good tumbles from refractory horses make hair-raising stories, as he tells them.

of seasons. He has never before played a part like The Virginian and, surprising as it may seem, had never even attempted anything in the line of dialect parts before. In connection with this cow-boy role, it is rather a coincidence that he is exceedingly fond of horseback riding, having ridden many hundreds of miles, both in the West and in the East, and some of his experiences in the way of good tumbles from refractory horses make hair-raising stories, as he tells them.

With a view to constant improvement Farnum has, at the close of his regular season, often spent his summer in stock company engagements, for they not only afforded him the relief desired from the one part idea of his regular season, but gave him an opportunity for gaining facility in every line that does not persent itself in any other branch. When asked about his ideals as to the parts he would like to play in the future, Mr. Farnum said: "Of course I have them, but I haven't nerve enough to tell them to people just yet. Up to the present, however, this is my favorite role, so far as I have gone." Mr. Farnum's family are all more or less connected with the theatrical profession, one brother being in a stock company in San Francisco and his brother Will, having played the title role in Ben Hur for the last two years.

FROM JULY 30, 1904 ISSUE

LEW M. FIELDS.

One of the most prominent comedians now seeking histrionic fame is Mr. Lew M. Fields, who recently became the junior member of the firm of Hamlin, Mitchel and Fields. Mr. Fields has leased of Oscar Hammerstein the new theatre he is building on Forty-second-st., near Eight-ave., New York City. The new theatre is to be christened the Lew Fields' Theatre and the style of entertainment will be along the same lines as became so popular at Weber and Fields' Music Hall. The new theatre will be opened Thursday, Nov. 17, with a burlesque on Sweet Kitty Bellairs to be called Sneck Kitty Beware.

Mr. Fields was associated with Mr. Weber longer than any other two comedians ever cast their lot together. Their rise was simultaneous and their names will ever be linked together as a popular combination. Business now causes a separation and their attentions in the future will be cast in different directions.

The new theatre is to be christened the Lew Fields Theatre . . . the style of entertainment will be along the same lines as became so popular at Weber & Fields Music Hall.

Mr. Fields will be associated on the stage the coming season with Marie Cahill who also occupies a lofty position in theatrical circles. A strong company will support them. Extensive preparations are being made to provide the company with every minor equipment and no work nor money is being spared to provide the highest class entertainment in a palace specially provided with comfort giving conveniences.

LEW M. FIELDS
Actor, Producer and Manager. formerly of Weber & Fields.

GEO. M. COHAN,
Who will Star in Little Johnny Jones.

FROM AUG. 27, 1904 ISSUE

GEO. M. COHAN.

Mr. George M. Cohan, whose portrait appears on the title page of this issue of "The Bill board," will star this season in his newest musical play. Little Johnny Jones. In this tour he will be supported by one of the strongest musical organizations that was ever selected for a traveling company. It is also worthy of note that his father and mother, Mr. and Mrs. Jerry J. Cohan, will be in his supporting company. Among others will be Tom Ryan, Sam T. Ryan, Miss Ethel Levey, C. Jack Harrington, and others who will be announced later. A chorus of fifty pretty girls that can sing and dance will be carried with the show

. . . a chorus of fifty pretty girls that can sing and dance will be carried with the show. Mr. Cohan celebrated his twenty-sixth birthday, July 4, and is joyful over the prospects of the coming season.

Mr. Cohan celebrated his twenty-sixth birthday. July 4. and is joyful over the prospects of the coming season.

FROM MAGIC LANTERNS
TO MOTION PICTURES

FROM DEC. 15, 1900 ISSUE

PICTURE OF THE WAGON,

Birthplace of Animated Picture Machine ; built
by Burg & Sons, Burlington, Iowa ;
used by Bonheur Bros.
for 13 years.

FROM MARCH 19, 1904 ISSUE

BOSWELL, JR., STEREOPTICON, $20.

Price includes Two 4½-inch Condensing Lenses; one-half size Bausch & Lomb Objective Lens, and either Electric, Calcium or Acetylene Burner. The above Outfit will be shipped C. O. D. and allow examination at express office upon receipt of $2.00 to guarantee express charges.

Russia-Japan War—20 colored slides with lecture, $7.50.

Iroquois Theatre Fire—20 colored slides with lecture, $7.50.

Baltimore Fire—12 colored slides with lecture, $4.50.

We are the Largest Manufacturers of Stereopticon Goods in the World and **our prices are** the Lowest. We have no junk or second-hand goods to dispose of, but are **selling only** New, First-Class Goods that you can depend upon. Remember, we can save **you money on anything** in the Stereopticon and Moving Picture Machine line.

Boswell Electric and Optical Co., —1610— Michigan Ave. Chicago.

FROM APRIL 12, 1902 ISSUE

The Cheapest and Most Reliable
House in New York

FOR THE RENTING OF

Machines and Films

with or without operators.

A Large Stock of Machines, Films
and Slides always on hand. Send
for catalogue ALFRED L. HARSTU
& CO., 136 and 138 E. 14 Street,
New York, N. Y.

FROM DEC. 8, 1900 ISSUE

That great boon to the vaudeville manager, the biograph or motion pictures, by whatever name they are called, are now taking up mysticism, and the result is most wonderful, amusing and interesting. If they keep on making improvements with this machine it will be no wonder that the "waybacks" will declare it bewitched. It is claimed it is to be introduced into the lecture field to illustrate talks instead of the lime-tight stereoptican.

FROM APRIL 27, 1901 ISSUE

A Great Picture Machine.

The Edison Manufacturing Company has an announcement in this number of "The Billboard" which will attract the attention of those persons who are looking for money-making features. The Edison Projecting Kinetoscope is a moving picture machine which has a reputation of being the best made. It combines accuracy with brilliant and satisfying results. It is both a projecting machine and stereopticon, thus saving the extra expense of separate apparatus, and also the cost of extra light. Every detail of the Edison machine has been worked out with the greatest of care, and its simplicity is best shown by the fact that one person can work the whole machine. It can be packed in one case or in an ordinary trunk, and can be shipped as personal baggage. The take-up device winds up the film automatically while it is being exhibited, thus avoiding kinks, snarls or the possibility of fire. The lamp house is the most complete of its kind ever put on the market, and must be seen to be appreciated. It is planned for any illuminant known to moving pictures and stereopticon exhibits. There are many other points of superiority in the Edison machine which an intending buyer will realize on an examination of the catalogue of the 1901 model, and "The Billboard" advises all of its readers who are interested to send at once for this catalogue.

FROM MARCH 21, 1903 ISSUE

STEREOPTICON, $12.50

Complete with Electric, Calcium or Acetylene Burner.

Illustrated Song Slides, beautifully colored, 25c each. Hand Feed Arc Lamp, $3.50. Rheostat, $3.50. 4½ inch Condensers, 90c. We manufacture everything in the Stereopticon and Moving Picture Machine line, and will save you money. Write for confidential price list.

Boswell Electric & Optical Co., 1725 Wabash Ave., Chicago
After May 1st, 1610 Michigan Avenue.

131

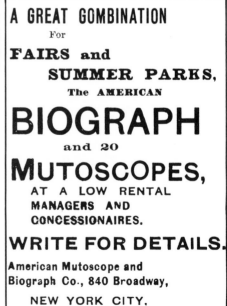

FROM JULY 11, 1903 ISSUE

EDISON FILMS

Send for New Film Supplement, No. 175, giving titles and descriptions of over One Hundred New Subjects. Following are a few of the latest: Shamrock III. and Sir Thomas Lipton's Fleet leaving Scotland, en route to America, Sleeping Beauty, The Enchanted Cup, Little Willie's Last Fourth of July, Happy Hooligan's Fourth of July, Blasting Rocks in Harlem, Washerwoman and Chimney Sweep, Soap vs. Blacking, Daylight Burglary, London Zoological Garden, Shooting the Rapids, Luna Park, Rattan Slide and General View of Luna Park, Mary Jane's Mishap, Glimpses of Venice, The Vatican and St. Peter's Church, Rome, Street Scene in Hyderabad, King Edward and President Loubet Reviewing French Troops, King Edward's Visit to Paris, Egyptian Fakir with Dancing Monkeys, Eating Macaroni in the Streets of Naples, Egyptian Boys in Swiming Race, Feeding Pigeons in Front of St. Mark's Church, Venice.

EDISON MANUFACTURING CO. MAIN OFFICE AND FACTORY, Orange, N. J., U. S. A.
NEW YORK OFFICE, 83 Chambers Street.

Office for United Kingdom: 52 Gray's Inn Road, Holborn, London, W. C., England. European Office: 32 Rempart Saint Georges, Antwerp, Belgium. Selling Agents: The Kinetograph Co., 41 E. 21st St., New York City; Kleine Optical Co., 52 State St., Chicago, Ill.; Peter Bacigalupi, 933 Market St., San Francisco, Cal.

FROM DEC. 3, 1904 ISSUE

....WANTED IMMEDIATELY....

For Ford & Wilson's Train Robbery Show

MOVING PICTURE

MACHINE OPERATOR.

Good treatment; salary rain or shine. No time to correspond; must join on wire. Address TOMMY WILSON, Great Train Robbery, Yazoo, Miss.

FROM SEPT. 17, 1904 ISSUE

Sensational Films.

THE STRIKE, 435 feet, Price, $52.20
INDIAN MASSACRE, 585 ft , " $70.20
Greatest Headliners since the Train Robbery.
THE GREAT TRAIN ROBBERY [Edison] $111.00

EUGENE CLINE & CO., - - 59 Dearborn St., CHICAGO, ILLS.

FROM JULY 18, 1903 ISSUE

WANTED

Picture Machine Operator. Must be capable of running with calcium or electric current, and must be an expert electrician. Will buy a few second-hand films. Address

H. SNYDER,

Champaign, Ill. - July 13-18.
Edwardsvilie, Ill. - July 20-25.

FROM SEPT. 24, 1904 ISSUE

WANTED
Great Train Robbery Film

BLACK TOP and PICTURE MACHINE. State all in first letter; write at once. CHAS. NAILL, Ferari Bros. Shows United.

Per Route:—Madison, Wis., Sept. 28 to Oct. 1; Cedar Rapids, Iowa, Oct. 3 to 9; Galesburg, Ills., Oct. 10 to 15.

FROM JAN. 30, 1904 ISSUE

WANTED

A Hustling Manager to put Big Life Motion Picture Show on the road, featuring
MR. BLUE BEARD,
(900 feet).
Reproduction of Chicago Fire Play; 15,000 feet of films; Illustrated Songs; Three Championship Fight Pictures, including Jeffries-Corbett. Liberal percentage.
DAN CONNORS, care "Billboard."

FROM AUG. 29, 1903 ISSUE

WANTED

Picture Machine Operator and Pianist.
ALSO
SINGER.

Address H. SNYDER, - Winchester, Ill
Until Aug. 29.

FROM JULY 23, 1904 ISSUE

SHOWMEN, LOOK!

WANTED WANTED

MOVING PICTURE SHOW featuring Trip to the Moon or Great Train Robbery. GLASS BLOWER'S SHOW.

Good Plantation, or can use good show other than electric theatre. Want addresses of JOE MARTINTET, DOC JACOB EDMONDS, WINDY HUGHES. All Privileges, $10.00, except Confetti and Novelties. No exclusives come on.
WM. H. SWANSON GALA WEEK AMUSEMENT CO., Mannington, W. Va., July 18-23.

W. H. SWANSON, Genl. Mgr.   D. G. HARTMAN, Bus. Mgr.   DOC N. C. WATTS, Genl. Contractor.

FROM OCT. 29, 1904 ISSUE

All our Films
Come With
Red Titles,
and Show our
Trade Mark.

TRADE MARK

PATHE FILMS.

SELLING AGENT:
KLINE OPTICAL CO.
CHICAGO.

LATEST NOVELTIES

12 CENTS PER FOOT.

Come and Look at Our Original Films and You Will Never Buy "Dupes."

We Recommend Our Great
Series of Biblical Subjects

The Passion Play	-	1410 feet
Joseph sold by his Bros.		623 feet
Sampson & Delilah	-	459 feet
The Prodigal Son		475 feet
The Strike (A Social Drama)	-	442 feet
Indians and Cowboys (Attack On a Coach)		590 feet
Annie's Love Story,	-	754 feet

Christopher Columbus	-	869 feet
Tour in Italy	-	787 feet
Barnum's Trunk	-	410 feet
Outlook on Port Arthur		131 feet
Ascending Mount Pilate		508 feet
Wrestling Donkey	-	114 feet
Japonaiserie	-	262 feet
Around Port Arthur	-	246 feet
Fantastic Fishing	-	98 feet
Fight on Yalu	-	131 feet
Ruffian's Dance	-	131 feet
Drama in the Air (Sensational)		196 feet

Nest Robbers	-	164 feet
Dogs and Cats	-	65 feet
Opera Hat	-	82 feet
Butterfly	-	114 feet
Boar Hunt	-	328 feet
Falls of Rhine	-	131 feet
Across the Alps	-	164 feet
Park in Barcelona	-	131 feet
Orla and His Dogs	-	147 feet
Japanese Ambush	-	131 feet
Greedy Cat	-	82 feet
Bathers at Joinville		131 feet

PATHE CINEMATOGRAPH CO.,
42 East 23rd Street, - - NEW YORK.

FROM MARCH 19, 1904 ISSUE

FILMS FILMS FILMS

Carnival Conpanies and Others Take Notice.
We have the FEATURE Films for you
This Season.

Japanese-Russian War Films
WE HAVE THEM

Torpedo Boats Attacking Port Arthur, Length 75 ft.
The Attack on Port Arthur,   -   "   100 ft.
Battle at Entrance to Harbor of Chemulpo "   100 ft.

Send for list and full description of these wonderful films.   Write at once and
don't delay order.   Don't forget we have the best and only Moving Picture
Machine that will make good and stand hard knocks without getting out of
order.   Send for description of the New Polyscope.

THE SELIG POLYSCOPE CO.,
43-45 Peck Court, Chicago, Ill., U. S. A.
H. H. BUCKWALTER, Gen. Western Agent,   -   DENVER, COLO.

FROM OCT. 15, 1904 ISSUE

BOLD BANK ROBBERY

The Greatest Production in 30 Motion Tableaux.

Length, 600 Feet.   **Price, $66.**

Send for Illustrated Catalogue, which contains
30 Half Tones and Full Description.

Lubin's 1905 Exposition Model Cineograph and
Stereopticon combined, together with Electric
Lamp, Adjustable Rheostat and Calcium Light,
                   $75.00

Two Cineograph Films (100 ft. each), 200
ft. films at $11.00 per 100 ft. - - **$22.00**

Two Monarch Records, playing the music
for the above Cineophone, Films $1. each   **$2.00**

TOTAL,   **$99.00**

With this Outfit Complete for $99.00 we will give

Free of Charge Victor Talking Machine,
complete, including horn
and sounding box. This
Victor Outfit is the latest improved model and could
not be purchased at retail for less than $37.50.

S. LUBIN,

23 South Eigth Street. PHILADELPHIA, PA.

FROM AUG. 27, 1904 ISSUE

PICTURES THAT SPEAK.

An Interesting Combination of the Cinematograph and Phonograph.

An apparatus which combines the cinematograph and phonograph, so that a moving picture of the human figure seems to talk, has been perfected in France and is described by La Nature. To accomplish the desired effect, it was necessary to connect the two systems by a combined transmission absolutely automatic. Of the two systems, the cinematograph requr's the greater power, the phonograph being actuated by a minute force in comparison. Therefore, while the vibrations of the figure movement may vary considerably without notice, a slight change in the speed of the phonograph materially affects the pitch of the vocal reproduction. The inventors appealed to electricity for a solution of the problem, with ready and perfect success.

The motor which controls the cinematograph is composed of a stationary inductor of the Gramme ring form, divided into a number of sections; the other member is a Siemens coil. When a current from an electric source is sent successively through the different sections of the inductor, the Siemens bobbin presents its poles, successively, in front of each of the section receiving the current, and rotates under its influence. But the current is sent to the inductor by a distributor, which may be some distance apart from the other apparatus. The distributer is formed of contacts, arranged on the shaft of phonograph, which successively touch the fixed brushes, each of which is connected to one of the sections of the inductor.

Necessarily, the motor of the cinematograph is absolutely dependent on the movement of the phonograph axle, and perfect synchronism must be had, positive and absolutely automatic, in order to render the illusion as perfectly lifelike as possible, and make the sounds from the phonograph appear to come from the lips of the image on the opaque screen. The phonograph should be concealed behind the representation. The connecting cable between the two instruments has not proved detrimental to the perfect success of the combination.

The next step in advance is already in the dreams of inventors, and we shall not be surprised at any time if some one of the color schemes should be attached, contributing to the screen representation a still further lifelike character.

FROM MAY 28, 1904 ISSUE

COLORED FILMS

THE NEW DISCOVERY

THE SUPREME NOVELTY IN MOVING PICTURES.

SEND FOR SAMPLE FREE

ALL OUR LIFE MOTION PICTURES are now put through the new process of artistic color effects, the brightest tints are used in making the pictures more lifelike than ever before. The effect is magnificent, and the monotony of one colored moving picture is done away with. * * * * * * * * * * * * * *

PRIDE SAME AS BEFORE.   **NO EXTRA CHARGE FOR COLORED FILMS.**

II Cents, Per Foot; 100 Feet $II

"THE SLEEP WALKER'S DREAM," Beautifully Colored in 4 Tints. . . . .200 ft. $22.00
"THE FIGHT on the BRIDGE BETWEEN RUSSIA and JAPAN," Colored 50 ft. $5.50
"KING OF SPADES" (Comic), Colored. . . . . 85 ft. $9.35
"DIFFICULTIES OF THE RUSSIANS' ADVANCE IN KOREA," Colored. .100 ft. $11.00
"THE WINDOW WASHER" (Comic), Colored. 42ft. $4.62
"SCENES ON EVERY FLOOR" (Comic) Colored. . . . . .390 ft. $42.90

The Great Port Arthur Naval Battle (COLORED) $22. 200 feet.

====ALSO 500 NEW SUBJECTS.====

When ordering Films please state whether plain or colored ones are wanted.

☞ALL SUBJECTS ALSO IN 50ft. LENGHTS.☜

====SPECIAL INDUCEMENT.====

We will give one of these remarkable colred naval battle films, 200 feet long, and one of our Celebrated

1904 Exhibition Model Cineograph, with Stereopticon Combined, including a Calcium Lamp, Electric Lamp, and and a Adjustable Rheostat, for $75.00.

THIS OFFER IS GOOD FOR ONE WEEK MORE.

Here is an opportunity to obtain a complete moving show for a small price.
Be Quick The Time is Short. Big and
easy money will be made with Colored films.

S. LUBIN,

Largest Manufacturer of Life Motion Machines and Films, Philadelphia. Pa.

A CAPSULE HISTORY

To identify individual show business areas see two-letter code descriptions below:

AP —Amusement Parks
BU —Burlesque
CA —Carnivals
CH —Chautauqua
CI —Circus
FA —Fairs
MI —Minstrelsy
MO —Motion Pictures
MU —Music
NC —Night Clubs, Supper
        Clubs, Cabarets
RA —Radio
RE —Recordings
SH —Showboats
ST —Stereorama and
        Panstereorama
TH —Legitimate Theatre
TV —Television
VA —Vaudeville
WA —Wagon Shows

1894

William H. Donaldson and James F. Hennegan publish first issue of *Billboard,* November 1. It is called *Billboard Advertising* and treats entertainment enterprises — such as traveling dramatic shows, circuses, et al. — only tangentially because they are major users of outdoor billboard advertising.

MO/TH/VA Novelist Alexander Black combines stereopticon slides — heretofore used to illustrate lectures — with drama and produces a "picture play" about *Miss Jerry,* a female reporter. By projecting slides illustrating the story line (at the rate of four slides a minute) he gives the illusion of movement. Black is considered by some historians to be the father of the photoplay and was known on the lyceum lecture cricuits as "the picture-play man."

TH Sam Shubert buys the road rights for New England and New York to a Charles Hale Hoyt play, *A Texas Steer,* with money borrowed from J. W. Jacobs, a Syracuse haberdasher, and Jess Oberdorfer, a foundry owner.

MO The Holland Brothers open the first Kinetoscope Parlor at 1155 Broadway in New York marking the official start of the motion picture business. Edison has invested approximately $24,000 in the project from 1887 to 1894. The Hollands have ten kinetoscope machines. In less than six months the "wizard's" peep show machines are pulling in money in parlors all over the U.S. and Europe. Each machine holds fifty feet of film.

MO Heavyweight boxing champion, Gentleman James Corbett, signs the first exclusive star contract with the Kinetoscope Exhibition Company (a Latham-Rector-Tilden firm) which owned six peep-show machines. A fight was staged and timed to last six one-minute rounds, so that each round could be shown on one of the machines.

RE Thomas MacDonald, Columbia Phonograph Company engineer, develops a hand-wind spring motor for the graphophone. Columbia markets this new machine for eighty dollars, less than half the price of earlier phonographs.

RE Berliner hires a Columbia Phonograph record producer, Fred Gaisberg. In addition to a number of unknown performers, Gaisberg signs two leading entertainers of the era, singer George Casken and Monologist Russell Hunting, to make flat disks for the Gramophone Company.

1895

TH Seven powerful figures in the theatre decide to form a combine to bring order to the chaotic conditions then existing. They are Charles and Daniel Frohman, Sam Nixon, Alf Hayman, J. F. Zimmerman, Marc Klaw, and Abe Erlanger. They control a majority of theatres in key cities, as well as production, plays, and actors. The company is called Klaw and Erlanger and becomes the theatre's trust. Erlanger runs the operation.

TH David Belasco presents Mrs. Leslie Carter in *The Heart of Maryland,* his own play. It is his first success as an independent producer and makes Mrs. Carter a star.

CI The *Cleopatra* spectacle is presented by the Ringling Brothers. The cast of 1,250 includes 300 dancers, 500 mounted soldiers, 200 foot soldiers, plus every animal in the show's menagerie. Such spectacles are a major feature of the big shows of the day.

MO Grey and Otway Latham of Northcliffe, Va. hold a press showing of the Pantoptikon, a moving picture projection machine, at 35 Frankfort Street in New York. A month later they introduce it at their store show at 153 Broadway, New York.

MO Thomas Armat runs a test of his projection machine, the Vitascope, in his shop in Washington, D.C. In September it is exhibited at the Cotton States Exposition in Atlanta, Ga. The machine is publicly promoted as an invention of Edison's (with his permission) because of the commercial value of his name.

MO Louis and Auguste Lumiere of Lyon, France, demonstrate their Cinematographe, a screen projection machine, in December and present the first commercial showing in Paris at the Cafe Grand.

MO Robert Paul of London completes work on his screen projection machine, the Theatrograph, and shows it to the Royal Institution in February, 1896.

RE Berliner organizes Berliner Gramophone Company, licensed by his own U.S. Gramophone Company.

RA In Bologna, Italy, young Guglielmo Marconi sends and receives the first wireless signals across the large Marconi estate.

RE By the end of this year a syndicate of Philadelphia businessmen buy stock in the Berliner Gramophone Company for $25,000, giving the flat disk firm badly needed financing.

RE Prevented from making phonographs or cylinders by legal entanglements resulting from North American bankruptcy, Edison develops a spring-driven motor for phonographs. He sets up the National Phonograph Company to sell the new spring-driven machine and cylinders as soon as legal matters are settled. The phonograph reaches the market a year later and sells for forty dollars.

1896

CI James A. Bailey acquires the Adam Forepaugh Circus, and arranges partnership with the Sells brothers, to combine the Forepaugh and Sells shows. The move is dictated by the rapid growth of Bailey's competitors, the Ringling Brothers.

VA "The Trocadero Vaudevilles," ten European novelties — starring Sandow, the strong man, and comedian Billy Van — are a hit variety company playing the Grand Opera House in New York in a show "conceived, organized and promoted by F. Ziegfeld, Jr."

MO The Thomas Armat Vitascope makes its debut at Koster & Bial's Music Hall in New York. The first bill features brief film glimpses of the Butterfly Dance, the Skirt Dance, a boxing bout and "Kaiser Wilhelm reviewing his troops." By the following year screen-projected movies are showing in every big city in the U.S. and abroad.

VA/MO Vaudeville theatres, in increasing numbers, add the Vitascope to their programs. Described as "life-size photographs projected upon a screen and going through movements so natural that it is difficult to believe they are not living persons," Vitascope is billed as Edison's Latest Marvel, though it was invented by Thomas Armat in Washington, D.C.

MU Twenty-nine-year-old Amy Marcy Beach is the first American woman to write a symphony, *Gaelic Symphony.*

MO In a one reel film May Irwin and John C. Rice repeat a scene from their Broadway show *The Widow Jones* — a kissing scene. *The Kiss* shocks audiences everywhere and is a big hit.

RE Berliner organizes the National Gramophone Company, to sell gramophones and flat disks. Sales manager for the new company is Frank Seamon. Hired to develop overseas operations is William Barry Owen.

RE With many local phonograph firms, once affiliated with the defunct North American Phonograph Company, now tied up by law suits and with Edison similarly handcuffed, Columbia Phonograph takes a big lead in record industry. It issues a catalog, offering more than a thousand selections on cylinders, and introduces a new graphophone to sell for fifty dollars.

1897

Billboard Advertising changes its name to *Billboard.*

TH The Shuberts buy the road rights for the entire U.S. to *The Belle of New York* from Charles Lederer for $8,000. They make big profits touring the show and also make theatre owner friends across the country who prove to be invaluable allies.

TH With the financial backing of Oberdorfer and Jacobs, the Shuberts buy their first theatre, the Bastable Theatre in Syracuse; Sam is the manager. The brothers build a new theatre, the Baker Theatre, in

Rochester. Erlanger makes a deal to book their theatre with top attractions for only five percent. He uses the deal to whip the leading theatre in town, the Lyceum, into line. He makes a new, more profitable deal with the Lyceum and reneges on his deal with the Shuberts.

CI Barnum and Bailey Circus goes to England and Europe and plays in major cities for five uninterrupted years, until 1902.

MO According to film historian Kemp Niver, Marc Klaw and Abraham Erlanger produce the first American film with a story line, *The Passion Play,* this year. Utilizing a new process for restoring and making copies of heretofore undiscovered paper prints registered with the Library of Congress by Klaw and Erlanger, Niver — in a 1977 book — claims that the Klaw-Erlanger film should supercede *The Great Train Robbery* as the first movie to tell a story. This is not generally recognized.

MO The first heavyweight championship prize fight between James Corbett and Bob Fitzsimmons is filmed by Edison films for screen projection. At ringside, three specially designed Enoch Rector cameras are used for the filming.

MU "Harlem Rag," written by Tom Turpin, is the first published ragtime tune.

RA The Marconi (wireless) Company is organized in England.

RE Berliner Gramophone Company makes deal with Camden (N.J.) machine shop operator Eldridge Johnson to manufacture handwound gramophones to retail for twenty-five dollars. The new gramophone, along with shellac disks instead of rubber disks, make the Berliner records totally competitive to the Columbia and Edison cylinders. The flat versus cylinder record is under way.

RE William Barry Owen sets up the Gramophone Company, Ltd. in England as nucleus for Berliner's European operations.

RE Among early performers to make flat disks are George Gasken, Thomas Butt, Tom Wooly, Ed Francis and Will Nankerville.

1898

WA Approximately 150 wagon medicine shows are still traveling various sections of the country.

TH Bob Cole writes *A Trip to Coontown,* the first black musical comedy to depart totally from the basic minstrel format. Cole is a black and his effort is a milestone step for blacks in American show businesses.

TH Marion Cook, black composer, writes *Clorindy, the Origin of the Cakewalk,* a black revue. It is the first production based on ragtime and black dance routines to play Broadway.

CI Ringling Brothers lease one of the most popular competitive circuses of the day, the John Robinson Circus, but the Robinson family takes back control after one year.

RE Edison introduces a home phonograph to sell for twenty-five dollars, and begins to compete successfully with Columbia. Both firms are still selling machines which play cylinder disks.

RE Gramophone Company launches branch operations in Germany, Austria, and Russia. The German organization is Deutsche Gramophone.

1899

VA George M. Cohan has a dispute with B. F. Keith and vows never to play a Keith-Albee house again. Neither he nor any member of the Cohan family ever does.

TH The Shuberts acquire the Grand Opera House in Syracuse and lease the Wieting, giving them total control of the city's theatres. They also take over a theatre in Utica.

TH/MO William S. Hart, first of the great cowboy superstars, plays Messala in a stage production of *Ben Hur.* Hart at that time specialized in Shakespearean roles.

RA Marconi transmits first wireless signals across the English Channel.

RE Johnson's Consolidated Talking Machine Company issues an improvement in flat disks over Berliner's earlier zinc records. The Johnson disks, called Improved Records, are wax recording blanks, thinly coated with graphite to conduct electrical current. The new records, featuring such stars as Dan Quinn, Sousa's Concert Band, basso Geroge Broderick and the Haydn Quartet are very successful.

RE In the course of a complicated series of legal actions involving the Tainter-Bell and Berliner patents and other matters, Seamon and Berliner split; Berliner is restrained from making Gramophones; Johnson sets up his own Consolidated Talking Machine Company; Seamon joins Columbia Phonograph Company.

1900

Bill Donaldson acquires Hennegan's interest in *Billboard.* Donaldson's policies now broaden the publication to include all entertainment fields. Beginning in May, *Billboard* goes from monthly to weekly.

TH The Shuberts lease the Herald Square Theatre at 35th St. & Broadway, New York. It is considered a "jinx" theatre — too far uptown. In spite of that, they book Richard Mansfield to play the house, assuring a successful run. They make another deal with Erlanger and the trust and cut them in for twenty-five percent.

TH Another hit, Augustus Thomas's *Arizona*, makes the Herald Square one of the most successful houses on Broadway. The show stars Kirk LaShelle with a young actor named Lionel Barrymore in a bit part. The play also sets off a vogue for "westerns" in drama, fiction, etc.

TH At the Bastable Theatre, Syracuse, Sam Shubert suggests to coatroom attendant that he keep a saucer filled with dimes and quarters on the coatroom counter. If people ask whether there is a checking charge, the coatroom attendant is to say "No, never in a Shubert theatre, but if people don't ask, and see the saucer, then . . ."

TH New York is star-struck this year. Among the acclaimed "star turns" are William Gillette in *Sherlock Holmes;* Richard Mansfield, whose revival-repertory includes *Dr. Jekyll and Mr. Hyde;* Julia Marlowe in *Barbara Frietchie;* and Sarah Bernhardt in *L'Aiglon.*

TH David Belasco discovers Blanche Bates and stars her in *Naughty Anthony* and as Cho Cho San in *Madam Butterfly.*

TH Olga Nethersole stars in *Sappho,* written by one of the day's most popular playwrights, Clyde Fitch; she is arrested for appearing in an "indecent" play.

TH The famous Floradora Sextette introduces "Tell Me Pretty Maiden" in the musical hit, *Floradora.*

VA B. F. Keith, E. F. Albee, F. F. Proctor and handful of other theatre owner/managers form the United Booking Office. Proctor drops out within a year, and Albee becomes the dominant operator of the combine. UBO takes five percent of the ten percent commission that acts must pay and adds an additional two and a half percent for collecting the agents' five percent. Contracts permit cancellation anytime at sole discretion of house manager up to the third performance. Many routes are poorly booked at an act's cost. The acts rebel.

VA William Morris opens his own booking office at 102 East 14th Street, New York. He is the only independent agent successfully bucking the United Booking Office.

VA The White Rats, an actors union, is organized by George Fuller Golden. Seven other founding members are Dave Montgomery, Fred Stone, Sam Morton, Tom Lewis, Sam J. Ryan, Mark Murphy and Charles Mason. Gypsy Dolan, on tour at the time of formation, attends the next meeting and is considered a charter member.

VA White Rats strike against managers, but disloyalty of many actors and fear of the managers' blacklist quickly defeats the fledgling actors' union.

RE Berliner establishes "His Master's Voice" as registered trademark for gramophones. He purchases the Francis Barraud painting of dog with his ear cocked at gramophone speaker horn.

MO Movies have become a standard entertainment commodity in museums, arcades, and vaudeville theatres but the public is beginning to tire of their sameness (vaudeville acts, circus turns, scenic views, etc.).

1901

By October of this year Bill Donaldson has launched complete departments in *Billboard* that cover dramatic stock and repertoire, music and opera, minstrelsy, vaudeville, burlesque, circuses, carnivals, street fairs, and amusement parks.

TH New York is the number-one theatre city with forty-one legitimate playhouses, a world record.

TH The Shuberts (Sam and Jacob) go into their own productions. Sam opens a play at the Herald Square and Jacob another at the Baker in Rochester. These are the first of what would be more than 1,000 Shubert productions of over 600 individual plays and musicals.

TH Making their debuts in New York as stars this year are twenty-one-year-old Ethel Barrymore in Clyde Fitch's *Captain Jinks of the Horse Marines;* David Warfield in *The Auctioneer;* and William Faversham in *A Royal Rival.*

TH Among the successful shows this season are *When Knighthood Was In Flower* with Julia Marlowe; Richard Mansfield in Booth Tarkington's *Beaucaire;* John Drew and his nephew, Lionel Barrymore, in *The Second in Command;* Maude Adams in *Quality Street; Under Two Flags* with Blanche Bates; and Ada Rehan in *Sweet Nell of Old Drury.*

RE Rudolph Wurlitzer Company introduces a new coin-operated music machine, The Tonophone, via an ad campaign in *Billboard.*

RA Reginald Fessenden conducts first successful experiments with transmission of a human voice.

RE Berliner and Johnson reunite to form the Victor Talking Machine Company. Berliner contributes his patents and owns forty percent of the company stock; Johnson brings in his thriving Camden plant and owns sixty percent of the stock.

1902

TH David Belasco, who has been paying the trust fifty percent of his plays' earnings, tires of this; he files suit against the trust demanding an accounting and charges them with anti-trust violations. His attorney

is Samuel Untermeyer, one of the Shubert backers.

TH Shuberts take over Theatre Comique on 29th Street and the Casino Theatre on 39th Street to give them four houses in Manhattan.

TH The Shuberts buy American rights to the English hit, *Chinese Honeymoon,* and open it at Casino Theatre. It is their first smash hit and tours the entire country successfully after its New York run.

TH England's George Arliss makes his New York debut with Mrs. Patrick Campbell's company and later appears with Blanche Bates in her hit *The Darling of the Gods.*

TH Blanche Ring introduces "In the Good Old Summer Time" in the musical *The Defender.* It was written by George "Honey Boy" Evans and Ben Shields.

MO The first science fiction movie, *A Trip To the Moon,* is filmed by George Melies in France. An ex-magician, Melies invented many special effects with and for the camera.

RE Fred Gaisberg, American record producer for HMV (His Master's Voice), records ten songs with Enrico Caruso in Milan, Italy. Caruso is paid one hundred pounds sterling for the recording — the largest sum paid a performer to that date. The records are released in London in May timed to tie in with Caruso's live concert at Covent Garden. These records account for the huge rise in sale of phonographs, until then considered a toy rather than a device for legitimate musical entertainment.

MO The Electric, the first motion picture theatre, opens April 16 on Main Street in downtown Los Angeles. More nickelodeons, most of them narrow stores with rows of chairs and a pianist to accompany screen action, are opened around the country. By 1907 there are 5,000 movie theatres in the U.S. Patrons are mainly blue collar, many illiterate. The Electric, owned by Thomas Tally, charges ten cents for "a vaudeville of motion pictures lasting one hour."

RE Victor Talking Machine Company and Columbia Phonograph Company pool all their player and record patents.

RE Victor begins importing Red Seal records made in various countries in Europe with leading operatic and concert stars. First Red Seal record made by Gramophone Company, Ltd. in Russia with basso Feodor Chaliapin. Records are very expensive for times, $5 each.

RE Johnson designs the tone arm for players. It shifts most of the weight from the surface of the record to the chassis of the machine. It not only improves sound quality, but reduces wear on record.

1903

CI Barnum and Bailey present one of finest forty-horse teams ever seen. Forty-horse teams previously featured with Dan Rice Circus (1873); Yankee Robinson (1866); and as early as 1848, with the Spalding and Rogers Circus. The Barnum and Bailey team is driven by Jim Thomas with two assistants.

TH The Shuberts make their first New York real estate buy, the property opposite the Casino Theatre on 39th Street, running from 107th to 113th.

TH Erlanger approaches the Shuberts and offers them the trust's best rate for participation, only twenty-five percent of any Shubert show and the minimal fee for booking all the shows in the Shubert theatres which now number about ten. The offer is attractive to the Shuberts and they sign. Shortly after contracts are signed Erlanger insists a new clause be added in which Shuberts agree they will not buy, lease, or erect any more theatres of their own. The Shuberts refuse.

TH The Iroquois Theatre, Chicago (playing *Mr. Bluebeard,* starring Eddie Foy) burns down in middle of holiday matinee performance; 602 people are burned or crushed to death. It is a trust house and newspapers across the country denounce Erlanger and the trust and insist on new safety laws for theatres.

TH This is the year of the musical and two of the biggest are *The Wizard of Oz* and Victor Herbert's *Babes In Toyland.*

TH Fritzi Scheff deserts the Metropolitan Opera to make her Broadway debut in the operetta *Babette.*

TH John Barrymore, formerly a commercial artist, makes his New York debut in Clyde Fitch's *Glad of It.*

RE First Red Seal records on Victor are recorded in a studio at Carnegie Hall, New York.

MO Marcus Loew, Adolph Zukor (both furriers), and Mitchell Mark become partners in a penny arcade on 14th Street in New York. Their firm is called the Automatic Vaudeville Company, and the peep show, kinetoscope movie machines are one of their best money-makers. Stage star David Warfield, a friend of Loew's, joins them in setting up additional arcades in Boston, Newark, and Philadelphia.

MO Harry Warner and his brothers open the Cascade Theater, a ninety-nine seat store, in their home town of Newcastle, Pa. The chairs are rented from a local funeral director and must be returned on burial days.

MO The success of Edwin Porter's Edison Film, *The Great Train Robbery* (which runs eleven minutes) sets the standard film length of one reel — from eight to twelve minutes long. This film revives interest in motion pictures, and also creates a role-model for western movies for years to come.

MU Scott Joplin writes the first ragtime opera, *A Guest of Honor.*

RE C. G. Childs, Victor record producer, begins to record many opera stars at the company's studios in Carnegie Hall. In order to hold on to the exclusive services of major artists, he institutes a system whereby they are paid a royalty on each record sold. It is the first royalty arrangement in the record business and is not adopted widely, nor in popular records for many years.

1904

MI Lew Dockstader and his partner, George Primrose, agree to disagree and Dockstader forms his own minstrel company.

TH Sam Shubert offers Erlanger use of the Shubert house in Chicago until the Iroquois can be rebuilt; Erlanger accepts. Two weeks later, Erlanger forces trust member Nirdlinger (now named Nixon) to pull out of Shubert production, *The Girl from Dixie,* which he is helping to finance. Shubert is furious at this new double cross.

TH The Shuberts set up new arrangements with their first politically influential and extremely wealthy associates, attorney Samuel Untermeyer and general financier Andrew. Freedman. Among other properties, Freedman owns the New York baseball Giants and is part of a group building the IRT subway. The arrangement allows the Shuberts to make deals they could never make before.

TH George M. Cohan becomes a star in *Little Johnny Jones,* which he also wrote. His score includes "Give My Regards to Broadway."

TH E. H. Sothern and Julia Marlowe play together for the first time in Shakespearean repertory, winning much acclaim for their *Romeo and Juliet.*

TH Ethel Barrymore appears in *Sunday* and utters her famous line "That's all there is, there isn't anymore." Other hits include Dustin Farnum in *The Virginian; Mrs. Wiggs of the Cabbage Patch;* and David Warfield's durable vehicle *The Music Master* produced by David Belasco.

MO Loew takes his money out of the Automatic Vaudeville Company and he and Warfield open another arcade of their own on 23rd Street. This firm they call the People's Vaudeville Company.

MO *Bold Bank Robbery,* produced by Sigmund Lubin, is featured in *Billboard* Oct. 15 in an ad offering the 600-foot film for sixty-six dollars plus a free RCA Victor Talking Machine if buyer also purchases two **Cineograph** films, plus "two Monarch records playing the music for above." This was one of several early experiments in synchronizing film and phonographs to produce "talking" pictures.

MO For the first time a well known stage star, Kyrle Bellew, agrees to appear in a movie, *A Gentleman of France,* a drastically condensed version of one of his stage vehicles.

MO The first chase scene is featured in *Personal,* a Biograph movie directed by Wallace McCutcheon. Plot concerns the (then) infamous personal ads in the *New York Herald.* Policemen, workmen, and others are involved in a wild chase scene at the end.

RA John Fleming perfects a glass-bulb "detector" of radio waves in England.

RE Until this date all flat records have been cut on one side only. Odeon in Berlin introduces first disks recorded on both sides.

RE The first two-sided disks are placed on the market in the United States by Columbia, retailing for a dollar and a half.

PART THREE

1905–1918

1905 Lee and Jake Shubert form the Shubert Theatrical Corporation, the first serious challenge to Klaw-Erlanger legitimate theatre syndicate.

1906 Earthquake and fire wipe out San Francisco's entire theatrical district. When smoke clears, show business goes on in tents.

1906 Shubert-sponsored Sarah Bernhardt tour (226 performances) grosses over $1,000,000, a record for its day.

1906 Eldridge Johnson introduces the Victrola, first phonograph with playback horn enclosed in body of machine, and turntable and tone-arm covered by a lid.

1907 Florenz Ziegfeld produces his first Follies.

1907 Edwin Porter gives D. W. Griffith (then called Lawrence) his first job in motion pictures as a ten dollar per day actor.

1907 DeForest Radio Telephone Company inaugurates broadcasts in New York City.

1907 Ringling Brothers buy Barnum and Bailey Circus for $410,000.

1908 D. W. Griffith directs his first movie, one -reeler *Adventures of Dolly.*

1908 Movie trust, the Motion Picture Patents Company, is formed.

1908 Columbia Phonograph Company releases first two-sided records.

1909 Griffith hires Mary Pickford, age sixteen, as $10 per day actress for Biograph.

1912 Adolph Zukor, Edwin Porter, and Joe Engel buy American rights to French-made four-reel film starring Sarah Bernhardt. It is first big ticket ($1) multiple-reel film hit.

1912 Columbia discontinues cylinder records; only Edison still makes them. Flat records have won battle versus cylinders.

1912 Federal government passes laws requiring licenses to broadcast.

1912 Young David Sarnoff, manning wireless at Wanakmaker's department store during sinking of *Titanic*, achieves first public recognition.

1912 Charlie Chaplin signs his first film contract with Mack Sennett's Keystone Company for $150 per week.

1912 Joint venture of Chicago *Tribune* and Selig Film Company produces first movie serial, *The Adventures of Kathlyn.*

1913 Palace Theatre opens in New York, becoming mecca of two-a-day vaudeville.

1913 Dance craze sweeps the nation.

1913 Edwin H. Armstrong invents radio feedback circuit.

1915 Charles Frohman, legendary producer-manager of the theatre, dies when German submarine sinks the *Lusitania.*

1915 D. W. Griffith produces and directs his masterpiece film, *The Birth of a Nation.*

1915 Ohio political boss George Cox dies; he was world's largest single owner of theatrical real estate.

1915 David Sarnoff, working for American Marconi, submits a proposal to manufacture "radio music boxes." Company rejects proposal.

1917 The Shuberts buy out the George Cox estate and surpass the Klaw-Erlanger combine as the most powerful trust in the theatre.

1917 First Pulitzer Prize for drama goes to a light comedy, *Why Marry?*

1917 Chaplin signs $1,075,000 contract with First National Pictures, a new producing company formed by exhibitors.

1917 Navy takes over all radio equipment and activity as U.S. declares war on Germany.

OF TRUSTS AND STARS

The first census in 1790 said there were 3,929,000 people in America. The 1910 count showed 91,972,266, fifteen million more than a decade earlier. In the depression year of 1907 a new immigration record was set: 1,285,349 men, women and children came from Europe and other foreign lands. The first ghettos scarred the faces of the larger cities. There were great extremes of ugly poverty and obscene wealth. The affluent and the upper-middle classes found their pleasures in the theatre and, in growing numbers, in vaudeville. The lower-middle class—and particularly the uneducated, non-English speaking poor—patronized the nickelodeons and the most moderately priced traveling outdoor shows, parks, and fairs.

A COSMIC CUE

The tempo of the times increased at a dizzying rate. Like a symbolic cue from the gods, Halley's Comet zoomed across the skies in 1910, the first visit of the fireball since 1759. The Wright brothers got their airplane off the ground at Kitty Hawk, N.C., in 1904. In an Edison film of tests the Wrights made for the Federal Government in 1909, they flew at speeds of forty-two miles per hour during a sustained ten-hour flight. That same year Henry Ford introduced his Model T. Within two years millions of Americans were bumping and rolling around the countryside.

While Benjamin Franklin in the eighteenth century had spent a *mal de mer*-ish two days at sea trying to get from Boston to Philadelphia, in 1905 a Pennsylvania Railroad or New York Central train could make the New York to Chicago run in eighteen hours. Both these rail lines introduced their fast trains in June of that year. In the first week of their runs, they each had wrecks; nineteen people were killed.

Two venerable old stars of the theatre, Maurice Barrymore and Joseph Jefferson III, died in 1905. Barrymore's children, however, were in good hands. Their uncle, John Drew, and producer-manager Charles Frohman guided their careers with affection and expertise. The same year that their father died, Ethel, John and Lionel all appeared on the same bill at the Criterion Theatre in New York. Ethel and John starred in *Alice-Sit-By-the-Fire*, the first play on the program; and Lionel appeared in *Pantaloon*, the evening's second drama.

PRODUCERS AND STARS, NEW AND OLD

Joseph Jefferson's son, Thomas, played in his father's classic, *Rip Van Winkle* that same year. Charles Frohman and his brother Daniel were two of the leading producer-managers of the day. David Belasco wrote and produced a string of successful plays, developing stars as he went. A teen-age girl named Gladys Smith worked for him. When she entered the infant movie industry in 1909 she became known as "Little Mary," derived from her new stage name, Mary Pickford.

George M. Cohan was the popular king of Broadway with an astonishing string of musicals and dramas, featuring some of the most memorable songs ever written—a number of which he recorded. Sarah Bernhardt not only continued as one of the brightest stars of all time but also expanded her influence to the American and world theatre, into the burgeoning vaudeville area, and to the bumbling but increasingly popular motion picture field.

A BATTLE OF THEATRE GIANTS

In 1905 the legitimate theatre was still the most prosperous segment of American entertainment. The dominant behind-the-scenes force continued to be the Klaw-Erlanger combine. Erlanger was more powerful than ever, and he ruled with an iron fist. The decade to come, however, was to witness one of the most incredible developments of a new ruling group, and a classic struggle between two giant show business organizations for control of the theatre.

Early in 1905, Sam, Levi (now Lee) and Jacob Shubert formed the Shubert Theatrical Corporation with a couple of new partners. They were George Cox, Republican leader in Cincinnati and a wealthy real estate operator, and Joseph Rhinock of Kentucky, a rich speculator and financier. Another important man in the company was the Shubert attorney, William Klein.

SEPT. 5, 1908 ISSUE   MARK KLAW AND ABRAHAM ERLANGER

In a relatively short time, by mid-1905, the Shuberts had already acquired thirteen theatres, and held contracts with some of the leading actors and composers of the day. With this new political power and financing they intended to accelerate their expansion. In May, they learned that the Duquesne Theatre in Pittsburgh was available. Sam decided to rush to Pittsburgh and close a deal for the house immediately. The fast new trains were the speediest way to go. And the time-saving, efficient procedure was to take the night train. You slept on the train, did your business first thing in the morning, got on another train and were back on Broadway before anyone even realized you'd left. Attorney Klein and another New York theatrical man, Abe Thalheimer, accompanied Sam on the trip.

TRAGEDY ON THE NIGHT TRAIN

Some time before midnight near Harrisburg, Pa., Sam Shubert, his colleagues, and most of the other passengers were asleep (or trying to sleep) in their berths on the rocking, clattering train. No one could say which came first: the three successive loud blasts, like amplified cannon shots, or the furious fire which, all at once, enshrouded most of the cars on the passenger train.

Newspaper reports later explained that the passenger train had been running at an excessive speed when it hit a jutting portion of a car on a work train which was loaded with dynamite. The dynamite exploded on impact, and within seconds large sections of both the passenger train and the work train were ablaze.

Sam Shubert was pinned in his lower berth. The crash had battered him into bleeding semi-consciousness. Abe Thalheimer staggered through the smoke and flames to Sam's berth, and after a struggle managed to free him. He dragged Shubert to the side of the track and covered Sam with his coat, and went back into the train and rescued Willie Klein, who was injured and burned, but not seriously.

They took Sam Shubert to the Commonwealth Hotel in Harrisburg. He lapsed into a coma. His brother, Lee, was in London opening a new theatre. Jacob rushed to Harrisburg with his mother and other members of the family. Shortly after they arrived, at nine-thirty in the morning, Sam Shubert was pronounced dead. He was thirty years old, although the newspapers listed his age at twenty-seven.

NO DEAL WITH DEAD MEN

Sam and his brother, Lee, had been extremely close. When Sam's will was probated, it was discovered that he left his entire estate to Lee. Lee and Jacob reacted differently to Sam's death. Lee was determined to sell out and get out of show business. Jake was determined to drive ahead, more aggressively than ever. Lee made the decision. He went to Abe Erlanger, the head of the theatrical trust and told him that the Shuberts would make any reasonable deal for their holdings. Only one condition had to be met. Sam had made a deal with David Belasco, guaranteeing Belasco's shows bookings in certain cities. Erlanger would have to honor Sam's agreement with Belasco.

As mentioned earlier, Belasco was one of the independent producers who fought the Erlanger combine most aggressively. At the time of Lee's visit to Erlanger, Belasco had a lawsuit pending against Klaw and Erlanger.

Erlanger stared stonily at Lee Shubert as Shubert detailed the Belasco deal.

"I don't honor dead men's contracts," said Erlanger.

Without another word, Lee Shubert left Erlanger's office. He became even more determined than the aggressive Jake to buck the Erlanger forces. The brothers worked eighteen to twenty hours a day, seven days a week. In 1906, Lew Fields—no longer partnered with Weber, but a star actor-manager in his own right—left Erlanger to sign with the Shuberts. E. H. Sothern and Julia Marlowe also left the Erlanger Trust to join the brothers.

INCREDIBLE SARAH'S INCREDIBLE TOUR

But the biggest triumph of all for the Shuberts in that year came with the booking of one of the most remarkable women who ever lived—in the theatre or anywhere else at any time. Sarah Bernhardt was sixty-one years old in 1906.

She looked thirty. She was a Parisienne of such charisma and talent that despite being unable to speak English (her manager, Frank Connors, served as interpreter), and acting solely in French she was an international favorite. She was as great an entertainment and cultural legend in the United States—she had made her New York debut in 1880—as in France. Her private life was as spectacular as her performances.

It is a measure of her power as a star that she became a focal point in key events in American entertainment in three separate and major areas of show business: the legitimate theatre, vaudeville, and motion pictures. We will come back to the latter two in due course. Now, in 1906, she was to embark on one of her several American "farewell" tours for the Shuberts.

ANOTHER ANTI-ERLANGER CAMPAIGN

Erlanger was enraged. He issued a loud and clear edict to all houses who had signed with the Klaw and Erlanger Trust that if they played Bernhardt, they were through forever as far as the trust was concerned. Never again would they get a single act or show from the trust! The Shuberts were delighted. The newspapers across the land still had vivid memories of the Iroquois holocaust. Encouraged by an alert Shubert press department, headed by Channing Pollock, they now began to run stories and editorials castigating the monstrous Erlanger trust for trying to deprive the American people of seeing one of the great cultural performances of the time, the divine Sarah.

In one northeastern city, where the trust controlled every theatre, the Shuberts requested permission from the Mayor to play the show in the City Hall. Erlanger's people protested that public facilities should not be used for the private gain of the Shuberts. The Mayor and the City Council denounced the Erlanger trust, and turned the City Hall over to Madame Bernhardt and her troupe.

In a southwestern city, where Erlanger controlled all the houses, the Shuberts rented a large circus tent from the Barnum and Bailey Circus. The tent held almost three times as many people as the largest theatre in town. And every seat in the tent was sold, at the same prices as would have been charged for theatre tickets. The Shubert publicity people, of course, lamented to the press that they were forced to make the great woman work in a tent because of the ruthless attitude of Abe Erlanger.

MADAME'S MILLION-DOLLAR GROSS

The fact was that on subsequent stops on the tour, even in cities where a theatre was available, the Shuberts would claim they were barred by the trust and were forced to present Madame Bernhardt in a tent. The tour was the most spectacularly successful of any made by a theatrical star in that era. The sixty-one-year-old French woman played 226 performances and grossed over $1,000,000. She got more than $300,000 of the million, and richly deserved it. The

AUG. 10, 1907 ISSUE   LEE SHUBERT

Shuberts made a huge profit and garnered publicity they could not buy at any price, depicting them as the guys in the white hats, tilting with the mighty and monstrous bad men of the syndicate.

Less than two years after Sam's death, Lee and Jake Shubert had built a minor empire that seriously threatened the long-entrenched Klaw and Erlanger group. They owned and/or controlled over a hundred theatres and a substantial amount of real estate. They had contracts with a number of leading producers, and they, themselves, produced twelve shows in 1907, a record number. They had more than one hundred employees. And they had just taken over the largest theatre in New York City, the Hippodrome, on a lease that cost them more than a quarter million dollars per year. All this activity was organized into thirty corporations by attorney Klein. Lee Shubert held the controlling vote, fifty-one percent or more, in each of the thirty corporations.

ALBEE AND THE VAUDE TRUST

By 1907, vaudeville was coming ever closer to challenging the theatre as America's most popular and lucrative form of entertainment. The Vaudeville Managers' Association—which had been formed in 1900, and out of which had evolved the United Booking Office—was now in almost complete control of one man, E. F. Albee. Albee's partner,

PRICE 10 CENTS
THEATRES ~ CIRCUSES
FIFTY-SIX PAGES.
FAIRS ~ MUSICIANS

The Billboard

America's Leading   Theatrical Weekly
REGISTERED IN UNITED STATES PATENT OFFICE.
Volume XVIII. No. 35.   CINCINNATI NEW YORK CHICAGO   September 1, 1906.

SEPT. 1, 1906 ISSUE   DAVID BELASCO

B. F. Keith, was in semi-retirement, and Albee had been running not only the Keith-Albee operations but masterminding the control and/or absorption of one regional or rival vaudeville theatre chain after another. His dictatorship in vaude matched and, in some ways, surpassed that of Erlanger in the theatre.

The United Booking Office booked all the acts, not only in its own theatres, but in hundreds of other theatres around the country. Albee virtually held the destiny of thousands of acts in his hands. The UBO took a five percent commission on the salaries of the acts it booked. It took an additional two and one half percent for collecting a second five percent for the individual booking agent involved.

It moved acts in and out of theatres around the country with no other consideration than what was most desirable for the theatre owner or manager. Performers' contracts provided they could be cancelled any time through the first three performances. Thus, if an act were playing "two-a-day," it could be cancelled after the first performance of the second day, without notice or penalty payment of any kind; if the house policy was three-a-day or continuous performance, the act could be cancelled on the first day.

Frequently acts were routed poorly. An act would play a week in an eastern city, then be required to fill a week in a midwestern town, then come back to do two weeks in another eastern city that neighbored the first eastern town. The act was required to pay the excessive transportation costs involved in such helter-skelter routing. Agents were never penalized. The theatre managers never picked up a penny in travel costs. The control held by Albee also tended to keep performers' prices down to sensible levels (with the exception of a handful of developing stars), unlike the sky-rocketing talent costs brought about by the Erlanger-Shubert rivalry in the theatre.

WILLIAM MORRIS BUCKS THE TRUST

Only one man seemed to give the Keith-Albee vaude trust any problems at all. He was William Morris, an independent booking agent, promoter, and sometimes manager-producer. He somehow retained booking contracts with some of the key theatre chains of the day, notably the Percy Williams and the F. F. Proctor groups of theatres. He was well-liked and respected by countless numbers of acts of all kinds from standard attractions to stars. However, in 1906 Proctor had dropped Morris and signed with Albee, and in 1907 Albee brought out the Percy Williams theatres.

Erlanger and the Shuberts were aware of all this. They liked what they saw in the fast-growing vaudeville field, and in mid-1907 they went into business together. The lust for power and money has often made strange bedfellows. Erlanger and the Shuberts formed the United States Amusement Company to produce vaudeville shows with capital of about $100,000,000. Its president was Abe Erlanger, and its vice president, Lee Shubert. They signed William Morris to a contract as their chief booker for five years at $200,000 per year.

In 1904, the budget for the entire bill at the number-one vaude house in New York, Willie Hammerstein's Victoria Theatre, was $1900 per week. The shows Morris began to book into U.S. Amusement-owned houses were soon costing up to $10,000 per week. That was what he spent to put together a show at the Chestnut Street Opera House in Philadelphia. The theatre was a few doors up the street from the B. F. Keith Chestnut Theatre. The Keith house tried to buck the Erlanger/Shubert theatre by boosting their advertising budget to $1500 per week. The Opera House upped theirs to $3000 per week.

Within three months Morris had signed United States Amusement Company contracts for $1,500,000 worth of acts. The entertainment sections of the newspapers also carried stories saying the U.S. Amusement was going into a new multi-million dollar theatre building program. It may be assumed that Albee was becoming concerned, as perhaps were Erlanger and the Shuberts.

AN ALBEE/ERLANGER/SHUBERT DEAL

The country was in a serious depression, which seemed to be getting worse by the day. Theatre grosses were dropping alarmingly. Inasmuch as the machinations of moguls, since time immemorial, have been planned and executed in rooms behind closed doors (today carefully checked for bugging), it is impossible to say precisely what brought about the sudden demise of the United States Amusement Company.

Six months after it was formed, Albee, Erlanger and Lee Shubert met and, with their appropriate attorneys and aides, worked out this arrangement:

In return for liquidating their company and for Erlanger's and Shubert's agreement to stay out of vaudeville for the next ten years, Albee would take over and honor the $1,500,000 in talent contracts to which U.S. Amusement Company had committed itself.

Albee would also pay to Erlanger and Shubert $250,000 in cash (presumably to be split between the two).

Albee would agree to hire William Morris as chief booker for the United Booking Office at up to $50,000 per year.

When Erlanger reported the deal to Morris, the agent told him what he could do with his United Booking Office proposal. He would not work for Albee under any circumstances. He also tore up his U.S. Amusement contract and threw it in Erlanger's ample lap—much to the tycoon's relief.

No one can say who benefitted, and to what degree, from the Erlanger/Shubert fling in vaudeville. It is a fair guess that several hundred performers did. In the meantime Erlanger and the Shuberts went back to their own war in the world of the theatre, all the time keeping an eagle eye on the rest of the entertainment business. Albee went back to dominating vaudeville more aggressively than ever before.

ALLIANCES AND MISALLIANCES

Lee Shubert tried, within the limits of a twenty-four hour day, to have a hand in any and every area of show business in which a reasonably honest dollar could be made. In 1908 he made his first deals with Marcus Loew, a struggling pioneer in the movie business. He leased four unprofitable Shubert theatres in upper Manhattan and the outer reaches of Brooklyn to Loew, who converted them into "electric" theatres showing movies. Two years later Loew formed a corporation called Loew's Theatrical Enterprises. With capital of $5,000,000, it had on its board Lee and Jake Shubert and their backer Joe Rhinock, as well as Loew's friend, Joe Schenck.

Shifts in alliances were common. In 1910, William Brady, a highly successful legitimate theatre producer, left Klaw and Erlanger and formed a new company with the Shuberts. That same year the independent arch-enemy of Abe Erlanger—the bosom buddy of the Shuberts—none other than David Belasco, left the brothers and signed on with Erlanger.

JULY 20, 1912 ISSUE   SARAH BERNHARDT

In 1916, one of the Shuberts' most influential partners, George Cox of Cincinnati, died. His will revealed that he was the largest single holder of theatrical real estate in the world, and that he was a major stockholder in almost every Shubert enterprise. In 1917, the Shuberts bought the Cox estate for $10,000,000. The deal was partially financed by Joe Rhinock. By 1918, Lee and Jake Shubert had exclusive booking contracts with more than forty independent theatrical producers. At the same time they, themselves, were producing a larger number of shows than any other producing combine in theatre history.

SHAW ON INDEPENDENTS AND TRUSTS

George Bernard Shaw had a number of plays produced in America in the first two decades of the twentieth century. Among them were *Mrs. Warren's Profession*, which was closed by the police as being too naughty; *You Never Can Tell*; *John Bull's Other Island*; *Candida*; and, much later, *Pygmalion* with Mrs. Patrick Campbell as Liza Doolittle.

During the time when the Klaw and Erlanger trust reigned supreme, and the Shuberts were considered struggling trust-busters, Shaw was asked his opinion of the situation in America.

A playwright has three choices, he said. *He may have his work produced by some obscure speculator, seedy, illiterate, shabby and opportunistic; or by a municipal theatre, politically run for and by Puritans, to whom thought is frightening; or by the trust—organized, financed, competent, and competed with by rival managers like Belasco or the Shuberts, whose anti-trust is nothing but a new trust.*

By 1918 the Shuberts were a theatrical empire such as the theatre had never seen. People other than Shaw called them the new trust.

Their power was based on the same solid foundation as that of the Erlanger syndicate, Albee's empire, and other controlling combines still to come: ownership and/or control of the show places (i.e., the theatres) and the facilities. But no customer ever walked up to a box-office and laid down hard cash to look at a bare stage, or even one populated by untalented amateurs. The Shuberts and other show business moguls learned early that control of outstanding creative talent—from producers through stars, writers, directors, set designers, et al.—was a most important, even if secondary, step to dominance in the entertainment industry.

ROMANCING THE CREATIVE TALENT

These moguls spent as much time, brain power, and money cultivating such talent as they did developing profitable property transactions. They utilized whatever devices served best in each individual case. They threw lavish parties for, and bestowed elegant gifts on, certain stars and managers. When necessary they cut a major talent or manager in on a lucrative real estate or other business deal. They gave superstars a percentage of their gross, all the while maintaining the right to do the arithmetic by which the percentage was ultimately determined. In some cases they even named a theatre after a star—e.g., the Ethel Barrymore Theatre. They specialized in loaning money to improvident stars who have always lived beyond their means.

The Shuberts made a success of their first New York theatre—the Herald Square on 34th Street (considered by the shrewdest people of the day as an out-of-the-way jinx house)—by flattering Richard Mansfield into starring for them.

BELASCO'S PLAYS AND THE FROHMANS

David Belasco probably was the Shuberts' single best weapon in the days when they desperately needed his shows for their houses. His plays were excitingly staged, and he developed some of the leading stars of the day. In 1905 he starred Blanche Bates in *The Girl of the Golden West,* which he wrote as well as produced. Puccini wrote an opera based on this Belasco work five years later. Mrs. Bates also starred in the Belasco play *The Darling of the Gods.* Among the showman's other hits were *Adrea,* starring

NOV. 18, 1911 ISSUE   ETHEL BARRYMORE

Mrs. Leslie Carter; *The Rose of the Rancho,* with Frances Starr; Nance O'Neill in *The Lily;* and Gladys Hanson and Milton Sills in *The Governor's Lady.* Mary Pickford worked for Belasco in her teenage years before she ever made a motion picture.

Probably the key factor in enabling the Klaw-Erlanger combine to dominate the theatre for so many years were the Frohman brothers, Charles and Daniel. Charles, the younger of the two, was a total theatre man, incredibly able and tireless. He owned and operated theatres in New York and London. In an average Broadway season he produced approximately twenty-five plays, calling upon the talents of 800 actors. He was manager for some of the most powerful box-office names of the day: Maude Adams, Marie Doro, Otis Skinner, John Drew—and Drew's niece and nephews, Ethel, Lionel and John Barrymore. Frohman managed their careers shrewdly, developing them in vehicles carefully selected to fit their performance capabilities.

In 1907 Frohman starred Marie Doro in *The Morals of Marcus.* In 1908 he cast Maude Adams in the lead of *What Every Woman Knows* by James Barrie. In that same year, among two dozen shows, he also starred Otis Skinner in *The Honor of the Family,* and Ethel Barrymore in W. Somerset Maugham's *Lady Frederick.*

FAREWELL AT THE PIER

To the younger Frohman, the theatre was the only legitimate form of entertainment. He frowned on vaudeville and held the budding movie industry in complete contempt. In 1911, he included in his contracts with each of his artists a clause expressly forbidding them to make films. The year 1914 was one of his busiest and most successful. Maude Adams starred in another Barrie play, *The Legend of Leonora*. John Drew did two shows that season. He co-starred with his niece, Ethel Barrymore, in a revival of *Scrap of Paper* and later with Helen Hayes in *The Prodigal Husband*.

But 1914 was to be the producer-manager's last season. Frohman was one of the 1,198 people who died when a German submarine sank the *Lusitania* on her way back to New York from London.

Daniel Frohman, nine years older than his brother, began his career as business manager for the Madison Square Theatre in New York. Although he, too, produced many plays, he was interested in other areas of show business as well. He was a key element in the multiple reel feature breakthrough in the film industry in 1912.

YOUNG GEORGE M. AND MR. KEITH

The actor-manager who was the most popular of all the stars of the day was George M. Cohan. Cohan had almost literally been cradled in a trouper's trunk. As a youth, he worked in vaudeville with his father, Jerry; his mother, Helen; and his sister, Josephine. In the years from 1897 through 1899, the "four act" played eight weeks each year for B. F. Keith's houses. At the end of the third year—when they had completed twenty-two of their twenty-four total weeks—they arrived in Boston to play their last two weeks at the Keith theatre. The act was so strong that in the three years since they signed the Keith contract, their salary had increased threefold. When George, then twenty years old, went to the theatre to check the act's billing, he discovered they were bottom-lined instead of top-lined, as they had been across the country for the entire previous year.

Cohan went to see Keith to straighten the matter out and was unceremoniously brushed off. He vowed that no Cohan would ever play a Keith house again and none did. A couple of years later, young George and the family left vaudeville and moved into the legitimate theatre. As mentioned earlier, George's *Little Johnny Jones*—featuring "I'm a Yankee Doodle Dandy" and "Give My Regards to Broadway"—was a 1904-1905 hit.

GET-RICH-QUICK COHAN

From that time on, George M. wrote and/or produced (with partner Sam Harris) and/or acted in a new play almost every year. In 1906, it was *George Washington, Jr.* In 1908, he and the entire family were reunited in George's play *The Yankee Prince*. The biggest hit of the 1910 season was *Get-Rich-Quick, Wallingford*. George did not act in it, but he wrote the play, and he and Harris produced it. It ran for 428 performances. That same year, the prolific young showman took *The Yankee Prince* on the road and did a land-office business with tickets selling at a five-dollar top. It was a price only leading stars of the day could command.

Get-Rich-Quick was followed by *The Little Millionaire* in 1911 and *Broadway Jones* in 1912. In 1913, George wrote a mystery farce called *Seven Keys to Baldpate* and it was a smash hit. Three years later Artcraft Films released it as a motion picture.

Many of Cohan's songs were the big hits of their day. In addition to "Give My Regards to Broadway" and "I'm a Yankee Doodle Dandy," several others were "You're a Grand Old Flag"; "Mary, It's a Grand Old Name"; and (as America went to war against Germany in 1917) "Over There," which literally became the nation's war song.

After his experience with Keith in the family's vaudeville days, Cohan never made a long-term alliance with any trust. He and his partner, Sam Harris, not only produced shows on Broadway, but they formed their own music publishing company and operated other entertainment enterprises.

So popular was Cohan as an entertainer that Marcus Loew offered him $10,000 per week to return to vaudeville in Loew's Theatre at a time when expensive stage presentations were being offered along with motion pictures. Cohan rejected the offer. He did make phonograph records for the Victor Talking Machine Company, at a price approximately ten times what the company was paying its top artist, Enrico Caruso.

MUSIC AND CHORUS GIRLS

Cohan's light, bright song and dance approach to entertainment, briskly mixed with cocky patriotism, was precisely what the audiences of the day demanded. Musicals were bigger than ever. Beauteous chorus girls found much employment. In the spectaculars at the New York Hippodrome they worked in an ingeniously designed underwater tank. In Jake Shubert's musical, *Lady Teazle*, in 1905, eighty-six lovely young ladies earned eighteen dollars per week displaying their charms. In 1907, Flo Ziegfeld produced his first *Follies*. The cast included Helen Broderick, Grace LaRue, Emma Carus, Harry Watson, Jr. and a horde of befeathered, bespangled show girls.

The biggest musical hit of 1907 (and destined to become an all-time classic) was Franz Lehar's *Merry Widow*. Another classical musical was produced in 1917, when Jake Shubert presented Sigmund Romberg's *Maytime*. It was so popular that a second company was formed to play it at the 44th Street Theatre, in addition to the original company's performances at the Shubert.

In 1918, brother Lee produced a musical "turkey" called *Over the Top*, starring Justine Johnson, a young lady with whom he was romantically involved. The single virtue of the show was a young dance team, Fred and Adele Astaire, who had worked as a child "two act" in vaudeville and were making their Broadway debut.

Perhaps the best indication of the preference of audiences for light fare was the fact that in 1917 the first Pulitzer Prize for drama was awarded. It went to a frothy comedy, *Why Marry?*, written by a short story author, Jesse Lynch Williams.

SOME SERIOUS THEATRE

There was some serious theatre. George Bernard Shaw was consistently produced. In 1916—the year of William Shakespeare's 300th anniversary—*Macbeth, The Merchant of Venice, The Merry Wives of Windsor, The Tempest* and *King Henry VII* were all presented on Broadway.

The Provincetown Players were organized on Cape Cod, Massachusetts, in 1915. Among other works, they offered the first plays (one-acters) of Eugene O'Neill. That same year the Washington Square Players were formed at the Band Box Theatre in New York, and three years later Lawrence Langner and other Washington Square founders organized the Theatre Guild. Two other serious groups were a band of millionaires and their wives—the Astors, the Vanderbilts, Otto Kahn, et al.—who formed the New Theatre, and a bunch of theatrically inclined social workers who created The Neighborhood Theatre. The former's presentations leaned toward Louis Calvert, Pedro de Cordoba and Beatrice Forbes-Robertson. The latter presented, as its maiden effort, a play dealing with the revolutionary movement in Russia.

No one paid it too much attention in 1906, but a Reverend Thomas Dixon wrote a play called *The Clansman,* which opened at the Walnut Street Theatre in Philadelphia. It caused riots similar to those which had developed earlier at certain showings of *Uncle Tom's Cabin.* We will hear more about *The Clansman* under another name, and in another show business sphere, some nine years later.

In one corner of the nation in the Far West in 1906, a classic example of the credo that the show must go on took place. It was the San Francisco earthquake and fire in which every theatre in the city was destroyed. The smoke had hardly blown into the Pacific, the embers hardly cooled, when showmen began presenting their productions in tents. In October, 1907, the first newly built playhouse, the Colonial Theatre, opened.

VAUDEVILLE'S OWN STARS

Vaudeville began to develop its own stars, as the "refined" variety bills matched and surpassed the theatre as the nation's number one form of mass entertainment. Acts of every description struggled to make it from the small time, to the big small time, to the big time itself. An increasing number did make it and from these the stars emerged.

Eva Tanguay, who billed herself as "The Girl Who Made Vaudeville Famous," was not exaggerating too greatly. Her brash, sexy, comedy and song act was im-

mensely popular. Nora Bayes (and her husband Jack Norworth) stopped many a show. Elsie Janis was a big favorite.

There were the headlining monologists: Will Rogers, Chic Sale, Jim Thornton, and Clark and McCullough. The star comics included Ed Wynn, Joe Cook, Doc Rockwell, Herb Williams, Eddie Cantor, and George Jessel. Ethnic comedy acts were extremely popular. There was no audience resentment when actors burlesqued Jewish, Dutch, Irish, or any other ethnic characters in outlandish make-up and outrageous accents. Julian Rose and Joe Welch did a Jewish act; Weber and Fields portrayed Irish lads. Honey Boy Evans and Frank Tinney worked in blackface. Bert Williams and his partner, George Walker, were black stars.

Toplining tramp acts were W. C. Fields and Nat Wills. Character vaude artists who rated top money and billing were Walter C. Kelly, "the Virginia Judge"; George Beban; and Junie McCrea. Magicians were big. Star prestidigitators included Harry Houdini, Howard Thurston, Harry Kellar, and Carl Hermann (better known as Hermann, the Great). "Two" to "five" act headliners were Van and Schenck; the Avon Comedy Four with Smith and Dale; and the Marx Brothers (five in their early days).

VAUDE STARS TO LEGIT AND VICE VERSA

As their popularity increased a number of the top vaudeville stars succumbed to the lure of the Broadway legitimate theatre. Ziegfeld (being an old vaudeville man himself) particularly raided the "two-a-day heavens" for stars for his *Follies*. In 1908 he featured Nora Bayes and Jack Norworth, doing their own song, "Shine On Harvest Moon." In 1910, he starred Fannie Brice. In 1918 three vaude headliners topped the *Follies* cast: Will Rogers, Eddie Cantor, and W. C. Fields.

But vaude soon reached the point where it paid so well it began to attract stars of the theatre. And so, once again, enter Madame Sarah Bernhardt, the divine one—this time to play the heroine in a real-life drama in which the Palace Theatre in New York becomes "the Everest" of two-a-day vaudeville.

E. F. Albee had pursued his implacable course of swallowing one competitor after another. He had outbid Morris Meyerfeld and Martin Beck of the mid-west Orpheum circuit for the eastern Percy Williams chain. Now Beck had moved into New York and was building a new theatre on the corner of 47th Street and Broadway. It was to be called the Palace. The Orpheum operators were obviously determined to try to establish a string of theatres in the East. Albee considered this an affront. Meyerfeld owned seventy-five percent of the Palace, and Beck twenty-five percent. Albee persuaded Meyerfeld to sell his share. Then it was easy to get Beck out.

Beck moved over to the legitimate theatre to produce and direct shows for Klaw & Erlanger, retaining control of his Western operations where the flagship house was the Majestic Theatre in Chicago.

NO ACTS FOR THE PALACE

In 1912, Albee bought the Majestic. But Albee's acquisition of the Palace left him with one more major problem. The Albee-controlled United Booking Office had a franchise agreement with Oscar Hammerstein, which gave Hammerstein exclusive rights to all UBO acts in the midtown theatre district—running as far north as 59th Street—for his Victoria theatre. This meant that Albee could not book any of his own acts into the Palace, and since the UBO controlled a large percentage of all the better acts, the Palace was doomed to failure without access to these performers.

Albee learned that Hammerstein was eager to build a new theatre in London, but was hard pressed for cash and/or financing. He bought back Hammerstein's franchise agreement for over $200,000 and his act problems for the Palace were solved. Or so he thought.

When the Palace opened on March 24, 1913, the show business trade press, and virtually all insiders, predicted it would not be able to compete successfully with Hammerstein's Victoria. *Billboard's* review of the opening said:

The show offered can be called nothing else but a vaudeville show, altho if a regular vaudeville theatre were to offer it as a regular bill patronage would undoubtedly be small after the Monday matinee.

The only generally remembered name on the bill was Ed Wynn in a skit, *The King's Jester,* and of him the *Billboard* reviewer said:

Wynn has been funny in the past and is undoubtedly a good comedian; but his present offering will in no way tend to increase his reputation as a funmaker.
(The entire review—along with the review of the show presented at the end of the Palace's glorious two-a-day period on May 7, 1932—is included in the Palace chapter of original material from Billboard.)

Attendance at the new showcase house of vaudeville ranged from poor to terrible for the first month and a half of its existence.

SRO WITH THE DIVINE SARAH

Before Albee acquired control of the Palace, Martin Beck had booked a number of acts into that house which he expected to operate for many years. Among other attractions, he had signed Sarah Bernhardt. She had never played a New York vaudeville house.

On May 5, 1913, she opened at the Palace. Mme. Bernhardt and her company were expensive, but she was unstinting in what she gave the customers. Included in her repertoire were a one-act play, *Une Nuit de Noel sous la Terreur,* a tear-jerker about a Christmas night under the Terror; one act from *Lucrezia Borgia* by Victor Hugo; two scenes from Racine's *Phedre;* a tabloid (condensed) version of Sardou's *Theodora.* Then came the feature which left

DEC. 13, 1913 ISSUE   SOPHIE TUCKER

strong men (not to mention women) weeping: the last act of Alexander Dumas' *The Lady of the Camellias,* better known to all as *Camille.*

Now it was SRO at the Palace! The remarkable Sarah's stay was extended until May 15. It ended then only because she had to leave the following day for a previous commitment in Paris.

Bernhardt got $1000 per day, but she was worth every dollar. The Palace's break-even point in 1913 was estimated at approximately $15,000 per week, but in the first week of Sarah's engagement the house grossed close to $30,000 and that business continued during her entire run. Thus the incredible Mme. Bernhardt, then sixty-eight years old, had set the Palace solidly on its way to becoming the legendary theatre of the glory days of American vaudeville.

THE WHITE RATS TRY AGAIN

Now vaudeville matched the legitimate theatre dollar for dollar at the box office in most major cities, and surpassed it as the number-one entertainment form in many smaller towns around the country. The stars did well (Eva Tanguay, for example, was earning $2500 per week and more), but most of the other acts on a vaude bill found themselves more than ever at the mercy of the managers.

MARCH 13, 1915 ISSUE   CARL LAEMMLE

In 1910, Harry Mountford—an English song-talk vaude-villian, who had served as chairman of the National Alliance of Actors, Stagehands and Musicians in London (and was now working in America)—succeeded in getting an American Federation of Labor charter for the White Rats, the vaudeville actors union. He had become head of the White Rats in the United States. Albee and his manager colleagues got nervous. They began to blacklist the most active White Rats members. In 1916, they organized the National Vaudeville Artists, a "company" actors' union. A new clause appeared in UBO contracts. It said:

. . . the actor guarantees that he is not a member of the White Rats Actors Union and that he is a member of the National Vaudeville Artists. In the event that either of these statements is found to be untrue, this contract is automatically cancelled.

Mountford called a national strike. He sought the support of the Stagehands' and Musicians' Unions, but in January, 1917, the stagehands signed a new agreement with the New York managers, and the White Rats' strike collapsed. Once again the trust had prevailed.

THE MOVIES STUMBLE FORWARD

In spite of the continuing wars between the trusts and the rank and file actors in both vaudeville and the legitimate theatre, these two segments of live show business dominated the first two decades of the twentieth century. It was not until the movies stumbled along to challenge them that their popularity declined. And stumbled is the right word.

From the day Edwin Porter's *Great Train Robbery* created a resurgence of interest in motion pictures in 1903, and for several years thereafter, the men who ran the industry liked it just the way it was—in most respects. They liked the fact that no stars existed in the movies. Actors were paid five dollars a day. Writers, directors, wardrobe people, cameramen and crews were all paid proportionately low wages. The cost of turning out the one-reel (approximately 1000 feet) films was being neatly held to a minimum. The nickelodeons and few "electric" theatres, parks, traveling showmen, and others who used films were increasing in numbers daily, as was the audience.

Only one cloud marred the blue skies of filmdom from the standpoint of the movie moguls. There were endless and expensive lawsuits over patents. Edison had failed to protect his original patents around the world and conflicting film and projection claims kept sprouting like weeds in a neglected garden. Edison's own film company and the Biograph Company were the main contestants in the court wars. Other film makers, however, were expensively and not infrequently involved.

BIRTH OF THE FILM TRUST

Sharp attorneys have always played a part in American industry, and show business was no exception. Biograph's chief counsel was Jeremiah Kennedy and he conceived the idea for the Motion Picture Patents Company (MPPC), which was organized in January, 1909. Unlike the theatre and vaudeville trusts, the film trust did not have to concern itself with the dirty, odiferous stores which were the nickelodeon show places, or even the small "electric" theatres, which were showing their one-reelers. The film trust had total and absolute control of the one-reel films and the machines with which the film was projected onto the screen.

The Patents Company was a combine of all the leading film makers of the day including Edison, Biograph, Vitagraph, Selig, Essanay, Kalem, Lubin, Kleine (all U.S. firms) and two French firms, Pathé and Melies. This potent group announced that they held *all* patents to the manufacturing of motion pictures (shooting through developing and projecting prints) in the United States, Canada, France, Great Britain, Italy and Germany, and that any theatre owner or exhibitor would henceforth have to be licensed by the MPPC.

Indicative of the extent to which the MPPC milked the exhibitor was the two dollar per week rental fee the exhibitor was required to pay for the right to use the projector—

OCTOBER 23, 1915 **The Billboard** PRICE 10 CENTS

IT KEEPS THE SHOW WORLD POSTED

WILLIAM FOX
PRESIDENT
FOX FILM CORPORATION

OCT. 23, 1915 ISSUE WILLIAM FOX

over and above the fee the exhibitor paid for rental of the films he showed. It is estimated that the $104 per year, per theatre projector rental alone brought the trust well over $1,000,000 yearly.

PRESERVATION OF THE ONE-REELER

The film trust was also dedicated to the preservation and continuation of the one-reeler. They believed the attention span of the average nickelodeon customer could not last more than ten or twelve minutes, without the relief of a song slide, interlude, or some other distraction from the flickering motion picture itself.

The MPPC formula worked so well that Jeremiah Kennedy soon set up a distributing organization, the General Film Company. At that time exhibitors were supplied with movies by distribution companies called "exchanges." General devised a simple formula for buying up all the nation's exchanges. They merely determined the amount of money each exchange spent on film per year, and offered the exchange that amount in General Film stock and twenty quarterly payments in cash over a five-year period. Thus they were buying the exchanges with the exchanges' own money. Since the exchanges required MPPC licenses to

exist, there was little opposition. In less than two years (from April, 1910, to January, 1912) the General Film Company acquired the fifty-seven principal distribution firms in the country for about $2,500,000 in cash and $794,000 worth of preferred stock.

FOX, THE LONE HOLDOUT

The only large licensed exchange the film trust was unable to acquire was the Greater New York Film Rental Company, owned by William Fox. Fox had enough clout in his own right to do prolonged battle with the MPPC and General. He owned many theatres around New York City and had strong political and financial connections, including Tim Sullivan, a Tammany Hall force. Almost every other exhibitor in the country knuckled under to the trust.

Almost! A handful, such as Carl Laemmle, William Swanson and a few others, decided to fight the powerful group. Laemmle, who had moved into the motion picture business in Chicago from his father-in-law's clothing store in Oshkosh, Wis., started as an exhibitor. Then he became a leading exchange operator, went into production, and finally founded Universal Studios, which is a major force in motion picture and television production today. Laemmle, Fox, Swanson, and their colleagues fought one of the longest, most bitter battles against the film trust in the entire history of entertainment.

LAEMMLE'S BILLBOARD CAMPAIGN

Laemmle's advertising in *Billboard* and some other film trade publications set the tone of the independents' battle strategy. The ads were written by Robert Cochrane, who ran an advertising agency in Chicago. His agency had handled the advertising for the Oshkosh clothing store which Laemmle had managed. Cochrane joined Laemmle in the film business and was a major executive in every Laemmle enterprise. Laemmle, Fox, Swanson, and other independents somehow found ways of securing more and better films as their battle with the film trust raged on. They organized the Motion Picture Distributing & Sales Company to meet the challenge of General Film.

Despite the might of the MPPC and its members, the independents stood up well and made constant progress. In October, 1910, a year and a half after the MPPC had been formed, there were 9,480 motion picture theatres in the United States and of those 4,199 were independent, as opposed to the 5,281 which were operating under licenses granted by the trust.

At the same time that the independents battled the film trust, within each camp there was a struggle for leadership and profits among individual members and companies.

Some of Laemmle's fiercest competitive tilts were against Harry Aitken, who organized the Mutual Film Company with Wall Street support in March, 1912; and against P. A. Powers from whom Laemmle finally won complete control of Universal. At one point Aitken seduced the Independent Motion Picture Company's (Laemmle's firm, IMP) general manager, Tom Cochrane, away from Laemmle.

Adam Kessel of Bauman & Kessel took Laemmle's number-one director, Thomas Ince, by paying him $150 per week ($90 more than the $60 per week Laemmle had been paying Ince).

COMPETITION MAKES STARS

Indeed, it was this very struggle between and within the two groups which eventually ripped through the curtain of anonymity behind which the film makers of the trust attempted to "hide" their stars in order to avoid "star" salaries. Despite the film makers' refusal to bill the players, the nickelodeon public soon "selected" its favorites. Not knowing the players' names, the movie-goers supplied them with appellations of their own. Florence Lawrence, the unbilled star in Biograph films, became known as "the Biograph girl." Mary Pickford, also working for Biograph, became "Little Mary" to her fans.

The film makers of the trust and the independents were aware of this situation. Carl Laemmle decided to take advantage of it. In 1910, he "stole" Florence Lawrence and her husband, Harry Salter, from Biograph by giving Miss Lawrence $125 per week. Soon after, he "stole" Mary Pickford from the same company, and ran ads saying: "Little Mary is an IMP now."

FILMDOM'S STAR SYSTEM ERUPTS

Now that the independent film makers had begun bidding for the services of the most popular players, it did not take too long for the star system to develop in the motion picture business, even more rapidly than it had ever developed in vaudeville or the legitimate theatre. Late in 1910, Mary Pickford went from Laemmle's firm to the Reliance-Majestic Film combine for $275 per week. From Majestic she returned to Biograph where David Wark Griffith had assembled a potent group of players which included her brother, Jack; Henry B. Walthall; and Owen Moore, whom Mary later married.

Before she was twenty years old, Miss Pickford was working for Adolph Zukor at his newly formed Famous Players Film Company and getting $20,000 per year. From that figure she moved up to $100,000 per year, and in gradual steps climbed to $500,000 per year. When she reached the half million mark, she decided she was worth another increase to $675,000. Zukor tried to convince her she needed a rest and offered to pay her a thousand dollars a week for five years, if she would temporarily retire and preserve her beauty and talent. In spite of this opportunity to take a vacation with pay, Miss Pickford told the shrewd producer that she would rather work for $675,000 per year than loaf for $50,000. Zukor saw her point.

JAN. 20, 1917 ISSUE   MARY PICKFORD

THE "LITTLE TRAMP'S" BIG MONEY

Little Mary's success in winning salary increases was in some measure due to similar experiences Charlie Chaplin was having during the same era. Adam Kessel of the theatrical firm of Bauman & Kessel discovered Chaplin in 1913, while the comedian was working with an English vaudeville act called Fred Karno's *A Night in an English Music Hall*. He offered Chaplin $100 per week to go to California and make pictures with Mack Sennett. Chaplin held out for $150 per week. When his one-year contract with Sennett expired, Essanay signed the comedian for $1,000 per week for the year 1915. At the end of 1915, he signed a new contract with the Mutual Film Corporation for $10,000 per week for a guaranteed fifty-two weeks per year. The $520,000 figure nudged Little Mary into requesting another small boost from Mr. Zukor.

Among other early stars created by the nickelodeon fans were John Bunny, Maurice Costello, Francis X. Bushman, and Charles Ray. *Billboard* made its own significant contribution toward winning recognition for players by running their names in player directory features and their photos in portraits and still shots from films they were making.

DEMISE OF THE NICKEL AND DIME DAYS

Just as actors of the theatre had once scorned vaudeville, they initially scorned the movies as well. And vaudeville actors, by and large, matched them in their contempt for the flickering films. But, by 1911, there was a strong trend toward ten-cent admissions. And soon big box office profits would produce the big salaries needed to lure actors from theatre and vaudeville. More and more theatres were being built and many were playing motion pictures exclusively.

The following year, 1912, the movies took the first big step toward leaving the nickel-and-dime days behind forever. And we flash back, now, to our all-around superstar, Sarah Bernhardt. In Paris in 1912, a Frenchman, Louis Mercanton, starred the divine Sarah in a four-reel film, *Queen Elizabeth*. Her leading man was Lou Tellegen. Enthusiastic word about the film reached the United States and such entrepreneurs as Adolph Zukor, who had prospered and become increasingly important in the movie business with his early buddy and partner, Marcus Loew. Zukor was treasurer of Marcus Loew Enterprises but was looking for new worlds to conquer. Another was Edwin Porter, who had put the movie business back on the track with his 1903 hit, *The Great Train Robbery*. Since then, Porter had hired a young actor named Lawrence Griffith (later to use his real name, David Wark Griffith) for five dollars a day to work as the woodsman hero in an Edison film called *The Eagle's Nest*. At the time of Madame Sarah's movie triumph, Porter was making films for Universal. He, another Universal man, Joe Engel, and Zukor bought the American rights to *Queen Elizabeth* for $18,000.

THE TRUST TURNS DOWN THE QUEEN

Zukor took the film to the film trust and attempted to make a distribution deal. They figuratively threw him out. To the fat, secure, rich members of the MPPC, these multiple-reel films were a nuisance and a threat. They felt that the soundest product for the movie business was the one-reel film.

Zukor had bought Bernhardt's *Queen Elizabeth* as a first test for a new concept in films: to star great stage players in great plays. He now took his idea to Daniel Frohman and Frohman enthusiastically joined the Zukor group. In the United States, Bernhardt's *Elizabeth* was now sold as "Presented by Daniel Frohman." A young film salesman named Al Lichtman went on the road and sold the film's rights, state by state, to individual distributors who in turn made their own deals with exhibitors in each of their own states. The Bernhardt four-reel film brought the Zukor group—now called the Famous Players Film Company—$80,000 in states rights sales.

Queen Elizabeth had its initial showing at the Lyceum Theatre in New York City on July 12, 1912, with tickets at one dollar. From that day until 1915, four, five and more multiple-reel, feature-length films—shown at increasingly higher prices—grew in popularity until they completely changed the basic nature of the film industry.

SEPT. 29, 1906 ISSUE   LILLIAN RUSSELL

SARAH'S LARGEST AUDIENCE

Once again the incredible Sarah Bernhardt had starred in an event which marked a significant turning point in American entertainment. What could the lady do for an encore? In 1915, she was slightly injured in a minor rail accident; gangrene infected one of her legs and it had to be amputated. In 1916, at age seventy-two, wearing an artificial limb, she made another American "farewell" tour. The largest audience to which she ever "played" was the 250,000 people of Paris who paid her their affectionate respects when she died in 1923.

The success of *Queen Elizabeth* was followed by another foreign film, *Quo Vadis*, made by Cines in Italy. George Kleine bought the rights to this eight reel feature. He booked it into the Astor Theatre on Broadway in New York City April 21, 1913. It ran for 22 weeks at a $1 admission charge and was extremely successful.

The old-line film makers fought the multiple-reel feature trend bitterly. They abhorred the tremendous cost involved in making these films. The powers at Biograph—most successful of the trust's original film making group—were horrified when D. W. Griffith budgeted *Judith of Bethulia* (a four-reel feature starring Blanche Sweet) at $18,000. They were virtually apoplectic when the film wound up actually costing $36,000.

THE GREAT D. W. GRIFFITH

Griffith had begun directing films at Biograph in 1908 with a movie called *The Adventures of Dolly,* and between that time and 1913 he had developed the art of movie making to a greater degree than any practitioner before or since. There is disagreement among film historians as to whether or not Griffith actually "invented" the close-up, the medium shot, the extreme long shot, the fade, the flashback and other dramatic film devices. For example, the close-up was used as early as 1894 in the Edison kinetoscope film in which Fred Ott did *The Sneeze.* Edwin Porter used the close-up in showing a hand turning the handle on a fire-alarm in *The Life of an American Fireman* in 1903. George Melies used camera tricks like double-exposure and fade-outs in some of his earliest films in the first years of the twentieth century.

But there is broad agreement that Griffith developed the most artful and meaningful manner of utilizing all these devices, and more, in telling a story on the screen. At Biograph he pressed his bosses to permit him to make more expensive and ambitious films. However when the company did decide to produce "stage-quality" features with outstanding actors, they went into a partnership with Klaw and Erlanger and used Broadway theatre directors. This partnership between Biograph and Klaw and Erlanger produced two feature-length films with black star Bert Williams, and they tried to persuade exhibitors to pay fifty dollars per day to play these five-reel films. Few were interested, and the Williams pictures were finally cut to two and three reels and sold at whatever price they could bring.

THE BIRTH OF A NATION

If Biograph failed to appreciate Griffith's talents, others did not. Zukor offered him $50,000 per year at a point when Famous Players could ill afford to pay a director such a salary. Griffith turned the offer down and went to work on October 1, 1913, for Harry Aitken of the Mutual Film Corporation. Mutual gave Griffith a huge salary, stock participation, and the right to make two movies of his own each year.

The first of these independent ventures was *The Birth of a Nation,* a film which made motion picture history. Working with cameraman William (Billy) Bitzer—who taught Griffith a great deal about shooting pictures during his five years at Biograph—Griffith assembled a cast that included Lillian Gish, Henry Walthall, Mae Marsh, Elmer Clifton, Joseph Henabery, Donald Crisp, Jennie Lee, and Sam de Grasse along with literally thousands of extras who played soldiers and officers of the Confederate and Union armies. He rented horses by the hundreds and risked Billy Bitzer's life by having Bitzer lie on his back in a ditch and film the horses as they leaped over him. Griffith exploded spectacular fireworks so close to Bitzer's camera that Billy wound up with powder burns all over his hands.

RENEWAL OF RACE RIOTS

Nothing like *The Birth of a Nation* had ever been seen on a movie screen before. In addition to its unquestioned excellence as a motion picture, it was the most controversial film of its time—perhaps one of the most controversial of all time. It dealt with the Civil War and the Reconstruction days immediately following, showing blacks as uniformly stupid and violent. It glorified the Ku Klux Klan and presented a totally one-sided picture of the humiliation and degradation of the South at the hands of blacks and Northerners.

Liberals everywhere protested the film. Blacks rioted in many places where it was shown—just as they had when the play from which it derived, *The Clansman,* played the Walnut Street Theatre in Philadelphia nine years earlier.

FROM UNCLE TOM TO ROOTS

Griffith had paid the Reverend Thomas Dixon—author of the novel and the play, *The Clansman*—$25,000 and agreed to give Dixon twenty-five percent of the profits of the film for the rights to Dixon's story. No one can estimate what the Reverend ultimately collected. Griffith and his associates sold distribution rights to *Birth of a Nation* for varying flat fees to independent companies in the United States and abroad, rather than on a royalty or percentage basis. According to Richard Griffith and Arthur Mayer in their book, *The Movies,* the film earned $18,000,000 by 1939. The film had its first showing at Clune's Auditorium in Los Angeles, February 8, 1915, and its New York opening on March 3 at the Liberty Theatre with an admission charge of two dollars top.

(It is an interesting commentary on the American psyche, black and white, that four of the most successful "entertainments" of their day, and of all time, dealt with slavery and black and white relationships: *Uncle Tom's Cabin, The Birth of a Nation* [*The Clansman*]*, Gone With the Wind,* and *Roots.* It is particularly interesting that the latter two—with their totally opposite depictions of the attitudes and conditions of life for black slaves—were among the most successful popular dramatic works of all time.)

MULTIPLE-REEL FEATURES TAKE OVER

The Birth of a Nation ended whatever question remained about the viability and profitability of multiple-reel, feature-length motion pictures. By 1916 the William Fox Film Company was producing one five-reel film every week. By 1918 Famous Players-Paramount was turning out two full length plays per week, or 104 per year.

The Fox schedule for that same year included seventy-eight full-length, multiple-reel features under the Standard, Victory, and Excel banners with such stars as Theda Bara, William Farnum, Tom Mix, Gladys Brockwell, George Walsh, Virginia Pearson, Peggy Hyland, Jewel Carmen, and many others.

AUG. 29, 1914 ISSUE   ADOLPH ZUKOR

NEW MOVIE TEMPLES

The success of the multiple-reel features was so great and consistent that soon the movie moguls began to build elegant new theatres. On May 14, 1914, the Strand opened on Broadway in New York City. *Billboard* said of the opening:

It would vastly profit every exhibitor in America if he could attend this highly modernized theatre and observe the methods of its management . . . . The Strand supplements the benefits of the moving picture business that the multiple reel has begun.

Soon thereafter other motion picture palaces were built. The Rialto, the Rivoli, and the Roxy were super houses, and showmen such as Samuel Rothafel (better known as Roxy) helped to build them into the nation's premiere entertainment centers, showing the finest in films and vaudeville presentations.

Long before the development of the multiple-reel feature film, some showmen were attempting to add voice and color to the movies. Some exhibitors hired acting companies to stand behind the screen and speak in synchronization with the lip movements of the actors in the film. Needless to say this took much rehearsal, and at best did not work too well. Many efforts were made to synchronize the phonograph, if only via music, with the action on the screen. Presently some mechanical inventions evolved, but none were satisfactory.

ENTER THE CLIFF-HANGERS

About the same time that multiple-reel features became the concept which established films as the nation's most popular form of mass entertainment, two other types of motion picture also came into being: the weekly cliff-hanger serial and the newsreel. The first serial, *The Adventures of Kathlyn,* was a joint venture of Colonel William Selig (an honored member of the film trust) and *The Chicago Tribune.* As a circulation builder, *The Tribune* printed daily the continuing story of Kathlyn's adventures while the film was showing in local theatres. The serial took its name from its star, Kathlyn Williams. The first theatre showing and first installment in *The Tribune* appeared on December 29, 1913. The Selig-*Tribune* serial was an unqualified success. Movie-goers could not wait to return to their favorite theatres each week to see how Kathlyn escaped from her latest dilemma. *The Tribune's* circulation jumped by 50,000 readers, almost ten percent of its total patronage. Other producers followed with serials which developed such stars as Pearl White, Ruth Roland, and others.

Newsreels, pioneered by Laemmle and Pathé among others, also became a weekly feature in movie theatres.

EARLY LIFE AND DEATH OF COLOR

Color efforts were more successful. A process called Kinemacolor was developed in England in July, 1906, but its first public demonstration did not take place until May 1, 1908, at the Urbana House in Wardour Street in London. It had its commercial debut at the Palace Theatre in London on February 26, 1909.

Efforts were made to introduce the color process to American film makers, but these were overtly and covertly sidetracked by the members of the film trust who saw no reason to add what would be another expensive cost to film making. Black and white American films were doing nicely at ten cents a foot, and color could only cut profits and create new problems. The English development of color was halted by the nation's declaration of war on Germany in 1914, so it was not until many years later that color became a meaningful factor in the motion picture business.

World War I had another highly significant effect on the American movie business. With England, France, Germany, Italy, and all the rest of Europe at war, commercial film making came to a halt in those countries. American film makers had the most profitable areas of the world film market all to themselves. They established a global dominance that was to last for generations.

SEPTEMBER 16, 1916 **The Billboard** PRICE 10 CENTS
72 PAGES
IT KEEPS THE SHOW WORLD POSTED

FRANCIS X. BUSHMAN
AS ROMEO IN METRO'S PRODUCTION OF
ROMEO AND JULIET

SEPT. 16, 1916 ISSUE   FRANCIS X. BUSHMAN

THE MOVIE GOLD RUSH

At home, between 1912 and 1918, a veritable gold rush took place in the movie business. Stars of the theatre and vaudeville, who had once been scornful of the flickering film medium, flocked to it. When Frohman joined Zukor at Famous Players in 1912, he brought in such stars of the legitimate theatre as John Drew, Maude Adams, David Warfield, George Arliss, the Barrymores, Nazimova, and others. Interestingly enough, the films of many of these stage luminaries were flops, while Mary Pickford, Charlie Chaplin, and other stars created by the films themselves became and remained the superstars of the motion picture medium. It became apparent that many in the film audience were not devotees of live drama.

In 1914, Jesse Lasky and his brother-in-law, Sam Goldfish (who later became Sam Goldwyn), set up a production company. Lasky made a deal to film David Belasco's plays. In 1915, the Shuberts and William Brady allied with movie men Arthur Spiegel and Lewis Selznick (father of David and Myron, two latter-day movie tycoons) to form the World Film Company. Metro Pictures was formed that same year by Richard Rowland, who hired Louis B. Mayer. Among their stars were Francis X. Bushman and Mary Miles Minter.

DIRECTORS' COMPANIES

The leading directors of the day—now fully aware of their power—formed their own companies. D. W. Griffith, Thomas Ince, and Mack Sennett organized Triangle Productions. They signed the biggest western star of the day, William S. Hart, along with Billie Burke, Frank Keenan, Eddie Foy and others. At this time, Cecil B. De Mille directed his hit film, *Carmen*, with Geraldine Farrar and Wallace Reid.

W. W. Hodkinson—a former owner of one of the exchanges acquired by the Patents Company—organized Paramount, which was originally a distribution firm created to handle the product of Zukor's Famous Players and Lasky Feature Plays.

By the end of 1915 Hollywood had become the film capital of the world. Many of the earlier film makers had come out to the West Coast from their studios in Fort Lee and West Orange, N.J., various locations in New York City, and numerous production plants around Chicago to escape the harassment of litigation. They soon discovered that both nature's climate and the economic climate in Hollywood were far more favorable to movie making than the East or Midwest. The sun supplied excellent lighting for long, uninterrupted periods of time, and the labor and tax laws in California were much more attractive than those in New York or Chicago.

The stars of the day, in addition to those mentioned, included Fatty Arbuckle, Beverly Bayne, Clara Kimball Young, Blanche Sweet, Marie Doro, Marguerite Clark, Thomas Meighan, Sessue Hayakawa, Marguerite Fisher, and a handful of others.

TYCOON ALLIANCES

Alliances between the tycoons shifted with as great a frequency as those in the legitimate theatre. There are countless stories of venal double-crosses, back-stabbings, and vendettas in movieland. In 1916, Famous Players and Lasky merged. They took over their distribution organization, Paramount, and acquired a half dozen smaller production companies. In 1917, Sam Goldwyn formed Goldwyn Pictures with theatre man Edgar Selwyn and playwright Margaret Mayo. That same year Mack Sennett moved over to Paramount and brought with him such outstanding comedians of the day as Buster Keaton, Ben Turpin and Chester Conklin. Paramount also signed Fatty Arbuckle.

EXHIBITORS REVOLT

The leading producers were not only gaining control of distribution outlets, but were building and acquiring control of theatres. In 1917, the veteran movie exhibitors revolted. Among the rebels was Tom Talley, who had opened the first "electric" motion picture theatre in Los Angeles in 1902. The exhibitors' group formed a corporation called First National Film, and another called the National Exhibitors' Circuit. Their first move was to go after the top stars of the day. They made a deal with Chaplin to make eight two-reel films for which they agreed to pay him $1,075,000.

Meanwhile Adolph Zukor, who had become the single most potent force in the industry, joined with Lewis Selznick to form Select Pictures. Zukor also arranged for Paramount to take over Artcraft Pictures, a company he had organized for Mary Pickford. In addition to Mary herself, Artcraft had Douglas Fairbanks, William S. Hart, Thomas Ince and D. W. Griffith (all formerly of Triangle) under contract.

Zukor also made a new deal with "Little Mary" in 1917, which paid her $1,040,000 and many extra benefits. But a year later, in 1918, Miss Pickford left Zukor to sign with the exhibitors' company, First National. She agreed to make three pictures for them at $350,000 per picture.

The war that would never end, between producers and exhibitors in the movie business, was well under way. And the happy beneficiaries, as always, were the stars.

THE UNBELIEVERS VANISH

By 1918 almost all of the original members of the Motion Picture Patents Company were out of business. Most of them had retired or sold out. Edison, Biograph, Lubin, and Kalem had already departed. Selig and Essanay were about to disappear. In the light of their steadfast refusal to recognize the desirability of producing dramatic multiple-reel features, it seems mildly ironic that the last movie made by the Edison Film Company was *The Unbeliever*.

In any event the film trust was long dead, and the new tycoons ruled. The simple fact was that by 1918 the movies had stumbled their way to total dominance as the leading form of mass entertainment in America. The film industry was the first of the mechanical forms of show business to achieve that distinction. The legitimate theatre retained its basic audience. Vaudeville would still enjoy another decade of popularity which would almost match that of the movies.

BEYOND LEGIT, VAUDE, AND FILMS

Other branches of live show business fared more or less well, depending on how directly competitive they were to vaudeville and silent movies. Minstrelsy went into somewhat of a decline, although it was absorbed in part by films and vaudeville.

On April 17, 1909, the last performance of a minstrel show was presented at the old Eleventh Street Opera House in Philadelphia. The theatre had played minstrel shows for fifty-four consecutive years. In 1906, Lew Dockstader's Minstrels were still operating and carrying seventy performers. In December, 1907, Dockstader made his first movie, *Minstrel Mishaps*, for the Edison Film Company.

In October of 1917, Al G. Fields' Minstrels completed their thirty-first year. Lowery's Greater Minstrels, an all-

black organization, wound up the 1917 season with the most successful tour in its history; it carried thirty-five people.

Eddie Leonard, one of the best-loved of the white minstrels, was booked on a solid tour of vaudeville theatres by the United Booking Office in 1915. When America's entry into World War I appeared imminent, women's minstrel organizations were formed. One of these was the Lady Bountiful Minstrel Company.

THE BURLESQUE CLEAN-UP

The same kind of struggle for control of theatres that had occured in the legitimate stage, vaudeville, and ultimately the movie business was taking place in burlesque. The two major burlesque chains were the Columbia and the Empire circuits. In March, 1913, they merged to form a combine of forty-four theatres. They exercised their power against independent burlesque theatre operators in the field in much the same manner as their counterparts in the other entertainment areas.

In 1915, an industry organization, the American Burlesque Association, initiated a clean-up campaign in the field. It came out strongly against "bare legs" and "smutty dialogue and vulgar jokes." The campaign was not very successful. In November of that year, the licenses of the Garrick and the Olympic theatres—the two leading burlesque houses in New York—were revoked for "indecent performances."

LASKY PIONEERS NIGHT CLUBS

Jesse Lasky (partnered with a theatre man, Henry B. Harris) introduced a new form of entertainment to show business on April 6, 1911. Lasky and Harris opened the Folies Bergere, the smartest restaurant and music hall seen to that date.

Of course, there had been roof gardens and theatre-restaurants which featured entertainment, but never on the lavish scale of the Folies Bergere. Folies was the forerunner of the smart night clubs and supper clubs which proliferated in subsequent years and which today still exist in entertainment centers such as Las Vegas. The Folies Bergere was a financial failure, but the basic idea caught on.

Within a year a number of cabarets, playing name acts and lesser performers, were operating. Louis Martin's Parisiene, Maxim's and Shanley's were the most prominent. Other successful, though less elaborate, clubs were the College Inn, the Carlton Terrace, the Ritz Grill, Rector's, Churchill's Gardens, Pabst's, the Old Vienna, the Cafe Revue and the Cafe Boulevard. The Carlton Terrace, at one point, played a revue based on Shakespeare's *Twelfth Night*. It was not too well received.

In 1917, *Billboard* wrote a review of one of the smart supper clubs, the Palais Royal. Fritzi Scheff headlined the show, but *Billboard* objected to the one-dollar cover charge made after 10:00 P.M. and said:

DEC. 5, 1914 ISSUE   JESSE L. LASKY

... strongarm methods strongly approaching deliberate theft are resorted to by the waiters.

That same year the Broadway Association persuaded the New York Police Department to launch a vice clean-up against the cabarets. It was temporarily successful.

TRAVEL TRAVAILS

Traveling dramatic shows found it most difficult to compete with vaudeville and motion picture operations. Those which were able to buck the movies and vaude most successfully were the newly formed "tab companies"—shows which performed one-hour or ninety-minute condensed versions of successful musical comedies. These tab companies charged ten, twenty, and thirty-cent admissions and did fairly well. In 1913, there were almost a hundred such companies in operation.

Least affected by the enormous growth of stage and film theatres were the standard outdoor areas of entertainment: the circuses, carnivals, fairs, and amusement parks. These areas of show business had an appeal all their own, and their audiences stood up well during the rising popularity of films and vaudeville. The one exception to this seemed to be the Wild West shows. Perhaps the 376 Western one-reelers made by Broncho Billy, and the thousands

of movies like it, took their toll. By 1908, the Pawnee Bill Wild West Show was still operating, but it was selling off substantial quantities of equipment. In 1910, Pawnee Bill and Buffalo Bill had joined forces in organizing a film company.

RINGLING BUYS BARNUM AND BAILEY

The circuses had not yet hit their peak period—which would not begin until early in the second decade of the twentieth century—but attendance at the big tops was generally excellent. James A. Bailey of Barnum and Bailey died in 1905, and two years later the Ringling brothers bought their major rival for $400,000. They continued to operate the two circuses completely separately, and each did extremely well.

In 1908, in order to avoid wipe-outs by bad weather, the two giant circuses played their major city engagements indoors. The Ringling Show played the Coliseum in Chicago and Barnum & Bailey had a magnificent New York opening at Madison Square Garden. These indoor performances were the first harbingers of times to come—the end for huge traveling tent shows.

JOAN OF ARC AND MAY WIRTH

Two of the most sensational performances of the era were the *Joan of Arc* spectacular, featured by the Barnum & Bailey show in 1913, and the riding of a sixteen-year-old Australian girl, May Wirth, who had been with the same show in the previous year. Miss Wirth was hailed as the finest equestrienne in the world. The *Joan of Arc* spectacular featured 1,200 people, including 650 soldiers mounted on fine horses, and forty elephants—among other personnel, animal and human. It was costumed and staged magnificently.

Other lesser circuses also did well. The Al G. Barnes Circus featured Mabel Stark, the only woman animal trainer in the world who worked with a pride of Bengal tigers. The Sells-Floto Show drew substantial crowds, as did the Hagenbeck-Wallace Shows. This latter ill-starred organization, however, once again encountered disaster in the form of man-killing, property-destroying floods in Indiana and Ohio. A young man named George Hamid toured successfully with George Hamid's Oriental Circus. Hamid was later to become a major figure in the outdoor show business world, heading the largest booking agency for outdoor attractions and acquiring ownership of the Steel Pier in Atlantic City and other important show properties.

The Shuberts were managing the Hippodrome Theatre in New York in 1915 and in February they booked a circus into that house. It did not run too long, since the Shuberts were not ready for some of the problems of the circus world which were unknown to the legitimate theatre.

A CARNIVAL CLEAN-UP

Carnivals, whether playing fairs or under other auspices, prospered. In 1912, the Carnival Managers' Association of America was formed. Its aim was to create "a better, cleaner, carnival business." One of the problems which plagued the traveling carnivals was the tendency of local politicians to rip them off in however petty a fashion. In Pikesville, Ky., for example, a clerk in the license department insisted a carnival representative come in each day to pay the two-and-a-half dollar per day license fee, rather than paying seventeen and a half dollars for the entire week on one visit. The reason was that the clerk received fifty cents each time he wrote a license.

Among the most ambitious of the carnival projects of the period was the Rice & Doar Floating City Shows. Showboats — like Wild West shows and, to a lesser degree, minstrel shows — had declined, but carnival entrepreneurs Rice and Doar set up a complete carnival with shows, games, and rides on twenty-four mammoth barges and floated it from town to town.

In March, 1917, the most important outdoor showmen's organization to date was formed. It was the National Outdoor Showmen's Association (NOSA). Sam Gumpertz, a well-known outdoor showman of his day, was elected first vice president of the NOSA and decided, as a top priority, to attempt to wipe out "the privilege car" on carnivals. The privilege car was that car, truck, wagon, or trailer which less scrupulous carnival owners leased to crooked gamblers. In these privilege cars, the gamblers ran roulette, faro, dice and other games of chance—most frequently rigged so that the players had little chance of winning. Most privilege car operators not only victimized local citizens in the towns they played, but also cheated their colleagues in the carnival itself. Gumpertz succeeded moderately in reducing this practice.

THE SENSATIONAL AEROPLANE

Kewpie dolls and Sayso Ice Cream cones were two new features to be found on most carnival midways and at fairs and amusement parks. But the most exciting new attraction at countless outdoor events were the daring young men, and women, in their flying machines. In July, 1909, a *Billboard* editorial predicted that "the aeroplane will be the great sensational attraction of the year at State Fairs . . ."

By March, 1911, there were approximately 1,800 aeroplanes in use, flown by about 1,000 birdmen and/or women of whom 450 were licensed. The plane replaced the balloon ascensionists as a parks-fairs attraction and just as many birdmen and women were killed as balloon ascensionists before them. Among the better known women flyers was Ruth Law, billed as *Queen of the Air,* and the Stinson sisters, "who never disappoint." Women were extremely active in every area of entertainment. In 1912 the woman's suffrage movement was at its peak, and male chauvinists referred to women as "broilers" at their own

risk. Willie Hammerstein ran a big "Women's Suffragette Week" at his Victoria Theatre. There were suffragette plays. Women could be found in almost every occupational stratum of show business. Nellie Revel was one of the leading press agents of the day; Lois Weber was probably the first woman film producer-director. In 1912, *Billboard* ran a pro-suffragette editorial.

Other new attractions at parks were auto polo and automobile and motorcycle stunts to replace the earlier bicycle daredevils. And, of course, many parks featured a kinodrome, where patrons could see the latest one-reel movies.

DANCERS AND ROLLER SKATERS

A number of relatively new entertainment forms arrived on the scene, caught on momentarily, reached a peak of acceptance, and then went into decline. From about 1909 through 1916, there was keen interest in the dance. Americans danced and became avid fans of leading dance acts. Dance halls (sometimes referred to as "dansants") opened by the hundreds. Couples whirled and pirouetted, kicked and dipped, slithered and hopped to the one-step, the turkey trot, the hesitation waltz, and the tango. In 1915 the dance of the day was the cakewalk, and every dance palace held cakewalk contests. In 1913 Victor Talking Machine Company produced a series of dance records, under the supervision of the celebrated team of Vernon and Irene Castle.

Roller skating also caught on briefly. It, too, was an amusement form in which the people both participated and became eager afficionados of skating performers. There were roller skating rinks by the thousands, and roller skate dance acts, and roller skate daredevil acts. Hillary Long was one of the latter. He did a vaudeville "turn," in which he skated down a sharp, looping incline on a roller skate attached to his head! The roller craze began in 1907 and peaked about 1914.

A SPAN FOR CHAUTAUQUAS

In 1909, an odd new mixture of entertainment, with an accent on education and enlightenment, began to proliferate. This was the chautauqua. Chautauqua started as an adjunct to Sunday schools and gradually absorbed what were until then called "camp meetings." A major chautauqua attraction was the lecturer. Speakers would deliver sermons on an infinite variety of topics ranging from the virtues of Teutonic discipline, to abstract philosophies, to the natal and death rites of the aborigines. There were also musical programs, stereopticon travel discourses, magic performances, and a truly mixed bag of many varieties. Chautauquas thrived from approximately 1909 to 1917.

In the meantime, two other forms of mechanical entertainment which were to have vast impact on each other, and on American show business as a whole, were taking shape.

MUSIC/RECORD HIGHLIGHTS

In 1914 a truly momentous achievement came about in the music industry. Victor Herbert and a group of colleagues were successful in establishing the American Society of Composers, Authors and Publishers (ASCAP), a performing rights society empowered to collect fees from most users of music for public performance for profit. Scores of authors, composers, and publishers have since collected hundreds of millions of dollars from persons and organizations who have used their music since that day. Twenty-two publishers, 170 composers and lyricists made up ASCAP's original membership. George Maxwell was its first president; Victor, first vice president.

The formation of ASCAP and the passage of the Copyright Law in 1909 were two of the most vital developments in the music business.

Records were not thought of as serious competition to the theatre, vaudeville, motion pictures, and other segments of entertainment simply because they, and the record players, were relatively expensive. Nevertheless the industry made remarkable progress.

Although the Victor Talking Machine Company and the Columbia Phonograph Company had pooled their patents, there was still a considerable difference of opinion in the record business as to the relative merits of Edison's phonograph and its cylindrical disks and the Victor machine and its flat records.

Until 1905, the battle seemed to be fairly even. While the flat disk had captured the greater portion of the urban market, the cylinder was still the preferred record in rural areas. For both camps business was good. Even in the depression year, 1907—when virtually all business in the nation, and particularly the entertainment business, was suffering—Edison's phonograph operations had their biggest year to that date, grossing about $7,000,000.

THE VICTROLA AND AMBEROLA

Victor's business was also healthy. From a gross of about $3,000,000 in 1905, it climbed to more than $30,000,000 by 1917. Victor's success was due to both the excellence of its Red Seal recordings and, on the equipment side, to the Victrola, which was introduced in 1906. The Victrola became so popular that all playback equipment came to be referred to by that trade name during that period. It sold for $200. In 1907, Edison introduced a competitive phonograph called the Amberola, featuring extra-large cylinder records which had four minutes of playing time. The Amberola also sold for $200.

One contributing factor to the success of the Victrola and other phonograph sales was the flat record that could be played on both sides which Columbia had introduced in the United States in August, 1904. This flat record sold for a dollar and a half.

The flat versus cylinder record contest staggered to its conclusion in 1912 when Columbia discontinued manufac-

APRIL 12, 1906 ISSUE   BUSTER KEATON

ture of the cylinders. Edison brought out a new flat disk that year, called the Diamond Disc Record, playable on a new phonograph also called Diamond Disc. The great inventor, however, continued to make and sell his cylinder disks until 1929.

NEW RECORD COMPETITION

Competition in the record industry accelerated in the years between 1914 and 1916 when the majority of the original Columbia and Victor patents expired. Before that year was out, such aggressive new manufacturers as Brunswick-Balke-Collender, Aeolian, Vocalion and Sonora entered the fray. The great classical artists and orchestras were still the major sellers of the day. Alma Gluck, a Red Seal artist, sold 1,000,000 copies of a record, "Carry Me Back to Old Virginny." That same year an American named Louis Sterling, heading up the English branch of Columbia, recorded the first complete show revue, *Business as Usual*. George M. Cohan made ten records for Victor. In 1917, Victor made the first "jass" (as they spelled it) record. The Original Dixieland Jass Band was working at Reisenweber's in New York, and Victor made "Livery Stable Blues" with them. It was released in May and was an immediate hit.

THE FIRST DISK JOCKEYS

No disk jockey played the record, of course, although for at least ten years previous to 1917 one or two people had been broadcasting music to distant points. Reginald Aubrey Fessenden was a Canadian electrical engineer deeply involved in experimentation with wireless telegraphy. On December 24, 1906, he broadcast records of a female vocalist and a violin player. He, or another male voice, also read passages from Luke. He was broadcasting from the National Electric Signaling Company at Brant Rock, Mass., and his program was picked up clearly enough, except for a measure of static, by wireless operators bobbing about on their ships in the Atlantic Ocean.

Fessenden's work led to the manufacture of the transmitter-receiver device which utilized various kinds of crystals. These crystals detected radio waves and turned them into electrical currents when the waves were touched in the precisely correct places with thin wires, called "cat's whiskers."

Lee De Forest brought radiophone development to its next level. De Forest, a scientist working with Western Electric, invented a device in 1907 called the Audion tube. The tube was a glass-bulb gadget which could not only detect but actually generate and amplify radio waves. De Forest's work derived, to a degree, from earlier experiments by John Ambrose Fleming, an engineer working for the British Marconi Company.

De Forest, in 1907, began broadcasting phonograph records from his "studio" in New York City. In 1908, he broadcast similar "shows" from the Eiffel Tower in Paris, and in 1910 came back to the United States and broadcast a program featuring Enrico Caruso from the stage of the Metropolitan Opera House. In 1916, De Forest broadcast the Presidential election returns. In that year he was broadcasting on a more or less consistent schedule. In one program his mother-in-law made a dramatic speech for the women's suffragette cause.

In 1916, young David Sarnoff, working for American Marconi, suggested to his superiors that the company produce what he called "radio music boxes." He felt there would be a great market for an instrument through which people could hear music and other entertainment and educational presentations transmitted from distant points. He was told that his idea was hare-brained, and he should forget it.

SHOW BUSINESS AT WAR

On April 6, 1917, the United States declared war on Germany. *"God Damn the Kaiser,"* wrote Bill Donaldson with fervent passion in *Billboard*. Show business, virtually to a man and woman, in every branch and in every way, went into battle, either literally or figuratively.

Vernon Castle was injured while teaching flying and was later killed. Arturo Toscanini led his orchestra in the midst of the Italian offensive at Monte Santo. George M. Cohan wrote "Over There."

Stars from every segment of the entertainment industry toured the country for the Red Cross. To name just a few: Cohan, Elsie Janis, Mary Pickford, George Arliss, Laurette Taylor, Chauncey Olcott, H. B. Warner, Ethel Barrymore, Maude Adams, John Drew, and Douglas Fairbanks. Fairbanks alone raised $6,400,000 in War Bond rallies.

The Rainbow Division of the Theatrical Allied Interests Committee of the Liberty Loan raised over $200,000,000. Klaw and Erlanger contributed $150,000; Martin Beck, $100,000; the Shuberts, $50,000; and Albee, $50,000.

Thousands upon thousands of show people from every branch of entertainment enlisted. Many of them were killed, or injured, or reported missing in action.

Their willingness to serve was touchingly described in Bill Donaldson's report in *Billboard* of a rally at the Palace Theatre in New York, under the simple heading, "Fine."

Just before America's entry into the war, American Telephone and Telegraph Company, fearing the expansion of the American Marconi Company, bought up a number of Lee De Forest's patents. Other major corporations, notably Westinghouse and General Electric, also stepped up their experiments and production, not only in electric light bulbs, but in vacuum tubes and similar equipment.

NO MORE HAMS

When the Yank war effort got under way radio ceased to be a plaything of the "ham" operators. All amateurs were forbidden to continue broadcasting to avoid interference with vital telegraphic communications. The Assistant Secretary of the Navy, Franklin Delano Roosevelt, signed an order setting aside all patent claims for the war's duration. Under the leadership of the Navy, the government went to the large manufacturing corporations and placed rush orders for hundreds of thousands of wireless transmitters and receivers. These were to be used on planes, ships, and automobiles. More sophisticated equipment had to be developed for "pack" transmitters and "trench" transmitters—which were capable of picking up and sending a signal by utilizing barbed wire as an antenna. Even more advanced electronic devices were urgently required for recording and breaking enemy codes. Radio direction finders and electronic submarine detectors were needed and delivered.

In short, the War did for radio in little more than a year what would possibly have taken another decade or more to develop in peace time. And when the Armistice was declared on November 11, 1918, a new and vital entertainment medium was ready to get under way.

The Navy, which had done such a magnificent job in the development and utilization of radio during the war, caused a bill to be introduced into the Congress. It called for total, monopolistic control of all radio by the Navy. Joseph Daniels, the Secretary of the Navy, testifying before a Congressional committee in December, 1918, said:

This bill will secure for all time to the Navy Department the control of radio in the United States, and will enable the Navy to continue the splendid work it has carried out during the war.

The bill was supported by the Department of State. The Navy and the State Department were only two of the potent backers of this bill to make radio a government monopoly.

"HAMS" VERSUS THE NAVY

In 1912, the government had passed a law requiring "ham" operators of radio equipment to secure a license to broadcast. Most of the operators ignored this requirement and simply took their chances, transmitting illegally. About the time America entered the war, 8,562 "hams" held licenses. A number of them had organized a body called the American Radio Relay League (ARRL). Its president was Hiram Percy Maxim. Maxim mounted his steed, positioned his shield and lance and charged full speed at the governmental dragon. When the proponents for Navy control pooh-poohed his insignificant membership, Maxim claimed he was speaking not only for the operators in the ARRL, but for more than 100,000 amateur wireless and radio enthusiasts who represented the nation's best brains in this field—and who were largely responsible for the nation's victory in the war by their many contributions in manufacturing, developing, and operating radio equipment all the way from the factories to the front.

Maxim won the support of many, among them Massachusetts congressman William S. Greene. Greene denounced the effort to create a governmental monopoly. "It would indeed be ironic," he said, "if having just won a fight against autocracy, we would start an autocratic movement with this bill."

The proposed Navy legislation failed to come out of committee and died. But the Navy now pushed to create another monopoly, a trust of the huge corporations with whom the military had naturally developed the most intimate and friendly relationships during the war. This monopoly became a reality.

HEAR THIS!

The story of this new trust in radio is the beginning of our next era and will be covered in Part Four. It was an era in which the *sound* of entertainment—in radio, in motion pictures, and on records—brought about some of the most dramatic and startling changes in show business.

MAY 11, 1918 ISSUE   MAY WIRTH AND MISS LEITZEL

ORIGINAL BILLBOARD MATERIAL
1905–1918

HIGHLIGHTS

You will find many words in the *Billboard* stories of this part spelled in a strange, condensed manner. Before you yell, "enuf, enuf," please read the explanation from the January 3, 1914 issue. And as you read some of the peculiarly spelled articles, remember that Carnegie "forct" them to it.

BLACK-HANDING ANDY

We have been pioneering for Andrew Carnegie's reformed spelling for two years.

We have been aggressiv, consistent and ultra-radical supporters of the movement.

Other papers, it is true, have loaned their support, but it has been reluctantly and conservativly given—rendered with apologies, misgivings, stinginess and qualifications.

They tackled the task gingerly.

We went the limit.

Expostulation, recrimination, abuse, sarcasm have been our portion and worst of all—we have been the butt of near-humorists.

Thruout it all we have stood manfully by our colors hoping against hope that Andy would toss something our way before he completely beggared himself.

But it has been no use.

He has not even noticed us.

Hoping to attract his attention we made our fonetics noisier and noisier and noisier.

But he heard not—just went on handing out chunks of scads to etymologists and pedants.

So he has forct us to it at last. We've got to black-hand him with this ultimatum—**Take the $30,000 worth of non-interest bearing bonds necessary to start the building of The American Theatrical Hospital in Chicago, Mr. Carnegie, or we tie a can to your fonetics—and with this, our last issue of the old year."**

THE BILLBOARD'S STAFF.

Mr. Carnegie's address is 2 E. 91st Street, New York City.

TRAGEDY IN A
PROGRESSIVE ERA   166
112,000 Americans died and 237,000 were wounded in World War I;
500,000 died in the 1918-1919 influenza epidemic. In 1906 the San
Francisco earthquake killed 400 and wiped out the theatre and business
districts of the city. Blacks continued to riot.

POWER STRUGGLE
IN THE THEATRE   168
The Shuberts gradually mounted an increasingly successful war against the
dominant Klaw and Erlanger "syndicate." Legendary producer-manager
Charles Frohman was a K & E stalwart; David Belasco was the key Shubert
producer-manager.

STARS OF THE
THEATRE'S GLORY DAYS   171
Sarah Bernhardt, George M. Cohan, and other stars made the theatre the
nation's most elegant and prosperous area of entertainment.

THE MEN WHO MADE VAUDEVILLE   174
Tony Pastor, B.F. Keith, E.F. Albee, William Morris, Martin Beck, and Percy
Williams were among the tycoons who brought vaudeville to the point where
it rivalled the theatre as America's favorite entertainment.

WHEN THE LAST
BIG BILL IS MADE UP   177
Small time novelty acts, dumb acts, animal acts, standard "turns" of every
description, and stars—all contributed to the variety stage's growing
popularity. The Majestic in Chicago was "big time"; but the pinnacle was
New York's Palace Theatre.

NICKELODEONS, TEN-CENT THEATRES,
ONE-REELERS AND UNBILLED PLAYERS   182
Movie actors got five dollars per day and no billing in the one-reelers, which
sold for four cents to fifteen cents per foot. Yet the movies had enormous
appeal, particularly to non-English-speaking immigrants and the poorly
educated masses. Each "studio" had its own stock company of players.

MOVIEGOERS MAKE
THEIR OWN STARS   189
The star system in films was created by the sheer public appeal of certain
players and the fierce competition between the movie trust, the independents
and rivals within each faction. Soon there were many stars and two
superstars, Mary Pickford and Charlie Chaplin.

STAGE AND VAUDEVILLE STARS
SUCCUMB TO MOVIES   193
Films became increasingly popular and more and more stars of the legitimate
theatre and vaudeville climbed on the movie bandwagon.

TRAGEDY IN A PROGRESSIVE ERA

FROM OCT. 6, 1906 ISSUE

The race riots in Atlanta, Ga., during the past fortnight go far to emphasize the deplorable conditions that prevail throughout the South.

Race Riots In The South. It is not our purpose here to enter into a learned dissertation on the general status of affairs on the equatorial side of Mason and Dixon's line, but it is opportune to outline a few of the difficulties that beset the theatre manager in this territory.

The average manager believes it is absolutely essential to the highest attainable degree of prosperity that he maintain harmony between his patrons of the two opposing races.

FROM MARCH 2, 1918 ISSUE

LEAVING STAGE TO SERVE UNCLE SAM

Eddie Leonard (shown on the left) will leave the vaudeville stage April 22, having enlisted to serve in the Aviation Division of the Signal Corps. It was necessary that he pass a very difficult and exacting examination before he was accepted, the tests being particularly stiff because he is over the age limit. However, his previous service in the army and his experience with airplanes made the tests comparatively easy. Mr. Leonard spent some time studying aviation from every angle under the capable tutorage of Chris Starvnson (shown on the right), the aviator, who was killed in an airplane accident last June.

FROM NOV.. 2, 1918 ISSUE

MASKED AGAINST THE "FLU"

The State Board of Health of Georgia ordered everyone attending the Southwestern Fair at Atlanta to wear "flu" masks. This picture shows Johnny J. Jones and his staff made up to resemble the old Jesse James gang. From left to right they are: A. H. Barkley, Johnny J. Jones, Ed R. Salter, Ed Kennedy and Ed Madigan.

FROM MARCH 23, 1918 ISSUE

IN U. S. NAVAL BAND

Six former Barnum & Bailey musicians, who are now in the service of Uncle Sam. Left to right: James J. Faricy, flute; Ed R. Swanson, clarinet; Henry Wook, tuba; Del Fields, bassoon; Loy Evans, trombone; John W. Drake, cornet.

FROM APRIL 28, 1906 ISSUE

SAN FRANCISCO THEATRES ALL GO DOWN IN DISASTER

Both Playhouse Districts Are Wiped Out

Many Companies Lose Scenery and Properties When Earthquake and Fire Visit the Metropolis of the Great Pacific Slope—Two Performers Reported Killed.

SAN FRANCISCO is a memory. At five o'clock Wednesday morning, April 18, a terrible earthquake visited the city and surrounding country, and the strongest buildings in the business portion of the town were reduced to heaps of debris. Numerous fires developed, and soon a hellish holocaust was eating away the city, consuming everything that had been left intact or partially so by the seismic shock.

Without the slightest warning people were thrown from their beds, is many cases, to find their hotels and homes tumbling about them. In the old mission district, where the houses were of ancient construction and rickety from age, hundreds were killed. Then came the fire. The relentless flames ate on, reaching farther and farther like the tentacles of some fiendish demon. Panic stricken crowds thronged the streets where tottering buildings waited only the work of the flames to complete their destruction. The tall frame work of sky-scrapers, the stone work and masonry having tumbled away from the shock, pierced the smoke-clouded sky. In such sections the streets were impassible. Few will ever realize the horror of the scene. The earthquake had burst the watermains and fire engines were useless. In a very short time the section where the handsome office buildings had reared their heads proudly was a roaring, seething, smoking furnace.

In lieu of water, dynamite was called into use, and many blocks of buildings were razed to create gulfs over which the flames could not pass, but in spite of those heroic measures, the fire burned on, leaping these improvised chasms, progressing steadily and surely from a common center. The business section south of Market and east of Ninth streets was soon reduced to ashes. The Claus Spreckles Building, the home of the San Francisco Call; The Chronicle Building, the Phelan Building, in which The Billboard's San Francisco office was located, all withstood the shock in a greater or less degree, only to be destroyed by fire. For a time it was believed that the Palace Hotel would be saved. It was a sort of refuge, but after awhile the heat and danger rendered it untenable and the guests fled farther from the center of destruction. Among them were the members of the Conried Grand Opera Co., which had put in two days of the two weeks' engagement, at the Grand Opera House on Mission street. The historic old playhouse, with all the scenery and properties of the Conried company was destroyed.

Practically not one San Francisco Theatre was saved. The Columbia, where The Babes in Toyland Co., was filling an engagement was probably the first to go, being located at Powell and Market streets, only a few blocks from the place from which the greatest fire radiated. Around the corner, on O'Farrell street, the Orpheum Theatre, Fisher's Theatre and the Alcazar were soon rendered a prey to the flames. The Orpheum and Fisher's were both vaudeville houses, while the Alcazar was the home of a well-known stock company.

It is impossible at this time to ascertain the exact extent of the damage done to San Francisco playhouses. The telegraph wires are kept so busy with messages to friends and relatives from people in the stricken city that other reports are held in abeyance. However, it may be assumed from reports that not one single theatre was left standing. The Market street Rialto, between Sixth and Ninth streets, and where were located the Lyceum, the Central, the new Belle, the Empire, the Majestic, and near by the Alhambra was swept clean by the all-consuming fire. The Tivoly, on Mason and Eddy streets, the California on the street of the same name, the Novelty on Powell street were the playhouses in the district that is now a smoking heap of ashes.

In the destruction of property, it was the greatest disaster that has ever visited this country, surpassing the Chicago, the Boston and the Baltimore fires; and though the loss of life was not so great as at Galveston where fifteen thousand people were drowned, the property loss was much greater.

> San Francisco was the gayest city in America . . . but now all those elegant cafes and elaborately decorated theatres have been leveled. There is desolation beyond description. Where once the streets were alive with the gayest of the gay crowds, they are now buried beneath piles of smoke-blackened masonry. All, all is gone . . .

San Francisco was the gayest city in America, it was cosmopolitan and metropolitan. There was an air of Orientalism about it that is not found anywhere else in the United States. Its people were amusement loving. It was a much bigger city than its population figures would indicate, there being no suburbs. The city was all built close together, the business streets running out into the residential districts without any definite lines of demarcation. Its restaurants, which are not surpassed anywhere, were the scenes of gayety and social enjoyment. Its many theatres were well patronized. There was nothing of the frugal spirit that characterizes so many other town. It may almost be said that everyone in San Francisco lived well. This may be generalizing in too great a degree, but certainly in comparison with other cities. The people of San Francisco were the freest spenders in the world. This liberal circulation of money naturally conduced to prosperity.

But now all those magnificent office buildings, all those elegant cafes and elaborately decorated theatres have been leveled. There is desolation beyond description. Where once the streets were alive with the gayest of gay crowds, they are now buried beneath piles of smoke-blackened masonry. All, all is gone.

The magnificent St. Frances Hotel, which was being greatly enlarged to accommodate the rapidly increasing patronage, was shaken by the quake and consumed by the fire. The New Fairmount, on Nob Hill, which would have been the grandest, most elaborate, and, at the same time, most expensively equipped hostelry in America, was level in the dust. The millionaire residence district was not spared; the Hopkins Institute, the Stanford residence and the Crocker residence went along with the rest.

But San Francisco, like another Phoenix, will rise from the ashes. She will be greater, more beautiful and more worthy of admiration than ever. But a large percentage of the new construction will be consummated by outside capital. Countless are individual fortunes and lesser interests that have been swept away in the recent disaster.

Never was the brotherhood of man more thoroughly established. Appeals for aid were unnecessary. Gratuitous gifts, voluntary subscriptions and unasked donations were immediately forthcoming from all the cities all noble-hearted, wealthy individuals and all the charitable masses of this country. None were more ready to meet the emergency than the professional benefit performances were announced in nearly every town, while those actor folks and managers who were able, affixed their names to their local subscription lists. Benefit performances are still being given, and they will probably continue throughout the next fortnight. The noble-hearted player folk have responded admirably with all their characteristic generosity, and there is little doubt that as soon as the individual losses of the members of the profession are ascertained, other benefits will follow, and many a heart made sad by disaster and suffering will pound with delight from receiving that which shall be given in great cheerfulness. It is to be hoped that every actor and every performer shall be entirely reimbursed for his whole loss.

Col. William Cody (Buffalo Bill) cabled one thousand dollars from France, for the relief of the sufferers, as soon as he learned of the disaster.

The New York Hippodrome subscribed the receipts of both Saturday performances to the list, and there is not a big city in America that is not holding its own performances for the same cause. As a free-giving institution in such exigencies the theatre leads them all. On page 14 of this issue will be found a list of the attractions that were filling engagements in San Francisco at the time of the catastrophe. Details are meager, and it is impossible to say at this writing what companies lost their effects or even what members of the profession lost their lives. Yet it is known that no manager, local or producing, that no actor whether he suffered personal and immediate loss, has come out without losses of some kind. Let the great world of the profession rehabilitate each one who has suffered. Small and from the many means the essence of hope to the unfortunate.

It is reported that Artie May Hall, the coon singer and one of the Agoust Sisters, of the Agoust Family of acrobats, were killed when the Orpheum Theatre collapsed, and that Harry Ourdorf, the stage manager of the Orpheum, had both legs broken and sustained other injuries.

The Jewish Theatrical Co. of Chicago lost all their effects and are stranded.

As the details of the San Francisco disaster are difficult to obtain so are they from the other points that were within the radius of the seismic disturbance. San Jose, Monterey, Santa Cruz, Vallejo, Oakland and all the other towns in the vicinity of the Golden Gate suffered to a greater or less extent. Just what theatres were injured is not known at this time, but for many moons the remembrance of the disaster will cast a pall over the theatrical business in that section. Rejuvenation will come, rehabitation is inevitable, but at the present time amusement is stretched in its temporary shroud. Interest has been drawn away from it; fear, superstition and other agencies of that character will militate against the spirit of enjoyment.

On the other hand, San Francisco will be filled with thousands of workmen and artisans engaged in the mammoth work of reconstruction. They will demand amusement, and in all probability vaudeville shows under canvas will be numerous in all the nearby towns, where the armies of workmen will sojourn.

POWER STRUGGLE IN THE THEATRE

FROM DEC. 10, 1910 ISSUE

THE SHAKE-UP IN THE BOOKING FIELD.

IT is a wise manager who knows his own booking agent these days. The shake-up in the booking field that occurred the latter part of last season and which has extended into this season in an even more aggravated form, has managers of theatres and attractions in different sections of the country guessing as to what attractions they are going to get. At times, they do not even know whether they are going to get any. The traveling manager for his part does not know from one town to another in several sections of the country whether he is going to play one house or another until he gets into the city where the engagement is to be filled. Wrangling often occurs. Sometimes the traveling manager will find that if he plays according to contract, he will see-saw back and forth between Klaw and Erlanger's and The Shuberts' theatres indefinitely.

The latest development is the consummation of a sort of protocol between the antagonistic factions, which it is believed will result in a final arrangement by which the attractions of both big booking agencies will be reciprocally booked into the houses one of the other. If this condition is brought about, it will be the nearest approach to the ideal that we have made in this country. It is difficult to anticipate just what the effect of an amicable arrangement of this kind would be. One contingency is almost assured: a good many houses would be eliminated, for whereas there were too many attractions and not enough houses before the Messrs. Shubert broke away from the syndicate, so many houses have been built and opened since that time that there are now too many first-class houses for the attractions that are available. It is more than probable that a great many of these houses will go over to vaudeville.

On the other hand, some observers of the situation maintain that the conditions will revert to first principles; that is, that the situation will resolve itself again so that managers of theatres will book their own attractions—that is, make their contracts direct with the managers of the attractions, and disregard altogether the booking agents. Whether this condition would be healthy or not is a question. It would mean long jumps and uncertain engagements unless each manager of an attraction should maintain a regular booking staff on his own account. This would be so difficult as to be almost impossible.

So the situation stands chaotic in the extreme, with no immediate prospect of order. The syndicate bookings have reached a very high state of system.

It is hardly probable that, as some contend, the day will come again when managers will book their attractions independently. This plan would entail too much expense and involve too much uncertainty. It would, of course, restore the old order of competition, but competition in the amusement business is usually accompanied by a degree of chaos and extravagance of expenditure that, coupled with the essential absence of rules for success, precipitates affairs into the states alternately of feverish panic and passive indifference.

Individual bookings are more consistent with the successful conduct of vaudeville than of the "legitimate." This is because it is more expensive for entire companies to travel than it is for individual acts to find their way from town to town.

There would be little chance for big companies employing barnstorming methods. In the days and in the districts of barnstorming, salaries were as uncertain as the weather in April, and where salaries are uncertain conditions are unhealthy.

In any contingency, somebody is sure to get the worst of it. The very secret of all perpetuation is natural selection.

FROHMAN ATTRACTIONS

JOHN DREW in THE SINGLE MAN

MAUDE ADAMS' in CHANTICLER

JULIA SANDERSON in THE SIREN

MME. NAZIMOVA in THE OTHER MARY

FRANCIS WILSON in THE BACHELOR'S BABY

ETHEL BARRYMORE in THE WITNESS for the DEFENSE

HATTIE WILLIAMS

DONALD BRIAN in THE SIREN

BILLIE BURKE in THE RUNAWAY

KYRLE BELLEW in THE MOLLUSC

MARIE POKO in A SUMBODDY ON THE WHEEL

DAVID BELASCO.

DAVID BELASCO'S
·STUYVESANT·THEATRE·
44TH ST. NEAR B'WAY.

BELASCO'S NEW STUYVESANT THEATRE.

THE SEASON'S SUCCESSFUL PLAYWRIGHTS

RICHARD CARLE
THE SPRING
CHICKEN

WILLIAM DEMILLE
THE GENIUS

CECIL DEMILLE
STRONGHEART

HARRY B SMITH
THE PARISIAN MODEL

DAVID
BELASCO
THE
GIRL OF
THE GOLDEN WEST

STARS OF THE THEATRE'S GLORY DAYS

FROM OCT. 6, 1906 ISSUE

FROM MARCH 6, 1915 ISSUE

ROBERT GRAU

Intimate and Important Revelations Appertaining to the Larger and Finer Phases of the Business

On the day these lines are written that illustrious French woman, known to fame as the Divine Sarah, is in the public eye the world over. With that courage and optimism which has characterized her amazing artistic career the Bernhardt has announced, on the eve of facing the surgeon's knife, that she has hastened the operation because she wishes to resume her career—that she will immediately prepare a spectacle at her Paris playhouse where many destitute players and not a few convalescents will find lucrative employment.

Only those who know Paris can conceive how the French people are grieving for their beloved Sarah. One may also only conjecture as to what the morrow holds forth for the brave woman who is already planning to trod the boards with but one leg, but why not? Surely the consummate artistry that has been hers will not be affected in the least. On the contrary if Sarah emerges from the operating table in triumph, as she believes she will, what a magnificent spectacle her return to the boards will present.

Once in a great while there is revealed in show business a genius in self-exploitation, who so manipulates the cards that no manager has ever been found ingenious enough to "play the game" with her (for it is invariably a woman) and win out.

Never in the world's history of the theater has there been recorded such a triumph as that one Sarah will achieve when, God willing, she faces the American public on one leg. The rush to see her on her first tour of the States will be as nothing compared to what will happen in 1915. The writer has been intimately associated with Bernhardt tours, and therefore comprehends the nature of her appeal with the people. To this day Sarah holds the world's record for a dramatic attraction for a week, accomplished at the Tremont Theater, Boston, on her fourth tour, when the gross for the six days was $42,000, including the auction sales.

It is understood that William M. Connor has Sarah's word—they never had a contract—that she will come hither under his management if all goes well with the knife. Connor knows how to conduct a Bernhardt tour, but even he probably has no conception of what will be the public response to this wonderful woman's triumphal re-entree. The Caruso-Farrar furor, great as it was, will look like a mere incident. I am not even sure that Connor could not adopt grand opera scale of prices. Surely Sarah's past scale will not be lowered. Once in a great while there is revealed in this "show business" of ours a genius in self-exploitation, who so manipulates the cards that no manager has ever been found ingenious enough to "play the game" with her (for it is invariably a woman) and win out.

FROM MARCH 23, 1912 ISSUE

BERNHARDT AS CAMILLE.
Last Act—Taken from the Film.

FROM OCT. 21, 1905 ISSUE

SARA BERNARDHT

FROM OCT. 12, 1907 ISSUE

EDDIE FOY,
Now appearing in The Orchid.

WILLIAM GILLETTE

FROM DEC. 4, 1909 ISSUE

DOUGLAS FAIRBANKS AND THOS. A. WISE.

As they appear to the artist in their successful company, A Gentleman From Mississippi.

FROM JULY 7, 1906 ISSUE

VICTOR MOORE

Who has scored a tremendous hit in George Cohan's musical play, Forty-five Minutes From Broadway.

THE MEN WHO MADE VAUDEVILLE

FROM SEPT. 5, 1908 ISSUE

"Tony" Pastor, the Father of Modern Variety

Just a mention of Tony Pastor. Just an idle thought in this busy day of ours, when money-grubbing crowds out the better thoughts, the kindly little tributes that are due to our betters. Tony Pastor lies in his last resting place. Medicines are not meant to heal a broken heart, and that is what poor old Tony died of. For twenty-seven years, Tony Pastor's name glistened over a theatre door on Fourteenth street. It is there no longer. Some one outbid Tony. The place will go into burlesque. The old haunts are gone, the old familiar office—its quaint and sentimentally priceless treasures are packed. Tony Pastor treasured nothing more than the photographs of his old friends, the faces of those who started on the road to fortune under his direction. The little stage where he had won renown, the little theatre that he cleansed in a moral sense, for be it forever understood that to Tony Pastor is due the credit for elevating the variety stage. It was he who prohibited smoking and drinking in his theatre, prohibited profanity and indecent comedy. It was he who innoculated the germ of ambition in a hundred players whose names to-day are niched in the theatric hall of fame. This was his life's struggle. Years ago he fought the winning battle and years ago the halo of success, gratitude and honor was wreathed for him.

Tony Pastor's Martyrdom.

Time rolled on; the stream of events entered another channel; the theatrical center shifted—commercial interests drove it up town. Tony stuck to the little playhouse that made him famous, that he made famous. His stars reached out—Broadway wanted them—Broadway got them. Tony valiantly kept his pace. New faces came, but the old audiences were gone. One by one they drifted with the current. Broadway was the whirlpool of theatricalism. And Fourteenth street was far away from Broadway. Tony reduced his prices, then changed the policy of his theatre, always stemming the tide of adversity with an indomitable pluck and courage.

Finally, vaudeville was overdone, moving pictures swept the field. They invaded Tony Pastor's famous little theatre. It was a set-back to poor old Tony's pride. But the worst was yet to come. The lease expired last month. It expired as it did for twenty-seven years before, and for twenty-seven years before Tony simply sent his check and thought no more about it. This year he did the same. The check was returned. Something must be wrong. Tony called up. He had been outbid. The blow was a staggering one.

Gray haired doctors shook in pity and wonder as they gazed at the venerable veteran Tony. Their prescriptions had no effect. Science has found nothing yet that will soothe a bleeding heart. Tony, in his intermittent consciousness, pressed his faithful wife's hand. The priest knelt at the bedside. Grief choked every heart.

Such is martyrdom—a grand and goodly soul crucified on the cross of commercialism.

"TONY" PASTOR.

FROM DEC. 11, 1909 ISSUE

Advanced Vaudeville

By

Martin Beck——*William Morris*

VAUDEVILLE OF TO-DAY AND YESTERDAY.

By Martin Beck.

The inspiration for whatever I write here may be attributed to a recent article in the columns of this valued publication on Edwin Forrest. In reading that interesting biography, this thought occurred to me: "The drama has in its history 'of yesterday' much of note and real dignity, but the history of vaudeville must yet be written."

In vaudeville we never hear the phrase, "Those were the Good Old Days," for, as a matter of fact, the earlier years in this field of endeavor are not associated with great achievements and only the more recent years have seen this splendid amusement claim a dignified place in theatricals. We are living in the most promising and healthful period vaudeville has experienced up to this time, but, as a matter of fact, I believe the real history of vaudeville will be a matter of future development. It has established a standing; has created a big, wholesome clientele, and has become an institution of wide proportions and magnificent importance, but it has not reached the zenith of its power and influence.

❧ ❧ ❧

William Harris, the well-known theatrical manager of New York and Boston, who is now intimately associated with Charles Frohman, began his career as a "variety performer," and his early experiences, as retold recently at a public banquet were not only excruciatingly funny, but they call to mind in a happy manner the conditions in American vaudeville, or, more properly, in "variety," some twenty years ago.

Most of the older vaudeville artists remember well when all those employed on the variety programs were required to black up for the minstrel first-part and appear in the after-piece.

Aside from the distinguished artists that made up the personnel of the Tony Pastor programs, I think the Cohan Family set the high-salary mark about 1895, when a Boston manager paid them $350. Another family, the Four Mortons, were later paid about the same.

One thing I recall, which shows how rapidly vaudeville has improved is that the first ensemble act ever played was as recently as 1900, when The Beaux and Belle Octet was sent to the Coast. The act consisted of four ladies, four men and a wardrobe mistress, and the price of this feature was $400 a week, the payment of which almost caused a sensation among the managers—and that was about ten years ago. Since that time rapid strides have been made by vaudeville producers, encouraged by the more ambitious of our managers, until to-day nothing is too pretentious to be considered as a part of the composite bills.

These past ten years have seen the expansion of the Orpheum from a single house on the Pacific Coast to a circuit which, with its valuable affiliations in the Middle West, joins hands with the Eastern Circuit at Cincinnati and makes it possible to book vaudeville acts for three consecutive years without a single repeat.

. . . The time has come when the most brilliant musical, dramatic, and operatic stars find it to their advantage to play our theatres, while still at the height of their popularity.

The time has come when the most brilliant musical, dramatic and operatic stars find it to their advantage to play our theatres while still at the height of their popularity; our producers devote the same thought, care and lavish investment to thirty-minute sketches and novelties as the producing manager does to a complete play; our resources give us a command of the world's markets for a variety of offerings and our own native artists are on the constant qui vive to better their material.

In short, vaudeville to-day is being taken seriously. It has approached a glorious era, and its destiny is in the hands of the present-day managers to mould and shape. All our most ambitious hopes may be realized if all interested in this very important branch of the theatre will make the most of the rich opportunities which the year 1910 will afford. If these are embraced the history of vaudeville a decade from now should be unique.

VAUDEVILLE—PAST AND PRESENT.

By William Morris.

The rapid development of the present-day vaudeville from the old-time "variety" has no analogy in theatrical history. There was a time when most of the theatre-going public looked askance at the style of entertainment offered in the so-called music halls of New York and other metropolitan centers; and there was some reason for the prevalence of these ideas, for they were not patronized by such people as now attend vaudeville houses. It is doubtful if the audiences of those days cared for anything more than the singing of spicy songs, buck dancing, or the antics of a couple of dialect comedians: but the time did come when they wanted something better, and were willing to pay more for it. The sketches began to take on a different tone, and here and there an act was presented which seemed more suitable for legitimate audiences, but when it was found that variety patrons not only appreciated but wanted these better kind of turns, the managers naturally responded to their desires.

Now, the same audiences who, on Monday nights, patronize a $2.00 Broadway opening, on Tuesday will readily, and with considerable pleasure, attend one of the music halls in the city, and the attitude of criticism will be on the same plane as that for a probably higher grade of attraction. The day of distinction, or a line of differentiation by theatre patrons has not only passed, but it is so completely submerged that there is no discriminating between legitimate musical comedy and the better kind of vaudeville.

FROM DEC. 19, 1914 ISSUE

THE FUTURE OF THE SHOW BUSINESS

By E. F. ALBEE

AMONG the ruling customs of the amusement world is one that calls upon showmen at Christmas time to express their opinion of show business, past, present and to come. As a rule there is little to say other than to report the procedure of a business now happily well regulated in nearly every branch. This year, however, showmen are faced by extraordinary conditions that have no precedent in the past and which will be recorded as unique in the history of the theater. We are all involved in the iron grip of a world-wide unsettled condition, and as war is said to try men's souls so certainly it tries men's business. At such a time it is well to take stock and to consider basic facts of amusement conditions and to endeavor to predict from a study of the past and present what the future holds of ill or good.

The war is not the only cause of the present difficulties in the vaudeville business. There has been an overproduction in all branches of the business. There are too many theaters, many of which have been built by people who were not previously identified with theatricals in any way, purely as a speculation. The temptations held out to outside capital to invest in theaters have been alluring. Glowing prospectuses have been issued by promoters showing large profits which are alleged to have been made in vaudeville and other theaters. Stock companies have been incorporated and stock in theaters sold to the public on the strength of these highly-colored prospectuses, and the law of supply and demand has been entirely disregarded in the wild scramble of these theatrical promoters to float their stock. For such schemes of financiering there must always be a day of reckoning.

A. Paul Keith and I, who acquired the B. F. Circuit, are interested in forty-eight theaters in large Eastern cities. Before going further, I wish to speak in praise of my associate, A. Paul Keith, son and heir of vaudeville's founder. He is a young man of sterling worth with whom it is a genuine joy to work. He possesses a sturdy, dependable personality, and has inherited the persistence in right policies that made B. F. Keith great. It is rarely that a theatrical manager's son develops the qualities for business and sticks to the detail part of it with the hard-headedness and great interest that A. Paul Keith has shown from his early boyhood. He was brought up in the business and, blessed in possessing his father's strong qualities, and his mother's lovable character, he adds to them a complete knowledge of present-day theatricals which makes him a showman to be reckoned with in the future. Our associates are all men of great experience in the show business, and many of them own and operate theaters of their own. All these men make a combined strength for legitimate vaudeville which was created by them, own theaters built by the money they have earned in over thirty years of struggle and saving. The foundation of their business was built on rock, and nursed with intelligence and care and frugality, and what they earned they put back into the business, until today they represent the great, solid circuits of the United States. That represents the vaudeville circuits east of Chicago. West of Chicago the late Charles E. Kohl started in the museum business at the same time as Hr. Keith and I, with George Castle and Mr. Middleton, developed in Chicago the vaudeville business from the old museum business up to the present high standard. Max Anderson and Henry Ziegler, at about this time, started in Cincinnati, Indianapolis and Louisville. They built beautiful theaters, ran them on a legitimate basis, using their own money and combining their own strength with others of equal experience who had gone through the same hardships and from no other source did they receive or ask for help.

PROMINENT THEATRICAL MAGNATES, PRODUCERS AND MANAGERS IN NEW YORK WHO ARE GRADUATES OF THAT GREATEST TRAINING SCHOOL FOR SHOWMEN "THE CIRCUS"

B. F. KEITH

E. F. ALBEE

M. C. ANDERSON

SAM SCRIBNER

F. F. PROCTOR

JAMES JAY BRADY

WHEN THE LAST BIG BILL IS MADE UP

FROM OCT. 9, 1915 ISSUE

The Vaudeville Artist's Creed

By HERBERT MOORE

I believe in my Profession—in my Act—in Myself. I believe in Sunshine and Smiles, Laughter and Jest, Beauty, Grace and Song. I believe that the chap who makes a Nation forget its griefs is greater than he who leads it into battle. I believe that the Great Stage Manager is not without a *sense of humor*, Himself, or He would not have bestowed it on so many of His own.

I believe in Humanity—ALL Humanity. I believe in the Divinity of Motherhood, the sanctity of Little Children, and the wholesome fineness of the Women of the Stage. I believe it is my Professional Duty to defend their good name. I believe the best about my Fellow Players—the worst about those who run them down. I believe in a Hell for Knockers—a Heaven for those apostles of Charity and Cheer whose hearts and hands are always open to the needy, whose lives are fragrant with good deeds quietly performed.

I believe in The Billboard, in its honesty, in its fairness, in its teachings and the things it stands for.

And I believe that when the last Big Bill is made up those who Make Good *here* needn't worry much about their "spot" up There.

————————————————
(YOUR NAME)

(For the top o' your trunk or your dressing room mirror.)

FROM MARCH 30, 1907 ISSUE

Doing a One-Night Stand.

FROM MAY 11, 1918 ISSUE

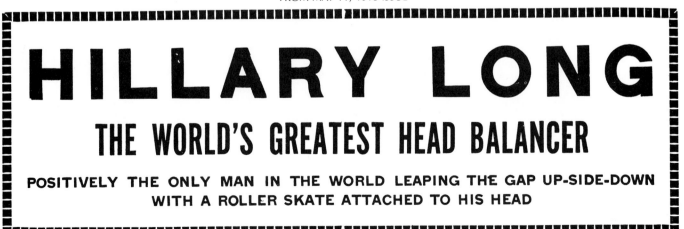

HILLARY LONG
THE WORLD'S GREATEST HEAD BALANCER
POSITIVELY THE ONLY MAN IN THE WORLD LEAPING THE GAP UP-SIDE-DOWN WITH A ROLLER SKATE ATTACHED TO HIS HEAD

FROM DEC. 18, 1915 ISSUE

MINNIE PALMER
—PRESENTS—

FROM DEC. 27, 1913 ISSUE

THE THREE KEATONS

One of vaudevil's standard comedy trios, who are received with appreciation wherever they appear.

4 MARX BROS.
PALACE THEATER, : : CHRISTMAS WEEK

"NAT BRAHAM'S EDUCATED FLEAS."

FROM AUG. 9, 1913 ISSUE

MAE WEST

Miss West is generally acknowledged to be one of vaudevil's cleverest singing singles.

BIG NAMES IN VAUDEVILLE

HINES & FOX — SAMUEL LIEBERT — BERT ERROL — ROGER IMHOF — TONY E. HUNTING & Corinne Frances

FLYING MARTINS — MAYME REMINGTON — CHARLIE AHEARN — BELLE BAKER — ETHEL GREEN

FOSTER BALL & FORD WEST — Miss Julia Nash — Mrs. W. H. RICE & Her Diving Dog CHAPPIE III — Harry B. Lester — MERCEDES

DARRELL AND CONWAY — MARY ELIZABETH — BLANCHE MEHAFFEY — BOBBIE HEATH & FLORRIE MILLERSHIP

FROM DEC. 29, 1934 ISSUE

The SPAN of the Big Time

BRIDGED BY THE BILLBOARD'S OPENING AND CLOSING REVIEWS OF THE PALACE, NEW YORK, AS THE ACE HOUSE OF THE TWO-A-DAY

From the Issue of April 5, 1913

OPENING OF THE PALACE.

NEW YORK, March 25.—(Special to *The Billboard*).—The much speculated upon and talked of opening of the new Palace Music Hall happened Monday afternoon, but it was not until the night show that the elite of showdom were on hand to witness the opening.

The show offered can be called nothing else but a vaudeville show, altho if a regular vaudeville theater were to offer it as a regular bill patronage would undoubtedly be small after the Monday matinee.

Viewing the show from the vaudeville standpoint:

The show is opened by the Eight Palace Girls. The girls are good to look upon and have a routine of dance steps which they show in a snappy manner. There is no change of costume and taken as a whole the act would not get far in the regular vaudeville theaters.

Hy Mayer was on in the number two position, the place assigned on the program to McIntyre and Hardy, who were out of the bill after the Monday afternoon show. Mayer is undoubtedly a master caricaturist, but as a vaudeville act he is terrible. There have been many acts of the kind in the two-a-day theaters, but seldom has there been anything offered that was as poorly conceived as is the act of Mr. Mayer's. He puts a teacup on his head and does an imitation. When nobody laughs he consults his written notes for the next funny (?) one. He tells some atrocious jokes and tells them about as poorly as could be told. Mr. Mayer is much too big and too clever a man to make such a spectacle of himself on the stage.

Ed Wynn is a regular vaudevillian and the idea of the new skit which he is offering is a good one. That is about the best thing that can be said about the act. Wynn has been funny in the past and is undoubtedly a good comedian; but his present offering will in no way tend to increase his reputation as a funmaker. As said before, the idea is there for a good comedy act, but the material now offered is about as funny as a funeral. Wynn is assisted by two other men. They fit into the action of the act all right, but there is nothing for them to do save to enhance the general gloom.

The Eternal Waltz is mostly froth. There is a great big flash, 30-odd people being used in the ensembles. The offering bears the names of a number of very clever poeple and is disappointing only because so much more is to be expected of the people connected with it. The music is by Leo Fahl, who has to his credit *The Dollar Princess* and *The Siren*. In spots the music is catchy, the waltz number being the most notable, but the work, as work of Leo Fahl, is very disappointing. Auston Hurgon is responsible for a book that is very ordinary and the whole thing is produced by Joseph Hart under the direction and patronage of Martin Beck. Cyril Chadwick and Mabel Berra are among the principals. Enough names, truly. Chadwick is funny at times in the role of an English actor, and Miss Berra is seen as a Viennese singer with yearning to be heard in London. The piece is not up to expectation by any manner of means and is not worth the amount of money, time and trouble spent on it.

Taylor Holmes was engaged after the Monday matinee to appear during the remainder of the week. Holmes is doing about half of the act which was reviewed in these columns last week, and much to the improvement of the said offering. Even so, the applause that greeted his efforts on Tuesday night was barely sufficient to cover a single legitimate bow.

Milton Pollock and Company in George Ade's comedy-playlet, *Speaking to Father*, was the only comedy to be found on the bill. That everybody loves to laugh was testified to by the amount of applause tendered the Pollock aggregation at the fall of the curtain.

The Four Vannis have a crackerjack wire offering, the work of the male member who dresses as a woman being particularly worthy of note. Not only is he a wonderful wire worker, but his makeup as a woman will pass muster almost anywhere and puts him in the Julian Eltinge class as far as looks are concerned. The four members of the Vannis troupe are all workers, not a staller among them, and they put up a brand of entertainment that is second to none of the kind.

The applause hit of the bill was the violin playing of one Ota Gygi, billed as "Violinist of the Spanish Court." In rather ill-fitting evening clothes and with no make-up to disguise the natural pallor of his face, Gygi came on and walked away with the honors of the bill. To be sure he didn't offer the kind of music that is attempted by every other violinist playing vaudeville, but it doesn't matter in the least what Gygi plays. It is very much the way he plays it. Gygi will be a great big hit anywhere from vaudeville up to the highest of the high-brow concerts. So well was he appreciated that the applause ran well into the long introductory music of the dancing act that followed.

La Napierkowska is offered as a pantomimist and dancer. The truth of the matter is that La Napierkowska is a mighty good-looking and shapely dancer of the "cooch" variety, formerly so often seen in the Oriental shows on the midway of a fair. But the young lady is some dancer of the kind. There isn't a portion of her body that she cannot make wiggle at will and there is very little of it that isn't constantly wiggling during the time which she spends on the stage in her offering, *The Captive*. She is supposed—so the story of the program runs—to have been stung by a bee and the gyrations that follow the stinging are consequent of the pain she feels. It must be some pain, for such wriggling has never before been seen on a high-grade vaudeville stage.

From the Issue of May 14, 1932

The Palace, New York

(Reviewed Saturday Afternoon, May 7)

Make way for the grind, you slow pokes. The sooner the better. Let's get that box office out in the street and maybe add a barker or two to the front-of-the-house staff. The Palace's quiet, pleasing days are over. Now the radio titan can gird his loins and give battle to civilized entertainment, decent conditions for actors, select audiences; in fact, everything that stands for that detestable institution known as the two-a-day. It is fitting and proper that the rapid-fire word slinger, Floyd Gibbons, who recently returned from the job of staging the big show in Manchuria, should be included among the personalities chosen to join the chorus in the swan song of the Palace that will soon be no more. Gibbons lined up against a Jim Thornton, the Pat Rooney of the old days, Leo Beers and countless others so closely identified with real vaudeville in its heyday makes an incongruous setup. So would a pair of youngsters who stopped the show cold this afternoon and had them hee-hawing at a gag that is dirtier than the stuff they pump out of constipated sewers.

The Palace of Elmer Rogers and weekly subscribers who supported the showcase of vaudeville since they wore knee pants is being thrown into the scrapheap. George Godfrey lined up a good show, even if plenty of self-conscious backs of seats greeted the performers at the opening show. The lineup is weak on "names," a chronic failing in a house that has paralysis of the purse strings, but it plays superbly. Specialties are well balanced and laughs are never lacking. Bill Demarest did well as m. c., as was proved by the great reception he got in his own act after squeezing out plenty of laughs via the introducing route.

ALLAN MANN AND DOROTHY DELL, assisted by Helen O'Shea, dished out a cleverly staged combo of song and dance in the opener. Miss Dell, monikered "Miss Universe" in the windup of a beaut tourney and late of the *Follies*, has very pleasing pipes, a professional beauty face and an attractive figure. Mann and Miss O'Shea are capable steppers, and Miss O'Shea is particularly skillful at toe work. The various specialties are dotted by special material that fits in nicely with the scheme of things. The trio went off to a great hand.

ADA BROWN, the capacious sepia warbler and a familiar item here, was handed the deuce spot and show-stopped with little effort. In fine voice and spirit, Miss Brown did more than her share to give the show a great start. Harry Swanagan at his old ivories position.

HENRY SANTREY is staging a comeback with a band that beats by a wide margin anything that he has done within this reviewer's memory. Bill Demarest made his first appearance preceding Santrey and gave the erstwhile world traveler a fitting sendoff. Santrey's act is dotted with swell music, punch specialties and—more important than these—is beautifully staged. A special attraction for this engagement is John Pio, of all things, a performing parrot who sings, talks, whistles and does authentic imitations. Other outstanding bits are a brass display by the 15 bandsmen and a punchy finale to the circus idea, wherein a girl appears in the back inset as a Roman rider astride two white horses galloping away on a revolving treadmill. Santrey should hit the high spots with this one. His reception was sensational here.

ROSETTA (TOPSY) DUNCAN had a clear field ahead of her all the way and wound up with an even better reception than on the occasion of her debut here as a single March a year ago. Opened with topical special and fairly slew them next with her Maypole number. Pat Casey filled part of a wait with a solo, and then some clowning with Demarest. Miss Duncan's Topsy interlude was considerably heightened in comedy effect this time by new material and gorgeous ad libbing. Her sob number in this guise apparently stirred the audience deeply, and she wound up with a rendering of *Waltz in Three-Quarter Time*, reminiscent of the bit with Ed Wynn that wowed them here last season. Another show-stop. Miss Duncan is one of the cleverest singles in her line today.

WILLIAM DEMAREST AND ESTELLE COLLETTE did surprisingly well as follow-up laugh contenders to Miss Duncan. Demarest took more and harder falls than his *Vanities* colleague, Mahoney, and rarely failed to get his full measure of laughs. Demarest is sometimes not quite as refined as he might be, but he is almost always funny. The pair play violin and cello capably, but the net results would have been the same had these been omitted. Just a decoration like buttons on sleeves.

FLOYD GIBBONS made his fast gab do 10 minutes as faked talk for a series of newsreel clips on the Sino-Japanese trouble before he came out on the apron for an informal chat on his experiences. The clips were interesting, but most of them had been seen at one time or another by fairly steady moviegoers. Gibbons had a sermon to preach in his exposition of conditions in the Far East. Floyd says: "Keep your heads, but keep your powder dry." Apparently he has been imbued with a few grains of Hearst political philosophy. Outside of his cocksureness about the archaic thing known as preparedness, Gibbons reflects a likable personality, and his seven minutes on were evenly interesting.

FRANK MITCHELL AND JACK DURANT, pioneers of the break-your-neck school of hoke, are opening the second half on their second week, and not less careless about their well-being. With Demarest handy, they put on their sensational knockabout antics in a setting similar to that used in *Vanities*, with Bill playing the role of the person who is auditioning their "play." The boys drew a deafening hand and deserved everything they got and more.

CHARLIE JORDAN AND JOHNNY WOODS, a pair of very capable youngsters, whose stock in trade is burlesquing radio personalities and commercial features, experienced no difficulty in retaining interest in their vast array of impersonations, both straight and clowned. Others are working along their line, but not as intensely and with considerably less display of mimicking versatility. With that one gag out in the Amos 'n' Andy takeoff, they should meet with more than passing approval anywhere.

DAVE APOLLON'S third week finds him ready with new tidbits of dialectic clowning and sock specialties. Augmenting his Filipino ensemble on this lap are eight Negro rhythmicians and a quartet of Albertina Rasch Girls doing well by a Chopin waltz. An unbilled adagio team also did well, and the usual warm reception awaited the dancing of Danzi Goodell and Nora Williams' warbling.

Martin Beck came back to save vaudeville. The Palace is going into a grind. And Martin Beck is in Europe with Roxy lining up talent. The Palace is dead. Long live the International Music Hall. ELIAS E. SUGARMAN.

NICKELODEONS, TEN-CENT THEATRES, ONE-REELERS AND UNBILLED PLAYERS

FROM JUNE 4, 1910 ISSUE

THE IDOL OF THE MIOGRAPH, OR THE UNKNOWN BELOVED.

I.

Oh, he's a handsome gallant
  He has sweethearts by the score
And ev'ry day and ev'ry night
  He always wins some more;
And, no wonder, now if you saw him
  I know you would agree,
In all the land from East to West
  No finer could you see!

II.

And yet of these admiring maids,
  Not any does he know,
Not one knows him nor yet his name,
  Still does their rapture flow;
"Oh, ain't he swell, gee, but he's great,
  Oh, Kid he sure is fine!"
And from the maidens more refined—
  "He simply is divine!"

III.

And so they rave and fast do gaze,
  And feast their eyes on him,
Upon his face of beauty rare
  His form so tall and slim.
Oh, sometimes he a soldier is
  In uniform and sword
And then again in curls and frills
  He does the noble lord.

IV.

And now and then he is a monk
  In habit and in cowl
But let him be what e'er he may
  They love him still in all.
His every trick of face they know,
  His frown, his smile so bright,
And every turn of foot and hand
  As he moves there plain to sight.

V.

And yet not one has heard him speak,
  Or seen him in the flesh,
But just the same with silent spell
  He's caught them in his mesh.
Just let some certain places put
  A placard at the door,
With magic words "A Miograph"
  And they need say no more.

VI.

For if they've but a nickel left,
  Out goes each maiden's hand,
They'll enter if the place be packed—
  Aye if they've room to stand.
And who, you ask, can be this one
  Who lures and charms them so—
Why, he's the leading man, you see,
  Of a moving picture show.
              HORTENSE M. LANAHAN,
                            1910.

FROM SEPT. 14, 1912 ISSUE

FROM MARCH 6, 1909 ISSUE

NICKELODEON, KEWANEE, ILL.

The Nickelodeon Theatre, of Kewanee, Ill., shown above, is the oldest of the moving picture houses in the city. It was opened in the spring of 1907, and has had a prosperous career, under the able management of Mr. Chris Taylor.

FROM MARCH 20, 1909 ISSUE

THE NOVELTY THEATRE.

The Novelty Theatre and Arcade is located at 38 Washington Ave. South, Minneapolis, Minn., and is owned and managed by Mr. L. E. Lund. This theatre seats 400 people and plays four shows daily, consisting of continuous vaudeville, motion pictures and illustrated songs. It is the intention of Mr. Lund to reinstate stock at this theatre in the course of about six weeks' time. This theatre enjoys an excellent patronage at all times, and the arcade run in connection with it has many entertaining and amusing devices which also show lucrative results.

FROM MARCH 16, 1907 ISSUE

EXTERIOR OF THE VITAGRAPH COMPANY'S PLANT ON LONG ISLAND.

INTERIOR OF THE SAME BUILDING SHOWING THE STUDIO WITH ITS ACCESSORIES.

FROM FEB. 3, 1912 ISSUE

PROMINENT IMP PLAYERS

GRACE LEWIS   H. L. MACK   MARGARET FISCHER

EDWARD LE SAINT

FARREL MAC DONALD   KING BAGGOT   HARRY POLLARD

WILLIAM SHAY   JOHN R CUMPSON   WILLIAM R. DALI

MEMBERS OF THE REX FAMILY.

LOIS WEBER.   PHILLIP SMALLEY.   HELEN REX ANDERSON.   CHAS. DeFOREST.   EDA AUGVALL.

184

FROM FEB. 3, 1912 ISSUE

FROM DEC. 2, 1905 ISSUE

FROM DEC. 9, 1905 ISSUE

MOVIEGOERS MAKE THEIR OWN STARS

FROM DEC. 9, 1911 ISSUE

FROM AUG. 17, 1912 ISSUE

FLORENCE LAWRENCE

FROM JULY 15, 1911 ISSUE

FROM DEC. 24, 1910 ISSUE

MARY PICKFORD

Known as the Biograph Comedy Girl, is Engaged by Carl Laemmle—She is One of the Best Known Picture Actresses in the Profession

New York, Dec. 19 (Special to The Bill-board).—Quite the most important event in the film gam• last week was the acquisition by Carl Laemmle to his company of Miss Mary Pickford, prominently known as the "Biograph Comedy Girl."

For some time past Miss Pickford has ap-peard in Biograph pictures, giving remarkably clever portrayals in all instances. Especially pleasing were her efforts in Biograph pictures taken during that company's stay in Cali-fornia not so very long ago. Miss Pickford is one of the most prominent of motion picture actresses by reason of her long association with the Biograph Company. In roles such as she has portrayed with the Biograph Company, Miss Pickford is the peer of her profession.

MARY PICKFORD,

The Biograph Comedy Girl, who has been engaged by Carl Laemmle. The little Lady is endearingly referred to as "Little Mary" and she is on intimate terms with every person who patronizes the moving picture theatre.

FROM MAY 1, 1915 ISSUE

FRANCIS X. BUSHMAN

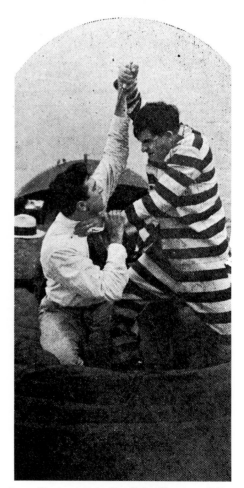

An exciting moment in The Stolen Woman, a Reliance two-reel subject. to be released Sept. 20.

FROM AUG. 26, 1916 ISSUE

Mary Pickford Film Corporation

World's Foremost Star of Motion Pictures Supreme Heads Her Own Company

ANNOUNCEMENT

"IN announcing the formation of the MARY PICK-FORD FILM CORPORATION, I want to first express my gratitude for the co-operation of the exhibitors, everywhere, and also for the generous response of the public in bringing success to my efforts and various creations on the screen. Surely without either no one can have progressed and in my instance our work together has been so full of happiness that it makes doubly treasured the success that has come to us.

"IN the selection of scenarios, the casting of companies, the direction, production and character creating of motion pictures I am sure that I have learned something every day and that I will keep on acquiring this knowledge. And that is just why I want to use it to the best advantage in guiding my own company, which will now produce all of the plays in which I am to be seen. It is our purpose not only to give every detail of the Mary Pickford Film Corporation our unfaltering direction, but to surround ourself with the best brains, ability and skill in this wonderful art industry.

"IT will be our purpose and endeavor to make most complete, elaborate and art harmonizing productions—each of which is to stand out pre-eminently as a master work. The productions will be the best that are made.

Each will have a cast of distinction, a direction of originality and creativeness, fine environment, its own especially written music—all with that dignity, simplicity and artistic ensemble that will make the best in motion pictures and attract the largest and most discriminating audiences. I want the Mary Pickford pictures to be seen in every theatre and playhouse in the country. We are delighted with the arrangements and broad plan of distribution made by the Artcraft Pictures Corporation which has been formed to handle them.

"PROMPTED by your encouragement of the past, and for which I feel that I owe so much to you in aiding me to reach an ambitious attainment, I feel now that with this incentive and with the ever present confidence with which you have approved and admired my work that I can now reach still higher, giving you the supreme of our art endeavor—but always depending on your affectionate interest, for which I am now and always—   Gratefully,

Mary Pickford.

To Be Distributed Everywhere and Alone by the ARTCRAFT PICTURES CORPORATION

"WITH full confidence the ARTCRAFT PICTURES CORPORATION makes its entry into the film industry announcing that it has been organized to present and distribute film attractions that will evidence the highest attainments of the cinematographic art. For its initial undertaking it now offers to the exhibitors of America the productions of THE MARY PICKFORD FILM CORPORATION, in which will be presented exclusively the greatest artist in the history of the world of amusements.

MARY PICKFORD

No personality is so dominant in motion pictures as that of Mary Pickford. It is the crystallization of magnetism without a parallel in the history of either the spoken or the silent stage.

Every exhibitor knows that the advent of a new Mary Pickford picture means an event in the season of his theatre or playhouse. This has been the unfailing rule.

NOW, heading her own film corporation, Mary Pickford with her wonderful art and great experience will bring to these productions a new life, a stronger drawing power and a more lasting charm. Being alone and on no programme she will com-

pletely pervade the entertainment presented, making its attractiveness to the marvelous and almost uncounted Mary Pickford following all the stronger.

IT is Mary Pickford's desire that these new productions shall be the best ever presented on the screen; they will be limited in number, but unlimited in cost. She will be surrounded by the best brains, skill and creative resourcefulness obtainable in this art industry. Each production will be a master-work and artistic ensemble beyond compare—that will in every detail have the wondrous touch and never failing appeal of Mary Pickford.

IT is the purpose to present the Mary Pickford pictures everywhere. It is her own desire that they shall be seen in every theatre and motion picture house in the land. She comes to you alone with productions surpassing anything yet done on the screen, supporting casts of distinction, master direction—in all a complete harmonizing of every detail of the art in which she stands alone as its most popular and favored star—the incomparable Mary Pickford.

YOU owe it to your patrons to immediately arrange for these new and all-appealing Mary Pickford productions in your theatre.

ARTCRAFT PICTURES CORPORATION, 729 Seventh Ave., New York City.

191

FROM JULY 7, 1917 ISSUE

CHARLES CHAPLIN

The screen's most famous comedian, who has contracted to do a series of pictures for Nat'l Exhibitors' Circuit.

FROM SEPT. 1, 1917 ISSUE

Scene in The Adventurer, Mutual-Chaplin Special. Released by Mutual Film Corp.

FROM MARCH 31, 1917 ISSUE

Scene in The Cure, forthcoming Mutual-Chaplin production, with Charles Chaplin. Released by Mutual Film Corporation.

FROM OCT. 7, 1916 ISSUE

Scene in The Pawnshop, with Charlie Chaplin. Released October 2 by the Mutual Film Corporation.

STAGE AND VAUDEVILLE STARS SUCCUMB TO MOVIES

FROM JULY 20, 1912 ISSUE

PROMINENT THEATRICAL STARS IN FILMS

New Company Is Formed To Be Known as Famous Players Film Company Which Will Produce Pictures in Which the Most Celebrated Actors in America and Europe Will Appear—Daniel Frohman, A. Zukor and Other Well-Known Theatrical Men Interested in Project

New York, July 13 (Special to The Billboard). —The famous theatrical stars of both America and Europe have entered the film end of the theatrical business, under the banner of a newly-formed organization, whose offices and headquarters are in New York.

The organization is known as The Famous Players Film Company, and has no less distinguished a name among its members than that of Daniel Frohman, who holds the office of managing director. A. Zukor, treasurer of the Marcus Loew enterprises, and prominent theatrical man of New York City, is president of the company, and is in charge of its offices in the Times Building.

While many of the names of those connected with the company are being kept in the dark, it is stated by the officers above-named that a large number of the most prominent theatrical men in the business are affiliated with the concern, and will soon let their identity be known.

The plan of the company is to produce feature films, using the big stars in the main roles. In many instances the same plays in which the players have become famous will be filmed, or else some production in which that star has recently appeared. In other instances new productions will be written in which the prominent people will appear.

The first production to be finished is a three-reel, one of Queen Elizabeth, in which Sarah Bernhardt plays the title role. This production was made in Paris recently in an especially equipped studio near the Sarah Bernhardt Theatre. The staff of that theatre, as well as some of the scenery and property, were utilized, while the entire company, which is maintained at the Sarah Bernhardt, was at the command of the producers, and many of them appear in the picture.

The films are to be sold on the state-right basis, but in many instances will be booked directly by the Famous Players Company into the houses controlled by its members. State-right purchasers will also be assured of good booking in houses controlled by the members of the company, and co-operation between state-right purchaser and producer will always be encouraged.

Popular exhibition of the films, that is, showing them at popular prices, will be prohibited by the company, as only the finest of houses are desired. The exhibition of the films in small theatres, the producers declare, will injure the results of the general plan of exhibition. No five and ten-cent houses or even 10, 20 and 30 houses will be permitted to use the films. It is likely that dollar prices will prevail wherever the films are shown.

The new company is capitalized at $25,000 and is going at each and every phase of the business, with the end in view of making the production strictly first-class and on a higher plane than pictures have ever been put before. Besides the organization in America, a European branch or connection has been established so that the films will be handled in Europe the same as they are in America. The shows will be put on as regular theatrical productions, billed as such, and run for long periods wherever possible. Special music for each production will be prepared, so that each orchestra where the films are shown will have the advantage of expert selection of music in creating the effects for the pictures.

The first showing of the Queen Elizabeth production took place at the Lyceum Theatre, New York, Friday afternoon, June 12, before a large and enthusiastic gathering of newspaper men and critics, as well as members of the Famous Players Company, who had not seen the work of the producing artists.

The setting and costuming of the production are exquisite in every sense of the word, while the photography and other technical points in the production are practically perfect. As to the acting displayed by the famous collection of players, it is, like all film productions in which legitimate people appear, a little too stiff and not quite as natural as that displayed by artists trained well in the art of pantomime, but, nevertheless, of a high quality, and free from all pretense and any display of amateurishness. Of all the films now made in which big people appear, Queen Elizabeth can easily be said to be the best.

Bernhardt is said to have realized that she was undertaking a very difficult thing in trying to act before the camera, and gave every possible attention to the producing manager who directed the play. Other people in the case also seem to be possessed with a willingness to make the film a success, and the original difficulty which legitimate people experience in a case of this kind is very much overcome in this production.

The scenery and settings, as stated above, have been prepared with wonderful care. In accomplishing this, many of the original letters and paintings which form a part of the story of Queen Elizabeth and her death have been utilized and are seen photographed in the picture.

The production of Queen Elizabeth will be followed by regular releases, made perhaps as often as once each month. In these, other stars of renown will appear. These stars have been definitely engaged and the productions arranged, but the Famous Players Company will not announce their names until just prior to the launching of each film on the market.

A peculiar state of affairs incident to the formation of the Famous Players Company is the bringing together of the legitimate interests which have for so long been at war. In the new company, it will soon be learned, men who have long fought each other in the legitimate producing field will be working side by side in the production of the feature films. These names will be announced later, and in the list, it is strange to say, will appear the names of men who for some time have been strongly antagonistic to the motion picture industry, and who have at every turn refused admittance into their houses to the picture companies.

DANIEL FROHMAN

Managing Director of the newly formed Famous Players Film Company.

FROM MARCH 21, 1914 ISSUE

ETHEL BARRYMORE

Engaged by All-Star

Famous Actress Will Make Her Debut in Pictures Under Direction of Augustus Thomas

New York, March 13.—Setting at rest the consistent and persistent rumor that this or that concern had secured the services of the greatest and most popular of modern-day theatrical stars of the gentler sex, comes the authorized announcement from the offices of the All-Star Feature Corporation, that contract has been entered into by that concern for the initial appearance before the moving picture camera, of the only and inimitable Ethel Barrymore.

Miss Barrymore's success as a theatrical star is world wide and probably she has enjoyed an almost unique distinction in the matter of record runs. She will be best remembered from her performances in Vera, the Medium, Miss Civilization, The Witness for the Defense, Mid-Channel, Cousin Kate, Captain Jinks, Carrots, Sunday, Alice, Sit by the Fire and her present success, Tante.

It is the plan of the All-Star Company that immediately upon the close of her present starring tour, Miss Barrymore will make her initial bow before the camera in the leading role of a prominent Broadway play, probably one in which she has before appeared, the title of which will be announced at an early date.

Miss Barrymore's services have been claimed from time to tim by nearly every large producer of moving pictures in America, and considerable speculation has been rife as to where and with whom her first appearance in photoplays was to be made, and with this, the first definite and authortative statement, rumor is set at rest.

That a pronounced success awaits Miss Barrymore in the field of moving pictures can not be denied, and it is more than probable that this may be but the first of a series of pictures in which this talented artist will appear.

Although the figure Miss Barrymore is to receive has not been disclosed it is freely rumored that it is well in excess of five figures and in all probability she will receive a greater amount than any artist has ever received for appearance in moving pictures. It is probable that in this agreement between the All-Star Feature Corporation and Miss Barrymore a new mark has been set.

Augustus Thomas, director general of the All-Star concern, will be in personal supervision of the picture in which Miss Barrymore will make her debut as an artist of the silent drama, and with the tremendous success with which he accredited himself in his company's latest release, Paid in Full, exhibitors, distributors and public may well expect another masterpiece to be added to the list of successes which have been produced by the All-Star Corporation.

FROM DEC. 20, 1913 ISSUE

LASKY ENTERS M. P. FIELD.

New York, Dec. 11.—Jesse L. Lasky, the well-known vaudevil producer and conceiver of the famous Follies Bergere, has entered the motion picture game at the head of a corporation under the laws of New York State, to be called the Jesse L. Lasky Feature Motion Picture Co.

Cecil De Mille, prominent playwright and director, who, for the past few years has been connected with Belasco productions, will be associated with Mr. Laskey as general stage director and will have full charge of the production end.

Oscar Apfel, the well-known director, having formerly been with the Majestic, Reliance, Edison and lately with Pathe-Freres, will assist Mr. De Mille in the technical part of the picture game with which he is not quite familiar.

> Cecil B. DeMille, prominent playwright and director . . . will be associated with Mr. Lasky as general stage director and will have full charge of production.

The sales department of the new company will be in charge of Frank A. Tichenor, widely known among manufacturers and exhibitors, and as the head of the Manhattan Slide and Film Co. Samuel Goldfish, as treasurer and business, manager will look after the commercial end.

The first production of the Lasky corporation will be Edward Milton Boyle's The Squaw Man, with as many of the original cast as can be secured. Dustin Farnum has already been engaged and with Messrs. Boyle and De Mille left for the West in search of the exact spot upon which Mr. Royle based the action of his drama, where the production will be enacted.

FROM SPEPT. 12, 1914 ISSUE

MODERN STUFF.

Mrs. Fiske thinks. It is one of her peculiarities. Big things interest her. Recently she had her first experience in the moving picture business. To a friend, she said, "I confess I approached it with a touch of contempt. I soon learned better. It is the great new art. Mighty things are to come from it. You will not see them, nor I. The beginnings are crude and the best is far off. But in the future is an art of wonderful spirituality. To the actor, it brings freedom from restrictive and artificial influences and tempts him to his largest possiblities."

FROM APRIL 17, 1909 ISSUE

GAUMONT'S NEW CHRONOPHONE AND FILM SUBJECTS.

The Harry Lauder Series.—Series of pictures sung and acted by Harry Lauder, the famous comedian. The subjects of this artist below listed are amongst his most successful numbers. Inverary, Wedding of Lauchie McGraw, Stop Your Tickling Jock, Rising Early in the Morning, Aye Waken O, and We Parted on the Shore.

Miss Victoria Monks.—Another well-known vaudeville artist in two of her best numbers. Love Song and Give My Regards to Leicester Square.

Will Evans.—The popular star in his screaming sketch, Invasion 1910.

Faust.—The great French opera sung by the exquisite talent of the Paris Opera House. Faust—Duet from the first act; Faust—First act, third part; Faust—My beloved; Faust—Church scene, first; Faust—I greet thee.

Carmen.—The great French opera Carmen rendered by the greatest Paris talent. Carmen—Mother I see thee; Carmen—Habanera; Carmen—The duel.

Dragons de Villars.—French opera. Moi, jolie, Duet. The Awakening.

Hannah, Won't You Open That Door, a funny darky story; Xylophone Solo; Pagliacci, Vesti la Giubba, by Signor Corradetti; O Sole Mio, a beautiful melody by a great artist; Every Little Bit Helps, funny darky songs and says; and others.

FROM JAN. 17, 1914 ISSUE

"Good-by, Old Man"—John Barrymore in An American Citizen, by the Famous Players Film Co.

THOS. H. INCE

BILLIE BURKE'S CAPITULATION TO THE LURE OF M. P. CAMERA

As Engineered by the Indefatigable Thos. H. Ince

It's all over. The story of it was told in a news dispatch that emanated from New York some weeks ago. Therefore, it's all over—all over the country. It took a long time and a bundle of money and cost at least one man many hours of sleep. But it's all over now and the man sleeps peacefully.

Billie Burke has succumbed to the lure of the camera. Her dainty signature has long since dried on the parchment, and before many fortnights she will have commenced to arise with the sun out in the fragrant fastnesses of the canyons on the Southern California Coast.

Director-in-chief of the New York Motion Picture Corp., the man who won Billie Burke to the "movies."

NAZIMOVA
Signed by Triangle
$60,000 Reported Salary of Famous Emotional Actress for Four Weeks' Work Before the Camera

New York, Oct. 22.—What is undoubtedly one of the biggest transactions in the field of motion pictures of recent date, so far as the signing of artists is concerned, probably is that this week of the Triangle Film Corporation in inducing Mme. Nazimova, the famous Russian tragedienne to affix her signature to a contract, calling for her exclusive services for film purposes for a period of four weeks for a consideration of $60,000.

The deal for Nazimova's services was closed by the Triangle representatives with her New York agent, M. S. Bentham, and calls for a weekly salary of $15,000, believed to be the largest sum ever paid for a motion picture artist for a stated period.

Nazimova created a furore upon her initial vaudeville appearance here this year, when she played to capacity audiences for three weeks in War Brides at the Palace Theater. Later she played the Keith Circuit in the vehicle, since which time she has been resting.

As an emotional actress few there are who can compare with Mme. Nazimova, and Triangle must be given unstinted praise and credit for their foresight and success in securing her for their photoplays. Just in what photodrama Mme. Nazimova will make her initial screen appearance has not yet been determined, but it undoubtedly will be some strong play, in which unlimited opportunities will be afforded her to display her truly marvelous histrionic ability.

Anna Pavlowa

A NEW WAVE OF MOVIE MOGULS, MULTIPLE-REEL FEATURES AND THE FIRST SERIALS

FROM JUNE 12, 1915 ISSUE

ADOLPH ZUKOR LEAVES FOR LOS ANGELES

President of Famous Players Will Remain at Coast Studios One Month—Three Separate Studios Will Be Erected in Western City

New York, June 2.—Adolph Zukor, president of the Famous Players Film Co., left last Saturday for the Coast studios of his company, accompanied by Mrs. Zukor and his son and daughter, Eugene J. and Mildred Zukor. It is said that Mr. Zukor's object for the trip is a very important one, and the fact that he contemplates remaining at Los Angeles for about a month lends an added significance.

Mr. Zukor's purpose, as indicated in a statement from the Famous Players Film Co., is no less than the purchase of a large tract of ground in or about Los Angeles for the erection of three separate studios. The Famous Players Film Co. has maintained a studio on the Pacific Coast for the past year, where most of the recent Mary Pickford subjects were produced. The satisfactory photographic and scenic results obtained by the Western company, it is inferred, have now encouraged the Famous Players to expand their producing activities in Los Angeles.

Under the management of Albert A. Kaufman, who has been acting as Western manager since the Famous Players invaded Los Angeles, the studio resources of this company have steadily accumulated to such an extent that but for the physical space required the Famous Players' Western organization is now fully equipped with lights and incidental paraphernalia to occupy two or more studios. It is to obtain the ground whereby to fill this need that caused Mr. Zukor to undertake this trip.

It is possible that in the future several other companies will be sent to the Coast, and the original plans for the Western productions are now being magnified to take in the added possibilities that will thus be supplied.

It is said that another factor that has actuated the Famous Players in the intention to perfect permanent studios on the Coast is the long duration of the present European war. Before the outbreak of hostilities abroad the Famous Players had concluded a policy of producing a number of elaborate feature subjects in the various countries of Europe each year. It is supposed that, with the elimination of the possibility of producing pictures in Europe for some time to come, the Famous Players intend to culminate their plans for these massive productions in California. When the European invasion was determined upon a series of great spectacular subjects were secured, which it would now be difficult to produce in the East. These plays, however, will have ample productive opportunities when Mr. Zukor's plans for the new Coast studios are matured.

FROM FEB. 5, 1916 ISSUE

SELZNICK HEADS MILLION DOLLAR PICTURE COMPANY

Clara Kimball Young Film Corporation Will Feature Star of That Name in What Are Expected To Be Classics of Screen— Initial Release in October Next

New York, Jan. 31.—Statement is made today by Lewis J. Selznick, former vice-president and general manager of the World Film Corporation, of the organization of the Clara Kimball Young Film Corporation, capitalized at $1,000,000, he to be president and general manager. Executive offices and the principal studios will be located in New York City. The initial release in which Miss Young will be starred in common with all of the forthcoming features will be made in October next, with one release each month thereafter.

Clara Kimball Young is one of the popular stars of the screen world, and features in which she is to have first prominence will be based on scenarios especially written for her by some of the best-known authors.

Work on the new company's studios here, in the South and in Cuba, is being rushed.

Selznick, who in the last few years has forged rapidly to the front rank of motion picture manufacturers, wishes to be quoted as saying that he will personally supervise every foot of film to bear the Clara Kimball Young brand.

Two noted directors have been placed under contract, and the work of engaging a picked company of well-known stage and screen favorites to support Miss Young is now in progress. Commenting on the new concern Selznick said: "It is my aim to make our features distinctive in every way. The photography will be the very best that masters of the art can produce, and the direction will be in the hands of the best producers I can obtain. Money and brains will be used lavishly to make these features of the Clara Kimball Young Corporation classics of the screen in every sense." In an interview Miss Young said: "My ambition is even higher than that. I want to be the founder of a studio which shall be to the film industry of America that the classic Theatre Francaise of Paris is to Europe. Among my plans is included a training school for young actresses, who will be taught the technique of the screen."

FROM OCT. 11, 1913 ISSUE

FROM JUNE 16, 1917 ISSUE

GOLDFISH DESCRIBES PLAN OF GOLDWYN PRODUCTIONS

Head of Big Producing Concern Tells How "The New Idea" Behind the Organization Has Succeeded Beyond All Expectations

New York, June 11.—Practically on the eve of showing the first of the Goldwyn productions to the nation's exhibitors at the various Goldwyn branches in the United States and Canada, Samuel Goldfish, president of Goldwyn Pictures Corporation, has for the first time talked personally about his organization's productions.

Goldwyn's first trade showings at its exchanges will be held in July and not less than four pictures, with as many stars, will be ready for inspection.

"We have deliberately set out in our Goldwyn Pictures," says Mr. Goldfish, "to show both exhibitors and the public that there is a great deal more that can be put in a motion picture than the featured personality known as the 'star.'

"I have a feeling now that goes much deeper than the feeling I had four years ago when I founded and organized the Lasky Company, whose productions were innovations in the film industry. I believe that today and for a long time into the future the quality of the story and the manner of its production will be the essentially big factors of successful pictures.

"I make no prediction about the lessening influence of stars, nor do I foresee the elimination of the star system. In Goldwyn we frankly recognize what we term star values by having exclusively in our service immensely popular women known everywhere and having box-office value everywhere. We expect exhibitors to advertise and exploit these stars because of their powers of audience attraction, but we know from within our organization that we can make the production itself our greatest mercantile asset. Incidentally we make the stars themselves much better thru the medium of powerful stories produced and directed by important artists.

"The splendid successes achieved by Edgar and Archibald Selwyn, Margaret Mayo, Arthur Hopkins, who are the associated owners of Goldwyn, as well as the achievements of the other distinguished factors we have enlisted with us, could not fail to exert a great influence for good in the world of motion pictures.

"In this alliance we have not been scared or even slightly influenced by precedent—which is the dangerous obstacle to progress in any art or industry. We have defied all of the established picture conventions as well as the business conventions of the industry. We have resisted from the beginning any and all influences that cause a producer to make time-clock pictures. We prefer to make pictures slowly.

"We have inventive, creative, imaginative artists in our service and we have not wanted them to think and work under excessive pressure. In other words we have taken our time and will continue to do so.

FROM SEPT. 1, 1917 ISSUE

SAY, MR!

Would You Read This If It Showed You How To Gather Some Money?---THEN DO!

Sarah Bernhardt has just transferred her divine genius and marvelous power of interpretation to a half-mile of wonderful celluloid with her latest and greatest success— "Queen Elizabeth"

THE DEATH OF THE QUEEN. ONLY ONE OF THE PAINTINGS IN THE PRODUCTION.

In which Bernhardt is supported by her all-star company with which she is now taking Europe by storm in the same play—the absorbing story of Queen Elizabeth's passionate attachment to her foolish young lover, Lord Essex, and his tragic death, one of the strangest and strongest stories history has ever written in tears and blood, in

THREE ARTISTICALLY TINTED AND TONED REELS OF MOVING PAINTINGS

SARAH BERNHARDT had only to be **herself** to be QUEEN ELIZABETH. The interpretation is so realistic, so inherently exact and astoundingly faithful, that it will go down in histrionic history as the most marvelous detail of Sarah Bernhardt's genius. Oh, we know you think **we must** say so, but suppose we appoint YOU as judge; the "Court" scenes themselves would win the trial.

The sovereign pride of Elizabeth, the haughty wit, the sincere pathos of her sorrow and her pathetic devotion to the fickle man she loved—after all so weakly human and humanly weak—are all suggested in the gifted art and astonishing skill of Bernhardt's delineation of the Lonely Queen.

The producers of "QUEEN ELIZABETH" were assisted by THE ENGLISH GOVERNMENT, which surrendered priceless documents from the British Museum (the originals of Elizabeth) for the purposes of the production. Every detail is a faithful reproduction of the Elizabethan period, and the dresses, armor, furniture and buildings bring you back over the road to yesterday to five hundred years ago!

Your State wants to see BERNHARDT as QUEEN ELIZABETH! Let your bank-roll toward a million! Express your thoughts in dots and dashes! Don't wait for a stamp or a stampede!—WIRE!

The U. S. Government Assures Protection To State-Right-Buyers!

FAMOUS PLAYERS FILM COMPANY
TIMES BUILDING
42nd St. and Broadway, - - N. Y. C.
DANIEL FROHMAN, MANAGING DIRECTOR.   A. ZUKOR, PRESIDENT.

OH, YES! If the fine assortment of seven-colored lithographs and artistically printed booklets were printed on the yellow silk paper used by the Government, they couldn't be worth any more money to you!

FROM DEC. 19, 1914 ISSUE

THE SUPREMACY OF THE FEATURE FILM AT LAST CONCEDED

By ADOLPH ZUKOR

President Famous Players' Film Co.

FROM the inception of the feature film to its present day of supreme advancement the theory has constantly been abroad in the land that the popularity of the multiple-reel production was non-endurable and destined for an early termination. In spite of the great number of these threnodizing theorists however, the feature production has steadily increased in importance and prestige until today it represents, more than any other form of the motion picture, the true dignity and power of the silent drama. That the feature has not only elevated the industry, but possibly actually perpetuated it, is a conclusion more and more commanding attention and credence.

Today no film program is complete without a feature, though this great phase of the motion picture industry is as yet in its initial stage, the first advance in the direction of a feature program having been made only two years ago, when the Famous Players inaugurated a service of three features a month.

The greatest glories of the silent drama, the highest artistic power attained by it, and its furthest possible future advancement, are all represented in the feature. Great as always were the mechanical and artistic possibilities of the screen, it remained for the feature films to utilize and extend to the fullest degree these possibilities.

Next in numbers to those who pessimistically forecasted the early demise of the feature film, was the army of calamity howlers who have always contended that European features are far superior to American productions and that American film could never reach the standard set by the more important foreign producers. While we have not yet produced a Cabiria in America, or a Quo Vadis, American concerns have produced a series of features during the past year that, on an average, more than measure up to those productions. For consistency of merit and regularity of standard, American features have already far surpassed the European product, and indeed it is a tenable statement that if one of the few leading American feature concerns devoted the physical time necessary for the production of a stupendous feature, such as Cabiria, it would very nearly reach the standard established by this subject.

Without wishing to devote this article to anything but a general survey of the feature situation, I might still say that two forthcoming Famous Players' productions, The Sign of the Cross and The Eternal City, approach the standard of the best European features yet presented to the public, and while the latter subject was produced in Italy, it must still be called an American feature because it was directed by American producers (Edwin S. Porter and Hugh Ford), with the leading role portrayed by an American star (Pauline Frederick). The Sign of the Cross, which has already been released in Europe, has been termed by the leading European trade journals, conspicuous among them being The London Bioscope, "The greatest Roman classic that ever appeared on the screen."

In this connection it should be remembered that The London Bioscope is a conservative journal, not given to fulsome praise of a production unless said production is absolutely deserving.

This would encourage us to conclude that the American feature is today in the first rank of universal multiple-reel productions. That we will go still further in the future, mechanically, artistically and dramatically, is a conservative statement, and that the American feature will place the domestic manufacturer far in advance of his foreign colleagues is a result at last visible to the majority associated with motion pictures.

FROM JULY 24, 1915 ISSUE

FROM JULY 24, 1915 ISSUE

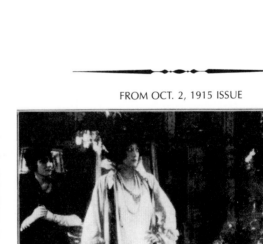

Douglas Fairbanks in The Lamb, one of the initial Triangle releases to be seen at the Knickerbocker Theatre, New York City.

FROM OCT. 2, 1915 ISSUE

Pauline Frederick in Zaza, the only one of eleven completed features wholly saved from the recent fire in the Famous Players Studios. Zaza will be released October 4 on Paramount program.

DAVID W. GRIFFITH

Producer of The Birth of a Nation, the first motion picture to play a lengthy engagement at $2 prices.

FROM OCT. 16, 1915 ISSUE

HIGH-WATER MARK SET IN PURCHASE OF STATE RIGHTS

Elliott-Sherman Film Co. Secure Privilege of Showing

The Birth of a Nation in Seventeen Western States

The Deal Involving a Cash Outlay of $250,000

New York, Oct. 9.—Rights for the exclusive showing privilege in seventeen Western States of the famous film production, The Birth of a Nation, have just been secured by General Manager H. A. Sherman, of the Elliott-Sherman Film Company, with headquarters in Minneapolis. A total

of $250,000 in cash is the sum involved in the transaction, which is one of the biggest State-right deals in motion pictures ever made. Joseph Friedman, an associate of the firm, accompanied Mr. Sherman to New York to complete the deal.

The States for which the Elliott-Sherman Company have purchased the rights for the Griffith picturization are Minnesota, Iowa, Kansas, Nebraska, North Dakota, South Dakota, New Mexico, Colorado, Wyoming, Montana, Nevada, Idaho, Utah, Wisconsin, Arizona, Oregon and Washington.

FROM MARCH 20, 1915 ISSUE

ROBERT GRAU

Intimate and Important Revelations Appertaining to the Larger and Finer Phases of the Business

David W. Griffith's pictorial cycle had two premiers this week, one on Monday afternoon for the press, while the general public saw The Birth of a Nation on Wednesday evening. Ever since the Liberty Theater has been practically sold out twice daily. One may see at any hour of the day a long line approaching the box-office, purchasing seats days in advance. In the balcony and gallery particularly the capacity has been tested, thus proving that the masses will pay "theater prices" to see a photoplay.

No previous film production has ever been exploited with such total disregard of expense. Never in the history of the theater has such an advertising campaign been attempted. The late J. M. Hill's exploitation of Denman Thompson, wherein he spent $10,000 in the New York dailies in one issue, no longer holds the record, for at least $25,000 was spent by the Mutual Film Corporation before the opening.

At the private showing it was observed that not one person left his or her seat until the final reel had been completed. For two hours and forty minutes an audience representing the best brains of the metropolis sat under the spell Griffith had woven. In the foyers during the one short intermission the predominating opinion expressed was that this Griffith effort created an epoch of greater significance than either Quo Vadis or Cabiria.

But in the second part of The Birth of a Nation the daring nature of this pictorial recital caused not a few eminent writers to shake their heads ominously. Said one:

"As recently as ten years ago this picture would have created a race war, twenty years ago it would never have been presented a second time, but today I wonder only at the intrepidity of the entire undertaking. If the films are not censored in part, if the public is permitted to see it as shown here today, even if in America snags are encountered the final result will be the greatest financial success in film history."

At the conclusion of the tense performance on the screen there gathered in the rear of the orchestra a group of stars and musicians from the Metropolitan Opera House. The discussion became so animated that a crowd soon gathered to listen to what was as heated an argument as even grnd opera singers of foreign characteristics can indulge in. "Griffith is the Toscanini of motion pictures," remarked one of the prima donnas of the opera house.

Immediately came a ponderous figure to the fore gesticulating wildly: "Bah," says he, "Griffith is more than a genius. He is to be compared with no mere man. When Toscanini can make men and women sing without voices, when he can make them live a story in two hours and a half, like this one today, then, and not before, will he be entitled to rank as the 'Griffith of Grand Opera.'"

After such a poignant disposition of the merits of the two masters there came a babble in several languages simultaneously. Griffith must have heard it all, for he was but a step away.

FROM SEPT. 11, 1915 ISSUE

500TH FOR THE NATION FILM

New York, Sept. 4.—The Birth of a Nation passed its 500th presentation in New York on last Tuesday night. The run at the Liberty Theater was marked last week by the fourth largest number of admissions of the twenty-seven weeks that the picture has been on Broadway. It is said that 453,000 people have seen the picture here, and that the gross receipts have been considerably over $300,000.

CLEAN-UPS IN NIGHT CLUBS
AND BURLESQUE

FROM APRIL 22, 1911 ISSUE

THE FOLIES BERGERE

Henry B. Harris and Jesse L. Lasky Offer New York a New Form of Enchantment—Production a Triumph of Artistic Construction

Henry B. Harris and Jesse L. Lasky have invested more than one million dollars in the Folies Bergere and its companies, which opened April 16.

The house as seen from Broadway and 46th street is an architectural exotic, with its rich front of glazed tiles, set in Louis Seize designs and inset with an $8,000 mural painting, depicting the origin and development of comedy, from the open air theatres of the Greeks to the stage of the Folies Bergere. This colored outside is illuminated at night by blazing gas torches softened with steam.

The Folies Bergere aims to be the smartest restaurant and the smartest music hall in the world. It is not a huge, garish resort. Its founders have achieved a triumph of artistic construction in every detail, and have exacted of the architect and decorators plans that call for the very quintessence of beauty, charm and studiously refined elegance. The orchestra de luxe of the Folies Bergere has no seats, as in the ordinary theatre. Instead, the entire space is taken up by movable tables and chairs, made in Paris from exclusive designs, together with the entire restaurant equipment. By a patented arrangement, all chairs and tables face the stage, and tables can instantly be set in units for parties of any size; thus one can dine alone at one's own table, or with any number of guests or companions at a private table set as a unit and independent of its neighbors. There are boxes with chairs and tables in the box circle, and behind them more restaurant room. There are theatre seats in the balcony and grand circle. The kitchens, wine cellars and storerooms are cut out of the solid rock beneath the street and alleys. The space directly beneath the auditorium is given to two Louis Seize dressing rooms, bath rooms, barber shop, manicures, valets and other comforts of a club or hotel.

The Folies Bergere opens for dinner at 6 P. M. During dinner, mandolin and guitar players, violinists, singers and dancers from Madrid, Vienna, Paris and Buda-Pesth go from table to table, giving tabloid shows, full of verve and sensation. At 8:15, when the diners have reached their coffee and cigarettes, the curtain goes up on a revue, which is followed by a ballet and then by another revue. At 11 P. M., the first show of the evening is over, and at 11:15 there begins supper and the Cabaret show, made up of sensational novelties from Europe, in which pretty women predominate. This runs until 1 A. M.

The second or Cabaret show has nothing to do with the first entertainment, and to see both it is necessary to purchase two sets of coupons. Prices range from $1 to $2.50 at the early show, and $1 to $1.50 at the second. One may buy for either show or for both.

There will be the fullest possible service at all times, and smoking will be permitted all over the house. It is expected, however, that during the actual progress of the first show that dinner will be over and only light refreshments be called for until the supper hour arrives. There will be matinees on Tuesday, Thursday and Saturdays, at which ladies' teas will be a special feature.

FROM APRIL 28, 1917 ISSUE

Worse Than a Spendery

New York, April 23.—Another strongarm holdup cafe and cabaret has just been installed on Broadway for the illumination and enlightenment of New York night life. It is the Palais Royal at Broadway and Forty-eighth street, where Fritzi Scheff, late of musical comedy and vaudeville, has installed what she terms a revue, but which in reality is nothing more than a standard vaudeville show. Exorbitant prices are asked for food and liquid refreshments. A couvier charge of one dollar per person is exacted after 10 p.m. and strongarm methods, strongly approaching deliberate theft, are resorted to by the waiters. Wine is sold at thirteen dollars a bottle, coffee at fifty cents per cup, Swiss cheese sandwiches at seventy-five cents each, half a grapefruit at sixty-five cents, a cup of clam broth at fifty cents, and so on. The interior has been lavishly decorated, with private stalls and a small dance floor whereon the denizens of Broadway night life may trip the light fantastic to the accompaniment of a really meritorious orchestra. The fact that one is in for a couvier charge is not sprung on you until after you have ordered and can not escape.

FROM MAR. 11, 1924 ISSUE

Evelyn Law.

FROM MARCH 31 , 1917 ISSUE

GAY WHITE WAY AND CABARETS SLATED FOR A VICE CLEANUP

Broadway Association, Backed by Police, To Take Action

Plan To Rid Famous Thoroughfare of Crime Pestilence

License Commissioner Bell To Make Test of His Powers

New York, March 26.—Broadway, the "Gay White Way" of New York, and admittedly the most famous thoroughfare in the world, is to be given a thorough cleaning to rid it of vice and crime, according to plans just formulated by the Broadway Association, which will have the backing of Police Commissioner Woods, Chief Magistrate McAdoo, License Commissioner Bell and other prominent officials in its campaign to improve the moral tone of the "old cowpath." At a meeting of the Executive Committee of the Broadway Association held on Thursday a decision was reached to take immediate steps to rid Broadway of vice, with which it has long run rampant, and to this end has called a conference for tonight at the Hotel Martinique, when a committee will be named to take charge of the campaign.

THE RINGLINGS DOMINATE
THE CIRCUS WORLD

FROM DEC. 10, 1910 ISSUE

LTOGETHER the circus season just passed has been among the most successful ones on record. First, there were more big circuses en tour throughout the season than there have ever been before in America. Ringling Brothers had three big circuses out this season: the one that bears their own name, the Barnum & Bailey, and the Forepaugh-Sells Show, the last named having been sent out for the first time since it was bought in by James A. Bailey at the Columbus, Ohio, sale, in 1905. The Hagenbeck-Wallace Show and the John Robinson Ten Big Shows took the road in their usual magnitude and magnificence. The wild west contingent was strongly and adequately represented by the Buffalo Bill-Pawnee Bill Wild West and Great Far East, and the Miller Bros. and Arlington's 101-Ranch Wild West. Numerous shows of smaller size were represented in the circus horoscope.

Another notable incident of the season was the testing out of the Texas license by the Ringling Brothers. The state revenue agent protested against the continuous performance device which the Messrs. Ringling instituted while the Forepaugh-Sells Show was in Texas, as a justifiable means of evading the enormous and exorbitant license fee levied by the Lone Star State, and the case was tried. No final decision has been heard on this matter, but inasmuch as the Federal court issued an injunction restraining the state revenue agent from interfering through arrests and other persecution with the continuous performance arrangement, there is little doubt that the Ringling Brothers will win out in the final hearing. This will mean a victory for all circuses which will naturally adopt the same means of evading the exorbitant license in Texas if the state does not revise its laws affecting them. It is estimated that for the Forepaugh-Sells Show alone the Ringling Bros. saved more than $14,000 by the continuous performance device.

Mr. H. H. Tammen, proprietor of the Sells-Floto Shows, endeavored, during the early part of the season, to induce the city councils in territory booked by his competitors to pass ordinances by which shows would be taxed on a graduated scale in ratio to the number of cars carried. Mr. Tammen's efforts were generally recognized as a subterfuge for the purpose of making licenses prohibitive in the towns included in the itinerary of his competitors

The circus business is peculiar in many of its aspects. Its beginnings were devoid of all dignity, but through the perseverance of its pioneer promoters, and through the prosecution of those principles of progression and reform that underlay even its humble station it has taken on the dignity of a legitimate form of business that has a virtue peculiar to it through its mission to amuse and entertain.

The menagerie feature of the big circus attaches to it an educational feature that, whether real or imagined, is responsible in large degree for its success.

Already preparations are under way for next season, and the mammoth scale with which they are being carried on indicates that those who are in the highest degree responsible for the circus business in its chief essentials are inspired by true optimism by the prospect upon which they are looking out.

1914

EVANS AND SISTER Foot Juggling Act

AERIAL MACKS

World's Greatest Aerialists

RODRIGUES

Mexican Wire Wizard

Third Season with Ringling Brothers.

FORTUNE de LEPOMME TROUPE

COMEDY BAR ACT.
THAT'S ALL.

3—JAHNS—3

Alfred Brothers

HAND TO HEAD
EQUILIBRISTS

INAS TROUPE

CHAMPION TUMBLERS
OF THE WORLD

Nelson Troupe

LADY and GENTLEMAN
AERIALIST

RETURN ACT

FEATURE ATTRACTIONS WITH THE RINGLING BROTHERS' WORLD'S GREATEST SHOWS

FAMOUS LLOYDS

THE MOST ORIGINAL
AND SENSATIONAL
RIDING ACT IN THE
LAST HALF CENTURY

McCREE DAVENPORT TROUPE

5 People — 4 Horses — 1 Dog
.. COMBINATION RIDING ACT ...
TAKES IN EVERYTHING IN ONE, FINISHING WITH
FOUR PEOPLE AND DOG STANDING ERECT
ON FAST RUNNING HORSE
RINGLING BROTHERS SEASON 1914

THE CLARKONIANS

ON THE

FLYING TRAPEZE

FEATURE ATTRACTION SEASON 1914
RINGLING BROTHERS

CLOWN ALLEY

JIM SPRIGGS
The Old Cop

FRED STELLING
7th Year with Ringling Bros.

PAUL MINNO
Clown and Augouste
That's All   Enough Said

JULES TURNOUR
The Great Pantomimist Clown

BILLY JAMESON
One Real Clown

JOHNIE TRIPP
Originator of the Scenery Bottles

ROY McDONALD
CLOWN
Originator of the X-Ray Skirt

OTHER FEATURE ACTS

MANOLA
Mijares' Brother. Only one doing a somersault on the Slack Wire without a support

Melnotte Lanole Troupe
Comedy Acrobatic Wire Walkers

GEO. HARTZELL
Principal Producing Clown

MAX DILLAE
The Clown with the Novel Ideas

Joe and Andrew Casino
The All-Feature Clowns

AL MIACO
The world's most versatile Clown

FROM AUG. 26, 1911 ISSUE

ELBA REINE HAFLEY
The smallest equestrienne in the world on Onion, horse trained by Miss Ada Sommerville of the California Frank Show.

MAMIE FRANCIS
(Mrs. C. F. Hafley)
Celebrated horse-back rifle shot.

MISS GEORGIE MULHALL
Chief of the cowgirls. She is working the high-school horse, San Jose, and has the reputation of being one of the greatest lady riders in the business.

MISS MILDRED MULHALL
Handsome little Oklahoma lady and her wonderful menage horse, Bill Oliver. An act near perfection, combining perfect horsewomanship, years of study and schooling a matchless bred Kentucky horse.

JOHNNIE McCRACKEN
105-lb. cowboy. Fourth season with California Frank's Show. He is riding bucking steers and the high-jumping horse, Geat.

CHAS. J. MULHALL
All around Wild West man, greatest sensational bucking horse rider and pony express rider. Featured with the famous Mulhall Family for the past eight years.

LORETTE
That "Little Dutch Cop." Formerly with Barnum & Bailey and Blake's Comedy Circus. Stands in class by himself as a clown. He is making good with California Frank.

GEO. M. BURK
Sole owner of Burk's Wild West, featuring his tandem high-school team, Alice and Margie. Mr. Burk was formerly with the John Robinson 10 Big Shows.

SOME OF THE BIG ACTS WITH THE BARNUM AND BAILEY SHOWS

PRINCE YOUTURKEY
In a class by himself.

HARRY LaPEARL
As foolish as ever.

GREAT EVERETT AND ORIGINAL LADY RAFFLES
Featuring their 20th century barrel escape.

LEACH-LaQUILLYN TRIO
Doing "some" novelty wire act and slide for life.

4—COMRADES—4
American representatives of acrobatic comedy.

AMERICAN FLORENCE TROUPE
Known the wide world over.

CAMILLE TRIO
Comedy bar acrobats unsurpassed.

NEW THRILLS IN THE GREAT OUTDOORS

FROM MARCH 18, 1911 ISSUE

By ROY KNABENSHUE.

N December 17, 1903, a telegram was received at the Wright Bros.' home, which announced that they had made a success of the aeroplane.

In 1904 and 1905, flights were made at Dayton on a lot which is now the proving grounds of the Wright Company.

The enormous possibilities were at once made apparent, especially from the showman's point of view, and propositions came pouring in daily for the exhibition of the Wright Brothers' aeroplane from all parts of the world, but the brothers were busy in France, Italy and Germany and at Washington, D. C., where demonstrations were made for the United States Government.

A number of American promoters during 1909 and 1910 had manufactured and also brought into this country, foreign makes of machines, all of which were considered more or less infringements on the Wright Brothers' scheme of control. Exhibitions of minor importance were held, and on account of inexperience of the aviators and being unskilled in the use of that particular type of machine, these exhibitions were more or less a disappointment to both the promoters and the public at large, especially the public.

At the Hudson-Fulton celebration in 1908, flights were made by Wilbur Wright in which he circled the Statue of Liberty and sailed up the Hudson river to Grant's Tomb, and returned to Governor's Island. These flights took place in winds of moderate veloc-

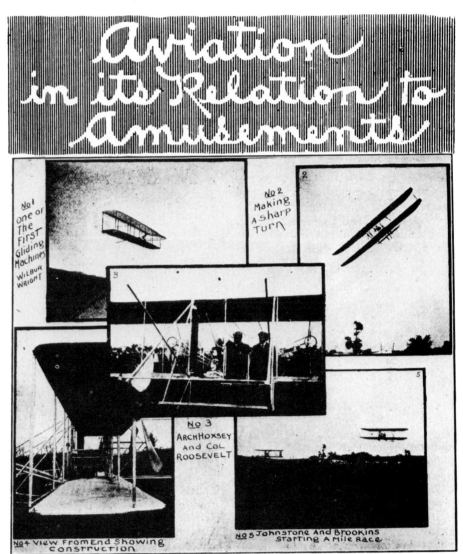

ity which in no way hampered the flight or caused any uneasiness on the part of Mr. Wright.

Immediately following this demonstration, the Wright Brothers received hundreds of applications for the ex-

hibition of their machine, but at that time did not deem it advisable to go into the show business, and it was not until March 1, 1910, that arrangements were completed for giving these public exhibitions.

FROM SEPT. 30, 1911 ISSUE

AIRMAN INCINERATED

Unable to Endure Jeers of Onlookers, Youthful Aviator Makes Flight, Although Knowing His Machine Was Unfit for Sailing—Is Burned to Death in Air

Troy, O., Sept. 22 (Special to The Billboard). —Another aviator was forced into the air by the jeers of the crowd, and Frank Miller, aged 23 years, a Toledo (O.) aviator, was burned to death in midair before the eyes of the terrified spectators on the Miami County Fair Grounds here. The aviator lost control of his machine when about two hundred feet in the air. As it started to fall the engine caught fire and communicated the flames to the gasoline tank, which exploded, wrapping Miller in flames. The craft struck the ground with great force, Miller's already charred body being buried underneath the motor.

Miller's engine had been acting badly in previous flights, and he had refused to make an ascent until the crowd started to jeer and call him coward.

It is only a few weeks ago that John J. Frisbie, one of the leading aviators, stung by the taunts of the crowd, made an ascent in a damaged machine at Norton, Kan., and was killed.

FROM MAY 2, 1914 ISSUE

BARNEY OLDFIELD AND LINCOLN BEACHEY

Barney Oldfield (with cigar), the famous auto racer, and Lincoln Beachey, the loop-the-loop aviator, have teamed for a tour of the larger cities of the United States in a series of contests for the "championship of the universe."

FROM OCT. 14, 1911 ISSUE

IGNORES THE LAW

Moisant Aviators, Despite Edict Prohibiting Sunday Flying, Make Ascensions at Nassau Boulevard, and Narrowly Escape the Sheriff's Clutches—Riot Is Precipitated

New York, Oct. 8 (Special to The Billboard). —With the issuance of an edict against Sunday flying at the Nassau Boulevard aviation meet, the Aero Club officially declared the meet off, but the Moisant Aviation Co. placed themselves above the law of the land, and despite the warnings of Sheriff De Mott of Nassau County, Miss Matilda Moisant made a flight in her machine, circling the grounds and then flying to Mineola. In the attempt to arrest her at this point, the deputies were opposed by a number of spectators and a small-size riot was on, resulting in a number of the participants being badly bruised. Miss Moisant was shaken up and slightly bruised in the fracas.

Earle Ovington also made a flight but succeeded in eluding the sheriff.

FROM JAN. 14, 1911 ISSUE

YOUTHFUL AVIATOR DEAD

Cromwell Dixon, Eighteen Year Old Birdman, Receives Injuries while Giving Exhibition at Spokane Interstate Fair, Which Result in His Death

Spokane, Wash., Oct. 3 (Special to The Billboard).—Cromwell Dixon, the 19-year-old aviator who has been thrilling the crowds at the Interstate Fair for the past few days with his daring flights, fell 100 feet to death yesterday. He was fatally hurt and died soon after the fall. Dixon was a native of Columbus, O., and made his first aerial flight in a dirigible balloon of his own making at the Ohio State Fair a Columbus in 1907, when he was but 15 years old.

Dixon has been flying an aeroplane but a short time, but had already achieved such success as to place him in the first rank of flyers.

His death was witnessed by several thousand people.

A CAPSULE HISTORY

To identify individual show business areas see two-letter code descriptions below:

AP —Amusement Parks
BU —Burlesque
CA —Carnivals
CH —Chautauqua
CI —Circus
FA —Fairs
MI —Minstrelsy
MO —Motion Pictures
MU —Music
NC —Night Clubs, Supper Clubs, Cabarets
RA —Radio
RE —Recordings
SH —Showboats
ST —Stereorama and Panstereorama
TH —Legitimate Theatre
TV —Television
VA —Vaudeville
WA —Wagon Shows

1905

TH The New York Hippodrome opens April 12.

TH Four George Bernard Shaw plays are produced in New York by actor/manager Arnold Daly: *Mrs. Warren's Profession, You Never Can Tell, John Bull's Other Island,* and *Candida.*

TH The classic *Rip Van Winkle,* which Joseph Jefferson III had introduced, is revived with his son, Thomas, in the title role.

TH Playwright Richard Ferris of Minneapolis sues James Glass for infringement on his play *Way Out West.* Jury in Keokuk, Iowa, finds in Ferris's favor. First case of successful prosecution of copyright infringement of a play.

TH Ethel, John, and Lionel Barrymore all appear on the same theatre bill on the same evening. Ethel and John star in first play, *Alice-Sit-by-the-Fire* and Lionel in second play, *Pantaloon,* at the Criterion Theatre in New York.

TH Blanche Bates stars as *The Girl of the Golden West,* written and produced by David Belasco. Puccini later bases his opera on the play.

TH Shubert Theatrical Corporation is formed. In addition to old associates (attorney Willie Klein, et al.) two very wealthy, politically influential midwesterners are key stockholders: George Cox, Republican leader in Cincinnati, and Joseph Rhinock of Kentucky.

TH Erlanger seems to control *The Morning Telegraph,* which runs constant vituperative campaign against the Shuberts. So in April, Shuberts launch own publication, *The Show,* edited by Channing Pollock, who has been handling press for them.

TH Sam Shubert, age thirty, is mortally wounded in a train wreck while on his way to Pittsburgh. He dies next day, May 12.

TH At time of Sam Shubert's death, the Shuberts own thirteen theatres. Lee Shubert takes over the Shubert operations and in the next two years achieves the greatest expansion in the history of the theatre.

RE The first "long playing" record is released. It is a twenty-inch disk released by the Neophone Company in London.

MO Before the year is out, Marcus Loew has opened and is operating four arcades — one in an uptown, prosperous section of New York City called Harlem.

MO Vitagraph produces *Raffles, the Amateur Cracksman,* with Jimmy Sherry as Raffles and G. M. Anderson as director. The 1,000-foot (one reel) film is based on a hit stage show. Vitagraph obtained the screen rights (a first) merely by giving the legit producers' name credit on the main title. The film is the most elaborately produced American movie drama to date.

1906

TH/VA The great San Francisco earthquake and fire destroy all of the city's theatres. A gigantic building program is undertaken and the Colonial Theatre is the first playhouse to re-open in October, 1907. Meanwhile, the "show goes on" in tents.

TH *The Great Divide* by William Vaughan Moody, starring Henry Miller and Margaret Anglin, is presented at the Princess Theatre. It is regarded by some historians as the first serious drama by an American playwright.

TH Shuberts book Sarah Bernhardt, at age sixty-one, for another American "farewell" tour. Erlanger forbids any trust house to play her. Lee Shubert rents tents from the Barnum and Bailey Circus and other sources, and Bernhardt plays in these. Since they seat three times as many people as the average theatre, and sell out just as quickly, Erlanger's move backfires. He is severely criticized in the press.

TH Battle for control of the theatre now at its peak. Both Klaw and Erlanger and Shuberts are building and leasing theatres, and bucking each other even in towns which can hardly support one theatre. They also drive up the salaries of performers by raiding each other's talent. Lew Fields leaves Klaw and Erlanger to join Shuberts. E. H. Sothern and Julia Marlowe also join Shuberts.

TH Bernhardt/Shubert tour closes in Springfield, Mass., in a tent performance. Tour report shows: 226 performances, grossing slightly more than $1,000,000. Ms. Bernhardt gets $305,000 for her share. The Shuberts get the rest, less expenses plus national publicity, which makes them the new power in the American theatre for years to come.

TH James J. Corbett, heavyweight boxing champion, stars in adaptation of G. B. Shaw's novel, *Cashel Byron's Profession.*

TH Lillian Russell does her first non-musical play, *Barbara's Millions.*

MO Growing out of the penny arcades, nickelodeons (or store shows) begin to spring up all around the country. They project movies onto a screen. William Fox, a cloth sponger, opens a group of store shows and joins Loew and Zukor in the ranks of pioneer movie entrepreneurs.

MO German immigrant Carl Laemmle — a former clothing salesman from Oshkosh, Wis. — opens a movie theatre in Chicago and six months later is operating a film exchange. His associate is a shrewd Chicago advertising man, Robert Cochrane.

MO Florence Turner, later known as The Vitagraph Girl, is paid $18 a week by Vitagraph as wardrobe mistress. She gets $5 a day when used as an actress. Maurice Costello is said to be the first actor who — when he joined Vitagraph — refused to double as set painter or grip.

RE Eldridge Johnson introduces the Victrola. It is the first phonograph with the playback horn enclosed in the body of the machine, and the turntable and tone arm covered by a lid. It sells for $200 and is such a hit that for years afterwards the public calls all players by the Johnson trade name, "Victrola."

RE On Victor's Red Seal label, Enrico Caruso and Antonio Scotti record their first duet.

RE A full length opera, *Aida,* is recorded and released for the first time by Zonophone. It takes twenty-three individual disks.

RE/RA Reginald Fessenden broadcasts a record of Handel's *Largo.* It is one of the first times that a record has been played on radio.

RA Dr. Lee De Forest invents a three-element vacuum tube, which he calls the Audion. It contains a filament, a plate, and a grid.

RE Victor cuts prices on flat disks: seven-inch, 50¢ to 35¢; ten-inch, $1 to 60¢; twelve-inch, $1.50 to $1. This signals a trend toward flat disk in preference over cylinders.

CI While strolling in the Barnum and Bailey backyard in New York, James Bailey is bitten by a flea. Infection sets in and within a few days he is dead.

1907

TH Severe national depression makes continuing costly rivalry between Klaw and Erlanger and the Shubert organization impractical. They announce sudden partnership called United States Amusement Company with Abe Erlanger, president and Lee Shubert, vice president; it is capitalized at $100,000,000. There is some trade talk that William Morris (battling B. F. Keith in vaudeville) is mastermind of the move.

VA/TH After a brief, fierce, and costly struggle between the Klaw-Erlanger-Shubert-Morris vs. Keith-Albee forces an agreement is reached in November whereby Albee is to honor $1,500,000 worth of vaude act contracts and pay the Shuberts and Klaw and Erlanger $250,000. In return, the theatrical giants agree to stay out of vaudeville for ten years. Morris goes out on his own again.

TH Ziegfeld produces first of his *Follies,* July 8. Cast includes Helen Broderick, Grace La Rue, Emma Carus and Harry Watson, Jr.

TH Franz Lehar's *The Merry Widow* opens at the New Amsterdam Theatre in New York, October 21. It runs 416 per-

formances and becomes a classic of the musical theatre.

MO Edwin S. Porter hires stage actor Lawrence Griffith for the role of a woodsman in Edison's *The Eagle's Nest.* Thus, the man credited with inventing motion pictures as an art form, director D. W. Griffith, begins his remarkable screen career. From there he goes to Biograph, still as an actor.

MO Essanay Films is formed by George M. Anderson and Chicago film producer George K. Spool, and the Kalem Company is founded by Frank Marion, George Kleine, and Samuel Long.

MO Kalem films its own version of the Lew Wallace stage play, *Ben Hur,* without permission. The author's estate and play's producers sue. Kalem loses and in 1911 settles for $25,000.

MO Francis Boggs, a Selig director, and Thomas Persons, an all-purpose camera-man-prop-man-you-name-it, make the first movie in Los Angeles, *The Count of Monte Cristo.* It is a one reeler, with a hypnotist in the title role. Later this year the two men open the first studio on a rooftop in downtown Los Angeles.

RE Though flat disks are gaining, cylinders dominate the rural markets. Edison phonograph operation grosses $7,000,000 this year, but depression soon hits and changes the entire phonograph picture.

RE Edison phonograph company markets a player in competition to the Victrola. It is called the Amberola, plays extra-large size cylinders, running four minutes each. The Amberola is priced precisely the same as the Victrola, $200.

RA The De Forest Radio Telephone Company inaugurates broadcasts in New York City.

CI The Ringling brothers buy the Barnum and Bailey show for the bargain price of $410,000, but for the time being continue to operate the shows as separate entities.

1908

TH Lee Shubert introduces female ushers for first time in a theatre at Casino, New York. Also introduces sale of orange-flavored water and coin-operated drinking cup dispensers.

TH Nora Bayes and her husband Jack Norworth are the hit of the 1908 *Ziegfeld Follies.* They sing their own song, "Shine On Harvest Moon."

TH/MO Marcus Loew, who operates two nickelodeons in penny arcades (one in Cincinnati, the other in New York) visits Lee Shubert. He leases a number of unprofitable Shubert Theatres in remote areas of

Brooklyn and upper Manhattan and converts them to "electric" theatres showing movies.

MO Florence Lawrence, who is earning $15 a week at Vitagraph, moves over to Biograph for a $10 raise. Film stars still aren't billed by name, but her movies are so popular that she is billed as The Biograph Girl. In 1910 when Florence signs with Carl Laemmle's IMP Company the public is told her real name.

MO G. M. Anderson makes the first western in California when he sets up a studio at Niles. He makes a "Broncho Billy" western virtually every week for the next seven years.

MO D. W. Griffith directs his first movie for Biograph, *The Adventures of Dolly,* with his wife Linda Arvidson and Arthur Johnson, who later becomes one of the movie's first matinee idols. During the next year Griffith directs 100 one-reelers for Biograph.

MO Billy Bitzer, most famous of early cameramen, works with Griffith for the first time on *The Adventures of Dolly.* Bitzer works with Griffith for the next sixteen years, helping him create such basic film techniques as the use of different camera angles for the same scene, dramatic lighting, the close-up, etc.

MO On December 18, the Motion Picture Patent Company is formed by Edison, Biograph, George Kleine, Essanay, Selig, Vitagraph, Lubin, Pathe, Melies and Kalem to pool their patents. They believe that films should be limited to one reel because movie goers only have an attention span of ten minutes.

MU/VA The use of stereopticon slides to illustrate popular songs sung in movie theatres and vaudeville houses reaches its peak this year. Many of the slides are elaborately produced on special locations. A cast of sixty appears in a slide series for composer Charles K. Harris' "Linda, Can't You Love Your Joe?"

RE Columbia issued two-sided flat disks. Edison holds out against idea until some fifteen years later, but Columbia's step is another indication that flat disks are winning the war against the cylinders.

RE Rudolph Wurlitzer Company introduces a complete line of "Modern Automatic Musical Instruments with Slot Attachments" for use in hotels, cafes, restaurants, etc. *Billboard* carries the first of these ads.

RE Edison releases campaign speeches of William Jennings Bryan and William Howard Taft, presidential candidates, on Amberola records. These are the first documentary disks in record business.

RA De Forest broadcasts from Paris, France atop the Eiffel Tower.

1909

AP Roller coasters in amusement parks across the country are extremely popular.

TH John Barrymore opens in *The Fortune Hunter.* It is his first hit play.

MO Singer-actor Mack Sennett goes to work at Biograph as an actor-writer and, in vain, tries to convince D. W. Griffith that a story about a funny policeman would be good box office. Years later, he proves his point with the Keystone Kops.

MO Two photographer's models start bright movie careers. Mabel Normand joins Vitagraph, but leaves shortly to join Biograph and meet her mentor, Mack Sennett. Alice Joyce is hired to make westerns for Kalem.

MO Mary Pickford, at sixteen an established stage actress, is hired by Griffith at Biograph. Her first released movie is *The Violin Maker of Cremona.* Her second is *In a Lonely Villa,* written by Mack Sennett. One of the *Villa* actors is Owen Moore, who becomes her first husband.

MO *Gertie The Dinosaur* is the first animated cartoon.

RE Odeon in Berlin records the entire *Nutcracker Suite,* the first major orchestral work to be done from first note to last.

RE/RA In San Jose, California, Charles Herrold broadcasts record concerts once a week over his wireless transmitter.

MU *Billboard* becomes the first trade newspaper to publish reproductions of sheet music (both words and music) of leading songs of the day as a new editorial feature.

1910

TH Stock companies are thriving, with more than 2,000 presenting dramatic offerings across the country.

TH Shifts in producing alliances accelerate. William Brady leaves Erlanger trust and forms new corporation with Shuberts. David Belasco, arch enemy of Erlanger, leaves Shuberts and forms new firm with Klaw and Erlanger.

TH/MO Marcus Loew incorporates Loew's Theatrical Enterprises for $5,000,000. On the board are Joseph Rhinock, active with the Shuberts, and Joseph Schenck. Loew now has fourteen theatres and is building three new ones. He is still working closely with Lee Shubert.

TH/MO J. J. Shubert, running the Lyric Theatre in Chicago with motion pictures, is losing money. He hires Samuel Rothafel (Roxy) of Minneapolis to come in and run the theatre. Roxy brings in a big orchestra and stage shows. Although attendance is increasing, Shubert fires him, because of the extra costs Roxy creates.

TH Sarah Bernhardt makes another of her "farewell" tours of the U.S. On this trip she brings with her, as her leading man, Lou Tellegen, who later stars opposite her in the French-made film, *Queen Elizabeth.*

TH Fannie Brice makes her *Ziegfeld Follies* debut singing Irving Berlin's "Goodbye Becky Cohen."

TH George M. Cohan and his partner Sam Harris produce *Get-Rich-Quick Wallingford.* It is biggest hit of the season.

MO Charlie Chaplin, twenty-one, leaves his native England for the first time on a cross-country tour of the U.S. with a music hall company owned by Fred Karno. Hollywood doesn't spot him, though, until he returns with Karno in 1913. He signs a contract with Keystone late that year.

MO The same powers behind the Motion Picture Patents Company, the film trust, organize General Film Company. In two years General buys up fifty-seven of the largest distribution firms in the movie business, for approximately $2,500,000 and almost $800,000 worth of stock. The only distributor to resist and refuse to sell out is William Fox, owner of the Greater New York Film Rental Company.

MO Robust John Bunny leaves the stage to join Vitagraph and becomes the first famous movie comedian. Paired with Flora Finch, Bunny's fame lasts until his death in 1915. He is one of the first film stars to have his name listed in the title.

MO *Ranch Life In the Great Southwest* is filmed in Oklahoma by Selig. A local United States Marshal, Tom Mix, plays a role in the film and is slated to become one of the all-time great western stars.

RA De Forest, using his radiophone, broadcasts Enrico Caruso and Emmy Destin from backstage at the Metropolitan Opera House. They are heard by ham operators in Connecticut and by at least one ship at sea, the S.S. Avon.

1911

AP Leading amusement parks of the day are Dreamland, Coney Island, New York; Coney Island, Cincinnati; White Park, Chicago; Luna Park, Los Angeles; Willow Park, Philadelphia. All play many vaudeville and circus acts, and feature newest rides of the day, including Ferris wheels, roller coasters, magician Howard Thurston's "Kiss" ride (a mild variation of the later Whip).

TH Richard Mansfield stars in Booth Tarkington's *Beaucaire.* The costume drama is a smash.

MO D. W. Griffith makes a two-reeler, *Enoch Arden,* violating the trust's one-reel length rule for movies. Biograph thwarts him and releases it as two separate films. Nevertheless, two reels become the standard length for serious dramas by the following year.

MO Unnamed cameraman for Champion Film Company shoots the first film from the air, on a flight with aviator Robert Fowler from Beaumont, Texas to New Orleans.

MO The first dog star is seen on the screen when Larry Trimble brings his pet collie, Jean, on the set to substitute for a temperamental Pomeranian. Vitagraph pays Jean $25 a week, $10 more than her master receives as an actor-writer. In 1923 Trimble will train one of the most famous dog stars, Strongheart.

MU Scott Joplin's all-black opera, *Treemonisha,* opens in New York and is unsuccessful. (It is revived in New York in 1976, and becomes a hit.)

CI One of the first and most successful women wild animal trainers is Mabel Stark, who leaves nursing this year to join the Al G. Barnes show. Miss Stark wrestles a full-grown Bengal tiger, and as the act's finale sticks her head in the tiger's mouth.

1912

FA/CA Stunt flying is the current sensation at many of the nation's fairs and other outdoor amusement events. Scores of men and women flyers are killed doing their "acts."

CA Leading carnival companies form the Carnival Managers' Association of America in Chicago. Association slogan: "A Better, Cleaner Carnival Business."

TH Max Reinhardt builds an apron out from center stage over several rows of seats, in his presentation of *Sumurun* at the Shuberts' Casino Theatre in New York. Lee is furious because of the seat loss, but J. J. adopts it at the Winter Garden, and has his eighty chorus girls strut down it, to the delight of the audience. It is the first use of a burlesque runway.

TH Weber and Fields, who have operated independently of one another for years, re-unite for musical *Hokey Pokey.* In the show with them are Lillian Russell, Fay Templeton, William Collier, Ada Lewis and other colleagues of their earlier variety days.

TH Laurette Taylor's husband, J. Hartley Manners writes *Peg O' My Heart* and it turns out to be Miss Taylor's biggest hit, running for 603 performances.

MO Improvised store-front movie houses begin to disappear and small film theatres, specially designed to show pictures, open up in cities throughout the U.S. Admission is now as much as 10¢ or 15¢.

MO The independent film makers band

together to form independent film exchanges (patterned after General Film, organized in 1910). Mutual is set up to distribute films by Majestic, Reliance, Thanhouser, and American. Carl Laemmle forms Universal to distribute his own IMP films, plus products from Nestor, Victor, Eclair, Rex and Powers.

MO   Adolph Zukor, an ex-furrier and treasurer of the Marcus Loew Enterprises, buys the American rights to Sarah Bernhardt's four-reel French film *Queen Elizabeth*. The Motion Picture Patent Company refuses to distribute the picture because of its length. Zukor arranges with Daniel Frohman to show the Bernhardt film at a legitimate house, the Lyceum Theatre, in New York. The Lyceum charges one dollar to see the Divine Sarah.

MO   Zukor forms the Famous Players Film Company with Frohman and Loew. The stigma of being a movie actor disappears and more and more big Broadway stars — John Drew, Maude Adams, David Warfield, George Arliss, Nazimova, the Barrymores, and Douglas Fairbanks — sign picture contracts.

MO   Mary Pickford, who left Biograph for IMP in 1911, returns to the former studio and makes *The New York Hat* with Lionel Barrymore from a script by teenager Anita Loos. Pickford is instrumental in Griffith signing Lillian and Dorothy Gish.

MO   Bison Film Company owners, Adam Kessel and Charles Bauman, back Mack Sennett with $2,500 to set up the Keystone Company in Los Angeles. Sennett's stock company for his slapstick comedies includes Mabel Normand, Ford Sterling, and Fred Mace. The first Keystone Comedy is *Cohen At Coney Island*.

RE   Columbia Phonograph discontinues manufacture and sale of cylinder records. It is the beginning of the end for the cylinder records, but Edison continues to manufacture them until 1929.

RE   Edison introduces new improved cylinder record called the Blue Amberola. It is the finest record made to date, utilizing celluloid and cut via the hill and dale method, as opposed to the lateral grooving method. At the same time Edison makes and markets his first flat disks, called the Diamond Disc Record.

RA   New laws are passed requiring licenses to broadcast.

RA   David Sarnoff, twenty-one-year-old Marconi operator at Wanamaker's Department Store in New York City, stays at his post for seventy-two hours passing information from operators at sea to newspapers in the city about the Titanic disaster. It is the first public awareness of a man who becomes a major force in radio, movies, and television.

CI   May Wirth, at the age of sixteen, makes her American debut with Barnum and Bailey at Madison Square Garden in New York. She is acknowledged as the world's greatest equestrienne.

1913

BU   Columbia Amusement Company absorbs the Empire Circuit to form combine which controls all burlesque in the United States and Canada. Value of forty-four theatres involved is estimated at $15,000,000. New trust employs about 4000 people.

VA   Marking the early years of vaudeville's glory days, the Palace Theatre opens on Broadway in New York. Every act aspires to play the Palace.

TH/VA   For the second time the Klaw and Erlanger syndicate and the Shuberts sign an agreement to work together. Lee Shubert also makes separate deals on theatres with Marcus Loew, while both he and Erlanger make special deals with Albee. As actors' salaries are driven down, Actors' Equity is organized.

TH   Shuberts open the first Sam Shubert Memorial Theater on October 28 with Sir Johnston Forbes-Robertson in *Anthony and Cleopatra*. Word "Memorial" is later dropped from theatres named in Sam's memory, because the somber sound of the word is bad for business.

TH   Doris Keane stars in Edward Sheldon's *Romance*, one of the biggest hits of the decade.

TH   Mary Pickford stars in Rostand's *A Good Little Devil*. Lillian Gish has a supporting role.

MO   Charlie Chaplin is signed by Keystone for $150 a week. Mack Sennett had seen his drunk act in Karno's *A Night In a London Club* vaudeville turn and thought he'd be a good replacement for Keystone comic Ford Sterling if the latter left the studio. Little more than a year later Chaplin signs with Essanay for $1250 a week.

MO   Kathlyn Williams stars in *The Adventures of Kathlyn* for Selig. It is the first serial, although Mary Fuller had starred in a forerunner of the serial, a series of films titled *What Happened to Mary?*

MO   The Vitagraph Company publishes a house newspaper, the first film fan magazine. *Photoplay*, which began as a theatre program in 1912, becomes the first professional screen publication in 1914.

MO   Mabel Normand throws the first custard pie during the shooting of a Keystone Comedy for Mack Sennett. On the spur of the moment during shooting she picks up the pie (dessert for the crew) and tosses it at comedian Ben Turpin.

VA   Evelyn Nesbit (whose husband Harry Thaw killed Stanford White) is teamed (by Willie Hammerstein) with Jack Clifford, ex-fighter, as a dance act. During their second week at Hammerstein's, Thaw escapes from prison and threatens to kill his wife. The public flocks to the theatre and Nesbit breaks house attendance records.

RE   A dance craze sweeps the nation. The tango, the hesitation waltz, the one-step, and the turkey trot are among the most popular dances. Victor releases a series of records made specifically for dancing. They are produced by Vernon and Irene Castle, leading dance team of the day.

RE   British recording engineers working for the Gramophone Company, Ltd. (Victor's English affiliate), record delicate stringed instruments with great fidelity and clarity for the first time. Among the violin virtuosos recorded are Mischa Elman and Fritz Kreisler.

RA   Edwin H. Armstrong invents feedback circuit.

RE   Odeon, Berlin achieves another first and records Beethoven's Symphonies Nos. Five and Six, first works of their kind recorded in their entirety.

MU   *Billboard* publishes first song popularity chart in July, called "Last Week's Ten Best Sellers in Popular Songs." In August, it initiates another chart, "Songs Heard in Vaudeville Last Week."

MU   Duke Ellington, fourteen years old, writes his first song, "Soda Fountain Rag."

1914

CI   Emil Pallenberg comes from Germany with his trained bear act to make history with attractions of this kind. His bears are the first to roller skate, ride bicycles, walk the tightrope, and play musical instruments. Pallenberg's bears are a feature with the Ringling Brothers & Barnum and Bailey show for thirteen consecutive seasons.

TH   Dance teams are in high favor. Irene and Vernon Castle star in musical, *Watch Your Step*. Other highly successful teams: John Murray Anderson and wife, Genevieve; Carl Hyson and Dorothy Dickson; and Maurice and Florence Walton. Fred and Adele Astaire are popular child-team in vaudeville.

TH   George Bernard Shaw's *Pygmalion*, with Mrs. Patrick Campbell as Eliza Doolittle, is presented for the first time in America.

MO   World War I starts in Europe and production is suspended abroad. U.S. film makers become dominant in the world film market.

MO   Ex-trapeze artist, Pearl White — who does her own stunts — stars in the best-known serial of all, *The Perils of Pauline*.

MO Motion picture companies are being formed and reformed in the rush to cash in on the lucrative medium. Jesse Lasky sets up his own company with his brother-in-law Samuel Goldfish (later to become Samuel Goldwyn) as an associate. Cecil B. De Mille directs Lasky's first film *The Squaw Man,* which is shot on Vine Street in Hollywood. Prior to that, Goldwyn was a glove salesman and Lasky a vaudevillian-producer who pioneered the night club concept in America.

MO/TH Broadway invades the motion picture industry. Lasky makes a deal to produce film versions of David Belasco plays.

MO The first palatial movie house, The Strand, opens on New York's Broadway with elegant decor, a thirty-piece orchestra (to provide background music for the movies) and only a twenty-five cent admission charge. It is such a hit that similar houses are opened (including the Rivoli and Rialto) around the country.

MO Paramount Pictures is set up to distribute Lasky, Famous-Players, and Bosworth films. Zukor is president, Lasky vice-president. William Fox makes his first picture, *Life's Shop Window.*

MO Mutual Films-Chicago *Tribune* combine offers Mary Pickford $208,000 per year to make a serial, *The Diamond in the Sky.* She decides instead to re-sign with Adolph Zukor at Paramount for $104,000 per year plus many other benefits. Five years earlier she was earning $10 per day playing her first film roles for Biograph. Her sister, Lottie Pickford, gets the *Diamond* part.

MO Chaplin's second picture is *Kid's Auto Races.* He creates his own film costume — baggy pants, cane, derby, big shoes and a small mustache. The legendary "little tramp" is born. One of his biggest hits is *Tillie's Punctured Romance,* Sennett's first six-reeler, co-starring Marie Dressler and Mabel Normand.

MO Chicago *Tribune/*Selig's second serial, *The Million Dollar Mystery,* successfully follows *The Adventures of Kathlyn.* Its twenty-three episodes cost about $125,000 and it grosses $1,500,000 playing in some 7,000 theatres. To producers hesitant about making multiple-reel features instead of one- and two-reelers, the serial seems a good compromise.

MO First great movie fight between two individual antagonists is staged in Rex Beach's *The Spoilers* between actors William Farnum and Tom Santschi. Fight scene lasts one complete reel of film.

MO Wallace Beery scores in a series of *Sweedie* shorts for Essanay as a Swedish house maid — in drag, of course. He is married to a beautiful extra, Gloria Swanson, who later becomes one of silent pictures' biggest stars.

RE Operatic and other recordings are made at Victor's New York studios in far greater numbers than ever before. Up to this time, Europe has been the center of classical recording.

1915

BU Charles Barton, manager of the American Burlesque Association, sends a letter to all house managers requesting elimination of four "objectionable" features in shows. They are: cooch and oriental dances; bare legs; smutty dialogues; vulgar jokes and actions.

MO Triangle Films is formed by D. W. Griffith, Mack Sennett and Thomas Ince, a powerhouse trio. They sign many big stage names — Billie Burke, Frank Keenan, Eddie Foy, etc. Their most important acquisitions are Douglas Fairbanks and William S. Hart, who becomes so famous as a cowboy star that in 1922 he refuses to make any pictures because he'll have to pay too much income tax — this in days when income taxes were insignificant.

MO/TH William A. Brady and the Shuberts form World Film Corporation with Arthur Spiegel as president and Lewis J. Selznick, a former jeweler, as general manager. The latter is the father of David and Myron.

TH *Lusitania* sunk by a German submarine. One of those drowned is Charles Frohman, leading producer/manager and key producer in the Klaw and Erlanger trust.

TH Sarah Bernhardt, at age seventy-one, has her leg amputated but keeps working.

TH The Provincetown Players are organized in Cape Cod, Mass., and are the first to present the works of Eugene O'Neill, a group of one-act plays titled *Bound East for Cardiff.* In 1916 they move to Macdougal Street in New York.

TH The Washington Square Players are organized in the Bandbox Theatre in New York.

MO America is movie-star crazy. Frances X. Bushman, Beverly Bayne, Clara Kimball Young, Marguerite Clark, Pauline Frederick, Marie Doro, Hazel Dawn, Blanche Sweet, Thomas Meighan, Sessue Hayakawa, Margarita Fischer and many others all have their fans.

MO Hollywood becomes the capitol of American movie production when film producers move their studios out to California. They soon discover that Hollywood is superior because of the climate and has more lenient tax and labor laws.

Half of the films made in America in 1915 are filmed in California.

MO Mary Pickford and Charlie Chaplin are the most popular movie stars in the world. America's Sweetheart makes five films this year, including *Madam Butterfly* and *Mistress Nell.* Chaplin is at Essanay with his new comedy stock company which includes leading lady Edna Purviance and Ben Turpin. The Crystal Hall Theatre in New York features a Chaplin short every week (with the exception of one four-day period) from 1913 to 1923 when the place burns down.

MO Thomas Ince invents the factory system of movie production which is utilized by major studios until the 1950s. To obtain maximum production output, he devises the system of assigning different "producers" to supervise production on a group of pictures, each reporting back to him. Thus shooting schedules are set up on a rotating basis, enabling Ince to utilize all studio facilities most of the time.

MO D W. Griffith produces and directs his masterpiece, *Birth of a Nation* (originally titled *The Clansman,* from the Thomas Dixon novel and play of the same name). The twelve-reeler opens at the Liberty Theatre in New York. In spite of its controversial treatment of blacks and sympathetic attitude towards the Klu Klux Klan (during the Civil War), the film is considered the most famous American movie of the silent era. Its cast includes Lillian Gish, Mae Marsh, Henry B. Walthall and Wallace Reid.

MO One infrequently observed virtue of D. W. Griffith's *Birth of a Nation* is the utilization of a special symphonic score, written for seventy players by Joseph Carl Breil. Symphony orchestras of this size play the score at the movie's initial showings.

MO Metro Pictures, forerunner of MGM, is set up. Richard Rowland is president and Louis B. Mayer (the man who will rule MGM through most of its glory years) is secretary. Their roster of players includes Ethel Barrymore, Lionel Barrymore, Francis X. Bushman, and Mary Miles Minter.

MO Cecil B. DeMille makes his first mark as a "name" director with *Carmen,* starring a mute Geraldine Farrar of opera fame and Wallace Reid.

MO Stage actress Theodosia Goodman changes her name to Theda Bara and starts the vamp craze. She makes forty pictures in three years, starting with *A Fool There Was* (from the Kipling poem "The Vampire") for Fox. Other "vamp" stars of the era are Louise Glaum, Nita Naldi, Olga Petrova, and Valeska Suratt. The vamp fad continues through 1917.

MO Harold Lloyd makes his first *Lonesome* comedy, *Just Nuts,* directed by Hal

Roach. Lloyd is still imitating Chaplin, and doesn't develop his tortoise-shell glasses character until later.

RE Louis Sterling, an American (who is head of Columbia in England) records the first complete musical revue with original cast. It is a show called *Business As Usual.* It is so well-received that Columbia follows with two more original cast albums: *Watch Your Step* written by Irving Berlin and *Cheep,* starring Beatrice Lillie.

RE Decca Record Company, England, manufactures a small portable phonograph. It is a favorite of British soldiers at the front.

RA The American Telephone & Telegraph Company, having acquired some of De Forest's patents, uses vacuum tube amplifiers to create long distance service from New York to San Francisco.

MU The first jazz arrangement ever published is made available by the man who wrote it: Ferdinand Morton's arrangement of his own composition, "Jelly Roll Blues."

1916

RA De Forest broadcasts frequently but on an irregular schedule from New York. Among other features, some musical, he broadcasts a speech by his mother-in-law on women's suffrage, and presidential election returns picked up from newspapers.

TH Ohio political boss George Cox dies. It is learned that he is largest single theatrical real estate owner in the world, with theatres in every large city, and is a major stockholder in Shubert properties.

TH Sarah Bernhardt makes another "farewell" tour of the U.S. This time she has an artificial leg to replace the limb she lost.

TH The 300th Anniversary of William Shakespeare's death sees *Macbeth, The Merchant of Venice, The Merry Wives of Windsor,* and *The Tempest,* all produced on Broadway.

MO Charlie Chaplin signs a contract with the Mutual Film Corporation for $670,000 a year, now making more money than any other film star. *The Floor Walker* is the first in his Lone Star series. By the end of the year he is no longer considered by the critics just a slapstick comic.

MO Mary Pickford signs new contract with Zukor for $1,040,000 for two years, plus many extras. Zukor forms Artcraft Pictures to distribute her films.

MO D. W. Griffith's *Intolerance* opens at the Liberty Theatre, New York. Admission is $2, but the three-and-a-half hour film is not as big a hit as *Birth of a Nation.*

MO Lewis J. Selznick leaves World and forms the Clara Kimball Young Film Corpo-ration. Young had been World's biggest star. Selznick also signs Norma Talmadge and Alla Nazimova. The Russian actress stars in *War Brides,* a skit in which she has been appearing on the Keith vaudeville circuit.

MO Bert Williams, the first great black star, makes a series of shorts for Klaw and Erlanger at Biograph. His comedy genius is undeniable, but at this time it is impossible for a black to become a movie star. One of his films, *Darktown Jubilee,* was initially a success, but a race riot broke out during its showing at a Brooklyn theatre and two men were killed.

MO Lois Weber, an ex-actress, produces a film about abortion, *Where Are My Children?* starring Tyrone Power (father of the talkies' Tyrone) for Universal. She is the first successful woman movie producer.

MO *The Heart of Paula,* starring Lenore Ulrich (a Pallas Pictures five reeler) is the first film shot with two different endings, a sad one and a happy one. Twenty-four critics vote on which ending they prefer and the vote turns out dead even. Consequently a coin is tossed to decide, and the happy ending wins.

RA American Marconi has been formed and David Sarnoff submits a proposal to its general manager, Edward Nally, that the company manufacture "radio music boxes." The recommendation is rejected.

CI Ringling Brothers introduce *Cinderella,* one of the most lavish "Spectacles" ever seen. It has a cast of 1,370 people, 735 horses and five herds of elephants. Its presentation takes more than a half-hour of the show's running time.

MU In April, *Billboard's Song Hits,* spotlighting "best songs in the catalogs of leading publishers," is introduced. Other charts follow, keeping pace with changes in show business' use of popular music and records.

1917

CI James Robinson, generally recognized as greatest bareback rider of all time, dies at age eighty-two in French Lick, Indiana.

CH One of most successful chautauqua producers of the season is Louis Runner. He is a slide trombonist, who left the Gentry Dog and Pony show to come into the chautauqua field, and this season produces fourteen concert companies, mainly musical groups.

CH One of the most controversial lecturers on the chautauqua circuit this season is a Chinese, Dr. Ng Poon Chew. Among other points, his talk stresses: "The Chinese people hope to a man for the success of Germany. Not that we love Ger-many more, but that we love her foes less. . . ."

TH With Joseph Rhinock putting up part of the money, the Shuberts buy out the theatrical holdings of the Cox estate for $10,000,000. They now own and/or control the largest theatrical empire in America. The Klaw and Erlanger trust now runs a poor second.

TH Sigmund Romberg writes the operetta *Maytime.* Produced by J. J. Shubert, it is such a big hit that, after opening at the Shubert Theatre, another company opens at the 44th Street Theatre.

TH First Pulitzer Prize for drama awarded to light comedy, *Why Marry?,* written by short story writer Jesse Lynch Williams.

MO From this year through 1919 almost every star makes at least one war film. Mary Pickford, *The Little American;* Lillian Gish, *Hearts of the World,* directed by Griffith; Alla Nazimova, *War Brides;* Charlie Chaplin, *Shoulder Arms;* Sarah Bernhardt, *Mothers of France;* etc. Griffith actually took his company behind the lines in France.

MO Zukor becomes kingpin of the industry. He becomes partners with Lewis J. Selznick in Select Pictures and arranges for Paramount to acquire control of Pickford's Artcraft Pictures. Meanwhile Artcraft has signed Douglas Fairbanks, Thomas Ince, Griffith, and Hart — all formerly with Triangle.

MO Paramount acquires the enormously popular Fatty Arbuckle, whose comedy company includes a young acrobat, Buster Keaton. Sennett also moves over to Paramount, taking with him Ben Turpin, Teddy and Pepper (a dog and cat), Louise Fazenda, Chaplin's brother Sidney, Chester Conklin, and Mack Swain.

MO Mack Sennett's Bathing Beauties are to World War I soldiers what Betty Grable was to World War II G.I.s. Daring in their knee-high, voluminous bathing costumes, they include Gloria Swanson, Phyllis Haver and Marie Prevost. All become prominent later, with Swanson obtaining legendary star status.

MO Irked by the rising cost of big name films, Thomas L. Tally, who opened America's first movie theatre, joins with other independent theatre owners around the country to form First National Films and the National Exhibitors Circuit to make their own film deals. Chaplin is the first star signed, followed by Mary Pickford, Norma and Constance Talmadge, and director Thomas Ince.

MO Charlie Chaplin makes deal with First National for $1,075,000 to make eight two reel films.

MO Samuel Goldfish forms Goldwyn Pictures with legit producer Edgar Selwyn and playwright Margaret Mayo. Their first release is *Polly of the Circus* with Mae Marsh. They sign leading Broadway stage players and the opera star Mary Garden.

MO Marion Davies, a former Follies girl, makes her first picture, *Runaway Romany,* with Pedro de Cordoba for Pathe.

MO Veteran actor Edwin August stars in one of the first all-color (other than the early hand-tinted reels) movie, *Tale of Two Nations.*

MO George Westmore founds the first movie make-up department at Selig Studios in Los Angeles. Selig specializes in animal films, so Westmore makes up beasts as well as actors. Later he helps Mary Pickford supplement her own "long but fine hair" by making false sausage curls at $50 per curl. Westmore also founds a make-up dynasty with his sons who — at one time or another — head the make-up departments of most of the top studios.

RE Victor makes first "jass" records, with a white band called, The Original Jass Band of New Orleans.

RE Conductor Leopold Stokowski makes his first recordings with the Philadelphia Orchestra. The musicians had to assemble in front of a large acoustic horn and play into it. Forty-nine years later, at the age of ninety-four, Stokowski will sign with Columbia to record four albums a year until 1982.

RA All radio equipment is taken over by the Navy as the United States declares war on Germany.

1918

CH A star chautauqua performer of the day is William Sterling Battis, who is billed as "the greatest living interpreter of the characters of Charles Dickens." Battis also

records for Victor Records, such "readings" as *Paul Revere's Ride* and *The Spirit of '76.*

TH Now more than forty leading theatrical producers book exclusively through the Shuberts, while at the same time the Shuberts themselves are producing more shows than any other production company before or since.

TH The Theatre Guild is formed by a group from the Washington Square Players — including Lawrence Langner, Helen Westley and later Theresa Helburn. They adopt a subscription plan which builds from an initial list of 135 to 50,000.

TH Sergeant Irving Berlin writes *Yip, Yip Yaphank,* a musical produced and played by soldiers at Camp Upton. He sings "Oh How I Hate To Get Up In the Morning" in the show.

TH John, Lionel, and Ethel Barrymore are all in hit shows: John, Tolstoi's *Redemption;* Lionel, *The Copperhead;* Ethel in two successive hits: *The Off Chance* and *Belinda.*

TH Will Rogers, Eddie Cantor, W. C. Fields, and Marilyn Miller are among the stars of the *Ziegfeld Follies of 1918.* George Gershwin is rehearsal pianist for the show.

TH Fred and Adele Astaire make their Broadway dancing debut in *Over the Top,* a "turkey" Lee Shubert produces. The show is a flop but later in the year Shubert stars the Astaires in *The Passing Show of 1918,* which is a hit.

MO One by one the pioneer film firms are disappearing from the scene. Kalem, Biograph, and Lubin have closed. Essanay, Mutual and Selig are on their way out, and Edison has shut down. *The Unbeliever* is the last Edison movie.

MO Herbert Kalmus begins experiments with process he calls Technicolor.

MO Mary Pickford signs a contract with First National Pictures to make three films for $350,000 each, or total of $1,050,000. This is the year Mary makes her famous *Rebecca of Sunnybrook Farm* and *The Little Princess,* both to become vehicles for Shirley Temple in the '30s.

MO Dual roles are in vogue. Mary Pickford is a hit as a beautiful woman and an ugly servant in *Stella Maris.* Her rival, Marguerite Clark, plays both Topsy and Little Eva in still another version of the durable *Uncle Tom's Cabin.*

MO Tallulah Bankhead makes her first picture for Goldwyn, *Thirty A Week,* a flop. Also a flop is famed opera star Enrico Caruso who makes two pictures for Zukor, *My Cousin* and *The Splendid Romance* (the latter is never even released). More and more producers are learning that an actor's magnetism on stage doesn't always come through on film.

MO Elmo Lincoln is Hollywood's first "ape man" in Edgar Rice Burroughs' *Tarzan of the Apes* with Enid Markey as Jane.

RA With the war at an end, the Navy proposes to Congress that it be granted total, monopolistic control over radio in the nation. Thanks to resistance of a few congressmen, supported by the country's amateur radio operators, the Navy proposal is defeated.

RA For the first time an American president's message is broadcast throughout Europe as the war ends and President Woodrow Wilson broadcasts his "fourteen points" from New Brunswick, N.J.

PART FOUR

1919–1946

1919 Actors' Equity wins first performers' strike against producers.

1919 British Marconi, parent company of American Marconi, gives over control of company to General Electric. GE, Westinghouse, A.T.&T. and United Fruit form Radio Corporation of America.

1919 Ringling Brothers and Barnum & Bailey are combined into one giant circus.

1920 Landmark year in legitimate theatre, with emergence of Eugene O'Neill as America's first great serious playwright.

1920 KDKA, Pittsburgh and WWJ, Detroit go on the air as the nation's first radio stations.

1922 Maj. Edwin H. Armstrong invents the superheterodyne broadcast receiver.

1923 Lee De Forest develops method of recording sound directly on film.

1923 ASCAP wins court decision requiring broadcasters to pay for right to play copyrighted music over the air.

1924 Record business severely hurt by increasing sale of radio sets.

1925 Victor and Columbia both release first electrically recorded disks.

1926 Vaudeville and some areas of the legitimate theatre severely hurt by phenomenal growth of radio and motion pictures.

1926 There are 14,500 movie houses in the country, and producers are turning out 400 films per year.

1926 RCA launches the National Broadcasting Company (NBC).

1927 Broadway's biggest boom season despite continuing popularity of radio and motion pictures.

1927 Warner Brothers' *Jazz Singer*, starring Al Jolson is an instant smash hit. It launches the talkies.

1927 Keith-Albee and the Orpheum circuits merge, representing a combine of 535 theatres.

1928 General Electric telecasts first drama over experimental station W2AXD, Schenectady, New York.

1928 Movie producers and exhibitors rush to convert from silent to sound operations.

1929 The stock market crash of Black Thursday, October 24, signals the beginning of the great depression.

1930 NBC puts the first experimental television station in New York city, W2XBS, into operation.

1931 Thomas A. Edison dies at age eighty-four in West Orange, N.J.

1931 CBS puts its first experimental television station in New York City, W2XAB, into operation.

1931 The great depression continues and many show business enterprises are thrown into bankruptcy and receiverships.

1932 In May, last two-a-day show opens at the Palace on Broadway, signalling the demise of big-time vaudeville.

1933 Major Edwin H. Armstrong gets frequency modulation broadcasting patents.

1933 Juke boxes spring up all across the country following the repeal of prohibition.

1936 First magnetic tape recording is done by Sir Thomas Beecham.

1936 The Big Band vogue gets underway.

1937 Guglielmo Marconi dies in Rome at age sixty-three.

1937 Hollywood turns out more films (778) than in any year since 1928.

1938 Railroad strikes cause eight circuses, including Ringling Brothers and Barnum & Bailey to close early in the season.

1939 One of Hollywood's greatest years. Among major film hits is *Gone With the Wind*.

1939 Two major Fairs open: The World's Fair in New York, and the Golden Gate Exposition in San Francisco.

1940 Broadcasters form their own music performance rights organization, Broadcast Music, Inc. (BMI) in opposition to ASCAP.

1941 In spite of imminent entry of U.S. into War, FCC approves black and white television standards.

1942 Radio disk jockeys become increasingly powerful force in record industry. New company, Capitol, recognizes this, courts the jockeys and wins quick success.

1943 NBC sells its Blue Network to Edward Noble, president of Life Savers. Noble converts it into the American Broadcasting Company.

1945 ABC network begins its television operations.

1945 Male and female vocalists take over as pop music favorites, as big band era wanes.

1946 RCA markets 10" television set for $375. It is first big commercial receiver success.

THE SOUND OF A NEW SHOW BUSINESS

By the end of World War I, the only area of American entertainment in which mechanical sound was a key factor was the record business. Despite the limitations on fidelity posed by still primitive acoustical recording and playback methods, the disk industry was well on its way to achieving its first $100,000,000 sales year. By 1921, as a matter of fact, record sales hit $106,000,000.

Otherwise, silent, feature length movies (now being made for the most part in Hollywood, the film—and sin, sex and glamour—capital of the world) and live show business dominated the entertainment scene. Movies had become so popular that film companies were listed on the stock exchanges. The big producer-exhibitor combines which controlled the major portion of the film business were recognized as multi-million dollar, solid growth investments. Movies were vying with the theatre and vaudeville for the still-exploding population's entertainment dollar.

The star system, opposed so aggressively for so long by the early film pioneers, was basically responsible for the movies' surging popularity. In addition to Mary Pickford and Charlie Chaplin, some other silent film luminaries were Lillian Gish, Gloria Swanson, Norma Talmadge, Rudolph Valentino, Mae Murray, Bebe Daniels, Clara Bow, Corrine Griffith, Billie Dove, Theda Bara, Harold Lloyd, Nazimova and Rin Tin Tin.

THE ACTORS WIN

In the theatre, the first successful actors' strike in 1919 was only a temporary, and ultimately insignificant, setback to the producers. The Actors' Equity victory corrected many abuses and achieved a new dignity and basic wage minimums for actors, but the producers soon learned to live with the upgraded conditions. The Shuberts made increasing inroads against the Klaw-Erlanger combine. By 1920 they not only had thirty of their own stage plays or musicals in production, but decided to make another aggressive try to cut into the Keith-Albee vaudeville empire. Apart from the Shuberts' commercial activities, 1920 was also considered by many a landmark year in the theatre.

An increasing number of plays treated mature themes. Eugene O'Neill won recognition as America's first truly important playwright.

NEW PEAKS FOR VAUDE STARS

In vaudeville, once again, salaries rose to new highs as the Shuberts signed many of the day's ranking stars such as Al Jolson, Jack Benny, Nora Bayes, the Marx Brothers, Eddie Cantor, Eva Tanguay and Will Rogers. They paid Rogers $5000 per week, which was $1500 more than the $3500 Ziegfeld had paid him for his last Follies appearance. And the Albee trust countered with equally inflated offers.

Elegant new film and vaudeville theatres opened; among them, on Broadway in New York were the Capitol with Major Edward Bowes as managing director in 1919, and Loew's State, the new flagship of the extensive chain built by Marcus Loew in 1921. In that same period, Loew acquired Metro Pictures and Goldwyn Pictures, Inc. and brought in independent producer Louis B. Mayer as studio chief for the powerful new combine, Metro-Goldwyn-Mayer.

The overall trend was increasingly toward "bigger and better." Finally, in 1919, the Ringling brothers, who had purchased the Barnum & Bailey circus in 1907 but had continued to operate the two shows as separate entities, combined the circuses, making the joint extravaganza truly "the greatest show on earth."

CHANGE AND GROWTH

It was a time of change as well as growth. Despite the horrendous loss of lives in the World War, the Spanish influenza epidemic, and lesser tragedies—such as the San Francisco earthquake, the Titanic disaster, the usual number of floods, fires, cyclones and such—the population soared from the 97,000,000 of 1910 to more than 105,000,000 in 1920. There was also a shift in the population to the cities. For the first time, *less* than fifty percent of the people lived on farms.

By 1920, both the eighteenth (Prohibition) and the nineteenth (Women's Suffrage) amendments were operative. The eighteenth amendment created organized crime on a scale never known before. Among other nefarious activities, the mobs moved into the night club business and into union activities. They gained domination of the stagehands union in the film industry and muscled producers out of some $2,500,000. A wave of gangster films eventually became big box-office.

Strangely enough, women, having won the right to vote, failed to effectively exercise that right to achieve broad equality. There were a variety of recognized (and unrecognized) reasons for this.

SMALL BLACK BREAKTHROUGH

There was a break-through of sorts and some continuing progress for blacks in show business. In 1921, Eubie Blake and Noble Sissle wrote, acted in, and produced a musical, *Shuffle Along*. Florence Mills had her first important role in the show and its score included "I'm Just Wild About Harry." It opened in Harlem but word of its virtues soon spread, and it moved to Broadway. It was enthusiastically received by both critics and audiences. It was the first all-black musical to make it to the main stem, and opened a few new doors for some talented black writers and performers.

Billboard played a part in helping black talent win acceptance in American entertainment. In the November 6, 1920 issue there appeared a new feature called *Jackson's Page*, a department written and edited by a black man, James Albert Jackson. *Billboard* was the first show business trade paper to search out, report on, and encourage black performers.

Nevertheless, change continued to be tortuously slow in matters of racial equality. Technological, economic, and other social changes moved at a faster pace.

THE SOUND OF PROGRESS

In the Bell laboratories, work was going forward on electrical recording processes. New sound-recording-for-film experiments were being conducted at Western Electric, GE, Westinghouse, RCA and in many other research and development centers.

On the highest management levels of the largest corporations in the United States and England, a power struggle which was to lead to the formation of a gigantic military-industrial radio and electronics trust was taking place. In its initial form, this trust had nothing to do with show business *per se*, although its ultimate directions were to determine the nature of much of American entertainment.

When the U.S. Navy failed to gain monopolistic control of wireless telegraphy and radio after World War I, Rear Admiral William Bullard met with E. W. Rice, Jr., president, and Owen Young, vice president and legal counsel of Gen-

OCT. 15, 1938 ISSUE   KATHARINE CORNELL

eral Electric. The men believed it vital that the United States secure control of the American Marconi Company, then owned by British Marconi.

THE BIRTH OF RCA

Young sent GE executives Edward Nally and Albert Davis to England to negotiate a deal. They acquired American Marconi for 364,000 shares of General Electric stock. Young now felt that it was necessary to devise a means of pooling the electric and electronic patents held by several American companies, so that expensive, destructive, and endless litigation in the development of wireless might be avoided. He was aware of the disastrous effects of such patent struggles in the early motion picture and other industries. Thus was the Radio Corporation of America created.

General Electric joined with three other large corporations, American Telephone and Telegraph (with its allied companies such as Western Electric, Bell, Electrical Research Products, Inc.); Westinghouse; and United Fruit (which had its own wireless company in Central America, the Tropical Radio Telegraph Company). By 1921, when the wheeling and dealing was completed, the ownership of RCA was: GE, 30.1%; Westinghouse, 20.6%; AT&T, 10.3%; United Fruit, 4.1%. Among them they controlled about

2000 electric and electronic patents. RCA's original function was primarily to serve as a selling agent for machines and equipment manufactured by General Electric and Westinghouse.

The first president of RCA was Edward Nally, the gentleman who had turned down David Sarnoff's suggestion that the company manufacture "radio music boxes" in 1916. Nally was not alone among the top brass in the RCA combine who felt the idea of using radio for entertainment purposes was frivolous, if not impractical. Their concentration was on the use of wireless for transoceanic and national telegraphy. They felt electric and electronic advances should be used in improving refrigeration, heating, and other basic needs of mankind.

THE SARNOFF INFLUENCE

It is difficult to compare the influence of one man versus another in the evolution of American entertainment. The dimensions of Edison's contributions are unquestioned. If any other man's influence came close to that of the genius from Menlo Park, it was David Sarnoff's. When Nally became president of RCA in December, 1919, Sarnoff was twenty-eight years old. Two years later, Nally retired. General James Harbord became president of the corporation, and Sarnoff, at age thirty, became general manager.

Sarnoff initially moved RCA into every vital area of radio. Even more significantly, over the years he utilized every strategy a brilliant field general could employ—including turning a Department of Justice anti-trust suit against the original RCA monopoly to his own purposes. He succeeded in making RCA a powerful, individual entity, independent of AT&T, GE, Westinghouse and all other corporate influence. Sarnoff and the new RCA were key factors in the development of radio, motion pictures, records and, eventually, the major force in the evolution of television.

THE VISIONARY GAMBLER

Sarnoff was no Barnum. His strength lay in his capacity to work with, inspire, and get results from (sometimes by instilling fear) scientists and engineers. He was also an administrative and organizational genius, a visionary, and a gambler. RCA poured $50,000,000 into television before the first dollar in profits came back. However, in the areas of understanding and evaluating show business talent Sarnoff was deficient. It was in these areas that William Paley frequently bested Sarnoff in battles between CBS and Columbia Records, and RCA and NBC. But those battles were yet to come.

In 1920, Sarnoff once again urged the corporation to go into the manufacture of radio music boxes. This time the board approved a budget of $2000 with which Sarnoff could build a prototype model of this box he was advocating so relentlessly.

CONRAD'S CONCERTS

Meanwhile, radio broadcasting as entertainment was coming to life in various parts of the country. Facilitating the birth were select members of an ingenious group of "hams," who had played so strong a part in preventing the Navy from securing a government monopoly in radio a few years earlier. Outstanding among these was Frank Conrad, assistant chief engineer at the Westinghouse plant in East Pittsburgh, Pa. During the war, Conrad had headed a manufacturing unit which made Army and Navy transmitters and receivers for the Signal Corps.

With the more sophisticated equipment developed during the War, notably vacuum tubes, Conrad resumed his favorite pastime of amateur broadcasting from "station" 8XK, in his garage in Wilkinsburg, Pa., near the Westinghouse plant in East Pittsburgh. On a more or less regular schedule, he broadcast phonograph record concerts. Soon he began to receive enthusiastic letters from fellow "hams." Many requested special musical selections.

On September 29, 1920, the Joseph Horne Department Store in Pittsburgh ran the following ad in *The Pittsburgh Sun:*

AIR CONCERT 'PICKED UP' BY RADIO HERE

Victrola music, played into the air over a wireless telephone, was "picked up" by listeners on the wireless receiving station which was recently installed here for patrons interested in wireless experiments. The concert was heard Thursday night about 10 o'clock and continued 20 minutes. Two orchestra numbers, a piano solo—which rang particularly high and clear through the air—and a juvenile 'talking piece' constituted the program. The music was from a Victrola pulled up close to the transmitter of a wireless telephone in the home of Frank Conrad, Penn and Peebles Avenues, Wilkinsburg. Mr. Conrad is a wireless enthusiast and 'puts on' the wireless concerts periodically for the entertainment of the many people in the district who have wireless sets. Amateur Wireless Sets, made by the maker of the Set which is in operation in our store, are on sale here $10 up. —West Basement

KDKA IS ON THE AIR

Conrad's boss, Westinghouse vice president Harry Davis, saw the advertisement and recognized the commercial potential for radio and the "music boxes" which Sarnoff had been urging since 1916. Davis put Conrad in charge of building a more powerful transmitter to broadcast commercially, and on November 2, 1920, radio station KDKA, Pittsburgh, went on the air with the Warren G. Harding-James M. Cox election returns.

Other amateur operations soon went on the air as "commercial" stations, one or two, possibly, even before

RADIO —— STAGE —— NIGHT SPOTS —— PICTURES —— OUTDOOR

The Billboard

The World's Foremost Amusement Weekly

DEC. 5, 1937 ISSUE   NELSON EDDY

took the same attitude many of the early film makers had adopted. They paid the performers nothing. The "free" exposure to thousands of people was worth a great deal to the performer, they insisted. And many players bought the idea—some because they believed in the value of the exposure, or because they had faith in the future of radio and wanted the experience, or both. Among the earliest announcers and performers were Eddie Cantor, John Charles Thomas, Milton Cross, the Vincent Lopez Orchestra, and Ethel Barrymore.

RECORDS SKID; THEATRE FINE

The record business was seriously affected by radio's emergence. Industry sales dropped steadily from $106,000,-000 in 1921 to $92,000,000 in 1922; to $79,000,000 in 1923; to $68,000,000 in 1924; to $59,000,000 in 1925. In 1925, the end of the recession along with the introduction of electrical recording techniques reversed the trend.

In January, 1925, Eldridge Johnson's Victor Talking Machine Company sponsored a radio show featuring John McCormack and Lucrezia Bori in a one-hour concert. Programs of this type convinced many record buyers that there was no need for them to spend money for music. Vincent Lopez's radio shows resulted in a successful six-week vaudeville run at New York's Palace Theatre.

Vaudeville, theatre and motion pictures were not adversely affected by radio until the end of the decade. Indeed in radio's earliest show business years, both vaude and the legitimate theatre were at a peak.

In 1923, the Palace Theatre operations showed a profit of over $500,000. Four years later the Keith-Albee and the Orpheum circuits were merged. The combine brought 535 theatres under one roof. A *Billboard* story estimated that the theatres represented more than seventy-five percent of all the houses in the country playing vaude.

KENNEDY MOVES IN

As indicated, Wall Street had moved into show business, and one of the shrewdest financiers to see exceptional financial opportunities in entertainment was Joseph P. Kennedy, father of John, Robert, and Ted. In 1926, he formed a syndicate which acquired control of a motion picture producing company, inaccurately named the Film Booking Office. It produced low-budget Westerns and held contracts with such stars as Tom Mix, Richard Talmadge, Evelyn Brent, and others. Kennedy sold RCA's Sarnoff a $500,000 share of the company.

THE SHUBERTS' DOMINANCE

During this time, in the legitimate theatre the Shuberts continued to do well. Their profits from producing and theatre

KDKA. Transmitters and receivers were built. The great majority of the builders completely ignored the patents rights of the members of the RCA trust. In fighting to have those rights recognized, the colossal monopolistic nature of the trust was dramatically exposed. And as radio's commercial potential became increasingly obvious, the individual companies within the trust began a fierce competition with each other for control of the various areas of the overall broadcasting scene. It was not until 1926 that the issue was substantially resolved. AT&T and its allied firms retained control of the nation's transmission lines. GE, Westinghouse, and RCA all continued in station ownership, transmitter and receiver manufacturing, and programming.

SOME STARS "TRY" RADIO

But in the interim, commercial radio, as part of the American entertainment scene, grew. Its acceptance was aided in 1920 by the fact that a severe economic recession set in. Putting together a radio receiver or purchasing a "set" was relatively inexpensive, and from that point on the entertainment was free. Some of the day's leading entertainers rushed to the stations to broadcast. The station operators

operations from 1919 through 1924 ran over $1,000,000 per year except for 1922. In that year they spent staggering sums trying unsuccessfully for the second time to buck the Keith-Albee trust in vaudeville. But their vaude fiasco was insignificant compared to their financial achievements in the legitimate theatre.

By 1924, the Shuberts owned or controlled eighty-six first class theatres in New York, Chicago, Philadelphia, Boston, and twenty-seven other major cities. These theatres included thirty in New York alone. The Broadway houses represented more than half of the seating capacity of all theatres on Broadway.

Together, the Shubert-owned houses could seat 130,000 customers per performance. It was not uncommon for the box-office "take" for a single week to reach $1,000,000. Typical profits of some of their own productions ran high: Romberg's *Blossom Time,* $700,000; *Bombo,* starring Al Jolson, $445,000; and Jake's *Artists and Models,* $196,000.

BOOKINGS, COSTUMES AND SCENERY

In addition to their theatre operations and their own productions, they booked (at rates ranging from 30% to 50% of the tenant show's receipts) 750 theatres, representing about 60% of all the legitimate theatre activity in the United States and Canada. Some outside producers whose shows they booked regularly included the Theatre Guild, William Brady, Sam Harris, Morris Gest, Winthrop Ames and William Morris. The Shuberts also had many top stars of the day under exclusive contract. In addition to all this, they had accumulated the largest scenery, costume and theatrical equipment inventory in the world. Almost all producers bought or leased substantial materials from the Shubert stockpiles.

All these holdings were revealed in a prospectus for a stock issue floated for the Shuberts by J. & W. Seligman, the Wall Street brokerage firm. The stock was made available on June 25, 1924, and by June 29 it was completely sold out. That same year Abe Erlanger sued his partner, Marc Klaw, for $200,000 which he claimed was interest on excess capital he (Erlanger) had put into the corporation. Erlanger won the suit, and the partnership was dissolved.

MOVIE MAKERS INTO RADIO

Some film makers moved quickly into radio, recognizing the new medium as a powerful exploitation device. In 1924, Marcus Loew inaugurated broadcasts which emanated from his own New York City station, WHN, atop the building which housed Loew's State Theatre. Loew's performance contracts with vaudeville acts stipulated that the acts would perform, gratis, via radio station WHN during their Loew's State engagements.

Harry Warner wrote an article for *Billboard* in 1928, in which he said:

AUG. 10, 1940 ISSUE   JOHN BARRYMORE

When the 1924 craze for radio swept the country, we installed a radio station (KFWB) at our studios in Hollywood . . . Strange trails have a way of leading to unexpected lands.

Warner was referring to the seemingly predestined way in which his company got into the talking pictures business at precisely the right time through contacts and experiences developed during their involvement in radio.

Technological experimentation and development were continuing, not only in sound motion pictures but in a number of other areas which would ultimately be vital influences in the evolution of show business.

A LIFT FOR SOTTO VOCE

J. P. Maxfield, an electronics and acoustics scientist, and his colleagues in the Bell Laboratories developed electrical recording and reproducing techniques which eliminated much of the distortion common to mechanical recording. They developed microphones and vacuum tube amplification of the original recorded sound (among other techniques) to a degree which eliminated forever the awkward, cumbersome pick-up horn.

Now, for the first time, an arranger-conductor could place musicians as he desired, and violins, flutes and other

RADIO ···· STAGE ···· NIGHT SPOTS ···· PICTURES ···· OUTDOOR

The Billboard
The World's Foremost Amusement Weekly

DEC. 11, 1937 ISSUE   ALFRED LUNT AND LYNNE FONTANNE

of the *sotto voce* instruments could be recorded as faithfully as the heavy brass. And now, for the first time, vocalists could sing softly—even "whisper" as did Art Gillham, the "Whispering Pianist," when he made the first electrical records for Columbia. The delicate harmonies as well as the more robust sounds of the University of Pennsylvania Mask & Wig Club were the first electrical recordings made by Victor.

A *Billboard* story in 1925, when the first electrical recordings were released, said:

It is generally felt that this radical advance in recording came too late in view of the disastrous inroads on the record business made by radio . . . Some companies, more optimistic, are inclined to believe that the new process may go a long way to restoring the industry to its former prestige.

In 1923 ,the leading record firm, Columbia Phonograph Company, had gone into receivership, and Victor sales were dropping alarmingly, so the pessimistic view could be appreciated.

SOUND FOR FILM

Lee De Forest developed a system for recording sound directly on film in 1923 and some film makers began to utilize the method in producing shorts of stars doing their vaudeville acts. These included Eddie Cantor, Weber and Fields, and others, but they created little excitement. Western Electric and Electrical Research Products, Inc. engineers developed a synchronized sound-on-disk system for films and produced a demonstration feature film starring Maude Adams. In 1924, they invited movie makers to see the talking film but the movie makers were not enthusiastic.

A NETWORK AND SPONSORS

AT&T took the first steps toward creating a radio network. In 1923 it linked WCAP in Washington, D.C., with its station WEAF in New York City. It licensed other stations to join the chain. The conditions of joining required a station to buy Western Electric transmitting equipment and pay AT&T a license fee, ranging from $500 to $3000.

Earlier AT&T, through WEAF, had learned how to earn money from radio through sponsorship. In 1922, it charged the Queensboro Corporation, a real estate firm in New York, $50 for ten afternoon minutes, and $100 for ten evening minutes. During this time the firm delivered selling talks for rental apartments.

Soon sponsors of all kinds were all over the air waves. On the AT&T network, The Cliquot Club Eskimos, The Ipana Troubadors, The A & P Gypsies and The Browning King Orchestra were heard regularly. On Westinghouse's WJZ in New York, The Schrafft's Tearoom Orchestra, The Rheingold Quartet, and The Wanamaker Organ Concert were regular attractions.

Other popular pioneer programs included "The Lucky Strike Show"; "Dr. Walter Damrosch and his Orchestra"; "Joseph White, the Silver-Masked Tenor"; "The Happiness Boys" (Billy Jones and Ernie Hare); and "Roxy and His Gang" ("coming to you direct from the stage of the Capitol Theatre"). Most sponsors paid the program costs but did not pay for time.

Sales of radio sets increased steadily: from $60,000,000 in 1922; to $123,000,000 in 1923; to $350,000,000 in 1924. The Department of Commerce issued licenses to some 600 stations in that period. Among the pioneers (along with KDKA, Pittsburgh, and WEAF and WJZ mentioned earlier) were WWJ, Detroit; KNX, Hollywood; WDAP, Chicago; KWCR, Cedar Rapids, Ia.; WCN, Worcester, Mass.; WOR, Newark, N.J., and WCAU, Philadelphia.

RADIO PAYS FOR MUSIC

WOR, Newark and WCAU, Philadelphia played extraordinary roles in radio's development. Music, as noted, was a staple of early radio fare. Broadcasters did *not* pay for the right to perform copyrighted music. But in 1923, the National Association of Radio Broadcasters suggested that music publishers turn over to the broadcasters all record

RADIO — STAGE — NIGHT SPOTS — PICTURES — OUTDOOR

The Billboard

The World's Foremost Amusement Weekly

JULY 2, 1938 ISSUE   LUCILLE BALL

RICH AND THE WARNERS

In 1925, a young promoter named Walter Rich made a deal with Western Electric (Electrical Research Products, Inc, ERPI) for the exclusive right to promote and sell their sound-on-disk system in the motion picture industry for a nine-month period. Although there were isolated instances of a drop in attendance at movies, the major film makers were doing well. The number of movie theatres had increased from 15,156 in 1924 to 20,189 in 1925. In that year, H. M. Lord, director of the Federal Budget, announced that the motion picture industry had become the fourth largest in the nation. People were standing in line to see Lon Chaney in *The Phantom of the Opera;* John Gilbert in *The Big Parade;* John Barrymore in *The Sea Beast;* and Charlie Chaplin in *The Gold Rush.*

It was little wonder that the major film maker and exhibitor combines paid scant attention to the people who were trying to sell them on the idea of adding sound to movies. However, Warner Brothers was not doing as well as Paramount, Loew's-MGM, Fox and some of its other competitors. Early in 1926 Walter Rich sold the brothers a 50% interest in his exclusive sound-on-disk system agreement with ERPI. Rich and the Warners formed the Vitaphone Corporation, and in August the Warners released their first sound feature movie, *Don Juan,* starring John Barrymore. There was no talking in the picture, but it had a synchronized musical score. The film was moderately successful.

2,000,000 PEOPLE "CATCH" A SHOW

In 1926, Sarnoff's RCA launched the first extensive radio network. The National Broadcasting Company presented its inaugural broadcast on November 15 over a chain of twenty-five stations in twenty cities. The program featured Will Rogers; Weber and Fields; the Ben Bernie, George Olsen, B. A. Rolfe, and Vincent Lopez orchestras; Walter Damrosch and the New York Symphony; and Mary Garden and Titta Ruffo of the Metropolitan Opera Company. It was estimated that 2,000,000 people tuned in to the show—a number considerably larger than had ever seen or heard an entertainment event at any time.

The debut of NBC caused great excitement in entertainment circles, and particularly in music. A leading musical entrepreneur of the day was Arthur Judson. Judson promoted concerts and was manager for many leading musical personalities. Among these were Jascha Heifetz, Vladimir Horowitz, George Szell, Ezio Pinza, Bruno Walter and both the New York and Philadelphia Philharmonic Orchestras.

RE-ENTER WCAU

Shortly after the formation of NBC, Judson visited Sarnoff and proposed that he, Judson, set up and supervise an artists' bureau for the network. Sarnoff expressed interest but

and piano roll royalties they received for songs played on radio. The broadcasters, said the Association, would be happy to use the money to pay performers.

The American Society of Composers, Authors and Publishers (ASCAP) sued station WOR on the grounds that because its broadcasts emanated from Bamberger's Department Store in Newark and advertised the store's wares, WOR was, therefore, using copyrighted music for public performance for profit. The court found in ASCAP's favor; from then on, radio stations were required to pay ASCAP performance rights fees. Initial payments were $250 per year.

The part WCAU played in the evolution of radio and show business ultimately had even broader significance. Two young Philadelphia law partners, Isaac (Ike) Levy and Daniel Murphy, and a dentist (Ike's younger brother, Leon) bought WCAU in 1922 for $25,000. They conducted their established practices and ran WCAU in their spare time. By 1925 the station was profitable, but its operation required much hard work and ingenuity. The Levys' development of WCAU was the first in a series of unrelated occurrences which took place over the next several years and changed the complexion of American show business.

MAY 7, 1938 ISSUE   GERTRUDE LAWRENCE

network with ten hours of programming per week for $10,000.

The network name was changed to the Columbia Phonograph Broadcasting System and in September it broadcast a distinguished inaugural program. A company of Metropolitan Opera artists under the direction of Howard Barlow presented *The King's Henchmen* by Edna St. Vincent Millay and Deems Taylor. The program was an artistic success but high production costs—and an incredible amount of technical difficulties encountered in broadcasting it—apparently terrified the record company owners.

TAKE BACK YOUR NETWORK

Within months, they sold the network back to Judson and his group for $10,000 and thirty hours of broadcast time. They agreed to permit Judson to retain the new name. He dropped the word "Phonograph," and thus was born the Columbia Broadcasting System.

Columbia or United, the struggling network continued to be plagued by financial problems. Before 1927 had ended, Judson sold a controlling interest in CBS to Ike and Leon Levy and their wealthy friend, construction millionaire Jerome Louchheim. That same year one of the most lucrative program and time sales the Levys made on their WCAU station was a $50,000 schedule to La Palina Cigars. La Palina's advertising manager was twenty-six year old William Paley. His father, Sam, owned the highly successful cigar firm. That same year Leon Levy married Paley's sister, Blanche. Ike's law partner and one-third WCAU owner, Dan Murphy, had become increasingly disturbed by the amount of his time the station was taking from his law practice, so, in 1927, he sold out his one-third interest to young Paley.

PRESIDENT PALEY OF CBS

Less than a year later, Louchheim, in poor health, sold out his share of the controlling interest in CBS to Paley. On September 26, 1927, Paley became president of the CBS Radio network. He had found his niche. Although NBC had a tremendous initial advantage over CBS, in due time the Paley-Levy network became a strong competitor. In radio, in records, and in television the battles between Sarnoff and Paley were to become "executive suite" entertainment industry classics.

In the same year that Paley became president of CBS, Warner Brothers, utilizing the Vitaphone sound-on-disk system, made *The Jazz Singer* with Al Jolson. It was an instantaneous smash hit. It did for the motion picture industry in its day what Porter's *The Great Train Robbery* and Griffith's *Birth of a Nation* did in theirs. The talking picture era was under way in earnest. Warners pulled out all stops in promoting their blockbuster. Among other elements of the campaign, they bought a $750,000 advertising campaign on the CBS radio network. It was a time and program purchase, which the struggling network sorely needed at the time.

was soon immersed in his countless other activities and operations and forgot about Judson. When Judson attempted to pin Sarnoff down some time later, the RCA head rejected him. A stubborn, proud and talented man, Judson decided to start a radio network of his own.

Before the year was out he organized the United Independent Broadcasters, Inc. With the help of Leon Levy—the young Philadelphia dentist who moonlighted by operating WCAU—Judson put together a network of sixteen stations and arranged with AT&T for connecting lines. Judson, with associates George Coats and Major J. Andrew White, and modest financing from a wealthy patron of classical music, Mrs. Betty Fleischmann Holmes, pressed ahead with the development of the network. They soon discovered that it was a most difficult and expensive task.

In the meantime the financially distressed Columbia Phonograph Company—taking advantage of the end of the recession, the new and growing prosperity, and the introduction of electrical recording—had made a considerable comeback. Early in 1927, Arthur Judson sold the United Independent Broadcasters, Inc. radio network to the Columbia Phonograph Company for $163,000, and a contract for the Arthur Judson Radio Program Corporation to supply the

Thus a chain of unrelated events created the dawn of the talking picture and the rivalry of the two networks. The complexion of show business was about to change.

A NEW ERA IN VAUDEVILLE

For the time being, through all this, the legitimate theatre and vaudeville continued to prosper. In full page ads in *Billboard* in 1926, Keith-Albee declared the 1926–1927 season "vaudeville's centennial year."

One hundred years of variety in America make this season the epoch-making period in the history of vaudeville.

Joseph Kennedy seemed to support this contention. In 1928, he persuaded Albee to sell his majority stock holdings in Keith-Albee-Orpheum to Kennedy's Wall Street syndicate for $21 per share. Its price at the time was $16 per share, so Albee made millions in the transaction. However, in three months the stock climbed to $50 a share.

After purchasing Albee's share, the Kennedy syndicate floated a $100,000,000 Keith-Albee-Orpheum stock issue at an asking price of $101 per share. A *Billboard* story reported that on the second day of the sale the issue was over-subscribed. In another 1928 *Billboard* ad—announcing Kennedy as Chairman of the Board, and Albee as President—Keith-Albee-Orpheum said,

"THIS IS A NEW ERA IN VAUDEVILLE"

It was indeed, as the world was to learn very shortly in a most stunning manner!

BIG DEALS AND RCA VICTOR

In 1927–1928, and through the first three quarters of 1929, the business boom was at its wild peak. President Calvin Coolidge had said that "the chief business of the American people is business." And everybody was doing it—on an ever grander scale.

In 1929, John, the last surviving member of the legendary Ringling brothers, bought the American Circus Corporation for $2,000,000. ACC was a conglomerate of a number of the leading circuses of the day: Hagenbeck-Wallace, Sells-Floto, Al. G. Barnes, and Sparks and John Robinson. The new corporation employed over 4000 performers, featured 2000 animals, and owned 150 railroad cars.

In 1927, two giant Wall Street firms—the Seligman organization, which was involved in many major entertainment industry deals, and Speyer & Company—bought the Victor Talking Machine Company of Camden, N.J.; its subsidiaries in South America, Canada and Japan; and its one-half ownership in Gramophone Company, Ltd. of England for $68,000,000. Eldridge Johnson and his family received $22,229,960 of that amount. Two years later David Sarnoff took over Victor and incorporated the RCA Victor Company.

OCT. 21, 1933 ISSUE   GEORGE BURNS AND GRACIE ALLEN

MORE RADIO PROGRESS

At the same time, NBC was progressing much to Sarnoff's satisfaction. Leading stars of vaudeville and the theatre had flocked to network radio. In 1926, Eddie Cantor, one of the most popular comedians of the day, signed with the network, and over the next decade many other stars launched their own shows on both networks. They included Bing Crosby, Jack Benny, Ed Wynn, Groucho Marx, Kate Smith, Rudy Vallee, Edgar Bergen and his dummy Charlie McCarthy, Jimmy Durante and George Burns and Gracie Allen.

But first NBC lured a blackface comedy act, *Sam and Henry* (actually Freeman Fisher Gosden and Charles Correll, who wrote and starred in the show) away from station WGN in Chicago, and built a new radio comedy strip, running from 7:00 to 7:15, five nights weekly. The story of the Fresh Air Taxicab Company, "Incorpulated," titled *Amos 'n Andy* began on NBC March 19, 1928 and was the entertainment sensation of the era. It seemed as though the entire nation tuned it in. Another tremendously popular situation comedy was *The Rise of the Goldbergs*, starring its creator and writer, Gertrude Berg.

The radio audience was growing at a fantastic rate. Royalty collections from radio patents paid to RCA by other

RADIO ——— STAGE ——— NIGHT SPOTS ——— PICTURES ——— OUTDOOR

The World's Foremost Amusement Weekly

NOV. 20, 1937 ISSUE   JACK OAKIE

receiver manufacturers were skyrocketing. In 1927, car radios had been introduced to add to the already huge horde of listeners and sponsor customers.

The upstart CBS network also was making progress. Within months after assuming the presidency, Paley had increased the number of stations affiliated with Columbia from twenty-two to forty-seven stations. Paley also seemed to be demonstrating a fine instinct for recognizing appealing talent, but Sarnoff was hardly aware of this.

SOUND-ON-DISK VS. SOUND-ON-FILM

In only one area in entertainment did RCA have severe problems. The success of The Jazz Singer and subsequent talking pictures created a tremendous demand for sound equipment. By early 1928, nearly all of the 20,000 movie theatres were rushing to install sound. Sarnoff's problem was that the favored movie sound system was the sound-on-disk Vitaphone. RCA had bought a sixty-percent controlling interest in Photophone, a sound-on-film system, which Sarnoff considered superior to the sound-on-disk method.

When The Jazz Singer created the sound explosion, however, the RCA Photophone had not been sufficiently refined to be acceptable to most film makers. A few producers, such as Pathe and Mack Sennett, contracted for use of the Photophone but Vitaphone installations were far in the lead. Vitaphone installations were costing theatre operators between $16,000 and $25,000, and Sarnoff felt he could beat those prices and supply a superior system.

"YOU'RE THROUGH, ED"

Shortly after he incorporated RCA Photophone in March, 1928, he met with Joseph Kennedy again, and RCA bought a major interest in the Keith-Albee-Orpheum theatre chain. In a single maneuver, Sarnoff now had almost 600 theatres, which would install the RCA Photophone sound-on-film system. The corporate name of Keith-Albee-Orpheum was changed to Radio-Keith-Orpheum. The omission of the name "Albee" was significant. The "new era in vaudeville" to which the Billboard ad referred seemed to be in the making. Kennedy visited Albee in his office at KAO one day and said, "You're through, Ed." Thus ended the long career of a man who had played a major part in vaudeville history.

Albee died shortly after his elimination from the company he had created. He left an estate of over $3,000,000. The bulk of that fortune, of course, was represented by the sale of his stock to the Kennedy syndicate. But Albee was not the only showman to earn millions through the stock market.

RCA stockholders in the period from early 1928 to July, 1929, saw their shares climb steadily from 85 to 500. While Sarnoff was making alliances and acquisitions in records, motion pictures, and other areas, Paley was working to further strengthen a thriving CBS. In 1929, he worked out a deal with Adolph Zukor, head of Paramount Pictures. Zukor had just opened the most elegant of all movie show palaces, the Paramount Theatre on Broadway in New York. He was considered by many the single most powerful man in the motion picture production and exhibition business. Paley sold Zukor fifty percent of the stock in the CBS radio network for 58,823 shares of Paramount Pictures stock. The Paramount stock was valued at $3,800,000 at the time.

THE BLACK THURSDAY OVERTURE

The Zukors, Paleys, Sarnoffs and their colleagues and competitors in show business were not the only people trading in stock. More than 1,500,000 Americans had accounts with brokerage firms. Over a third of them were buying on margin (putting up their stocks as collateral for bank loans). RCA was the pride of the bull market. When it reached 500 it was split five for one. And then came Black Thursday, October 24, 1929—the overture to the Great Depression. That day RCA opened at 68¾ and dropped steadily until it reached a 1929 low of 28 on November 13. And kept plummeting. So did American business.

DEC. 5, 1942 ISSUE KATE SMITH

What would have happened to the various segments of show business if the prosperity of the mid-twenties had continued no one knows. What did happen was fascinating, and in some ways surprising.

DEPRESSION-PROOF RADIO

Radio, no doubt, would have continued to grow, but it is unlikely that its rise would have been as meteoric had not the depression come along. What little money people had to spend for anything but the bare necessities, they seemed to spend for radio receivers. By 1931, the second year of an increasingly severe economic crisis, the Census Bureau reported that 12,078,345 American homes out of a total of 29,980,146 homes (two out of five) had radio receivers.

Billboard stories revealed the extent of radio's continuing prosperity in the teeth of the depression. In 1934, NBC grossed $28,062,885 and CBS $14,822,675. Paley had reacquired the fifty percent of the network's stock from Zukor and had returned the depressed Paramount stock to the film company. The networks ran up high profits not only from their broadcast operations, but also from allied activities. Both of them ran talent and booking agencies and sold pro-

grams in the form of electrical transcriptions to independent stations.

In 1931, the NBC Artists' Bureau did $10,000,000 in booking commissions.

One week in 1932, the CBS Artists' Bureau had eleven acts working in theatres in the metropolitan New York area alone, earning a total of $25,000 for the week. At salaries ranging from $4000 per week and up, the acts and the houses they played included Kate Smith (Madison, Brooklyn); Boswell Sisters (Paramount, New York); Mills Brothers and the George Olson orchestra (Palace, New York); Vaughan DeLeath (Regent, Patterson, N.J.); Arthur Tracy, the Street Singer (Hippodrome, New York); Singin' Sam (Academy of Music, New York). The average commissions paid the CBS Artists' Bureau by the performers was twelve and one-half percent.

It was apparent that in spite of the anti-trust efforts and accomplishments of the Department of Justice in the case of the Motion Picture Patents Company and other trusts, the Federal government was not inclined nor able to move too rapidly against present major entertainment industry trusts. The Department had filed a suit against RCA, GE, Westinghouse and other members of the radio patents trusts in 1931, and in 1932 the corporations signed a consent decree which dissolved the patents pool. It was this decree which gave Sarnoff and RCA complete freedom from the other corporations.

However the Government did not move against the talent booking, programming, and other allied operations of the radio networks, or against the major motion picture producer-exhibitor organizations on anti-trust charges until some time later. In the meantime radio boomed. In *Billboard* stories in 1935, the NBC Artists' Bureau brass announced that "it was the largest talent organization of its kind in the world," and the CBS Artists' Bureau reported a record gross of $3,500,000, a substantial increase over the previous year. Only Jules Stein's Music Corporation of America and the William Morris Agency rivaled the two network bureaus.

FINE DRAMA AND BOWES

At the heart of radio's depression-proof performance, of course, was the continuing development of exceptional entertainment. By 1935, virtually every important comedian or comedy team and every musical attraction of consequence was appearing regularly on either the NBC Red or Blue or the CBS network. In 1935, another tremendously popular show, *The Major Bowes Amateur Hour,* made its bow, and the following season a number of outstanding dramatic programs were introduced. These included Cecil B. De Mille's *Lux Radio Theatre,* the *First Nighter* with Don Ameche, and the *Columbia Workshops.* John Barrymore did a series of six Shakespearean plays.

OCT. 31, 1942 ISSUE   OLSEN AND JOHNSON

MOTION PICTURE CHAOS

The combined impact of the enormous public acceptance of radio and the deepening national depression was devastating on vaudeville and the legitimate theatre, two of the three most popular segments of American entertainment. Motion pictures again seemed to have been saved from a serious decline by a minor miracle; this time it was a technological one. In the first several years of the depression the movies prospered thanks to the introduction of "the talkies." Nevertheless, sound's debut created internal chaos on every level of the film business.

The public had shown a quick response to the talkies. From 60,000,000 paid admissions in 1927, attendance almost doubled to 110,000,000 by the end of 1929. Up to this time producers faced the dilemma of whether they should continue to make silent or sound pictures. Most straddled the fence and went into the expensive procedure of making each movie in a silent and a sound version. Exhibitors, from the giant combines to the smallest independents, struggled with the question of whether or not they should wire their houses to play the talkies—and if so, whether they should install a sound-on-disk or sound-on-film system.

Their decisions were apparent in the unfolding statistics: At the beginning of 1929 only 1,300 theatres of the 20,500 in the country had installed sound. By the end of the year, 9000 houses were wired. And before the end of 1930, 83 percent of all the houses in the nation showed talking pictures. The movement was spurred by the reduction in installation prices. Where the original Vitaphone system cost a theatre owner between $16,000 and $25,000, by 1929 RCA Photophone was advertising installations of its sound-on-film system for smaller theatres in *Billboard* for $2,995.

THE FINANCING PROBLEM

What the sound movement did to the film industry's largest corporations, however, was to put them deeper and deeper into debt to the bankers. Loew and MGM, Twentieth Century Fox, Paramount, and the Warners themselves, as well as RKO had borrowed heavily to finance the construction of new theatres and acquisition and control of others of the thousands they now operated along with their production activities. To a lesser degree this was also true of United Artists, Columbia, and Universal. Now they were faced with spending additional millions to wire these houses for talkies.

Another problem they faced was discussed in a *Billboard* article by Louis B. Mayer.

The old silent screen was international in scope . . . We must now find ways to make the new talking screen internationally acceptable.

On the creative level the upheaval was equally seismic. Screen stars whose voices did not match their silent image were suddenly doomed. The classic example was John Gilbert. In 1929, he had just signed a new million-dollar contract with his studio, MGM. His torrid love scenes with Garbo and other female favorites in the silent era had made him (along with Rudolph Valentino and a handful of others) the great lover of the day. His virile image thrilled thousands. When audiences saw (and *heard*) his first talkie, they were shocked. Gilbert's voice was thin and high-pitched, contradicting his physical virility. The unfortunate star soon sank into oblivion. His first talking picture was ironically titled, *His Glorious Night.*

THE FLOW OF FILM HITS

Some silent film stars died with sound; new stars ascended to their places. As in the case of radio, it was outstanding new entertainment, like talking pictures (many of them dazzling new musicals) which carried the movies through the first several years of the depression. In 1929, the Marx Brothers made *Cocoanuts;* MGM scored with the Oscar winning musical *Broadway Melody;* and Mary Pickford won an Oscar for her first talking picture, *Coquette.*

The following year, Greta Garbo was an instant success in *Anna Christie; All Quiet On The Western Front* with Lew Ayres, and Jean Harlow in *Hell's Angels* were part of a

RADIO —— STAGE —— NIGHT SPOTS —— PICTURES —— OUTDOOR

The Billboard

he World's Foremost Amusement Weekly

FEB. 26, 1938 ISSUE   FRED ALLEN

World War I film trend; Clark Gable became a star by socking Norma Shearer in *A Free Soul.*

The gangster era was heralded by Edward G. Robinson in *Little Caesar* (1930), James Cagney in *Public Enemy* (1931) and Paul Muni as *Scarface* (1932). Musicals exploded into popularity again in 1933, headed by *Forty Second Street* and *Gold Diggers of 1933.*

1934 was a vintage year. Shirley Temple, America's darling, became the number-one box office draw. One of her closest competitors was Mae West. Frank Capra's *It Happened One Night,* with Clark Gable and Claudette Colbert, made a clean sweep of the top Academy Awards.

AND MORE BOX OFFICE WINNERS

1934 was also the year of W. C. Fields. Fred Astaire and Ginger Rogers, Hollywood's most famous dance team, made their first movie as co-stars, *The Gay Divorcee.* Bette Davis appeared in *Of Human Bondage* with Leslie Howard; the first *Thin Man* picture with William Powell and Myrna Loy was released.

In 1935, Gable and Charles Laughton's *Mutiny on the Bounty;* John Ford's *The Informer; Alice Adams* with Katharine Hepburn; and Errol Flynn in *Captain Blood* all

contributed to keeping a financially hard-pressed populace spending some of their money at the movies.

In 1936, Gary Cooper brought them in with *Mr. Deeds Goes to Town* and Charlie Chaplin—still silent—with *Modern Times.* Clark Gable, Spencer Tracy and Jeanette MacDonald were devastated by the San Francisco earthquake; Greta Garbo was exquisite as Camille, and Humphrey Bogart became a star in *The Petrified Forest.*

ADVANCES IN COLOR

Experimentation also continued in the use of color in films. Herbert Kalmus had begun research in a process called "Technicolor" in 1918. By 1923, he introduced a two-color process to the market. This was used in occasional sequences in a film. One of the most effective early applications was in Lon Chaney's *The Phantom of the Opera* in 1925.

In 1926, the two-color process was used throughout *The Black Pirate* starring Douglas Fairbanks.

By 1935, Kalmus had improved the system to the point where it delivered a highly acceptable full color print. Director Rouben Mamoulian made the first full-length feature in the perfected Technicolor process that year, *Becky Sharp,* starring Miriam Hopkins. Studios produced more and more color films from that time on, but the impact of the addition of color did not match the overwhelming initial impact of the conversion to talkies.

Forceful new production and administrative personalities were beginning to make their marks in the movie business. In 1923, at the age of twenty-four, Irving Thalberg left Carl Laemmle's Universal studios to join Louis B. Mayer at MGM. When Thalberg died of pneumonia in 1936 at the age of thirty-seven, he was earning $400,000 per year plus bonuses and had become a legendary figure. By 1933, Darryl Zanuck had worked his way up from writing Rin-Tin-Tin scripts to head of production at Warner's. David Selznick, son of Lewis, after a bitter battle with young Thalberg at MGM, had moved to Paramount in 1929 to work under B. P. Schulberg. New generation moguls, as well as the veterans, were producing outstanding films and corresponding profits.

FROM FREE DISHES TO RECEIVERSHIPS

But from Black Thursday in 1929 until the late 30s, the nation sank deeper and deeper into joblessness and despair. And—in due time—despite these fine pictures and their brilliant writers, directors and stars; despite the dedicated efforts of the industry's moguls, both rookie and veteran; despite the "miracle" of the talkies and the additional appeal of color; despite *"Free Dishes," "Bingo," "Bank Night"* and a hundred-and-one other promotional allurements— almost all the film companies went into bankruptcy and operated under receiverships, just as did countless thousands of other American businesses.

The legitimate theatre succumbed considerably sooner than films. The talkies, along with radio and the depression, contributed to the woes of the stage. As early as the spring of 1929, *before* the depression hit, *Billboard* reported that of the eighteen theatres on Broadway from 42nd to 53rd Street, seventeen were showing talking pictures. Most of these had previously housed legitimate attractions. The sole exception was the Palace, which continued to play two-a-day vaudeville.

THE SHUBERTS "SPARE A DIME"

The Shuberts, Ziegfeld, and most of the other producers were writing clauses into their actor contracts which forbade the performer to make movies while employed by the legit producer. Then came the depression and matters went from bad to impossible. Producers cut ticket prices from a three-dollar top, to two dollars, then to a dollar—to no avail.

William Klein, the Shuberts' attorney, revealed that the brothers lost over $3,000,000 in 1931. In the 1932–1933 season, the Shuberts brought in only five shows and produced none of their own. One of the productions, a musical revue, *Americana,* introduced a theme song for the times, E. Y. Yip Harburg's, "Brother, Can You Spare a Dime." A man named Rex Weber sang it.

On New Year's Day, 1933, the Court ordered the Shuberts to liquidate the assets of the Shubert Theatres Corporation. Lee Shubert, himself, ultimately bought the bankrupt corporation bearing his name for $400,000. The Shuberts, along with the Irving Trust Bank and others, had conducted the affairs of the corporation through its days of receivership. The courts, of course, considered them—as they indeed were—best qualified. This practice prevailed in most bankruptcies and receiverships. When the Paramount organizations went into bankruptcy, Zukor and his chief lieutenants conducted the company's affairs in receivership, and in due time, reorganized the corporation, with Zukor again at its head.

$5,000,000 AND SOME GOOD PLAYS

How many millions the Shuberts made in the theatre before the depression no one knows. But between the worst years of the economic crisis, from 1931 to 1937, they poured over $5,000,000 into theatre operations. Knowledgeable Broadway observers insist to this day that the Shuberts virtually kept the theatre alive in that period. The observers add: *They could afford it!*

Surely contributing to keeping the theatre alive were the outstanding dramas, comedies, and musicals which continued to be produced through the depression. The years 1931–1937 saw George M. Cohan in Eugene O'Neill's *Ah! Wilderness; Tobacco Road,* a play condemned as "vulgar," but which ran seven years, depression or no depression; Maxwell Anderson's *Winterset; Of Mice and Men;* Maurice Evans in Shakespeare's *Richard II;*

OCT. 2, 1937 ISSUE   GEORGE M. COHAN

Katharine Cornell in *The Barretts of Wimpole Street;* Lunt and Fontanne in Robert Sherwood's Pulitzer Prize winner, *Idiot's Delight;* Clifford Odet's *Awake and Sing!;* Lillian Hellman's *The Children's Hour; Room Service;* and such popular musicals as Jerome Kern's *Roberta;* Gershwin's Pulitzer Prize winner, *Of Thee I Sing;* Fred and Adele Astaire in *The Band Wagon;* Billy Rose's *Jumbo* with a Rodgers and Hart score; and Ethel Merman in Cole Porter's *Anything Goes.*

JUKE BOXES AND DECCA

The depression, talkies, and radio pushed the record business to the brink of oblivion. Beginning in 1925, with the introduction of electrical recording and improvements in playback equipment, records had made a steady, healthy climb back to a $75,000,000 sales year in 1929. Then with blood-chilling precipitousness industry grosses streaked downward: $46,000,000 in 1930; $18,000,000 in 1931; $11,000,000 in 1932, and an all-time modern era low of $5,000,000 in 1933.

A combination of forces rode to the rescue in 1934. Prohibition was repealed, and thousands upon thousands of cafes, saloons, bars and restaurants installed juke boxes. They

AUG. 24, 1940 ISSUE   MAXWELL ANDERSON

radio stations from playing records. Paul Whiteman and Fred Waring were in the forefront of these movements. Supporting these name bandleaders were some of the powerful attorneys and show businessmen of the day.

VAUDEVILLE'S BAD DAYS

If the record industry escaped extinction, vaudeville did not. It had gone into decline even before the beginning of the depression. *Billboard* reported a drop of seventy percent in national vaude grosses from 1927 through 1932. On May 14, 1932, the two-a-day era ended at the Palace Theatre, and the legendary temple of vaudeville went into a grind policy of continuous shows, five a day.

Perhaps Martin Beck spelled out the basic reason for vaude's demise when he said, in an article in *Billboard* in 1932:

Vaudeville and its performers are still riding high bicycles . . . Less innovation and less originality is displayed in vaudeville than in any form of stage presentation.

George Jessel, one of vaude's veteran stars, in another *Billboard* article, detailed one part radio had played in vaude's decline. Said Jessel:

Radio offered a problem similar to nothing ever previously encountered. Material had to be changed with every performance. The good old days when a standard act could play for years without altering a line or changing a gag were gone. The small towns and the big towns, which formerly it took two years to cover completely, now were covered in two minutes . . . .
Those script writers from whom the continuity was purchased soon exhausted their own ideas, and fell back on good old Joe Miller with a vengeance. Vaudeville was being brought back without a credit line.

OTHER AREAS, OTHER PROBLEMS

All other show business areas experienced hardships during the great depression. A large number of night clubs were owned or controlled by racket people, and before and during the depression, they opened and closed in helter skelter fashion. During prohibition the clubs were frequently raided by Federal agents, only to open again under new names and disguised "new" management.

Burlesque turned increasingly to ever more naked bump and grind but to little avail. The 1933–1934 season was burlesque's worst year to date.

Outdoor shows were hard hit, but state and county fairs did surprisingly well. Ralph Ammon, manager of the Wisconsin State Fair, conducted a survey in 1930 comparing attendance at eight state fairs (Wisconsin, Iowa, Illinois, Minnesota, Ohio, Indiana, Missouri, Nebraska) and found that patronage had almost doubled, from 1,502,000 in 1915 to 2,870,000 in 1930. This was due in part to the continuing population increase. The 1930 census showed over

became not only important buyers of millions of records, but also popularizers of songs and artists.

A second key factor in the industry resurgence was the formation of American Decca. E. R. Lewis, founder of Decca in England, hired Jack Kapp who, along with E. F. Stevens, launched Decca in the United States. Kapp signed important new artists, among them Bing Crosby, the Andrews Sisters, the Mills Brothers, and the Guy Lombardo band. He produced top hit records with them. Stevens created a sales and merchandising structure. The records retailed for 35¢, as opposed to the going price of 75¢ for most popular records. Decca's emergence and the proliferation of juke boxes brought the record business back to good health.

Record sales climbed from $7,000,000 in 1934 to $9,000,000 in 1935; $11,000,000 in 1936; $13,000,000 in 1937 and doubled to $26,000,000 in 1938.

By 1940, a *Billboard* survey estimated that there were 400,000 juke boxes on location. They represented an operator investment of over $60,000,000 and these operators were buying 720,000 records per week.

The record industry, manufacturers and artists alike, considered radio such a mortal enemy that they attempted in 1935, and for a number of years thereafter, to prevent

RADIO — STAGE — PICTURES — OUTDOOR

15 Cents   MARCH 21, 1936

The Billboard

The World's Foremost Amusement Weekly

HORACE HEIDT
Of Horace Heidt and His Alemite Brigadiers
Broadcasting CBS Weekly

MARCH 21, 1936 ISSUE   HORACE HEIDT

123,000,000, 18,000,000 more than the 105,000,000 of 1920.

Almost all travelling shows, circuses, carnivals, and tent shows of every description experienced great problems. Amusement parks suffered.

At parks, fairs and carnivals the most popular merchandise prizes were Lindbergh dolls and boxes of candy, and Madam Queen and Amos and Andy dolls. In 1935, the Shirley Temple doll was the number-one prize item.

The most vivid symbol of the depression in show business was the danceathon or walkathon. Dancing couples staggered and stumbled their way through endless hours of physical torture to earn pitifully small cash prizes. The public wearied of these sad, masochistic spectacles by the mid-thirties, long before the depression itself ended.

UNCLE SAM TIME

Franklin Delano Roosevelt took over the presidency from Herbert Hoover in 1932. Soon the Federal Government, under FDR, was the major employer in show business. The Federal Theatre Project supplied work to thousands of actors and other craftsmen. It also supplied the longest route for dramatic and variety travelling shows, *Uncle Sam Time,*

embracing Civilian Conservation Corps camps and other Federal institutions. Acts and shows played a string of sixty-five consecutive weeks: twenty in New York City and forty-five on the road from coast to coast.

TV'S FAR-OFF CORNER

Back in 1928, a year before the great depression began, at the tail end of that swinging era of Coolidge prosperity, a handful of men began to preach television. Sarnoff was the high priest. That year—while almost all radio broadcasters, movie moguls, theatre tycoons, and showmen in every area were building bigger grosses and net earnings—Sarnoff made a speech at the Harvard Business School. He told the undergraduates that a great future lay ahead in television, that the new sight and sound medium was "just around the corner."

He was more aware than most, of course, of the experimental work in video which had been and was being carried on. In the AT&T research labs, which Sarnoff watched closely, H. E. Ives was developing a TV-by-wire transmission system. Ives actually sent a picture of Secretary of Commerce Herbert Hoover from Washington, D.C. to New York in 1927. In New Jersey, Allen B. Du Mont was already manufacturing picture tubes and other components. In California, Philo Farnsworth was working on a transmitting system.

By 1928, General Electric began television program experiments in Schenectady, N.Y., at their experimental station W2XAD. On September 11 that year, they telecast the first drama, *The Queen's Messenger.* In 1929, Dr. Vladimir Zworykin, now working for RCA, demonstrated his kinescope and the cathode ray television tube before the Institute of Radio Engineers.

In 1930, NBC went on the air in New York City with its experimental TV station, W2XBS. Farnsworth's electronic TV transmission system patents were approved. A year later CBS put its experimental station, W2XAB, into operation in New York.

In 1935, Sarnoff announced plans to spend $1,000,000 on television program experimentation. Up to this time, in an arrangement with RCA, Major Edward H. Armstrong had been conducting frequency modulation (FM) static-free radio broadcast experiments from the RCA transmitter atop the Empire State Building. Now Armstrong was requested by RCA to remove his FM equipment to make room for the television experiments. Armstrong built his own FM transmitter atop the Palisades at Alpine, N. J., and began much-praised, static-free broadcasts of classical music. It is ironic that many years after Armstrong's tragic suicide, FM radio achieved its widest acceptance and growth by serving as the prime medium for popularizing "hard," "acid," and other forms of rock music.

NO MOVIE SUPPORT

But Sarnoff had decided that television must take priority over any further development of radio. It was believed in

JULY 27, 1940 ISSUE   VIVIEN LEIGH

is Born; Nothing Sacred with Carole Lombard; and Cary Grant in *The Awful Truth*.

Business slowed up in some areas in 1938, but the new prosperity of the Big Five (Paramount, Warner Brothers, MGM, RKO, and Twentieth Century Fox) and the Little Three (Universal, Columbia, and United Artists) once again attracted the attention of the Department of Justice. In 1938, the Department filed a new anti-trust suit against the movie makers objecting to their dual control of production and exhibition. But this suit dragged on for years.

News of the government action did not slow up the release of some outstanding films that year. Bette Davis in *Jezebel* and James Stewart and Jean Arthur in *You Can't Take It With You* were just two of the big box office films of 1938. Judy Garland was teamed with Mickey Rooney for the first time in *Love Finds Andy Hardy*, the fourth in the series. And a young actor named Ronald Reagan had a part in *Brother Rat*.

GONE WITH THE WIND

In 1939, David Selznick produced one of the greatest box-office successes of all time, *Gone With the Wind*. Clark Gable as Rhett Butler, Vivien Leigh as Scarlett O'Hara, Olivia DeHavilland and Leslie Howard starred in the film. Hattie McDaniel, as Mammy, won an Oscar for Best Supporting Player, the first black ever to win the Academy's prize.

The picture, which cost $4,500,000, had grossed close to $175,000,000 by 1975. In 1976, NBC paid $5,000,000 for the right to show it on television. Running two nights, it played to the largest viewing audience of any film in TV history. Achieving successes of these dimensions, the film makers saw no good reason to get involved with television.

RADIO BOOMS ON

Radio continued to grow, attract and absorb stars and other performers from all the entertainment media. By the end of 1939, there were 743 AM and 9 FM radio stations. That year, an incident occurred which gave fresh evidence of the power of the medium. One of the highest rated network shows of the day was the Edgar Bergen-Charlie McCarthy program on NBC. On the night of October 30, the CBS show opposite Bergen-McCarthy was a dramatic presentation by Orson Welles' Mercury Theatre players of H. G. Wells' *War of the Worlds*. So realistic was the Welles radio play that it caused a national panic. Listeners by the thousands called police stations, convinced that an invasion of the Earth by Martians was in progress. Even shows bucking radio's number one program found millions of listeners.

Bing Crosby and Kate Smith had both been presented on CBS by Paley in the time slot opposite the top-ranked *Amos 'N Andy* show on NBC. And both found sufficient audiences to boost them into stardom. Broadcasters felt they had it made, and most of them were disinclined to get involved with TV.

some quarters that the major reason for this decision was that many of RCA's patents in radio had expired or were nearing expiration dates, and that the RCA engineering staff, led by Dr. Zworykin, had developed important new patents in television.

Sarnoff's TV drive received little support from any entertainment quarter. The movie industry, of course, was aware of the early activity in television. But apart from Adolph Zukor's purchase of an interest in the Allen B. Du Mont television laboratories in 1938, and some tentative, soon-aborted moves into the new medium by the Warner Brothers, film leaders stuck to their own thriving field.

A *Billboard* story suggested that one reason for this was that almost all of the movie people had such enormous investments to recoup that they were reluctant to put themselves in the position of making additional heavy financial commitments to television. And the movies were once again doing well. By 1937, Hollywood was turning out a greater number of films, 778, than at any time since the pre-depression year, 1928. These included *A Family Affair*, the first of the highly successful *Andy Hardy* series, starring Mickey Rooney; Walt Disney's first feature length cartoon, *Snow White and The Seven Dwarfs*; Fredric March in *A Star*

PALEY HURLS A RECORD CHALLENGE

The record business also continued to prosper. In 1938, Paley decided to challenge RCA and Sarnoff in this arena. The operating head of RCA Victor in that year was Edward (Ted) Wallerstein. Wallerstein had taken the company to the top position in the industry. Decca was a strong second and Columbia Records trailed in third place. Over the years since the Columbia Phonograph Record Company had hastened to give back the radio network to Judson and his associates, the disk operation had been sold and resold a number of times. In 1934, the Majestic Radio Company had sold it to American Record Company for $70,000.

Now in 1938, Wallerstein was dissatisfied with conditions at RCA, despite the company's success. He resigned and persuaded William Paley to buy Columbia Records for $700,000, ten times the price of the last sale. Under Wallerstein's leadership, the competitive battle between Columbia and RCA began in earnest. It would continue into the next decade, marked by a technological confrontation which in its own way matched the more immediate upcoming war in television. In 1938–1939, however, the competitive struggle in the record industry on the creative and technological levels sparked the boom in big bands, and subsequently the era of the superstar vocal soloist.

HERE COME THE BANDS

While the Paul Whiteman, Vincent Lopez, Fred Waring, Ben Selvin and other orchestras had been important, popular entertainment features since the early 1920s, and while Decca's mid-1930s recordings of bands such as Guy Lombardo were strong sellers, the big bands did not reach their mass popularity period until 1939. That year, Wallerstein at Columbia introduced a new laminated record with considerably improved sound and longer life than the commonly used shellac disks.

He featured bands such as Count Basie, Benny Goodman, and Duke Ellington on these new disks at the lowered price of 50¢. That same year the CBS radio network carried programs featuring the Goodman, Cab Calloway, Sammy Kaye, Kay Kyser, Hal Kemp, and Paul Whiteman orchestras. On NBC, more than forty big bands were programmed, including Glenn Miller, Artie Shaw, Jimmy and Tommy Dorsey, Horace Heidt, and Charlie Barnett.

CROSBY, SINATRA, LEE, AND SHORE

At their peak, the bands developed the vocal soloists who soon became the kings and queens of popular music. Bing Crosby, prior to the big bands' golden days, had sung with the Paul Whiteman orchestra as a member of the Rhythm Boys. Frank Sinatra joined the Harry James band in 1939. He left James after less than a year to join Tommy Dorsey, and soon left Dorsey to embark on his own spectacular career.

JULY 13, 1940 ISSUE   BING CROSBY

Other big band singers were Perry Como, Dick Haymes, Peggy Lee, Jo Stafford, Helen O'Connell, and Doris Day. The emergence of many of these band singers as long reigning superstars in several show business areas surprised some observers. Now in 1939, and for the next several years, the record business and the big bands were literally swinging.

Vaudeville continued its decline. In 1939, RKO, which had operated over 300 show houses as late as 1929, was down to a single theatre playing vaudeville. However, the Golden Gate in San Francisco continued to run one-week variety bills.

OUTDOORS' TRADITIONAL GROOVES

Like the legitimate theatre, the outdoor areas of American entertainment were settling more firmly into their niche in the overall scheme of show business. Apart from the introduction of a new act or feature here, a new thrill ride there, they went along in their traditional, well-loved grooves. In 1938, Ringling Brothers and Barnum & Bailey starred Gargantua, a fierce-looking gorilla and *Bring-Em-Back-Alive*

OCT. 22, 1938 ISSUE   BOB HOPE

Frank Buck. A railroad strike that year resulted in setbacks for most travelling shows. Only two circuses, Al G. Barnes and Sells-Floto, made it through the entire season. The rest, including the Big One, folded early—but they were to bounce back. Some carnivals found a solution in mergers. Three large midway companies, Rubin & Cherry, Beckman-Gerety, and Royal American combined forces to make up a large new enterprise, Amusement Corporation of America.

In 1939, two of the most ambitious fairs of all time opened their gates: The New York World's Fair and the Golden Gate Exposition in San Francisco.

FDR'S TV BOW

Sarnoff chose the New York World's Fair, at Flushing Meadows, Long Island, in New York City as the forum from which to launch the RCA-NBC campaign to introduce television. President Roosevelt spoke on the opening day of the fair, April 30, and his talk was telecast over NBC's experimental station. On display in the RCA exhibit was a "full" line of television sets. Their picture tube sizes were 5", 9" and 12" and they retailed from $199.50 to $600. RCA rushed 25,000 to the market.

A combination of forces and events conspired against television's early acceptance and development. Most important of all, of course, was World War II. Roosevelt's picture had hardly faded from the tube when the government called upon Sarnoff and all other electronics industry leaders to prepare to convert their facilities from consumer goods to production of war materials of all kinds.

TELEVISION'S "ICE AGE"

Just as World War I had resulted in numerous technological advances in radio, so did World War II speed up technological improvements in television. However, the situation in TV at war's end in 1945 was quite different from that of radio in 1918. Television, to begin with, presented more complex scientific problems than radio. There was no all-powerful monopoly in control of video to the extent there had been in radio. The Federal Communications Commission's regulatory position was far more stringent and sophisticated. Television's early progress, consequently, was impeded by an ice age, a series of "freezes" ordered by the Federal Communications Commission while it studied the question of standards, utilization of the very-high (VHF) and ultra-high (UHF) frequencies for video and other claimants for the air space.

It was not until 1940 that the FCC gave approval for limited commercial telecasting; not until 1941 that the Commission set standards of 525 lines, 30 frames, FM sound for black and white video transmission.

NBC, CBS, and Dr. Allen Du Mont's station, WABD, began more or less regular schedules of telecasting, and by 1941 the first sponsors—Procter and Gamble, Lever Bros., and Sun Oil—were buying time on WNBT at a rate of $120 per evening hour.

PALEY WANTS COLOR

Although CBS was operating in black and white television, in 1940 Paley—through his chief engineer, Peter Goldmark—demonstrated a mechanical, spinning-disk type *color* television system for the FCC and began his campaign to have standards set and channels assigned for color immediately. Sarnoff and his RCA engineers charged that CBS was introducing an inadequate, incompatible color system primarily for the purpose of throwing the TV situation into a state of confusion, so that the advance of black and white television would be slowed down.

This marked the beginning of a sustained battle between Sarnoff and Paley on the color system to be adopted in television. The struggle went on, with a continuing series of demonstrations of the incompatible mechanical system by CBS, and later by Du Mont, and of a compatible electronic system by RCA. RCA did not have its color system ready for demonstration until 1945, and then the FCC felt it required refinement. The color issue was not to be resolved for some time.

Whatever Paley's intentions were in introducing the mechanical color system immediately after Sarnoff launched his all-out black and white drive—and in doggedly pushing the color issue in the year thereafter—there is no question that the strategy played a part in impeding the development of commercial black and white television.

WAR'S BROAD EFFECTS

The CBS color effort contributed to the need for the continuing freeze orders by the FCC, and these, combined with the electronic industry's conversion to war production, effectively delayed television's growth for at least half a decade. Of course, World War II had other effects on show business, just as it had on every aspect of American life. For one thing, it created an unprecedented boom.

In 1941, 90,000,000 people heard President Roosevelt, broadcasting over some 800 radio stations, denounce the infamy of Pearl Harbor. By 1945, there were 943 AM radio stations, practically all doing extremely well; there were 46 struggling FM stations; and 9 television stations, struggling even harder.

There were 56,000,000 radio sets in use. One sponsor alone, Procter and Gamble, was spending $11,000,000 per year for radio time, plus another $11,000,000 for the talent to create and perform its major sponsored show form, the soap operas. In addition to the "soaps," war time radio favorites included Fibber McGee and Molly, Bob Hope, Abbott and Costello, Red Skelton, Walter Winchell, Arthur Godfrey, and quiz shows.

Even though the Department of Justice had filed anti-trust suits against both NBC and CBS, forcing them to give up their non-broadcast activities, the networks and all of their affiliated stations continued to show handsome profits. In 1943, NBC sold its Blue network to Edward Noble, president of Life Savers, for $8,000,000 and the American Broadcasting Company came into existence.

HOLLYWOOD'S CONTINUING HITS

The movie industry had ultimately ridden out the storms of both radio competition and the severe depression, and only a few of its leaders took television seriously. In the years from 1939 through 1946, Hollywood presented some of its most successful films and glittering stars. To name a representative few, there were Gunga Din with Cary Grant; Chaplin's The Great Dictator; Hitchcock's Rebecca, with Joan Fontaine; John Wayne in Stagecoach; Merle Oberon and Laurence Olivier in Wuthering Heights; Goodbye, Mr. Chips; The Wizard of Oz; Mrs. Miniver; The Lost Weekend; Samuel Goldwyn's The Best Years of Our Lives; Henry Fonda in The Grapes of Wrath; Katharine Hepburn and James Stewart in The Philadelphia Story; James Cagney in the story of George M. Cohan's life, Yankee Doodle Dandy; Bing Crosby in Going My Way; Humphrey Bogart and In-

AUG. 20, 1938 ISSUE   JOAN FONTAINE

grid Bergman in Casablanca; and Gene Kelly and Frank Sinatra in Anchors Aweigh.

THE MAGNIFICENT SURVIVOR

The legitimate theatre had long since adjusted to its unique position. It was content to supply that special entertainment which only live actors, performing well written and directed plays or musicals on a stage before an audience, can achieve. It had reached a point where it was not truly competitive to the giant mechanical show business forms, nor did it pretend nor aspire to be. It continued to develop fine actors, directors, writers and other craftsmen of entertainment, only to have many of the best of them move on to radio and movies.

During the 1939–1946 heyday period of network radio and blockbuster movies, the legitimate stage remained a magnificent survivor. Some of the outstanding plays included William Saroyan's The Time of Your Life; Lillian Hellman's Little Foxes with Tallulah Bankhead; Cabin in the Sky with Ethel Waters; Rodgers and Hammerstein's Oklahoma and Carousel; One Touch of Venus with Mary Martin; Ethel Merman in Irving Berlin's Annie Get Your Gun; Pal Joey with Gene Kelly; Moss Hart's Winged Victory; George M. Cohan's last stage appearance in The Return of

OCT. 10, 1942 ISSUE   RITA HAYWORTH AND XAVIER CUGAT

OCTOBER 10, 1942   The Billboard   25 Cents

the Vagabond; Berlin's *This Is The Army;* Tennessee Williams' *The Glass Menagerie;* Leonard Bernstein's *On The Town;* Judy Holliday in *Born Yesterday; Harvey; The Skin of Our Teeth;* and Robert Sherwood's Pulitzer Prize-winning *There Shall Be No Night* with Lunt and Fontanne.

MUSIC/RECORD CHANGES

In music and records, in addition to the successive emergence of the big bands and solo vocalists, other changes developed. ASCAP raised the performance fees they charged broadcasters to such heights that in 1940 the broadcasters formed their own performing rights society, Broadcast Music, Inc.

In the meantime, after many legal bouts and decisions the courts had decided that radio stations were free to play phonograph records without payment of any performance fee to artist or record company. In 1941, the Department of Justice filed anti-trust suits against both ASCAP and BMI, and the two music organizations quickly agreed to sign consent decrees, outlining operational procedures and setting forth methods of logging and paying for performances. In years to come, as late as 1977 some music/record industry leaders continued to seek performance royalty payments from broadcasters.

CAPITOL'S METEORIC RISE

In 1942, the shellac shortage caused by the war, and the atmosphere created by the fierce battle most record companies were fighting to prevent radio stations from playing records, resulted in virtually overnight success for an aggressive, imaginative, and talented new record company, Capitol Records. It was launched by Glenn Wallichs, a Los Angeles record retailer; Buddy De Sylva, songwriter and film producer; and Johnny Mercer, another outstanding songwriter of the day, with capitalization of $10,000. Capitol romanced disk jockeys and radio stations, while the rest of the industry fought them.

With aggressive leadership by Wallichs; with excellent records produced (and some written) by Mercer; with limitations on record quantities that established competitive companies could produce, caused by the shellac shortage; and brilliant promotion of disk jockeys and radio stations by a young ex-newspaperman, Dave Dexter, Capitol became an important factor in the record business in a stunningly short time. It was the first of what, in years to come, would be a long parade of successful "independent" record companies, challenging the established, so-called "majors."

BUGSY'S FLAMINGO

Night club entertainment stood on the threshold of a new plateau in 1946, when a mobster, Benjamin (Bugsy) Siegel and his associates opened a hotel-casino, the Flamingo, in Las Vegas. Siegel was murdered in due time, but not until he had seen the desert resort well on its way to becoming the new night club-supper club entertainment center of the world. Even Siegel could not have imagined the stratospheric heights Vegas would reach as the nation's live show business capital, paying stars and superstars salaries undreamed of in 1946, and creating the format to be followed by other resort centers, such as Atlantic City, N.J., in 1977.

THE BIG CIRCUS TRAGEDY

Outdoor shows continued to have their own problems. Most tragic was the disaster which befell the Ringling Brothers and Barnum & Bailey circus in 1944. The Wallendas were performing their high wire act in Hartford, Conn. when a fire broke out; 168 people, more than 100 of them children, were burned, crushed or trampled to death and 487 were injured. Six executives of the greatest show on earth went to prison; the circus was fined $10,000, and paid more than $4,000,000 in damages to people injured, or relatives and families of those who died. In 1946, John Ringling North, John Ringling's nephew, was made president of the circus and embarked on an aggressive and successful campaign to bring the shows back to their high place in American entertainment.

TV'S MODEL T AND JOE LOUIS

And all the while—in the absence of interest or support from show business; in the face of the ice age created by the FCC freezes; in spite of fighting the color battle against Paley and CBS—Sarnoff and his RCA and NBC associates pushed ahead to gain a foothold for black and white commercial television. In 1946, there were at least three signs that TV's day was near at hand.

Bristol-Myers, the pharmaceutical company, sponsored the first network television show, *Geographically Speaking* on *two* NBC stations.

RCA introduced a new ten-inch television set to sell for $375. The corporation's chief engineer Elmer (Shorty) Engstrom—who was later to be appointed RCA president—called the set "the Model T" of television. It was immediately and enormously successful. Other receiver manufacturers rushed to the market with their own TV sets for the first time.

When Joe Louis successfully defended his heavyweight boxing championship against Billy Conn, surveys showed that more than 100,000 people watched the fight, sponsored by the Gillette Safety Razor Company, on a *four* station NBC television network.

Suddenly a lot of people in show business said, "*Here comes television!*"

AUG. 28, 1943 ISSUE OZZIE NELSON AND HARRIET HILLIARD

ORIGINAL BILLBOARD MATERIAL
1919–1946

HIGHLIGHTS

RADIOPHONE CUTS INTO SHOW BUSINESS

FROM MARCH 4, 1922 ISSUE

RADIOPHONE CUTS INTO SHOW BUSINESS

Vaudeville Exchanges First To Realize Artists Hurt Their Value by Wireless Appearances

Why bother to rush thru dinner and get into tuxedo or claw-hammer and suffer insults of taxi drivers and ticket speculators and then find the seats are not on the aisle when in slippers and smoking jacket one can sit at home and get the whole show over the radiophone—for nothing?

Hundreds of thousands of persons thruout the country have answered that question by buying radiophone home outfits and hundreds of thousands more are likely to answer the same question or a paraphrase of it when it is put to them in the advertising of the manufacturers of these compact little instruments which bid fair to become as popular as the Victrola and other commercially improved offshoots of the original Edison phonograph.

It is not the intention of The Billboard to belittle the tremendous importance of the radiophone. There is no lack of appreciation of what this little instrument is bound to mean to millions who otherwise would never have the entertainment this comparatively inexpensive invention affords.

Warning to Actors

It comes within the province and becomes the duty of The Billboard to sound a warning, however, altho full credit for the suggestion is not claimed. The idea of opening the eyes of artists came as a result of the following report, which was brought to the Vaudeville Department of The Billboard by a big-time artist:

"The Keith Circuit has suggested that appearing for the radiophone lessens the value of a vaudeville artist as a box-office attraction."

An effort was made to learn if this suggestion had been made officially, but, there being too little time before going to press, it was not possible to get confirmation, and so the report is printed as a rumor only and for what it is worth, which this department considers is this:

Whether the Keith offices made this suggestion to their artists or not, it might be accepted as a warning to those who contemplate making an appearance "for publicity." It is human nature to get as much for nothing as possible, and if a vaudeville artist can be heard at home over the phone why pay money to hear him in a theater?

It is known that certain artists have taken up the matter among themselves and it is expected that they will make some effort to see that others who have been "invited" to appear for the radiophone get the proper box-office angle on the new fad.

"Publicity" the Bait

It is not difficult to understand how easy it is to influence an artist to sing or talk for the radiophone, for he feels that his fame will be spread thru the air to hundreds of thousands of potential playgoers, and this may be true. Old showmen, however, do not forget that the box-office is placed in a convenient location in the theater lobby to make it easy for people to pay money to see and hear artists.

That the radiophone fad is sweeping the country is proven by the published fact that between the Battery and Fourteenth street in New York City there are 60,000 home wireless instruments and that the number of outfits used for picking up government weather forecasts, music entertainments and even entire Broadway productions and excellently programmed concerts from the W. J. Z. radio station in Newark, N. J., runs into hundreds of thousands.

It is said that 300,000 amateur radio licenses have been granted in the area supplied with entertainment from the Newark station, and when it is remembered that thousands who have made their own instruments have not bothered to take out licenses some idea of the number of persons who "get more fun" out of staying at home and getting their entertainment by wireless may be had.

Radio departments have become a daily feature of large newspapers thruout the country and The New York Globe and Commercial Advertiser publishes, on Saturdays, The Radio Globe, a 32-page supplement. With such publicity the success of the radiophone is assured, and those who laugh at the suggestion that this home entertainment fad will have no effect on the show business might be interested in studying the varied programs clipped at random from the newspapers.

Hourly news service and music, from 11 a.m. to 8 p.m.

Agricultural reports at 12 m. and 6 p.m.

Arlington official time, 11.55 a.m. to 12 m. and 9.52 to 10 p. m.

Weather reports, 11 a.m., 12 m., 5 p.m. and 10.01 p.m.

Shipping news at 2.05 p.m.

7 p.m., "Man-in-the-Moon Stories" for the children.

7.30 p.m., "First Aid to the Injured," an address by Dr. Eric S. Greene, first aide specialist of the American Red Cross Society.

8.15 p.m. (Dance Night), "The Empire State Novelty Six" will supply the music for the many clubs holding dances tonight. This dance program will be longer than usual by request of the radio dance clubs.

Music at 10 a.m. to 10.15 a.m., 12.30 p.m. to 1 p.m., to 2 p.m., 2.20 p.m., and 4 p.m. to 4.20 p.m.

7.30 p.m., Music and Uncle Wiggily's Bed time Story.

7.45 p.m., Government market reports and a report of the New York Stock Exchange.

8.00 p.m., "Better Architecture," by Henry Hornbostel, Professor of Architecture, College of Fine Arts, Carnegie Tech. Designer of Soldiers' Memorial and many bridges, including the East River, Manhattan and Hell Gate bridges in New York.

242

8.30 P.M.—MUSIC SELECTIONS.

Piano Solo—Country Dances Nos. 1, 2, and 3.. Beethoven

Miss Eleanor Shaw.

Violin Solo—Old Refrain.............Kreisler

The Duo Art reproducing the playing of Rudolf Ganz, St. Louis Symphony Orchestra.

Baritone Solos (a) Lungi Del Caro Bene..Secchi
(b) Invictus.............Huhn

Mr. George L. Kirk, accompanied by H. H. Fleer.

Piano Solo (a) On Wings of Song............
'Mendelssohn-Liszt

(b) Hungarian Dance No. 5 (arranged for four hands) Brahms

Miss Shaw at the first piano, the Duo Art reproducing the playing of Harold Bauer.

(c) Bagatelle No. 1—Dambois

Miss Shaw playing alternately with the recorded playing of the composer as reproduced by the Duo Art.

(While "On Wings of Song" is being played radio operators will be asked to guess when Miss Shaw is playing and when the Duo Art is in operation.)

Baritone Solo (a) At Dawning........Cadman

George L. Kirk, accompanied by Duo Art reproducing the recorded playing of Cadman.

(b) Ishtar.............Sproas

George L. Kirk, accompanied by Duo Art reproducing the recorded playing of Shauffler.

Piano Solo—Romance........Frank La Forge

Miss Eleanor Shaw.

Piano Solo—Orientale..................Amani

Miss Eleanor Shaw.

Piano Solo—Scherzo E Minor......Mendelssohn

Miss Shaw playing alternately and with her own recording on the Duo Art.

The chief objection to performing for the radiophone seems to be that the remuneration is publicity and not money. When the players are paid then perhaps it will be realized that the radiophone will become just another field for employment.

Meantime there will be plenty who agree with the music publishers and others that the radiophone accelerates business and will more and more.

Without desiring to get into a controversy The Billboard repeats that the reported warning to vaudeville artists is printed for what it is worth.

FROM APRIL 22, 1921 ISSUE

NO RADIO FOR "ZIGGY"

New York, April 14.—Florenz Ziegfeld, Jr., will not stand for any of the artists under contract to him exercising their talents via radio. He claims that broadcasting cheapens them and a clause is to be added to all contracts forbidding the practice. Ziegfeld has always been strict about his artists working elsewhere than with him and a conflict over Eddie Cantor making records is said to have been one of the reasons for the comedian leaving his employ. Fannie Brice has started recording for the Victor and Van and Schenck record for Columbia, and it was figured from this that Ziegfeld had modified his views on the matter. The radio order would seem to put the quietus on that.

FROM MARCH 18, 1922 ISSUE

WANT PAY FOR RADIO CONCERTS

Actors' Equity Association Adopts Resolution Advising Members To Seek Compensation

Following the publication in The Billboard two weeks ago of a warning to the effect that the free concerts sent broadcast by the radiophone companies were injuring show business, the Actors' Equity Association last week went on record as opposed to its members giving ethereal performances without proper compensation. A resolution to this effect, adopted by the council of the Actors' Equity, read:

RESOLVED: That the attention of our members be drawn to the fact that the radiophone is a profitable commercial enterprise, which also in a way enters into competition with the theater, and that therefore our members be advised to seek proper compensation for any services they may be invited to give to the radiophone companies.

In explaining the Equity stand in regard to what they term the "radiograft," Mr. Paul Dullzell, assistant executive secretary, says:

"The General Electric Company and the Westinghouse people have been getting in on a lot of good stuff for nothing. Also the general electrical appliance houses. The radio concerts are a money making scheme and the artists who make them possible should be compensated.

"Heretofore the understanding has been that the advertising afforded the actor and the singer is of great advantage to them. For instance, they are told impressively that an audience of 400,000 has its ears clamped to the receiving apparatus all over the land and sea.

"I can see where the vaudeville managers already have just complaint. If this thing grows—and it bids fair to assume enormous proportions—there will soon be no incentive to go to the theaters. When audiences can hear everything in their own homes they won't have to go out to be entertained. What they will miss in stage settings and the personality of the actor will be made up by the novelty of the radiophone itself.

"We considered this a matter of such importance that at the meeting of the council last week it was resolved to suggest to our members that they seek compensation for ethereal performances."

E. F. Albee, head of the Keith Circuit, in an interview with a daily paper this week was quoted as saying that appearances for the radiophone by Keith artists was a violation of contract.

FROM MAY 7, 1921 ISSUE

MUSIC BY WIRELESS

Schenectady, N. Y., April 30.—An unique stunt will be staged by the Union College Radio Club in connection with the musical program to be given by Dabney's Syncopated Orchestra from Ziegfeld's Midnight Frolics at the junior prom on May 6. The music will be sent by wireless to 2,000 operators in the United States and Canada. Twelve hundred miles will be the sending distance. The orchestra will play from 10 in the evening to 5 in the morning. The club has become famous for its weekly concerts, which have been heard by operators in 22 States of the union, as well as by stations in Canada and ships at sea.

FROM FEB. 18, 1922 ISSUE

TO RADIO SHOWS

New York, Feb. 10.—Both "Tangerine" and "The Perfect Fool" will be broadcasted by wireless telephone. "Tangerine" will be the first to try, the whole company going to the Newark Westinghouse Station on February 12 and doing the complete show thru radio. "The Perfect Fool" will do the same stunt the following Sunday night. It is estimated that there are nearly 150,000 receiving stations able to pick up this station and the shows will get much publicity thru it.

FROM FEB. 28, 1925 ISSUE

Hotel McAlpin Opens Broadcasting Studio

Many Theatrical and Newspaper Notables Take Part in Opening Program

New York, Feb. 23.—Still another broadcasting station was added to the large number already in this city when the Hotel McAlpin opened its own broadcasting studio last night, under the call letters of WMCA. The station has been testing for the past few weeks under the test letters of 2XH. It operates on a 428.6 meters wave length, making it one of the most powerful in the city.

Many theatrical and newspaper notables attended the opening and did bits for the program. Among them were: Irving S. Cobb, Harry Hirschfield, Walter Catlett, Ed Squires, Harry Archer, John P. Medbury, Constance Mering, Louis John Bartels, Franklyn Bauer, Holbrook Blinn, Countess Peggy Hopkins Joyce Morner, Al Piantadosi, Louis Bave, Joe Meyers, Joe E. Brown, Martha Pryor, Harry Puck, John Burke, Earl Carroll, Vladimir Radeef, Florence Richardson, John Carroll, Eva Clark, Henry Clark's Hawaiians, Don Roberts, Carson Robison, Milton Sills, Walter Donaldson, Josephine Davis, Harry Fox, Cliff Edwards, George Gershwin, Olga Steck, Abner Silver, Duncan Sisters, "Rube" Goldberg, Nell Brushingham Starr, Marguerite Sylva, Harry Von Tilzer, Ernie Golden and Band, Harmon's Cinderella Orchestra, Milt Gross, Mary Hay, Edna Hubbard, Johnny Hines, Lou Holtz, Henry Hull, Madge Kennedy, William Kent, Fay King, Geo. McManus, Nydia Westman, Sigrid Holmquist, Fred Klem, Jimmie Murphy, Wynn's Orchestra, Mary Young, Yerkes' Happy Six, Louis Wolheim, Kenneth Webb, Maj. J. A. White, Milton Wallace, Genevieve Tobin and Dolores Cassinelli.

FROM FEB. 24, 1923 ISSUE

VALENTINO PANS ZUKOR OVER RADIO

Suddenly Cut Off When Language Waxes Hot—Big Draw in St. Louis

St. Louis, Mo., Feb. 19.—While appearing at the Delmonte Theater last week with Winifred Hudnut, Rodolph Valentino made a special trip to the Post Dispatch radio broadcasting station, KSD, one of the largest sending stations in the country, and made a speech in which he vigorously and in no uncertain terms panned the motion picture "trust" for keeping down the real artistic pictures to which the public is entitled, and producing which he termed "nothing but cheap trash." When he started on Adolph Zukor, president of the Famous Players-Lasky Corporation, his language waxed so strong that he was suddenly cut off as tho the main broadcasting switch had been pulled.

FROM MAY 2, 1925 ISSUE

$300,000 Profit for Loew's Radio Station

WHN Credited With Cleanup Thru Broadcasting on Commercial Basis---Specialized on Supper Clubs

New York, April 27.—Many broadcasting stations are making tremendous profits and can afford to pay for their program talent, according to a report made to the Radio Artists' Association by Richard B. Gilbert, chairman of the Investigating Committee of that organization. He stated that WHN, the Loew's State station, has a yearly income of more than $300,000, while its operating expenses are not more than $50,000. WFBH, the Hotel Majestic station, he stated, has a net annual income of $90,000, and operating expenses of not more than $35,000.

The committee reported that WEAF also is making money, tho it could not secure any definite information regarding expenses or profits. The advertising rates of WEAF, operated by the American Telephone & Telegraph Company, are given (and verified) as $500 an hour, $312.50 per half hour and $195.35 per quarter hour. It is reported, however, on good authority, that the expenditures of WEAF are not equaled by the receipts. WHN until recently had a long list of clients, mostly cabarets and supper clubs, which used the service to advertise their entertainment. These paid according to how many half-hour periods they broadcast a week, the Loew station receiving an average of a few hundred dollars a week each.

FROM APRIL 21, 1923 ISSUE

WANTS BROADCASTERS TO LET COPYRIGHTED MUSIC ALONE

Would Save Members Money, Says Executive of Composers' Society—Several Angles to Broadcasting Situation

NEW YORK, April 14.—Declaring that the royalty statements received by song writers from the phonograph record and piano roll manufacturers covering the last twelve months show a decrease of nearly 20 per cent in sales as a result of radio broadcasting, J. C. Rosenthal, executive chairman of the American Society of Composers, Authors and Publishers, asserted this week that he hoped that all the broadcasting stations in the country would refuse to use the copyrighted songs belonging to members of the society.

"I am sure that we can save for our members, during the next few years, fifty times as much money as we are asking the broadcasting stations to pay if they will only leave our music alone," said Mr. Rosenthal.

The Westinghouse Electric and Manufacturing Company, operating Station WJZ, in Newark, N. J., stopped broadcasting all musical compositions belonging to the society last Wednesday night. This was done after announcements to the effect that it had refused to pay the annual fee demanded by the society. The Westinghouse Company operates three other stations in Pittsburg, Chicago and Springfield, Mass.

Following upon the heels of this statement it was learned that the American Telephone & Telegraph Co., operating Station WEAF, in New York, had accepted the terms of the society and had taken out a license for one year, giving it permission to use all the songs copyrighted by members of the society. The fee to be paid is said to amount to more than $2,000, altho Mr. Rosenthal would not make it public.

Four other broadcasting stations have also taken out licenses from the society. They are: The Kansas City Star, newspaper; I. R. Nelson Co., Newark, N. J., manufacturers of radio apparatus; the Earl C. Anthony Co., Los Angeles, Calif.; Packard Motor Co., agents for the State of California, and Erner & Hopkins, Columbus, O., apparatus makers.

The WEAF Station of the American Telephone & Telegraph Co., which is the largest to take out a license so far, is one of the few broadcasting stations to earn a direct revenue. This station is rented to any person or firm at the rate of $600 an hour, or $10 a minute.

Issued 600 Licenses

When the Composers' Society sent out licenses to more than 600 broadcasting stations several months ago at fees ranging from $200 to $5,000 yearly, depending upon the size of the station, it stated that after March 15 strict watch would be kept on all programs and use of copyrighted music by non-licensed stations would be prosecuted. The WJZ plant in Newark was asked to pay $5,000 a year, but after several conferences between Mr. Rosenthal and J. Townley, vice-president of the Westinghouse company, the price of $14,000

for all four of the company's stations was made by Rosenthal. This was refused by the Westinghouse Company.

"We want to protect ourselves from loss of income," said Mr. Rosenthal to a Billboard reporter. "The tremendous spread of the radio is already hurting our interests, and the time seems approaching when the radio will take a still more important part in the public's entertainment.

"Of my own knowledge, many people who are owners of phonographs and formerly regular buyers of records no longer use them now. They have radio sets installed in their machines. In a number of cities new apartment houses are being built with wireless instruments constructed right in the walls."

The Broadcasting Society of America, at a meeting held this week, announced that it would ignore the demands for license fees. This seems to point to a string of litigations between the radio broadcasters and the Society of Composers, as both are ready to take their dispute to the courts.

Another angle on the situation which may lead to litigation over the question of broadcasting copyrighted music was uncovered on Saturday when Arthur Hammerstein, musical comedy producer, speaking for the Producing Managers' Association, announced that only the producers of musical shows had the right to permit broadcasting of music from these shows, and not the composers of the music or the American Society of Composers, Authors and Publishers.

This announcement was sharply contradicted by Mr. Rosenthal, of the society, who told The Billboard that producers have control only over the theatrical performing rights of music and over the broadcasting of an entire show, but that the society, as the instrument of the composers, controlled the rights to broadcast individual numbers from any show.

"Furthermore, the society holds an assignment for five years of the public performing rights of all songs written by its members, and these assignments antedate any contracts with composers that Mr. Hammerstein or other producers may have," said Mr. Rosenthal. "We stand ready to indemnify any radio broadcaster who holds a license issued by the society from any litigation resulting from the stand taken by Hammerstein and the Producing Managers' Association."

FROM APRIL 7, 1928 ISSUE

Film Star Radio Hour Was Flop In Opinion of Many Listeners

Charlie Chaplin and John Barrymore Only Ones To Make Real Impression—Theaters Generally Reported Gross Slumps —Some Put in Wireless To Draw Patrons

NEW YORK, March 31.—Theaters generally reported a falloff in grosses on Thursday night, when the second of the Dodge Brothers' radio hours, this time with several motion-picture lights taking part, went on the air thru Station WJZ and 51 other stations of the National Broadcasting network. It was generally agreed by those who listened in that the hour was far inferior in entertainment value to the first Dodge Brothers sponsored, and that of the film luminaries heard over the ether, only Charlie Chaplin and John Barrymore made any impression.

Paul Whiteman played several numbers, with an unnamed soloist heard in vocal bits. The orchestra was not heard to advantage thru Station WJZ.

Douglas Fairbanks was master of ceremonies. He made a brief address, dwelling on athletics, and talked so fast and with such poor enunciation that it was difficult to get the words. He introduced Norma Talmadge, who expatiated on women's fashions. D. W. Griffith indulged in a preachment on the influence of motion pictures, and Dolores Del Rio sang *Ramona* in a poor voice.

Several theaters thruout the country installed radios in their theaters as an added attraction for the patrons who wanted to see a show and listen to the Dodge hour besides, to protect themselves against empty houses on that night.

FROM JAN. 1, 1927 ISSUE

RADIO
ENTERTAINERS
Conducted by WILLIAM SACHS
Communications to 25 Opera Place, Cincinnati, O.

NATHANIEL SHILKRET'S Orchestra will present a program made up entirely of the works of French composers over WJZ Wednesday night, December 29, at 9 o'clock.

JACK DENNY and His Orchestra, together with Frank Munn and Virginia Rea, were scheduled to be heard over WJZ Tuesday night, December 28.

GODFREY LUDLOW, Australian violinist and staff artist of WJZ, and Lolita Cabrera Gainsborg, Spanish pianist, were heard in a joint sonata recital thru WJZ, WGY and WBZ Sunday night.

THE COMMODORE ENSEMBLE, under the direction of Bernhard Levitow, on Sunday night entertained the listeners of WJZ and WGY with a rendition of *The Nutcracker Suite* of Tschaikowsky. On Wednesday night of this week at 7 o'clock the Commodore Ensemble is scheduled to present a number of selections from Franz Lehar's operetta, *The Merry Widow*, over WJZ.

WALTER DAMROSCH and the New York Symphony Orchestra will be heard thru WEAF, WEEI, WGR, WTAM, WFI, WSAI, WGN, WOC, WCCO and WCAE Saturday night, January 1, at 8 o'clock, Eastern standard time. George Gershwin, widely known pianist and popular songwriter, will be the soloist of the evening and will play his *Concerto in F*, accompanied by the New York Symphony Orchestra.

FROM FEB. 12, 1927 ISSUE

A. & P. Gypsies
Nationally Famed String Orchestra Under the Personal Direction of Harry Horlick

Reviewed at the B. F. Albee Theater, Brooklyn. Style — Orchestra novelty. Setting—In two (special). Time—Fifteen minutes.

This eight-man string unit of national fame, when reviewed, was greeted at the opening with an enthusiastic reception. This aggregation, in the reviewer's opinion, is the finest of its kind utilized for commercial radio purposes today. On the stage it loses none of the appeal which has earned for it such a large radio following. Horlick, who plays the violin, is a leader of the restrained type—letting his organization speak for itself—and this it does eloquently. The routine comprises pop. and semi-classical numbers, the latter of the more conservative genre. The secret of the beautiful quality of its air concerts is given away after hearing the unit in the flesh. The tuneful melody poured out thru all its numbers is directly attributable to the man who plays the zither-like arrangement. The player of this instrument is given due acknowledgment of his importance in the act since he is heard in several obbligatos, as are, to a lesser extent, the other instrumentalists. **E. E. S.**

FROM JULY 6, 1929 ISSUE

Don'ts for Air Talent

NEW YORK, June 29.—RKO artists doing their bit toward selling the circuit and themselves to the public via the radio mike are finding that etherized entertainment is considerably more of an exacting art than work in the varieties. At least from the standpoint of prohibitions. Before they go on the air for the RKO hour, artists chosen for the institutional broadcast are being handed a set of six rules telling exactly what they may not do. These rules apply not only to etherized RKO folk, but also to all artistes appearing before NBC mikes.

The six rules of verbotens follow:

1—No songs, material, stories, gags or speeches can be broadcast without being passed on by an authorized representative of the NBC.

2—After an act has been rehearsed and timed, no extra material may be inserted.

3—Messages or greetings to personal friends or relatives are prohibited under a ruling of the Federal Radio Commission.

4—No material that can be construed as an unauthorized advertising plug will be permitted.

5—Avoid all references that may be offensive on moral, religious or racial grounds.

6—Positively no visitors allowed in the studio during broadcasting.

FROM APRIL 7, 1928 ISSUE

Device Records Laughs During Run of Picture

NEW YORK, April 2.—The Laugh Recorder, a new device calculated to record the laughter of the theater crowd witnessing a picture by means of cues imposed on the recording medium, the action which brought the laughs, was tried out at a recent preview of a two-reel comedy.

The apparatus consists of a radio broadcasting studio microphone to which is attached an amplifying device, the output of which is fed into a mechanism which transfers it to a phonograph record. The speed of the recording machines can be synchronized with the speed of the projection machine, so that the reproduction of the laughter occurs at the correct time when the picture is later projected in the exhibition rooms at the studio.

The Laugh Recorder is the invention of Freeman Lang, radio engineer of Los Angeles.

THE RADIO NETWORKS BOOM THROUGH THE DEPRESSION

FROM SEPT. 18, 1926 ISSUE

New Broadcasting Corporation May Revolutionize Radio Methods

NEW YORK, Sept. 13..—After November 13 Station WEAF will be controlled by the National Broadcasting Company, Inc., which has been organized to take over the plant, which was recently bought by the Radio Corporation of America from the American Telephone and Telegraph Company for $1,000,000. The purpose is said to be the broadcasting of the best programs available in the United States and nation-wide tie-ups with any other stations interested and willing to share the expense. In the official announcement signed by General James G. Harbord, chairman and president of the Radio Corporation of America, and Owen D. Young, one of the main objects is to stimulate the sale of radio parts and sets. M. H. Aylesworth will head the new organization, and he stated that in order that the public will be assured of the best possible programs an advisory board of 12 would be chosen.

Coincident with the announcement of the new arrangement, *The Billboard* learns that revolutionary methods in selling radio advertising is in the wind. The new plans call for the selling of complete series of programs of entertainment to the advertiser as well as the use of the station. In the past the usual way was to sell the use of the station for so much per hour or, according to a longer contract, it may be so many hours per week at a cheaper rate. The advertiser had to supply his own orchestra or other talent.

In the new scheme, one of the leading concert bureaus will act as a sort of booking office and supply entire programs, any one of which a prospective advertiser may choose, either moderate in price or expensive, and this, with the use of the station, will come under one complete charge. Better shows and a less obnoxious way of advertising is expected of the new plan. The concert bureau will be used by the largest broadcasting organization in the country as its source of supply for talent to sell the advertisers.

FROM DEC. 14, 1929 ISSUE

M-G-M $500,000 Radio Hookup Starts January 6

NEW YORK, Dec. 7.—M-G-M will begin broadcasting a weekly radio program over the Columbia System weekly, beginning January 6, it was learned today upon the signing of a contract between Columbia, M-G-M and the Purity Broadcasting and the Carter Manufacturing companies, the latter two being tied up in conjunction with the broadcast and who will sponsor the programs.

This series of broadcasts will be the most widely advertised radio broadcasts yet attempted and will involve an expenditure of more than $500,000 in addition to the expense of the radio hookup.

A remote control station has been installed in the M-G-M studios, from which place the stars and talent furnished by M-G-M will broadcast the program, which will be picked up and rebroadcast over the Columbia net work by Station KHJ in Los Angeles. The broadcast is unique inasmuch as it is the first time a movie program will be broadcast directly from the studio of the company.

FROM JAN. 9, 1932 ISSUE

Big Progress In Past Year

Major radio chains add to network and gain in all directions

NEW YORK, Jan. 4.—The steady absorption of indie stations by CBS and NBC, the increasing number of performers used by radio, the steady gain in commercial programs, the larger and international broadcasts and the making of new stars by radio seem to be the outstanding points in the history of radio for 1931. During the past year, radio went a long way toward stabilizing its position in spite of the depression and in gaining commercal sponsors at the expense of other forms of advertising. NBC and CBS continued as the largest broadcasting systems.

NBC alone handled 33,000 broadcasts, involving more than 250,000 participants this past year. Network programs increased in popularity, half of the total remaining commercial. NBC increased the number of associated stations from 73 to 85 the past year, while CBS begins the new year with 90 member stations.

International broadcasts on both networks increased, while several important advances were made in radio engineering, including station synchronization, improved wire transmission, reflector microphones, improved television and the study of transoceanic conditions.

Radio programs have been speeded up and the 15-minute period has become increasingly popular. Morning programs are finding commercial sponsors and the woman audience is recognized as important.

Music continued to corner the most time on the radio. NBC reports that a typical broadcasting month showed these program percentages: Music, 62.9 per cent; literature, 11.8; educational, 21.3; religion, 2.5, and novelties, 1.5.

Both CBS and NBC's artists' bureaus expanded. Besides signing up many "names," both landed franchises to sell acts to RKO and have perfected their contacts to take care of almost every kind of booking.

FROM OCT. 27, 1945 ISSUE

In the Beginning . . .

MAY 1932—*In 1932 NBC pioneered with a new type of satiric comedy program in contrast to the broader slapstick variety of air humor then prevalent. Its hero* *was over-endowed with the most common failings of the man-on-the-street. He was vain, penurious, boastful, and absurdly anxious to please. His name was Benny.*

13 Years Later . . .

OCTOBER 7, 1945—*Jack Benny is starting his fourteenth year on NBC—the network's oldest comedian in point of service.* **TO SUM IT UP**—*During his thirteen years on NBC, Jack Benny has piled up more rating points than any other entertainer on the air.*

FROM OCT. 28, 1933 ISSUE

Bing Crosby

Reviewed Monday, 8:30-9 p.m. Style— Baritone and orchestra. Sponsor—John H. Woodbury, Inc. Station—WABC (CBS network).

Selling a product to the women must of necessity use a program of definite appeal to them, and in Crosby Woodbury soap has chosen wisely. For Bing is in the midst of a brilliant career and the motion picture successes in which he appears add to his strength as a radio draw. Further, he has not been heard too often of late and his performance is better than ever as to both voice and choice of selections. On this particular program he neither whistled nor dabbled in his famous impromptu obbligatos. Lennie Hayton, an able accompanist, arranger and conductor, has always shown a distinctive style about his work, and Crosby, thru past association, naturally feels at home when Hayton wields the baton or is at the piano. All of which makes for efficiency.

> ## Crosby is in the midst of a brilliant career and the motion picture successes in which he appears add to his strength as a radio draw.

With Crosby and Hayton is a chorus of mixed voices that comes in occasionally, while a good piece of showmanship was a solo by a feminine vocalist about the middle of the program which seemed to offer the precise bit of relief and contrast. Hayton also injected some piano parts played by himself for further diversity of the musical end of the half hour. Crosby himself offered an excellent selection of ballads, mostly of the romantic type, and closed with *The Last Roundup* for good measure. Orchestral interludes were well done, smooth and soft, plus plenty of rhythm. Show originated on the Coast, where Crosby, of course, is making pictures. Credits, done against a partly faded out musical background with the theme *Beautiful Lady*, leaned toward the lower price of the product and its value as a complexion requisite. These were not overdone considering the background of Woodbury, which was used by many grandmothers of today when they were girls. **M. H. S.**

FROM JUNE 10, 1933 ISSUE

"One Man's Family"

Reviewed Wednesday, 9:30-10 p.m. Style—Dramatic sketch. Sustaining, on WEAF (NBC network).

This series of episodes that might take place in the daily lives of an average family has been a feature on the West Coast for some time, originating as it does from NBC San Francisco studios. Recently it has been piped east to cover this part of the country and it seems that the effort is well worth while as a program to interest the average listener who may think untoward circumstances crop up is his immediate circle only. Family in question, however, may be said to be in better than moderate circumstances inasmuch as the head of the house is a stockbroker; yet, they are everyday folks as the script reveals.

Characters are the two parents, a disabled war veteran who was an aviator in the war evidently at a tender age since his years are but 31, according to the script on the first Eastern program, which would have him as 16 years old while flying around the Western front. Also, there is the studious son, one not so studious, a set of twins (boy and girl) and an eldest daughter.

Trend of the yarns, each broadcast being a separate episode in the Barbour family, seem to lean toward the fact that only rare good luck keeps the family name out of the daily papers for some mischief or crimes committed by the offspring and the psychology ought to take with many dial turners. Thus the old man is tipped off one night that a shooting has taken place and it turns out that while at a house party the daughter while fooling around in the gun room of the host's establishment saw fit to take a shot at a fresh young egg and the said shot knocked him off. Matter is hushed up, but the worries of the head of the house are plainly indicated. Then there is the proposition accepted by the family aviator to run a little liquor into the U. S. from Canada, while still another time dad actually gets a little lesson in treating ma with more consideration from none other than one of the kids.

Organ music works in and out of the program taking the curse off the dialog and indicates lapse of time as well as ushering the program in and out. Acting is in good hands, the various roles being smoothly done in the usual quiet matter of fact style of the stage. In fact, it seems at times the characters might talk a little louder, or, arrange the acoustics of the studios to cut out the echo-like interference. It is possible that the long-distance wire helps to distort the voices occasionally. However, the series of sketches would not make the worst program for a sponsor seeking a script, altho the colder months would make it much more attractive.

J. Anthony Smythe plays the part of Henry Barbour, head of the family; Minetta Ellen, Mrs. Barbour; Kathleen Wilson, the daughter, Claudia; Barton Yarborough, one of the happy-go-lucky twins; Billy Paige, Jack Barbour; Bernice Berwin, eldest daughter, Hazel, and Michael Rafetto, the crippled war veter-

an. Carlton E. Morse is author of the scripts. One of the artists is said to be none other than the son of Don Gilman, v.-p. in charge of West Coast operations for NBC (possibly Billy Paige). **M. H. S.**

FROM JUNE 18, 1932 ISSUE

Ed Sullivan-Jack Denny

Reviewed Sunday 10-10:30 p.m. Style—Dramatic bits, interviews and orchestra. Sponsor—Gem Safety Razor Corporation. Station WABC (CBS network).

Highlights of Broadway, sport and music are the theme of this program, and Ed Sullivan, newspaper columnist, seems to have achieved his purpose well enough on the initial broadcast of this new account. Sullivan had on hand Georges Carpentier to represent the sports end of the program and, of course, he was interviewed on his Dempsey fight, bringing out several very interesting items and choice bits of conversation. Dramatization of part of the fight, excitement of the crowd, etc., was worked up nicely, but it seems that it would have been better to have let the Frenchman do the telling instead of splitting this portion of the program up so that it became momentarily incoherent. On the other hand, perhaps it is Sullivan's unusual sense of dramatic values that keys his listeners to the point where they resent any break in the continuity.

For Broadway, Sam H. Harris, producer, and Irving Berlin were taken back to the opening night of the first *Music Box Revue*, and this was dramatized in good style, altho neither of them actually took part in the skit. Later they both cried a little, Sam stating he had the two outstanding musical hits, but wondered if he would get his money back; while Berlin admitted everybody played his songs, but nobody was buying them.

> ## Sullivan went through his stuff in his aggressive style. He has a good radio voice and is not a poor salesman at all.

Jack Denny was on the job as usual and gave Berlin a great plug on his tunes, both new and old, and, of course, whatever he played was faultless from any angle. Sullivan went thru his stuff in his same aggressive style. He has a good radio voice and is not a poor salesman at all. Sponsor grabbed his credits, not only with the aid of one man but with the additional help of a stooge or kibitzer, who insisted on getting the last word. We doubt the efficacy of the copy handed out in such fashion. Male voice singing with the band is worthy of mention, and the three-way program should prove a popular one. **M. H. S.**

FROM MAY 7, 1932 ISSUE

Program Reviews

Ed Wynn

Reviewed Tuesday, 9:30-10 p.m. Style —Comedy, orchestra and male voices. Sponsor—The Texas Company. Station —WEAF (NBC network).

Ed Wynn, w.-k. comedian, makes his radio debut as the Texaco Fireman, with Graham McNamee doing the announcing and playing straight for him, in addition to Don Vorhees and a 35-piece band and a double male quartet.

This ever-funny clown, of course, does not come into the category of those who have to be seen in order to be fully appreciated. Wynn and his lisp, his comedy talk and style of putting a gag over hops thru the ether in no uncertain manner. Sure-fire hit as long as he has any kind of material at all, and there is no danger of him running out of gags or stories. His personality is well suited to the mike.

An intimate atmosphere is created, with Wynn as the local fire chief and gagging with McNamee. He also did the letter answering stuff, which is not strictly original with him, of course, and showed his strength by launching into an opera piece-by-piece, and after each short narration had the orchestra interpret it. This was built up cleverly. Interspersed at another period was selections by the singers and Vorhees with an excellent combination offered a few selections on his own, as well as clowning pieces for Wynn.

FROM JULY 15, 1933 ISSUE

RADIO BOYS EYE HOLLYWOOD
Pearl, Wynn, Cantor and Jolson Lead Way; Others Get Buildups

●

Crosby and Burns and Allen set by Paramount for special featuring—lesser radio names hit Hollywood trail to cash in on latest musical film cycle

●

NEW YORK, July 8.—Radio talent is in for its biggest movie year since the original talkie hysteria. The advance lists of major film product for the new season have four radio stars (Jack Pearl, Ed Wynn, Eddie Cantor and Al Jolson) slated for a minimum of one feature each, in which each will star. Two radio acts, Burns and Allen and Bing Crosby, are listed as feature names and will do at least two pictures each, while other radio artists are slated for roles in coming features. The producers' desperate search for new stars and the latest cycle of musical films combine to pave the way for a new rush to Hollywood. The last big rush was headed by legit and vaude people. Now the radio boys will be up in front.

Pearl, of course, is the new shining star, the other three having made pictures before. Pearl is now in Hollywood to start work on *The Big Liar* for MGM and will follow this with a role in *The Hollywood Party*, into which MGM will throw 15 of its stars. Wynn has just arrived in Hollywood and begins work on *The Fire Chief* immediately. He will continue his NBC broadcasts from Hollywood. Eddie Cantor's first for United Artists will be *Roman Scandals*.

FROM NOV. 12, 1932 ISSUE

Eddie Cantor

Reviewed Sunday 8-9 p.m. Style — Comedian and orchestra. Sponsor— Standard Brands, Inc. Station—WEAF (NBC network).

As the saying goes, considerable water has flowed under the bridge since Cantor was last heard on the air. Fans have been taught to gather many laughs in the course of a half-hour period, more or less, and the prestige of this outstanding comedian is seriously threatened as a radio attraction unless he has some better material under his belt for future broadcasts. His return has proved a disappointment to a vast army of eager followers, this reviewer included. He may bust out with a terrific sock at subsequent broadcasts, and, being scheduled for the road, will no doubt prove an asset for his sponsor, as most radio troupes en tour usually are. But it is rather disconcerting to have a comedian return who had months in which to line up a few laughs and then appear in the studio with a script that sounded as tho he had just typed it out a little while before rehearsal without worrying about its effectiveness.

Perhaps it was but natural that he should do the usual Hollywood stuff, because he has recently arrived from there, and in case the dial-turners thought it was someone else, decided to sound off with the same family mentions, money situation and boost for his latest picture.

POST-DEPRESSION RADIO HITS

FROM MAY 21, 1938 ISSUE

26,666,500 U. S. Families Own Radios; 82% of Nation's Total

NEW YORK, May 14.—Joint Committee on Radio Research this week made public its figures on home radio set ownership of the United States. Committee, organized by broadcasters, advertisers and advertising agencies, figures that there are now 26,666,500 radio families as of January 1 this year.

State	July, 1937, Families	Total % Ownership	1938 Radio Families
Alabama	670,000	56	375,200
Arizona	104,000	77	79,600
Arkansas	501,000	51	254,800
California	1,818,000	95	1,719,800
Colorado	288,000	81	233,500
Connecticut	437,000	92	402,100
Delaware	67,000	86	57,600
District of Columbia	168,000	91	152,900
Florida	443,000	67	297,900
Georgia	716,000	52	370,800
Idaho	124,000	80	98,700
Illinois	2,063,000	90	1,857,100
Indiana	934,000	87	816,800
Iowa	680,000	85	577,800
Kansas	501,000	73	367,800
Kentucky	708,000	70	494,900
Louisiana	510,000	58	297,400
Maine	221,000	91	201,100
Maryland	401,000	87	355,100
Massachusetts	1,104,000	92	1,019,200
Michigan	1,220,000	92	1,122,200
Minnesota	652,000	85	556,900
Mississippi	494,000	42	207,000
Missouri	1,072,000	77	822,800
Montana	142,000	81	114,600
Nebraska	352,000	81	284,100
Nevada	30,000	95	28,500
New Hampshire	136,000	92	124,400
New Jersey	1,098,000	93	1,022,500
New Mexico	102,000	61	62,300
New York	3,372,000	93	3,132,300
North Carolina	736,000	55	408,600
North Dakota	156,000	77	119,600
Ohio	1,777,000	92	1,641,500
Oklahoma	619,000	73	454,300
Oregon	299,000	95	285,400
Pennsylvania	2,452,000	90	2,206,400
Rhode Island	169,000	92	155,500
South Carolina	407,000	51	207,300
South Dakota	167,000	80	132,900
Tennessee	689,000	67	459,900
Texas	1,516,000	68	1,033,500
Utah	123,000	90	111,000
Vermont	99,000	90	88,600
Virginia	613,000	65	400,200
Washington	468,000	95	443,300
West Virginia	417,000	84	348,300
Wisconsin	735,000	83	612,700
Wyoming	62,000	80	49,800

FROM SEPT. 9, 1939 ISSUE

Estimated Talent Costs .Of Leading Network Shows

Program	Sponsor	Estimated Talent Costs	
Charlie McCarthy	Chase & Sanborn Coffee	$16,000	
Good News	Maxwell House	15,000	
Bing Crosby-Bob Burns	Kraft	14,000	
Jack Benny	Jello	13,500	
Fred Allen	Ipana, etc.	12,500	
Burns & Allen	Lehn & Fink	12,500	
Kate Smith	General Foods	12,500	
Fred Waring	Chesterfield	12,500	
Radio Theater	Lever Brothers	10,000	
Big Town	Lever Brothers	10,000	
Major Bowes	Chrysler	10,000	
Star Theater	Texas Company	9,000-$10,000	
Bob Hope	Pepsodent	9,000	
Orson Welles	Campbell Soup	8,000	
Hit Parade	Lucky Strike	7,500	
Kay Kyser	Lucky Strike	6,000	
Walter O'Keefe	Lever Brothers	6,000	
Professor Quiz	Procter & Gamble	6,000	
Fibber McGee	Johnson's Wax	6,000	
Joe E. Brown	Post Toasties	5,000-$ 6,000	
Ben Bernie	American Tobacco	5,000	
Information Please	Canada Dry	5,000	
Wayne King and his Ork	Colgate-Palmolive-Peet Co. Cashmere Bouquet Products & Halo)	5,000	
Guy Lombardo	Lady Esther	5,000	
One Man's Family	Chase & Sanborn Tea	5,000	
Tommy Riggs	Quaker Oats	5,000	
Screen Guild	Gulf	5,000*	
Artie Shaw-Bob Benchley	Old Gold	5,000	
Phil Baker	Dole	4,000-$ 5,000	
Tune Up Time	Ethyl Gas	4,000-$ 5,000	
Joe Penner	Ward Baking Co.	4,200	
Benny Goodman	Camel	4,000	
Horace Heidt	Tums	3,500-$ 4,000	
Hour of Charm	General Electric Co.	3,500-$ 4,000	
Hal Kemp	Griffin	3,000-$ 4,000	
Blondie	Camel	3,500	
Jean Hersholt	Chesebrough Mfg. Co.	3,500	
Sherlock Holmes	Grove Laboratories	3,500	
Mr. District Attorney	Pepsodent	3,500	
Philip Morris Program	Philip Morris	3,500	
Ripley	Royal Crown	3,500	
Shelton and Howard	U. S. Tobacco	3,500	
Woodbury Hollywood Playhouse	Andrew Jergens Co.	3,500	
Bob Crosby	Camel	3,000	
For Men Only	Vitalis	3,000	
Hobby Lobby	Fels	3,000	
Metropolitan Auditions of the Air	Sherwin-Williams Co.	3,000	
Alec Templeton Time	Miles Laboratories	3,000	
Strange as It Seems	Colgate-P-P	2,500	
Easy Aces	Anacin	2,500	
Manhattan Merry-Go-Round	Sterling Products	2,000-$ 2,500	
Larry Clinton	Sensation	2,000	
Enna Jettick Melodies	Dunn & McCarthy Standard Brands	2,000	
Those We Love	R. L. Watkins Co.	2,000	
Jimmie Fiddler	Procter & Gamble (Drene Shampoo)	1,500	
Grand Central Station	Listerine	1,500	
The Parker Family	Andrew Jergens Co.	1,200	
Battle of Sexes	Molle	750-$ 1,000	

*Not including donation to Motion Picture Relief Fund.

Bing Crosby

Fred Waring

Guy Lombardo

KATE SMITH

BENNY GOODMAN

FROM OCT. 16, 1937 ISSUE

Kate Smith

Reviewed Thursday, 8-9 p.m. Style —Variety program. Sponsor—General Foods Sales Co., Inc. Agency—Young & Rubicam. Station—WABC (CBS network).

Kate Smith is one of the few who could even attempt to oppose the strongly intrenched Rudy Vallee program playing at this same time on the NBC Red network. Miss Smith's own draw, plus an apparently unlimited budget for guest stars, will unquestionably get the show an audience of no mean caliber. Judging from this program, the second, the Vallee opera maintains a much better pace all around than the opposition does. Guestees were Lefty Gomez, Yankee pitcher; Jim Crowley, Fordham football coach; Ruth Gordon, Dennis King, Sam Jaffee, and Paul Lukas, from the stage and pictures. Henny Youngman is back again as the comedy element on the program. Ted Collins, Miss Smith's manager, is the announcing gentleman, with Jack Miller's Orchestra and a chorus rounding up the lengthy roster of performers. With all of that talent the program should have been far more diverting than it was; certainly it shouldn't have dragged out so that it seemed much more than 60 minutes.

Gomez and Crowley contributed a satisfactory cross-fire interview, with Collins foiling, each arguing for his own game. It is quite apparent than an attempt is being made to get the same effective lightness into the dialog as is used on both the Vallee and Bing Crosby shows. When light dialog flops it falls plenty hard and it produced as many goose eggs in this case as did Gomez's pitching against the Giants or more.

> Miss Smith's own draw, plus an apparently unlimited budget for guest stars, will unquestionably get the show an audience of no mean caliber.

The four name performers did an adaptation of Ibsen's *Doll's House*. Only the inherent power of the story saved it from complete disaster, due to a combination of poor scripting and unsatisfactory acting.

Musically, the program is quite good, with Miller's Orchestra delivering quite well and the choral work standing out, both on its own and in background. Miss Smith's singing is in her usual style, but in one number, which she introduced as a first rendition, she was trying much too hard.

Youngman has yet to hit his stride in radio. A sock stage or floor-show worker, he hasn't as yet been able to produce laughs in the abundance he does in flesh dates, altho he did fairly well on this program.

Commercials quite palatable and unobtrusive. *J. F.*

FROM OCT. 8, 1938 ISSUE

Bob Hope

Reviewed Tuesday, 10-10:30 p.m. Style—Variety. Sponsor—Pepsodent Co. Agency—Lord & Thomas. Station—WEAF (NBC Red network).

First of Bob Hope's programs for Pepsodent indicated a few minor bugs to be straightened out, but also that a good laugh session is in store for this radio season. A deft and expert comic, with a trigger-like socko delivery, aided by years of vaude and theater experience, Hope, when he really gets going in his groove, should deliver handsomely. Considerable help comes from his current picture build-up by way of Paramount.

Initial program had a flock of laughs, including the ever-present Hope ad libbings, or what certainly seemed to be extempore nifties. Bug number one was that Hope himself didn't have enough time, what with Constance Bennett and Jerry Colonna guesting. Glamour girl's spot, a visit to a ladies' baseball team, was a weakie. Looks like someone pulled a boner, since Miss Bennett had guested two days before on Chase & Sanborn. Colonna's screwball singing, or yowling, is funny, but there was too much of it, another bug.

Final bug came thru having the show open with Skinnay Ennis giving a long-drawn-out version of *Change Partners* in his whispered baritone. Otherwise band did okeh. Bill Goodwin sells the Pepsodent stuff forcefully, as required.

On against Hal Kemp (CBS), Ennis' former boss. *Franken.*

FROM SEPT. 17, 1938 ISSUE

"Lum and Abner"

Reviewed Wednesday, 6:45-7 p.m. Style—Hillbilly serial. Sponsor—General Foods. Agency—Young & Rubicam. Station—WABC (CBS network).

This type of hoke comedy serial has been going on long enough to require no apologies. Wednesday session, tho, seemed a dull, plodding 15 minutes of hayseed chatter by characters usually referred to, for some vague reason, as "lovable."

Situation this time presented the Pine Ridge philosophers in the light of potential educators. This miscarriage comes about when Lum, who recently made a European trip and is being built up into a travel lecturer, claims he feels the need of a "dee-gree." Abner, aware that Lum has just inherited some 6,000 fish, suggests he build a University and make himself president and dean.

Program ends on this happy note, with Lew Crosby, announcer, trying to instill some interest into the question of whether Lum and Abner will make Pine Ridge the home of a University.

While lines and dialect are reminiscent of bad vaudeville, the boys do a good job in a very difficult medium. They not only play the Lum and Abner leads, but portray all the other personalities in the script. This is no mean talent.

Commercials are well done, opening one a testimonial. *Ackerman.*

FROM SEPT. 24, 1938 ISSUE

Lux Radio Theater

Reviewed Monday, 9-10 p.m. Style —Drama. Sponsor—Lever Brothers. Agency—J. Walter Thompson, Inc. Station—WABC (CBS network).

For some time now, especially in the last months of its career before taking a summer layoff, the Lux dramatic stanzas have built to a steady position among the first four or five shows in radio, including both half and hour periods. With nothing socko in the way of opposition, Lux attraction dominates Monday night, as amply proved by *The Billboard* and other radio program surveys. Re-enacting pic and stage hits with film biggies in one of the few good dramatic sessions—especially by comparison with other ether drayma—looks like a foolproof formula.

> Starting this season was a radio version of Paramount's *Spawn of the North*, as crummy a choice for the inaugural clambake as could be selected.

Starting this season was a radio version of Paramount's *Spawn of the North*, as crummy a choice for the inaugural clambake as could be selected, a sprawling he-man thing about salmon fishers. Pal A finally sacrifices his life for Pal B to the heartbreak of all concerned and especially Dorothy Lamour, who vocally wept thruout and all over the place. Cast had George Raft, Fred MacMurray, Akim Tamiroff and John Barrymore, in addition to Miss Lamour, with Cecil B. DeMille directing and welcoming all hands. Performances hit par—par being fromagenous. But the commercials don't even make par.

Will Hays, during an entr'acte, gave speech No. 7 on the glories of the film industry. *Franken.*

LAST DAYS OF THE SILENTS

FROM JAN. 16, 1926 ISSUE

Famous Plans To Control All Movie Houses in the U. S.

New York, Jan. 11.—The ultimate consolidation of all the 3,000 first-run motion picture theaters in the United States into one huge organization, under the control of the Famous Players-Lasky Corporation, is the aim of its president, Adolph Zukor.

A new step toward the realization of that aim was taken within the last few days, when it was announced that the intention of Famous is to have the Publix Theaters Corporation, which it formed recently to manage its theater properties, own the theaters outright as well as manage them.

To that end a stock issue is being planned whereby the public will become shareholders in the theaters, the estimated aggregate worth of which is $200,000,000.

When the Publix Theaters was organized by Famous there was placed at the head of it a man who with his partner is the controlling hand of more than 700 theaters thruout the country, especially in Chicago, where the firm of Balaban & Katz practically controls the theater situation. That man is Sam Katz, said to be a wizard in the handling of theaters. But a not inconsiderable feature of the alliance between Famous and Balaban & Katz was that the latter brought with them their enormous chain of theaters, and also those of the Lubliner & Trinz chain, which B. & K. recently acquired.

Ostensibly, Famous took Balaban & Katz into the fold in order that the theater managing and production departments of the gigantic organization might be kept apart as separate entities, and on the theory that it was a sounder banking principle to have the assets of the two departments segregated.

The thought has been expressed in banking circles that this general merger of theaters would not get by the Federal Trade Commission, because primarily it would be in the nature (in its eyes) of an order in direct disobedience of the commission's demand that the leading motion picture producers divest themselves of their theater holdings and stick to the production end of the business solely. In addition to that, it is pointed out, it would be regarded as a move toward controlling the price of admissions to theaters and the price of films as well.

FROM DEC. 25, 1926 ISSUE

Universal Floats $5,000,000 Issue To Finance New Theater Chain Company

Will Buy Outright Sparks, Hostetler and Shine Interests From Universal Pictures, Inc., and Will Start Immediate Acquisition of New Theater Chains Thruout the Country

NEW YORK, Dec. 7.—The Universal Chain Theaters Corporation, organized last week by Universal Pictures Corporation, to acquire and operate a chain of 1,000 picture theaters thruout the country, has floated a new stock issue in the amount of $5,000,000, with which to finance the project. Carl Laemmle, president of the motion picture corporation, is also president of the new company.

A banking syndicate, headed by Shields & Company, will handle the financing, and last week an offering of $4,000,000 of eight per cent preferred stock of Chain Theaters was announced at $100 par and accrued interest. Each share will carry one share of the common stock as a bonus.

The proceeds of this sale, with the sale of $1,000,000 of eight per cent convertible second preferred, will be used to buy the theaters.

Mr. Laemmle will purchase at par $1,000,000 of the second preferred stock, while Universal Pictures, Inc., will take the same amount of second preferred stock in return for its interest in the Sparks, Hostetler and Shine properties, in the Southeast and Southwest, which control 91 houses and in which Universal has a large interest. After the purchase outright of this circuit, the corporation will immediately set out in search of other properties.

The first public financing of Universal Pictures, Inc., was done last year thru a banking syndicate headed by Dillon-Read Company and Shields & Company. At that time, a $3,000,000 issue of eight per cent preferred stock was sold, carrying with it option warrants on the common stock of the company.

Universal thus, with its latest project, lines up with the other big motion picture producing companies. A few years ago Famous Players-Lasky floated $10,000,000 of preferred stock for the same purpose, while Loew, Inc., almost doubled its capital stock to finance a widespread extension of its theater operations.

FROM MAY 23, 1925 ISSUE

Harold Lloyd and his wife, Mildred Davis.

"BROKEN BLOSSOMS"

A. D. W. Griffith Production, adapted from a story by Thomas Burke. In M. P. Repertory at Cohan's Theater, New York

Reviewed by W. STEPHEN BUSH

Pure tragedy, rousing alternately the pity and terror of the audience. Direction will add to Griffith fame; acting superb thruout.

THE STORY IN SKELETON FORM

A young Chinaman leaves his country to come to England, continuing his Oriental dreams in the sordid surroundings of a very poor quarter in London. In the same quarter lives a low and brutal thug, with a reputation as a prizefighter. He has a little girl whom he ill-treats. One night he drives the girl out of the house, after beating her cruelly. The girl finds refuge in the house of the young Chinaman, who has seen and admired her as she passed his store. He bathes her wounds, takes her to his rooms, where he clothes and adorns her like a princess, lighting the joss in her honor and treating her generally as a most precious and loved guest.

The prizefighter hears of his daughter being with the Chinaman ... and after he gets her in his power, beats her to death.

The prizefighter hears of his daughter being with the Chinaman, and despite her protestations that there had been nothing wrong drags her thru the streets, and after he gets her in his power beats her to death. The Chinaman, who had been out when the girl was taken away, follows the thug to his house and confronts him. As the fighter is about to assault him with an ax he fires his pistol at him, killing him. The Chinaman then takes the dead body of the girl to his home, again places it on the couch, once more clothes and adorns her and once more burns the joss in her honor. Then he lingers over her most tenderly and finally stabs himself to death.

THE CRITICAL X-RAY

I can not attempt to assess the commercial value of this play, only the public may do that, and as the play is only a few days old no judgment on the attitude of the public will be attempted. Judged as a production of the screen Broken Blossoms measures up to the great fame of its producer. It is tragedy on the ancient Greek pattern, showing that Fate is blind and relentless, that human beings are but the toys of a higher power, which delights to mock the importance of mortals. The building up to the plot is perfection itself. Tho the somberness of theme and atmosphere is never relieved for one moment the audience is held spellbound from start to finish and the climax finds the crowd silent, deeply stirred and in a mood which is not eager for utterance. The performance lasted from 8:55 to 10:35, with not a minute's intermission, but the attention of the audience never wavered for an instance. The spell of Griffith's name had brought the crowds to the theater. The spell of his genius held them captive every minute they were there.

WALTER HUSTON

Made his debut on the legitimate stage in "Mr. Pitt" at the 39th Street Theater, New York. He comes from vaudeville, where he sang or danced for ten years, and never appeared in a dramatic sketch. He walked right into the title role of "Mr. Pitt", and into the approval of New York's sophisticated critics, who proclaim him a genius. Mr. Huston is a brother of Mrs. Carrington, with whom John Barrymore studied diction before playing Hamlet.

HUMPHREY BOGART

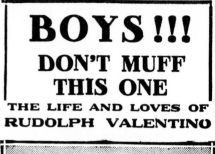

—Photo by James Margis Connelly, Chicago. One of the most promising members of the younger generation of actors. He is of the dark and romantic type, lending the requisite touch of youth to "Meet the Wife", which has been holding forth at the Klaw, New York, since November 26.

TALKIES' LANDMARK: THE JAZZ SINGER

FROM OCT. 15, 1927 ISSUE

Al Jolson Opens In First Picture

NEW YORK, Oct. 8.—Al Jolson opened Thursday night at the bullet-shaped Warner Theater in *The Jazz Singer*, his first picture, scored by Vitaphone and with several vocal numbers and a bit of dialog interpolated in the action. This is the same Jolson who several months ago, in defending a suit for breach of contract brought by D. W. Griffith, admitted he was a poor screen actor. The former Shubert star was quite right. He's as flat on the screen as a glass of tepid beer.

Were it not for the novelty of the Vitaphone numbers, sung from the screen, the picture could hardly stand comparison with the average program effort. Vitaphone practically saves the day for this reason, but the picture is still a disappointment. Hearing Jolson from the screen is not hearing him from the stage. There is a big difference, and the metallic reproduction by Vitaphone, like a phonograph, is partly to blame.

The songs Jolson offers outside of *Kol Nidre*, Yiddish number, are *Dirty Hands, Dirty Face; Toot, Toot, Tootsie, Good-By; Blue Skies; Mother o' Mine, I Still Love You*, and *Mammy*, all green with age. Cantor Josef Rosenblatt is seen and heard singing a Yiddish work in a synagog shot, and a kid star early in the picture is heard singing a number in a voice that sounded suspiciously like that of Jolson's, somewhat faked.

The story of *The Jazz Singer* is banal and depends largely on excellent acting, which the screen version does not have. The direction, by Alan Crosland, who has done some fine work in his career, is not particularly inspired, and the subtitles, besides being in excess, are lacking in taste and intelligence.

A $2 special should have much more than *The Jazz Singer* can offer outside of the name of Al Jolson, which, indubitably, will act as a draw. Its appeal, no doubt, to the Jews will be strong, but for the average picturegoer it is rather stale entertainment based on a stale situation in the life of a cantor's son who was driven from home by his fanatically orthodox father and became a "jazz singer".

The cast in support of Jolson includes May McAvoy, who is practically negative as a dancer; Warner Oland, Eugenie Besserer, Otto Lederer, Richard Tucker, Nat Carr, William Demarest and others.

At the Warner the picture alone is given. There are no preliminary Vitaphone numbers or other program matter, not even a newsreel, with the consequence that the show is comparatively short.

Vitaphone Opens New Field to Acts

The Aristocrats, String Band, First Picture House Act Booked

NEW YORK, Sept. 6.—A new field, and one that promises to afford a good outlet for vaudeville and picture house acts, is being opened by Vitaphone, which plans using as many artistes with vocal, musical and novelty offerings as it can obtain, booking men declare. The Aristocrats, which toured with a Publix unit and since has been playing the picture houses, including the Rivoli and the Metropolitan, Boston, have just been signed to do a Vitaphone film, which will open at the Colony early next month in conjunction with *The Better 'Ole*. Benjamin David negotiated the booking of the Aristocrats, string orchestra, with the Vitaphone people, and indicated he had a number of other acts under his direction "penciled in".

The booking of the Aristocrats, an attraction that was developed by David strictly for the picture houses, turns the tide of Vitaphone requirements to this and the vaudeville field. With the premiere of Vitaphone recently at the Warner Theater, its sponsors offered short films introducing Anna Case, Giovanni Martinelli, Mischa Elman, Marion Talley and other renowned concert stars, in brief vocal or musical numbers, and for the opening of *The Better 'Ole* next month they have obtained Al Jolson, Elsie Janis and the Howard Brothers. The booking of these "names", costing considerable money, has been done by Warner Brothers, it is generally admitted, to put the Vitaphone over on a grand scale, and while Warners will continue to engage artistes from the concert and musical comedy fields, it will also find it necessary to "fill in" open spots with acts of less importance and cost. These will have to be found in the vaudeville and presentation fields.

Vitaphone Declared On Opposition List

Proctor, Moss and K.-A. Circuits Will Fire Artistes for Violation

NEW YORK, Feb. 12.—Vitaphone or any other synchronizing device has been declared strict opposition to vaudeville by the Keith-Albee Circuit, with immediate cancellation of contracts to the artiste the penalty for violation. The ink has hardly dried on the new form of contract incorporating a clause to this effect. It reads:

"It is understood that the theaters of the F. F. Proctor Circuit, the B. S. Moss Circuit and the Keith-Albee Circuit are booked together as one chain, and the artiste agrees that the aforesaid act will not, nor will any member thereof, perform for any person between the date hereof and the end of this engagement, either privately or publicly (including Sunday concerts and clubs), in any city where a theater of any one of the above-mentioned circuits is located, or anywhere by or thru the means of radio or broadcasting or the use of the Vitaphone or any other device for synchronizing moving pictures and the voice and action of the artiste without the writen consent of the booking manager of said circuit, and in the event of a breach of this covenant the manager may forthwith cancel this agreement."

The clause heretofore has been worded similarly, imposing the same penalty, to cover radio broadcasting.

Early this week, before the new form of printed contract was off the press, a rubber stamp prohibiting Vitaphone or any other "talking picture" engagement was used on the face of the contracts.

In time Vitaphone is looked on as serious competition to straight vaudeville because of the probability whole shows of acts can be booked by the theater owner much in the same manner that he books films. Vitaphone is busy engaging artistes so that many shelves of "film acts" may be in readiness for this day.

De Forest Phonofilm has also been engaging many acts known to the two-a-day and musical comedy world. Photophone and numerous other devices for synchronization, under development, will bring competition even to the "talking picture" field.

Vitaphone at Popular Prices Is Presented in Providence

First Showing of Talking Films at Low Scale of 40 Cents Top Is Given by Edward M. Fay in His Majestic Theater—Other Synchronized Productions To Follow

PROVIDENCE, Dec. 25.—What is announced as the first showing of the Vitaphone at the low scale of 40 cents top took place here today when the new talking film was presented at Edward M. Fay's Majestic Theater.

The opening picture program included the Warner Bros.' feature, *The Third Degree*, and other novelties. The Vitaphone artists announced include Giovanni Martinelli, Roy Smeck, Anna Case, Mischa Elman, Marion Talley, Will Rogers, Al Jolson and others.

Considerable anticipation has been aroused over the arrival of the Vitaphone in Rhode Island, and a large crowd was on hand to witness the initial showing. At the popular prices quoted, the attraction is expected to go big.

RCA Photophone

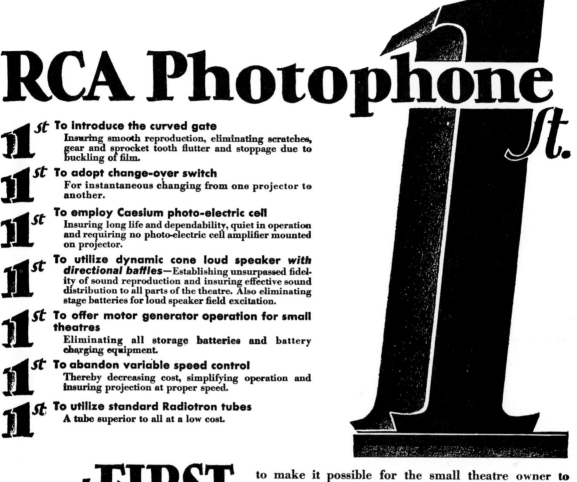

1st To introduce the curved gate
Insuring smooth reproduction, eliminating scratches, gear and sprocket tooth flutter and stoppage due to buckling of film.

1st To adopt change-over switch
For instantaneous changing from one projector to another.

1st To employ Caesium photo-electric cell
Insuring long life and dependability, quiet in operation and requiring no photo-electric cell amplifier mounted on projector.

1st To utilize dynamic cone loud speaker *with directional baffles* —Establishing unsurpassed fidelity of sound reproduction and insuring effective sound distribution to all parts of the theatre. Also eliminating stage batteries for loud speaker field excitation.

1st To offer motor generator operation for small theatres
Eliminating all storage batteries and battery charging equipment.

1st To abandon variable speed control
Thereby decreasing cost, simplifying operation and insuring projection at proper speed.

1st To utilize standard Radiotron tubes
A tube superior to all at a low cost.

and FIRST

to make it possible for the small theatre owner to install the finest sound equipment at a price he can afford to pay.

1st *in Sound Satisfaction!*

Today, more than ever before, the patron of the motion picture theatre demands "sound satisfaction," and the installation of RCA Photophone sound reproducing equipment is the exhibitor's best guarantee of sound reproduction of the highest quality.

The trend nationally and internationally is toward RCA Photophone!

Back of every installation made by RCA Photophone, Inc., lies the unmatched prestige of the world's foremost electrical engineering organizations and their strength and stability are reflected in the performance of RCA Photophone sound reproducing equipment.

SMALL THEATRE TYPE A. C. EQUIPMENT
FOR SIMPLEX PROJECTORS

SOUND ON FILM AND DISC

FOR THEATRES UP TO 1,000 CAPACITY

$2995.00

(Deferred Payment Plan for best equipment available)

THE EMBLEM OF — PERFECT SOUND

RCA PHOTOPHONE, INC.

Executive and Commercial Offices
411 Fifth Avenue, New York City
Installation and Service Department
438 W. 37th Street, New York City
United States Branch Offices

Albany, N. Y. . . . . State and Eagle Sts.
Atlanta, Ga. . . . . 101 Marietta St.
Boston, Mass. . . . Room 706 Statler Office Bldg., 20 Providence St.
Chicago, Ill. . . . . 100 W. Monroe St.
Cleveland, Ohio . . . . Suite 203 Film Bldg.
Dallas, Texas . . . . Room 824, 1700 Commerce St.
Denver, Colo. . . . . . . Room 1014 U. S. National Bank Bldg.
Detroit, Mich. . . . . Suite 608 Fox Theatre Bldg.
Kansas City, Mo. . . . . 1717 Wyandotte St.
Los Angeles, Calif. . . . . 811 Hollywood Bank Bldg.
Philadelphia, Pa. . . . . 261 North Broad St.
Pittsburgh, Pa. . . . . William Penn Hotel
San Francisco, Calif. . Room 2012 Russ Bldg., 235 Montgomery St.
Seattle, Wash. . . . . Suite 506 Orpheum Theatre Bldg.
Washington, D. C. . . . . 1910 K St. N.W.

MOVIE MOGULS' REACTION TO THE TALKIES

FROM NOV. 5, 1927 ISSUE

Big Film Companies Ready To Bow to Talking Pictures

Committee of Five Investigating All Available Inventions, New and Old—Said To Represent Paramount, M.-G.-M., United Artists Pathe and First National

NEW YORK, Oct. 31.—The representative film producer-distributing companies controlling theaters have not gone cold on talking pictures. A committee of five, representing that number of big companies, is investigating every new talking picture device on the market, going into full details concerning the inventions, their patents, practicability, etc.

This committee of five is said to represent Paramount, Metro-Goldwyn-Mayer, Pathe, United Artists and First National, whose interests are interlocked in some manner or other, either thru picture or chain connections.

The big film interests have faith in talking pictures, even tho the developments and reactions in the field thus far have been slower and less spirited than anticipated at first. In a recent interview, Adolph Zukor was quoted as having said the talking picture is here to stay.

From one company with a talking picture open for backing, it was learned the committee of five was ready to sign up but not ready to dole out capital, taking the position this would not be done until product on which the companies would have to pass was available.

Keith-Albee, in control of Pathe, has a device of its own under option on which it is experimenting, but is said to be represented, nevertheless, on the committee of five. K.-A.'s invention is Audiophone, which has been tried out privately and publicly sans advertising, with results that have not been announced by the circuit.

Vitaphone is going along, making a few installations, but is failing to arouse the keen interest that was anticipated for it, while Fox-Case, with Movietone (hooked up by license agreement with Vitaphone), is planning to start a big campaign in the near future to place Movietone thruout the country on a large basis, following successful showings here.

FROM DEC. 1, 1928 ISSUE

U. A. To Remake Talkies as Silents

NEW YORK, Nov. 24. — Because the majority of theaters are not wired now, United Artists will remake every one of their talkies in silent versions, according to Al Lichtman, who has given instructions to begin selling all 17 of the U. A. pictures, of which more than 50 per cent have talking sequences.

The 17 include two all-dialog films, seven part talking and eight synchronized with music and sound effects. Those with dialog will be made first as talkies and then made over again as silents.

Mary Pickford's *Coquette* and the Roland West production, *Nightstick*, are the 100 per cent talkies being sold now.

The seven part-talkies are Gloria Swanson in *Queen Kelly*, Charlie Chaplin's *City Lights*, Douglas Fairbanks' *The Iron Mask*, Ronald Colman in *The Rescue*, Lupe Velez and others in *Masquerade* (D. W. Griffith production with 65 per cent dialog), *Lummox*, Fannie Hurst story and *She Goes to War*, Henry King production.

FROM SEPT. 1, 1928 ISSUE

Talkies Doomed, Says Joe Schenck

Head of United Artists Insists That Voice Synchronization Is Not Successful

NEW YORK, Aug. 25.—Talking films are doomed to fade from vogue in about six months, according to Joseph M. Schenck, president of United Artists, who discussed his views with newspapermen early this week following his return from a trip abroad. Tho he feels that canned musical accompaniment to films and synchronization of sound effects are an aid to the better appreciation of films, Schenck states that the so-called all-talking pictures are a passing novelty and are not meeting with public favor.

Altho United Artists will go in for the talkie racket this season, Schenck said that this will be done only to satisfy a passing fancy. It would be foolhardy, he added, to make elaborate plans for the development of the production of talking pictures when even at this early time the public is showing keen disappointment over heavily ballyhooed all-talking pictures. "No talking picture is any good . . . they are uniformly uninteresting."

FROM OCT. 20, 1928 ISSUE

U. A. Strong on Talkies Despite Schenck's Views

NEW YORK, Oct. 15.—Despite Joseph M. Schenck's avowed lack of faith in the future of sound pictures, United Artists are out with a program of sound pictures that include the present and forthcoming productions of their bevy of stars. Mary Pickford, Gloria Swanson, Douglas Fairbanks, Ronald Colman, Lili Damita, Lupe Velez, Walter Byron, Harry Richman and others will be heard talking in new U. A. pictures now in various stages of production.

Mary Pickford's *Coquette* will be 100 per cent talkie and Herbert Brenon's *Lummox* will be partly with dialog. Gloria will do some talking in *Queen Kelly*, and *Nightstick*, another all-talkie, goes into production November 1.

"WITH CASTS THAT CAN TALK"

FROM OCT. 27, 1928 ISSUE

Lasky Slogan Spells Danger To Film Star Who Can't Talk

Realizes Difference Between Average Voice and That of Stage-Trained Artistes—"Interference" and Research Decided Him—Paramount's Test To Be Severe

NEW YORK, Oct. 22.—The Paramount slogan, as approved by Jesse Lasky, for all future talkies from this company will be "With Casts That Can Talk". The decision was made following the private viewing of *Interference*, 100 per cent talkie, by Lasky, and carries with it the strong probability that Paramount stars, no matter how big they are, will not have a ghost's chance in talking roles if their voices are not sufficiently trained for proper reproduction.

Before Lasky saw *Interference*, his opinion was that the average star's voice would record satisfactorily and that the difference between the voice of an untrained film star and that of an artiste who has had stage experience or is particularly adapted to histrionics, was not so great.

He has now changed his mind. With the cast of *Interference* all having had previous stage experience and time having given him a chance to make comparisons with the voices of regular film stars, he has decided that the legit. training is highly essential. One of the chief reasons why he signed Maurice Chevalier as a star is that he has a fine stage voice.

Interference proved to Lasky, it is understood, that only the best trained voices are of any use. The cast of this picture includes Clive Brook, English actor for more than 10 years; William Powell, who was long on the dramatic stage before going in pictures a few years ago; Evelyn Brent, who had experience on the English stage, and Doris Kenyon, who has been in various Broadway plays in recent years.

Under the Lasky slogan, the most severe tests are facing those who would play in Paramount talkies. Paramount has proceeded very cautiously with its talking picture plans and has made test after test before releasing product or hollering about it.

The first in the East, *The Letter*, stars Jeanne Eagels, whose excellent stage voice was quickly o. k.'d for a talking role.

FROM OCT. 13, 1928 ISSUE

Strain of Acting in Talkies Awful, Says William Haines

M-G-M Star, in Exclusive Interview With "Billboard" Says He Nearly Fainted Doing His First—Hints Actors May Become Nervous Wrecks
By ROY CHARTIER

NEW YORK, Oct. 6.—Working in talking pictures is terribly nerveracking, and is liable to make physical wrecks out of some of our stars, according to William Haines, M-G-M star, who discussed the talkies freely this week in an interview for *The Billboard*, giving his views as well as experiences.

Thus far, the front-line star has worked in only one picture with talking sequences, *Alias Jimmy Valentine*, but according to his version of the ordeal he went thru he would be just as happy if talkies did a nosedive. From his account of the restrictions and limitations of production methods in the filming of sound, only the toughest of constitutions will survive the strain of making "canned" movies.

"You are confined to working quarters in the studios that are almost airtight," Haines stated. "You can hardly breathe, and in the hot weather it's like working in a boilerroom. When I was making the talking sequences for *Alias Jimmy Valentine* the sweat rolled off me until I could hardly stand it, and once I nearly felt like fainting, it was so uncomfortable and nerveracking."

Haines went on to point out that he was not generally a nervous type, and laughingly predicted what might happen to some of the more temperamental stars, especially the women.

The M-G-M star brought in the camera-grinding angle in discussing the talkies and the revolutionary effect they are having on motion picture production and methods.

"In making silent pictures, I personally sense the grinding of the camera, and know, perhaps by intuition, when it runs out of film and I am to stop acting," he pointed out. "With talkies and the camera as a result in a glass cage, where you can't hear it grinding, the suspense is annoying, and makes it more difficult to give a really good performance. The quiet finally gets on your nerves."

Haines also stated that the making of talkies places hardships on the directors as well as artistes. Everything has to be laid out beforehand, and the director, sitting above the scene somewhere, pressing buzzers, has to keep his voice to himself. M-G-M's big star also dwelt on the caution that must be exercised in not making noise, pointing out that a paper being torn, for instance, makes a terrible sound when reproduced.

FROM MARCH 30, 1929 ISSUE

Menjou and Others In Doubt With Para.

Future of Beery, Vidor, Wray, Jannings, Holt, Loder Also Question—Others in Strong, Including Talkie Finds —Bancroft, Powell, Brook, Bow Lead in Favor

NEW YORK, March 25.—The future of Adolphe Menjou, Wallace Beery, Florence Vidor, Fay Wray, John Loder, Jack Holt and Emil Jannings is somewhat in doubt so far as Paramount is concerned. Talkies have brought about a considerable change in the complexion of things with the company, as it has with others, and with certain of its high-salaried stars and players virtually on the skids now. new talent, especially from the legit., is coming in to fill the gap that may be left.

Menjou's next picture is to be a talkie entitled *The Prince Consort*. It will be directed by Ernst Lubitsch, who did *Forbidden Paradise*, one of Menjou's outstanding pictures, several years ago. This will be the last picture under Menjou's present contract, which calls for a reported salary of $5,500 a week. A renewal of this contract is largely dependent on the results from *The Prince Consort* and even then may mean a slash in Menjou's salary owing to the feeling that he is beginning to slip.

Wallace Beery, big moneymaker for the company in comedies of recent years, has only a few more pictures to make on his present contract and it is understood voice tests he has made are not up to expectations. In view of the heavy salary Beery is getting, the problem with Paramount is whether he is now worth it.

Miss Vidor's future is almost entirely dependent, it is said, on the results of *Chinatown Nights*, new talkie in which she appears.

Jannings, one of the biggest of the Paramount stars until the advent of talkies, but still fairly strong, has stirred considerable speculation because of his German accent. Paramount is making a talkie with him entitled *The Concert* and on this will hinge the possibility of a renewal of his contract, which expires after two or three pictures.

Fay Wray is said to be washed up because she has not "clicked" as anticipated. The same is reported to be the case with John Loder, English actor imported by Jesse Lasky and recently loaned to M-G-M. Jack Holt is thru as a result of the abandoning of Westerns.

Already definitely out of Paramount are Bebe Daniels and Louise Brooks. The former has signed with Radio Pictures.

The actors on Paramount contracts that lead in the company's favor (including sales organization) are George Bancroft, William Powell, Clive Brook and Clara Bow. Those whose value has not been entirely proven, but nevertheless rank high in Paramount's graces are Jeanne Eagels, Maurice Chevalier, O. P. Heggie and Ruth Chatterton, all of these having come from the legit.

JOHN BOLES, former musical comedy star, who has become more firmly established in the movie firmament since the advent of talking pictures. He has been placed under a five-year contract by Universal after a period of free-lancing.

FROM MAY 4, 1929 ISSUE

Powell a Star

NEW YORK, April 29.—William Powell has risen from a good villain to a star, thru talking pictures. As a result of his work in *Interference* and *The Canary Murder Case*, Paramount has decided to give Powell the rating of star, starting with his next release, *The Greene Murder Case*.

Powell originally hailed from the speaking stage. He entered pictures four or five years ago and, because he was a "type" was made a villain.

His perfect stage voice has made him a star.

FROM FEB. 2, 1929 ISSUE

Marion Davies Has Lisp; Talkie Film Suspended

NEW YORK, Jan. 26.—The future of the latest Marion Davies' production for M-G-M, *The Five o'Clock Girl*, is open to conjecture. It is thought quite probable production may be shelved permanently. No particular reason is proffered by the film company for the apparent fizzle of the Davies' picture, which was expected to be one of her best. More than $100,000 had been expended on the production.

At the home office the only information to be gleaned was that production had been "suspended temporarily", according to advices from the West Coast. The picture was first made as a silent and then scrapped. It was then tried as a talkie and this also proved unsatisfactory. The report has gotten out that Miss Davies has a pronounced lisp, which may have caused the scrapping of the talkie version.

MARION DAVIES

MOVIES ARE RADIO- AND DEPRESSION-PROOF — FOR A WHILE

FROM JUNE 22, 1929 ISSUE

Fox Lists Imposing Program

NEW YORK, June 17.—Fox, which has come forward with marked strides in the past year and since the advent of talking pictures has chalked up a number of outstanding hits, is individual in its program offering for 1929-'30, with dialog product only to be produced and sold.

The 48 dialog features on the Fox program embrace 19 all-talking dramas, 7 talking feature comedies, 6 dialog plays with music and songs, 4 musical comedies, 4 musical revues, 3 operettas and 5 synchronized and sound productions with dialog sequences.

Paramount Schedule Big One

NEW YORK, June 17.—With the opening of the Paramount convention (Western Division) this week at the Coronado Hotel, St. Louis, Jesse Lasky announces a program for 1929-'30, including feature and shorts material, of 200 individual pictures.

The number includes 65 features, 80 one and two-reel short features and 52 issues of the new Paramount Sound News and marks the most ambitious talking picture program yet made public.

332 Films All Told From U.

NEW YORK, June 24.—Under the direct supervision of Carl Laemmle, Jr., now in charge at Universal City, Calif., 332 subjects, varying in length from 12-reel superproductions to single-reel cartoons, will be included in Universal's 1929-'30 program. Both sound and silent pictures appear in the list. There will be 55 features made, including three superspecials, six Carl Laemmle special productions, seven star series, totaling 19 features, five all-star features, 16 Westerns divided between two stars and six other Westerns representing the pick of the reissue material. With the exception of reissues all other productions will be in both sound and silent form.

M-G-M Is Plunging With 63

NEW YORK, June 17.—With the largest number of productions it has yet listed for exhibitor consumption, Metro-Goldwyn-Mayer comes into the field for the 1929-1930 season with a grand total of 63 productions, silent and sound. This announcement was made public today by Nicholas M. Schenck, president of the organization.

Metro has listed 47 features of dialog or synchronization variety, with 16 silents designated for those theaters without equipment. M-G-M is expected to release a greater number of silent films than any other of its recognized competitors.

RKO Bows With 30 On Tap

NEW YORK, June 24.—Radio Pictures, new self-styled "titan" in the business, today will officially announce the lineup of 30 pictures for the 1929-'30 season. The list looks imposing and highly worthwhile and demonstrates the genius that has had a hand in the formation of an outgrowth of FBO over a comparatively short period, with stars, directors, writers and stories of the first rank lined up for its debut.

261

FROM DEC. 21, 1929 ISSUE

New $1,000,000 Plant
For Technicolor on W. C.

Demand for Technicolor Films Makes Fifth Laboratory Necessary—Day and Night Camera Shifts Busy in West

NEW YORK, Dec. 16.—From the Technicolor offices in New York comes the announcement that so heavy is the demand for Technicolor productions for next season that a fifth Hollywood plant is being rushed to completion at a cost of more than $1,000,000. Technicolor now has four plants, two in Hollywood and two in Boston, working at a heavy schedule to complete current releases. With more than 100 films, either all in Technicolor or carrying color sequences, set for next season, the demand for greater manufacturing facilities made the building of the new structure a necessity.

The new laboratory will be in operation early next month. It is a concrete three-story-and-basement structure and will contain 53,820 square feet of floor space. Daily and rush prints will be developed there within a few hours after the negative has been exposed for the studios using Technicolor. These rushes will have the color on one side of the film only. At present, rushes are printed on double-coated positive stock, with emulsion holding the color on both sides of the celluloid. Then the release prints with the emulsion all on one side of the film are turned out at the Boston plants.

Eventually, this new Technicolor plant will have a capacity of 47,000 feet of colored celluloid every day, or about 75,000,000 feet a year. All of the Technicolor plants in Hollywood and Boston are working triple shifts and the 30 or more Technicolor cameras are grinding night and day, being rushed from one studio to another at the close of each day's work.

FROM NOV. 9, 1929 ISSUE

50 Color Productions
Announced for 1930-'31

NEW YORK, Nov. 4.—That the Technicolor film will be more in demand during the approaching season and even more popular as the musical type film production is advanced, is borne out by the announcement that there are now 14 new color productions headed for Broadway.

The first of these, Paris, starring Irene Bordoni, will have its premiere this week at the Central Theater. The productions practically all come from the Paramount, M-G-M, Warner and First National studios, the Warner outfit having led with color production. This is due to the fact that they had the forethought to tie up the Technicolor apparatus at the start of the sound vogue and now have full use of about 80 per cent of the Technicolor apparatus.

The productions in color or with color sequences that are headed for Broadway include Cotton and Silk, M-G-M production, starring the Duncan Sisters; Footlights and Fools, First National, starring Colleen Moore; Glorifying the American Girl, Paramount, featuring Mary Eaton; Golden Dawn, Warners, with Vivienne Segal and Walter Woolf; General Crack, Warners, starring John Barrymore; Pointed Heels, Paramount, with William Powell and Helen Kane; Sally, First National, starring Marilyn Miller; Show of Shows, Warners, with an all-star cast; Son of the Gods, First National, starring Richard Barthelmess; Song of the West, Warners, John Boles and Vivienne Segal; The Vagabond King, Paramount, starring Dennis King, and The Rogue's Song, M-G-M, starring Lawrence Tibbetts. Gold Diggers of Broadway, from Warners, and Rio Rita, from RKO, have already been seen on Broadway and will shortly have a general release.

Eleven other feature productions are now being made with Technicolor sequences. These films are being produced by Paramount, Warner Bros., First National, Metro-Goldwyn-Mayer and Radio Pictures.

When On With the Show, the first all-color production, was made less than eight months ago there were only eight Technicolor cameras in operation. Now there are 34 and working both day and night shifts on account of heavy production they are doing the work of 68.

More than 50 color productions are expected for release from the combined studios during the coming year.

FROM FEB. 16, 1929 ISSUE

"Broadway Melody"
(M-G-M-MOVIETONE)
At the Astor

Chalk up for M-G-M a talking picture that presents every indication of being one of its best money makers this year. The picture is one of the most entertaining and best made talkies thus far from any company and is the first to really offer musical comedy scenes that combine showmanship with excellent photography and sure-fire audience appeal.

Harry Beaumont, the director, who with this and *Dancing Daughters* to his credit becomes one of the best on the M-G-M roster, has done exceptionally fine work, particularly in the sequence in technicolor in which an entire scene in a musical comedy is offered as Ziegfeld would have desired it done. For the first time in history a scene of a musical show in action is done so that it looks real.

> **Harry Beaumont, the director . . . has done exceptionally fine work, particularly in the sequence in technicolor in which an entire scene is offered as Ziegfeld would have done it.**

Altho *Broadway Melody* is a so-called all-talkie, the action is relieved every now and then with music and singing, with the result that a happy combination of entertainment has been provided.

The chief songs are *Broadway Melody, You Were Meant for Me* and *The Wedding of the Painted Doll*. The latter is done during the technicolor scene and is a particularly catchy tune. *Broadway Melody* also is a number that pleases song-tired ears. Charles King, featured with Bessie Love and Anita Page, sings this song several times. The girls, playing a sister team in vaudeville, also do it pleasingly.

King, as a songwriter-hoofer in love with one of the girls in the sister act, gives an unusually fine account of himself. As does Bessie Love, who has not been heard of much lately. Talkies ought to make her a reigning favorite again. Miss Page, too, is heard to advantage and proves very effective in scenes in which bursts of anger figure. On the opening night there was discernible a slight lisping sound in two or three parts of the picture, but it is possible this was caused by faulty operation, since it occurred only in spots.

Besides sob stuff there is considerable comedy in *Broadway Melody*. Jed Prouty, playing a stuttering vaudeville agent, is the chief comedy relief.

This picture marks a very definite step ahead in talking picture production and deserves to be one of the 10 best photoplays for 1929.　　R. C.

FROM APRIL 12, 1931 ISSUE

GLORIA SWANSON, appearing in "Trespasser", her first talkie, that opened November 1 at the Rialto Theater, New York.

FROM APRIL 25, 1931 ISSUE

ALICE FAYE, who will step out of a chorus line in a Loew presentation unit to take a featured spot in a new unit opening June 1 at the Capitol, New York. Attractive little dancer is now touring with "Rolling Along."

FROM MAY 2, 1931 ISSUE

"City Lights"
(UNITED ARTISTS)
At the George M. Cohan

Producer's footage, 7,650. Running time, 85 minutes.
(Release date not set)

Altho there have been ideas promulgated that Charlie Chaplin's *City Lights* might be the turning point in bringing silence back to the screen, after viewing it one feels that those who held such thoughts were very much error.

This is purely a picture for Chaplin. Silence is his forte, and this "comedy romance in pantomime", as he chooses to term it, proves to be a hilarious bit of tomfoolery with a touch of the dramatic so beautifully blended that the transitions are almost indistinguishable.

There is something pathetic about Chaplin's art—even in his comedy moments—and with a little more body to the story than there has usually been to other of the Chaplin films, this one stands almost alone. Coming as it does in an era of dialog it is really refreshing in its silence, and this great pantomimist has touched the risibilities with a bit of original and whimsical comedy at the same time playing a miserere on the heartstrings. And without a discordant note.

There is mirth supreme in situation after situation, the various sequences seeming like scenes from a silent play, yet all knitted together with an excellent continuity. Slapstick comedy, as one would expect, but done with the finesse of this great artist that puts it in a class of artistic slapstick.

Story concerns Chaplin's love for a blind flower girl, whom he befriends. When he finds she is in need of money, he sets out to get it. He takes it from a millionaire, who is Charlie's pal when he is intoxicated, but denies any knowledge of his acquaintance when sober. Chaplin gives the money to the girl so that she can take treatment from a famous specialist. Chaplin serves time for the theft, and when he gets out he finds the girl, with her eyesight regained, established in a neat florist shop. They meet, and she recognizes the tramp, who, in her blindness, she believed a millionaire, as her benefactor. Somehow we wish that Chaplin had moved on before the recognition was established. It would have made for a more pathetic ending.

Chaplin wrote, directed and produced the film and has done a good job. His supporting cast is perfect, with Virginia Cherrill, newcomer to the screen, as the blind girl, anad Harry C. Myers, an old favorite of the silent screen, as the millionaire, giving excellent performances.

　　　　　　H. DAVID STRAUSS.

8 Color Films From Warners

NEW YORK, Nov. 4.—Warners will release eight Technicolor specials during the season of 1929-'30. Six of these will be entirely in colors, while the remaining two will carry color sequences.

The all-color productions are *Song of the West*, the screen version of the musical comedy, *Rainbow*, with John Boles and Vivienne Segal; *Under a Texas Moon*, with Frank Fay; *Golden Dawn*, with Walter Woolf; *Hold Everything*, with Winnie Lightner, Georges Carpentier and Sally O'Neil; *Shows of Shows*, featuring Warner and First National stars, and *Gold Diggers of Broadway*, which is now having its Broadway showing.

The two with color sequences will be *General Crack*, starring John Barrymore, and Al Jolson's next vehicle, *Mammy*.

MAE WEST

"The Public Enemy"
(WARNER-VITAPHONE
At the Strand
Producer's footage, 8,766.   Time, 97 minutes.
(Release date, May 15)

James Cagney, a new star, is born in this one. It is another one of the racketeer-hoodlum stories, from an original by Kubec Glasmon and John Bright, that is said to be based on an actual occurrence.

Cagney hails originally from vaudeville, from where he went into a Broadway revue, and finally drifted to the movies. After seeing his portrayal in this one movie audiences will have no reason to forget him, but will want to see him again. Starting as a kid of 17 in 1917, Cagney goes thru the role and ages up to today, giving a portrayal that is realistic, natural and powerful. Outstanding performance of all newcomers to the screen in the last few years is this one, and one that will take its place among the finest of those offered by favorite names of the screen.

James Cagney, a new star, is born in this one.

In making this picture the Warner organization no doubt has begun to fear that the public is not reacting any too kindly to the gangster-racketeer film. They offer a foreword that is a sort of an apology stating that this picture depicts a phase or condition in American life of today, an actual occurrence, and is not intended as the glorification of the hoodlum or the racketeer.

At the start of the film we find two young lads in a large city, evidently Chicago, as the names of the streets, hotels and telephone exchanges are distinctive to the Windy City, learning thieving and nefarious trades from a gang of older crooks. This is in 1917. Thru the years we see these two kid boys drift, getting deeper and deeper into the mire. Tom, played by Jimmy Cagney, has an elder brother, Mike, played by Don Cook, who is a street-car conductor. Kids start burglarizing fur shops and finally drift into the beer racket. Finally, the elder brother enlists for service overseas, and the bad brother decides he must remain home with his mother, when he really wants to continue in his game, where he is becoming rich, owning fine autos and apartments. He has a pal, played by Eddie Woods, and the two of them get mixed up with numerous women. Cagney treats his women rough and finally, when one of his chief men is killed, goes out to get the other gang himself.

He is severely wounded and, as he falls unconscious, mumbles "I'm not so tough." He is beginning to improve in a hospital when word is received that he has been kidnaped by the rival gang. Proposition is made by one of his leaders that if the boy is returned home safe that they will quit the racket and leave the town to the rival gang. A phone message to the older brother brings the news he is coming home, and as the mother commences to prepare for his return, there is a knock at the door. She opens it, and the boy, bound hand and foot, falls into the doorway face down, dead.

Story is inclined to be episodic, but the direction by William Wellman and the characterization by James Cagney will take the picture out of the ordinary. Edward Woods, as the pal-in-crime, also proves himself a worthy player, as do Leslie Fenton and Robert Emmett O'Connor. Women's roles are subordinate, Jean Harlow being featured, but making her appearance after picture is half over and then having little to do. Beryl Mercer, Joan Blondell and Mae Clark have the other feminine roles.

H. DAVID STRAUSS.

"GINGER" ROGERS, formerly with Paul Ash in Chicago, who is in at the Paramount, New York, for an indefinite run. Publix thinks she's another "find". Miss Rogers was in one of the new Publix units in New Haven, but was taken out due to overloading of talent and put into the Paramount last week.

FROM JAN. 22, 1938 ISSUE

"Snow White and the Seven Dwarfs"

(RKO-RADIO PICTURES)

Time, 80 minutes. Directed and conceived by Walt Disney. Adapted from the famous Grimm Brothers' story. Supervising director, David Hand. Reviewed at Radio City Music Hall, New York.

As hokey as it may sound, this is really a milestone in the development of pictures. Disney's first full-length cartoon comedy, in color and set to music, *Snow White* ought to be a box-office smash.

For those patrons who stay away, fearing a full-length cartoon couldn't possibly be worth the money, there will be many more who will be attracted to see this genuine novelty and truly a work of art.

The story of the little Princess Snow White who runs away from her jealous sister, the Queen, and enters the home of the seven dwarfs is well known and provides the frame for Disney's high imagination. The story, interesting in itself, is given magnificent pictorial background, exquisite coloring, tuneful music, rollicking comedy and genuine characterizations. For the first time cartoon characters achieve flesh and blood quality, the dwarfs coming to life in amazing fashion. Of course, there are the usual flock of forest animals in fantastic actions satirizing us humans. But the most startling fact of all is that the picture is so effective that you will forget it's a cartoon. And that is the greatest praise anyone can give Disney and his staff. *Paul Denis.*

LILA LEE, who has staged an outstanding comeback to the screen via talkies and makes her latest hit in "Flight", Columbia special current at the Cohan, New York. This is Miss Lee's fourth talkie and her first with Columbia. She made her best hit in "Drag", First National talkie, starring Richard Barthelmess, and one of the best pictures this year.

FROM DEC. 30, 1939 ISSUE

"Gone With the Wind" Opens In Blaze of Lights and Glory

NEW YORK, Dec. 23.—With simultaneous showings at two major Broadway houses, a gathering of celebrities thicker than a pest of locusts, and such mobs that a block on the Main Stem had to be closed to all pedestrians except those who held tickets to the show, *Gone With the Wind* finally opened in New York Tuesday evening (19). The world premiere had taken place the previous Friday in Atlanta, scene of much of the action in the mammoth spectacle.

The picture takes almost four hours to unwind, and was greeted with long paeans of praise by all reviewers.

The double opening took place at the Astor and Capitol Theaters, the former playing to $2.20 top and the latter to $1.65. Following the opening, the Astor plays two shows daily to reserved-seat audiences, while the Capitol features continuous showings with no reserved seats, at the same $2.20 and $1.65 scales, respectively. The claim is made that the film will not be shown at pop prices during 1940, and there is talk of converting several other houses in the metropolitan area to the Capitol's three-shows-a-day, advanced-price policy, to give it added showings.

The openings were terrific, rating as the biggest since Radio City Music Hall first threw open its doors back in 1932. The block between 50th and 51st streets, in front of the Capitol, was so jammed that police had to throw a cordon around it and refuse access to all but holders of tickets. Down at the Astor, between 45th and 46th, cops lined the middle of the sidewalk, dividing passers-by into two packed, sluggish streams and keeping them constantly moving. The openings were the first at which television played a part. Tele apparatus picked up the attending celebs and cornered them for brief interviews, in the old radio technique. Top names from all walks of life were a dime a dozen.

The previous night (18) a press preview was held at the Astor to take care of the newspaper boys and gals. The house was packed then, too.

Success of the big film seems assured, with crowds mobbing both houses ever since the twin premieres.

"A Star Is Born"

(UNITED ARTISTS)

Time, 111 minutes. Release date, April 30. Producer, David O. Selznick. Director, William A. Wellman. Screen play by Dorothy Parker, Alan Campbell and Robert Carson. Cast—Janet Gaynor, Frederic March, Adolphe Menjou, May Robson, Lionel Stander, Andy Devine, Elizabeth Jenns, Edgar Kennedy, Owen Moore, J. C. Nugent and others.

Cheers upon cheers for this picture of pictures, one of Hollywood's greatest efforts. Surprisingly it's a story of the movie industry, a back-yard product. For sheer honesty, deepness of emotion, brilliant play-acting and ever so many excellent qualities there's none better. It's done in technicolor, but there is no scenic buildup and, in fact, the color is unobtrusive. Box office is written all over it, and the "can't miss it" buildups from reviewers will bring 'em in.

It's Gaynor's best, in a role that makes her the envy of all femme flickerites. The story's all hers, but March does his usual grand job, giving his dramatic role, and a difficult one, outstanding treatment. Rest of cast works in excellently as well. Not only the cast but the story and direction rate equal buildups.

A young miss from the sticks dreams of movies and is encouraged by her philosophical granny. She finds the movie field a tough nut to crack when she hits the Coast, with the usual struggle for room rent, meals, etc., but she meets up with a male star, a boozer, who gets her a test and speaks up for her because he's in love with her. She clicks right from the start, but her star lover is on the skids.

They marry, she climbs to fame and he hits the gutter. His come-down sets him on drunken sprees frequently, but the love of the two is great. On one too many an escapade, he learns that she's to give up the movies just for him. He takes an out by drowning himself, and deep in sorrow she's still resolved to quit but hangs on thru a pep talk from her old granny.   *Harris.*

"Monkey Business"

(PARAMOUNT)
At the Paramount

Producer's footage, 6,947. Time, 77 minutes.
(Release date, September 19)

The Four Marx Brothers romp, cavort, frolic and just cut up generally thruout the full running time of this film. It is by far the fastest paced of the three movies that these irrepressible comics have done for Paramount. It keeps going at a steady, snappy pace from start to finish. There are laughs galore—nonsensical stuff, it is true, but just the type of material that one would expect from these four rowdy comics.

Then, too, the picture is an improvement over former vehicles, for the sound pictures have learned how to wait for and space laughs. It has been a hard proposition to gauge this heretofore, but someone with a fine sense of what audiences will find rip-roaring laughs has managed to keep the dialog and action so spaced that not one line is lost by actors stepping on a roar, as has been the case in former comedy pictures.

The picture is somewhat lunatic. It could not be otherwise with Groucho, Chico, Harpo and Zeppo appearing in the chief lunacies. And for once the films have found something for Zeppo, the juvenile of the four, to do. Previously Zeppo has just appeared in the Marx Brothers' vehicles both on stage and screen because he was one of the four. In this one he has much more footage and goes thru a rough and tumble battle with the villain, in which a double works for Zeppo, but which keeps his character before the camera, much more than it has in earlier vehicles. Groucho is immense, and naturally has the fattest lines in the film, tho Chico and Harpo come thru, with the latter chasing the stunning-looking girls hither and yon as he has been accustomed to in other films. Chico plays the piano, and Harpo manipulates his harp as one might expect, all to good comedy results. All in all, the picture is the best that has come from the Marx Brothers.

> **Groucho is immense, and naturally has the fattest lines in the film ... the picture is the best that has come from the Marx Brothers.**

The story was written by S. J. Perelman and Will B. Johnstone and has been fashioned to fit the four. Norman McLeod directed and has done an excellent piece of work. The story starts with the four Marx Brothers as stowaways on an ocean liner. The entire crew chases them in and about the ship, from hold to top deck, and in the meantime they get mixed up with a couple of gangs of crooks, two of the brothers, Groucho and Zeppo, aligning themselves with one faction, while Harpo and Chico become the bodyguard of the chief of the opposing forces. Naturally this lends to some excruciatingly amusing situations and sure-fire horseplay. The daughter of one of the gangsters is kidnaped by the rival gang with the Marx Brothers arriving in time for the rescue and Zeppo, who has fallen hard for the girl, going thru a real battle in an old barn to save her, while Groucho sits on the rafters, changing from one corner to another, and faking radio announcement of a prizefight. The supporting cast includes Thelma Todd, Ruth Hall, Rockcliffe Fellowes, Tom Kennedy, Ben Taggart and Harry Woods. If audiences have liked the Marx Brothers in their previous vehicles they will go stronger for them in this one. Their comical eccentricities have been enhanced by the lack of musical numbers to break into the story. The music interludes seemed to break the continuity of their former vehicles.

VILMA BANKY, Samuel Goldwyn's Hungarian star, who, thru a special arrangement with Goldwyn, has been engaged for one picture by M-G-M. She will appear in an original story by Sidney Howard, author of "They Knew What They Wanted" and "The Silver Chord", stage successes. Miss Banky became a star with "The Awakening" and did her first talking role in "This Is Heaven".

ARCHIE LEACH, a young song and dance artiste who is making his second Broadway appearance in "Boom, Boom", at the Casino Theater, New York, and attracing favorable attention. Last season he appeared under the Arthur Hammerstein banner in "Golden Dawn". He is now under contract to the Shuberts.

THE THEATRE'S VERY SPECIAL PLACE

FROM SEPT. 13, 1919 ISSUE

EQUITY'S VICTORY

A Triumph of the Loftier Aims and Nobler Impulses of

THE PLAYERS

Over the Hard, Sordid Business Considerations Which Alone Interested and Concerned

THE PRODUCERS

The Theater Gains Immeasurably by the Outcome and the Profession Wins an Honorable and Respected Status That Otherwise Might Have Taken Generations To Secure

THE FINEST RESULT OF ALL,

Though, Is the Strong Bond of Sympathy and Understanding Established Between Musicians, Stage Hands, Billposters, Electricians and Actors and Actresses — It Needs Only the Inclusion of the Agents and, All in Good Time, the Vaudeville Artists and the Outdoor Following To Make It Perfect

DEMOCRACY HAS ROUTED CLASS PREJUDICE, SNOBBERY, SELFISH BARRIERS AND ALL THE EVILS THAT OVERCOMMERCIALI-ZATION WAS BUILDING UP AND RE-ESTABLISHING

The actors' strike was won —not settled—on Saturday, September 6, along about 3 o'clock in the morning.

It lasted 31 days—one long month.

It was won because the Actors' Equity Association secured all of its original demands, and more—ALL, IN FACT, THAT THE PRODUCERS OFFERED THE RUMP LEAGUE, and these were many and important.

It was won in a remarkably clean fight by the actors and their loyal supporters, the stage hands, the musicians, billposters and a handful of guerilla radical vaudeartists against as unscrupulous tactics and methods as men can well stoop to.

It was won decisively.

There must be no mistake about that. It was a victory— a triumph for the players.

They deserved it, moreover.

Their magnificent solidarity —their oneness—their singleness of purpose deserved it.

Their sacrifices deserved it.

But, thank heaven, it is over, and the services of the players, so important in these trying days of reconstruction, may again be devoted to the highly valuable work of entertaining the people.

267

FROM AUG. 15, 1925 ISSUE

INTERESTING FACTS
About the
NEW YORK THEATRICAL SEASON
of 1924-1925

(As Revealed by The Billboard Index of New York Theatricals)

Most Prolific Actor—James Meighan, who appeared in nine productions.

Most Prolific Playwright—Eugene O'Neill, who had four full-length plays and one short play produced. Ernest Vadja, Hungarian author, had four plays presented. Aside from O'Neill, no American playwright had more than two pieces produced during the season.

Number of Producers With Only One Show to Their Credit for the Season—109, indicating considerable activity on the part of non-established producers.

Percentage of Failures—Dramatic, about 75 per cent; musical comedy, about 35 per cent.

Suddenness of Failures—In the dramatic line, out of 194 new shows, 51 closed within two weeks, 75 within three weeks, 90 within four weeks and 110 within six weeks; therefore, more than half of the dramatic shows FAILED WITHIN SIX WEEKS. In the musical comedy line, out of 50 shows, 4 closed within two weeks, 6 within three weeks and 9 within six weeks; but 35 ran beyond 100 performances.

Total Number of New Productions for the Season—244, including 194 dramatic shows and 50 musical comedies. In addition to this, 11 dramatic and 9 musical attractions were held over from the previous season; making a grand total of 264 productions on view the past season.

HELEN HAYES

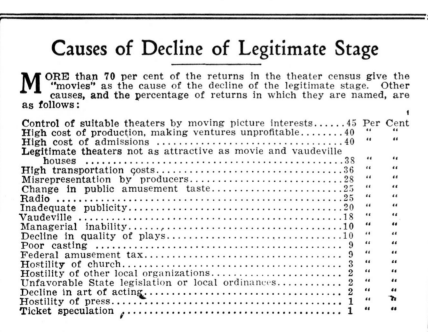

One of our youngest actresses, who has one of the finest acting opportunities of her brilliant career as the pert flapper in "Dancing Mothers", the new play by Edgar Selwyn, written in collaboration with Edmund Goulding, and produced under the personal direction of Edgar Selwyn at the Booth Theater, New York.

FROM AUG. 14, 1926 ISSUE

Causes of Decline of Legitimate Stage

MORE than 70 per cent of the returns in the theater census give the "movies" as the cause of the decline of the legitimate stage. Other causes, and the percentage of returns in which they are named, are as follows:

Control of suitable theaters by moving picture interests......45 Per Cent	
High cost of production, making ventures unprofitable........40 " "	
High cost of admissions ....40 " "	
Legitimate theaters not as attractive as movie and vaudeville houses ....38 " "	
High transportation costs....................................36 " "	
Misrepresentation by producers...........................28 " "	
Change in public amusement taste........................25 " "	
Radio ....25 " "	
Inadequate publicity..20 " "	
Vaudeville ....18 " "	
Managerial inability.....................,..................10 " "	
Decline in quality of plays.................................10 " "	
Poor casting ....9 " "	
Federal amusement tax......................................9 " "	
Hostility of church..3 " "	
Hostility of other local organizations.......................2 " "	
Unfavorable State legislation or local ordinances...........2 " "	
Decline in art of acting....................................2 " "	
Hostility of press ....1 " "	
Ticket speculation ....1 " "	

GEORGE ABBOTT

Who makes the character of "Sid" Hunt in Hatcher Hughes' stirring comedy-drama, "Hell-Bent-fer-Heaven", at the Frazee Theater, New York, a constant source of pleasure to the audience. His portrayal of a young mountaineer who, coming out of the caldron of the great world war, realizes the futility of family feuds, and treats his antagonist with genial humor, is sincerely done, even to the humorous twinkle in the eye.

FROM DEC. 26, 1925 ISSUE

THE DECLINE OF "THE ROAD"

A Comparative List of Theaters Available for Legitimate Attractions in 1910 and in 1925

NEW YORK, Dec. 21.—The decline of "the road", the great decrease in the number of theaters available for legitimate attractions thruout the country today as compared to the number available 15 years ago, is shown in a report just compiled by *The Billboard* from authentic sources, which report is set forth below.

While the figures in some cases must be considered as approximate, the compilation as a whole is about as near correct as it is possible for it to be.

The principal point about the situation is that in 1910 there were no restrictions whatever on traveling shows, while at present almost every town is more or less restricted—not a single one can be considered "wide open" to road attractions. The restrictions are of several kinds. In some places there are only certain days in the week when legitimate shows are permitted to come in. This is true almost everywhere, even in the towns that are "open". There also is discrimination as to the nature of the attractions. Farces and musical productions are in greatest demand. In fact, there is very little call for dramatic shows. Then the terms under which the attraction can play in the town are invariably such that a legitimate production cannot live up to them. With the advent of motion pictures, together with vaudeville, it has become increasingly harder to bring theater managers to terms. Many of the legitimate houses now play vaudeville and pictures on the days when legitimate shows are restricted and the theater manager figures that if he plays a road show he will have to lose on his vaudeville and picture business, therefore he wants to make up for this loss by getting more out of the legitimate show.

The figures show that the number of legitimate theaters on the road has decreased by more than one-half in the past 15 years, and of those remaining open there are so many restricted locations that the decrease amounts to practically two-thirds. Most of this loss has been suffered by the very small town, which, since motion pictures came along, has practically gone out of existence as far as road shows are concerned. There is no call any more for the very small show that used to play the rural districts of less than 5,000 population.

STATE	OPEN IN 1910	OPEN IN 1925	RESTRICTED AND CLOSED
New York.....About	85	12	About 6 closed and 67 badly restricted
Alabama	20	15	5 closed
Mississippi	24	20	4 (very choosy territory)
Arkansas	16	12	4
Louisiana	15	11	4
Arizona	8	5	3 (hard going)
Utah	9	4	5
Nevada	3	3	..
California	42	18	4 closed and 20 badly restricted
Colorado	24	10	6 closed and 8 badly restricted
New Mexico	10	6	4
Connecticut	25	4	12 closed and 9 badly restricted
Rhode Island	7	..	5 closed and 2 badly restricted
Delaware	10	5	5
Maryland (including Washington, D. C.)	12	3	9
Florida	29	3	26
Georgia	24	9	15
Idaho	14	5	9
Montana	18	3	15
Wyoming	10	3	7
Illinois	75	28	12 closed and 35 badly restricted
Indiana	56	9	10 closed and 37 badly restricted
Kansas	44	22	5 closed and 17 badly restricted
Iowa	55	18	37
Kentucky	26	9	5 closed and 12 badly restricted
Tennessee	16	10	3 closed and 3 bad'y restricted
Maine	28	3	12 closed and 13 badly restricted
Massachusetts	50	8	42 closed
Michigan	56	10	2 closed and 44 badly restricted
Minnesota	35	14	21
Missouri	28	14	14
Nebraska	38	14	24
Vermont	25	7	18
New Hampshire	26	7	19
New Jersey	44	9	35
North Carolina	36	29	7
South Carolina	28	20	8
North Dakota	10	10	..
South Dakota	10	8	2
Ohio	74	33	41
Oklahoma	42	32	10
Oregon	21	15	6
Pennsylvania	110	70	40
Texas	60	..	All badly restricted
West Virginia	28	18	10
Washington	28	20	8
Virginia	36	24	12
Wisconsin	30	22	8
	1,540	674	

FROM JAN. 13, 1923 ISSUE

HELEN GAHAGAN

The girl who looks like Ethel Barrymore. She glided gracefully from the cast of "Shoot!" produced by the Inter-Theater Arts, at the McDowell Galleries in June, into the cast of "Manhattan"; thence into the feminine lead of "Dreams for Sale", and into a contract with William A. Brady. Yes, she is both fortunate and beautiful!

FROM DEC. 10, 1921 ISSUE

LIONEL BARRYMORE

As he appears in the last act of "The Claw."

FROM NOV. 26, 1938 ISSUE

Repertory--'38

By ORSON WELLES AND JOHN HOUSEMAN

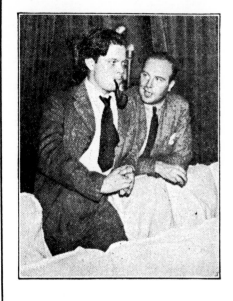

ORSON WELLES, directory of the Mercury Theater, New York, was born in Kenosha, Wis. After appearing at the Gate Theater in Dublin, Ireland, he joined Katharine Cornell's company for two seasons. For the Federal Theater Project he directed the Negro *Macbeth, Horse Eats Hat, Dr. Faustus* and *The Cradle Will Rock.* For the Mercury he has staged *Julius Caesar, The Shoemakers' Holiday* and *Heartbreak House.*

* * *

JOHN HOUSEMAN, co-director of the Mercury Theater, began his association with the theater by reviewing London productions for various English publications. After an interlude as a grain broker Houseman became an active participant in theatrical affairs by collaborating on several plays. Subsequently he turned to direction, staging Gertrude Stein's *Four Saints in Three Acts* and Ibsen's *Lady From the Sea* and acting as co-director for the Theater Guild's production of Maxwell Anderson's *Valley Forge.*

FOR the first time in many years—only the Lord and *The Billboard's* staff of statisticians can give you the exact figure—Broadway is faced with the prospect of having several repertory companies within its orbit.

Maurice Evans, who got off to an excellent start with his production of *Hamlet* in its entirety, plans to follow up with a new production of *Henry IV* and to revive his successful *Richard II*—all on the stage of the St James Theater. The Lunts, now touring with *Amphitryon 38* and *The Sea Gull,* are planning a tour and a spring season in New York with revivals of those two attractions, plus *Taming of the Shrew, Idiot's Delight, Reunion in Vienna* and *Elizabeth the Queen,* a venture which also comes under the heading of modified repertory. And at this point we also might mention the Mercury Theater, which last season played the first full season of repertory in New York since the Le Gallienne era.

The Le Gallienne era, incidentally, might well be a convenient landmark with which to launch this discussion of a system of theatrical production which again seems to be coming into favor. Miss Le Gallienne's Civic Reper-

tory Theater broke the ground for the popular-priced classical theater in New York. She introduced the works of Chekov, Ibsen and other European dramatists to thousands of playgoers. Had it not been for Miss Le Gallienne it is doubtful that Jed Harris would have produced *Uncle Vanya* or, more recently, *A Doll's House,* or that the Lunts would include a play by Chekov with those of Robert Sherwood and William Shakespeare in their current plans.

The Civic Repertory was a heavily subsidized institution. The sale of tickets might pay running expenses, but it was not sufficient, even with near-capacity audiences, to pay for the expense of new productions, a stumbling block which even now looms large on the none too smooth path of a repertory enterprise. Miss Le Gallienne's wealthy patrons did not seem to mind the necessity of contributing the production costs, looking upon the Civic Repertory as a philanthropist might view his donations to a library, art museum or symphony orchestra. Had it not been for the repercussions of the depression the Civic might have continued for years beyond its life span; but there came a time

when even Miss Le Gallienne's generous backers felt they could not afford further contributions, even for such a worthy cause.

The Mercury must pay its own way. The small profit we rolled up on the performances of *Caesar* paid for the production of *Shoemakers' Holiday,* and these two in turn paid for the production of *Heartbreak House.* It might be more comfortable to enjoy a liberal endowment, but perhaps there is some virtue in the fact that each production is as important to us as a single production would be to a manager who operates in the usual Broadway manner. When so much depends on your next show it is apt to have a greater quality of excitement and individuality than if you are turning out plays in the manner of a stock company or a Grade B picture-producing unit.

* *

For seven months last season we presented our plays in repertory, and we discovered for ourselves what everyone told us before we started: That repertory in New York is an enormously expensive business. The technical expense of shifting scenery frequently is high, but we were prepared for that and planned our productions accordingly. We spent a lot of money publicizing the details of a repertory system which the New York public (accustomed as it is to the long runs of successful plays) continued to find vaguely incomprehensible and disturbing. We were prepared for that, too. What we were not prepared for was the agony of deliberately slashing the runs of our two most successful productions at the peak of the season in order to conform with our repertory schedule.

It may be, as so many of our friends have maintained, that we have laid too much stress on a strict adherence to the repertory form. We can remember night after night of meetings, from the time the curtain rang down until the following dawn, at which we debated whether we should take advantage of the good notices on *Shoemaker* to split our company and move one show into a separate theater, thus certainly doubling our receipts. For better or worse, we decided that, having announced repertory, we would stick to it. In consequence, *Shoemakers' Holiday* closed to standing room after only 64 performances to make room for *Heartbreak House.*

Late in the season we did separate *Julius Caesar* and *Heartbreak House* for 20 performances, partly as an experiment. The substantial build in business on the part of both shows as the result of their having been able to play continuous runs was an eloquent altho not necessarily convincing argument against too slavish an adherence to the repertory system.

A similar problem arose in the matter of casting. Strict observance of orthodox repertory practice entails the use of the same cast in every production We do not believe that the New York public, accustomed as it is to a very specialized system of casting, is willing to accept the sort of stock-company atmosphere that inevitably results from the unquestioning use of the same actors in every play. In each of our successive productions we have chosen the best available actors for each part, even if in special cases we had to go outside of our own organization to find them.

As a result, last season we consistently carried in our company a number of actors receiving full pay but playing only three or four performances a week. With the opening of *Heartbreak House* last April we were carrying 28 *Julius Caesar* actors who only performed three times in two weeks. It was then that we sent *Caesar* into another theater for its final weeks. Lest this sound too tragic a story, let us add that, for all of our problems, we emerged from our first season a few dollars ahead of the game.

* * *

Now let us examine another phase of this business of running a repertory theater—the audience. We did not start the Mercury—nor did Mr. Evans begin his repertory season—without some conviction that an audience already existed for the type of production planned.

We laid the groundwork for the Mercury by producing *Macbeth, Dr. Faustus, Horse Eats Hat* and *The Cradle Will Rock* for the Federal Theater. We knew that we had aroused a certain interest for great plays of the past which have some emotional bearing on the present.

Our pre-Mercury following was a heterogeneous group of playgoers. It included thousands of intelligent, appreciative persons who, according to the answers to the questionnaires we distributed, had never attended a theatrical performance — young people who had keen kept away from the Broadway theater by the bugaboo of high prices for the kind of plays which normally would have attracted them. It included numerous seasoned theatergoers who came by subway, taxi or in their private limousines to the Lafayette in Harlem to see *Macbeth* or to the Maxine Elliott on 39th street to see *Dr. Faustus*

With the establishment of our own theater we were able to give even more attention to two other types of playgoers who now form an important and amazingly large segment of our audience. The first group consists of those associated, either as teachers or students, with the universities, colleges, high schools, grammar schools and private schools of Greater New York and its environs. Last season, and again this season, we distributed thousands of student discount cards at educational institutions, and we believe that 40 per cent of our audience came from this source.

Another important segment of our audience is that which comes to the theater in groups—the theater party. In the highly complex social and political life of the metropolis there are thousands of organizations consisting of persons who are bound together by some common interest. By organizing a theater party the executives of these organizations can improve their financial status or raise funds for a special purpose while at the some time providing an enjoyable evening for their members at a cost no greater than if the member were to go to the theater by himself. To the theater the advantage of theater parties is obvious. In addition to disposing of tickets in bulk and building of a certain kind of good will, the theater party practice gives the box office a fairly accurate view of the prospects of a play—which makes it possible to synchronize advertising and publicity efforts more exactly.

But no matter how well a theater may succeed in organizing the organizable audience, its success or failure must be measured to a great degree by the desire of the casual theatergoer to see its individual productions. This type of theatergoer doesn't particularly care whether you're playing repertory or not. He wants to see a good show at the least possible expense with the greatest possible convenience. The practice of rotating plays may seem to him like an annoying innovation—until he gets used to the idea.

FROM JULY 23, 1932 ISSUE

FROM DEC. 1, 1934 ISSUE

ETHEL MERMAN, who has speedily become one of Broadway's most popular songstresses. She will be seen and heard next season in the Schwab-DeSylva musical, "Humpty-Dumpty."

Robert Stolz has made a career out of "The Merry Widow" ever since he introduced it in 1905.

Cole Porter score has a better than 50-50 chance to win a good press for any production on Broadway.

FROM AUG. 10, 1946 ISSUE

Donaldson Awards on the Air

AMERICAN BROADCASTING COMPANY
Saturday, July 27, 1946
7:30-8 p.m.

RADIO again offers congratulatory palm to season's "bests" in the legitimate theater. ABC network airs presentations of scrolls and gold keys to winners of Third Annual Donaldson Awards (sponsored by *The Billboard*) over a Coast-to-Coast hook-up.

(1) Myron McCormick and Ralph Bellamy in a scene from *State of the Union*, year's best play.

(2) Ray Bolger, best musical actor and dancer, sings *Old Soft Shoe* from *Three To Make Ready*.

(3) Bert Lytell and Frank Fay cross-fire in emsee chores.

(4) Carol Bruce, best supporting actress, sings *Bill* from *Show Boat*.

(5) Betty Garrett, best musical actress, contributes *South America, Take It Away* from *Call Me Mister*.

(6) Pearl Bailey chants *A Woman's Prerogative* from *St. Louis Woman*, which brought her best Broadway debut award.

(7) Judy Holliday and Paul Douglas in a tense scene from *Born Yesterday*, rated best "first" play. She won scroll and key as season's best actress and he took "best debut" honors.

"THAT ENDEARING MERRY-GO-ROUND CALLED VAUDEVILLE"

FROM DEC. 26, 1936 ISSUE

"Twenty-Six Weeks in Vaudeville -- Learning Things I Have Never Forgotten"

By Alfred Lunt

IN MOURNING the death, or at least the virtual disappearance of vaude-ville, as I am about to do, I do not speak as one of the immediate family but rather as an admiring friend. It is true that for 26 weeks—probably the most exciting weeks of my life—I was a vaudeville actor. But I was an adopted child, whisked away from Greek tragedy for my fling and returned, when it was over, to Tarkington comedy and all that has followed since.

But I must say that I enjoyed my Orpheum Time when I had it. I was a vaudeville fan before I became a vaude-villian and my experience as such did nothing to disillusion me. On the con-trary, I have been a more ardent fan ever since. During my brief career in vaudeville I saw and met some of the finest artists that have ever graced the American stage. That is a completely sincere statement. That this particular field or artistry has declined is a major tragedy.

When I say artists, I do not mean it as it is used by an agent seeking his 10 per cent. I use it in the true sense of the word. And I mean not only men and women, but animals, for they were in-cluded in vaudeville. I remember one week in Winnipeg when Lady DeBathe (that would be Mrs. Langtry, the Jersey Lily, for it was she who gave me the op-portunity to see and know and work with these amazing people of vaudeville by en-gaging me as "leading man" for her vaudeville sketch) shared honors with Fink's Mules.

Mrs. Langtry thought the combination entirely irreconcilable. She told the booking office so in notes that probably should have been written on asbestos rather than hotel stationery. I never could understand why. The mules, it seemed to me, were unusually talented. They behaved admirably about the whole business. They made no objection at all to her sharing their billing.

I spent my entire 26 weeks in vaude-ville learning things I have never for-gotten. I was fascinated from the begin-ning by the sincerity of these performers and have never ceased to be fascinated.

I would rush to the theater on Monday —when we joined a new bill—hurry into my makeup and stand in the wings watching the other acts. In fact, I was seldom out of the wings except for the 15 minutes when I had to be on the stage myself.

Those 15 minutes were not always easy. Our sketch was called *Ashes*. I played the role of the man with whom Mrs. Langtry was in love. Inasmuch as Mrs. Langtry, at that time, was 63 and I was 21, audiences were inclined to be somewhat bewildered. Usually they be-gan by thinking that I was her son, so it must have seemed a little odd to them when I suddenly began to make violent love to her. But they were really very nice about it all.

Even after my own career in vaudeville ended, my interest in it did not. I was, for years, a regular Monday matinee patron at the Palace. And no matter where I happened to be on tour, I never failed to find the vaudeville house and see a matinee. Even today I never miss a bill at Loew's State—altho it seems rather sad to me that such acts as Al Trahan and Lady Yukona Cameron must share headline honors with a mere mo-tion picture. It isn't right.

So when I say that vaudeville actors were intrinsically the finest artists I have ever known, I speak as one who has not only worked with them but watched them from out front. Vaudeville was a real show business. I have never seen any phase of the theater in which every-thing counted so much. Vaudeville actors never let down for a minute. They fought to score each individual point and, if they failed to do it, they took the act apart to find out what was wrong and worked until it was right.

If a team of dancers found that their routine wasn't going well, you would find them at the theater early the next morning, rehearsing. Sometimes it was just that they had gone stale. Some-times it was that they had taken too much for granted.

I've always tried to remember that lesson. Miss Fontanne and I feel that

any audience which pays to see a play in which we are appearing is entitled to the best we know how to give them. So when we feel that the edge of any play in which we are appearing has be-gun to dull, we call rehearsals, too, and at least try to sharpen it as the vaude-ville actors used to do.

We only play performance a day, ex-cept for regular matinees, but vaude-ville actors, playing two performances a day, which is a task in itself, managed to be good consistently. I know of no group in the theater in my time who have given, day after day and night after night, better performances.

Many of these actors have been lost to the theater thru the fading of vaudeville, which is unfortunate. Some have remained in other branches—the legitimate theater, night clubs, radio, motion pictures—and, with rare exception, their vaudeville training shines thru.

There were so many of them that I hesitate to mention even a few for fear of leaving out, inadvertently, some equally as good. I am sure that as soon

ALFRED LUNT as he looks in his portrayal of the part of Harry Van, the world-traveling vaudevillian in the Theater Guild's production of "Idiot's Delight."

as I finish my list and find it in cold type, too late to amend, I shall remember many more names that should be on it.

Perhaps the first names that come to my mind are those of Sophie Tucker and Nora Bayes. Altho each had her individual style, they could do more with a song than any one I have ever known. Another act comes to mind immediately. I will never forget the afternoon I sat at a vaudeville theater laughing immoderately, to say the least, at an act known—but not then very well known—as Burns and Allen. I'm very proud of them now—even tho I don't know them. For I have a feeling that I discovered them. Of course I didn't, but at least I recognized them long before the world at large did, and that gives me a great personal pleasure.

I've followed Jim Barton from theater to theater when he was doing his mad-dog routine. I think it was one of the finest things I've ever seen on the stage. And it didn't surprise me a bit when Mr. Barton stepped into the legitimate theater and made a place and a name for himself. I was sure he would.

I remember, with shivers still ascending and descending along my spine, the mind-reading act of Harry and Emma Sharrock—the only word for which is great. They were so good that when I was on the same bill with them I was actually afraid to think, so sure I was that they could read my mind right thru the dressing-room walls.

Harry Lauder stands out in my mind

as perhaps the greatest vaudevillian, because his comedy had a touching quality that was irresistible. I remember Nazimova when she played vaudeville in an act called *War Brides* and gave a performance which was magnificent under extremely trying conditions. In a play, Nazimova had time to establish and build a character. But in a vaudeville sketch, she had to establish that character at once, for her entire sketch ran only 12 minutes. And yet she did it.

Stan Kavanaugh is perhaps the last of the jugglers with charm. There was once a school of them in vaudeville. I can name two of them whose charm has carried them thru to even greater triumphs since, altho they've dropped their juggling long ago—W. C. Fields and Jimmy Savo. And, if you remember, Fred Allen started out as a juggler, too.

There are so many of them that defy classification—they were great for different reasons. The best I can do is list a few of them, in the hope that I will not offend anyone by an unintended omission:

There was Rae Samuels, the "Blue Streak of Vaudeville," and Willard, "The Man Who Grows," and Long Tack Sam, and Lew Hearn and Bonita, and Montgomery and Moore, and Stan Stanley and his bouncing act, and Van and Schenck, and Frank Van Hoven, "The Dippy Mad Magician," and Pauline, the hypnotist, and Bert Fitzibbon, who was, perhaps, the first of the "nut" comedians.

There was Julius Tannen and Doyle and Dixon, a great dancing team, and Avon Comedy Four and the Three Sailors, and Shaw and Lee, and the Dancing Kennedys, and Victor Moore and Emma Littlefield in *Change Your Act,* and the enchanting clown Toto, and Edna Aug, and Brice and King, and Ted Healy and his stooges, and Mr. and Mrs. Jimmy Barry, Eddie Leonard, McIntyre and Heath, and the Ponselle Sisters—that would be Rosa and Carmela Ponselle.

There was Emma Carus, and Vernon and Irene Castle, who started the country dancing, and Joe Jackson, the bicycle rider, and the incomparable Eva Tanguay, and the drawling Moran and Mack, and the completely mad Mr. Duffy and Mr. Sweeney, Al and Fanny Steadman, Mason and Keeler, Elsie Janis, Gertrude Hoffman, Dainty Marie, Barry and Whitlege, Walter C. Kelley, Marie Lloyd, Chic Sale anad the brilliant Grock.

An all-inclusive list would require a special edition of *The Billboard.* I only hope that I have not left out too many of those who never failed to give me great pleasure in the theater.

Where is vaudeville now? The only place you can get a real vaudeville bill today is on the radio—and even then, you must keep twirling a dial for an entire evening, picking up a bit of this program and a bit of that one and piecing them together to form a vaudeville bill, which, in the old days, you could get perfectly balanced in any one of a thousand theaters in the United States.

Will it come back? That is a question the answer of which is unpredictable. My guess would be in the negative, for the world has changed in the few years since vaudeville has slipped. Perhaps it may come back in some small form with television, when you can actually see the

things which now you only hear on the radio. For all comedy is not meant for the ear—nor is all music, for that matter. It would not have been enough, for instance, to hear Nora Bayes. She had to be seen to be fully appreciated.

Whether or not it ever returns, vaudeville was great entertainment. And many of the people who provided it were great artists. Even those who were not so truly great had a greatness of spirit and a sincerity that made them a real part of the theater.

Of this type was "Harry Van," the

ALFRED LUNT as himself—one of the most successful actors of America's legitimate stage and husband of the equally successful Lynn Fontanne, his co-star in outstanding Guild productions.

character I have the privilege of playing in *Idiot's Delight.* Harry was the sort of performer who never quite made the grade, who never got east of the Alleghenies. He never worried about his own billing but resented bitterly the fact that an act, which he thought was really good, was forced to take second billing. He was full of the appreciation of talent, altho he didn't possess it in any marked degree himself. And he didn't worry about the fact that he didn't possess it himself. It just didn't occur to him to worry about that, or even to think of it.

He would have fought for rooms for the girls in his act and then slept on the hotel pool table because there wasn't a room for him. There was a great many like him in vaudeville—people who never quite came thru. But they had their place and they filled it. They kept theaters open.

Those pan-timers, those interstate-timers, those four-a-dayers, those six-a-dayers, those Harry Vans—they were an integral part of that endearing merry-go-round called vaudeville.

Their sincerity was greater than their artistry—their eagerness to please was beyond their capacity to please—but they gave their hearts and their lives and it was not their fault that that was not enough. God bless them, every one.

FROM MAY 19, 1928 ISSUE

Joseph P. Kennedy Is Negotiating To Take Over All Interests of Keith-Albee-Orpheum Organization

Radio Corporation Also Reported Involved — Principals Withhold Confirmation, But "Inside" Information Points to Deal

By ROY CHARTIER

NEW YORK, May 14.—Joseph P. Kennedy, president of FBO Pictures and the corporation doctor in attendance upon Pathe for several months, and his associates are negotiating to take over the entire Keith-Albee-Orpheum interests, according to reports that have been unofficially confirmed. A deal is expected to be consummated shortly placing Kennedy at the helm of the great vaudeville organization dominated by E. F. Albee, with the transaction involving the Pathe Company, controlled by K-A-O.

Kennedy has been reorganizing Pathe both here and on the Coast, spending most of his time in connection with this work. A merger of FBO and Pathe has long been hinted as a result of the assistance he has been giving the ailing picture concern, but all inquiries concerning such a move have met with quick denials. The first inkling that any negotiations were on to take over K-A-O came to *The Billboard* on reliable authority from an "inside" source that the biggest surprise in national vaudeville and picture circles would be sprung shortly with the passing of the recently merged Keith-Albee and Orpheum circuits to another company or individuals. Investigation of the report resulted in the information that Kennedy and his associates were the prospective purchasers of the K-A-O interests and that definite negotiations were in progress.

Kennedy declines to make any statement one way or another concerning the report he is to gain control of the big-time vaudeville interests and its picture company holdings. He refuses to discuss the matter, but from a source close to the FBO Company it was learned that negotiations were well under way and that formal announcement of results may be made in a week or two. One source familiar with the pourparlers declared that it was not exactly certain what present negotiations would lead to, but that dickering was on, nevertheless.

FROM FEB. 26, 1938 ISSUE

When Bernhardt Got $7,000 and Benny, Bergen, Burns-Allen $350

PITTSBURGH, Feb. 19.—Consideration of the shuttered Davis Theater as a site for a retail store revived thought that the landmark of the city's vaude heydays was once one of the country's most profitable spots for flesh entertainment. Built by Arch Kennedy for Harry Davis in 1915, the house was a hub for big-time Keith bookings. Leased by Warner Brothers for pix-vaude combo in 1929, the theater went dark a few years ago except for occasional openings.

The files of Eugene Connolly, who handled publicity for the theater, reveal that 14 years ago Edgar Bergen and Jack Benny played the Davis for $350 apiece a week, while opera singer Johanna Gadski pulled down $3,250. Bill Robinson danced two-a-day for $450 a week, while Clark and McCullough netted $2,250 in 1925. Twelve years ago Burns and Allen were worth $350 together weekly.

The roster of acts 10 and more years ago that anticipated Davis bookings was a directory of footlight elite. It included Ina Claire ($2,500 weekly), Joe Cook ($2,500), Alice Brady ($2,500), Herman Timberg ($2,500), El Brendel and wife ($2,000), Florence Reed ($1,650), the Albertina Rasch Ballet ($1,600), Mrs. Leslie Carter ($1,250), Benny Rubin ($1,250), Charlie Ruggles ($1,200), Dr. Rockell ($1,050), Leo Carrillo ($1,000), East and Dumke ($350), William Gaxton, Fannie Brice, Sophie Tucker, Dave Apollon, Belle Baker, the Coogan Family, Ned Wayburn, Douglas Fairbanks, Robert Benchley, James Barton, Richard Bennett, William Farnum, Gus Edwards with George Jessel and Eddie Cantor, and many others still in show business.

Top all-time salary went to Sarah Bernhardt, who received $7,000 for her six days' emoting.

Will Rogers, Chic Sale, Theodore Roberts, Eva Tanguay, Lillian Leitzel, Beverly Bayne and Bernhardt were among the stage immortals who drew pay envelopes from Manager John P. Harris.

When built the 2,000-seat house was planned as a stock company. But despite an opening cast that included William Powell, Edward Everett Horton and Nance O'Neill the rep idea folded in three months.

In 1925 it was the first theater in America to install a cooling system.

In 1927 the theater was sold to the Stanley Company of America and two years later it was taken over by Warner Brothers, who found a pix-flesh policy unprofitable.

"Vaudeville declined," claims Connelly, "because of its prosperity. Business became so good and the auditoriums then built were so large that some of the acts' intimate and informal tricks were missed by too many people who had to sit too far away from the stage."

FROM SEPT. 22, 1923 ISSUE

NAZIMOVA TRIES VAUDEVILLE

FROM JAN. 5, 1924 ISSUE

FANNIE BRICE SAYS A FEW THINGS ABOUT HER NOSE
Provided by the FAMOUS FACIAL SURGEON, DR. HENRY J. SCHIRESON, of Chicago.

"I am making this, statement of my own free will and spending my own money to correct a wrong that I believe has been done a veritable genius in his specialization in surgery, because I personally feel I am indebted to Dr. Henry J. Schireson to that extent for the splendid work that he has done for me in operating on my nose.

"Prior to consulting Dr. Schireson I satisfied myself of his surgical abilities in facial corrections through viewing the physical miracles that he performed for the Brill Sisters, Frankie James, Minnie Allen, Stepanoff the dancer, Senator Murphy, Rubini Sisters, Ben Bard of Bard and Pearl, and Weston and Elaine, all of whom he successfully operated on and who are to my own personal knowledge not only entirely satisfied with his work, but also feel deeply indebted to him for what he accomplished for them.

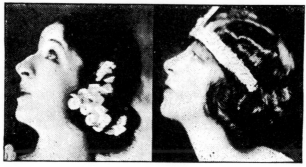

"I believe that the greatest expression of undoubted faith that I have in Dr. Schireson is shown in the fact that I insisted that my brother, Lew Brice, have his nose operated on by him, and now, despite all disclosures regarding the doctor, I am having my second brother undergo an operation as soon as the doctor returns to his offices at the State Lake Bldg. in Chicago.

"My principal reason for making this statement, in addition to public expression of my faith in the doctor, is to assure well-meaning friends, who have been incessantly telephoning me and expressing their condolences—while I thank them for their interest, I wish to assure them that I have no need for expressions of sympathy—that I'm satisfied, and I believe that is sufficient."

(Signed) FANNIE BRICE.

FROM DEC. 30, 1939 ISSUE

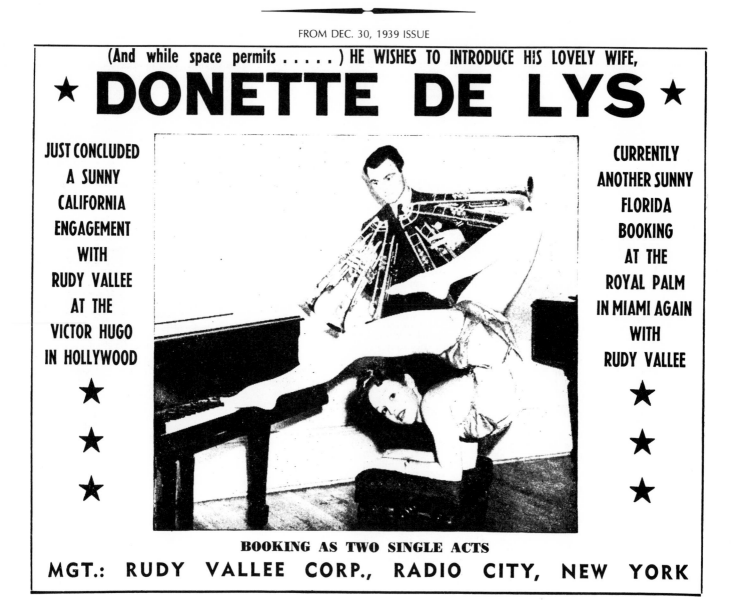

FROM JUNE 23, 1923 ISSUE

EDDIE CANTOR

Reviewed Monday afternoon, June **11**, *at Palace, New York. Style—Black-face comedy and singing. Setting—One. Time—Twenty-three minutes.*

Eddie Cantor is one of the snappiest black-face comedians the writer has ever seen. He enters with spirit, pep, effervescence and gusto. He is unique in a style of his own as he rattles off one joke after another, ad lib., all over the place and sings song after song with a rapidity that would leave many another breathless. He is absolutely sure-fire in his delivery and has few contemporaries who can equal him in putting over a number. He claps his hands and dances around as if he were happy, and obtrudes his remarkably optimistic personality to the furthermost corners of the auditorium. Despite the fact that paging the majority of the staff of any of the New York music publishers would in all probability have resulted in a negation of response, Cantor would more than likely have been just as big a hit without the claque, or the frequent requests from the gentlemen referred to in theatrical argot under a vegetarian nomenclature.

Cantor facetiously referred to the army of "song pluggers" who had met him at the stage entrance with requests to "Give us a break"—and just to give a few of them a break, Eddie put over "How Are You Goin' to Keep Your Mind on Dancing", "Yes, We Have No Bananas", "Oh Gee, Oh Gosh, Oh Golly, I'm in Love", "Be Be Bebe", "Eddie Steady, Steady Eddie", and for encores a special version of "You Know You Belong to Somebody Else" and "Runnin' Wild".

A riot of a hit that will live in the memories of the oldest habitues of the Palace as unique.

FROM APRIL 9, 1927 ISSUE

Geo. N. Burns and Grace Allen
— in —
LAMB CHOPS
By Al Boasberg

Reviewed Monday matinee, March 28, at the Palace Theater, New York. Style —Comedy, chatter and dancing. Setting —In one. Time—Fifteen minutes.

This is an act that should register anywhere. The cross-fire banter is mostly original and delivered with a punch. Miss Allen has a winning personality of the ingenue brand; she takes the middle course of the quiet girl who knows her way around, altho she inclines toward lamb chops as her "piece de resistance". She interprets the role of the sophisticated Dumb Dora—if there could be such a combination—in such manner that Burns gets most of his laughable bits successfully. The girl is a neat stepper and the man has several attributes that help make the act click. The turn opens with the trite "Didn't I see you in Atlantic City?", but diverges from that point into something really interesting in chatter and comedy. For a closing bit Miss Allen brings on a book which she proposes reading—it will take only a matter of 5 or 10 hours—and Burns brings his rug and pillow and reclines on the stage while the girl gets off some wise cracks which Burns sends home with a good wallop. **J. W. R.**

FROM DEC. 17, 1927 ISSUE

Jack Benny
and the
NEW YORKERS

Reviewed Monday evening, December 5, at Fox's Savoy Theater, New York. Style—Band specialties and comedy. Setting—In one and full stage (cyc.). Time —Thirty minutes.

Benny didn't show up well earlier in the season as master of ceremonies for six-act bills, but in this new act, wherein he is joined by the 13 instrumentalists of the defunct Frank Fay night club and a shapely girl specialty dancer, he is at his best. At this show the act was given the best reception accorded an offering since this house opened early last season. Benny is on alone at first, gagging along in his subtle manner and expressing a desire to do an act with a band. While this is going on, strains of music are heard from behind the drop, and when the curtain rises there is a single violinist. This business was good for plenty of laughs. The boys prelude their corking ensemble work by clowning, producing noise when Benny attempts to wield the baton and getting down to earnest work when the fiddler nonchalantly waves his baton. Benny leads the boys thru a corking arrangement of what he calls a Chinese lullaby, containing the familiar strains from *East Is West.* Don Murray, sax. player, is introduced as responsible for arranging most of the unit's selections. John Griffin, tenor, is given two solo assignments, both well received. Benny plays his violin in several bits and the girl is seen in a toe routine and a novelty bit which punctuates the orchestra's rendering of an Indian medley called *Rhapsody in Red* in Benny's announcement. The violinist used in the prolog clowning and a guitarist give a short and snappy duo, and the encore piece, *Annabelle Lee*, is marked by comedy and a singing chorus. Benny's personable clowning is interwoven thruout and is responsible for the wallop carried by the turn. **E. E. S.**

FROM AUG. 18, 1928 ISSUE

Paul Whiteman's Rhythm Boys

Reviewed Thursday evening, August 9, at Keith's 81st Street Theater, New York. Style—Singing. Setting—In one. Time—Twelve minutes.

Harry Barris, Bing Crosby and Al Rinker, billed as the Paul Whiteman Rhythm Boys, have personality, good voices and a way of putting their song numbers over effectively. Enough comedy is introduced to keep things moving rapidly while they are on the stage.

They have the art of rhythm perfected to a stellar degree and add a brilliant touch to the song numbers constituting their repertoire. An act worthy of big-time booking and a distinctive asset to any bill. **J. P.**

FROM DEC. 10, 1927 ISSUE

Fred Allen and Company
— in —
THE DISAPPOINTMENTS OF 1927
Reviewed Tuesday afternoon, November 29, at Moss' Jefferson Theater. Style— Comedy. Setting—In one. Time—Twelve minutes.

This turn is a travesty on the usual run of girl flash acts. Allen does an "I-am-prolog" introduction, with reverse English, a bit of broad burlesque that is a positive ribtickler. The act takes its billing from the fact that none of the big-name turns announced for small-bit parts in Allen's revue are able to appear for one reason or another. Despite the "disappointment", Allen carries on very well with a snappy line of laugh-winning gags, broken now and then with a bit of song. He is assisted by an unbilled girl, who breaks the single routine twice—the first time to engage in a bit of cross-fire, and the second time to display a nifty set of underpinning. It's too bad he doesn't give her more to do, especially after her second appearance. It might serve to roll the hand up a bit more. **E. H.**

FROM NOV. 23, 1929 ISSUE

Bob Hope

Reviewed at Keith's Jefferson. Style— Comedy, singing and dancing. Setting— In one. Time—Sixteen minutes.

Discovered here recently by Lee Stewart when he was with the *WLS Show-boat Revue*, Bob Hope, youthful entertainer, showed great promise to the RKO bookers, who promptly signed him to the circuit for a year, with an option on his services for two years more. And certain it is that they were not wrong in their judgment of him. He stepped into the show-stopping category here with a consistently appealing line of chatter, warbling and eccentric stepping. The way he puts over his material with a winning personality boosts him high in the estimation of his auditors. Capable assistance is given by an unbilled, pretty girl in several laugh-provoking dumb-Dora bits.

Opens with a few preliminary and unoffending gags on the preceding acts, and breaking into *The Pagan Love Song*, getting loud and discordant co-operation from the pit, which pulled many hearty laughs here. A session of rapid-fire chatter which sounded like a reading of a gangsters' catalog, from auto jokes to synthetic Scotch witticisms, socked in heavy on the laugh register. Follows some cross-fire talk with the pretty girl, who retains well but tardily, and for no reason at all steps off with a well-placed punch gag to big laughs. Hope warbles *True Blue Lou*, putting a recitative paraphrase to it with an "Off to Buffalo" finish, which solidified the show stop. Encored with an eccentric soft shoe which he calls *Collegiate Sam*. This revealed him as a versatile footologist. Okeh for the best of them. **C. G. B.**

THE NIGHT CLUB OPERATORS

FROM FEB. 6, 1926 ISSUE

Cabaret and Orchestra Reviews

Fifth Avenue Club, N. Y.

Various men and women of wealth have brought homes, shops and famous institutions to Fifth avenue, and Billy Rose, best known on Broadway for his song-writing proclivities, has given it a night club which upholds the traditions of the avenue in every way. There have been and are clubs and cabarets just off the avenue, but it remained for the enterprising Rose to open one in no less a place than the quarters formerly occupied by the exclusive Criterion Club, directly opposite the University Club and within the very shadow of the Vanderbilt mansions. What's more, Samuel Untermyer lives right next door—so that's that.

Billy Rose has given it (Fifth Avenue) a night club which upholds the traditions of the avenue in every way.

Class and nothing else but, is the keynote from street door to the wall back of the stage. No expense has been spared in any direction to make the club an artistic triumph as to mural and other decorations, surpassing anything ever seen here or abroad. Clara Tice has covered the walls with sketches expressing no less than 45 moods and longing for personal liberty, both from social restraint and clothes—all feminine, of course. As marvelous an array of nymphs as one would wish to see. There is a "perfumed garden" away from the dining and dance room which is presided over by a harem tender, who stands guard at the iron gate. The garden has a blue-sky effect, gold columns, flowers, and neither chairs nor tables, but a lounge built around the walls, plentifully supplied with luxurious cushions. Richard Bennett is credited with the work of art.

Needless to say, the other rooms are well ventilated and unlike the usual night-club atmosphere. There is a stage at one end of the dining room fully equipped as to mechanical and lighting effects, as well as curtains and drops. The show's cast and material reads like another *Sunny* and, comparatively speaking, it is even better. The *Fifth Avenue Follies* runs nearly two hours, every moment of it sparkling with brilliant talent, comedy, singing and dancing.

The cast needs no further words of description. Cecil Cunningham heads the feminine entertainers who, with the rest of the company, offer about 18 numbers.

There is Doris Canfield (she whom K.-A. Vaudeville sought the courts to restrain from leaving the two-a-day), Bert Hanlon, Bobbie Clif, Edith Babson, Richard Bennett (not the legit. actor), Johnnie Claire, Elizabeth Brown and Dan McCarthy; Mabel Olsen and Albert Burke; Adler, Weil and Herman; Dorothy Deeder, Gelen Sheperd, Maryland Jarboe, Ednor Frilling, Mignon Laird and the Fifth Avenue Girls (musical comedy specialty chorus) and the Third Avenue Girls, who do but one number for laughs.

Seymour Felix conceived and staged the show, Richard Rodgers did the music and Lorenz Hart the lyrics (last two of *Dearest Enemy* and *Garrick Gaieties* fame); Harold Atteridge wrote two original comedy sketches, the material being as funny as his Winter Garden show contributions, and Jack Donahue wrote the mammy songs for Hanlon. Harry Archer's Fifth Avenue Club Orchestra, under the direction of Harold Childs, played the show and put it over marvelously well. Not an easy feat. There are seven pieces in the band, which does not shine so strongly as a straight dance combination, but there is a melodious saxophone and the tempo is fair. The chief objection probably is that they do not offer any fancy style in the way of arrangements, which may be negligible to many.

Each number of the show was not only an effort to be different but a distinct hit when reviewed. The finale uncovers the bit of plot, and it seems the chorus was not singing "We are the feature of the show" in vain. The finale was a sensational show in itself, the specialty chorus getting down on the dance floor and vying with the rest of the company in doing solos. This attained almost superhuman momentum and brought forth cheers from all parts of the club. There never was a more talented or better costumed hand-picked bevy of beauties. Prior to the finale was a wow of the first water in the way of the Third Avenue Girls coming out as a surprise following a snappy number by the regular chorus. They did a regulation military drill number as was the case with every burlesque show of about 25 years ago, and the "girls" were all nearly five feet nine tall and weighing well over 160 pounds. The drill was balled up and the skinny member was always caught in the crush.

Cover charge is $5, and considering what the best of any two clubs are offering, the price is cheap. Clubs with similar or $3 couvert are offering an imported dance team, or a straight cabaret floor show, in comparison. This show is different from any other ever seen in town. The food may be safely compared to any club on the avenue, which also goes for the efficient and polite service. Who's Who in the Social Register will all take the place in eventually. It is worth $5 of anybody's money to see the resort and catch the show. Rose has spent in excess of $50,000 in merely bringing the club up to his idea of what it should be—all before opening the

doors. And he states there will be no attempt to dictate what the patrons should wear. However, the bluest blood in town blew in on the opening night and it looked like the diamond horseshoe section of the Metropolitan Opera House. Wiseacres are worried as to how Rose can make it pay, even with the high cover charges. Those who know Rose best, however, also remember him as a youth in a cap who revolutionized the method of payment on songwriter's royalties, managing to get them months in advance, instead of after, from powerful publishers. Which means he will put his club over.   M. H. S.

Rendezvous Cafe, Chicago

With the departure of Van and Schenck the show at the Rendezvous Cafe appears drab. The dinner performance that this reviewer caught consisted of a few song and dance numbers and not much of either to cause the most ardent cafe fan to look up from his ginger ale.

The dinner performance consisted of a few song and dance numbers and not much of either to cause the most ardent cafe fan to look up from his ginger ale.

The cast of this floor show consisted of a tenor, prima donna, soubret and a sister act. The tenor's voice was voluminous, tho not too melodious, but effective for this cabaret. The dancing and singing of the female members was none too bright, possibly because of its being the first show of the evening. The chorus of 10 or 12 appear to splendid advantage, being rather pretty in form and face and well drilled.

The one redeeming feature of this cafe was the splendid playing of Charlie Straight and His Orchestra, a Music Corporation of America attraction. This aggregation has been playing here for about four years and is booked indefinitely, and is really the reason this place attracts a fairly large and classy clientele. It surely isn't the show, the food (and this place is only a seven-cent fare from the stockyards) nor the couvert charge that is slapped on, even tho remaining but 15 minutes beyond the dinner to see the dinner show.
                MAX GALLIN.

FROM APRIL 16, 1938 ISSUE

BILLY ROSE is shown signing the contract with the American Federation of Actors providing for improved working conditions for chorus girls of his Casa Manana night club, New York. The signing ceremonies were the climax of the AFA mass meeting in the Edsion Hotel and made the Casa Manana the first night club using chorus girls to operate 100 per cent union. Left to right are Gladys Feldman Braham, vice-president of the Ziegfeld "Follies" Girls Club; Billy Rose, Ralph Whitehead, AFA executive secretary; Sally Rand, member of the AFA Council and also featured at the Casa Manana, and Harry R. Calkins, chief organizer for the AFA. The girls standing are Casa Manana chorines.

FROM JAN. 2, 1932 ISSUE

TEXAS GUINAN and her "Too Hot for Paris" Gang as they appeared on their transcontinental tour. They are now holding forth at the Planet Mars, Chicago, for what looks like a winter's engagement.

FROM FEB. 26, 1927 ISSUE

Whiteman's Own Club Has Grand Opening

NEW YORK, Feb. 19.—Paul Whiteman opened at his own restaurant, 48th street and Broadway, last night, and played to a packed house, numbering approximately 900 friends, admirers and prohibition agents, at $10 per head. The old Cinderella Ballroom has been renovated at a big expense and is beautifully decorated in black and gold.

A host of prominents of the stage, screen and music circles was on hand to welcome Paul back to Broadway, including Texas Guinan, Charles Chaplin, Mr. and Mrs. Gerson, Ernie Golden, Jack Golden, Jack Robbins, Nat Shilkret, Joe Higgins, L. Wolfe Gilbert, Mr. and Mrs. Joe Neuman, Mr. and Mrs. Charles Lynch, Phil Kornheiser, Julius Tannen, George Piantadosi, Elliott Shapiro, Edgar Leslie, Lew Brown, Lawrence Wright, Billy Stone, Mr. and Mrs. Joe Hillerna, Walter Douglas, Adelaide Ambrose, Harry Warren, Solly Cohen, Arthur Piantadosi, Joseph Gilbert, Cliff Friend, Bobby Crawford and scores of others.

In the way of entertainment, Whiteman offered Les Murrays, dancers, who made quite a hit, and Ruth Eddy, a "blues" singer from Chicago. A tiny colored "kid" in a red uniform danced and strummed a ukulele and got a big hand and many laughs. Jimmy Durante horned into the spotlight, with Paul's permission, and directed the orchestra for a few minutes. The way the boys and girls crowded about Jimmy made one think he was doubling in the home-coming act with Whiteman. Several members of the orchestra entertained from the dance floor and helped to round out a night's entertainment for the crowd.

The opening was a great success for Whiteman, and the ticket committee could have sold twice the number of tickets it did. The consensus of opinion is that Whiteman will clean up a small fortune in his new enterprise.

Texas Guinan's Club Raided

NEW YORK, Feb. 19.—Texas Guinan and three of her employees of her 300 Club, 151 West 54th street, were arrested Wednesday night, during a raid conducted by Federal prohibition officers. Three of the raiding party charged they had visited the club and purchased liquor. The other prisoners were Henry Littwin, 111 West 111th street; John Golden, 1140 President street, Brooklyn, and Charles Miller, 890 Fox street, the Bronx. After spending a short time in jail, Texas and her employees were released on bail. Her case will come up next Wednesday.

THE QUEEN OF THEM ALL

FROM OCT. 3, 1936 ISSUE

GYPSY ROSE LEE

The news of last night's harlequinade might well be cloaked about the aspen body of Miss Gypsy Rose Lee. In their constant quest for hidden talent the Messrs. Shubert reached into burlesque for Miss Lee, where, as an awakener of fundamental passion, she is justifiably rated a flaming sensation.

WORLD-TELEGRAM, 9/15/36, Douglas Gilbert.

★

Immensely entertaining as are both Miss Brice and Mr. Clark, the production boasts other features which are rewarding. Certainly from the visual side (and not only from the side) Gypsy Rose Lee is once the Bernhardt, the Duse and the Joan Crawford of Strip-Tease girls, is given many intellectual verses to sing. But in spite of her efforts as Class Odist, she remains less interesting to the L. L. D. than to the student of anatomy. She has beauty and manner, a walk of which both goddesses and peacocks should be envious, and a philanthropic spirit. What she succeeds in adding to the new "Follies" is essentially the same appeal Miss Baker failed to add to last year's edition.

**NEW YORK POST, 9/15/36,
John Mason Brown.**

ZIEGFELD FOLLIES
Winter Garden, New York

FLOSSIE EVERETTE

"The Little Mamzelle", leading lady-ingenue-soubret, now being featured in Irons & Clamage's "Temptations of 1923" on the Columbia Circuit.

FLOSSIE EVERETTE

Temperamental Artiste Resents Our Review

We first met Flossie Everette some five years ago on an annual outing of the Burlesque Club and conceded her to be one of the most personally attractive girls that we had ever met.

Since then we have reviewed her personal appearance and work in various shows on the Columbia Circuit, likewise in burlesque stock companies, and always commended her for her pleasing personality, talent and ability as a singing and dancing soubret of exceptional vivaciousness and versatility; for Flossie in her fascinating Frenchified facetiousness is irresistible and admirable, and noting that she was to be the featured feminine in Irons &

Clamage's "Temptations of 1923" at the Columbia Theater, New York City, we looked forward with anticipations of delight to seeing Flossie disporting herself about stage as a singing and dancing soubret in all her numbers. But, alas and alack, instead of the Flossie we have known in the past some irresponsible ill-adviser foisted onto us a new and altogether different leading-lady-ingenue Flossie with a Mary Marble bobbed head and ingenue gown, who changed to male attire for a song recital that didn't mean a thing to anybody, least of all to Flossie, who didn't get anything out of it for the reason that the expectant audience, including ourself, missed our former jazz-baby-dancing Flossie with her short-skirt costumes and slender, symmetrical limbs that have always twinkled in dances as Flossie's eyes have twinkled in her flirtations with the audiences.   **NELSE.**

Billy "Beef Trust" Watson Knows What Burlesque Fans Want

New York, June 15.—When Billy "Beef Trust" Watson opened at the Columbia Theater this season his revival of "Krousmeyer's Alley", with its Dutch and Irish heroes, and the alley kids, with brickbats and cats, the censors were against the use of the brickbats and cats, and decided to rule them out of the show, but after careful consideration it was decided to let the mstay, and, as we predicted in our review at the Casino, if they did stay they would in all probability prove a box-office attraction, which the close of the season proved conclusively. Be that as it may, Billy Watson has proved his showmanship and "brought home the bacon" and he has been doing it for over forty years, and saving it instead of wasting it, with the result that Billy "Beef Trust" Watson or, as we personally prefer to title him, Paterson Billy Watson is now enjoying the reapings of his harvest in burlesque, with two theaters, an office building, a hotel and other realty holdings in Paterson that make some of the Wall Streeters appear like pikers. Supplementary to his holdings in Paterson is a beautiful estate that he calls a summer home at Belmar, N. J., where the Watson children (including three hopefuls) enjoy their summers in company with their dad, whose head and social advancements will not interfere with their aspirations for the stage, for all of the Watson kiddies are talented, and the ability that they have shown at charitable affairs preassures a future stage career.

Billy "Beef Trust" Watson (Gee, how he must love that title!) is the same genial fellow that he was when coffee and sinkers were a treat and "beef and" down on the Bowery a feast. But now he is eating lobsters, peaches and cream, riding around in autos when he isn't out on Shark River fishing or in his Paterson office with Dan Guggenheim figuring out his income tax, which runs up into four figures.

LENA DALEY

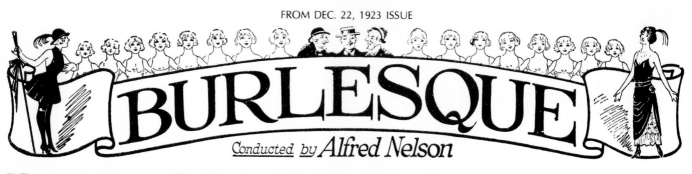

BURLESQUE

Conducted by *Alfred Nelson*

Mutual Shows Polluting Public Morals

Louisville Puts Ban on Lewdness—Police Place Ban on Performance—Little Napoleon of Burlesque on Verge of a "Waterloo"—Scribner Hailed as a Salvationist

New York, Dec. 11.—The chief topic of conversation among burlesquers on Columbia Corner this morning was what effect the stopping of the performance of "Step Lively Girls" at the Gayety Theater, Louisville, Ky., Sunday night will have on burlesque in general.

Reports from Louisville indicate that Sam Reider, manager of the Gayety Theater, playing shows booked by the Mutual Burlesque Association of this city, in an effort to increase receipts, has gone over the top with dirty shows; at least this is the claim of a member of the Police Department, who has been a regular attendant at the Sunday shows for some time past, and his reports, confirmed by his superiors, resulted in a ban being placed on the performance Sunday night, when Captain Larkin, chief of detectives, and Maj. Ben F. Griffin, assistant chief of police, headed a party of twenty-five detectives and patrolmen in taking charge of the theater and preventing a performance by having the patrol wagon backed up in front of the house.

Capt. Larkin attended a performance Sunday afternoon, and what he says he saw and heard decided him in stopping the night performance.

No one but employees of the house were permitted to enter the theater, and when the company, in twos and threes, arrived for the night performance they were ordered away from the theater by the police.

We have reviewed many Mutual Circuit shows since the opening of the season at the Star Theater, Brooklyn, N. Y., and Julius Michaels' "Step Lively Girls" was, for the most part, clean, altho we did have occasion to criticize the soubret on the runway for her "grind", but this was eliminated from the show and reports from houses on the circuit indicated that it was one of the cleanest shows among the Mutuals, therefore it is hard to understand why it became sufficiently indecent to warrant the police in putting the ban on it in Louisville. It would not have been surprising if it had been some one of the other Mutual shows that are notorious for their filth-slinging self-termed comics.

MIDGIE GIBBONS

The Passing of Billy Minsky

LAST week a colorful figure in New York burlesque circles died. Conservative daily papers, such as The Herald-Tribune, devoted an entire column to his obituary. Marcus Loew, E. F. Albee and other noted leaders in the theatrical industry did not command any more space in the local papers of the day, despite their having amassed a vast fortune as well as having been instrumental in founding nation-wide theater circuits. Billy Minsky had a few houses around New York, and some of these were not above reproach of merchant and other organizations. What was there about Billy Minsky that drew him such full attention when he passed on?

First and last he was a showman. When he put burlesque into the National Winter Garden, down on the East Side, the whole city knew about it. Park avenue trade filtered pass the turnstile. He never failed to take full advantage of every publicity angle. When a bystander inquired as to why all the hundreds of electric lights still lit on signs long after the house was sold out, and why it was necessary on an out-of-the-way street where few transients would notice it, he gleefully replied that the mere fact that he was being asked was sufficient reason. He wanted people to wonder, ask questions and talk about it. His name became synonymous with anything staged in torrid style.

Burlesque had been uptown in the Times Square sector, playing the Columbia Theater for years. Yet when he took over a house on 42d street, he staged an opening like a Hollywood premiere. Everybody forgot burlesque was playing five blocks north up Broadway. His was the reign that started regulation-sized chorus girls in shows in place of the beef trusts. No name in theatricals was too good for burlesque if the salary fitted into his scheme of things. He surrounded fast-fading burly entertainment with a new glamour—in fact, gave new life as well as impetus to many independent stock stands still running.

AN OUTDOOR SHOWMAN'S GOODBYE

FROM OCT. 24, 1931 ISSUE

THOMAS ALVA EDISON

With tear-dimmed eyes and heads bowed in sorrow, the whole world mourns your fading out of this life's picture. The world to which you brought perpetual sunshine is darkened, as your passing has cast a shadow over all the earth, from the Siberian wastes to the banks of the Zambesi.

Words fail to express the priceless honor you bestowed upon me when you first called me your friend. The memory of the hours spent in your distinguished company as we wandered down among the wagons and in to the shows and on the rides, or as we sat and confabbed in my office on the midway—while I reveled in the majesty, sublimity and graudeur of your presence—can never, never, be effaced from my mind. You, Tom Edison, whose beautiful life seemed to be reflected in the halo surrounding you and which apparently awed all who approached you.

You took the "blossoms from the lovely stars and the forget-me-nots of the angels" and converted the earth's darkness into light. Savage tribes, with no language but a gibberish confusion of tongues, have been known to shout "Edison" at the sign of a flashlight.

Your earthly bulb has burned out, but the memory of your dear self and your achievements is imperishable. The nobility of your life "as chaste as unsunn'd snow" has clothed the name of Edison with a luster that will brilliantly shine thru all the centuries to come. Kings, presidents and others of today's notables will long be forgotten when the memory of you will still reign as the greatest benefactor of all mankind.

Your discoveries are giving employment to millions thruout the world. Just as it is impossible to paint the lily or as it is impossible to add luster to the Koh-i-noor—so it is impossible for my feeble pen to paint the Edison that I knew. In my humble opinion America has produced three really great men—Washington, Lincoln and Edison—and now, my dear friend, you with them have solved the biggest of all problems.

Undaunted by the lure of lucre, disdaining all mercenary affiliations, and living a life, pure and wholesome, with never a whisper of scandal, you have accomplished untold benefits for mankind and endeared your memory in the hearts of the highest and lowliest of this earth.

We of the great outdoor show world offer our sincere condolence to Mrs. Edison in the passing of her glorious husband. Lovely, charming and fascinating, Mrs. Edison has been the great inventor's pal, counselor and guide (altho always retiring to the background in the fierce light of publicity) for more than 40 years, and as a hostess at the Edison estate in Florida she made me feel that I was one of the family.

I shall cherish and revere until my last breath Mr. Edison's autographed photograph: "To our good friend Hilliar," which stands on my desk, draped in crepe today as I record these few words of eulogy to the memory of the world's greatest genius who called me friend.

"To live in hearts we leave behind is not to die"

WILLIAM J. HILLIAR.

UPS AND DOWNS IN THE CIRCUS

FROM APRIL 19, 1924 ISSUE

Time Tests All Things and Ringling Bros. and Barnum & Bailey Has Stood the Test of 90 Years

THE RINGLING BROS. WORLD'S GREATEST SHOWS with a record of 40 years behind it.

THE BARNUM & BAILEY GREATEST SHOW ON EARTH with its record of 50 years.

Severally and jointly they have during this period of time entertained

EIGHT HUNDRED MILLION PEOPLE

being a conservative estimate of the grand total of their combined and world-wide audiences.

There must be a reason.   There IS a reason.   It is here set down in a single sentence:

RINGLING BROS. and BARNUM & BAILEY COMBINED IS NOW AND EVER HAS BEEN THE WORLD'S GREATEST AMUSEMENT INSTITUTION

While you are reading this, thousands upon thousands are daily thronging Madison Square Garden, New York. For it is there—in the Biggest City in the World—that the Biggest Circus on Earth annually opens its season.   It, alone, exhibits in the great metropolis.

IT, ALONE, IS THE ONE BIG SHOW

Beginning its 1924 tour under canvas
at Brooklyn, April 28th

Traveling thence and elsewhere throughout America

**ON TRAINS MORE THAN ONE AND ONE-THIRD MILES LONG
LOADED WITH 10,000 WONDERS FROM EVERY LAND**

FROM NOV. 13, 1937 ISSUE

'BIG SHOW" IN OLD HANDS
Ringlings Regain Management
Of Ringling - Barnum Circus

●

Mortgage for $800,000 held by Allied Owners, Inc., is satisfied and mortgagors released from further supervision—several changes in board of directors hinted

●

SARASOTA, Fla., Nov. 6.—The operation and management of the Ringling Bros. and Barnum & Bailey Combined Circus reverted to the estate of John Ringling at a meeting in Washington, D. C., on Thursday when Allied Owners, Inc., holder of a mortgage against the Ringling ownership of the circus, was paid off and the mortgage, already paid down to $800,000, satisfied. Among those at the meeting were representatives of various interested corporations and John Ringling North and Henry Ringling (Buddy) North, nephews of John Ringling. The $800,000

was paid off thru a refinancing program and also thru co-operation of the government, which held large bond and stock assets of the Ringlings. A new note and mortgage has been issued to the Manufacturers Trust Company of New York.

With the mortgage being satisfied, Allied Owners, Inc., was released from all further supervision and management of the circus. The mortgage was originally held by the old Prudence Company. It was given by John Ringling when he purchased from Mugivan & Bowers a number of large circuses some years ago for incorporation under a master company.

FROM FEB. 26, 1938 ISSUE

North Bitten By Huge Ape At Sarasota

SARASOTA, Feb. 19.—John Ringling North sustained a painfully injured arm at quarters here last Tuesday when he came too close to the cage of Gargantua the Great, new Ringling gorilla, and was seized and bitten by the huge ape.

The gorilla grabbed North's arm, pulled it thru the bars of his cage and bit his victim three times on the wrist and forearm before Keeper Richard Kroener was able to club the beast away from the circus executive.

After first-aid cauterization to the ugly tooth wounds by Dr. Joe Bergin, show physician, North was rushed to the Joseph Halton Hospital for further treatment and observation.

Following a telephone consultation with Prof. Robert M. Yerkes, head of the Yale University department of primate biology and foremost American authority on anthropoids, Dr. Halton injected 1,500 units of anti-tetanus serum in North's arm to check any possible lockjaw infection.

North was able to go to his home but was kept under medical observation for any sign of infection. Circus men recalled that it was similar wild-animal bites that caused the death of John H. Sparks.

FROM FEB. 10, 1934 ISSUE

TOM MIX patting an elephant as he conversed with Sam B. Dill at the quarters of the Dill-Mix Circus and Roundup at Dallas, Tex.

PARKS, FAIRS, CARNIVALS RUN THE ENTERTAINMENT GAMUT

FROM DEC. 30, 1939 ISSUE

Bee Kyle Universal Titlist

FINAL STANDING

Pos. Name	Points
1. Bee Kyle	32,728
2. Mabel Stark	26,071
3. Four Aerial Apollos	22,363
4. Four Jacks (Aces)	20,190
5. Flying Valentinos (George Valentine)	16,007
6. Harold Barnes	14,874
7. Great Wilno	14,833
8. Dime Wilson	13,992
9. Marjorie Bailey	13,346
10. Flying Behees	12,412
11. Frank Shepherd	12,384
12. Flying Valentines (Roy G. Valentine)	12,207
13. Mickey King	11,116
14. Flying Fishers	10,879
15. Zacchini Bros.	10,832
16. Hubert Castle	10,486
17. Ollie Hager	10,458
18. Harry Clark	10,423
19. Frank Cushing	10,320
20. Marlo and LeFors	10,297
21. Hazel Cotter	10,233
22. Jack Starry	9,897
23. Blondin Rellim Troupe	9,827
24. The Stratosphere Man	9,812
25. Dave Geyer	9,615
26. Emmett Kelly	9,503
27. Shorty Flemm	9,408
28. Rita and Dunn	9,399
29. *Lionel Legare	9,374
30. Terrell Jacobs	9,341
31. Schaller's Four Queens	8,198
32. Connors Trio	7,584
33. Sol Solomon	7,441
34. Clyde Beatty	7,354
35. Speedy Phoenix	7,242
36. Dorothy Herbert	6,986
37. Peerless Potters	6,959
38. Lucky Teter	6,799
39. Roman Proske	6,759
40. Ethel Jennier	6,552
41. Fearless Flyers	6,545
42. English Macks	6,485
43. Jamie Graves	6,285
44. Cheerful Gardner	6,266
45. Mary Erdlitz	6,241
46. Mary Gordon	6,220
47. Hunt Sisters	6,206
48. Three Milos	6,164
49. Captain Mars	6,120
50. Great Wallendas	6,073

*Deceased (See Rolling Globe Class for Details)

*   *   *

Diver Rules 3,756 Artists for Whom Ballots Were Cast—Mabel Stark Takes No. 2 Spot and Wild Animal Crown—Apollos Win High Act Title and Jacks Excel in First-Place Votes

●

VALENTINOS, BARNES BEAT OTHERS TO TAPE

●

Cushing Is Thriller King, Bailey High Pole Queen—Wilno, Behees, Shepherd, Blondins, King, Selden, Marlo and LeFors, Yacopis Are Best in Their Brackets

FINAL RESULTS

The Billboard

FAVORITE OUTDOOR PERFORMER CONTEST

With an Album of Artists Declared Universal and Divisional Titleholders

FROM DEC. 30, 1939 ISSUE

BEE KYLE

1st Place: All Divisions
(Universal Title)

Automatic Winner: High Diving Title

Bee Kyle started professional diving at the age of 12, having done her first plunging from the cliffs of the old St. Croix River in Eastern Maine, neighboring on her birthplace in Calais. She has worked for Diamond Lew Walker, Harry Dore, C. A. Wortham, Johnny J. Jones and W. H. (Bill) Rice on water shows. Her manager is her husband, W. B. Wecker, of St. Louis. Her engagements have taken her as far as Japan, Australia and the Philippine Islands. Miss Kyle's top trick is a back somersault from a 100-foot ladder into a tank of fire. Since 1927 hers has been a standard free act and this year she took out her own act, appearing on Gold Medal Shows and also at parks and fairs.

STANDING

1, Bee Kyle (automatic winner), 32,-728; 2, Sol Solomon, winner Male Division, 7,441; 3, Speedy Phoenix, winner Net Diving Class, 7,242; 4, Jamie Graves, 6,285; 5, Peggy Hale, 3,597; 6, Charles Sauterberg, 3,588.

MABEL STARK

Winner: Wild Animal Training Division
2d Place: Universal Title

Mabel Stark, who is from Princeton, Ky., is one of the best known trainers in the world. She was featured on the Al G. Barnes Circus for 11 years running, 1911-1921, then for seven years, 1930-1936, and again in 1938 when the Barnes title was merged with that of Sells-Floto. During the period 1922-1927 she was on the Ringling-Barnum show, spent the season of '28 with John Robinson, the next year with Sells-Floto. In 1937 she joined John T. Benson's Wild Animal Farm. A dozen years ago she was engaged by the Bertram Mills Olympia Circus in London. The wild animals used in her act were raised and broken by Louis Goebel, of Goebel's Lion Farm, on the West Coast. Miss Stark was a feature of C. F. Zeiger United Shows the past season.

Terrell Jacobs

STANDING

1, Mabel Stark, 26,071; 2, Terrell Jacobs, winner Male Division, 9,341; 3, Clyde Beatty, 7,534; 4, Capt. Roman Proske, 6,759; 5, Bert Nelson, 5,938; 6, Dolly Jacobs, 3,062.

4 AERIAL APOLLOS

Winner: High Rigging Division

3d Place: Universal Title

Four Aerial Apollos line up with Jean LeMarr, of Kansas City; Bill Brick, San Francisco; Robert Perry, Denver, and Jack Brick, owner of the act, who was born in Ireland. Intact since 1937, contingent works on a 120-foot double ladder and features hand balancing, including one-arm handstand, routines on traps and rings, a breakaway and a 20-foot swaying perch and flagpole.

FROM SEPT. 11, 1937 ISSUE

FROM DEC. 22, 1917 ISSUE

WHEELS THEN AND NOW, 1897 AND 1937. One on left is the first wheel to be operated at the Old Home-Coming Celebration, Lebanon, Kan., and on right is the last, a Big Eli Wheel No. 5, operated by W. E. West, of W. E. West Motorized Shows, who is shown on the right standing by the ticket box. Note the interested spectators and riders, locations on streets, the difference in mechanical construction and mentally that "Ferris" Wheels have retained their popularity for 40 years in this community as attested above.

FROM JUNE 1, 1935 ISSUE

LEFT TO RIGHT: Mrs. Emma Parker, mother of the late Bonnie Parker; J. W. Dillinger, father of the late John Dillinger; Mrs. Henrietta Barrow, mother of the late Clyde Barrow, all with Mrs. John R. Castle's "Crime Does Not Pay" attraction with United Shows of America.

OLD FORMS AND NEW VOGUES

FROM FEB. 21, 1920 ISSUE

The MOST PLEASING, SATISFYING and SURPRISING of ALL MINSTRELS

HARVEY'S GREATER MINSTRELS

The Biggest and Best Colored Show ever organized. Billed in circus style, managed by circus men and moves with circus pep. Presenting a charming Octoroon Chorus and an Olio of highest class Vaudeville superior to that offered by any minstrel, white or black.

The MANAGERS' ASSOCIATION'S REPORTS all testify without a single exception to the unusual merit of this attraction, that it pleases the most refined of white audiences and is appropriate for any theatre in any city. The *Only Colored Show* being booked by KLAW & ERLANGER, New Amsterdam Theatre Bldg., New York.

We are always ready to hear from ambitious, clever, sober, energetic, genuine minstrel people who will prove to be worthy of recognition by this, the Greatest of Colored Attractions, and who will appreciate the accommodations afforded by our two steel Palace Stateroom Pullman Cars and good treatment. We never close, and show theatres exclusively.

Address R. M. HARVEY, Manager, as per route.

FROM SEPT. 13, 1919 ISSUE

INTERESTING CHAUTAUQUA FIGURES

1 **PURPOSE**—The best interests of all the people, all the time.
2 **CONTINENTS** have chautauquas, Australia and North America.
4 **COUNTRIES** have chautauquas, Alaska, Australia, Canada and United States.
48 **STATES** in the Union have chautauquas—every State.
20,000 **TOWNS** have chautauquas and lyceum courses.
500,000 **GUARANTORS** underwrite chautauquas and lyceum courses.
8,500,000 **PEOPLE** are season ticket holders.
20,000,000 **PEOPLE** attend chautauquas and lyceum courses every year.

Interesting Figures About the Chautauqua Association of Pennsylvania

In 1912 we had 41 chautauqua towns in 4 States.
In 1913 we had 103 chautauqua towns in 7 States.
In 1914 we had 218 chautauqua towns in 13 States.
In 1915 we had 250 chautauqua towns in 13 States.
In 1916 we had 290 chautauqua towns in 13 States.
In 1917 we had 387 chautauqua towns in 13 States.
In 1918 we had 420 chautauqua towns in 14 States and Canada.
In 1919 we had 460 chautauqua towns in 15 States and Canada.
In 1919 we had 175 music festivals in 6 States.

The CHAUTAUQUA ASSOCIATION
SWARTHMORE, PA.

FROM DEC. 26, 1936 ISSUE

I wish to thank all the individuals and magic societies that joined in the final Houdini seance that encircled the world October 31, 1936.

Those names and records will live forever in the Houdini room in the Congressional Library at Washington, D. C.

Since the failure of the ten-year test and the seventeen seances held simultaneously in all parts of the world with Hollywood, it is my opinion that all concerned have struck a mighty world-wide blow at superstition.

MRS. HARRY HOUDINI

EDW SAINT, Director
Final Houdini Seance.

CRYSTAL WILLIAMS

Miss Williams is now in her sixth season as leading lady with Richards, "The Wizard," and his big mystery show, which is the largest, most costly and elaborate popular priced production of its kind in America.

How many of our readers remember seeing the exhibitions given years ago by S. S. Baldwin the White Mahatma? Perhaps some of the newcomers in magic have never heard his name, but Baldwin was the most traveled artist of his time, and created a world-wide sensation twenty-five years ago with his mental work or mind reading. It is conceded by searchers after truth regarding the origin of many occult feats that Baldwin was the inventor and originator of the style of mind reading practiced by hundreds today, he first having presented it in 1873 in New Orleans. Baldwin, now in retirement, is living quietly in San Francisco, with his daughter, Shadow, a very accomplished medium. Once in a while the Doctor is persuaded to give a demonstration of his powers for some private affair.

We were honored by being invited to spend an evening at the Doctor's home, and enjoyed beyond expression every minute of the three hours we were in his company. He has a scrap book, probably unequaled in the world, filled with newspaper clippings and photos of every town he has ever visited. After Miss Baldwin had entertained us with music and song, Mr. Baldwin bewildered us with just a little of his mental work or Psychometric Picturations, and we can safely say that we have never before quite realized the possibilities of this style of intuitional delineations.

Dr. Baldwin is going back into the business. He feels that a wave of occultism and magic is sweeping the world, and that the time is now ripe for him to return to the footlights. And what a merry chase he will lead some of the mind readers of today.

† † †

Walter Baker was featured at the Hippodrome in Chicago, doing a new act that is making a hit with magicians as well as laymen, but a bigger hit still with the agents, for they have him booked solidly away up till

(Continued on page 80)

HOUDINI · **THURSTON** · **HARRY KELLAR** · **MALINI** · **GOLDIN**

In the above group of photographs are shown the leaders in the magical world of today: Harry Kellar, dean of American magicians, and idolized by the magical fraternity of the world; Houdini—his very latest picture—showing how he looked when Famous Players-Lasky told him they wanted him to make another movie; Howard Thurston, the Master Magician, now enjoying the most successful season of his entire career, after putting magic on Broadway at $2 per; Malini, the king of drawing room prestidigitateurs, just returned from the Orient, and Horace Goldin, the world toured illusionist, who has taken magic into every crevice and corner of this earth.

FROM AUG. 1, 1925 ISSUE

The Billboard's
FREE SHOPPING SERVICE

A Gown From the Vanities
And a Charleston Costume
For the Peppy Steppet

FROM APRIL 11, 1925 ISSUE

In response to numerous requests for particulars concerning the Dancelette step-in girdle, mentioned in this column last week, the above sketch of this article is shown. It was designed to emphasize the slim silhouet, first by eliminating diaphragm and hip bulging and second by reducing the number of undergarments worn usually. Its maker also tells us that it meets the present need of the woman who, after going corsetless for several years, finds the lines of her figure aging, especially at the hips. In this dancing age, you know, wobbly hips are, to say the least, considered vulgar.

You step into the Dancelette as you would step into a teddy. You may still roll your stockings, for the garment has no garters attached and you will feel just as comfortable in it as when you were corsetless, as it has no boning. Made of brocade, with insets of strong rubber webbing at the hips, $3.50; in Rayon silk, with rubber webbing, $5.

As buck and wing dancing gains in speed and versatility the agile dancer substitutes for the heavy fiber sole commonly worn a new patented aluminum tip which is fastened to the sole of the shoe at the toe. Altho small and light in weight it may be depended on for a good volume of sound. Worn by some of the most skilled exhibition dancers in Broadway shows. They are but $1.65—a decided saving when one considers that fiber soles cost at least $3. For both men's and women's shoes.

Oh, Charleston steppers, every clever little step will gather added audacity if you wear a gay Charleston costume like the one illustrated, for instance. The designer had just added the finishing touch to this sketch when we walked in and bore it off in triumph as a new wrinkle in costuming for our readers. To begin with it costs but $35. It is made in either red or white baronet satin, the vest, collar and band of black velvet. Rhinestone buttons add a bright touch.

BALLROOM ACTS TAKING FIRST PLACE AS POPULAR OFFERING

Classy Dancers With or Without Own Music From Night Clubs in Greatest Demand Since Vogue of Castles---Replacing Straight Orchestra Craze

NEW YORK, April 6.—Vaudeville bookers and patrons seem to have decided on one definite type of entertainment to succeed the rapidly dying craze for orchestra and jazz bands, with the result that ballroom dancers, particularly from night clubs and productions, are in demand.   Not since the Castles were last seen together in vaudeville have as many ballroom dancers been playing the local theaters, or as many negotiating for bookings.   Last week, at the Hippodrome alone, were two ballroom dance acts on the same bill, being Adelaide and Hughes and Addison Fowler and Florence Tamara.

The popularity of these dancers at their various night clubs is largely responsible for the increasing vogue of that type of entertainment in vaudeville. Clifton Webb and Mary Hay, from Ciro's, scored such a hit at the Palace last week that they have been held over for the current week. The De Marcos, who were formerly in vaudeville in unimportant spots, ofttimes opening bills, returned to vaudeville after playing productions and this week are one of the big features at the Hippodrome. Sielle and Mills returned to the big time with a new dance, this time assisted by the Knickerbocker Grill Orchestra. Moss and Fontana, from the Club Mirador, are going into vaudeville shortly. Cortez and Peggy, from the Trocadero

Club, are also candidates for the two-a-day. Edythe Baker, who has won a big reputation as a pianist, is now one of the recognized ballroom dancers of the city, and is the partner of William Reardon at the Club Lido. She will be seen with him in a vaudeville act, it is reported. Reardon was formerly dancing partner to Irene Castle.

Most of these dancers carry orchestras with them, but merely as a background. The orchestras are generally the same ones that play for them at the various clubs in which they appear. Incidentally, those playing at clubs who are going into vaudeville are permitted to double during their vaudeville engagements to the club from which they come, altho the rule regarding artistes who originally play vaudeville and wish to double in a club at the same time, is strictly adhered to.

A BREAKTHROUGH FOR BLACKS

FROM JUNE 4, 1921 ISSUE

NOBLE SISSLE AND EUBIE BLAKE

Who wrote the music for the "Shuffle Along" show and are working in the cast as co-stars with Miller and Lyles. Reviewed in musical comedy section of this issue.

FROM DEC. 13, 1924 ISSUE

"FROM DIXIE TO BROADWAY"

WM. VODERY
MUSICAL DIRECTOR

FLORENCE MILLS
STAR

DANNY SMALL
JUVENILE LEAD

SHELTON BROOKS
COMEDIAN

KOVAN & THOMPSON
DANCERS

HAMTREE HARRINGTON
COMEDIAN

Florence Mills, star of "From Dixie to Broadway", and some of the members of the company whose offering has been receiving the unanimous praise of the critics. It is the first colored attraction ever to command a $3 top price of admission. Now playing at the Broadhurst Theater, New York.

293

FROM AUG. 6, 1921 ISSUE

A Survey Of The Negro In American Life And In The Amusement World
By J.A. Jackson

THE LAFAYETTE PLAYERS

And Their Development of the Drama Among Negroes

By LESTER A. WALTON
(General Manager Quality Amusement Company and For Ten Years Dramatic Critic of New York Age)

It is beginning to dawn on the American public that the Negro, in a none too distant future, is destined to command respectful attention and win favorable consideration in the realm of drama. In the past the theatergoer has visualized the Negro on the stage only in comedy, dance and song, and colored comedians have made enviable reputations as exponents of buffoonery; but today there is every indication that the Negro is soon to invade the legitimate field.

The pronounced success scored last season on Broadway by Charles S. Gilpin in "The Emperor Jones" did enough to bring the public to the realization that the time has come to regard the Negro as a dramatic potentiality.

The expression is often heard: "There is nothing new under the sun." This certainly is true as far as relating to the Negro in drama. For six years colored actors, namely, the Lafayette Players, have been appearing with great success in stock at the Lafayette Theater, Seventh avenue, between 131st and 132nd streets, New York. These performances have been attended by white theatrical managers and actors of note, who have had nothing but praise for the efforts of the colored artists.

Robert Hilliard expressed himself "especially pleased" and was in a complimentary mood after witnessing a performance by the Lafayette Players of "A Fool There Was," and so enthused was Miss Marjorie Rambeau at the close of the presentation of "Eyes of Youth" by the colored actors that she went back stage and uttered words of commendation with such earnestness that the Lafayette Players were as deeply impressed with Miss Rambeau's talk as she was with their acting. Sir Beerbohm Tree, the noted English actor, also has been a visitor to the Lafayette Theater to get an idea of what the colored American is doing for the stage. He, too, left Harlem profuse in encomiums as to the Negro's ability as an actor and entertainer.

It has been the mission of the Quality Amusement Corporation, owned and operated by colored Americans, to present the Lafayette Players during the season outside of New York. Companies also have been appearing with success in Philadelphia, Washington, D. C., Chicago, Norfolk and Newport News. Baltimore, where the corporation is erecting a theater to cost nearly half a million dollars; Richmond, Pittsburg and Indianapolis are seen to be included in the Quality Circuit.

The Quality Amusement Corporation has been owned by colored capitalists since the summer of 1919, and Negroes of this country generally regarded this big theatrical project as the most comprehensive and constructive inaugurated by the race since the period of rehabilitation. The fact that some of the leading colored financiers in America were behind the project— E. O. Brown, of Brown & Stevens, bankers, Philadelphia, and L. E. Williams, president of the Wage Earners' Savings Bank, Savannah, insured confidence, that has been manifest in all sections.

Many artists have passed thru the Lafayette as players for varying lengths of service; some to greater rewards, and even distinction, the experience acquired no doubt being of material assistance to their progress.

Chas. S. Gilpin, who as "The Emperor Jones" at the Provincetown, the Selwyn and the Princess theaters, New York, acquired more publicity than ever before was bestowed on an actor in a single season, has been a Lafayette player.

> For six years colored actors, namely the Lafayette Players, have been appearing with great success in stock at the Lafayette Theatre, Seventh Avenue, between 131st and 132nd streets, New York.

Miss Anita Bush, a clever little artist, who was an enthusiastic pioneer in the dramatic field, was another.

Clarence E. Muse, now a director for a large motion film producing company, was another. The late Tom Brown was an early member of the company and was a finished character actor, measured by any standard. Walker Thompson played many leading parts while with the company. Lawrence Chenault graduated from the players to the motion picture field, leaving happy recollections with an audience that is glad to see him on his occasional return.

Abbie Mitchell is today as great a success in the London halls as she was with the players; She is a vocalist who can act. Charles Olden was, and is, a finished actor, as is Mrs. Mattie Wilkes, now in the Broadway "Shuffle Along." In the present organizations are four groups of artists, some of whom exhibit all of the well-rounded artistry that marks the experienced professional.

Barrington Carter, who made a Broadway debut in the deservedly unfortunate "Goat Alley," is a Lafayette product. He was the redeeming feature of the show, according to critics.

Mrs. Chas. J. Anderson, Miss Cleo Desmond, Miss Evelyn Ellis and Miss Edna Thomas are four entirely different types of capable leading ladies.

Andrew Bishop, Babe Townsend, Arthur Simmons, J. Lawrence Criner and Sydney Kirkpatrick are leads whose names have box office value.

Inez Clough, Laura Bowman, Susie Sutton, Elizabeth Williams, Alice Gorgas and Elizabeth Jackson, of the present units, are meritorious delineators of character parts. Arthur Ray, Harry Plater, A. B. DeComithere, Lionel Monagas, Richard Gregg, H. L. Pryor and J. F. Mores are others. David K. Brisbane, a young and quietly serious Negro, is the assistant director who has successfully handled the multitude of details essential to the productions offered. Sam Craig, in charge of the stage, has probably built, with less assistance, more stage effects than have many stage managers better known to fame.

While the Lafayette Theater is known as "the home of the Lafayette" to players, the Dunbar Theater, Philadelphia, which was opened in January, 1920, and created at a cost of over $400,000, is the largest house on the circuit. It is one of the finest houses in the Quaker City.

ANITA BUSH

FROM AUG. 6, 1921 ISSUE

THE NEGRO

And the Film Industry—Some Actors and Producers

By CLARENCE E. MUSE

At last the Colored Motion Picture game has been organized. The producing concerns have definite plans and are working on a schedule, releasing regularly. The distributing end of the industry is well prepared to market the products while the exhibitors are fully convinced that colored pictures for colored patrons are the best attractions they can secure.

To date there are over a dozen corporations that are producing pictures, specially for the colored trade, namely The Micheaux Film Corporation, Reel Productions, The Blue Ribbons Pictures, Inc.; The Delsarte Film Corporation, Bookertee Film Company, Norman Film Co., Democracy Film Co., Monumental Pictures Corporation, with a weekly release of Negro news; Maurice Film Co., Royal Garden Film Co., Lincoln Motion Picture Co., Chas. Holman White Film Co., Dunbar Theatrical and Amusement Co., Louis DeBulger Co., the Peacock Film Co. and others the writer does not know enough about to mention. Nine of these are capitalized by Negroes.

On first glance one might think this is a large number of concerns, or the field is crowded. The fact that there are over six hundred theaters in this country that cater to colored people makes it very clear that it will require between 3,600 and 4,200 pictures per week to supply the first-class houses with a colored feature each day. Of course, it will be fully five to ten years before the producing concerns can provide such a large output; however, the future prospects are assured, in that the demand is greater than the output.

The most important requirement in the producer's program, to my mind, is the quality of this product. By this I mean that every element of picture making must receive judicial attention. Perhaps we can amplify by discussing the principle. First the story, the scenario, camera technique, director, action, actors, interior and exterior atmospheres, together with elasticity of funds.

The story must be clean, entertaining, devoid of odorous propaganda and above all a Negro tale, with Negro heroes and heroines in a natural atmosphere.

Apart from the story, is the scenario or continuity. The sequence of the scenes must be natural, easy to follow, allowing the theme to flow in one continuous stream so that the most ordinary patron can enjoy the author's intention without straining the imagination, or with pain await the arrival of poorly written titles to explain the action. Short, snappy titles with carefully studied sequence are a guarantee that the continuity is par excellence.

In speaking of the camera technique; it will surprise a great many producers to know that the colored artist is the best screen type obtainable; the darker the skin tone the greater the objective; hence, in the photograph when finished instead of a ghostly white against a dark background, you will have delightful studies in all shades blending harmoniously from black to a soft white tint. This cannot be accomplished with cheap, ordinary camera men, or poor laboratory work, but there are some concerns, to my knowledge, which have proven that it is an advance to photographic art to study the black face, and its possibilities.

The director is one of the most important executives in this great game of picture making. In handling colored artists, he must thru experience learn to feel with the Negro.

> **Any people who have suffered because of oppression hold the secret of their lives and aspirations close to their hearts ... the Negro can play the entire gamut of emotions with perfect ease.**

Any people who have suffered because of oppression hold the secrets of their lives and aspirations close to their hearts. Then they wonder when it is said that 75 per cent of the Negro race are natural born actors, and when aroused can play the entire gamut of the emotions with perfect ease. Their whole existence has been one of continuous acting.

The "pent-up" things within the soul, instead of rushing out, seem to mark time until a well ordered crescendo is reached without guidance. Such is the wealth of material among Negro actors. Select your cast with a fine regard for types.

A very striking evidence that the Negro actor in pictures is a success is the long list of popular artists already on the screen: Messrs. Harold C. Jackson, J. Kenneth Goodman, Lawrence Chenault, Jim Burroughs, Walker Thompson, Abe De Cemathiere, Eddie Gray, Francis Perkins, Eddie Brown, Alfred Dawning, Kelly Thompson, Leon Williams, Harry Haynes, Richard Abrams, Dink Stewart, William Manlif, Arthur Ames, Robert Billeups, Will A. Cook. Among the ladies, Iris Hall, Mabel Young, Susie Sutton Brown, Evelyn Preer, Mattie Wilkes, May Frances, Albe Lessens, Ruby Mason, Edith Payne, Ursals Hill, Mrs. Harper Brown, Elizabeth Boyer, Bettie Stewart and many others.

Among those whose work has been favorably reviewed as members of an otherwise all white cast are: Huel Brooks, Thurston Brooks, Will H. Herman, Howard Palmer, McHenry, Happy Bud Joyner, George Reed, Thurston Briggs, John Williams, Zack Williams, J. Wesley Jenkins, Anthony Byrd, Noble Johnson, Pauline Demsey, Mrs. Mines, Mercedes Gilbert and Mrs. Gabriel Jackson. Noble Johnson, Huel Brooks, Reid and Wesley Jenkins being especially prominent in general releases.

Interior and exterior scenes should be artistically selected. Backgrounds in "interiors" should blend with the actors and the atmosphere suggestive of the theme portrayed. The same scheme can be followed with success in exterior scenes.

PROMINENT IN MOTION PICTURE FIELD

Left to right: (1) Clarence E. Muse, director of the Del Sarte Film Co., and a former member of the Lafayette Players. Mr. Muse has had fifteen years' experience in Negro amusements. (2) Elizabeth Boyer, the clever little leading lady in Reol Production Company's release of Paul Lawrence Dunbar's "The Sport of the Gods." (3) Sydney P. Dones, the lead in the Bookertee Film Company's "Loyal Hearts," "The Reformation" and "My First Love"

SHOW BUSINESS AND WORLD WAR II

FROM DEC. 25, 1943 ISSUE

Showbusiness at War

SCREENDOM'S SPECIAL SKILLS FOR ASSIGNMENT TO MORALE

By James Cagney
President Screen Actors' Guild

Even before America was directly engaged in the war, members of the Screen Actors' Guild willingly placed at the disposal of the government their special skills. At least a skeleton program of camp entertainment, activated in large part by screen celebrities, was under way before the attack on Pearl Harbor.

When the nation became directly involved in the war, the actor, doubly eager to serve his country, increased the momentum of his work for the war program. Members of Screen Actors' Guild have made two major contributions to the fighting war: the direct contribution of man power and the indirect but equally potent contribution of morale-building activities.

More than 1,300 members of the Guild are serving in the armed forces. Approximately 650 members have temporarily suspended their professional careers in order to work in war industries. Hundreds of other actors are contributing their time and talent on civilian fronts—notably

by making personal appearances on morale-stimulating assignments.

Second only to the magnificent record which has been achieved by actors in entertaining members of the armed services in camps in this continent and overseas has been their contribution to the Treasury Department's bond-selling campaigns.

On the three major War Loan drives, the government has asked for and received the full-hearted co-operation of actors, who have proved to be extraordinarily successful salesmen in eliciting generous financial support for the war program. For the Third War Loan Drive in September, Hollywood's now-famous Bond Cavalcade, made up of 12 stellar personalities, toured 15 cities, more than doubled the half-billion-dollar quota which had been set for them.

HOLLYWOOD WRITERS MOBILIZED

Robert Rosson
Chairman of Steering Committee, Hollywood Writers' Mobilization

Ever since the evening of December 8, 1941 —the day following the attack on Pearl Harbor —the Hollywood Writers' Mobilization has functioned actively in carrying out the writer's part in the war effort. Starting with a mass meeting on that evening two years ago, the HWM quickly settled down to the job of contributing material of all kinds, and hundreds of assignments a month have been produced consistently ever since.

Since the Hollywood Writers' Mobilization is made up of members of the Screen Writers' Guild, Radio Writers' Guild, Screen Publicists' Guild, Screen Readers' Guild, Screen Cartoonists' Guild, American Newspaper Guild, Independent Publicists' Guild and the Songwriters' Protective Association, the organization has been able to expeditely handle any request.

A steering committee under Chairman Robert Rosson and Vice-Chairman Paul Franklin sifts and assigns requests. More than 1,000 men and women have written camp show en-

tertainment, speeches, radio programs and spot announcements, complete publicity campaigns, newspaper features, advertising and booklets for innumerable agencies engaged in the war effort. All of this goes on as routine contributions every week in the year.

The Hollywood Writers' Mobilization has also instituted activities, particularly the Writers' Congress, which it co-sponsored with the University of California. The entire field of the writer, educator, film maker and other creative artists in the war was exhaustively discussed at general meetings, seminars and panels over a period of three days. Results and resolution of this congress, chairmaned by Marc Connelly and Ralph Freud, are now being carried out in committee work which will continue for the duration. This comprises group research and discussion seminars, committee to conduct writer participation nationally and internationally, and the publication of a volume embracing the whole Writers' Congress.

BONDBARDMENT NUMBER
DECEMBER 25th 1943

KATE SMITH
THE ONE-MAN FOOTLIGHT FRONT
By Ted Collins

ASCAP MARCHES TO MUSIC BATONED BY BONDS, SCRIPTS AND CONCERTS

By John G. Paine
Ceneral Manager, American Society of Composers, Authors and Publishers

Figures speak louder than words, and so the scope of Kate Smith's tour of army, navy and marine posts and training centers can be judged by the fact that we covered approximately 50,000 miles. We visited camps in practically every part of the country and even made some trips to Canada. These were no brief hops involving just a few persons. We took our entire entourage with us, a caravan of some 60 people, including a full-sized orchestra, entertainers and our general staff. What complicated it was the matter of our daily noontime broadcast, which we had to do no matter where we were. It meant paying monumental line charges, not only for the daytime program, but for **our two Friday broadcasts (early and repeat).**

Needless to say, it gave us a tremendous thrill to visit the boys and entertain them. There were many difficulties caused by weather, transportation and other factors. We went out in all kinds of temperatures, ranging from frigid zero winds at Lakehurst to the tropical heat of the California desert. All of us had colds and Kate was frequently under a doctor's care. Sometimes transportation difficulties were a nightmare. We used anything we could get—trains, cars, busses. Sometimes the bus broke down and there were many nervous moments for fear we wouldn't get to the camp in time for the broadcast. Many of the camps were in out-of-the-way spots difficult of access.

Because of limited facilities in many camps, we put on our shows under primitive conditions. For example, our broadcast from the Army Air Depot in Rome, N. Y., was staged in an enormous hangar converted for the occasion into an auditorium. Our stage was roped off so that it looked like a boxing ring. We had an audience of 9,000 at each performance.

Few of the camps have auditoriums, and none of them is air-conditioned. The temperature was flirting with 100 when we did a program at the Navy Receiving Station in Brooklyn. The boys in the troupe did the broadcast in their shirt-sleeves. Kate sweltered, but she never was in better voice.

Our audiences at these camp appearances have totaled approximately 1,640,000. We are particularly careful to see that the enlisted men get the best seats and the majority of the seats at each show. After the show, Kate signs autographs for an hour or more. The boys' delight and apparent gratitude for our entertainment has given us extreme pleasure.

During the Third War Bond Drive which ended October 5, the American Society of Composers, Authors and Publishers was chosen by the Bond Committee as the organization to head the drive in the music business in New York State. The Society promptly contacted its publisher members and requested that some member of each firm be appointed chairman of the drive. At the same time the writer membership was asked to purchase bonds thru the Society by authorizing deduction of the cost of a bond from their royalty distribution. Eighty-one of our members purchased $10,075 worth of bonds in this manner. The publisher members reported a sale of $355,875. Some of the publishing houses had made their reports to the film industry with which they are affiliated and, therefore, did not report to ASCAP. Within the organization itself, the

Society's employees bought $6,819 worth of bonds. This included the New York office and branch offices. The grand total reported to the Treasury was $372,769.

At the present time there are 108 members of the Society serving in the armed forces; 31 men and four women employees are also in the service.

In the ASCAP radio scripts, which are sent without charge to the Society's licensed stations, the Society has developed a program called "Marching to Music." This program is based on the common man who inadvertently has contributed his small part to the progress of American democracy.

MARSHALING MUSIC IN TUNE WITH THE ALL-OUT HYMN

By Max Targ
President, Music War Council of America

On March 24, 1942, a group of Middle Western music industry leaders met in Chicago for the purpose of determining how they might co-operate to solve their problems arising out of the war. It was about three and one-half months after Pearl Harbor, and there was talk of relegating music to the limbo of non-essential luxuries for the duration.

But those music industry leaders who met in Chicago believed in music's importance in wartime as well as in peace. They realized that the productive facilities of the industry were needed for the manufacture of war materials, and pledged their aid to effect as quick a conversion to war work as possible; but, believing whole-heartedly in music's ability to help the war effort, they were determined to oppose, with all the power at their command, any attempt to curtail musical activity as non-essential.

With the organization a few days later of the Music War Council of America they pledged themselves to mobilize all forms of music for the national effort, that our armed forces, civilian workers and children might have the advantage of the recreational and educational benefits and the patriotic inspiration that music affords.

Imbued with a strong will to carry out its self-appointed mission the new organization moved forward swiftly. Within a week of the first preliminary meeting its delegates to the Music Educators' National Conference meeting in Milwaukee had a hand in securing the passage of a list of recommendations by that body's council of past presidents calling for the maximum possible utilization of music to bolster morale on the home front and in the armed forces. These recommendations were transmitted to the President of the United States, who, in turn, endorsed music as a wartime essential.

As a result, after two years of war, instead of being curtailed, music organizations have been revitalized, and hundreds of thousands of musicians have been encouraged to play for bond rallies, for draftee send-offs, for the entertainment of servicemen in camps and on leave, and for work-weary employees of war plants.

HERE COMES TELEVISION

FROM AUG. 18, 1928 ISSUE

First Radio Movies Shown in Pittsburgh

PITTSBURGH, Aug. 11.—The first transmission of movies by radio took place here Wednesday in the television laboratory of the Westinghouse Electric and Manufacturing Company. The demonstration was witnessed by scientists and other notables, including David Sarnoff, president, and other officials of the Radio Corporation of America. Regular transmission of motion pictures from KDKA will begin in a few months, Westinghouse officials announce, and it was said that in the near future it will be possible to enjoy movies at home by merely plugging in the television apparatus just as people now tune in on radio programs. The Radio Corporation will be the selling medium for the television apparatus.

Those present at the demonstration expressed the opinion that television has the same extensive possibilities as the movies and the radio had in their early days.

FROM SEPT. 28, 1929 ISSUE

To Television Show Notables

NEW YORK, Sept. 23.—A large number of notables from pictures, legit. and other fields have been lined up to be televisioned this week at the Madison Square Garden, where the Radio World's Fair opens. Among them are Claudette Colbert, Charles Ruggles, Walter Huston, Paul Ash, Ray Sinnott, Babe Ruth, Yascha Bunchuk, Vincent Lopez, John Murray Anderson, Bebe Daniels, Patricia Barclay and Clayton, Jackson and Durante.

The RCA television apparatus with sound is being demonstrated. The performers will stand in front of the tubes, which are synchronized with a mike placed just at the top of the tubes, and will be seen and heard from a ground glass screen, size 14x14. This apparatus is cumbersome and for laboratories only, but is to be eventually built for the home, it is understood

FROM SEPT. 20, 1930 ISSUE

U. S. Television Looms As English Steal March

2,000 home sets in England receiving television programs daily—American interests hustling to meet competition—RCA erects Broadway television studio

NEW YORK, Sept. 13.—Officials of Baird Television, the English company which is developing television from patents taken out 15 years ago, and which differ basically from American television patents, told a representative of *The Billboard* that television in the home in England was not a dream, but a fact, that over 2,000 television home receptors had been sold and that television programs were being broadcast daily from two studios. Reception of programs occurs all over England and as far away as Berlin.

It was pointed out that American television interests, controlled by RCA, have not progressed as far towards the popularization of television as the English company, altho their experiments equal the progress of the English ones. No reasons for slowness of American interests could be obtained from their English rivals other than that the history of RCA was an indication of its policy regarding giving publicity to new discoveries and that full-grown television might be suddenly sprung on the public in the same manner as a more proficient radio tube was suddenly put on sale after an official of the radio company announced at a public banquet it would be several years before the tube in question would progress beyond the laboratory state.

In answer to the many rumors rife concerning what it is doing with television, RCA made public this week plans for the erection of a television broadcasting station on top of the New Amsterdam Theater, drawing theatrical material from the stage, screen and radio thru the Times Square studio of NBC. Equipment to be used will come from General Electric, under the supervision of Dr. E. F. W. Alexanderson, television engineer.

Officials of the Baird office admitted the commercialization of television would offer the talkies serious competition, with the possibility of finally obliterating them since television programs are so similar in nature to talkies. Just what television would do to the legitimate stage was not indicated, altho it was implied television interests would lean heavily on the Broadway stage for programs, possibly cutting out the road, but not the New York theater, the inevitable source of supply for writing, acting and producing talent.

FROM AUG. 1, 1931 ISSUE

FRC Sets Television

Will have own high kilocycle area — new station opens in New York

NEW YORK, July 25.—Federal Radio Commission is already making plans to take care of television when it comes in. Things are being fixed so that there will be no interference with the now-existing radio stations, it being planned to put all television outfits in the high channel of between 43,000 and 80,000 kilocycles. This kilocycle band does not interfere at all with present radio bands. Commission's plans for future were made after recent telly developments and interest shown in them.

There are 27 experimental telly stations now operating in United States, of which 16 are in low kilocycle band of between 2,000 and 5,000. This conflicts with amateur territory, but times on air are so worked out that there have been no kicks from the non-pros as yet. As soon as television stations increase in number so that they can't be fitted into low channel, high band will be used for them exclusively.

Meanwhile, Tuesday night here saw opening of new television station of Columbia Network. It is sixth television station in metropolitan area, and will be known as W2XAB, working in conjunction with W2XE, which will transmit sound portions of program. Mayor Walker drew the curtain concealing the television eye, and a program was broadcast immediately thereafter. W2XE's short wave carried sound portion to Europe.

W2XAB and W2XE are broadcasting sight and sound programs every night between 8 and 11. Between 2 and 6 in the afternoon W2XAB works alone, sending visual program only, as experimental aid to Columbia Broadcasting engineers.

FROM AUG. 6, 1932 ISSUE

Television

By Benn Hall

The first column to be devoted to news of television—its entertainers, mechanical advancements and general news—commences with this issue of *The Billboard*. Television is still in the experimental stage, comparable to the radio of some 10 years back, and to the now quaint moving pictures of about two decades ago. But television is just as sure to develop and expand as films and radio have done. *The Billboard* and this columnist have faith in the future of television.

Those who were in on the ground floor of the picture and radio industries were in favorable spots to reap the harvest that followed the engineering perfections and public demands for these new entertainment mediums. So will it be with television.

Television will be of far greater appeal than radio or pictures.

Television will call for experienced performers. Today the experienced entertainer appearing in television programs has a great advantage over the amateur. Stars of radio, movies and legit will undoubtedly be recruited to television. But, more important, new stars will be developed. Names scarcely known now will be names when the perfecters of the Magic Eye have achieved their purpose. The performer who is now in a flesh show or in pictures or radio will be wise in following the advancement of television. He will be much wiser, however, in keeping in step with this new magic. The player who appears in television gains a world of experience with each performance.

Television will call for a new technique. Makeup, directing, use of props, mechanical limitations, and a hundred other considerations all will call for a new, a different treatment. Material, particularly skits and plays, will require a handling different from that employed in the present branches of show business.

Television will be of far greater appeal than radio or the pictures. It will be in the home and will appeal to two senses—sight and hearing—rather than hearing alone. It is doubtful today if there is as much fan interest in radio personalities as there is in film personalities. The fan's interest is accentuated when he, or she, sees as well as hears the player. Witness the number of movie fan mags. Compare the number of these publications with the radio fan mags.

But with the coming of television the fan will have a new idol to burn incense before. Performers who learn television technique and secure some public in-

terest while television is still in the toddling stage will be that much ahead in the game.

Television offers a broad, unlimited, unexplored field for the performer and producer. There are few rules to follow, no traditions. It is a place, much the same as radio, for young blood and young ideas. But, to acquire a sense of showmanship and entertainment values, be they in the established show business or the new and untried field of television, requires experience and observation.

So, showfolk, watch television. Get in on the ground floor. Get on the band wagon. Let's go!

FROM OCT. 3, 1931 ISSUE

Many Acts Rush To Be Televised--- Show Great Interest at Experiment

NEW YORK, Sept. 28.—With television as a medium for vaudeville entertainment receiving tremendous impetus last week at the Madison Square Garden Radio-Electrical Show, the rush of vaude and radio performers to get in on the ground floor of television is on. Scores of well-known stage people appeared briefly on the Sanabria 10-foot screen, the largest and most perfect yet achieved, and huge crowds viewed sound-and-vision images.

The great public interest shown in television and the William Morris Agency's preparation of television acts for theater stage demonstrations are two indications of the closeness of television as practical entertainment. Stage and radio performers are striving hard to make connections with television broadcasting and many performers are working without pay in television experiments just so that they would be there when television is ready to pay good money.

The eagerness to be televised is so strong that many vaude "names" appeared on the Radio Show screen with absolutely no previous experience and without the least idea as to how they would go over. They took the chance with no hesitation, tho most of them would never think of going on the air without rehearsing and testing their voice, or opening cold with a new act.

Like the famous gold rush to Hollywood of songwriters and stage people when the talkies broke out, stage performers are toeing the mark and keeping their ears open for the television rush. Instead of waiting patiently, as with radio, for developments, performers are trying to establish themselves firmly with the television before it has even left the experimental period.

Among those who were televised at the Radio Show are George Jessel, Mae Murray, Sophie Tucker, Borrah Minevitch, Paul Ash, Lester Allen, Ben Bernie, Ted Healy and Alice White.

FROM JULY 22, 1933 ISSUE

Film Stars Doubt Telly's Future

HOLLYWOOD, July 15.—Commenting on television in a recent Coast interview, Merlin H. Aylesworth, head of NBC, said: "In connection with the RKO radio studio there will be an experimental laboratory for the perfection of television." Since then Hollywood film stars have been wondering just what effect the so-called development of this new science might have upon films and their present standing in show business.

A *Billboard* reporter caught a number of the film stars at the various studios and asked them what they thought of television, what bearing it might have on the theater and what effect it might have on motion pictures. Eddie Cantor thinks the theater will never be replaced by television because "people are gregarious." Jack Oakie and the Marx brothers laughed at the idea of television ever affecting pictures.

W. C. Fields, a veteran of stage and films, said with a twinkle in his eye: "Well, it's like this. People laughed at Galileo when he invented the telescope, people laughed at Columbus when he said the world was round, people laughed at Marconi when he invented wireless, people laughed at Philadelphia when it was last in the American League. And now we are approaching television! Ha! ha! I'm laughing."

Work is going ahead on the television experimental studios on the RKO lot and will be ready for use shortly. In building the studios here, it is the belief of NBC officials that Hollywood, with its vast array of talent of all descriptions, will be the home of television chain broadcasts to the entire country.

FROM JULY 6, 1929 ISSUE

Television
Step Ahead

NEW YORK, June 29.—Color television was demonstrated last week at the laboratories of the Bell Telephone Company, when images were transmitted thru the ether from one end of a large auditorium to the other which housed the mechanism of the apparatus.

Al Jolson's singing of *Sunny Boy* was the subject used for demonstration. Experiments will continue until "television adds materially to human comfort and happiness," it was said.

FROM NOV. 14, 1936 ISSUE

RCA-NBC TELE PROGRESS
First Demonstration of Show Set for Entertainment Value

•

Forty-minute program held talks by Sarnoff and Lohr, also live talent acts and motion pictures—experiment for further perfection—no "arrival" dates predicted

•

NEW YORK, Nov. 7.—First demonstration of television under practical working conditions, as developed by RCA and NBC, was given for the press yesterday afternoon when a 40-minute program of live talent and films illustrated the extent of the RCA experimental developments. Altho previous laboratory television has been shown by RCA, yesterday's show before some 200 guests represented the first showing of a complete program built for entertainment value as well as a demonstration of transmission. A new 12-inch receiving tube, which reproduces a picture on a 7½ by 10-inch screen, the largest screen yet employed capable of commercial adaptation, was demonstrated.

Program originated on the third floor of NBC studios via coaxial cable to the top of the Empire State Building, about three quarters of a mile away. From the transmitter atop the Empire the sound and images were sent thru the air, the former on 52 megacycle channel and the latter on 49.75 megacycles. Normal range of the transmitter is 25 to 30 miles, altho an outpost in Connecticut 45 miles away picks up the programs clearly. The television "theater" was on the 62d floor of the RCA Building which also houses the NBC studios. While the demonstration used 343-line tele-pictures, David Sarnoff, RCA president, who took part in the show, stated that the Federal Communications Commission had recommended the adoption of 441-line definition as a standard for commercial television programs.

FROM SEPT. 23, 1933 ISSUE

Television
By Benn Hall

Hello, Minny!

Minneapolis is on our list. Dr. George W. Young, owner of local Station WDGY, now has a television license. Station is W9XAT, a 500 watter and given unlimited time. Sound will come from WDGY.

Young has been trying to secure a federal license for television for about two years. His station will be a pioneer picture-sending depot in the Northwest. Altho at present there are but few television receiving sets in the Minneapolis zone, fan and experimental interest should stimulate and increase the demand and sale of sets and parts.

Don Lee television stations . . . are experimenting with televising full-length films. . . . De Mille's *This Day and Age* and *The Texan* with Gary Cooper were the first two features televised.

Full-Length Films Televised

Don Lee television stations on the West Coast, W6XS and W6XAO, are experimenting with televising full-length films, as well as trailers, newsreels and closeups. De Mille's *This Day and Age* and *The Texan* with Gary Cooper were the two features first televised under the new arrangement.

Television Director Harry R. Lubcke reports that forward-looking m. p. producers are co-operating with these experiments. Images of 80 lines at 15 frames each second are televised from 7 to 9 p.m. (Pacific Coast time) daily and from 9 to 11 a.m. Monday, Wednesday and Friday.

FROM OCT. 23, 1937 ISSUE

Large Tele

NEW YORK, Oct. 16.—NBC and RCA gave a demonstration of large television on a 3 by 4-foot screen this week before the Society of Motion Picture Engineers and newspaper men. This is the first time this size has been shown. Pictures were fairly clear but quite yellow in tint, altho there seemed to be little flicker compared to earlier smaller screen shows.

RCA tele receivers with 7 by 10-inch screens gave excellent results, both on studio shows and newsreel film. Latter was much clearer. Makeup problem is far from being solved.

General reaction is that major advances have been made.

FROM JUNE 29, 1946 ISSUE

Ad-Less Video?

To the Editor:

For 20 years I have been reading articles in the daily press and in national magazines telling how television was just around the corner. . . . Most of the articles I have read indicate that the advertisers of America are going to foot this enormous bill of providing television entertainment. I do not believe it. I do not believe they will, any more than the advertisers financed the movies, and that was tried once.

The sooner we can persuade the technical talent of our industry that the advertisers are not going to pay for television, the sooner they will get busy and develop a means of technically obtaining a box office which will pay for the entertainment necessary to be offered by this great new industry.

E. F. McDONALD JR.,
President,
Zenith Radio Corporation.

FROM MAY 13, 1939 ISSUE

TELEVISION REVIEWS

Reviewed Wednesday, 8-9:30 p.m. EDST. Style—Variety, using both film and live talent. Reviewed on RCA Television Receiver Style TRK 12, with 7½ by 10-inch screen. Station — W2XBS.

Inaugurating regular television service, RCA-NBC presented a program Wednesday evening, including an especially made newsreel, Fred Waring's Orchestra; Helen Lewis, emsee; Richard Rodgers, composer, and Marcy Westcott from the *Boys From Syracuse;* Bill Farren, the Three Swifts; a Donald Duck cartoon, *Donald's Cousin Gus;* Earle Larimore and Marjorie Clarke in an Aaron Hoffman sketch, Lowell Thomas and a New York Port Authority trailer.

The program was a complete technical success, especially in view of unfavorable reception conditions obtaining in Radio City, with its many steel buildings. It showed, too, that television has a long way to go to solve its programing, production and talent problems. It showed, too, that a 7½ by 10-inch screen makes for poor watching. Altho there was no semblance of flicker, the 90 minutes resulted in eyestrain.

The punch of the program was probably the actual pick-up from the New York World's Fair. Bill Farren, regular staff NBC announcer, interviewed fair visitors. These interviews showed where television's most important drawing power will come from. There was tremendous impact seeing and hearing Farren and his interviewees as they spoke. Oddy enough, the strong lights needed by tele cameras did not seem especially troublesome, altho they were of enormous power.

The small screen and the difficulty yet to be solved of how to get greater scope from the cameras handicapped practically all of the other acts, except Rodgers, the composer, and Miss Westcott. Camera moved from one to another, and since neither required considerable range the problem was easy to solve. But in handling the Waring troupe and the Three Swifts the tele camera showed that its directors and producers have far to go. The Swifts are a strong act in any theater, but in trying to show the three of them working simultaneously the punch of the act was lost. When just two or so of the Waring menage were working it was again okeh, but when the ensemble was on the screen the camera's weakness was apparent.

Greatest sign that NBC is slow on television production came in *The Unexpected,* a playlet by Aaron Hoffman—an antique if ever there was one. There was no need for doing the piece, and the newness of television is no excuse.

Reviewed Friday, 8 to 9:30 p.m. Style—Variety, using both film and live talent. Reviewed on Dumont Television Receiver Style No. 183, with 8x10-inch screen. Station— W2XBS.

Second of NBC's regular television programs had Mitzi Green, Ed Herlihy; Novello Brothers, whistling act; Roy Post and his lie detector, a newsreel; a play with Josephine Huston and seven girl emsees, each of whom introduced one act. Girls, who are being tried out for a permanent spot, were Muriel Fleit, Joan Allison, Mary McCormack, Louise Illingston, May Stuart, Evelyn Holt and Sandra Ramoy. Warren Wade, Burk Grotty and Eddie Padula shared the direction.

Television production methods are unprofessional.

Eschewing actual comment on the performances, none of which were especially noteworthy, this second program solidified opinion that television's present production methods can be compared only to those of a kindergarten play. Obvious things such as moving out of focus and other roughness in performances seem to this reviewer to be unnecessary. Unnecessary because NBC has had time during the past year or so, at least, to improve methods. Experimentation on television technically was done in the studios and laboratories, and the same thing should have been done insofar as production is concerned. A purchaser of a $400 television set is not going to feel any great love for television when the shows provided are about on a par with not very good amateur stuff.

While all television receivers have screens more or less the same size, the 8-by-10 or 7-by-10 screens do not make for much comfort when watched for more than very short times. An offhand opinion, then, is that unless the screens sizes are made larger only outstanding programs will attract audiences as matters now stand. Radio allows for casual listening, but television does not. An hour or more of poor programs will only backfire against television itself.

Dumont receiver model, which sells for $435, gave good reproduction. Altho the screen is a bit larger than the RCA screen on which Wednesday's program was reviewed, the slightly larger area made scant difference. Dumont does not use a mirror as the RCA sets do, and the direct method seems preferable.

But it is still a puzzle to this reviewer that television production methods are so unprofessional.   *Franken.*

FROM JUNE 29, 1946 ISSUE

45,266 There---141,375 Looked In

SAMPLING THE LOUIS-CONN TELE-VIEWERS

The first telephone rating of any video program by the C. E. Hooper organization, an exclusive feature of The Billboard, being a 101-call sample in the Metropolitan New York Area.

Call No.	Using Set	Time Set Turned On	Time Set Turned Off	Number of People Viewing Before Louis-Conn Fight	Number of People Viewing During Louis-Conn Fight	Is Set Converted?
1.	Yes	8:30	11:00	4	6	Yes
2.	Yes	8:30	11:05	6	10	Yes
3.	Yes	7:00	11:00	6	15	Yes
4.	Yes	8:15	11:00	15	15	No
5.	Yes	7:30	11:15	10	12	Yes
6.	Yes	9:00	11:30	28	28	Yes
7.	Yes	8:00	11:15	17	17	Yes
8.	Yes	7:30	After Fight	Don't Know	25	Yes
9.	Yes	7:30	11:30	13	13	Yes
10.	No					
11.	Yes	8:30	11:30	Don't Know	250*	Yes

*This television set put up in a church for the men's club.

Call No.	Using Set	Time Set Turned On	Time Set Turned Off	Number of People Viewing Before Louis-Conn Fight	Number of People Viewing During Louis-Conn Fight	Is Set Converted?
12.	Yes	7:30	11:15	14	14	Yes
13.	Yes	7:35	After Fight	9	9	Yes
14.	Yes	8:30	"	34	34	Yes
15.	Yes	8:00	"	50	60	Yes
16.	Yes	8:30	"	6	6	Don't Know
17.	Yes	9:00	"	17	17	Yes
18.	Yes	9:00	"	Don't Know	49	Yes
19.	Yes	8:00	"	20	22	Yes
20.	No					
21.	Yes	8:00	"	Don't Know	25	Yes
22.	Yes	8:15	"	30	60	No
23.	Yes	8:30	"	15	15	Yes
24.	Yes	Don't Know*	Don't Know*	Don't Know*	Don't Know*	Don't Know*

*Respondent reached during daytime said we could get information during evening. We were unable to re-contract.

Call No.	Using Set	Time Set Turned On	Time Set Turned Off	Number of People Viewing Before Louis-Conn Fight	Number of People Viewing During Louis-Conn Fight	Is Set Converted?
25.	Yes	8:30	10:00	15	15	Yes
26.	Yes	8:00	After Fight	20	20	Yes
27.	Yes	8:00	11:00	7	7	Yes
28.	Yes	When Fight Started	Don't Know	6	6	Don't Know
29.	Yes	7:30	After Fight	30	30	Yes
30.	Yes	8:30	11:15	30	30	Yes
31.	Yes	8:45	After Fight	30	30	Yes
32.	No					
33.	Yes	8:30	11:00	25	25	Yes
34.	Yes	8:30	11:00	12	12	Yes
35.	Yes	8:00	11:00	30	30	Yes
36.	Yes	8:00	11:00	6	20	Yes
37.	Yes	9:00	11:00	60	60	No
38.	Yes	7:30	11:00	6	26	Yes
39.	Yes	9:00	11:00	40	40	Yes
40.	Yes	9:30	11:00	50	50	Don't Know
41.	Yes	10:00	11:00	30	30	Yes
42.	No					
43.	Yes	8:15	11:00	10	10	No
44.	No					
45.	Yes	7:30	11:00	15	15	Yes
46.	No					
47.	Yes	8:30	10:45	9	9	Yes
48.	No—Not ready in time					
49.	Yes	8:30	11:00	40	40	Don't Know
50.	Yes	8:30	11:00	15	15	No
51.	Yes	8:00	11:00	6	6	Yes
52.	Yes	Don't Know*	Don't Know*	Don't Know*	Don't Know*	Don't Know*

*Respondent says set was in use, but was at country home and she did not know answers to other questions.

Call No.	Using Set	Time Set Turned On	Time Set Turned Off	Number of People Viewing Before Louis-Conn Fight	Number of People Viewing During Louis-Conn Fight	Is Set Converted?
53.	No					
54.	Yes	8:30	11:00	24	40	Yes
55.	Yes	8:00	11:00	20	30	Yes
56.	No					
57.	Yes	8:30	10:45	35	35	Yes
58.	Yes	7:00	11:00	7	7	Yes
59.	Yes	7:30	11:00	6	60	Yes
60.	Yes	Start of Fight	End of Fight	—	35	Yes
61.	Yes	8:00	After Fight	20	175 (Guests)	Yes
62.	Yes	7:30	10:45	10	19	Yes
63.	Yes	8:00	11:00	4	15	No
64.	Yes	8:00	10:45	15	20	No

Hooper Tabs Fight Viewers

●

Average of 32.5 persons per set builds terrific audience for Louis-Conn battle

●

NEW YORK, June 22.—Video set owners are television's best boosters. That was the reaction of the Hooper

interviewers upon the occasion of the first telephone checking of a scanned program. They are just as great rooters as were the first autoists, without any feeling that guests will ever call out "get a radio."

The average receiver tuned in on the fight, in the sample taken in the metropolitan area, had 32.5 people viewing the battle. The sample eliminated pubs and public places except in a few cases where the set-owner had moved the receiver over to the YMCA, church, club or some other community center. In these cases, as many as 250 people viewed the heavyweight championship fight from a single kinescope (complete report on the 101 interviews on this page).

101 Interviews

The sample, 101 interviews, while not large represented the greatest index of viewing from any concentrated area since the birth of air pix, the mail surveys of the past hitting that 100 figure, but from areas including Philadelphia, Schenectady, etc., only two respondents reported their sets were not in working order, altho a number (10) stated that their equipment had not been set for the new wavebands. It's possible, of course, to look in on channel 4 (WNBT's allocation) without the receivers being reset for the rest of the channels (old channel 3 is present channel 4).

A CAPSULE HISTORY

To identify individual show business areas see two-letter code descriptions below:

AP —Amusement Parks
BU —Burlesque
CA —Carnivals
CH —Chautauqua
CI —Circus
FA —Fairs
MI —Minstrelsy
MO —Motion Pictures
MU —Music
NC —Night Clubs, Supper Clubs, Cabarets
RA —Radio
RE —Recordings
SH —Showboats
ST —Stereorama and Panstereorama
TH —Legitimate Theatre
TV —Television
VA —Vaudeville
WA —Wagon Shows

1919

TH Actors' Equity calls its strike against the producers after months of fruitless negotiations. They are joined by the AFL stagehands union. Theatres are closed down in New York, Boston, Chicago, Los Angeles, and San Francisco.

VA Although the Actors' Equity strike is directed against legitimate theatre owners and managers, Albee participates, along with legitimate operators, by serving as vice president of the United Managers Protective Association of the Amusement Interests of the United States. One of their objectives is to resist "the unreasonable demands of labor unions."

TH At an Actors' Equity strike benefit show at Lexington Avenue Opera House in New York, Ed Wynn does his entire act from his seat in the audience, because a judge rules that he cannot perform on any stage for anyone except the Shuberts to whom he is under contract.

TH Actors' Equity wins complete victory in the strike and William H. Donaldson, editor-publisher of *Billboard*, is cited for his

publication's great contribution to the actors' victory.

VA Walter Winchell — a hoofer in the two-act, Winchell and Green — begins writing a column for *Billboard* called "Stage Whispers;" it is by-lined, "by The Busybody," and is the columnist's first literary effort.

TH Among most successful plays of the season: Ethel Barrymore in *Declassee;* John and Lionel Barrymore co-star in *The Jest.* Comedy hits include Helen Hayes and Alfred Lunt in *Clarence* and *Up In Mabel's Room,* destined to be a stock company favorite.

TH George White produces first of his series of *Scandals* starring Ann Pennington and himself.

MO Movie company stocks are listed on Wall Street exchanges and handled by major brokerage firms. Films are recognized as an important new industry.

MO Griffith's big hit this year is *Broken Blossoms* with Lillian Gish and Richard Barthelmess as "the chink and the child." It is shot in eighteen days. Germ-shy Griffith insists that Gish wear a medical mask between shots, because she is recovering from the Spanish Flu. Adolph Zukor, unhappy with the film which he considered "uncommercial," sells it to Griffith for $250,000. The film is United Artists' first release.

MO Cecil B. De Mille sets off trend toward sophisticated films of sex life of the rich with *Male and Female; For Better, For Worse;* and *Don't Change Your Husband,* (all starring Gloria Swanson). He will make the last of this type, *Adam's Rib,* in 1923.

MO In January the industry's three most popular stars — Mary Pickford, Douglas Fairbanks and Charles Chaplin — form United Artists Corporation. Comment of Richard Rowland, president of Metro Pictures, upon hearing of this event: "So the lunatics have taken over the asylum!" Company attorney is William McAdoo, former Secretary of the Treasury of U.S., whom they pay $100,000 per year. He leaves in April.

MO Marcus Loew acquires Metro Pictures, giving the latter a theatre chain. In 1924, Lee Shubert, a board member of both Loew's, Inc. and Goldwyn Pictures,

suggests Metro merge with Goldwyn. Shortly thereafter, Louis B. Mayer — then an independent film producer — is signed as studio chief and the studio becomes Metro Goldwyn Mayer. Ironically, Sam Goldwyn, who left Goldwyn Pictures in 1922, was never a part of MGM.

MO Nazimova is Metro's top star. Her hits include *The Red Lantern* and *Out of the Fog.*

MO Triangle, Mutual, and Thanhouser go out of business.

MO Adolph Zukor, head of Paramount, conducts aggressive campaign to build and acquire theatres. By late 1920s, Paramount owns or controls more than 600 theatres, including the strong Chicago-based Balaban & Katz chain. The company's only serious rivals are Fox, Loew's and Warner's.

RA British Marconi, parent company of American Marconi, gives over control to General Electric. Radio Corporation of America is formed; GE, Westinghouse, American Telephone & Telegraph and United Fruit own blocks of its stock. Between them they control approximately 2000 electronic patents.

RE First work in U.S. is done on electrical recording in experiments conducted at Bell Telephone Labs.

TV At Westinghouse, engineer Vladimir Zworykin conducts his first television experiments.

CH Diverse summer assembly entertainments called chautauquas thrive this year. 6,200 chautauquas run 100,000 sessions playing to an estimated 15,000,000 people this summer.

MI Minstrel man George Primrose dies.

CI The Ringling Brothers and the Barnum & Bailey Circuses are combined into one super-colossal show for the first time, although they have been owned by the Ringlings for a number of years.

CA Typical of growth of successful carnival companies of the day are the Greater Sheesley Shows (which travel in twenty cars) and the Johnny J. Jones Exposition Shows, which travel on twenty-seven all-steel flat cars, five all-steel stock cars and eight Pullmans.

1920

TH This is a landmark year for the American theatre, marking the turning point toward more mature themes and the emergence of the first great American playwright, Eugene O'Neill. The season also witnesses the worldwide premiere of George Bernard Shaw's *Heartbreak House.* Shaw shrewdly insists that the Theatre Guild postpone opening his play until after the Presidential election.

TH Eugene O'Neill has two plays produced with spectacular success. His first full length work, *Beyond the Horizon,* starring Richard Bennett wins the 1919-1920 Pulitzer Prize. *Emperor Jones* wins acclaim for its star Charles Gilpin but work is still scarce for black actors; Gilpin returns to his job as an elevator operator after the run of the play. Paul Robeson will revive *Jones* with great success.

TH John Barrymore plays his first Shakespearean role, *The Tragedy of Richard III.*

TH James Cagney, destined to become the quintessential movie tough guy, makes his Broadway debut as a chorus boy in *Pitter Patter.* Cagney started out in show business as part of a female impersonator vaudeville act, Every Sailor, dancing the Peabody. He later replaced Cary Grant (then named Archie Leach) in a vaude act — Parker, Rand and Cagney.

TH/VA At the same time they are acquiring new theatres for vaudeville presentations and lining up top vaudeville acts, the Shuberts have thirty legitimate theatrical productions in preparation for the 1920-1921 season.

MO Movie industry is now largely centered in Hollywood. Laemmle's Universal City has grown to a vast operation; Chaplin has opened own studios on La Brea Ave.; Paramount operates on an entire city block of stages. Industry contributes approximately $30,000,000 per year in salary and materials to community prosperity.

MO Star system in ascendancy. Average cost of feature film is approximately $115,000.

MO Increasing numbers of film studios provide cue sheets of standard musical numbers which they suggest should be played with their silent features. Erno Rapee and Hugo Riesenfeld are two of the composer/conductor/arrangers who develop such musical accompaniment cue sheets.

MO Griffith films his classic *Way Down East* with Lillian Gish and Richard Barthelmess. The valiant cast works during a blizzard and Gish almost loses her life when Barthelmess almost fails to catch her before the floe goes over the falls. Fifty years later Gish declares that her hand,

which floated in the icy water for hours, still hurts in cold weather. No stunt men for Griffith in those days.

MO Chaplin discovers a waif-like child actor, Jackie Coogan, and makes him a star in the classic comedy, *The Kid.*

MO *Passion,* a German movie starring Pola Negri, is a success in the U.S. In a few years Hollywood imports both Negri and the film's director, Ernst Lubitsch, who lends his name to a unique style of frothy sophisticated comedy.

MO Two of the year's most successful pictures are *Dr. Jekyll and Mr. Hyde* starring John Barrymore, and *Madam X* with Pauline Frederick.

RA Substantial acceleration in "ham" radio activity, notably on part of Frank Conrad, a Westinghouse engineer, who broadcasts records and live music from workshop over his garage in Wilkinsburg, Pa. Other "hams" are broadcasting in Madison, Wisc.; Hollywood; Charlotte, N.C.; and Detroit.

RA Joseph Horne Department Store runs ad in *Pittsburgh Sun,* offering Amateur Wireless Sets for $10. Ad refers to music from Victrola played by Frank Conrad over his 8XK transmitter in Wilkinsburg.

RA Harry Davis, Westinghouse vice president, asks Frank Conrad to build more powerful transmitter for regular programming atop tall Westinghouse building in East Pittsburgh. Conrad sets up 100-watt transmitter and broadcasting shack, which becomes radio station KDKA.

RA A station in Detroit, WWJ, and KDKA, Pittsburgh, both claim to inaugurate regular broadcasting. WWJ's "show" airs in August; KDKA broadcasts the Harding-Cox election returns in November.

RA Two Philadelphia brothers, Isaac (Ike) and Leon Levy and their partner, Daniel Murphy, buy radio station WCAU, Philadelphia for $25,000. They and their station are destined to play a key part in the birth of the Columbia Broadcasting System network.

RE Arturo Toscanini makes his first record for the Victor Talking Machine Company in December.

RE Mamie Smith records "Crazy Blues" on the Okeh label, the first vocal blues record by a black singer.

CI Young, attractive Bird Millman is the first American tightwire performer to work without a balancing umbrella. She also sings as she walks the wire.

1921

TH Musicals are big this season. Al Jolson stars in *Bombo;* Ed Wynn in *The Perfect Fool.* Sigmund Romberg's *Blossom Time* is

so popular that the Shuberts send out road company versions of the musical for years thereafter.

TH *Shuffle Along* moves from Harlem to Broadway and is the first Broadway musical hit acted, produced, and written by blacks — starting a trend for all-black shows. Noble Sissle and Eubie Blake double as performers and writers of the score which includes, "I'm Just Wild About Harry." Florence Mills has first major role.

TH The critics are excited about the performances of five young actresses: Lynn Fontanne in *Dulcy,* Katharine Cornell in *A Bill of Divorcement,* Eva Le Gallienne in Molnar's *Liliom,* with Joseph Schildkraut and Francine Larrimore in *Nice People,* supported by Miss Cornell and Tallulah Bankhead.

TH Four Eugene O'Neill plays are produced this season: *Diff'rent, Gold, The Straw* and *Anna Christie,* starring Pauline Lord. The last wins O'Neill his second Pulitzer Prize.

MI Minstrel man Al G. Field dies.

MO Metro Pictures makes *The Four Horsemen of the Apocalypse* starring new matinee idol Rudolph Valentino. By 1925 film grosses $4,000,000.

MO George Arliss is a critical success in a film version of his stage hit *Disraeli.* In the thirties he scores even a greater hit in a sound version of the same play.

RA David Sarnoff, age thirty, becomes general manager of RCA and launches manufacture of "radio music boxes," an idea which had been rejected in 1916.

RA KDKA broadcasting operation so successful that transmitter wattage is increased to 500, and Westinghouse opens similar radio stations in Newark, N.J. (WJZ); Springfield, Mass. (WBZ); and Chicago (KYW).

RA Vincent Lopez is first bandleader to broadcast on radio, when he fills in for cancelled show as a favor to his friend, Tommy Cowan, program director for WJZ.

RA A great promotion event for radio is the broadcast of the Dempsey-Carpentier heavyweight championship fight from Boyle's Thirty Acres in Jersey City, N.J. The fight announcer is Major J. Andrew White, later a partner in United Independent Broadcasters, Inc. and CBS.

MU/MO M. F. Gaillard writes first score ever composed expressly for a film, *El Dorado.*

1922

TH *Abie's Irish Rose,* written and financed by Anne Nichols, opens and becomes a box office phenomenon; it runs 2,327 performances on Broadway and later plays to millions on the road for many years.

TH John Barrymore plays *Hamlet* for the first time. Blanche Yurka and Tyrone Power are also in the cast. Barrymore's is the longest running *Hamlet* in Broadway history, until Richard Burton breaks the record with his version of Shakespeare's tragedy in 1964.

TH *The Torchbearers*, George Kelly's farce about amateur theatre groups (starring Mary Boland and Alison Skipworth) reflects a growing trend. As motion pictures continue to make inroads on touring companies, the "little theatres" take over the professionals' territory. By 1925, there are 1900 little playhouses registered with the Drama League of America.

TH Three perennial favorites have their first presentations: *Rain*, starring Jeanne Eagels as Sadie Thompson; Glenn Hunter in *Merton of the Movies;* and Eugene O'Neill's *The Hairy Ape* which makes a star of Louis Wolheim.

MO The public's impression of the wild and immoral lifestyles of movie stars reaches peak with the murder-rape trials of comedian Roscoe (Fatty) Arbuckle (after two hung juries he is acquitted); the murder of director William Desmond (unsolved) involving stars Mary Miles Minter and Mabel Normand; and recurring cases of drug abuse by such stars as Wallace Reid who died trying to kick the habit.

MO Tragic decline and fall of D. W. Griffith as premier film maker begins with release of *Orphans of the Storm*, followed in 1924 by other box office failures: *America* and *Isn't Life Wonderful*. Finally (in sound) *Abraham Lincoln* and *The Struggle* made in 1931, 1932 respectively, also fail.

MO The first *Our Gang* comedies are produced by Hal Roach. The popular shorts feature a varying group of youngsters (Farina, Joan Darling, Joe Cobb, Johnny Downs, Jackie Cooper, etc.) over the years.

MO *Nanook of the North* is Robert J. Flaherty's first documentary and one of the great films of this genre.

MO Big stars of this year are Strongheart, a German police dog; Norma and Constance Talmadge; Tom Mix and Buck Jones in Fox westerns; Douglas Fairbanks in *Robin Hood;* and Mary Pickford in *Tess of the Storm Country*.

CA Two important carnival companies merge: Wortham's World's Greatest Shows with Morris & Castle.

RA Edwin H. Armstrong invents the superheterodyne broadcast receiver.

RA Over 500 radio stations go into operation and are licensed by Department of Commerce. Many originated as "ham" transmitters.

RA $60,000,000 worth of radio receivers are sold in the U.S., and $50,000,000 of that amount is in parts for sets put together by hams.

RA Among earliest performers and shows on air this year and in 1923 are: *The Lucky Strike Radio Show* sponsored by American Tobacco; *The Happiness Boys*, Ernie Hare and Billy Jones, sponsored by Happiness Candy Co.; *Roxy and His Gang*, a broadcast from stage of the Capitol Theatre by veteran theatre man S.L. Rothafel; Dr. Walter Damrosch and his orchestra; and Joseph White, "The Silver Masked Tenor."

RA First comedy broadcast is by Ed Wynn who does program for WJZ. He is appalled by the lack of audience, because his jokes get no response. The show's announcer rounds up everyone around the studio to sit in as audience and their laughs bring show to life.

RA Radio's first commercial is for a real estate firm, the Queensboro Corporation. The ten-minute commercial sells apartments over station WEAF, New York. WEAF charges $50 for ten minutes in afternoon; $100 for ten minutes in evening.

RA AT&T and RCA have been linking up stations they own to form the beginnings of radio networks. Sarnoff suggests combining all stations into one network and RCA buys AT&T-owned WEAF for $200,000 for facilities and $800,000 for goodwill and WEAF's clear channel. In the first year AT&T grosses over $800,000 by leasing telephone lines to the newly linked stations. What later becomes NBC begins to take form.

RA Manager of station WEAF rejects first commercial for toothpaste, telling the salesman that "care of the teeth" is too delicate a matter to be discussed on the air.

MU *Billboard* publishes charts featuring songs performed by artists in burlesque, stock companies and in concerts. *Billboard* also predicts ". . . radio holds great possibilities for popular song publishers."

1923

TH A number of top comics star in musicals: Eddie Cantor in *Kid Boots;* Joe Cook in Earl Carroll's *Vanities;* Frank Fay in *Artists and Models;* Fannie Brice in Ziegfeld *Follies*. Arthur Schwartz and Howard Dietz have their first Broadway tune, "Alibi Baby," in *Poppy* starring W. C. Fields as Professor Eustace McGargle.

TH The Theatre Guild has one of its most successful years. It presents G. B. Shaw's

Saint Joan, The Devil's Disciple, and Ibsen's *Peer Gynt*. Russia's famous director, Stanislavsky, (inventor of "the method" school of acting) presents his famous Moscow Art Theatre.

TH Owen Davis's play *Icebound* wins Pulitzer Prize. Classic performances are given by Jane Cowl as Juliet and Walter Hampden in *Cyrano de Bergerac*. A tacky contrast is offered by the melodrama *White Cargo*, famous for the slinky leading lady's opening line, "I am Tondelayo."

TH Eleanora Duse's American tour, billed as her "farewell" tour, turns out to be truly that. She dies of pneumonia in Pittsburgh mid-tour.

TH Jake Shubert opens his *Artists and Models* at the Shubert Theatre. A throwback to old burlesque, featuring a large chorus of bare-breasted girls, it is the sensation of the Broadway season. It also sets off a new censorship drive.

MO De Forest develops method of recording sound directly on film. Method is used in producing shorts featuring vaudeville stars, such as Eddie Cantor and Weber and Fields.

MO Mary Pickford buys up large number of negatives of her old films for $10,000. Purpose is to keep re-issues of these films off the market, and from competing with her current movies. Fortunately she decides, in mid '70s, to release them for use in retrospectives of her remarkable career.

MO Cecil B. De Mille makes *The Ten Commandments*, a biblical spectacular and sharp departure from his previous work. This film and *King of Kings* (1927) are big money-makers.

MO First of the Western epics, *The Covered Wagon*, (produced by Jesse Lasky, directed by James Cruze) starring James Kerrigan, Ernest Torrence and Lois Wilson, is a huge success. It sets pattern for films dealing with pioneer life in U.S., stressing story rather than stars, and is followed a year later by John Ford's epic *The Iron Horse*.

MC New performers this year who will later reach stardom in silent and/or talking pictures include: Jean Arthur; Clara Bow in *Down to the Sea in Ships;* England's Ronald Colman in *The White Sister* with Lillian Gish; and Norma Shearer. In Sweden, Greta Garbo (then Greta Gustaffson) films *The Saga of Gosta Borling*.

MO Several comedians vie with Chaplin for billing as comic superstars. Among them: Ben Turpin, Harold Lloyd (*Safety Last*, 1923; *Girl Shy*, 1924; *The Freshman*, 1925; *Speedy*, 1928, etc.); Buster Keaton (*The Boat*, 1923); Harry Langdon; and Laurel and Hardy.

RA/MO/RE Vast improvements in many types of electronic equipment (microphones, loud speakers, vacuum tubes, etc.) this year (and several years immediately following) bring acceptable sound to silent films; greatly enhance quality of records; and eliminate screeches and howls of radio reception. Western Electric subsidiary, Electrical Research Products, Inc. (ERPI) and RCA Photophone, among others, develop keen rivalry in supplying quality sound for all media.

RA Radio receiver sales for entire industry climb to $123,000,000. RCA's share is only $22,500,000 and Sarnoff considers this inexcusably low for a company which (with GE and Westinghouse) controls more than 2000 basic radio patents.

RA/RE For the first time Victor Talking Machine Company puts phonographs on the market with built-in space for customer to insert a radio set.

RA WJZ-WJY, Radio Corp. of America station, goes on the air May 15. Stations do not pay performers, not even their own announcers. Announcers, such as Norman Brokenshire, are identified only by code letters. Brokenshire's is "AON," but the appeal of his voice is such that he is soon getting as many as 100 fan letters daily — all addressed to "AON."

RA ASCAP wins court decision in suit against WOR, Newark, N.J., on grounds that broadcast is "public performance for profit," since mention is made that it originates at Bamberger's, one of the nation's great stores. Broadcasters begin to pay ASCAP $250 per year for right to play music.

RA Ethel Barrymore, appearing on Broadway in The Laughing Lady, performs the play on radio station WJZ, one of the first dramatic broadcasts.

RE Severe post-war depression. Columbia Records files bankruptcy and goes into the hands of receivers who struggle to keep the company alive.

VA This is, perhaps, the peak year of two-a-day vaudeville. The Palace shows a profit of over $500,000 for the year.

RA/RE J. C. Rosenthal, executive chairman of ASCAP, claims royalty payments received by songwriters from phonograph record and piano roll sales dropped twenty percent in past year because of radio. Wants broadcasters to stop playing ASCAP songs.

1924

TH Actors' Equity Association's five-year contract with Producers' Association approaches an end and a group of important producers (Erlanger, Ziegfeld, Sam Harris, Charles Dillingham and others) decide to try to destroy the union by refusing to sign

new agreement. Lee Shubert negotiates independently with Equity and brings a deal to producers' group. They reject it.

TH Shuberts formally resign from Producers' Association; the weakened association signs new contract with Actors' Equity on same terms originally worked out by Shuberts.

TH Eugene O'Neill's All God's Chillun Got Wings, produced by the Provincetown Players, is a landmark treatment of a mixed marriage between a black man (Paul Robeson) and a white woman (Mary Blair). It makes Robeson a star. However, blacks resented O'Neill's apparent assumption that only tragedy could result from such a union.

TH The Student Prince by Sigmund Romberg and Dorothy Donnelly opens and is a smash hit. It becomes the biggest moneymaker in the history of the musical theatre to date. It derives from an old Shubert flop, Old Heidelberg, originally produced in 1902. The Shuberts fight the Romberg "unhappy" ending, but Romberg stands pat.

TH Other popular musicals are I'll Say She Is with the Marx Brothers, and Fred and Adele Astaire in Lady Be Good!, with a great score by George Gershwin, including the standard "Fascinating Rhythm." Ira Gershwin provides all the show's lyrics for the first time.

TH Alfred Lunt and Lynn Fontanne score first great success as a team in Molnar's The Guardsman. Other important shows: Pulitzer Prize winner They Knew What They Wanted by Sidney Howard; Eugene O'Neill's Desire Under the Elms starring Walter Huston; Alfred Lunt and Leslie Howard in Outward Bound; the Maxwell Anderson-Laurence Stallings World War I play, What Price Glory?; and Beggar on Horseback by George Kaufman and Marc Connelly.

TH A Shubert stock-issue prospectus reveals that they own thirty theatres in New York (half of all of Broadway's total seating capacity), plus fifty-six other theatres in major cities throughout the country. Also have largest scenery, costume, and equipment inventory in the world. Earnings for each of five previous years (excepting 1922) $1,000,000 or more.

TH/VA The Klaw-Erlanger partnership is dissolved and winds up with Erlanger suing Klaw for $200,000 in interest on excess capital Erlanger claims he put into the firm. Erlanger wins the case.

MO The influence of European motion pictures on U.S. film makers — which began in 1919 with Germany's classic The Cabinet of Dr. Caligari starring Conrad Veidt — continues throughout the early and mid 20's. By dint of artful direction of Germany's F. W. Murnau and revolutionary

camera work, The Last Laugh (starring Emil Jannings) tells a complete story without any explanatory titles. Russian film makers develop the "montage" with new editing techniques.

MO Big flashy costume pictures are in demand — Fairbanks in The Thief of Bagdad; Rudolph Valentino in Monsieur Beaucaire; John Barrymore in Beau Brummel; Lon Chaney in He Who Gets Slapped; Milton Sills in The Sea Hawk; Romola with Lillian Gish. Nevertheless one of the most popular stars wears no costume at all — Rin Tin Tin, the all-time greatest dog actor.

MO Eric Von Stroheim produces his masterpiece, Greed, a forty-two reel epic based on Frank Norris' McTeague, and refuses to cut more than twenty-two reels. Metro takes it away from him and releases it in ten reels. It's a flop, but later considered a classic by film buffs. Zazu Pitts, the fluttery comedienne, stars in a straight dramatic role.

RA/MO Western Electric, showing talking film using Maude Adams and other celebrities, demonstrates its sound-on-disk system for leading motion picture executives. There is little interest in it.

MO Thomas Meighan is the most popular star this year according to Photoplay magazine, followed by Norma Talmadge, Harold Lloyd, Tom Mix, and Mary Pickford. Cecil B. De Mille is the number one director.

RA/RE Radio sales make a phenomenal leap from $60,000,000 in 1923 to $350,000,000 in 1924. Columbia Records had already gone into receivership; now Victor's record sales drop another twenty percent in a steady decline attributed to the popularity of radio.

RA Among earliest musical aggregations on radio are the Cliquout Club Eskimos, the Ipana Troubadors, the A&P Gypsies, the Browning King Orchestra, all on the AT&T chain; Schrafft's Tearoom Orchestra, the Wanamaker Organ Concert, and Rheingold Quartet on WJZ, the Westinghouse station. Sponsors pay program but not time costs.

RE A Western Electric engineer, H. C. Harrison, patents an electrical recording process.

RE Louis Sterling (head of British Columbia) with some financial help from U.S. sources buys American Columbia for $2,500,000. Purpose is to get the right to use Bell Laboratories' new electrical recording process which Bell was licensing only to American firms.

RE/RA First loudspeakers are manufactured in the U.S. by B. Grigsby.

MU George Gershwin's most famous composition, "Rhapsody In Blue," is presented for the first time by Paul Whiteman and his orchestra in an "all American music concert." It marks Gershwin's acceptance as a "serious" composer. Whiteman's initial recording of "Rhapsody In Blue" sells 1,000,000 copies.

CI Lillian Leitzel, queen of the aerialists with Ringling Brothers & Barnum and Bailey Circus, does 239 planges (swinging her body in complete circular revolutions by throwing herself over her own shoulder, while hanging from a rope with her right hand and wrist in a loop). No other aerialist has ever come close to matching this record.

1925

TH England's triple threat, (writer, actor, composer), Noel Coward invades Broadway. Age twenty-five, he has three plays opening: *Vortex,* in which he plays lead; *Hay Fever,* starring Laura Hope Crews; and *Easy Virtue* with Jane Cowl.

TH Comedy musical hit of the season is *The Coconuts,* which establishes the Marx Brothers' unique brand of zany comedy. Book is by George Kaufman, score by Irving Berlin.

TH Jerome Kern writes another hit score for a Marilyn Miller musical, *Sunny,* with Jack Donahue and Clifton Webb. His first Miller musical for Ziegfeld in 1920, *Sally,* introduced the classic "Look for the Silver Lining." Other musical hits include Dennis King in *The Vagabond King* and *No, No Nanette* ("Tea for Two").

TH Theatre Guild presents Richard Rodgers-Lorenz Hart's *Garrick Gaieties,* with the standard "Manhattan." It's the team's first hit show. They write score for *Dearest Enemy* (hit tune: "Here In My Arms") the same year.

MO Radio is the big new entertainment novelty and Hollywood blames it for sagging box office returns. But some films are still bringing in people: Lon Chaney's *Phantom of the Opera; The Big Parade,* which starts a new vogue for World War I movies; John Barrymore in *The Sea Beast;* that early soap opera *Stella Dallas;* Chaplin's *The Gold Rush* which contains his priceless shoe-eating pantomine; and Mae Murray in *The Merry Widow.*

MO United Artists hires Joseph Schenck as chief administrator. He signs John Barrymore, Gloria Swanson, Buster Keaton, and Norma and Constance Talmadge.

MO Warner Brothers takes over Vitagraph, last of the pioneer film companies. Cecil B. De Mille leaves Paramount to set up his own independent production company.

MO A young Metro actress, Lucille le Sueur, is named Joan Crawford by a fan magazine contest. Playing small parts or extra roles at this time are such future stars

as Clark Gable, Carole Lombard, Gary Cooper, and Janet Gaynor.

RA The first presidential inaugural address is broadcast by Calvin Coolidge over a twenty-four station transcontinental network.

RE Victor Talking Machine Company shows deficit of $141,000 this year, dropping from earnings of $1,300,000 the year before; and $17,500,000 in 1923. These are indications of inroads radio has made on phonograph and record business.

RE Victor releases first electrically recorded sides in April, a performance by University of Pennsylvania Mask & Wig Club.

RE Art Gillham, known as "The Whispering Pianist," makes the first electrical recordings in the Columbia studios.

RE New electrical recording techniques (utilizing microphones, etc.) are changing performing styles drastically. No longer do singers need powerful voices to be picked up by the horns. Now the "Whispering Jack Smiths" and "Little Jack Littles," the "soft" vocalists and instrumentalists, come into popularity. Strings and other softer sounding instruments may be recorded effectively.

RE Eldridge Johnson, who has fought the radio invasion, finally decides to join up. He makes a deal with RCA to purchase Radiolas from them, which he installs in Victor phonographs. RCA also manufactures the Electrola, Victor's first electric record player. Victor's business booms.

RE A twelve-inch, long-playing record is produced experimentally by Brunswick-Balke-Collender. It has forty minutes of material recorded at 78 rpm.

CI Con Colleano, an Australian with the Ringling Brothers and Barnum & Bailey Show, is the day's premier tightwire performer. He originates the forward, feet-to-feet somersault; does Spanish dancing; and removes his trousers on the wire.

NC Night club business is booming. Some more notable owners and/or operators: Paul Whiteman, who has his own club on 48th Street and Broadway; Roger Wolfe Kahn, son of millionaire financier, not only has his own club but his own band; and Texas Guinan, whose clubs are frequently padlocked by Federal officers for various violations. Biggest Chicago night club star is Joe E. Lewis, who is almost killed by local hoodlums.

BU Top star of the day in burlesque is Carrie Finnell, billed as "the girl with the $100,000 legs." Later in her career, Finnell adds a spectacular routine in which she twirls tassles suspended from her breasts and buttocks.

RA/VA Loew's, Inc., which owns and operates radio station WHN in New York, stipulates in its vaudeville contracts that acts must do radio shows when requested by WHN.

TV Francis Jenkins conducts successful television transmitting and receiving experiments at laboratories in Washington, D.C.

TV Ernst Alexanderson and Jenkins in the U.S. and John Baird in England all conduct public demonstrations of rotating-disk television, similar to earlier experiments by Paul Nipkow.

1926

TH Eva Le Gallienne's Civic Repertory Theatre opens. Located on 14th Street in New York, it features excellent plays and players at low prices ($1.50). It opens with Nazimova in *The Cherry Orchard* and presents 1,581 plays from 1926 to its demise in 1932.

TH Dramatic highlights this year: Eugene O'Neill's *The Great God Brown,* produced by O'Neill and featuring his first use of dual-personality characters, utilizing masks; Florence Reed in *The Shanghai Gesture;* and one of the first plays to describe an adoring mother in unflattering terms, Sidney Howard's *The Silver Cord.*

TH Other popular shows this season are Romberg's *The Desert Song* with Vivienne Segal; Anita Loos' *Gentlemen Prefer Blondes;* and Gertrude Lawrence in *Oh Kay!* with a Gershwin score.

TH Mae West writes and stars in *Sex.* She becomes the sex symbol of the era. The play is closed by police and Miss West serves ten days in the workhouse.

MO According to *Motion Picture News,* there are over 14,500 movie houses in the U.S. Hollywood is turning out 400 films this year. Movies are America's favorite entertainment — a major influence on the mores and morals of the country.

MO Paramount Theatre in New York opens. It is one of Adolph Zukor's outstanding achievements and the most elegant of the movie houses.

MO Joseph P. Kennedy and an investors' syndicate acquire control of British-owned Film Booking Office, a producing company specializing in low-budget Westerns, with Tom Mix and his horse Tony, Richard Talmadge, Evelyn Brent, and other stars under contract. After Kennedy's acquisition of the company, Sarnoff buys into FBO for RCA to the extent of $500,000. It is the first transaction between Sarnoff and Kennedy.

MO Walter Rich and Warner Brothers form Vitaphone Corporation which is the licensor to the motion picture industry for the Western Electric (ERPI) sound-on-disk system.

MO Warner Brothers premieres Vitaphone sound systems. Program presents Giovanni Martinelli, Mischa Elman, the New York Philharmonic Symphony Orchestra, and Eddie Foy and is introduced — in a filmed talk — by Will Hays. Feature picture is *Don Juan* (starring John Barrymore), a silent film with symphonic musical score.

MO Sound is still considered a novelty. The big pictures, all silent of course, are MGM's smash remake of *Ben Hur* with Ramon Navarro and Francis X. Bushman; *What Price Glory*, another World War I film; Ronald Colman as *Beau Geste* and Chaplin's *The Circus*.

MO Greta Garbo, Swedish star, makes first American film, *The Torrent*. She plays a Spanish peasant. She follows this with *Flesh and the Devil* (1927); *The Mysterious Lady* (1928); and *Wild Orchids* (1929) to become one of the superstars of the era.

MO Technicolor achieves first important success in *The Black Pirate*, starring Douglas Fairbanks.

MO Rudolph Valentino's death and funeral create an incredible situation. More than 100,000 people line both sides of the streets down which his funeral procession proceeds. There are even reports that some women commit suicide over his death. Fans still visit his grave more than fifty years later.

RA The Federal Radio Commission is created in Coolidge's administration, ending a period of confusion resulting from radio's phenomenal growth and spread.

RA Radio Corporation of America announces formation of the National Broadcasting Company, Inc. NBC is owned 50% by RCA, 30% by General Electric and 20% by Westinghouse. Merlin (Deacon) Aylesworth, former president of National Electric Light Association, becomes NBC president; George McClelland, a WEAF time salesman, is in charge of programming. NBC soon has two networks, the Red and the Blue.

RA Inaugural broadcast of NBC, November 15, includes Will Rogers, Weber & Fields, Ben Bernie, George Olsen, B. A. Rolfe, Vincent Lopez, Walter Damrosch and the New York Symphony Orchestra, Mary Garden, Metropolitan Opera's Titta Ruffo, and others. Twenty-five stations in twenty-one cities carry the broadcast to an estimated audience of 2,000,000 people.

RA/MO/TH/VA Inroads of radio and movies on entertainment audiences have begun to seriously hurt vaudeville. Top stars in those fields sign with networks. Eddie Cantor signs with NBC in 1926; Al Jolson in 1928; followed by many others including Jack Benny, Groucho Marx, Ed Wynn, Bing Crosby, Jimmy Durante, George Burns and Gracie Allen.

RA Station WGN in Chicago introduces new situation comedy, called *Sam and Henry*, a story of two blacks in the taxi-cab business, played by two white men, Charles Correll and Freeman Gosden. Two years later show moves to WMAQ, the NBC affiliate in Chicago, and name is changed to *Amos 'n Andy*.

RA Arthur Judson — concert entrepreneur and manager of Ezio Pinza, Yascha Heifetz, Vladimir Horowitz, George Szell, Bruno Walter and both the New York and Philadelphia Philharmonic Orchestras — proposes to David Sarnoff that he head an artists' bureau for Sarnoff's new radio network. Sarnoff indicates an interest in the plan, but later rejects Judson. Judson organizes a network, United Independent Broadcasters, Inc., forerunner of CBS.

CI Charles Ringling dies. John is the last of the five brothers to survive. That year he builds a home in Sarasota, Florida, at a cost of over $1,000,000.

CI Ala Naitto is the only woman who does a forward feet-to-feet somersault on the tightwire. She is also a hoop juggler and a head-to-head balancer.

1927

TH Biggest boom in the history of the American theatre takes place: 280 shows open during the 1927-28 season — a number never equalled before or since. A greater number are hits than ever before: *Burlesque* with Hal Skelly and Barbara Stanwyck; *The Barker* (Walter Huston and Claudette Colbert); *Coquette* (Helen Hayes); and *The Trial of Mary Dugan* (Ann Harding).

TH Florenz Ziegfeld opens his Ziegfeld Theatre in February with a hit musical, *Rio Rita*, followed by an even greater hit, *Show Boat*, in December. The latter, which set a precedent by integrating book with score, is considered the outstanding musical achievement of the twenties. The great Jerome Kern-Oscar Hammerstein II score includes "Old Man River," "Why Do I Love You" and "Can't Help Lovin' That Man." Cast: Helen Morgan, Norma Terris, Charles Winninger, and Edna May Oliver.

MO Warner Brothers' *Jazz Singer*, starring Al Jolson in the role George Jessel played on Broadway, opens on Broadway in New York. It only contains four talking or singing sequences but is immediate smash hit. It does for talking-musical films approximately what *The Great Train Robbery* did for early one-reelers.

MO The huge success of Warner Bros. *Jazz Singer* results in majority of important film studios adopting (Western Electric-ERPI developed) Vitaphone sound-on-disk system for talking pictures. RCA Photophone left with handful of lesser studios.

MO General Electric, which controls Photophone (sound-on-film) system at this time, arranges for Paramount to use the system in production of *Wings*.

MO Film producers add sound sequences to silent films, calling them "part-talkie." Audiences are offered *Abie's Irish Rose* two ways, "silent or with sound."

MO Cecil B. De Mille makes what he considers his best picture, *The King of Kings*, with H. B. Warner as Jesus. It is an international hit, acclaimed by both audiences and religious authorities.

MO The Academy of Motion Picture Arts and Sciences, representing the industry's actors, producers, directors and writers, is formed this year. Originally conceived in late 1926 — by Louis B. Mayer, director Fred Niblo and actor Conrad Nagel — the Academy is founded in January, 1927, by thirty-six industry figures, including Mary Pickford, Douglas Fairbanks, Sid Grauman, Jack Warner, Raoul Walsh, and Henry King. In May a gala banquet is held to announce the Academy's formation; 231 become members. At the start all the voting is done by five people (Pickford, Fairbanks, Mayer, Grauman and Joe Schenck) but that soon changes.

MO The 1927 Academy Awards (later dubbed Oscars), presented in 1928, go to Emil Jannings for his first U.S. film, *The Way of All Flesh*; and to Janet Gaynor for three pictures, including the memorable *Seventh Heaven* with Charles Farrell. *Wings*, a pioneer aviation film (with Richard Arlen, Charles "Buddy" Rogers and "It Girl" Clara Bow) is voted "best picture."

MO The Roxy Theatre, named after Samuel Rothafel, opens in New York City. Called "The Cathedral of the Motion Picture," it is the most elegant and flamboyant of all the new theatres.

VA Keith-Albee and Orpheum circuits merge. The combine now owns and/or controls 535 theatres, more than seventy-five percent of all the vaude theatres in the country. They are said to constitute assets of close to $100,000,000.

MO A Warner's Vitaphone sound installation costs a theatre approximately $16,000 to $25,000. This year only 185 houses are wired.

MO Sam Warner, who was in active charge of developing Warner's acquisition and utilization of Vitaphone, dies on October 5 at age forty of pneumonia. He does not live to see the great triumph of Vitaphone and talking pictures.

RA Ike and Leon Levy sell La Palina Cigars a $50,000 advertising deal on WCAU.

La Palina is a Philadelphia company owned by Sam Paley. His son, William, is advertising manager of the company. His daughter, Blanche, is newly married to Leon Levy.

RA The Levys' partner in WCAU, Dan Murphy, wants to get out of the radio business. Meanwhile, the La Palina advertising campaign on WCAU proves startlingly successful. Young William Paley buys Murphy's one-third share in WCAU.

RA With the help of WCAU's Leon Levy, United Independent Broadcasters, Inc. puts together a network of sixteen radio stations. UIB also has an arrangement with AT&T for long lines to interconnect the stations. But Judson's network is having desperate financial problems.

RA The UIB network sells out to the Columbia Phonograph Company for $163,000. A new company, the Columbia Phonograph Broadcasting System, is set up. Arthur Judson's Radio Program Corporation is contracted to supply ten hours of programming a week, for $10,000 per week.

RA In September the Columbia Phonograph Broadcasting System broadcasts its first network program, *The King's Henchmen*, by Edna St. Vincent Millay and Deems Taylor, performed by a Metropolitan Opera company of artists under the direction of Howard Barlow. The broadcast encounters technical difficulties, but is an artistic success. However the company is virtually out of funds.

RA Columbia Phonograph Broadcasting System sells the network back to UIB for $10,000 and thirty hours of broadcasting time. It permits the network to retain the name, which becomes the Columbia Broadcasting System. The Phonograph Company's proprietorship lasted less than four months.

RA Owning the radio network once again, the original founders of UIB — Arthur Judson, Major J. Andrew White and George Coats (plus investor Betty Fleischmann) — continue to experience severe financial difficulties. The Levy brothers and a close friend, Jerome Louchheim (a Philadelphia construction tycoon), buy controlling interest in the network.

RA Shortly after the Levy/Louchheim purchase of controlling interest in CBS, the Warner Brothers' subsidiary company, Vitaphone, buys a $750,000 advertising campaign on the network. La Palina cigar sales skyrocket from 400,000 to 1,000,000 per day, largely due to its campaign on CBS.

RA Earliest sponsors and their shows on the NBC Red and Blue networks include Palmolive Hour, Atwater Kent Hour, the Ampico Hour, the Cities Service Orchestra, the General Motors Family Party and veteran favorites the Cliquout Club Eskimos, the Ipana Troubadors and the A&P Gypsies.

RA First car radios are introduced.

RA NBC broadcasts the Rose Bowl football game in Pasadena for the first time. Same year the Gene Tunney-Jack Dempsey heavyweight fight is carried by sixty-nine stations on both the Red and Blue networks.

RA The Federal Radio Act passed this year stipulates that broadcasters may have "the use of" channels to which they are assigned, but "not the ownership thereof." Station requirement to operate in "the public interest" is also spelled out for the first time.

TV Herbert Hoover, leading contender for 1928 Presidential nomination, speaks on experimental television broadcast conducted by AT&T.

RE Victor markets the first phonograph to feature an automatic record changer.

RE Edison Phonograph Company markets its own long-playing, forty-minute records. It is a failure because an inadequate number of machines are able to play the 80 rpm speed required.

RE/MO Brunswick Records cashes in on Al Jolson's smash "talkies" motion picture hit, *The Jazz Singer*, by releasing disks of songs he sings in the film. They are all hits, including "Mother of Mine, I Love You," a tune written specifically for the movie.

1928

TH Clark Gable makes Broadway appearance in play by Sophie Treadwell, *Machinal*.

TH Bonanza year for comedy stars in the theatre: Marx Brothers in *Animal Crackers*; Eddie Cantor, *Whoopee*; Victor Moore and Bert Lahr, *Hold Everything*; Joe Cook, *Rain or Shine*; W. C. Fields, *Vanities*; and Will Rogers, *Three Cheers*.

TH Eugene O'Neill's *Strange Interlude*, starring Lynn Fontanne, wins Pulitzer Prize. Produced by the Theatre Guild, it is first play to open at 5:15 p.m., adjourn after the fifth act for dinner intermission, and resume at 8:30.

TH Biggest dramatic-comedy hit of the year is Charles MacArthur and Ben Hecht's *Front Page*, starring Lee Tracy.

TH Mae West has another hit, *Diamond Lil*. She is author and star. Again she and entire cast are hauled off to jail.

TH Musical hits include Bill Robinson and Adelaide Hall in *Blackbirds of 1928*, score by Dorothy Fields and Jimmy McHugh ("I Can't Give You Anything But Love Baby"). It is the first Broadway hit for "Bojangles" and one of the biggest all-black revues.

MO Films go into one of the industry's more chaotic periods, with every major studio rushing to make its own all-talking films. Many movies are made both with sound and in silent versions as theatres attempt to convert to various competitive sound systems offered.

MO Mickey Mouse makes his debut in Walt Disney's animated cartoon (silent) *Plane Crazy*. His first talkie, *Steamboat Willie*, appears the following year. Disney records Mickey's voice himself.

MO Encouraged by the phenomenal success of *The Jazz Singer*, Warners release first full-length, all-talking picture, a poorly produced quickie called *The Lights of New York* with Helene Costello.

MO/RA In a deal arranged between Joseph Kennedy and Sarnoff, RCA buys into Keith-Albee-Orpheum theatre chain and changes its name to RKO, short for Radio-Keith-Orpheum. Major purpose of move is to gain foothold for RCA Photophone sound-on-film system for theatres. Pathe, Mack Sennett, other producers using RCA Photophone.

MO Walter Rich sells Vitaphone's exclusive rights for films in ERPI-produced sound-on-disk system back to ERPI for $1,000,000. Vitaphone (Rich and Warners) retains non-exclusive rights to the system.

MO ERPI, having reacquired control of its own sound-on-disk system, makes royalty arrangement with film producers. They pay $1000 per negative reel for rights to use ERPI sound-on-disk system. This means studios would pay maximum of $10,000 for a ten-reeler. If it was a big hit, it would earn millions. Bargain deal is brought about through desperate rivalry between ERPI (Western Electric-AT&T) and RCA (GE) Photophone.

MO Major Hollywood film companies send group of technical experts to New York to analyze and make recommendations on the competing Vitaphone and Photophone sound systems. Group feels RCA and GE not ready with Photophone, recommends Vitaphone.

RA From early 1928 to July, 1929, RCA stock climbs from 85 to over 500. Then, in 1929, comes the market crash, and within one month the stock drops to 20.

RA Jerome Louchheim's health is not too good and William Paley buys out the greater part of his interest in CBS. The Levys and the Paleys now substantially own the network, and William Paley is elected president on September 26.

RA *Amos 'n Andy* begins airing on NBC March 19. Pepsodent sponsors the show at 7 to 7:15 p.m. five nights weekly. It is by far the most successful show in the history of radio to date. It is written and performed by its originators, Freeman Fisher Gosden (Amos) and Charles Correll (Andy). Although not publicized, black actors are regularly used as members of the cast.

RA First dramatic and melodramatic shows presented include *Real Folks, Main Street Sketches*.

MU/RA RCA buys two important music publishing companies: Leo Feist, Inc. and Carl Fischer, Inc.

TV General Electric begins television program experiments. First drama to be telecast is *The Queen's Messenger*, September 11, via experimental TV station, W2XAD, in Schenectady. Show is shot with three cameras, utilizing close-ups only.

MU *Billboard* publishes new feature: "Popular Numbers Performed by Famous Singers and (Orchestra) Leaders."

RE/MO RCA Victor records Fannie Brice doing tunes from her movie, *My Man*. They are almost as successful as the Jolson records from *Jazz Singer* on Brunswick.

RE Almost every record company records both vocal and instrumental versions of "The Wedding of the Painted Doll," "You Were Meant For Me" and other tunes from the hit MGM singing-talking movie *Broadway Melody*. However, no one has yet made an original sound track album.

VA Vaudeville magnate F. F. Proctor dies. Leaves $1,000,000 to Actors' Fund.

VA Keith-Albee-Orpheum stock issue of $100,000,000 is floated at $101 per share. On the second day of the sale the issue is oversubscribed. Joe Kennedy is the man behind the promotion.

MO Talkies are highly successful but only 500 theatres out of a possible 20,000 are wired for sound. Others are converting as rapidly as possible.

TV Carl Laemmle includes a clause in all his movie contracts, which gives him rights to use stories, plays, etc. in television, as well as movies.

TV In August, Westinghouse transmits movies by television at its laboratories in Pittsburgh. Among those in attendance at the demonstration is David Sarnoff of RCA.

CI The most spectacular highwire act of all time, the Wallendas, makes its debut with Ringling Brothers and Barnum and Bailey. There are only four family members in the act at this time (Helen, Joe, Carl and Herman). As the family grows, nine Wallendas will walk, ride bicycles, and create formations two and three high, forty feet above the circus floor.

CI Alfred Cordona, greatest of all the "daring young men on the flying trapeze," marries aerial star, Lillian Leitzel.

1929

TH Two all-Negro shows — a revue called *Hot Chocolates* and a play about a rent party, *Harlem* — are hits.

TH Archie Leach appears in two musicals, *A Wonderful Night* and *Boom Boom*, starring Jeanette MacDonald. When the ex-Coney Island stilt-walker goes to Hollywood he changes his name to Cary Grant.

TH *Street Scene*, a social commentary on the plight of the poor in a big city by Elmer Rice, is first big hit of the season and wins Pulitzer Prize.

TH *Show Girl*, Ruby Keeler's first starring role, is not a success but her husband, Al Jolson, helps business during the run by appearing nightly in the aisle to sing "Liza" while his wife tap dances to the Gershwin standard.

TH Laurence Olivier plays for first time in the U.S. in *Murder on the Second Floor*.

MO The incredibly costly struggle in the film industry for supremacy in sound is primarily responsible for the strong position (never relinquished) of the banks and Wall Street financiers in the industry.

MO At beginning of year only 1300 theatres of 20,500 in U.S. have sound installations. By end of 1929 more than 9000 houses can show sound films.

MO Public response to sound films results in record-breaking 110,000,000 paid admissions in 1929. Two years earlier the figure was 60,000,000. Sound's arrival is probably responsible for carrying industry through the depression, which begins this year.

MO Warners releases first all-talking, all-singing, all-color (also all-star) feature film, *On With the Show*. Musicals are big box office. "Singing In the Rain" is introduced in MGM's *Hollywood Revue of 1929*; Jolson sings "Sonny Boy" in *The Singing Fool*; Jeanette MacDonald is teamed with Maurice Chevalier for the first time in *Love Parade*; and the biggest smash is Academy Award winner, *Broadway Melody*.

MO Ernst Lubitsch, Rouben Mamoulian, King Vidor, and Lewis Milestone are among first directors to use sound in post-synchronization, i.e., shoot much of the film as a silent, and add sound and music after silent filming is completed.

MO Stars who make their talkie debuts this year include the Marx Brothers, *Coconuts*; Gloria Swanson, *The Trespasser*; Joan Crawford, *Untamed*; and Mary Pickford, *Coquette*, for which she wins an Oscar.

MO Fox releases first all-talking film made outdoors, *In Old Arizona*. Its star, Warner Baxter, wins an Oscar.

MO Director King Vidor makes first major all-talking film with an all-black cast, *Hallelujah!*, headed by Nina Mae McKinney.

MO John Gilbert's unfortunately thin voice (a pathetic mismatch for his visual image as the screen's great lover) ruins his career with the release of his first talking picture, *His Glorious Night*.

MO Mary Pickford and Douglas Fairbanks team for *The Taming of the Shrew*, mainly remembered for its title-credit line, "Play by William Shakespeare; Additional dialogue by (Director) Samuel Taylor."

MO Some of the most successful and/or critically acclaimed talkies this year are *Disraeli*, for which George Arliss wins an Oscar; Helen Morgan in *Applause*; and Ruth Chatterton in *Madam X*.

BU Ann Corio is one of first burlesque strippers to move on to Broadway musicals. She appears in Earl Carroll's *Vanities* to good notices.

MO/TH/VA All but one of the eighteen theatres on Broadway in New York between 42nd and 53rd Streets are showing talkies, either at popular prices or a $2 admission. Only exception is the Palace, which is playing vaudeville. Not a single house is showing legitimate productions.

MO Darryl Zanuck becomes head of production at Warner Brothers and continues in that key post until 1933. Salary: $5000 per week.

RA Shortly after Paley takes the reins as CBS's president (via a new deal for affiliated stations), he increases the CBS station line-up from twenty-two to forty-seven stations. All of them are committed to carry network shows in prime time; in exchange, the network furnishes them with free sustaining programming.

MO/RA Paley sells 50% of CBS stock for 58,823 shares of Paramount Pictures stock, value $3,800,000, in a deal with Paramount head, Adolph Zukor.

RA Paley uses 7–7:15 p.m. time slot to test new talent against powerful *Amos 'n Andy*. None surpass the black situation comedy, but among stars developed in that time slot are Bing Crosby, the Mills Brothers, Kate Smith and others.

RA One of most successful of all ethnic family situation comedies, *The Rise of the Goldbergs*, debuts November 20 on NBC. Show runs until 1946, and in 1949 is revived as a television show. Gertrude Berg is writer, producer, and star of the show.

RA Rudy Vallee makes his radio debut on The Fleischmann Hour in October. Kate Smith; Arthur Tracy, the Street Singer; Jan Garber and Wayne King also make their first radio appearances in this year. Arthur Godfrey makes his initial radio appearance on station WTOP, Baltimore.

RA/MO First National's film *Fast Life*, a $2 ticket in New York City, is the first movie to be serialized on the radio. Fifteen-minute installments are aired over WGBS, New York, starting in August.

TV Vladimir Zworykin, engineer, spells out his ideas for a television development for Sarnoff. Estimates costs would run about $100,000. Before TV reaches acceptable commercial entertainment quality, RCA has spent $10,000,000. By time it shows first profits, RCA has invested $50,000,000.

TV Al Jolson sings "Sonny Boy" in color television demonstration at Bell Telephone Company laboratories.

TV The Institute of Radio Engineers gets the first demonstration of Vladimir Zworykin's cathode ray television receiver (the kinescope).

RE Decca Records is organized in England by E. R. (Ted) Lewis.

CI Last surviving Ringling, John, buys the American Circus Corporation for $2,000,000. It is a conglomerate of some of the outstanding shows in the country, including Hagenbeck-Wallace, Sells-Floto, Al G. Barnes, Sparks, and John Robinson. The combine owns 150 railroad cars, 2000 animals, and features more than 4000 performers. Within months after the purchase the stock market crashes and the banks take over the shows.

CI Acrobat and ground leaper Billy Pape with the Sparks-Downie Circus springboard-leaps into a forward somersault over five elephants and two camels, a distance estimated at forty-one feet.

CI A favorite old spectacular circus act is revived by Hugo Zacchini. He is shot from a cannon by compressed air to a height of about seventy feet and a distance of almost 150 feet.

CI/CA Cowboy movie stars get into circus-carnival business. Tom Mix takes out his own circus; Jack Hoxie joins Dodson's World's Fair Shows carnival company.

1930

TH/MO Talking pictures and the depression begin to take their toll on the legitimate theatre. Fewer houses become available for live theatre. Stock companies go into decline. Traveling shows are seriously hurt.

TH Hit musicals include *Girl Crazy* in which Ethel Merman, making her Broadway debut, and Ginger Rogers sing the Gershwins' great score. Miss Merman scores by holding a high C for sixteen bars on "I've Got Rhythm." Miss Rogers croons the standard "Embraceable You." Other musicals: *Three's a Crowd,* with Fred Allen, Libby Holman and Clifton Webb; Bert Lahr

and Kate Smith in *Flying High*.

TH Other successful and/or interesting productions this year are Spencer Tracy in *The Last Mile;* Lunt and Fontanne in Maxwell Anderson's *Elizabeth the Queen; Once In a Lifetime,* the first Moss Hart-George Kaufman play, a farce about the advent of sound in Hollywood; and Helen Gahagan and Melvyn Douglas in *Tonight or Never,* the last play produced by the venerable David Belasco before his death in 1931.

TH Vicki Baum's *Grand Hotel,* produced by Herman Shumlin, and Marc Connelly's *The Green Pastures,* with an all-black cast, are two of biggest successes of the year. Latter wins Pulitzer Prize.

MO Hollywood masters sound in 1930 and talkies begin to develop an art of their own. By the following year sound is installed in 83% of the nation's theatres. Silent stars who can talk go on to new fame. Actors who could always talk (those recruited from the theatre) become instant film stars in some cases. Movies include *The Big House; Min and Bill* (teaming Marie Dressler and Wallace Beery for the first time); and Lon Chaney's first and only talkie, a remake of *The Unholy Three.* He dies on August 26.

MO World War I films are hot — Howard Hughes' *Hell's Angels, Journey's End* and Oscar winner *All's Quiet on the Western Front* with young Lew Ayres. Jean Harlow becomes a star when she replaces a foreign actress in *Hell's Angels,* after Hughes decides to make the film with sound midway through production.

MO Greta Garbo makes her first talkie, Eugene O'Neill's *Anna Christie,* advertised with the line "Garbo Talks!" Marie Dressler almost steals the picture, but final honors go to Garbo, whose husky Swedish accent suits her enigmatic star quality. Her first words on the screen are "Gif me a viskey, and don't be stingy, baby." The previous year, 1929, she made her last silent film, *The Kiss,* which was also MGM's last silent film.

MO Busby Berkeley (formerly a Broadway choreographer) directs musical sequences for Eddie Cantor's *Whoopee* and introduces his unique technique of filming such scenes using a variety of dizzying camera angles. Heretofore, musical numbers were filmed as though viewed on a legit stage.

TV NBC puts the first experimental television station into operation in New York. Call letters are W2XBS.

RA/RE Department of Justice brings antitrust action against RCA, GE, Westinghouse, and AT&T.

RE Depression and radio's inroads con-

tinue to take their toll in the record industry. Industry sales drop from $75,000,000 in 1929 to $46,000,000 in 1930. This is only the beginning of a calamitous slide which continues till 1938.

MU The era of the big bands has not yet begun. But a midwestern band, Glen Gray and his Casa Loma Orchestra, is attracting wide attention among musicians and young people.

TV Philo T. Farnsworth electronic television transmission system patent approved.

VA E. F. Albee dies of a heart attack March 11.

FA Ralph Ammon, manager of Wisconsin State Fair, makes a survey of attendance at eight fairs for the last fifteen years. It shows that in eight states surveyed (Wisconsin, Ohio, Minnesota, Indiana, Missouri, Nebraska, Iowa, Illinois) attendance climbed from 1,502,000 in 1915 to 2,870,000 in 1930.

1931

RE/MO Edison, whose contributions to American entertainment were as great as his work for society as a whole, dies October 18 in West Orange, N. J. at the age of eighty-four.

TH The Group Theatre, whose members will have a deep impact on the American theatre for the next forty years, is organized by thirty-one actors and directors. They include such pacesetters as John Garfield, Stella and Luther Adler, playwright-actor Clifford Odets, Elia Kazan, Lee Strasberg, and Cheryl Crawford. The Theatre Guild helps by presenting the Group's first production, *The House of Connelly* by Paul Green, under the Guild's sponsorship.

TH The Shubert Theatre Corporation goes into receivership with Irving Trust Bank and Lee Shubert as receivers.

TH Theatre Guild produces O'Neill's *Mourning Becomes Electra,* another lengthy trilogy with an intermission for dinner. It stars Alla Nazimova and Alice Brady. O'Neill considered it his best play.

TH *Of Thee I Sing* is political satire with Victor Moore and William Gaxton (score by the Gershwins, book by George Kaufman and Morrie Ryskind). It is the first musical ever to win a Pulitzer Prize. Strong season for musicals with Fred and Adele Astaire in *Band Wagon* with an Arthur Schwartz-Howard Dietz score ("Dancing in the Dark"); *The Cat and the Fiddle;* Ethel Waters in *Rhapsody in Black;* and *Laugh Parade* with Ed Wynn.

TH Noel Coward's *Private Lives,* starring himself and Gertrude Lawrence, is the outstanding hit of the year.

TH Katharine Cornell, in her first venture as actress-producer, presents *The Barretts of*

Wimpole Street. Brian Aherne plays Robert Browning to her Elizabeth Barrett. Director is her husband, Guthrie McClintic.

TH David Belasco dies May 15.

MO An obscure silent picture extra, Clark Gable, makes a hit in a road company prison drama and is signed by MGM to slap Norma Shearer around in *A Free Soul*, resulting in instant stardom. Bing Crosby croons in some Mack Sennett shorts in his film debut.

MO Two classic horror films are box office hits this year: *Frankenstein* with Boris Karloff as the monster and Colin Clive as the title role scientist; and *Dracula* with Bela Lugosi as the vampire, a role he originated on Broadway.

MO This year and 1932 mark the peak of the popularity of gangster films, including *Public Enemy* with James Cagney; *Scarface* with Paul Muni and George Raft; *The Big House* with Wallace Beery and Chester Morris; and *The Last Mile* with Preston Foster and George E. Stone. *Little Caesar* with Edward G. Robinson had been released in 1930.

MO Ethel Waters appears in a short, *Rufus Jones for President*, and is upstaged by a singer-tap dancer, five-year-old Sammy Davis Jr.

MO *Flowers and Trees*, Walt Disney's first Silly Symphony technicolor cartoon, wins an Oscar. The following year Disney is awarded a special citation by the Academy for creating Mickey Mouse. An Oscar also goes to Wallace Beery for *The Champ*, introducing one of the great child actors, Jackie Cooper.

MO Helen Hayes wins an Oscar for *The Sin of Madelon Claudet*, but fellow stage stars Lynn Fontanne and Alfred Lunt make their first and last movie, *The Guardsman*, and return to Broadway.

MO Bette Davis is recruited from Broadway by Universal where one unknowing executive describes her as having "as much sex appeal as Slim Summerville." After several forgettable roles, she is discovered by George Arliss and featured in his 1932 Warner Brothers film, *The Man Who Played God*. She remains with Warners for eighteen years.

MO/RA The depression has severely damaged Paramount Pictures, but CBS has prospered. In a deal made possible by the contract in which Paramount initially bought into CBS, the film company now sells back its 50% share of CBS to Paley for $5,200,000 — and Paramount buys back its shares still held by the network for $4,000,000.

RA U.S. Census Bureau reports that 12,078,345 American homes out of a total number of 29,980,146 have radio receivers, or about two out of every five.

RA Eddie Cantor makes his network radio debut this year. In the next five years other leading comedians of vaudeville, Broadway, and films get their own shows, including George Burns and Gracie Allen, Jack Benny, Bob Hope, Goodman Ace and wife Jane as *Easy Aces*, Ed Wynn, Jack Pearl, Joe Penner, and Fibber McGee and Molly.

TV Columbia Broadcasting System sets up W2XAB in New York as its first experimental television station.

RE RCA Victor introduces the 33⅓ rpm long-playing record, but does not manufacture phonographs to play the new speed. There are some 78 rpm players, convertible to 33⅓, but not enough. After an effort of less than one year, RCA Victor drops the 33⅓ disk.

RE English Columbia and His Master's Voice are combined and become EMI (Electric & Musical Industries). New company is largest international record operation in the world. It is headed by American Louis Sterling, who has become a British citizen. In Britain, EMI's only competition is English Decca.

RE American Record Company secures from Warner Brothers the non-exclusive right to use the Brunswick trademark, and to sell a substantial portion of the records in the Brunswick catalog.

CI Clyde Beatty, one of the outstanding wild animal trainers of all time, makes his debut with the Ringling Brothers and Barnum & Bailey show. His is the first wild animal act with the show since 1926, when John Ringling dropped such acts. Beatty works a dozen lions and tigers in a single cage, using gun, whip, and chair.

CI Lillian Leitzel, doing her spectacular aerial act in Copenhagen, Denmark, falls to the circus floor and is killed.

VA Kate Smith sets all-time long-run record at the Palace, New York, playing eleven consecutive weeks. A previous long-run show (starring William Gaxton, Lou Holtz and Lyda Roberti) played eight weeks.

NC Texas Guinan opens her newest club, the Planet Mars.

RA/VA Artists' bureaus operated by NBC and CBS are highly profitable. This year NBC Artists' Bureau grosses approximately $10,000,000 by selling acts to vaudeville, legit producers, et al. Much younger CBS Artists' Bureau does over $500,000.

1932

TH In the 1932–1933 season, the Shuberts bring in only five shows, none of their own. *Autumn Crocus*, marking Francis Lederer's first American apperance, is the only success.

TH A flock of Broadway actors destined to become Hollywood's brightest stars is still on the boards this year: Katharine Hepburn in *The Warrior's Husband*; Humphrey Bogart and Margaret Sullavan in *Chrysalis*; James Stewart in *Goodbye Again*; Leslie Howard in *The Animal Kingdom*; Basil Rathbone in *The Devil Passes*; and Grace Moore in *The Du Barry*.

TH *Face the Music*, a musical-comedy with a depression theme and an Irving Berlin score, is a hit. Berlin's "Let's Have Another Cup of Coffee" becomes an anthem of the thirties.

TH A Lee Shubert musical revue, *Americana*, introduces E. Y. Harburg's "Brother, Can You Spare a Dime," theme song of the depression, sung by Rex Weber.

TH Other outstanding plays this season are Noel Coward's *Design For Living* with Lunt, Fontanne and the playwright himself and Helen Hayes in *Mary of Scotland*.

TH Adele Astaire marries and retires from the stage. Her brother Fred makes his first and last Broadway appearance without her in *The Gay Divorcee* with Claire Luce as his new dancing partner and a Cole Porter score ("Night and Day"). Astaire goes to Hollywood the following year and — in 1934 — makes a film version of the show, *The Gay Divorcee*, with Ginger Rogers.

MO/RA *The Big Broadcast* is the first film to feature stars created primarily by radio: Bing Crosby, Kate Smith, the Mills Brothers, the Boswell Sisters, Arthur Tracy, the Street Singer, and others.

MO Garbo's closest rival is Marlene Dietrich — equally mysterious but with an earthier appeal. Scoring first in the German film *Blue Angel* with Emil Jannings, Dietrich makes *Morroco* with Gary Cooper in 1930. This year she is big box office in *Blond Venus* with Cary Grant and *Shanghai Express*.

MO Lavish productions this year include *Grand Hotel*, featuring MGM'S top stars: Wallace Beery, Joan Crawford, Greta Garbo, John Barrymore, etc. *Dr. Jekyll and Mr. Hyde* wins Fredric March an Oscar and Cecil B. De Mille's *Sign of the Cross* stars Claudette Colbert, Charles Laughton and March. *Rasputin and the Empress* is the only movie made featuring all three Barrymores — Ethel, John, and Lionel.

MO Ex-swimming champion Johnny Weismuller, the most famous Tarzan of all, makes his first jungle movie, *Tarzan, the Ape Man*, with Maureen O'Sullivan as Jane.

MO Katharine Hepburn makes a smash movie debut in *A Bill of Divorcement* with John Barrymore. The following year she gives an Oscar-winning performance in *Morning Glory* and is the definitive Jo in *Little Women.*

MO The romanticized image of the solid citizen cowboy — as compared to the "good bad" reformed outlaw character epitomized by William S. Hart — was established in the twenties and continues throughout the talkies. Popular exponents this year are Tom Mix, Buck Jones, Ken Maynard and Tim McCoy.

MO Charles Boyer, a star in his native France, makes his U.S. debut in a bit part as Jean Harlow's chauffeur-lover in *Red-Headed Woman* and becomes the new matinee idol.

RA RCA, GE, AT&T and Westinghouse sign consent decree to settle U.S. Department of Justice 1930 anti-trust suit brought against them to dissolve patent agreements they made in the 1919–1921 period. RCA, with Sarnoff as president, emerges as major broadcasting power, owning two networks, numerous radio stations, manufacturing plants, experimental labs, and international wireless communications facilities.

RA Radio's power is demonstrated by the fact that one of nation's largest advertisers, Lehn & Fink, put their entire advertising budget for Pebeco Toothpaste into the medium.

RA *One Man's Family,* among the earliest soap operas, debuts in April. It becomes one of the longest-running shows of its kind on the air.

RA Fred Allen's first show, *The Linit Revue,* debuts October 23, 1932. (The last Fred Allen Show was carried June 26, 1949.) Allen's cast includes: his wife (Portland Hoffa); Titus Moody (Parker Fennelly); Mrs. Nussbaum (Minerva Pious); Senator Claghorn (Kenny Delmar); and Ajax Cassidy (Peter Donald).

RE EMI sells the American Columbia record operation to Majestic Radio.

RE Edward (Ted) Wallerstein, sales manager of Brunswick Records, leaves to take over as chief operating officer of RCA Victor records. He makes the decision to discontinue the 33⅓ long-playing disk. He also introduces a record player, the Duo, Jr., that has no tubes or speaker, but contains a jack which enables the user to plug it into a radio set. Retail price is $16.50. It's a tremendous success, since there are 20,000,000 radio sets in use.

RE A new company, Birmingham Sound Reproducers, puts a line of amplifiers and loud speakers on the market.

RE The first separate automatic record changer for players is introduced by Garrard.

BU Burlesque's most successful stripper is Gypsy Rose Lee. She opens a new act at the Republic Theatre and gets rave reviews.

VA Pallbearers at William Morris' funeral reflect the esteem in which he was held in show business. Among them are George M. Cohan, Joe Weber, Lew Fields, Arthur Hammerstein, Martin Beck, Adolph Zukor, Irving Berlin, Sam Harris, Walter Kelly, Henry Chesterfield, Izzy Herk, Gene Buck, Sime Silverman, and David Warfield.

TV *Billboard* runs its first regular television column, written by Benn Hall, in August 6 issue.

VA Final two-a-day all-vaudeville show at the Palace opens in May and closes July 9, a victim of increasing competition from talking motion pictures, radio, and the depression. It had a nineteen-year run as the Mecca of class, two-a-day vaudeville. Now, the Palace goes to mixed film-vaude grind policy.

1933

TH Half of New York's theatres are dark. Impresarios Arthur Hammerstein, A. H. Woods, and other prominent theatrical people go into bankruptcy.

TH On New Year's Day the court orders the Shubert Theatre Corporation to be liquidated and its assets offered at public sale. Lee Shubert resigns as co-receiver so that he may bid on assets at the public sale. The corporation is broke, but Lee and Jake Shubert are financially secure and independent. At the public sale Lee Shubert, representing the newly organized Select Theatres, Inc., buys the bankrupt Shubert Theatre Corporation for $400,000. He is the only bidder.

TH Maxwell Anderson's *Both Your Houses* wins the 1932–1933 Pulitzer, while Sidney Kingsley's *Men in White,* one of the Group Theatre's biggest hits, captures the prize for the 1933–34 season.

TH *Tobacco Road,* a melodrama about poor Southern whites, begins its historic run. Cast: Henry Hull, Sam Byrd, Dean Jagger, and Margaret Wycherly. Although called vulgar by critics, the play runs for seven years.

TH *Roberta,* Jerome Kern's fine musical ("Smoke Gets In Your Eyes"), is the top hit of the year. Cast: George Murphy, Ray Middleton, Bob Hope, Tamara, Fay Templeton, sax player Fred MacMurray, Sydney Greenstreet, and Lyda Roberti. Other major musicals: *Let 'em Eat Cake, As Thousands Cheer, Hold Your Horses.*

TH After Flo Ziegfeld's death, his widow, Billie Burke, arranges to have Lee Shubert produce the *Ziegfeld Follies.* Its cast includes Fred Allen, Willie and Eugene Howard, Fannie Brice, Vilma and Buddy Ebsen, and Jane Froman.

MO Walt Disney helps people laugh at their depression troubles with his Oscar-winning cartoon *The Three Little Pigs,* featuring a defiant little ditty, "Who's Afraid of the Big Bad Wolf." Ginger Rogers warbles another depression-inspired song "We're In The Money" in *Gold Diggers of 1933.*

MO Lay members and officials of the Catholic church form the Legion of Decency to set up a new Production Code for the film industry. Most Protestant religious groups support the code the following year. The Code includes such prim requirements as the use of twin beds rather than double.

MO The year of the musical. Warner Brothers features Busby Berkeley's flamboyant choreography in *Forty-Second Street* with Ruby Keeler, Dick Powell, Warner Baxter; *Footlight Parade* with James Cagney and Joan Blondell; and *Gold Diggers of 1933* in which Ginger Rogers has a small role. Joan Crawford dons her dancing shoes at MGM for *Dancing Lady,* featuring Fred Astaire and Nelson Eddy in their film debuts.

MO Musical history is made late this year when Fred Astaire and Ginger Rogers dance together for the first time in RKO's *Flying Down to Rio,* starring Dolores Del Rio. Their one number together, "The Carioca," is the film's top spot.

MO Mary Pickford makes her last picture, *Secrets,* this year. Her leading man is a young English actor, Leslie Howard, who also appears in a film version of his Broadway hit, *Berkeley Square.* The following year her ex-husband Douglas Fairbanks makes his last film, *The Private Life of Don Juan.*

MO Schenck drops D. W. Griffith from United Artists; signs Darryl Zanuck as producer-director.

MO The classic version of *King Kong,* in which the giant ape carries Fay Wray to the top of New York's Empire State Building, is big box office.

MO Two quality English pictures are hits in the United States — Noel Coward's *Cavalcade,* which wins an Academy Award, and *The Private Life of Henry VIII,* with an Oscar-winning performance by Charles Laughton. Other hit movies are MGM's all-star *Dinner at Eight;* Will Rogers in *State Fair;* Capra's *Lady For A Day* with May Robson; Margaret Sullavan's first film, *Only Yesterday;* and Greta Garbo's *Queen Christina.*

MO Mae West, who made her film debut in George Raft's *Night After Night* in 1932, becomes a big star in *She Done Him Wrong.* Her subsequent films, kidding sex with double-entendres, are box office hits but unpopular with the Hayes office and state censorship boards.

RA Edwin H. Armstrong gets Frequency Modulation broadcasting patents.

RA NBC occupies the world's largest broadcasting facility as it moves into Radio City headquarters and studios in New York.

RA Ed Wynn's new radio network, Amalgamated Broadcasting System, goes on the air in September and is bankrupt by November. Just one of numerous efforts to establish radio networks in competition to NBC and CBS, virtually all of them costly failures.

RE Record sales hit an all-time low of $5,500,000, having dropped from $106,000,000 in 1921.

RE Prohibition is repealed and new bars, saloons, cocktail lounges and other such establishments open in great numbers. Coin-operated juke boxes are placed in almost all of them. Within a two-year period drug stores, restaurants, and diners are also installing juke boxes. They are a major factor in the ultimate resurgence of the record business.

RE Fritz Pfleumer, working with BASF, conducts experiments fastening iron oxide onto paper strips and evolves magnetic tape.

CI The Flying Concellos is the only trapeze act to feature two triple somersaults from trapeze to catcher. One is performed by Art Concello, the other by his wife, Antoinette. She is the only woman to perform the triple.

VA Final combination film and vaude show at the Palace, January 7, features light-weight boxing champion Benny Leonard and prima ballerina Marie Gambarelli. Legendary house now goes to straight film policy.

1934

TH Ethel Merman sings Cole Porter's score in *Anything Goes* ("I Get a Kick Out of You") with Victor Moore and William Gaxton. Other big musicals are Noel Coward's *Conversation Piece,* and *Life Begins at 8:40* with Bert Lahr, Ray Bolger, and Frances Williams.

TH Lillian Hellman's *The Children's Hour* and Walter Huston in Sinclair Lewis's *Dodsworth* are two of the big hits of the year.

MO The most famous child star of all time, Shirley Temple, becomes a top attraction with *Stand Up and Cheer* and — especially — *Little Miss Marker.* She reigns as No. 1 — or thereabouts — at the box office for the next few years.

MO Frank Capra makes *It Happened One Night* which wins five Oscars, including

best picture, best director and best actor (Clark Gable) and actress (Claudette Colbert). It won't happen again until 1975 when *One Flew Over the Cuckoo's Nest* makes a similar sweep.

MO Significant movie events this year include the first of the popular *Thin Man* pictures with William Powell and Myrna Loy as Dashiell Hammett's Nick and Nora Charles; Donald Duck's first cartoon appearance in Disney's *The Orphan's Benefit;* Wallace Beery in *Viva Villa!;* Grace Moore in *One Night of Love;* John Barrymore and Carole Lombard in *20th Century;* and Robert Donat in *The Count of Monte Cristo.*

MO *Imitation of Life,* starring Claudette Colbert, is the first significant "black" movie of the thirties. By standards of the day it presents the first dignified portrait of a black woman, played by Louise Beavers, with Fredi Washington as her defiant daughter who elects to "pass" as white.

MO Bette Davis gives the first of her exciting star performances as Mildred in *Of Human Bondage* with Leslie Howard. It is her twenty-first film.

MO Fred Astaire and Ginger Rogers make the first (*The Gay Divorcee*) of their big box office musicals as co-stars, followed, in 1935, by their classic *Top Hat* with Irving Berlin's great score ("Cheek To Cheek"). Astaire brings dancing maturity to films, filming dance routines with full-figure shots, and integrating musical numbers into the plot.

RA Transmitting from the Empire State Building in New York to a receiver seventy miles away in Long Island, Armstrong sends totally static-free FM sound for first time. Tests are made by agreement with RCA.

RA/MU ASCAP is charged with being an illegal monopoly in a suit filed by the Department of Justice in September.

RA All three networks — NBC, CBS and ABC — are linked into a chain of one hundred-eighty stations to broadcast the World Series, sponsored by Ford Motor Company. Ford pays $100,000 for these radio rights.

RA Mutual Broadcasting System is the new name adopted by a network of major market stations (WOR in New York; WGN in Chicago; WLW in Cincinnati; and WXYZ in Detroit) which originally called themselves the Quality Group network.

RA WTMJ, Milwaukee, produces a half-hour program which it sells to six sponsors instead of a single advertiser, the first instance of this practice.

RE E. R. (Ted) Lewis, head of British Decca, buys from Warner Brothers the rights to the Brunswick trademark, and a portion

of the Brunswick catalog still owned by Brunswick. With this initial catalog he organizes American Decca, and makes Jack Kapp, creative director of Brunswick, head of the U.S. operation.

RE Majestic Radio sells Columbia to the American Record Company for $70,000.

CI The original four Wallendas, on the wire, have one of their numerous spills in Akron, Ohio. The wire sags and they tumble off. Carl grabs the wire, and manages to hold Helen by the neck with his feet; Herman gets a foot stranglehold on Joe and all four make it back to the platforms and descend safely.

CI Western movie star Tom Mix organizes his own circus. He and his horse, Tony, Jr. are the show's stars. It is a truck show, carrying 150 people and for several years is quite successful.

1935

TH The Federal Theatre Project, a nationwide activity of the Works Progress Administration (WPA), comes to the aid of unemployed actors. Under the leadership of Hallie Flanagan, the Project employs more than 12,000 theatre people (50% in New York) the following year.

TH *Porgy and Bess* (a musical version of Dorothy and DuBose Heyward's *Porgy*) with music by George Gershwin and featuring Todd Duncan and John Bubbles, is produced by the Theatre Guild. Critics are cool to the folk opera and it runs only 124 performances. Seventeen years later it runs eight months on Broadway, a record run for revivals at that time, and is acclaimed as Gershwin's masterpiece.

TH Billy Rose's spectacular mix of musical comedy and circus, *Jumbo,* is the last show at the Hippodrome before the famous entertainment palace is torn down. It is directed by George Abbott, written by Ben Hecht and Charles MacArthur with a score by Rodgers and Hart. Staging is by John Murray Anderson. Cast: Jimmy Durante, Donald Novis, clown "Poodles" Hannaford and 1,000 animals! Show is reminiscent of earliest mixed entertainments which played the old Hippodrome.

TH The Group Theatre raises audiences' social consciousness with Clifford Odet's searing one-acter *Waiting For Lefty* and his first full-length play, *Awake and Sing!* with the Adlers, John Garfield, and Morris Carnovsky.

TH *Jubilee* with Mary Boland and fifteen-year-old Montgomery Clift is a musical comedy hit. Cole Porter's score includes "Begin the Beguine" and "Just One Of Those Things."

TH Helen Hayes' *Victoria Regina* and Leslie Howard in *The Petrified Forest* are two of a crop of exceptionally strong plays in this suddenly revitalized legit year.

TH New York drama critics, unhappy with recent Pulitzer Prize selections, form the Drama Critics' Circle to present their own annual dramatic awards. First one goes to Maxwell Anderson's *Winterset* with Burgess Meredith. The Pulitzer for this year is won by Zoe Akins' *The Old Maid.*

VA/TH Longest route for vaude and legitimate theatre acts is the Federal Government route of Civilian Conservation Corps (CCC) and other federal institutions. Route runs sixty-five weeks (twenty in New York City and forty-five on the road).

MO William Fox chain of theatres and Hollywood studios are merged with Twentieth Century pictures, a new company formed by Darryl Zanuck and Joseph Schenck in 1933. Fox had been forced out of his own company in 1931.

MO After two years of receivership in bankruptcy, Paramount Pictures is reorganized. Zukor is chairman of the board; Barney Balaban, president; Y. Frank Freeman, vice president in charge of production.

MO *The Informer,* which wins Oscars for director John Ford and star Victor McLaglen, features a symphonic score by Max Steiner. Full-scale musical accompaniment is now an accepted component of most dramas as well as musicals.

MO Will Rogers and aviator Wiley Post are killed in a plane crash in August.

MO English director Alfred Hitchcock makes his first big impact on the American market with the British-made thriller, *The 39 Steps,* starring Robert Donat.

MO Miriam Hopkins stars as *Becky Sharp* in the first U.S.-made Technicolor feature. Director: Rouben Mamoulian.

MO *Naughty Marietta* revives operetta as successful film fare. Nelson Eddy and Jeanette MacDonald become a hot box office team.

MO Film debuts this year include Errol Flynn in *Captain Blood* with teenager Olivia De Havilland; Noel Coward in *The Scoundrel.* Important pictures are Oscar-winner *Mutiny on the Bounty* with Clark Gable and Charles Laughton; Max Reinhardt's all-star *A Midsummer Night's Dream* with Mickey Rooney as Puck and James Cagney as Bottom; Laughton in *Ruggles of Red Gap;* and *David Copperfield* with W. C. Fields as Micawber.

RA/RE New organization, American Society of Recording Artists, asks radio stations to pay royalty for right to broadcast phonograph records.

RA NBC inaugurates recorded transcription library program service, Thesaurus.

RA Major Bowes' *Amateur Hour* debuts and becomes one of the most popular shows on the air.

RA A young industrial psychologist sends his Ph.D. dissertation, "A Critique of Present Methods and a New Plan for Studying Radio Listening Behavior" to CBS, in applying for a job. Paul Kesten, CBS advertising/public relations V.P., hires the young man for $55 per week. He is Frank Stanton, who later becomes president of CBS.

RA/TV RCA announces plan to spend $1,000,000 on television program experiments. At approximately the same time, RCA requests Armstrong to remove his FM equipment from Empire State Building studios, and drops FM development in favor of aggressive TV expansion.

TV Farnsworth, working with Philco; Allen B. DuMont, working with Francis Jenkins; and Don Lee in California are all experimenting with television programming.

RE American Decca, under Jack Kapp and E. F. Stevens, sells records for retail list price of 35¢, as opposed to 75¢ price of most other popular records. Kapp signs Bing Crosby, Guy Lombardo, the Andrews Sisters, the Mills Brothers, Tommy and Jimmy Dorsey, Fletcher Henderson, and other top artists. Record sales climb from the 1933 low of $5,500,000 back up to $9,000,000 and continue upward.

CA Unique "act" of the day is the *Crime Does Not Pay* show with the United Shows of America Carnival. It stars Mrs. Emma Parker (mother of Bonnie); Mrs. Henrietta Barrow (mother of Clyde); and J. W. Dillinger (father of John).

MU The Benny Goodman orchestra does a Saturday night coast-to-coast network radio show, and the big band era is under way. Other bands attracting attention are those fronted by Ray Noble and the Dorsey brothers, Tommy and Jimmy.

1936

TH Federal Theatre Project produces its first plays, among them, T. S. Eliot's *Murder in the Cathedral, The Living Newspaper* and *Class of 1929.* It is poet Eliot's worldwide debut as a playwright. Playwright Elmer Rice, who conceived *Newspaper,* resigns when government officials censor its reports.

TH Musicals thrive. Bob Hope and Ethel Merman warble Cole Porter's "It's Delovely" in *Red Hot and Blue;* Ray Bolger and Tamara Geva dance to the torrid "Slaughter On Tenth Avenue," from the Rodgers-Hart score for *On Your Toes.* Josephine Baker returns to the U.S in the current *Ziegfeld Follies,* also starring Gypsy Rose Lee, moving up from burlesque.

TH Noel Coward and Gertrude Lawrence score a triumph in Coward's *Tonight at 8:30,* a program of nine short plays. Other hits include Claire Booth Luce's *The Women; Ethan Frome* with Pauline Lord, Raymond Massey and Ruth Gordon; Katharine Cornell in Maxwell Anderson's *The Wingless Victory.*

TH Two *Hamlets* play Broadway this season, one month apart. The first, starring John Gielgud, supported by Judith Anderson and Lillian Gish, runs for 132 performances. The second, starring Leslie Howard, closes after thirty-nine shows. However, some critics prefer the "subtlety" of Howard's Prince.

TH At the age of eighty, veteran star William Gillette plays in a revival of *Three Wise Fools.*

TH The 1935–1936 Pulitzer goes to Robert Sherwood's *Idiot's Delight,* starring Lunt and Fontanne, and for 1936–1937 to George Kaufman's and Moss Hart's *You Can't Take It With You.*

MO The depression is still with us and America chases the blues with such popular comedies as Frank Capra's *Mr. Deeds Goes To Town* with Gary Cooper and Jean Arthur; Carole Lombard and William Powell in *My Man Godfrey;* Charlie Chaplin's last silent film, *Modern Times,* introducing Paulette Goddard; and *Ehhh, What's Up Doc?,* Bugs Bunny's first cartoon. Giveaways — dishes, bank nights, etc. — are used to entice customers, and most theatres show double — in some cases even triple — features.

MO Costume movies are big this year. They include: Greta Garbo and Robert Taylor in *Camille;* Frederic March in *Anthony Adverse;* Clark Gable, Spencer Tracy and Jeanette MacDonald in *San Francisco;* Katherine Hepburn in *Mary of Scotland;* and Norma Shearer and Leslie Howard in *Romeo and Juliet.*

MO Irving Thalberg dies at thirty-seven. The following year the Academy establishes an Irving Thalberg Memorial Award. His last picture, *The Good Earth* with Paul Muni, is dedicated to his memory, one of the few times the modest tycoon's name was seen on the screen.

MO After thirty years in the business, Carl Laemmle sells Universal to Charles R. Rogers.

RA At a meeting of the Association of National Advertisers, A. C. Nielsen demonstrates his research firm's audimeter and proposes method of measuring program audiences. It is the system which will largely decide the fate of performers and shows in radio and television for years to come.

RA/RE In August, a new organization, National Association of Recording Artists (whose president is Fred Waring) wins an injunction against radio station WDAS, Philadelphia, forbidding the station to play records. NARA now files suits against three other stations, WHN, WNEW and WEVD, all in New York City.

RA/MU ASCAP cancels temporary licenses of broadcasters in mid-January, demands new, five-year contracts at current rates, despite absence of Warner copyrights from ASCAP repertoire. Broadcasters hold talks among themselves to establish their own music performing rights society.

RA Mutual Broadcasting System becomes a national network, when the Don Lee west coast web joins it.

RA In the biggest single station deal to date, CBS buys KNX, Los Angeles for $1,300,000.

TV RCA demonstrates its television system for radio manufacturers with telecasts from atop the Empire State Building.

RA Both NBC Red and NBC Blue networks go national with addition of Pacific Coast chain of stations.

RA This year the Lux Radio Theatre with Cecil B. De Mille is introduced, and for the next several years dramatic programs achieve great popularity. Among them are *The First Nighter*, starring Don Ameche. Leading Broadway players appear on these programs. John Barrymore does six Shakespeare plays in a special series.

TV Television programming experiments struggle with previously undreamed-of staging problems: excessive heat of lights needed for proper pictorial effect; green lipstick and purple pan creams are used in efforts to get "natural" look.

TV First coaxial cable is laid by AT&T between Philadelphia and New York, permitting remote telecasts and expanding video programming experiments.

RE The increasing popularity and usage of juke boxes throughout the U.S. and Decca's low-priced 35¢ record — featuring stars like Bing Crosby, the Andrews Sisters, Guy Lombardo — are credited with the revival of the record industry.

RE The superiority of magnetic tape recording is vividly demonstrated when Sir Thomas Beecham and the London Philharmonic record on magnetic tape at a concert in Ludwigshaven, Germany.

RE *Billboard* introduces a record chart, "10 Best Records for Week Ending. . . ." The list is supplied by RCA Victor, Decca, Brunswick and Vocalion.

MU The vogue for big bands continues. Soon on the scene are: Glenn Miller, Artie Shaw, Charlie Spivak, Will Bradley, Count Basie, Red Norvo, Charlie Barnet, Harry James, Gene Krupa, Lionel Hampton, Freddy Martin, Claude Thornhill, Eddy Duchin, Les Brown, Larry Clinton, Raymond Scott, Stan Kenton, Duke Ellington, Sammy Kaye, Kay Kyser, Guy Lombardo, Woody Herman, Vaughn Monroe, Hal McIntyre and many others.

1937

TH Orson Welles' and John Houseman's production of *Dr. Faustus,* a revival, is the outstanding Federal Theatre presentation of the year. Later Welles and Houseman leave the Project and form the Mercury Theatre, which presents a modern-dress version of *Julius Caesar* (comparing Mussolini with the Roman ruler) starring Welles and Joseph Cotten. It is the beginning of Welles' "stock" company.

TH *I'd Rather Be Right,* starring George M. Cohan, is the biggest hit musical of the season. The George Kaufman-Moss Hart book satirizes Roosevelt's new deal. Score is by Rodgers and Hart, who also have another hit show this year — *Babes in Arms* ("The Lady is a Tramp," "Where or When," "My Funny Valentine").

TH Other important shows are John Steinbeck's first play, *Of Mice and Men,* the 1937–1938 Pulitzer Prize winner; Luther Adler in *Golden Boy,* Clifford Odets' most commercial vehicle; and *Room Service,* with master comedy director George Abbott at the helm.

MO Hollywood turns out more films (778) than in any year since 1928. "Firsts" include Lana Turner's debut in *They Won't Forget;* the first Andy Hardy movie (*A Family Affair* with Mickey Rooney); Hedy Lamarr's startling "topless" debut in the Czechoslovakian film *Ecstasy,* and the Dead End Kids in *Dead End,* starring Humphrey Bogart and Sylvia Sidney.

MO Walt Disney makes another landmark cartoon, his first full-length feature, *Snow White and the Seven Dwarfs,* which will still delight youngsters forty years later. The score includes "Whistle While You Work." Disney Studios will make more than $22,000,000 on the picture.

MO Teenage and sub-teen stars are big box office this year. Shirley Temple still tops the list, which includes little Jane Withers. Two fifteen-year-old singers click: Deanna Durbin in *One Hundred Men and a Girl* and Judy Garland (singing her memorable "You Made Me Love You" to Clark Gable's photo) in *Broadway Melody of 1938.*

MO Paul Muni makes his Oscar-winning movie, *The Good Earth,* and receives an Oscar for his 1936 film *The Life of Emile Zola.* His co-star, Luise Rainer, wins an award for her 1936 film *The Great Ziegfeld* and a second Oscar (for *The Good Earth*) the next year.

MO At the insistence of Leslie Howard, Humphrey Bogart plays his same stage role as a cynical killer in *The Petrified Forest* — the beginning of his phenomenal career in hardboiled roles. MGM loans out teenager Judy Garland for her first feature, *Pigskin Parade,* which also features Betty Grable.

MO Frank Capra's *Lost Horizons* with Ronald Colman is a hit. Capra shoots the film's authentic-looking snow scenes of Tibet's arctic Himalayas at sub-zero temperatures in a converted ice house.

MO Fredric March and Janet Gaynor make what many consider the all-time best version of *A Star Is Born,* as compared to Constance Bennett in *What Price Hollywood* in 1932, and two musical versions (Judy Garland and James Mason in 1954; Barbra Streisand and Kris Kristofferson in 1976).

MO The original platinum blonde, Jean Harlow, dies June 7 of uremic poisoning at twenty-six. Her last picture is *Saratoga* with Clark Gable. After her death, a double completed her remaining scenes in long shots.

MO Classic comedy hits this year include Oscar-winning director Leo McCarey's *The Awful Truth* with Irene Dunne and Cary Grant, and Carole Lombard and Fredric March in *Nothing Sacred.* One of MGM's top comedy actors, Robert Montgomery, takes a drastic gamble and wins with his highly acclaimed portrayal of a psychotic in *Night Must Fall.*

RA Guglielmo Marconi dies of a heart attack in Rome at age sixty-three.

RA/RE NBC signs Arturo Toscanini to organize and conduct the NBC Symphony Orchestra.

RA The American Federation of Radio Artists is formed, and Actors' Equity relinquishes its right to represent talent in broadcasting.

TV NBC puts first mobile television truck into operation.

RE Philharmonic Radio Company is organized by Avery Fisher to manufacture the first high fidelity phonographs.

MU *Billboard* initiates feature, "Songs With Most Radio Plugs." It is based on reports from Accurate Reporting Service and covers airplay on stations WEAF and WJZ (both NBC), WABC (CBS) and New York independent stations WOR, WNEW, WMCA and WHN.

1938

TH Two contrasting works are produced without scenery and with an on-stage narrator — *Our Town* by Thornton Wilder; and the Mercury Theatre production of *The Cradle Will Rock*, a political musical with composer Marc Blitzstein playing his score on stage and explaining the plot between scenes. *Our Town* wins the 1937–1938 Pulitzer Prize.

TH It is a big season for hit musicals. Among them are Cole Porter's *Leave It To Me*, starring Victor Moore, William Gaxton and Sophie Tucker. Young Mary Martin stops the show with "My Heart Belongs to Daddy." Gene Kelly is in the chorus. Walter Huston, one-time song and dance man turned legit, sings Kurt Weill's haunting "September Song" in *Knickerbocker Holiday*. Rodgers and Hart have another hit in *The Boys From Syracuse* ("Falling In Love With Love") with Jimmy Savo.

TH Maurice Evans stars in Broadway's first full length production of *Hamlet*. Show starts at 6:30 p.m. With time out for dinner it runs almost six hours.

TH Veteran vaudeville stars Ole Olsen and Chic Johnson star in *Hellzapoppin'*. It is a smash hit, runs 1404 performances. The bombastic burlesque-like revue has men in gorilla suits running up the aisles, balloons bursting, guns booming and pigeons soaring over the audience.

TH Other important shows this year are *Oscar Wilde* with England's Robert Morley making his Broadway debut and 1938–39 Pulitzer Prize winner *Abe Lincoln In Illinois* by Robert Sherwood with Raymond Massey in the title role. Success of the latter enables Sherwood to form the Playwrights Company with fellow scribes S.M. Behrman, Elmer Rice, Maxwell Anderson, and Sidney Howard to produce their own plays.

MO The government files the first of its on-going anti-trust suits which ultimately result in studios having to divest themselves of theatre chains. Box office returns are lagging, but audiences are turning out for new stars Mickey Rooney, Alice Faye, Tyrone Power as well as durable Spencer Tracy, Clark Gable and Myrna Loy. Last named three have a hit with *Test Pilot*.

MO F. Scott Fitzgerald receives his only screen credit as a writer on *Three Comrades*, co-starring Margaret Sullavan and Robert Taylor, plus Franchot Tone and Robert Young.

MO Judy Garland teams with Mickey Rooney for the first time in *Love Finds Andy Hardy*, fourth in the hit series.

MO Bette Davis makes *Jezebel*, a Civil War costume drama, with her favorite director William Wyler, and wins her second Oscar. Her first was for *Dangerous* in 1935.

MO Director Frank Capra makes his sixth smash hit, *You Can't Take It With You* (from the Pulitzer Prize winning play), starring Jean Arthur and James Stewart. The film wins Capra his third Oscar; (his second was for *Mr. Deeds Goes to Town* with Gary Cooper in 1936).

MO The classic comedy *Bringing Up Baby*, with Katharine Hepburn and Cary Grant, is made this year. "Baby" is a pet leopard whose favorite song is "I Can't Give You Anything But Love, Baby." One of the best of the "screwball" comedy genre.

MO Newcomers registering this year include William Holden in *Golden Boy* with Barbara Stanwyck; John Garfield in *Four Daughters* with the Lane Sisters; Ronald Reagan as one of the juveniles in *Brother Rat*; and Europe's Hedy Lamarr in *Algiers* with Charles Boyer.

RA Orson Welles and his *Mercury Theatre of the Air* throw the nation into a panic the night of October 30, with a CBS broadcast of H. G. Wells' *War of the Worlds*. Thousands of listeners believe there is an actual invasion of earth by Martians and flee their homes, call police, etc. Strangely, the show was broadcast against one of the highest-rated opposition shows of the day, *The Chase & Sanborn Hour* with Edgar Bergen and Charlie McCarthy on NBC.

RA/TV After RCA discontinues Armstrong FM transmissions from the Empire State Building, to begin testing TV, Armstrong builds his own 400-foot transmitter on the Palisades at Alpine, N. J., and begins FM broadcasting, mostly classical music. John Shepherd III builds another FM transmitter atop Mt. Asnebumskit in Massachusetts.

RA/MO Paramount Pictures buys an interest in Allen B. Du Mont television laboratories.

VA Still another indication of vaudeville's decline: RKO is down to one booker. In 1928 company had thirty-five bookers, booking approximately 300 houses.

RA/RE Paul Whiteman sues WNEW, New York, and RCA in turn sues Whiteman in separate litigation to attempt to establish whether record artists, record companies, or either, have the right to forbid stations to play records without fee.

RE Garrard introduces a turntable that automatically flips a record over, so that it plays both sides.

RE RCA Victor does first film (partial) sound track album, three tunes from Walt Disney's *Snow White and the Seven Dwarfs*. Jack Kapp covers the tunes with Decca artists, and his album almost matches the original sound track version in sales.

MU/RE In March, *Billboard* discontinues using best-selling record lists supplied by record companies and compiles new opinion chart of records with strongest potential for juke box play. In October this feature becomes The *Billboard* Record Buying Guide.

RE Although RCA Victor is number one in record sales (with Decca a strong number two) and Columbia trailing in third position, Ted Wallerstein leaves RCA Victor. He persuades William Paley, head of the now thriving CBS radio network, to buy Columbia Records for $700,000. It is ten times the price American Record Company paid four years earlier. Wallerstein now heads up Columbia.

CI The giant gorilla, Gargantua, is introduced in the Ringling Brothers and Barnum & Bailey show, in a parade featuring Frank "Bring 'Em Back Alive" Buck. The gorilla's extraordinarily fierce and vicious look was caused by a scar resulting from acid thrown in his face, when he was much younger.

CI Ringling Brothers and Barnum & Bailey, experiencing financial problems, ask employees to take 25% pay cut during run in Scranton, Pa. Employees refuse and show closes.

CI This is possibly the worst year in circus history. Eight shows, including the Big One, Ringling Brothers and Barnum & Bailey, and the recently formed Tom Mix Circus, close early in the season. The Al G. Barnes and the Sells Floto Shows are the only ones to make it through the season. Railroad strikes are basic cause of the closings.

CA Three of the largest carnival companies merge. Rubin & Cherry, Beckman-Gerety, and Royal American Shows combine to form giant Amusement Corporation of America.

1939

TH *The Time of Your Life* by William Saroyan is winner of both the Drama Critics Circle Award and the Pulitzer Prize. The play has formidable competition: Lillian Hellman's *The Little Foxes* starring Tallulah Bankhead; Philip Barry's *The Philadelphia Story* with Katharine Hepburn; Monty Woolley as *The Man Who Came to Dinner*; Ethel Waters in her first non-musical role, *Mamba's Daughters*; and *No Time For Comedy* with Katharine Cornell and Laurence Olivier.

TH From a longevity point, the most important play this season is *Life with Father*, Howard Lindsay's and Russel Crouse's nostalgic family play, starring Lindsay and his wife Dorothy Stickney. It ultimately runs for seven and a half years on Broadway, and has countless road companies and little theatre presentations.

MO This is considered by many historians to be Hollywood's finest year. Quality productions — led by David Selznick's legendary *Gone With the Wind* — include *Wuthering Heights* with Laurence Olivier and Merle Oberon; Capra's *Mr. Smith Goes To Washington* with James Stewart; John Ford's *Stagecoach,* which makes a star of John Wayne; *Goodbye Mr. Chips* with Oscar-winner Robert Donat, introducing Greer Garson; Judy Garland in *The Wizard of Oz;* Greta Garbo in her first comedy, Lubitsch's *Ninotchka;* and Bette Davis in *Dark Victory.*

MO Hollywood largely ignores the fact that NBC starts regular TV transmissions this year. Most studio moguls consider the advent of television a threat to radio rather than films. Radio, in fact, is a strong factor in Hollywood's sagging box office. According to a *Fortune* magazine poll, almost 80% of the public would rather listen to the radio than see a movie.

MO *Gone With the Wind,* one of the all-time hit movies, stars Clark Gable, Vivien Leigh, Leslie Howard and Olivia De Havilland. Hattie McDaniel — as Mammy — is first black to win an Academy Award. The three hour and forty-two minute film version of the Margaret Mitchell novel is produced by David Selznick at a cost of $4,500,000. By 1974 it will have grossed more than $150,000,000. In 1976 it will be sold to TV for one showing for $5,000,000 and become television's most watched feature film.

MO The bread and butter productions are low-budgeted but big box office series: Lionel Barrymore and Lew Ayres in *Dr. Kildare;* the *Andy Hardy* films; Ann Sothern as *Maisie;* the *Thin Man* mysteries; *Tarzan; Charlie Chan;* and Peter Lorre's *Mr. Moto* series, which is dropped in 1942 after Pearl Harbor.

MO Carl Laemmle dies at seventy-two of a heart attack.

RA/RE Federal district court in New York decides that a record company (RCA in this case) owns performance rights to its records, unless artist contract specifically turns rights over to artist. Decision orders WNEW to cease playing RCA and Bluebird records. RCA plans to license stations to play records.

RA/MU National Association of Broadcasters hires copyright attorney Sydney Kaye to help radio owners set up their own organization for securing and controlling music copyrights. Broadcast Music, Inc. (BMI), only major performing rights organization since ASCAP, eventually results from this move.

VA Vaudeville reaches its lowest ebb. RKO, which operated approximately 300 vaude houses in 1929, now has one theatre, playing one-week vaude bills. It is the Golden Gate in San Francisco.

FA New York World's Fair opens at Flush-ing Meadows, Long Island, New York, April 30.

FA Golden Gate International Exposition opens in San Francisco, February 18.

CI Winners in *Billboard* Favorite Outdoor Performer Contest are: 1. Bee Kyle, woman high diver; 2. Mabel Stark, wild animal trainer; 3. Four Aerial Apollos, high wire act.

TV *Billboard* runs first television review. Special program presents Richard Rodgers, Fred Waring, Helen Lewis, Marcy Westcott, Bill Farren, the Three Swifts, and a Donald Duck cartoon, *Donald's Cousin Gus.*

TV After long court battles Dr. Vladimir Zworykin's patents for iconoscope-kinescope tubes are established as his own. These are the basis for electronic television.

TV President Franklin D. Roosevelt speaks over NBC television at opening of N.Y. World's Fair on April 30. RCA receivers with 5", 9" and 12" picture tubes are on display. Retail prices range from $199.50 to $600.

TV Television's progress completely halted as Germany invades Poland, and President Roosevelt calls on Sarnoff and other leaders in electronic and other manufacturing areas to come to Washington to discuss shift from civilian to military usage of all resources. Radar is one new electronic device the military is planning.

RE At the New York World's Fair, Bell Laboratories demonstrates a stereo recorder, using steel tape.

RE Wallerstein signs a number of the big bands of the day to Columbia. They include Benny Goodman, Duke Ellington, Count Basie. He releases their records on a new laminated disk, with superior sound quality, and longer life than the shellac records of the day. At 50¢ retail list, they are an immediate success. He also makes inroads into RCA Victor's classical business.

MU Indicative of the great popularity of the big bands is the fact that on its Red and Blue networks, the National Broadcasting Company carries summer shows featuring more than forty of the orchestras. They include Glenn Miller, Artie Shaw, Jimmy and Tommy Dorsey, Horace Heidt, and Charlie Barnet. CBS presents Benny Goodman, Cab Calloway, Sammy Kaye, Kay Kyser, Hal Kemp, Paul Whiteman and others.

MU Frank Sinatra joins the Harry James band. He stays with the band less than a year and leaves to join the Tommy Dorsey band in 1940.

CI The foremost wild animal trainer of the day, a Frenchman, Alfred Court, joins Ringling Brothers and Barnum & Bailey. Without gun, whip, or chair and never speaking in any but a soothing, conversational tone, he works lions, tigers, leopards and Great Danes all in the same cage. A woman trainer, May Kovar, also works his animals.

RE *Billboard* publishes first special section on records for juke boxes. Called "Talent and Tunes on Music Machines," the special supplement is a first major step in promoting a link between juke box operators and record industry.

1940

TH Ethel Barrymore gives one of her most memorable performances in *The Corn Is Green* by young Emlyn Williams. The Pulitzer Prize this year, though, goes to Robert Sherwood's *There Shall Be No Night* with Alfred Lunt, Lynn Fontanne and twenty-year-old Montgomery Clift. Other successful shows are *My Sister Eileen* with Shirley Booth, and the Laurence Olivier-Vivien Leigh version of *Romeo and Juliet.*

TH *The Return of the Vagabond* stars George M. Cohan in his last stage appearance. The same year he receives, by a special act of Congress, a gold medal from President Roosevelt. The event makes a heart-warming finale scene for Jimmy Cagney's film version of Cohan's life, *Yankee Doodle Dandy* in 1942. Cohan died a few months after the film was released.

TH Broadway discovers Gene Kelly as the heel-hero of the Rodgers-Hart musical, *Pal Joey,* with Vivienne Segal and June Havoc. Van Johnson is in the chorus. Another future Hollywood star, June Allyson, gets her big break this year when she is hired to understudy Betty Hutton in *Panama Hattie,* starring Ethel Merman.

TH Ethel Waters gives a glowing performance of Vernon Duke's score in *Cabin In The Sky* ("Taking a Chance On Love").

MO Although the U.S. is still not at war, American film makers are turning out anti-Nazi pictures. Outstanding is *The Great Dictator,* Chaplin's first talkie, in which he plays Hitler (and his double). Jack Oakie in Mussolini. Memorable sequence: Chaplin, as "Der Phooey" doing a ballet dance while balancing a globe.

MO Bing Crosby and Bob Hope make the first of their box office bonanza "Road" pictures. It's *The Road to Singapore,* with, of course, Dorothy Lamour.

MO Two of Hollywood's greatest and most durable directors make classic films this year. John Ford directs John Steinbeck's harrowing account of the dust-bowl disaster of the thirties, *The Grapes of Wrath* with Henry Fonda. Alfred Hitchcock makes the Oscar-winning suspense film *Rebecca* with Laurence Olivier and Joan Fontaine.

MO In *Fantasia,* Disney combines his cartoon characters with classical music, via "Fantasound," which utilizes a multi-track stereo sound system. *Pinocchio,* another Disney cartoon feature, is an even bigger audience pleaser. Gus Edwards, as the voice of Jiminy Cricket, introduces the hit song "When You Wish Upon A Star." In 1942 *Bambi,* perhaps Disney's most beloved feature, is released.

MO Ginger Rogers deserts her longtime partner Fred Astaire for non-musicals and gives an Oscar-winning performance as a typical "white collar" girl, *Kitty Foyle.* Her "last" picture with Astaire was *The Story of Irene and Vernon Castle* (1939) until they were reunited for their final movie, *The Barkleys of Broadway* in 1949.

MO Katherine Hepburn makes a film version of the Broadway hit, *The Philadelphia Story,* also starring Cary Grant and James Stewart. Stewart wins an Oscar for his portrayal as a newspaperman.

RA Chain Monopoly Committee of the Federal Communications Commission recommends that networks dispose of their ownership in talent management operations, transcription companies, and make less severe contracts with affiliated stations.

RA/TV The Federal Communications Commission assigns thirty-five channels to FM and approves commercial operation of FM stations. At the same time, it halts television development until industry agreements on technological standards are reached. This is the first of the incidents which "freeze" television.

RA As the year opens there are 743 AM radio stations, and nine experimental FM stations operating in the U.S.

RA/MU At a special convention called to meet radio industry's music problems with ASCAP, National Association of Broadcasters creates $1,500,000 fund to establish its own supply of music. It is another step toward the upcoming formation of the broadcaster's own performing rights organization, Broadcast Music, Inc.

RA/MU Broadcast Music, Inc. (BMI) is formed by broadcasters to create and control music copyrights for performance. BMI buys the catalog of M. M. Cole Music Publishing Company, Chicago. It is first substantial step in the operation of the new performing rights organization.

RA/MU BMI achieves its most meaningful coup to date with acquisition of old-line ASCAP music publishing catalog owned by E. B. Marks. Marks' catalog contains more than 15,000 copyrights, many of them great standards.

RA/RE In September BMI supplies its member radio stations with transcription records containing fifty non-ASCAP musical numbers.

RA/RE The U.S. Circuit Court of Appeals overrules the findings of the lower court in the RCA-Whiteman case, and establishes that broadcasters have right to use records on the air without permission of, or payment of fee to, either the record company or the recording artist.

RA Among most successful of newer shows this year, and the years immediately following, are the *Ed Sullivan Show; Duffy's Tavern; Your Hit Parade; Arthur Godfrey Time; Take It or Leave It; Abbott and Costello; The Garry Moore Show; Henry Morgan* and *Red Skelton; Suspense; My Friend, Irma;* and a number of big band shows with orchestras such as Glenn Miller, Benny Goodman, Artie Shaw and others.

RA New group called FM Broadcasters, Inc. is founded in New York.

TV "Limited commercialization" of television is approved by the Federal Communications Commission.

TV Dr. Peter Goldmark, chief engineer of CBS, demonstrates the Paley network's color television system for the FCC.

TV RCA makes all-out drive to establish television in New York market by drastically slashing prices of sets. Announced goal is to have 25,000 sets in metropolitan homes before end of year.

TV First sponsor of regularly telecast programs is Sun Oil. They simulcast Lowell Thomas's Monday through Friday news program on NBC Blue radio network and on TV station W2XBS.

TV CBS and Du Mont also telecasting on more or less regular schedules, along with NBC. By May of this year twenty-three television stations are operating throughout the country.

TV The first color telecast is demonstrated to the press and the FCC by CBS for a period of three months this year, and to the public in January, 1941.

TV The first commercially licensed TV transmitters — NBC's WNBT and CBS's WCBW — start broadcasting in New York City on July 1.

FA International Association of Fairs and Expositions celebrates its 50th anniversary.

MU After forty years as head of the American Federation of Musicians, Joseph Weber retires, and James C. Petrillo becomes head of the musicians' national union. He has been head of the Chicago local, and has established himself as a tough negotiator and fighter for rights of musicians.

RE *Billboard* introduces first full-fledged record charts. Tommy Dorsey's "I'll Never Smile Again" with vocal by the Pied Pipers; Bing Crosby's "Only Forever"; and Artie Shaw's "Frenesi" are among the leading records on the first charts.

1941

TH Lillian Hellman's *Watch on the Rhine,* about the Nazi regime, wins the Drama Critics' Circle Award. Other hits include: *Claudia,* with Dorothy McGuire; Noel Coward's *Blithe Spirit;* and *Arsenic and Old Lace.*

TH The big discovery this year is comedian Danny Kaye supporting Gertrude Lawrence in the musical, *Lady In The Dark.* Kaye stars later this year in *Let's Face It.*

TH Canada Lee, an ex-vaudevillian, gives a shattering performance as a black man fighting to survive in the Chicago slums in *Native Son,* adapted by Paul Green and Richard Wright from the latter's novel.

MU/MO Films, like all other entertainment media, move to cash in on the popularity of the big bands. Virtually every name band makes at least a two-reel short and many make feature films.

MO Orson Welles makes his landmark film debut as director, writer, producer and star of *Citizen Kane.* Acclaimed by critics for its innovative use of the camera and — especially — brilliant new sound techniques, the film is considered controversial because it is, allegedly, a thinly veiled version of the life of newspaper tycoon William Randolph Hearst. The following year Welles directs another classic *The Magnificent Ambersons.*

MO Greta Garbo retires at thirty-six after making *Two-Faced Woman,* a box office fiasco. Although she never won an Oscar, the Academy does present her with a special award years later.

MO John Huston directs the all-time classic private eye film, *The Maltese Falcon* with Humphrey Bogart as Sam Spade. Veteran director Raoul Walsh makes another memorable Bogart film, *High Sierra.*

MO Frank Capra makes his first independent film, *Meet John Doe,* with Gary Cooper. The director shoots five different endings for the movie and lets preview audiences help him decide which one to use. Cooper also appears in *Sergeant York,* which wins him an Oscar.

MO Red Skelton, former burlesque comic, vaude and radio star, has his first hit movie, a sleeper comedy, *Whistling In the Dark,* which becomes a series.

RA/TV In spite of imminence of U.S. entry into war, Federal Communications Commission approves full commercial operaton of TV and sets standards at 525 lines, 30 frames, FM sound. FCC also issues monopoly report in which it recommends banning of option time, exclusive station affiliations, sets limit on station ownership and rules that same interests may not operate more than one network.

RA/MU At the beginning of the year, Department of Justice prepares anti-trust suits against ASCAP, BMI, and the networks. Supreme Court begins review of state anti-ASCAP laws.

RA/MU Late in January the Department of Justice and BMI come to terms on a consent decree.

RA/MU Late in February, ASCAP accepts a Department of Justice consent decree. Broadcasters may now contract for ASCAP controlled copyrights either on a per-song, or a blanket basis, covering all of the songs ASCAP controls.

RA NBC creates complete separation between its Red and Blue networks, with totally different managements operating each.

RA According to listener surveys, President Franklin D. Roosevelt's address to the nation on Dec. 9 (the day after his declaration of war) is heard by largest audience in the history of radio, 90,000,000 people.

RA Dr. Frank Conrad, Westinghouse engineer and important factor in earliest days of radio, dies of heart attack on December 15 at sixty-seven.

RA/MU BMI growth is substantial. By mid-year it is supported by almost 700 radio stations, and now has 190 affiliated music publishers, many of them owned by important recording artists, composers, etc.

RA CBS gets out of the talent management and booking business. It sells its Columbia Concerts Corporation to an employee group, who have been operating that firm, and its powerful Columbia Artists Bureau to the Music Corporation of America for $250,000. MCA is already the major band booking organization of the day, and becoming increasingly powerful in all areas of talent management and booking.

RA At this time there are 103 stations affiliated with the NBC Blue network, seventy-six with the Red network, and sixty-four supplementary stations, using NBC programs, but on a non-affiliated basis.

RA First FM radio "network" connects New York, Boston, Schenectady, and Hartford.

RA Another oil company, Socony-Vacuum, becomes the first sponsor to use FM radio. And again it buys a news show. Time is purchased on the American Network, an FM chain in New England.

TV First sponsors in commercial television buy time on WNBT(TV), New York NBC station (which was formerly W2XBS).

They are Procter and Gamble, Lever Bros. Co., and Sun Oil. They pay $120 per evening hour for the time.

RE One of first effects of World War II, in which U.S. is not yet directly involved, is restriction on usage of aluminum. This affects manufacture of recording blanks, among other usages.

1942

TH Irving Berlin's World War II musical *This Is The Army,* with a G.I. cast, is a hit on Broadway. Berlin sings his World War I hit "Oh How I Hate To Get Up In the Morning." Other big musicals are *By Jupiter* starring Ray Bolger, the last Rodgers and Hart musical, and a revival of George Gershwin's *Porgy and Bess.*

TH Tallulah Bankhead, Fredric March, Montgomery Clift, and Florence Eldridge star in Thornton Wilder's *The Skin of Our Teeth,* a Pulitzer Prize winner. It is Wilder's tribute to the indestructibility of man.

MO Hollywood goes to war and eighty movies this year have a war theme. Greer Garson stars in *Mrs. Miniver,* about bravery on the home front in England. Both she and the film win Oscars.

MO Carole Lombard is killed in a plane crash while on a bond tour.

MO Escapist films are also in demand, particularly musicals. Jimmy Cagney wins an Oscar for his portrayal of George M. Cohan in *Yankee Doodle Dandy.* Bing Crosby and Fred Astaire introduce Irving Berlin's Oscar-winning song "White Christmas" in *Holiday Inn.* Astaire has a new dance partner, new star Rita Hayworth, in *You Were Never Lovelier.* Bud Abbott and Lou Costello, slap-stick comedy team, are big box office.

MO MGM imports Vincente Minnelli from Broadway to direct *Cabin In the Sky,* the third all-black movie filmed by Hollywood. *Hallelujah!* was first in 1929; *Green Pastures,* second in 1936.

MO Two men, destined to become big stars, make their debuts this year — Gene Kelly as Judy Garland's leading man in *For Me and My Gal* and Alan Ladd as the "hit man" in *This Gun For Hire* with Veronica Lake.

RA U.S. Department of Justice files anti-trust suits against NBC and CBS.

RA FCC rules (and is upheld by U.S. Supreme Court) that RCA may not operate two radio networks. RCA agrees to dispose of the Blue network. Mark Woods, NBC executive, runs the Blue while attempting to find a buyer for it.

RA/RE The disk jockey is becoming a powerful factor in the record business and Capitol Records is the first to recognize his

influence on record buyers by giving "deejays" free records to play. Martin Block's *Make Believe Ballroom* on WNEW, New York, is the powerhouse disk jockey show in the country, although Al Jarvis actually originated the format with his own *Make Believe Ballroom* on KFWB, Los Angeles, in the mid-thirties.

MU/RE The American Federation of Musicians' strike against the recording companies, the entry of a number of big bands into the armed forces, and other factors mark the beginning of the end of the big band era, although efforts are made periodically thereafter to revive the popularity of the orchestras. Vocalists begin to gain in popularity.

RE War Production Board restricts phonograph record companies use of shellac to thirty percent of what they used in previous year. Since transcriptions use vinyl, which is not in such short supply, there are no restrictions on that ingredient for present time.

RE/RA Radio stations begin to play more and more popular records and disk jockeys become important radio and entertainment personalities. Many recording artists, and some record companies (notably Decca) make strong efforts to prevent radio stations from playing records, without paying for the rights. Record labels clearly state that the records are for home use only and forbid broadcasting.

RE In spite of material shortage (or perhaps because of it) Glenn Wallichs, a Hollywood music/record retailer, Buddy De Sylva, a film producer and songwriter, and Johnny Mercer, a leading songwriter of the day, launch Capitol Records, with $10,000. In a day when record companies and recording artists are trying to stop radio stations from playing records, Capitol woos the stations and their disk jockeys. The label is quickly successful.

RE Among Capitol's earliest hits are "Cow Cow Boogie" by Ella Mae Morse with the Freddie Slack orchestra; "Queenie, Queen of Them All," a song about a burlesque stripper by Johnny Mercer; and a Paul Whiteman record.

MU Frank Sinatra leaves the Tommy Dorsey Orchestra and goes out on his own. His first club date in New York is at the Rio Bomba in a show starring Walter O'Keefe. Sinatra is a smash.

1943

TH *Oklahoma!* with Alfred Drake and Celeste Holm — the Rodgers and Hammerstein hit — pioneers a new style in musical comedy and is the biggest success on Broadway. Other musical hits include Mary Martin in *One Touch of Venus* and

Ethel Merman in *Something For the Boys.* Billy Rose produces an unusual adaptation of Bizet's opera, *Carmen,* with libretto by Oscar Hammerstein II and an all-black cast headed by Muriel Smith and Muriel Rahn, who alternate in the title role.

TH Larry Hart dies on Nov. 17, five days after a revival of the Rodgers and Hart musical, *A Connecticut Yankee,* opens on Broadway. Pessimistic Hart had a favorite phrase — "Just because you're paranoid doesn't mean they're not out to get you."

TH Moss Hart's *Winged Victory,* an air force dramatic counterpart to Berlin's *This Is The Army,* is a hit. The top comedy is a three-character play, John Van Druten's *Voice of the Turtle,* starring Margaret Sullavan. Sidney Kingsley's *The Patriots,* a Revolutionary War drama, wins the Drama Critics' Circle Award.

TH The Theatre Guild presents *Othello,* starring Paul Robeson with Jose Ferrer as Iago. Robeson had played the role in London, with Maurice Evans as Iago. This role marks Robeson's first Broadway appearance since 1932.

MO War films continue to bolster morale. Among the best this year is Oscar winning *Casablanca,* starring Humphrey Bogart, Ingrid Bergman and the haunting theme song "As Time Goes By." Other popular war theme movies are *Hitler's Children, A Guy Named Joe, Destination Tokyo,* and two musicals — Irving Berlin's *This Is The Army* and *Stage Door Canteen,* featuring Katharine Cornell's one and only film appearance.

MO Important movies this year include Ernest Hemingway's *For Whom the Bell Tolls* with Gary Cooper and Ingrid Bergman; Greer Garson and Walter Pidgeon in *Madame Curie; Watch on the Rhine* with Bette Davis and Paul Lukas, who wins an Oscar for the film.

MO Newcomers making an impact this year include Jennifer Jones and her Academy Award winning performance in *The Song of Bernadette;* Roddy McDowell, Elizabeth Taylor and a transvestite collie in *Lassie Come Home.* Frank Sinatra makes his movie debut in *Higher and Higher.*

MO Betty Grable, the G.I.'s favorite pin-up; and Greer Garson are the only women in the box office Top Ten.

MO Ex-Al Capone mobsters move in on International Alliance of Theatre and Stage Electricians (IATSE) and milk the stagehands union and movie producers for $2,500,000.

RA Just as Mark Woods is about to close a deal to sell the NBC Blue network to a syndicate formed by the Wall Street firm of Dillon & Read, Sarnoff sells the network to Ed Noble, head of Life Savers, and James

McGraw of McGraw-Hill for $8,000,000. Woods becomes president of the new network, which becomes the American Broadcasting Company. Before deal is finalized, McGraw drops out for reasons of poor health.

RA In October the Department of Justice drops its anti-trust suits against NBC and CBS, since the former has disposed of its Blue network, and both major networks have dropped a number of non-broadcast operations.

RE/MU *Billboard* two-page chart feature, "Music Popularity Charts," embraces "Best Selling Retail Records." "Most Played Juke Box Records;" "Records Most Played on the Air;" "Record Possibilities;" "Record Reviews;" "Songs with Most Radio Plugs;" "Best Selling Sheet Music;" "Lucky Strike Hit Parade (CBS);" "All-Time Hit Parade (NBC)" and "Harlem Hit Parade" are all introduced. All these are thoroughly researched and are the forerunners of the charts in the present publication.

RE The record companies, utilizing masters in the "can" (previously recorded but unreleased), hold out against the musicians union strike for thirteen months. Then Decca (having less backlog than either RCA or Columbia) capitulates. They sign an agreement with the AFM to pay, into a special fund, a royalty on every record they sell. RCA and Columbia hold out for another fourteen months.

1944

TH Frank Fay scores the hit of his career in Mary Chase's *Harvey,* which wins the Pulitzer Prize. Josephine Hull co-stars in the comedy about a six-foot rabbit visible only to Fay.

TH The Edvard Grieg show, *Song of Norway; Bloomer Girl,* starring Celeste Holm; and *On the Town* are musical hits. *On The Town,* with lyrics by Betty Comden and Adolph Green, is composer Leonard Bernstein's first musical comedy.

TH *Billboard* creates its own version of Hollywood's Academy Awards by instituting the Donaldson Awards. Actors, producers, stagehands, etc. vote for their favorites in the Broadway theatre. The first awards — for the 1943–44 season — go to Paul Robeson, and Margaret Sullavan, along with her play *Voice of the Turtle.*

MO Many of Hollywood's established male stars (Clark Gable, Jimmy Stewart, Robert Taylor, Robert Montgomery, Mickey Rooney, etc.) have gone to war. "Star" directors Frank Capra, John Ford, William Wyler, John Huston also have enlisted and are responsible for some of the finest documentaries and combat footage produced by the various branches of the armed services.

MO War stories and religious themes dominate. The former include *Thirty Seconds Over Tokyo* with Spencer Tracy, Van Johnson and Robert Walker, and David Selznick's *Since You Went Away.* Latter include *Going My Way,* which wins an Oscar for Bing Crosby playing a priest, and *Keys of the Kingdom,* Gregory Peck's first starring role.

MO Other outstanding films this year are *Laura* with its haunting title theme, Gene Tierney, and Clifton Webb; Ingrid Bergman's Oscar-winning performance in *Gaslight* with Charles Boyer; Humphrey Bogart in *To Have and Have Not,* introducing Lauren Bacall; *Double Indemnity* with Barbara Stanwyck and Fred MacMurray; Judy Garland's classic musical *Meet Me In St. Louis,* featuring "The Trolley Song"; and Mickey Rooney in *National Velvet* in which Elizabeth Taylor, age twelve, makes her first impact on film audiences.

MO Danny Kaye makes his first movie for Sam Goldwyn, *Up In Arms* with Dinah Shore. MGM promotes swimmer Esther Williams from featured player to star status in *Bathing Beauty* with Red Skelton.

RE American troops invade Germany and, among other prizes, capture magnetic tape recorders. Although these are bulky and unwieldy for use in commercial recording, they do form base of subsequent magnetic tape recording in the U.S.

RA NBC and CBS AM radio station affiliates supply network programs to their FM stations. Networks permit them to use shows on FM without charge to help build FM audiences.

RE Columbia and RCA Victor both sign new agreements with the American Federation of Musicians on the same terms signed a year earlier by Decca.

MU Frank Sinatra appears at the Paramount Theatre, New York, on Columbus Day and 30,000 fans, many of them swooning bobby soxers, acclaim the hottest new star of the era.

CI In Hartford, Conn., during a matinee performance of the Ringling Brothers and Barnum & Bailey Circus on July 6, the worst disaster in circus history takes place. The Wallendas are doing their high wire act, when a fire breaks out; 168 people, more than 100 of them children, are burned or trampled to death; 487 are injured. Six circus executives go to prison, the show is fined $10,000 and pays more than $4,000,000 in damage awards.

CI In August the Ringling Brothers and Barnum & Bailey Show, having pulled itself together in winter quarters in Sarasota, goes back on the road, playing only stadiums, ball parks and other locations, without a tent of any kind. Work is being done to develop flame-proof tents after the Hartford tragedy.

1945

TH Tennessee Williams' first hit, *The Glass Menagerie,* with a stunning comeback performance by Laurette Taylor, wins the Drama Critics' Circle Award. Also starred are Julie Haydon and Eddie Dowling. At the same time, another playwright destined to be a major force in the theatre, Arthur Miller, has his first play, *The Man Who Had All the Luck,* on Broadway, but it closes in four days.

TH Rodgers and Hammerstein have another hit with *Carousel,* a musical treatment of *Liliom.* It is — and remains — Rodgers' favorite score ("You'll Never Walk Alone," "Soliloquy," "If I Loved You"). It wins eight of *Billboard's* Donaldson Awards.

MO Fred Astaire dances with Gene Kelly for the first and only time in MGM's musical revue *Ziegfeld Follies.* Kelly also does an innovative dance with animated figure of a mouse, Jerry of the Oscar winning Hanna-Barbera cartoon shorts, *Tom and Jerry.* MGM has another musical hit in *Anchors Aweigh,* starring Kelly and Frank Sinatra.

MO Industrialist Eric Johnston becomes Hollywood's new "watchdog," succeeding Will Hays as Motion Picture Producers and Distributors of America president, a post Hays had held for thirty-three years. The organization's name is changed to the Motion Picture Association of America.

MO *The Lost Weekend,* about the downfall of an executive-alcoholic, is the picture of the year, winning Oscars for star Ray Milland and director Billy Wilder. Joan Crawford makes a stunning comeback in *Mildred Pierce* and wins an Oscar after twenty years in films.

MO Roy Rogers, king of Republic's low-budget westerns, (featuring Dale Evans, Gabby Hayes and Rogers' horse, Trigger) makes the box office Top Ten, following in boot-steps of another singing cowboy, Gene Autry, who made the Top Ten in 1941.

RA At the beginning of the year there are 943 AM radio stations, forty-six FM radio stations and nine TV stations on the air. Magnetic wire recorders are now available on the consumer market.

RA There are now over 56,000,000 radio sets in American homes, and approximately 16,500 television sets.

MU "Boy" and "girl" singers, almost all alumni of the big bands, dominate the popular music scene on records and radio. Among them are Frank Sinatra, Perry Como, Dick Haymes, Peggy Lee, Jo Stafford, Doris Day, Helen O'Connell, and Kay

Starr. Many, if not all of them, attribute their success to their experiences with the big bands.

RA Number one advertiser in radio is Procter & Gamble. A *Broadcasting* magazine survey indicates company spends about $11,000,000 per year for time, and another $11,000,000 per year for talent. A large portion of the budget is spent on soap operas.

RA All commercial programs are dropped for the day as radio covers the death of President Franklin Delano Roosevelt in April.

TV CBS demonstrates its mechanical color TV system for the FCC. Although it is incompatible with current black and white sets, it does produce a good quality color picture. RCA claims CBS is pushing its mechanical color to slow up the commercialization and progress of black and white television.

TV ABC starts its TV operation this year. Programming includes Don McNeill's *Breakfast Club, Ladies Be Seated,* and *The Singing Lady.* All the existing TV stations give heavy coverage to the end of WW II and the nationwide celebrations of VE and VJ Days.

TV RCA holds first public demonstrations of its color television in their Princeton, N.J. laboratories.

CI The Ringling Brothers and Barnum & Bailey Show opens in New York City with a benefit for the Seventh War Loan. The show stages an old-time parade, the first the big town has seen in twenty-five years.

1946

TH The American Repertory Theatre is formed by Eva Le Gallienne, Margaret Webster, and Cheryl Crawford. Their initial productions include *What Every Woman Knows* with Le Gallienne and Walter Hampden, and Victor Jory as *Henry VIII.*

TH Critics are indifferent to *The Iceman Cometh,* Eugene O'Neill's first play since 1934. More than ten years will pass before the O'Neill work will receive the acclaim it deserves, when Jason Robards Jr. stars in an off-Broadway production of the play.

TH Ethel Merman is a smash in Irving Berlin's musical, *Annie Get Your Gun,* about the legendary sharpshooter Annie Oakley. The score includes "There's No Business Like Show Business." Betty Garrett becomes a star, warbling Harold Rome's "South America, Take It Away" in *Call Me Mister;* Pearl Bailey sings a soaring Harold Arlen-Johnny Mercer score in *St. Louis Woman* ("Come Rain or Come Shine").

TH Marlon Brando — his *Streetcar Named Desire* hit still ahead — plays Marchbanks in a revival of *Candida* starring

Katharine Cornell. Ingrid Bergman stars in Maxwell Anderson's *Joan of Lorraine.* Patricia Neal and Mildred Dunnock are in Lillian Hellman's *Another Part of the Forest.*

TH Judy Holliday is discovered in the Garson Kanin hit comedy, *Born Yesterday.* She had replaced Jean Arthur out-of-town. Paul Douglas co-stars.

MO The happiness and trauma of a returning serviceman in this first post-war year is captured in Samuel Goldwyn's *The Best Years of Our Lives* which wins Oscars for director William Wyler, star Fredric March, and supporting actor Harold Russell, a non-professional and an amputee veteran of the war.

MO Hollywood is still largely unaware of the coming competitive threat of TV, and business is booming. Paramount, as one example, with such hot stars as Crosby, Bob Hope, and Oscar-winner Olivia DeHavilland (for *To Each His Own*), registers a $39,000,000 profit.

MO Newcomers (insofar as America is concerned) include James Mason, a hit in the English film *The Seventh Veil;* and English star Rex Harrison in his first U.S. movie, *Anna and the King of Siam* with Irene Dunne; also Larry Parks in the box office hit *The Jolson Story,* with Parks miming to Al Jolson's vocals.

MO Other important, and/or, big box office pictures this year are Rita Hayworth's sizzling *Gilda* with Glenn Ford; *The Yearling;* Walt Disney's full-length "live" film, *Song of the South;* and four remarkable imports: Laurence Olivier's *Henry V,* and *Caesar and Cleopatra* (Vivien Leigh and Claude Rains) from England; France's classic *Children of Paradise;* and Italy's *Open City* with Anna Magnani.

NC Mobster Bugsy Siegel and associates open the Flamingo in Las Vegas, marking the beginning of the desert town as the "entertainment capital of the world."

RE Jack Mullin demonstrates Magnetophon tape and recorder on a machine he shipped back from Europe during the war for the Society of Motion Picture and Television Engineers.

RA Bing Crosby signs new deal with Philco to do weekly show for $30,000 per program. The unique feature of the deal is that Crosby has permission to tape the show in advance. This is the first time this has ever been done. The contract provides that if the quality is not satisfactory, Crosby will return to doing the show live. It is satisfactory.

RA Many radio manufacturers go into production of FM receivers after the War.

RA/MU AFM president Petrillo calls a strike against WAAF, Chicago, because the fuses to hire three extra local musicians to serve as music librarians.

MU In this year more than a half dozen of the country's top big bands dissolve. They include the orchestras of Tommy Dorsey, Benny Goodman, Woody Herman, Harry James, Les Brown and Benny Carter. A number of them reorganize at a later date, and continue to operate, but the golden days of the big bands are finished.

RE It is the day of the popular vocalists. Frank Sinatra leaves the Tommy Dorsey band to go out on his own. Dick Haymes, with the Harry James band, leaves to launch a solo career. Other band singers who leave to become stars on their own are Doris Day and Perry Como.

RE With the end of World War II, shellac is again readily available, and in great quantities. The record business soars to new heights, achieving sales of $218,000,000 by the end of this year.

RE The General Electric Company secures patents on a magnetic phonograph cartridge.

TV RCA Victor markets a television set with a ten-inch picture tube to sell for $375. Engineer Elmer Engstrom calls it the Model T of television. It is a tremendous success. Other manufacturers rush out with TV sets and by the end of 1947, 175,000 TV sets are in use.

RA/TV Charles R. Denny, Jr. is appointed head of the Federal Communications Commission, when its chairman Paul Porter leaves to head up the Office of Price Administration. Denny's chairmanship covers the period of the introduction of competitive color systems by NBC and CBS.

TV The CBS and Du Mont networks demonstrate their own color television systems for the Federal Communications Commission.

TV In April CBS telecasts a color film show from its UHF transmitter and issues a statement maintaining that color TV can be a practical reality in one year.

TV CBS transmits color show over co-axial cable link between New York and Washington.

TV In September CBS asks the FCC to set standards and permit color telecasting in UHF frequencies immediately.

TV In November RCA demonstrates its all-electronic color TV system for the FCC.

TV An audience survey shows that more than 100,000 viewers watch Joe Louis-Billy Conn heavyweight title bout, telecast on four-station network. The show, sponsored by Gillette Safety Razor Company, convinces skeptics that television has truly arrived.

TV First sponsor of a TV network program is Bristol-Myers, which bankrolls *Geographically Speaking* on two-station NBC-TV hook-up.

CI John Ringling North, old John's nephew, is made president of the circus corporation. He embarks on an aggressive campaign to bring the shows back to their former high place in the world of entertainment.

PART FIVE

1947-1977

1947 Work on tape recorders/players, dynaural noise suppressors, amplifiers, new speeds, etc. mark beginning of high fidelity era in recorded music.

1948 FCC freezes all television station licensing.

1948 Columbia Records introduces 33 1/3 rpm, long playing disks.

1949 RCA introduces 45 rpm disks.

1949 First cable TV services go on the air.

1950 FCC authorizes first experimental over-the-air pay TV systems.

1951 United Paramount Theatres buys ABC.

1952 FCC lifts freeze on TV station licensing.

1953 FCC approves RCA compatible color TV system as industry standard.

1954 First color TV sets are introduced.

1954 Disney and Warner Bros. are first major film companies to produce shows for televisions.

1955 First theme park, Disneyland, opens in Anaheim, Ca.

1956 Shuberts sign Consent Decree, agreeing to sell twelve theatres.

1956 Great acceleration of sale of pre-1948 movies to television.

1958 Disk jockeys hold first national convention.

1959 Most record companies now releasing monoraul and stereophonic disks. Mono is on way out.

1965 Sales of color television sets double over previous year.

1966 Era of conglomerate control of much of show business begins.

1966 Breakthrough year for tape cartridges. Stereo cassette decks introduced.

1966 Three TV networks buy vast numbers of post-1948 films from major producers.

1967 After 100 years of family ownership, Ringlings sell circus to Irvin Feld.

1969 In one of most phenomenal events of the era, Woodstock Music Festival draws almost 500,000 young people.

1971 Over 5,000,000 families now subscribe to CATV systems.

1972 First quadraphonic records are released.

1974 Record and tape sales this year exceed $2,000,000,000 for first time.

1975 Film box office receipts set new record, $1,900,000,000.

1975 *Billboard* shows top record stars for 1945-1975 era: 1. The Beatles; 2. Elvis Presley; 3. Frank Sinatra.

1975 Sony introduces videocassette recorder/player.

1977 Theatre has record-breaking season. Between Broadway and the road, receipts are over $175,000,000.

1977 100th Anniversary of recorded sound is celebrated by all facets of the industry.

1977 First FCC approved over-the-air pay TV system is launched by National Television Subscription in Los Angeles.

1977 Alex Haley's *Roots*, as eight part mini-series on ABC-TV, sets all time viewing record. 130,000,000 people estimated to have seen one or more episodes.

1976 (MCA) Universal and Disney sue Sony and others to stop sale of videotape recorders, players and cassettes.

1976 Two night showing of *Gone With the Wind* on NBC-TV draws highest ratings to date.

1976 MCA-Phillipps and RCA demonstrate videodisk players for trade, but do not introduce them to consumer market.

TECHNOLOGY, CONGLOMERATES AND SUPERSTARS

Continuing and relentless technological advances of every description; the ascendancy of conglomerates; and the emergence of unprecedented numbers of superstars—these were the three hallmarks of the 1947–1977 era in American entertainment

In addition to the technological miracle of television itself (to which present generations quickly became accustomed), scientists and inventors made advances which improved and altered many phases of show business and affected the impact of one evolving entertainment medium upon one or more others.

The day of the trusts, when individuals and small groups controlled entire industries, was long gone. Now major entertainment organizations diversified their activities within show business and into many other spheres of industry. Some show business operations, in turn, were swallowed up by conglomerates which wielded power in numerous areas foreign to entertainment.

More stars were created and developed (the term superstars came into common usage) than had ever existed before. These stars had an appeal to greater masses of people than had their illustrious predecessors and their earnings reached astronomical proportions. There were more multimillionaire entertainers and entertainment entrepreneurs ("teens" through septuagenarians) than ever before.

THE SPECTACULAR CYCLORAMA

All this evolved in show business against a national and international socio-economic cyclorama that was frequently exciting and stunning; often depressing and frightening; sometimes all simultaneously. There were the Cold War and the Red-Under-Every-Bed periods of the '50s when the House Un-American Activities Committee, Senator Joe McCarthy, and other self-appointed guardians of democracy hunted "witches" and destroyed a number of lives in the radio-movie-television communities.

There were the civil rights marches of the mid-'50s, led by the gallant Martin Luther King; the Korean "police action" which became a war; and the Vietnam catastrophe in which a handful of American military advisors

metamorphosed into a half million American soldiers, large numbers of them fighting a war they didn't understand or believe in. And there were the constantly growing, "hell-no-we-won't-go" protests against the war.

There was the Soviet-U.S. space race, blasted off with the Russians' first man-made satellite, Sputnik I, in 1957, eventually followed by Neil Armstrong taking man's first step on the moon, and shots to Mars and beyond.

The "drop-out, turn-on" drug era was fed by Dr. Timothy Leary's League for Spiritual Discovery, the Beatles' "Lucy in the Sky with Diamonds" and sundry movements and groups proselytizing LSD and other hard drugs designated by many alphabetical combinations.

Hordes of young people, disenchanted and even more confused than their parents, went to "pot." They created drug culture capitals on both coasts (Haight-Ashbury in San Francisco and the East Village in downtown Manhattan) and celebrated their flower-bedecked, free-love, freaked-out high-decibel life styles at festivals like Altamont and Woodstock.

In 1967 the second feminist revolution began with the formation of the National Organization for Women. Minority groups (blacks, Chicanos, Indians) stepped up their struggles.

Intermittent murder—ugly, bigot-based and insane—smeared these restless years: the Kennedys and Martin Luther King and Medgar Evers; the three young civil rights workers in Mississippi; the four young students at Kent.

THE 200,000,000 AUDIENCE

Through all this, as they had from the very beginning, Americans kept procreating. The 1950 census showed 150,697,361; in 1960, 179,323,175; and by 1970, 203,211,926. The best estimates were that by the end of 1977, there would be 218,364,000 Americans.

The vastness of their numbers and the diversified range of their tastes—with their changeable, unpredictable nature—made show business in modern times a multi-billion dollar guessing game. The entertainment focal point was television.

DRESS REHEARSAL FOR TV

It was certainly not the intention of the Federal Communications Commission in 1948 to stage a show business dress rehearsal for television, but that is precisely what the Commission achieved. By September 30, 1948 there were 108 television stations on the air. Most cities had one station, but the nation's two largest markets, New York and Los Angeles, had seven stations each. At that point the FCC declared a total freeze on new station licenses, because the agency was having difficulty allocating channels in a rational manner. That freeze was not lifted until April, 1952.

In that three years and seven months interval, a 108 station, four network television industry operated. (For practical purposes, it was really two networks, NBC and CBS, since ABC and DuMont were extremely hard pressed to compete with the long established Sarnoff and Paley networks.)

In 1948 show business, generally, was in good health. Tennessee Williams and Arthur Miller were enjoying successful runs of *A Streetcar Named Desire* and *All My Sons,* respectively. Cole Porter's *Kiss Me, Kate* followed Alan Jay Lerner's and Frederick Loewe's first hit musical, *Brigadoon.* Henry Fonda was starring in *Mister Roberts;* Rex Harrison was playing Henry VIII in *Anne of the Thousand Days,* among other excellent Broadway theatre attractions.

The Supreme Court in 1948 ruled that block booking of films was restraint of trade and ordered the producer-exhibitor film companies to divest themselves of their theatre operations.

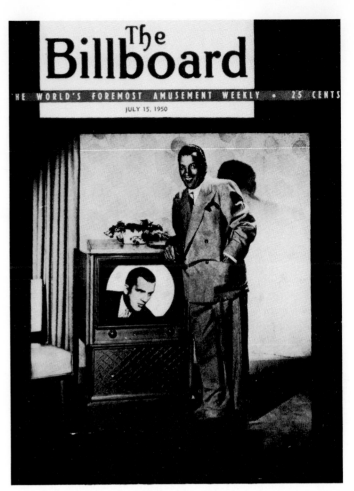

JULY 15, 1950 ISSUE   ED SULLIVAN

BASIC CHANGES IN FILMS

In time, of course, this decision was to create basic changes in the movie industry. No longer would a small handful of all-powerful men, running a few film companies, be able to decide what the movie-going public would like—take it or leave it. While the major movie makers owned or controlled most of the theatres in the major markets, they made what they felt like making, secure in the knowledge that their theatres would exhibit the films. Once exhibitors could book or reject films, the moguls automatically lost a substantial part of their power. Up to this point, of course, there had been no significant television competition.

So the film tycoons were not too worried. They felt they would have ample time to sell off the movie houses, and in the meantime their good pictures were registering huge grosses.

RADIO AND RECORDS THRIVE

Radio was thriving. Ninety-three percent of all American homes (35,900,000) in the late '40s owned at least one radio set. Record sales had hit the $200,000,000 mark for the second year in a row in 1947, although the industry was being shaken up by the introduction of a new 33⅓ rpm record by Columbia in 1948 and an American Federation of Musicians strike against the record companies. Other areas of entertainment, indoor and out, were holding their own.

Predictably, television drew upon all of show business for its programs. In converting audio-only players and shows to video-audio, TV encountered none of the difficulties that the movie people had run up against in the earlier reverse conversion from silents to talkies.

PALEY'S TALENT RAIDS

Within the space of a year, beginning in 1948, William Paley opened a battle on yet another front in his war with Sarnoff and RCA/NBC. He "stole" Amos 'n' Andy, Jack Benny, Edgar Bergen and Charlie McCarthy, and Red Skelton from NBC, by making them multi-million dollar capital gains offers they could not refuse. He also brought Bing Crosby back to CBS. Not only did these maneuvers enable CBS to overtake NBC in key prime time periods in radio, but they simultaneously gave Paley the nucleus of a potent talent line-up for the budding television network.

NBC, of course, quickly countered. In the next several years they signed long-term, multi-million dollar deals with Fred Allen, Groucho Marx, Bob Hope and Kate Smith, among others.

Television also invaded the theatre by presenting excellent anthology drama in shows such as *Kraft Theatre, Philco Playhouse, Studio One* and others with scripts by new playwrights Paddy Chayefsky, Horton Foote, Reginald Rose, Rod Serling, and new young actors like Kim Stanley, Grace Kelly, Joanne Woodward and Paul Newman.

TV, THE NEW VAUDE STAGE

To paraphrase what George Jessel said of radio—television brought back vaudeville, but without a credit line. In 1948, the *Texaco Star Theatre* made Uncle Miltie (Berle), "Mr. Television." Columnist Ed Sullivan booked every conceivable variety act on his new TV *Toast of the Town* show. And the following season, another variety show, starring Sid Caesar and Imogene Coca, which began as *Friday Night Frolics* and became *Your Show of Shows,* won high ratings.

When any of these shows was on the air, attendance in movie theatres, legit houses, even restaurants in television cities fell off. Of course, there were also the roller derby and wrestling and some more credible sports shows, news, cooking and kiddie programs.

INSULATED FROM REALITY

But one type of show was conspicuous in its absence from TV—the full length motion picture. *Los Angeles Times* entertainment editor and motion picture critic Charles Champlin in his book, *FLICKS, or Whatever Became of Andy Hardy,* commented on filmdom's attitude toward television:

Only an industry as obsessed with itself, as savagely competitive within itself, and as self-satisfied and insulated from much other reality as Hollywood, could have ignored so successfully, and then underestimated so drastically, the invention that spelled revolutionary change.

The evidence during TV's "dress rehearsal" period was all there. By mid-1951, every television city, without exception, reported decreases ranging from twenty percent to forty percent in movie attendance. Movie theatres were closing in these same cities. But the film makers would neither make movies for TV nor sell movies to TV.

David Sarnoff went to the West Coast to meet with Louis B. Mayer to work out a production arrangement between MGM and NBC. Mayer turned him down.

NO SCARCITY OF HITS

After all, the movie men could point to such box office hits in the 1949–1952 period as *Adam's Rib* with Spencer Tracy and Katharine Hepburn; Tracy with a beautiful new star, Elizabeth Taylor, in *Father of the Bride;* Hepburn and Bogart in *The African Queen;* blockbusters like Gloria Swanson in *Sunset Boulevard;* Bette Davis in *All About Eve;* George Gershwin's *American in Paris,* starring Gene Kelly; and Kelly and Sinatra in *On the Town* and *Take Me Out to the Ball Game.* Mario Lanza in *The Great Caruso; Show Boat*

with Ava Gardner, Kathryn Grayson and Howard Keel; the picture version of *A Streetcar Named Desire* with Vivien Leigh and a forceful young new actor named Marlon Brando; and the Hope and Crosby pictures were some more of these hits.

Or you could look at Broadway. How badly were the seven television stations in New York hurting shows like Arthur Miller's *Death of a Salesman; South Pacific* with Mary Martin and Ezio Pinza; Carol Channing in *Gentlemen Prefer Blondes;* Frank Loesser's *Guys and Dolls;* William Inge's *Come Back Little Sheba; The King and I* with Gertrude Lawrence and Yul Brynner; Maureen Stapleton in Tennessee Williams' *The Rose Tattoo;* Sidney Kingsley's *Darkness at Noon?* How much was TV really hurting?

Right there in New York, in 1951, with seven TV stations giving away all kinds of free shows, vaudeville was coming back, believe it or not. Judy Garland was doing two-a-day at the Palace. She'd gone in for four weeks and had run nineteen. And when she closed, they booked in new shows. It looked like vaudeville was back and would run forever. (It actually did continue for seven more years.)

The movie people were not afraid of TV, but they were certainly not going to help it. They were busy with other matters—as Champlin had put it, "savage competition," among other things. In 1951, Mayer resigned as head of MGM, and Dore Schary took over. One of Schary's early moves was to announce pay cuts for more than 4,000 MGM employees.

ENTER LEONARD GOLDENSON

Meanwhile each of the individual major studios that had signed the consent decree with the Department of Justice to divest themselves of their theatre holdings were planning their own sell-off schedules. MGM-Loew's was the last to achieve divestiture in 1954. Among the first was Paramount. In 1951, Paramount split into two companies, Paramount Pictures and United Paramount Theatres. Heading the United Paramount Theatres operation was a brilliant young attorney, Leonard Goldenson. Goldenson did not feel about television the way so many movie people did.

In 1951, against the strong objections of many members of his own Board of Directors, and the advice of most Wall Street experts, Goldenson acquired the ABC radio and television networks for United Paramount Theatres. Ed Noble, who had originally bought ABC (then the NBC Blue network) for $8,000,000 acquired eight and a half percent of UPT stock in a $25,000,000 transaction. Goldenson became president of UPT-ABC; Robert Kintner, president of the ABC Broadcasting Division; and Ed Noble, chairman of the Finance Committee.

Goldenson's entry into the television business was to make ABC a viable competitor of the solidly entrenched NBC and CBS networks. And one of the key weapons Goldenson used in the early stages of television was motion pictures. Du Mont dropped out of the TV network competition after a long and valiant struggle against hopeless odds.

NEW TV PRODUCERS

While the major studios refused to produce films for television, enterprising new organizations filled the production vacuum. The talent agency, Music Corporation of America (MCA), had begun to "dabble" in program production to the point where the Department of Justice was considering a suit to force MCA to give up either its booking or its production activities. In the meantime, the agency had developed its Revue Productions into one of the most active TV show producers. Lucille Ball and her husband, Desi Arnaz, had launched their own Desilu Productions and developed *I Love Lucy* into a top program. Ziv Television Productions, originally a radio program syndicator, turned out such series as *I Led Three Lives* and *A Man Called X,* spy-action-adventure shows. Hal Roach and Screen Gems, a subsidiary of Columbia Pictures, were the first two movie-oriented firms to go into TV show production.

NEW LOOK FOR RADIO

As TV's three year, seven month dress rehearsal proceeded, it quickly became apparent that radio was going to be drastically altered by television. Just one example: the Bob Hope radio show's rating on NBC was cut in half from 1949 to 1951, dropping from a 23.8 to 12.7. Network radio and affiliated stations, as well as independents, frantically searched for new formats. And the local stations found a foolproof program structure that was ideal in every sense: (1) it was incredibly inexpensive; (2) it attracted a demographically desirable audience—young people; and (3) the audience it attracted tended to have a high degree of loyalty to its favorite station. The format, of course, was recorded music.

In 1940, when BMI and external non-show business events created a situation in which country music and rhythm and blues or soul music became important parts of the popular music mainstream, new record stars, singing and playing all of these various musical styles, developed. The record companies, which had proliferated to a point where the competition between literally scores of companies was fierce, had long since discovered that performance of their records on radio was by far the most effective sales and promotion tool available to them. And, of course, the radio stations played their records free.

Television's dress rehearsal period created the greatest acceleration of radio play for all types of recorded music in radio or recording history. Meanwhile Paley and Sarnoff were engaged in a bitter battle to establish the new rpm record speeds they had introduced. RCA refused to go along with Columbia's 33⅓ rpm LP, and in February, 1949, introduced its own large-hole, seven inch 45 rpm disk. But radio play on hit records continued unabated.

RECORDS SLOW DOWN AND SURGE

Record sales dropped from $224,000,000 in 1947 to $189,000,000 in 1948; and dropped farther to $173,000,000 in 1949, but this was clearly attributable to the chaos created by the three different speeds situation. Distributors, dealers, and consumers did not know whether to buy the old 78 rpms, or the Columbia 33⅓ or RCA's 45. It was a fierce and costly technological war, but one which ultimately proved to be the first step in creating a giant record industry. By mid-1950, it was becoming apparent that all record companies would be producing albums in the 33⅓ long playing speed, and singles in the 45 rpm speed; the 78 rpm speed would be phased out.

The radio networks—owned and operated, of course, by the same people who were making the major investments in television—found themselves in the position of having to cut time rates drastically to advertisers to allow for the audiences they were losing to TV in the 108 television cities.

In programming, the radio networks were aware that their radio stars and top radio shows would sooner or later be converted to television, and they concentrated on developing radio formats consisting largely of worldwide news services, "name" commentary, and other service features, plus supplementing the recorded music formats most of their affiliated stations were building so successfully.

NOW THE TV DELUGE

So went the three year, seven month television dress rehearsal from 1948–1952. It was obvious that American entertainment had a new monster hit on its hands. In 1948, there were approximately 250,000 TV sets in use in the 108 television cities. By 1952, there were 15,000,000 sets in homes in those cities. And then on April 14, 1952, in its "Sixth Report and Order" the FCC lifted its freeze. The order provided for 617 new VHF and 1436 UHF stations in 1,291 cities. The Commission, as expected, was literally deluged with applications for channels from every section of the country.

The battle in color television continued. CBS and NBC pushed their respective systems; others, including Du Mont, demonstrated systems of their own. In 1950, it appeared as though this was another battle Paley was to win. The FCC approved the CBS non-compatible color system, but Sarnoff's attorneys immediately got a restraining order, halting the Commission's ruling and continuing the color fight.

CATV AND OTHER ADVANCES

Technological advances continued in other areas. As early as 1949, the first Community Antenna Television systems (CATV) went on the air. They did not originate programming, but carried TV signals to communities beyond the reach of the originating stations via radio relay. In 1950, the FCC authorized over-the-air pay television, and the Skiatron Corporation introduced such a system, called Subscriber-Vision. A year later, Zenith launched a pay-TV experiment in Hartford, Conn., wiring 300 homes, and charging $1 for telecasts of such current movies as they could acquire and of other special events.

Until 1951, virtually all television programming was done live, but that year in Hollywood, Lucille Ball and Desi Arnaz (Desilu Productions) filmed their *I Love Lucy* show. The show was the number one rated program in TV, and marked the beginning of filming TV series. That same year, the first theatre telecast (again featuring Joe Louis, this time beating Lee Savold) was promoted. Nine theatres in six cities carried the fight, and they were all sold out.

MOVIES' TECHNOLOGICAL RESPONSE

Many movie people were seeking technological answers to the TV competition. In 1952, inventor Fred Aller's Cinerama was introduced at the Broadway Theatre in New York. It was a curved screen, six times larger than the regular sized screen of the day, and gave a strong dimensional effect. The show, called *This Is Cinerama*, featuring an exciting roller coaster ride and spectacular scenic effects, ran for 122 weeks and clearly heralded the coming of large screens.

In radio, as early as 1947, Bing Crosby taped his *Philco Show* on John T. Mullin's magnetic tape. It was the first radio network show which dared venture away from live broadcast and began the trend to taping radio programs. Ampex introduced its tape machines. Tape was also introduced into the recording business. Two small companies, Vox and Livingston, released the first pre-recorded magnetic tapes in 1950. Other technological advances in recorded music preceded and followed the introduction of the new speed disks by Columbia and RCA Victor. In 1947, H. H. Scott was demonstrating its first noise suppressors and high fidelity amplifiers. And, by 1949, much experimentation in stereo was going on.

AN EARLY CONGLOMERATE MOVE

One of the earliest examples of a non-show business organization sweeping an entertainment firm into its conglomerate house occurred in 1951, when the General Tire & Rubber Corporation bought the Don Lee Broadcasting network.

With the end of the freeze, television really erupted. Stations went on the air across the country as fast as licenses were granted and construction could be completed. New coaxial cable and radio relay installations tied them together. The 15,000,000 sets in American homes in 1952 more than doubled by 1955 to 32,000,000, and, in the single year that followed, climbed to 37,000,000. Sponsors bought millions of dollars worth of time and talent. In 1953, Ford, celebrating its fiftieth anniversary, presented a two-hour special starring Mary Martin and Ethel Merman on both the NBC and the CBS TV networks. Phillip Morris signed Lucille Ball and Desi Arnaz to a thirty month contract for $8,000,000. Procter and Gamble spent

MAY 1, 1948 ISSUE   MICKEY ROONEY

$36,000,000 in TV and radio in 1953. Where broadcasters couldn't build stations, they bought them. Westinghouse paid Philco $8,500,000 for WPTZ-TV in Philadelphia.

SARNOFF WINS COLOR WAR

In 1954, Sarnoff won the color battle. The FCC approved the RCA compatible color system as the standard for the industry. RCA introduced its first all-electronic color tubes, and Emerson Radio and Television brought out the first color sets to sell for $700. RCA brought out its own color set, retailing for $1000. NBC telecast the first color show, the *Tournament of Roses,* from Pasadena, Ca.

Under new NBC-TV president Pat Weaver, the network began to produce more and more "spectaculars." And in 1954, for the first time, television showed a greater total industry gross than radio: $595,000,000 to radio's $449,500,000. In 1955, NBC's telecast of Mary Martin in *Peter Pan* drew 65,000,000 viewers. Weaver also launched the *Tonight Show.* The eclectic tastes of TV audiences included Gertrude Berg's *The Goldbergs; The Arthur Murray Dance Party* with Kathryn Murray; Jackie Gleason and Art Carney in *The Honeymooners; What's My Line;* Groucho Marx's *You Bet Your Life;* Bishop Sheen, and pianist Liberace.

STILL NO MOVIES

Movies were still not available to TV. Movie men refused to sell films to television. Many film leaders felt the answer to television competition was in technological improvements of their own. Following Cinerama, there were the three-dimensional (3-D) films. Audiences were supplied with colored spectacles to view these movies; *Bwana Devil* was the first movie shown in 3-D. 20th Century Fox introduced Cinemascope. Other film makers promoted Todd-AO, Vistavision, Warnerphonic, and Glamorama. In spite of some excellent movies in 1953 and 1954, attendance by the following year had dropped to its lowest point since 1923. In 1955, the majors produced fewer than 200 films; yet they would have nothing to do with television.

DISNEYLAND'S TV IMPACT

Leonard Goldenson finally changed that. Walt Disney was seeking financing for Disneyland and invited all three of the television networks to participate. NBC and CBS passed, but Goldenson bought a 34.48% interest in the new theme park for $500,000 and guaranteed loans to the park of up to $4,500,000. In exchange for ABC's support, Disney agreed to produce shows for the ABC television network. The Disneyland programs were an immediate hit. One early three-part series—*Davy Crockett*, starring Fess Parker—became so popular that it spun off millions in merchandising profits. Among numerous other items, 10,000,000 Davy Crockett coonskin caps were sold, and the record "The Ballad of Davy Crockett" was a multi-million copy best seller.

Once having won over Disney, Goldenson next persuaded Jack Warner to produce films for ABC for the 1955–1956 season.

Warners produced a number of series for the network; among them was a western, *Cheyenne*. *Cheyenne* was so successful it kicked off a new string of cowboy shows including *Maverick, Sugarfoot, Colt .45, Lawman, Wyatt Earp* and *Gunsmoke*, the eventual long-running hit, starring James Arness.

An English organization, J. Arthur Rank, finally made the first substantial batch of feature films available to TV in 1955, when it sold 100 full length movies to ABC-TV.

THE PRE-48 MOVIE DAM BURSTS

And then, in 1956, the pre-1948 dam burst. More than $100,000,000 worth of pre-1948 film shorts and features were sold or leased to television. After demonstrating the success Disney and Warner Brothers were having by producing shows for television, Goldenson succeeded in making deals with MGM and 20th Century Fox to go into production for ABC. The first signs of major film company total participation in the television business began to appear. In 1960, United Artists bought Ziv Television Productions and a year later 20th Century Fox sold thirty of its post-1948 feature films to NBC for $6,000,000, and announced its plans to go into television production.

TV CARBON COPIES FILMS

By 1958, it was becoming apparent to everyone that the most successful shows on television were the same kind of entertainment the film companies had been producing and showing in theatres. The family situation comedies, for example, were all offspring of moviedom's *Andy Hardy* and similar films. This was particularly true in action/adventure, crime and western shows. In 1959, Quinn Martin produced a new crime show for ABC, *The Untouchables*. It went on the air in October, and by the spring of 1960 it was number one in the ratings. Other crime shows were also among the most watched. They included *Peter Gunn, 77 Sunset Strip* and *Hawaiian Eye*. Many civic and religious groups set up loud screams against the excessive violence on TV, but to little avail.

While ABC was still the number three network—primarily because it still did not have nearly as many VHF affiliates in major markets as either CBS or NBC—the rating studies showed that in most three network station markets, ABC was consistently topping its two established rivals in the ratings.

MOVIES' "MATURE THEMES"

The creative and business leaders of the film industry finally realized they must make movies which television could not duplicate. Since television was accountable to the FCC, and stations could lose their licenses for telecasting shows of questionable moral content, the film makers went to sex. (Some of them also tried to "out-violence" television.)

In 1960, one expensive call girl and one less elegant hooker won Oscars for best actress and best supporting actress, respectively. The call girl was Elizabeth Taylor in *Butterfield 8*, and the strident hooker was Shirley Jones in *Elmer Gantry*, starring Burt Lancaster. Melina Mercouri did excellent business as a carefree hooker in a Greek import, *Never On Sunday*. Jack Lemmon and Shirley MacLaine in *The Apartment* won the Oscar for "Best Picture of the Year." It told the story of a young executive, who climbs the corporate ladder by loaning his apartment to his superiors for the purposes of hanky-panky. For violence, Alfred Hitchcock's *Psycho*, with Tony Perkins playing the weird killer, set a blood-splashed pace. Many female moviegoers were afraid to take a shower for months after seeing the vicious stabbing scene.

It is nice to note that even in that year of new peaks in sex and violence, Walt Disney's Buena Vista Films remained unsullied. Disney's *Pollyanna* was a box-office success, and won a special Oscar for English child star Hayley Mills. Perhaps the Academy was attempting to show that you didn't have to be a hooker to win.

QUIZ SHOWS

In 1955, independent TV producer Louis G. Cowan and Walter Craig of the Norman, Craig and Kummel ad agency sold Revlon a show titled *The $64,000 Question*. It was an overnight sensation, and, by 1957, three big money quiz shows were among the Top Ten rated shows in television. *Question* was number one, *Twenty-One* was fifth, and *The $64,000 Challenge* eighth. Other shows in the top ten were *Gunsmoke*, *I've Got a Secret*, *Ed Sullivan*, *Lawrence Welk*, *Alfred Hitchcock*, *Studio One* and *What's My Line.*

The following year, the New York District Attorney's office launched an investigation of the quiz shows. *Twenty-One* was abruptly cancelled, and its producer was indicted. A House Legislative Oversight Committee opened hearings on the high-rated quiz programs, and the nation was shocked when Charles Van Doren, member of a distinguished family of scholars and an English professor at Columbia, confessed that the producers of *Twenty-One* reviewed with him questions he was asked, and gave him the answers, before a number of the shows. He "won" $129,000 before it was decided by the producers that he should be defeated by another contestant. Van Doren was only one of several contestants who testified to rigging of big money quiz shows. A major and long-lasting effect of the quiz show scandals was that the networks took back control of programming.

RECORD BUSINESS PAYOLA

In 1960, the House Legislative Oversight Committee began hearings into rumored payola in the record industry. These hearings resulted in the ruination of some of radio's leading disk jockeys, notably Alan Freed, one of the most powerful deejays of the day.

But, of course, the era was not all graft and corruption. In spite of TV's tremendous public acceptance, radio was bigger and better than ever on the local level. In 1956, more radio sets (8,332,077) were sold—not counting auto radios—than in any other year in history. In 1960, George Storer paid $10,000,000 for station WINS, New York, and Crowell-Collier bought WMGM, New York, for $11,000,000.

In spite of vociferous protests from dealers, Columbia Records launched its record club in 1955. The new mail-order record sales operation was so successful that RCA and eventually Capitol, among other record companies, followed suit. In 1955, Colonel Tom Parker became Elvis Presley's manager, made a deal for the young singer with RCA, and "Heartbreak Hotel" became the Tupelo, Miss. truck driver's first national smash hit.

PRESLEY AND OTHER MUSIC STARS

By 1957, Presley had not only had a string of million selling singles and albums, but had made several motion pictures. His 1957 film, *Jailhouse Rock* (while rapped by the critics), put him in motion pictures' Top Ten. The potency of music names was building. In addition to Presley, ex-big band singers Sinatra and Doris Day were earning big money for movie exhibitors.

Two more major record acts emerged in the early '60s. In 1961, *New York Times* music critic Robert Shelton wrote a rave review about Bob Dylan, an unknown songwriter-singer he had seen at a folk club, Gerde's. John Hammond, talent acquisition executive for Columbia Records (who had previously discovered and launched some great jazz names—Benny Goodman, Count Basie and Billie Holiday, among others—signed the twenty-year-old Dylan to a record contract. His first album, simply titled *Bob Dylan*, was made at a cost of $400 and sold about 5000 copies. By 1965, Dylan's albums were selling by the millions, and his songs ("Blowin' in the Wind," "The Times They Are A-Changin'," "A Hard Rain's A-Gonna Fall" and others) were rallying themes for the era's protesting youth.

THE BEATLES' POTENT IMPACT

In 1962, young Brian Epstein had taken on management of a scruffy English vocal group, The Beatles, working in a Liverpool dive, appropriately enough named The Cavern. After being turned down by a number of record companies, Epstein finally persuaded George Martin, of Parlophone—one of the Electrical Musical Industries (EMI) record companies—to sign and record the Beatles. By 1964, "I Want to Hold Your Hand," their first record on Capitol (owned by EMI)—supported by a $50,000 promotion campaign—turned into one of the biggest single record hits of all time. Within a year, the Beatles had not only become the most potent popular musical attraction in America, but were well on their way to spearheading a drastic change in life style for millions of young people around the world.

The two-speed record war had resolved itself, and a new technological advance, stereophonic recordings, had been introduced. By 1951, industry sales had climbed back to a new high of $199,000,000; by 1959, almost all companies were releasing LPs both monaurally and in stereo (mono's days were numbered). By 1962, sales had skyrocketed to $687,000,000.

DEATH STRIKES THE SHUBERTS

From the early '50s to the mid-'60s, the old order gave way to the new in some areas of the theatre. In 1953, Lee Shubert died of a stroke at eighty. It was common knowledge on Broadway that he and his brother, Jake, disliked each other heartily, but theatre people were still surprised and shocked when Lee's will was probated and it was learned that he had left not one penny to Jake. Jake was surprised and shocked, too. And bitter! Lee's multi-million dollar affront kicked off a family feud and a series of lawsuits and counter suits, which went on for years.

As Jake, himself, grew increasingly senile, his son, John, a gentle and non-aggressive man, took over as head of the organization. In 1956, the Department of Justice filed anti-trust charges against the Shuberts. Jake, John and their advisors signed a consent decree, in which they agreed they would get out of the booking business and sell off twelve of their theatres in six cities, within two years. Among the houses they were forced to relinquish were the St. James, the National, and the Imperial on Broadway in New York.

In 1962, John Shubert, fifty-three, died of a massive coronary while en route by train from New York to Miami. It was discovered that John had two wives and families, one of which he had kept completely secret. More bitter and lengthy litigation commenced. Jake was still alive, but was so senile by this time that he was not even told of John's death. Jake, himself, died a year later. The company, nevertheless, continued as an important force in the theatre.

PRINCE PRODUCTIONS

In the meantime, new producers, playwrights and stars made their marks. Harold Prince, with partner Robert Griffith—under the tutelage of writer-producer-director George Abbott, whom everyone in the theatre referred to only as Mr. Abbott—produced a string of hits, beginning with *Pajama Game* in 1954.

Vying with Prince for production honors in this era was David Merrick. He, too, had a long string of hit shows, including *Gypsy* with Ethel Merman in 1958 and culminating in *Hello, Dolly,* musical adaptation of *The Matchmaker* with a score by Jerry Herman, book by Michael Stewart, and starring Carol Channing in 1964.

ALBEE, HANSBERRY AND SIMON

Edward Albee emerged as an important playwright in this period. His off-Broadway dramas, *The American Dream* and *The Death of Bessie Smith,* won critical approval in 1961, and his first Broadway play, *Who's Afraid of Virginia Woolf?* was an outstanding hit of 1962. In 1959, Lorraine Hansberry became the first black playwright to turn out a hit Broadway play, *A Raisin in the Sun.* The play had Sidney Poitier, Ruby Dee, Claudia McNeil and Diana Sands in the cast.

Neil Simon had successive hits in 1963 and 1965 with *Barefoot in the Park* and *The Odd Couple,* respectively.

O'NEILL, WILLIAMS, INGE AND PINTER

Eugene O'Neill, Tennessee Williams, William Inge and Harold Pinter plays were great successes. O'Neill's posthumous *A Long Day's Journey Into Night,* directed by José Quintero with Frederic March, Florence Eldridge and Jason Robards, Jr. was one of 1956's exceptional hits. O'Neill's *Moon for the Misbegotten* in 1957 and *A Touch of the Poet* in 1958 were less successful. Tennessee Williams' *Cat on a Hot Tin Roof* was one of 1955's big hits followed by *Sweet Bird of Youth,* starring Paul Newman and Geraldine Page in 1958, and *The Night of the Iguana* starring Bette Davis in 1961. William Inge's *Dark at the Top of the Stairs* and Harold Pinter's *The Caretakers* were other outstanding plays of the period.

NOV. 8, 1947 ISSUE   FRANK SINATRA

HOTEL SUPPER CLUBS AND NIGHTSPOTS

Nightclubs, somewhat in the fashion of the legitimate theatre, had found an affluent audience of their own. The bulk of the nation's clubs were the supper club showrooms in first rate hotels in the larger cities across the country. Their cover charges were more than the average person could afford. In New York there was the Empire Room in the Waldorf-Astoria, the Persian Room in the Plaza, the Maisonette in the St. Regis, and others. The Copacabana and several other non-hotel clubs still ran. In Chicago, the deluxe supper club was the Empire Room in the Palmer House, while Los Angeles boasted the Cocoanut Grove in the Ambassador, along with a handful of non-hotel clubs along the Sunset Strip such as Mocambo and Ciro's.

Hotel entrepreneur Raymond Swig featured supper club-showrooms in his Fairmont Hotels in San Francisco, Dallas and Atlanta. In each of the Swig hostelries the clubs were called The Venetian Room.

Among the stars of the day who played the clubs were singers—Sinatra, Tony Martin, Mel Torme, Peggy Lee, Ella Fitzgerald—and comics—Milton Berle, Dean Martin and Jerry Lewis, Jackie Mason, Joe E. Lewis and others.

These and many other stars also played the really lucrative areas of the nightclub scene, the showrooms in the hotels in Las Vegas. Salaries for the Las Vegas clubs were already high, ranging from $25,000 per week up to as much as $100,000 per week for top acts, and still climbing. In the second half of the '60s and through the '70s, these salaries were to reach figures undreamed of in the '50s and early '60s.

There was little left of the burlesque business by the '60s, unless one considered the *Folies Bergere* and other shows of that type, which played the Tropicana and other hotel rooms in Las Vegas.

By the mid-'60s, outdoor show business—the circuses, carnivals and fairs—were doing healthy business in their established, traditional fashion commensurate with the growth of the population, increased leisure time and spendable income.

CONGLOMERATES' GROWTH

In 1955, conglomerate General Tire made its second show business acquisition. Howard Hughes had tired of his fling in the film business, and sold RKO to General. But the trend toward conglomeratization really began in 1966.

Conglomerate acquisitions sparked the sale of post-1948 and specially produced films to television. The television networks (which had purchased some post-1948 films on a film-by-film basis) now succeeded in buying huge blocks of movies made after 1948. In a single week in 1966, ABC bought thirty-two post-1948 films from Paramount; CBS bought seventeen from 20th Century-Fox, and NBC purchased sixty-three from MGM. The total paid by the television networks for these 112 films was over $9,000,000.

In 1966, an ABC-TV showing of *The Bridge on the River Kwai*, starring Alec Guinness, pulled a television audience of 65,000,000 viewers. ABC had paid $2,000,000 for TV rights to the film. The networks began to run feature films five nights a week.

A year later, in 1967, motion picture studios began to produce full length (two hour or more) films specifically for television.

Two major conglomerate developments in 1966 were takeovers by Gulf & Western and Seven Arts. Doing over a billion dollars a year in 1967 in numerous non-show business manufacturing, natural resources, mining and other fields, Gulf & Western acquired Paramount Pictures and a year later, Desilu Productions. G&W also acquired theatre chains and the Simon & Schuster publishing operations. By 1976, G&W's net sales had hit $3,395,600,000.

THE WARNER CASE

Seven Arts, in 1966, acquired Warner Brothers. The Warner takeover is an interesting example of conglomerate evolution. In 1967, the company's income was $193,300,000. By 1976, it had climbed to $826,770,000. In the interim,

Seven Arts had been absorbed by the National Kinney Corp., and in time, a new corporation, Warner Communications, Inc., became the conglomerate parent, and absorbed forty-seven percent of Kinney's common stock and acquired beneficial ownership of 1,500,000 shares (100 percent) of Kinney's convertible preferred stock.

Along the way the company had absorbed the Reprise, Atlantic, Elektra, Nonesuch and Asylum record operations.

These acquisitions brought into their management fold some of the outstanding creative and sales executives in the record industry: Mo Ostin of Reprise, Joe Smith and Joel Friedman of Warners, Ahmet and Nesuhi Ertegun and Jerry Wexler of Atlantic, Jac Holzman of Elektra, David Geffen of Asylum, and others. They were manpower acquisitions of immeasurable value.

By 1976, Warners had become one of the two or three leading companies in the record business (if not the leading company). It had also become one of the biggest cable television operators in the country, with ownership of 138 cable systems, with more than 500,000 subscribers. And it owned numerous non-show business operations.

THE RCA, CBS, ABC EXPANSIONS

The broadcasting-telecasting networks "conglomerated" into many other areas. RCA, which, of course, had long been in the consumer and government materiels manufacturing business, acquired Hertz, the rent-a-car company; Banquet Frozen Foods; Coronet Industries; carpet manufacturing; and the Random House publishing company, for which Bennett Cerf and his associates got more than $40,000,000 worth of RCA stock. RCA's gross income for the year ending December 31, 1976, was $5,328,500,000, with the broadcasting-telecasting divisions representing only eighteen percent of the total.

William Paley's original Columbia Broadcasting System also diversified into many areas. The corporation in 1977 was called CBS, Inc. and was divided into four groups: the CBS/Broadcast group, embracing all radio, TV activities; the Columbia Records group, all record and music publishing operations; the CBS/Columbia group, covering the record and tape clubs, musical instrument, toy and music/record/tape retail divisions; and the CBS book and magazine publishing group. In January, 1977, CBS bought Fawcett Publications for $50,000,000 in cash, adding tremendous strength to this division. Fawcett's own 1976 gross was $135,000,000. CBS, Inc.'s total net income in 1976 was $2,230,600,000.

The bulk of ABC's 1976 gross revenue of $1,342,-180,000 still came from its radio and television operations (seventy-six percent), but the Goldenson organization, too, diversified into records and music publishing (fourteen percent of its gross); consumer and specialty magazines; and three scenic attractions, Weeki Wachee Spring and Silver Springs, Florida and the restored Colonial village of Smithville near Atlantic City, N.J.

333

THE MCA STORY

One of the most meaningful of all the show business conglomerate developments from the standpoint of the kinds of films and TV shows which reached the public, was that of MCA, Inc., originally Music Corporation of America. Founded in the early 1920s by Jules Stein, as a band booking agency, MCA had a remarkable growth. By the early 1930s, it was the biggest band booking agency in the entertainment industry. By 1976, the company showed gross revenues of $802,920,000. From the standpoint of what the American movie-going and TV audiences would see, it had become one of the major forces in the entertainment industry.

In 1962, given the choice by the Department of Justice of divesting itself of its production or of its booking operations, MCA opted for production. By 1977, through its Universal TV, MCA was producing more than twenty television series (representing more than twelve hours weekly) for the networks, plus an appreciable number of full length movies for television, plus a number of mini-series, high-budget programs in a venture aimed at supplying top programming via syndication to independent stations.

MCA had achieved conglomerate status by acquiring Decca Records, which had previously bought up Universal Pictures—and many other operations.

A CONGLOMERATE SWALLOWS THE CIRCUS

Master showmen were no longer the major factors in deciding show business's direction or destiny. They were essential elements, to be sure, but the shots were called by the financiers, who controlled the conglomerates.

Even the Greatest Show on Earth, the Ringling Bros. and Barnum & Bailey Circus, was taken over by a conglomerate. Initially acquired in 1967 by Irving Feld from the Ringling family, the shows were sold to Mattel, Inc., with Feld continuing as president and producer. Mattel was the largest American manufacturer of toys.

THE EX-AGENT MOGULS

But conglomerate control of the Ringling show is only a wistful footnote to this phase of the development of American entertainment. The significance of the situation was that the conglomerates now controlled the two show business areas which spoke most frequently and forcefully to almost every person in the United States: television and motion pictures. And conglomerate control made ex-talent and booking agents increasingly dominant in determining what American people would see on their theatre and home screens.

The best of the agents not only knew how to make solid, profitable deals but, more important, they were intimately acquainted with all of the industry's creative community, the top independent producers, directors, writers, choreographers, set and costume designers, stars and sup-

porting players. They knew how to package a combination of these talents into a blockbuster whole. And such agents had long since learned how to nurse the delicate creative temperament. They were past masters at dealing with the unique amalgam of megalomania, insecurity and the insatiable hunger for adoration and applause, which roils forever in the guts of so many creative geniuses.

Thus it came about that six of the seven production heads of the major film companies in 1977 were ex-agents. They were: Mike Medavoy, senior vice president in charge of production for United Artists; Ned Tanen, president of Universal Pictures, who had started in the mailroom of MCA; Richard Shepherd, production head of MGM; Alan Ladd, Jr., president and production chief of 20th Century Fox Films; David Begelman, president and production head of Columbia Pictures; and Martin Elfand, production head of Warner Bros. Pictures. In October of 1977, Begelman was ousted as Columbia's president and production chief, when he admitted having forged and cashed three company checks and embezzling other funds totalling $61,000. He repaid these monies, and was reinstated in his job, but later resigned. The Begelman affair caused an avalanche of stories in newspapers and magazines, concerning alleged scandalous wheeling and dealing in moviedom.

THE MULTI-MILLION DOLLAR GAMBLES

The task of these contemporary moguls was not an easy one. They earned the $150,000 to $300,000 per year, plus limos and other "perks" they commanded. Unlike their predecessors—Sam Goldwyn, Louis B. Mayer, Jesse Lasky, Adolph Zukor, Jack Warner, David Selznick, Darryl Zanuck, Dore Schary, to name a handful—they did not have the luxury of calling the shots without accountability to anyone but a generally sympathetic and often controlled Board of Directors. In every case, they had conglomerate brass, approving or disapproving their initial decisions. The turnover in film studio heads was considerable.

RISING COSTS AND BOX OFFICE RECORDS

Although the average cost of producing a motion picture in 1977 was $4,000,000, many films exceeded that. *Star Wars* and *The Deep* both ran about $10,000,000; *New York, New York,* $9,000,000; *A Bridge Too Far,* $24,000,000, which included $1,000,000 for William Goldman's screen play, $9,000,000 for the cast—of which Robert Redford got $500,000 per week for four weeks work, or $2,000,000.

Budgets frequently got out of hand. Production costs on Francis Ford Coppola's *Apocalypse Now,* in late 1977, were up to $26,000,000 of which United Artists had put up $7,000,000. As alarming as rising production costs was the fact that, by the late 1970s, it had often become desirable or necessary to spend as much advertising and promoting a film as to produce it. Faced with sharply rising costs, the movie makers produced fewer and fewer films, but their track record was quite good.

TV PAYS NEW HIGHS

There were various approaches for contending with the wild inflation in production and promotion costs. One was the sale of a film to television even before it was put into theatrical release. United Artists chairman Arthur Krim told Wall Street analysts in 1977 that UA had sold TV rights to five new films, not yet in theatrical release, to the networks for broadcasting over a three-year period for $15,000,000. The five films cost UA $27,000,000 to produce.

Krim said that the networks, in 1977, were willing to pay as high as $1,000,000 for TV rights to a film before release. Before the intense network competition of the 1975–1977 period for ratings (more about this later), $300,000 was the top figure for films prior to release. On one new UA film, *Convoy*, a TV network paid $3,300,000, the full production costs of the movie before release.

Of course, in the case of films which became big hits after release the TV networks paid staggering sums: NBC paid $15,000,000 for TV rights to *The Godfather*. (This was for two Oscar-winning feature films and a subsequent nine part mini-series, made up of *Godfather I* and *II* plus much material not previously used.) CBS paid $5,000,000 for *Network*; NBC, $7,000,000 for *A Bridge Too Far*, $4,500,-000 for *MacArthur*, etc.

The movie business prospered in the period from the mid-'60s to the end of 1977. 1969 was a poor year, with attendance down sharply, but by 1975, *Variety's* highly regarded annual Box Office study showed that the year had set an all-time record gross of $1,900,000,000. By the end of 1977 *Variety* estimated the year's box office gross would hit a new high of $2,300,000,000.

THE PORNO AGE

In 1967, State Censorship Boards were discontinued around the country, to be replaced by the movie industry's own rating system (G-General; PG-Parental Guidance; R-Restricted to people over 17; *X-horrors, all those under 18 stay out!*). In 1969, the first outright pornographic film, the Swedish import, *I Am Curious Yellow*, became a box office hit.

Sex and pornography had an orgy. The Motion Picture Association of America ratings report for the period from November, 1968 (first year of the ratings) to October, 1976, showed a huge increase in R and X rated movies. In the November, 1975, to October, 1976, period, fifty-five percent of all films produced by the majors, secondary majors and independents were either R or X rated. Only thirteen percent were G rated. In brief, on eighty-three percent of all films, people under seventeen required parental guidance or, theoretically, could not see the movie at all.

This was the period (1972 to be specific) when Linda Lovelace made *Deep Throat* for Damiamo Films. Produced

APRIL 19, 1947 ISSUE   FRANZ ALLERS, DAVID BROOKS, MARION BELL, AND PAMELA BRITTON

for $25,000 (reputedly "mob" money), the porno landmark film had distributor rentals of $4,000,000 by 1973, and was still showing in 1977. Two other low budget, multi-million dollar porno hits were *The Devil in Miss Jones,* with distributor rentals of $2,000,000, and the Mitchell Brothers' *Behind the Green Door,* on which distributors took in over $1,000,000.

In 1973, many critics hailed porno as a new art form when, in Bernardo Bertolucci's *Last Tango in Paris,* superstar Marlon Brando simulated frenetic intercourse so realistically, that an unsimulated coupling could hardly have been more convincing. Brando made the film for a percentage of the gross, and was reported to have earned $1,600,000 for his portrayal of the existentialistic, loveless fornicator.

DISASTERS AND OTHER HITS

Disaster movies proved a film form which played more effectively on the theatre screen than on the TV tube. *The Poseidon Adventure, Towering Inferno* and *Earthquake* were three examples of all-star disaster epics. Producer Irwin Allen proved a master of this style.

There were many other outstanding films in the period from the mid-'60s to the late '70s. Audiences were turning out for *All the President's Men,* starring Robert Redford and

Dustin Hoffman; *Network,* a strong and successful satire on network TV news operations, with Peter Finch, Faye Dunaway and William Holden; Ellen Burstyn's Oscar-winning performance in the feminist film, *Alice Doesn't Live Here Anymore;* Jane Fonda in *Klute;* Al Pacino in *Dog Day Afternoon;* the 1975 Oscar winner, *One Flew Over the Cuckoo's Nest* with Jack Nicholson; Liza Minnelli's *Cabaret;* Woody Allen's *Annie Hall* with Diane Keaton; George Burns and Walter Matthau in Neil Simon's *The Sunshine Boys;* Paul Newman and Robert Redford in *Butch Cassidy and the Sundance Kid; Love Story;* Barbra Streisand in *Funny Girl;* and Julie Andrews in *The Sound of Music.* Violence was king at the box office with such hit films as *Bonnie and Clyde, The Wild Bunch, The French Connection; Straw Dogs* and *The Godfather,* Parts I and II, starring Marlon Brando, Al Pacino, Robert DeNiro, and James Caan.

ROCKY AND *STAR WARS*

Two of the most interesting blockbusters were *Rocky* and *Star Wars. Rocky* was written by a struggling journeyman actor and new screenwriter, Sylvester Stallone, who refused to permit his screenplay to be made unless he himself could play the lead in the film. He won his point and the movie was made on a tight budget of $1,000,000. By mid-1977, it had grossed $50,000,000 in distributor rentals and made an overnight star out of Stallone.

Star Wars was written and directed by another young talent, George Lucas, who had previously made the hit film, *American Graffiti.* His twelve page outline of the science fiction story was turned down by several studios before Alan Ladd, Jr. at 20th Century Fox decided to gamble on making it. Lucas brought it in for about $10,000,000, but with that $10,000,000 he took advantage of every technological trick, audio and visual, which had ever been invented. Using the latest hardware in computers, optical devices, matteing techniques, recording and sound systems, he created a space opera—pitting plain old good against nasty old evil—of such power and excitement that it captured the affection of millions of moviegoers. It was such a tremendous hit that in the first two weeks of its release, 20th Century Fox stock doubled from approximately $10 to $20 per share. In less than a year, *Star Wars* surpassed the staggering distributor rentals and box office grosses of director Steven Spielberg's *Jaws* to become the number one money-making film of all time. Its box office gross at the end of 1977 was over $200,000,000.

Toward the end of 1977, another science fiction film, *Close Encounters of the Third Kind,* written and directed by *Jaw's* director Steven Spielberg was released and was doing exceptional business.

A NOSTALGIC NOTE

In 1975 and 1976, a nostalgic movie note was struck with the celebration of D. W. Griffith's 100th birthday, and a filmed appearance by Mary Pickford at age eighty-three on

APRIL 24, 1948 ISSUE GOODMAN ACE (WITH CIGAR), JANE AND "BROTHER-IN-LAW" PAUL

the 1976 Academy Awards TV show. Old timers recalled the days when Miss Pickford had persuaded Griffith to pay her $10 per day, rather than the standard rate of $5, because she was a Belasco trained actress; and the time when the bosses at Biograph hit the ceiling when Griffith budgeted the four-reeler *Judith of Bethulia* at $18,000 and turned purple when the movie actually cost $36,000.

But let us not linger longer than a paragraph on those somehow pleasant, if penurious, times. Let us zoom back to the contemporary multi-billion dollar show business world of rampant technology, devouring conglomerates and Croesus-style superstars.

While television seemed a dire threat and actually hurt the movie business for a number of years, eventually TV became the movies' best customer. The two giant entertainment areas discovered they needed each other. Fierce, go-for-the-jugular competition existed within each of the industries.

TV'S FANTASTIC GROWTH

By 1970, there were TV sets in 59,300,000 American homes. Many homes had two sets; 25,300,000 of these were color sets.

By 1977, there were about 120,000,000 sets in 79,200,000 American homes. This number represented almost all the homes in the nation, some ninety-eight percent, and still growing. More than half these homes had two or more sets, and among them there were 55,000,000 color sets. About 10,935,000 of these homes were tied into one cable system or another; ninety percent of them could receive UHF as well as VHF signals. And an average of 2.3 people in each of these homes watched television programs an average of six hours per day, according to the latest authoritative studies.

The three networks had by far the biggest sales years in their histories. In 1976, a year before celebrating its fiftieth anniversary, Paley's CBS became the first advertising medium in the nation's history to achieve more than a billion dollars in sales ($1,045,550,700) in a single year. Although General Sarnoff had retired as Chairman of the Board of RCA in 1970 (to be succeeded by his son, Robert), the NBC network he had created (which celebrated its fiftieth year in 1976) had sales of $991,748,300. But the shocker of the season was the stunning figure turned in by Leonard Goldenson's traditional third-running ABC: $954,312,100.

The percentage gains of each of the three networks told an even more dramatic story than the figures themselves. CBS's gain over the previous year had been 19.8 percent; NBC's, 17.8 percent; and ABC's 33.2 percent. The fierce competition between the three networks was plain for all to read.

TV'S THREE BILLION DOLLAR SPENDERS

The top hundred sponsors in television in 1976 spent $3,811,881,800. Procter & Gamble alone spent $339,183,600; General Foods, $192,275,500 and American Home Products, $130,955,700. Prices of TV spots soared from $65,000 per full minute in 1969 on such high-rated shows as *Mission Impossible*, *Mayberry RFD* and *Laugh-In* to $130,000 for top-rated 1977 shows such as *Happy Days*, *Laverne and Shirley* and *Three's Company*. Thirty-second spots were up to $55,000 for the average show and ranged all the way from $40,000 on less successful programs to $90,000 on the highest-rated sports shows and specials.

Bob Howard, president of NBC-TV, in 1976, told a Congressional committee that costs of programming were skyrocketing. In 1977, one episode in a half hour series cost the network about $155,000; a full hour series episode, $335,000; a two hour movie-for-TV, $882,000. Still the independent producers of the programs were complaining that they could not make any money on the shows unless they went into successful syndication after their network runs, which the best of them did. And syndication prices for off-network shows were hitting new highs. WPIX-TV, New York, made a deal agreeing to pay Paramount $35,000 per episode to carry *Happy Days*, the ABC hit featuring Henry Winkler as The Fonz, beginning in 1979. MCA's

Universal TV budgeted $200,000,000 for television program production for the 1977–1978 season.

TV'S PROBLEMS

These bedazzling numbers may give the impression that television's path from the mid-'60s to 1977 was strewn with roses. Not so. There were as many trying periods in the video area of the show world as in any other. In 1971, television took a staggering financial blow when legislation was passed prohibiting TV stations from carrying cigarette advertising. This cost the networks and stations $236,000,000 in revenue. In an industry which was grossing a little over $3,000,000,000 (station and network income combined), this was more than a mere puff of smoke.

New rules and legislation restricting the amount of time networks could take from stations in prime time (7 to 11 p.m.), and limitations on single ownership of communications media (TV stations, radio stations, newspapers) in single markets were among other problems faced by the era's broadcasters.

THE TV SHOWS AND STARS

As always, in television as in all of show business, from the very beginning it was the shows and stars who were at the heart of the continuing boom. In earlier years, *I Love Lucy* and *The Dick Van Dyke Show* (with Mary Tyler Moore in support) were long-running favorites. *Gunsmoke* with Jim Arness was a western leader. Red Skelton and Jackie Gleason and Danny Thomas hovered near the top of the ratings, season after season. Ed Sullivan (who ultimately ran for twenty-three successful years) continued his mix of variety and circus acts, the latest new music stars, and celebrities from all fields, on stage and in his studio audience.

For many years through the early and mid-'60s the public seemed happy with TV's innocuous simple-minded situation comedies. *The Beverly Hillbillies* and *Petticoat Junction* were frequently one and two in the ratings. *The Andy Griffith Show*, *Gomer Pyle*, *Mayberry RFD* all presented countrified "aw-shucks" comedy every week.

Throughout the day, the soap operas and the game shows had their loyal and substantial followings. The movies made for television, plus the films the studios were releasing without restriction, provided varied, popular movie fare. In 1969, there was a unique television special. We saw men in space suits (live) bunny-hopping around on the moon.

THE DRIVE FOR NEW VIEWERS

Then suddenly the networks, led by CBS, changed their popular programming direction. It was simply a matter of demographics; the agencies and sponsors were not happy with the rural audiences, the too young or too old people, the not-too-affluent viewers the most popular shows had been pulling. CBS dropped such old time favorites as

Gleason, Skelton, and Danny Thomas. Cancelled were *The Andy Griffith Show, Mayberry RFD, The Beverly Hillbillies,* and *Petticoat Junction.* Programming for the viewers who reflected more education and sophistication was substituted.

More mature themes and less cartoon-like characters dominated the situation comedies for a time. One of the most outstanding was *The Mary Tyler Moore Show,* with Ms. Moore as a production assistant in the television news department of a Minneapolis video station. Ms. Moore's supporting cast was one of the finest ever put together. *The Mary Tyler Moore Show* was created by a producer-writer hyphenate team of the kind which had become the backbone of much of television programming in the '70s. The MTM hyphenates were James Brooks and Allan Burns, working under MTM head, Grant Tinker. Among other highly successful producer-writer creative combinations and individuals were: Danny Arnold and Theodore Flicker *(Barney Miller);* Larry Gelbart *(M.A.S.H.);* James Komack *(Chico and the Man,* starring ill-fated Freddie Prinz and Jack Albertson); *Welcome Back, Kotter;* and Norman Lear.

THE LEAR BREAKTHROUGH

It was Lear who, in 1972, after trying for many years, sold CBS a show called *All in the Family.* It was a program of English derivation, featuring a blue-collar bigot, Archie Bunker, and it dealt with such subjects as homosexuality, rape, impotence and other matters previously considered taboo on TV and certainly not proper material for situation comedy.

All in the Family became the number one rated show in television, and made a superstar out of Carroll O'Connor, playing Archie. Also starring was Jean Stapleton as his loveable, pixilated wife, Edith; and supporting were Sally Struthers as daughter, Gloria; and Rob Reiner (son of Carl) as her husband.

Lear (originally with partner Bud Yorkin, then on his own or with Yorkin or other associates) created many series following *All in the Family.* Spinoffs from the Bunker show were *Maude* and *The Jeffersons.* Lear shows were assigned to various producing-writing teams, some of whom became highly successful in their own rights. Typical of these was the team of Don Nichols, Mickey Ross and Bernie West. Having worked with Lear on *All in the Family,* they developed *The Jeffersons* and other shows and by 1977 were producing a number of successful shows, among them a new hit, *Three's Company. Three's Company* was originated in England by Thames TV and brought to America by Ted Bergmann and his partner, Don Traffner.

By 1977, there had been an ever-increasing number of shows treating subjects such as transvestitism, homosexuality, impotence, and combinations thereof. Lear dealt with many of them once again in his successful, syndicated soap opera spoof, *Mary Hartman, Mary Hartman,* starring Louise Lasser.

A number of new police and crime shows were high in the ratings, as always, in the mid-'70s. Among them were *Starsky and Hutch, Baretta, Kojak, Police Woman,* and *Police Story.*

BIKINI ANGELS AND INNOCENT SEX

The successful *Charlie's Angels*—which made a superstar out of Farrah Fawcett-Majors, and on which Ms. Majors and her "two co-angels," Kate Jackson and Jaclyn Smith, frequently performed their derring-do as private investigators in bikinis and other revealing attire—was a contemporary era television "sex" show. Ms. Majors left and was replaced by another curvaceous young beauty, Cheryl Ladd. *Three's Company* was also a rather innocent sex comedy series stressing the charms of a new young star, Suzanne Somers.

Again in the 1976–1977 period, many civic groups were protesting the excessive violence in television. The networks made an aborted and highly unpopular move to satisfy the anti-violence forces by creating the "Family Hours" segment of prime time. They announced that in the hours from 7 to 9 p.m. only programs suitable for viewing by the entire family would be shown. The idea was alternately laughed at and vociferously criticized by leading producers and others in television and proved ludicrously ineffective.

INTENSIFIED NETWORK COMPETITION

The 1975–1976, 1976–1977 and 1977–1978 seasons saw the most intensive competitive struggle between the three networks in the history of television. It might be said that the wheels for this fierce battle were set in motion as early as 1962, when Mike Dann, then head of programming for CBS-TV, hired twenty-four-year-old Fred Silverman as head of daytime programming for the network. Silverman's doctoral thesis at Ohio State had been an in-depth analysis of the ABC-TV network's program schedule. The daytime soap operas and game shows, and the lush Saturday morning periods were low cost, high profit segments of the network operation. Silverman did spectacularly well in the job. In 1970, when Dann resigned to go to work for the Children's Television Workshop (then developing *Sesame Street*), Fred Silverman replaced him as head of programming for the CBS-TV network.

For the previous sixteen or seventeen years, under the program leadership of Lou Cowan, Jim Aubrey and Mike Dann, CBS had been the consistent ratings leader among the three networks, with NBC running a close second (even occasionally sweeping by CBS into first place). Silverman added to CBS's long-established strength. ABC had always been a poor to middling third.

ABC STREAKS TO NUMBER ONE

In 1975, ABC-TV president Fred Pierce hired Fred Silverman away from CBS with a three-year contract at $250,000 per year. In two years, Silverman and his colleagues at ABC turned the network picture completely around. By the end of the 1976–1977 season, ABC had racked up a Nielsen rating average of 21.5, compared to 18.7 for CBS and 18.0 for NBC. Week in and week out during the season, ABC had the top three shows (and sometimes the top four) in the weekly Top Ten Nielsen ratings. The two leaders were *Happy Days* and *Laverne and Shirley* (a spinoff from *Happy Days*). In the 1977–1978 season, these two hits were followed by *Three's Company,* which often ranked number three, and the controversial *Soap.* Oddly enough, *Happy Days* and *Laverne and Shirley* were rather simple-minded situation comedies, with the added basic nostalgic appeal of being set in the '50s.

Silverman's genius lay not only in the programs he selected and shepherded, but in his scheduling strategies. This was demonstrated by the *Roots* mini-series. It was Silverman who decided to run the dramatization of the Alex Haley novel on eight consecutive nights. Seven of the *Roots* showings were the number-one rated programs of their evenings, which gave ABC the highest ratings for the week ever achieved by any network to that date.

Silverman's spectacular success was most strikingly spelled out in "bottom-line" dollars. The difference in the ratings positions of the three networks led to a profit-spread for ABC over CBS for 1976 of over $100,000,000. It enabled ABC to achieve billings of over a billion dollars in 1977, for the first time in its history.

ABC CLOSES AFFILIATES GAP

Equally important, the shift in leadership enabled ABC to lure a number of affiliated stations away from CBS and NBC. Within a year after Silverman's ratings' coups, fifteen stations switched their affiliations to ABC from either CBS or NBC. The affiliated station line-up as of the fall of 1977 was NBC, 208; CBS, 204; and ABC, 195 with the gap closing.

NBC and CBS were not accepting the ABC surge passively. Both networks altered their upper echelon executive structures in 1977. And both were using every conceivable programming and promotion approach to try to recapture their once-dominant positions.

On January 20, 1978 NBC made a competitive move which came as a surprise to most of show business. On that date, Edgar Griffiths, president of NBC's parent, RCA Corp., announced that the network had hired Fred Silverman as president and chief executive officer of NBC, replacing Herb Schlosser. No details of Silverman's contract were released. Since Silverman's contract with ABC did not expire until June of 1978, he could not actively nor openly begin his new task of attempting to move NBC into ratings leadership in television. His move to the RCA-owned network merely intensified the already white-hot competition between the three networks.

In the meantime, the Department of Justice, in the fall of 1977, stepped up its anti-trust suit against the networks.

Filed in 1974 against all three networks, the Department had secured NBC's agreement to a consent decree, wherein the network stipulated it would restrict its prime time production to two and one half hours and cut its option term on series it purchased to four years. CBS and ABC had not signed the consent decree.

In September, 1977, the Department submitted to U.S. District Court Judge Robert Kelleher in Los Angeles testimony from almost every leading producer in Hollywood, indicating that the networks' positions of power should be curtailed.

SIGNS OF NETWORK POWER

The producers charged that the networks were signing more and more star and other key performers and creative talent to exclusive contracts; had vast control over most production facilities; used various methods to prevent spinoffs from hit shows from going to any network other than the one carrying the originating show; and utilized procedures for tying up TV series for many years with inadequate increases in production costs.

If any appreciable number or all of these charges were eventually proved, and the Court ruled against the networks, changes in television show production would come about. But in the meantime the networks, and television as a whole, were experiencing their most profitable years, just like the motion picture industry.

NEW PEAKS FOR SUPERSTARS

TV superstars were receiving compensation never before seen in the entertainment industry. Mention has already been made of the percentage deals of Marlon Brando in *The Godfather* and *The Last Tango in Paris,* which earned him close to $4,000,000—and Robert Redford's $2,000,000 (or $500,000 per week for four weeks) for *A Bridge Too Far.* And a genuine superstar didn't have to make a motion picture or do a TV series to make a million dollars. In late 1977, John Wayne signed a deal to do commercials for Great Western, a California savings and loan institution. Wayne received $1,000,000 for the first three-year period of the contract. In television, as early as the heyday of *Gunsmoke,* series stars such as James Arness not only received five-figure weekly salaries ($25,000 and up), but were given part ownership of the series in which they were starring.

At the beginning of 1978, however, Johnny Carson signed the superstar deal of the era with NBC. Starting his sixteenth year as host of the *Tonight Show,* Carson was to be paid between $2,500,000 and $3,000,000 per year. Of course, he would not work full weeks for this money. Every Monday of the year, the show would have a guest host, cutting Carson's work week down to four days. About twenty-five weeks of the year, a compilation of previously aired shows, called *The Best of the Tonight Show,* would be assembled for Tuesday showings, cutting Carson's work week down to three days. And to be sure he wasn't over-worked, Carson would have fifteen weeks of vacation per year.

RADIO AND RECORDS HIT NEW HIGHS

The prosperity of TV and films, interestingly enough, did not cut into any of the other areas of show business. Radio and the pre-recorded music industry danced down through the years, arm in arm, reaching new peaks from one era to the next. By 1977, there were 425,000,000 radio sets in American homes; very few autos were without radios, and many also had radio/tape cassette combinations.

From a 1965 industry gross for pre-recorded music of $862,000,000, the record business climbed uninterruptedly each year until, in 1967, it reached its first $1,000,000,000-plus year and, in 1974, its first $2,000,000,000-plus year. In 1974, the industry gross was $2,200,000,000; in 1975, $2,360,000,000; in 1976, $2,737,000,000; and there was no question in the minds of industry leaders that the 1977 figure would surpass three billion and keep climbing.

Much of this was attributable to the constant play of all music styles on thousands of radio stations around the country, around the clock. By 1977, there were 8,240 radio stations: 4497 AM, 2873 commercial FM and 870 non-commercial FM.

FM'S FIRST "TOPPERS"

FM stations had become a vital factor. In 1970, two FM stations—WOOD, Grand Rapids, Mich. and WEAT, West Palm Beach, Fla.—became the top-rated stations in their markets. It was the first time any FM stations had achieved this. Since that time many FM stations in key markets have become the dominant music stations in their areas.

Stations which were not programming music formats were doing talk shows, all-news, or combinations of these, and some music. By 1977, about twenty percent of all the nation's stations were completely automated, i.e., computer-programmed via cartridges, with just one engineer pushing appropriate buttons as required.

RECORDS' OWN SUPERSTARS

Record superstars were among the highest-paid and most idolized of the mid-'60s to late '70s. Capitol Records signed ex-Beatle Paul McCartney and his new group, Wings, to a five-year contract, guaranteeing McCartney $8,000,000 in record royalties over the period; MCA wrote a similar contract for Elton John; Stevie Wonder was given a $13,000,000 guarantee over a five-year period by Motown, and again for artist royalties only. Royalties from songwriting and publishing for all three of these artists were paid them over and above their earnings in artist royalties.

Million selling LPs continued to be common, and many artists were now selling five million, ten million and

MAY 10, 1947 ISSUE   BUD ABBOTT AND LOU COSTELLO

more records per LP release. Among these were McCartney, Elton John, Stevie Wonder, Peter Frampton, Carole King, Fleetwood Mac, Chicago, Kansas, and numerous others.

Two of the all-time record greats, Elvis Presley and Bing Crosby, who had also achieved general superstardom, died within months of each other in 1977. Bing, of course, had been a legendary superstar for forty years. He died of a heart attack on a golf course in Spain. Zero Mostel, Groucho Marx and Alfred Lunt were among the superstars who died that same year. All the theatres on Broadway observed a minute of darkness and silence as a tribute to Lunt. On Christmas day in 1977, the most legendary of filmdom's superstars, Charlie Chaplin, died in his sleep at age eighty-eight at his home in Switzerland.

TRIPLE MEDIA EXPOSURE

The proliferation of stars and superstars was due to the existence of three major entertainment media—television, movies and records—through which performers could reach ten, fifty, occasionally even a hundred million people or more in a single showing. Prior to television and the enormous expansion of the record/tape industry, stars could be made via films, radio or records. However, television—

particularly in series shows in which performers were seen every week—added new dimensions to the impact an entertainer could make on the public. And, of course, the impact a performer could make by working in a combination of two or three of these major media in concurrent periods (which many did) was truly stunning.

THE THEATRE'S BIG SEASON

The legitimate theatre continued to develop stars, even as it had in the earliest days of entertainment history, and stage stars soared to superstardom when they moved beyond the theatre into films or television or both.

The theatre, on its own levels, reached new box office peaks. According to *Variety* an all-time record (up to that date) was set in the 1975-1976 season. Broadway grossed $70,841,738 and the road had its second best year ever, hitting $52,587,985. The following seasin, 1976-1977, set a new record: Broadway hit $93,406,082 and the road turned in $82,627,309.

As in other show business fields, inflation was a factor in setting these new financial records. By the mid-'70s, orchestra and front row mezzanine tickets on Broadway ran generally from a low of $10 to about $17 per ticket. In 1977, when Cy Feuer and Ernie Martin brought in *The Act*, a Liza Minnelli *tour de force*, a new high was set. Orchestra and front row mezzanine tickets went for $20 on weekday evenings and $22.50 on Saturday nights.

PLAYWRIGHTS, HOT AND COLD

The most prolific, certainly the most successful, playwright in the mid-'60s to the mid-'70s was Neil Simon.

Edward Albee won two Pulitzer Prizes during this same period, one for *A Delicate Balance* in 1966 and another for *Seascape* in 1975. Ironically, neither of these two works was even remotely as successful commercially as Albee's earlier *Who's Afraid of Virginia Woolf?* Two other major playwrights had flops during this period. In 1972, Tennessee Williams' *Small Craft Warnings* and Arthur Miller's *The Creation of the World and Other Business* were poorly received by the critics and folded after short runs.

Several newer playwrights broke through in this decade. Paul Zindel won recognition with *The Effects of Gamma Rays on Man-in-the-Moon Marigolds* and David Rabe with *Sticks and Stones*. Two black playwrights also made strong impressions: Lonnie Elder III with *Ceremonies in Dark Old Men* and Charles Gordone with *No Place to be Somebody*. Contemporary rock musicals came into their own. *Hair* in 1968 was followed by *Jesus Christ, Superstar, Godspell* and *Pippin*.

Hal Prince, David Merrick and Joseph Papp continued to be among the most active producers of the time. Beginning in 1966 with *Cabaret*, Prince had a string of exciting, innovative productions including *Company* in 1970, *Follies* in 1971, *A Little Night Music* in 1973 and *Pacific Overtures*

in 1976. Scores for all these, except *Cabaret*, were written by the vastly talented Stephen Sondheim. Fred Ebb and John Kander wrote the *Cabaret* score.

Among Merrick's outstanding productions were *Promises, Promises* and *Sugar*, an adaptation of the Marilyn Monroe, Jack Lemmon, Tony Curtis film, *Some Like It Hot*. Both Prince and Merrick involved themselves with motion pictures during this period—Prince as both producer and director, and Merrick as producer.

Papp was by far the most venturesome, innovative and *avant garde* producer of the day. He worked with new playwrights, many of them blacks, Hispanics, etc. He concerned himself more with experimentation in broadening the theatre as an art form than with commercial success. Nevertheless, he did have a number of commercial hits, including Jason Miller's *That Championship Season*.

A GREEN HEAVEN FOR SUPERSTARS

By 1977, Las Vegas, the isolated Nevada desert community where mobster Bugsy Siegel and his friends had opened the Flamingo thirty years earlier, had become a veritable green heaven for superstars in nightclubs. In 1976, 10,000,000 people from all over the world visited the twenty-four hour live entertainment capital and spent $2,400,000,000 playing the town's games and seeing the shows. The $25,000 per week that singer Johnny Ray received at the Desert Inn in 1952, and the $50,000 weekly wage paid Liberace by the Riviera in 1955 were moderate salaries by the mid-'70s.

Large corporations had taken over ownership of most of the hotel-casino operations from the mobsters. Among them were the Del Webb Corporation, Hilton and Howard Hughes. Hughes' Summa Corporation had acquired the Sands, the Desert Inn, the Frontier, the Landmark, Castaways and the Silver Slipper. Walter Kane, talent buyer for the Hughes' spots, with an annual act budget of $20,000,000, competed with Sid Gathrid of Caesar's Palace, Jack Eglash of the Sahara, Dick Lane of the Hilton, Bernie Rothkopf of the MGM Grand and other key buyers for the "names" most likely to draw people to their respective hotels.

Some of the other major hotel-casino operations—such as the Tropicana, the Flamingo and the Dunes—had dropped out of the bidding for the superstars and were presenting extravagant girlie shows, ice revues, or plays (usually comedies) in dinner theatre formats.

LURE FOR HIGH ROLLERS

The task of the talent buyers was always further complicated by the fact that they needed acts which would not only draw large numbers of people but the right kind of people—notably the "high rollers." Performers who could draw these big spenders could virtually name their own price. And the Vegas talent buyers sought them in every area of entertainment.

First, of course, were the old standbys, the entertainers who had long since proven that they were loved by the boys with the big bundles. These were the established saloon singers and club comics; among them Frank Sinatra, Dean Martin, Sammy Davis, Jr., Shecky Greene, Buddy Hackett, and Don Rickles. They commanded anywhere from $150,000 to $250,000 per week. In some cases the management got back a considerable part of the salary when the entertainer decided to have a shot at the dice or roulette tables.

FILMDOM'S GLAMOUR GIRLS

Beyond the standbys, the Vegas talent moguls invaded filmdom, television and the record world. At one point, Debbie Reynolds played the Hughes hotels sixteen weeks per year for $75,000 per week plus a number of extras, including the use of the palatial home of Robert Maheu (one-time head of the Hughes' Vegas operations) and housing for every member of the cast of Ms. Reynolds' show. When her contract with the Summa Corporation ran out, Ms. Reynolds built an entirely new act (which cost her well over $100,000) and took it to the Riviera, where she got $105,000 per week for a seven-week run. Ann-Margret, Shirley MacLaine and Mitzi Gaynor were three other movie glamour names who earned more than $100,000 per week playing Vegas clubs, but brought in extraordinarily expensive shows.

Recording stars also helped fill the gambling resort showrooms. Helen Reddy played the Celebrity Room of the MGM Grand Hotel in 1977. Ms. Reddy was getting $125,000 per week for a six-week run, but her elegant act cost almost $200,000 to put together. Elvis Presley, right up to 1977, played to packed houses at the Hilton International and was paid well over $100,000 per week with many extras, although Elvis did not draw a particularly high rolling crowd. Most of his fans were Coke drinkers.

MORE MUSIC ACTS

Other music acts who played the major Vegas spots ranged from Barbra Streisand, who got $250,000 per week at the International (when she played there in 1969), to Sergio Franchi and Bert Bacharach, who received $50,000 to $75,000 per week—and a long list of in-betweeners who were paid from $100,000 to $200,000 weekly. These included Paul Anka, Neil Diamond, Neil Sedaka, Glen Campbell, Bette Midler, Engelbert Humperdinck, Barry Manilow, Steve Lawrence and Eydie Gorme, Diana Ross, Olivia Newton-John and Tom Jones. Possibly the most unique example of a record star who became a Vegas superstar was Wayne Newton. Ranked by show business experts on the Vegas scene as the third most potent draw in the town (behind only Sinatra and Presley), Newton was under contract to the Summa Corporation to play their hotels an average of thirty-six weeks per year at approxi-

mately $150,000 per week, for a total of more than $5,000,000 per year.

TV STARS: HITS AND FLOPS

The Vegas talent buyers played numerous television stars in their showrooms. The surprising aspect of this development was the large number of such stars who flopped on the Vegas stages. Notable among these were Carroll O'Connor (Archie Bunker of *All in the Family*) and Telly Savalas, better known as *Kojak*. Neither one drew well in his Vegas nightclub debut, and Vegas experts maintained that the reason was simply that they put together live acts which were completely at variance with their familiar television characters.

HERE'S JOHNNY IN VEGAS

The outstanding superstar of television, who quickly became a superstar of equal magnitude on the stage of Caesar's Palace, was Johnny Carson. Carson was getting $225,000 per week for two-week runs at Caesar's Palace when he decided he did not wish to play fourteen shows. He switched to the Congo Room in the Sahara Hotel, where he played weekends only (four shows) at the same pro rata price he was earning at Caesar's (i.e., about $65,000 for the two days).

Obviously, if there were several hundred or several thousand Las Vegases around the country, the nightclub business would become a truly major force in live American entertainment. As it stood in the late '70s, there were a few gambling resort areas, notably nearby Reno and Lake Tahoe, which had hotel-gambling casino showrooms that played and paid superstars on a near-Vegas level. Owner Bill Harrah was the outstanding operator in these two resort locations. Here and there around the country, by the late '70s, there were still a few supper clubs which played major attractions. The Miami Beach hotels were among these, until the resort area went into a sharp decline in the late '70s. A handful of isolated spots such as the Latin Casino in Cherry Hill, N.J., the Beverly Hills Supper Club in Covington, Ky., etc., still played name acts. The Beverly Hills club was the site of one of the worst tragedies in recent entertainment memory. On May 28, 1977 a fire in the club's Zebra Room killed 161 people. Singer John Davidson was starring in the show.

ATLANTIC CITY, EAST COAST VEGAS?

There was a strong possibility in 1977 that the nation's East Coast might develop a Las Vegas of its own. New Jersey legalized gambling in Atlantic City, a long-established beach resort. By fall of 1977, powerful and wealthy financial forces were competing for hotels or beachfront properties on which to construct hotel-gambling casinos.

JUNE 5, 1948 ISSUE   FLETCHER MARKLE AND ROBERT MITCHUM

THE 1977 CIRCUS PICTURE

In outdoor show business the Ringling Bros. and Barnum & Bailey circus thrived under the direction of Irvin Feld, operating the shows for the Mattel conglomerate. Feld's major coup was the purchase of the Circus Williams, a German show owned by Gunther Gebel-Williams. There was unanimous agreement that Williams was the greatest animal trainer the world had ever seen. He, his wife, and young son and daughter worked with tigers, lions, panthers and elephants, and, without whip or gun, put the beasts through incredible routines. Williams and his family were frequently featured as the major segment of network television specials.

Feld also brought a contemporary musical touch to the Big One. A standout number was the Elephant Disco in which the pachyderms danced to records by Barry Manilow, Elton John, and other rock stars.

However, there were fewer than 100 circuses still operating in 1977, and only eighteen playing in tents. Among the more successful of the surviving tent shows were the Clyde Beatty-Cole Bros. Circus, the Carson-Barnes Shows, the Hoxie Show and Circus Vargas. The last was somewhat typical of these shows. Run by owner Clifford Vargas, the circus had thirty-three trucks, a staff of about 150, nine

elephants and eight Andalusian horses. Vargas travelled about 35,000 miles per year, crossing the country four or five times. The Circus Vargas usually pitched its tents in shopping centers. Admission was $2.75 for children and $4.75 for adults.

FAIRS AND CARNIVALS PROSPER

The carnivals, whose destiny was always directly connected to state and county fairs, saw little change through the mid-'60s and '70s. The larger organizations, who had contracts with the long-established giant fairs, did well since the attendance at fairs held up and increased in the mid-'70s. In 1976, the State Fair of Texas did 3,000,000 admissions for its seventeen-day run. The Los Angeles County Fair drew more than 1,000,000. The Iowa State Fair—one of the nation's largest, longest established and most successful—drew 6,000,000 customers from August 18 to 28 in 1977.

Many fairs were playing "name" acts, and paying top salaries. Jeff Wald, manager of Helen Reddy, maintained that Ms. Reddy got more for a week at a major state fair than the $125,000 per week she received in Las Vegas. Fairs were also featuring modern events, such as skateboard contests, rock dances, etc.

Amusement Business magazine studies showed that the fair and carnival industries grossed about $1,000,000,000 in 1976, with total attendance exceeding 160,000,000 compared to 149,000,000 in 1975.

DISCOS AND THEME PARKS

Two of the more recent innovations in entertainment in the '60s and '70s highlighted the tremendous variations in the tastes of the mass audience. The discotheques, a hybrid of the earlier dance halls and nightclubs, had a hedonistic appeal to swinging couples, single or otherwise, and often of the same sex. The use of cocaine and other drugs around the clubs was not unknown. The theme parks, on the other hand, attracted mom, pop, grandma, grandpa and the kids, frequently all in the same party. The highs in the parks came from the roller coaster rides, and the most potent drug was the caffeine in the hot coffee. Yet both the discos and the theme parks reached new peaks of commercial success by 1977.

The disco's mother was an exotic dancer; its father a disk jockey. It was conceived in a technological boudoir where mind-melting strobe and laser beam lighting effects and ultrahigh decibel, heavy backbeat music wiped out reality and created a fantasy world of erotic pleasure.

The discos had been a fixture in Europe for many years. Regine, operator of one of New York's most exclusive discos, had been running one in Paris since the mid-1950s. In the early '60s, the discos made a faltering start in the United States, hit a modest peak, and slowed down to a point of near-extinction. In those days, male homosexuals were mainly responsible for keeping the movement alive. But, in 1973, there was a resurgence. That year there were about 1500 discos; by 1975, the number had increased to some 3000; and, by 1977, there were close to 15,000 discos operating across the country.

By 1977, every major city in the country had one or more high class discotheques. In Los Angeles, Hugh Hefner, founder of *Playboy,* and Stan Herman, a Beverly Hills real estate man, opened Pip's. A board of directors had to approve members for Pip's, and after such approval the members paid a $1000 membership fee and monthly dues of $30. Members of Pip's were many of the top stars (Lucille Ball, Sinatra, Peter Falk, Tony Curtis) and wealthy professional and business people, who liked to consort with the entertainment leaders.

Los Angeles also had a four-floor disco, Dillon's, where customers could watch the dance floor action via closed circuit TV. Some disco patrons came to see the show which, of course, was watching other patrons performing on the dance floor. Bathed in an infinite variety of multi-colored, kaleidoscopic lighting—weaving, bumping, grinding, kicking, prancing to the sensuous supersound—every dancer was a performer. During all but the slowest of the slow dances (when some dancers actually held their partners), each dancer entertained him or herself and the observers. There were some structured dances—such as the hustle, the roach, the rope, and the bus stop—but by 1977 most of the dances were free form.

THE HOTELS JOIN THE MOVEMENT

Holiday Inns and other moderately priced hotel chains across the country installed their own discos, some using small groups of live musicians, some records and some combinations of both. Some of the more expensive hotel chains installed elaborate disco operations. In the New York Hilton, Martin O'Hara created one called Sybil's in the summer of 1977. The hotel gave O'Hara a budget of $500,000 to set up the new, quietly elegant and sophisticated disco club/restaurant.

Late in 1977, the Loew's-Hilton chain spent $1,000,000 in its Drake Hotel in New York to create an elegant Egyptian motif disco, Shepheard's.

THE SMALL TIME

Discos also proliferated on a small-time, neighborhood level. Special services sprung up for these operations. Three disco jockeys, Bobby Guttadaro, Tom Savarese and Kevin Guilmet, who had been named "Disk Jockeys of the Year" in a *Billboard* poll, set up a special service for discos. They offered to send the dance spots a new 12'', 33⅓ rpm record programmed with their own selections of six to ten sides released by top record companies each week. Their service was called Disconet. One of the old-line radio disk jockeys, Murray Kaufman, set up a mobile *Murray the K*

disco franchise operation. Mobile disco operators serviced parties such as bar mitzvahs, weddings, and private get-togethers of all kinds, held in church halls, school gyms, etc. They simply moved in sound and lighting equipment and a disk jockey to play the records.

PATRON SAINT WALT

The theme park, it will be recalled, was launched in 1955 by the patron saint of wholesome, "mom's apple pie, Old Glory" show business, Walt Disney. Just as Disney set the pace for clean, G-rated entertainment in motion pictures, so did he (and the organization he created) set the style for America's theme parks. The idea of Disneyland with five distinct theme areas, *Main Street, U.S.A., Adventureland, Frontierland, Fantasyland* and *Tomorrowland,* each with its own rides, restaurants, shows and other attractions, had great appeal. And the extra touch of having life-size Mickey and Minnie Mouse, Donald Duck, Goofy and all the other Disney characters roaming the park, greeting and mingling with the visitors proved irresistible. The cross-merchandising of Disney's creations between motion pictures, television and the parks was an entertainment industry model.

The Disney theme park idea was a stupendous success. Yet it took some time before other operators put together outdoor theme entertainment centers. In 1961, a southern group opened *Six Flags Over Texas,* on a multi-acre site about twenty miles from the Dallas-Fort Worth airport. It was the first theme park to celebrate local history. The Six Flags group opened another theme park in 1966, *Six Flags Over Georgia,* on 276 acres ten minutes from downtown Atlanta, at an initial construction cost of $13,700,000. The pride of the Georgia "local history" theme park was *The Great American Scream Machine,* the world's highest and longest roller coaster ride. It also featured a twenty-two story parachute drop ride.

TAFT BUYS YOGI BEAR

The Six Flags group built another park, *Six Flags Over Mid-America,* at Eureka, Mo., outside St. Louis, and took over Astroworld in Houston and Great Adventure in Jackson, N.J. This gave the Six Flags organization a network of five parks. The Taft Broadcasting Corporation acquired the Hanna-Barbera animated film production company, and utilized Yogi Bear and all the Hanna-Barbera television characters in the same way Disney had used Mickey et al. in their theme parks. They created King's Island in Kings Mill, Oh., near Cincinnati, and King's Dominion in Doswell, Va., near Richmond. Taft also acquired a third park, Carowinds, in Charlotte, N.C.

THE MARRIOTT MOVE

Beer manufacturer Anheuser-Busch developed theme parks called The Dark Continent in Tampa, Fla. and the Old Country in Williamsburg, Va. And a highly successful conglomerate, the Marriott Corporation, moved into the theme park picture. Marriott had worldwide sales of $890,000,000 in 1976. The organization employed more than 60,000 people in 825 hotels, restaurants, in-flight catering services and leisure time operations. The corporation began planning its first theme park, Great America, in Gurnee, Ill., near Chicago and Milwaukee, in 1972. Four years and $75,000,000 later, on May 29, 1976, the Great America theme park opened. Its theme areas were Hometown Square, the Great Midwest Livestock Exposition & County Fair, Yankee Harbor, Yukon Territory and Orleans Place. Marriott had also worked out an arrangement with Warner Brothers for the rights to use Bugs Bunny, Porky Pig, Foghorn Leghorn, Tweety, Roadrunner, Will E. Coyote and other WB cartoon characters.

In its first year, 1976, it drew 2,350,000 people. The Gurnee Great America is one of the majority of theme parks which operate on a one-admission-covers-all policy. Adults pay $8.95 and children, $7.95, which covers all rides and shows. Interestingly enough, even though the theme park leader, Disney, still operates on an admission charge at the gate, *plus* books of tickets which must be purchased for rides and shows, only fourteen percent of all theme parks follow the Disney policy. Marriott opened a second park in Santa Clara, Ca. near San Francisco, and was planning a third park in the Washington, D.C. area in 1977.

THE BIG FIVE

Disney, Six Flags, Taft, Anheuser-Busch and Marriott are considered the Big Five of the theme park industry. Single park operations—so-called independents, playing to more than 2,000,000 people per year—include two other California parks, Knott's Berry Farm in Buena Park, and Magic Mountain in Valencia; as well as Opryland in Nashville and Cedar Point in Sandusky, Oh. Disney, however, continued to set the pace for theme park operations. Walt Disney World in Lake Buena Vista, Fla., which opened in 1972, is unlikely to be matched as a show business project for some time to come. It covers forty-three square miles of land, and consists not only of the Magic Kingdom, the theme park *per se*, but of hotels (the Contemporary and the Polynesian Village), condominiums, shopping centers, golf courses, campgrounds and restaurants. The total cost of creating Disney World was $750,000,000, of which $400,000,000 was spent on the park itself. The operation employs about 12,000 people. According to a *Fortune* magazine study, in 1976 Disney World and Disneyland combined drew more than 22,000,000 people. The annual revenue for the two parks for the year was $360,000,000 which represented forty percent of the total revenues of the Big Five and the four leading independent theme parks all put together!

SMALLER PARKS

A number of old established amusement parks switched to the theme concept. Notable among these was the seventy-one year old Hersheypark in Hershey, Pa. At present it has six theme areas: Tudor England, eighteenth century Germany, and American sections featuring a Pennsylvania Dutch, a contemporary America, a nostalgic area and a children's pet zoo. Its attendance runs 1,000,000 or more annually.

An interesting theme park concept which had not proved too successful by early 1977 was Circus World, twelve miles west of Disney World, in Haines City, Fla. It was a spinoff enterprise of Irvin Feld's operation of the Ringling Bros. and Barnum & Bailey circus. There were about forty theme parks around the country by the end of 1977.

Technological advances in the outdoor show world were seen primarily in some of the thrill rides in the theme parks. Roller coasters such as the Texas Cyclone at Astroworld in Houston; The Great American Scream Machine at Six Flags Over Georgia; Willard's Whizzer at the Gurnee Great America; the Screamin' Eagle at Six Flags Over Mid-America; and the Great American Revolution at Magic Mountain in Valencia, Ca., were true engineering marvels. Their construction costs ran between $1,000,000 and $3,000,000. Because the Disneyland roller coaster rockets through the "universe" of the park's Space Mountain, 260 tons of steel were required to support the Mountain's roof construction alone.

MORE MIND-BOGGLING TECHNOLOGICAL ADVANCES

In the decade between 1967 and 1977, technological developments generally—and in records, radio, films and television in particular—were mind-boggling. In music and records, innovations in musical instruments (synthesizers, electronic sounds, i.e., the Fender bass guitar, the Rhodes piano, et al.), recording studio inventions, and record and tape reproduction advances not only created huge new markets but also literally changed the very sound of music.

In the mid-'60s, a configuration war similar to that between the 33⅓ and 45 rpm speeds heated up. This one was between four-track, eight-track, reel-to-reel and cassette tape. By 1967, eight-track had emerged as the dominant form.

In 1970, quadraphonic recording was introduced, but even though some radio stations experimented with quad broadcasting, the idea was slow in catching on.

Many new techniques were introduced in film-making and exhibition. Producers moved from the optical stereo of Walt Disney's *Fantasia* to magnetic stereo, beginning with *The Robe;* then to six-track, 70 mm audio as in *Oklahoma!;* thence to Sensurround, an all-enveloping sound technique used in films such as *Earthquake* and *Roller Coaster;* and finally the dynamic Dolby 70 mm employed in *A Star is Born, Star Wars, Close Encounters of the Third Kind* and other films of the later '70s.

PIRATES AND COUNTERFEITERS

An ironic price the record and film industries were paying for their technological progress was the fantastic amount of duplication of their product, legal and illegal, which was taking place by late 1977. Taping records off radio broadcasts was, of course, completely legal and by 1977 the International Federation of Phonographic Industries (IFPI) announced that it estimated that the practice of recording music off the air onto tapes and cassettes was costing the industry $500,000,000 on a worldwide basis.

In addition to this perfectly legal duplication practice, the growth of record and film piracy and counterfeiting reached staggering proportions by 1977. The ease with which long playing records or tapes could be duplicated; the low cost of such duplication; and duplication of record jackets, tape cartons, as well as motion pictures, made the business of pirating and counterfeiting records, tapes and motion pictures a billion dollar industry.

The IFPI began working with Interpol, the international police organization, and their efforts were coordinated with those of the Record Industry Association of America and the Motion Picture Association of America. An increasing number of tape and film pirates were arrested, many were convicted, but the rip-off was still in the billion dollar area, and no end was in sight.

CABLE AND PAY TELEVISION

The entertainment area in which technological advances promised the most dramatic change for the future was, of course, television. As has been noted, various forms of theatre, cable and pay television had been operating for many years. Literally billions of dollars had been invested on one new TV concept or another. As 1977 came to a close, the stakes grew ever larger, as continuing progress was made in a number of video areas.

There were several indications that over-the-air and/or cable pay television was at a point of near-eruption. Jerry Perenchio set up a new corporation with Oak Industries, and they purchased UHF station KBSC-TV in Los Angeles from Kaiser Broadcasting for $1,200,000 and secured an FCC license to convert it to National Subscription Television, an over-the-air pay-TV operation. It went on the air in November, 1977, programming twenty-eight hours weekly of specially produced entertainment, sports and film shows. Cost to the viewer was $24.95 for installation, $25 for a decoder, and $17 per month to cover all programs.

HOME BOX OFFICE AND SATELLITES

The Time-Life pay-TV operation, Home Box Office, was making progress. In addition to producing a substantial number of shows, many using established "name" talent, the HBO operation was developing its satellite communications network. By early 1977, HBO was transmitting movies, sports shows, and other specials to about 350 cable

TV and multi-point distribution systems in forty-five states, reaching over 500,000 subscribers.

In early summer of 1977, Southern Satellite Systems, Inc. of Tulsa, Okla., launched the first FCC licensed satellite-distributing television station in the nation, WTCG in Atlanta.

At the Western Cable Television Show and Convention in San Diego that November, Edward Taylor, president of Southern Satellite, said that 106 cable systems were using the independent station distribution service, and reaching over 750,000 subscribers. Taylor also claimed that about 70,000 new homes were signing up for the service each month. Other independent TV stations were expected to become satellite distributing points over the next several years.

While the average citizen was not particularly aware of these space-age TV developments, some entertainment industry executives were not only aware but concerned about them. At another convention, in Miami Beach, Martin Firestone, communications counsel for the National Association of Theatre Owners, told the motion picture exhibitors:

The future is now! A nationwide cable pay TV network, relying primarily on the exhibition of theatrical films to attract subscribers . . . is no longer decades or even a few years away. It is in operation here and now.

$894,000,000 CABLE GROSS

The FCC reported that for the twelve-month period ending October, 1976, the cable television business in the United States had grossed $894,000,000. Monthly subscriber rates ranged from $5.19 to $8.03. (Of course, these figures had no particular bearing on pay-cable, since the majority represented cable subscribers, whose service merely gave them a better, interference-free signal, and the capacity to receive some UHF stations they could not receive without the cable hookup.) Further development of pay TV, cable or over-the-air, would depend on many factors, not the least of which were lobbying efforts and resulting legislation, as well as continued technological advances.

THE QUBE EXPERIMENT

In the same general "space-age" category as satellite distribution of pay-television programs were two other technological achievements. On December 1, 1977, in Columbus, Oh., Warner Cable Corporation launched its QUBE experiment. QUBE television gave the viewer a choice of thirty channels. These were equally divided into four sections:

1. Nine orthodox television stations, four local, and five imported;
2. Community channels, offering a package of programs each day on local matters, *Columbus Alive;* or special programming for pre-school children, on a feature called *Pinwheel;*

SEPT. 27, 1947 ISSUE   SAM GOLDWYN, LIONEL HAMPTON, & BENNY GOODMAN

3. Premium programs, consisting of a wide selection of old and new feature length films, sports shows, art programs and educational courses, at prices running from $1 to $3.50;

4. Audience participation selections, consisting of five response buttons on the right of the selection mechanism, which permitted subscribers to participate in local game shows, answer quiz questions, vote on issues presented, or actually purchase products being offered for sale by advertisers.

The Warner QUBE operation began on December 1, 1977. It was offered to Warner Cable's 26,500 established subscribers for an installation charge of $9.95. New subscribers were asked to pay $19.95 for installation. There was a regular monthly charge of $10.95, plus whatever special programming the subscriber chose to buy.

The QUBE offered an additional radio service. For an extra $10 per month, six stereo radio stations would be piped in on a twenty-four hour per day basis. Warner's QUBE experiment represented an investment of $10,000,000 by the time it was activated in December, 1977. How quickly it would catch on, and to what degree, even Gus Hauser, chairman and chief executive officer of Warner Cable, would not say.

Perhaps the most stunning futuristic technological development in TV was the announcement by the Japanese electronic giant, Matsushita, that it had developed a television receiver which could deliver an exact reproduction of the full color picture on the television tube, into your hands, in a matter of minutes.

THE VIDEOCASSETTE DRIVE

In the much more immediate future of mass entertainment via television technology were the videodisk and the videocassette player and recorder. Matsushita and its major competitor, the Sony Corporation, were in the forefront of this development. Immediately after Thanksgiving of 1977, and continuing through Christmas, every major American consumer electronics producer and distributor introduced and promoted its own version of either the Matsushita (sometimes in coordination with JVC, Japan Victor Company), or the Sony videocassette player and recorder. The two systems were technologically incompatible. And the development struggle, prior to the all-out American debuts, had been fierce.

Sony introduced its Betamax recorder and player in April, 1975 in a combination console with a Trinitron TV receiver, priced at $2300. The purpose of the combination introduction was to demonstrate how effectively a videocassette recorder/player could work in conjunction with a regular TV receiver.

The viewer could set a timer and record one full hour of any program on any station, to be played back on the videocassette deck at any time. Or one could be watching a television show on Channel 2, and taping any other show on any other channel at the same time, for playback at a later time. There was also a camera, with which one could shoot one's own TV program, and play the recorded tape back whenever desired. And the shows on a tape could be erased, so that another show could be recorded on the same tape.

The $2300 price, of course, kept the Sony Betamax out of reach of the vast majority of potential buyers. But it made its point. In March, 1976, Sony brought out the Sony Betamax recorder/player deck for $1300, suggested list price. Its tape recording capacity was still one hour. Three months later Matsushita brought out a unit with a two-hour tape recording capacity. Five months after that, in November, 1976, Sony debuted its own two-hour tape deck. Matsushita, shortly thereafter, introduced a four-hour unit, followed, of course, by a Sony Betamax with a four-hour capacity.

AMERICAN FIRMS LEAP IN

In the meantime, feverish negotiations between the two Japanese electronic giants and American producers and distributors were being conducted. By the opening of the Christmas selling season of 1977, the line-up was as follows.

RCA, with a unit called Selectavision, Sylvania, Magnavox, Curtis Mathis, Panasonic, JVC and Sharp were having videocassette recorder/players produced to their specifications either by Matsushita or the Matsushita/JVC combination. In addition to its own Betamax, Sony was producing recorder/players to their individual designs for Zenith, Sears, Sanyo, Pioneer, Toshiba, and, as of late 1977, was negotiating with Admiral.

Possibly even more significant was the fact that these producer-distributors were spending millions of dollars advertising their units during the pre-Christmas season. RCA announced that its budget for the RCA Selectavision recorder/player was about $5,000,000. Sony itself planned to spend another $4,000,000. Conservative estimates were that more than $25,000,000 would be spent in one form or another of advertising/publicity and/or promotion of the videocassette recorder/players in the last forty-five days of 1977.

A typical co-op ad by an established retailer, the May Company department stores in Los Angeles, offered Quasar's The Great Time Machine, with two-hour capacity for $799.95 and the MGA home video system and the Sony Betamax (both with two-hour capacities) for $1095. And most interesting was the fact that all the producer-distributors were stressing the same basic theme. It was a theme which had proved a major factor in the salvation of the record industry, when it seemed on the brink of extinction in the face of the introduction of radio. The videocassette sellers were saying:

See the television programs you want to see, when you want to see them. You need no longer be a slave to the TV schedules. You need never again miss another favorite show because of another engagement, or because it conflicts with another desirable show.

PRE-RECORDED TAPES

In addition to the appeal of being able to tape any program a viewer cared to, there was, of course, the additional attraction of pre-recorded tapes. A small nucleus of pre-recorded cassette material had been created with the release of some educational and instructional films and some high-priced, deluxe packages. Time-Life, seemingly active in every area of broadcast information and entertainment, had released a series of tapes called the Time-Life *Great Programs Collection* on the Sony Betamax configuration. It featured such classic Time-Life TV program series as *The Ascent of Man* and *Ten Who Dared*. Some 500 sets were sold at $340 per set.

A number of motion picture companies, notably Columbia Pictures and Twentieth Century Fox, were leasing videocassette rights to various companies. Magnetic Video Corp. of Farmington Hills, Mi., acquired rights to more than fifty such feature films and launched the Video Club of America. Operating on the same principle as the record and book clubs, Video Club of America offered a charter membership for $10. With the charter membership, one received a $10 discount certificate, which could be applied toward the purchase of any videocassette or videocassette player/recorder.

In full page ads in such media as *The New York Times Book Review*, *TV Guide* and others, Video Club of America offered "for as little as $39.95" videocassettes of feature films including *Patton, Hello Dolly, The French Connection, M.A.S.H., Hombre, Dr. Doolittle, The Sand Pebbles, Von Ryan's Express, The Longest Day* and *The Seven Year Itch*. The member could also return any cassettes he had purchased and receive a fifty percent credit on the purchase of another film.

SHIRLEY TEMPLE OR LINDA LOVELACE

Stranger feature film videocassette propositions seemed to be available. In Daily *Variety's* September 16, 1977 issue International Video and Cable Network of Beverly Hills offered "Copyright Movies on ¾'' & ½'' videocassette from $69." Listed were *Deep Throat, The Devil in Miss Jones, Confessions of Linda Lovelace*, Shirley Temple in *The Little Princess*, the Beatles' *Magical Mystery Tour*, Bob Hope in *My Favorite Brunette*, the Laurel and Hardy *Flying Deuces*, and several others. The ad said there were "over 200 titles to choose from."

In the waning months of 1977, it was impossible to foretell the consumer response to the $25,000,000 worth of advertising the producers were using to persuade consumers to buy videocassette recorders. It was also difficult to predict whether the caution, which appeared in very small type (about the size of type the cigarette companies use to warn against cancer), would discourage buying. A typical notice read:

The legality of recording copyrighted material for private use has not been clarified at this time. By the sale of this equipment we do not represent that copyrighted materials can be recorded.

THE ANTI-RECORDING SUIT

The reason for this statement was a lawsuit filed late in 1976 by MCA's Universal Studios and Walt Disney Productions in the U.S. District Court in Los Angeles against the Sony Corp. of America, Sony Corp. of Japan, retail outlets including the Carter Hawley Hale Stores, J.W. Robinson Co., Bullock's, Inc., Henry's Camera Corp., the Doyle Dane Bernbach advertising agency and William Griffiths, a consumer who purchased a Sony Betamax. The suit charged copyright infringement and intentional interference with the studios' contractual and business relationships with networks, independent TV stations and others. The studios asked for undetermined financial damages.

Just before Christmas, in 1977, Sony issued its financial statement. It showed that the company's sales had increased from $1,920,000,000 to $2,100,000,000 despite a drop in television set sales. The brightest spot in the Sony financial picture was that sales of its line of videotape recorders, including the Betamax home system, had increased 50% in the fiscal year to $296,200,000.

Some observers maintained that the MCA-Universal-Disney suit was filed not so much in the hopes of a victory, as for the purpose of hampering the efforts of the video-cassette producers to promote and sell their product. MCA itself, as noted earlier, had been working with the international conglomerate, Phillips, developing DiscoVision, a videodisk recorder/player. On a number of occasions, beginning in 1976, it had announced that the recorder/player, which operates a laser beam which scans the record, would be introduced to the market. For some time in 1975 and 1976, RCA, too, announced that it was on the verge of marketing a videodisk recorder/player called Selectavision, but this, too, was never introduced.

IS THERE A PLACE FOR BOTH?

And to add another titillating touch to the competitive videocassette-videodisk picture, in late November, 1977, Adam Yokoi, general manager of product engineering for Panasonic (one of Matsushita's American companies) introduced a new videodisk system called VISC. It was a "mechanical system using a 'twist' stylus technique which permits a much faster direct-cutting method for the master disk." Yokoi claimed this new technique would help solve the problems both RCA and MCA-Phillips had been having in getting their respective videodisk units on the market. Yokoi said that Matsushita had not yet developed marketing plans for its VISC system—and he said he believed there

was ample room in the marketplace for both videocassettes and videodisks.

In the booming, inflated show business of 1977, two small grey clouds in the otherwise brilliant blue sky were being largely ignored. One was that for the first time in television history viewing was down. Nielsen studies for the period November, 1976 to November, 1977 showed a decline from 1976 to 1977 of 6.4 percent for daytime viewing and 3.1 percent for prime time viewing; Arbitron showed a nine a.m. to noon drop of 11 percent and a prime time drop of 5 percent. While these percentage numbers are small, they represent millions of viewers.

The other dark cloud was the announcement in January, 1978 that the Radio City Music Hall in New York City would close down after Easter due to severe losses sustained for some time. This 6200 seat motion picture and live entertainment palace symbolized one phase of motion pictures' glory days. When the closing announcement was made, Disney's *Pete's Dragon* was showing on the screen, and the world-famous Rockettes were still precision-dancing across the huge stage. Whether these two incidents were portents of the future remained to be seen.

In the meantime, the effort to establish the new TV entertainment devices; the competitive battle constituting that effort; the continuing struggle for supremacy among the three television networks; the reactions of the film industry to all this on several levels; the fresh approaches in the old established areas of American entertainment—all these will have the same quality of excitement, the same vitality and suspense that every entertainment development since Thomas Edison's phonograph and motion picture has had. The shows we see and hear (in whatever form) will be ever more varied, bigger and better. That's show business!

ORIGINAL BILLBOARD MATERIAL
1947–1977
HIGHLIGHTS

As mentioned in Roger S. Littleford, Jr.'s article, "A Man Who Loved Show Business," *Billboard's* management and editors in the early '50s found it increasingly difficult to adequately cover and properly service every area of the entertainment industry in a single publication. The concerns and interests of outdoor showmen had long since reached the point where they were far removed from those of the Broadway theatrical producer, the Hollywood film maker, the television executive or the record people. The decision was made to discontinue the outdoor show business departments in *Billboard* and to cover these segments of American entertainment in two new publications, *Fun Spot* and *Amusement Business.*

Some time later, in January, 1961 — for reasons having to do with the phenomenal growth of the pre-recorded music industry (tapes and records) and *Billboard's* unique position in music/records — it was decided to concentrate *Billboard's* coverage on those music industries. Radio, films, TV and other show business fields were covered only as they related to music and records. Thus, for the greater part of the 1947–1977 period (and particularly, the eventful second half of that era), *Billboard's* stories and ads obviously did not reflect historical developments in the overall entertainment industry.

The original material from *Billboard* for the 1947–1977 period is consequently limited to a few ads, stories and appropriate photographs published during those years.

EARLY TV BRINGS BACK VAUDEVILLE; DRAWS ON THE THEATRE

FROM JUNE 12, 1948 ISSUE

The curtain rings up on

TELEVISION'S GREATEST SHOW

A full hour of All-Star

VAUDEVILLE

every Tuesday

Created by KUDNER AGENCY, Inc.

Arthur Godfrey was a major talk show personality in radio's heyday, and continued as one of TV's superstars through the '50s and '60s. Here he discusses show plans with producer Ted Bergmann.

Dick Van Dyke and Mary Tyler Moore in a scene from *The Dick Van Dyke Show,* another top-rated show of the mid-60s on CBS. Van Dyke continued as a superstar in films and the theatre as well as TV. The *Mary Tyler Moore Show* of the '70s was one of the most popular series of its time.

Photo courtesy CBS Television Network

Carroll O'Connor and Jean Stapleton played Archie Bunker and his wife, Edith, in the Norman Lear situation comedy, *All In The Family.* The Tandem Production, aired on CBS, blazed numerous television trails by building plots around prominent and/or controversial themes.

Young LeVar Burton played his first starring role (with dozens of other new and veteran superstars) in Alex Haley's *Roots,* the highest-rated television program in history as of its showing on ABC in 1977.

Photo Courtesy Warner Bros. Television

353

MOVIE HITS, ORIGINAL CAST AND SOUND TRACK ALBUMS, THEME PARKS

FROM MAY 21, 1977 ISSUE

Familiar movies (clockwise from above) Robert Redford and Barbara Streisand in *The Way We Were;* Joel Gray in *Cabaret;* Topol in *Fiddler On The Roof;* Diana Ross in *Mahogany;* and Natalie Wood in *West Side Story.*

© WALT DISNEY PRODUCTIONS

© WALT DISNEY PRODUCTIONS

Walt Disney's *Swiss Family Robinson*, starring John Mills and Dorothy McGuire developed into part of the Adventureland area, and his full-length classic, *Peter Pan,* inspired a section of Fantasyland, when Disney-land opened in 1955. Disneyland in Anaheim, Ca. (first them park ever created) and Walt Disney World in Buena Vista, Fla. were by far the two most successful theme parks in the world.

© WALT DISNEY PRODUCTIONS

© WALT DISNEY PRODUCTIONS

The Marriott Corporation's two highly successful Great America theme parks (one in Gurnee, Ill., the other in San Jose, Ca.) used Warner Bros. cartoon characters Bugs Bunny and Yosemite Sam in the same way the Disney parks used Mickey and Minnie Mouse and the Disney characters. In addition to shows like Bugs Bunny's Bourbon Street Follies, the parks featured Willard's Whizzer speedracer roller coaster, and the Great America Scenic Railway, among many other rides.

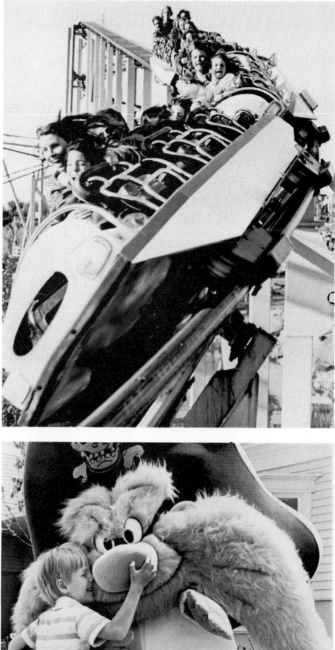

GREEN HEAVEN FOR SUPERSTARS

FROM JULY 4, 1976 ISSUE

Howard Hughes six Las Vegas hotels had a talent budget of $20,000,000 per year.

Las Vegas News Bureau Photo

Frank Sinatra and Sammy Davis, Jr. were two of the established Las Vegas superstar standbys, favorites of the high rollers.

Las Vegas News Bureau Photo

Although Elvis Presley fans were largely Coke drinkers, he sold out practically every show at the International.

RCA Photo

Las Vegas News Bureau Photo

Johnny Carson was getting $225,000 per week, but he didn't want to work that hard.

Las Vegas News Bureau Photo

Dean Martin was another gambling resort standby who made the high rollers happy.

Las Vegas News Bureau Photo

Liza Minnelli (left) was always a sure-fire Vegas drawing card.

Las Vegas News Bureau Photo

Liberace, his piano and his candelabra were one of the longest-running superstar attractions in Las Vegas.

MCA Artists Photo

PONDERING THE PROBLEMS OF ENTERTAINMENT'S NEW TECHNOLOGY

FROM APRIL 23, 1977 ISSUE

ITA SEMINAR HIGHLIGHTS:
Home Video Systems, Copyrights, New A/V Duplication, Technology

Biggest draw at seventh ITA seminar, April 4-6 at Hilton Head Is., S.C., was consumer video panel. From left are Frank McLaughlin, Office of Consumer Affairs; Bob Cavanagh, North American Philips; moderator Bill Madden, 3M; chairman Nick Denton, Reader's Digest; Irwin Tarr, Panasonic; Norman Glenn, MCA Disco-Vision, Harvey Schein, Sony.

Billboard photos by Stephen Traiman

First demonstration of 2-hour institutional model of Panasonic VHS video-cassette player-recorder, by Irwin "Skip" Tarr, left, video systems general manager, and Ted Kasuga, sales engineer, also included a player-only model. Main feature is built-in tuner/timer.

Showing off new 2-hour JVC VHS HR-3300 to be sold later this year in the U.S. is Dick O'Brion, JVC Industries, and current ITA president.

359

A CAPSULE HISTORY

To identify individual show business areas see two-letter code descriptions below:

AP —Amusement Parks
BU —Burlesque
CA —Carnivals
CH —Chautauqua
CI —Circus
FA —Fairs
MI —Minstrelsy
MO —Motion Pictures
MU —Music
NC —Night Clubs, Supper Clubs, Cabarets
RA —Radio
RE —Recordings
SH —Showboats
ST —Stereorama and Panstereorama
TH —Legitimate Theatre
TV —Television
VA —Vaudeville
WA —Wagon Shows

1947

TH More than a third of the Broadway shows for the 1947–48 season are revivals. More than half (forty-seven) are flops totaling $4,500,000 in losses.

TH The two most important American playwrights since Eugene O'Neill have hits (commercially and artistically) on Broadway. Tennessee Williams' *A Streetcar Named Desire* stars Marlon Brando, Jessica Tandy, Kim Hunter, Karl Malden and wins the Pulitzer Prize. Arthur Miller's *All My Sons* stars Ed Begley and Arthur Kennedy. Both plays are directed by Elia Kazan.

TH Alan Jay Lerner and Frederick Loewe have their first hit score in *Brigadoon*, a fantasy set in Scotland and featuring "Come to Me, Bend to Me" and "Heather on the Hill." Other hit musicals are *Finian's Rainbow* with Ella Logan, David Wayne and such hit tunes as "How Are Things in Glocca Morra" and "High Button Shoes," with Nanette Fabray singing "Papa Won't You Dance With Me."

MO/TV/TH The House of Representatives' Un-American Activities Committee (HUAC) begins investigation of suspected communist infiltration in films, theatre, and TV. Their witch hunt will ultimately end in blacklisting of hundreds and conviction of the famous "Unfriendly Ten," a group of writers and directors who went to jail because they refused to testify. Many never worked again.

MO *Gentlemen's Agreement,* starring Gregory Peck and John Garfield, is an Oscar-winning film treatment of anti-Semitism. Charlie Chaplin has a flop for the first time, *Monsieur Verdoux,* in which he plays a murderer instead of his beloved tramp character.

MO Solid "no-message-just-entertainment" this year is provided by *Life With Father* with William Powell, Irene Dunne and Elizabeth Taylor; Claudette Colbert and Fred MacMurray in *The Egg and I;* Crosby and Hope in *Road to Rio; Miracle on 34th Street;* and *The Ghost and Mrs. Muir* with Rex Harrison and Gene Tierney.

RE Ampex begins work on its first tape recorders. By the following year, it produces the Ampex model 200.

RE First dynaural noise suppressors and first high fidelity amplifiers are demonstrated by H. H. Scott. This, along with the introduction of tape recorders and other developments, marks the beginning of a tremendous surge in audio and high fidelity technology.

RE Record sales pass $200,000,000 mark for the second successive year. They increase steadily, with minor declines in 1954 and 1960, until they pass $1,000,000,000 mark in 1967.

RE/RA John T. Mullin, who brought Magnetophone tape recorders back from Germany as World War II souvenirs, tapes a network radio show, *The Philco Show,* starring Bing Crosby. It's the first successful taping of a major radio show and eliminates the need for doing shows live.

RA A. C. Nielsen survey shows 93% of all U.S. homes (35,900,000) now have radios, and total number of listening hours per day is a staggering 150,000,000. New favorites include *My Friend Irma* with Marie Wilson and Arthur Godfrey's *Talent Scouts.*

TV Quiz shows and panel discussion programs are extremely popular in early television. NBC this year has *Leave It To The Girls,* and Jack Barry's *Juvenile Jury.*

TV *Meet the Press,* the first regularly scheduled public affairs television show, debuts on NBC. Moderators are Lawrence Spivak and Martha Roundtree.

TV Two all-time great puppet shows for children make their TV debuts: Burr Tillstrom's *Kukla, Fran and Ollie* with Fran Allison, and "Uncle" Bob Smith's *Howdy Doody* on NBC. The former starts on WBKB, Chicago, but will move to NBC in 1949 and to ABC in 1954.

1948

TH Ray Bolger clicks in *Where's Charley?,* a musical version of *Charley's Aunt.* Frank Loesser's melodic score includes "Once In Love With Amy."

TH Henry Fonda stars in his most memorable stage role as *Mister Roberts* with David Wayne in support. Rex Harrison is Henry VIII in Maxwell Anderson's *Anne of the Thousand Days.*

TH The year closes in a blaze of musical glory with Cole Porter's *Kiss Me, Kate,* one of the great musical comedies of the decade, starring Alfred Drake. Score includes "So In Love," "Wunderbar," and "Another Openin', Another Show."

MO The Supreme Court this year rules that block booking is in restraint of trade. The studios also are ordered to divest themselves of their theatre chains. By 1954 all the majors except for MGM have sold off their movie houses. MGM will resist the edict until 1959.

MO TV is beginning to make inroads on films and business is off this year. MGM profits are at their lowest ebb since 1932–33. Dore Schary moves over from RKO to become production head of MGM. Universal and Walt Disney studios are in the red.

MO David Wark Griffith dies in Hollywood on July 23; some said he died from a broken heart. Many of the movie moguls who attended his funeral — some serving as honorary pallbearers — had refused to give him work during his last unhappy years.

MO/RE Big band singer Doris Day makes her first picture, *Romance on the High Seas,* for Warner Brothers and has a million-selling single record, "It's Magic" from the score. She will make seventeen more films for Warners (all but two will be musicals) until her contract ends in 1955.

MO *The Treasure of Sierra Madre* wins Oscars for director John Huston, supporting actor Walter Huston, and acclaim for Humphrey Bogart in an unusual "desert rat" role. However, the "best picture" Oscar is won by *Hamlet* as played by Laurence Olivier, who also wins an Oscar. Jane Wyman wins for *Johnny Belinda*.

MO Judy Garland is at her peak this year in *The Pirate* with Gene Kelly and a Cole Porter score, and in *Easter Parade* with Fred Astaire and seventeen Irving Berlin songs.

RA Following its acquisition of NBC's *Amos 'n Andy* for $2,000,000 in October, CBS, late in November, acquires *The Jack Benny Show* from NBC. It runs in same time period (Sunday, 7–7:30 p.m.) and with same sponsor, American Tobacco, as on NBC. It represents the second major talent raid by Paley against Sarnoff's network. There will be more.

RA Walter Winchell has the number-one rated program this year, followed by *Lux Radio Theatre*. Also in the Top Ten are *Irma, Arthur Godfrey Show, Duffy's Tavern,* and the *Phil Harris-Alice Faye Show*.

RA/TV First regular commercially sponsored simulcast is *We, the People,* bankrolled by Gulf Oil on both CBS radio and CBS-TV networks.

TV Vaudeville makes a spectacular comeback on television as Texaco kicks off a sixty-minute series starring Milton Berle. It becomes the smash hit of the early TV era. Arthur Godfrey's *Talent Scouts* bows on CBS-TV. Perry Como makes his first video appearance on NBC's *Chesterfield Supper Club*. Ed Sullivan's long-running *Toast of the Town* debuts on CBS.

TV The official FCC freeze of TV this year leads to a peculiar period in entertainment history. New York and Los Angeles each have seven operating TV stations. In all, there are 108 stations across the country, with most cities having only one. But in all these cities TV's impact quickly becomes evident. Ratings of top radio shows in TV cities drop; business falls off in theatres and restaurants when popular video shows are on the air.

TV Arturo Toscanini conducts the NBC Symphony from Carnegie Hall in his live TV debut on March 20 in a simulcast with NBC radio. NBC radio's long-time favorite musical series, *Voice of Firestone,* makes its television bow as a simulcast with one telecast this year. It will become a weekly simulcast in September, 1949.

TV Some of television's most memorable dramatic shows debut this year. NBC introduces *Kraft Television Theatre* as a network series and, in October, *Philco Playhouse.*

CBS bows with *Studio One* in November.

TV Veteran film actor Bill Boyd has a whole new career when his old *Hopalong Cassidy* movies become TV's first hit western series. *The Lone Ranger* is also a favorite for children.

RE In June, Columbia Records introduces its long-playing (LP) 33⅓ rpm microgroove disk. It plays twenty-three minutes per side, and has high audio quality. Ted Wallerstein, Columbia president, attempts to persuade RCA to go along with the new speed, but RCA refuses. It marks the beginning of the war in records between Sarnoff and Paley, and the beginning of a chaotic period in the record industry.

RE Record sales drop from $224,000,000 in 1947 to $189,000,000 this year. It's the first decline in record sales since 1933, the year the industry hit its rock bottom low of $5,500,000. The drop is partially due to Columbia's introduction of the LP, partially to some TV activity.

1949

TH Arthur Miller's tragedy, *Death of a Salesman* — starring Lee J. Cobb, Mildred Dunnock, and Arthur Kennedy — wins the Drama Critics' Circle Award. Also impressive is Sidney Kingsley's *Detective Story* with Ralph Bellamy and Lee Grant.

TH Carol Channing becomes a star as Lorelei Lee in a musical version of Anita Loos' *Gentlemen Prefer Blondes*. A startling contrast is offered by another musical hit, *Lost In the Stars,* a moving tragedy about the plight of South African blacks, starring Todd Duncan, book and lyrics by Maxwell Anderson, music by Kurt Weill.

TH Pulitzer Prize-winning musical *South Pacific* opens in April with the biggest advance sale in Broadway history. The landmark show stars Mary Martin, Metropolitan basso Ezio Pinza, and a glorious score by Rodgers and Hammerstein ("Some Enchanted Evening," "There Is Nothing Like A Dame," "Younger Than Springtime").

MO Mario Lanza, billed as "the new Caruso," makes his film debut in *That Midnight Kiss*. Judy Holliday registers strongly on film for the first time in *Adam's Rib* starring Katharine Hepburn and Spencer Tracy. John Wayne and Gary Cooper continue to be big-money stars.

MO Comedy teams are big box office — Hope and Crosby, Dean Martin and Jerry Lewis, Abbott and Costello. Frank Sinatra and Gene Kelly hit with two musicals, *On the Town* and *Take Me Out to the Ball Game*.

MO Oscar winners this year include Olivia De Havilland for *The Heiress,* and Broderick Crawford for *All the King's Men*. De Sica's *The Bicycle Thief* is awarded a special Oscar.

MO Racial prejudice is the theme of several important pictures this year — Stanley Kramer's *Home of the Brave, Pinky, Intruder in the Dust, Lost Boundaries* and a documentary, *The Quiet One*.

RE After keeping the industry in suspense for many months, RCA introduces its new 45 rpm player and records in February. The record is a seven-inch, large hole disk. The battle of record speeds starts in earnest with RCA and Columbia each spending millions to attempt to establish respective new speeds. Some player manufacturers introduce three-speed (33⅓, 45, 78 rpm) phonographs.

RE Record sales drop another 8.5%, from $189,000,000 in 1948 to $173,000,000 this year. The decline is attributed to the raging battle of the speeds between RCA and Columbia with rest of industry undecided, and dealers required to carry triple inventories. 78 rpm sales dwindle significantly, and it is apparent that new speeds are here to stay.

RA By mid-January, the ratings show that *The Jack Benny Show* and *Amos 'n Andy* in the Sunday, 7 to 8 p.m. period on CBS top NBC in the ratings for the first time in the rivalry between the two networks.

RA Two more major stars take their shows from NBC to CBS in late January: Edgar Bergen-Charlie McCarthy, et al., plus Red Skelton. Paley is still working to lure other top shows away from NBC.

RA/TV Bing Crosby, who started in radio on CBS, then switched to NBC, returns to CBS under the terms of a new contract, which gives the Paley network his exclusive services for both radio and television.

RA/TV Fred Allen, one of top stars of the day, signs exclusive contract for both radio and TV with NBC.

RA Other radio favorites this year include Eve Arden in *Our Miss Brooks; Inner Sanctum; The Garry Moore Show;* and *The Quiz Kids.*

TV Early video dramatic shows tend to be stock, proven radio shows with pictures. Crime series are prime examples. One of earliest successes of the genre is *Man Against Crime,* starring Ralph Bellamy. Shows are produced by ad agencies, and writers must follow rigid rules: cigarette sponsors insist that "heavies" or other unattractive characters must never be shown smoking; plots must deal with murder rather than other less gripping crimes, etc. Live production costs about $15,000 per show.

TV First cable TV services go on air. They originate no programming, but merely bring TV to homes outside the reach of regular TV stations, via microwave radio relay.

TV The first Emmy awards — telecast on KTSL-TV, Los Angeles — are made in January by the newly formed National Academy of Television Arts and Sciences. Only six Emmys are presented. Winners include ventriloquist Shirley Dinsdale and *Pantomime Quiz Time.*

TV *Arthur Godfrey and His Friends,* a variety hour, starts on CBS. *The Friday Night Frolics,* a musical-revue starring Sid Caesar and Imogene Coca, plus dance team Marge and Gower Champion, is sponsored on both the Du Mont and the NBC-TV networks.

TV Other notable network video debuts this year are (Dave) *Garroway at Large, Ted Mack's Original Amateur Hour,* and Allen Funt's *Candid Camera.* Ed Wynn has first major network show produced on the West Coast.

1950

TH Television is making inroads on the theatre. A survey reveals that less than 2% of Americans are theatregoers, and of that group less than 1% are younger than twenty-five. The dearth of Broadway touring companies, however, is a boon to regional theatres. Arena Stage is formed in Washington, D.C. and similar local groups of professional stature are organized across the country.

TH It's a year of exciting performances: Ethel Waters and Julie Harris in Carson McCullers' *The Member of the Wedding;* Shirley Booth and Sidney Blackmer in William Inge's *Come Back Little Sheba;* Alec Guinness and Cathleen Nesbitt in T.S. Eliot's *The Cocktail Party;* Clifford Odets' *The Country Girl* with Uta Hagen and Paul Kelly; Jean Arthur and Boris Karloff in *Peter Pan;* and Katharine Hepburn in Shakespeare's *As You Like It.*

TH Another landmark musical is presented this year: *Guys and Dolls,* starring Robert Alda, Sam Levene, and Vivian Blaine. Frank Loesser's score includes "Fugue For Tinhorns" and "Luck Be a Lady Tonight."

MO Although movie attendance is at a "1933 low," the big pictures still do business. Gloria Swanson makes a stunning comeback in *Sunset Boulevard;* Bette Davis scores in an Oscar winner, *All About Eve.* Judy Holliday wins an Oscar for *Born Yesterday.* Marlon Brando makes a strong impression in his first film, *The Men.* Orson Welles and Joseph Cotten are reunited for *The Third Man* with its haunting theme.

MO Two actresses destined to become all-time glamour stars score this year. Elizabeth Taylor displays her classic beauty in *Father of the Bride,* starring Spencer Tracy. Marilyn Monroe attracts attention in a bit part in *The Asphalt Jungle.* Debbie

Reynolds also shows star potential in the Fred Astaire-Red Skelton musical *Three Little Words.*

MU/RE/MO Frank Sinatra's career goes into a serious decline. His record sales drop and Columbia does not pick up his option. He blames Columbia artists-and-repertoire head Mitch Miller for forcing him to record poor songs, including a duet called "Mama Barks" with non-singer sex symbol, Dagmar. He revitalizes his record career by signing with Capitol Records.

RE Folk music continues to be strong factor in pop sales. Hits such as The Weavers' "Good Night, Irene" are among the biggest sellers of the day.

RA TV is making inroads on network radio, but nevertheless Tallulah Bankhead scores a hit with her new NBC Sunday night variety hour, *The Big Show.* Also still drawing listeners are *Bob Hope Show, The Great Gildersleeve,* and *Fibber McGee and Molly.*

TV/RA Blacklisting of performers and others with alleged communist affiliations and/or sympathies reaches a peak. CBS requires signing of a loyalty oath.

TV In one of the first instances of the anti-communist hysteria of the day, General Foods drops actress Jean Muir from *The Aldrich Family,* because of allegations that she was sympathetic to communist causes; she denies all such allegations.

TV On Oct. 16, FCC approves CBS color effective November 20, but at RCA's request a Chicago federal court initially issues a temporary restraining order halting the FCC's ruling. In December, same federal court bans operation of CBS color, pending decision by the U.S. Supreme Court.

RA/TV In a stepped-up counterattack in the battle for top talent, NBC makes a $3,000,000 capital gains deal for an eight-year term with Groucho Marx. One week later the network signs Bob Hope to a five-year contract.

TV Popular with viewers are Emmy winner Gertrude Berg in *The Goldbergs; Time for Beanie,* a children's show; Groucho Marx on his own with the new quiz show, *You Bet Your Life;* comedian Alan Young; Ralph Edwards' *Truth or Consequences;* and *I Remember Mama* with Peggy Wood. Burns and Allen make their TV debut as a regular comedy series.

TV FCC authorizes first experimental, over-the-air pay TV subscription systems, wherein scrambled signals are transmitted over the air. Signals may then be unscrambled by deciphering equipment attached to subscriber's set. Skiatron Corporation announces its pay-TV system, Subscriber-Vision.

TV *What's My Line,* one of the most durable game shows, starts its long run. Kate Smith begins a four-year run with an afternoon show.

1951

TH Yul Brynner makes a smash debut as the magnetic monarch of Siam in Rodgers and Hammerstein's *The King and I.* For star Gertrude Lawrence, it is her best and last performance. She dies during the show's long run on September 6, 1952. Score includes such classics as "Hello Young Lovers," "Getting to Know You," and "I Have Dreamed." A revival of the musical — still starring Brynner — will be one of Broadway's biggest hits in 1977.

TH Maureen Stapleton becomes a star as the earthy heroine of Tennessee Williams' *The Rose Tattoo* with Eli Wallach. Claude Rains stars in Sidney Kingsley's adaptation of Arthur Koestler's *Darkness at Noon,* which wins the Drama Critics' Circle Award.

TH A star-studded First Drama Quartette (Charles Boyer, Charles Laughton, Agnes Moorehead and Sir Cedric Hardwicke) gives readings of Shaw's *Don Juan in Hell.* The touring foursome, who work on a bare stage, are a sell-out.

VA In a startling revival of the two-a-day vaude policy at the Palace, New York (after many years of showing films only), Judy Garland breaks all long-run records at the legendary house. Booked for four weeks, she plays nineteen. Among other supporting acts are Smith and Dale, a comedy team. Potent revival enables Palace to operate straight two-a-day vaude policy for seven more years.

MO The major studios are still resisting TV by refusing to sell their old films to the medium, and banning TV appearances for their contract players. However, some of the majors (Paramount, Universal and Columbia) are setting up TV film operations.

MO A quality year for Hollywood. Vivien Leigh wins an Oscar for *A Streetcar Named Desire,* which makes Marlon Brando a star. Humphrey Bogart gives an Oscar-winning performance in the classic *The African Queen* with Katharine Hepburn. Other superior films are Montgomery Clift, Elizabeth Taylor, and Shelley Winters in George Stevens' *A Place in the Sun,* a remake of *An American Tragedy;* and Alfred Hitchcock's *Strangers On a Train* with Robert Walker, who dies the same year.

MO Vincent Minnelli's innovative musical, *An American in Paris* — starring Gene Kelly, a great Gershwin score, and an eighteen-minute ballet sequence — wins a "best picture" Oscar. MGM paid $300,000

to the Gershwin estate just to use the title. Mario Lanza scores as *The Great Caruso.*

MU Duke Ellington and his orchestra play a new long work — a suite, *Harlem* — at the Metropolitan Opera House in New York. It is the latest in a succession of longer works which Ellington has written and performed in concert. Among them: *New World A-Comin', Deep South Suite, Blutopia,* and *Tattooed Bride.*

TV Zenith Radio Corporation launches its pay-TV system, Phonevision, in Chicago. 300 homes are wired into the system, and asked to pay $1 to see current, major films.

TV Winners of 1951 Emmy Awards include Red Skelton, *Studio One;* Sid Caesar and Imogene Coca in *Your Show of Shows;* and the Kefauver hearings on organized crime, which draw 20,000,000 viewers. Menotti's *Amahl and the Night Visitors,* first opera commissioned for TV, debuts Christmas night.

TV Lucille Ball finds her greatest medium as the star of *I Love Lucy,* which debuts on Oct. 15 on CBS. Her real life husband, Desi Arnaz, is her co-star.

TV Up to this year, the great majority of series have been produced "live." Now Lucille Ball and Desi Arnaz do *I Love Lucy* on film, and it quickly climbs to number one in the ratings. Other shows begin to go to film, including a new crime series, *Dragnet,* which first airs in Jan., 1952. When *Man Against Crime* goes on film, the handwriting is truly on the wall. The production of such series swings to Hollywood from New York.

TV/MO United Paramount Theatres buys ABC for $25,000,000. Leonard Goldenson, UPT president, heads a new combine, with Robert Kintner, president of ABC, heading the broadcasting division. Edward Noble, who originally purchased Blue network from NBC and formed ABC, is chairman of the finance committee of the new organization.

1952

TH Rodgers and Hart's *Pal Joey* is revived with Harold Lang, Helen Gallagher, and Vivienne Segal in her original role. The revival, which runs longer than the original, is acclaimed by the critics this time and wins eleven of *Billboard's* sixteen Donaldson Awards.

MO The circus forms a glittering backdrop for Cecil B. De Mille's Oscar-winning film, *The Greatest Show On Earth* and for Charlie Chaplin's movie, *Limelight,* in which he plays an aging clown. Two hit films have a Hollywood background — Gene Kelly's all-time great musical, *Singin' In the Rain* with Debbie Reynolds and Donald O'Connor; and *The Bad and The Beautiful* with Dick Powell, Lana Turner, and Kirk Douglas.

MO Gary Cooper wins an Oscar for *High Noon,* introducing Grace Kelly. Shirley Booth is also an Oscar winner in *Come Back Little Sheba.* Other outstanding performances are Fredric March in *Death of a Salesman,* Marlon Brando in *Viva Zapata!,* Alec Guinness in *The Lavender Hill Mob,* John Wayne in *The Quiet Man.*

MO In an effort to combat the lure of television, Hollywood introduces *This Is Cinerama,* featuring a curved screen about six times as large as a regular screen. The three-dimensional effect was invented by Fred Waller. The accompanying "Stereophonic" sound system was developed by Hazard Reeves. *This Is Cinerama,* featuring roller coaster rides and various scenic experiences, runs for 122 weeks at the Broadway Theatre in New York.

RE Record Industry Association of America is organized. Milton Rackmil, head of Decca Records, is its first president. A *Billboard* editorial campaign urging the formation of the organization is partially responsible for the Association's existence.

TV Emmy-winning TV shows and performers for 1952 include *What's My Line?;* Bishop Fulton J. Sheen; and Helen Hayes as *Victoria Regina* on *Robert Montgomery Presents,* Emmy's "best dramatic series."

TV New TV favorites include Wally Cox in *Mr. Peepers;* Jack Webb's *Dragnet;* Edward R. Murrow's *See It Now;* and *The Jackie Gleason Show. Victory at Sea,* a World War II documentary, features a highly acclaimed Richard Rodgers score.

TV *Ozzie and Harriet* begins this year and David and Ricky Nelson grow up on camera over the years. Liberace's syndicated show is a spectacular hit. *Your Hit Parade,* which debuted in 1950, continues to be a musical favorite, starring Dorothy Collins, Snooky Lanson, Russell Arms, and Gisele Mackenzie.

TV NBC-TV launches the *Today Show.* First host is Dave Garroway, and the chimp, J. Fred Muggs, is one of its early stars.

TV On April 14, the FCC lifts the Sept. 30, 1948, freeze on TV station licenses. The order provides for 617 VHF and 1436 UHF stations in 1,291 cities. Many of the 108 TV stations that had gone into operation prior to the 1948 freeze are already showing a profit. It is apparent that television station operation is a highly lucrative enterprise. It is not surprising that the Commission is deluged with applications for licenses.

TV Ted Bergmann is appointed managing director of the Broadcast Division of Du Mont.

TV New production companies are estab-lished in TV-film production. Among them are Revue Productions, a subsidiary of MCA; Ziv Television, a radio producer moving successfully into video; Desilu, the Ball-Arnaz company; and Screen Gems, a subsidiary of Columbia Pictures. Film production costs per half-hour show climb to $25,000 per episode vs. $15,000 for live production.

TV *Amos 'n Andy,* first TV situation comedy with an all black cast, wins an Emmy nomination.

1953

TH Gwen Verdon makes her first show-stopping impression in Cole Porter's musical *Can-Can* ("I Love Paris"). Rosalind Russell is the toast of Broadway in *Wonderful Town* with music by Leonard Bernstein and lyrics by Comden and Green. Borodin's lush classical themes are adapted by Robert Wright and George Forrest in *Kismet,* starring Alfred Drake. Result: two pop hits, "A Stranger in Paradise" and "This Is My Beloved."

TH Deborah Kerr makes a striking Broadway debut in Robert Anderson's sensitive drama, *Tea and Sympathy,* but most of the hits this year are comedies—Josephine Hull in *The Solid Gold Cadillac,* Margaret Sullavan in *Sabrina Fair.*

TH Arthur Miller's *The Crucible,* an indictment of witch-hunting, is courageously presented at the height of the McCarthy era, but has a short run. The 1952–53 Pulitzer Prize and Drama Critics' Circle Award go to William Inge's *Picnic.* David Wayne clicks in John Patrick's comedy hit, *The Teahouse of the August Moon,* which wins a Pulitzer and Critics' Circle Award for the 1953–54 season.

MO Outstanding films this year include *Julius Caesar* with Marlon Brando; *Shane,* George Stevens' classic western, starring Alan Ladd and Jean Arthur; the charming *Lili* with Leslie Caron; and *Moulin Rouge* with Jose Ferrer.

MO The ageless Fred Astaire scores in a film version of his old stage musical *The Band Wagon* with Cyd Charisse, Jack Buchanan, and Nanette Fabray. Other musical hits are Doris Day in *Calamity Jane; Gentlemen Prefer Blondes* with Marilyn Monroe and Jane Russell; *Kiss Me, Kate,* starring Kathryn Grayson, Howard Keel, and Ann Miller, with an outstanding dance by young Bob Fosse; *Easy to Love,* with Esther Williams' startling water ballet choreographed by Busby Berkeley.

MO Hollywood has to have a gimmick this year. Audiences don special glasses to watch the first 3-D (three-dimensional) movie, *Bwana Devil.* 20th Century Fox introduces wide-screen Cinemascope with *The Robe* starring Richard Burton. Other novelties include Todd-AO, VistaVision,

Warnerphonic, and Glamorama. Only Cinemascope has a lasting effect.

MO/RE/MU With his career still at a low ebb, Frank Sinatra prevails upon Columbia studio head Harry Cohn to give him the part of Maggio in *From Here to Eternity*. He wins a "best supporting actor" Oscar for his performance, and his career reaches new heights.

RE Elvis Presley, an eighteen-year-old truck driver, pays $4 to cut a record at the Memphis Recording Service (a division of Sun Records) as a birthday present for his mother, Gladys. He records "My Happiness." Sam Phillips, Sun Records owner, hears the tape and records Presley a year later. "That's All Right, Mama" becomes a regional hit, and Presley is on his way to becoming an all-time superstar.

TV This year, and the next two, witness a golden era of dramatic anthology series in television. *Philco Playhouse, Goodyear Playhouse, Kraft Theatre, Studio One, Robert Montgomery Presents* and the *U.S. Steel Hour* are among the leaders. Such outstanding players as Rod Steiger, Paul Newman, Kim Stanley, Joanne Woodward, and Sidney Poitier participate, as do directors Sidney Lumet, Arthur Penn, and Del Mann.

TV Among the top new shows and stars this year are Danny Thomas in *Make Room For Daddy;* Donald O'Connor; the cerebral *Omnibus,* hosted by Alistair Cooke, which debuts late in 1952; Edward R. Murrow's *Person to Person;* and Ralph Edwards' durable *This Is Your Life* which started in October, 1952.

TV The famous Mary Martin-Ethel Merman special for Ford's 50th Anniversary two-hour show is aired by both NBC and CBS. Only when the stars compare notes shortly before the show goes on, do they discover that each has been guaranteed "total control" of the program.

TV CBS and cigarette manufacturer Philip Morris sign Lucille Ball and husband Desi Arnaz to thirty-month contract for $8,000,000.

TV Viewers are also watching *The Arthur Murray Dance Party* with the dancing school tycoon's vivacious wife Kathryn as host; Dr. Frances Horwich's *Ding Dong School;* and *Coke Time With Eddie Fisher.*

TV *The Goodyear Playhouse* presents two classic TV dramas this year: Paddy Chayefsky's *Marty* with Rod Steiger; and Horton Foote's *A Trip To Bountiful* with Lillian Gish and Eva Marie Saint. Although this is the golden era of video drama, many advertisers are unhappy with the realistic plays, theorizing that more simple-minded, happy-ending comedies sell products more effectively.

TV FCC approves standards for RCA's compatible color television system.

TV Sylvester (Pat) Weaver, who left the Young & Rubicam advertising agency in 1949 to head up NBC's television department, is named president of NBC-TV. During his tenure at NBC, Weaver creates the idea of big specials, which he called "spectaculars." He also promotes the "magazine concept" (sponsors buying inserts on shows controlled by the network) and those high-profit earners *The Today Show* (1952) and *The Tonight Show* (1954).

1954

TH Two intense dramas are the top Broadway offerings this year. Herman Wouk's *The Caine Mutiny Court Martial* stars Henry Fonda and a riveting performance by Lloyd Nolan as Captain Queeg. Maxwell Anderson's *The Bad Seed* stars Nancy Kelly with child actress Patty McCormack remarkable as a pre-puberty murderess.

TH Ezio Pinza stars in a Harold Rome musical, *Fanny,* which introduces Florence Henderson. Mary Martin is youth incarnate in a musical version of *Peter Pan,* later to become a perennial on TV, and Julie Andrews makes her Broadway debut in an English import, *The Boy Friend.*

TH The season's top musical is *Pajama Game* which makes overnight successes of heretofore unknown choreographer Bob Fosse and producers Frederick Brisson, Harold Prince, and Robert Griffith. Score includes "Hey There" and "Hernando's Hideaway." It also makes a star of Shirley MacLaine; as an understudy for Carol Haney, she goes on one night and is discovered by Hollywood.

MO Outstanding films this year are Bing Crosby in *Country Girl,* which wins an Oscar for Grace Kelly; Hitchcock's *Rear Window* with James Stewart and Grace Kelly; *The Caine Mutiny* with Humphrey Bogart.

MO *On The Waterfront,* 1954's Oscar-winning film, also brings Oscars to its star Marlon Brando, director Elia Kazan, and supporting actress Eva Marie Saint. Brando, who also stars in *The Wild One,* is in the Top Ten at the box office, but John Wayne is number one again.

MO The musical, *Carmen Jones,* is the most lavish all-black film of the decade. Dorothy Dandridge plays the title role. Cast also includes Harry Belafonte, Pearl Bailey, and Diahann Carroll.

MO Judy Garland makes an exciting comeback in a musical remake of *A Star Is Born* with James Mason. Other hit musicals are *Seven Brides for Seven Brothers* with Jane Powell and Michael Kidd's great

choreography; Bing Crosby and Danny Kaye in Irving Berlin's *White Christmas.*

RE "Sh-Boom," in versions by the Chords and the Crew Cuts, and "Gee" by the Crows are among the earliest rock and roll hits. "Rock Around the Clock" by Bill Haley has been released, but is ignored until a year later when it is heavily reprised in the film, *The Blackboard Jungle.* The Haley record is then re-released and becomes a major rock smash.

TV/RA Official FCC report shows that TV passes radio in total industry gross for the first time: TV, $595,000,000; radio, $449,500,000. It is also first year combined broadcasting-telecasting industries pass the billion dollar gross mark.

TV First network colorcast is the New Year's Day Tournament of Roses Parade on NBC.

TV RCA introduces first TV color sets: 15" open-face console retails for $1000. RCA also makes first all-electronic color tube available to all set manufacturers.

TV/AP Walt Disney, one of the first film makers to go with TV, bargains that whichever network invests in the Disneyland theme park wins his video show. Disney signs with ABC, which buys 34.48% of Disneyland for $500,000 and guarantees loans up to $4,500,000. The *Disneyland* TV show is an instant hit, particularly its *Davy Crockett* three-parter. *Crockett* is a merchandising bonanza. More than 1,000,000 Crockett hats and a like number of "The Ballad of Davy Crockett" recordings are sold.

MO/TV Jack Warner, shortly thereafter, makes arrangements to produce a series of films for ABC-TV for the 1955–56 season. Warner's deal stipulates that each show carrys a ten-minute segment promoting Warner theatrical film product.

TV Emmy-winning personalities this year include Perry Como, Dinah Shore, Lassie, and Loretta Young, famous for her sweeping entrance. The year's dramatic highlight is Reginald Rose's *Twelve Angry Men* on *Studio One.*

TV NBC-TV launches *The Tonight Show.* Steve Allen is first host; followed by Jack Paar (in 1957) and Johnny Carson (in 1962).

TV Comedy rules TV this year. Video favorites include Jimmy Durante, Martha Raye, George Gobel, Red Buttons, Ann Sothern, Eddie Cantor. Audience participation shows are also big — Bert Parks' *Stop the Music;* Art Linkletter's *People Are Funny;* and *Name That Tune.*

1955

TH Two Pulitzer Prize winners are presented this year. For the 1954–55 season,

Tennessee Williams' *Cat On A Hot Tin Roof* with Burl Ives as Big Daddy; and, for 1955–56, the moving *Diary of Anne Frank* with Susan Strasberg as the tragic victim of the Nazis, and Joseph Schildkraut as her father. Young Ben Gazarra is in *Cat* and also stars in *A Hatful of Rain* with Shelley Winters and Anthony Franciosa.

TH Star performances this year are given by Paul Muni in *Inherit the Wind;* new-comer Kim Stanley in William Inge's *Bus Stop;* Ruth Gordon in Thornton Wilder's *The Matchmaker* (supported by Robert Morse); and Julie Harris as Joan of Arc in *The Lark. The Desperate Hours* lists Paul Newman in a supporting role. Andy Griffith makes his Broadway debut in *No Time for Sergeants.*

TH Cole Porter celebrates his fortieth year as a Broadway composer with his twenty-fifth show, *Silk Stockings,* adapted from Greta Garbo's 1939 movie *Ninotchka.* Don Ameche and Hildegarde Neff star and show's hit song is "All of You."

TH Musical smash of the season is *Damn Yankees,* starring Gwen Verdon and Ray Walston, and directed by George Abbott. Score, by Richard Adler and Jerry Ross, includes "Whatever Lola Wants." TV's Jean Stapleton has a small role in the play.

MO Attendance is at its lowest ebb since 1923. Only slightly more than 200 films are released this year by the key studios. General Tire and Rubber Company buys RKO from Howard Hughes.

MO Walt Disney releases the first all-cartoon Cinemascope feature, *Lady and the Tramp.*

MO Paddy Chayefsky's *Marty* wins a flock of Oscars: for "best picture;" "best actor," Ernest Borgnine; and "best director," Delbert Mann. Anna Magnani wins an Oscar for *The Rose Tattoo* and Jack Lemmon receives a supporting Oscar for *Mr. Roberts,* starring Henry Fonda, James Cagney and William Powell.

MO Sidney Poitier, destined to become Hollywood's number one black star, scores in *Blackboard Jungle* with Glenn Ford. Poitier's first movie was *No Way Out* in 1950.

MO James Dean dies in an auto crash at the age of twenty-four and becomes a cult hero of teenagers. He only made three pictures. Two of them — *Rebel Without a Cause* and *East of Eden* — are released this year; both are hits, as is his third film, *Giant* (starring Elizabeth Taylor and Rock Hudson) released posthumously in 1956.

RE Tom Parker acquires management contract on Elvis Presley from disk jockey Bob Neal. He immediately makes a deal with Steve Sholes, RCA Victor's country and western artists-and-repertoire director,

for RCA to buy Presley's record contract and all masters from Sam Phillips at Sun. Over the objections of some of his executive colleagues at RCA, Sholes pays Phillips $35,000 for the contract, and gives Presley an extra $5000 for signing.

RE Elvis Presley's first record on RCA, "Heartbreak Hotel," is a national smash hit. It launches Presley on a phenomenal career as a record, movie, and personal appearance star. Sholes' $40,000 gamble turns into one of the greatest investments RCA ever made, since Presley earns the company many millions.

TV Louis G. Cowan, Inc., independent producer, and Walter Craig of the Norman, Craig & Kummel agency sell Revlon a show called *The $64,000 Question,* produced by Steve Carlin. The show gets high ratings and kicks off the big-money quiz era in television.

RA NBC Radio network introduces its major network program scheduling and selling format. It is called *Monitor,* a forty-hour show carried weekends only. Time is sold on the magazine concept—another prime example of network radio's efforts to find place for itself in booming TV period.

TV Westerns are hot this year and the next — *Gunsmoke* with Jim Arness; *Maverick* with James Garner; *Wyatt Earp; Lawman; Colt 45; Death Valley Days;* and *Texas Rangers. Gunsmoke* has the longest run.

TV Memorable series introduced this year include Walt Disney's *Mickey Mouse Club;* Phil Silvers as Sgt. Ernest G. Bilko; *The Lawrence Welk Show* (bigger than ever in 1977 on the syndicated circuit); *The Ernie Kovacs Show; Tennessee Ernie Ford Show; Alfred Hitchcock Presents;* and the long-time favorite of children, *Captain Kangaroo* (Bob Keeshan).

TV *Father Knows Best,* starring Robert Young and Jane Wyatt, which began in 1954, is cancelled by CBS in March, but so many viewers protest that NBC picks it up in August and the series becomes one of television's longest running situation comedies.

RE To the dismay of record dealers, and in spite of their protests, Columbia Records launches its Record Club. The club is highly successful. RCA Victor and Capitol follow with clubs of their own.

AP Walt Disney's dream, inspired by his visit to Tivoli Gardens in Copenhagen, becomes a reality when Disneyland, the nation's first theme park, opens July 17 in Anaheim, Calif. Each park area has a theme: Fantasyland, Frontierland, Main Street U.S.A., etc. Disney insists on absolute cleanliness and wholesome entertainment. "If you keep a place clean," he said,

"people will respect it. If you let it get dirty, they'll make it worse."

1956

TH Anti-trust suit against Shuberts culminates in consent decree requiring Shuberts to get out of the booking business and sell off twelve theatres in six cities within two years. Theatres include the St. James, the Imperial and the National on Broadway, among others.

TH It's a vintage year for musicals. *My Fair Lady,* based on Shaw's *Pygmalion,* is one of the all-time greats. Rex Harrison and Julie Andrews star. Lerner-Loewe score includes "I Could Have Danced All Night," and "On the Street Where You Live." The show had only one angel (CBS) and the gamble is still paying off. The year's other "class" musical is Frank Loesser's *Most Happy Fella,* adapted from Sidney Howard's drama, *They Knew What They Wanted.*

TH Paddy Chayefsky, fresh from his TV triumph with *Marty,* has his first play produced on Broadway. It's *Middle of the Night,* starring Edward G. Robinson and Gena Rowlands in a May-December romance.

TH *Long Day's Journey Into Night,* starring Fredric March, Florence Eldridge, and Jason Robards, Jr., wins the Pulitzer Prize. Eugene O'Neill wrote the searing story of his family in 1940, but forbade production until after his death. In sunny contrast to O'Neill is another show this season, Rosalind Russell in her biggest comedy hit, *Auntie Mame.*

MO There are 37,000,000 TV households this year and moviegoers have dwindled to less than half their number in 1946.

MO Film production is beginning to move away from Hollywood. More than 50 of some 290 films this year were produced out of the country, including two blockbusters — Mike Todd's Oscar-winning *Around the World in Eighty Days* and Cecil B. De Mille's remake of *The Ten Commandments,* his last and greatest movie.

MO Marilyn Monroe gives her best performance in *Bus Stop* under Josh Logan's direction. Logan also directs another William Inge play for the screen, *Picnic,* starring William Holden and newcomer Kim Novak.

MO Other interesting films this year are Otto Preminger's *The Man With the Golden Arm* with Frank Sinatra impressive as a drug addict; Marlon Brando in *The Teahouse of the August Moon;* and *Lust For Life* with Kirk Douglas in his best role, as Vincent Van Gogh, and Anthony Quinn's Oscar-winning performance as Gauguin.

MU After a period of relative quiet and unproductivity, Duke Ellington scores a major triumph at the Newport Jazz Festival, signs a new recording contract with Columbia, and, the following year, does a TV special on CBS, *A Drum Is a Woman*. The Duke reaches new peaks of popularity and successful creativity.

MO/TV This year witnesses a tremendous acceleration of the sale of pre-1948 movie features and shorts to TV — and the beginning of television's drive to acquire post-1948 films.

MO Elvis Presley's first film, *Love Me Tender*, a 20th Century Fox release, gets mixed-to-poor reviews, but is a tremendous box office hit. He makes a string of films in the next decade, most under contract to producer Hal Wallis. They are all big money-makers.

MU/RE Elvis's early smash hits include "Heartbreak Hotel," "I Was The One," "Don't Be Cruel," "Hound Dog," "Love Me Tender," "Are You Lonesome Tonight," "All Shook Up," "Teddy Bear," "Loving You" and many others. His albums are all huge sellers, and his films big money-makers.

MU/RE Beginning this year and continuing until he joins the Army in 1958, Elvis Presley firmly establishes himself as the "king" of rock and roll. He virtually establishes a style, originally called "rockabilly." It's a combination of southern black rhythm and blues, gospel, and country. In live performances, he plays his guitar waist-high, grinding and swiveling his pelvic area, as he sings with great emotion. He's a potent sex symbol to young females.

RE Magnecord markets the first stereo tape recorder.

RA Despite incredible growth of TV, more radio sets (8,332,077 — not counting auto radios) are sold than ever before in a single year.

CA Many carnivals are putting together spin-off units made up of a few rides and small shows to play shopping center parking lots. It's a profitable new form of "small" show business for the carnival operators.

CI This season is one of worst in circus history. The Clyde Beatty Circus goes into bankruptcy, but is reorganized and goes out to complete a dismal year. All smaller shows struggle against weather and economic handicaps.

CI John Ringling North decides to abandon tents completely. The Ringling Brothers and Barnum & Bailey Circus plays only in huge indoor arenas and ball parks.

TV Two new giveaway shows draw audiences: *Queen for a Day* and *The Price Is Right*. Also popular is the panel program *To Tell The Truth*.

TV The outstanding drama this year is Rod Serling's *Playhouse 90* production, *Requiem for a Heavyweight*, which wins a flock of Emmys, including one for star Jack Palance.

TV Ampex and CBS win a 1956 Emmy for their development and use of video tape, marking the turning point away from live television in prime network time.

TV *The Nat "King" Cole Show*, first regularly scheduled network variety TV program with a black star, begins on NBC. However, it only runs a year, and several years will pass before black artists achieve major success as series stars.

TV Dick Clark takes over a local Philadelphia deejay show, *Bandstand*, on WFIL-TV. The following year he goes network as *American Bandstand* on ABC, complete with teenagers dancing to rock and roll records.

1957

TH William Inge has another hit with *The Dark at the Top of the Stairs*, but the works of two other distinguished playwrights fare less well. Eugene O'Neill's tragedy, *A Moon for the Misbegotten*, starring Wendy Hiller and Franchot Tone, and Tennessee Williams' *Orpheus Descending* have brief runs. The Pulitzer Prize is won by Ketti Frings' *Look Homeward, Angel* with Anthony Perkins playing the young Thomas Wolfe. England's "angry young man," playwright John Osborne, has a hit with *Look Back In Anger* with Alan Bates and Kenneth Haigh.

TH Another vintage year for musicals. *West Side Story*, a modern teenage-gangland version of *Romeo and Juliet*, with score by Leonard Bernstein and Stephen Sondheim is a smash. Score includes "Tonight," "Maria" and "Somewhere." Critics acclaim its new projection of drama through dance. More conventional, but equally successful, is Meredith Willson's *Music Man* with Robert Preston at his vital best in his first musical role.

MO *The Bridge Over the River Kwai* wins Oscars as "best picture" and for director David Lean and actor Alec Guinness. Newcomer Joanne Woodward wins an Oscar for *Three Faces of Eve*. Supporting Oscars go to comedian Red Buttons and Miyoshi Umeki for *Sayonara*, starring Marlon Brando. Elvis Presley makes *Jailhouse Rock*, which gives him a multi-million record seller and a place on Hollywood's box office Top Ten.

MO Durable dancer Fred Astaire is still a leading man at fifty-eight — starring in *Funny Face* with Audrey Hepburn and in *Silk Stockings* with Cyd Charisse. Other musicals include *Pal Joey* with Frank Sinatra and Rita Hayworth; *Les Girls* with Gene Kelly, Kay Kendall, and Cole Porter's last film score; and Doris Day in *Pajama Game*.

TV Three major quiz shows are in the Top Ten in the ratings: *$64,000 Question* is number one; *Twenty-One* is number five and *The $64,000 Challenge* is number eight. *Gunsmoke*, *I've Got a Secret*, *Ed Sullivan*, *Lawrence Welk*, *Alfred Hitchcock* and *Studio One* are other shows in the group.

RA/TV/RE Arturo Toscanini dies at ninety. The NBC Symphony Orchestra, created especially for the great conductor, was under his direction from 1937 until his retirement in 1954.

TV New TV stars and series this year are Raymond Burr as *Perry Mason*, *Little Beaver*, and Richard Boone in *Have Gun, Will Travel*.

MO/TV By this year more and more major film producers move into TV production. MCA is turning out shows such as *Wagon Train*, *M Squad*, and *Tales of Wells Fargo* for NBC-TV and *Schlitz Playhouse* for CBS-TV. CBS is also buying shows from Desilu: *I Love Lucy*, *December Bride*; as well as *Perry Mason* from 20th Century Fox.

1958

TH The Lunts star in Friedrich Durrenmatt's grim drama, *The Visit*. It is one of their rare departures from comedy, and, many critics think, one of their most impressive performances. Another remarkable performance is that of Laurence Olivier — marvelously tacky in the title role of *The Entertainer*.

TH Other successful shows are poet Archibald MacLeish's *J.B.*, a Pulitzer Prize winner with Pat Hingle as Job; Ralph Bellamy as Franklin D. Roosevelt in *Sunrise at Campobello*; O'Neill's *A Touch of the Poet* with Helen Hayes, Kim Stanley, and Eric Portman; and *Two For the Seesaw* with Henry Fonda and Anne Bancroft.

MO The hit musical *Gigi* wins ten Oscars including "best picture," "best director" (Vincent Minnelli) and best song (the title tune). Cast includes Leslie Caron, Louis Jourdan, and Maurice Chevalier. The Lerner-Loewe score also features "Thank Heaven For Little Girls" and "I Remember It Well."

MO Film versions of two Broadway plays are popular this year. Elizabeth Taylor and Paul Newman star in Tennessee Williams' *Cat On a Hot Tin Roof*. English actors David Niven and Wendy Hiller win Oscars for *Separate Tables*. The "best supporting actress" award goes to Susan Hayward for her powerful portrayal of a condemned murderess in *I Want to Live*.

MO Mitzi Gaynor plays the Mary Martin role in Rodgers and Hammerstein's *South Pacific,* one of the all-time money-making musicals. Rossano Brazzi has the Ezio Pinza role.

MO/TV Paramount Pictures, which had sold only short subjects to TV, now releases its entire pre-1948 catalog of feature pictures for $50,000,000.

RE Technological improvements continue in the record industry, particularly in stereo areas. This year Fairchild and Electro-Voice produce new equipment to play back stereo records; John Koss develops stereo headphones; Shure Brothers develop moving magnet stereo pickup; London Records and Audio Fidelity both release their first high fidelity stereo disks.

RE/RA Disk jockeys, who have become a dominant force in radio, hold their first national convention.

RE At age eighteen, Phil Spector writes and produces his first rock hit, "To Know Him Is To Love Him" with the Teddy Bears. By the time he is twenty-one, Spector is the record industry's youngest millionaire, having written and produced a string of hits, among them "Spanish Harlem," one of the biggest sellers of 1960.

TV The District Attorney's office in New York City launches an investigation of the *Twenty-One* quiz show, when a contestant claims procedures are rigged. In November, show is cancelled and its producer is indicted for perjury.

TV One of TV's most successful shows, *The Burns and Allen Show,* ends as Gracie Allen retires. Burns continues a spectacularly successful career as a single.

TV *An Evening With Fred Astaire* is a smash video debut for the star, winning eight Emmys. Another exciting dance show is *Dancing: A Man's Game,* starring Gene Kelly, on *Omnibus.*

TV New video series this year include Craig Stevens as *Peter Gunn; The Donna Reed Show;* and *77 Sunset Strip.* Hallmark's *Hall of Fame* wins an Emmy with *Little Moon of Alban,* starring Julie Harris. Bob Hope wins the "Trustees Award" Emmy.

1959

TH For the first time a black playwright, Lorraine Hansberry, has a hit on Broadway, *A Raisin In The Sun,* with Sidney Poitier, Ruby Dee, Diana Sands, and Claudia McNeil. Other strong offerings are the moving story of Helen Keller, *The Miracle Worker,* with Anne Bancroft and Patty Duke; and Tennessee Williams' flamboyant *Sweet Bird of Youth* with Geraldine Page and Paul Newman.

TH Mary Martin opens late this year in Rodgers and Hammerstein's *The Sound of Music* ("Climb Every Mountain"). The critics are lukewarm, but audiences love it.

TH Ethel Merman has the best part of her career as Gypsy Rose Lee's mother in *Gypsy* with a memorable score by Jule Styne and Stephen Sondheim ("Everything's Coming Up Roses"). However, the Pulitzer Prize this year goes to another musical, *Fiorello!* with Tom Bosley as the exuberant mayor of New York City.

TH Two TV personalities are also "hot ticket" musical stars — young Carol Burnett in *Once Upon A Mattress* and Jackie Gleason in *Take Me Along,* a musical version of O'Neill's *Ah, Wilderness.*

MO In an effort to combat the effect of TV on their box office, films are spicier this year, albeit cautiously. Doris Day and Rock Hudson (a top box office figure) team for the first time in *Pillow Talk.* Jack Lemmon and Tony Curtis are in drag for Billy Wilder's *Some Like It Hot* with Marilyn Monroe. Cary Grant romances Eva Marie Saint in *North by Northwest,* one of Hitchcock's best. *Anatomy of a Murder,* with James Stewart, contains some blunt language.

MO Highly regarded actresses this year include Shelley Winters for her Oscar-winning performance in *The Diary of Anne Frank,* Elizabeth Taylor and Katharine Hepburn in *Suddenly Last Summer,* and Dorothy Dandridge in *Porgy and Bess* with Sidney Poitier, Pearl Bailey and Sammy Davis, Jr.

RA/TV Two government agencies, FTC and FCC, go after illegal practices in radio and TV. FTC claims record companies have been bribing disk jockeys and other radio station personnel to play records. FCC alleges illegal plugs on both radio and TV for many products. At the end of the year RCA Victor signs consent judgment with the FTC, stipulating it will not pay disk jockeys to play records, unless such payment is disclosed.

TV House Legislative Oversight Subcommittee holds hearings on rigged quiz shows. A number of contestants testify they were given answers in advance. CBS drops major big-money shows.

TV Charles Van Doren, English instructor at Columbia College, confesses to House Committee that producers of *Twenty-One* (on which he made fourteen appearances and won $129,000) gave him questions and answers in advance of shows. The dramatic confession gets nationwide attention and sounds the death knell for big-money quiz shows.

RE Most record companies now releasing LPs on stereo and mono. *Persuasive Percussion* is one of earliest hit stereo LPs.

TV Two great actors make their U.S. TV debuts and win Emmys: Laurence Olivier for *The Moon and Sixpence;* Ingrid Bergman in *The Turn of the Screw.* Also an Emmy winner is Harry Belafonte for his variety special on CBS, *Tonight With Belafonte.* He is the first black to win an Emmy.

TV *Bonanza,* a western starring Lorne Greene, is the first series to be telecast regularly in color. By 1965, practically the entire NBC schedule is being telecast in color. There are thirty-two western series on the three networks this year.

TV One of the most talked about 1959 shows is *The Untouchables* with Robert Stack as FBI agent Elliot Ness and Walter Winchell as narrator. Stack wins an Emmy. Another Emmy winner is *Huckleberry Hound,* one of the first animated cartoon series produced specially for television (by Hanna-Barbera).

1960

TH Richard Burton wins a Tony for his first musical role in Lerner and Loewe's *Camelot* with Julie Andrews and Robert Goulet. Tammy Grimes scores with Meredith Willson's *The Unsinkable Molly Brown. An Evening With Mike Nichols and Elaine May* showcases one of the all-time great comedy duos. Dick Van Dyke stars in the Tony-winning musical *Bye, Bye Birdie.*

TH Tad Mosel's *All The Way Home,* a dramatization of James Agee's *A Death In the Family,* starring Arthur Hill, wins the Pulitzer Prize but still loses money. Other quality dramas: Lillian Hellman's *Toys In the Attic* with Maureen Stapleton, Anne Revere and Jason Robards Jr.; and *A Taste of Honey* with Angela Lansbury and Joan Plowright. Laurence Olivier demonstrates his brilliant versatility by playing the elegant title role in *Becket,* and then switching to the earthy part of Henry II during the play's run.

TH Off-Broadway theatre this year features such innovative works as Edward Albee's *The Zoo Story,* Jean Genet's *The Balcony* and the long-running musical *The Fantasticks.*

MO Hollywood's entry into the more sexually permissive sixties is signaled by many films with more adult themes. The Oscar-winning film is Billy Wilder's *The Apartment* with Jack Lemmon and Shirley MacLaine. Burt Lancaster wins an Oscar for *Elmer Gantry.* Shirley Jones wins a "supporting actress" Oscar as a prostitute in the same film. Elizabeth Taylor wins the "best actress" award playing a call girl in *Butterfield 8.*

MO Hitchcock makes his most horrifying film, *Psycho,* this year with Tony Perkins in the title role. It's a smash. Perkins also stars in *Tall Story*, notable because it introduces Jane Fonda in her first film role. Making her last movie appearance is Judy Holliday in *Bells Are Ringing* with Dean Martin.

MO One of Hollywood's best science fiction films is made this year — George Pal's production of H.G. Wells' *Time Machine*, which wins a best "special effects" Oscar. Most popular film epics this year are *Spartacus* with Kirk Douglas and *Exodus* with Paul Newman.

MO Death comes to Mack Sennett and Clark Gable, still a leading man at fifty-nine years of age. Gable's last picture is *The Misfits* with Marilyn Monroe, which is released in 1961.

TV/MO RKO and Zenith team up to launch $10,000,000 test of on-air pay television in Hartford, Conn.

NC/MU An unknown Brooklyn teenager wins the Thursday Night Talent Contest at an obscure Greenwich Village nightclub, The Lion, with a sock rendition of Harold Arlen's "A Sleepin' Bee." Her name is Barbra Streisand.

RE Young Berry Gordy and his sister, Gwen, write "Lonely Teardrops." It's recorded by Jackie Wilson and becomes a big hit. Gordy quits his job on the assembly line at Ford Motor Company, to spend his full time writing and producing records.

RE Berry Gordy borrows $800 from his family and starts Motown Records in Detroit. Berry and his sister Loucye run the company. They are joined by record exec, Barney Ales. In the next ten years, Motown not only becomes one of the most phenomenally successful independent companies in record history, but actually creates a total music sound and style, "the Motown sound."

RE Motown hits, beginning with "Shop Around" this year, continue at an incredible pace. In 1962, the label has seven Top Ten records by Mary Wells and the Coutours; in 1963, Stevie Wonder, then thirteen, and Martha and the Vandellas hit with nine songs in the Top Ten and seventeen in the Top Forty. The streak continues through the sixties and beyond.

RE/RA House Legislative Oversight Subcommittee opens payola hearings; accuses WBZ-AM, Boston and KYW-AM, of accepting bribes to play records.

CA A greater degree of stability exists this year in the carnival business than ever before in carnival history. Shows have been cleaned up to a great extent with few exceptions. Fairs are booking established carnivals long in advance. Trade now calls the top carnivals "Sunday school" shows.

TV Network control of TV shows increases. In the new season, it's estimated networks control more than 75% of all shows they carry. In earlier years, ad agencies controlled network programming to great extent.

1961

TH Two English imports enrich the year. Young playwright Harold Pinter introduces unique new style in *The Caretaker*, starring Alan Bates, Robert Shaw and Donald Pleasence. Paul Scofield gives a Tony-winning performance in *A Man For All Seasons* as the martyred Thomas More. Other notable dramas are Tennessee Williams' *Night of the Iguana* with Bette Davis, Patrick O'Neal and Margaret Leighton; Zero Mostel in Ionesco's *Rhinoceros*.

TH The smash musical this season is *How To Succeed In Business Without Really Trying*, with Robert Morse and Rudy Vallee, and a Frank Loesser score ("I Believe In You"). Jean Kerr's *Mary, Mary*, starring Barbara Bel Geddes, is a non-musical comedy hit.

TH Among the most impressive off-Broadway dramas are Edward Albee's *The American Dream*; *The Death of Bessie Smith*; and *The Blacks*, which features in its cast James Earl Jones, Louis Gossett, Cicely Tyson, Godfrey Cambridge, Maya Angelou, playwright Charles Gordone, Roscoe Lee Browne and Raymond St. Jacques.

MO Both the New York Film Critics and the Academy give their "best picture" awards to the musical *West Side Story*, which also wins ten other awards, including "best supporting" Oscars to George Chakiris and Rita Moreno.

MO Other important movies are *The Hustler* with Paul Newman and Piper Laurie; *The Guns of Navarone* with Gregory Peck; Audrey Hepburn in Truman Capote's *Breakfast at Tiffany's*; *Splendor in the Grass*, with Natalie Wood and introducing Warren Beatty; and this year's epic, *El Cid*, with Charlton Heston and Sophia Loren.

MU/RE A customer comes into the North End Music Store in Liverpool, England, and asks for a record, "My Bonnie," by a group called The Beatles. Twenty-seven-year-old Brian Epstein, who manages the family store, does not have the record in stock but tells the customer he will try to find it. He discovers The Beatles are playing a local club, The Cavern, and the record was made a year earlier in Germany. He becomes the group's manager in January, 1962.

RE Bob Dylan gets his first recording opportunities, but strictly as backup harmonica player with a black blues singer, Victoria Spivey, as well as Lonnie Johnson, Carolyn Hester and other folk artists.

RE Israel Young, who runs Village Folk Center, promotes first Bob Dylan concert at Carnegie Chapter Hall, a large room (seating 200) on the fifth floor of the building housing Carnegie Hall. At $2 per ticket, concert is a flop. Only fifty people show up.

MU/RE *New York Times* music critic Robert Shelton catches new singer-songwriter Bob Dylan at Gerde's, a Village folk club, and writes a rave review of his performance. Shortly after, John Hammond, who had also given the first important recording opportunities to many black artists and other jazz and blues performers, signs Dylan to a Columbia Records contract. Dylan is twenty at the time.

RE/RA FCC okays stereophonic broadcasting by FM stations.

TV Class comedy series this year are *The Dick Van Dyke Show* with Mary Tyler Moore, and Bob Newhart's first show. Other new comedy programs include *Hazel* with Shirley Booth, and the *Andy Griffith Show* with Emmy-winning Don Knotts. Carol Burnett wins an Emmy for her performance on *The Garry Moore Show*.

TV Law and medicine are important series themes this year. *The Defenders*, created by Reginald Rose with E.G. Marshall and Robert Reed as a father and son legal team, garners 1961 Emmys. Medics include Vince Edwards as (Dr.) *Ben Casey* and Richard Chamberlain as *Dr. Kildare*.

1962

TH Edward Albee's first Broadway play is the powerful *Who's Afraid of Virginia Woolf?*, starring Uta Hagen and Arthur Hill. The play and stars all win Tonys. Barbara Harrison makes a vivid debut in Arthur Kopit's off-Broadway hit, *Oh Dad, Poor Dad, Mama's Hung You In The Closet And I'm Feelin' So Sad*, starring Jo Van Fleet.

TH Following Oscar Hammerstein's death, Richard Rodgers becomes his own lyricist for the first time and writes the score for *No Strings*, an innovative musical starring a black actress, Diahann Carroll, in an interracial romance with Richard Kiley. Rodgers moves his orchestra out of the pit, behind a scrim on stage, and integrates the musicians with the action. Hit song: "The Sweetest Sounds."

TH Elliott Gould is the star of the Harold Rome show, *I Can Get It For You Wholesale*, but the real news is a nineteen-year-old supporting player, Barbra Streisand as "Miss Marmelstein"; Zero Mostel is a smash in *A Funny Thing Happened On The Way To The Forum*, directed by George Abbott, score by Stephen Sondheim. England's Anthony Newley sings his own score ("What Kind Of Fool Am I") as star of *Stop The World I Want To Get Off*.

MO Gregory Peck wins an Oscar for *To Kill a Mockingbird*. Anne Bancroft and Patty Duke receive "best actress" and "best supporting" Oscars for their remarkable portrayals of the blind deaf mute Helen Keller as a child and her first teacher Annie Sullivan, in *The Miracle Worker*.

MO *Lawrence of Arabia*, one of the great adventure films, wins an Oscar for English director David Lean (his second) and one for "best picture." Peter O'Toole stars. The film introduces Egyptian actor Omar Sharif to U.S. audiences.

MO Other interesting films this year are *Lolita* with James Mason and Sue Lyons as his barely adolescent love interest — a shocker for its day; the low-budget, big box office horror movie *What Ever Happened to Baby Jane?*, teaming movie greats Bette Davis and Joan Crawford for the first time; and *How the West Was Won*, with an all-star cast, the first Cinerama saga. Musicals include *Gypsy* with Rosalind Russell instead of Merman, and *Music Man* with Robert Preston in his Broadway role.

MO Marilyn Monroe dies at the age of thirty-six under tragic circumstances.

RE Ted Taylor, leader of a group called the Dominoes, records his group at the Star Club in Hamburg, Germany with a simple one-microphone-hooked-into-a-tape-recorder setup — and he also records another group on the bill, The Beatles. In 1977, Larry Grosberg, producer-engineer, working technological magic, gets the tape in shape to release as an acceptable album. Thus, *The Beatles Live! at the Star-Club in Hamburg, Germany; 1962* reaches the international market and does well.

MU/RE After being turned down by English Decca and other record companies, Brian Epstein plays The Beatles' demo records for George Martin, producer at Parlophone, one of the EMI labels. Martin likes the group and signs them. Contract calls for royalty of 1c per side, i.e., 2c on a single record; 10c on a ten-song album. In October, "Love Me Do" is released, makes English charts and, in 1963, EMI increases their royalty to 2c per side.

RE Bob Dylan records first album for Columbia, called simply *Bob Dylan*. Produced by John Hammond, album costs only $400 to make, but also sells only 5000 copies.

RE Herb Alpert and Jerry Moss launch A&M Records, which develops into one of the most successful of the newer independents. In 1966, the company buys the old Charlie Chaplin film studio lot in Hollywood for its headquarters.

RE Phil Spector launches his Philles label. In quick succession he has million-selling singles with a group, The Crystals, on "There's No Other Like My Baby" and "He's a Rebel." In 1963, he continues his string of smashes with "Be My Baby" by the Ronettes, and many other big records.

TV Carol Burnett comes into her own this year with the Emmy-winning special *Julie (Andrews) and Carol at Carnegie Hall*, followed by another award-winner, *Carol and Company* in 1963.

TV The AT&T orbiting satellite, Telstar, makes its global television debut, as the means of "instant TV communication between the peoples of the world." The first shot beamed by Telstar, on July 10, is of an unfurled American flag.

TV/RA/MO/RE MCA gives up talent agency operations to concentrate on production, mainly in TV. It also acquires controlling interest in Decca Records, which in turn owns majority stock in Universal Pictures.

TV Colonel John Glenn's flight in orbit is the first space shot to be seen on TV. Cost of the coverage to networks is about $3,000,000. Nielsen estimates 135,000,000 people watch the history-making flight.

1963

TH Although Broadway has a bad year, regional theatre is booming. The Tyrone Guthrie Theatre opens in Minneapolis with Jessica Tandy and Hume Cronyn in the company, under the supervision of England's Sir Tyrone Guthrie. Morris Carnovsky is a memorable *King Lear* for the American Shakespeare Festival Theatre at Stratford, Conn.

TH Vivien Leigh does a Charleston and wins a Tony for her first performance in a musical, *Tovarich*. Hal Prince has another award-winning show in *She Loves Me*, a musical version of *The Shop Around The Corner* with a Tony-winning supporting performance by Jack Cassidy. *Oliver!*, an English import, starring Clive Revill as Fagin, is a solid hit.

TH Geraldine Page shines in an interesting revival of *Strange Interlude*, the marathon O'Neill drama. Albert Finney gives a powerful performance in John Osborne's *Luther*, an English import.

MO The most expensive film ever made to this date, *Cleopatra*, starring Elizabeth Taylor, Richard Burton and Rex Harrison, is released and 20th Century must gross well over $40,000,000 to break even. Stockholder disapproval brings about the departure of company president Spyros Skouras.

MO England sends over the first James Bond movie, *Dr. No*, with Sean Connery as the irresistible spy — part Casanova, part comic strip hero. Two other unusual foreign films register with the critics — Fellini's autobiographical *8-1/2* and Roman Polanski's *Knife in the Water*.

MO A bawdy British historical comedy, *Tom Jones*, starring Albert Finney, wins the "best picture" Oscar this year. Sidney Poitier is the first black to win a "best actor" Oscar in *Lilies of the Field*. Oscars also go to Patricia Neal and Melvyn Douglas (supporting) for *Hud*, starring Paul Newman as an anti-hero. Newman makes the Top Ten box office this year along with Jack Lemmon, whose 1963 film is *Irma La Douce* with Shirley MacLaine.

MO Among U.S. box office favorites are Doris Day, Frank Sinatra, Elvis Presley, and Ann-Margret. The last two score as a duo in *Viva Las Vegas*.

RE Bob Dylan's second album, *Freewheelin' Bob Dylan* is released in May. It includes "Blowin' In the Wind," "Hard Rain's A-Gonna Fall," "Don't Think Twice, It's All Right," and several others of Dylan's best songs. It sells several 100,000 copies and sparks new sales of his first album.

MU/RE At Newport Folk Festival this year Bob Dylan is recognized as the folk superstar of the period. Introduced by top folk singer, Joan Baez, he is the hit of the Festival.

RE/TV Ed Sullivan books Dylan for his TV show, but when CBS refuses to permit him to sing his "John Birch Society Talking Blues," Dylan refuses to do the show.

MU/RE By August, "She Loves You" by The Beatles is released, and their incredible popularity is demonstrated in London, when thousands of hysterical, crying, screaming fans jam the Palladium, where the group is doing a Sunday night concert, which is being televised.

TV First pictures from outer space are sent back to earth by astronaut Gordon Cooper.

TV The new *Danny Kaye Show*, a prolific 1963 Emmy winner, is the big news in variety shows. Other new shows are Judy Garland's problem-laden variety hour; *McHale's Navy* with Ernest Borgnine; and the controversial *East Side, West Side* dramatic series with George C. Scott and Cicely Tyson. One of its episodes, *Who Do You Have to Kill?* with James Earl Jones and Diana Sands, wins an Emmy.

TV Top Ten shows this season are: *Beverly Hillbillies*; the *Andy Griffith Show*; the *Red Skelton Hour*; *Candid Camera*; *Ben Casey*; *Bonanza*; the *Lucy Show*; the *Dick Van Dyke Show*; the *Danny Thomas Show*; and *Gunsmoke*. Also popular is Mitch Miller's *Sing Along With Mitch*.

1964

TH New York City's Lincoln Center Repertory Theatre is formed and — pending the construction of Lincoln Center — opens its first production in the Village at the ANTA Washington Square Theatre. Their first production is Arthur Miller's first play in nine years, *After The Fall*, with Jason Robards Jr. and Barbara Loden as a Miller-Marilyn Monroe pair. In December, another Miller play, *Incident at Vichy*, is presented.

TH One of the all-time memorable musicals, *Fiddler On The Roof*, opens with Zero Mostel as star and a haunting score by Sheldon Harnick and Jerry Bock ("If I Were a Rich Man," "Sunrise, Sunset"). Barbra Streisand becomes an instant star with her portrayal of Fanny Brice in *Funny Girl*. The Bob Merrill-Jule Styne score includes "People." Carol Channing wins a Tony for *Hello Dolly*, musical version of *The Matchmaker*, with a score by Jerry Herman.

TH Frank Gilroy's Pulitzer Prize-winning drama, *The Subject Was Roses*, stars Jack Albertson, former song and dance man, Martin Sheen and Irene Dailey. Richard Burton appears in a limited, but box office smash, version of *Hamlet*.

MO The Beatles make their first film, *A Hard Day's Night*. They follow it a year later with a second film, *Help!*

MU/RE After enormously successful national tours by The Beatles in England and on the Continent, plus continuing top record sales in England, EMI persuades two American record labels, Swan and Vee Jay, to release Beatles records which have been rejected by Capitol. (Capitol, owned by EMI, had first refusal rights on all EMI artists.) The Swan record, "She Loves You," makes the charts, and Capitol releases the group's next record, "I Want to Hold Your Hand" and backs it with $50,000 promotion campaign.

MU/RE Brian Epstein takes "short" money, $2400 for the Beatles' first appearance on U.S. television on the *Ed Sullivan Show*. He feels the TV exposure, plus the $50,000 Capitol push, which has been under way, will get the group off to a big start in America. But the group is already under way as proved by a reception committee of 10,000 teen-agers, who meet the group as they arrive at Kennedy Airport in February.

MU/RE It is estimated by the *Wall Street Journal* that sales of Beatles merchandise (t-shirts, other clothing, wigs, etc.) worldwide this year will amount to $100,000,000, with $50,000,000 accounted for by sales in the U.S. where Beatlemania has taken hold.

RE Bob Dylan's two Columbia albums this year (*Times They Are A-Changin'*, in January, and *Another Side of Bob Dylan*, in August) are both huge sellers. Dylan is now a full-fledged star with his album sales running in the millions.

RE Phillips introduces its tape cassette player.

FA More than 300 companies and sixty-six countries participate in the New York World's Fair, which opens in Flushing Meadows on April 22. About 27,000,000 visitors attend the Fair until its closing on October 18, but 40,000,000 had been expected. Fair's theme is "Peace Through Understanding." The Fair's most popular attractions are the industrial exhibits of Ford, Bell Telephone, General Electric, and others.

TV The top-rated new shows include *Bewitched* with Elizabeth Montgomery as a domesticated witch; *The Man From U.N.C.L.E.*, in the James Bond genre; David Janssen in *The Fugitive*; and a nighttime soap opera, *Peyton Place*, with Ryan O'Neal, Mia Farrow and Lee Grant.

1965

TH Comedies predominate this year, including Neil Simon's smash, *The Odd Couple* with Art Carney and Walter Matthau; Lauren Bacall in *Cactus Flower*; Henry Fonda in *Generation*.

TH Richard Rodgers works with a new lyricist, Stephen Sondheim, on a musical version of *Time of the Cuckoo*, starring Elizabeth Allen and Sergio Franchi, titled *Do I Hear A Waltz?* The previous year, Rodgers had become head man of Lincoln Center's new Music Theatre, featuring revivals of great musicals. Thus there are now separate Lincoln Center companies for ballet, opera, drama, concert music and musical comedy.

TH Liza Minnelli, nineteen, makes her Broadway debut in *Flora, The Red Menace* and wins a Tony. The Fred Ebb-John Kander score includes "A Quiet Thing." Richard Kiley also wins a Tony for his performance in the Tony-winning musical *Man Of La Mancha*. Book and score (including the memorable "The Impossible Dream") are by Mitch Leigh, Dale Wasserman, and Joe Darion.

TH The Royal Shakespeare Company of London presents the powerful Tony-winning drama, *The Persecution and Assassination of Marat as Performed By the Inmates of the Asylum of Charenton Under the Direction of the Marquis De Sade*, with Glenda Jackson, Ian Richardson, and Patrick Magee. It is the longest title ever listed on a U.S. theatre marquee.

TH New York City's Lincoln Center Repertory Theatre Company moves into its permanent headquarters, the Vivian Beaumont Theatre, and its original co-directors, Robert Whitehead and Elia Kazan, are replaced by Jules Irving and Herbert Blau, founders-directors of San Francisco's Actors Workshop.

TH Faye Dunaway becomes a star in the poetic off-Broadway production of *Hogan's Goat*. Jason Robards, Jr. stars in the two-man drama *Hughie*, first and only part of a planned series by Eugene O'Neill of eight plays.

MO The Supreme Court hands down a decision on censorship whereby most state and local film censorship boards are eliminated, including those in New York.

MO In September, President Lyndon Johnson signs the National Foundation on the Arts and Humanities Act, which includes a provision for the formation of an American Film Institute.

MO *Cat Ballou*, a western spoof, stars Jane Fonda and Lee Marvin who wins an Oscar for his performance. The "best actress" Oscar goes to England's Julie Christie in *Darling*. Other strong acting jobs are contributed by Rod Steiger in *The Pawnbroker*, Oskar Werner and Simone Signoret in *Ship of Fools*, and Shelley Winters who wins a "supporting" Oscar for *A Patch of Blue*, starring Sidney Poitier.

RE/MO A new noise-reduction unit is demonstrated by Ray Dolby. It is later widely used, not only in the record business but in high fidelity sound systems in motion pictures.

RE Prolific inventor William Lear introduces eight-track cartridge player for cars. RCA, Motorola, and Ford get behind the eight-track effort.

MU/RE The Beatles' tours in the U.S. are among the most successful in popular music entertainment history. Sid Bernstein, promoter, who presented them for the first time on their arrival in America at Carnegie Hall, this year presents them at Shea Stadium. His deal with Brian Epstein is that the group gets $100,000 or 65% of the gross, whichever is greater. The Beatles collect $180,000 for the show. The figure could have been double that, but Epstein would not permit a $10 top, insisting that tickets sell for $3 to $5.

TV For the first time, FCC accepts authority over Community Antenna Television (CATV). In early action, Commission freezes CATV microwave applications in major markets.

TV First commercial communications satellite, Early Bird, goes into orbit. Trans-Atlantic circuits are opened up for video usage.

TV Bill Cosby, destined to receive many Emmy awards, is the first black actor to co-star in a network dramatic series, *I Spy*, with Bob Culp. Other popular new series are *Hogan's Heroes*, Ben Gazzara in *Run For Your Life*; *Green Acres*, a bucolic comedy with Eddie Albert and Eva Gabor; and Barbara Stanwyck in a western, *The Big Valley*.

TV Barbra Streisand's Emmy-winning special, *My Name is Barbra*, is a smash. Other 1965 specials which rate Emmys are *Frank Sinatra: A Man and His Music*; the charming cartoon, *A Charlie Brown Christmas*; and the Lunts in *The Magnificent Yankee*.

TV Tremendous surge of color TV indicated by fact that set sales this year double sales of 1964. NBC airs 95% of its shows in color; CBS, 50%; and ABC, 40%. By fall 1966, all three networks will be virtually 100% color in evening time periods.

1966

TH It's a good year for musicals. Angela Lansbury wins a Tony for *Mame*, musical version of *Auntie Mame*, with Beatrice Arthur (TV's *Maude*) and Jerry Herman's score. Gwen Verdon stars in *Sweet Charity*, score by Dorothy Fields and Cy Coleman ("If My Friends Could See Me Now," "Hey Big Spender"). Mary Martin and Robert Preston are showmanship personified in *I Do! I Do!*, a two-character musical with score by Tom Jones and Harvey Schmidt ("My Cup Runneth Over").

TH Harold Prince's *Cabaret* is the musical of the year, winning eight Tony awards. The outstanding performer is Joel Gray as a sinister song and dance man in Berlin during 1930–31, just before the Nazi reign. The Ebb-Kander score includes the title song and "Willkommen."

TH Edward Albee's Pulitzer Prize-winning drama, *A Delicate Balance*, stars Jessica Tandy and Hume Cronyn. Other notable dramas are James Goldman's *The Lion in Winter*; Lee Remick in *Wait Until Dark*; British import *The Killing of Sister George* with Tony-winner Beryl Reid as a lesbian soap-opera actress; and Hal Holbrook's one-man show, *Mark Twain Tonight!*, another award winner.

TH Ellis Rabb's cooperative repertory company, A.P.A., which moves to Broadway in 1965, has a series of successful revivals, including *School For Scandal* with Rosemary Harris and Helen Hayes, who joins A.P.A. this year.

MO The old order changes and it's the era of the conglomerate. Paramount becomes a subsidiary of Gulf & Western Industries and Jack Warner, the "last tycoon," sells Warner Brothers to Seven Arts. Before the year is out, Warner-Seven Arts is taken over by Kinney National Service, Inc. The

following year, 1967, Transamerica Corporation absorbs United Artists.

MO Studios become financially deeply dependent upon the networks this year. In addition to making multi-million dollar sales of old films to TV, studios begin making feature films specially *for* TV. The first deal is made by NBC with MCA-Television for thirty two-hour films. The first, *Fame Is the Name of The Game*, airs in November. ABC-TV makes a similar arrangement with MGM.

MO Still riding the crest of the 1965 *Sound of Music*, Julie Andrews is number one at the box office, but Sean Connery's sex-charged James Bond pictures put him in second place and the trend is definitely towards more permissive film treatments — the kind you couldn't see on TV in 1966. A new sex symbol, Raquel Welch, makes an exciting debut as a prehistoric beauty in *One Million Years B.C.*

MO *Who's Afraid of Virginia Woolf?*, with Richard Burton and an Oscar-winning performance by Elizabeth Taylor, is a landmark picture in that it breaks several Production Code taboos with the use of (to 1966 audiences) "shocking" language. Refused a Seal, Jack Warner counters by advertising the picture as "Suggested for Mature Audiences" and insisting that theatre owners refuse admission to anyone under eighteen unless accompanied by parents.

MO Jack Valenti, new president of the Motion Picture Association of America (MPAA), adopts Warner's compromise as part of a new Production Code calling for voluntary classification of all films by studios rather than arbitrary one-standard censorship. The first movies tagged by MPAA as "Suggested For Mature Audiences" are two English films, both hits — *Georgie Girl* with Lynn Redgrave and Alan Bates, and *Alfie*, starring Michael Caine.

TV Strong new series include the surprise hit *Batman*; Jim Nabors as *Gomer Pyle*; *The Monkees*; a secret agent adventure, *Mission Impossible*; and TV's most successful science fiction show, *Star Trek* with William Shatner and Leonard Nimoy as the alien Mr. Spock.

TV Emmy-winning specials this year are Arthur Miller's *Death of a Salesman*, starring Lee J. Cobb; the Truman Capote-Eleanor Perry dramatization of *A Christmas Memory* with Geraldine Page; Bob Hope's annual Christmas tour of GI bases; and Sir John Gielgud in *Ages of Man*.

TV Falling victim to new California legislation outlawing pay-TV, Subscription TV operation folds.

MO/TV TV networks spend heavily in October to buy major post-1948 feature films. In one week this year, ABC-TV buys

thirty-two films from Paramount; CBS-TV purchases seventeen 20th Century Fox pictures; and NBC-TV acquires sixty-three MGM movies. Total cost runs to well over $90,000,000.

RE It's a breakthrough year for tape cartridges. Ampex and Norelco are among the manufacturers who introduce stereo cassette decks.

1967

TH Ingrid Bergman returns to Broadway in *More Stately Mansions*, an unfinished Eugene O'Neill play completed by director Jose Quintero. Comedy hit of the season is Robert Anderson's *You Know I Can't Hear You When The Water's Running*. It poses the then unbelievable question: will an actor actually take off his clothes on stage to get a part? The answer is "yes."

TH British playwright Harold Pinter has two hits on Broadway. His enigmatic *The Homecoming* is a multi-Tony winner. Cast includes Ian Holm, Paul Rogers and Vivien Merchant. *The Birthday Party* is also stimulating in the same mysterious fashion. Other British imports are Tom Stoppard's brilliant *Rosencrantz and Guildenstern Are Dead* and *Black Comedy* with Lynn Redgrave and Michael Crawford.

TH *Hallelujah Baby!*, a musical spanning the black experience in and out of show business over a sixty-year period, wins a Tony, as do its stars, Leslie Uggams and Lillian Hayman. Score: Comden, Green and Styne. Marlene Dietrich wins a special Tony for her Broadway debut in an S.R.O one-woman show. One of the biggest hits this year is an off-Broadway musical version of *Peanuts*, the Schultz cartoon strip. It's *You're a Good Man, Charlie Brown* with Gary Burghoff (Radar on TV's *M.A.S.H.*) in the title role and a score by Clark Gesner.

MO Violence abounds in films this year, including *Bonnie and Clyde*, gory saga of the depression-era killers, played by Warren Beatty and Faye Dunaway; Robert Altman's *Dirty Dozen*; and *In Cold Blood*, introducing former child star Robert Blake, as part of a murderous duo.

MO Mike Nichols' witty *The Graduate* makes a star of Dustin Hoffman, and, as of 1977, is the number eleven box office movie of all time. Other successful films this year are Paul Newman in *Cool Hand Luke*; Julie Andrews' musical, *Thoroughly Modern Millie*; Disney's full-length cartoon, *The Jungle Book*; John Wayne's *El Dorado*; and Robert Redford in *Barefoot in the Park*.

MO *Guess Who's Coming to Dinner* is a landmark film in interracial romance themes. Sidney Poitier's romance with the daughter of Katharine Hepburn and Spencer Tracy is accepted by practically all audiences. It's Tracy's last movie. He dies shortly after its completion. Hepburn wins the "best actress" Oscar. Poitier also stars in *In the Heat of the Night* with Rod Steiger who wins the "best actor" Oscar.

TV/MO CBS purchases Republic Studios, Hollywood acreage, and sound stages for $9,500,000 and changes its name to CBS Studio Center.

RE In the tape area there has been a struggle for supremacy among several configurations: four-track, eight-track cassettes, and reel-to-reel. By the end of this year, eight-track emerges as the dominant configuration. It accounts for $60,000,000 worth of sales, as opposed to $36,000,000 for four-track, $20,000,000 for reel-to-reel. Ten years later eight-track is totally dominant, with $687,000,000 in sales.

MU/RE The Beatles sign a new contract with EMI. The royalty in the new agreement is seventeen percent of the wholesale price in America, ten percent in the rest of the world. This, of course, is only the artist royalty and has nothing to do with what they are paid as writers and publishers of the songs they record.

RA *Billboard* launches first annual International Radio Programming Forum. Event becomes major yearly meeting of record and radio executives.

RE/CI After 100 years of ownership, Ringling family sells the Ringling Brothers and Barnum & Bailey Circus to Irvin Feld, former record retailer, early rock concert promoter and talent manager. Feld makes many changes in circus operation and policy. Eventually he sells the "big one" to conglomerate Mattel (major U.S. toy manufacturer), but Irvin and son Kenneth continue to produce the show with Richard Barstow as line producer and director.

AP Six Flags Over Georgia, another new theme park, opens near Atlanta. Initial investment is $13,700,000 and in the following ten years an additional $10,000,000 is spent on the park. In 1976, the park will draw 2,300,000 people.

TV The Public Broadcasting Act is signed on November 7 by President Lyndon Johnson. For the first time, a federal subsidy is provided for TV programming. The Act, recommended by the Carnegie Foundation, sets up a fifteen-man Public Broadcasting Corporation.

TV Movies are chalking up such strong ratings in prime time six nights a week that CBS and ABC decide to produce films on their own. Major Hollywood producers ask Justice Department to investigate possible anti-trust implications.

TV Topical humor is hot this year. *The Smothers Brothers Comedy Hour* debuts.

The Rowan and Martin Laugh-In special wins an Emmy and starts its phenomenal run as a series in January '68. Other audience favorites among new shows are Raymond Burr in *Ironsides* and *The Flying Nun* with Sally Field.

1968

TH Washington, D.C.'s historic Ford Theatre, where President Abraham Lincoln was assassinated by actor John Wilkes Booth, is reopened after 103 years.

TH James Earl Jones gives a powerful performance as the first black heavyweight champion, Jack Johnson, in Howard Sackler's *The Great White Hope* with Jane Alexander as his tragic white mistress. The play wins all three awards: Pulitzer, Tony and Critics' Circle. Charismatic performances are also given by Zoe Caldwell in *The Prime of Miss Jean Brodie;* Donald Pleasence as *The Man In the Glass Booth* by Robert Shaw; and Arthur Kennedy and Pat Hingle in Arthur Miller's *The Price.*

TH *Promises, Promises,* a musical version of the Jack Lemmon film *The Apartment,* is a hit. Jerry Orbach and Marian Mercer win Tonys. The Burt Bacharach-Hal David score includes "I'll Never Fall In Love Again." *Hair,* one of the first anti-establishment rock musicals, moves uptown from off-Broadway and is first to present a mass nude scene. The score by Gerome Ragni and James Rado and Galt MacDermot includes hit song "Aquarius." Rado and Ragni also appear in the cast which includes young Ben Vereen.

TH Audience participation is rampant now and during the late '60s. The *Hair* cast troops down, into — and sometimes over — the audience. The Living Theatre, which started at Yale, invites New York audiences to improvise dialogue, touch and be touched, as actual participants in on-stage happenings.

TH Comedy hits include Tony-winner Julie Harris in *Forty Carats,* Neil Simon's *Plaza Suite* with George C. Scott and Maureen Stapleton, and the bittersweet off-Broadway play about homosexuals, *The Boys In The Band.*

MO Nudity, homosexuality, more explicit heterosexuality, and violence abound this year. Nevertheless, the "best picture" Oscar goes to *Oliver,* a wholesome family musical.

MO The MPAA devises a new rating system, thereby acknowledging that films are no longer designed for every moviegoer. The categories: G, for general audiences; PG, parental guidance suggested; R, restricted, no one under seventeen admitted unless accompanied by parent or guardian; X, no one under eighteen admitted at all.

However, it is still voluntary and MPAA has no control over "sexploitation" producers, or non-members.

MO Cliff Robertson wins the "best actor" Oscar for his role as a mentally retarded young man in *Charly.* For the second time in Academy history, a "best actress" Oscar is split between two performers: Katharine Hepburn (for the third time) in *The Lion in Winter,* and Barbra Streisand's debut in *Funny Girl.* "Supporting" Oscars go to Jack Albertson for *The Subject Was Roses* (with Patricia Neal) and to Ruth Gordon, as — literally — a witch in Roman Polanski's satanic hit, *Rosemary's Baby,* with Mia Farrow.

MO More and more pictures are aimed at young audiences, who constitute 48% of the market. Youth favorites this year include two science fiction films: Kubrick's landmark *2001: A Space Odyssey* and *Planet of the Apes;* as well as Zeffirelli's *Romeo and Juliet,* and *Bullitt* with Steve McQueen and the definitive auto chase scene. Other interesting films are *Rachel, Rachel,* starring Joanne Woodward and directed by her husband Paul Newman; and *The Odd Couple,* with Jack Lemmon and Walter Matthau.

MU/RE The Beatles release their first single, "Hey, Jude," backed with "Revolution" on their own label, Apple. It's one of the biggest hits of the year. The members of the group, however, continue in individual projects as well.

MU CBS files suit against ASCAP seeking the right to pay the performing rights society only for such of its music as the network uses, rather than the blanket license now in effect. Blanket license permits user to play anything in ASCAP repertoire, but network must pay percentage of its gross earnings for the right.

TV/RA/MU Broadcasters, who created BMI some twenty years earlier, now claim BMI's demands for performance rights payments are exorbitant, and break off negotiations to establish new rates. However, before the end of the year broadcasters settle for a ten percent-and-up increase.

TV Comedy and variety shows dominate ratings with such stars as Lucille Ball, Dean Martin, Rowan and Martin, Carol Burnett, Red Skelton, Jim Nabors, Andy Griffith, Jackie Gleason, Art Carney and Bob Hope. Popular variety specials star Fred Astaire, Elvis Presley, Frank Sinatra, Barbra Streisand and Ann-Margret.

TV Among the most interesting new shows are *Julia* with Diahann Carroll as a chic nurse (a far cry from TV's first black female series star, *Beulah,* played during the early '50s by Louise Beavers, Hattie McDaniel and Ethel Waters at various times); Hope Lange in *The Ghost and Mrs. Muir*; and *The Name of the Game*.

TV This is the first year in which American-made color TV sets outsell black and white receivers, 6,000,000 to 5,500,000.

TV FCC approves over-the-air pay television as a permanent service, even though WHCT-TV, UHF channel 18 experiment in Hartford, Conn., which began in 1962, is faring poorly. WHCT-TV ends experiment, January, 1969.

TV/MO/RE/RA Creative Management Associates and General Artists Corporation merge to form talent agency challenging the William Morris Agency as industry's biggest booking office.

1969

TH Two new black playwrights score with off-Broadway productions: Lonnie Elder III's *Ceremonies in Dark Old Men* and Charles Gordone's angry *No Place To Be Somebody* which wins the Pulitzer Prize for drama.

TH A "sleeper" musical, *1776*, with book, music and lyrics by ex-high school teacher Sherman Edwards, wins the Tony and Drama Critics' awards. Katharine Hepburn scores a personal triumph in her first musical, *Coco*, based on the life of the famous French designer, with score by Alan Lerner and Andre Previn. *Oh Calcutta!*, a revue featuring total nudity by some members of the cast, is a box office, albeit not a critical, hit.

TH Woody Allen and Diane Keaton team for the first time in Allen's *Play It Again, Sam*, in which Humphrey Bogart's ghost advises Allen on ways to "play it cool" with women.

MO Movie attendance is sharply down this year and the studios are still emphasizing violence and sex in an effort to sell their product. *Midnight Cowboy* starring Dustin Hoffman and Jon Voight is the first X-rated picture to win an Oscar. The super-violent *The Wild Bunch*, directed by Sam Peckinpah, is big box office as are *Bob and Carol and Ted and Alice*; Swedish porno film *I Am Curious Yellow*; and *Easy Rider*, starring Peter Fonda, which makes a star of Jack Nicholson in a supporting role.

MO Two performers destined to be superstars make their film debuts this year. Liza Minnelli, daughter of Vincent Minnelli and Judy Garland, stars in *The Sterile Cuckoo*; Woody Allen displays his unique brand of comedy in *Take the Money and Run*.

MO Robert Redford becomes a full-fledged star in *Butch Cassidy and the Sundance Kid* (co-starring Paul Newman), as of 1977 the number fourteen all-time box

office hit. Other solid grossers are *Goodbye, Columbus* starring Richard Benjamin and introducing Ali MacGraw; Richard Burton in *Anne of the Thousand Days*; *Last Summer*, introducing Richard Thomas (later star of TV's *The Waltons*); and *Cotton Comes to Harlem*.

MO English actress Maggie Smith wins an Oscar for *The Prime of Miss Jean Brody*. Veteran superstar John Wayne wins his first Oscar in *True Grit* in which he does a superb parody of his long-time cowboy career. Supporting Oscars go to Gig Young for *They Shoot Horses, Don't They?*, starring Jane Fonda in a bitter drama about marathons in the thirties; and to Goldie Hawn in her first film role in *Cactus Flower*, starring Ingrid Bergman.

MU/RE *Billboard* holds its first annual International Music Industry Conference (IMIC). IMIC quickly becomes, and continues to be, the major summit meeting of top music/record industry leaders.

MU Rock music festivals become incredible "happenings." Of a number of such events held this year, the most exceptional is the Woodstock Festival held on Max Yasgur's farm in Bethel, N.Y. (fifty-five miles from Woodstock). Audience estimates vary from 300,000 to a half million young people. They spend a weekend getting high on grass and various drugs, making love in the open, and occasionally listening (if they're within hearing distance) to one of the parade of rock groups and singers on the bill.

MU/RE Elvis Presley had been comparatively quiet for some time prior to this year, but Col. Tom Parker now launches him on what might be called Phase 2 of a phenomenal career. This year he has three hit singles, "In the Ghetto," "Don't Cry, Daddy," and "Clean Up Your Own Backyard." He also has three gold albums. His concerts break records everywhere.

AP/RA In a diversification move, the Taft Broadcasting Company builds a theme park, King's Island, near Cincinnati, and plans another, King's Dominion, in Virginia.

MO/TV/RE/NC An overdose of sleeping pills ends the tragic life of Judy Garland.

TV An estimated 700,000,000 (125,000,000 in the U.S. alone) viewers watch man's first lunar landing on July 20. Neil Armstrong's "first step" on the moon is telecast by all three networks and seen around the world.

TV Comedy continues strong this year. Among the most popular new shows are *The Bill Cosby Show*, and *Marcus Welby, M.D.*, marking a big comeback for Robert Young. Highly lauded specials include *Teacher, Teacher* about retarded children,

and *Artur Rubinstein*, the fabulous concert pianist.

TV There are now three late-night network talk shows — Johnny Carson, NBC; Dick Cavett, ABC; and Merv Griffin, CBS. However, only Carson will survive. Griffin becomes a syndicated series host. Cavett ultimately returns to television in 1977 with a late-night interview show on public television. Mike Douglas continues his successful daytime talk show in syndication.

TV National Educational Television (NET) has an impressive lineup for its first year, highlighted by the British import *The Forsyte Saga*, forerunner of the mini-series trend; and the $8,000,000 series which revolutionized pre-school children's education, *Sesame Street*. The award-winning children's series is carried daily by 250 public TV stations. The Muppets, including Big Bird and puppet Kermit the Frog, debut on this show.

1970

TH Sada Thompson wins a flock of awards in *The Effect of Gamma Rays on Man-in-the-Moon Marigolds* by Paul Zindel, who later wins the Pulitzer Prize. Other successful plays are *Child's Play* with Tony-winning Fritz Weaver and Pat Hingle; Neil Simon's *The Gingerbread Lady* with Tony-winning Maureen Stapleton; and British imports *Sleuth* and David Storey's *Home* with brilliant performances by John Gielgud and Sir Ralph Richardson.

TH Hal Linden gives a Tony-winning performance ('70-'71) in *The Rothschilds*. Danny Kaye returns to Broadway, after twenty-nine years, in Richard Rodgers' *Two By Two*.

TH Lauren Bacall makes a vibrant musical debut, winning a Tony for *Applause* (based on the movie *All About Eve*), with score by Lee Adams and Charles Strouse. Hal Prince's innovative *Company* with Stephen Sondheim's witty, sophisticated score, wins Critics' Circle Awards.

MO Economy is the catchword for Hollywood in 1970. Production is down both in the U.S. and abroad. Warners and MGM shut down their New York offices. MGM stuns the industry by auctioning off all its props, costumes, and furnishings, including Judy Garland's ruby red slippers from *The Wizard of Oz* and Fred Astaire's top hat. The studio also sells its fabled Lot 3, where the *Tarzan* pictures were made, to a housing developer.

MO Significant U.S. film debuts are made this year by Robert De Niro in the low-budget *Bloody Mama* with Shelley Winters; Peter Boyle in *Joe*. Jack Nicholson becomes an established star in another low-budget film, *Five Easy Pieces*, which wins the New York Film Critics award. James

Earl Jones repeats his masterful performance in *The Great White Hope.*

MO War movies are big box office this year, particularly the Oscar-winning film *Patton,* starring George C. Scott as the World War II General; and *M*A*S*H,* Robert Altman's black comedy about the Korean War, which makes stars of Elliott Gould and Donald Sutherland. Scott was awarded the "best actor" Oscar but refused to accept it at the 1971 ceremonies.

MO Hits of the year are *Love Story* with relatively unknown stars Ryan O'Neal and Ali MacGraw, as of 1977 the number nine all-time box office champ; and the number fifteen film *Airport,* an all-star spectacular, which wins Helen Hayes a "best supporting actress" Oscar. Dustin Hoffman gives a versatile performance in *Little Big Man,* Arthur Penn's western spoof; and Disney has still another hit with *The Aristocats.* *Woodstock,* a wild rock concert documentary, is also a big grossing movie.

MO/RE The Beatles make another film, *Let It Be,* an album, and a hit single of the same title. Nevertheless rumors that the group will split continue and in 1971, they indeed make an official announcement that they have decided to pursue individual careers.

RE RCA and Motorola introduce another technological advance: a compatible, eight-track cartridge system. It is called Quad 8.

RA Two FM stations (WOOD, Grand Rapids, Mich. and WEAT, West Palm Beach, Fla.) lead their individual markets in share of audience. It is the first time FM stations have accomplished this against AM opposition.

RA Black civil rights groups step up their demands for recognition, insisting stations be forced to hire more blacks. Black-oriented AM station WVON, Cicero, Ill. is sold for $9,000,000, biggest sale for station of its type in broadcasting history.

TV There are now 59,300,000 TV sets in American homes, of which 25,300,000 are color sets.

TV There are now 3,700,000 American homes which subscribe to one or another CATV system.

TV Zenith pay-TV system, Phonevision, is the first to get official FCC approval.

TV CBS-TV drops Jackie Gleason and Red Skelton, but Skelton is picked up by NBC-TV. The CBS move is dictated by the network's desire to go after younger audiences.

TV *The Flip Wilson Show* is a hit of the new season. It's the first weekly network variety show starring a black comic to score consistently high ratings.

TV A one-minute commercial on top prime-time shows now runs about $65,000. Among programs charging this are *Mission Impossible, Mayberry RFD,* and *Laugh-In.*

MU/RE Janis Joplin, rock singer phenomenon, is found dead in a Hollywood motel room at twenty-eight.

1971

TH Dramatic blockbuster this year is David Rabe's bitter satire *Sticks and Bones* about a blind Vietnam veteran. Produced by Joseph Papp's New York Shakespeare Festival Public Theatre, the play wins both the Critics' Circle and Tony Awards as "best play." Tonys also go to Sada Thompson in George Furth's *Twigs;* Cliff Gorman as tragic comedian Lenny Bruce in *Lenny;* and Mike Nichols as director of Neil Simon's *Prisoner of Second Avenue* with Peter Falk and Lee Grant.

TH An opulent, unusual musical, *Follies,* wins the Critics' Circle Award. Sondheim's score is suitably nostalgic and star Alexis Smith wins a Tony for her first performance in a musical. In the fall, another hit musical, *Two Gentlemen From Verona* (based on Shakespeare's comedy and produced by Joseph Papp) wins a Tony. Ruby Keeler, at sixty, taps up a box office storm in a revival of *No, No Nanette.*

TH *Hair* director Tom O'Horgan creates a flamboyant stage version of *Jesus Christ Superstar* by Andrew Lloyd Weber and Tim Rice, a rock opera originally released as a record album in England. Another musical this year is also based on the life of Christ — *Godspell,* an off-Broadway production.

TH Other quality offerings this year include the Royal Shakespeare Company of England's presentation of Harold Pinter's *Old Times* with Mary Ure, Rosemary Harris and Robert Shaw; Edward Albee's *All Over* with Colleen Dewhurst and Jessica Tandy; and Paul Zindel's *And Miss Reardon Drinks a Little* with Julie Harris and Estelle Parsons.

TH Off-Broadway flourishes. John Guare's *The House of Blue Leaves* receives the Critics' Circle's "best American play" award.

MO Excessive violence is the keynote of many hit movies this year, including *The French Connection,* which wins five Oscars ("best picture"; "best actor," Gene Hackman; "best director," William Friedkin, etc.); Dustin Hoffman in *Straw Dogs;* Tom Laughlin's *Billy Jack;* and *Willard,* a low-budget horror film about man-killing rats. One of the most violent and sex-oriented films is *A Clockwork Orange,* Stanley Kubrick's horrific image of the future.

MO Sexual candor dominates in Mike Nichols' *Carnal Knowledge,* starring Jack Nicholson; *Klute,* with Jane Fonda's Oscar-winning performance as a call girl; and, from England, a tasteful study of homosexuality, *Sunday, Bloody Sunday* with Glenda Jackson and Peter Finch.

MO This is the first year in which hardcore pornographic movies establish themselves as "legitimate" entertainment in nation's larger cities. Leading porno film makers are Alex de Renzy, producer of *Censorship in Denmark, A History of the Blue Movie, Powder Burns* and *Group Encounter.* Bill Osco is also a major maker in this area with *Hollywood Blue, Harlot, Flesh Gordon* and others.

MO Black-oriented films are gaining more and more success at the box office as Hollywood finds a new audience. *Shaft,* Gordon Park's second film, makes a star of Richard Roundtree as the tough, super cool title character. Isaac Hayes' title theme wins an Oscar. Melvin Van Peebles' *Sweet Sweetback* is a big money-maker.

RE Congress passes legislation enabling manufacturers to copyright records for seventy-five years. It is part of a strong anti-piracy bill. In the next several years a number of states also pass anti-piracy legislation. The Record Industry Association of America campaign, spearheaded by president Stan Gortikov, is credited with bringing about this important action on the legislative front.

RE Again a configuration war looms, this time in quadraphonic recording. CBS and Sony introduce the SQ record, a compatible four-channel system, as opposed to the previously introduced eight-track, RCA-Motorola system.

RA As rock music becomes the basic format for an increasing number of stations, the FCC warns broadcasters against playing records with lyrics that might "glorify the use of illegal drugs." Songs such as "Acid Queen" and "Cocaine Blues" are cited as examples.

AP On October 1, Disney opens Walt Disney World in Florida. It is an extension of the original theme park idea, and becomes known as "the vacation kingdom of the world."

NC Academy of Variety and Cabaret Artists is formed in Las Vegas to bring attention to creative talent working in the area, and, not too coincidentally, to form the basis for a network television special.

TV A re-evaluation of demographic studies results in a record number of shows (some high-rated) being dropped by the networks, particularly CBS. Attempting to appeal to younger, more affluent viewers, programs cancelled include *Lawrence*

Welk Show, Jim Nabors Show, Andy Griffith Show, Danny Thomas, Beverly Hillbillies, Green Acres, and even the *Ed Sullivan Show,* which has had a twenty-three year run.

TV Cable television (CATV) now has over 5,000,000 customers in 2500 towns and smaller cities across the land, but there is still an FCC freeze on cable service in some of the larger cities.

RE/RA/TV/MO General David Sarnoff dies at eighty.

1972

TH Joseph Papp continues to present his New York Shakespeare Festival performance for free in Central Park. Stacy Keach is a moving *Hamlet* with James Earl Jones as Claudius. Regional theatres benefit from the National Endowment for the Arts' generous allotment of almost $3,000,000.

TH *That Championship Season* by Jason Miller and produced by Joseph Papp's New York Shakespeare Festival, wins a Tony and moves up from off-Broadway. Miller later wins a Pulitzer Prize. Alan Bates gives a powerful Tony-winning performance in British playwright Simon Gray's *Butley.* Julie Harris wins her Tony for *The Last of Mrs. Lincoln.*

TH The most successful comedy is Neil Simon's *The Sunshine Boys* with Sam Levene and Jack Albertson. Unsuccessful are works by two of America's best playwrights — Tennessee Williams' *Small Craft Warnings* and Arthur Miller's *The Creation of the World and Other Business.*

TH *Pippin,* a joyous costume musical set in the days of Charlemagne, stars John Rubinstein and Ben Vereen, who wins a Tony for his outstanding performance. Other successful musicals include Micki Grant's *Don't Bother Me, I Can't Cope,* about the black experience; *Grease,* a rock and roll tribute to the fifties; and Robert Morse in *Sugar,* a musical version of the movie *Some Like It Hot.* Phil Silvers wins a Tony for his revival of the 1962 hit *A Funny Thing Happened on the Way to the Forum.*

MO Francis Ford Coppola's violent *The Godfather* is the Oscar-winning film and the biggest money-maker of the year. As of 1977, it's the number three all-time box office hit. The movie makes a star of Al Pacino and wins an Oscar for Marlon Brando (as an aging Mafia Don) which he refuses. The picture also draws critical acclaim for newcomer James Caan.

MO Liza Minnelli wins an Oscar for the R-rated musical *Cabaret,* as do director Bob Fosse and supporting actor Joel Gray. The most moving moment in all Oscar history happens this year (at the presentation of the 1971 awards) when eighty-three-year-old Charlie Chaplin is finally honored by the industry for the "humor and humanity" he gave to films for more than fifty years.

MO Black films continue to be big box office. Quality black movies this year include *Sounder* with Cicely Tyson and Paul Winfield; Diana Ross as Billie Holliday in *Lady Sings the Blues;* and *Buck and the Preacher* starring Sidney Poitier and Harry Belafonte. Other successful black films are *The Legend of Nigger Charley* with Fred Williamson; *Shaft's Big Score;* the controversial *Superfly* with Ron O'Neal as an enigmatic drug "pusher-hero;" *Blacula* and *Blackenstein.*

MO Successful movies this year include new matinee idol Robert Redford in *The Candidate;* Barbra Streisand and Ryan O'Neal in *What's Up Doc?;* Hitchcock's thriller, *Frenzy;* Clint Eastwood in the violent *Dirty Harry;* the latest James Bond, *Diamonds Are Forever;* Woody Allen in *Play It Again, Sam;* and *Deliverance* with Jon Voight and Burt Reynolds.

MO In a year when pornographic films, such as *Deep Throat,* find wide audience acceptance, it's not surprising that the first X-rated cartoon — *Fritz the Cat* — scores at the box office.

MU/RE Elvis Presley continues his string of hit singles and albums this year and in the year following. Among his big sellers are: *Elvis at Madison Square Garden, Elvis Now, I Got Lucky,* and *Burning Love and Hits From His Movies.* Biggest album is the recording of his TV special, in 1973, *Aloha from Hawaii Via Satellite.* It does more than $1,000,000 in tape sales alone.

RE RCA, Panasonic, and the Japan Victor Company introduce a four-channel discrete disk system. Sansui introduces a quadraphonic matrixed disk.

MU/RE Jamaican Chris Blackwell releases reggae singer Bob Marley on Blackwell's Island label. It represents the first international distribution for the reggae star and creates a minor trend toward reggae music. In a few years, name acts like Barbra Streisand, Johnny Nash and others are recording Marley songs and Marley and his group, the Wailers, are the top reggae act in the country.

RE RCA releases its first two quadraphonic records: *Love Theme from the Godfather* with the Hugo Montenegro Orchestra, and *The Fantastic Philadelphians.*

RA What critics call "audio pornography" erupts as radio programming with sex-slanted talk shows achieve high audience shares. Most successful of these shows is that of Bill Ballance on KGBS, Los Angeles. Female listeners talk with Ballance about intimate details of their sex and love lives. Other major radio markets feature similar shows and win audiences.

TV/RA Frank Stanton retires as president of CBS. Working with William Paley, Stanton is credited with CBS's success to a great degree. He is considered to have been one of the most statesmanlike executives in broadcasting history.

TV *All in the Family,* an Emmy-winning situation comedy in 1971, deals with heretofore untouchable adult subjects such as homosexuality, impotence, and bigotry, and becomes the top-rated show of the year. It leads the way to a new "maturity" and/or "permissiveness" in television entertainment. Producer is Norman Lear, and stars are Carroll O'Connor as Archie Bunker and Jean Stapleton as his wife, Edith.

TV The trend towards ethnic humor and "adult" themes in situation comedy is also reflected in two other new shows, *Sanford and Son,* with Redd Foxx as a bigoted black; and *Maude* starring Beatrice Arthur. Both are in the Top Ten. One of the most sophisticated situation comedies is also a critic's favorite, *The Mary Tyler Moore Show,* which debuted in 1970.

1973

TH More than a third (twenty) of shows produced on Broadway this year are revivals. One of the most successful is *Irene,* which chalked up the longest run of its day in 1919. Debbie Reynolds becomes a new Broadway star in *Irene.* Score includes "Alice Blue Gown." *Irene* is the first play presented in the new Minskoff Theatre on the site of the old Hotel Astor.

TH Tony-winning musicals this year are Hal Prince's *A Little Night Music* with Stephen Sondheim's score ("Send In the Clowns"), starring Glynis Johns ('72–'73 season); and *Raisin,* a musical version of *Raisin In the Sun,* starring Tony winner Virginia Capers ('73–'74).

TH The "best play" Tony goes to The Negro Ensemble Company's *The River Niger* by Joseph A. Walker, which moves up to Broadway in March. British import, *The Changing Room* by David Storey wins a Critics' Circle Award for best foreign play. Off-Broadway *Hot L Baltimore* by Lanford Wilson, produced by The Circle Theatre Company, is the Critics' choice as best American play.

TH Musical Tonys also go this year to Christopher Plummer for *Cyrano;* the score of Lerner and Loewe for *Gigi,* based on their hit movie; and Tommy Tune, "best supporting actor," in *Seesaw,* with direction and choreography by Michael Bennett.

TH For the first time, road show companies make more money than Broadway attractions. Subscription theatre clubs — such as Kennedy Center in Washington, D.C.; Fisher Theatre in Detroit; Music Center, Los Angeles — guarantee solid box office returns. New York City companies — off and on Broadway — also find security in subscription plans — Circle in the Square, New Phoenix, New York Shakespeare Festival at Lincoln Center, Negro Ensemble, etc.

TH Lincoln Center hands over operational reins of the Vivian Beaumont Theatre and the Forum Theatre to Joseph Papp and his New York Shakespeare Festival company. Papp promptly renames the Forum, the Mitzie E. Newhouse Theatre, which henceforth features Shakespeare year-round. Mrs. Newhouse donated $1,000,000 to Papp's fund-raising drive for the new playhouse.

MO The landmark picture this year is *Last Tango in Paris* starring Marlon Brando, directed by Italy's Bernardo Bertolucci. Although acclaimed as a masterpiece by many critics, the film — the most erotic movie to date featuring a major star — is the object of legal action seeking to ban it in many communities. In June, the Supreme Court declares that community, not national, standards should be used to define "obscenity."

MO Hard-core pornographic films are now quite frequently big box office. Damiamo Films' *Deep Throat*, starring Linda Lovelace, is the most successful of all. *Variety* credits it with distributor rentals of $4,000,000, a figure surpassing hundreds of important straight movies. Two other porno hits are *The Devil In Miss Jones* (distrib. rental, $2,000,000) and Mitchell Brothers' *Behind the Green Door*, (distrib. rental, well over $1,000,000).

MO One of the top superstar incomes for year is racked up by Marlon Brando. His deal for 10% of the gross on United Artists' porno-flavored *Last Tango In Paris* earns him $1,600,000. In the previous year, his percentage deal of *The Godfather* had earned him $3,000,000.

MO Violence and adventure dominate the box office. *The Poseidon Adventure*, about a ship overturned at sea, is a big money-maker, as are Sam Peckinpah's wild *The Getaway* with Steve McQueen and Ali MacGraw; *Live and Let Die*, with Roger Moore as the new James Bond; and the first *Kung Fu* imports.

MO Glenda Jackson wins her second Oscar for *A Touch of Class*, a comedy. Jack Lemmon wins the "best actor" award for *Save the Tiger*. Quality performances are given by England's Laurence Olivier and Michael Caine in *Sleuth*. The outstanding musical is *Jesus Christ Superstar*.

MO Among remarkable performances by

new actors and directors this year are Robert De Niro in *Bang the Drum Slowly* and Martin Scorsese with his *Mean Streets;* Terrence Mallick's *Badlands* with Martin Sheen; and Al Pacino in *Serpico*. Woody Allen has another satirical hit with *Sleeper*.

MO New young directors click this year. George Lucas scores with *American Graffiti;* Peter Bogdanovich introduces child star Tatum O'Neal, who wins an Oscar for *Paper Moon,* starring her father Ryan O'Neal. *American Graffiti* is the number twelve all-time box office champion as of 1977.

MO Top box office films include the Oscar-winning *The Sting* (number seven all-time box office champ as of 1977) with Robert Redford and Paul Newman; and *The Way We Were* with Redford, Barbra Streisand, and an Oscar-winning title theme by Marvin Hamlisch.

MU/RE Clive Davis, president of Columbia Records who has led the company to new high sales, is suddenly fired. Davis was indicted for failing to report $8,800 in income, in a year in which he did report $320,000. He was fined $10,000 and cleared of all other charges. In June, 1974 (after writing a successful book on the record industry) he launches Arista Records and builds it into an important, profitable factor in the industry.

RA The sex-slanted talk shows — variously called "audio pornography" and "topless radio" — bring a mounting storm of protest from listeners. The FCC fines station WGLD-FM in Oak Park, Ill., $2000 for broadcasting two such shows the Commission calls "obscene." The jockeys and stations carrying these shows tone them down considerably.

TV The Watergate hearings telecasts, carried by all three networks, are the programming sensation of the season. Surveys show that people watched the telecasts for a total of more than a billion and a half hours on the three networks alone; plus an additional 400 million hours for taped replays on public television in the evenings.

TV Two vastly different types of shows dealing with families are among the most discussed and highly rated of the year. *The Waltons*, a wholesome drama about a rural family in the depression years, wins six Emmys; *An American Family*, a documentary, *cinéma verité* series about a troubled real-life family, the Louds, wins huge audiences. The number-one rated show, however, is *All in the Family*, the situation comedy.

TV Law and order shows dominate, with more than half the new fall shows featuring cops, lawyers, or private eyes. Best of the

genre are *Columbo* with Peter Falk, *Police Story*, and *Hawaii Five-O*.

1974

TH Revivals dominate Broadway this year. Colleen Dewhurst, Ed Flanders, and director Jose Quintero all win '73–'74 Tonys for their revival of O'Neill's *A Moon For the Misbegotten*, also starring Jason Robards Jr. William Gillette's 1899 play, *Sherlock Holmes*, is a hit again with England's John Wood in the title role. Elizabeth Ashley scores as Maggie in Tennessee Williams' 1955 drama, *Cat On A Hot Tin Roof*.

TH A revival of Leonard Bernstein's satiric musical, *Candide*, off-Broadway at the Chelsea Theatre Center, is so successful that director Harold Prince moves the show to the Broadway Theatre. It wins a flock of Tonys. Another revival, *Gypsy*, brings a Tony to star Angela Lansbury. The surviving Andrew Sisters, Patti and Maxine, revive their heyday, World War II, in a new musical, *Over There*.

TH Foreign plays and performers are a rich source of entertainment this year. From England comes Peter Shaffer's *Equus*, starring Anthony Hopkins and Peter Firth, a Critics' Circle winner; Tom Stoppards' *Jumpers;* and *Scarpino*. From South Africa: the '74–'75 "best actor" Tony is split between John Kani and Winston Ntschona, black stars of *Sizwe Banzi is Dead* and *The Island*.

MO A group of big money-making films this year marks a worldwide upturn for the industry. All-star disaster films are hot at the box office — *Towering Inferno, Airport 1975,* and *Earthquake*, which features a new process, Sensurround, which sumulates tremor experiences for audiences. Supernatural violence is represented by *The Exorcist*, a controversial shocker about demonic possession of a child (as of 1977 it's the number four all-time box office champ).

MO Although MGM has few films in release, the studio celebrates its fiftieth anniversary in style with *That's Entertainment,* a compilation of clips from MGM's greatest musicals ranging from *Broadway Melody* in 1929 to the great Garland, Kelly, Sinatra, and Astaire films of the forties and fifties. It's a dazzling critical and audience success.

MO *The Godfather, Part II* wins the "best picture" Oscar for 1974, marking the first time a sequel to an Oscar-winning film also wins an award. Robert De Niro, playing the title role as a young man, wins a "best supporting actor" Oscar and Francis Ford Coppola wins as "best director."

MO Feminist themes are featured in several films this year. Ellen Burstyn wins an

Oscar as a widow on her own in *Alice Doesn't Live Here Anymore*. Gena Rowland is outstanding as a pressured housewife having a breakdown in *Woman Under the Influence*. Liv Ullman gives what should have been an Academy nomination performance in Bergman's *Scenes From a Marriage*, but is disqualified because the picture was edited down from a six-hour series made for Scandinavian TV.

MO *Benji*, a low-budget family movie starring a talented mongrel dog in the title role, is big box office, as is Mel Brooks' outrageous comedy *Blazing Saddles*. Another low-budget film, *Lords of Flatbush*, is notable in that its cast includes Henry "The Fonz" Winkler and Sylvester Stallone.

MO Veteran Art Carney pulls an upset by winning the "best actor" Oscar for *Harry and Tonto*, besting such tough competition as Jack Nicholson in *Chinatown*, Al Pacino in the *Godfather* sequel, and Dustin Hoffman in *Lenny*, the Lenny Bruce biofilm. Another veteran, Ingrid Bergman, wins "best supporting actress" for her role in the all-star *Murder on the Orient Express* with Albert Finney impressive as Agatha Christie's detective hero, Hercule Poirot.

MO The American Film Institute presents its "Life Achievement Award" in March to James Cagney in tribute to his forty-year career. In accepting the award, Cagney wryly attributes his success in part to "a touch of the gutter."

RE Continuing steady annual increases, record sales hit over two billion dollars for first time in 1974. Actual figure is $2,200,000,000.

MU/RE Stevie Wonder, whose first record, "I Call It Pretty Music," was released in 1963 when he was twelve, wins Grammy Awards for Best Male Pop Vocal ("You Are the Sunshine of My Life"), Best Song, and Best R&B Male Vocal ("Superstition") and Best Album (*Innervisions*). Following year, when Paul Simon wins award, he thanks Stevie for not having made an album during the year.

TV There are now 120,000,000 television sets in American homes.

TV *Upstairs, Downstairs*, a British series which tells a continuing story from the Edwardian days to the 1929 stock crash, debuts on the public broadcasting system. It becomes a multi-Emmy winner and a cultural landmark in the U.S. as well as England. Its final episode concludes in 1977.

TV Among the top new series are two cop shows — Angie Dickinson in *Police Woman*, *Kojak* with Telly Savalas — and three ethnic comedies — Valerie Harper as *Rhoda*; *Good Times*, introducing young comedian Jimmie Walker; and *Chico and the Man*, starring veteran actor Jack Al-

bertson and Freddie Prinze, who dies under tragic circumstances in 1977.

TV The year features some outstanding drama. Among exceptional specials are *The Autobiography of Miss Jane Pittman*, starring Cicely Tyson; *Tell Me Where It Hurts*, starring Maureen Stapleton; *A Case of Rape*, starring Elizabeth Montgomery; *The Execution of Private Slovik*, starring Martin Sheen; Henry Fonda's one-man show portraying Clarence Darrow; and the $2,500,000 two-part, *QB VII*.

TV Lucille Ball retires as a regular series star (three shows over the past twenty-three years) but will return in specials.

VA/TH/MO/MU/RA/TV All show business mourns the death of beloved comedian Jack Benny who dies at eighty. Other prominent entertainment figures who die this year are Katharine Cornell, Samuel Goldwyn, Duke Ellington and Ed Sullivan.

1975

TH In anticipation of the Bicentennial, which begins July 4, theatres across the country are reviving old American plays — ranging from the works of nineteenth century playwrights Dion Boucicault and William Gillette to O'Neill, Miller, Williams, Wilder, and Hellman. One of the most successful is the Circle in the Square's Broadway production of Miller's *Death of a Salesman* (1949) with George C. Scott as Willy Loman.

TH Although a twenty-five day musicians strike results in a loss of more than $3,000,000 at the box office, it's still a vintage year for musicals. After six months as an off-Broadway hit, Michael Bennett's *A Chorus Line* (score by Marvin Hamlisch and Edward Keban) moves up to Broadway and wins the Pulitzer Prize, Critics' Circle Award, and nine Tonys. The show, in effect, is a consciousness-raising session by eight dancers auditioning for a director.

TH Other musical hits this year is *The Wiz*, an all-black, rock version of *The Wizard of Oz*, directed by Geoffrey Holder with a spirited score by Charlie Smalls. It wins a Tony. Gwen Verdon stars in a musical version of the 1926 comedy hit, *Chicago*, with a John Kander-Fred Ebb score. John Cullum wins a Tony for his performance in *Shenandoah*, which features a nostalgic score based on Civil War tunes.

TH Edward Albee wins his second Pulitzer Prize, for *Seascape*, starring Deborah Kerr. Ironically, his acknowledged masterpiece, *Who's Afraid of Virginia Woolf?*, was rejected in 1962 by Pulitzer's advisory board, whereas *Seascape* receives lukewarm reviews.

TH Among hit plays this year are the comedy *Same Time Next Year* with a

Tony-winning performance by Ellen Burstyn; Tom Stoppard's brilliant *Travesties* which wins Tonys as "best play" and for star John Wood; and Ed Bullins' *The Taking of Miss Janie*, which wins the Critics' Circle "best American play" award.

TH In his sixties, and now a grandfather, Frank Sinatra reaches new heights in his concert career. Young producer Jerry Weintraub puts Sinatra, Ella Fitzgerald, and Count Basie's orchestra into the Uris Theatre on Broadway and sells tickets at $40 each. The show grosses $1,088,000 in a two-week run.

MO *Variety* Box Office Index shows that this year breaks all film box office records, hitting $1,900,000,000.

MO Another rich year for performances by male actors. Jack Nicholson wins the Oscar for *One Flew Over the Cuckoo's Nest*, which also wins "best director" (Milos Forman) and "best screenplay." Al Pacino is a fascinatingly inept bank robber in *Dog Day Afternoon*.

MO There are few strong roles for women this year. Louise Fletcher wins her "best actress" Oscar for a role in *One Flew Over the Cuckoo's Nest*, which many considered a supporting part. Lee Grant plays a role of equal size in *Shampoo*, and wins the "best supporting" Oscar.

MO Robert Altman's *Nashville*, a critical hit but a box office disappointment, wins an Oscar for "best song," actor Keith Carradine's "I'm Easy." The most popular Oscar win is that of eighty-four-year-old George Burns as "best supporting actor" in *The Sunshine Boys*.

MU/RE *Billboard's* recapitulation of all record charts from 1946 through 1975 shows the top three artists through that period to be: Number 1, The Beatles; Number 2, Elvis Presley; and Number 3, Frank Sinatra.

RE Clive Davis, ex-Columbia Records head, sets up new record company, Arista, for Columbia Pictures. In less than three years Davis makes Arista an important label in the industry, developing such key artists as Barry Manilow, Bay City Rollers, and others.

NC *Billboard* launches first annual discotheque industry conference, in recognition of the spectacular growth of the dance establishments, and their influence on the recording industry.

NC *Billboard* launches first annual International Talent Forum, designed to deal with problems of producers, promoters, performers, personal managers, bookers, et al., in live areas: nightclubs, concerts, etc. Top industry leaders participate.

NC/MO The MGM Grand Hotel in Las Vegas, built at a cost of $120,000,000 in

January 1974, accounts for more than 66% of MGM's record net this year of almost $31,900,000.

AP A *Funspot Directory* survey, published by *Amusement Business* magazine, shows theme parks attracted 64,100,000 people this year for a gross income of $372,500,000. The parks spent $10,800,000 on live entertainment. The theme parks employed 8575 people on year-round basis; 70,000 people full-time during seasons. All other outdoor attractions (zoos, museums, state and national parks, kiddielands, etc.) drew 516,736,000 people for a gross income of $1,400,806,500.

FA There are approximately thirty-five state fairs and 2350 county fairs operating in the U.S. These draw 149,900,000 people in 1975. The fairs spend close to $50,000,000 for talent for grandstand shows this year. Top acts from all areas of show business are now playing fairs in ever-increasing numbers. Salaries to some top-name acts reach and surpass the astronomical salaries paid by Las Vegas nightclubs.

CA Only a handful more than 200 carnivals still travel the country, most of them on a regional basis. The few largest — such as Royal American Shows and World of Mirth — play the larger fairs; but the smaller carnivals play important lesser fairs, celebrations, festivals, church and school promotions, shopping centers, some military bases, etc. Show of this type generally carries six to eight rides, some games, booths, etc.

TV Sony introduces its videocassette recorder-player. Built into the Pioneer TV console, it sells for $2295. It does not do well. In 1976, Sony brings out its Betamax videocassette tape deck for $1300 including timer.

TV Fred Silverman, thirty-seven, resigns as vice president in charge of programming for CBS-TV, to become president of ABC Entertainment. He has a three-year contract at $250,000 per year. At end of 1975–1976 TV season, ABC climbs from third place in network ratings to first place, by half a rating point. Change in ratings positions are estimated by *Variety* and other trade sources to represent $40,000,000 in additional corporate profits to ABC.

TV Under severe pressure from many viewers protesting excessive sex and violence on TV programs, the FCC persuades the networks to institute a procedure called Family Time. Networks agree that between the hours of 7–9 p.m. only shows suitable for general family viewing will be shown. The experiment is an unpopular flop. Most of the Family Time shows are low-rated.

TV Moving into the Top Ten this year are *M*A*S*H* starring Alan Alda; *The Six Million Dollar Man* with Lee Majors; and *Phyllis* with Cloris Leachman. There are twenty ethnic series in the fall, but the only new entry showing strong rating potential is the violent *Starsky and Hutch*.

TV *Gunsmoke*, shot down by the ratings after twenty years, is dropped, as is *The Odd Couple*, which has garnered Emmys for stars Jack Klugman and Tony Randall.

TV Specials include the multi-Emmy-winning *Love Among the Ruins*, starring Katharine Hepburn and Sir Laurence Olivier; *Fear On Trial*; and *Queen of the Stardust Ballroom* with Maureen Stapleton. Quality public television series include *Nova*, *The Ascent of Man*, and Frederick Wiseman's grim special *Welfare*.

1976

TH Black performers and playwrights invade Broadway, on and off, with increasing success. Black playwrights include Ntozake Shange *(For Colored Girls Who Have Considered Suicide When the Rainbow Is Enuf)*, Richard Wesley, and Ed Bullins. Black actors and singers score in musical revivals of *Guys and Dolls* and *Bubbling Brown Sugar*. Most impressive of all is the Houston Grand Opera's revival of *Porgy and Bess*.

TH Other successful and/or important plays include Neil Simon's *California Suite*, and two impressive English playwrights' works — Harold Pinter's *No Man's Land*, starring John Gielgud and Ralph Richardson, and Tom Stoppard's *Dirty Linen*.

TH A record number of musicals (seventeen), old and new, are running on Broadway by November. The new shows include Hal Prince's *Pacific Overtures*, which wins the Drama Critics' "best musical" award; and *Chicago*, starring Gwen Verdon. Also scoring with the critics are revivals of *Three Penny Opera* and *My Fair Lady*.

TH According to *Variety*, the Broadway theatre for the 1975–1976 season had its biggest year in the history of the theatre, grossing $70,841,738. The road had its second best-ever season with a gross of $52,587,985.

TH Vietnam veteran playwright David Rabe wins a "best American play" award from the New York Drama Critics' Circle for his bitter *Streamers*. His first anti-war play, *The Basic Training of Pavlo Hummel*, will be revived in 1977 and win a Tony for star Al Pacino.

MO Male Cinderella story of the year is *Rocky*, a low-budget fight film written by an unknown actor, Sylvester Stallone, who wins an Oscar nomination in the title role. The film wins "best picture" Oscar and "best director" (John G. Avildsen).

MO The top box office picture — and, according to many critics, the greatest artistic triumph — is *All The President's Men* starring Robert Redford and Dustin Hoffman as the *Washington Post* reporters who exposed the Watergate cover-up. Jason Robards wins "best supporting" Oscar for his role in the film.

MO Paddy Chayefsky's satire on television, *Network*, features Faye Dunaway, William Holden and Peter Finch, who dies after completing the film. Its Oscar wins include "best writer," "best actress" (Dunaway), and (for Finch's performance) the first posthumous award for "best actor."

MO Other big box office films this year are Barbra Streisand in *A Star Is Born*; *Silent Movie*; a $24,000,000 remake of *King Kong*; Neil Simon's *Murder by Death*; Tatum O'Neal in *The Bad News Bears*; and Gregory Peck in *The Omen*.

MO Critical acclaim goes to Robert De Niro as a psycho and Jodie Foster as a twelve-year-old prostitute in *Taxi Driver*; *Road to Glory* with David Carradine as folk singer Woody Guthrie; and masterful performances by Dustin Hoffman and Sir Laurence Olivier in William Goldman's thriller, *Marathon Man*.

MO Producer Joseph Levine spends $25,000,000 to turn out *A Bridge Too Far*. Unusual aspect of the budget is that $9,000,000 of the total goes to the cast, with Robert Redford, only one of many stars in the film, getting $500,000 per week for four weeks' work.

MO/TV "America's Sweetheart," Mary Pickford, now eighty-three and virtually in seclusion, makes a rare appearance via a poignant interview on film when the industry honors her on its annual Oscar Awards telecast.

MO Adolph Zukor dies in his sleep at the age of 103. Until just before his death, Zukor reported regularly for work at Paramount's New York office.

MU ASCAP's gross receipts for the year are $94,055,000. $80,336,000 of this is domestic, and $13,719,000 foreign. Television pays $42,916,000 to play ASCAP songs; radio pays $24,401,000. Broadcasters pay more than 70% of the Society's total income.

MU National Music Publishers Association reports sales of printed music of $211,000,000 for the year. Surge in printed music is largely due to increased usage in schools and colleges.

RE Record Industry Association of America figures show phenomenal growth of tape sales vs. disks in past ten years. In 1967, tape represented 10% of total prerecorded music sales, and by 1976 tape represented 30% of total. 1976 figures: disks,

$1,908,000,000; tape, $829,000,000. 1967 figures: disks, $1,051,000,000; tape, $122,000,000.

MU/RE After sixty-seven years, the U.S. House and Senate pass a new copyright law, updating the original legislation which became operative in 1909. Among other provisions the new law (effective January, 1978) increases publisher/writer royalty on records from 2¢ to 2¾¢ per song, and, for the first time, calls upon jukebox operators to pay a performance fee for the use of music, just as broadcasters and all other users pay such fees.

MU/RE A surge of raucous, rough, earthy, super-rebellious rock begins to spread in New York, Los Angeles, Boston, and gathers momentum in London. It is called "Punk" rock by many, though its own advocates prefer to call it "New Wave" rock. Most successful exponents of the genre are the Sex Pistols, the Ramones, Patti Smith, and the Talking Heads. Radio does not play the new wave material, just as in the early days of rock many refused to air rock records.

NC/RE Discos, which have been popular in various European countries for a number of years, proliferate here. For first time, the dance-to-records establishments are considered important areas for "making" record hits. Record company promotion departments service many of them in a manner similar to that in which they service radio stations.

NC Atlantic City, N.J., legalizes gambling. Many expect it to become an eastern version of Las Vegas, and possibly keen competition to the Nevada gambling area and stage show resort.

TV Universal Studios and Walt Disney Productions file suit against Sony Corp. of America and Sony Corp. of Japan; the Hale Stores; J.W. Robinson Co.; Bullocks, Inc.; Henry's Camera Corp.; Doyle, Dane, Bernbach ad agency; and William Griffiths to stop sale of Betamax videotape recorders and pre-recorded videotape cassettes. Ultimate outcome of the suit will have substantial bearing on recording video shows off the air for home use and other aspects of videotape recording and cassette sales.

TV All three of the networks have big sales years. CBS becomes the first network — and the first advertising medium in any area — to gross over a billion dollars. CBS does $1,045,550,700; NBC, $991,748,300; ABC, $954,312,100. Although ABC is third, its percentage gain over the previous year is greatest of all three, 33.2% — as opposed to gains of 19.8% for CBS and 17.8% for NBC.

TV In November NBC-TV telecasts its four-and-a-half-hour anniversary show, *The First Fifty Years*. Orson Welles, narrating

the show, says: "History is made right here in this magic box . . . stars are born between station breaks." George C. Scott calls TV a "superb and unique training ground for actors."

TV Sponsors break new records in spending on TV. Procter & Gamble — the biggest broadcast advertiser dating back to early days of network radio — spends $339,183,600 in TV alone. General Foods is second with a budget of $192,275,500, and American Home Products third with a $130,955,700 expenditure. Total spent by top 100 sponsors is $3,811,881,800.

TV Syndication wing of Paramount TV gets a record price for syndicated series from WPIX-TV, New York, which pays $35,000 per episode for *Happy Days*, series starring Henry Winkler as "The Fonz" on ABC-TV. Syndication showings to begin in 1979.

TV By mid-season of the 1976-1977 TV years, ABC-TV's ratings lead over CBS and NBC is almost three points, and one minute of prime time on a top show on ABC sells for as much as $130,000.

TV Commercial TV adopts public video's mini-series concept this year. A twelve-hour, $4,500,000 adaptation of Irwin Shaw's novel *Rich Man, Poor Man* makes the Top Ten every week of its run. Other mini-series include *Captains and the Kings*, *Executive Suite*, and — on public television — Emmy-winning *Adams Chronicles*, a $6,000,000 production, and *Madame Bovary*.

TV Cream of the specials are Julie Harris in PBS's *The Last of Mrs. Lincoln*; Emmy-winning Anthony Hopkins in *The Lindbergh Kidnapping Case*; Jane Alexander in *Eleanor and Franklin* (Roosevelt); Susan Clark as sports star, Babe Zaharias; *Judge Horton and the Scottsboro Boys*; and the first live telecast of a full-length ballet, *Swan Lake*, on public television.

TV Relevancy is out, and simple-minded situation comedy is back in this year. Topping the rating pools are two campy series set in the '50s: *Happy Days*, which makes a teenage idol out of Henry Winkler as "The Fonz," and *Laverne and Shirley* with Penny Marshall and Cindy Williams. Both shows will continue to dominate the Top Ten through 1977.

TV Also high on the charts this year are Lindsay Wagner as *The Bionic Woman*; *Charlie's Angels* with a trio of beautiful women as special agents; and *All In the Family*, the only irreverent series still in the Top Ten. One of the "angels", Farrah Fawcett-Majors, becomes show business' new glamour symbol, but she leaves the show in '77.

TV Two outrageous new series thrive out-

side of prime time. *Mary Hartman, Mary Hartman*, a satirical soap opera starring Louise Lasser, is an overnight sensation on the syndication circuit. NBC's live *Saturday Night*, a far-out revue headed by comedian Chevy Chase, is aired from 11:30 p.m. to 1 a.m. Both series win Emmys.

TV Two-night (Sunday and Monday) TV showings of the legendary MGM film *Gone With the Wind* on NBC-TV win spectacular ratings: 49.3 and 66 share vs. ABC-TV with 14.7 and CBS-TV, 9.3.

TV RCA and Phillips-MCA both demonstrate color videodisk systems.

TV By end of this year, there are about 30,000 Sony Betamax videocassette recorders in use. In December, Sony sells almost 150,000 cassettes.

TV/RA The last radio soap opera went off in 1960 (two years earlier there were sixty hours of soaps on network radio). However, soap opera is alive and well on TV in 1976, with forty-five hours (fourteen shows) on daytime video each week, watched by more than 20,000,000 people from housewives to college professors.

TV/AP TV puppet show producers plan to open first indoor theme park, and first such entertainment center located in downtown section of major city. It is *The World of Sid & Marty Kroft*, and will occupy eight floors of the new $70,000,000 Omni International megastructure being built in downtown Atlanta. Cost of the Kroft entertainment center will run $14,000,000.

AP Marriott Corporation opens Great America Theme Parks in Gurnee, Ill., near Chicago; and Santa Clara, Calif., near San Francisco. The two parks draw more than 4,500,000 in 1976.

CI There are only eighteen traveling circuses still playing under tents. Four of the most successful are Clyde Beatty-Cole Bros.; Hoxie Bros.; Carson-Barnes; and Circus Vargas. The latter, a typical show, treks cross-country four times annually and usually plays shopping centers. Ticket prices: $2.75 for children, $4.75 for adults.

1977

TH Julie Harris wins a Tony for *The Belle of Amherst*, giving her five Tony awards, a record for performers. Other outstanding performances of the '76–'77 season are given by Robert Duvall in *American Buffalo*; Liv Ullman in *Anna Christie*; Tom Courtenay in *Otherwise Engaged*; George C. Scott in *Sly Fox*, and Estelle Parsons in *Miss Margarida's Way*.

TH The fall season is distinguished by Anne Bancroft as *Golda* (Meir); Frank Langella brilliant in the funny, opulent production of *Dracula*; Neil Simon's latest, *Chapter Two*, with Judd Hirsch and Anita

Gillette; and Hume Cronyn and Jessica Tandy in *The Gin Game.*

TH New playwright Michael Cristofer's drama, *The Shadow Box,* wins both the Pulitzer Prize and a Tony as best play. Director Gordon Davidson also receives a Tony award.

TH Also scoring this year on Broadway and off are new playwright Albert Innaurato with *Gemini;* Colleen Dewhurst in *An Almost Perfect Person;* Lily Tomlin's smash one-woman show, *Appearing Nightly;* and Irene Worth in *The Cherry Orchard.*

TH Zero Mostel receives one of highest salaries ever paid an actor in the legitimate theatre, when he gets $30,000 per week for twenty-two-week limited engagement run of revival of *Fiddler on the Roof.* Later, in September, playing in pre-Broadway tryout of *The Merchant* in Philadelphia, Mostel dies of cardiac arrest.

TH In June (citing financial and artistic differences with emphasis on the latter) Joseph Papp resigns from Lincoln Center. His New York Shakespeare Festival company had operated the Center's theatres since 1973.

TH Child performer Andre McArdle stars in the Tony-winning musical (Little Orphan) *Annie,* but co-star Dorothy Loudon wins the "best musical actress" Tony. Score by Strouse and Charnin. Other hit musicals include *I Love My Wife, Side by Side by Sondheim,* and one of the first hit musicals since the twenties with a score written by a black (Alex Bradford), *Your Arm's Too Short to Box With God,* with book and direction by Vinnette Carroll.

TH In a rare tribute, Broadway theatres black out marquees on August 5 at 7:55 p.m. in honor of Alfred Lunt who died August 3 at age of eighty-four. Helen Hayes, Lillian Gish and other theatre luminaries gather in front of the Lunt-Fontanne Theatre to mourn one of America's most distinguished actors. Miss Hayes co-starred with Lunt in *Clarence,* his first major Broadway role, in 1919, also the year he met his future wife and acting partner, Lynn Fontanne.

TH The Shubert Organization is still a major force in the theatre. Today's operators: Warren Caro, Director of Theatre Operations; Philip Smith, General Manager; and Lee Silver, Director of Management. Chairman of the Board is Gerald Schoenfeld; President, Bernard Jacobs. The Board consists of John W. Kluge, Helen Hollerith, Lee Seider, Kerttu H. Shubert, Irving Wall, along with Schoenfeld and Jacobs.

TH Ticket prices for Broadway shows (both musical and straight plays) which have been rising for years reach new highs. *The Act,* starring Liza Minnelli at the Majestic Theatre, charges $22.50 per Saturday evening seat, $20 week nights.

TH The theatre has an all-time record-breaking season (1977-1978), surpassing the high figures of the previous season. Broadway does $93,406,082 while the road accounts for $82,627,309 — according to *Variety.*

MO The big picture this year is director George Lucas' smash science fiction film *Star Wars.* By fall it is the all-time box office champ, topping even *Jaws.* It heralds the first major science fiction trend in industry since *2001: A Space Odyssey.*

MO Steven Spielberg's science fiction film, *Close Encounters of the Third Kind* opens in November and early box office returns indicate that the mystic UFO film could give *Star Wars* a run for number one honors. The movie's star, Richard Dreyfuss, also wins fine reviews for his comedy performance in Neil Simon's *The Goodbye Girl* with Marsha Mason. Veteran George Burns stars in the title role of *Oh God!,* another fantasy.

MO Women are big box office again. Diane Keaton becomes a star in Woody Allen's funny, yet moving, *Annie Hall,* one of the year's top money-makers. Other women performers scoring include Kathleen Quinlan in *I Never Promised You A Rose Garden;* Shelley Duvall and Sissy Spacek in *3 Women;* Lily Tomlin in *The Late Show* with Art Carney; Ms. Keaton in *Looking For Mr. Goodbar;* Jane Fonda and Vanessa Redgrave in *Julia;* and Anne Bancroft and Shirley MacLaine in *Turning Point.*

MO The David Fishman study for Arthur D. Little consulting firm, issued only to subscribers of company's Impact Services, predicts drastic shrinkage in number of theatres that will be in operation by 1985. Fishman says possibly as few as 3500. Major cause will be growth of various home movie sources: videocassettes; video disks; CATV, or other forms of Pay-TV.

MO Thirty theatres in the U.S. are now equipped with the Dolby noise reduction, high fidelity sound system. Major films are now releasing with Dolby encoded versions in 70 mm six-track; 35 mm four-track, and 35 mm stereo optical prints as well as conventional prints. There is little doubt that more and more top films (particularly those utilizing music to any great extent) will use improved high fidelity encoding in prints.

MO Francis Ford Coppola, whose *Godfather* films were huge successes, encounters unusual difficulty producing-directing *Apocalypse Now,* his Vietnam war picture, shooting in the Philippines. Originally budgeted at $12,000,000, costs have mounted to more than $25,000,000 by summer of this year. Coppola is said to have hocked personal holdings to cover the overage.

MO The fiftieth anniversary of the Academy of Motion Picture Arts and Sciences is celebrated in May. Of the thirty-six original founding members, the only survivors are Mary Pickford, Henry King, Raoul Walsh and Jack L. Warner.

MO A new sex symbol explodes on the screen in December when young John Travolta makes the transition from "sweathog" on TV's *Welcome Back Kotter* to disco dance idol in *Saturday Night Fever.*

MO Macho heroes as personified by Burt Reynolds, Clint Eastwood, and Charles Bronson are still big box office. Reynolds' *Smokey and the Bandit* is second only to *Star Wars* as a top money-maker in 1977.

MO The entire world mourns the death of Charlie Chaplin who dies in his sleep on Christmas Day at the age of eighty-eight.

MO According to a Motion Picture Association survey, a sizeable percentage of those forty years of age and over never go to the movies. The age range for the average moviegoer (about 90% of current audiences) is older than twelve but younger than thirty-nine, even though those age groups represent less than 60% of the total U.S. population.

MO/RA/RE/TV Elvis Presley dies at forty-two of cardiac arrythmia, extremely irregular heartbeat. It is said that he has been ailing for more than a year. Hypertension, a twisted colon and some eye trouble plagued him. More than 80,000 people crowd around his Graceland mansion in Memphis. Almost 30,000 of them are admitted into the house to view the body. He is buried near his mother.

MO/RA/RE/TV Bing Crosby, seventy-three, completes a "good" round of golf on a course outside Madrid, Spain, October 14 and dies of a heart attack on his return to the clubhouse. The long-time star began his career in the late '20s as one of the Rhythm Boys with the Paul Whiteman band.

MO/RA/RE/TV In marked contrast to the Elvis Presley funeral, Bing Crosby is buried at the Holy Cross Cemetery in Culver City, Calif., just before dawn on October 18. The only persons present are his immediate family (his six sons are pallbearers) and a few intimate friends including Bob Hope, Phil Harris, and Rosemary Clooney.

MO/RE Interpol (the International Crime Police organization) adopts a resolution at its forty-sixth general assembly in Stockholm, Sweden urging its 125 affiliates around the world to help fight record and film pirating. Interpol has worked with the Record Industry Association of America and the Motion Picture Association of America to stem the rising tide of piracy and counterfeiting of films and disks.

NC Bidding for choice hotel locations and jockeying for gambling casino licenses begins in Atlantic City. Some top people encounter "conflict of interest" problems.

NC Among major organizations establishing early footholds in Atlantic City, where gambling has been legalized, are Resorts International, which buys 1000-room Chalfonte-Haddon Hall hotel for $5,200,000; Playboy Enterprises, which owns boardwalk site next to Convention Hall and plans $50,000,000 hotel there; and the Loew's hotel and theatre chain. I.G. Davis, president of Resorts International, says they are ready to pay acts $250,000 per week to play A.C. hotel.

NC The disco craze spreads. It is estimated that there are now more than 15,000 discotheques in the U.S. today. It has become a $4,000,000,000 per year business.

NC New York Hilton Hotel spends $500,000 to build experimental private disco/club/restaurant complex in the hotel. To be called Sybil's, disco will be operated by director Martin O'Hara. If successful, Hilton chain plans discos in more of their hotels.

NC 900 people attend *Billboard's* Disco III, third annual discotheque conference in New York. Speaker Larry Harris, V.P. of Casablanca Records, attributes success of many record artists — such as Donna Summer, KC and the Sunshine Band — to the fact that their records have been disco-oriented, i.e., strong dance records.

NC The greatest nightclub disaster in years occurs at the Beverly Hills Supper Club in Covington, Ky., May 28, when fire breaks out and sweeps through showroom; 161 persons die in the fire. John Davidson was the club's attraction.

MU There's a true electronic explosion in music. More and more electronic instruments (synthesizers — the Moog, the Polymoog, the ARP, Sel-Sync, etc.) are being used in recording. The 1977 Music Educators National Conference in Washington, D.C., has more exhibits and workshops featuring electronic music instruments and equipment than ever before. Some trace this back to the hit *Switched-On Bach* LP in 1969.

MU Nine years after the original CBS suit was filed, the U.S. Appeals Court finds that the ASCAP blanket licensing system constitutes illegal price-fixing. For the moment CBS seems to have won its battle to pay only for music used, instead of blanket license, but ASCAP asks for hearing before full nine-member Court of Appeals, and plans to take case to Supreme Court if necessary.

MU Paul McCartney (ex-Beatle) and his wife, Linda — through their MPL Communications company represented by Linda's father, veteran music industry attorney Lee Eastman — buy the long-established E.H. Morris Music publishing catalog for $9,000,000. Formed only three years earlier, MPL has previously purchased the Buddy Holly and Morley Music catalogs and published all of McCartney's own songs, written since 1973.

MU Neil Sedaka pays $2,000,000 to Kirshner Entertainment Corporation to buy 116 copyrights of his own songs, held by Kirshner. Kirshner published Sedaka's first song in 1967.

MU Industry leaders predict music folio sales this year will reach $300,000,000. 1976 totals were $211,000,000.

MU/TV NBC-TV runs a two-hour "big event" show, *The Billboard Awards*, Dec. 11, featuring awards made to top record artists in all music categories as determined by *Billboard* charts.

RE Record albums reach new sales peaks this year; twenty-six albums on *Billboard's* top LP chart in mid-October show the Recording Industry Association of America's seal for certified sales of 1,000,000 or more units. Many are selling three, four, five or more million units. Joel Friedman, President of Warner-Elektra-Atlantic distribution organization, predicts that the next precious metal "identification" of monster sellers will be titanium, signifying sales of 10,000,000 or more units.

RE Home recording of commercial records onto blanks tapes and/or cassettes directly off radio programs is skimming $1,000,000,000 a year off the sales of record albums and pre-recorded tapes, according to the International Federation of Phonographic Industries. The IFPI is studying possible measures for checking the burgeoning practice of home taping. Some countries such as Germany and England license people to tape music off the air, but systems are said to be unsatisfactory.

RE U.S. Copyright Office holds record industry hearings to consider once again the question of whether radio stations should pay a royalty fee to record companies and performers for right to play records. Resolution of the matter seems distant.

RE It is the 100th anniversary of recorded sound. *Billboard* publishes outstanding special issue on history of recorded sound. All industry organizations celebrate the event.

RE More and more record companies are raising the suggested retail price of their albums to $7.98. Large record retail chains, however, continue to sell "$7.98" LPs in the $3.93-$4.69 range.

RE After technological evolution, which saw recording up to twenty-four and thirty-two tracks, some companies go back to direct-to-disk recording for first time in years.

RE/RA New Government hearings and trials on payola take place this year, but do not reach the dimensions of the payola scandals of 1960.

MU/RE/TH Producers Steven Leber and David Krebs present four young musicians — who look, play, and sing like The Beatles — in a Broadway production called *Beatlemania*. At a $10 (orchestra) ticket price, the show does well.

RA/RE *Billboard* Broadcasting division introduces first five-hour syndicated music special for radio. Titled *Sound of '77*, the show features year's top personalities and hits as well as many other features.

RA The FCC issues a sweeping new policy statement on radio, upsetting most of the network radio rules passed in 1941. Any network program may now be rejected by an affiliate station. The FCC also stresses broadcasters' community service obligations.

RA At the beginning of this year there are approximately 425,000,000 radio sets in the country, 73% of them in homes.

RA Fantastic growth of FM is indicated in comparative figures for the increasing number of stations in FM from 1959 to present. In 1959 there were 3,318 AM stations, which increased to 4,513 by 1977; in 1959 there were 571 FM stations, which increased to 3,927 by 1977; 1,148 of the FM stations are now broadcasting in stereo.

RA At the end of the year, there are 4,513 commercial AM radio stations, 3,001 commercial FM radio stations and 926 non-commercial FM operations. Total number of stations: 8,441.

RA Independent radio station formats have stabilized across the country. The most popular formats (in rank order) are: Contemporary/Rock Music; Middle of the Road (MOR) and/or Beautiful Music; News, Information and/or Talk Shows; Country Music; Black (or soul) Music; and Classical Music.

RA Approximately 20% of all the radio stations in the country are completely computerized, i.e., automated, and operate without engineers, disk jockeys and other live on the air personnel. Many of them are the highest-rated stations in their markets.

TV/RA William Paley, seventy-five, retires as chief executive officer of CBS. At this point he is, of course, the company's largest single stockholder, owning 1,700,000 shares (6% of the total corporate stock) worth almost $90,000,000. John D. Backe, forty-four, who joined CBS in 1973 as V.P. in charge of the book division, becomes CBS's chief executive. It is expected Paley will maintain an active part in the corporation's operation.

TV/RA CBS celebrates its fiftieth anniversary. From net sales of $1,300,000 in 1928 (first full year in action) the original radio network has grown to a conglomerate that had net sales of $2,230,000,000 in 1976.

TV/RE In one of first instances of a live concert filmed for and presented on pay-TV and recorded for release by a major record label, Bette Midler does a show at the Cleveland Music Hall. National Subscription Television, through its ON service, shows it as a bonus on four nights in June and July; Atlantic releases it as a two LP set.

MO/TV Although the film *Network* highlights the most unattractive aspects of the television business, all three TV networks bid for TV rights to the Paddy Chayefsky movie. CBS wins, paying $5,000,000 for rights to televise the movie three times.

TV At the beginning of 1977, 97% of all American homes (approximately 71,500,000) have television sets. Almost half of these have more than one set; about 54,000,000 are color sets. More than 90% of TV homes can receive UHF signals, and approximately 15% are linked to a cable system. The average American home has the TV set on more than six hours per day. By year's end there are 72,900,000 sets in the nation's homes.

TV At the end of the year, there are 727 commercial TV stations (516, VHF; 211, UHF). There are also 259 non-commercial TV stations (101, VHF; 158, UHF). Total TV stations: 986.

TV FCC's first report on financial picture in CATV shows that the cable TV business grossed $894,000,000 in twelve-month period ending October, 1976. Operating expenses were $560,000,000; pre-tax income estimated at $27,000,000. Total assets of all cable operations close to $2,000,000,000. Monthly subscriber rates run from $5.19 to $8.03.

TV Although networks have been signing exclusive contracts with talent for some time, ABC goes on a talent-buying binge beginning July of this year and signs exclusive deals with Cloris Leachman, Peter Strauss, Cher, Mary Kay Place, among many others.

TV Two great pioneer inventors in television are voted into the National Inventors Hall of Fame: Dr. V.K. Zworykin, eighty-seven, inventor of iconoscope and kinescope tubes; and the late Dr. Lee De Forest, creator of scores of major broadcasting innovations.

TV The Johnny Carson *Tonight Show* celebrates its fifteenth anniversary. Carson's new deal, signed in 1978, gives him a shorter work week, but jumps his salary from approximately $1,000,000 per year to $3,000,000 per year.

TV Current TV thirty-second commercial spots on individual stations range from as little as $5 per spot in the least populated markets to $15,000 per spot in top-rated shows in major markets. However, full-minute commercials in the 1977 Super Bowl telecast went for $250,000. The show was seen by approximately 75,000,000 people. The average prime-time network television thirty-second spot now costs about $50,000.

TV The phenomenal mini-series about slavery, *Roots*, which runs eight nights in a row in January, is the most-watched TV show in history; 130,000,000 watch at least part of the series. The eighth episode draws a 71% audience share, making it the all-time, number one video show, a title formerly held by *Gone With the Wind*, Part Two. *Roots* receives a record number of Emmy nominations (thirty-seven) including all four selections for lead actor. Louis Gossett, Jr. is the winner.

TV The success of *Roots* changes network TV programming concepts. In a bid for ratings, all three networks schedule a record number of specials — more than 100 for each network, including triple the number of mini-series they ran in 1976.

TV Other popular mini-series include the $7,500,000 six-part *Washington: Behind Closed Doors*; Jim Arness in *How the West Was Won*; *The Trial of Lee Harvey Oswald*; Franco Zeffirelli's *Jesus of Nazareth*; the nine-hour *Godfather Saga*; and three PBS series: *The Pallisers*, Ingmar Bergman's six-part *Scenes From a Marriage* with Liv Ullman, and *I, Claudius*.

TV Robert T. Howard, NBC-TV president, tells Congressional subcommittee about high costs of current programming: for two showings, one episode in a half-hour series, $155,000; for average one hour program, $335,000; for average feature movie made for TV, $882,000.

TV Universal TV (MCA subsidiary) allocates $200,000,000 for programming for 1977–1978 season. Record-breaking expenditure includes production costs of a number of mini-series based on important novels, such as *79 Park Avenue* (six parts); *Wheels* (twelve parts); *Aspen* (six parts); *Centennial* (twelve parts); as well as

weekly series shows: *Kojak, Switch, Bionic Woman, Rockford Files, Quincy, Oregon Trail,* and others.

TV NBC-TV signs deal with Soviet Union for 1980 Summer Olympic Games in Moscow. Network pays $35,000,000 for TV rights, plus $50,000,000 for production and equipment costs. Additionally it pays West German TV entrepreneur Lothar Bock $1,000,000 fee (plus guarantee to carry Bock programs in U.S.) for arranging the deal with the Russians. ABC-TV had paid $25,000,000 for the 1976 Olympics in Montreal.

TV A surge in original production for cable-TV is taking place. Columbia Pictures, 20th Century Fox Telecommunications, Showtime (a subsidiary of Viacom), and Home Box Office are among the producing companies actually doing shows or announcing plans for the immediate future.

TV Minority performers are making progress. Shows featuring black stars include *The Jeffersons, Good Times, What's Happening!!, The Redd Foxx Show, The Richard Pryor Show,* and *Sanford Arms*. The last three series have limited runs.

TV Among the impressive 1977 specials are *Eleanor and Franklin: The White House Years;* Peter Boyle as *Tail Gunner Joe* (McCarthy); and the last performances of Elvis Presley and Bing Crosby. Quality public TV series include *Visions,* featuring the works of new playwrights, and John Kenneth Galbraith's *The Age of Uncertainty*.

TV Increased pressure by advertisers, Congress and various medical, religious and educational groups to eliminate violence on TV gets some results from the networks. Action-oriented shows (*Serpico, The Streets of San Francisco,* etc.) are dropped or — like Robert Blake's *Baretta* — their level of mayhem is reduced.

TV The fall schedule is dominated by family and fantasy shows, mostly youth-oriented. In addition to oldies like *One Day at a Time,* new youth-oriented shows include *Three's Company,* about a young man with two pretty roommates, and *On Our Own*. Other popular series are *Family, Alice, Barney Miller* starring Hal Linden, and — often in the Top Ten — the documentary, *60 minutes*.

TV The most controversial new show is *Soap,* a raunchy soap opera spoof which almost didn't go on the air because of a write-in campaign protesting its sexy content. However, its initial ratings are high.

TV *The Mary Tyler Moore Show,* which won numerous awards including twenty-nine Emmys during its seven-year run, goes off voluntarily in March. Louise Lasser also resigns as the star of the 1976 smash *Mary Hartman, Mary Hartman,* but the show returns in the fall as *Fernwood U.S.A.* with most of the original cast.

TV U.S. Presidents, past and present, are served up as TV fare this year. President Jimmy Carter makes more video appearances in '77 than any other President. Former President Richard Nixon stars in a series of startling syndicated interviews with David Frost for $600,000 plus a percentage. Ex-President Gerald Ford and his wife Betty sign a five-year contract with NBC for $1,500,000.

TV International Video & Cable Network, a Beverly Hills, Calif. firm, advertises ¾" and ½" videocassettes of copyrighted movies for $69 and up in *Daily Variety.* Among features advertised are *Deep Throat;* Beatles' *Magical Mystery Tour; The Devil in Miss Jones;* and Bob Hope in *My Favorite Brunette.*

CI/FA Kenneth and Irvin Feld produce a special unit, The Ringling Thrill Circus, to play big state fairs. Unit makes first appearance at Ohio State Fair and does sensational one week business, playing to 2,600,000 people at raised admission charge of $3 for adults and $1 for children. Karl Wallenda Family and the Hugo and Edmundo Zacchini cannon act are major features of the minicircus.

CI Marcella, star elephant ballerina of the Ringling Brothers and Barnum & Bailey Circus, retires from the ring to Circus World, Florida. The dancing elephant, who joined the circus in Ceylon back in 1922, is feted at a farewell party with a bouquet of roses and an elephant-shaped cake, both of which she eats.

TV Conservative estimates are that more than 250,000 videotape recorder/players will be sold in the October–December period this year. It is considered possible that by the end of 1978 1,000,000 video-

tape recorders may be in use. Tremendous sale in blank videocassette tape is anticipated in spite of pending suit seeking to make home taping illegal.

TV Twentieth Century Fox makes deal licensing Magnetic Video to use fifty pre-1972 feature films for conversion to ½" videocassettes for use in Sony Betamax (and similar players). Deal is non-exclusive. Earlier, Twentieth had made similar license deal with RCA for its videodisk system. MGM had also made deal with RCA for its videodisk players. All deals are non-exclusive.

TV After buying UHF station KBSC-TV from Kaiser Broadcasting Corp. for $1,200,000, National Subscription Television announces it will launch the first over-the-air pay television system in history. Operating with FCC approval over Channel 52, Los Angeles, NST will program minimum of twenty-eight hours weekly (7:30 p.m. to midnight) current films, sports events, etc. Subscribers pay $24.95 installation charge, plus $25 for decoder and $17 per month to receive all programs.

TV Warner Communications' CATV division inaugurates QUBE thirty-channel service to its 100,000 CATV subscribers in Columbus. With new electronic service, subscribers will be able to tune in more than two dozen video programs, select special programs, play games, take various tests and participate directly in TV programs right from their homes via two-way communication. The system is developed by Warners and Pioneer Electronic Corp. of Japan.

TV In October, North American Philips and MCA Disc-Vision announce that their laser playback videodisk player will not reach the market until fall, 1978, at the earliest. Original introduction was scheduled

for the end of 1977. RCA also announces delay on the introduction of its SelectaVision videodisk system. Industry feels delays by these two majors gives videotape systems (Beta, etc.) decided advantage in the configuration struggle.

MO/TV Columbia Pictures steps up production of features for cable and pay-TV. Kip Walton Productions is producing series of music shows, featuring stars such as Johnny Mathis, Seals and Crofts, Kenny Rankin, Paul Williams, Sarah Vaughn, Carmen MacCrae, Diahann Carroll and Henry Mancini. Marti-Trachtenberg Productions is producing cabaret type shows, called *No Cover, No Minimum,* for the Columbia pay and cable catalogue.

MO/TV Martin Firestone, counsel for National Association of Theatre Owners, tells NATO convention in Miami Beach that a national pay-cable TV network linked by domestic earth satellites is an imminent and major threat to theatre owners. He points out that cable pay systems have increased from 190 to 364 in past year, and that subscribers have jumped from over 600,000 to close to 1,000,000.

TV In the pre-Christmas selling season (from Thanksgiving Day to December 14), almost every major American manufacturer/distributor of television receivers is advertising its own brand name version of videocassette recorder/players. Two Japanese firms, Sony and Matsushita (sometimes tied in with JVC) are making the units to the specifications of the American manufacturers. The systems, the Sony Betamax and the Matsushita and/or JVC VHS, are incompatible, and approximately the same number of American firms are utilizing the one system as the other. More than $25,000,000 in advertising is being spent by the American firms, with RCA budgeting about $5,000,000 for its campaign, and Sony itself about $4,000,000.

PART SIX

THERE WAS ALWAYS MUSIC

━━━━━━━━━━━━◆━●━◆━━━━━━━━━━━━

The history of popular music as it affected, or was affected, by developments in other areas of show business has been told in the introductory essays as well as the chronological histories in each of the preceding five parts of American Entertainment. *The technological advances in recording and tape; the highlights of the big band era; the emergence of the star vocalists; and activity in the musical theatre have all been detailed. But music is unique in that it is the only segment of show business which has been an important supportive element in every branch of entertainment, while growing into a major show business area in its own right. Therefore, this* Coda *which briefly summarizes music's role in American entertainment is presented here.*

CODA

There was always music!

"I heard good Musick," Benjamin Franklin wrote in 1743, on a visit to the colonial Pennsylvania settlement of Bethlehem, ". . . the Organ being accompanied with Violins, Hautboys, Flutes and Clarinets."

Originally there were the religious songs, brightened with up-tempo treatments by America's first songwriter, William Billings. And there were the political and patriotic songs of the colonial days, "The Liberty Song," "Jefferson and Liberty," and such. Then came the first sentimental ballads, "The Banks of the Dee," "The Minstrel's Return from the War." In the new nation music was unfailingly an integral part of entertainment as the nation struggled through its formative years.

The circus band sang notice that the show was in town as the parade of performers and animals marched down the dusty village streets. Every carnival, every minstrel, vaudeville and burlesque show had its singers and musicians, although they were frequently required to double not only on several instruments, but also as janitors, barbers and assorted odd-job functionaries. The "Jenny Linds" toured triumphantly.

SONGS OF THE NEGRO

The minstrel shows of the first half of the nineteenth century gave us a special type of Negro song, many written by whites, based on Negro themes and melodies. Dan Emmett created a long string from "Ol' Dan Tucker" in 1843 to "Dixie" in 1859. Stephen Foster called these "Ethiopian" songs and for a time considered having his works in this category published under a pseudonym. In the openly bigoted manner of the day, these and similar songs came to be referred to as "coon songs." Among Foster's works were "De Camptown Races" and "Massa's in de Cold, Cold Ground." Foster's successor, as a leading writer of Negro songs, was a Howard College-educated black, James Bland. He wrote "Carry Me Back to Old Virginny," "Oh! Dem Golden Slippers" and "Hand Me Down My Walking Cane," among others from 1875 to 1879.

OCT. 1, 1910 ISSUE

RECORDS, MOVIES AND PIANOS

When the first mechanical forms of show business, movies, and records came into being, music played an increasingly important role. In the dark and smelly storefront theatres, the piano player's *allegro* rush of sixteenth-note bars, punctuated with crashing major and minor chords, gave excitement to the chase scenes and depth to the vile mis-

385

behavings of the villains on the silent screen. His lilting *andante* melodies tenderized the love scenes.

One could have wished for greater fidelity, less blare and squawk, from the Edison cylinders or the Berliner flat disks. Still the singing and playing were remarkable. Of course, only the more affluent could afford the phonographs, or for that matter the pianos, which were even more popular. Yet by the turn of the nineteenth century several million people had pianos—many of them player pianos—in their homes and a full-fledged music/record industry was blossoming.

The most meaningful single advance of the period in records was Eldridge Johnson's new wax recording blanks, coated with graphite (for more effective conduction of electric current). The wax disks were a vast improvement over Berliner's zinc records. Johnson introduced a new line of records, called Improved Records, with a strong line-up of vocalists and bands. Among them were the Metropolitan Orchestra, which recorded such current favorites as "The Mandalay Two Step," "The Koonville Koonlets," "The Swell Irish Waltz" and "The Girl in the Barracks." Vocal star Dan Quinn recorded "The Mick Who Threw the Brick," and "Pletty Little Chinee from San Toy," among other hits. A duo, E. M. Favor and Arthur Collins, specialized in "coon" songs such as "I Ain't Seen No Messenger Boy," "Cindy, I Dreams About You," and "My Honey Lou." George Broderick's records featured "Father O'Flynn" and "The Turnkey's Song."

Sousa's Concert Band and the Haydn Quartet also recorded for Johnson's Improved label. Johnson, of course, was later to found the Victor Talking Machine Company.

OCT. 1, 1904 ISSUE   LEO FEIST

PIONEER PUBLISHERS

The publishers' and writers' road to gold was sheet music sales. With the majority of the nation still largely oriented to self-entertainment, a favorite American family pastime was to gather around the piano for a sing-along. Record and piano royalties accounted for some writer/publisher earnings, but a million-copy selling song would earn $200,000, which would be divided equally between writer and publisher. There were no earnings from public performance for profit, since the copyright law was not passed until 1909, and the Society of Composers, Authors and Publishers was not formed until 1914. It wasn't until years later that the word "American" was added to the name of that organization to make it ASCAP.

A single million-copy hit launched some of the most successful publishing firms of the day. "And Her Golden Hair Was Hanging Down Her Back" established the Leo Feist firm. It was written by Monroe Rosenfeld, a *New York Herald Tribune* reporter, who is generally credited with coining the phrase "Tin Pan Alley" in the days when the music business was centered around Union Square in New York City. "The Picture That Is Turned Toward the Wall" by Charles Graham was the first big hit for M. Witmark & Sons.

Edward B. Marks (lyrics) and Joseph Stern (melody) wrote "The Little Lost Child" to send Joseph Stern & Co. on its way. "The Little Lost Child" was the first song to use the newly introduced song slides. Joseph Stern & Co. became E. B. Marks Publishing Co., one of the industry's largest.

EARLY SONG PLUGGING

A viable pattern of song plugging evolved. Ed Marks, or any other active writer/publisher, would set out, after a day in the office, to make the rounds of the vaudeville and burlesque theatres and concert halls, calling on singers and musicians, distributing copies of his latest song. Frequently the song plugger would take a singer or band leader to an expensive restaurant for dinner—one where a meal might cost as much as two dollars—or make a gift of a bottle of fine whiskey to a popular baritone, or give a vial of expensive perfume to a vaudeville or burlesque soubrette. Later, and gradually, more blatant forms of persuasion came into use. Some important singers were put on a publisher's weekly payroll; some, who could not write a note of music nor spell cat, had their names put on hit songs as co-writers and shared in the royalties.

GUMM AND BALINE

The pluggers' rounds were not limited to the theatres. During that time, restaurants, beer gardens, even some of the more exclusive brothels featured singing waiters, piano players or musical groups. Irving Berlin (whose real name was Israel Baline) was a singing waiter on the Bowery and worked as a song-plugging stooge for Harry Von Tilzer, singing the works of that prolific and highly successful composer from the balcony at Tony Pastor's. It was common practice for publishers to plant a stooge in a theatre. When the singer on stage finished a song, the stooge would rise in the audience and sing another chorus, urging the audience to sing along with him. In the restaurants and beer gardens, the plugger would give each of the customers a lyric sheet with the words of the chorus of the song so that they could sing along with the performer or the waiters.

Von Tilzer was the writing-publishing phenomenon of his day. His real name was Harry Gumm (Tilzer was his mother's maiden name and he inserted the Von for distinction). At fourteen he joined the Cole Bros. Circus as a tumbler. He left the circus and worked with a traveling repertory company and later in burlesque as a piano player. In 1892 he was playing piano in a Brooklyn saloon for $15 per week.

SHAPIRO, BERNSTEIN AND VON TILZER

In 1896, while working in an act with George Sidney at Tony Pastor's, he wrote over 100 songs. He sold many of them outright, for two dollars each. His first hits were "I'd Leave My Happy Home for You" and "My Old New Hampshire Home." Publishers Lewis (sometimes spelled "Louis") Bernstein and Maurice Shapiro had bought the last song outright, but when it showed signs of becoming a hit, they gave Von Tilzer an additional $4000 and made him a partner in the firm. Shortly after the formation of Shapiro, Bernstein & Von Tilzer, the writer wrote "She's Only a Bird in a Gilded Cage" with lyrics by Arthur Lamb. It became the biggest hit of its time, selling over 2,000,000 copies. Von Tilzer left Shapiro and Bernstein and formed his own publishing company.

Until his young employee, Israel Baline, who had already changed his name to Irving Berlin, developed his spectacular career, Von Tilzer was unquestionably the most prolific and successful writer/publisher in the history of popular music. His catalogue of songs was awesome. It included "I Want a Girl Just Like the Girl That Married Dear Old Dad," "That Old Irish Mother of Mine," "Down on the Farm," among scores of other hits.

INCREDIBLE IRVING BERLIN

Berlin, of course, exceeded not only the accomplishments of Von Tilzer, but of any other single person in the history of popular music. Jerome Kern was asked his opinion of Berlin's contributions to American music, and replied: "Contributions!? He *is* American music!" One need only ponder the fact that among his thousands of songs are the nation's definitive patriotic song, "God Bless America"; its definitive Christmas song, "White Christmas"; and its definitive Easter song, "Easter Parade." Or that when no less a superstar writing/producing team than Richard Rodgers and Oscar Hammerstein II were seeking a composer for the score of their musical comedy production, *Annie, Get Your Gun*, they asked Berlin to do the job. That score included "They Say It's Wonderful," "Doin' What Comes Naturally," "The Girl That I Marry," "Anything You Can Do, I Can Do Better," "You Can't Get a Man With a Gun," "An Old Fashioned Wedding," and "There's No Business Like Show Business." And it took Berlin all of three months to write the words and music for that hit Ethel Merman show!

FROM "MARIE" TO RAG

In 1907, he wrote his first song (lyrics only) to a melody by a saloon pianist, Nick Michaelson. It was "Marie from Sunny Italy." Ragtime, along with sentimental ballads and novelty songs, was popular in the late 1800s and early 1900s. Scott Joplin wrote "Maple Rag" and other outstanding rag tunes in 1899. That same year Joe E. Howard used the syncopated rag format for the hit song, "Hello, Ma Baby," and in 1902 Hugh Cannon wrote "Bill Bailey, Won't You Please Come Home." But by 1910 Irving Berlin was considered the leading writer of ragtime songs. That year he wrote "Play Some Ragtime," "Stop That Rag," and "Yiddle on Your Fiddle," and all became rag hits. The following year he wrote "Alexander's Rag Time Band," which was not really a rag.

VICTOR HERBERT AND ASCAP

In the meantime, the musical theatre had made some progress since *The Black Crook's* strange debut. In 1894, Victor Herbert, a man destined to become a major force in music (not only as a composer, but as a key factor in creating ASCAP), had his first show produced in the United States. It was *Prince Ananias*, which he wrote for a touring company, The Bostonians. Herbert was said to have been the inspiration for many another composer, including Jerome Kern. Kern was ten years old when he saw Herbert's second light opera, *The Wizard of the Nile*, in 1895. In the 1899–1900 season Herbert wrote the scores for four operettas: *Cyrano de Bergerac*, *The Singing Girl*, *Ameer* and *The Viceroy*.

In 1914, Herbert, his attorney Nathan Burkan, his collaborator Glen MacDonough, composer Raymond Hubell, George Maxwell and producer John Golden met at the Hotel Claridge and formed the Society of Authors, Composers and Publishers (later ASCAP). Herbert declined the presidency, and Maxwell became the performing rights society's first president. Twenty-two publishers and 177 composers and lyricists constituted the Society's charter membership.

HERBERT TO KERN TO RODGERS TO GERSHWIN

That same year Jerome Kern wrote the score for his first Broadway success, *The Girl From Utah*. "They Didn't Believe Me" was the hit song from the show. Kern, in turn, inspired later writers for the musical theatre. Richard Rodgers was fourteen when he saw Kern's musical, *Very Good, Eddie*. George Gershwin also drew inspiration from Kern's works. All of the composers of this era, however, owed a debt to one of the outstanding publishers of the day, Max Dreyfus. Dreyfus, as head of J. H. Remick & Company—later the Harms-Witmark-Remick combine of leading publishers—gave jobs as house pianists, demonstrators, or salesmen to Kern himself, as well as Vincent Youmans, Gershwin and many others.

With the formation of ASCAP, the popular music industry fell into a comfortable groove. A half dozen of the larger publishing organizations had the great majority of the most successful and prolific writers of popular songs under contract. These publishers and writers worked very closely with the artist-and-repertoire and production heads of the record companies and the piano roll companies. Through ASCAP they policed the other users of music (nightclubs, restaurants, theatres, beer gardens, et al.) ever more effectively.

ENTER RADIO

Then came World War I and at its conclusion, radio! The relationship between music and radio was strange and frequently paradoxical. From the time in 1920, when Westinghouse engineer Frank Conrad broadcast his "air concerts" from his garage in Wilkinsburg, Pa., music had been an essential element of radio, frequently its very heart. Yet by 1923, ASCAP was screaming that radio was wrecking the music industry. Record and piano royalties dropped drastically, and (until ASCAP finally won a lawsuit against WOR) radio was not even paying publishers and/or writers for the use of their music. For years, in the late 1930s (and in some instances, the early 1940s) record companies, led by Decca and recording artists, spearheaded by Fred Waring, Paul Whiteman and others, waged legal war against the broadcasters, insisting that they should pay performers and record companies as well as music publishers and writers for the right to play records.

FROM HATE TO LOVE

Nevertheless when the development of television created a situation which found some eighty percent of all radio stations utilizing records for virtually all their programming (still without any payment except to publishers and song writers), artists and record companies spent vast sums of money in myriad ways to court radio's program directors and disk jockeys. Some forms of this courtship became known as payola. In the 1960s congressional hearings on corrupt practices of this kind led to Federal anti-payola legislation.

From 1921 to 1925, however, it was true that radio (plus an economic recession) threatened the music/record industry. Sales dropped steadily until a technological miracle, electrical recording, saved the day. The new recording technique created whole new musical styles and opportunities, since the newly invented microphones enabled soft-voiced singers and the more delicate instruments to be recorded well for the first time. No longer did the vocal bellowers and booming brass dominate recorded music. Record sales climbed again until 1929.

NEW THREAT TO RECORDS

A combination of external (non-show business) and internal (entertainment) forces conspired to wipe out the record industry. Beginning in 1929, the external force, of course, was the great depression. The internal entertainment developments were the launching and subsequent phenomenal growth of the NBC and CBS radio networks, and the public acceptance of talking pictures. By the end of 1933, record sales had plummeted to a modern era low of some $5,000,000, and many record people felt certain the end was near.

The repeal of prohibition and the subsequent opening of thousands upon thousands of bars, small clubs and restaurants—most of which installed juke boxes—and a new record company, Decca, stemmed the recording industry's decline. E. R. Lewis of London Records and Jack Kapp, E. F. Stevens, Milt Rackmil and their colleagues at Decca produced and marketed low-priced (thirty-five cents), high-quality records by stars such as Bing Crosby, the Andrews Sisters, Guy Lombardo and his orchestra and others. The work of these men was an early example of the vital influence that so-called "independents" (i.e., non-establishment, smaller new record companies) had on the destiny of the music/record industry.

The juke box operators bought Decca records by the millions; in an amazingly short time there was a big three rather than a big two—just Columbia and RCA Victor—in the record industry, although both companies pushed hard against their brilliant and aggressive new competitor. At that point, the record industry started its successful climb. In 1977, it reached almost $3,000,000,000 in sales—a truly superstar-making, major entertainment business.

A MUSIC PANTHEON

From 1934 to 1940, the combination of potent network radio, increasingly appealing records, and spectacular movie and legitimate theatre musicals created a pantheon of musical superstar performers, writers, and all-powerful publishing and recording executives. For example, Bing Crosby became a superstar through such a combination. William Paley presented Bing Crosby on the CBS radio network; Jack Kapp made one hit record after another with Bing, and the movies added luster to his name and spread his fame around the world. Similar combinations of exposure made superstars of Frank Sinatra, Perry Como, Dinah Shore, Peggy Lee, Doris Day, Mary Martin, Ethel Merman, to name a few. Such exposure also created an era of never yet equalled popularity for the big bands of Glenn Miller, Benny Goodman, Artie Shaw, Tommy and Jimmy Dorsey, Duke Ellington, Count Basie, Horace Heidt, Charlie Spivak, Les Brown, Glen Gray, Xavier Cugat, Fletcher Henderson, Cab Calloway, Guy Lombardo, Gene Krupa, Jimmy Lunceford, Kay Kyser, Freddy Martin, Sammy Kaye, Chick Webb, Lawrence Welk, Paul Whiteman, Woody Herman, Vaughn Monroe, Harry James and scores of others.

The writers of the movie and Broadway musicals, as well as the writers of pop hit songs recorded by the stars, became rich and renowned. Among them were Irving Berlin, George Gershwin, Ira Gershwin, Richard Rodgers and Lorenz Hart, Oscar Hammerstein II, Vincent Youmans, Cole Porter, Arthur Schwartz and Howard Dietz, "Yip" Harburg, Vernon Duke, Burton Lane, Harold Rome, Kurt Weill, Julie Styne, Alan Jay Lerner and Frederick Loewe, Frank Loesser, Buddy DeSylva, Lew Brown, Ray Henderson, Sammy Cahn, Adolph Green, Betty Comden, Harold Arlen, Johnny Mercer, Otto Harbach, Irving Caesar, Jimmy Van Heusen, Johnny Burke, Ned Washington, Jimmy McHugh, Leo Robin, Harold Adamson, P. G. Wodehouse, and Dorothy Fields.

THE POTENT POP PUBLISHERS

The publishers who handled the copyrights of these composers and their batteries of song pluggers (called contact men) pursued a well-defined, foolproof system of making popular song hits. The major publishers included the Music Publishers Holding Corporation, a combine of firms acquired by Warner Bros.; Chappell; the big three of Robbins-Feist-Miller (partly owned by MGM and 20th Century-Fox); Shapiro-Bernstein; Santly-Joy; Famous (owned by Paramount); and Bourne and Bregman, Vocco and Conn. These behemoths each selected a song, written by a favorite writer or team of writers to be their "plug" song for a given period, three to six months generally. The "plug" song would receive the full promotional attention and be backed by the total resources of the publisher for the "plug" period.

The publisher informed the artist-and-repertoire heads of the three major record companies (RCA Victor, Columbia and Decca) and a few of the more aggressive independents of the plug song, and the record companies dutifully recorded it, each with one of their top artists. In the meantime, the publisher's contact men supplied copies of the song to every bandleader and/or singer who controlled radio air time, such as a Bing Crosby or orchestra leader like John Scott Trotter on a high-rated commercial program, or a Tommy Dorsey (with Sinatra in the band) who did nightly "remotes" from the Cafe Rouge of the Pennsylvania Hotel in New York City.

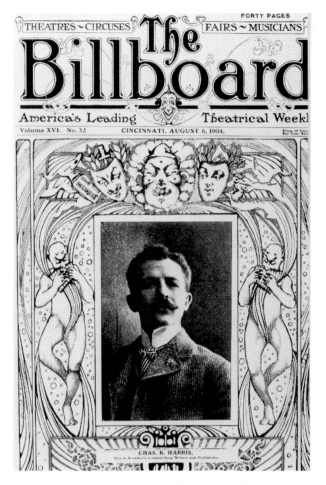

AUG. 4, 1904 ISSUE   CHAS. K. HARRIS

NO ROOM FOR HILLBILLY AND RACE

The bandleaders and singers were persuaded to play the "plug" tune heavily and repeatedly by whatever means the song plugger found necessary; for the most part, the tunes got played. Not all of the songs turned out to be Top Ten hits, but a large number did. A song which did not have the benefit of this organized, establishment plugging treatment did not stand too much chance of becoming a hit. Country and western songs (called "hillbilly" tunes) and rhythm and blues (R&B), or soul tunes (called "race" songs), had no chance at all for national mass popularity.

It was a prosperous, well-oiled and organized music business, although somewhat closed and somewhat plastic. The hit songs were generally formula (ABAB, AABA, or whatever), precisely thirty-two bar works dealing with love, fulfilled or unrequited, with an occasional "Mairzy Doats," or "The Music Goes Round and Round" thrown in for comedy or novelty relief. This is not to say that hundreds of the songs by Rodgers, Porter, Kern, Youmans, et al. were not excellent (as their popularity through the years has proven). It was simply that songwriters at that time did not choose (nor had they any need) to deal with social problems of any kind.

AUG. 4, 1917 ISSUE   HARRY VON TILZER

ASCAP CREATES BMI

This situation derived basically from the fact that ASCAP was a monopoly, and the record companies and the major film makers were tight combines of powerful groups. In the way of monopolies, ASCAP raised its rates to music users each time a current two, three or five-year contract with the users expired. By 1939, the radio broadcasters, who had originally paid the Society $250 per year per station for the right to play ASCAP music, were paying millions of dollars annually to the publishers and writers. And as the December 31, 1939 expiration date of the then current contract approached, ASCAP notified the broadcasters that it wanted another increase in the rates.

The broadcasters said no, emphatically. As of January 1, 1940, not a single song represented by ASCAP could be heard on any radio station. The broadcasters "vamped" with sundry renditions of "Jeannie with the Light Brown Hair," and other Stephen Foster works, plus such acceptable musical material in the public domain as they could find. They formed their own music performing rights society, Broadcast Music, Inc. (BMI). They felt there was no reason why they couldn't find competent songwriters and intelligent music people who could operate music publishing firms.

RADIO PLAYS COUNTRY AND R&B

They discovered, somewhat to their surprise, that virtually every experienced, able writer of popular songs was a member of ASCAP and thus untouchable. They also discovered, to their considerable relief, that most hillbilly songwriters and publishers and most "race" songwriters and publishers did not belong to ASCAP. They had been unable to join. In Nashville and other southern and rural cities, BMI found publishing organizations with substantial catalogues of hillbilly songs, and elsewhere in the country they found people who had published hundreds of so-called race songs. BMI quickly signed these writers and publishers. And now, for the first time in radio/music history, the music which came to be known as country and western, rhythm and blues, and soul was played consistently, twenty-four hours a day, on America's radio stations. The music was played exclusively through the long months before the broadcasters worked out what they considered to be a satisfactory deal with ASCAP.

By the time the deal was worked out and the broadcasters began to play ASCAP songs again, country and western, rhythm and blues, and also soul music had begun to flow into the mainstream of the nation's popular music. For the first time, people across the country could hear various musical styles. In the south and in many rural areas, naturally enough, the stations playing country and soul won high ratings; in many of the larger cities, stations began programming all-black, soul music.

WARS MAKE NEW FANS

An external force (the series of wars beginning with World War II, and continuing through the Korean "police action" and the Vietnam catastrophe) swelled the flow of the once-secondary music styles into the pop mainstream. Down through those years from 1940 right up to the end of the Vietnam war in 1973, young Americans from all parts of the country, with widely diversified musical tastes, were thrown together. Far from home, frightened, bored and lonely, these men exchanged ideas and extolled their favorite entertainments to each other. Sophisticated city lads were exposed to country and soul music for the first time, and many of them became fans.

The major record companies, prior to World War II, had produced some country and soul records, just as they had turned out some jazz and classical records. But the big profits lay in the pop operations. So, when the shellac shortage developed early in the war, the big companies virtually dropped their activities in these secondary areas.

THE INDEPENDENTS MOVE IN

By the time the war ended in 1945, America had had almost five years of solid radio exposure to country and rhythm and blues (R&B) music. The market for this music had been substantially expanded, and a number of aggres-

390

sive, young, independent record makers moved into the picture. In the rhythm and blues and jazz fields, Atlantic, Chess, National, Aladdin, Black & White, Savoy, Imperial and RPM record companies launched hard-driving operations. They worked closely with the program directors and disk jockeys on the stations specializing in these musical styles. Similarly in the country field, labels such as King, Queen, Fabor and others moved in. They set up similar close relationships with the people who chose the records to be played on the country music stations. The major record companies, quite content with their thriving pop business, made few efforts to cultivate these special markets.

By the early 1950s, the R&B sound had caught on to such a degree that more and more top stations in major cities were adding an increasing number of these records to their playlists. The major record companies increased their efforts to cultivate these markets, but the independents had developed promotional techniques and relationships with the top artists, writers, producers and disk jockeys in this area, which made it difficult for the majors to compete successfully.

And more and more white artists, having been exposed since 1941, via radio and records, to the soul and country music, began to make records flavored with elements of both rhythm and blues and country. In 1954, Bill Haley and his group recorded "Rock Around the Clock," a tune which was featured in a youth-protest film, *The Blackboard Jungle.* Following the film's release the record became a big hit.

PHILLIPS AND PRESLEY

In Memphis, about the same time, another independent record man was readying what was to be a major contribution to the evolution of popular music. Sam Phillips of Sun Records had already made hit records with such artists as Johnny Cash and Jerry Lee Lewis. But in 1954 he recorded an eighteen-year-old truck driver from Tupelo, Mississippi, named Elvis Presley. Phillips released Presley's "That's All Right, Mama," followed by "Mystery Train" and "I Forgot to Remember"; these became moderate regional hits.

By 1956, Tom Parker had taken over Presley's career and signed him to RCA Victor where Steve Sholes, the company's head of country artists and repertoire, produced "Heartbreak Hotel" backed with "I Was the One." These were followed by "Don't Be Cruel" and "Hound Dog" and Presley was on his way to becoming one of American entertainment's major superstars and the generally acknowledged "King of Rock." The style Presley sang was "rockabilly," a combination of soul, gospel, rhythm and blues and country which he had absorbed by listening to records by Bo Didley and other black artists and by Eddy Arnold and other country stars.

Presley's phenomenal rise to superstardom easily matched that of Bing Crosby and Frank Sinatra in the generations just preceding him. And, like Crosby and Sinatra, he carried the banner for an entire new singing and musical style.

MARCH 20, 1937 ISSUE   VINCENT LOPEZ

ROCK AND THE VARIATIONS

In 1955 in New York, Alan Freed, one of the nation's most potent disk jockeys, who had been featuring rhythm and blues records for some time on his shows, began using the phrase "rock and roll" to describe that music. There were establishment protests against the use of that phrase, since it was a term used in some black quarters to describe the act of sexual intercourse. But the objections were no more effective than earlier protests against rag or jazz had been.

Rock, and a dozen or more variations or fusions of it with other musical styles, was here to stay. There developed numerous forms of rock. Some of these forms and the leading exponents of each form were:

Jazz/Rock—Chicago; Blood, Sweat & Tears; Chuck Mangione
Motown Rock—the Supremes; the Temptations
Soft Rock—the Carpenters; Carole King; James Taylor
Hard Rock—Grand Funk; Jefferson Starship; Black Sabbath
Classical Rock—Emerson, Lake & Palmer
Progressive Soul Rock—Earth, Wind & Fire
Latin Rock—Santana
Bubble Gum Rock—Jackson Five; the Osmonds
Unisex-Bisex Rock—David Bowie; Alice Cooper; the Kinks

In 1977–1978 a strong campaign was being waged to establish *Punk Rock* (or *New Wave Rock*). The leading group and exponent of this form was the Sex Pistols, an English band consisting of Johnny Rotten, Sid Vicious, Steve Jones and Paul Cook. The four lads made their American debut in January of 1978. They featured raw, basic rock accented with on-stage fighting, spitting, vomiting and foul language.

HOT JOCKEYS AND TOP 40

Freed and other disk jockeys, particularly in the major markets, became increasingly potent as the makers of hit records. Among the most powerful of these "platter spinners" in New York, in addition to Freed, were Martin Block (credited with originating the disk jockey programming concept, along with Al Jarvis in Hollywood), William B. Williams, Murray the K (Kaufman), Art Ford and Alan Courtney. In Chicago there was Howard Miller and Eddie Chase; in Hollywood, Jarvis, Peter Potter, Ira Cook and Gene Norman; in Cleveland, Bill Randle. Every major market and many secondary markets developed their own strong disk jockey personalities. Many of the disk jockeys ventured into other areas of show business. Many emceed stage shows presenting current record favorites in person; many conducted weekly "hops," or teen-age dance parties. Some wrote songs and recorded. The most successful in the writing/recording area was Jim Lowe, New York personality, who wrote songs such as "Gambler's Guitar," a major hit by Rusty Draper, and recorded one of the biggest hits of the early '50s, "Green Door" on the Dot label.

Radio's hit-making capacity was substantially stepped up when the heads of two independent broadcasting chains adopted the Top 40 format. They were Todd Storz of Omaha, Neb. and Gordon McClendon of Dallas. The Top 40 format consisted of forty records, determined to be the most popular in the station's area, which were played repeatedly all through the day and night. It was this repetition, this relentless playing of the same record over and over, which sold millions of records and created recording stars and superstars.

MUSIC AND TELEVISION

While television had been primarily responsible for converting independent radio into an incredibly effective promotion medium for music and records, by forcing radio to utilize records for the bulk of its programming, TV itself used music almost exclusively in a key supportive way. Just as motion pictures, and every other form of entertainment, bulwarked their appeal with theme music and other secondary usages, television programs also developed their own theme songs. Many of these became record hits, just as movie themes had become record hits down through the years. TV, of course, also featured recording stars in many shows and occasionally built important music-variety series around some of them.

But there were no TV disk jockeys. The closest kin to radio's record spinners were the hosts of the early TV teenage dance shows. On these programs a personality played records to which the youngsters danced. Interviews with guest record stars were also featured. By far the most successful of these was Dick Clark's *American Bandstand* on ABC. Other shows featuring record stars were the midnight-early morning rock programs—such as Don Kirshner's *Rock Concert* and Burt Sugarman's *Midnight Special*—and numerous syndicated country music shows.

Extremely important to record promoters were the highly popular TV "talk" shows. *The Tonight Show* on NBC, starring Johnny Carson, and top-rated syndicated shows, headlining Merv Griffin, Mike Douglas and Dinah Shore frequently featured record stars. The three syndicated show hosts had been record stars at one point in their careers. Griffin's vocal on "I've Got a Lovely Bunch of Cocoanuts" with the Freddy Martin Band was a 1949 smash. Mike Douglas's "The Men in My Little Girl's Life," and "Cabaret" were hits in 1965 and 1966, and Dinah Shore, of course, won early fame as one of the nation's top vocalists, and had many hit records.

THE SPEED BATTLE

In 1948, however, at the same time that the nation's 108 pre-freeze television stations were setting TV patterns, the two major record companies, RCA Victor and Columbia, made another vital contribution to the development of the record industry. There had been no monumental technological advances in records since the introduction of magnetic tape recording and laminated disks in the '30s. But the development of the 33⅓ rpm record by Columbia; the counterdevelopment of the 45 rpm disk by RCA Victor; and the multi-million dollar battle between the two giants to establish the new speeds had a strong (initially negative, ultimately positive) impact on the music/record business. The tremendous advertising, publicity and promotional barrage which the controversial issue of the speeds touched off called public attention to records to a degree never before witnessed. The introduction of the new speeds also marked the beginning of the spectacular high fidelity era in the record business.

A TECHNOLOGICAL DELUGE

The "battle of the speeds" was followed by a continuing series of technological advances which (along with drastic evolutionary changes in songs, performers and musical styles) brought the music industry to new days of glory by the end of 1977. There were stereophonic and the somewhat less successful quadraphonic records. Reel-to-reel, four-track, then eight-track tape and cassettes were introduced. Eight-track tape grew into an important configuration. There were tremendous studio advances: recording on four separate tracks, then eight, then sixteen, twenty-four and thirty-two separate tracks, as well as an amazing array of noise reduction devices, echo chambers, equalizers and mixers.

At the very root of music, in the instruments themselves, technology expanded. In 1929, Les Paul (who with his wife, Mary Ford, had a number of hit records) experimented with his guitar by driving a Victrola needle into the wood and hooking it up to a speaker. It was the first example of amplification of a musical instrument. In the years following 1948, all manner of amplification of acoustic instruments—the Fender bass guitar, the Rhodes piano, et al.—were developed. "Fuzz" and "wah-wahs" and other desirable distortions were achieved by foot pedal. From the outer-space sounds of the early theramin experiments, music advanced to Robert Moog's incredible synthesizer which could make the sounds of virtually every instrument ever known, and many that never before existed.

Home (and garage) recording activity began as recorder-players improved steadily in quality and decreased in price. Soon four-track recording units, produced by firms such as TEAC, represented the tools with which creative young people could produce and engineer their own hits.

NEW MUSIC, NEW STARS

The young writers and musicians, the exponents of rock, who had been severely criticized for their musical ignorance, their lack of refinement and sophistication, latched on to these instruments and recording units. The best of them frequently got their musical training by joining the progressive jazz bands and groups, the so-called stage bands, in the nation's high schools and colleges. By the mid-1970s, there were more than 20,000 such bands in the high schools, and over 1,000 in the colleges around the country. The young writers and performers learned their new, electronic instruments and their synthesizers; they experimented with sounds; they combined their technical knowledge and their growing skills with their non-establishment attitudes (in some cases with their inspirational reliance on drugs) to create an entire new world of popular music. Much of their music was based on the blues, gospel, and country music which had flowed into the mainstream when the floodgates were opened by the formation of BMI in 1940.

Extraordinary double-threat and triple-threat music stars emerged. In previous times in the music/record business, a songwriter wrote the songs; an arranger arranged them; a singer sang them; a band played them; a producer recorded them. Very occasionally a producer also wrote songs, and played or sang. In the '50s, as rock grew, a few writer/performers such as Paul Anka and Neil Sedaka made their debuts. But most of the stars were strictly performers. Presley was the king of rock but others wrote his songs and Sam Phillips and Steve Sholes produced his records. The Kingston Trio (who followed Presley as superstars in the brief 1958–1965 period during which folk music became a dominant style) performed the works of other writers and recorded under the direction of Voyle Gilmore and other Capitol producers.

RADIO — STAGE — PICTURES — OUTDOOR

15 Cents   The Billboard   MAY 9, 1936

The World's Foremost Amusement Weekly

TOMMY DORSEY
And His Orchestra

MAY 9, 1936 ISSUE   TOMMY DORSEY

The Kingston Trio—with records such as "Where Have All the Flowers Gone," a Pete Seeger, anti-war protest—was one of the first groups to bring social consciousness to popular music. But during the '60s and '70s, the trend toward double- and triple-threat talents exploded. Bob Dylan continued and expanded on the Kingston Trio's strong emphasis on social awareness and was also one of the earliest double-threat, later to become triple-threat, artists. Signed to Columbia and initially recorded by John Hammond, Dylan and his songs "Blowin' in the Wind," "The Times They Are A-Changin' " and many other tunes of social consciousness spoke for rebellious youth. Dylan also moved from the folk idiom into country and then rock, and eventually wrote, performed and produced his own records.

THE PHENOMENAL BEATLES

The same year, 1964, that Dylan wrote the prophetic "The Times They Are A-Changin' ", The Beatles had their first American hit record on Capitol, "I Want to Hold Your Hand." The Beatles (Paul McCartney, John Lennon, George Harrison and Ringo Starr) quickly became the most successful group in the history of American (or for that matter, international) entertainment. But, more importantly, they actually created a new lifestyle for young people around the world. Their young manager, Brian Epstein, had not been able to get them a record contract until 1962 when he signed them to EMI in London where George Martin produced their earliest records.

Even then they were writing their own songs. Paul McCartney and John Lennon continued to write and created a catalogue of exceptional songs to match those of any writers, anywhere in any time. Eventually the four young men from Liverpool also began to produce their own records. After they discontinued as The Beatles, and each recorded on his own, they all turned out to be extraordinary triple-threat writer/performer/producer talents.

THE BRITISH INVASION AND STEVIE WONDER

The unprecedented success of The Beatles set off a British invasion in the mid-'60s. And many of the new British groups and singers had developed styles similar to Presley's, based on black Southern blues and country songs which had become an increasingly important part of the popular American musical mainstream. One example was the Rolling Stones, whose eventual popularity almost matched that of The Beatles. Mick Jagger and his Stones basically played and sang Deep South blues. Another example, which erupted into full flower in the mid-'70s, was Fleetwood Mac. Mick Fleetwood and his original group also played in the blues style, particularly during their early days in 1964.

By the end of 1977, numerous solo artists and groups were writing, performing and producing their own hit records and albums. Possibly the most talented and successful of all was a blind, young black man, Stevie Wonder. Wonder not only wrote and produced his multi-million selling albums on Motown's Tamla label (among them *Songs in the Key of Life*, *Innervisions*, and *Fulfillingness' First Finale*), but he also played most of the instruments for the recording sessions.

Of course not all of the new recording stars wrote their own songs and produced their own records. Those whose talents were limited to performing were strongly supported by the efforts of a constantly growing number of contemporary writers, independent producers, aggressive record companies, and in some cases dedicated and shrewd personal managers. The degree to which each contributed to the star-making process varied, of course, with each individual.

ROAD MAP TO SUPERSTARS

It is generally recognized that Elvis Presley and The Beatles may not have become legendary superstars without the efforts of Tom Parker and RCA and Brian Epstein and EMI/Capitol, respectively. Scores of music stars owe their success largely to the promotion, distribution, and general support of their record labels.

A road map to the stars and superstars of each era can be found in the collection of music and record popularity charts that have been (and still are) published by *Billboard*. As early as 1903, in random news reports, *Billboard* published a virtual running record which documented the individual vaudeville and other singing stars who were successfully singing certain songs. In July, 1913, *Billboard* published its first formal music chart, *Last Week's Ten Best Sellers Among Popular Songs*. It was based on reports from twelve music retailers and department stores across the country.

Down through the years, as new developments occurred in music, additional charts were published. By 1945 weekly charts, tabulating best-selling and most played songs and records in every musical category, were being published. A recapitulation of these charts, many for the three decades from 1945 through 1975, appears in the section "Original *Billboard* Material" following this essay. These charts give a comprehensive picture of the most popular songs, artists, and record labels in pop, country, and rhythm and blues down through the years.

MORE NEW LABELS

These lists reveal the large number of new, independent record companies which came into the music industry. All of them made contributions in one fashion or another. Among the new labels were companies owned by motion picture firms: MGM, 20th Century Fox, United Artists, Warner Bros., Colpix and Arista (both Columbia Pictures firms). Warners (along with corporate sister firms, Elektra and Atlantic) developed into an industry giant and was responsible for a long list of contemporary superstars including Fleetwood Mac, Rod Stewart, Alice Cooper, and Shaun Cassidy. Atlantic was no doubt the greatest success story of the early independents; it started as a rhythm and blues and gospel record label in the early '50s. Scores of stars have been developed by the label, including Ray Charles, Aretha Franklin, Bobby Darin and countless top rock, soul and jazz names.

Twentieth Century Fox created one of the earliest disco stars, Barry White, and of course, acquired the original sound-track to the hit, *Star Wars*. MGM introduced and developed one of the all-time great country stars, writer-performer Hank Williams. United Artists had some of the nation's outstanding acts in Kenny Rogers, Brass Construction, Bill Conti, Crystal Gale, and the Electric Light Orchestra.

RECORD COMPANIES INTO FILM MAKING

By 1977, some of the more aggressive independent record companies were going into the motion picture business with considerable success. Fantasy, the jazz label, which developed the Credence Clearwater Revival group into a hit act, made the Oscar-winning film, *One Flew Over the Cuck-*

RADIO   STAGE   NIGHT SPOTS   PICTURES   OUTDOOR

★ *15* Cents   **The Billboard**   MARCH 6, 1937

The World's Foremost Amusement Weekly

BENNY GOODMAN
MANAGEMENT MUSIC CORPORATION OF AMERICA

MARCH 6, 1937 ISSUE   BENNY GOODMAN

television series, who had also had several hit records and made several feature and TV films. Stigwood also taped enough footage of the making of the film and its premiere screening (attended by scores of show business celebrities) to put together a television "special," which was carried by stations in major markets concurrent with the film's opening.

At the end of 1977, Stigwood was making another film, *Sergeant Pepper's Lonely Hearts Band,* based on the multi-million selling Beatles' album of the same name, using the same Paul McCartney-John Lennon songs, and starring A&M's superstar, Peter Frampton. The same high-powered promotional combination as was used for *Saturday Night Fever* was planned for the *Pepper* film.

At least one major artist ventured into picture making on his own. In early 1978, Bob Dylan released a four-hour film, *Renaldo and Clara,* which he wrote, directed and co-edited. John Rockwell, *New York Times* writer, described it as:

> a grandly ambitious, sometimes muddled effort to pose a complex of philosophical questions and to dig behind the outer reality of Mr. Dylan's life and career.

A&M, MOTOWN AND ARISTA

A&M, launched in 1962 by trumpeter Herb Alpert and Jerry Moss with a single hit, "The Lonely Bull" by Alpert, had become one of the most successful star-making labels in record history by 1977. Its line-up of stars and superstars, in addition to Frampton, included the Carpenters, the Captain and Tennille, Quincy Jones, Rita Coolidge, the Brothers Johnson, Supertramp and others.

One of the independents, Motown was organized in 1960 by Berry Gordy. It not only created an imposing line-up of major artists, beginning with Smokey Robinson, the Temptations, and Diana Ross and the Supremes, Stevie Wonder and many others, but actually originated a musical rock style, identified as "the Motown sound," which was emulated by many other record companies and artists.

Arista Records, launched in November, 1974 by Clive Davis, with financial backing by Columbia Pictures Industries, Inc., was an outstanding music/record business success story. Starting from absolute scratch, Arista became an important industry factor in less than three years. Davis had spent twelve years running Columbia Records before that major company fired him abruptly in the early '70s. John Hammond, who worked with Davis at Columbia, said, in *Billboard:*

> As far as I know, nothing that Clive ever did at Columbia was in any way unethical, and I can't conceive how a sensitive and dedicated employee could have been treated that way.

In any event, by 1977, Arista's net revenue for its last fiscal year was over $36,000,000. Davis and his Arista colleagues had created several new star and superstar acts, including Barry Manilow, Melissa Manchester, the Bay City Rollers, Eric Carmen, the Kinks, the Outlaws, Lou Reed and

oo's *Nest.* Motown produced *Lady Sings the Blues* and *Mahogany* with its superstar, Diana Ross, in the lead in both films. In partnership with Casablanca, Motown, in 1977, was making *Thank God, It's Friday,* with a disco-theme and Donna Summer and other stars. Casablanca also made *The Deep,* a strong box office film of 1977.

Another disco theme movie was *Saturday Night Fever,* produced by RSO Records. *Saturday Night Fever* was probably the most extraordinary example of multi-media film making and promotion of 1977. Produced by Robert Stigwood, head of RSO, it had a score of songs written by one or more of the Gibbs brothers—Barry, Maurice, Robin and Andy. Known as the Bee Gees, the Gibbs boys were one of the hottest contemporary acts in music in 1977. Stigwood was the Bee Gees' manager. Two of the songs from the picture, recorded by the Bee Gees on Stigwood's RSO label, became big hit single records. They were "How Deep Is Your Love" and "Stayin' Alive." A third tune from the film, "More Than a Woman"—written by Barry, Maurice and Robin and recorded by Tavares—was also a chart-making hit. The original soundtrack album, released on the RSO label and distributed by Polydor, was also among the top-selling albums on the charts. Starring in the film was young John Travolta of the *Welcome Back, Kotter*

others. Arista also recorded Lily Tomlin, who had won considerable television and motion picture fame, and the Muppets, Jim Henson's hit TV puppet group. Arista had also acquired the Savoy and Freedom labels and taken on distribution of the Passport and Buddah record labels.

COLUMBIA, RCA, CAPITOL AND DECCA (MCA)

The majors, of course, continued as the potent star-making force they had been for decades. Columbia boasted a wide range of superstars, such as Barbra Streisand, Boz Scaggs, the Emotions, James Taylor, Aerosmith, Chicago; Earth, Wind and Fire; Pink Floyd, Neil Diamond, Deniece Williams, Dave Mason, Kenny Loggins, Maynard Ferguson and others. RCA also maintained a high position with strong star and superstar acts including John Denver, veteran country superstar Eddy Arnold, Daryl Hall and John Oates, Waylon Jennings, Dr. Buzzard's Original Savannah Band, and David Bowie.

Decca, which had become MCA, contributed its share of superstars and major acts with Elton John, Rose Royce, Olivia Newton-John, B.J. Thomas, Conway Twitty, Loretta Lynn, Tanya Tucker and Mel Tillis. Capitol, too, maintained its position with a wide variety of strong-selling acts. Among them were the Steve Miller Band, Bob Seger and the Silver Bullet Band, Paul McCartney and Wings, Natalie Cole (daughter of the great Nat Cole, who had been a major star on Capitol in its early days), Maze, the Beach Boys, Glen Campbell and Helen Reddy. Of course, RCA continued to sell millions of Elvis Presley's albums after his death; just as Capitol continued to sell millions of Beatles albums long after the group broke up.

INDEPENDENT PRODUCERS AND WRITERS

Among the leading independent producers in 1977 were Richard Perry, Freddie Perren, Tom Dowd, Steve Miller, Bill Szymczyk, Peter Asher, Jeff Lynn and Norman Whitfield. Some performer-writers in addition to those already mentioned were Carole King, Boz Scaggs, Christine McVie of the Fleetwood Mac group, Paul Simon, Rod Stewart, Bob Welch, Neil Diamond, Kris Kristofferson, John Denver, Tom T. Hall, Jeff Barry, James Taylor, Smokey Robinson, David Gates, Alan O'Day, Henry Mancini, Burt Bacharach, and Carole Bayer Sager.

Non-performing writers of the mid-'70s included Al Kasha and Joel Hirschorn, Norman Gimble, Marvin Moore, Norman Petty, Tommy Boyce, Cynthia Weill and Barry Mann, Bernie Wayne, Joe Brooks and Hal David. Some successful film and television music writers of the period were Andre Previn, Johnny Green, Irwin Kostal, Saul Chaplin, Alan and Marilyn Bergman, Dave Grusin, Lalo Schifrin, Bill Conti, Jack Elliott and Allyn Ferguson, Pat Williams, Maurice Jarre, Nino Rota (who wrote the *Godfather* score),

MAY 24, 1941 ISSUE   GLENN MILLER

and John Williams, who wrote the scores for both *Star Wars* and *Close Encounters of the Third Kind.*

In the musical theatre, several writers joined the Rodgers, Harts, Hammersteins, Porters, et al. of earlier days. Among them were Leonard Bernstein, Meredith Wilson, Frank Loesser, Jerry Bock and Sheldon Harnick, Jerry Herman, Alan Jay Lerner, and Frederick Loewe (whose *My Fair Lady* precipitated a new rush of original cast albums and record company investment in Broadway shows, paced by Goddard Lieberson of Columbia), Fred Ebb and John Kander, and Stephen Sondheim.

Several writers of rock musicals made a mark in the late '60s and '70s. Most notable were Andrew Lloyd Weber (music) and Tim Rice (lyrics) who created *Jesus Christ, Superstar. Hair* by Gerome Ragni, James Rado and Galt McDermott had preceded it in 1968. Stephen Schwartz wrote *Godspell* in 1971.

NEW PUBLISHING POWERS

Many publishing organizations of the '70s were owned by record companies and recording artists. Firms such as Jobete (Motown), Warner Bros., United Artists, Almo and Irving (A&M), American Broadcasting, Stigwood, Duchess, were typical of these. In the country field the leaders included Tree Publishing, Acuff-Ross, Al Gallico and Algee, Hall-Clement, among many others. In the rhythm and blues (soul) category, Jobete, Sherlyn, Mighty Three, ABC-Dunhill, Jays Enterprises and Unichappel were among the most active firms. Paul McCartney bought one of the old established publishing houses, E.H. Morris, for $10,000,000 and added it to his already substantial publishing empire.

Although sheet music sales amounted to little in the last four decades from the mid-'30s to the '70s, print music in the form of folios and songbooks was making an astonishing comeback. Records, tapes, and performances were the major sources of publisher and writer income. As Joel Friedman, head of WEA, had predicted, an increasing number of artists were achieving sales of 5,000,000 and more per album and heading for the titanium classification (10,000,000 or more per album release). Fleetwood Mac's album, *Rumours,* sold more than 2,000,000 internationally outside the United States and double that amount in the United States. Recording deals reached staggering proportions: MCA guaranteed Elton John $8,000,000 when he signed his last contract; Paul McCartney got a similar guarantee from Capitol; Stevie Wonder got a $13,000,000 guarantee from Motown. And all these were for record royalties only. They did not include the publisher and writer royalties.

PERFORMANCES AND CONCERTS

ASCAP and BMI collected well over $150,000,000 in performances fees in 1976 which, after expenses, was paid out to writer and publisher members.

In January of 1978, the newly passed copyright law (the first change since 1909) went into effect. It could do nothing but make the music/record picture even brighter. Among other provisions it increased the statutory royalty rate record companies must pay music copyright owners from two cents per song per record sold to two and three-quarters cents. It also required that jukebox operators must pay for the right to play records. Up to this time they were the only users of music-for-public-performance-for-profit who did not pay for such use.

A *Billboard* study of contemporary music concert grosses in 1977 showed that of the top fifteen concerts at festivals or in stadiums with seating capacities of 20,000 or more, and in arenas with 6000 to 20,000 capacities, three rock shows did over $1,000,000 in one or two night concerts; thirteen shows did $250,000 to $500,000; and thirteen others did between $100,000 and $250,000. Projecting these figures on the most conservative scale, industry estimates are that rock concert shows do well over $100,000,000 in business annually. Since the top rock acts on the bills frequently get 50% of the gross or a fixed amount, whichever is higher, it is easy to understand why so many rock acts concentrated their efforts solely on making records and doing concert tours and paid scant attention to motion pictures and television.

NEW PEAKS FOR RECORDS AND TAPE

By the end of 1977, it appeared that the pre-recorded music industry would be grossing $3,000,000,000 for the year. And it was still growing. Industry organizations such as the Recording Industry Association of America and the National Association of Record Merchandisers were working with similar organizations in the hardware (players-recorders, etc.) fields to develop co-operative efforts to expand the market for pre-recorded music.

Videocassette players and recorders were being pushed by almost every major consumer electronics manufacturer. And while it remained to be seen whether there would be a substantial market for pre-recorded videocassettes of record stars and music acts, it was obvious that another dimension was being added to pre-recorded music. Many contemporary acts by 1977—virtually all who played concerts—featured visual gimmickry almost as much as they featured their music. Among these were the Rolling Stones, Kiss, Alice Cooper and Ted Nugent.

FERTILE ATMOSPHERE
FOR NEW TALENT

And, by 1977, it was a wide open, multi-faceted music world. ASCAP—which thirty-seven years earlier had a repertoire quite limited in rhythm and blues and country material—now boasted some of the greatest writers and publishers in those musical styles as members. BMI—which began life with nothing but country and rhythm and blues songs—boasted some of the outstanding writers and publishers for the musical theatre, films and television.

And both the performing rights organizations had a full share of the leading contemporary rock writers, easy-listening writers and publishers. It was a fertile atmosphere in which writers and performers could grow. Indeed, fresh talent was emerging daily. The industry was waiting for the next Presley or the next Beatles to take it to plateaus undreamed of, even in this period of achievement.

ORIGINAL BILLBOARD MATERIAL

HIGHLIGHTS

———◆—◆—◆———

PARADE OF SUPERSTARS 418
From Bing Crosby, Frank Sinatra, Perry Como, and Nat "King" Cole to Elvis Presley, Bob Dylan, Bobby Darin, The Beatles, the Rolling Stoes, ill-fated Janis Joplin and Jimi Hendrix, Elton John, Tom Jones, Helen Reddy, Fleetwood Mac and scores of others, the recording superstars created new excitement in popular music.

CHARTING THE BEST: POP, COUNTRY, SOUL 421

In 1940, broadcaster-created BMI was forced to concentrate on developing country and soul music, enabling these styles to flow into the popular music mainstream. By 1946, country and soul songs and their stars were making an increasingly strong impact, and the musical base for rock was taking form. By that time, too, the *Billboard* charts had been expanded and developed so that weekly tabulations of the best in all fields of music were published. Thirty years later, during the nation's bicentennial, *Billboard* recapped the best artists, songs, single records and albums in Pop, Country and Soul for three decades from 1946–1975.

IN THE '70s:
AN EXCITING, WIDE OPEN MIX 439
By the 1970s, both ASCAP and BMI had thousands of writer-members and hundreds of publisher-members turning out exciting material in every musical style. The newer "independent" record companies were in fierce competition with the long-established majors. Numerous network television specials honored music's superstars. The twenty-year old National Association of Recording Arts and Sciences *Grammy Awards Show* was the oldest of these shows, and the *Billboard Number 1 Big Event* two-hour special on NBC-TV the newest.

"MR. MERRY-GO-ROUND MAN, IN WHAT CONDITION IS YOUR ORGAN?"

FROM SEPT. 11, 1909 ISSUE

SAY, MR. MERRY-GO-ROUND MAN,
In What Condition is Your Organ ?

When the season is over, send your organ to me to be put in first-class shape. Have late popular music, that's the main thing! Have bass and snare drums attached, that's the only thing! Correspondence solicited. Satisfaction guaranteed. C. F. BATH, Abilene, Kansas.

FROM DEC. 24, 1904 ISSUE

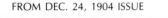

BARBER who plays B-flat Clarinet.

No Boozers. Address
FRANK MESSNER, Boswell, Ind.

FROM APRIL 25, 1903 ISSUE

YOUNG MUSICIAN
...WANTED...

To play instrument in Band, who is familiar with House Work. to act as Porter on Traveling Theatrical Car. Must be a young white man, strong and willing to work, and be perfectly sober and cleanly in his habits. A long engagement and a good position for the right party. Salary must be low and is paid promptly, the season to run forty weeks. Send full particulars as to age, height, weight and experience. Address WARREN NOBLE, Mgr. Noble's Theatre Company, No. 3 Broadway, (East), Winnipeg, Manitoba.

FROM APRIL 18, 1903 ISSUE

WANTED
Performers: also tuba for band and orchestra, baritone to double 2nd violin or clarinet, cornet to double 2nd violin or viola, porter on car to double alto: also first-class cook. State age, weight and height, and what show experience. Must be gentlemen. Open season latter part of April. **J. S. SWENSON, write.** Address,
BEACH & BOWER'S MINSTRELS, Maquaketa, Iowa

FROM MAY 16, 1903 ISSUE

MUSICIANS WANTED !

TO COMPLETE BAND TWENTY PIECES.

WRITE QUICK. MAY 11th, NORFOLK, VA.

GASKILL--MUNDY--LEVITT CARNIVAL CO.

FROM MARCH 17, 1906 ISSUE

Can offer 50 weeks work in the year
to good musicians. Parks in summer. Vaudeville and Concert in winter.

Will give a lady DIRECTOR who can lead a lady's band competently, a 5 year contract at a good salary.

Also want A 1 LADY VOCALISTS for Lady's Quartette. Address,

G. PRESTON,

Garden Theatre, Buffalo, N. Y.

WANTED

Lady Musicians and Vocalists.

FROM JUNE 7, 1902 ISSUE

VIOLINIST - LEADER
At Liberty for engagement, experienced in all branches. Fine repertoire of music, locate or travel. (Reference exchanged if desired. Box 235 Wilmington, Delaware.

AT LIBERTY
The petite singing, dancing and character soubrette
MISS RUBY ATKINSON.
Change specialties nightly for two weeks. Good worker in acts, afterpieces, etc Put on same if requested Play organ. Responsible Med. Co managers address Saxon, Wis. next two weeks, after that, the good old "Billboard" Office.

OBOE PLAYER AT LIBERTY
A Gentleman of experience. Address A. Perina, 903 E. 161st. New York City.

MECHANICAL MUSIC

FROM MAY 21, 1977 ISSUE

This sketch of Edison by James E. Kelly probably shows the inventor as he appeared that historic day in 1877 when he first recorded the words of the familiar nursery rhyme "Mary Had A Little Lamb . . ." on his tinfoil phonograph.

Edison demonstrates his tinfoil phonograph in Washington in April 1878 (right), for his host, Uriah Painter, left, and mechanical draftsman Charles Batchelor, one of his chief aids who designed phonets.

Edison National Historic Site

Emile Berliner's historic invention the "Gramophone," patented in 1887. The hand-cranked machine was the first to use disks—also Berliner's invention—instead of cylinders. Its success led to the foundation of the Deutsche Grammophon Gesellschaft, oldest established record manufacturing company in the world, in 1898.

Berliner Collection

Beginnings of the Victor Talking Machine Company, 1900. Eldridge R. Johnson took over the Berliner operation and renamed it the Consolidated Talking Machine Co.

401

FROM MAY 21, 1977 ISSUE

Also around 1900, vocalist Jacques Urlus makes a recording at Edison's Fifth Ave. studio in NYC.

FROM MARCH 21, 1908 ISSUE

PERFORATED MUSIC

FOR

Electric Pianos

Guaranteed.

From Manufacturer to Consumer, at **$1.50 each.**

UNITED STATES MUSIC CO.

Milwaukee and Western Ave.,   -   -   -   -   CHICAGO, ILL.

Send for Catalogue.

402

THE SIGN OF QUALITY

WURLITZER

UpTo-Date Automatic Musical Instruments With Slot Attachment

Not only entertain your customers, and increase your trade, but are Money-Making Propositions.

Past experience has proven that these instruments with slot attachment, will pay as high as 200 to 300 per cent. on the investment.

WE MANUFACTURE THE LARGEST LINE OF

Automatic Musical Instruments IN THE WORLD.

ALL STYLES, ALL SIZES, ALL PRICES.

We sell these Instruments on such easy terms that the receipts, in many cases. amount to 3 and 4 times as much as the monthly payments.

Handsome Illustrated Catalog free upon request.

THE Rudolph Wurlitzer Co.

121 East 4th St., Cincinnati, Ohio.

268 Wabash Ave., Chicago, Ills.

MONSTER MILITARY BAND ORGAN.

THE PIANINO

THE WURLITZER HARP

GREATEST LINE ON EARTH

MILITARY BAND ORGAN

WURLITZER PLAYER-PIANO

THE MANDOLIN QUARTETTE

THE PIAN-ORCHESTRA

$1,200 to $5,000

Wurlitzer Automatic Instruments make nickels grow into dollars.

TIN PAN ALLEY PIONEERS

FROM DEC. 14, 1912 ISSUE

Prominent Music Publishers and Song Writers

FROM JUNE 5, 1909 ISSUE

FROM DEC. 5, 1908 ISSUE

JOS. W. STERN.

EDW. B. MARKS.

FROM JULY 19, 1902 ISSUE

FROM MAY 17, 1902 ISSUE

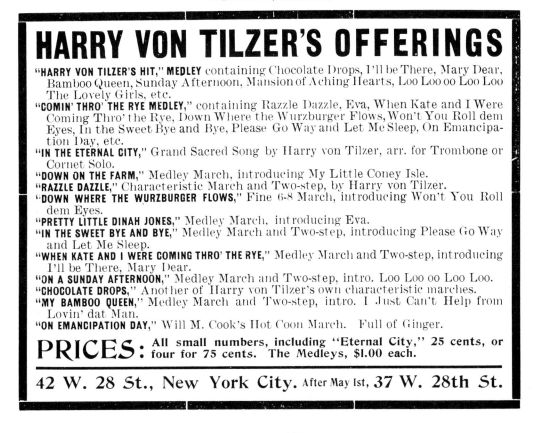

FROM DEC. 30, 1905 ISSUE

FROM MARCH 19, 1910 ISSUE

AGAIN WE SAY

"That Mesmerizing Mendelssohn Tune"

By IRVING BERLIN, is a Classic with a line under the first syllable. Get it and make your act classy; and,

"Next to Your Mother, Who Do You Love?"

By BERLIN AND SNYDER, has yet its first "flop" to experience. We dare you to "flop" with it; and,

"Yiddle On Your Fiddle, Play Some Rag Time"

By IRVING BERLIN. And--And--Well--Write down your own opinion of the only successor to Sadie Salome, by the same wr iter; and

"Ogalalla"

By BRYAN AND SNYDER. Have you heard them whistling an irresistible melody? Have you heard them shouting? Well. that's it---"Ogalalla"; and,

"Sweet Marie, Make-A Rag-A Time-A Dance Wid Me"

By BERLIN AND SNYDER. Three months before any of those "nifty" writers thought of Italian rags, Irving Berlin and Ted Snyder wrote this number for Emma Carus. She used same to great success in "The Jolly Bachelor Co." Get it while it's new---the original song; and,

——————————— THE ABOVE HITS ARE PUBLISHED BY THE ———————————

TED SNYDER CO. (Inc.), Music Publishers, 112 W. 38th

Chicago Office: Oneonta Bldg., Clark and Randolph Sts., Frank Clark

FROM MAY 1, 1909 ISSUE

LAEMMLE BRANCHES OUT INTO MUSIC PUBLISHING

The rumor which has been current in and around Chicago for the last few days that Carl Laemmle, the well-known factor in the moving picture business, had decided to enter the field of music publishers, was substantiated Saturday, April 24, by Mr. Laemmle himself, who admitted to a representative of The Billboard that he had yielded to the call of the harmony Muse and that shortly his ideas would be actively evidenced and in operation as a component part of his business organization. Mr. Laemmle stated during the interview that while at the present moment the project is practically in embryo it would be put a short while before his movements in the field will be on an extensive basis and of such strength as will make him one of the big factors in the business.

The practical man in charge, according to present plans, will be Mr. Homer Howard, formerly of Helf and Hager. Mr. Laemmle, with his usual discernment, will give Mr. Howard full sway in his department and will bow to his experience in this particular field of endeavor. However, the aggressive business policies of the Carl Laemmle Co.. will be the real power behind the throne and the music publishing of the company will be done on the same style of magnitude and thoroughness as has characterized their early efforts in the film business.

It is the intention not to confine their work merely to Chicago, although that city will be the fountain-head of their operations as heretofore, but to establish branch offices throughout the country and cover a national territory. It is inferred that even now they are under cover with several melodies of the popular sort that have all the earmarks of money-getting "hits" and that they have in mind some novelties that will be innovations indeed.

BUY COHAN-HARRIS CATALOGUE.

Maurice Shapiro. the New York music publisher. has bought the Cohan and Harris Music Publishing Co. catalogue including The Ham Tree. Steeplechasers. Whitewash Man and Meet Me in the Rose Time Rosie.

Chas. K. Harris has purchased the Little Nemo publishing rights from the same firm.

TED SNYDER

CARL LAEMMLE

THE PHONOGRAPH AS A FACTOR
AND PLUGGING BY RADIO

INTRODUCING OUR PHONOGRAPH DEPT.

Publishers' Song Values Will Be Gauged for Instrument Which Has Revolution-ized Music Sales

The phonograph is the greatest musical factor of all times—and it belongs to us.

We didn't invent it.

We don't own a record-making factory.

Yet the phonograph belongs to us—and by US we mean The Billboard and its family of readers and friends.

To say that the phonograph has revolutionized the music publishing field sounds like a mighty statement, but, as a matter of fact, its truth is almost self-evident. The phonograph performs an important double function. It takes songs which have earned their share of popularity on the regular sheet music market and repopularizes them in a field far more far-reaching and profitable. It also takes songs which would never experience spirited counter sales and popularizes them over the instrument.

Its accounting of royalties is exact and frequently publishers and writers make far more out of the phonograph earnings than thru counter sales. There are many phonograph companies working for the publishers at the same time, making the record sales possibilities of a song that takes hold almost unlimited. Yet, when all is said and done, the sheet music sales market is really a rather limited proposition.

Were the methods in vogue between the phonograph record manufacturers and the music publishers entirely above question we would stop this discussion with words of praise for the wonderful instrument and its makers.

But they aren't.

Knowing the ultimate reward, unscrupulous men have stooped to questionable methods in the all-important work of getting their songs upon the phonograph.

You probably know of yesterday's contemptible practice of bribing ten-cent store managers so that certain favored songs would see the light of day at sheet music counters. Incidentally it may be mentioned that few sheet-music salesmen now venture to shake hands with the girl demonstrators and leave $5 bills in their palms. This, too, has died with yesterday.

But, tho sheet music has eliminated graft, the phonograph, perhaps because its field is so new and undeveloped, has its fine springs of vitality besmeared with petty graft. We do not mean to insinuate that the men behind the phonograph are grafters. On the contrary we believe they are reputable business men. But the temptation to "put something over" is so alluring for certain small-calibered people placed in positions of confidence that the endeavors of the business-like directorate are thwarted. "I can get that song put on such and such record for a price" is a phrase which still rings in some publishers' ears.

The phonograph has not yet had an opportunity to test all the officials who prepare it and its records for the market. This opens up the avenues for graft.

Those of us who love popular music and are glad the sales counters are now clean are eager to see that the process of record making for phonographs be brought up to an equally clean standard, inasmuch as OUR phonograph now means more to us than the sales counters ever meant.

The phonograph people want to know what are the best songs for the phonograph. We intend to aid them. Making these recommendations will constitute part of our work.

In the long run this system of recommendation will reduce the opportunities for graft in the phonograph field.

The phonograph—the greatest of all musical carriers—covers too broad a field to be monopolized by any one interest. It belongs to all of us and we intend to treat it as a sacred trust.

If you are interested in songs you should be interested in the phonograph. What we have to say about the phonograph value (PV) of songs in our "Cold Type Review" of the music market's current issues should interest you.

PLUGGING BY RADIO

It looks as if radio may become a good thing for song publishers and a bad thing for song pluggers. Radio is gradually becoming a national pastime, and at present there are something like 250,000 licensed operators. There are five thousand active stations in this country owned and operated by men, women, boys and girls. Some radio clubs have as many as a thousand members.

About two weeks ago Bide Dudley of The New York World, Eddie Cantor, Vaugh De Leath, Louis Breau, Nat Sanders and Harry Garland gave a concert at Roselle Park, N. J. They sang and talked to listeners at hundreds of receiving stations, which means that numerous persons discussed what they did.

The radio concert is becoming quite a fad. While it is a fad for the public, and an entertaining one in the bargain, it should become a big asset for the music publishers. Just suppose every worth while music dealer in the country owned a receiving station. If this were the case all a publisher would have to do would be to engage a first-class singer to introduce his new numbers by radio, with the dealers listening in, and then wait for his orders to come thru. With this method of exploitation in practice a publisher would not have much use for a traveling salesman. And it might be a good plan for the publishers to talk dealers into purchasing a receiving outfit, which may be had for about $25. A dealer would not require any Government license to receive.

At the present time it takes a publisher weeks and months to cover the country with a new song, but via the radio method he could make thousands acquainted with a new number in an hour or so. Once the news got abroad that music publishers were giving free concerts at regular intervals there would be many new radio fans eager to obtain receiving stations. And it is not unlikely that the corporation that makes a specialty of manufacturing radio outfits would be willing to co-operate with publishers. Can you imagine a greater plug for a new number? Even performers near stations could listen to see what publishers had to offer. In any event, radio holds great possibilities for popular song publishers.

Paul Whiteman and NBC's "Romeo of Song," Russ Columbo

THE BIG BANDS

FROM JUNE 13, 1925 ISSUE

FROM DEC. 18, 1937 ISSUE

PARA THE BAND PALACE

•

Popularity Poll Indicates the Public Pulse on Music Faves

•

Shep Fields replaces Waring among 1936 top trio—no monopoly of swing at Paramount Theater—radio commercial counts most for booking

•

Tommy Dorsey

NEW YORK, Dec. 11.—With only two weeks to go, winners of the Paramount Theater band-popularity poll for 1937 will probably be Benny Goodman, Guy Lombardo and Shep Fields. Last year Lombardo, Fred Waring and Glen Gray grabbed the goblets. This time five prizes will be presented, with Eddy Duchin, Horace Heidt, Tommy Dorsey and Hal Kemp in a close race for fourth and fifth places. Importance of the Paramount poll as an accurate indication of the public pulse arises from the fact that during the last two years this theater has built up what is probably the most band-conscious audience in the country, consistently booking and featuring name bands, not merely as a side-dish for the picture but as the main attraction. Band leaders are prominently played up and top-billed on the marquee and lobby displays. Conscious of the powerful mass enthusiasm for orchestra styles and leader personalities, the management follows music trends and styles carefully, feeling that bands are the big draw in stage showmanship today.

"The public wants bands as never before," says Robert Weitman, Para manager. "The kids between 18 and 24 who make up the backbone of our audience demand dance bands on the stage. They want bands."

Fred Waring

Band Leaders in Para Poll

Standings, on December 10, of bands with 10,000 or more votes in the Paramount band-popularity contest:

Benny Goodman	27,051
Guy Lombardo	22,703
Shep Fields	18,874
Eddy Duchin	17,149
Tommy Dorsey	16,679
Horace Heidt	15,047
Hal Kemp	14,406
Glen Gray	13,122
Fred Waring	13,053
Sammy Kaye	12,048
George Hall	11,304
Ozzie Nelson	11,221
Rudy Vallee	11,052
Bunny Berigan	10,709
Wayne King	10,516
Phil Spitalny	10,439

Artie Shaw

Harry James   Guy Lombardo   Count Basie

FROM MARCH 5, 1949 ISSUE

Agency Band List Via $$$ Classification

"A" BANDS
(Those which grossed approximately $200,000 or more during 1948.)

Music Corporation of America
Charlie Barnet
Blue Barron
Tex Beneke
Carmen Cavallaro
Xavier Cugat
Tommy Dorsey
Eddy Duchin
Jack Fina
Shep Fields
Phil Harris
Skitch Henderson
Eddy Howard
Harry James
Spike Jones
Dick Jurgens
Gene Krupa
Ted Lewis
Guy Lombardo
Freddy Martin
Louis Prima
Three Suns
Ted Weems
Lawrence Welk
Bob Wills

General Artists Corporation
Desi Arnaz
Frankie Carle
Jimmy Dorsey
Woody Herman
Louis Jordan
Sammy Kaye
Elliot Lawrence
Ray McKinley
Tony Pastor
Henry Busse
King Cole Trio
Count Basie
Jan Garber
Cab Calloway
Art Kassel
Johnny Long
Hal McIntyre
Alvino Rey
Buddy Rich
Jan Garber

Associated Booking Corporation
Russ Morgan
Lionel Hampton
Louis Armstrong
Art Mooney
Les Brown
Gordon Jenkins

William Morris Agency
Duke Ellington
Charlie Spivak

Gale Agency
Lucky Millinder
Erskine Hawkins
Buddy Johnson
Illinois Jacquet

Willard Alexander Agency
Vaughn Monroe
Claude Thornhill
Dizzy Gillespie

"B" BANDS
(Those which grossed less than $200,000 but more than $100,000 during 1948.)

Music Corporation of America
Barclay Allen
Murray Arnold
Jan August
Johnny Bond
Nat Brandwynne
Emil Coleman
Chris Cross
Bernie Cummins
Al Donahue
Skinnay Ennis
Sherman Hayes
Henry King
Victor Lombardo
Matty Malneck
Frankie Masters
Buddy Moreno
Harry Owens
Joe Reichman
Benny Strong
Bob Strong
Al Trace
Orrin Tucker
Griff Williams
Sterling Young

General Artists Corporation
Ray Anthony
Ike Carpenter
Gay Claridge
Larry Clinton
Del Courtney
Hal Derwin
Sam Donahue
Sonny Dunham
Ray Eberle
Pee Wee Hunt
Red Ingle
Carlos Molina
Joe Sanders
Earl Spencer
George Towne
Jerry Wald
Frank Yankovich
George Olsen
Page Cavanaugh Trio
Bobby Byrne
Leighton Noble
Joe Venuti

Associated Booking Corporation
Ina Ray Hutton
Noro Morales
Charlie Ventura
Andy Kirk
Miguelito Valdez

William Morris Agency
Raymond Scott
Pupi Campo

Gale Agency
Bull Moose Jackson
Jimmie Lunceford
(Eddie Wilcox-Joe Thomas)
Lester Young

Willard Alexander Agency
Larry Green

"C" BANDS
(Those which grossed less than $100,000 during 1948.)

Music Corporation of America
Arnie Arnold
Dick Barlow
Denny Beckner
Mischa Borr
Johnny Bothwell
Russ Carlyle
Johnny Dee
Dick Dildine
Tony Di Pardo
George Duffy
Michael Durso
Roy Eldridge
Ziggy Elman (inactive)
Charlie Fisk
Dick Foy
Jerry Glidden
Cesar Gonzmart
Bob Grant
Glen Gray (inactive)
Ken Harris
Ernie Hecksher
Joel Herron
Henry Jerome
Don Kaye
Erwin Kent
Steve Kisley
Billy McDonald
Nicholas Matthey
Don McGrane
Bob Millar
Ray Morton
Freddy Nagel
Paul Neighbors
Red Nichols
Eddie Oliver
Leo Pieper
Emil Petti
Teddy Phillips
Gene Pringle
Ramon Ramos
Tommy Reynolds
Ray Robbins
Warney Ruhl
Freddie Shaffer
Bobby Sherwood
(inactive)
George Sterney
Ronnie Stevens
Eddie Stone
Nick Stuart
Joseph Sudy
Curt Sykes
Jimmie Tucker
Bud Waples
Sammy Watkins
Alvy West
Ran Wilde
Florian Zabach

General Artists Corporation
Jan Arnold
Will Back
Billy Bishop
Bob Bishop
Jay Burkhart
Billy Butterfield
Tony Cappa
Al Cassady
Dave Cavanaugh
Harvey Crawford
Michael Dunn
Hawaiian Sophisticates
Jack Emerson
Jimmy Featherstone

Ernie Fields
Johnny Gilbert
Albert Gomez
Chuck Gould
Wayne Gregg
Daryl Harpa
Will Hauser
Gray Gordon
Lenny Herman
Buddy Hisey
Johnny Hodges
Cee Pee Johnson
Austin Little
Del Lucas
Joe Lutcher
Dude Martin
Del Mason
Jose Melis
Deke Moffitt
Eddie Noel
Jimmy Palmer
Charlie Peterson
Hal Pruden
Ernie Ray
Pete Rubino
Tommy Reed
Shorty Sherock
Lyle Sisk
Deuce Spriggins
Jack Terrell
Thelma White
George Winslow
Al Jahns
Don Ricardo

Associated Booking Corporation
Randy Brooks (inactive)
Bob Berkey
Morrey Brennan
Don Bestor (inactive)
Jack Stallcup
Argueso
Tommy Ryan
Larry Fotine
Eddie Rogers
Johnny (Scat) Davis
Bob Chester (inactive)
Noble Sissle (inactive)
Sacasas
Pillado
George Paxton
(inactive)
Ray Herbeck
Dean Hudson

William Morris Agency
Carl Sands
Teddy Powell
Leonard Sues
Dick LaSalle

Gale Agency
Paul Williams

Shaw Artists Corporation
Hal Singer
Tadd Dameron
Charlie Parker
Cozy Cole
Thelonius Monk
Chubby Jackson

Universal Attractions
Nine (9) orks (names unobtainable at press time)

JUKE BOXES AND DISK JOCKEYS CREATE RECORD BOOM

FROM MAY 21, 1977 ISSUE

Alan Freed (left) was one of the most influential disk jockeys of the '60s. Wolfman Jack (top right) was one of the most widely heard "deejays" of the '70s.

Martin Block (circle) was the originator (with Al Jarvis) of the successful early deejay format, "Make Believe Ballroom." Al "Jazzbo" Collins (small box, left) is seen with pianist George Shearing. Dave Dexter (box, left), then with KFWB, is seen with West Coast "jocks" (left to right) Al Jarvis, Ira Cook, Gene Norman and Peter Potter.

FROM AUG. 2, 1947 ISSUE

The Billboard's First Annual Disk Jockey Poll—Part I
BEST-LIKED RECORDS
(FOR THE YEAR OF JUNE, '46, TO JUNE, '47)

GREATEST ALL-AROUND

To Each His Own—Eddy Howard (Majestic)....1,080

Heartaches—Ted Weems (Decca and Victor).... 908

Linda—Buddy Clark (Columbia) 572

For Sentimental Reasons— King Cole Trio (Capitol) 526

Anniversary Song—Al Jolson (Decca) 334

I Never Knew—Sam Donahue 241

Mam'selle—Art Lund (MGM) 241

Prisoner of Love—Perry Como (Victor)........ 241

Artistry Jumps—Stan Kenton (Capitol)...... 235

Anniversary Song—Dinah Shore (Columbia)..... 208

FOLK

Tim-Tay-Shun—Red Ingle (Capitol) 503
That's How Much I Love You—Eddy Arnold (Victor)............... 468
Cool Water—Sons of the Pioneers (Victor) 235
What Is Life Without Love—Eddy Arnold (Victor)............... 235
New Jole Blon—Moon Mullican (King) 151
Feudin', Fightin', Fussin'—Dorothy Shay (Columbia)............... 144
New Jole Blon—Roy Acuff (Columbia) 144
A Little Too Fer—Johnny Mercer (Capitol) 136
So Round, So Firm, So Fully Packed —Merle Travis (Capitol)....... 136
Eeny Meeny Dixie Deeny—Slim Bryant (Majestic) 123

POPULAR

To Each His Own—Eddy Howard (Majestic) 855
Linda—Buddy Clark (Columbia)... 672
Heartaches—Ted Weems (Decca).. 649
For Sentimental Reasons — King Cole Trio (Capitol)............. 511
Mam'selle—Art Lund (MGM)...... 368
Anniversary Song—Al Jolson (Decca) 353
Prisoner of Love—Perry Como (Victor) 317
That's My Desire—Frankie Laine (Mercury) 317
Anniversary Song—Dinah Shore (Columbia) 292
A Sunday Kind of Love—Claude Thornhill (Columbia).......... 286

RACE

Ain't Nobody Here But Us Chickens —Louis Jordan (Decca)........ 809
Choo Choo Ch Boogie—Louis Jordan '(Decca) 653
I Want To Be Loved—Savannah Churchill (Manor) 475
Open the Door, Richard — Three Flames (Columbia)............. 336
Open the Door, Richard — Charioteers (Columbia) 284
That's Good Enough For Me—Pearl Bailey (Columbia)............. 284
For Sentimental Reasons — King Cole Trio (Capitol)............. 262
I Ain't Mad At You—Jesse Price (Capitol) 262
Open the Door, Richard—Jack McVea (Black & White)........ 262
Gotta Gimme What You Got—Julia Lee (Capitol)................. 215
Texas and Pacific—Louis Jordan (Decca)..................... 215

POPULAR ALBUMS

Artistry In Rhythm—Stan Kenton (Capitol) 1,476
Songs By Sinatra—Frank Sinatra (Columbia) 1,223
Al Jolson Favorites—Al Jolson (Decca) 878
Tommy Dorsey All-Time Hits— Tommy Dorsey (Victor)........ 824
A Date With Dinah—Dinah Shore (Columbia) 824
Dorothy Shay Sings—Dorothy Shay (Columbia) 536
Harry James Favorites—Harry James (Columbia) 479
Glenn Miller—Glenn Miller (Victor) 425
Romance With Eddy Howard— Eddy Howard (Majestic)....... 404
Will Bradley-Ray McKinley Boogie Woogie—Will Bradley-Ray McKinley (Columbia)............. 397

CLASSICAL

Hora Staccato—Alfred Newman (Majestic) 447
Jalousie—Boston Pops (Victor).... 421
Polonaise—Jose Iturbi (Victor).... 334
Jalousie—Alfred Newman (Majestic 222
Warsaw Concerto—Boston Pops (Victor) 216
Clair de Lune—Jose Iturbi (Victor). 195
Warsaw Concerto—Carmen Cavallaro (Decca) 153
Whiffenpoof Song—Robert Merrill (Victor) 121
Clair de Lune—Oscar Levant (Columbia) 109
Our Waltz—James Melton (Victor) 98

HOT JAZZ

Artistry Jumps—Stan Kenton (Capitol) 239
Carle Boogie—Frankie Carle (Columbia) 207
Dark Eyes—Gene Krupa (Columbia) 207
Creole Jazz Album—Kid Ory (Columbia) 207
Sherwood's Forest—Bobby Sherwood (Capitol) 183
Trumpet No End—Duke Ellington (Musicraft) 183
Elks Parade—Bobby Sherwood (Capitol) 176
Lover—Gene Krupa (Columbia)... 176
The Good Earth—Woody Herman (Columbia) 176
Bill Bailey—Kid Ory (Columbia).. 165

CLASSICAL ALBUMS

1. Alfred Newman Conducts (Majestic) 1,243
2. Rachmaninoff Concerto In C Minor (Artur Rubenstein, pianist, and NBC Symphony, Vladimir Golshmann, conductor) (Victor)............... 346
3. Rhapsody In Blue (Oscar Levant, Philadelphia Ork, Eugene Ormandy, conductor) (Columbia) 268
4. Duel in the Sun (Victor)...... 237
5. A Night in Carnegie Hall (Columbia) 164

KIDDY ALBUMS

Tales of Uncle Remus (Capitol)... 732
Bozo at the Circus (Capitol)....... 397
Rusty in Orchestraville (Capitol).. 324
Margaret O'Brien—Stories for Children (Capitol)................. 324
Tubby the Tuba (Cosmo)........ 293

FROM AUG. 2, 1947 ISSUE

The Billboard's First Annual Disk Jockey Poll—Part I

BEST-LIKED VOCALISTS

(FOR THE YEAR OF JUNE, '46, TO JUNE, '47)

ALL-AROUND POPULAR MALE

Bing Crosby	2,994
Frank Sinatra	2,987
Perry Como	2,382
Dick Haymes	1,745
Art Lund	929
Buddy Clark	846
Frankie Laine	762
Mel Torme	611
Tony Martin	494
Andy Russell	397

MALE BAND VOCALIST

Stuart Foster	1,852
Eddy Howard	1,129
Harry Babbitt	715
Art Lund	667
Jack Hunter	640
Vaughn Monroe	593
Buddy DeVito	566
Jimmy Saunders	535
Frankie Lester	439
Bill Lockwood	421

CLASSICAL MALE-FEMALE

Lauritz Melchior	661
Robert Merrill	540
John Charles Thomas	538
Lily Pons	469
Nelson Eddy	456
Rise Stevens	456
Jan Peerce	375
James Melton	276
Ezio Pinza	240
Marion Anderson	216

ALL-AROUND POPULAR FEMALE

Dinah Shore	3,227
Jo Stafford	2,420
Peggy Lee	2,371
Margaret Whiting	1,542
Martha Tilton	886
Doris Day	684
Monica Lewis	522
Billie Holiday	519
Sarah Vaughan	519
Anita O'Day	502

FEM BAND VOCALIST

June Christy	2,695
Marjorie Hughes	1,377
Fran Warren	1,258
Doris Day	1,051
Rosalind Patton	909
Carolyn Grey	692
Anita O'Day	637
Marion Morgan	463
Peggy Lee	428
Jane Russell	331

SINGING GROUPS

Pied Pipers	3,237
Modernaires	1,773
Mills Brothers	1,441
Ink Spots	1,239
Dinning Sisters	1,193
Andrews Sisters	1,076
King Cole Trio	932
Charioteers	785
Starlighters	708
Mel-Tones	511

MOST PROMISING NEWER NAMES

BANDS

Elliot Lawrence	2,843
Sam Donahue	1,258
Eddy Howard	714
Boyd Raeburn	687
Ray McKinley	635
Johnny Bothwell	511
Herbie Fields	491
Skitch Henderson	462
Billy Butterfield	462
Art Mooney	386

MALE VOCALISTS

Frankie Laine	1,128
Art Lund	947
Mel Torme	660
Vic Damone	434
Buddy Clark	343
Joe Alexander	245
Gordon MacRae	245
Bill Lockwood	204
Clark Dennis	192
Johnny Desmond	192
Ray Dorey	192

FEMALE VOCALISTS

Fran Warren	493
Rosalind Patton	468
Jane Russell	444
Doris Day	387
June Christy	348
Monica Lewis	348
Sarah Vaughan	348
Betty Rhodes	255
Peggy Lee	228
Marjorie Hughes	211

BEST-LIKED BANDS

(FOR THE YEAR OF JUNE, '46, TO JUNE, '47)

SWEET

Eddy Howard	1,272
Tex Beneke	971
Claude Thornhill	679
Freddy Martin	648
Tommy Dorsey	612
Elliot Lawrence	540
Sammy Kaye	485
Frankie Carle	444
Les Brown	432
Guy Lombardo	423

SWING

Stan Kenton	2,196
Benny Goodman	1,308
Duke Ellington	660
Harry James	607
Tommy Dorsey	576
Woody Herman	529
Les Brown	405
Ray McKinley	384
Boyd Raeburn	384
Count Basie	361

LATIN-AMERICAN

Xavier Cugat	3,984
Enric Madriguera	745
Desi Arnaz	689
Noro Morales	623
Carlos Molinas	267
Lecuona's Cuban Boys	180
Jose Morand	156
Rafael Mendez	156
Emil Coleman	138
Carmen Cavallaro	122
Miguelito Valdes	122

400,000 MUSIC MACHINES

NEW YORK, Sept. 21.—The tremendous progress made by the record industry, to a large measure due to the Coast-to-Coast network of 400,000 music machines, necessitates the pressing of 720,000 records every week, according to information found in the second annual edition of the Talent and Tunes Supplement published in the current issue of *The Billboard*. The phonograph industry, representing an investment of $60,000,000, has been for the last several years a major stimulant in the rebirth of the popular music field, circulating tunes not only on the 400,000 locations but also stimulating record sales for home use.

It is no longer news that a phonograph can build a tune into a hit and a band leader into a drawing attraction. The ever-increasing popularity of the machine in locations ranging from luxurious night clubs to small taverns indicates that it will influence the rise of tunes and artists more than ever before.

For this reason, promotional campaigns of songs and leaders on records have reached a new high. They have united the music machine operator, comparatively new to the music industry, with the band leader, the music publisher, and allied forces in the field, all working for a common good. The phonograph today, for publicity purposes, finds itself in the lobby of a theater, building the records of an artist scheduled to play there, and in a ballroom publicizing the work of bands penciled in for engagements during the season.

For the sake of convenience and to increase the play the automatic phonograph industry of late has developed a number of improved accessory boxes and selector units installed in walls, booths, bars, and at tables.

New machine models are the latest word in design and light and color combinations. The industry estimates that between 70,000 and 90,000 new machines will be sold to operators by the end of this year, costing more than $21,000,000.

Never before have band leaders displayed so much concern over the tunes assigned to them for recording. They are well aware of the coverage each record will have and, naturally, want to land the best possible material. Major band booking office execs have given their publicity heads standing instructions to publicize the leaders' record and make as many tie-ups with phonograph operators as possible.

PARADE OF SUPERSTARS

FROM MAY 21, 1977 ISSUE

Emerging with folk-protest songs and paying homage to Woody Guthrie, Bob Dylan (circle) went on to become the leading spokesman for a musical generation, and something of a poet-laureate. Today, still touring, his name is almost synonymous with early rock'n'roll.

Elton John rocked the '70s, both in life style and in music. He's seen here with Bernie Taupin.

Como and Cole. Aside from both being immensely popular baritone pop singers, they have career highlights in common too. Both signed important recording contracts in 1943; Como with RCA where a year later he was the first popular singer to have a pair of million sellers at the same time; Cole with Capitol, where his "All For You" sold 100,000.

The same mothers who expressed shock when Elvis Presley went into those Bo Diddley hip moves in the early '50s are today queuing up for his performances and complaining they are all too infrequent. To say that he revolutionized a musical generation is to say too little, because as a white man with the music and moves of the black performer, he took r&b to still another level of acceptance, to say nothing of opening up the whole rock field to a flood of innovation that has really never ceased.

418

FROM MAY 21, 1977 ISSUE

The beginning of a rock and roll era for Decca Records in London. Picture shows Sir Edward Lewis, chairman of the company, meeting the Rolling Stones for the first time at a lunch party to celebrate the signing of the group's recording contract. The Stones were to match EMI's Beatles in terms of headlining-catching publicity. Left to right: Charlie Watts, drummer; Bill Wyman, bassist; Mick Jagger; Sir Edward Lewis; Keith Richard, guitarist, and Brian Jones, guitarist and founder member who died by drowning in his swimming pool at the height of the group's fame.

When Richard and Karen Carpenter's Spectrum group stopped the Whiskey-A-Go-Go dancers who wanted to listen in the late '60s, the two regrouped and A&M's Herb Alpert saw promise that was fulfilled almost immediately with "Ticket To Ride." The hits just kept on coming.

She rocked the rock world with her Southern Comfort whiskey voice and wild stage presence at the Monterey Pop Festival in 1967, a year after San Francisco had discovered her fronting before Big Brother & the Holding Co. She came out of Texas country and blues singing, this girl who would set new trends for female vocalists. Albert Grossman took one look and signed the Holding Co. and Janis Joplin, who later split with the group and whose death made her a rock martyr.

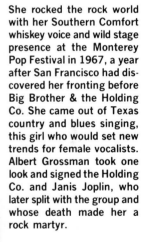

Until he commenced touring, David Bowie's (right) records on Mercury went largely unnoticed in America. Suddenly, everything came together for this immense glitter star.

Pre-glitter rock but with much of its flamboyance, the late Jimi Hendrix, who ex-Animal Chas Chandler introduced to England with fantastic success. A pioneering influence in establishing the rock trio format.

FROM MAY 21, 1977 ISSUE

Bill Graham, whose name has been synonmous with rock of the '70s (center) as a pioneering promoter of concerts. He's flanked by Atlantic luminaries Ahmet Ertegun (left) and Jerry Wexler.

Helen Reddy, she heralded the women's movement with her song "I Am Woman."
Combining elements of big band instrumentation with rock, Chicago has developed a unique sound with numerous steady selling albums over a long time since they were based in the city of their names as Chicago Transit Authority.

Fitting together easily on stage at Caesars Palace, Paul Anka and Tom Jones (left). Anka's "Diana" launched his amazing career in 1957 (he borrowed $100 from his father to make a trip to ABC in New York). He went from teen idol into a maturation that has rocketed him back to the chart tops in recent years. Jones, on the other hand, electrified American women when he hit the Copacabana in 1967 and was the first British entertainer to star in a regular TV show ("This Is Tom Jones" ABC-TV in 1969).

Fleetwood Mac: (shown below) English blues styled for a mass audience with enough repertoire scope to go well beyond the John Mayall and Eric Clapton influences the group reflects; perhaps unusual as a modern rock-blues group in that they feature three lead guitarists.

CHARTING THE BEST: POP

FROM JULY 4, 1976 ISSUE

This chart is based on *Billboard*'s year-end product recaps for the period 1946-1975, with individual products being inverted for point totals. These point totals were then tabulated, by artist, and the resulting totals ranked in descending order. Excluded from tabulation are seasonal products (e.g. Christmas) and specialty products (e.g. budget).

ARTISTS

1. BEATLES
2. ELVIS PRESLEY
3. FRANK SINATRA
4. KINGSTON TRIO
5. HERB ALPERT & THE TIJUANA BRASS
6. ELTON JOHN
7. JOHNNY MATHIS
8. PERRY COMO
9. BARBRA STREISAND
10. JOHN DENVER
11. ROLLING STONES
12. TEMPTATIONS
13. DIANA ROSS & THE SUPREMES
14. ANDY WILLIAMS
15. STEVIE WONDER
16. THREE DOG NIGHT
17. PETER, PAUL & MARY
18. MITCH MILLER
19. SIMON & GARFUNKEL
20. NAT KING COLE
21. HARRY BELAFONTE
22. NEIL DIAMOND

Early Beatles

Mel Schacher of Grand Funk.

23. PAT BOONE
24. HENRY MANCINI
25. BEACH BOYS
26. CREEDENCE CLEARWATER REVIVAL
27. SLY & THE FAMILY STONE
28. CHICAGO
29. MAMAS & THE PAPAS
30. TENNESSEE ERNIE FORD
31. EVERLY BROTHERS
32. PLATTERS
33. LED ZEPPELIN
34. JIM CROCE
35. TOM JONES
36. ROY ORBISON
37. HERMAN'S HERMITS
38. ROBERTA FLACK
39. ROGER WILLIAMS
40. RAY CHARLES
41. TONY BENNETT
42. TOMMY JAMES & THE SHONDELLS
43. BILL COSBY
44. MONKEES
45. CONNIE FRANCIS
46. LAWRENCE WELK
47. GLEN CAMPBELL
48. RICKY NELSON
49. BOBBY DARIN
50. PAUL McCARTNEY & WINGS
51. DOORS
52. AL GREEN
53. JACKSON 5
54. MANTOVANI

55. EAGLES
56. ASSOCIATION
57. PAUL ANKA
58. ARETHA FRANKLIN
59. TONY ORLANDO & DAWN
60. WAR

Neil Diamond

61. GRAND FUNK RAILROAD
62. CARPENTERS
63. JOAN BAEZ
64. RIGHTEOUS BROTHERS
65. FIFTH DIMENSION
66. BILLY VAUGHN
67. CHUBBY CHECKER
68. CAROLE KING
69. VAUGHN MONROE
70. FOUR TOPS
71. PATTI PAGE
72. AL HIRT

73. SAMMY KAYE
74. CAT STEVENS
75. DOOBIE BROTHERS
76. FRANKIE LAINE
77. SHELLEY BERMAN
78. CREAM
79. EDDIE FISHER
80. DINAH SHORE
81. PETULA CLARK
82. DEAN MARTIN
83. GLADYS KNIGHT & THE PIPS
84. SHIRELLES
85. AMERICA
86. BREAD
87. JAMES TAYLOR
88. EARTH, WIND & FIRE
89. ENOCH LIGHT & THE LIGHT BRIGADE
90. BLOOD, SWEAT & TEARS
91. DORIS DAY
92. NEIL SEDAKA
93. OLIVIA NEWTON-JOHN
94. JOHNNY HORTON
95. DIANA ROSS
96. YOUNG RASCALS
97. IRON BUTTERFLY
98. STYLISTICS
99. B. J. THOMAS
100. MARVIN GAYE
101. LLOYD PRICE

Andy Williams

102. MARTY ROBBINS
103. HELEN REDDY
104. SANTANA
105. BRENDA LEE
106. KINGSMEN
107. ISAAC HAYES
108. FREDDY MARTIN
109. BOB DYLAN
110. JIMI HENDRIX EXPERIENCE
111. GUESS WHO
112. TOMMY ROE
113. ROSEMARY CLOONEY
114. ISLEY BROTHERS
115. HIGHWAYMEN
116. FRANKIE VALLI
117. SAM COOKE
118. BING CROSBY
119. BOBBY VINTON
120. MOODY BLUES
121. S/SGT. BARRY SADLER
122. MINNIE RIPERTON
123. FREDDY FENDER
124. FOUR SEASONS
125. FERRANTE & TEICHER
126. PERCY FAITH
127. MAC DAVIS
128. BEE GEES

The late Jimi Hendrix

129. SEALS & CROFTS
130. DAVID BOWIE
131. ROGER MILLER
132. RAY STEVENS
133. BOX TOPS
134. OTIS REDDING
135. LES BAXTER
136. AWB
137. KAY KYSER
138. MR. ACKER BILK
139. CHARLIE RICH
140. KAY STARR
141. SERGIO MENDES & BRAZIL '66
142. KOOL & THE GANG
143. JANIS IAN
144. JETHRO TULL
145. DIONNE WARWICK
146. ANIMALS
147. COASTERS
148. LOGGINS & MESSINA
149. PINK FLOYD
150. EDDY HOWARD
151. JOHNNIE RAY
152. RARE EARTH
153. ALICE COOPER

Chicago

154. BILLY PRESTON
155. FRANKIE AVALON
156. NEW CHRISTY MINSTRELS
157. AMES BROTHERS
158. CHEECH & CHONG
159. LOVIN' SPOONFUL
160. JOHNNY CASH
161. BACHMAN-TURNER OVERDRIVE
162. LES PAUL & MARY FORD
163. FRANKIE CARLE
164. TERRY SNYDER & THE ALL STARS
165. CHUCK BERRY
166. LOUIS ARMSTRONG
167. FOUR LADS
168. DRIFTERS
169. NILSSON
170. GORDON LIGHTFOOT
171. MARY WELLS
172. FOUR ACES
173. O'JAYS
174. DEEP PURPLE
175. JOHNNY NASH
176. BOBBY SHERMAN
177. SWEET

Patti Page

178. SAM THE SHAM & THE PHARAOHS
179. Z. Z. TOP
180. LESLEY GORE
181. EDGAR WINTER GROUP
182. RAY CONNIFF
183. JAY & THE AMERICANS
184. DONOVAN
185. GORDON JENKINS
186. PARTRIDGE FAMILY
187. PREZ PRADO
188. JR. WALKER & THE ALL STARS
189. BILL WITHERS
190. MARTHA & THE VANDELLAS
191. EMERSON, LAKE & PALMER
192. VAN CLIBURN
193. NANCY SINATRA
194. JOHNNY RIVERS
195. TONY MARTIN
196. RASCALS
197. CROSBY, STILLS, NASH & YOUNG
198. CHER
199. STEPPENWOLF
200. BROOK BENTON

This chart is based on *Billboard*'s year-end product recaps for the period 1956-1975, with individual products being inverted for point totals. These point totals were then tabulated, by product, and the resulting totals ranked in descending order. Excluded is seasonal product.

SINGLES

RANK, TITLE—Artist (Label), year(s) in the top 10

1. **THE TWIST**—Chubby Checker (Parkway), 60 & 61-62
2. **HEY JUDE**—Beatles (Apple), 68
3. **MACK THE KNIFE**—Bobby Darin (Atco), 59
4. **DON'T BE CRUEL/HOUND DOG**—Elvis Presley (RCA Victor), 56
5. **TOSSIN' AND TURNIN'**—Bobby Lewis (Beltone), 61
6. **I WANT TO HOLD YOUR HAND**—Beatles (Capitol), 64
7. **BATTLE OF NEW ORLEANS**—Johnny Horton (Columbia), 59
8. **I'M A BELIEVER**—Monkees (Colgems), 66-67
9. **SINGING THE BLUES**—Guy Mitchell (Columbia), 56-57
10. **RAINDROPS KEEP FALLIN' ON MY HEAD**—B.J. Thomas (Scepter), 69-70
11. **LOVE LETTERS IN THE SAND/BERNADINE**—Pat Boone (Dot), 57

Connie Francis

12. **THEME FROM "A SUMMER PLACE"**—Percy Faith (Columbia), 60
13. **SUGAR, SUGAR**—Archies (Calendar), 69
14. **JAILHOUSE ROCK/TREAT ME NICE**—Elvis Presley (RCA Victor), 57-58
15. **AQUARIUS/LET THE SUNSHINE IN (Medley)**—5th Dimension (Soul City), 69
16. **ALONE AGAIN (Naturally)**—Gilbert O'Sullivan (MAM), 72
17. **THE FIRST TIME EVER I SAW YOUR FACE**—Roberta Flack (Atlantic), 72
18. **GREEN DOOR**—Jim Lowe (Dot), 56-57
19. **IT'S ALL IN THE GAME**—Tommy Edwards (MGM), 58
20. **LOVE ME TENDER**—Elvis Presely (RCA Victor), 56-57
21. **I HEARD IT THROUGH THE GRAPEVINE**—Marvin Gaye (Tamla), 68-69
22. **TIE A YELLOW RIBBON ROUND THE OLE OAK TREE**—Dawn (Featuring Tony Orlando) (Bell), 73
23. **AMERICAN PIE**—Don McLean (United Artists), 71-72
24. **LET'S GET IT ON**—Marvin Gaye (Tamla), 73
25. **JOY TO THE WORLD**—Three Dog Night (Dunhill), 71
26. **LOVE IS BLUE**—Paul Mauriat (Philips), 68
27. **I CAN'T STOP LOVING YOU**—Ray Charles (ABC-Paramount), 62
28. **ARE YOU LONESOME TONIGHT?**—Elvis Presley (RCA Victor), 60-61
29. **HELLO, DOLLY!**—Louis Armstrong (Kapp), 64
30. **I'LL BE THERE**—Jackson 5 (Motown), 70

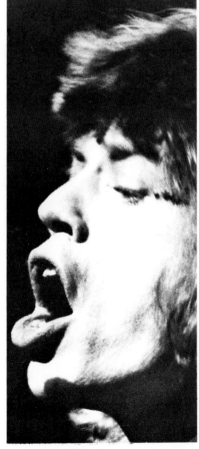

Mick Jagger

31. **HEARTBREAK HOTEL/I WAS THE ONE**—Elvis Presley (RCA Victor), 56
32. **SUGAR SHACK**—Jimmy Gilmer & The Fireballs (Dot), 63
33. **BIG GIRLS DON'T CRY**—Four Seasons (Vee Jay), 62
34. **MAGGIE MAY/REASON TO BELIEVE**—Rod Stewart (Mercury), 71
35. **IT'S NOW OR NEVER**—Elvis Presley (RCA Victor), 60
36. **RHINESTONE COWBOY**—Glen Campbell (Capitol), 75
37. **MONSTER MASH**—Bobby (Boris) Pickett & The Crypt Kickers (Garpax), 62 & (Parrot), 73
38. **SATISFACTION**—Rolling Stones (London), 65
39. **SHE LOVES YOU**—Beatles (Swan), 64
40. **BALLAD OF THE GREEN BERETS**—S/Sgt. Barry Sadler (RCA Victor), 66
41. **HONKY TONK WOMEN**—Rolling Stones (London), 69
42. **YOU'RE SO VAIN**—Carly Simon (Elektra), 72-73
43. **LISBON ANTIGUA**—Nelson Riddle (Capitol), 56
44. **ALL SHOOK UP**—Elvis Presley (RCA Victor), 57
45. **(Sittin' On) THE DOCK OF THE BAY**—Otis Redding (Volt), 68
46. **LOVE CHILD**—Diana Ross & The Supremes (Motown), 68
47. **WAYWARD WIND**—Gogi Grant (Era), 56
48. **TAMMY**—Debbie Reynolds (Coral), 57
49. **BIG BAD JOHN**—Jimmy Dean (Columbia), 61
50. **KILLING ME SOFTLY WITH HIS SONG**—Roberta Flack (Atlantic), 73
51. **BRIDGE OVER TROUBLED WATER**—Simon & Garfunkel (Columbia), 70
52. **HONEY**—Bobby Goldsboro (United Artists), 68

Carly Simon

53. **WINCHESTER CATHEDRAL**—New Vaudeville Band (Fontana), 66
54. **IT'S TOO LATE/I FEEL THE EARTH MOVE**—Carole King (Ode), 71
55. **I'M SORRY**—Brenda Lee (Decca), 60
56. **(They Long To Be) CLOSE TO YOU**—Carpenters (A&M), 70
57. **KNOCK THREE TIMES**—Dawn (Bell), 70-71
58. **TO SIR, WITH LOVE**—Lulu (Epic), 67
59. **AT THE HOP**—Danny & The Juniors (ABC-Paramount), 57-58

PART SIX   THERE WAS ALWAYS MUSIC

Monkees

Frankie Avalon

Eagles

142. **STUCK ON YOU**—Elvis Presley (RCA Victor), 60
143. **LITTLE DARLIN'**—Diamonds (Mercury), 57
144. **RETURN TO SENDER**—Elvis Presley (RCA Victor), 62
145. **I GOTCHA**—Joe Tex (Dial), 72
146. **WIPEPOUT**—Surfaris (Dot), 63 & 66
147. **COME SEE ABOUT ME**—Supremes (Motown), 64-65
148. **A HORSE WITH NO NAME**—America (Warner Bros.), 72
149. **BABY LOVE**—Supremes (Motown, 64
150. **SUKIYAKI**—Kyu Sakamoto (Capitol), 63
151. **FINGERTIPS (Part II)**—Little Stevie Wonder (Tamla), 63
152. **MY BOYFRIEND'S BACK**—Angels (Smash), 63
153. **THE PURPLE PEOPLE EATER**—Sheb Wooley (MGM), 58

The Carpenters

154. **WHERE DID OUR LOVE GO**—Supremes (Motown), 64
155. **MOONGLOW AND THEME FROM "PICNIC"**—Morris Stoloff (Decca), 56
156. **LET'S STAY TOGETHER**—Al Green (Hi), 71-72
157. **OH, PRETTY WOMAN**—Roy Orbison (Monument), 64
158. **YOU CAN'T HURRY LOVE**—Supremes (Motown), 66
159. **HELP!**—Beatles (Capitol), 65
160. **MR. LONELY**—Bobby Vinton (Epic), 64-65
161. **FLY, ROBIN, FLY**—Silver Convention (Midland International), 75
162. **WHATEVER WILL BE, WILL BE (Que Sera Sera)**—Doris Day (Columbia), 56
163. **KUNG FU FIGHTING**—Carl Douglas (20th Century), 74
164. **WE CAN WORK IT OUT**—Beatles (Capitol), 65-66
165. **APRIL LOVE**—Pat Boone (Dot), 57-58
166. **I WANT YOU BACK**—Jackson 5 (Motown), 69-70
167. **DIZZY**—Tommy Roe (ABC), 69
168. **BRANDY (You're A Fine Girl)**—Looking Glass (Epic), 72
169. **GO AWAY LITTLE GIRL**—Donny Osmond (MGM), 71
170. **INDIAN RESERVATION**—Raiders (Columbia), 71
171. **IT'S ONLY MAKE BELIEVE**—Conway Twitty (MGM), 58

Fifth Dimension.

172. **MONDAY, MONDAY**—Mamas & Papas (Dunhill), 66
173. **THEN CAME YOU**—Dionne Warwicke & Spinners (Atlantic), 74
174. **TEQUILA**—Champs (Challenge), 58
175. **MY GUY**—Mary Wells (Motown), 64
176. **I WILL FOLLOW HIM**—Little Peggy March (PCA Victor), 63
177. **DANCING MACHINE**—Jackson 5 (Motown), 74
178. **SHERRY**—Four Seasons (Vee Jay), 62
179. **CALCUTTA**—Lawrence Welk (Dot), 61
180. **PATRICIA**—Perez Prado (RCA Victor), 58
181. **EVERYBODY'S SOMEBODY'S FOOL**—Connie Francis (MGM), 60
182. **BYE BYE LOVE**—Everly Brothers (Cadence), 57

Chubby Checker

183. **YESTERDAY**—Beatles (Captiol), 65
184. **WAR**—Edwin Starr (Gordy), 70
185. **LOVIN' YOU**—Minnie Riperton (Epic), 75
186. **STAGGER LEE**—Lloyd Price (ABC-Paramount), 59
188. **I CAN'T GET NEXT TO YOU**—Temptations (Gordy), 69
189. **JUDY IN DISGUISE (With Glasses)**—John Fred & His Playboy Band (Paula), 67-68
190. **MAMA TOLD ME (Not To Come)**—Three Dog Night (Dunhill), 70
191. **JOHNNY ANGEL**—Shelley Fabares (Colpix), 62
192. **MAKE IT WITH YOU**—Bread (Elektra), 70

The Captain & Tennille

193. **MIDNIGHT TRAIN TO GEORGIA**—Gladys Knight & The Pips (Buddah), 73
194. **LEAVING ON A JET PLANE**—Peter, Paul & Mary (Warner Bros.), 69-70
195. **GYPSIES, TRAMPS & THIEVES**—Cher (Kapp), 71
196. **SUMMER IN THE CITY**—Lovin' Spoonful (Kama Sutra), 66
197. **STOP! IN THE NAME OF LOVE**—Supremes (Motown), 65
198. **PONY TIME**—Cubby Checker (Parkway), 61
199. **LAST TRAIN TO CLARKSVILLE**—Monkees (Colgems), 66
200. **ONE OF THESE NIGHTS**—Eagles (Asylum), 75

Guy Mitchell

This chart is based on *Billboard*'s year-end product recaps for the period 1956-1975, with individual products being inverted for point totals. These point totals were then tabulated, by product, and the resulting totals ranked in descending order. Excluded are seasonal products (e.g. Christmas) and specialty products (e.g. budget).

ALBUMS

Pos. TITLE, Artist (Label)
1. **MY FAIR LADY**—Original Cast (Columbia)
2. **SOUTH PACIFIC**—Soundtrack (RCA Victor)
3. **THE SOUND OF MUSIC**—Soundtrack (RCA Victor)
4. **THE SOUND OF MUSIC**—Original Cast (Columbia)
5. **WEST SIDE STORY**—Soundtrack (Columbia)
6. **OKLAHOMA**—Soundtrack (Capitol)
7. **JOHNNY'S GREATEST HITS**—Johnny Mathis (Columbia)

John Denver

8. **SING ALONG WITH MITCH**—Mitch Miller (Columbia)
9. **CAMELOT**—Original Cast (Columbia)
10. **KING AND I**—Soundtrack (Capitol)
11. **GREATEST HITS**—John Denver (RCA)
12. **LED ZEPPELIN**—Led Zeppelin (Atlantic)
13. **TAPESTRY**—Carole King (Ode)
13. **MOON RIVER AND OTHER GREAT MOVIE THEMES**—Andy Williams (Columbia)
15. **PETER, PAUL, AND MARY**—Peter, Paul, and Mary (Warner Bros.)
16. **WHIPPED CREAM AND OTHER DELIGHTS**—Herb Alpert's Tijuana Brass (A&M)
17. **HYMNS**—Tennessee Ernie Ford (Capitol)
18. **FIDDLER ON THE ROOF**—Original Cast (RCA Victor)
19. **GIGI**—Original Cast (MGM)
20. **THE MUSIC MAN**—Original Cast (Capitol)

Herb Alpert

21. **HELLO, DOLLY**—Original Cast (RCA Victor)
22. **FILM ENCORES, VOL. 1**—Mantovani (London)
23. **DR. ZHIVAGO**—Soundtrack (MGM)
24. **EDDIE DUCHIN STORY**—Soundtrack (Decca)
25. **GOING PLACES**—Herb Alpert and the Tijuana Brass (A&M)
26. **SGT. PEPPER'S LONELY HEARTS CLUB BAND**—Beatles (Capitol)
27. **INSIDE SHELLEY BERMAN**—Shelley Berman (Verve)
28. **TEMPTATIONS GREATEST HITS**—Temptations (Gordy)
29. **HAIR**—Original Cast (RCA)
30. **BLOOD, SWEAT & TEARS**—Blood, Sweat & Tears (Columbia)
31. **IN-A-GADDA-DA-VIDA**—Iron Butterfly (Atco)
32. **WEST SIDE STORY**—Original Cast (Columbia)
33. **MY FAIR LADY**—Soundtrack (Columbia)
34. **BELAFONTE AT CARNEGIE HALL**—Harry Bellafonte (RCA Victor)
35. **FROM THE HUNGRY i**—Kingston Trio (Capitol)
36. **THE BARBRA STREISAND ALBUM**—Barbra Streisand (Colmbuia)
37. **AROUND THE WORLD IN 80 DAYS**—Soundtrack (Decca)
38. **SOUTH PACIFIC**—Original Cast (Columbia)

Linda Ronstadt

James Taylor

39. **MODERN SOUND IN COUNTRY & WESTERN MUSIC, VOL. 1**—Ray Charles (ABC Paramount)
40. **MOVING**—Peter, Paul and Mary (Warner Bros.)
41. **DAYS OF WINE AND ROSES**—Andy Williams (Columbia)
42. **SWEET BABY JAMES**—James Taylor (Warner Bros.)
43. **CHICAGO**—Chicago (Columbia)
44. **THE KINGSTON TRIO AT LARGE**—Kingston Trio (Capitol)
45. **IF YOU CAN BELIEVE YOUR EYES & EARS**—Mamas and Papas (Dunhill)
46. **I LEFT MY HEART IN SAN FRANCISCO**—Tony Bennett (Columbia)
47. **CALYPSO**—Harry Belafonte (Victor)
48. **MAN OF LA MANCHA**—Original Cast (Kapp)
49. **BEST OF THE ANIMALS**—Animals (MGM)
50. **TALKING BOOK**—Stevie Wonder (Tamla)
51. **JOAN BAEZ IN CONCERT**—Joan Baez (Vanguard)
52. **HEAVENLY**—Johnny Mathis (Columbia)
53. **LONELY BULL**—Herb Alpert & The Tijuana Brass (A&M)
54. **FUNNY GIRL**—Original Cast (Capitol)
55. **PERSUASIVE PERCUSSION, VOL. 1**—Terry Snyder & The All Stars (Command)
56. **TCHAIKOVSKY: PIANO CONCERTO NO. 1**—Van Cliburn (RCA Victor)
57. **PARSLEY, SAGE, ROSEMARY & THYME**—Simon & Garfunkel (Columbia)
58. **HONEY IN THE HORN**—Al Hirt (RCA Victor)
59. **MARY POPPINS**—Soundtrack (Vista)
60. **JUDY AT CARNEGIE HALL**—Judy Garland (Capitol)
61. **GOODBYE YELLOW BRICK ROAD**—Elton John (MCA)
62. **MEET THE BEATLES**—Beatles (Capitol)
63. **ROY ORBISON GREATEST HITS**—Roy Orbison (Monument)
64. **ELVIS**—Elvis Presley (Victor)
65. **ELTON JOHN GREATEST HITS**—Elton John (MCA)
66. **THE KINGSTON TRIO**—Kingston Trio (Capitol)
67. **SONGS OF THE FABULOUS FIFTIES**—Roger Williams (Kapp)
68. **THE BEST OF THE KINGSTON TRIO**—Kingston Trio (Capitol)
69. **BELAFONTE**—Harry Belafonte (Victor)
70. **BAND ON THE RUN**—Paul McCartney (Apple)
71. **INNERVISIONS**—Stevie Wonder (Tamla)

72. **THAT'S THE WAY OF THE WORLD—** Earth, Wind & Fire (Columbia)
73. **YOU DON'T MESS AROUND WITH JIM—**Jim Corce (ABC)
74. **BACK HOME AGAIN—**John Denver (RCA)
75. **THE SECOND BARBRA STREISAND ALBUM—**Barbra Streisand (Columbia)
76. **PAT'S GREATEST HITS—**Pat Boone (Dot)
77. **AMERICAN GRAFFITI—**Soundtrack (MCA)
78. **PHOEBE SNOW—**Phoebe Snow (Shelter)
79. **LOVE IS THE THING—**Nat King Cole (Capitol)
80. **IMAGINATION—**Gladys Knight & The Pips (Buddah)
81. **HEART LIKE A WHEEL—**Linda Ronstadt (Capitol)
82. **RICKY—**Ricky Nelson (Imperial)
83. **TODAY—**New Christy Minstrels (Columbia)
84. **ON THE BORDER—**Eagles (Asylum)

Roy Orbison

103. **PETER GUNN—**Henry Mancini (RCA Victor)
104. **MY NAME IS BARBRA—**Barbra Streisand (Columbia)
105. **RUBBERSOUL—**Beatles (Capitol)
106. **DIANA ROSS & THE SUPREME'S GREATEST HITS—**Diana Ross and The Supremes (Motown)
107. **BREAKFAST AT TIFFANY'S—**Henry Mancini (RCA Victor)
108. **PERFECT ANGEL—**Minnie Riperton (Epic)
109. **BACHMAN-TURNER OVERDRIVE II—** Bachman-Turner Overdrive (Mercury)
110. **BAYOU COUNTRY—**Credence Clearwater Revival (Fantasy)
111. **A MAN AND A WOMAN—**Soundtrack (United Artists)
112. **HARVEST—**Neil Young (Reprise)
113. **WHAT NOW MY LOVE—**Herb Alpert & The Tijuana Brass (A&M)
114. **CALCUTTA—**Lawrence Welk (Dot)
115. **BRIDGE OVER TROUBLED WATER—** Simon & Garfunkel (Columbia)
116. **STEREO 35 MM—**Enoch Light & His Orchestra (Command)
117. **BETWEEN THE LINES—**Janis Ian (Columbia)
118. **COURT AND SPARK—**Joni Mitchell (Asylum)
119. **MORE JOHNNY'S GREATEST HITS—** Johnny Mathis (Columbia)
120. **S.R.O.—**Herb Alpert & The Tijuana Brass (A&M)
121. **IN THE WIND—**Peter, Paul & Mary (Warner Bros.)
122. **EXODUS—**Soundtrack (RCA Victor)
123. **LED ZEPPELIN II—**Led Zeppelin (Atlantic)
124. **DOORS—**Doors (Elektra)
125. **JESUS CHRIST, SUPERSTAR—**Various Artists (Decca)

126. **JOHNNY CASH AT FOLSOM PRISON—** Johnny Cash (Columbia)
127. **HAVE YOU NEVER BEEN MELLOW—** Olivia Newton-John (MCA)
128. **AMERICAN PIE—**Don McLean (United Artists)
129. **SUNDOWN—**Gordon Lightfoot (Reprise)
130. **BUTTON DOWN MIND OF BOB NEWHART—**Bob Newhart (Warner Bros.)
131. **GOLDFINGER—**Soundtrack (United Artists)
132. **FUNNY GIRL—**Soundtrack (Columbia)
133. **TEASER AND THE FIRECAT—**Cat Stevens (A&M)
134. **BLUE SKY NIGHT THUNDER—**Michael Murphey (Epic)
135. **GREAT MOTION PICTURE THEMES—** Various Artists (United Artists)
136. **PAL JOEY—**Soundtrack (Capitol)
137. **ABBEY ROAD—**Beatles (Apple)
138. **CLOSE TO YOU—**Carpenters (A&M)
139. **REVOLVER—**Beatles (Capitol)

Elton John

85. **MORE OF THE MONKEES—**Monkeys (Colgems)
86. **CAPTAIN FANTASTIC & THE BROWN DIRT COWBOY—**Elton John (MCA)
87. **BEHIND CLOSED DOORS—**Charlie Rich (Epic)
88. **SONGS FOR SWINGIN' LOVERS—**Frank Sinatra (Capitol)
89. **ARE YOU EXPERIENCED—**Jimi Hendrix Experience (Reprise)
90. **THE MONKEES—**Monkees (Colgems)
91. **AN EVENING WITH JOHN DENVER—** John Denver (RCA)
92. **THE STING—**Soundtrack (MCA)
93. **ELVIS PRESLEY—**Elvis Presley (Victor)
94. **THE GRADUATE—**Soundtrack (Columbia)
95. **GETZ/GILBERTO—**Stan Getz & Joao Gilberto (Verve)
96. **AVERAGE WHITE BAND—**Average White Band (Atlantic)
97. **TRES HOMBRES—**Z.Z. Top (London)
98. **DISRAELI GEARS—**Cream (Atco)
99. **LAWRENCE OF ARABIA—**Soundtrack (Colpix)
100. **MAGICAL MYSTERY TOUR—**Beatles (Capitol)
101. **BEATLES '65—**Beatles (Capitol)
102. **DARK SIDE OF THE MOON—**Pink Floyd (Harvest)

Earth, Wind & Fire

140. **SIXTY YEARS OF MUSIC AMERICA LOVES BEST, VOL. I**—Assorted Artists (RCA Victor)
141. **MARIA MULDAUR**—Maria Muldaur (Reprise)
142. **BLUE HAWAII**—Elvis Presley (RCA Victor)
143. **VANILLA FUDGE**—Vanilla Fudge (Atco)
144. **HOT ROCKS 1964-1971**—Rolling Stones (London)
145. **BEATLES**—Beatles (Apple)
146. **THE WORLD IS A GHETTO**—War (United Artists)
147. **MUSIC FROM EXODUS AND OTHER GREAT THEMES**—Mantovani (London)
148. **HERE WE GO AGAIN**—Kingston Trio (Capitol)
149. **SANTANA**—Santana (Columbia)
150. **COLOR ME BARBRA**—Barbra Streisand (Columbia)
151. **PEARL**—Janis Joplin (Columbia)
152. **PHYSICAL GRAFFITI**—Led Zeppelin (Swan Song)
153. **DEAR HEART**—Andy Williams (Columbia)
154. **I GOT A NAME**—Jim Croce (ABC)
155. **BLOOMING HITS**—Paul Mauriat & His Orchestra (Philips)
156. **KILLER**—Alice Cooper (Warner Bros.)

Paul Simon

167. **A SONG FOR YOU**—Temptations (Gordy)
168. **BARBRA STREISAND/THE THIRD ALBUM**—Barbra Streisand (Columbia)
169. **BOOKENDS**—Simon & Garfunkel (Columbia)
170. **BRAIN SALAD SURGERY**—Emerson, Lake & Palmer (Manticore)
171. **FIRST TAKE**—Roberta Flack (Atlantic)
172. **ASSOCIATION'S GREATEST HITS**—Association (Warner Bros.)
173. **EASY RIDER**—Soundtrack (Dunhill)

188. **MOON RIVER**—Lawrence Welk (Dot)
189. **STRANGERS IN THE NIGHT**—Frank Sinatra (Reprise)
190. **PETER, PAUL & MARY IN CONCERT**—Peter, Paul, and Mary (Warner Bros.)
191. **LADY SINGS THE BLUES**—Diana Ross (Motown)
192. **MUSIC**—Carole King (Ode)
193. **OLIVER**—Original Soundtrack (RCA Victor)
194. **LADY SOUL**—Aretha Franklin (Atlantic)
195. **TOMMY**—Original Soundtrack (Polydor)
196. **FAITHFULLY**—Johnny Mathis (Columbia)
197. **JOE COCKER!**—Joe Cocker (A&M)
198. **TEA FOR THE TILLERMAN**—Cat Stevens (A&M)
199. **PROVOCATIVE PERCUSSION, VOL. I**—Enoch Light & The Light Brigade (Command)
200. **THREE DOG NIGHT**—Three Dog Night (Dunhill)

Alice Cooper

The late Janis Joplin

157. **SUMMER BREEZE**—Seals & Crofts (Warner Bros.)
158. **DONOVAN'S GREATEST HITS**—Donovan (Epic)
159. **GET READY**—Rare Earth (Rare Earth)
160. **SOLD OUT**—Kingston Trio (Capitol)
161. **ABRAXAS**—Santana (Columbia)
162. **WHAT NOW MY LOVE**—Herb Alpert & The Tijuana Brass (A&M)
163. **BALLADS OF THE GREEN BERETS**—S/Sgt. Barry Sadler (RCA Victor)
164. **BILL COSBY IS A VERY FUNNY FELLOW, RIGHT?**—Bill Cosby (Warner Bros.)
165. **EXOTICA, VOL. I**—Martin Denny (Liberty)
166. **INTRODUCING HERMAN'S HERMITS**—Herman's Hermits (MGM)

174. **THE PARTRIDGE FAMILY ALBUM**—The Partridge Family (Bell)
175. **WONDERFULNESS**—Bill Cosby (Warner Bros.)
176. **SOUTH OF THE BORDER**—Herb Alpert & The Tijuana Brass (A&M)
177. **TIME OUT**—Dave Brubeck (Columbia)
178. **BEATLES VI**—Beatles (Capitol)
179. **NO SECRETS**—Carly Simon (Elektra)
180. **WAR CHILD**—Jethro Tull (Chrysalis)
181. **BY THE TIME I GET TO PHOENIX**—Glen Campbell (Capitol)
182. **AMERICA**—America (Warner Bros.)
183. **ROMEO & JULIET**—Soundtrack (Capitol)
184. **BUTCH CASSIDY & THE SUNDANCE KID**—Burt Bacharach/Soundtrack (A&M)
185. **SHIP AHOY**—O'Jays (Philly International)
186. **COME FLY WITH ME**—Frank Sinatra (Capitol)
187. **FLOWER DRUM SONG**—Original Cast (Columbia)

Lawrence Welk

CHARTING THE BEST: COUNTRY

This chart is based on *Billboard*'s year-end product recaps for the period 1946-1975, with individual products being inverted for point totals. These point totals were then tabulated, by artist, and the resulting totals ranked in descending order. Excluded from tabulation are seasonal products (e.g. Christmas) and specialty products (e.g. budget) country artists.

Eddy Arnold

ARTISTS

1. EDDY ARNOLD
2. BUCK OWENS
3. MERLE HAGGARD
4. RAY PRICE
5. JOHNNY CASH
6. SONNY JAMES
7. JIM REEVES
8. CHARLEY PRIDE
9. LORETTA LYNN
10. TAMMY WYNETTE
11. CONWAY TWITTY
12. WEBB PIERCE
13. MARTY ROBBINS
14. BILL ANDERSON
15. GEORGE JONES
16. ELVIS PRESLEY
17. GLEN CAMPBELL
18. JERRY LEE LEWIS
19. FARON YOUNG
20. CHARLIE RICH
21. KITTY WELLS
22. WAYLON JENNINGS
23. FREDDIE HART
24. LYNN ANDERSON
25. HANK WILLIAMS, SR.
26. HANK SNOW
27. PORTER WAGONER
28. DON GIBSON
29. DAVID HOUSTON
30. CARL SMITH
31. CONWAY TWITTY & LORETTA LYNN
32. JACK GREENE
33. TOM T. HALL
34. ROY CLARK
35. CONNIE SMITH
36. BOBBY BARE
37. RED FOLEY
38. ERNEST TUBB
39. ROBER MILLER
40. OLIVIA NEWTON-JOHN
41. MEL TILLIS
42. DONNA FARGO
43. JOHNNY RODRIGUEZ
44. STONEWALL JACKSON

45. ROY DRUSKY
46. DON WILLIAMS
47. LEFTY FRIZZELL
48. TANYA TUCKER
49. WARNER MACK
50. PORTER WAGONER & DOLLY PARTON
51. HANK THOMPSON
52. HANK WILLIAMS, JR.
53. RONNIE MILSAP
54. DOLLY PARTON
55. JOHN DENVER
56. PATSY CLINE
57. ERNEST ASHWORTH
58. HANK LOCKLIN
59. CAL SMITH
60. FERLIN HUSKY
61. BILLY "CRASH" CRADDOCK
62. EVERLY BROTHERS
63. MERLE TRAVIS
64. FREDDY FENDER
65. JOHNNY HORTON
66. JERRY REED
67. WILBURN BROTHERS
68. CHARLIE McCOY
69. SKEETER DAVIS
70. JERRY WALLACE
71. GEORGE HAMILTON IV
72. AL DEXTER
73. BOB WILLS
74. GEORGE MORGAN
75. BILLY WALKER
76. JEAN SHEPARD
77. LINDA RONSTADT
78. WILLIE NELSON
79. MICKEY GILLEY
80. WYNN STEWART
81. DAVE DUDLEY
82. LESTER FLATT & EARL SCRUGGS

83. ANNE MURRAY
84. STATLER BROTHERS
85. TEX RITTER
86. BOBBY HELMS
87. JEANNIE C. RILEY
88. CLAUDE KING
89. GENE AUTRY
90. DOTTIE WEST
91. LEROY VAN DYKE
92. JIMMY DEAN
93. TEX WILLIAMS
94. JIMMY WAKELY
95. JESSI COLTER
96. WILMA LEE & STONEY COOPER
97. DEL REEVES
98. GEORGE JONES & TAMMY WYNETTE
99. SAMMI SMITH
100. MOON MULLICAN
101. BOBBY GOLDSBORO
102. FREDDY WELLER
103. KRIS KRISTOFFERSON

Tammy Wynette

104. TOMMY OVERSTREET
105. T. G. SHEPARD
106. JOHNNY CASH & JUNE CARTER
107. JIMMY WAKELY & MARGARET WHITING
108. CHARLIE LOUVIN
109. PEE WEE KING

110. TENNESSEE ERNIE FORD
111. JEANNE PRUETT
112. BURL IVES
113. HENSON CARGILL
114. COWBOY COPAS
115. RED SOVINE
116. JIM ED BROWN
117. NARVEL FELTS
118. JOE STAMPLEY
119. NED MILLER
120. CLAUDE GRAY
121. THE BROWNS
122. RED FOLEY & ERNEST TUBB
123. JOHNNY & JACK
124. STUART HAMBLEN
125. SLIM WHITMAN
126. JEANNIE SEELY

Charley Pride

127. JOHNNY PAYCHECK
128. BARBARA FAIRCHILD
129. RICKY NELSON
130. GENE WATSON
131. FLOYD TILLMAN
132. ELTON BRITT
133. HOOSIER HOT SHOTS
134. JIM STAFFORD
135. WARREN SMITH
136. BILLY EDD WHEELER
137. MAC DAVIS
138. SPADE COOLEY
139. GARY STEWART
140. CRYSTAL GAYLE
141. RED FOLEY & KITTY WELLS
142. BRENDA LEE
143. RED SOVINE & WEBB PIERCE
144. B. J. THOMAS
145. LEON ASHLEY
146. SUSAN RAYE
147. JACK BLANCHARD & MISTY MORGAN
148. CARL PERKINS
149. GEORGE JONES & MELBA MONTGOMERY
150. HAWKSHAW HAWKINS
151. JIMMY NEWMAN
152. DAVID HOUSTON & TAMMY WYNETTE
153. MARION WORTH
154. MELBA MONTGOMERY
155. JIMMIE RODGERS
156. JAN HOWARD
157. EMMYLOU HARRIS
158. CHARLIE WALKER
159. CARL BUTLER

160. T. TEXAS TYLER
161. HARDEN TRIO
162. JOHNNY BOND
163. CHET ATKINS
164. WILMA BURGESS
165. RED SIMPSON
166. DOTTIE WEST & DON GIBSON
167. JERRY JORDAN
168. BILL PHILLIPS
169. GEORGE JONES & GENE PITNEY
170. BOBBIE GENTRY & GLEN CAMPBELL
171. BILLY SWAN
172. SIMON CRUM
173. DANNY DAVIS & THE NASHVILLE BRASS
174. FRANKIE MILLER
175. MARGIE SINGLETON & FARON YOUNG
176. LEWIS PRUITT
177. JOHNNY DARRELL
178. ZEKE MANNERS
179. MARVIN RAINWATER
180. SHEB WOOLEY
181. LOUVIN BROTHERS
182. BILLIE JO SPEARS
183. DICK CURLESS
184. DELMORE BROTHERS
185. RED INGLE NATURAL SEVEN & JO STAFFORD
186. RAY STEVENS
187. NORMA JEAN
188. ERIC WEISSBERG & STEVE MANDELL
189. DAVID WILLS
190. DAVID ALLAN COE
191. TOMMY COLLINS
192. MOM & DADS
193. DICK THOMAS
194. BOBBIE GENTRY
195. C. W. McCALL
196. ERNEST TUBB & LORETTA LYNN
197. BOB GILLION
198. ROY ACUFF
199. NAT STUCKEY
200. GRANDPA JONES

Listed below are the top 10 country singles, annually, for the period 1946-1975, based on *Billboard*'s year-end product recaps. Excluded is seasonal product.

Pos., TITLE, Artist (Label)

1946

1. NEW SPANISH TWO STEP—Bob Wills (Columbia)
2. GUITAR POLKA—Al Dexter (Columbia)
3. DIVORCE ME C.O.D.—Merle Travis (Capitol)
4. ROLY-POLY—Bob Wills (Columbia)
5. SIOUX CITY SUE—Zeke Manners (Victor)
6. WINE, WOMEN AND SONG—Al Dexter (Columbia)
7. SOMEDAY (You'll Want Me To Want You)—Elton Britt (Victor)
8. CINCINNATI LOU—Merle Travis (Capitol)
9. SIOUX CITY SUE—Hoosier Hot Shots (Decca)
10. THAT'S HOW MUCH I LOVE YOU—Eddy Arnold (Victor)

Loretta Lynn

1947

1. SMOKE, SMOKE, SMOKE (That Cigarette)—Tex Williams Western Caravan (Capitol Americana)
2. IT'S A SIN—Eddy Arnold (Victor)
3. SO ROUND, SO FIRM, SO FULLY PACKED—Merle Travis (Capitol)
4. WHAT IS LIFE WITHOUT LOVE—Eddy Arnold (Victor)
5. I'LL HOLD YOU IN MY HEART (Till I Can Hold You In My Arms)—Eddy Arnold & His Tennessee Plowboys (Victor)
6. TIMTAYSHUN—Red Ingle Natural Seven & Jo Stafford (Capitol)
7. NEW JOLIE BLONDE—Red Foley (Decca)
8. RAINBOW AT MIDNIGHT—Ernest Tubb (Decca)
9. NEW PRETTY BLONDE—Moon Mullican (King)
10. DIVORCE ME C.O.D.—Merle Travis (Capitol)

1948

1. BOUQUET OF ROSES—Eddy Arnold (Victor)
2. ANYTIME—Eddy Arnold (Victor)
3. JUST A LITTLE LOVIN'—Eddy Arnold (Victor)
4. TEXARKANA BABY—Eddy Arnold (Victor)
5. ONE HAS MY HEART—Jimmy Wakely (Capitol)
6. HUMPTY DUMPTY HEART—Hank Thompson (Capitol)
7. LIFE GETS TER-JUS DON'T IT—Carson Robison (MGM)
8. SWEETER THAN THE FLOWERS—Moon Mullican (King)
9. DECK OF CARDS—T. Texas Tyler (Four Star)
10. MY DADDY IS ONLY A PICTURE—Eddy Arnold (Victor)

1949

1. LOVESICK BLUES—Hank Williams & Drifting Cowboys (MGM)
2. DON'T ROB ANOTHER MAN'S CASTLE—Eddy Arnold (RCA Victor)
4. SLIPPING AROUND—Jimmy Wakely & Margaret Whiting (Capitol)
5. WEDDING BELLS—Hank Williams (MGM)
6. CANDY KISSES—George Morgan (Columbia)
7. WHY DON'T YOU HAUL OFF AND LOVE ME?—Wayne Raney (King)
8. BOUQUET OF ROSES—Eddy Arnold (RCA Victor)
9. I LOVE YOU SO MUCH IT HURTS—Jimmy Wakely (Capitol)
10. TENNESSEE SATURDAY NIGHT—Red Foley & Cumberland Valley Boys (Decca)

1950

1. I'm MOVIN' ON—Hank Snow (Victor)
2. CHATTANOOGIE SHOE SHINE BOY—Red Foley (Cecca)
3. I'LL SAIL MY SHIP ALONE—Moon Mullican (King)
4. WHY DON'T YOU LOVE ME?—Hank Williams (MGM)
5. LONG GONE LONESOME BLUES—Hank Williams (MGM)
6. GOODNIGHT, IRENE—Red Foley & Ernest Tubb (Decca)
7. CUDDLE BUGGIN' BABY—Eddy Arnold (Victor)
8. (Remember Me) I'M THE ONE WHO LOVES YOU—Stuart Hamblen (Columbia)
9. BIRMINGHAM BOUNCE—Red Foley (Decca)
10. LOVEBUG ITCH—Eddy Arnold (Victor)

1951

1. **COLD, COLD HEART**—Hank Williams (MGM)
2. **I WANT TO BE WITH YOU ALWAYS**—Lefty Frizzell (Columbia)
3. **ALWAYS LATE**—Lefty Frizzell (Columbia)
4. **RHUMBA BOOGIE**—Hank Snow (Victor)
5. **I WANNA PLAY HOUSE WITH YOU**—Eddy Arnold (Victor)
6. **THERE'S BEEN A CHANGE IN ME**—Eddy Arnold (Victor)
7. **SHOTGUN BOOGIE**—Tennessee Ernie (Capitol)
8. **HEY, GOOD LOOKIN'**—Hank Williams (MGM)
9. **MOM AND DAD'S WALTZ**—Lefty Frizzell (Columbia)
10. **GOLDEN ROCKET**—Hank Snow (Victor)

1952

1. **WILD SIDE OF LIFE**—Hank Thompson (Capitol)
2. **LET OLD MOTHER NATURE HAVE HER WAY**—Carl Smith (Columbia)
3. **JAMBALAYA**—Hank Williams (MGM)
4. **IT WASN'T GOD WHO MADE HONKY TONK ANGELS**—Kitty Wells (Decca)
5. **SLOW POKE**—Pee Wee King (Victor)
6. **INDIAN LOVE CALL**—Slim Whitman (Imperial)
7. **WONDERIN'**—Webb Pierce (Decca)
8. **DON'T JUST STAND THERE**—Carl Smith (Columbia)
9. **ALMOST**—George Morgan (Columbia)
10. **GIVE ME MORE, MORE, MORE OF YOUR KISSES**—Lefty Frizzell (Columbia)

Glen Campbell

1953

1. **KAW-LIGA**—Hank Williams (MGM)
2. **YOUR CHEATING HEART**—Hank Williams (MGM)
3. **NO HELP WANTED**—Carlisles (Mercury)
4. **DEAR JOHN LETTER**—Jean Shepard & Ferlin Huskey (Capitol)
5. **HEY, JOE**—Carl Smith (Columbia)
6. **MEXICAN JOE**—Jim Reeves (Abbott)
7. **I FORGOT MORE THAN YOU'LL EVER KNOW**—Davis Sisters (RCA Victor)
8. **IT'S BEEN SO LONG**—Webb Pierce (Decca)
9. **TAKE THESE CHAINS FROM MY HEART**—Hank Williams (MGM)
10. **FOOL SUCH AS I**—Hank Snow (Victor)

1954

1. **I DON'T HURT ANYMORE**—Hank Snow (Victor)
2. **ONE BY ONE**—Kitty Wells & Red Foley (Decca)
3. **SLOWLY**—Webb Pierce (Decca)
4. **EVEN THO**—Webb Pierce (Decca)
5. **I REALLY DON'T WANT TO KNOW**—Eddy Arnold (Victor)
6. **MORE AND MORE**—Webb Pierce (Decca)
7. **YOU BETTER NOT DO THAT**—Tommy Collins (Capitol)

8. **THERE STANDS THE GLASS**—Webb Pierce (Decca)
9. **ROSE MARIE**—Slim Whitman (Imperial)
10. **I'LL BE THERE**—Ray Price (Columbia)

1955

1. **IN THE JAILHOUSE NOW**—Webb Pierce (Decca)
2. **MAKING BELIEVE**—Kitty Wells (Decca)
3. **I DON'T CARE**—Webb Pierce (Decca)
4. **LOOSE TALK**—Carl Smith (Columbia)
5. **SATISFIED MIND**—Porter Wagoner (RCA Victor)
6. **CATTLE CALL**—Eddy Arnold & Hugo Winterhalter (RCA Victor)
7. **LIVE FAST, LOVE HARD AND DIE YOUNG**—Faron Young (Capitol)
8. **IF YOU AIN'T LOVIN'**—Faron Young (Capitol)
9. **YELLOW ROSES**—Hank Snow (RCA Victor)
10. **I'VE BEEN THINKING**—Eddy Arnold (RCA Victor)

1956

1. **CRAZY ARMS**—Ray Price (Columbia)
2. **HEARTBREAK HOTEL**—Elvis Presley (Victor)
3. **I WALK THE LINE**—Johnny Cash (Sun)
4. **BLUE SUEDE SHOES**—Carl Perkins (Sun)
5. **SEARCHING**—Kitty Wells (Decca)
6. **I WANT YOU, I NEED YOU, I LOVE YOU**—Elvis Presley (Victor)
7. **DON'T BE CRUEL**—Elvis Presley (Victor)
8. **WHY BABY WHY**—Red Sovine & Webb Pierce (Decca)
9. **I FORGOT TO REMEMBER TO FORGET**—Elvis Presley (Victor)
10. **SINGING THE BLUES**—Marty Robbins (Columbia)

1957

1. **GONE**—Ferlin Husky (Capitol)
2. **FRAULEIN**—Bobby Helms (Decca)
3. **BYE BYE LOVE**—Everly Brothers (Cadence)
4. **A WHITE SPORT COAT**—Marty Robbins (Columbia)
5. **YOUNG LOVE**—Sonny James (Capitol)
6. **FOUR WALLS**—Jim Reeves (RCA Victor)
7. **THERE YOU GO/TRAIN OF LOVE**—Johnny Cash (Sun)
8. **WAKE UP LITTLE SUSIE**—Everly Brothers (Cadence)
9. **GONNA FIND ME A BLUEBIRD**—Marvin Rainwater (MGM)
10. **JAILHOUSE ROCK**—Elvis Presley (RCA Victor)

1958

1. **OH, LONESOME ME/I CAN'T STOP LOVING YOU**—Don Gibson (RCA Victor)
2. **JUST MARRIED/STAIRWAY OF LOVE**—Marty Robbins (Columbia)
3. **GUESS THINGS HAPPEN THAT WAY/ COME IN, STRANGER**—Johnny Cash (Sun)
4. **CITY LIGHTS/INVITATION TO THE BLUES**—Ray Price (Columbia)
5. **DON'T/I BEG OF YOU**—Elvis Presley (RCA Victor)
6. **THE WAYS OF A WOMAN IN LOVE/ YOU'RE THE NEAREST THING TO HEAVEN**—Johnny Cash (Sun)
7. **BALLAD OF A TEENAGE QUEEN**—Johnny Cash (Sun)
8. **SEND ME THE PILLOW YOU DREAM ON**—Hank Locklin (RCA Victor)
9. **BLUE, BLUE DAY**—Don Gibson (RCA Victor)
10. **ALONE WITH YOU**—Faron Young (Capitol)

1959

1. **BATTLE OF NEW ORLEANS**—Johnny Horton (Columbia)
2. **THE THREE BELLS**—The Browns (RCA Victor)
3. **HEARTACHES BY THE NUMBER**—Ray Price (Columbia)
4. **WATERLOO**—Stonewall Jackson (Columbia)
5. **DON'T TAKE YOUR GUNS TO TOWN**—Johnny Cash (Columbia)

6. **WHITE LIGHTNING**—George Jones (Mercury)
7. **COUNTRY GIRL**—Faron Young (Capitol)
8. **I AIN'T NEVER**—Webb Pierce (Decca)
9. **WHEN IT'S SPRINGTIME IN ALASKA**—Johnny Horton (Columbia)
10. **BILLY BAYOU**—Jim Reeves (RCA Victor)

1960

1. **PLEASE HELP ME, I'M FALLING**—Hank Locklin (RCA Victor)
2. **HE'LL HAVE TO GO**—Jim Reeves (RCA Victor)
3. **ALABAM**—Cowboy Copas (Starday)
4. **ONE MORE TIME**—Ray Price (Columbia)
5. **ABOVE AND BEYOND**—Buck Owens (Capitol)
6. **ANOTHER**—Roy Drusky (Decca)
7. **JUST ONE TIME**—Don Gibson (RCA Victor)
8. **ON THE WINGS OF A DOVE**—Ferlin Husky (Capitol)
9. **EL PASO**—Marty Robbins (Columbia)
10. **EXCUSE ME (I Think I've Got A Heartache)**—Buck Owens (Capitol)

1961

1. **I FALL TO PIECES**—Patsy Cline (Decca)
2. **FOOLIN' AROUND**— Buck Owens (Capitol)
3. **WINDOW UP ABOVE**— George Jones (Mercury)

Conway Twitty

4. **TENDER YEARS**— George Jones (Mercury)
5. **THREE HEARTS IN A TANGLE**— Roy Drusky (Decca)
6. **HELLO WALLS**— Faron Young (Capitol)
7. **DON'T WORRY**— Marty Robbins (Columbia)
8. **HEARTBREAK U.S.A.**— Kitty Wells (Decca)
9. **SEA OF HEARTBREAK**— Don Gibson (RCA Victor)
10. **ON THE WINGS OF A DOVE**— Ferlin Husky (Capitol)

1962

1. **WOLVERTON MOUNTAIN**—Claude King (Columbia)
2. **MISERY LOVES COMPANY**—Porter Wagoner (RCA Victor)
3. **SHE THINKS I STILL CARE**—George Jones (United Artists)
4. **CHARLIE'S SHOES**—Billy Walker (Columbia)
5. **ADIOS AMIGO**—Jim Reeves (RCA Victor)
6. **A WOUND TIME CAN'T ERASE**—Stonewall Jackson (Columbia)
7. **SHE'S GOT YOU**—Patsy Cline (Decca)
8. **WALK ON BY**—Leroy Van Dyke (Mercury)
9. **TROUBLE'S BACK IN TOWN**—Wilburn Brothers (Decca)
10. **LOSING YOUR LOVE**—Jim Reeves (RCA Victor)

1963

1. **STILL**—Bill Anderson (Decca)
2. **ACT NATURALLY**—Buck Owens (Capitol)
3. **RING OF FIRE**—Johnny Cash (Columbia)
4. **WE MUST HAVE BEEN OUT OF OUR MINDS**—George Jones & Melba Montgomery (United Artists)
5. **LONESOME 7-7203**—Hawshaw Hawkins (King)
6. **TALK BACK TREMBLING LIPS**—Ernest Ashworth (Hickory)
7. **ABILENE**—George Hamilton IV (RCA Victor)
8. **DON'T LET ME CROSS OVER**—Carl Butler (Columbia)

9. SIX DAYS ON THE ROAD—Dave Dudley (Golden Wing)
10. YOU COMB HER HAIR—George Jones (United Artists)

1964

1. MY HEART SKIPS A BEAT—Buck Owens (Capitol)
2. WELCOME TO MY WORLD—Jim Reeves (RCA Victor)
3. TOGETHER AGAIN—Buck Owens (Capitol)
4. I GUESS I'M CRAZY—Jim Reeves (RCA Victor)
5. I DON'T LOVE YOU ANYMORE—Charlie Louvin (Capitol)
6. SAGINAW MICHIGAN—Lefty Frizzell (Columbia)
7. BURNING MEMORIES—Ray Price (Columbia)
8. UNDERSTAND YOUR MAN—Johnny Cash (Columbia)
9. DANG ME—Roger Miller (Smash)
10. MEMORY #1—Webb Pierce (Decca)

1965

1. WHAT'S HE DOING IN MY WORLD—Eddy Arnold (RCA Victor)
2. I'VE GOT A TIGER BY THE TAIL—Buck Owens (Capitol)
3. YES MR. PETERS—Roy Drusky & Priscilla Mitchell (Mercury)
4. BRIDGE WASHED OUT—Warner Mack (Decca)
5. THE OTHER WOMAN—Ray Price (Columbia)
6. THEN AND ONLY THEN—Connie Smith (RCA Victor)
7. BEFORE YOU GO—Buck Owens (Capitol)
8. KING OF THE ROAD—Roger Miller (Smash)
9. YOU'RE THE ONLY WORLD I KNOW—Sonny James (Capitol)
10. I'LL KEEP HOLDING ON—Sonny James (Capitol)

1966

1. ALMOST PERSUADED—David Houston (Epic)
2. THINK OF ME—Buck Owens (Capitol)
3. WAITIN' IN YOUR WELFARE LINE—Buck Owens (Capitol)
4. I WANT TO GO WITH YOU—Eddy Arnold (RCA Victor)
5. SWINGING DOORS—Merle Haggard (Capitol)
6. DISTANT DRUMS—Jim Reeves (RCA Victor)
7. GIDDYUP GO—Red Sovine (Starday)
8. OPEN UP YOUR HEART—Buck Owens (Capitol)
9. TAKE GOOD CARE OF HER—Sonny James (Capitol)
10. I LOVE YOU DROPS—Bill Anderson (Decca)

1967

1. ALL THE TIME—Jack Greene (Decca)
2. WALK THROUGH THIS WORLD WITH ME—George Jones (Musicor)
3. IT'S SUCH A PRETTY WORLD TODAY—Wynn Stewart (Capitol)
4. I'LL NEVER FIND ANOTHER YOU—Sonny James (Capitol)
5. WHERE DOES THE GOOD TIMES GO—Sonny James (Capitol)
6. I DON'T WANNA PLAY HOUSE—Tammy Wynette (EPic)
7. YOUR GOOD GIRL'S GONNA GO BAD—Tammy Wynette (Epic)
8. THERE GOES MY EVERYTHING—Jack Greene (Decca)
9. IT'S THE LITTLE THINGS—Sonny James (Capitol)
10. MY ELUSIVE DREAMS—David Houston & Tammy Wynette (Epic)

1968

1. FOLSOM PRISON BLUES—Johnny Cash (Columbia)
2. SKIP A ROPE—Henson Cargill (Monument)
3. D-I-V-O-R-C-E—Tammy Wynette (Epic)
4. MAMA TRIED (The Ballad From ''Killers Three'')—Merle Haggard (Capitol)

5. WORLD OF OUR OWN—Sonny James (Capitol)
6. I WANNA LIVE—Glen Campbell (Capitol)
7. ONLY DADDY THAT'LL WALK THE LINE—Waylon Jennings (RCA Victor)
8. HEAVEN SAYS HELLO—Sonny James (Capitol)
9. HONEY—Bobby Goldsboro (United Artists)
10. HARPER VALLEY P.T.A.—Jeannie C. Riley (Plantation)

1969

1. MY LIFE—Bill Anderson (Decca)
2. DADDY SANG BASS—Johnny Cash (Columbia)
3. I'LL SHARE MY WORLD WITH YOU—George Jones (Musicor)
4. HUNGRY EYES—Merle Haggard & The Strangers (Capitol)
5. STATUE OF A FOOL—Jack Greene (Decca)
6. (Margie's At) THE LINCOLN PARK INN—Bobby Bare (RCA Victor)
7. ONLY THE LONELY—Sonny James (Capitol)
8. I LOVE YOU MORE TODAY—Conway Twitty (Decca)

Sonny James

9. DARLING, YOU KNOW I WOULDN'T LIE—Conway Twitty (Decca)
10. THE WAYS TO LOVE A MAN—Tammy Wynette (Epic)

1970

1. HELLO DARLIN'—Conway Twitty (Decca)
2. FOR THE GOOD TIMES/GRAZIN' IN GREENER PASTURES—Ray Price (Columbia)
3. TENNESSEE BIRDWALK—Jack Blanchard & Misty Morgan (Wayside)
4. DON'T KEEP ME HANGIN' ON—Sonny James (Capitol)
5. IS ANYBODY GOIN' TO SAN ANTONE?—Charley Pride (RCA Victor)
6. WONDER COULD I LIVE THERE ANYMORE—Charley Pride (RCA Victor)
7. IT'S JUST A MATTER OF TIME—Sonny James (Capitol)
8. MY LOVE—Sonny James (Capitol)
9. FIGHTIN' SIDE OF ME—Merle Haggard & The Strangers (Capitol)
10. HE LOVES ME ALL THE WAY—Tammy Wynette (Epic)

1971

1. EASY LOVING—Freddie Hart (Capitol)
2. I WON'T MENTION IT AGAIN—Ray Price (Columbia)
3. HELP ME MAKE IT THROUGH THE NIGHT—Sammi Smith (Mega)
4. THE YEAR THAT CLAYTON DELANEY DIED—Tom T. Hall (Mercury)

5. WHEN YOU'RE HOT, YOU'RE HOT—Jerry Reed (RCA)
6. EMPTY ARMS—Sonny James (Capitol)
7. I'M JUST ME—Charley Pride (RCA)
8. HOW CAN I UNLOVE YOU—Lynn Anderson (Columbia)
9. GOOD LOVIN' (Makes It Right)—Tammy Wynette (Epic)
10. HOW MUCH MORE CAN SHE STAND—Conway Twitty (Decca)

1972

1. MY HANG UP IS YOU—Freddie Hart (Capitol)
2. THE HAPPIEST GIRL IN THE WHOLE U.S.A.—Donna Fargo (Dot)
3. IT'S FOUR IN THE MORNING—Faron Young (Mercury)
4. IT'S GONNA TAKE A LITTLE BIT LONGER—Charley Pride (RCA)
5. IF YOU LEAVE ME TONIGHT I'LL CRY—Jerry Wallace (Decca)
6. CAROLYN—Merle Haggard & The Strangers (Capitol)
7. KISS AN ANGEL GOOD MORNING—Charley Pride (RCA)
8. CHANTILLY LACE/THINK ABOUT IT DARLIN'—Jerry Lee Lewis (Mercury)
9. ONE'S ON THE WAY—Loretta Lynn (Decca)
10. WOMAN (SENSUOUS WOMAN)—Don Gibson (Hickory)

1973

1. YOU'VE NEVER BEEN THIS FAR BEFORE—Conway Twitty (MCA)
2. BEHIND CLOSED DOORS—Charlie Rich (Epic)
3. SATIN SHEETS—Jeanne Pruett (MCA)
4. TEDDY BEAR SONG—Barbara Fairchild (Columbia)
5. AMANDA—Don Williams (JMI)
6. YOU'RE THE BEST THING THAT'S HAPPENED TO ME—Ray Price (Columbia)
7. WHY ME—Kris Kristofferson (Monument—Columbia)
8. EVERYBODY'S HAD THE BLUES—Merle Haggard (Capitol)
9. SHE NEEDS SOMEONE TO HOLD HER—Conway Twitty (MCA)
10. THE LORD KNOWS I'M DRINKING—Cal Smith (MCA)

1974

1. THERE WON'T BE ANYMORE—Charlie Rich (RCA)
2. IF WE MAKE IT THROUGH DECEMBER—Merle Haggard (Capitol)
3. I LOVE—Tom T. Hall (Mercury)
4. THE GRAND TOUR—George Jones (Epic)
5. RUB IT IN—Billy ''Crash'' Craddock (ABC)
6. JOLENE—Dolly Parton (RCA)
7. MARIE LAVEAU—Bobby Bare (RCA)
8. A VERY SPECIAL LOVE SONG—Charlie Rich (Epic)
9. IF YOU LOVE ME (Let Me Know)—Olivia Newton-John (MCA)
10. ANOTHER LONELY SONG—Tammy Wynette (Epic)

1975

1. RHINESTONE COWBOY—Glen Campbell (Capitol)
2. RECONSIDER ME—Narvel Felts (ABC/Dot)
3. BLUE EYES CRYING IN THE RAIN—Willie Nelson (Columbia)
4. LOVE IN THE HOT AFTERNOON—Gene Watson (Capitol)
5. WASTED DAYS & WASTED NIGHTS—Freddy Fender (ABC/Dot)
6. FEELIN'S—Loretta Lynn & Conway Twitty (MCA)
7. IT'S TIME TO PAY THE FIDDLER—Cal Smith (MCA)
8. YOU'RE MY BEST FRIEND—Don Williams (ABC/Dot)
9. WRONG ROAD AGAIN—Crystal Gayle (United Artists)
10. LIZZIE & THE RAINMAN—Tanya Tucker (MCA)

ALBUMS

Listed below are the top 10 country albums, annually, for the period 1965-1975, based on *Billboard's* year-end product recaps. Excluded are seasonal products (e.g. Christmas) and specialty products (e.g. budget).

Pos., TITLE, Artist (Label)

1965

1. I'VE GOT A TIGER BY THE TAIL—Buck Owens (Capitol)
2. CONNIE SMITH—(RCA Victor)
3. THE JIM REEVES WAY—(RCA Victor)
4. RETURN OF ROGER MILLER—(Smash)
5. I DON'T CARE—Buck Owens & His Buckaroos (Capitol)
6. YOU'RE THE ONLY WORLD I KNOW—Sonny James (Capitol)
7. THE FABULOUS SOUND OF FLATT & SCRUGGS—Lester Flatt & Earl Scruggs (Columbia)
8. THE BEST OF JIM REEVES—(RCA Victor)
9. TOGETHER AGAIN/MY HEART SKIPS A BEAT—Buck Owens & His Buckaroos (Capitol)
10. THE EASY WAY—Eddy Arnold (RCA Victor)

1966

1. MY WORLD—Eddy Arnold (RCA Victor)
2. ROLL OUT THE RED CARPET FOR BUCK OWENS & HIS BUCKAROOS—(Capitol)
3. DISTANT DRUMS—Jim Reeves (RCA Victor)
4. I WANT TO GO WITH YOU—Eddy Arnold (RCA Victor)
5. CARNEGIE HALL CONCERT WITH BUCK OWENS & HIS BUCKAROOS—(Capitol)
6. BEHIND THE TEAR—Sonny James (Capitol)
7. ROGER MILLER/GOLDEN HITS—(Smash)
8. I LIKE 'EM COUNTRY—Loretta Lynn (Decca)
9. I LOVE YOU DROPS—Bill Anderson (Decca)
10. THE LAST WORD IN LONESOME IS ME—Eddy Arnold (RCA Victor)

Olivia Newton-John

1967

1. THERE GOES MY EVERYTHING—Jack Greene (Decca)
2. THE BEST OF EDDY ARNOLD—(RCA Victor)
3. TOUCH MY HEART—Roy Price (COLUMBIA)
4. LONELY AGAIN—Eddy Ernold (RCA Victor)
5. ALL THE TIME—Jack Greene (Decca)
6. SOMEBODY LIKE ME—Eddy Arnold (RCA Victor)
7. DON'T COME HOME A DRINKIN'—Loretta Lynn (Decca)
8. OPEN UP YOUR HEART—Buck Owens & His Buckaroos (Capitol)
9. THE BEST OF SONNY JAMES—(Capitol)
10. DANNY BOY—Ray Price (Columbia)

1968

1. BY THE TIME I GET TO PHOENIX—Glen Campbell (Capitol)
2. GENTLE ON MY MIND—Glen Campbell (Capitol)
3. PROMISES, PROMISES—Lynn Anderson (Chart)
4. BEST OF EDDY ARNOLD—(RCA Victor)
5. HEY LITTLE ONE—Glen Campbell (Capitol)
6. THE COUNTRY WAY—Charley Pride (RCA Victor)
7. HONEY—Bobby Goldsboro (United Artists)
8. NEW PLACE IN THE SUN—Glen Campbell (Capitol)
9. EVERLOVIN' WORLD OF EDDY ARNOLD—(RCA Victor)
10. JOHNNY CASH AT FOLSOM PRISON—(Columbia)

1969

1. WICHITA LINEMAN—Glen Campbell (Capitol)
2. JOHNNY CASH AT FOLSOM PRISON—(Columbia)
3. STAND BY YOUR MAN—Tammy Wynette (Epic)
4. JEWELS—Waylon Jennings (RCA)
5. CHARLEY PRIDE IN PERSON—(RCA)
6. YOUR SQUAW IS ON THE WARPATH—Loretta Lynn (Decca)
7. THE SENSATIONAL CHARLEY PRIDE—(RCA)
8. JOHNNY CASH AT SAN QUENTIN—(Columbia)
9. SAME TRAIN, DIFFERENT TIME—Merle Haggard (Capitol)
10. GALVESTON—Glen Campbell (Capitol)

1970

1. THE BEST OF CHARLEY PRIDE—(RCA)
2. OKIE FROM MUSKOGEE—Merle Haggard & the Strangers (Capitol)
3. JUST PLAIN CHARLEY—Charley Pride (RCA)
4. TAMMY WYNETTE'S GREATEST HITS—(Epic)
5. HELLO, I'M JOHNNY CASH—(Columbia)
6. CHARLEY PRIDE'S 10Th ALBUM—(RCA)
7. FIGHTN' SIDE OF ME—Merle Haggard & the Strangers (Capitol)
8. TAMMY'S TOUCH—Tammy Wynette (Epic)
9. THE WAYS TO LOVE A MAN—Tammy Wynette (Epic)
10. MY WOMAN, MY WOMAN, MY WIFE—Marty Robbins (Columbia)

1971

1. ROSE GARDEN—Lynn Anderson (Columbia)
2. FOR THE GOOD TIMES—Ray Price (Columbia)
3. I WON'T MENTION IT AGAIN—Ray Price (Columbia)
4. HAG—Merle Haggard (Capitol)
5. YOU'RE MY MAN—Lynn Anderson (Columbia)
6. FROM ME TO YOU—Charley Pride (RCA)
7. WHEN YOU'RE HOT, YOU'RE HOT—Jerry Reed (RCA)
8. HELP ME MAKE IT THROUGH THE NIGHT—Sammi Smith (MEGA)
9. I'M JUST ME—Charley Pride (RCA)
10. MAN IN BLACK—Johnny Cash (Columbia)

1972

1. BEST OF CHARLEY PRIDE VOL. 2—(RCA)
2. CHARLEY PRIDE SINGS HEART SONGS—(RCA)
3. EASY LOVING—Feddie Hart (Capitol)
4. FOR THE GOOD TIMES—Ray Price (Columbia)
5. REAL McCOY—Charlie McCoy (Monument)
6. HAPPIEST GIRL IN THE WHOLE U.S.A.—Donna Fargo (Dot)
7. CRY—Lynn Anderson (Columbia)
8. A SUNSHINY DAY WITH CHARLEY PRIDE—(RCA)
9. HOW CAN I UNLOVE YOU—Lynn Anderson (Columbia)
10. WE GO TOGETHER—Tammy Wynette & George Jones (Epic)

The late Jim Reeves as he appeared his very first day before the movie camera for "Strike It Rich."

1973

1. BEHIND CLOSED DOORS—Charlie Rich (Epic)
2. INTRODUCING—Johnny Rodriguez (Mercury)
3. SATIN SHEETS—Jeanne Pruett (MCA)
4. ALOHA FROM HAWAII VIA SATELLITE—Elvis Presley (RCA)
5. ENTERTAINER OF THE YEAR—Loretta Lynn (MCA)
6. CHARLIE MCCOY—Charlie McCoy (Monument)
7. THE BEST OF MERLE HAGGARD—Merle Haggard (Capitol)
8. THE HAPPIEST GIRL IN THE WHOLE U.S.A.—Donna Fargo (Dot)
9. SONG OF LOVE—Charley Pride (RCA)
10. JESUS WAS A CAPRICORN—Kris Kristofferson (Monument)

1974

1. BEHIND CLOSED DOORS—Charlie Rich (Epic)
2. LET ME BE THERE—Olivia Newton-John (MCA)
3. VERY SPECIAL LOVE SONGS—Charlie Rich (Epic)
4. THERE WON'T BE ANYMORE—Charlie Rich (RCA)
5. IF YOU LOVE ME LET ME KNOW—Olivia Newton-John (MCA)
6. YOU'VE NEVER BEEN THIS FAR BEFORE/BABY'S GONE—Conway Twitty (MCA)
7. A LEGENDARY PERFORMER VOL. I.—Elvis Presley (RCA)
8. STOP & SMELL THE ROSES—Mac Davis (Columbia)
9. SPIDERS & SNAKES—Jim Stafford (MGM)
10. BACK HOME AGAIN—John Denver (RCA)

1975

1. BACK HOME AGAIN—John Denver (RCA)
2. HEART LIKE A SHELL—Linda Ronstadt (Capitol)
3. BEFORE THE NEXT TEARDROP FALLS—Freddy Fender (ABC/Dot)
4. HAVE YOU NEVER BEEN MELLOW—Olivia Newton-John (MCA)
5. I'M JESSI COLTER—Jessie Colter (Capitol)
6. MERLE HAGGARD & THE STRANGERS—(Capitol)
7. AN EVENING WITH JOHN DENVER—John Denver (RCA)
8. KEEP MOVIN' ON—Merle Haggard (Capitol)
9. LINDA ON MY MIND—Conway Twitty (MCA)
10. SONGS OF FOX HOLLOW—Tom T. Hall (Mercury)

CHARTING THE BEST: SOUL

FROM JULY 4, 1976 ISSUE

This chart is based on *Billboard*'s year-end product recaps for the period 1946-1975, with individual products being inverted for point totals. These point totals were then tabulated, by artist, and the resulting totals ranked in descending order. Excluded from tabulation are seasonal products (e.g. Christmas) and specialty products (e.g. budget).

Stevie Wonder

ARTISTS

1. TEMPTATIONS
2. JAMES BROWN
3. ARETHA FRANKLIN
4. STEVIE WONDER
5. GLADYS KNIGHT & THE PIPS
6. DIANA ROSS & THE SUPREMES
7. LOUIS JORDAN
8. MARVIN GAYE
9. AL GREEN
10. JACKSON 5
11. RAY CHARLES
12. SMOKEY ROBINSON & THE MIRACLES
13. FOUR TOPS
14. ISLEY BROTHERS
15. SLY & THE FAMILY STONE
16. LOU RAWLS
17. FATS DOMINO
18. WILSON PICKETT
19. BROOK BENTON
20. ISAAC HAYES
21. O'JAYS
22. SAM COOKE
23. SPINNERS
24. DIONNE WARWICK
25. BARRY WHITE
26. B. B. KING
27. DELLS
28. OTIS REDDING
29. JACKIE WILSON
30. JERRY BUTLER
31. BOBBY WOMACK
32. CURTIS MAYFIELD
33. OHIO PLAYERS
34. ELVIS PRESLEY
35. EARTH, WIND & FIRE
36. JR. WALKER & THE ALL STARS
37. NAT KING COLE
38. SAM & DAVE
39. PLATTERS
40. WES MONTGOMERY
41. IMPRESSIONS

42. BOBBY (BLUE) BLAND
43. JOHNNY TAYLOR
44. EDDIE KENDRICKS
45. CLOVERS
46. LLOYD PRICE
47. RAMSEY LEWIS TRIO
48. KOOL & THE GANG
49. BILL WITHERS
50. NANCY WILSON
51. JOE SIMON
52. ROBERTA FLACK
53. DINAH WASHINGTON
54. DRIFTERS
55. CHI-LITES
56. WAR
57. STYLISTICS
58. IKE & TINA TURNER
59. JOE TEX
60. LITTLE RICHARD
61. MOMENTS
62. DIANA ROSS
63. MARTHA & THE VANDELLAS
64. BOOKER T. & THE M G's
65. STAPLE SINGERS
66. ETTA JAMES
67. AMOS MILBURN
68. ROY MILTON
69. MARVIN GAYE & TAMMI TERRELL
70. COASTERS
71. RUFUS featuring CHAKA KHAN
72. GENE CHANDLER
73. EVERLY BROTHERS
74. BLOODSTONE
75. MARVELLETTES
76. JOHNNY ACE
77. RUTH BROWN
78. CHUCK BERRY
79. BILLY PAUL
80. CHUCK WILLIS
81. CHUBBY CHECKER

82. FRIENDS OF DISTINCTION
83. AVERAGE WHITE BAND
84. RUFUS THOMAS
85. JOE TURNER
86. HANK BALLARD & THE MOONLIGHTERS
87. BILLY PRESTON
88. NEW BIRTH
89. DRAMATICS
90. JOE LIGGINS & HIS HONEYDRIPPERS
91. LOVE UNLIMITED
92. BLUE MAGIC
93. MAIN INGREDIENT
94. ROY HAMILTON
95. LAVERN BAKER
96. HONEY CONE
97. MFSB
98. CHARLES BROWN
99. SHIRELLES
100. FIFTH DIMENSION
101. QUINCY JONES
102. BULL MOOSE JACKSON
103. DELFONICS
104. IVORY JOE HUNTER
105. SANTANA
106. HERBIE HANCOCK

Aretha   Franklin

107. SOLOMON BURKE
108. MARY WELLS
109. LIONEL HAMPTON
110. CLARENCE CARTER
111. BILL BLACK'S COMBO
112. BEN E. KING
113. GROVER WASHINGTON, JR.
114. RARE EARTH
115. GRAHAM CENTRAL STATION
116. PERCY SLEDGE
117. ERNIE K-DOE
118. TYRONE DAVIS
119. HUGH MASEKELA

The Supremes

120. BARBARA MASON
121. LITTLE WILLIE JOHN
122. CLYDE McPHATTER
123. JOHNNY OTIS, LITTLE ESTHER & MEL WALKER
124. BLACKBYRDS
125. NELLIE LUTCHER
126. WYNONIE HARRIS
127. ROY BROWN
128. CARLA THOMAS
129. HAROLD MELVIN & THE BLUENOTES
130. DOMINOES
131. VAN McCOY & THE SOUL CITY SYMPHONY
132. JULIE LEE
133. BILL COSBY
134. BILLY STEWART
135. BARBARA LEWIS
136. B. T. EXPRESS
137. LITTLE MILTON
138. OTIS REDDING & CARLA THOMAS
139. DONNY HATHAWAY
140. EDDIE FLOYD
141. EDDIE HARRIS
142. DAVID RUFFIN
143. DONALD BYRD
144. ROSCOE GORDON
145. ERSKINE HAWKINS
146. LABELLE
147. ORIOLES
148. TEEN AGERS
149. SONNY THOMPSON
150. CHUCK JACKSON
151. CANNONBALL ADDERLEY
152. ROBERTA FLACK & DONNY HATHAWAY
153. MIDNIGHTERS
154. SMOKEY ROBINSON
155. MICHAEL JACKSON
156. EDWIN STARR
157. FAYE ADAMS
158. RICHARD (GROOVE) HOLMES
159. PEACHES & HERB
160. NINA SIMONE

161. COMMODORES
162. K. C. & THE SUNSHINE BAND
163. MILLIE JACKSON
164. FIVE ROYALES
165. PERCY MAYFIELD
166. ARCHIE BELL & THE DRELLS
167. MAJOR HARRIS
168. O. C. SMITH
169. CRUSADERS
170. UNDISPUTED TRUTH
171. GEORGE McCRAE
172. ORIGINALS
173. RICHARD PRYOR
174. LITTLE WALTER
175. ARTHUR CONLEY
176. FOUR SEASONS
177. LUCKY MILLINDER
178. MILLS BROTHERS
179. BILL DOGGETT
180. MARV JOHNSON
181. BIG JAY McNEELY
182. YOUNG RASCALS
183. LAMONT DOZIER
184. BAR-KAYS
185. LES McCANN & EDDIE HARRIS
186. FREDDY KING
187. JIMI HENDRIX EXPERIENCE
188. SHIRLEY & COMPANY
189. FIVE STAIRSTEPS
190. GWEN McCRAE
191. KING FLOYD
192. BETTY WRIGHT
193. JOE MORRIS
194. CAPITOLS
195. INTRUDERS
196. JOHN LEE HOOKER
197. LEE DORSEY
198. BETTYE SWANN
199. LARRY DARNELL
200. SLIM HARPO

Listed below are the top 10 rhythm & blues singles, annually, for the period 1946-1963 and 1965-1975. (There were no rhythm & blues singles charts published by *Billboard* during 1964); based on *Billboard*'s year-end product recaps. Excluded is seasonal product.

SINGLES

Pos., TITLE, Artist (Label)

1946

1. HEY-BA-BA-RE-BOP—Lionel Hampton (Decca)
2. CHOO CHOO CH'BOOGIE—Louis Jordan (Decca)
3. STONE COLD DEAD IN THE MARKET—Louis Jordan & Ella Fitzgerald (Decca)
4. THE GYPSY—Ink Spots (Decca)
5. R. M. BLUES—Roy Milton (Juke Box/Specialty)
6. BUZZ ME—Louis Jordan (Decca)
7. DRIFTING BLUES—Johnny Moor & His Three Blazers (Philo)
8. SALT PORK, W. VA.—Louis Jordan (Decca)
9. I KNOW—The Jubilaires & Andy Kirk Ork. (Decca)
10. AIN'T THAT JUST LIKE A WOMAN?—Louis Jordan (Decca)

1947

1. AIN'T NOBODY HERE BUT US CHICKENS—Louis Jordan (Decca)

2. BOOGIE WOOGIE BLUE PLATE—Louis Jordan (Decca)
3. I WANT TO BE LOVED—Savannah Churchill (Manor)
4. JACK, YOU'RE DEAD—Louis Jordan (Decca)
5. OLD MAID BOOGIE—Eddie Vinson Ork. (Mercury)
6. SNATCH AND GRAB IT—Julie Lee & Her Boy Friends (Capitol Americana)
7. LET THE GOOD TIMES ROLL—Louis Jordan (Decca)
8. TEXAS AND PACIFIC—Louis Jordan (Decca)
9. HE'S A REAL GONE GUY—Nellie Lutcher (Capitol Americana)
10. HURRY ON DOWN—Nellie Lutcher (Capitol Americana)

1948

1. LONG GONE—Sonny Thompson (Miracle)
2. GOOD ROCKIN' TONIGHT—Wynonie Harris (King)
3. TOMORROW NIGHT—Lonnie Johnson (King)
4. PRETTY MAMA BLUES—Ivory Joe Hunter (4 Star)
5. I CAN'T GO ON WITHOUT YOU—Bull Moose Jackson (King)
6. MESSIN' AROUND—Memphis Slim (Miracle)
7. MY HEART BELONGS TO YOU—Arbee Stidham (Victor)
8. CORN BREAD—Hal Singer Sextette (Savoy)
9. RUN, JOE—Louis Jordan (Decca)
10. BLUES AFTER HOURS—Pee Wee Crayton (Modern)

Ike & Tina Turner

1949

1. THE HUCKLEBUCK—Paul Williams (Savoy)
2. TROUBLE BLUES—Charles Brown (Aladdin)
3. SATURDAY NIGHT FISH FRY—Louis Jordan & Tympany Five (Decca)
4. AIN'T NOBODY'S BUSINESS—Jimmy Witherspoon (Supreme)
5. LITTLE GIRL, DON'T CRY—Bull Moose Jackson (King)
6. TELL ME SO—The Orioles (Jubilee)
7. DRINKIN' WIND, SPO-DEE-O-DEE—Stick McGhee & Buddies (Atlantic)
8. HOLD ME, BABY—Amos Milburn (Aladdin)
9. CHICKEN SHACK BOOGIE—Amos Milburn (Aladdin)
10. BOOGIE CHILLIN'—John Lee Hooker (Modern)

1950

1. PINK CHAMPAGNE—Joe Liggins (Specialty)
2. DOUBLE CROSSING BLUES—Johnny Otis, Little Esther, Mel Walker (Savoy)
3. I NEED YOU SO—Ivory Joe Hunter (MGM)
4. HARD LUCK BLUES—Roy Brown (DeLuxe)
5. CUPID'S BOOGIE—Little Esther, Johnny Otis, Mel Walker (Savoy)
6. I ALMOST LOST MY MIND—Ivory Joe Hunter (MGM)
7. WELL, OH, WELL—Tiny Bradshaw (King)
8. BLUE LIGHT BOOGIE—Louis Jordan (Decca)
9. FOR YOU MY LOVE—Larry Darnell (Regal)
10. MISTRUSTIN' BLUES—Johnny Otis, Little Esther, Mel Walker (Savoy)

1951

1. **SIXTY MINUTE MAN**—Dominoes (Federal)
2. **BLACK NIGHT**— Charles Brown (Aladdin)
3. **TEARDROPS FROM MY EYES**— Ruth Brown (Atlantic)
4. **CHAINS OF LOVE**— Joe Turner (Atlantic)
5. **DON'T YOU KNOW I LOVE YOU**— Clovers (Atlantic)
6. **PLEASE SEND ME SOMEONE TO LOVE**— Percy Mayfield (Specialty)
7. **I'M WAITING JUST FOR YOU**— Lucky Millinder (King)
8. **GLORY OF LOVE**— Five Keys (Aladdin)
9. **ROCKEY 88**— Jackie Brenston (Chess)
10. **ROCKIN' BLUES**— Johnny Otis, Mel Walker (Savoy)

1952

1. **LAWDY, MISS CLAWDY**—Lloyd Price (Specialty)
2. **HAVE MERCY, BABY**—Dominoes (Federal)
3. **FIVE, TEN, FIFTEEN HOURS**—Ruth Brown (Atlantic)
4. **GOIN' HOME**—Fats Domino (Imperial)
5. **NIGHT TRAIN**—Jimmy Forrest (United)
6. **MY SONG**—Johnny Ace (Duke)
7. **ONE MINT JULEP**—Clovers (Atlantic)
8. **TING A LING**—Clovers (Atlantic)
9. **THREE O' CLOCK BLUES**—B.B. King (RPM)
10. **JUKE**—Little Walter (Checker)

Little Richard

1953

1. **(Mama) HE TREATS YOUR DAUGHTER MEAN**—Ruth Brown (Atlantic)
2. **SHAKE A HAND**—Faye Adams (Herald)
3. **HOUND DOG**—Willie Mae Thorton (Peacock)
4. **CRYING IN THE CHAPEL**—Orioles (Jubilee)
5. **CLOCK**—Johnny Ace (Duke)
6. **I DON'T KNOW**—Willie Mabon (Chess)
7. **GOOD LOVIN'**—Clovers (Atlantic)
8. **BABY, DON'T DO IT**—Five Royales (Apollo)
9. **HELP ME, SOMEBODY**—Five Royales (Apollo)
10. **PLEASE LOVE ME**—B.B. King (RPM)

1954

1. **WORK WITH ME, ANNIE**—Midnighters (Federal)
2. **HONEY LOVE**—Drifters (Atlantic)
3. **WHAT A DREAM**—Ruth Brown (Atlantic)
4. **YOU'LL NEVER WALK ALONE**—Roy Hamilton (Epic)
5. **SHAKE, RATTLE AND ROLL**—Joe Turner (Atlantic)
6. **THINGS THAT I USED TO DO**—Guitar Slim (Specialty)
7. **HURTS ME TO MY HEART**—Faye Adams (Herald)
8. **ANNIE HAD A BABY**—Midnighters (Federal)
9. **LOVEY DOVEY**—Clovers (Atlantic)
10. **SEXY WAYS**—Midnighters (Federal)

TOP RHYTHM & BLUES SINGLES OF 1955

1. **PLEDGING MY LOVE**—Johnny Ace (Duke)
2. **AIN'T THAT A SHAME**—Fats Domino (Imperial)
3. **MAYBELLENE**—Chuck Berry (Chess)
4. **EARTH ANGEL**—Penquins (Dootone)
5. **I'VE GOT A WOMAN**—Ray Charles (Atlantic)
6. **WALLFLOWER**—Etta James (Modern)
7. **ONLY YOU**—Platters (Mercury)
8. **MY BABE**—Little Walter (Chess)
9. **SINCERELY**—Moonglows (Chess)
10. **UNCHAINED MELODY**—Roy Hamilton (Epic)

1956

1. **HONKY TONK**—Bill Doggett (King)
2. **I'M IN LOVE AGAIN**—Fats Domino (Imperial)
3. **LONG TALL SALLY**—Little Richard (Specialty)
4. **FEVER**—Little Willie John (King)
5. **GREAT PRETENDER**—Platters (Mercury)
6. **WHY DO FOOLS FALL IN LOVE**—Teen Agers (Gee)
7. **I WANT YOU TO BE MY GIRL**—Teen Agers (Gee)
8. **MY PRAYER**—Platters (Mercury)
9. **BLUE SUEDE SHOES**—Carl Perkins (Sun)
10. **LET THE GOOD TIMES ROLL**—Shirley & Lee (Aladdin)

1957

1. **JAILHOUSE ROCK/TREAT ME NICE**—Elvis Presley (RCA Victor)
2. **SEARCHIN'/YOUNG BLOOD**—Coasters (Atco)
3. **YOU SEND ME**—Sam Cooke (Keen)
4. **WAKE UP LITTLE SUSIE**—Everly Brothers (Cadence)
5. **ALL SHOOK UP**—Elvis Presley (RCA Victor)
6. **BLUE MONDAY**—Fats Domino (Imperial)
7. **HONEYCOMB**—Jimmie Rodgers (Roulette)
8. **DIANA**—Paul Anka (ABC-Paramount)
9. **SILHOUETTES**—Rays (Cameo)
10. **COME GO WITH ME**—Del Vikings (Dot)

1958

1. **WHAT AM I LOVING FOR/HANG UP MY ROCK & ROLL SHOES**—Chuck Willis (Atlantic)
2. **ROCK-IN' ROBIN**—Bobby Day (Class)
3. **DON'T/I BEG OF YOU**—Elvis Presley (RCA Victor)
4. **LOOKING BACK/DO I LIKE IT**—Nat King Cole (Capitol)
5. **ALL I HAVE TO DO IS DREAM**—Everly Brothers (Cadence)
6. **IT'S ALL IN THE GAME**—Tommy Edwards (MGM)
7. **JUST A DREAM**—Jimmy Clanton (Ace)
8. **YAKETY YAK**—Coasters (Atco)
9. **WITCH DOCTOR**—David Seville (Liberty)
10. **LITTLE STAR**—Elegants (Apt)

1959

1. **STAGGER LEE**—Lloyd Price (ABC-Paramount)
2. **IT'S JUST A MATTER OF TIME**—Brook Benton (Mercury)
3. **KANSAS CITY**—Wilbert Harrison (Fury)
4. **LONELY TEARDROPS**—Jackie Wilson (Brunswick)
5. **PERSONALITY**—Lloyd Price (ABC-Paramount)
6. **I CRIED A TEAR**—LaVern Baker (Atlantic)
7. **TRY ME (I Need You)**—James Brown & The Famous Flames (Federal)
8. **THERE GOES MY BABY**—Drifters (Atlantic)
9. **WHAT'D I SAY**—Ray Charles (Atlantic)
10. **THANK YOU PRETTY BABY**—Brook Benton (Mercury)

1960

1. **KIDDIO**—Brook Benton (Mercury)
2. **BABY**—Brook Benton & Dinah Washington (Mercury)
3. **FOOL IN LOVE**—Ike & Tina Turner (Sue)
4. **THE TWIST**—Chubby Checker (Parkway)
5. **CHAIN GANG**—Sam Cooke (RCA Victor)
6. **MONEY**—Barrett Strong (Anna)
7. **LET'S GO, LET'S GO, LET'S GO**—Hank Ballard & The Midnighters (King)
8. **FINGER POPPIN' TIME**—Hank Ballard & The Midnighters (King)
9. **A WOMAN, A LOVER, A FRIEND**—Jackie Wilson (Brunswick)
10. **SAVE THE LAST DANCE FOR ME**—Drifters (Atlantic)

Isley Brothers

1961

1. **TOSSIN' AND TURNIN'**—Bobby Lewis (Beltone)
2. **IT'S GONNA WORK OUT FINE**—Ike & Tina Turner (Sue)
3. **DON'T CRY NO MORE**—Bobby Bland (Duke)
4. **HIDEAWAY**—Freddy King (Federal)
5. **SHOP AROUND**—The Miracles (Tamla)
6. **MY TRUE STORY**—Jive Five (Beltone)
7. **I LIKE IT LIKE THAT**—Chris Kenner (Instant)
8. **STAND BY ME**—Ben E. King (Atco)
9. **MOTHER-IN-LAW**—Ernie K-Doe (Minit)
10. **ALL IN MY MIND**—Maxine Brown (Nomar)

1962

1. **SOUL TWIST**—King Curtis (Enjoy)
2. **I CAN'T STOP LOVING YOU**—Ray Charles (ABC-Paramount)
3. **TWIST AND SHOUT**—Isley Brothers (Wand)
4. **BRING IT ON HOME TO ME**— Sam Cooke (RCA Victor)
5. **LOST SOMEONE**— James Brown & The Famous Flames (King)
6. **MASHED POTATO TIME**— Dee Dee Sharp (Cameo)
7. **ANY DAY NOW**— Chuck Jackson (Wand)
8. **SNAP YOUR FINGERS**— Joe Henderson (Todd)
9. **PARTY NIGHTS**— Claudine Clark (Chancellor)
10. **YOU'LL LOSE A GOOD THING**— Barbara Lynn (Jamie)

1963

1. **PART TIME LOVE**—Little Johnny Taylor (Galaxy)
2. **MOCKINGBIRD**—Inez Foxx (Symbol)
3. **BABY WORKOUT**—Jackie Wilson (Brunswick)
4. **FINGERTIPS (Part II)**—Little Stevie Wonder (Tamla)
5. **HEAT WAVE**—Martha & The Vandellas (Gordy)
6. **PRIDE AND JOY**—Marvin Gaye (Tamla)
7. **THE LOVE OF MY MAN**—Theola Gilgore (Serock)
8. **CRY BABY**—Garnett Mimms & The Enchanters (United Artists)

9. **YOU'VE REALLY GOT A HOLD ON ME—** Miracles (Tamla)
10. **HELLO STRANGER—**Barbara Lewis (Atlantic)

There were no Rhythm & Blues Singles charts published by Billboard during 1964.

1965

1. **I CAN'T HELP MYSELF—**Four Tops (Motown)
2. **IN THE MIDNIGHT HOUR—**Wilson Pickett (Atlantic)
3. **SHOTGUN—**Jr. Walker & The All Stars (Soul)
4. **I DO LOVE YOU—**Billy Stewart (Chess)
5. **YES, I'M READY—**Barbara Mason (Alantic)
6. **PAPA'S GOT A BRAND NEW BAG—**James Brown (King)
7. **THE TRACK OF MY TEARS—**Miracles (Tamla)
8. **WE'RE GONNA MAKE IT—**Little Milton (Checker)
9. **TONIGHT'S THE NIGHT—**Solomon Burke (Atlantic)

1966

1. **HOLD ON! I'M COMIN'—**Sam & Dave (Stax)
2. **COOL JERK—**Capitols (Karen)
3. **BABY SCRATCH MY BACK—**Slim Harpo (Excello)
4. **AIN'T TOO PROUD TO BEG—**Temptations (Gordy)
5. **BAREFOOTIN'—**Robert Parker (Nola)
6. **634-5789—**Wilson Pickett (Atlantic)
7. **UP TIGHT—**Stevie Wonder (Tamla)
8. **WHEN A MAN LOVES A WOMAN—**Percy Sledge (Atlantic)
9. **WHAT BECOMES OF THE BROKENHEARTED—** Jimmy Ruffin (Soul)
10. **BEAUTY IS ONLY SKIN DEEP—**Temptations (Gordy)

1967

1. **RESPECT—**Aretha Franklin (Atlantic)
2. **SOUL MAN—** Sam & Dave (Stax)
3. **I NEVER LOVED A MAN THE WAY I LOVE YOU—** Aretha Franklin (Atlantic)
4. **MAKE ME YOURS—** Bettye Swann (Money)
5. **I WAS MADE TO LOVE HER—** Stevie Wonder (Tamla)
6. **COLD SWEAT—** James Brown & The Famous Flames (King)
7. **ARE YOU LONELY FOR ME—** Freddie Scott (Shout)
8. **TELL IT LIKE IT IS—** Aaron Neville (Parlo)
9. **SWEET SOUL MUSIC—** Arthur Conley (Atco)
10. **(Your Love Keeps Lifting Me) HIGHER AND HIGHER—** Jackie Wilson (Brunswick)

1968

1. **SAY IT LOUD—I'M BLACK AND I'M PROUD—** James Brown (King)
2. **SLIP AWAY—**Clarence Carter (Atlantic)
3. **(Sittin' On The) DOCK OF THE BAY—**Otis Redding (Volt)
4. **GRAZING IN THE GRASS—**Hugh Masekela (Uni)
5. **YOU'RE ALL I NEED TO GET BY—** Marvin Gaye & Tammi Terrell (Tamla)
6. **STAY IN MY CORNER—** Dells (Cadet)
7. **WE'RE A WINNER—** Impressions (ABC)
8. **I WISH IT WOULD RAIN—** Temptations (Gordy)
9. **TIGHTEN UP—** Archie Bell & The Drells (Atlantic)
10. **LOVER'S HOLIDAY—** Peggy Scott & JoJo Benson (SSS International)

1969

1. **WHAT DOES IT TAKE TO WIN YOUR LOVE—** Jr. Walker & The All Stars (Soul)
2. **I CAN'T GET NEXT TO YOU—**Temptations (Gordy)
3. **MOTHER POPCORN, Part 1—**James Brown (King)
4. **TOO BUSY THINKING ABOUT MY BABY—** Marvin Gaye (Tamla)

5. **IT'S YOUR THING—**Isley Brothers (T-Neck)
6. **ONLY THE STRONG SURVIVE—**Jerry Butler (Mercury)
7. **CHOKIN' KIND—**Joe Simon (Sound Stage 7)
8. **HOT FUN IN THE SUMMERTIME—**Sly & The Family Stone (Epic)
9. **JEALOUS KIND OF FELLOW—**Garland Green (Uni)
10. **GRAZING IN THE GRASS—**Friends of Distinction (RCA)

Isaac Hayes

1970

1. **I'LL BE THERE—**Jackson 5 (Motown)
2. **LOVE ON A TWO WAY STREET—**Moments (Stang)
3. **SIGNED, SEALED, DELIVERED (I'm Yours)—** Stevie Wonder (Tamla)
4. **THE LOVE YOU SAVE—**Jackson 5 (Motown)
5. **THANK YOU (Falletin Me Be Mice Elf Agin)—** Sly & The Family Stone (Epic)
6. **RAINY NIGHT IN GEORGIA—**Brook Benton (Cotillion)
7. **BALL OF CONFUSION (That's What the World Is Today)—**Temptations (Gordy)
8. **TURN BACK THE HANDS OF TIME—**Tyrone Davis (Dakar)
9. **COLE, COOKE & REDDING/SUGAR SUGAR—** Wilson Pickett (Atlantic)
10. **EXPRESS YOURSELF—**Charles Wright & The Watts 103rd Street Rhythm Band (Warner Bros.)

1971

1. **MR. BIG STUFF—**Jean Knight (Stax)
2. **WHAT'S GOING ON—**Marvin Gaye (Tamla)
3. **WANT ADS—**Honey Cone (Hot Wax)
4. **TIRED OF BEING ALONE—**Al Green (Hi)
5. **SPANISH HARLEM—**Aretha Franklin (Atlantic)
6. **JUST MY IMAGINATION (Running Away With Me)—**Temptations (Gordy)
7. **BRIDGE OVER TROUBLED WATER—**Aretha Franklin (Atlantic)
8. **THIN LINE BETWEEN LOVE AND HATE—** Persuaders (Atco)
9. **NEVER CAN SAY GOODBYE—**Jackson 5 (Motown)
10. **MAKE IT FUNKY, Part 1—**James Brown (Polydor)

1972

1. **LET'S STAY TOGETHER—**Al Green (Hi)
2. **I'LL TAKE YOU THERE—**Staple Singers (Stax)
3. **IF LOVING YOU IS WRONG, I DON'T WANT TO BE RIGHT—**Luther Ingram (Koko)
4. **IN THE RAIN—**Dramatics (Volt)
5. **OH GIRL—**Chi-Lites (Brunswick)
6. **BACK STABBERS—**O'Jays (Philadelphia International)

7. **THAT'S THE WAY I FEEL ABOUT'CHA—**Bobby Womack (United Artists)
8. **EVERYBODY PLAYS THE FOOL—**Main Ingredient (RCA)
9. **DO THE FUNKY PENGUIN—**Rufus Thomas (Stax)
10. **I GOTCHA—**Joe Tex (Dial)

1973

1. **LET'S GET IT ON—**Marvin Gaye (Tamla)
2. **SUPERSTITION—**Stevie Wonder (Tamla)
3. **NEITHER ONE OF US (Wants To Be The First To Say Goodbye—**Gladys Knight and the Pips (Soul)
4. **ME AND MRS. JONES—**Billy Paul (Philadelphia International)
5. **WHY CAN'T WE LIVE TOGETHER—**Timmy Thomas (Glades)
6. **ONE OF A KIND (Love Affair)—**Spinners (Atlantic)
7. **LOVE TRAIN—**O'Jays (Philadelphia International)
8. **DOING IT TO DEATH—**Fred Wesley & The JB's (People)
9. **MIDNIGHT TRAIN TO GEORGIA—**Gladys Knight and the Pips (Buddah)
10. **LOVE JONES—**Brighter Side of Darkness (20th Century)

1974

1. **FEEL LIKE MAKING LOVE—**Roberta Flack (Atlantic)
2. **BOOGIE DOWN—**Eddie Kendricks (Tamla)
3. **JUNGLE BOOGIE—**Kool and the Gang (De-Lite)
4. **BEST THING THAT EVER HAPPENED TO ME—** Gladys Knight & The Pips (Buddah)
5. **LOOKIN' FOR LOVE—**Bobby Womack (United Artists)
6. **ROCK YOUR BABY—**George McCrae (T.K.)
7. **THE PLAYBACK—**James Brown (Polydor)
8. **MIGHTY LOVE, Part I—**Spinners (Atlantic)
9. **DANCING MACHINE—**Jackson 5 (Motown)
10. **SEXY MAMA—**Moments (Stang)

Barry White

1975

1. **FIGHT THE POWER PT. I—**Isley Brothers (T-Neck) (Epic/Columbia)
2. **FIRE—**Ohio Players (Mercury) (Phonogram)
3. **GET DOWN TONIGHT—**K.C. & The Sunshine Band (TK)
4. **LOVE WON'T LET ME WAIT—**Major Harris (Atlantic)
5. **I BELONG TO YOU—**Love Unlimited (20th Century)
6. **LOOK AT ME (I'm In Love)—**Moments (Stand—All Platinum)
7. **THE HUSTLE—**Van McCoy & The Soul City Symphony (Avco)
8. **ROCKIN' CHAIR—**Gwen McCrae (Cat—TK)
9. **PICK UP THE PIECES—**Average White Band (Atlantic)
10. **SHINING STAR—**Earth, Wind & Fire (Columbia)

Listed below are the top 10 rhythm & blues albums, annually, for the period 1966-1975, based on *Billboard's* year-end recaps. Excluded are seasonal products (e.g. Christmas) and specialty products (e.g. budget).

ALBUMS

Pos., TITLE, Artist (Label)

1966

TITLE, Artist (Label)
1. **LOU RAWLS LIVE**—(Capitol)
2. **TEMPTIN' TEMPTATIONS**—(Gordy)
3. **GETTIN' READY**—Temptations (Gordy)
4. **LOW RAWLS SOULIN'**—(Capitol)
5. **CRYING TIME**—Ray Charles (ABC)
6. **THE MIRACLES GOING TO A GO-GO**—(Tamla)
7. **SUPREMES A GO GO**—(Motown)
8. **UP TIGHT**—Stevie Wonder (Tamla)
9. **SOUL ALBUM**—Otis Redding (Volt)
10. **THE EXCITING WILSON PICKETT**—(Atlantic)

1967

1. **THE TEMPTATIONS' GREATEST HITS**—(Gordy)
2. **I NEVER LOVE A MAN THE WAY I LOVE YOU**—Aretha Franklin (Atlantic)
3. **THE TEMPTATIONS LIVE!**—(Gordy)
4. **CARRYIN' ON**—Lou Rawls (Capitol)
5. **THE FOUR TOPS LIVE!**—(Motown)
6. **DIANA ROSS & THE SUPREMES' GREATEST HITS**—(Motown)
7. **HERE WHERE THERE IS LOVE**—Dionne Warwick (Scepter)
8. **THE SUPREMES SING HOLLAND-DOZIER-HOLLAND**—(Motown)
9. **ARETHE ARRIVES**—Aretha Franklin (Atlantic)
10. **WITH A LOT O' SOUL**—Temptations (Gordy)

1968

1. **LADY SOUL**—Aretha Franklin (Atlantic)
2. **IN A MELLOW MOOD**—Temptations (Gordy)
3. **A DAY IN THE LIFE**—Wes Montgomery (A&M)
4. **ARETHA NOW**—Aretha Franklin (Atlantic)
5. **THE HISTORY OF OTIS REDDING**—(Volt)
6. **ARE YOU EXPERIENCED**— Jimi Hendrix Experience (Reprise)
7. **THE TEMPTATIONS' GREATEST HITS**—(Gordy)
8. **THE ELECTRIFYING EDDIE HARRIS**—(Atlantic)
9. **DIOONE WARWICK'S GOLDEN HITS, PART I**—(Scepter)
10. **DOCK OF THE BAY**— Otis Redding (Volt)

1969

1. **CLOUD NINE**—Temptations (Gordy)
2. **ICE MAN COMETH**—Jerry Butler (Mercury)
3. **STAND**—Sly & the Family Stone (Epic)
4. **SOUL '69**—Aretha Franklin (Atlantic)
5. **MEMPHIS UNDERGROUND**—Herbie Mann (Atlantic)
6. **TCB**—Diana Ross & the Supremes & the Temptations (Motown)
7. **LIVE AT THE COPA**—Temptations (Gordy)
8. **HOT BUTTERED SOUL**—Isaac Hayes (Enterprise)
9. **PROMISES, PROMISES**—Dionne Warwick (Scepter)
10. **GRAZIN' IN THE GRASS**—Friends of Distinction (RCA)

1970

1. **THE ISAAC HAYES MOVEMENT**—(Enterprise)
2. **STAND**—Sly & the Family Stone (Epic)
3. **GET READY**—Rare Earth (Rare Earth)
4. **STILL WATER**—Four Tops (Motown)
5. **THIS GIRL'S IN LOVE WITH YOU**—Aretha Franklin (Atlantic)
6. **PSYCHEDELIC SHACK**—Temptations (Gordy)
7. **I WANT YOU BACK**—Jackson 5 (Motown)
8. **SWISS MOVEMENT**—Les McCann & Eddie Harris (Atlantic)

9. **ABC**—Jackson 5 (Motown)
10. **COMPLETELY WELL**—B.B. King (BluesWay)

1971

1. **TO BE CONTINUED**—Isaac Hayes (Enterprise)
2. **CHAPTER TWO**—Roberta Flack (Atlantic)
3. **WHAT'S GOING ON**—Marvin Gaye (Tamla)
4. **CURTIS**—Curtis Mayfield (Curtom)
5. **ARETHA LIVE AT FILLMORE WEST**—Aretha Franklin (Atlantic)
6. **MAYBE TOMORROW**—Jackson 5 (Motown)
7. **SHAFT**—Soundtrack/Isaac Hayes (Enterprise)
8. **THE SKY'S THE LIMIT**—Temptations (Gordy)
9. **MELTING POT**—Booker T. & the MG's (Stax)
10. **ABRAXAS**—Santana (Columbia)

1972

1. **REVOLUTION OF THE MIND/LIVE AT THE APOLLO**—James Brown (Polydor)
2. **LET'S STAY TOGETHER**—Al Green (Hi)
3. **SHAFT**—Soundtrack/Isaac Hayes (MGM/Enterprise)
4. **STYLISTICS**—(Avco)
5. **A LONELY MAN**—Chi-Lites (Brunswick)
6. **ALL DAY MUSIC**—War (United Artists)
7. **STILL BILL**—Bill Withers (sussex)
8. **FIRST TAKE**—Roberta Flack (Atlantic)
9. **THERE'S A RIOT GOIN' ON**—Sly & The Family Stone (Epic)
10. **SOLID ROCK**—Temptations (Gordy)

1973

1. **I'M STILL IN LOVE WITH YOU**—Al Green (Hi) (London)
2. **THE WORLD IS A GHETTO**—War (United Artists)
3. **TALKING BOOK**—Stevie Wonder (Tamla) (Motown)
4. **LADY SINGS THE BLUES**—Diana Ross (Motown)
5. **ROUND 2**—Stylistics (Avco)
6. **CALL ME**—Al Green (Hi) (London)
7. **I'VE GOT SO MUCH TO GIVE**—Barry White (20th Century)
8. **BACK STABBERS**—O'Jays (Philadelphia Int'l) (Columbia)
9. **360 DEGREES OF BILLY PAUL**—Billy Paul (Philadelphia Int'l) (Columbia)
10. **NEITHER ONE OF US (Wants To Be The First To Say Goodbye)**—Gladys Knight & The Pips (Soul) (Motown)

1974

1. **SHIP AHOY**—O'Jays (Philadelphia International)
2. **IMAGINATION**—Gladys Knight & The Pips (Buddah)
3. **HEADHUNTERS**—Herbie Hancock (Columbia)
4. **THE PLAYBACK**—James Brown (Polydor)
5. **LIVIN' FOR YOU**—Al Green (Hi)
6. **SKIN TIGHT**—Ohio Players (Mercury)
7. **LOVE IS THE MESSAGE**—MFSB (Philadelphia International)
8. **LET'S GET IT ON**—Marvin Gaye (Tamla)
9. **INNERVISIONS**—Stevie Wonder (Tamla)
10. **OPEN OUR EYES**—Earth, Wind & Fire (Columbia)

1975

1. **THAT'S THE WAY OF THE WORLD**—Earth, Wind, & Fire (Columbia)
2. **FIRE**—Ohio Players (Mercury) (Phonogram)
3. **A SONG FOR YOU**—Temptations (Motown)
4. **SUN GODDESS**—Ramsey Lewis (Columbia)
5. **EXPLORES YOUR MIND**—Al Green (Hi) (London)
6. **TO BE TRUE**—Harold Melvin & The Bluenotes (Philadelphia Int'l) (Epic/ Columbia)
7. **FLYING START**—Blackbyrds (Fantasy)
8. **MISTER MAGIC**—Grover Washington, Jr. (Dudu) (Motown)
9. **REFUSIZED**—Rufus Featuring Chaka Khan (ABC)
10. **FULFILLINGNESS' FIRST FINALE**—Stevie Wonder (Tamla) (Motown)

Temptations

IN THE '70s: AN EXCITING, WIDE OPEN MIX

FROM JULY 4, 1976 ISSUE

At the 2nd Annual awards dinner of the Songwriters Hall of Fame, the following are pictured: Mitchell Parish, Abe Olman, Hal David, Harold Adamson, Sammy Fain, Sheldon Harnick, Stanley Adams, Burton Lane, Paul Francis Webster, Sammy Cahn, Carl Sigman, Fred Coots, Ned Washington, Joe Meyer, E.Y. Harburg, Harold Arlen, Irving Caesar, Johnny Mercer, Jule Styne, Dorothy Fields, Andy Razaf.

PUBLISHER PANTHEON—Directors attending National Music Publisher's Assn. board meeting: standing, from left, Sidney Herman (Famous Music), Al Brackman (TRO Inc.), Ralph Peer II (Peer International), Wesley Rose (Acuff-Rose), Al Shulman (Belwin-Mills), Larry Shayne (Larry Shayne Music), Sidney Shemel (United Artists Music), Joseph Auslander (E.B. Marks Music), Jeff Rosen (NMPA counsel) and Ed Silvers (Warner Bros.). Seated, from left, Norman Weiser (Chappell), Irwin Robinson (Screen Gems-Columbia), John Taylor (NMPA general counsel), Sal Chiantia (MCA Music and NMPA president), Al Berman (Harry Fox Agency), Leonard Feist, (NMPA executive vice president), and Leon Brettler (Shapiro, Bernstein). Board members not present at the February meeting are Ernest Farmer (Shawnee Press), Al Gallico (Al Gallico Music), and Robert Gordy (Jobete).

FROM JUNE 25, 1977 ISSUE

BMI Honors Writers, Publishers

211 Feted At L.A. Event

The complete list of winners:

ALL BY MYSELF—CAM-USA, Inc., Eric Carmen

ALL THESE THINGS—Tune-Kel Publishing Co., Inc., Allen Toussaint

BETH—Under-Cut Publishing Co., Inc., Bob Ezrin (BMIC)

BLIND MAN IN THE BLEACHERS—Tree Publishing Co., Inc., Sterling Whipple

BOOGIE FEVER—Bull Pen Music Co., Kenny St. Lewis

BREAK AWAY—Irving Music, Inc., Benny Gallagher (PRS), Graham Lyle (PRS)

BREAKING UP IS HARD TO DO—(third award) Screen Gems-EMI Music, Inc., Howard Greenfield

BROKEN LADY—First Generation Music Co., Larry Gatlin

BUTTERFLY FOR BUCKY—Unart Music Corp., Douglas Cox, Bobby Goldsboro

THE CALL—Beechwood Music Corp., Gene MacLellan (BMIC)

CAN'T YOU SEE—No Exit Music, Toy Caldwell Jr.

COME ON OVER—Casserole Music Corp., Flamm Music, Inc., Barry Gibb (PRS), Robin Gibb (PRS)

COUNTRY BOY YOU GOT YOUR FEET IN L.A.—(second award), ABC/Dunhill Music, Inc., One of a Kind Music, Dennis Lambert, Brian Potter

CUPID—Kags Music Corp., Sam Cooke

DEVIL WOMAN—Unichappell Music, Inc., Christine Authors (BMIC), Terry Britten (PRS)

DISCO DUCK—Stafree Publishing Co., Rick Dees

DISCO LADY—Groovesville Music, Harvey Scales, Albert Vance

DON'T PULL YOUR LOVE—(second award), ABC/Dunhill Music, Inc., Dennis Lambert, Brian Potter

THE DOOR'S ALWAYS OPEN—Jack Music, Inc., Bob McDill, Dickey Lee

DREAM ON—Daksel Music Corp., Steve Tallarico

EVIL WOMAN—Unart Music Corp., Jeff Lynne (PRS)

FANNY BE TENDER WITH MY LOVE—Casserole Music Corp., Flamm Music, Inc., Barry Gibb (PRS), Maurice Gibb (PRS), Robin Gibb (PRS)

FASTER HORSES—Hallnote Music, Tom T. Hall

A FIFTH OF BEETHOVEN—RFT Music Publishing Corp., Walter Murphy

FIFTY WAYS TO LEAVE YOUR LOVER—Paul Simon Music, Paul Simon

GET CLOSER—Dawnbreaker Music, Jimmy Seals, Dash Crofts

GOLDEN RING—Tree Publishing Co., Inc., Bobby Braddock, Rafe Van Hoy

GOLDEN YEARS—Bewlay Bros. Music, Moth Music Ltd., Fleur Music, David Bowie (PRS) **A GOOD HEARTED WOMAN**—Baron Music Publishing Co., Willie Nelson Music, Inc., Willie Nelson, Waylon Jennings

GOT TO GET YOU INTO MY LIFE—Maclen Music, Inc., Paul McCartney (PRS), John Lennon (PRS)

HAPPY DAYS—Bruin Music Co., Norman Gimbel, Charles Fox

HEAVEN MUST BE MISSING AN ANGEL—Bull Pen Music Co., Kenny St. Lewis

HERE'S SOME LOVE—Screen Gems-EMI Music, Inc., Richard Mainegra, William Roberts

I DO, I DO, I DO, I DO, I DO—Countless Songs Ltd., Benny Andersson (STIM), Stig Anderson (STIM), Bjorn Ulvaeus (STIM)

I LOVE MUSIC—Mighty Three Music, Kenneth Gamble, Leon Huff

I'D REALLY LOVE TO SEE YOU TONIGHT—Dawnbreaker Music, Parker McGee

I'LL BE GOOD TO YOU—Kidada Music Co., Goulgris Music, Louis Johnson, George Johnson, Senora Sam

JUST TOO MANY PEOPLE—Braintree Music, Rumanian Pickle Works Co., Melissa Manchester, Vini Poncia

THREE POP WINNERS—John Sebastian, Neil Sedaka and Harry Casey celebrate their winning top pop honors at BMI's awards presentation in Los Angeles. Sebastian won for one song; Sedaka for four and Casey for two.

KILLING ME SOFTLY WITH HIS SONG—(fourth award), Fox-Gimbel Productions, Inc., Norman Gimbel, Charles Fox

KISS AND SAY GOODBYE—Blackwood Music, Inc., Nattahnam Music Co., Winfred Lovett

LET 'EM IN—MPL Communications, Inc., ATV Music Corp., Paul McCartney (PRS), Linda McCartney (PRS)

LET IT SHINE—Window Music Pub. Co., Inc., Linda Hargrove

LET YOUR LOVE FLOW—Loaves and Fishes Music Co., Inc., Lawrence Williams

LET'S DO IT AGAIN—Warner-Tamerlane Publishing Corp., Curtis Mayfield

LONELY NIGHT—Neil Sedaka Music, Neil Sedaka

LOVE HURTS—House of Bryant Publications, Boudleaux Bryant

LOVE IN THE SHADOWS—Neil Sedaka Music, Neil Sedaka

LOVE ROLLERCOASTER—Unichappell Music, Inc., Clarence Satchell, Leroy Bonner, Ralph Middlebrooks, Willie Beck, Marvin Pierce, Marshall Jones, James Williams

LOVE SO RIGHT—Stigwood Music, Inc., Barry Gibb (PRS), Maurice Gibb (PRS), Robin Gibb (PRS)

LOVE TO LOVE YOU BABY—Rick's Music, Inc., Peter Bellotte (GEMA), Donna Summer, Giorgio Moroder (SUISA)

LOVE WILL KEEP US TOGETHER—(second award), Neil Sedaka Music, Howard Greenfield, Neil Sedaka

MEXICO—Country Road Music, Inc., James Taylor

MISTY BLUE—Talmont Music, Inc., Bob Montgomery

MONEY HONEY—The Hudson Bay Music Company, Eric Faulkner (PRS), Stuart Woods (PRS)

NADIA'S THEME—Screen Gems-EMI Music, Inc., Perry Botkin Jr., Barry De Vorzon

NEVER GONNA FALL IN LOVE AGAIN—CAM-USA, Inc., Eric Carmen

NIGHTS ON BROADWAY—Casserole Music Corp., Flamm Music, Inc., Barry Gibb (PRS), Maurice Gibb (PRS), Robin Gibb (PRS)

ONE LITTLE PIECE AT A TIME—Tree Publishing Co., Inc., Wayne Kemp

ONE OF THESE DAYS—Altam Music Corp., Earl Montgomery

ONLY SIXTEEN—Kags Music Corp., Sam Cooke

OVER MY HEAD—Gentoo Music, Christine McVie

REMEMBER ME (WHEN THE CANDLE LIGHTS ARE GLEAMING)—Vogue Music, Inc., Scott Wiseman

RHIANNON—Gentoo Music, Stephanie Nicks

RIGHT BACK WHERE WE STARTED FROM—Unart Music Corp., ATV Music Corp., Pierre Tubbs (PRS), Vincent Edwards (PRS)

ROCK AND ROLL MUSIC—Arc Music Corp., Chuck Berry

RUBBERBAND MAN—Mighty Three Music, Thomas Bell, Linda Creed

SARA SMILE—Unichappell Music, Inc., Daryl Hall, John Oates

SAY IT AGAIN—Hall-Clement Publications, Bob McDill

SAY YOU LOVE ME—Gentoo Music, Christine McVie

(SHAKE, SHAKE, SHAKE) SHAKE YOUR BOOTY—Sherlyn Pub. Co., Inc., Harrick Music, Inc., Harry Casey, Richard Finch

SHE'S GONE—Unichappell Music, Inc., Daryl Hall, John Oates

SHOWER THE PEOPLE—Country Road Music, Inc., James Taylor

SILLY LOVE SONGS—MPL Communications, Inc., ATV Music Corp., Paul McCartney (PRS), Linda McCartney (PRS)

SING A SONG—Saggifire Music, Maurice White

SOMEWHERE IN THE NIGHT—Irving Music, Inc., Will Jennings, Richard Kerr (PRS)

SQUEEZE BOX—Towser Tunes, Inc., Peter Townshend (PRS)

STILL THE ONE—Siren Songs, John Hall, Johanna Hall

STRANGE MAGIC—Unart Music Corp., Jeff Lynne (PRS)

STRANGER—Resaca Music Publishing Co., Kris Kristofferson

SUSPICIOUS MINDS—(second award), Screen Gems-EMI Music, Inc., Mark James

TEDDY BEAR—Cedarwood Publishing Co., Inc., Red Sovine, Billy Joe Burnette, Dale Royal, Tommy Hill

THAT'L BE THE DAY—(second award), MPL Communications, Inc., Jerry Allison, Buddy Holly, Norman Petty

THAT'S THE WAY I LIKE IT—Sherlyn Publishing Co., Inc. Harry Casey, Richard Finch

THEME FROM MAHOGANY (DO YOU KNOW WHERE YOU'RE GOING TO)—Screen Gems-EMI Music, Inc., Gerry Goffin

THEME FROM S.W.A.T.—Spellgold Music, Barry De Vorzon

THINGS—(second award), The Hudson Bay Music Company, Bobby Darin

THIS MASQUERADE—Teddy Jack Music, Leon Russell

'TIL I CAN MAKE IT ON MY OWN—Altam Music Corp., Algee Music Corp., Billy Sherrill, George Richey, Tammy Wynette

('TIL)I KISSED YOU— (second award), Acuff-Rose Publications, Inc., Don Everly

(TILL THE RIVERS ALL RUN DRY—Maplehill Music, Vogue Music, Inc., Wayland Holyfield, Don Williams

TRYIN' TO GET THE FEELIN' AGAIN—Warner-Tamerlane Pub. Corp., Upward Spiral Music, David Pomeranz

WAKE UP EVERYBODY—Mighty Three Music, Gene McFadden, John Whitehead, Vic Carstarphen

WALK AWAY FROM LOVE—Charles Kipps Music, Inc., Charles Kipps Jr.

WELCOME BACK KOTTER—John Sebastian Music, John Sebastian

WHAT I'VE GOT IN MIND—House of Gold Music, Inc., Kenny O'Dell

WHITE KNIGHT—Unichappell Music, Inc., Jay Huguely

WINNERS AND LOSERS—Spitfire Music, Inc., Danny Hamilton, Ann Hamilton

WITH YOUR LOVE—Diamondback Music, Martyn Buchwald, Joey Covington, Victor Smith

YOU ARE SO BEAUTIFUL—(second award), Irving Music, Inc., Billy Preston

YOU ARE THE WOMAN—Stephen Stills Music, Richard Roberts

YOU SHOULD BE DANCING—Casserole Music Corp., Barry Gibb (PRS), Maurice Gibb (PRS), Robin Gibb (PRS)

YOU'LL LOSE A GOOD THING—(second award), Jamie Music Publishing Co., Crazy Cajun Music, Barbara Ozen

YOU'LL NEVER FIND ANOTHER LOVE LIKE MINE—Mighty Three Music, Kenneth Gamble, Leon Huff

FROM MAR. 5, 1977 ISSUE

TOP GRAMMY WINNERS AT L.A. CEREMONIES

Linda Ronstadt holds Grammy she won for Best Pop Female Vocal Performance. Ringo Starr is on her right, and Paul Williams on her left.

Bette Midler and Stevie Wonder's sister, Renee Hayward hold two of the four Grammys awarded to the incredible Stevie.

Ella Fitzgerald (left) accepts her Grammy from affectionate colleague Sarah Vaughan. Fitzgerald was honored for the best jazz vocal performance for her LP "Fitzgerald And Pass . . . Again."

Jazz guitarist George Benson (right) and producer Tommy Lipuma are presented record of the year Grammys by vocalist Barbra Streisand for the single "This Masquerade."

441

BIBLIOGRAPHY

Among the books we read in researching *American Entertainment,* the following were some of the most interesting and useful.

Allen, Frederick Lewis, *Only Yesterday* (Harper, 1931).

Astaire, Fred, *Steps in Time* (Harper, 1959).

Atkinson, Brooks, *Broadway* (Macmillan, 1974).

Barnouw, Erik, *A History of Broadcasting in the United States; Vol. 1 A Tower in Babel; Vol. 2 The Golden Web, 1968; Vol. 3 The Image Empire, 1970. Tube of Plenty* (Oxford University Press, 1975).

Bayer, William, *The Great Movies* (Ridge Press, 1973).

Benchley, Nathaniel, *Humphrey Bogart* (Little, Brown, 1975).

Blum, Daniel, *A Pictorial History of the American Theatre* (Grosset and Dunlap, 1953); *A Pictorial History of the Silent Screen* (G. P. Putnam, 1953); *A Pictorial History of the Talkies* (Grosset & Dunlap, 1958); *A Pictorial History of Television* (Chilton, 1959).

Bogle, Donald, *Toms, Coons, Mulattoes, Mammies & Bucks* (Viking Press, 1973).

Butterfield, Roger, *The American Past* (Simon and Schuster, 1957).

Cagney, James, *Cagney By Cagney* (Doubleday, 1976).

Capra, Frank, *Frank Capra: The Name Above the Title* (Macmillan, 1971).

Champlin, Charles, *The Flicks* (Ward Ritchie Press, 1977).

Chaplin, Charles, *My Autobiography* (Simon and Schuster, 1964).

Chindahl, George L., *A History of the Circus in America* (Caxton Printers, 1959).

Cleaver, James, *Theatre Through the Ages* (Hart, 1967).

Cooke, Alistair, *America* (Alfred A. Knopf, 1973).

Crowther, Bosley, *The Lion's Share* (E. P. Dutton, 1957).

Croy, Homer, *Star Maker, the Story of D. W. Griffith* (Duell, Sloan and Pearce, 1959).

Dannett, Sylvia and Rachel, Frank, *Down Memory Lane* (story of Arthur Murray) (Greenberg, 1954).

Dreher, Carl, *Sarnoff, An American Success* (Quadrangle/The New York Times Book Co., 1977).

Dunning, John, *Tune in Yesterday* (Prentice-Hall, 1976).

Durant, John and Alice, *A Pictorial History of the American Circus* (A. S. Barnes, 1957).

Eames, John Douglas, *The MGM Story* (Crown, 1976).

Ewen, David, *American Popular Songs* (Random House, 1966); *The Complete Book of the American Musical Theatre* (Holt, Rinehart, Winston, 1970); *Great Men of American Popular Song* (Prentice-Hall, 1970).

Fein, Irving, *Jack Benny* (G. P. Putnam, 1976).

Fielding, Raymond (Editor), *A Technological History of Motion Pictures and Television Anthology* (University of California Press, 1974).

French, Philip, *The Movie Moguls* (Henry Regnery, 1971).

Furnas, J. C., *The Americans* (G. P. Putnam, 1969).

Gilbert, Douglas, *American Vaudeville, Its Life and Times* (Whittlesey House, 1940).

Gish, Lillian and Pinchot, Ann, *The Movies, Mr. Griffith & Me* (Avon Books, 1969).

Green, Abel and Laurie, Joe Jr., *Show Biz, from Vaude to Video* (Henry Holt, 1951).

Griffith, Richard and Mayer, Arthur, *The Movies* (Simon and Schuster, 1970).

Hamid, George A., as told to his son, Hamid, George A., Jr., *Circus* (Sterling House, 1950).

Harrison, Harry P., as told to Karl Detzer, *Culture Under Canvas* (Hastings House, 1958).

Higham, Charles, *Cecil B. DeMille* (Charles Scribner, 1973).

Hornblow, Arthur, *A History of the Theatre In America,* Vols. 1 and 2 (Benjamin Bloom, 1919).

Hotchner, A. E., *Doris Day, Her Own Story* (William Morrow, 1976).

Isaacs, Edith J. R., *The Negro in the American Theatre* (Theatre Arts, 1947).

Johnson, E. R. Fenimore, *His Master's Voice Was Eldridge Johnson* (self-published, 1975).

Jordan, Rene, *The Greatest Star, The Barbra Streisand Story* (G. P. Putnam, 1975).

Josephson, Matthew, *Edison* (Eyre & Spottiswoode, 1959).

Kanin, Garson, *Garson Kanin's Hollywood* (Viking Press, 1974).

Kelly, Emmett with Kelly, F. Beverly, *Clown* (Prentice-Hall, 1954).

Kerr, Walter, *The Silent Clowns* (Alfred A. Knopf, 1975).

Knight, Arthur, *The Liveliest Art* (Macmillan, 1957).

Lahr, John, *Notes on a Cowardly Lion* (Alfred A. Knopf, 1970).

Laurie, Joe Jr., *Vaudeville: From the Honky Tonks to the Palace* (Henry Holt, 1953).

Logan, Joshua, *Josh: My Up and Down, In and Out Life* (Dell, 1977).

Mann, May, *Elvis and the Colonel* (Drake, 1975).

Martin, Mary, *My Heart Belongs* (William Morrow, 1976).

Marx, Groucho and Anobile, Richard J., *The Marx Brothers Scrapbook* (Darien House, 1973).

Marx, Samuel, *Mayer and Thalberg* (Random House, 1975).

Marx, Samuel and Clayton, Jan, *Rodgers & Hart* (G. P. Putnam, 1976).

May, Earl Chapin, *The Circus from Rome to Ringling* (Dover, 1963).

McCabe, Peter and Schonfeld, Robert D., *Apple To The Core (The Beatles)* (Pocket Book, 1972).

Metz, Robert, *CBS, Reflections in a Bloodshot Eye* (Playboy Press, 1975).

Morris, Ron, *Wallenda, A Biography of Karl Wallenda* (Sagarin Press, 1976).

Morrison, Samuel Eliot, *The Oxford History of the American People* (Oxford University Press, 1965).

Murray, Marian, *Circus!* (Appleton-Century, Crofts, 1956).

Pickford, Mary, *Sunshine and Shadow* (Doubleday, 1955).

Ramsaye, Terry, *A Million and One Nights* (Simon and Schuster, 1926).

Richard Rodgers Fact Book—The Lynn Farnol Group, 1965.

Rosenberg, Bernard and Silverstein, Harry, *The Real Tinsel* (Collier-Macmillan, 1970).

Schicke, Charles, *Revolution in Sound* (Little, Brown, 1974).

Schickel, Richard, *The Stars* (Dial Press, 1962).

Sennett, Mack, as told to Shipp, Cameron, *King of Comedy* (Doubleday, 1954).

Shanks, Bob, *The Cool Fire* (Norton, 1976).

Skinner, Cornelia Otis, *Madam Sarah* (Houghton-Mifflin, 1967).

Sobel, Bernard, *A Pictorial History of Vaudeville* (Citadel Press, 1961).

Spitzer, Marian, *The Palace* (Atheneum, 1969).

Stagg, Jerry, *A Half Century of Show Business and the Fabulous Empire of the Brothers Shubert* (Random House, 1968).

Sutton, Felix, *The Big Show* (Doubleday, 1971).

Taubman, Howard, *The Making of the American Theatre* (Coward, McCann, 1965).

Taylor, Deems, Peterson, Marcelene and Hale, Bryant, *A Pictorial History of the Movies* (Simon and Schuster, 1950).

Wallace, Irving, *The Fabulous Showman, the Life and Times of P. T. Barnum* (Alfred A. Knopf, 1959).

Westmore, Frank and Davidson, Muriel, *The Westmores of Hollywood* (Lippencott, 1976).

Windeler, Robert, *Sweetheart: The Story of Mary Pickford* (Praeger Publishers, 1974).

Billboard issues from November, 1894 to December, 1977.

Various issues of the following publications: weekly and daily *Variety; Broadcasting; Downbeat; High Fidelity; Hollywood Reporter;* the entertainment section of the Sunday edition of the *New York Times* and the "Calendar" section of the *Los Angeles Times.*

INDEX

The chronological capsule history sections of the book have not been included in this index since the items in the capsule history constitute a concise, albeit non-alphabetized index, *per se.*